# Collins
## ESSENTIAL ROAD ATLAS
# BRITAIN

D1283357

 Collins

Published by Collins
*An imprint of* HarperCollins Publishers
Westerhill Road, Bishopbriggs, Glasgow G64 2QT

www.harpercollins.co.uk

Copyright © HarperCollins Publishers Ltd 2011

Collins® is a registered trademark of HarperCollins Publishers Limited

Mapping generated from CollinsBartholomew digital databases

The grid on this map is the National Grid taken from the Ordnance Survey map with the permission of the Controller of Her Majesty's Stationery Office.

Printed in China

ISBN 978 0 00 742738 3   Imp 001

e-mail: roadcheck@harpercollins.co.uk

Information on fixed speed camera locations provided by PocketGPSWorld.Com Ltd.

With thanks to the Wine Guild of the United Kingdom for help with researching vineyards.

Information regarding blue flag beach awards is current as of summer 2009. For latest information please visit www.blueflag.org.uk

CASTLE COVER
The 50+ Insurance Specialists

**Europcar**

**See back pages for money-off vouchers and Castle Cover Insurance**

# Contents

## Route planning

| | |
|---|---|
| Route planning maps | ii-vii |
| Restricted motorway junctions | viii-ix |
| Motorway services information | x-xi |
| Orbital motorway maps - M25 & Birmingham | xii-xiii |
| Distance chart | xiv |
| National Rail network | xv |
| Risk rating of Britain's motorways and A roads | xvi-xvii |

## Urban approach maps (1 mile to 1 inch)   2-32

| | |
|---|---|
| Symbols used on maps | 2 |
| Plymouth | 2 |
| Bournemouth | 3 |
| Southampton & Portsmouth | 4-5 |
| Swansea | 6 |
| Cardiff & Newport | 7 |
| Bristol | 8 |
| Milton Keynes | 9 |
| London | 10-13 |
| West Midlands | 14-15 |
| Coventry | 16 |
| Leicester | 17 |
| Derby & Nottingham | 18-19 |
| Stoke-on-Trent | 20 |
| Sheffield | 21 |
| Merseyside | 22-23 |
| Greater Manchester | 24-25 |
| Leeds & Bradford | 26-27 |
| Newcastle upon Tyne & Sunderland | 28 |
| Middlesbrough | 29 |
| Glasgow | 30-31 |
| Edinburgh | 32 |

## Street maps   33-91

| | | | |
|---|---|---|---|
| Symbols used on maps | 33 | Hastings | 75 |
| Birmingham | 34-35 | Hereford | 75 |
| Edinburgh | 36-37 | Hull | 76 |
| Glasgow | 38-39 | Inverness | 76 |
| Leeds | 40-41 | Leicester | 77 |
| Liverpool | 42-43 | Lincoln | 77 |
| London | 44-45 | Middlesbrough | 78 |
| Manchester | 46-47 | Milton Keynes | 78 |
| Birmingham index | 48 | Newcastle upon Tyne | 79 |
| Edinburgh index | 49 | Norwich | 79 |
| Glasgow index | 51 | Nottingham | 80 |
| Leeds index | 52 | Oxford | 80 |
| Liverpool index | 54 | Perth | 81 |
| London index | 56 | Plymouth | 81 |
| Manchester index | 60 | Portsmouth | 82 |
| Aberdeen | 63 | Reading | 82 |
| Bath | 63 | Salisbury | 83 |
| Blackpool | 64 | Scarborough | 83 |
| Bournemouth | 64 | Sheffield | 84 |
| Bradford | 65 | Southampton | 84 |
| Brighton | 65 | Stoke-on-Trent | 85 |
| Bristol | 66 | Stratford-upon-Avon | 85 |
| Cambridge | 66 | Sunderland | 86 |
| Canterbury | 67 | Swansea | 86 |
| Cardiff | 67 | Swindon | 87 |
| Carlisle | 68 | Torquay | 87 |
| Cheltenham | 68 | Watford | 88 |
| Chester | 69 | Weston-super-Mare | 88 |
| Coventry | 69 | Winchester | 89 |
| Derby | 70 | Windsor | 89 |
| Dover | 70 | Worcester | 90 |
| Dundee | 71 | York | 90 |
| Durham | 71 | **Airport plans** | |
| Eastbourne | 72 | Birmingham International | 91 |
| Exeter | 72 | Gatwick | 91 |
| Folkestone | 73 | Glasgow | 91 |
| Gloucester | 73 | Heathrow | 91 |
| Guildford | 74 | Manchester | 91 |
| Harrogate | 74 | Stansted | 91 |

## Road maps   92-279

| | |
|---|---|
| Symbols used on maps & key to map pages | 92-93 |
| England, Wales & Southern Scotland (3.2 miles to 1 inch) | 94-253 |
| Northern Scotland (4.2 miles to 1 inch) | 254-279 |

## Index   280-318

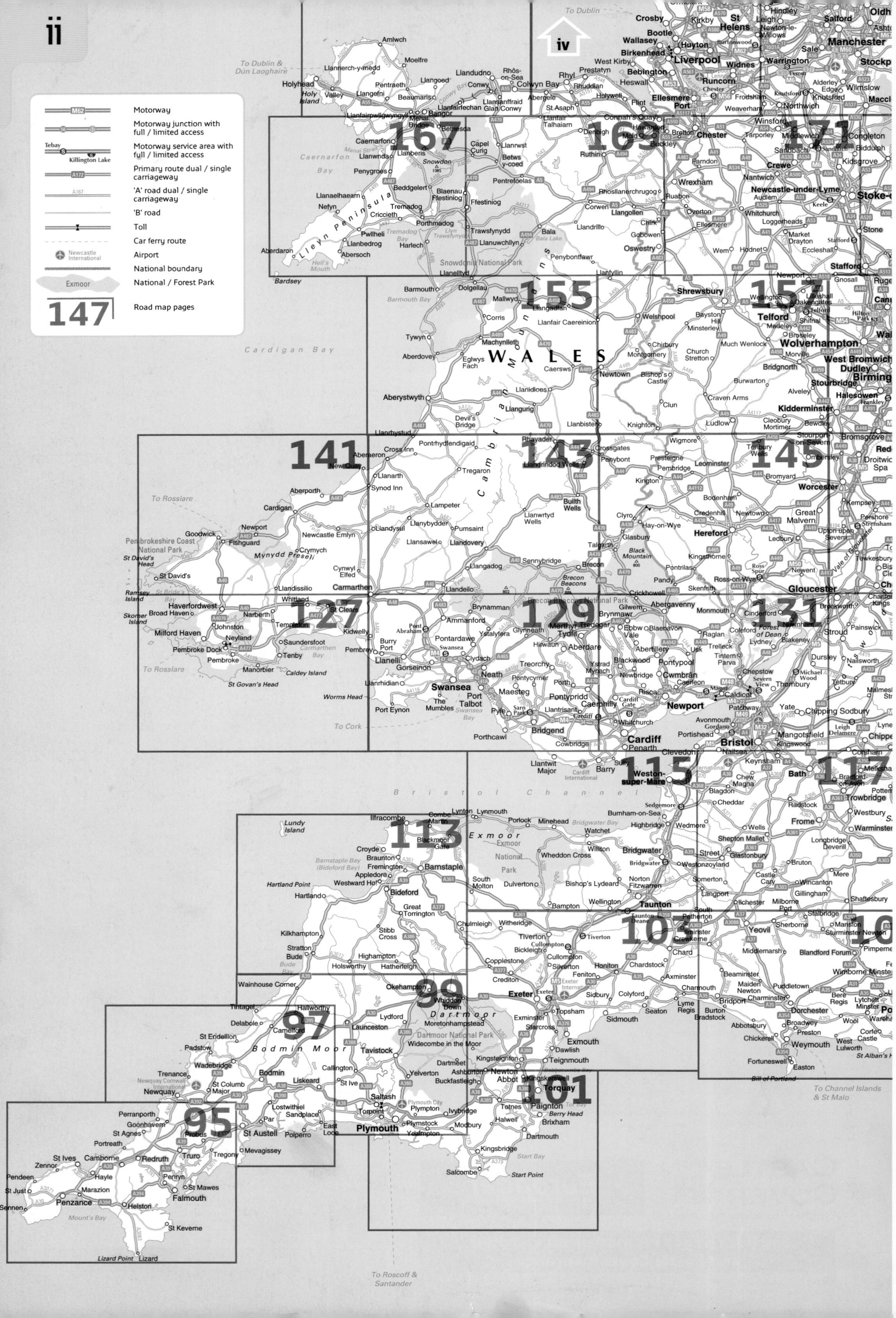

iv

**Motorway**

**Motorway junction with full / limited access**

**Motorway service area with full / limited access**

Tebay
Killington Lake

**Primary route dual / single carriageway**

**'A' road dual / single carriageway**

A167

**'B' road**

**Toll**

**Car ferry route**

Newcastle International

**Airport**

**National boundary**

Exmoor

**National / Forest Park**

147

**Road map pages**

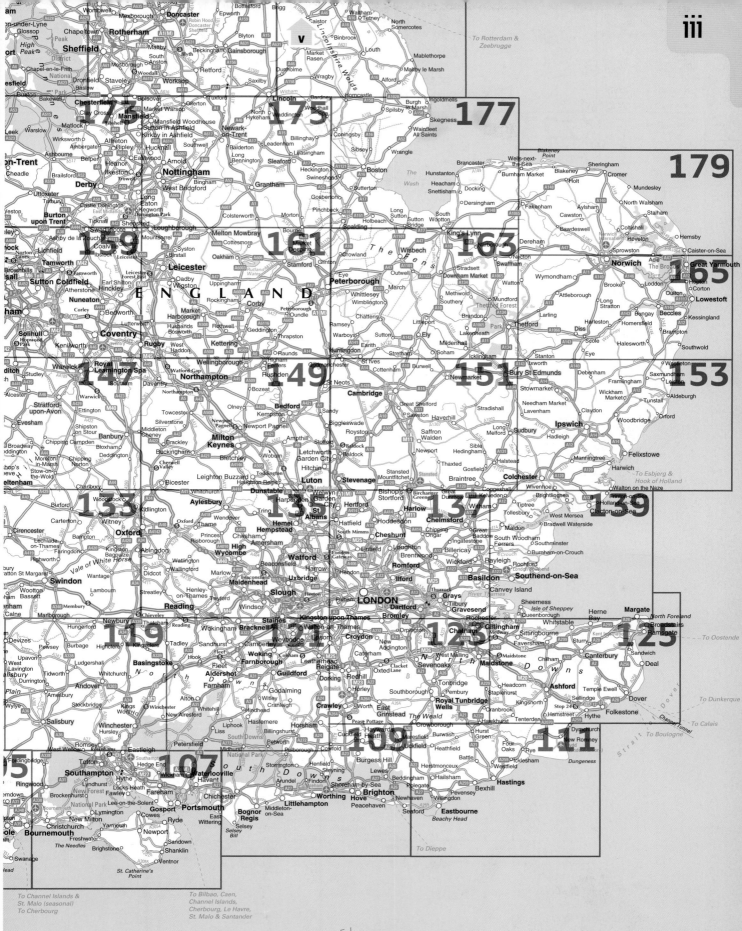

SCALE 1:1,408,450

0    10    20    30    40 miles

0   10   20   30   40   50   60 kilometres

22 miles to 1 inch / 14 km to 1 cm

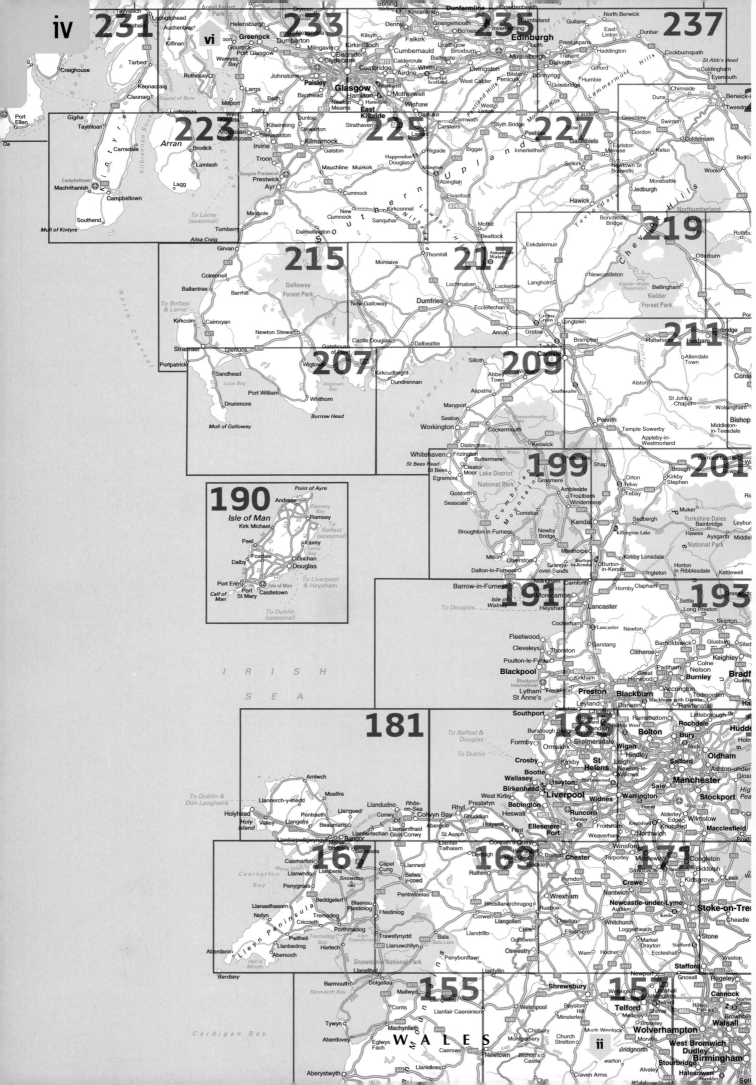

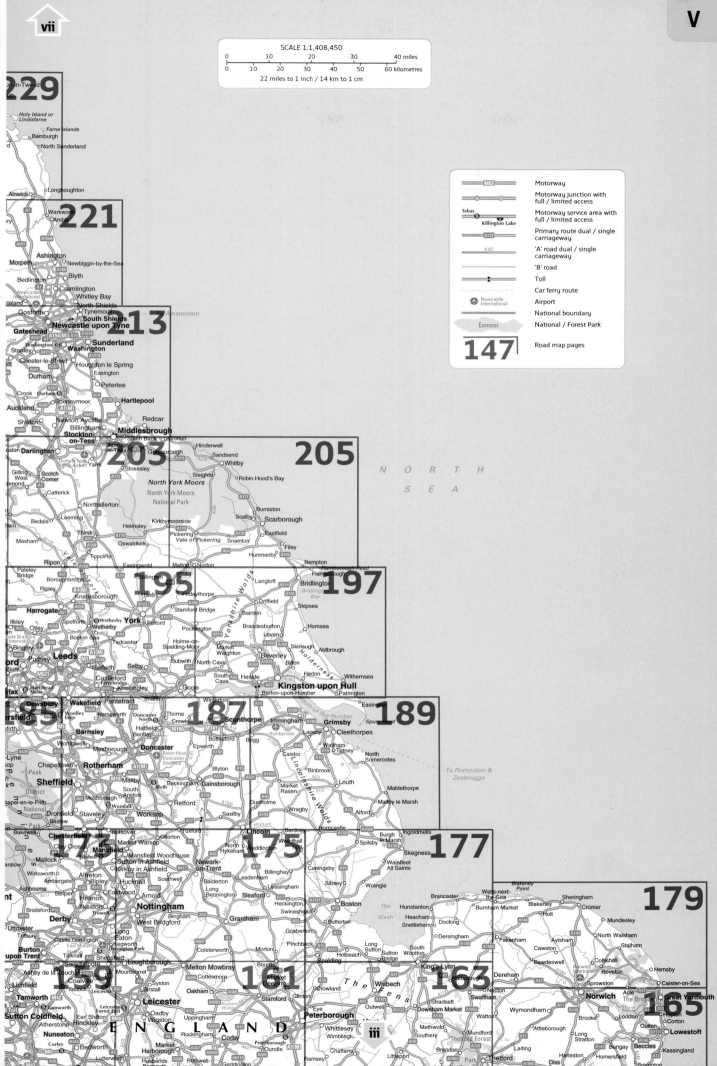

271
273
263
265
255
257
247
249
239
241
231
233
223
225
215

WESTERN ISLES

ATLANTIC OCEAN

SUTHERLAND

North West Highlands

Easter Ross

Wester Ross

Glen Albyn (Glen Mòr)

Monadhliath Mountains

Cairngorm

SCOTLAND

Argyll

Loch Lomond & the Trossachs National Park

Queen Elizabeth Forest Park

Argyll Forest Park

Galloway Forest Park

**Place names (selection):**

Butt of Lewis, Port of Ness, Portnaguran, Tolsta Head, Barvas, Carloway, Stornoway, Great Bernera, Miabhig, Garrynahine, Lewis, Scarp, Kebock Head, Loch Langavat

North Harris, Tarbert, Scalpay, Shiant Islands, South Harris, Northton, Pabbay, Berneray, Leverburgh, Rodel, North Uist, Lochmaddy, Monach Islands, Benbecula, Barra, Eriskay, Vatersay, Castlebay, Pabaigh, Mingulay, Lochboisdale

Cape Wrath, Durness, Kinlochbervie, Scourie, Laxford Bridge, Tongue, Bettyhill, Strathy Point, Strathy, Dounreay, Forsinard, Kinbrace, Altnaharra, Ben Hope 927, Unapool, Point of Stoer, Lochinver, Elphin, Ledmore, Summer Isles, Loch Shin, Strath Halladale

Ullapool, An Teallach, An Teallach 1062, Rubha Reidh, Aultbea, Poolewe, Gairloch, Loch Maree, Loch Fannich, Kinlochewe, Liathach 1054, Torridon, Shieldaig, Lairg, Invercassley, Pittentrail, Bonar Bridge, Ardgay, Brora, Golspie, Dornoch, Tarbat, Portmahomack, Tain, Hill of Fearn, Balintore, Garve, Dingwall, Strathpeffer, Achnasheen, Black Isle, Fortrose, Cromarty, Invergordon, Findhorn, Alness, Rosemarkie, Nairn, Muir of Ord, Beauly, Conon Bridge, Ardersier, Inverness

Sligachan, Sconser, Scalpay, Broadford, Portree, Raasay, Rona, The Storr 719, Uig, Loch Snizort, Dunvegan, Bracadale, Skye, Borve, Cuillin Hills, Bla Bheinn 928, Soay, Elgol, Ardvasar, Knoydart, Mallaig, Morar, Kilchoan, Tobermory, Coll, Tiree

Stromeferry, Lochcarron, Kyle of Lochalsh, Kyleakin, Dornie, Glen Affric, Cannich, Glen Shiel, Loch Quoich, Loch Hourn, Loch Morar, Drumnadrochit, Dores, Foyers, Invermoriston, Fort Augustus, Invergarry, Glen Garry, Glen Albyn, Glen Garry, Spean Bridge, Roybridge, Loch Lochy, Laggan, Newtonmore, Kingussie, Kincraig, Aviemore, Carrbridge, Grantown-on-Spey, Dulnain Bridge, Tomatin, Boat of Garten, Ben Macdui 1309

Arisaig, Glenfinnan, Fort William, Ben Nevis 1344, Loch Arkaig, Loch Shiel, Salen, Strontian, Kinlochleven, Glen Coe, Ballachulish, Bidean nam Bian 1150, Appin, Lochaline, Salen, Dalwhinnie, Loch Ericht, Rannoch Station, Kinloch Rannoch, Loch Rannoch, Rannoch Moor, Ben Lawers, Kenmore, Blair Atholl, Spittal of Glenshee, Pitlochry, Grandtully, Aberfeldy, Killin

Mull, Ben More 966, Pennyghael, Fionnphort, Iona, Ulva, Craignure, Oban, Taynuilt, Bridge of Orchy, Tyndrum, Dalmally, Crianlarich, Lochearnhead, Comrie, Crieff, Strathyre, Callander, Loch Awe, Kilmelford, Kilmartin, Inveraray, Arrochar, Ben Lomond 974, Loch Lomond, Aberfoyle, Doune, Dunblane, Bridge of Allan, Dollar, Stirling, Alloa, Clackmannan

Jura, Islay, Craighouse, Tarbert, Tayvallich, Ardrishaig, Lochgilphead, Auchenbreck, Kilfinan, Helensburgh, Duncon, Gourock, Greenock, Port Glasgow, Wemyss Bay, Dumbarton, Alexandria, Milngavie, Bearsden, Clydebank, Kirkintilloch, Cumbernauld, Caldercruix, Falkirk, Linlithgow, Bathgate, Whitburn, Broxburn, Coatbridge, Airdrie, Port Askaig, Bowmore, Portnahaven, Port Ellen, Mull Of Oa, Rothesay, Kennacraig, Claonaig, Millport, Largs, Johnstone, Paisley, Glasgow, Barrhead, Newton Mearns, Beith, Dalry, Hamilton, Motherwell, Wishaw, East Kilbride, Bothwell, Carluke, Strathaven

Gigha, Tayinloan, Arran, Brodick, Lamlash, Lagg, Lochranza, West Kilbride, Ardrossan, Saltcoats, Stevenston, Kilwinning, Irvine, Troon, Kilmarnock, Galston, Stewarton, Dunlop, Prestwick, Ayr, Mauchline, Muirkirk, Douglas, Happendon, Rigside, Abington

Carradale, Machrihanish, Campbeltown, Southend, Mull of Kintyre, Kintyre, Sound of Bute, Kilbrannan Sound, To Larne (seasonal), Ailsa Craig, Turnberry, Maybole, Glasgow Prestwick, New Cumnock, Cumnock, Sanquhar, Kirkconnel, Dalmellington, Girvan, Barrhill, Ballantrae, Colmonell, Thornhill, Moniaive, Galloway Forest Park

**Legend:**

- M62 — Motorway
- Motorway junction with full / limited access
- Tebay / Killington Lake — Motorway service area with full / limited access
- A172 — Primary route dual / single carriageway
- A167 — 'A' road dual / single carriageway
- 'B' road
- Toll
- Car ferry route
- Newcastle International — Airport
- National boundary
- Exmoor — National / Forest Park
- 147 — Road map pages

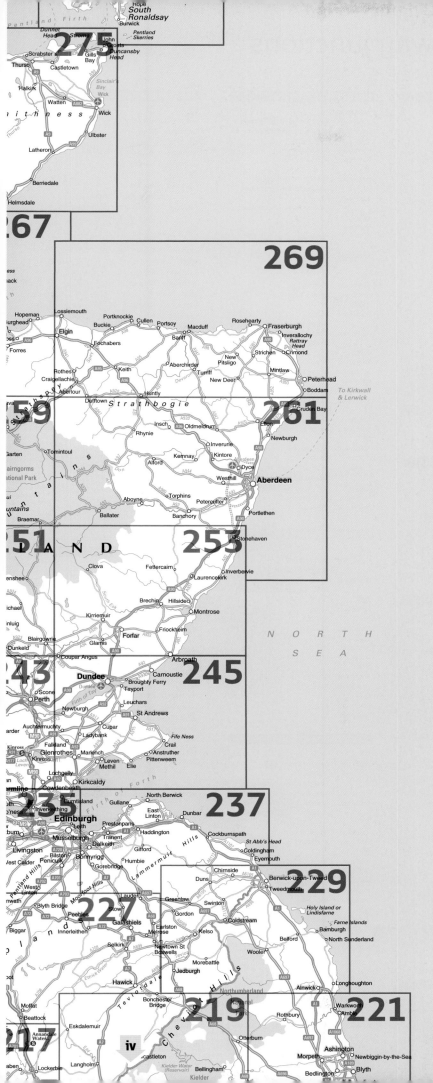

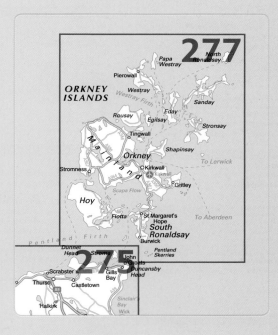

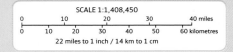

SCALE 1:1,408,450

22 miles to 1 inch / 14 km to 1 cm

# Restricted motorway junctions

## A1(M) LONDON TO NEWCASTLE

**(2)**
Northbound : No access
Southbound : No exit
**(3)**
Southbound : No access
**(5)**
Northbound : No exit
Southbound : No access
         : No exit
**(41)**
Northbound : No exit to M62 Eastbound
**(43)**
Northbound : No exit to M1 Westbound
**Dishforth**
Southbound : No access from A168 Eastbound
**(57)**
Northbound : No access
         : Exit only to A66(M) Northbound
Southbound : Access only from A66(M) Southbound
         : No exit
**(65)**
Northbound : No access from A1
Southbound : No exit to A1

## A3(M) PORTSMOUTH

**(1)**
Northbound : No exit
Southbound : No access
**(4)**
Northbound : No access
Southbound : No exit

## A38(M) BIRMINGHAM

**Victoria Road**
Northbound : No exit
Southbound : No access

## A48(M) CARDIFF

**Junction with M4**
Westbound : No access from M4 **(29)** Eastbound
Eastbound : No exit to M4 **(29)** Westbound
**(29A)**
Westbound : No exit to A48 Eastbound
Eastbound : No access from A48 Westbound

## A57(M) MANCHESTER

**Brook Street**
Westbound : No exit
Eastbound : No access

## A58(M) LEEDS

**Westgate**
Southbound : No access
**Woodhouse Lane**
Westbound : No exit

## A64(M) LEEDS

**Claypit Lane**
Eastbound : No access

## A66(M) DARLINGTON

**Junction with A1(M)**
Northbound : No access from A1(M) Southbound
         : No exit
Southbound : No access
         : No exit to A1(M) Northbound

## A74(M) LOCKERBIE

**(18)**
Northbound : No access
Southbound : No exit

## A167(M) NEWCASTLE

**Campden Street**
Northbound : No exit
Southbound : No access
         : No exit

## M1 LONDON TO LEEDS

**(2)**
Northbound : No exit
Southbound : No access
**(4)**
Northbound : No exit
Southbound : No access
**(6A)**
Northbound : Access only from M25 **(21)**
         : No exit
Southbound : No access
         : Exit only to M25 **(21)**
**(7)**
Northbound : Access only from A414
         : No exit
Southbound : No access
         : Exit only to A414

## M1 LONDON TO LEEDS (continued)

**(17)**
Northbound : No access
         : Exit only to M45
Southbound : Access only from M45
         : No exit
**(19)**
Northbound : Exit only to M6
Southbound : Access only from M6
**(21A)**
Northbound : No access
Southbound : No exit
**(23A)**
Northbound : No access from A453
Southbound : No exit to A453
**(24A)**
Northbound : No exit
Southbound : No access
**(35A)**
Northbound : No access
Southbound : No exit
**(43)**
Northbound : No access
         : Exit only to M621
Southbound : No exit
         : Access only from M621
**(48)**
Northbound : No exit to A1(M) Southbound
         : Access only from A1(M) Northbound
Southbound : Exit only to A1(M) Southbound
         : No access

## M2 ROCHESTER TO CANTERBURY

**(1)**
Westbound : No exit to A2 Eastbound
Eastbound : No access from A2 Westbound

## M3 LONDON TO WINCHESTER

**(8)**
Westbound : No access
Eastbound : No exit
**(10)**
Northbound : No access
Southbound : No exit
**(13)**
Southbound : No exit to A335 Eastbound
         : No access
**(14)**
Westbound : No access
Eastbound : No exit

## M4 LONDON TO SWANSEA

**(1)**
Westbound : No access from A4 Eastbound
Eastbound : No exit to A4 Westbound
**(2)**
Westbound : No access from A4 Eastbound
         : No exit to A4 Eastbound
Eastbound : No access from A4 Westbound
         : No exit to A4 Westbound
**(21)**
Westbound : No access from M48 Eastbound
Eastbound : No exit to M48 Westbound
**(23)**
Westbound : No exit to M48 Eastbound
Eastbound : No access from M48 Westbound
**(25)**
Westbound : No access
Eastbound : No exit
**(25A)**
Westbound : No access
Eastbound : No exit
**(29)**
Westbound : No access
         : Exit only to A48(M)
Eastbound : Access only from A48(M) Eastbound
         : No exit
**(38)**
Westbound : No access
**(39)**
Westbound : No exit
Eastbound : No access
         : No exit
**(41)**
Westbound : No exit
Eastbound : No access
**(42)**
Westbound : No exit to A48
Eastbound : No access from A48

## M5 BIRMINGHAM TO EXETER

**(10)**
Northbound : No exit
Southbound : No access
**(11A)**
Northbound : No access from A417 Eastbound
Southbound : No exit to A417 Westbound

## M6 COVENTRY TO CARLISLE

**Junction with M1**
Northbound : No access from M1 **(19)** Southbound
Southbound : No exit to M1 **(19)** Northbound
**(3A)**
Northbound : No access from M6 Toll
Southbound : No exit to M6 Toll
**(4)**
Northbound : No exit to M42 Northbound
         : No access from M42 Southbound
Southbound : No exit to M42
         : No access from M42 Southbound
**(4A)**
Northbound : No access from M42 **(8)**
          Northbound
         : No exit
Southbound : No access
         : Exit only to M42 **(8)**
**(5)**
Northbound : No access
Southbound : No exit
**(10A)**
Northbound : No access
         : Exit only to M54
Southbound : Access only from M54
         : No exit
**(11A)**
Northbound : No exit to M6 Toll
Southbound : No access from M6 Toll
**(24)**
Northbound : No exit
Southbound : No access
**(25)**
Northbound : No exit
Southbound : No access
**(30)**
Northbound : Access only from M61 Northbound
         : No exit
Southbound : No access
         : Exit only to M61 Southbound
**(31A)**
Northbound : No access
Southbound : No exit

## M6 Toll BIRMINGHAM

**(T1)**
Northbound : Exit only to M42
         : Access only from A4097
Southbound : No exit
         : Access only from M42 Southbound
**(T2)**
Northbound : No exit
         : No access
Southbound : No access
**(T5)**
Northbound : No exit
Southbound : No access
**(T7)**
Northbound : No access
Southbound : No exit
**(T8)**
Northbound : No access
Southbound : No exit

## M8 EDINBURGH TO GLASGOW

**(8)**
Westbound : No access from M73 **(2)**
          Southbound
         : No access from A8 Eastbound
         : No access from A89 Eastbound
Eastbound : No access from A89 Westbound
         : No exit to M73 **(2)** Northbound
**(9)**
Westbound : No exit
Eastbound : No access
**(13)**
Westbound : Access only from M80
Eastbound : Exit only to M80
**(14)**
Westbound : No exit
Eastbound : No access
**(16)**
Westbound : No access
Eastbound : No exit
**(17)**
Eastbound : Access only from A82,
          not central Glasgow
         : Exit only to A82,
          not central Glasgow
**(18)**
Westbound : No access
Eastbound : No access
**(19)**
Westbound : Access only from A814 Eastbound
Eastbound : Exit only to A814 Westbound,
          not central Glasgow

## M8 EDINBURGH TO GLASGOW (cont)

**(20)**
Westbound : No access
Eastbound : No exit
**(21)**
Westbound : No exit
Eastbound : No access
**(22)**
Westbound : No access
         : Exit only to M77 Southbound
Eastbound : Access only from M77 Northbound
         : No exit
**(23)**
Westbound : No access
Eastbound : No exit
**(25A)**
Eastbound : No exit
Westbound : No access
**(28)**
Westbound : No access
Eastbound : No exit
**(28A)**
Westbound : No access
Eastbound : No access

## M9 EDINBURGH TO STIRLING

**(1A)**
Westbound : No access
Eastbound : No exit
**(2)**
Westbound : No exit
Eastbound : No access
**(3)**
Westbound : No access
Eastbound : No exit
**(6)**
Westbound : No exit
Eastbound : No access
**(8)**
Westbound : No access
Eastbound : No exit

## M11 LONDON TO CAMBRIDGE

**(4)**
Northbound : No access from A1400 Westbound
         : No exit
Southbound : No access
         : No exit to A1400 Eastbound
**(5)**
Northbound : No access
Southbound : No exit
**(8A)**
Northbound : No access
Southbound : No exit
**(9)**
Northbound : No access
Southbound : No exit
**(13)**
Northbound : No access
Southbound : No exit
**(14)**
Northbound : No access from A428 Eastbound
         : No exit to A428 Westbound
         : No exit to A1307
Southbound : No access from A428 Eastbound
         : No access from A1307
         : No exit

## M20 LONDON TO FOLKESTONE

**(2)**
Westbound : No exit
Eastbound : No access
**(3)**
Westbound : No access
         : Exit only to M26 Westbound
Eastbound : Access only from M26 Eastbound
         : No access
**(11A)**
Westbound : No exit
Eastbound : No access

## M23 LONDON TO CRAWLEY

**(7)**
Northbound : No exit to A23 Southbound
Southbound : No access from A23 Northbound
**(10A)**
Southbound : No access from B2036
Northbound : No exit to B2036

Restricted motorway junctions are shown on the maps as:

## M25 LONDON ORBITAL MOTORWAY

**(1B)**
| | |
|---|---|
| Clockwise | : No access |
| Anticlockwise | : No exit |

**(5)**
| | |
|---|---|
| Clockwise | : No exit to M26 Eastbound |
| Anticlockwise | : No access from M26 Westbound |

**Spur of M25 (5)**
| | |
|---|---|
| Clockwise | : No access from M26 Westbound |
| Anticlockwise | : No exit to M26 Eastbound |

**(19)**
| | |
|---|---|
| Clockwise | : No access |
| Anticlockwise | : No exit |

**(21)**
| | |
|---|---|
| Clockwise | : No access from M1 (6A) Northbound |
| | : No exit to M1 (6A) Southbound |
| Anticlockwise | : No access from M1 (6A) Northbound |
| | : No exit to M1 (6A) Southbound |

**(31)**
| | |
|---|---|
| Clockwise | : No exit |
| Anticlockwise | : No access |

## M26 SEVENOAKS

**Junction with M25 (5)**
| | |
|---|---|
| Westbound | : No exit to M25 Anticlockwise |
| | : No exit to M25 spur |
| Eastbound | : No access from M25 Clockwise |
| | : No access from M25 spur |

**Junction with M20**
| | |
|---|---|
| Westbound | : No access from M20 (3) Eastbound |
| Eastbound | : No exit to M20 (3) Westbound |

## M27 SOUTHAMPTON TO PORTSMOUTH

**(4) West**
| | |
|---|---|
| Westbound | : No exit |
| Eastbound | : No access |

**(4) East**
| | |
|---|---|
| Westbound | : No access |
| Eastbound | : No exit |

**(10)**
| | |
|---|---|
| Westbound | : No access |
| Eastbound | : No exit |

**(12) West**
| | |
|---|---|
| Westbound | : No exit |
| Eastbound | : No access |

**(12) East**
| | |
|---|---|
| Westbound | : No access from A3 |
| Eastbound | : No exit |

## M40 LONDON TO BIRMINGHAM

**(3)**
| | |
|---|---|
| Westbound | : No access |
| Eastbound | : No exit |

**(7)**
| | |
|---|---|
| Westbound | : No access |
| Eastbound | : No exit |

**(8)**
| | |
|---|---|
| Northbound | : No access |
| Southbound | : No exit |

**(13)**
| | |
|---|---|
| Northbound | : No access |
| Southbound | : No exit |

**(14)**
| | |
|---|---|
| Northbound | : No exit |
| Southbound | : No access |

**(16)**
| | |
|---|---|
| Northbound | : No exit |
| Southbound | : No access |

## M42 BIRMINGHAM

**(1)**
| | |
|---|---|
| Northbound | : No access |
| Southbound | : No exit |

**(7)**
| | |
|---|---|
| Northbound | : No access |
| | : Exit only to M6 Northbound |
| Southbound | : Access only from M6 Northbound |
| | : No exit |

**(7A)**
| | |
|---|---|
| Northbound | : No access |
| | : Exit only to M6 Eastbound |
| Southbound | : No access |
| | : No exit |

**(8)**
| | |
|---|---|
| Northbound | : Access only from M6 Southbound |
| | : No exit |
| Southbound | : Access only from M6 Southbound |
| | : Exit only to M6 Northbound |

## M45 COVENTRY

**Junction with M1**
| | |
|---|---|
| Westbound | : No access from M1 (17) Southbound |
| Eastbound | : No exit to M1 (17) Northbound |

**Junction with A45**
| | |
|---|---|
| Westbound | : No exit |
| Eastbound | : No access |

## M48 CHEPSTOW

**M4**
| | |
|---|---|
| Westbound | : No exit to M4 Eastbound |
| Eastbound | : No access from M4 Westbound |

## M49 BRISTOL

**(18A)**
| | |
|---|---|
| Northbound | : No access from M5 Southbound |
| Southbound | : No access from M5 Northbound |

## M53 BIRKENHEAD TO CHESTER

**(11)**
| | |
|---|---|
| Northbound | : No access from M56 (15) Eastbound |
| | : No exit to M56 (15) Westbound |
| Southbound | : No access from M56 (15) Eastbound |
| | : No exit to M56 (15) Westbound |

## M54 WOLVERHAMPTON TO TELFORD

**Junction with M6**
| | |
|---|---|
| Westbound | : No access from M6 (10A) Southbound |
| Eastbound | : No exit to M6 (10A) Northbound |

## M56 STOCKPORT TO CHESTER

**(1)**
| | |
|---|---|
| Westbound | : No access from M60 Eastbound |
| | : No access from A34 Northbound |
| Eastbound | : No exit to M60 Westbound |
| | : No exit to A34 Southbound |

**(2)**
| | |
|---|---|
| Westbound | : No access |
| Eastbound | : No exit |

**(3)**
| | |
|---|---|
| Westbound | : No exit |
| Eastbound | : No access |

**(4)**
| | |
|---|---|
| Westbound | : No access |
| Eastbound | : No exit |

**(7)**
| | |
|---|---|
| Westbound | : No access |
| Eastbound | : No exit |

**(8)**
| | |
|---|---|
| Westbound | : No exit |
| Eastbound | : No access |

**(9)**
| | |
|---|---|
| Westbound | : No exit to M6 Southbound |
| Eastbound | : No access from M6 Northbound |

**(15)**
| | |
|---|---|
| Westbound | : No access |
| | : No access from M53 (11) |
| Eastbound | : No exit |
| | : No exit to M53 (11) |

## M57 LIVERPOOL

**(3)**
| | |
|---|---|
| Northbound | : No exit |
| Southbound | : No access |

**(5)**
| | |
|---|---|
| Northbound | : Access only from A580 Westbound |
| | : No exit |
| Southbound | : No access |
| | : Exit only to A580 Eastbound |

## M58 LIVERPOOL TO WIGAN

**(1)**
| | |
|---|---|
| Westbound | : No access |
| Eastbound | : No exit |

## M60 MANCHESTER

**(2)**
| | |
|---|---|
| Westbound | : No exit |
| Eastbound | : No access |

**(3)**
| | |
|---|---|
| Westbound | : No access from M56 (1) |
| | : No access from A34 Southbound |
| | : No exit to A34 Northbound |
| Eastbound | : No access from A34 Southbound |
| | : No exit to M56 (1) |
| | : No exit to A34 Northbound |

**(4)**
| | |
|---|---|
| Westbound | : No access |
| Eastbound | : No exit to M56 |

## M60 MANCHESTER (continued)

**(5)**
| | |
|---|---|
| Westbound | : No access from A5103 Southbound |
| | : No exit to A5103 Southbound |
| Eastbound | : No access from A5103 Northbound |
| | : No exit to A5103 Northbound |

**(14)**
| | |
|---|---|
| Westbound | : No access from A580 |
| | : No exit to A580 Eastbound |
| Eastbound | : No access from A580 Westbound |
| | : No exit to A580 |

**(16)**
| | |
|---|---|
| Westbound | : No access |
| Eastbound | : No exit |

**(20)**
| | |
|---|---|
| Westbound | : No access |
| Eastbound | : No exit |

**(22)**
| | |
|---|---|
| Westbound | : No access |

**(25)**
| | |
|---|---|
| Westbound | : No access |

**(26)**
| | |
|---|---|
| Southbound | : No access |
| | : No exit |

**(27)**
| | |
|---|---|
| Northbound | : No exit |
| Eastbound | : No access |

## M61 MANCHESTER TO PRESTON

**(2)**
| | |
|---|---|
| Northbound | : No access from A580 Eastbound |
| | : No access from A666 |
| Southbound | : No exit to A580 Westbound |

**(3)**
| | |
|---|---|
| Northbound | : No access from A580 Eastbound |
| | : No access from A666 |
| Southbound | : No exit to A580 Westbound |

**Junction with M6**
| | |
|---|---|
| Northbound | : No exit to M6 (30) Southbound |
| Southbound | : No access from M6 (30) Northbound |

## M62 LIVERPOOL TO HULL

**(23)**
| | |
|---|---|
| Westbound | : No exit |
| Eastbound | : No access |

**(32A)**
| | |
|---|---|
| Westbound | : No exit to A1(M) Southbound |

## M65 BURNLEY

**(9)**
| | |
|---|---|
| Westbound | : No exit |
| Eastbound | : No access |

**(11)**
| | |
|---|---|
| Westbound | : No access |
| Eastbound | : No exit |

## M66 MANCHESTER TO EDENFIELD

**(1)**
| | |
|---|---|
| Northbound | : No access |
| Southbound | : No exit |

**Junction with A56**
| | |
|---|---|
| Northbound | : Exit only to A56 Northbound |
| Southbound | : Access only from A56 Southbound |

## M67 MANCHESTER

**(1)**
| | |
|---|---|
| Westbound | : No exit |
| Eastbound | : No access |

**(2)**
| | |
|---|---|
| Westbound | : No access |
| Eastbound | : No exit |

## M69 COVENTRY TO LEICESTER

**(2)**
| | |
|---|---|
| Northbound | : No exit |
| Southbound | : No access |

## M73 GLASGOW

**(1)**
| | |
|---|---|
| Northbound | : No access from A721 Eastbound |
| Southbound | : No exit to A721 Eastbound |

**(2)**
| | |
|---|---|
| Northbound | : No access from M8 (8) Eastbound |
| Southbound | : No exit to M8 (8) Westbound |

**(3)**
| | |
|---|---|
| Northbound | : No exit to A80 Southbound |
| Southbound | : No access from A80 Northbound |

## M74 GLASGOW

**(2)**
| | |
|---|---|
| Westbound | : No access |
| Eastbound | : No exit |

**(3)**
| | |
|---|---|
| Westbound | : No exit |
| Eastbound | : No access |

## M74 GLASGOW (continued)

**(7)**
| | |
|---|---|
| Northbound | : No exit |
| Southbound | : No access |

**(9)**
| | |
|---|---|
| Northbound | : No access |
| | : No exit |

**(10)**
| | |
|---|---|

**(11)**
| | |
|---|---|
| Northbound | : No exit |
| Southbound | : No access |

**(12)**
| | |
|---|---|
| Northbound | : Access only from A70 Northbound |
| Southbound | : Exit only to A70 Southbound |

## M77 GLASGOW

**Junction with M8**
| | |
|---|---|
| Northbound | : No exit to M8 (22) Westbound |
| Southbound | : No access from M8 (22) Eastbound |

**(4)**
| | |
|---|---|
| Northbound | : No exit |
| Southbound | : No access |

**(6)**
| | |
|---|---|
| Northbound | : No exit to A77 |
| Southbound | : No access from A77 |

**(7)**
| | |
|---|---|
| Northbound | : No access |
| | : No exit |

**(8)**
| | |
|---|---|
| Northbound | : No access |
| Southbound | : No access |

## M80 STIRLING

**(3)**
| | |
|---|---|
| Southbound | : No access |

**(5)**
| | |
|---|---|
| Northbound | : No access |
| | : No access from M876 |
| Southbound | : No exit |
| | : No exit to M876 |

## M90 EDINBURGH TO PERTH

**(2A)**
| | |
|---|---|
| Northbound | : No access |
| Southbound | : No access |

**(7)**
| | |
|---|---|
| Northbound | : No exit |
| Southbound | : No access |

**(8)**
| | |
|---|---|
| Northbound | : No access |
| Southbound | : No exit |

**(10)**
| | |
|---|---|
| Northbound | : No access from A912 |
| | : No exit to A912 Southbound |
| Southbound | : No access from A912 Northbound |
| | : No exit to A912 |

## M180 SCUNTHORPE

**(1)**
| | |
|---|---|
| Westbound | : No exit |
| Eastbound | : No access |

## M606 BRADFORD

**Straithgate Lane**
| | |
|---|---|
| Northbound | : No access |

## M621 LEEDS

**(2A)**
| | |
|---|---|
| Northbound | : No exit |
| Southbound | : No access |

**(5)**
| | |
|---|---|
| Northbound | : No access |
| Southbound | : No exit |

**(6)**
| | |
|---|---|
| Northbound | : No exit |
| Southbound | : No access |

## M876 FALKIRK

**Junction with M80**
| | |
|---|---|
| Westbound | : No exit to M80 (5) Northbound |
| Eastbound | : No access from M80 (5) Southbound |

**Junction with M9**
| | |
|---|---|
| Westbound | : No access |
| Eastbound | : No exit |

**(2)**
| | |
|---|---|
| Northbound | : No access |
| Southbound | : No exit |

# Motorway services information

All motorway service areas have fuel, food, toilets, disabled facilities and free short-term parking

**For further information on motorway services providers:**

| | | |
|---|---|---|
| Moto www.moto-way.com | RoadChef www.roadchef.com | Welcome Break www.welcomebreak.co.uk |
| Extra www.extraservices.co.uk | Westmorland www.westmorland.com | |

Motorway Services ½ m — Petrol

| Motorway | Junction | Service provider | Service name | Fuel supplier | Information | Accommodation | Conference facilities | Showers | M&S Simply Food | Costa Coffee | Starbucks | Burger King | KFC | McDonalds | Wimpy |
|---|---|---|---|---|---|---|---|---|---|---|---|---|---|---|---|
| **A1(M)** | 1 | Welcome Break | South Mimms | BP | ● | ● | ● | ● | | | ● | ● | ● | | |
| | 10 | Extra | Baldock | Shell | | ● | ● | | ● | ● | | | ● | ● | |
| | 17 | Extra | Peterborough | Shell | ● | ● | | ● | ● | | | | ● | ● | |
| | 34 | Moto | Blyth | Esso | ● | ● | | | ● | | | | | | |
| | 46 | Moto | Wetherby | BP | | | ● | ● | ● | ● | | ● | | | |
| | 61 | RoadChef | Durham | Total | ● | ● | ● | | | ● | | | | | |
| | 64 | Moto | Washington | BP | ● | ● | | | | ● | | ● | | | |
| **A74(M)** | 16 | RoadChef | Annandale Water | BP | ● | ● | | ● | | | | | | | |
| | 22 | Welcome Break | Gretna Green | BP | ● | ● | | ● | | | ● | ● | ● | | |
| **M1** | 2-4 | Welcome Break | London Gateway | Shell | ● | ● | | | ● | ● | | | ● | | |
| | 11-12 | Moto | Toddington | BP | | ● | | ● | ● | ● | ● | | ● | | |
| | 14-15 | Welcome Break | Newport Pagnell | Shell | ● | ● | | ● | | ● | | ● | ● | | |
| | 15A | RoadChef | Northampton | BP | | ● | | | | | | | | | |
| | 16-17 | RoadChef | Watford Gap | BP | ● | ● | | ● | | ● | | | | ● | |
| | 21-21A | Welcome Break | Leicester Forest East | BP | ● | ● | | ● | ● | ● | | ● | ● | ● | |
| | 22 | Moto | Leicester | BP | ● | ● | | ● | | ● | | | ● | | |
| | 23A | Moto | Donington Park | BP | ● | ● | | ● | ● | ● | | ● | | | |
| | 25-26 | Moto | Trowell | BP | ● | ● | | ● | ● | ● | | ● | | | |
| | 28-29 | RoadChef | Tibshelf | Shell | ● | ● | ● | | | ● | | | | | |
| | 30-31 | Welcome Break | Woodall | Shell | ● | ● | | | | | ● | ● | ● | ● | |
| | 38-39 | Moto | Woolley Edge | Esso | ● | ● | | ● | ● | ● | | ● | | | |
| **M2** | 4-5 | Moto | Medway | BP | | ● | | ● | | ● | | | | | |
| **M3** | 4A-5 | Welcome Break | Fleet | Shell | ● | ● | ● | | | ● | | ● | ● | ● | |
| | 8-9 | Moto | Winchester | Shell | | ● | | | ● | | ● | | | | |
| **M4** | 3 | Moto | Heston | BP | ● | ● | ● | ● | ● | ● | | ● | | | |
| | 11-12 | Moto | Reading | BP | ● | ● | ● | ● | ● | ● | | ● | | | |
| | 13 | Moto | Chieveley | BP | ● | ● | | ● | | ● | | | | | |
| | 14-15 | Welcome Break | Membury | BP | ● | ● | | ● | ● | ● | | ● | ● | ● | |
| | 17-18 | Moto | Leigh Delamere | Esso | ● | ● | ● | ● | ● | ● | | ● | | | |
| | 23A | First | Magor | Esso | ● | ● | | ● | ● | ● | | ● | | | |
| | 30 | Welcome Break | Cardiff Gate | Total | | ● | | ● | | | | ● | ● | | |
| | 33 | Moto | Cardiff West | Esso | | ● | | ● | | | | ● | | | |
| | 36 | Welcome Break | Sarn Park | Shell | | ● | | ● | | ● | | ● | | | |
| | 47 | Moto | Swansea | BP | ● | ● | | | | ● | | | | | |
| | 49 | RoadChef | Pont Abraham | Texaco | ● | | | | | ● | | | | | |
| **M5** | 3-4 | Moto | Frankley | Esso | | ● | | ● | ● | ● | | ● | | | |
| | 8 | RoadChef | Strensham (South) | BP | | ● | | | ● | | | | ● | | |
| | 8 | RoadChef | Strensham (North) | BP | | ● | ● | | | | ● | | | | |
| | 13-14 | Welcome Break | Michaelwood | BP | ● | ● | | ● | ● | ● | | ● | | | |
| | 19 | Welcome Break | Gordano | Shell | ● | ● | | ● | ● | ● | | ● | ● | | |
| | 21-22 | RoadChef | Sedgemoor (South) | Total | ● | ● | | ● | ● | ● | | | | | |
| | 21-22 | Welcome Break | Sedgemoor (North) | Shell | ● | ● | | ● | ● | ● | | ● | | | |
| | 24 | Moto | Bridgwater | BP | ● | ● | | | ● | ● | | | | | |
| | 25-26 | RoadChef | Taunton Deane | Shell | ● | ● | | | | | | | | | |
| | 27 | Moto | Tiverton | Shell | ● | ● | | | | ● | | | | | |
| | 28 | Extra | Cullompton | Shell | | | | ● | | | | | ● | | |
| | 29-30 | Moto | Exeter | BP | ● | ● | | ● | ● | ● | | ● | | | |
| **M6** | 3-4 | Welcome Break | Corley | Shell | ● | ● | | ● | | ● | | ● | ● | ● | |
| | 10-11 | Moto | Hilton Park | BP | ● | ● | | ● | ● | ● | ● | | | | |
| | 14-15 | RoadChef | Stafford (South) | Esso | ● | ● | ● | | ● | ● | | | | ● | |
| | 14-15 | Moto | Stafford (North) | BP | ● | ● | | ● | ● | ● | | | | | |
| | 15-16 | Welcome Break | Keele | Shell | ● | ● | | | | ● | | ● | ● | ● | |
| | 16-17 | RoadChef | Sandbach | Esso | | ● | | | | | | | | | |
| | 18-19 | Moto | Knutsford | BP | ● | ● | | ● | ● | ● | | | | | |
| | 20 | Moto | Lymm | Total | ● | ● | | ● | | | | | | ● | |
| | 27-28 | Welcome Break | Charnock Richard | Shell | ● | ● | | ● | | ● | | ● | | | |
| | 32-33 | Moto | Lancaster | BP | ● | ● | | ● | ● | ● | | | | | |
| | 35A-36 | Moto | Burton-in-Kendal (N) | BP | ● | ● | | ● | | ● | | | | | |
| | 36-37 | RoadChef | Killington Lake (S) | BP | ● | ● | | ● | | | | | | | |
| | 38-39 | Westmorland | Tebay | Total | ● | ● | ● | | | | | | | | |
| | 41-42 | Moto | Southwaite | Esso | ● | ● | | ● | ● | ● | | ● | | | |
| | 44-45 | Moto | Todhills | BP/Shell | ● | ● | | | ● | | | | | | |
| **M6 Toll** | T6-T7 | RoadChef | Norton Canes | BP | ● | ● | ● | | | | | | | | |
| **M8** | 4-5 | BP | Heart of Scotland | BP | | | | ● | ● | ● | | | | | |
| **M9** | 9 | Moto | Stirling | BP | ● | ● | | ● | ● | ● | | | | | |
| **M11** | 8 | Welcome Break | Birchanger Green | Shell | ● | ● | ● | ● | | | | ● | ● | | |
| **M18** | 5 | Moto | Doncaster North | BP | ● | ● | | | | ● | | | | | |
| **M20** | 8 | RoadChef | Maidstone | Esso | ● | ● | | | | ● | | | | ● | |
| | 11 | Stop 24 | Stop 24 | Shell | ● | ● | | | | ● | | | | | |
| **M23** | 11 | Moto | Pease Pottage | Shell | ● | | | | | ● | | | | | |
| **M25** | 5-6 | RoadChef | Clacket Lane | Total | ● | ● | | ● | | ● | | | | ● | |
| | 9-10 | Extra | Cobham (opening 2012) | Shell | ● | ● | | | | ● | | | ● | ● | |
| | 23 | Welcome Break | South Mimms | BP | ● | ● | ● | | | | ● | | | | |
| | 30 | Moto | Thurrock | Esso | ● | ● | | ● | ● | ● | | ● | | | |
| **M27** | 3-4 | RoadChef | Rownhams | Esso | ● | | | | ● | | | | | ● | |
| **M40** | 2 | Extra | Beaconsfield | Shell | ● | ● | | | | ● | | | ● | ● | |
| | 8 | Welcome Break | Oxford | BP | ● | ● | ● | | | ● | | | ● | | |
| | 10 | Moto | Cherwell Valley | Esso | ● | ● | | ● | | ● | | | | | |
| | 12-13 | Welcome Break | Warwick | BP/Shell | ● | ● | ● | | | ● | | ● | | | |
| **M42** | 2 | Welcome Break | Hopwood Park | Shell | ● | | | ● | | ● | | | ● | | |
| | 10 | Moto | Tamworth | Esso | ● | ● | | ● | ● | ● | | ● | | | |
| **M48** | 1 | Moto | Severn View | BP | | ● | | | | | | | | | |
| **M54** | 4 | Welcome Break | Telford | Shell | ● | ● | | | | ● | | | | | |
| **M56** | 14 | RoadChef | Chester | Shell | ● | ● | | | ● | | | | | | |
| **M61** | 6-7 | Euro Garages | Bolton West | BP | ● | ● | | ● | | | | | | | |
| **M62** | 7-9 | Welcome Break | Burtonwood | Shell | ● | ● | | ● | | ● | | ● | ● | | |
| | 18-19 | Moto | Birch | Esso | ● | ● | ● | ● | ● | ● | | ● | | | |
| | 25-26 | Welcome Break | Hartshead Moor | Shell | ● | ● | | ● | | ● | | ● | | | |
| | 33 | Moto | Ferrybridge | Esso | ● | ● | | | ● | ● | | | | | |
| **M65** | 4 | Extra | Blackburn with Darwen | Shell | ● | ● | | | | ● | | | | ● | |
| **M74** | 4-5 | RoadChef | Bothwell (South) | BP | ● | ● | | ● | ● | ● | | | | | |
| | 5-6 | RoadChef | Hamilton (North) | BP | ● | ● | | ● | ● | ● | | | | | |
| | 11-12 | Cairn Lodge | Happendon | Shell | ● | ● | | | | | | | | | |
| | 12-13 | Welcome Break | Abington | Shell | ● | ● | | ● | | ● | | | | | |
| **M90** | 6 | Moto | Kinross | BP | ● | ● | | ● | | ● | | ● | | | |

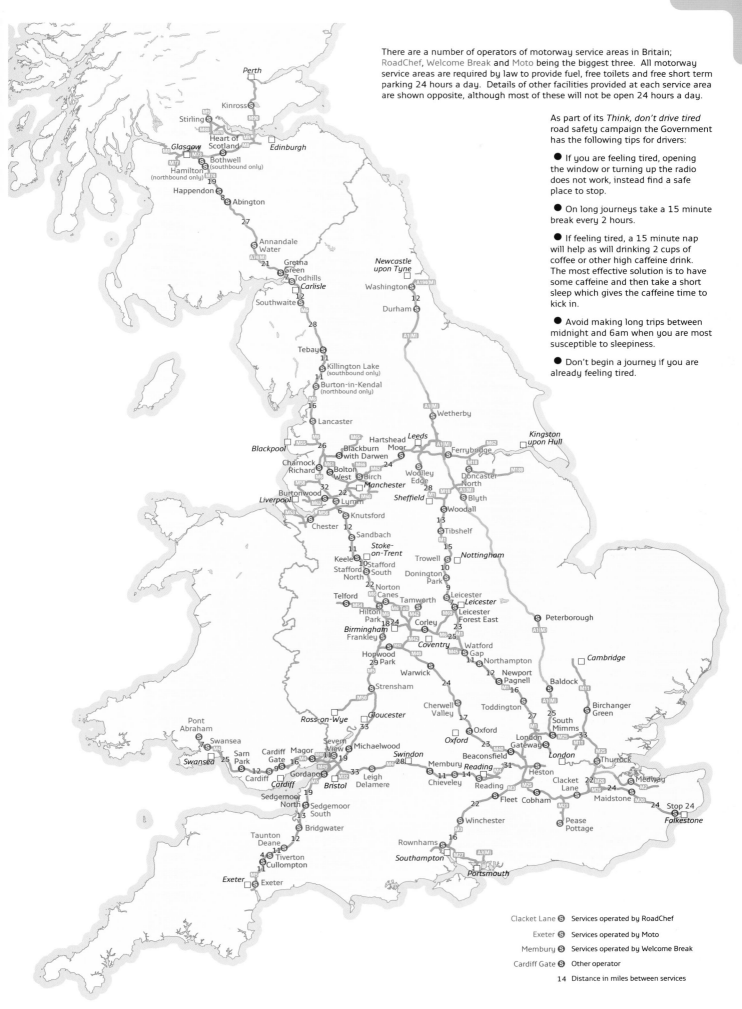

There are a number of operators of motorway service areas in Britain; RoadChef, Welcome Break and Moto being the biggest three. All motorway service areas are required by law to provide fuel, free toilets and free short term parking 24 hours a day. Details of other facilities provided at each service area are shown opposite, although most of these will not be open 24 hours a day.

As part of its *Think, don't drive tired* road safety campaign the Government has the following tips for drivers:

● If you are feeling tired, opening the window or turning up the radio does not work, instead find a safe place to stop.

● On long journeys take a 15 minute break every 2 hours.

● If feeling tired, a 15 minute nap will help as will drinking 2 cups of coffee or other high caffeine drink. The most effective solution is to have some caffeine and then take a short sleep which gives the caffeine time to kick in.

● Avoid making long trips between midnight and 6am when you are most susceptible to sleepiness.

● Don't begin a journey if you are already feeling tired.

Clacket Lane ⑤ Services operated by RoadChef
Exeter ⑤ Services operated by Moto
Membury ⑤ Services operated by Welcome Break
Cardiff Gate ⑤ Other operator
14 Distance in miles between services

# M25 orbital map

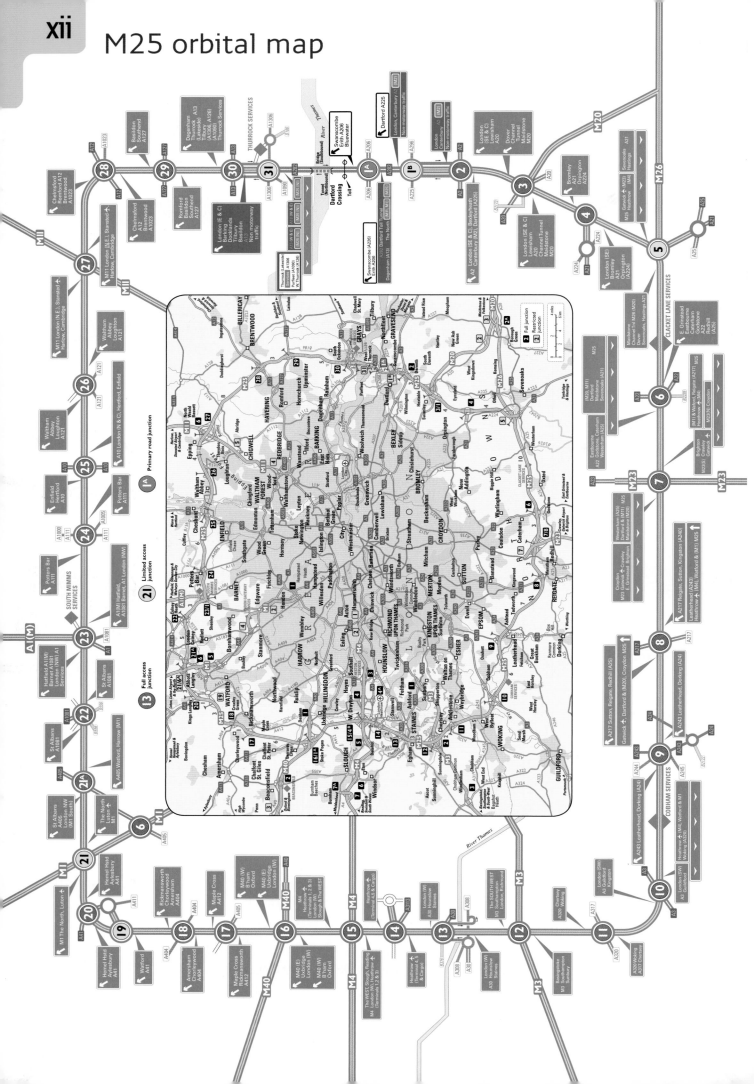

## M6 (North / left side, top to bottom)

**M6**

The SOUTH, B'ham
The S. WEST (M5)

The SOUTH M6 Toll

A4601

**11A** — A4601

A460 — M6 Toll

**T8** — A460

(M6 south)
A460 Wolverhampton

The NORTH WEST
(M6, North)
Stafford, telford — M6 Toll

**11**

A460 Wolverhampton
Cannock — A460

A460 Cannock

HILTON PARK SERVICES

**M54**

**10A**

M54 NORTH (& MID) WALES
Wolverhampton & Telford

The NORTH WEST & Stafford M6

A454 Walsall

**10** — A454

A454 — A454

A454 Walsall, W'hampton
(Cent. & East)

The North West, Telford (M54),
W'hampton (N) M6

A461 Wednesbury

The SOUTH & Birmingham M6

**9** — A4148

A461 — A461

A461 Wednesbury

The NORTH WEST,
Walsall & W'hampton M6

M6

London (M1 & M40)
Birmingham
(N, E & Cen.) N.E.C. & M6

The SOUTH WEST
M5 Birmingham (W & S)
West Bromwich

M5   M6   M6

**8**

**8**

M6
London (M1 & M40)
Birmingham (N & E)

The NORTH WEST
Walsall
Wolverhampton M6

**8** — A41 — A41

A41 West Bromwich,
Sandwell & B'ham (N & W)

The SOUTH WEST
& Birmingham (W & S) M5

**1**

A41 West Bromwich & B'ham (NW)

The NORTH (M1 & M6),
Birmingham (N), N.E.C. M5

M5

A4123 Birmingham (W)
& Dudley

The SOUTH WEST
& Birmingham (S) M5

**2** — A4123 — A4123

A4123 Dudley, W'hampton
& Sandwell

The NORTH (M1 & M6),
Birmingham (N) M5

A456 Kidderminster

The SOUTH WEST
& Birmingham (S) M5

**3** — A456 — A456

A456 Birmingham (W & Cen)

FRANKLEY SERVICES

A38 B'ham (SW)
Bromsgrove — A38

**4** — A491

A38 Birmingham (SW),
A491 Stourbridge

M42   M42   M5
London (M40)   &   The SOUTH WEST
N.E.C. &   M5   Worcester

**M5**

A38

**4A** — M42

M5   M5
The NORTH EAST (M1)   The NORTH WEST
London (M40)   (M6)
N.E.C. &   B'ham (W, N & Cen)

M42
The NORTH EAST (M1),   M42   M5
London (M40)   &   The NORTH WEST
N.E.C. &   M5   B'ham (W,N & Cen)
Stourbridge (M6)

A38 — A38 Bromsgrove

**M5**

## M6 Toll (North / top)

**M6 Toll**

A5148 Lichfield, (A38) Burton

The SOUTH, Tamworth M6 Toll

A5195 Brownhills, Burntwood

The SOUTH, Lichfield M6 Toll

A5   A460

**T7** — A34

Toll

NORTON CANES SERVICES

A5

A34

A5195 — A5195 Brownhills, Burntwood

**T6** — Toll

A34 Walsall, Cannock
A460 Rugeley
TOLLS

A34

**T5** — A5

Toll

The NORTH WEST
(M6 North), Cannock M6 Toll

A5   Tamworth (M42 North)

The SOUTH, Birmingham
Sutton Coldfield M6 Toll

A5   A38

**T4** — A5

Toll

A5127

A38 Burton, Lichfield
A5 Tamworth

The NORTH WEST
(M6 North), Cannock M6 Toll

A38
Birmingham
Sutton Coldfield

M6 Toll
London, Coventry,
(M6, M42)

A38

**T3** — Tolls — A38

A446
(M42 North)
Coleshill

M6 Toll
London, Coventry,
(M6, M42(S))

A446

**T2** — A4091

A446

## M42 (East / right side)

**T1** — A446   M42

A4097

**9** — A446

A446

**M42**

A4097   M42   The N. EAST (M1),   The NORTH WEST
A446   Tamworth   Cannock, Lichfield   M6 Toll

A38(M) & A38
B'ham (E, Cen, & NE)
& Lichfield

London (M1 & M40)
N.E.C. & B'ham M6

M42   M42   M6
The NORTH (M1)   &   LONDON (M1)
The SOUTH (M40)   M6   Coventry
&   N.E.C.

**8**
M6(N)   M42
Birmingham   The SOUTH WEST (M5)
(Cen, E, N & W)   (M6, South M40)
Birmingham (S), N.E.C.
& London, Coventry

A446
M42
The SOUTH WEST (M5)
B'ham (S), N.E.C. &
London, (S & W), (M40)
Coventry (S & W)

M42
London (N & E) (M1)
Coventry (N & E)

M6

**7A**

M6 London (M1), Coventry

The N. WEST (M6Toll)   M42
The N. EAST (M1), Tamworth

M6 The NORTH WEST, B'ham

The NORTH WEST (M6Toll)   M42
The NORTH EAST (M1)

**7** — **4** — M6 — **3A**

A446

A45 B'ham (S.E.)   N.E.C. Coventry

The SOUTH WEST (M5),
LONDON (M40),
Birmingham (SE), Solihull   M42

A45 B'ham (S.E.)
N.E.C., Coventry (S & W)

The NORTH, B'ham (E,N & Cen),
Coventry (N & E)   M42

**6** — A45

A41   Solihull

A41   Solihull

**5** — A4141

A3400   Henley-in-Arden

A34   Shirley

**4** — A3400

M42
London,
Warwick,
Stratford

M42
The SOUTH WEST
(M5),
Birmingham (S & W)

**M42**

## M42 (South / bottom)

The NORTH
M42 Solihull, B'ham (E)   M42   M42
N.E.C. &   &   Warwick
M40   Stratford

**3A** — **M42** — **M40**

A38

A441 Birmingham (S)

HOPWOOD PARK SERVICES

A435 B'ham (S), Redditch
Evesham

A435

**1** — **2** — **3**

A441   A441 Birmingham (S)   A435 B'ham (S), Redditch
Evesham

## Legend

**3** Full access junction

**4A** Limited access junction

**T4** Full access junction M6 Toll

**T1** Limited access junction M6 Toll

(Inset maps showing WALSALL, DUDLEY, WEST BROMWICH, BIRMINGHAM, HALESOWEN, SUTTON COLDFIELD, LICHFIELD, SOLIHULL, BIRMINGHAM INTERNATIONAL, etc.)

Full junction
Restricted junction

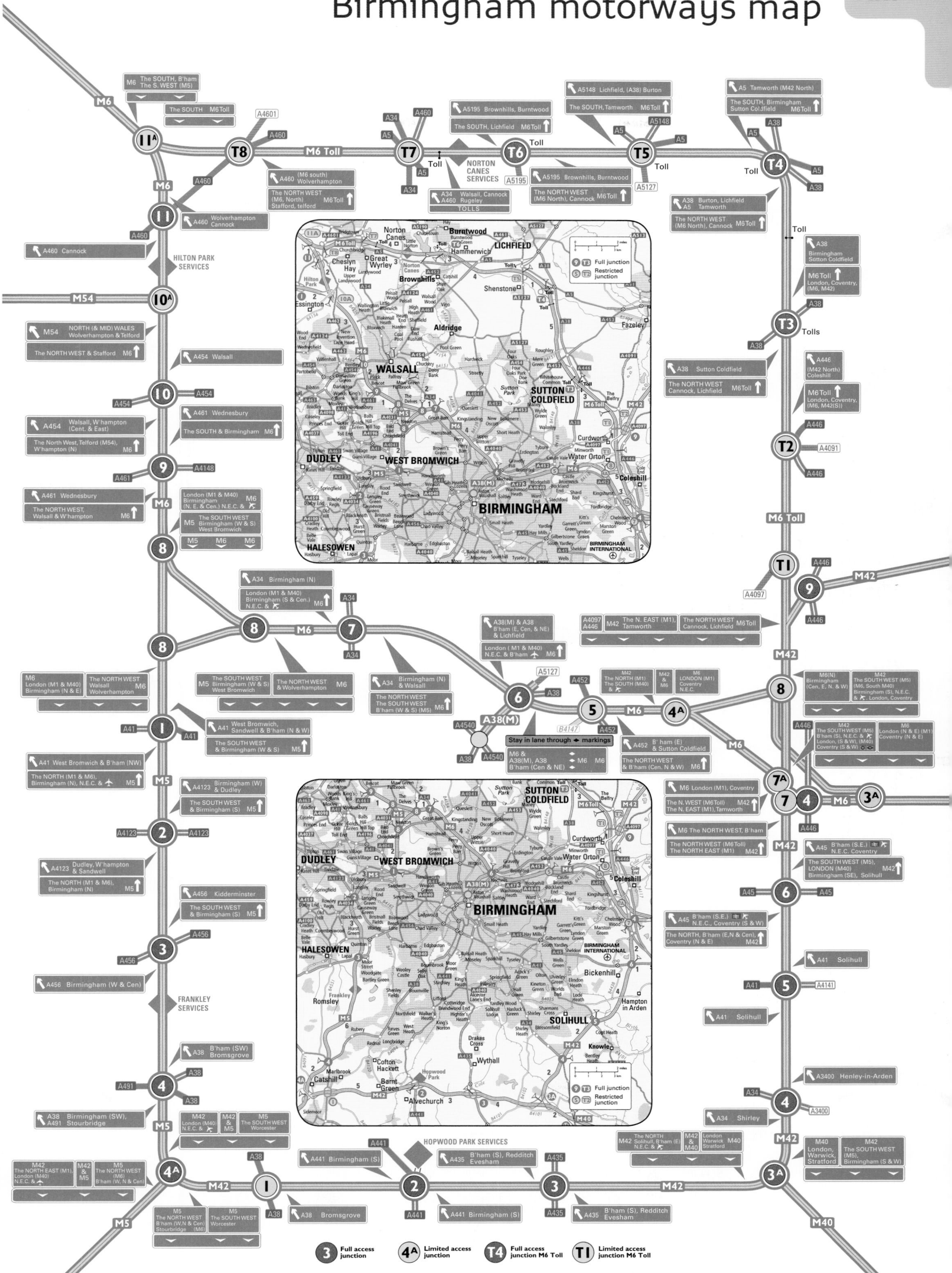

# Distance chart

Distances between two selected towns in this table are shown in miles and kilometres.
In general, distances are based on the shortest routes by classified roads.

## Distance in kilometres

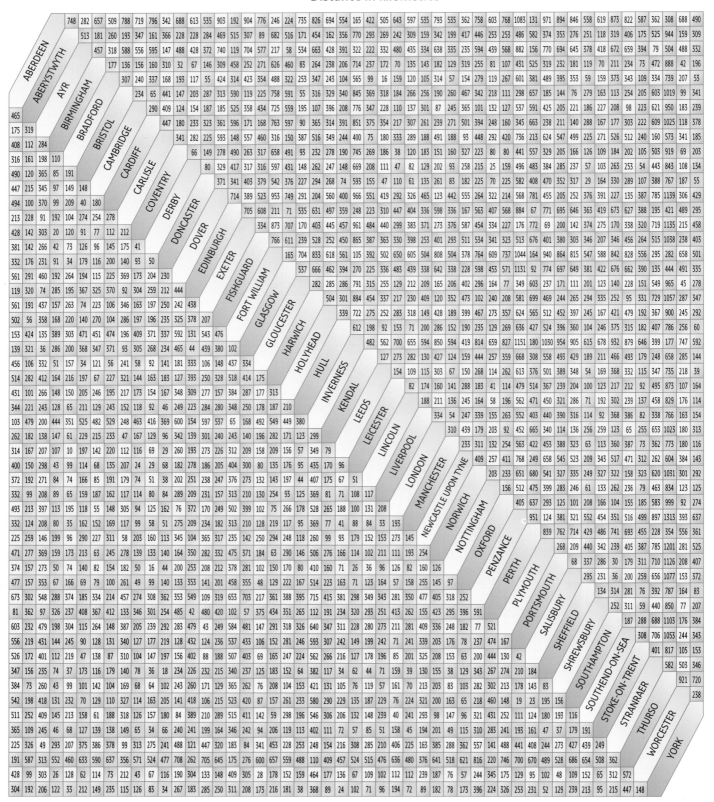

## Distance in miles

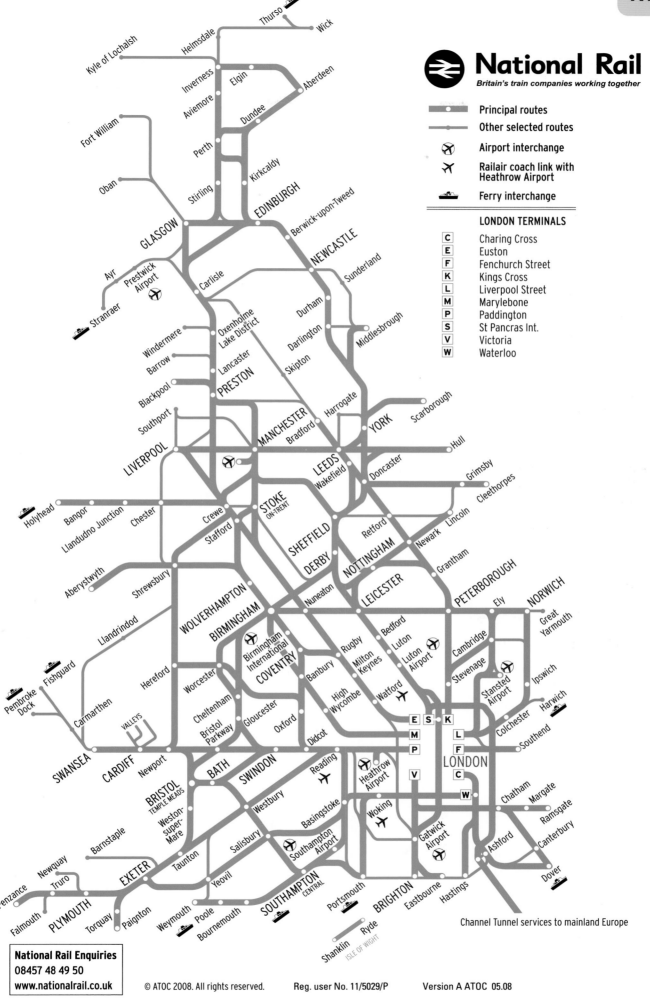

# Risk rating of Britain's motorways and A roads

EuroRAP
EUROPEAN ROAD ASSESSMENT PROGRAMME

This map shows the statistical risk of death or serious injury occurring on Britain's motorway and A road network for 2007-2009. Covering 45,000km in total, these roads represent just 11% of Britain's road length but carry 54% of the traffic. Half of Britain's fatal crashes occur on these roads.

The risk is calculated by comparing the frequency of road crashes resulting in death and serious injury on every stretch of road with how much traffic each road is carrying. For example, if there are 20 collisions on a road carrying 10,000 vehicles a day, the risk is 10 times higher than if the road has the same number of collisions but carries 100,000 vehicles.

Some of the roads shown have had improvements made to them recently, but during the survey period the risk of a fatal or serious injury collision on the black road sections was more than 30 times higher than on the safest (green) roads.

For more information on the Road Safety Foundation go to **www.roadsafetyfoundation.org.**

For more information on the statistical background to this research, visit the EuroRAP website at **www.eurorap.org.**

## Road Assessment Programme Risk Rating

Low risk (safest) roads

Low-medium risk roads

Medium risk roads

Medium-high risk roads

High risk roads

Motorway

Single and dual carriageway

Linking roads

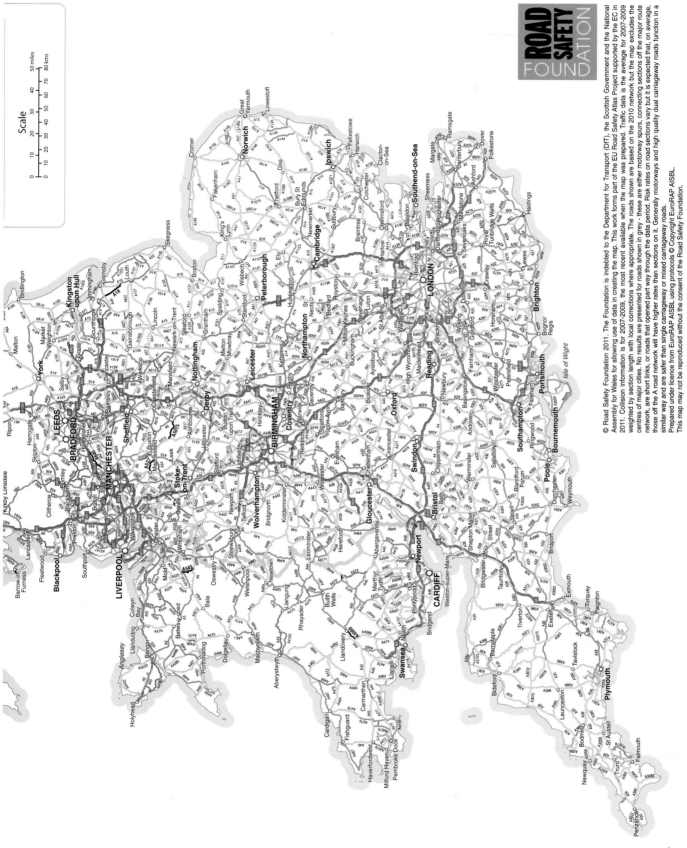

Scale

## Symbols used on the map

Blue place of interest symbols e.g ★ are listed on page 93

Motorway junction with full / limited access

Motorway service area

**M6 Toll** Toll motorway

**A316** Primary route dual / single carriageway / junction / service area

**A4054** 'A' road dual / single carriageway

**B7078** 'B' road dual / single carriageway

Minor road dual / single carriageway

Restricted access road

Road proposed or under construction

Road tunnel

Roundabout

Toll / One way street

Level crossing

National Trail / Long Distance Route

Fixed safety camera / fixed average-speed safety camera. Speed shown by number within camera, a V indicates a variable limit.

Park and Ride site operated by bus / rail (runs at least 5 days a week)

Car ferry with destination

Foot ferry with destination

Airport

Railway line / Railway tunnel / Light railway line

Railway station / Light rail station

London Underground / London Overground stations

Glasgow Subway station

Extent of London congestion charging zone

Notable building

Hospital

Spot height (in metres) / Lighthouse

Built up area

Woodland / Park

National Park

Heritage Coast

**BRISTOL** County / Unitary Authority boundary and name

**SEE PAGE 68** Area covered by street map

### Urban approach maps

| | | | |
|---|---|---|---|
| Birmingham | 14-15 | Merseyside | 22-23 |
| Bournemouth | 3 | Middlesbrough | 29 |
| Bradford | 26-27 | Milton Keynes | 9 |
| Bristol | 8 | Newcastle upon Tyne | 28-29 |
| Cardiff | 7 | Newport | 7 |
| Coventry | 16 | Nottingham | 18-19 |
| Derby | 18-19 | Plymouth | 2 |
| Edinburgh | 32 | Portsmouth | 4-5 |
| Glasgow | 30-31 | Sheffield | 21 |
| Leeds | 26-27 | Southampton | 4-5 |
| Leicester | 17 | Stoke-on-Trent | 20 |
| Liverpool | 22-23 | Sunderland | 28-29 |
| London | 10-13 | Swansea | 6 |
| Manchester | 24-25 | West Midlands | 14-15 |

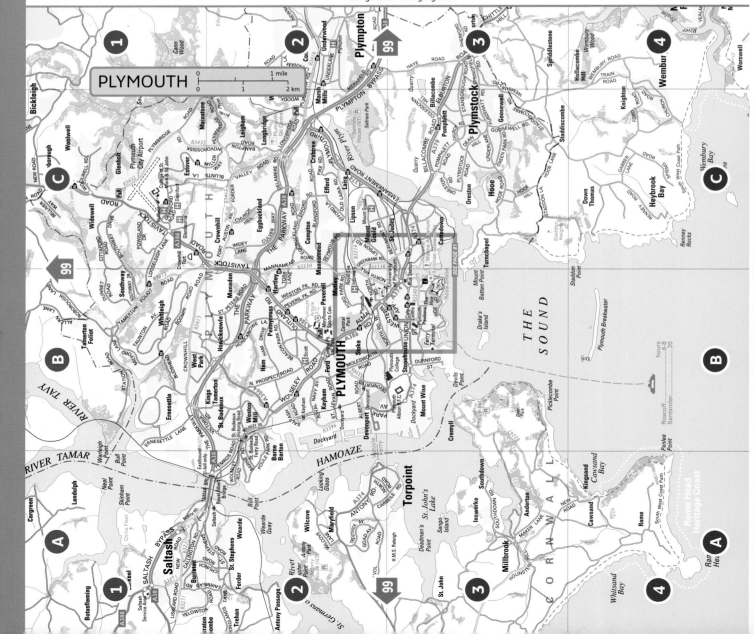

PLYMOUTH

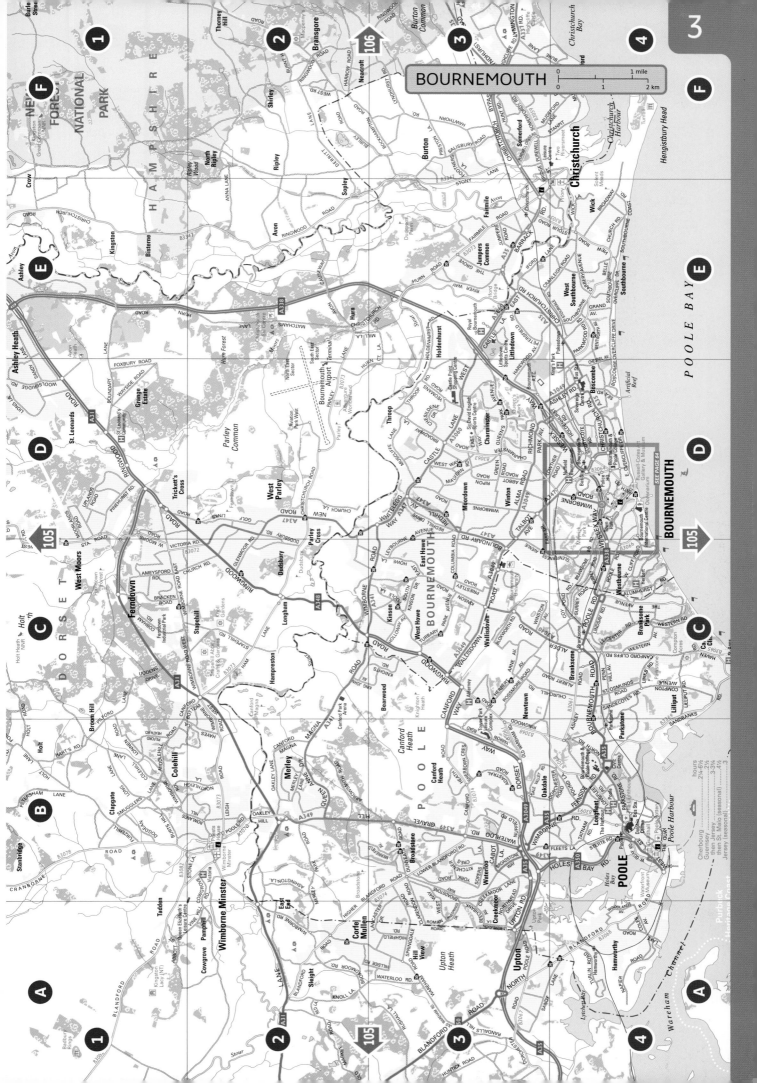

BOURNEMOUTH

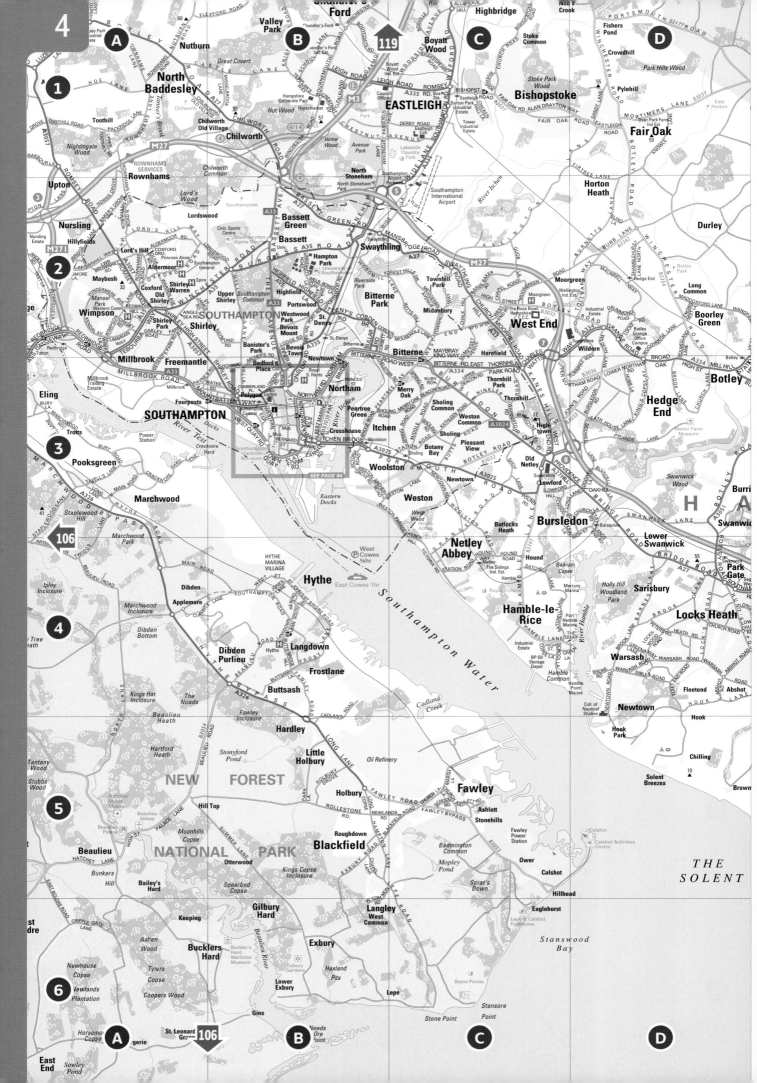

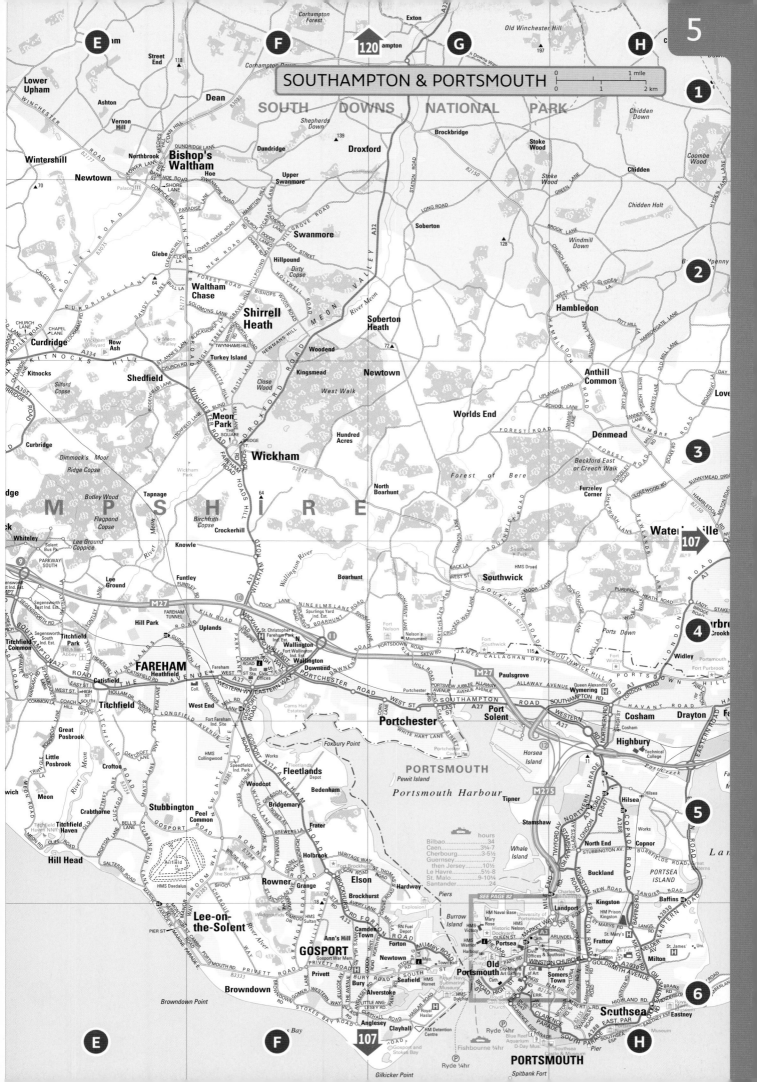

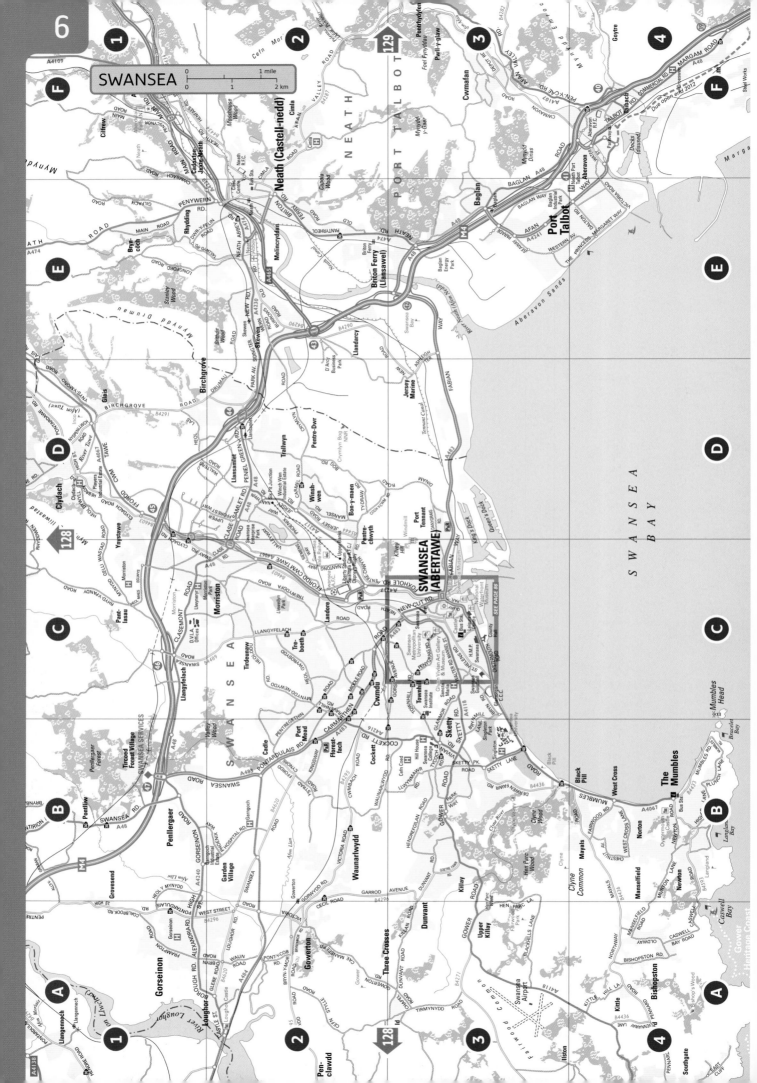

CARDIFF & NEWPORT

BRISTOL CHANNEL

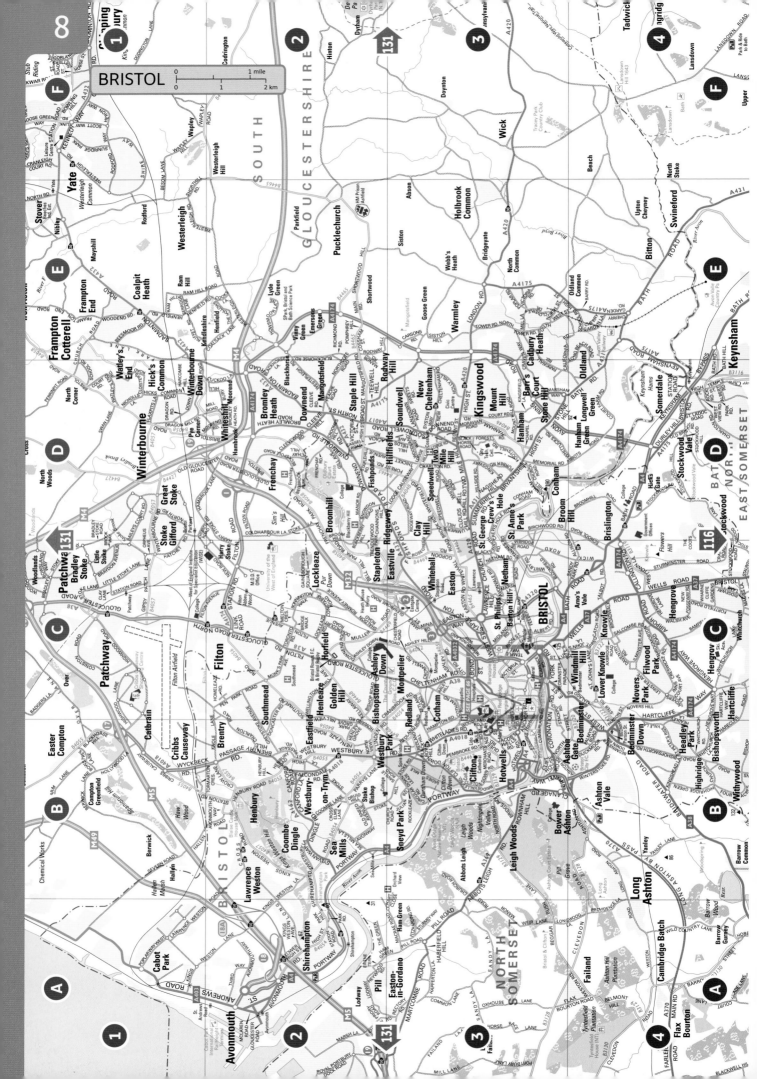

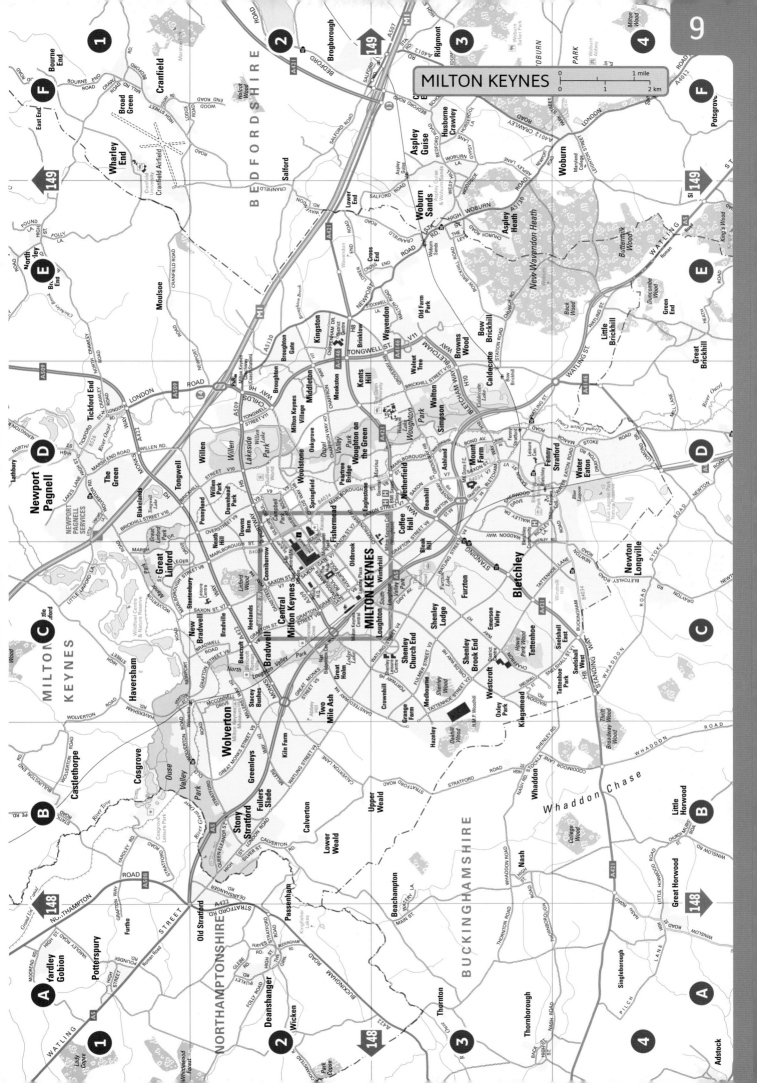

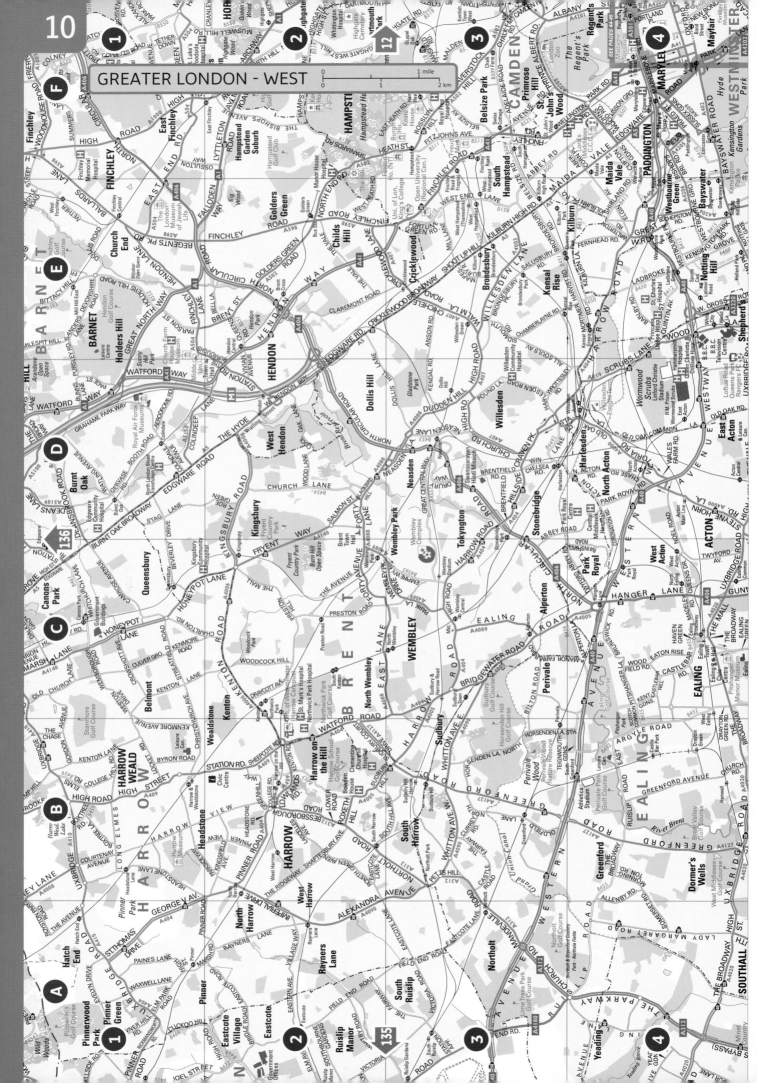

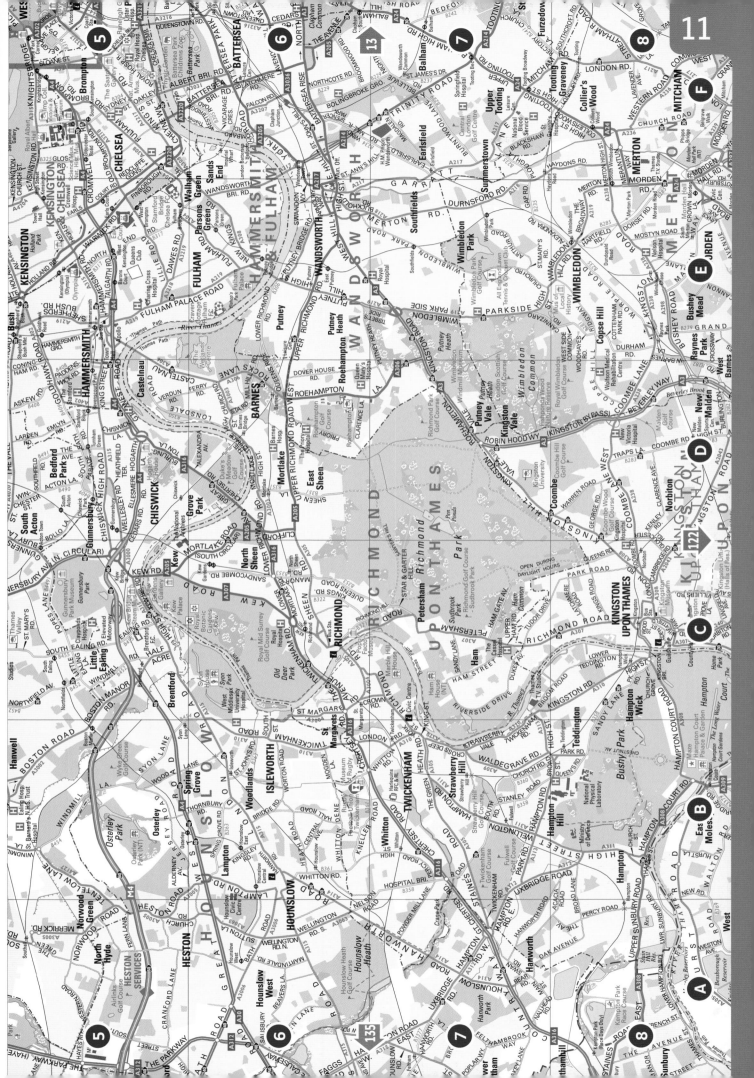

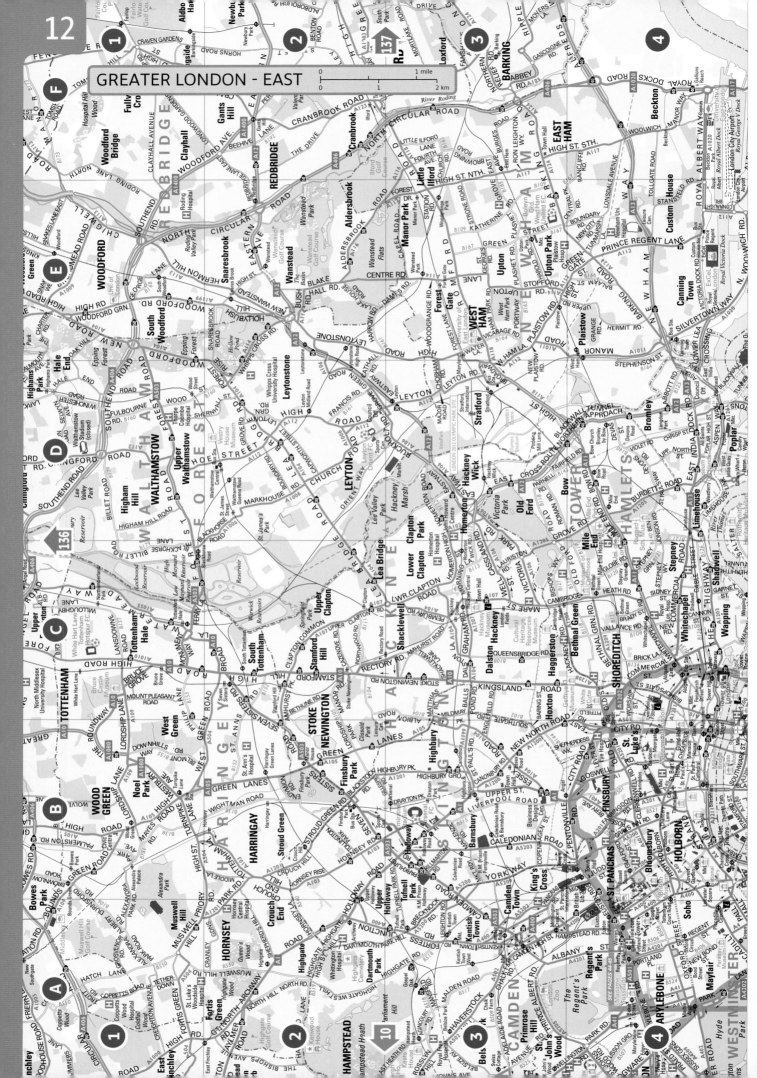

GREATER LONDON - EAST

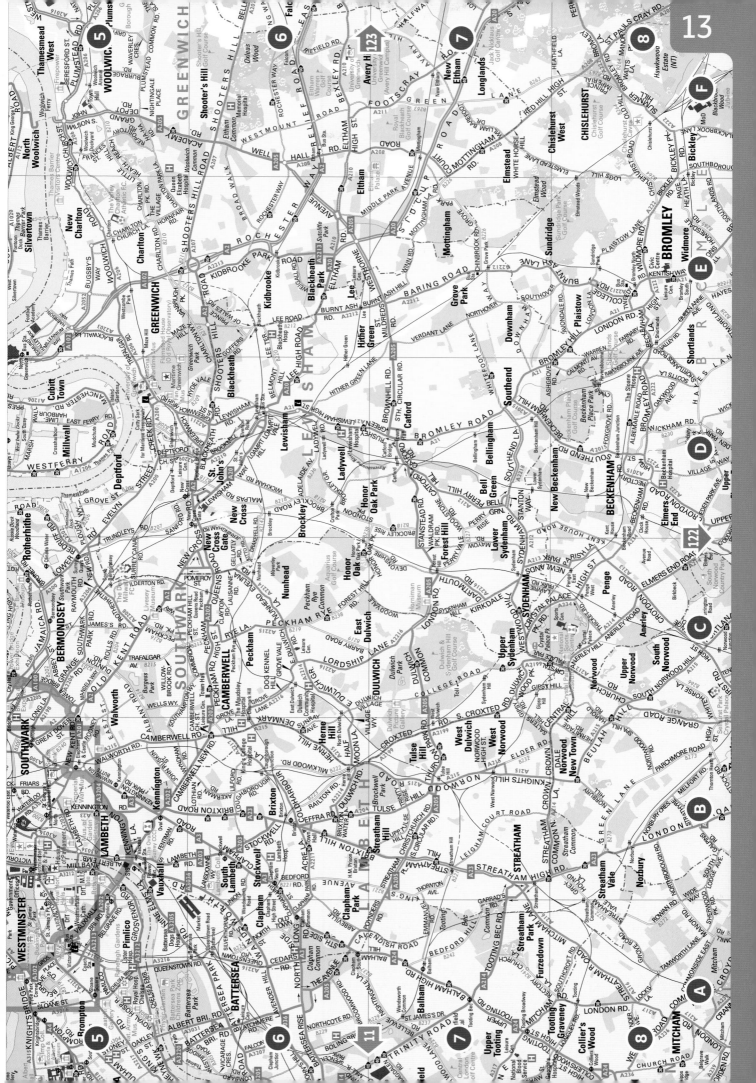

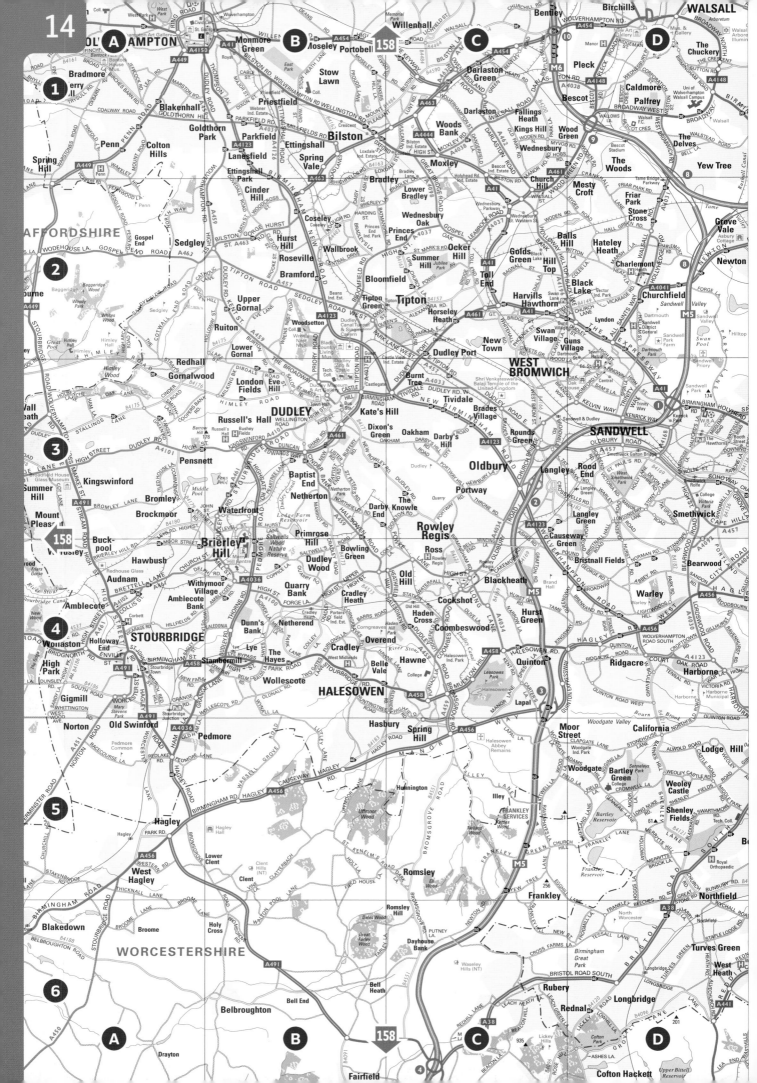

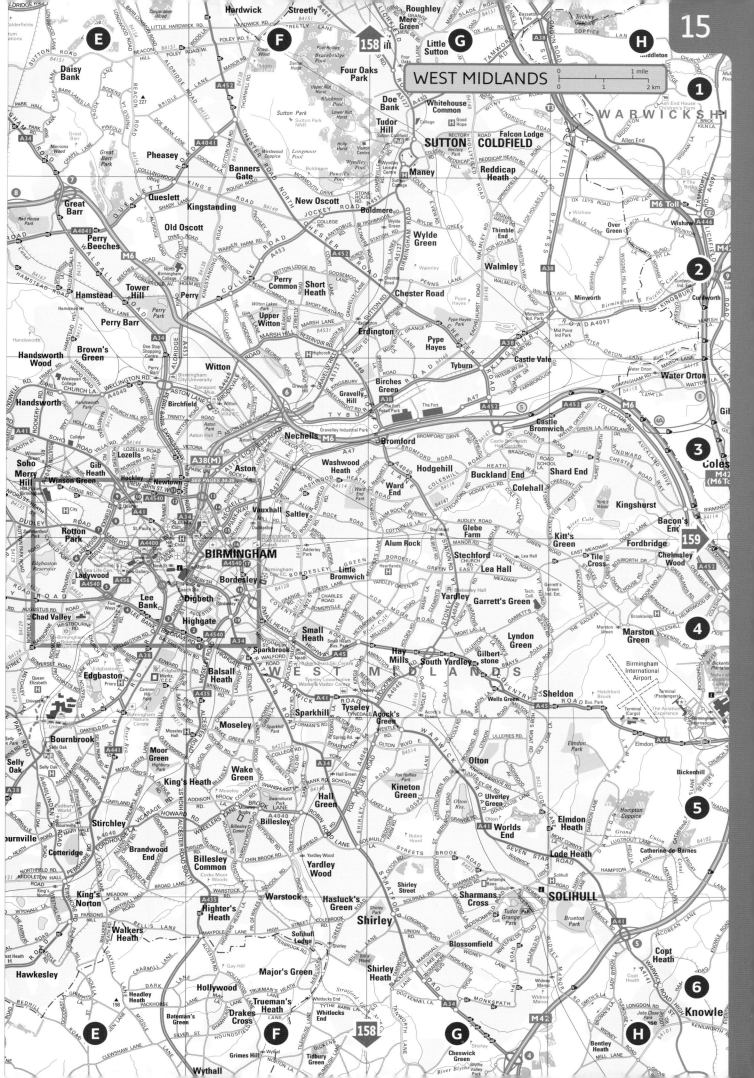

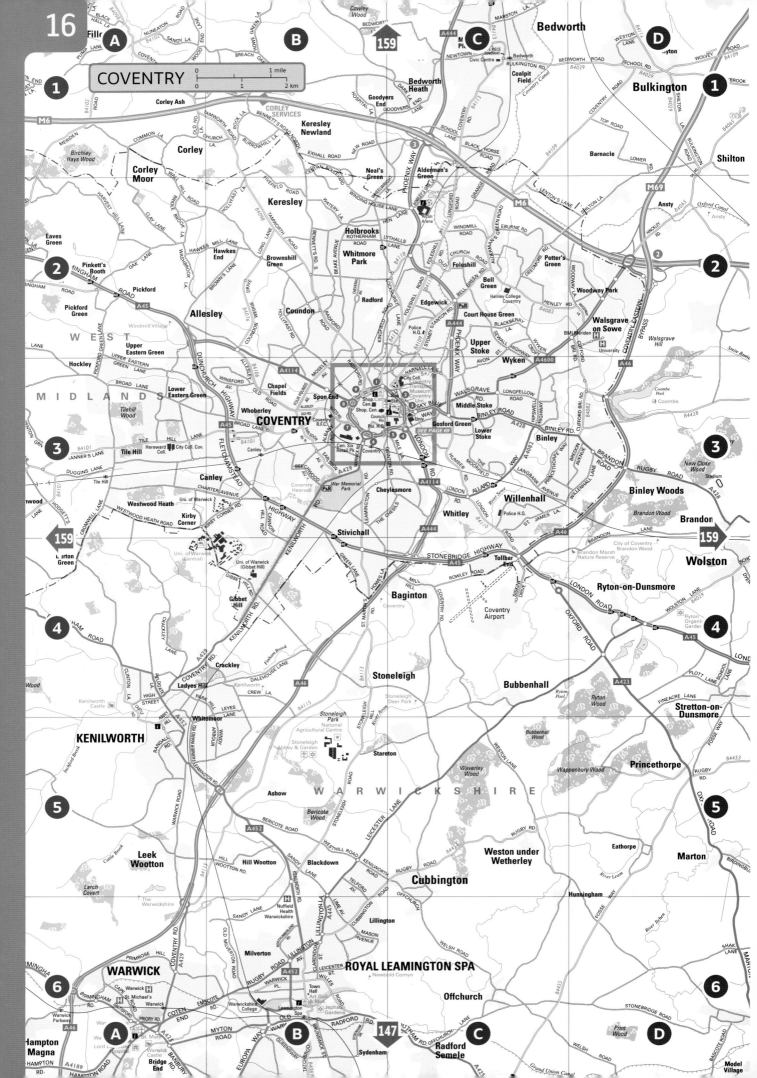

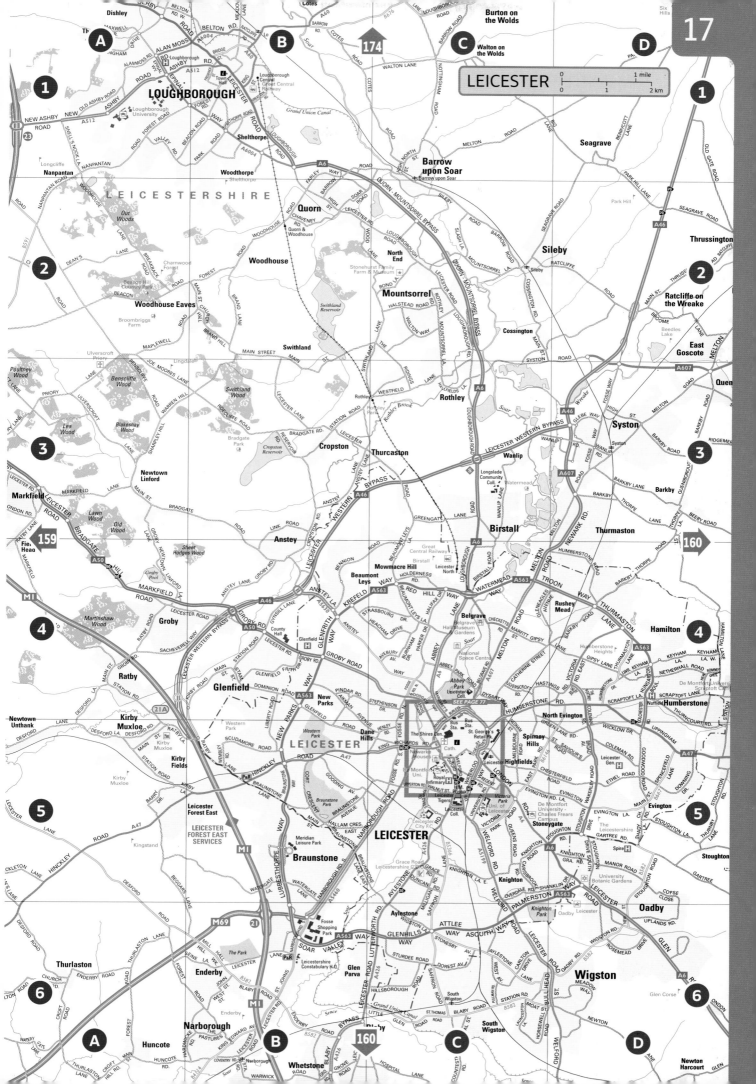

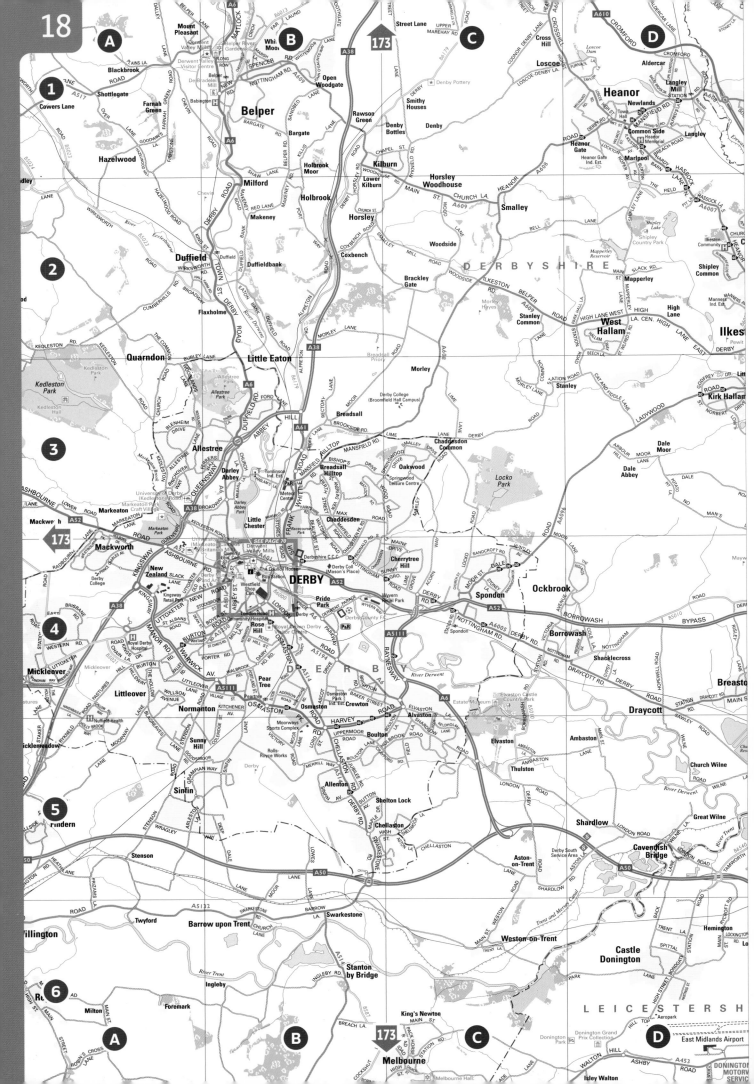

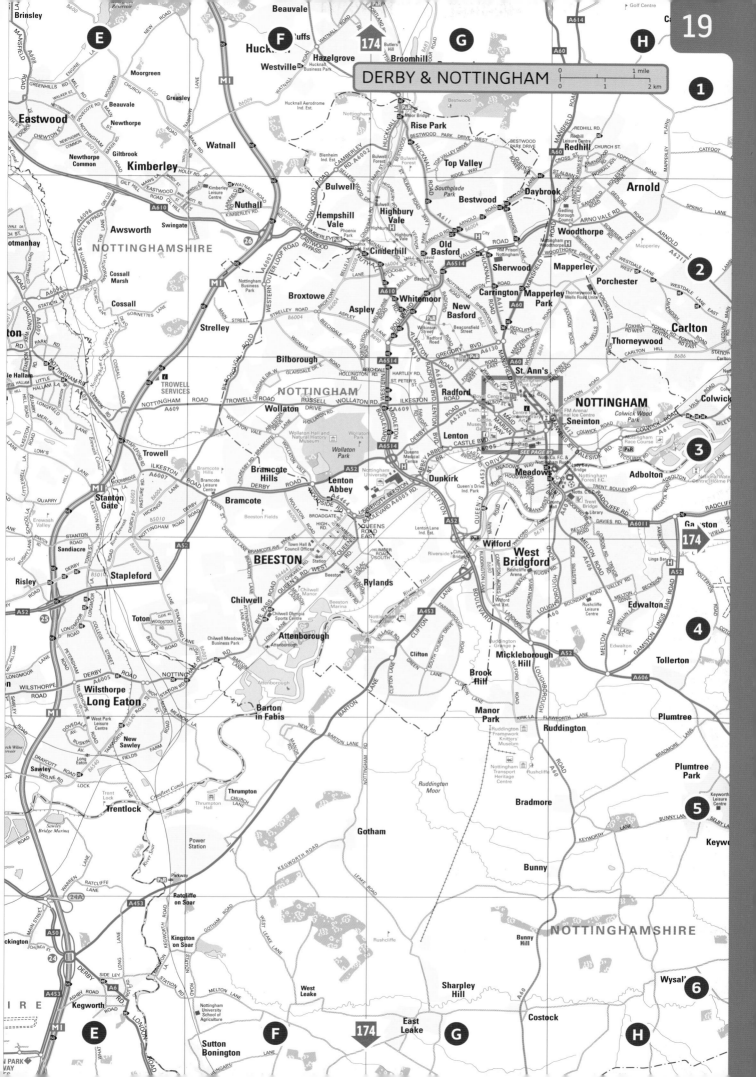

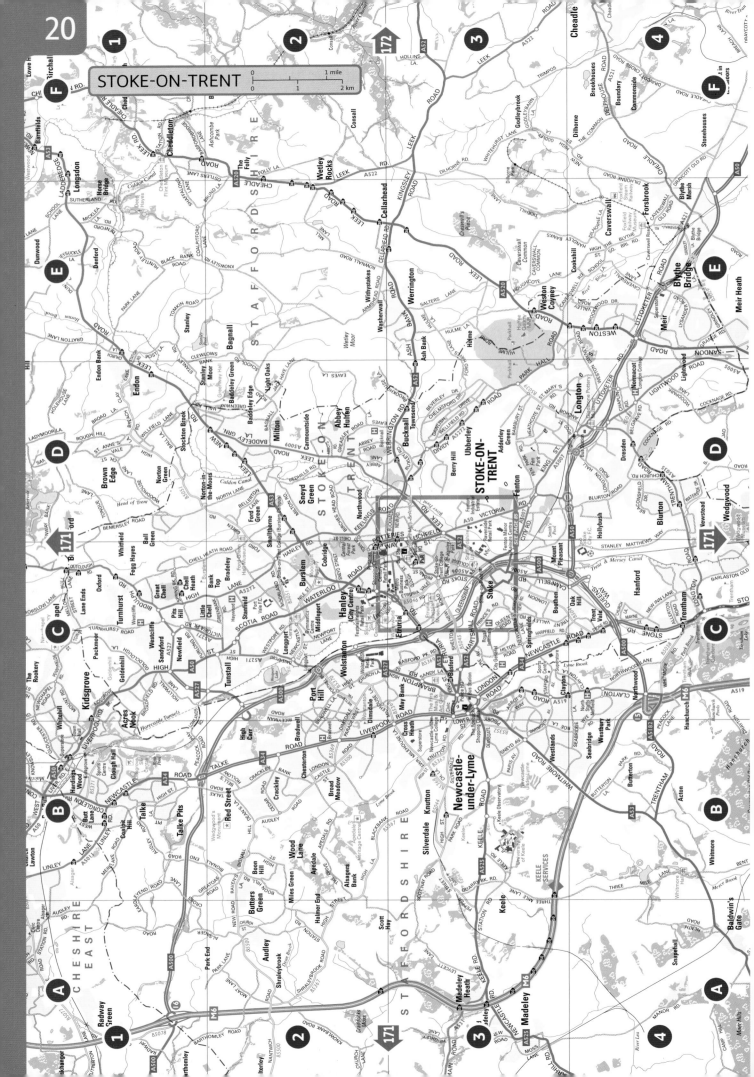

# STOKE-ON-TRENT

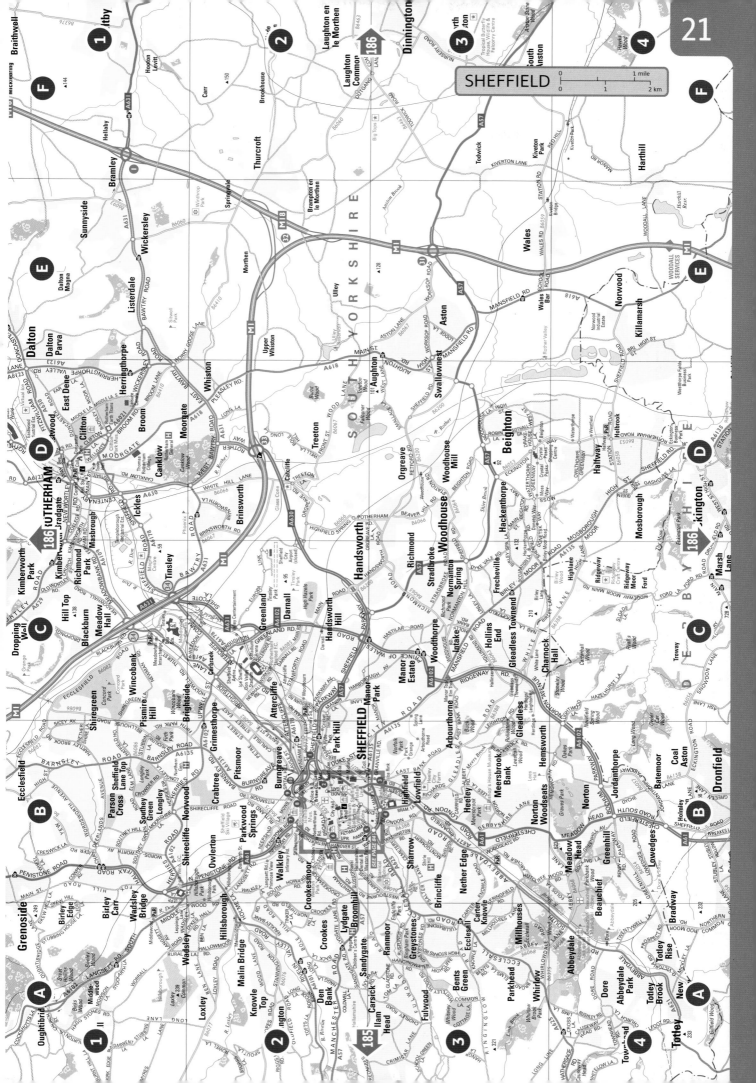

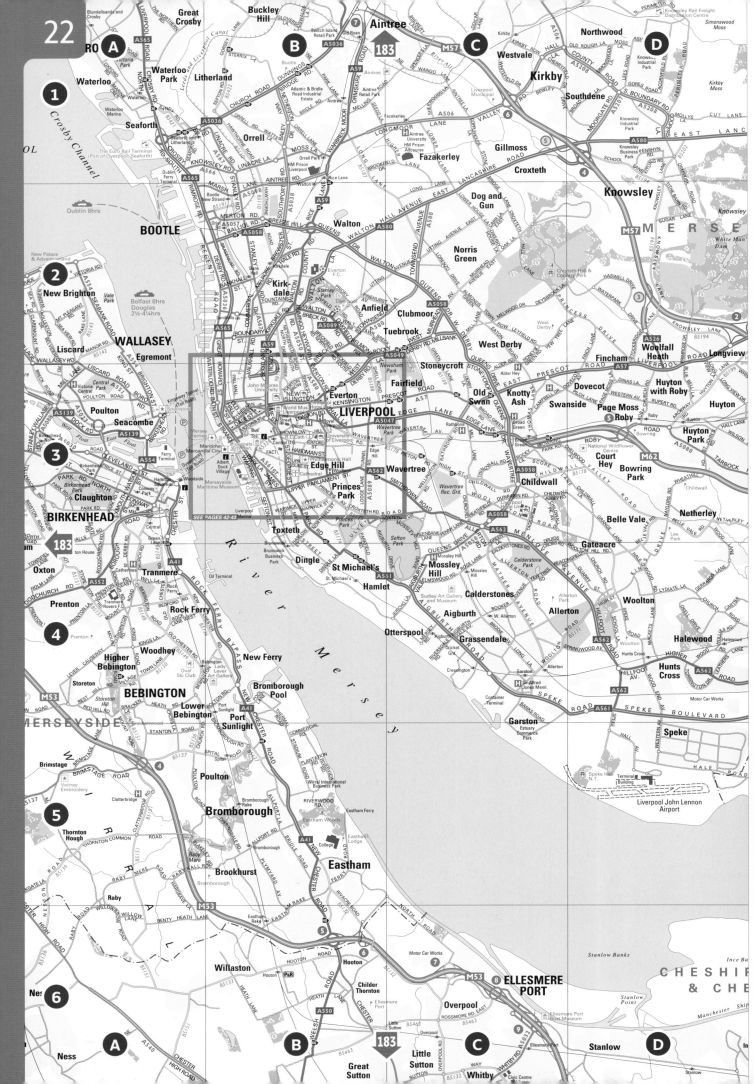

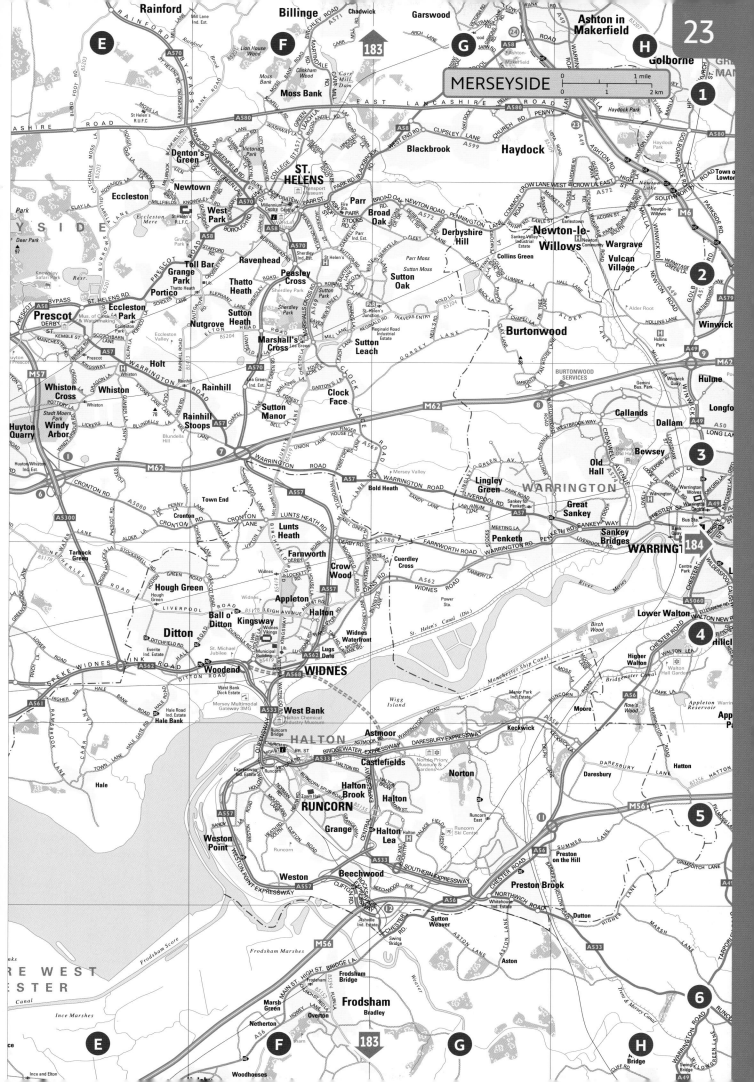

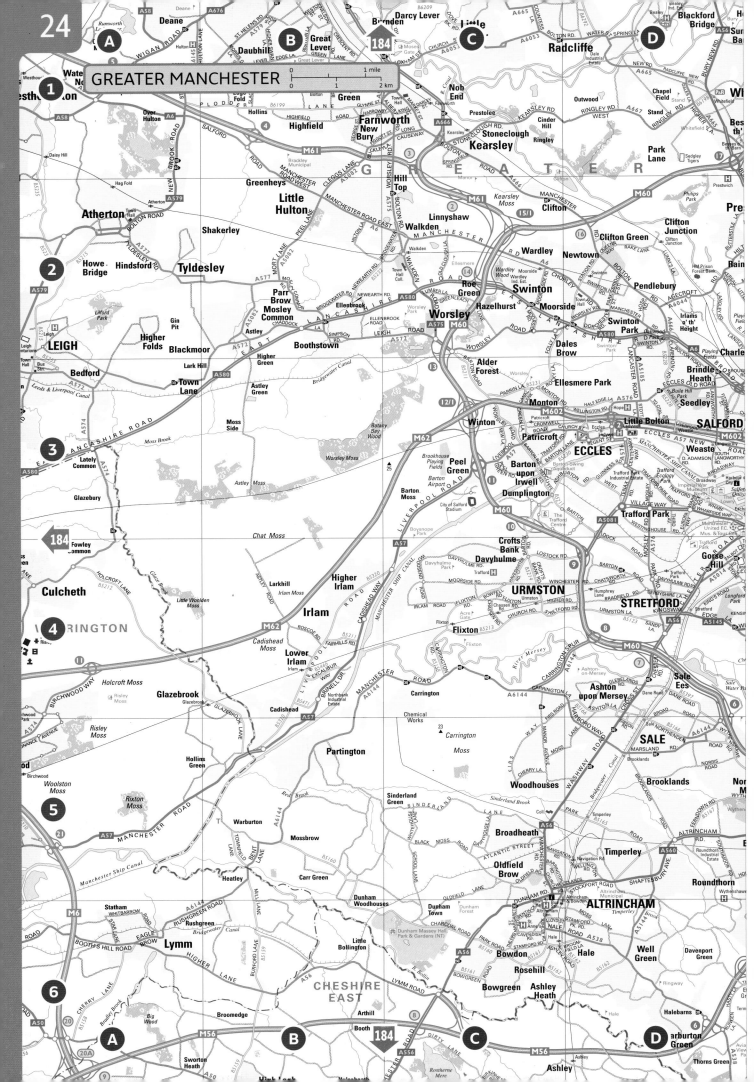

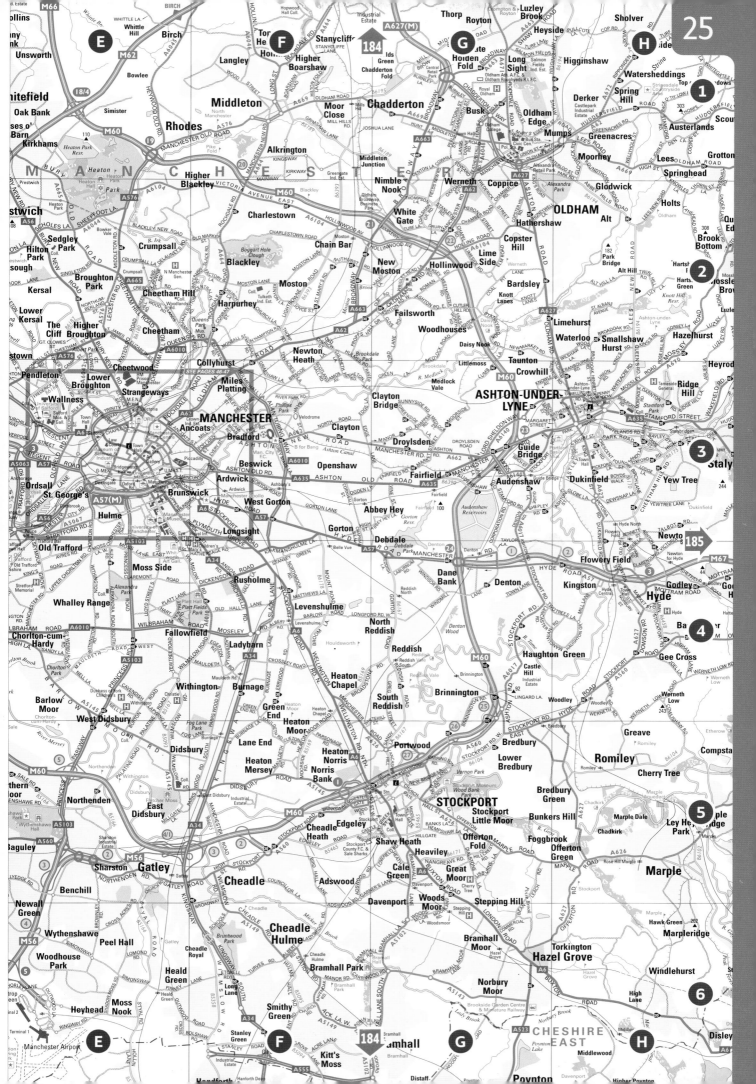

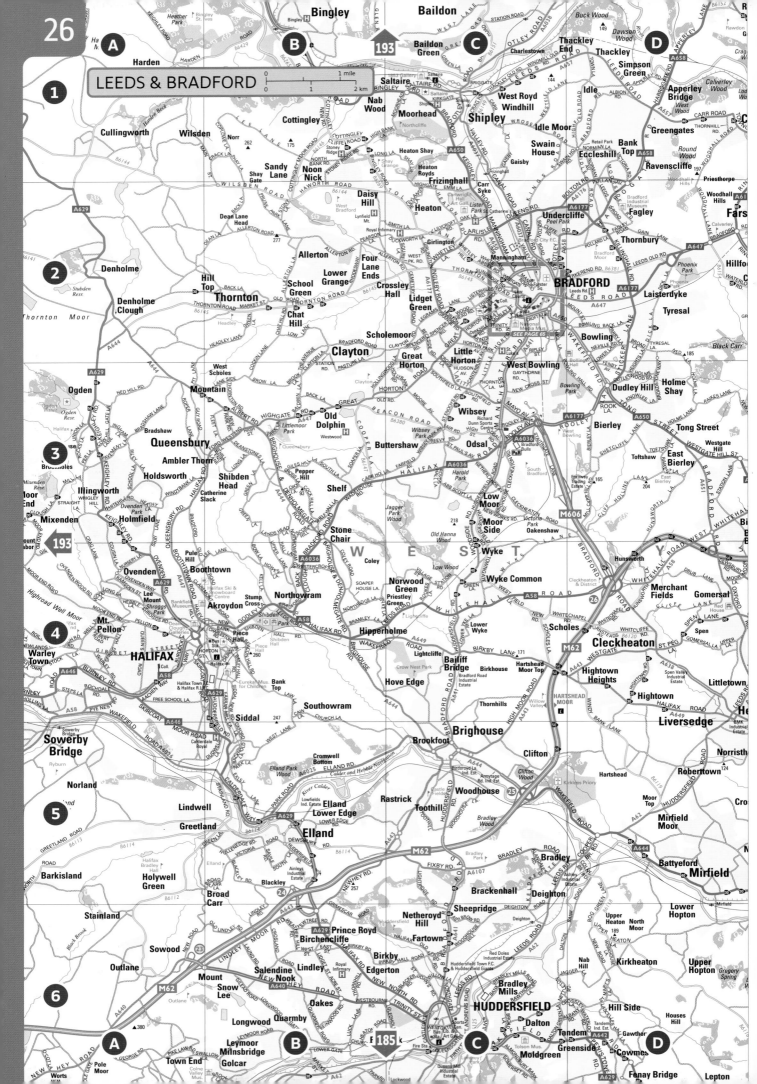

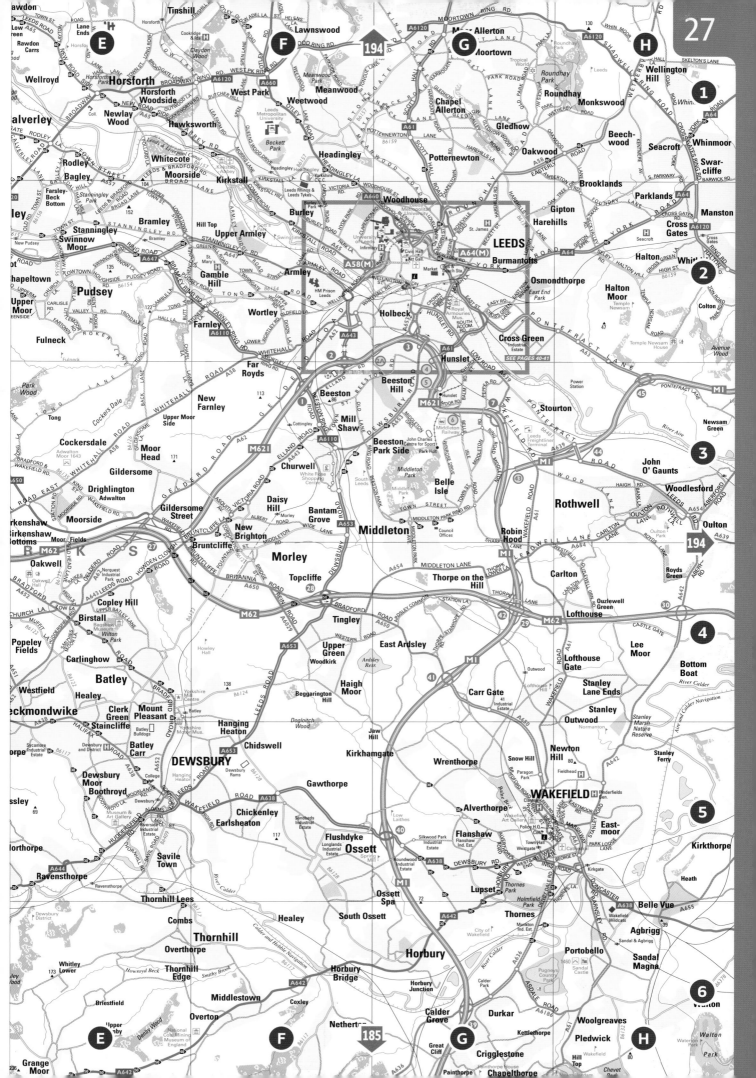

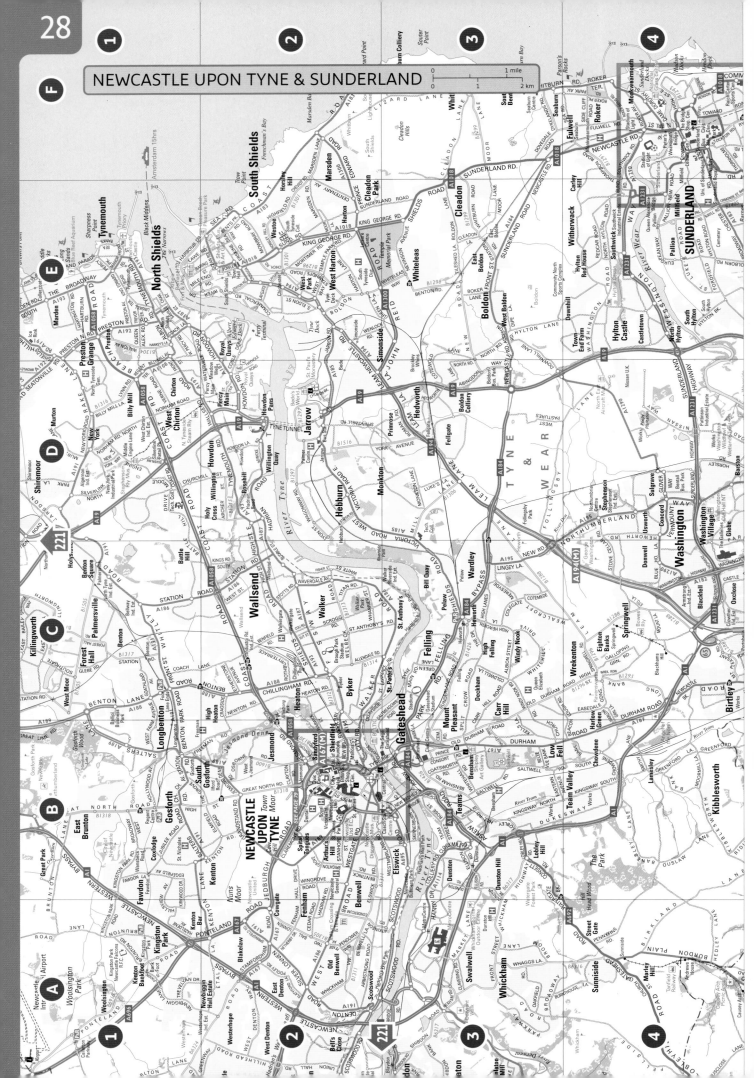

# NEWCASTLE UPON TYNE & SUNDERLAND

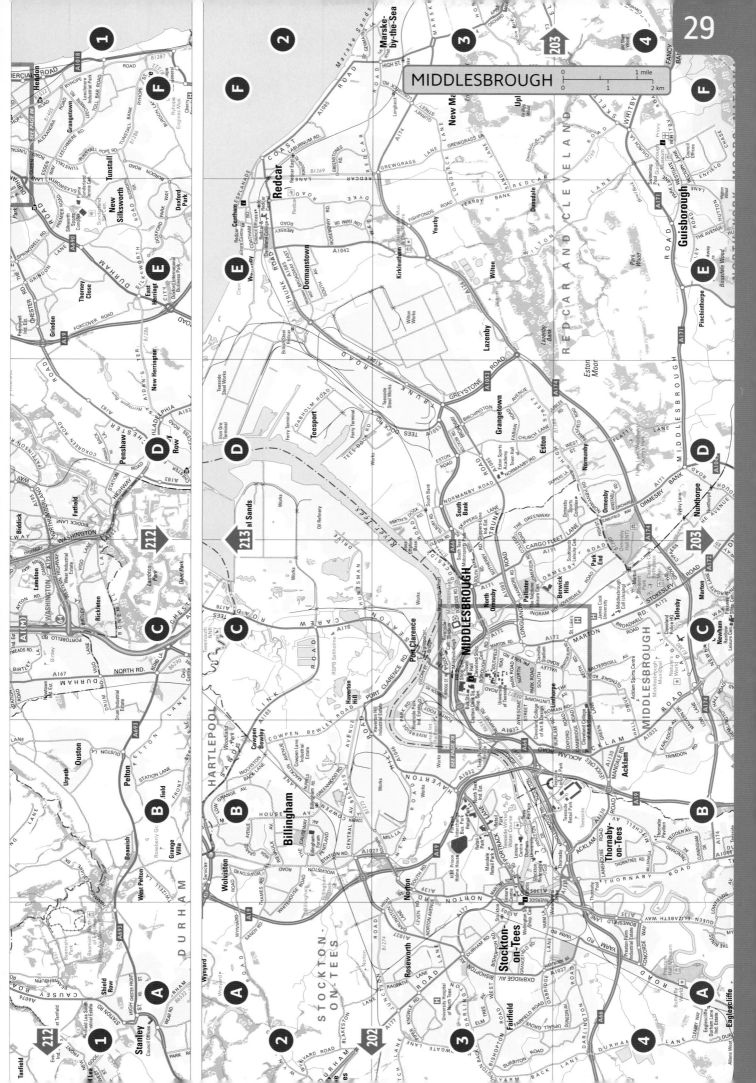

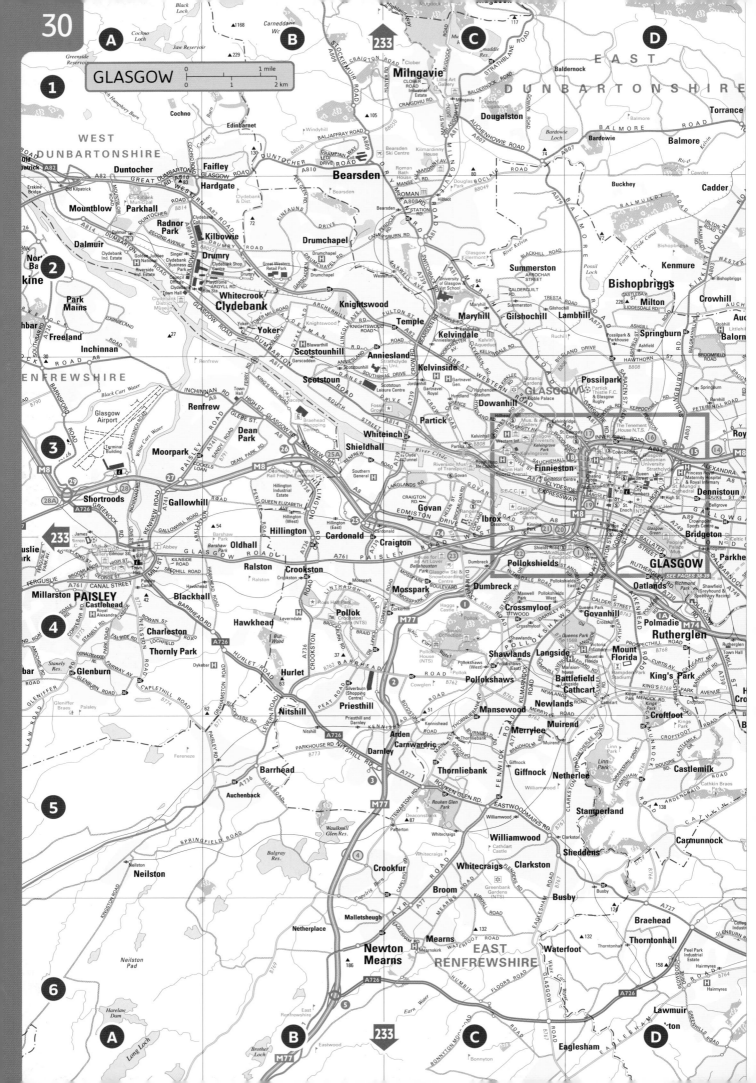

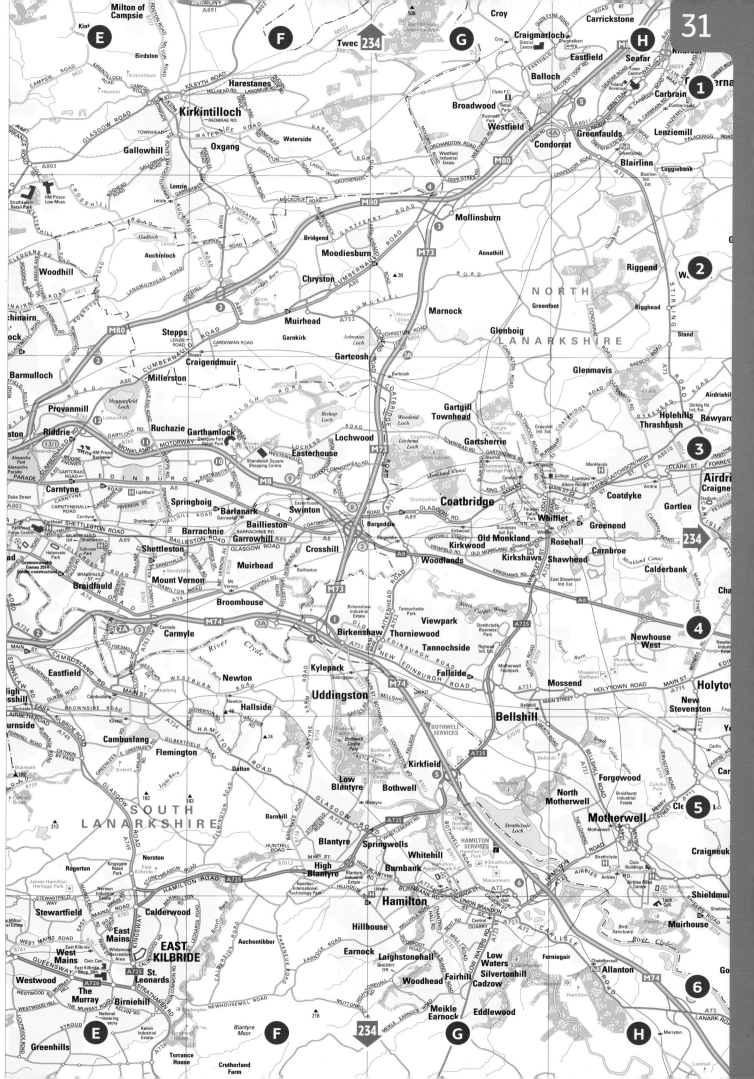

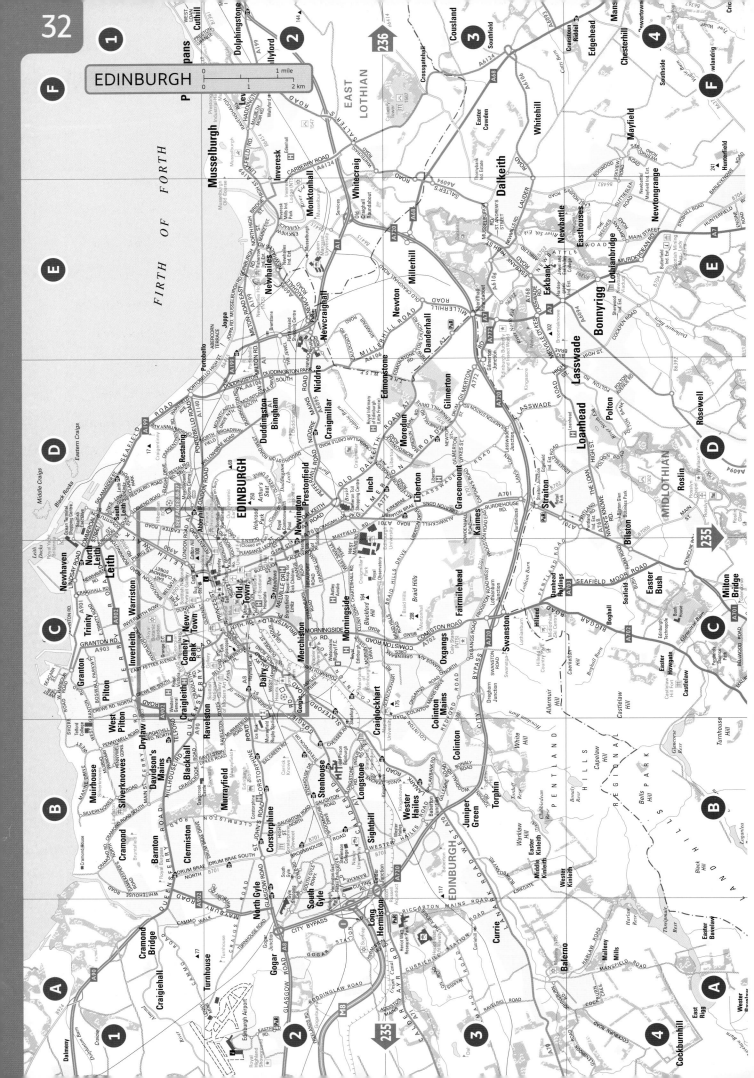

## Symbols used on the map

| | | | | | |
|---|---|---|---|---|---|
| **M8** | Motorway | ⬤ | Bus / Coach station | ⌐JAPAN | Embassy |
| **A4** ❶ | Primary route dual / single carriageway / Junction | P&R | Park and Ride site - rail operated (runs at least 5 days a week) | 🎥 🎥 | Cinema |
| **A40** | 'A' road dual / single carriageway | | Extent of London congestion charging zone | ⬛+ + | Cathedral / Church |
| **B507** | 'B' road dual / single carriageway | Dublin 8hrs ⬤ | Vehicle / Pedestrian ferry | ☽ ✡ ▪ Mormon | Mosque / Synagogue / Other place of worship |
| Toll | Other road dual / single carriageway / Toll | P P | Car park | | Leisure & tourism |
| → 7 | One way street / Orbital route | 🎭 | Theatre | | Shopping |
| • | Access restriction | 🏨 | Major hotel | | Administration & law |
| | Pedestrian street | 🍺 | Public House | | Health & welfare |
| | Street market | Pol | Police station | | Education |
| | Minor road / Track | Lib | Library | | Industry / Office |
| FB | Footpath / Footbridge | PO | Post Office | | Other notable building |
| | Road under construction | i i | Visitor information centre (open all year / seasonally) | | Park / Garden / Sports ground |
| ⬤ ⬤ | Main / other National Rail station | 🚻 | Toilet | ↑↑↑↑ | Cemetery |
| ⬤ ⬤ | London Underground / Overground station | | | | |
| ⬤ | Light Rail / Station | | | | |

## Locator map

| Street maps | | | |
|---|---|---|---|
| Aberdeen | 63 | Leeds index | 52 |
| Bath | 63 | Leicester | 77 |
| Birmingham | 34-35 | Lincoln | 77 |
| Birmingham index | 48 | Liverpool | 42-43 |
| Blackpool | 64 | Liverpool index | 54 |
| Bournemouth | 64 | London | 44-45 |
| Bradford | 65 | London index | 56 |
| Brighton | 65 | Manchester | 46-47 |
| Bristol | 66 | Manchester index | 60 |
| Cambridge | 66 | Middlesbrough | 78 |
| Canterbury | 67 | Milton Keynes | 78 |
| Cardiff | 67 | Newcastle upon Tyne | 79 |
| Carlisle | 68 | Norwich | 79 |
| Cheltenham | 68 | Nottingham | 80 |
| Chester | 69 | Oxford | 80 |
| Coventry | 69 | Perth | 81 |
| Derby | 70 | Plymouth | 81 |
| Dover | 70 | Portsmouth | 82 |
| Dundee | 71 | Reading | 82 |
| Durham | 71 | Salisbury | 83 |
| Eastbourne | 72 | Scarborough | 83 |
| Edinburgh | 36-37 | Sheffield | 84 |
| Edinburgh index | 49 | Southampton | 84 |
| Exeter | 72 | Stoke-on-Trent | 85 |
| Folkestone | 73 | Stratford-upon-Avon | 85 |
| Glasgow | 38-39 | Sunderland | 86 |
| Glasgow index | 51 | Swansea | 86 |
| Gloucester | 73 | Swindon | 87 |
| Guildford | 74 | Torquay | 87 |
| Harrogate | 74 | Watford | 88 |
| Hastings | 75 | Weston-super-Mare | 88 |
| Hereford | 75 | Winchester | 89 |
| Hull (Kingston upon Hull) | 76 | Windsor | 89 |
| Inverness | 76 | Worcester | 90 |
| Leeds | 40-41 | York | 90 |

| Airport plans | |
|---|---|
| Birmingham International | 91 |
| Gatwick | 91 |
| Glasgow | 91 |
| Heathrow | 91 |
| Manchester | 91 |
| Stansted | 91 |

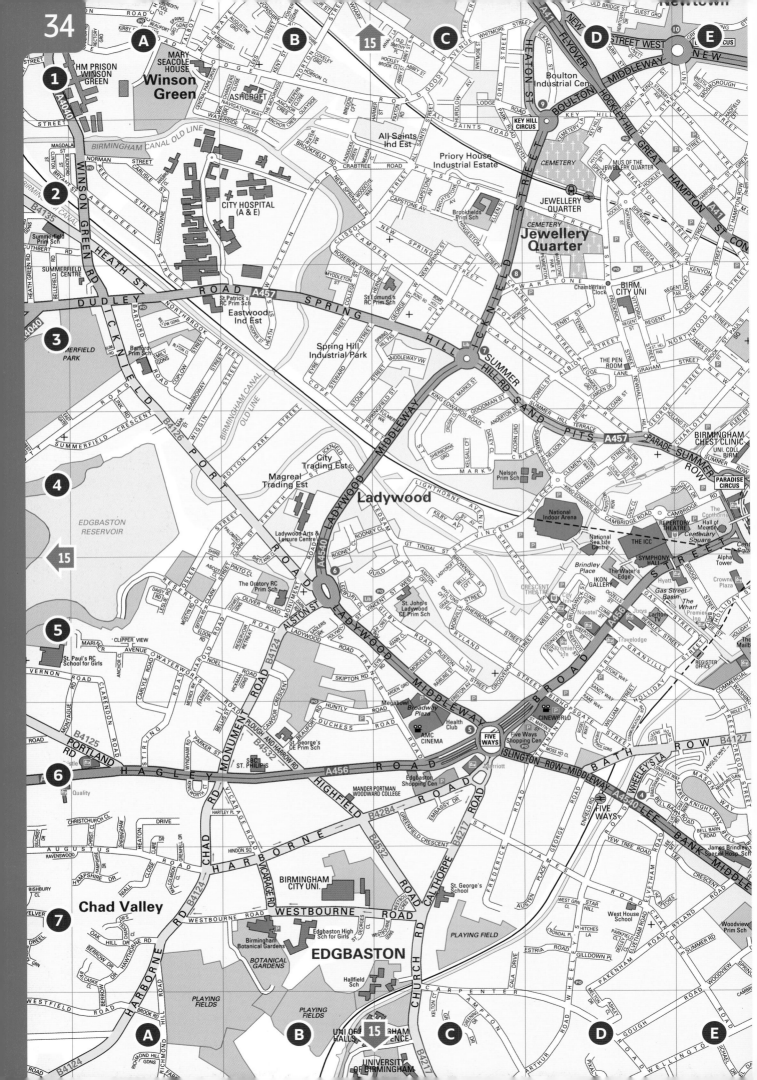

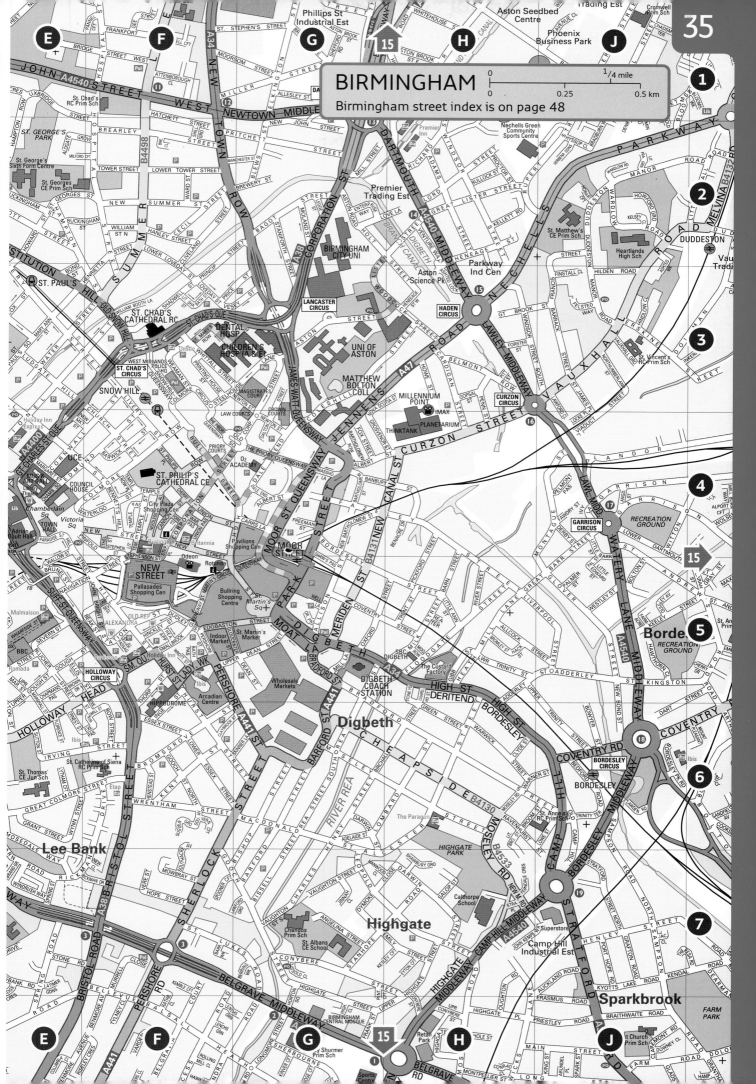

# BIRMINGHAM

Birmingham street index is on page 48

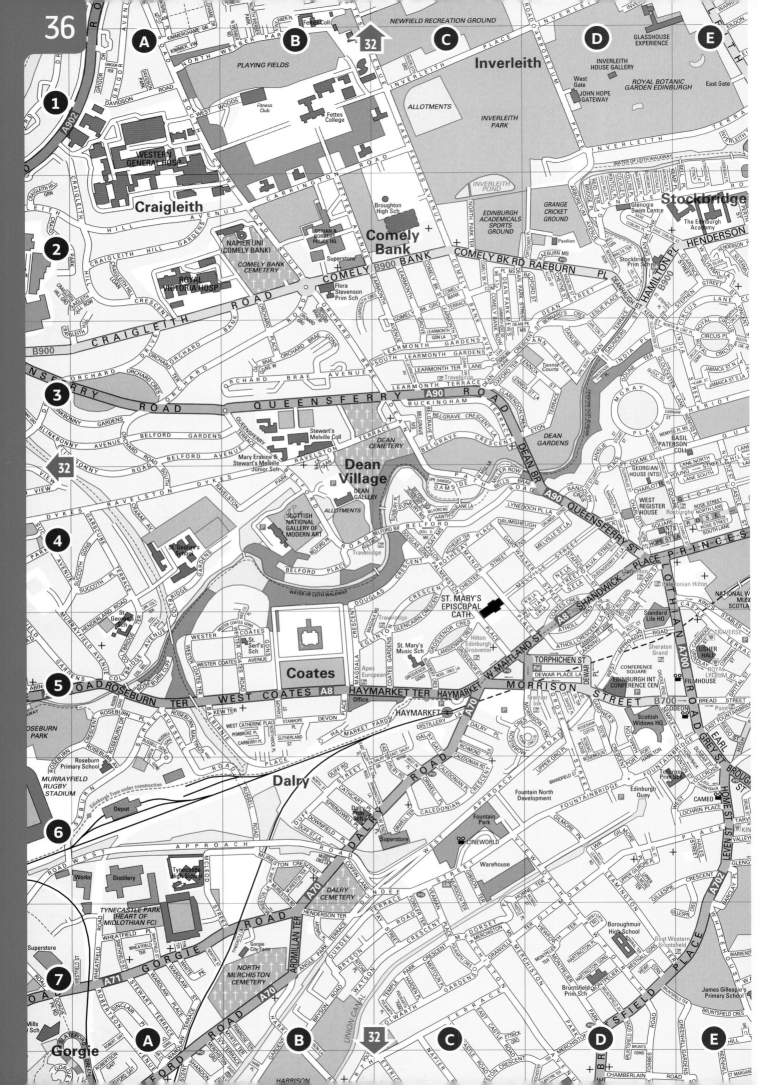

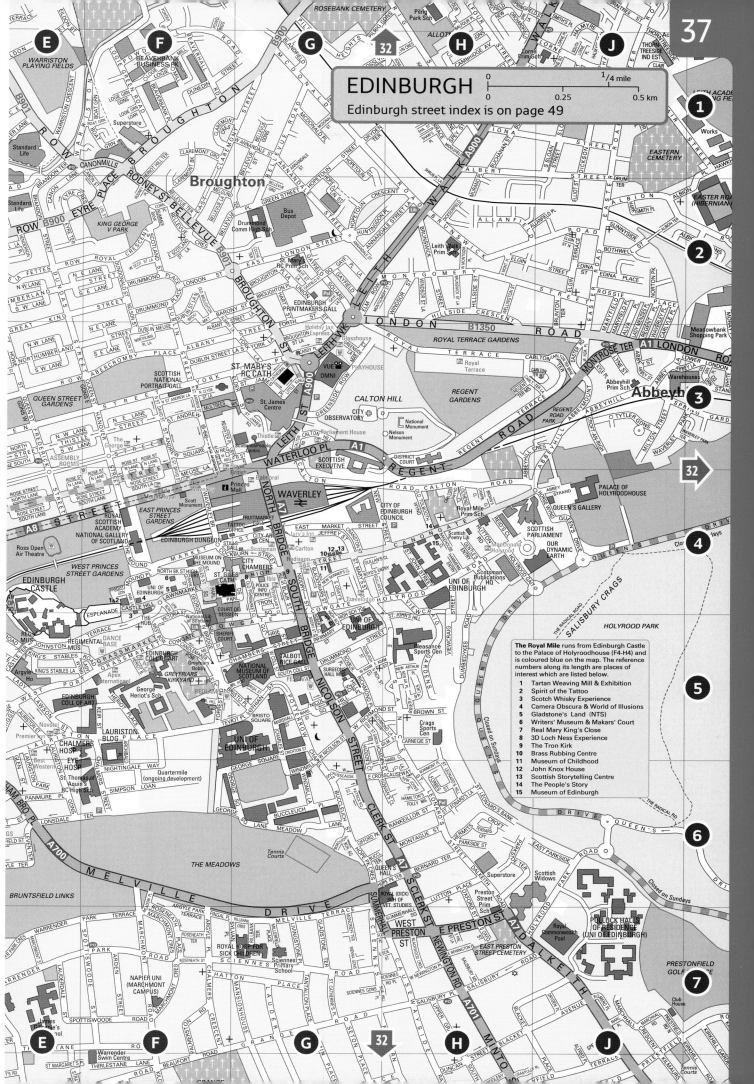

# EDINBURGH
Edinburgh street index is on page 49

0          1/4 mile
0     0.25     0.5 km

**Broughton**

**The Royal Mile** runs from Edinburgh Castle to the Palace of Holyroodhouse (F4-H4) and is coloured blue on the map. The reference numbers along its length are places of interest which are listed below.

1   Tartan Weaving Mill & Exhibition
2   Spirit of the Tattoo
3   Scotch Whisky Experience
4   Camera Obscura & World of Illusions
5   Gladstone's Land (NTS)
6   Writers' Museum & Makars' Court
7   Real Mary King's Close
8   3D Loch Ness Experience
9   The Tron Kirk
10   Brass Rubbing Centre
11   Museum of Childhood
12   John Knox House
13   Scottish Storytelling Centre
14   The People's Story
15   Museum of Edinburgh

THE MEADOWS

BRUNTSFIELD LINKS

HOLYROOD PARK

EDINBURGH CASTLE

WAVERLEY

PALACE OF HOLYROODHOUSE

SALISBURY CRAGS

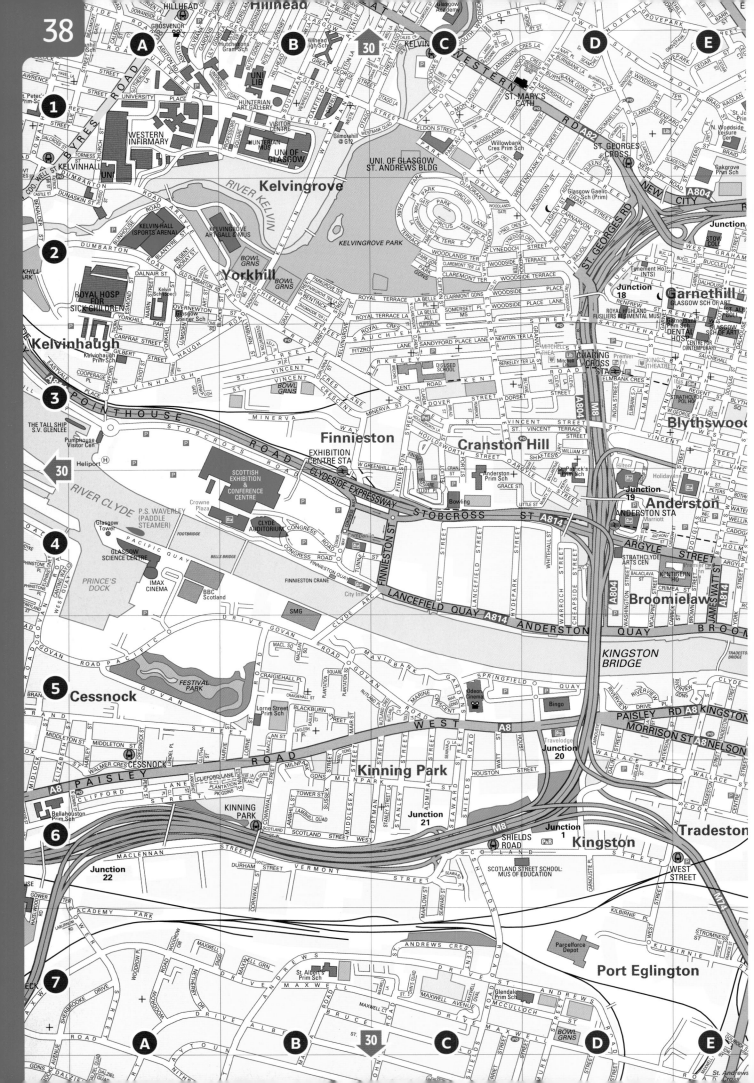

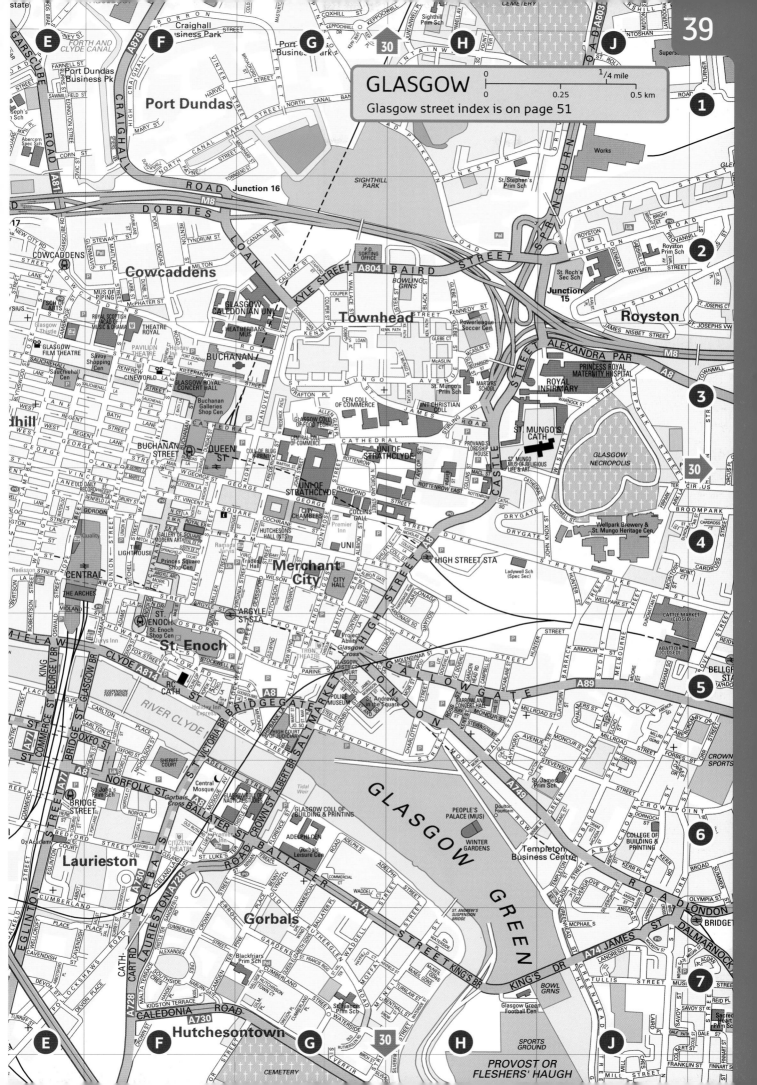

GLASGOW
Glasgow street index is on page 51

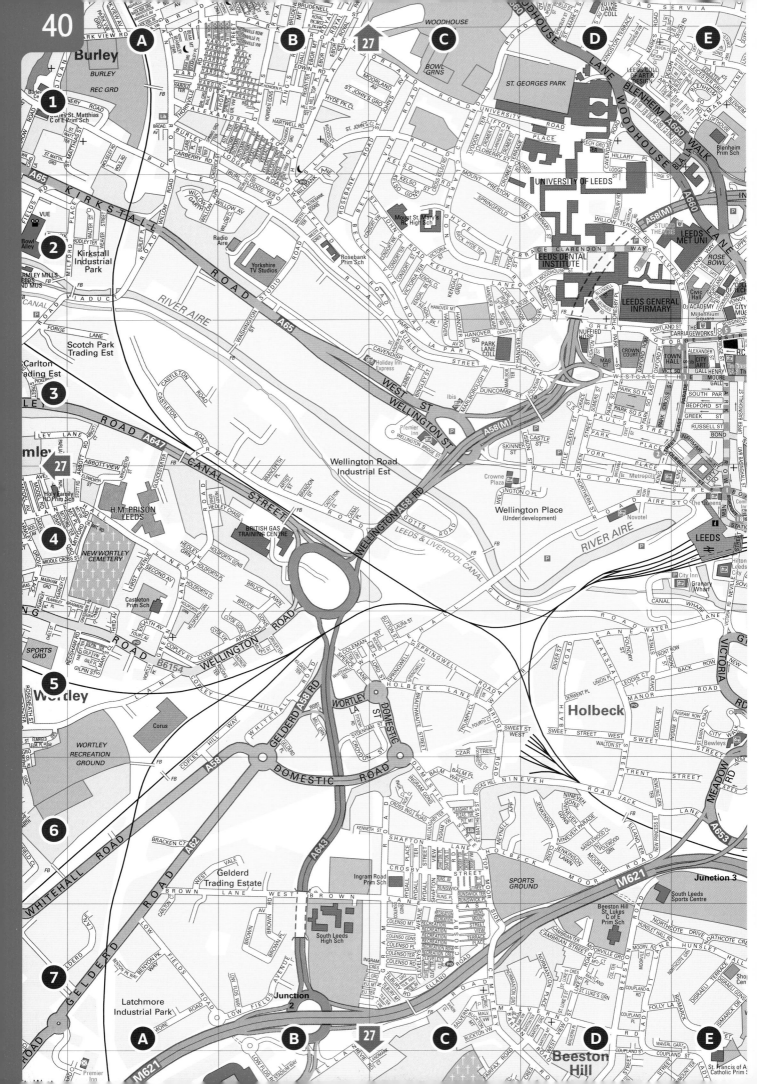

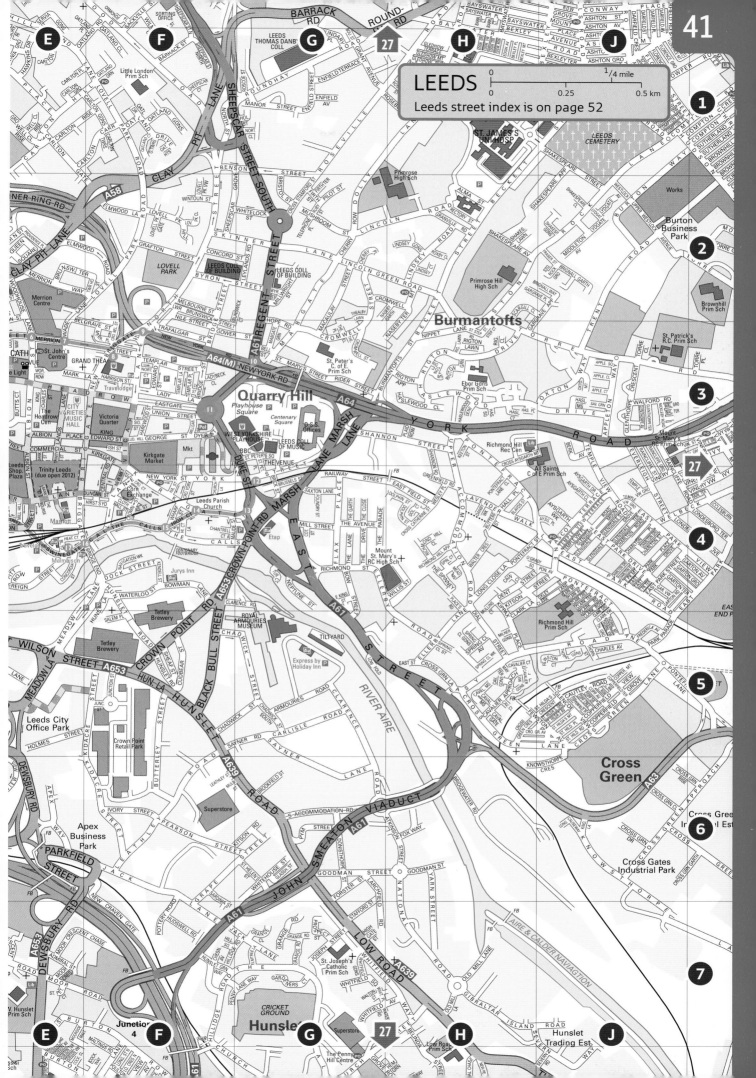

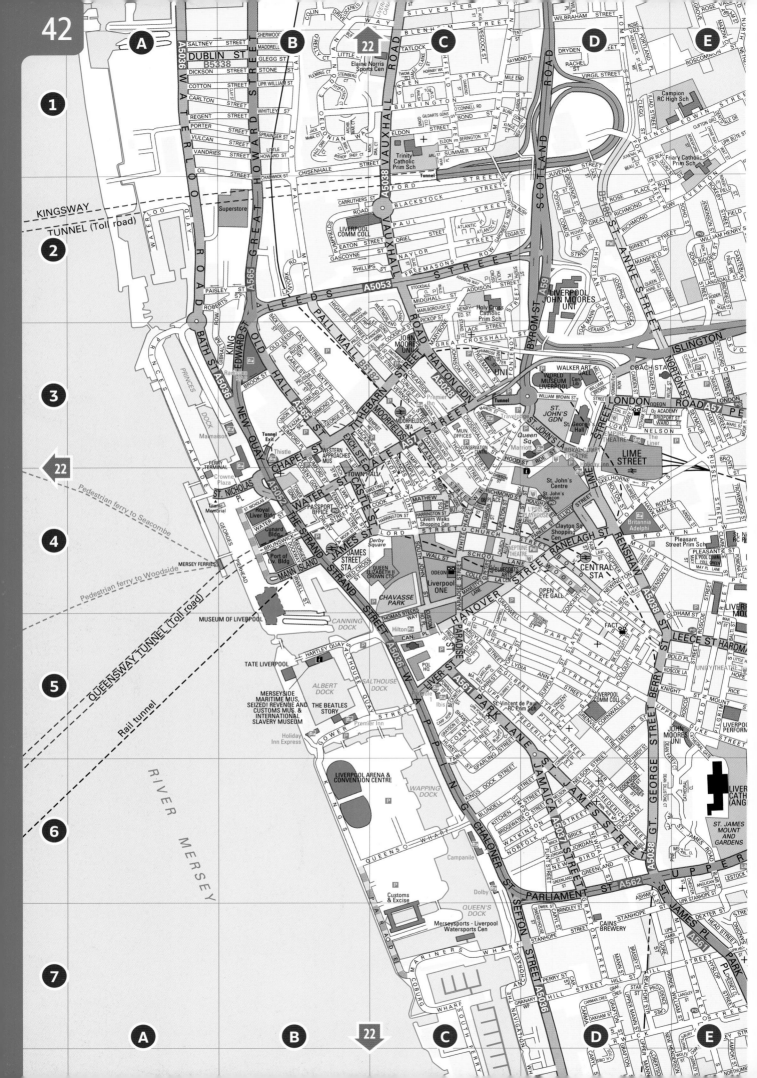

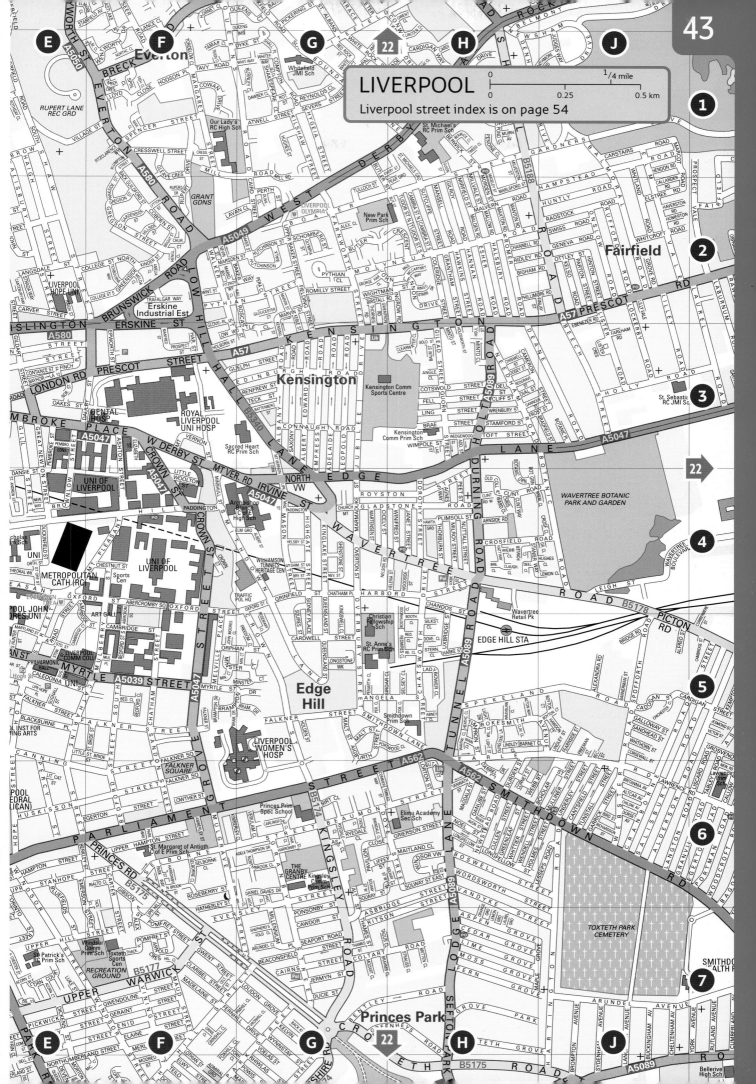

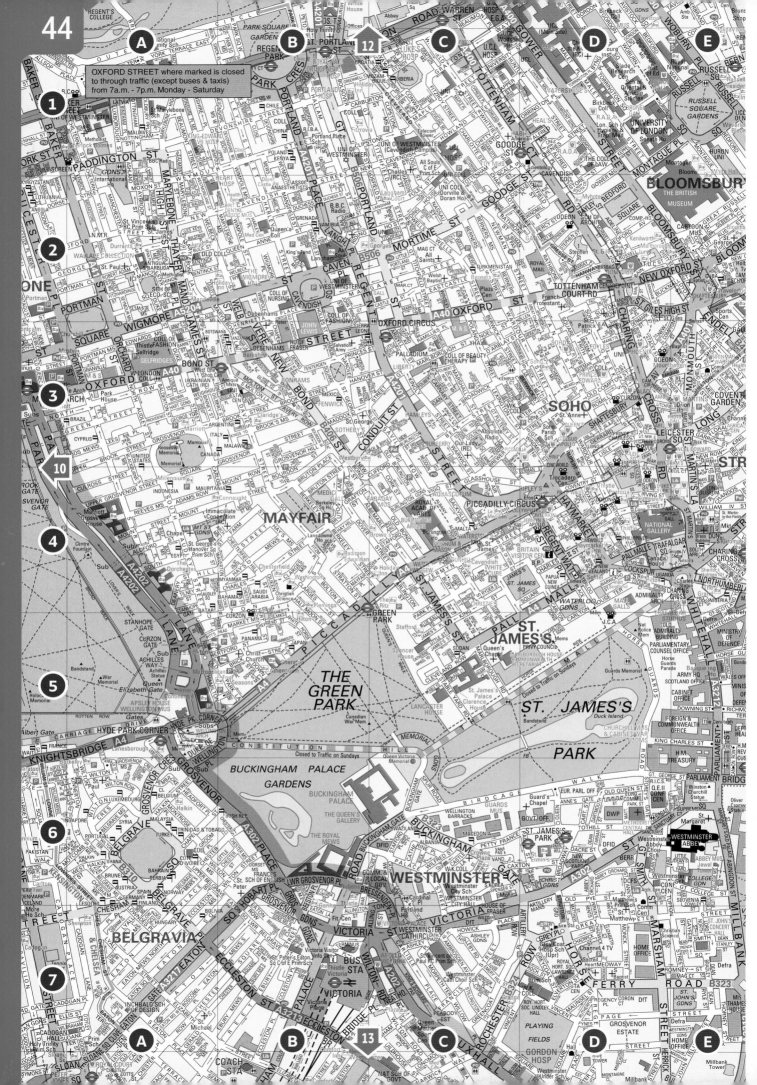

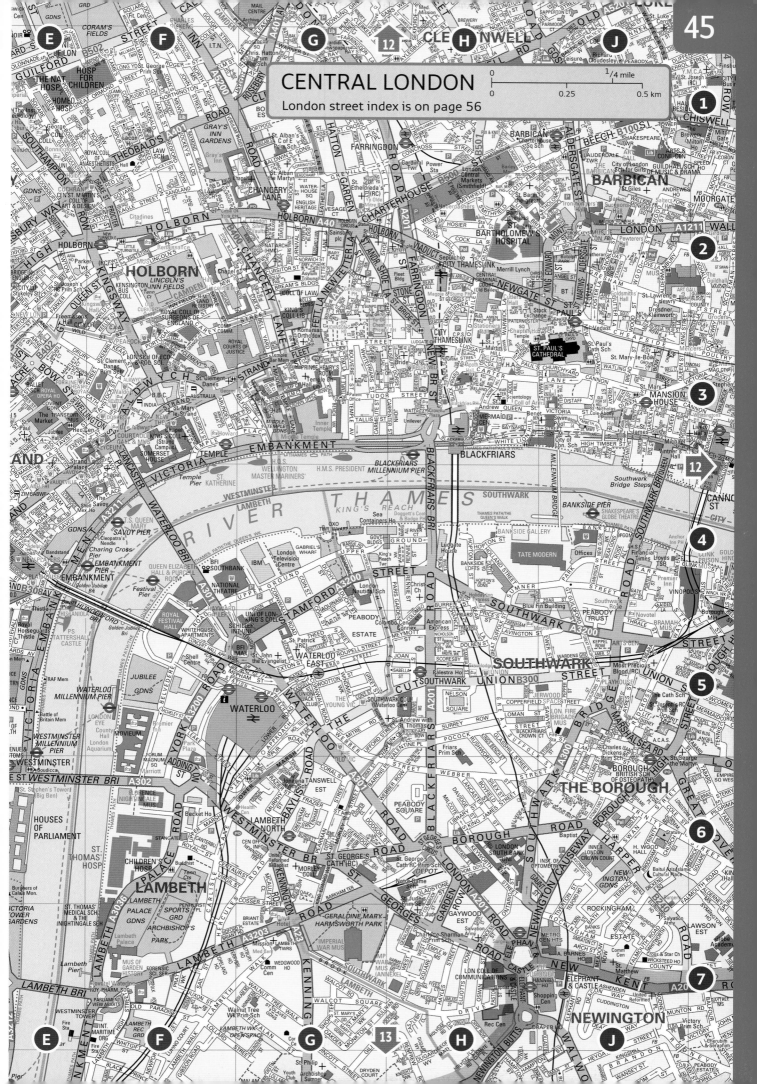

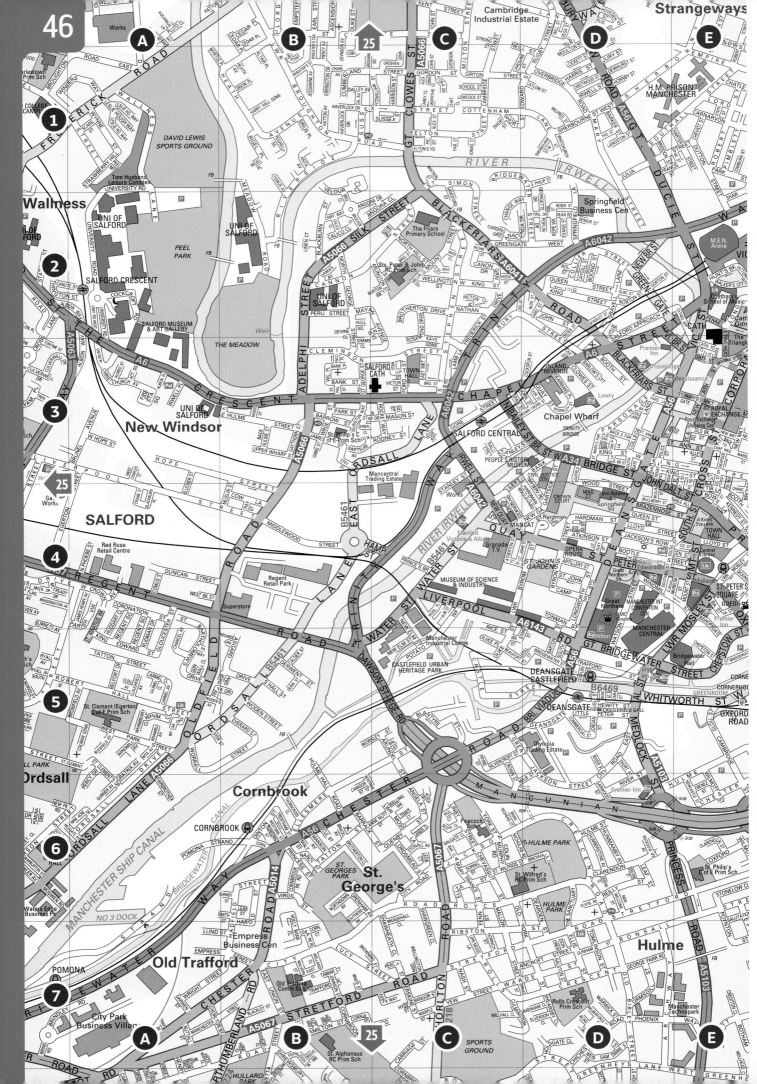

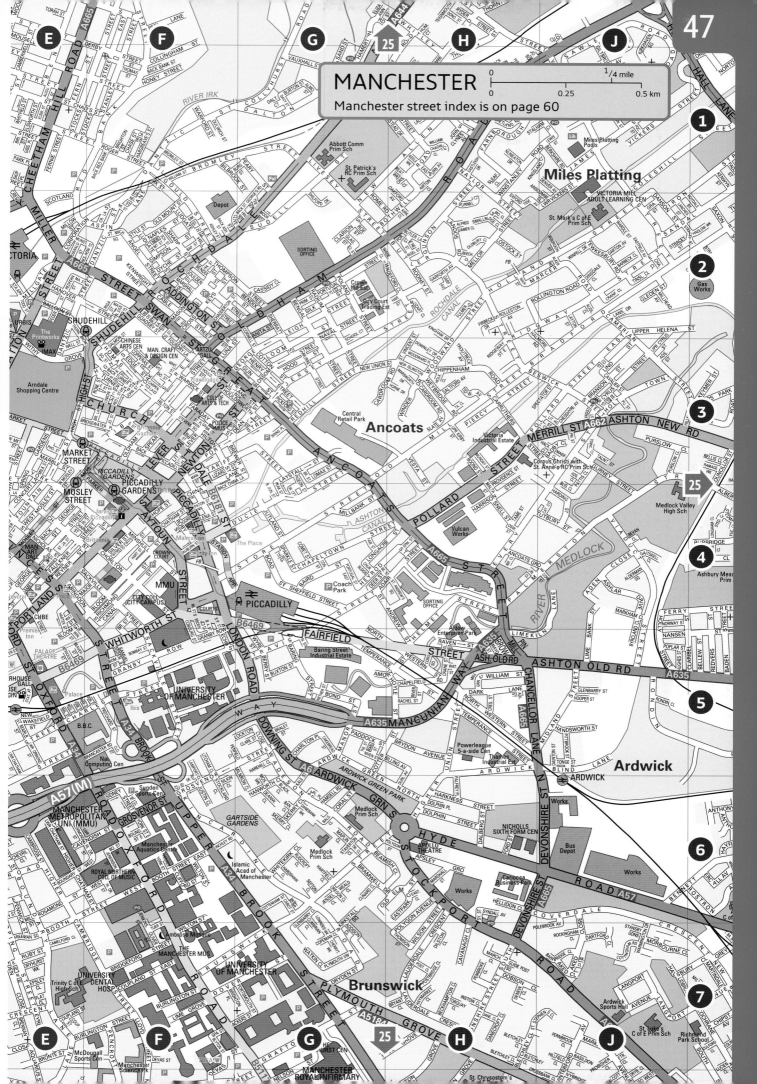

# Indexes to street maps

## General abbreviations

| | | | | | | | | | | | |
|---|---|---|---|---|---|---|---|---|---|---|---|
| All | Alley | Chyd | Churchyard | Embk | Embankment | La | Lane | Pl | Place | W | West |
| App | Approach | Circ | Circus | Est | Estate | Lo | Lodge | Rd | Road | Wf | Wharf |
| Arc | Arcade | Clo | Close | Flds | Fields | Mans | Mansions | Ri | Rise | Wk | Walk |
| Av/Ave | Avenue | Cor | Corner | Gdn | Garden | Mkt/Mkts | Market/Markets | S | South | Yd | Yard |
| Bdy | Broadway | Cres | Crescent | Gdns | Gardens | Ms | Mews | Sq | Square | | |
| Bldgs | Buildings | Ct | Court | Grd | Ground | N | North | St | Street | | |
| Br/Bri | Bridge | Ctyd | Courtyard | Grn | Green | Par | Parade | St. | Saint | | |
| Cen | Central, Centre | Dr | Drive | Gro | Grove | Pas | Passage | Ter | Terrace | | |
| Ch | Church | E | East | Ho | House | Pk | Park | Twr | Tower | | |

**Place names are shown in bold type**

## Birmingham street index


### A
Abbey St 34 C1
Abbey St N 34 C1
Aberdeen St 34 A2
Acorn Gro 34 C4
Adams St 35 H2
Adderley St 35 H5
Adelaide St 35 G6
Albert St 35 G4
Albion St 34 D3
Alcester St 35 G7
Aldgate Gro 35 E2
Alfred Knight Way 34 E6
Allcock St 35 H5
Allesley St 35 G1
Allison St 35 G5
All Saints Rd 34 C1
All Saints St 34 C2
Alston St 34 B5
Anchor Cl 34 A5
Anchor Cres 34 B1
Anderton St 34 C4
Angelina St 35 G7
Ansbro Cl 34 A2
Arden Gro 34 C5
Arthur Pl 34 D4
Ascot Cl 34 A5
Ashted Lock 35 H3
Ashted Wk 35 J2
Ashton Cft 34 C5
**Aston** 35 H1
Aston Br 35 G1
Aston Brook St 35 G1
Aston Brook St E 35 H1
Aston Expressway 35 G2
Aston Rd 35 H1
Aston St 35 G3
Attenborough Cl 35 F1
Auckland Rd 35 J7
Augusta St 34 D2
Augustine Gro 34 B1
Austen Pl 34 C7
Autumn Gro 34 E1
Avenue Cl 35 J1
Avenue Rd 35 H1

### B
Bacchus Rd 34 A1
Bagot St 35 G2
Balcaskie Cl 34 A7
Banbury St 35 G4
Barford Rd 34 A3
Barford St 35 G6
Barn St 35 H5
Barrack St 35 J3
Barrow Wk 35 F7
Barr St 34 D1
Bartholomew Row 35 G4
Bartholomew St 35 G4
Barwick St 35 F4
Bath Pas 35 F5
Bath Row 34 D6
Bath St 35 F3
Beak St 35 F5
Beaufort Gdns 34 A1
Beaufort Rd 34 B6
Bedford Rd 35 J6
Beeches, The 34 D7
Belgrave Middleway 35 F7
Bell Barn Rd 34 D6
Bellcroft 34 C5
Bellevue 35 F7
Bellis St 34 A6
Belmont Pas 35 J4
Belmont Row 35 H3
Benacre Dr 35 H4
Bennett's Hill 35 F4
Benson Rd 34 A1
Berkley St 34 D5
Berrington Wk 35 G7
Birchall St 35 G6
Bishopsgate St 34 D5
Bishop St 35 G7
Bissell St 35 G7
Blews St 35 G2
Bloomsbury St 35 J2
Blucher St 35 E5
Blyton Cl 34 A3
Boar Hound Cl 34 C3
Bodmin Gro 35 J1
Bolton St 35 J5
Bond Sq 34 C3
Bond St 35 E3
**Bordesley** 35 J5
Bordesley Circ 35 J6
Bordesley Middleway 35 J7
Bordesley Pk Rd 35 J6
Bordesley St 35 G4
Boulton Middleway 34 D1
Bow St 35 F6
Bowyer St 35 J6
Bracebridge St 35 G1
Bradburn Way 35 J2
Bradford St 35 G5
Branston St 34 D2
Brearley Cl 35 F2
Brearley St 35 F2
Bredon Cft 34 B1
Brewery St 35 G2
Bridge St 34 E5
Bridge St W 35 E1
Brindley Dr 34 D4
Brindley Pl 34 D5
Bristol St 35 F7
Broad St 34 D6
Broadway Plaza 34 C6
Bromley St 35 H5
Bromsgrove St 35 F6
Brookfield Rd 34 B2
Brook St 34 E3
Brook Vw Cl 34 E1
Broom St 35 H6
Brough Cl 35 J1
Browning St 34 C5
Brownsea Dr 35 E5
Brunel St 35 E5
Brunswick St 34 D5
Buckingham St 35 E2
Bullock St 35 H2
Bull St 35 F4

### C
Cala Dr 34 C7
Calthorpe Rd 34 C7
Cambridge Rd 34 D4
Camden Dr 34 D3
Camden Gro 34 D3
Camden St 34 B2
Camp Hill 35 J7
Camp Hill Middleway 35 H7
Cannon St 35 F4
Capstone Av 34 C2
Cardigan St 35 H3
Carlisle St 34 A2
Carlyle Rd 34 A5
Caroline St 34 E3
Carpenter Rd 34 C7
Carrs La 35 G4
Carver St 34 C3
Cawdor Cres 34 B6
Cecil St 35 F2
Cemetery La 34 D2
Centenary Sq 34 E4
Central Pk Dr 34 A1
Central Sq 34 E5
Chad Rd 34 A7
Chadsmoor Ter 35 J1
**Chad Valley** 34 A7
Chamberlain Sq 35 E4
Chancellor's Cl 34 A7
Chandlers Cl 34 B1
Chapel Ho St 35 H5
Chapmans Pas 35 E5
Charles Henry St 35 G7
Charlotte Rd 34 D7
Charlotte St 34 E4
Chatsworth Way 34 E6
Cheapside 35 G6
Cherry St 35 F4
Chester St 35 H1
Chilwell Cft 35 F1
Christchurch Cl 34 A6
Church Rd 34 C7
Church St 35 F3
Civic Cl 34 D4
Clare Dr 34 A7
Clarendon Rd 34 A5
Clark St 34 A5
Claybrook St 35 F6
Clement St 34 D4
Clipper Vw 34 A5
Clissold Cl 35 G7
Clissold St 34 B2
Cliveland St 35 F3
Clyde St 35 H6
Colbrand Gro 35 E7
Coleshill St 35 G4
College St 34 B3
Colmore Circ 35 F3
Colmore Row 35 F4
Commercial St 34 E5
Communication Row 34 D6
Constitution Hill 34 E2
Conybere St 35 G7
Cope St 34 B3
Coplow St 34 A3
Cornwall St 35 E4
Corporation St 35 F4
Coveley Gro 34 B1
Coventry Rd 35 J6
Coventry St 35 G5
Cox St 35 E3
Coxwell Gdns 34 B5
Crabtree Rd 34 B2
Cregoe St 34 E6
Crescent, The 34 C1
Crescent Av 34 C1
Cromwell St 35 J1
Crondal Pl 34 D7
Crosby Cl 34 C4
Cumberland St 34 D5
Curzon Circ 35 H3
Curzon St 35 H4

### D
Daisy Rd 34 A5
Dale End 35 G4
Daley Cl 34 C4
Dalton St 35 G4
Darnley Rd 34 B5
Dartmouth Circ 35 G1
Dartmouth Middleway 35 G2
Dart St 35 J6
Darwin St 35 G6
Dean St 35 G5
Deeley Cl 34 D7
Denby Cl 35 J2
Derby St 35 J4
Devonshire Av 34 B1
Devonshire St 34 B1
**Digbeth** 35 G6
Digbeth 35 G5
Dollman St 35 J3
Dover St 34 B1
Duchess Rd 34 B6
Duddeston Manor Rd 35 J2
Dudley St 35 F5
Dymoke Cl 35 G7

### E
**Edgbaston** 34 B7
Edgbaston St 35 F5
Edmund St 35 E4
Edward St 34 D4
Eldon Rd 34 A5
Elkington St 35 G1
Ellen St 34 C3
Ellis St 35 E5
Elvetham Rd 34 D7
Embassy Dr 34 C6
Emily Gdns 34 A3
Emily St 35 G7
Enfield Rd 34 D6
Enterprise Way 35 G2
Ernest St 35 E6
Erskine St 35 J3
Essex St 35 F6
Essington St 34 D5
Estria Rd 34 C7
Ethel St 35 F4
Exeter Pas 35 F6
Exeter St 35 F6
Eyre St 34 B3
Eyton Cft 35 H7

### F
Farmacre 35 J5
Farm Cft 34 D1
Farm St 34 D1
Fawdry St 35 J4
Fazeley St 35 G4
Felsted Way 35 J3
Ferndale Cres 35 H7
Finstall Cl 35 J3
Five Ways 34 C6
Fleet St 34 E4
Floodgate St 35 H5
Florence St 35 E6
Ford St 34 C1
Fore St 35 F4
Forster St 35 H3
Foster Gdns 34 B1
Fox St 35 G4
Francis Rd 34 B5
Francis St 35 J3
Frankfort St 35 F1
Frederick Rd 34 C7
Frederick St 34 D3
Freeman St 35 G4
Freeth St 34 B4
Friston Av 34 C6
Fulmer Wk 34 C4

### G
Garrison Circ 35 J4
Garrison La 35 J4
Garrison St 35 J4
Gas St 34 D5
Gas St Basin 34 E5
Geach St 35 F1
Gee St 35 F1
George Rd 34 D7
George St 34 D4
George St W 34 C3
Gibb St 35 H5
Gilby Rd 34 C5
Gilldown Pl 34 D7
Glebeland Cl 34 C5
Gloucester St 35 F5
Glover St 35 J5
Gooch St 35 F7
Gooch St N 35 F6
Goode Av 34 C1
Goodman St 34 C4
Gopsal St 35 H3
Gough St 35 E5
Grafton Rd 35 J7
Graham St 34 D3
Grant St 35 E6
Granville St 34 D5
Graston Cl 34 C5
Great Barr St 35 H5
Great Brook St 35 H3
Great Charles St Queensway 35 E4
Great Colmore St 34 E6
Great Hampton Row 34 E2
Great Hampton St 34 D2
Great King St 34 D1
Great King St N 34 E1
Great Lister St 35 H2
Great Tindal St 34 C4
Greenfield Cres 34 C6
Green St 35 H6
Grenfell Dr 34 A7
Grosvenor St 35 G4
Grosvenor St W 34 C5
Guest Gro 34 D1
Guild Cl 34 B5
Guild Cft 35 F1
Guthrie Cl 35 E1

### H
Hack St 35 H5
Hadfield Cft 34 E2
Hagley Rd 34 A6
Hall St 34 E3
Hampshire Dr 34 A7
Hampton St 35 E2
Hanley St 35 F2
Hanwood Cl 35 G7
Harborne Rd 34 A7
Harford St 34 E2
Harmer St 34 C2
Harold Rd 34 A5
Hartley Pl 34 A6
Hatchett St 35 F1
Hawthorn Cl 35 J5
Hawthorne Rd 34 A7
Heath Mill La 35 H5
Heath St S 34 B3
Heaton Dr 34 A7
Heaton St 34 D1
Helena St 34 D4
Heneage St 35 H2
Heneage St W 35 H3
Henley St 35 J7
Henrietta St 35 F3
Henstead St 35 F6
Herne Cl 34 C3
Hickman Gdns 34 B5
Highfield Rd 34 B6
**Highgate** 35 H7
Highgate St 35 G7
High St 35 G4
Hilden Rd 35 J3
Hill St 35 E4
Hinckley St 35 F5
Hindlow Cl 35 J3
Hindon Sq 34 B7
Hingeston St 34 C2
Hitches La 34 D7
Hobart Cft 35 J2
Hobson Cl 34 B1
Hockley Brook Cl 34 B1
Hockley Cl 35 F1
Hockley Hill 34 D1
Hockley St 34 D2
Holland St 34 D4
Holliday Pas 34 E5
Holliday St 34 E5
Holloway Circ 35 F5
Holloway Head 35 E6
Holt St 35 G2
Holywell Cl 34 B5
Hooper St 34 B3
Hope St 35 F7
Hospital St 35 F1
Howard St 35 E2
Howe St 35 H3
Howford Gro 35 J2
Hubert St 35 H1
Hunter's Vale 34 D1
Huntly Rd 34 B6
Hurdlow Av 34 C2
Hurst St 35 F5
Hylton St 34 D2
Hyssop Cl 35 J2

### I
Icknield Port Rd 34 A3
Icknield Sq 34 B4
Icknield St 34 C3
Inge St 35 F6
Inkerman St 35 J3
Irving St 35 E6
Islington Row Middleway 34 C6
Ivy La 35 J4

### J
Jackson Cl 35 J7
James St 34 E3
James Watt Queensway 35 G3
Jennens Rd 35 G4
**Jewellery Quarter** 34 D2
Jinnah Cl 35 G7
John Bright St 35 F5
John Kempe Way 35 H7

### K
Keeley St 35 J5
Keepers Cl 34 B1
Kellett Rd 35 H2
Kelsall Cft 34 C4
Kelsey Cl 35 J2
Kemble Cft 35 F7
Kendal Rd 35 J7
Kenilworth Ct 34 A6
Kent St 35 F6
Kent St N 34 B1
Kenyon St 34 E3
Ketley Cft 35 G7
Key Hill 34 D2
Key Hill Dr 34 D2
Kilby Av 34 C4
King Edwards Rd 34 D4
Kingston Rd 35 J5
Kingston Row 34 D4
Kirby Rd 34 A1
Knightstone Av 34 C2
Kyotts Lake Rd 35 J7

### L
Ladycroft 34 C5
Ladywell Wk 35 F5
**Ladywood** 34 C4
Ladywood Middleway 34 B5
Ladywood Rd 34 B5
Lancaster Circ 35 G3
Landor St 35 J4
Langdon St 35 J4
Lansdowne St 34 A2
Latimer Gdns 35 E7
Lawden Rd 35 J6
Lawford Cl 35 J3
Lawford Gro 35 G7
Lawley Middleway 35 H3
Ledbury Cl 34 B5
Ledsam St 34 C4
**Lee Bk** 35 E7
Lee Bk Middleway 34 D6
Lee Cres 34 D7
Lee Mt 34 D7
Lees St 34 B1
Legge La 34 D3
Legge St 35 G2
Lennox St 35 E1
Leopold St 35 G7
Leslie Rd 34 A5
Leyburn Rd 34 C5
Lighthorne Av 34 C4
Link Rd 34 A3
Lionel St 34 E4
Lister St 35 G3
Little Ann St 35 H5
Little Barr St 35 J4
Little Broom St 35 H6
Little Edward St 35 J5
Little Francis Grn 35 J2
Little Shadwell St 35 F3
Liverpool St 35 H5
Livery St 35 F3
Locke Pl 35 J4
Lodge Rd 34 A1
Lombard St 35 G6
Longleat Way 34 D6
Lord St 35 H2
Louisa St 34 D4
Loveday St 35 F3
Love La 35 G2
Lower Dartmouth St 35 J4
Lower Essex St 35 F6
Lower Loveday St 35 F2
Lower Severn St 35 F5

| Street | Ref | Street | Ref | Street | Ref |
|---|---|---|---|---|---|
| Lower Temple St | 35 F4 | New Bond St | 35 J5 | Pickford St | 35 H5 |
| Lower Twr St | 35 F2 | New Canal St | 35 G4 | Pinfold St | 35 E4 |
| Lower Trinity St | 35 H5 | Newhall Hill | 34 D3 | Pinto Cl | 34 B5 |
| Lowe St | 35 J6 | Newhall St | 34 E3 | Pitsford St | 34 C2 |
| Ludgate Hill | 35 E3 | Newhope Cl | 35 F7 | Pitt St | 35 H3 |
| Lytham Cft | 35 E6 | New John St | 35 G2 | Plough & Harrow Rd | 34 B6 |
| **M** | | New John St W | 34 E1 | Pool St | 35 G1 |
| Macdonald St | 35 G6 | New Mkt St | 35 E4 | Pope St | 34 C3 |
| Malcolmson Cl | 34 A7 | New Moseley Rd | 35 H7 | Port Hope Rd | 35 J7 |
| Manchester St | 35 F2 | New Spring St | 34 C2 | Powell St | 34 D3 |
| Margaret St | 35 E4 | New Spring St N | 34 B2 | Power Cres | 34 C5 |
| Mariner Av | 34 A5 | New St | 35 F4 | Price St | 35 F3 |
| Marroway St | 34 A3 | New Summer St | 35 F2 | Princip St | 35 F3 |
| Marshall St | 35 E5 | Newton St | 35 G4 | Printing Ho St | 35 F3 |
| Mary Ann St | 35 E3 | **Newtown** | 34 E1 | Priory Queensway, The | 35 G4 |
| Mary St | 34 E3 | Newtown Dr | 34 D1 | Pritchett St | 35 F2 |
| Mason Way | 34 E6 | Newtown Middleway | 35 F1 | Proctor St | 35 H2 |
| Masshouse La | 35 G4 | New Town Row | 35 F1 | **Q** | |
| Mearse Cl | 34 C2 | Niall Cl | 34 A7 | Quayside | 34 B1 |
| Melton Dr | 34 D7 | Noel Rd | 34 A5 | Queens Hosp Cl | 34 D6 |
| Meredith Pool Cl | 34 A1 | Norman St | 34 A2 | Quigley Av | 35 J5 |
| Meriden St | 35 G5 | Northampton St | 34 D2 | **R** | |
| Merryhill Dr | 34 A1 | Northbrook St | 34 A3 | Radnor St | 34 B1 |
| Meyrick Wk | 34 A6 | Northumberland St | 35 J3 | Radshaw Cl | 34 D6 |
| Middleway Vw | 34 C3 | Northwood St | 34 D3 | Rake Way | 34 D5 |
| Midford Grn | 34 E6 | Nova Scotia St | 35 G4 | Rann Cl | 34 C5 |
| Milford Cft | 35 E2 | Nursery Rd | 34 D1 | Ravenhurst St | 35 H6 |
| Milk St | 35 H5 | **O** | | Rawlins St | 34 C5 |
| Miller St | 35 F1 | Oak Hill Dr | 34 A7 | Rea St | 35 G6 |
| Mill La | 35 G5 | Old Br St | 34 D1 | Rea St S | 35 G6 |
| Mill St | 35 G2 | Old Camp Hill | 35 J6 | Rea Ter | 35 H5 |
| Milton St | 35 F1 | Old Smithy Pl | 34 C1 | Rectory Gro | 34 A1 |
| Moat La | 35 G5 | Old Snow Hill | 35 F3 | Regent Par | 34 D3 |
| Moland St | 35 G2 | Old Sq | 35 F4 | Regent Pl | 34 D3 |
| Montague St | 35 J4 | Oliver Rd | 34 B5 | Regent St | 34 D3 |
| Monument Rd | 34 B6 | Oliver St | 35 J1 | Reservoir Retreat | 34 B5 |
| Moore's Row | 35 H5 | Oozells St | 34 D5 | Reservoir Rd | 34 A5 |
| Moorings, The | 34 B1 | Orchid Dr | 35 E1 | Richard St | 35 H2 |
| Moorsom St | 35 F1 | Orwell Pas | 35 G5 | Rickman Dr | 35 E7 |
| Moor St Queensway | 35 G4 | Osler St | 34 A5 | Ridley St | 34 E6 |
| Moreton St | 34 C3 | Oxford St | 35 G5 | River St | 35 H5 |
| Morville St | 34 C5 | **P** | | Rocky La | 35 J1 |
| Mosborough Cres | 34 E1 | Paddocks Grn | 34 B2 | Rodney Cl | 34 B4 |
| Mosedale Way | 35 E6 | Pakenham Rd | 34 D7 | Rosebery St | 34 B2 |
| Moseley Rd | 35 H6 | Palmer St | 35 J5 | Roseland Way | 34 D6 |
| Moseley St | 35 G6 | Palomino Pl | 34 B4 | Rotton Pk St | 34 B4 |
| Moss Ho Cl | 34 D6 | Pannel Cft | 35 F1 | Rupert St | 35 H2 |
| Mostyn Rd | 34 A5 | Parade | 34 D4 | Ruston St | 34 C5 |
| Mott St | 34 E2 | Paradise Circ | 34 E4 | Ryland Rd | 34 D7 |
| Mowbray St | 35 F7 | Paradise St | 35 E4 | Ryland St | 34 C5 |
| Murrell Cl | 35 F7 | Parker St | 34 A6 | **S** | |
| Musgrave Rd | 34 A1 | Parkfield Cl | 34 D7 | Sadlers Wk | 34 B5 |
| Myddleton St | 34 B3 | Park Rd | 34 C1 | St. Andrew's Rd | 35 J4 |
| **N** | | Park Rd S | 34 C1 | St. Chad's Queensway | 35 F3 |
| Navigation St | 35 E5 | Park St | 35 G5 | St. Georges Cl | 34 B7 |
| Navigation Way | 34 B1 | Paxton Rd | 34 C2 | St. Georges St | 35 E2 |
| Nechells Parkway | 35 H3 | Peel St | 34 A2 | St. Helen's Pas | 34 D3 |
| Needless All | 35 F4 | Pemberton St | 34 D2 | St. James Pl | 35 J3 |
| Nelson St | 34 D4 | Penn St | 35 H3 | St. James Rd | 34 C6 |
| New Bartholomew St | 35 G4 | Pershore St | 35 F5 | | |
| Newbold Cft | 35 J1 | | | | |

| Street | Ref | Street | Ref | Street | Ref |
|---|---|---|---|---|---|
| St. Jude's Pas | 35 F5 | Stirling Rd | 34 A6 | Victor Rd | 34 A1 |
| St. Lukes Rd | 35 F7 | Stoke Way | 34 D5 | Vittoria St | 34 D3 |
| St. Marks Cres | 34 C4 | Stone Rd | 35 E7 | Vyse St | 34 D3 |
| St. Marks St | 34 C3 | Stone Yd | 35 H5 | **W** | |
| St. Martin's Circ Queensway | 35 F5 | Stour St | 34 B3 | Walter St | 35 J1 |
| St. Martin's Sq | 35 G5 | Stratford Pl | 35 H7 | Wardlow Rd | 35 J2 |
| St. Martin's St | 34 D6 | Stratford Rd | 35 J7 | Ward St | 35 F2 |
| St. Mary's Row | 35 F3 | Stratford St N | 35 J7 | Warner St | 35 H6 |
| St. Paul's Sq | 34 E3 | Suffolk St Queensway | 35 E5 | Warstone La | 34 C3 |
| St. Phillips Pl | 35 F4 | Sugden Gro | 35 F6 | Warstone Par E | 34 D2 |
| St. Stephen's St | 35 F1 | Summer Cft | 35 F1 | Warwick Pas | 35 F4 |
| St. Vincent St | 34 C4 | Summerfield Rd | 34 A3 | Warwick St | 35 H6 |
| St. Vincent St W | 34 B5 | Summer Hill Rd | 34 C3 | Washington St | 34 E5 |
| Salop St | 35 H7 | Summer Hill St | 34 D4 | Waterloo St | 35 E4 |
| Sampson Rd | 35 J7 | Summer Hill Ter | 34 D3 | Waterside Dr | 34 A1 |
| Sampson Rd N | 35 J6 | Summer La | 35 F3 | Waterside Vw | 34 B2 |
| Sand Pits | 34 C3 | Summer Rd | 34 E7 | Water St | 35 E3 |
| Sandy Way | 34 D5 | Summer Row | 34 E4 | Waterworks Rd | 34 A5 |
| Scotland St | 34 D4 | Sutton St | 35 E6 | Watery La Middleway | 35 J4 |
| Sefton Rd | 34 A5 | Swallow St | 35 E5 | Weaman St | 35 F3 |
| Severn St | 35 E5 | **T** | | Well La | 35 G5 |
| Shadwell St | 35 F3 | Talbot St | 34 A1 | Well St | 34 C7 |
| Shawbury Gro | 35 H7 | Temple Pas | 35 F4 | Westbourne Cres | 34 C7 |
| Shaw's Pas | 35 G4 | Temple Row | 35 F4 | Westbourne Gdns | 34 B7 |
| Sheepcote St | 34 C4 | Temple Row W | 35 F4 | Westbourne Rd | 34 A7 |
| Shefford Rd | 35 G1 | Temple St | 35 F4 | Western Rd | 34 B3 |
| Shepherds Gdns | 34 C4 | Tenby St | 34 D3 | West Grn Cl | 34 D7 |
| Sherborne Gro | 34 C4 | Tenby St N | 34 D3 | Westhorpe Gro | 34 E1 |
| Sherborne St | 34 C5 | Tennant St | 34 D6 | Westley St | 35 J5 |
| Sheringham | 34 A6 | Theatre App | 35 F5 | Wharf, The | 34 E5 |
| Sherlock St | 35 F7 | Theresa Rd | 35 J7 | Wharf La | 34 C1 |
| Shetland Cl | 34 B5 | Thomas St | 35 G1 | Wharfside St | 35 E5 |
| Shillcock Gro | 35 F2 | Thorp St | 35 F6 | Wharf St | 34 B1 |
| Shire Cl | 34 A4 | Tower St | 35 F2 | Wheeler St | 35 E1 |
| Shyltons Cft | 34 C5 | Townsend Way | 34 D4 | Wheeley's La | 34 D6 |
| Skinner La | 35 G6 | Trent St | 35 H5 | Whitehouse St | 35 H1 |
| Skipton Rd | 34 B5 | Trinity Ter | 35 J6 | Whitmore St | 34 C1 |
| Sloane St | 34 D4 | **U** | | Whittall St | 35 F3 |
| Smallbrook Queensway | 35 F5 | Unett St | 34 E1 | Wiggin St | 34 A4 |
| Smith St | 34 E1 | Union Pas | 35 F4 | William Booth La | 35 F3 |
| Snow Hill Queensway | 35 F3 | Union St | 35 F4 | William Henry St | 35 J1 |
| Soho Pool Way | 35 B1 | Upper Dean St | 35 F5 | William St | 34 D6 |
| Southacre Av | 35 F7 | Upper Gough St | 35 E6 | William St N | 35 F2 |
| South Rd | 35 J7 | Upper Marshall St | 35 E5 | Willow Gdns | 34 A3 |
| Spencer St | 34 D2 | Upper Trinity St | 35 H5 | Windmill St | 35 F6 |
| Spooner Cft | 35 F7 | Uxbridge St | 35 E1 | Windrush Way | 35 E7 |
| Springbank Rd | 34 B4 | **V** | | Windsor St | 35 H2 |
| Springfield St | 34 B4 | Vaughton St | 35 G7 | Windsor St S | 35 H3 |
| Spring Gro Gdns | 34 A1 | Vaughton St S | 35 G7 | **Winson Grn** | 34 A1 |
| Spring Hill | 34 B3 | Vauxhall Gro | 35 J3 | Witton St | 35 J4 |
| Spring Hill Pas | 34 C3 | Vauxhall Rd | 35 J3 | Woodcock St | 35 G3 |
| Spring St | 35 E7 | Venture Way | 35 H2 | Woodcote Way | 34 B2 |
| Stainsby Av | 34 D1 | Verbena Gdns | 35 J2 | Woodview Dr | 34 E7 |
| Stanhope Rd | 35 G7 | Vere St | 35 F7 | Wrentham St | 35 F6 |
| Staniforth St | 35 G2 | Vernolds Cft | 35 F6 | Wrottesley St | 35 F5 |
| Star Hill | 34 D7 | Vesey St | 35 F3 | Wyndham Rd | 34 A6 |
| Station St | 35 F5 | Viaduct St | 35 J4 | Wynn St | 35 E6 |
| Steelhouse La | 35 F3 | Vicarage Rd | 34 B6 | **Y** | |
| Stephenson Pl | 35 F5 | Victoria Sq | 35 E4 | Yew Tree Rd | 34 D6 |
| Stephenson St | 35 F4 | | | | |
| Steward St | 34 B3 | | | | |

## Edinburgh street index

| Street | Ref | Street | Ref | Street | Ref |
|---|---|---|---|---|---|
| **A** | | Archibald Pl | 37 F6 | Belgrave Cres La | 36 C3 |
| **Abbeyhill** | 37 J3 | Arden St | 37 F7 | Belgrave Ms | 36 C3 |
| Abbeyhill | 37 J3 | Ardmillan Pl | 36 B7 | Belgrave Pl | 36 C3 |
| Abbeyhill Cres | 37 H4 | Ardmillan Ter | 36 B7 | Bellevue | 37 F2 |
| Abbey La | 37 J3 | Argyle Pk Ter | 37 F7 | Bellevue Cres | 37 F2 |
| Abbeymount | 37 J3 | Argyle Pl | 37 F7 | Bellevue Gdns | 37 G1 |
| Abbey Strand | 37 J4 | Arthur St | 37 H1 | Bellevue Gro | 37 G2 |
| Abbey St | 37 J3 | Arthur St La | 37 H1 | Bellevue La | 37 F2 |
| Abercromby Pl | 37 F3 | Atholl Cres | 36 D5 | Bellevue Pl | 37 F2 |
| Admiral Ter | 36 D7 | Atholl Cres La | 36 D5 | Bellevue Rd | 37 G2 |
| Ainslie Pl | 36 D3 | Avondale Pl | 36 D1 | Bellevue St | 37 G2 |
| Albany La | 37 F2 | **B** | | Bellevue Ter | 37 F2 |
| Albany St | 37 F3 | Back Dean | 36 B4 | Bell Pl | 36 E1 |
| Albany St La | 37 F3 | Bakehouse Cl | 37 H4 | Bells Brae | 36 C4 |
| Albert St | 37 H1 | Balbirnie Pl | 36 A5 | Bell's Mills | 36 B4 |
| Albion Gdns | 37 J2 | Balmoral Pl | 36 D2 | Bernard Ter | 37 H6 |
| Albion Pl | 37 J2 | Bank St | 37 F4 | Blacket Av | 37 H7 |
| Albion Rd | 37 J2 | Barclay Pl | 37 E7 | Blacket Pl | 37 H7 |
| Albion Ter | 37 J2 | Barony St | 37 F2 | Blackfriars St | 37 G5 |
| Alfred Pl | 37 J7 | Beaverbank Pl | 37 F1 | Blackwood Cres | 37 H7 |
| Allanfield | 37 H2 | Beaverhall Rd | 37 F1 | Blair St | 37 G4 |
| Allanfield Pl | 37 H2 | Bedford St | 36 D2 | Blandfield | 37 G1 |
| Allan St | 36 D2 | Belford Av | 36 A3 | Boat Grn | 37 F1 |
| Alva Pl | 37 J3 | Belford Br | 36 C4 | Boroughloch | 37 G6 |
| Alva St | 36 D4 | Belford Gdns | 36 A3 | Boroughloch Sq | 37 G6 |
| Angle Pk Ter | 36 B7 | Belford Ms | 36 C4 | Borthwick St | 36 B5 |
| Annandale St | 37 G1 | Belford Pk | 36 B4 | Bothwell St | 37 J2 |
| Annandale St La | 37 G2 | Belford Pl | 36 B4 | Bowmont Pl | 37 H6 |
| Ann St | 36 D3 | Belford Rd | 36 B4 | Boyd's Entry | 37 G4 |
| Arboretum Av | 36 D2 | Belgrave Cres | 36 C3 | Brandfield St | 36 D6 |
| Arboretum Pl | 36 D1 | | | Brandon St | 37 E2 |

| Street | Ref | Street | Ref | Street | Ref |
|---|---|---|---|---|---|
| Brandon Ter | 37 E2 | Buckingham Ter | 36 C3 | Castle Ter | 36 E4 |
| Bread St | 36 E5 | **C** | | Cathcart Pl | 36 B6 |
| Bridge Pl | 36 D2 | Caledonian Cres | 36 C6 | Cathedral La | 37 G3 |
| Briery Bauks | 37 H5 | Caledonian Pl | 36 C6 | Causewayside | 37 H7 |
| Brighton St | 37 G5 | Caledonian Rd | 36 C6 | Chalmers Cres | 37 F7 |
| Bristo Pl | 37 F5 | Calton Hill | 37 G3 | Chalmers St | 37 F5 |
| Bristo Port | 37 F5 | Calton Rd | 37 G3 | Chambers St | 37 F5 |
| Brougham Pl | 37 E6 | Cambridge Av | 37 H1 | Chapel St | 37 G5 |
| Brougham St | 36 E6 | Cambridge Gdns | 37 H1 | Charles St | 37 G5 |
| **Broughton** | 37 F1 | Cambridge St | 36 E5 | Charlotte La | 36 D4 |
| Broughton Mkt | 37 F3 | Campbell's Cl | 37 H4 | Charlotte Sq | 36 D4 |
| Broughton Pl | 37 G2 | Candlemaker Row | 37 F5 | Chester St | 36 C4 |
| Broughton Pl La | 37 G2 | Canning St | 36 D5 | Cheyne St | 36 D2 |
| Broughton Rd | 37 F1 | Canning St La | 36 D5 | Chuckie Pend | 36 D5 |
| Broughton St | 37 G2 | Canongate | 37 G4 | Circus Gdns | 36 E3 |
| Broughton St La | 37 G3 | Canon La | 37 E2 | Circus La | 36 E3 |
| Brown's Cl | 37 H4 | Canon St | 37 E1 | Circus Pl | 36 E3 |
| Brown St | 37 H5 | Canonmills | 37 E1 | Claremont Bk | 37 F2 |
| Brunswick Rd | 37 H2 | Carberry Pl | 36 B5 | Claremont Cres | 37 F1 |
| Brunswick St | 37 H2 | Carlton St | 36 D3 | Claremont Gro | 37 F1 |
| Brunswick St La | 37 H2 | Carlton Ter | 37 H3 | Clarence St | 36 E2 |
| Brunton Ter | 37 J3 | Carlton Ter Brae | 37 J3 | Clarendon Cres | 36 C3 |
| Bruntsfield Av | 36 D7 | Carlton Ter La | 37 H3 | Clerk St | 37 G6 |
| Bruntsfield Cres | 36 E7 | Carlton Ter Ms | 37 H3 | **Coates** | 36 B5 |
| Bruntsfield Gdns | 36 D7 | Carlton Wynd | 37 H4 | Coates Cres | 36 D5 |
| Bruntsfield Ter | 36 D7 | Carlyle Pl | 37 J3 | Coates Gdns | 36 C5 |
| Bryson Rd | 36 B7 | Carnegie St | 37 H5 | Cochran Ter | 37 G2 |
| Buccleuch Pl | 37 G6 | Carrington Rd | 36 B2 | Cockburn St | 37 F4 |
| Buccleuch St | 37 G6 | Castle Hill | 37 F4 | Coffin La | 36 B6 |
| Buccleuch Ter | 37 G6 | Castle St | 36 E4 | Collins Pl | 36 D2 |
| Buchanan St | 37 H1 | | | Coltbridge Av | 36 A5 |

Coltbridge Gdns 36 A5
Coltbridge Millside 36 A5
Coltbridge Ter 36 A5
Coltbridge Vale 36 A5
Colville Pl 36 D2
**Comely Bk** 36 C2
Comely Bk 36 B2
Comely Bk Av 36 C2
Comely Bk Gro 36 C3
Comely Bk Pl 36 C2
Comely Bk Pl Ms 36 C2
Comely Bk Rd 36 C2
Comely Bk Row 36 C2
Comely Bk St 36 C2
Comely Bk Ter 36 C2
Conference Sq 36 D5
Cornwallis Pl 37 F2
Cornwall St 36 E5
Cowan's Cl 37 G6
Cowgate 37 F5
Cowgatehead 37 F5
**Craigleith** 36 A2
Craigleith Hill Cres 36 A2
Craigleith Hill Gdns 36 A2
Craigleith Hill Ln 36 A2
Craigleith Hill Row 36 A2
Cranston St 37 G4
Crarae Av 36 A4
Crewe Rd S 36 A1
Crichton St 37 G5
Croft-an-Righ 37 J3
Cumberland St 36 E2
Cumberland St N E La 37 E2
Cumberland St N W La 37 E2
Cumberland St S E La 37 E2
Cumberland St S W La 37 E2
Cumin Pl 37 G7

**D**
Dalkeith Rd 37 H6
Dalmeny St 37 H1
**Dalry** 36 B6
Dalry Gait 36 C5
Dalry Pl 36 C5
Dalry Rd 36 B7
Damside 36 C4
Danube St 36 D3
Darnaway St 36 D3
Davidson Pk 36 A1
Davidson Rd 36 A1
Davie St 37 G5
Dean Bk La 36 D2
Dean Br 36 C3
Deanhaugh St 36 D2
Dean Pk Cres 36 C3
Dean Pk Ms 36 C2
Dean Pk St 36 C2
Dean Path 36 C3
Dean St 36 D3
Dean Ter 36 D3
**Dean Village** 36 B4
Devon Pl 36 B5
Dewar Pl 36 D5
Dewar Pl La 36 D5
Dicksonfield 37 H2
Dickson St 37 J1
Distillery La 36 C5
Dorset Pl 36 C7
Douglas Cres 36 B4
Douglas Gdns 36 C4
Douglas Gdns Ms 36 C4
Doune Ter 36 D3
Downfield Pl 36 B6
Drumdryan St 36 E6
Drummond Pl 37 F2
Drummond St 37 G5
Drumsheugh Gdns 36 C4
Drum Ter 37 J2
Dryden Gait 37 G1
Dryden Gdns 37 G1
Dryden Pl 37 J7
Dryden St 37 G1
Dryden Ter 37 G1
Dublin Meuse 37 F3
Dublin St 37 F2
Dublin St La N 37 F2
Dublin St La S 37 F3
Duff Rd 36 B6
Duff St 36 B6
Duff St La 36 B6
Dumbiedykes Rd 37 H5
Dundas St 36 E2
Dundee St 36 B7
Dundee Ter 36 B7
Dundonald St 37 F2

Dunedin St 37 F1
Dunrobin Pl 36 D2

**E**
Earl Grey St 36 E5
East Adam St 37 G5
East Castle Rd 36 C7
East Claremont St 37 F2
East Crosscauseway 37 G6
Easter Dalry Dr 36 B6
Easter Dalry Pl 36 B5
Easter Dalry Rigg 36 B6
Easter Dalry Rd 36 C5
Easter Dalry Wynd 36 C6
Easter Rd 37 J3
East Fettes Av 36 C1
East Fountainbridge 36 E5
East London St 37 G2
East Mkt St 37 G4
East Montgomery Pl 37 H4
East Newington Pl 37 H7
East Parkside 37 H6
East Preston St 37 H7
East Preston St La 37 H7
East Sciennes St 37 G7
East Scotland St La 37 F2
East Silvermills La 36 E2
Edina Pl 37 J2
Edina St 37 J2
Edinburgh Quay 36 D6
Eglinton Cres 36 B5
Eildon St 36 E1
Eildon Ter 36 E1
Elder St 37 F3
Elgin Pl 37 H2
Elgin St 37 J2
Elgin St N 37 J2
Elgin Ter 37 J2
Elliot St 37 J2
Elm Row 37 G2
Eton Ter 36 D3
Ettrickdale Pl 36 E1
Ettrick Gro 36 C7
Eyre Cres 37 E2
Eyre Pl 37 E2
Eyre Ter 37 E2

**F**
Fettes Av 36 B2
Fettes Row 37 E2
Findhorn Pl 37 G7
Fingal Pl 37 F7
Forbes St 37 H6
Forres St 36 D3
Forrest Hill 37 F5
Forrest Rd 37 F5
Forth St 37 G3
Fountainbridge 36 D6
Fowler Ter 36 C6
Frederick St 37 E3

**G**
Gardner's Cres 36 D5
Garscube Ter 36 A4
Gayfield La 37 G2
Gayfield Pl La 37 G2
Gayfield Sq 37 G2
Gayfield St 37 G2
Gayfield St La 37 G2
Gentle's Entry 37 H4
George IV Br 37 F4
George Sq 37 F6
George Sq La 37 F6
George St 36 E4
Gibson Ter 36 C6
Gifford Pk 37 G6
Gillespie Cres 36 D6
Gillespie St 36 D6
Gilmore Pk 36 D6
Gilmore Pl 36 D7
Gilmour St 37 G5
Gladstone Ter 37 G7
Glencairn Cres 36 C5
Glenfinlas St 36 D4
Glengyle Ter 36 E6
Glenogle Rd 36 D2
Glen St 37 E5
Gloucester La 36 D3
Gloucester Pl 36 D3
Gloucester Sq 36 D3
Gloucester St 36 D3
Gorgie Rd 36 A7
Grange Rd 37 F7
Granville Ter 36 C7
Grassmarket 37 F5
Great King St 37 E3
Great Stuart St 36 D4
Greenhill Ct 36 E7
Greenhill Gdns 36 E7
Greenhill Pl 36 E7
Greenhill Ter 36 E7
Greenside La 37 G3
Greenside Row 37 G3

Green St 37 G2
Greyfriars Pl 37 F5
Grigor Av 36 A1
Grigor Dr 36 A1
Grigor Gdns 36 A1
Grigor Ter 36 A1
Grindlay St 36 E5
Grosvenor Cres 36 C5
Grosvenor Gdns 36 C5
Grosvenor St 36 C5
Grove St 36 D5
Gullan's Cl 37 G4
Guthrie St 37 G5

**H**
Haddon's Ct 37 G5
Hailes St 36 E6
Halmyre St 37 J1
Hamilton Pl 36 D2
Hamilton's Folly Ms 37 H6
Hammermen's Entry 37 H4
Hanover St 37 F3
Harden Pl 36 C7
Hardwell Cl 37 H6
Harrismith Pl 37 J2
Harrison La 36 B7
Harrison Rd 36 B7
Hartington Gdns 36 D7
Hartington Pl 36 D7
Hart St 37 G2
Hatton Pl 37 F7
Haugh St 36 D2
Hawthornbank La 36 C4
Hawthornden Pl 37 H1
Haymarket 36 C5
Haymarket Ter 36 B5
Haymarket Yards 36 A5
Henderland Rd 36 A5
Henderson Pl 37 E2
Henderson Pl La 37 E2
Henderson Row 36 E2
Henderson Ter 36 B7
Heriot Br 37 F5
Heriot Hill Ter 37 F2
Heriot Pl 37 F5
Heriot Row 36 E3
Hermits Cft 37 H6
High Riggs 36 E5
High Sch Wynd 37 G4
High Sch Yards 37 G5
High St 37 F4
Hill Pl 37 G5
Hillside Cres 37 H2
Hillside St 37 H2
Hill Sq 37 G5
Hill St 36 E3
Hill St La N 36 E3
Hill St La S 36 E4
Holyrood Gait 37 H4
Holyrood Pk Rd 37 H7
Holyrood Rd 37 G4
Home St 36 E6
Hope Pk Cres 37 G6
Hope Pk Ter 37 G6
Hope St 36 D4
Hope St La 36 D4
Hopetoun Cres 37 G2
Hopetoun St 37 G2
Horne Ter 36 C6
Horse Wynd 37 J4
Howden St 37 G5
Howe St 37 E3
Hugh Miller Pl 36 D2
Hunter Sq 37 G4
Huntingdon Pl 37 G2
Hutton Rd 37 H4

**I**
India Pl 36 D3
India St 36 E3
Infirmary St 37 G5
**Inverleith** 36 C1
Inverleith Gro 36 C1
Inverleith Pl 36 C1
Inverleith Ter 36 D1
Inverleith Ter La 36 E1
Iona St 37 H1
Ivy Ter 36 A7

**J**
Jamaica St 36 E3
Jamaica St N La 36 E3
Jamaica St S La 36 E3
Jameson Pl 37 H1
Jeffrey St 37 G4
Johnston Ter 37 E5

**K**
Keir St 37 F5
Kemp Pl 36 D1
Kerr St 36 D2
Kew Ter 36 A5
Kimmerghame Dr 36 A1
Kimmerghame Vw 36 A1

King's Stables La 37 E5
King's Stables Rd 36 E4
Kirkhill Rd 37 J7
Kyle Pl 37 J3

**L**
Lady Lawson St 37 E5
Lady Menzies Pl 37 J3
Lady Wynd 37 F5
Lamb's Cl 37 H6
Lansdowne Cres 36 C5
Lauderdale St 37 E7
Lauder Rd 37 G7
Lauriston Gdns 36 E5
Lauriston Pk 36 E5
Lauriston Pl 36 E6
Lauriston St 37 E5
Lawnmarket 37 F4
Leamington Rd 36 D6
Leamington Ter 36 D6
Learmonth Av 36 B2
Learmonth Cres 36 B3
Learmonth Gdn La 36 C3
Learmonth Gdns 36 C3
Learmonth Gdns Ms 36 C3
Learmonth Gro 36 C3
Learmonth Pl 36 C2
Learmonth Ter 36 C3
Learmonth Ter La 36 C3
Learmonth Vw 36 C3
Leith St 37 G3
Leith Wk 37 G3
Lennox St 36 C3
Lennox St La 36 C3
Leslie Pl 36 D3
Leven St 36 E6
Leven Ter 36 E6
Liddesdale Pl 36 E1
Little King St 37 G3
Livingstone Pl 37 G7
Lochend Cl 37 H4
Lochrin Pl 36 E6
Logan St 37 F2
Logie Grn Gdns 37 F1
Logie Grn Ln 37 F1
Logie Grn Rd 37 F1
Logie Mill 37 F1
London Rd 37 J3
London St 37 F2
Lonsdale Ter 36 E6
Lorne Pl 37 J1
Lorne Sq 37 J1
Lorne St 37 J1
Lothian Rd 36 D4
Lothian St 37 G5
Lower Gilmore Pl 36 D6
Lower London Rd 37 J3
Lutton Pl 37 H6
Lynedoch Pl La 36 C4
Lyne St 37 J3

**M**
McDonald Pl 37 G1
McDonald Rd 37 G1
McDonald St 37 G1
Mackenzie Pl 36 D3
McLeod St 36 A6
McNeill St 36 D6
Magdala Cres 36 B5
Magdala Ms 36 B5
Malta Grn 36 D2
Malta Ter 36 D2
Manor Pl 36 C4
Mansionhouse Rd 37 G7
Marchhall Cres 37 J7
Marchhall Pl 37 J7
Marchhall Rd 37 J7
Marchmont Cres 37 F7
Marchmont Rd 37 F6
Marchmont St 37 E7
Market St 37 F4
Marshall's Ct 37 G3
Marshall St 37 G5
Maryfield 37 J3
Maryfield Pl 37 J3
Meadow La 37 G6
Meadow Pl 37 F7
Melgund Ter 37 F2
Melville Dr 36 E6
Melville St 36 C4
Melville St La 36 D4
Melville Ter 37 G7
Merchant St 37 F5
Merchiston Av 36 C7
Merchiston Gro 36 A7
Merchiston Ms 36 C7
Merchiston Pk 36 C7
Mertoun Pl 36 C7
Meuse La 37 F4
Middlefield 37 H1
Millerfield Pl 37 G7
Miller Row 36 C4
Milton St 37 J3
Minto St 37 H7

Moncrieff Ter 37 G7
Montague St 37 H6
Montgomery St 37 H3
Montgomery St La 37 G2
Montpelier 36 D7
Montpelier Pk 36 D7
Montpelier Ter 36 D7
Montrose Ter 37 J3
Moray Pl 36 D3
Morrison Circ 36 C5
Morrison Cres 36 D5
Morrison Link 36 D5
Morrison St 36 C5
Mound, The 37 F4
Mound Pl 37 F4
Multrees Wk 37 F3
Murano Pl 37 H2
Murdoch Ter 36 C6
Murieston Cres 36 B6
Murieston Cres La 36 B6
Murieston La 36 B6
Murieston Pl 36 B6
Murieston Rd 36 B6
Murieston Ter 36 B6
Myrtle Ter 36 B7

**N**
Napier Rd 36 C7
Nelson St 37 F2
New Arthur Pl 37 H5
Newington Rd 37 H6
New John's Pl 37 H6
New Skinner's Cl 37 G4
New St 37 G4
Newton St 36 A7
Nicolson Sq 37 G5
Nicolson St 37 G5
Niddry St 37 G4
Niddry St S 37 G5
Nightingale Way 37 F6
North Bk St 37 F4
North Br 37 G4
North Castle St 36 D3
North Charlotte St 36 D3
North Clyde St La 37 F3
Northcote St 36 B6
North E Circ Pl 36 E3
North Pk Ter 36 C2
North Richmond St 37 G5
North St. Andrew La 37 F3
North St. Andrew St 37 F3
North St. David St 37 F3
Northumberland Pl La 37 F3
Northumberland St 37 E3
Northumberland St N E La 37 F3
Northumberland St N W La 37 E3
Northumberland St S E La 37 F3
Northumberland St S W La 37 E3
North Werber Pk 36 A1
North Werber Pl 36 B1
North W Circ Pl 36 D3
Norton Pk 37 J2

**O**
Old Broughton 37 F2
Old Fishmarket Cl 37 G4
Old Tolbooth Wynd 37 H4
Orchard Bk 36 A3
Orchard Brae 36 B2
Orchard Brae Av 36 B3
Orchard Brae Gdns 36 B3
Orchard Brae Gdns W 36 B3
Orchard Brae W 36 B2
Orchard Cres 36 A3
Orchard Dr 36 A3
Orchard Gro 36 B2
Orchard Pl 36 B2
Orchard Rd 36 A3
Orchard Rd S 36 A3
Orchard Ter 36 A3
Orwell Pl 36 C6
Orwell Ter 36 C6
Oxford St 37 H6
Oxford Ter 36 C3

**P**
Palmerston Pl 36 C4
Panmure Pl 37 E6
Papermill Wynd 37 G1
Parkside St 37 H6
Parkside Ter 37 H6
Parliament Sq 37 F4
Pembroke Pl 36 B5
Perth St 36 E2
Picardy Pl 37 G3
Pilrig Gdns 37 G1
Pilrig Glebe 37 H1
Pleasance 37 G5

Polwarth Cres 36 C7
Polwarth Gdns 36 C7
Polwarth Pk 36 C7
Polwarth Pl 36 C7
Ponton St 36 D6
Portgower Pl 36 D2
Port Hamilton 36 D6
Potterrow 37 G5
Powderhall Rd 37 F1
Priestfield Rd N 37 J7
Primrose Ter 36 B7
Princes St 36 D4

**Q**
Queen's Dr 37 H5
Queensferry Rd 36 B3
Queensferry St 36 D4
Queensferry St La 36 D4
Queensferry Ter 36 B3
Queen St 36 E3
Queen St Gdns E 37 F3
Queen St Gdns W 37 E3

**R**
Raeburn Ms 36 D2
Raeburn Pl 36 D2
Raeburn St 36 D2
Ramsay Gdn 37 F4
Ramsay La 37 F4
Randolph Cres 36 D4
Randolph La 36 D4
Randolph Pl 36 D4
Rankeillor St 37 H6
Ravelston Dykes 36 A4
Ravelston Pk 36 A4
Ravelston Ter 36 B4
Regent Pl 37 J3
Regent Rd 37 G3
Regent Ter 37 H3
Regent Ter Ms 37 H3
Register Pl 37 F3
Reid's Cl 37 H4
Reid Ter 36 D2
Richmond La 37 G5
Richmond Pl 37 G5
Richmond Ter 36 C5
Riego St 36 E5
Rillbank Cres 37 G7
Rillbank Ter 37 G7
Rintoul Pl 36 D2
Ritchie Pl 36 B7
Robertson Av 36 A7
Robertson Gait 36 A7
Robertson's Cl 37 G5
Rodney Pl 37 F2
Rodney St 37 F1
Romero Pl 37 J7
Rosebank Cotts 36 D5
Rosebery Cres 36 C5
Rosebery Cres La 36 C5
Roseburn Av 36 A5
Roseburn Cliff 36 A5
Roseburn Dr 36 A5
Roseburn Gdns 36 A5
Roseburn Maltings 36 A5
Roseburn Pl 36 A5
Roseburn Ter 36 A5
Rosemount Bldgs 36 D6
Roseneath Pl 37 F7
Roseneath St 37 F7
Roseneath Ter 37 F7
Rose St 36 E4
Rose St N La 36 E4
Rose St S La 36 E4
Rossie Pl 37 J2
Rosslyn Cres 37 G1
Rosslyn Ter 37 H1
Rothesay Ms 36 C4
Rothesay Pl 36 C4
Rothesay Ter 36 C4
Roxburgh Pl 37 G5
Roxburgh St 37 G5
Royal Circ 36 D3
Royal Cres 37 F2
Royal Ter 37 G3
Russell Gdns 36 A5
Russell Rd 36 A5
Rutland Ct La 36 D5
Rutland Sq 36 D4
Rutland St 36 D4

**S**
St. Andrew Sq 37 F3
St. Bernard's Cres 36 D3
St. Bernard's Row 36 D2
St. Catherine's Pl 37 G7
St. Clair Av 37 J1
St. Clair Pl 37 J1
St. Clair Rd 37 J1
St. Clair St 37 J1
St. Colme St 36 D4
St. David's Pl 36 D5
St. David's Ter 36 D5
St. Giles St 37 F4

St. James Pl 37 G3
St. James Sq 37 G3
St. John's Hill 37 H5
St. John St 37 H4
St. Leonard's Bk 37 H6
St. Leonard's Hill 37 H6
St. Leonard's La 37 H6
St. Leonard's St 37 H6
St. Mary's St 37 G4
St. Patrick Sq 37 G6
St. Stephen Pl 36 D2
St. Stephen St 36 D3
St. Vincent St 36 E2
Salisbury Ms 37 H7
Salisbury Pl 37 H7
Salisbury Rd 37 H7
Saunders St 36 D3
Saxe Coburg Pl 36 D2
Saxe Coburg St 36 D2
Sciennes 37 G7
Sciennes Gdns 37 G7
Sciennes Hill Pl 37 G7
Sciennes Ho Pl 37 G7
Sciennes Pl 37 G7
Sciennes Rd 37 F7
Scotland St 37 F2
Semple St 36 D5
Seton St 37 G7
Shandwick Pl 36 D5
Shaw's Pl 37 H1
Shaw's Sq 37 H1
Shaw's Ter 37 H1
Shrub Pl La 37 H1
Sienna Gdns 37 G7

Silvermills 36 E2
Simon Sq 37 G5
Simpson Loan 37 F6
Sinclair Cl 36 A7
Sinclair Gdns 36 A7
Sinclair Pl 36 A7
Sloan St 37 J1
Smithfield St 36 A7
South Br 37 G4
South Charlotte St 36 E4
South Clerk St 37 H6
South Coll St 37 G5
South E Circ Pl 36 E3
South Gray's Cl 37 G4
South Learmonth Av 36 C3
South Learmonth Gdns 36 C3
South Lorne Pl 37 J1
South Oxford St 37 H7
South St. Andrew St 37 F3
South St. David St 37 F3
South Sloan St 37 J1
Spence St 37 J7
Spey St 37 H1
Spey St La 37 H1
Spey Ter 37 H1
Spittal St 36 E5
Spottiswoode Rd 37 E7
Spottiswoode St 37 F7
Spring Gdns 37 J3
Springwell Pl 36 B6
Stafford St 36 D4
Stanhope Pl 36 B5
Stanhope St 36 B5

Stevenlaw's Cl 37 G4
Stewart Ter 36 A7
**Stockbridge** 36 E2
Succoth Gdns 36 A4
Succoth Pl 36 A4
Summer Bk 37 F2
Summerhall 37 G6
Summerhall Sq 37 H7
Sunbury Ms 36 C4
Sunbury Pl 36 C4
Sunbury St 36 C4
Sunnyside 37 J2
Sutherland St 36 B5
Sylvan Pl 37 G7

**T**
Tantallon Pl 37 G7
Tarvit St 36 E6
Tay St 36 C7
Temple Pk Cres 36 C7
Terrars Cft 37 H6
Teviotdale Pl 36 D1
Teviot Pl 37 F5
Thirlestane Rd 37 E7
Thistle Pl 36 C7
Thistle St 37 E3
Thistle St N E La 37 F3
Thistle St N W La 37 E3
Thistle St S W La 37 E3
Thornybauk 36 E6
Torphichen St 36 D5
Tron Sq 37 G4
Tynecastle La 36 B7
Tynecastle Ter 36 A7

Tytler Gdns 37 J3

**U**
Union St 37 G2
Upper Bow 37 F4
Upper Coltbridge Ter 36 A4
Upper Damside 36 C4
Upper Dean Ter 36 D3
Upper Gilmore Pl 36 D6
Upper Gilmore Ter 36 D6
Upper Gray St 37 H7
Upper Gro Pl 36 D6

**V**
Valleyfield St 36 E6
Veitch's Sq 36 D2
Victoria St 37 F5
Viewcraig Gdns 37 H4
Viewcraig St 37 H5
Viewforth 36 C6
Viewforth Gdns 36 D7
Viewforth Sq 36 D7
Viewforth Ter 36 D7

**W**
Walker St 36 C4
Wardlaw Pl 36 A7
Wardlaw St 36 A7
Warrender Pk Cres 36 E7
Warrender Pk Rd 36 E7
Warrender Pk Ter 37 E7
Warriston Cres 37 E1
Warriston Rd 37 E1
Washington La 36 B6

Waterloo Pl 37 G3
Watson Cres 36 B7
Waverley Br 37 F4
Waverley Pk 37 J3
Waverley Pk Ter 37 J3
Waverley Pl 37 J3
Wellington St 37 H2
Wemyss Pl 36 E3
Wemyss Pl Ms 36 D3
West Adam St 37 G5
West Annandale St 37 F1
West App Rd 36 D5
West Bow 37 F5
West Bryson Rd 36 B7
West Castle Rd 36 C7
West Catherine Pl 36 B5
West Coates 36 A5
West Coll St 37 G5
West Crosscauseway 37 G6
West End Pl 36 C6
Wester Coates Av 36 A5
Wester Coates Gdns 36 A5
Wester Coates Pl 36 B5
Wester Coates Rd 36 B5
Wester Coates Ter 36 A5
Westfield St 36 A7
Westhall Gdns 36 D7
West Maitland St 36 C5
West Mill La 36 C4
West Montgomery Pl 37 H2
West Newington Pl 37 H7
West Nicolson St 37 G5
West Norton Pl 37 J3
West Pk Pl 36 C6

West Port 37 E5
West Preston St 37 H7
West Register St 37 F3
West Register St La 37 F3
West Richmond St 37 G5
West Scotland St La 37 F2
West Silvermills La 36 E2
West Tollcross 36 E6
West Wds 36 A1
Wheatfield Pl 36 A7
Wheatfield Rd 36 A7
Wheatfield St 36 A7
Wheatfield Ter 36 A7
Whitehouse Ln 36 E7
White Pk 36 A7
William St 36 C5
William St N E La 36 D4
William St N W La 36 D4
William St S E La 36 D4
William St S W La 36 D5
Windmill La 37 G6
Windmill St 37 G6
Windsor St 37 H2
Windsor St La 37 H2

**Y**
Yeaman Pl 36 C6
York La 37 G3
York Pl 37 F3
Young St 36 D4
Young St La N 36 E4
Young St La S 36 E4

# Glasgow street index

**A**
Abbotsford Pl 39 E7
Abercromby Dr 39 J5
Abercromby Sq 39 J5
Abercromby St 39 J6
Academy Pk 38 A7
Adams Ct La 39 F5
Adelphi St 39 F6
Admiral St 38 C6
Aird's La 39 G5
Albert Br 39 G6
Albert Dr 38 B7
Albion Gate 39 G4
Albion St 39 G5
Alexander Cres 39 F7
Alexandra Par 39 J3
Allen Glen Pl 39 G3
Anchor La 39 F4
**Anderston** 38 E4
Anderston Quay 38 C5
Anson St 39 J7
Anthony St 38 D4
Arcadia Pl 39 J6
Arcadia St 39 J6
Argyle St 39 F4
Argyll Arc 39 F4
Ark La 39 J4
Arlington St 38 D2
Armour St 39 J5
Arthur St 38 A2
Ashley La 38 D2
Ashley St 38 D2
Ashton La 38 A1
Ashton Rd 38 A1
Auchentoshan Ter 39 J1

**B**
Bain St 39 H5
Baird St 39 H2
Balaclava St 38 D4
Baliol La 38 D2
Baliol St 38 D2
Ballantrae Ct 38 D4
Ballater Pl 39 G7
Ballater St 39 F6
Bank St 38 B1
Barrack St 39 J5
Barrington Dr 38 C1
Bath La 38 D3
Bath St 38 D3
Beaumont Gate 38 A1
Bedford La 39 F6
Bedford St 39 E6
Bell St 39 G4
Beltane St 38 D3
Benny Lynch Ct 39 G6
Benthall St 39 G7
Bentinck St 38 B2
Berkeley St 38 C3
Berkeley Ter La 38 C3

Binnie Pl 39 H6
Bishop St 38 D4
Blackburn St 38 B5
Blackfriars St 39 G4
Blackie St 38 B3
Black St 39 H2
Blantyre St 38 A2
**Blythswoodhill** 38 E3
Blythswood Sq 38 E3
Blythswood St 38 E4
Bothwell La 38 E4
Bothwell La (Hillhead) 38 C1
Bothwell St 38 E4
Braid Sq 38 E1
Braid St 38 E1
Breadalbane St 38 C3
Brechin St 38 C3
Bridgegate 39 F5
Bridge St 39 E6
Bridgeton Cross 39 J6
Bright St 39 J2
Broadford St 39 G1
Broomielaw 38 E5
Broompark Dr 39 J4
Brown St 38 E5
Bruce Rd 38 B7
Brunswick St 39 G4
Buccleuch La 38 E2
Buccleuch St 38 D2
Buchanan St 39 F4
Bunhouse Rd 38 A2
Burnbank Gdns 38 D1
Burnbank La 38 D1
Burnbank Pl 38 D1
Burnbank Ter 38 D1
Burns St 39 E1
Bute Gdns 38 B1
Bute La 38 B1

**C**
Cadogan St 38 E4
Cadzow St 38 D4
Caledonian Cres 38 C1
Caledonia Rd 39 F7
Caledon La 38 A1
Caledon St 38 A1
Calgary St 39 G2
Cambridge St 38 E3
Camden Ter 39 F7
Canal St 39 G2
Candleriggs 39 G5
Cardwell St 38 E7
Carfrae St 38 A3
Carlton Ct 39 E5
Carlton Pl 39 F5
Carnarvon St 38 D2
Carnoustie Pl 38 D6
Carnoustie St 38 D6
Carrick St 38 E5
Carrington St 38 D1

Castle St 39 H4
Cathcart Rd 39 F7
Cathedral Sq 39 H4
Cathedral St 39 F3
Cavendish Pl 38 E7
Cavendish St 38 E7
Cecil St 38 B1
Cedar Ct 38 E1
Cedar St 38 E1
Centre St 38 E6
**Cessnock** 38 A5
Chalmers St 39 J5
Charles St 39 J2
Charlotte St 39 H5
Cheapside St 38 D5
Chisolm St 39 G5
Church St 38 A2
Circus Dr 39 J4
Citizen La 39 F4
Civic St 39 E2
Clairmont Gdns 38 C2
Claremont Pl 38 C2
Claremont St 38 C3
Claremont Ter 38 C2
Claremont Ter La 38 C2
Clarendon Pl 38 D1
Clarendon St 38 D1
Clayslaps Rd 38 B2
Claythorn Av 39 H6
Claythorn Circ 39 H5
Claythorn Pk 39 H6
Claythorn St 39 J5
Claythorn Ter 39 J5
Cleland La 39 F6
Cleland St 39 F6
Cleveland La 38 D3
Cleveland St 38 D3
Clifford La 38 A6
Clifford Pl 38 A6
Clifford St 38 A6
Cliff Rd 38 C1
Clifton Pl 38 C3
Clifton St 38 C2
Clutha St 38 A6
Clyde Arc 38 B5
Clyde Pl 38 E5
Clydeside Expressway 38 B4
Clyde St 39 F5
Cobden Rd 39 J1
Coburg St 39 E6
Cochrane St 39 G4
College La 39 H4
College St 39 G4
Collins St 39 H4
Commerce St 39 E5
Commercial Ct 39 G6
Commercial Rd 39 G7
Congress Rd 38 B4
Congress Way 38 B4
Cook St 38 E6

Cooperage Pl 38 A3
Corn St 39 E1
Cornwall St S 38 B7
Corunna St 38 B3
Couper Pl 39 G2
Couper St 39 G2
Cowan La 38 C1
Cowan St 38 B1
**Cowcaddens** 39 F2
Cowcaddens Rd 39 E2
Cownwall St 38 B6
Cragmaddie Ter La 38 B2
Craighall Rd 39 F1
Craigiehall Pl 38 B5
Craigiehall St 38 B5
**Cranston Hill** 38 C3
Cranston St 38 C4
Cressnock St 38 A5
Crimea St 38 D4
Cromwell La 38 D1
Cromwell St 38 D1
Crownpoint Rd 39 J6
Crown St 39 F7
Cumberland Pl 39 G7
Cumberland St 39 E6

**D**
Dale Path 39 J7
Dalhouse St 38 E3
Dalhousie La 38 E2
Dalintober St 38 D6
Dalmarnock Rd 39 J7
Dalnair St 38 A2
Derby St 38 B3
Devon Pl 39 E7
Devon St 39 E7
Dixon St 39 F5
Dobbies Ln 39 F2
Dobbie's Ln Pl 39 G3
Dornoch St 39 J6
Dorset St 38 C3
Douglas La 38 E3
Douglas St 38 E4
Dover St 38 C3
Drake St 39 J6
Drury St 39 F4
Drygate 39 H4
Duke St 39 H4
Dunblane St 39 F2
Dunchattan Pl 39 J5
Dunchattan St 39 J4
Dundashill 39 F1
Dundas La 39 F3
Dundas St 39 F3
Dunearn St 38 D1
Dunlop St 39 F5
Durham St 38 B6

**E**
Eaglesham Ct 38 B5

Eaglesham Pl 38 B5
Eagle St 39 F1
Earlston Av 39 J2
Earlston Pl 39 J2
East Bath La 39 F3
East Campbell St 39 H5
Edington St 39 E1
Edwin St 38 B6
Eglinton Ct 39 E6
Elcho St 39 J5
Elderslie St 38 C2
Eldon St 38 C1
Elie St 38 A1
Elliot Pl 38 C4
Elliot St 38 C4
Elmbank Cres 38 D3
Elmbank St 38 D3
Elmbank St La 38 D3
Errol Gdns 39 F6
Esmond St 38 A2
Eton La 38 B1
Exchange Pl 39 F4

**F**
Falfield St 38 E7
Farnell St 39 E1
**Finnieston** 38 B3
Finnieston Quay 38 B4
Finnieston Sq 38 C3
Finnieston St 38 C4
Firpark St 39 J3
Firpark Ter 39 J4
Fitzroy La 38 B3
Florence St 39 G6
Forbes Dr 39 J6
Forbes St 39 J5
Fountainwell Av 39 H1
Fountainwell Dr 39 H1
Fountainwell Pl 39 H1
Fountainwell Rd 39 H1
Fountainwell Sq 39 H1
Fountainwell Ter 39 H1
Fox St 39 F5
Francis St 38 E7

**G**
Gadshill St 39 J2
Gallowgate 39 H5
**Garnethill** 38 E2
Garnethill St 38 E2
Garnet St 38 D3
Garscube Rd 38 E2
Garth St 39 G4
George Sq 39 F4
George St 39 G4
Gibson St 39 H5
Gibson St (Hillhead) 38 B1
Gilbert St 38 A3
Gilmour Pl 39 G7
Gladstone St 38 D1

Glasgow Br 39 F5
Glassford St 39 G4
Glebe Ct 39 H3
Glebe St 39 H2
Glenbarr St 39 J2
Glenfarg St 38 D1
Glenmavis St 39 E2
Gloucester St 38 D6
Goosedubbs 39 G5
**Gorbals** 39 G7
Gorbals St 39 F7
Gordon La 39 F4
Gordon St 39 E4
Gourock St 38 E7
Govan Rd 38 A5
Grace St 38 C4
Grafton Pl 39 G3
Graham Sq 39 J5
Graignestock St 39 J6
Granby La 38 B1
Grant St 38 D2
Granville St 38 D3
Gray St 38 B3
Great Dovehill 39 H5
Great George St 38 B1
Green, The 39 J7
Greendyke St 39 G5
Greenhead St 39 J6
Green St 39 J6
Grovepark Ct 38 D1
Grovepark Gdns 38 D1

**H**
Hallside Pl 39 G7
Handel Pl 39 F7
Hanover St 39 F4
Harley St 38 A6
Harvey St 39 F1
Harvie St 38 B5
Hastie St 38 A2
Haugh Rd 38 A3
Hayfield Ct 39 G7
Hayfield St 39 G7
Herbertson St 39 E6
High Craighall Rd 39 F1
High St 39 G5
Hillhead St 38 B1
Hill St 38 D2
Holland St 38 D3
Holm St 38 E4
Holyrood Cres 38 C1
Holyrood Quad 38 D1
Hopehill Rd 38 D1
Hope St 39 E4
Houldsworth La 38 C3
Houldsworth St 38 C3
Houston Pl 38 C5
Houston St 38 C6
Howard St 39 F5
Hunter St 39 H5

Huntingdon Rd 39 H1
Huntingdon Sq 39 H1
Hutcheson St 39 G5
**Hutchesontown** 39 G7
Hutchinson Town Ct 39 G7
Hydepark St 38 C5

**I**
India St 38 D3
Ingram St 39 G4

**J**
Jamaica St 39 F5
James Morrison St 39 G5
James Nisbet St 39 J3
James St 39 J7
James Watt St 38 E5
Jocelyn Sq 39 G5
John Knox St 39 J4
John St 39 G4

**K**
**Kelvingrove** 38 B2
Kelvingrove St 38 B3
**Kelvinhaugh** 38 A3
Kelvinhaugh Gate 38 A3
Kelvinhaugh Pl 38 B3
Kelvinhaugh St 38 A3
Kelvin Way 38 B2
Kennedy Path 39 G3
Kennedy St 39 G3
Kent Rd 38 C3
Kent St 39 H5
Keppochhill Pl 39 G1
Keppochhill Way 39 G1
Kerr Dr 39 J6
Kerr Pl 39 J6
Kerr St 39 J6
Kidston Pl 39 F7
Kidston Ter 39 F7
Kilbarchan St 39 E6
Kilbirnie Pl 38 D7
Kilbirnie St 38 D7
Killermont St 39 F3
King George V Br 39 E5
King's Br 39 H7
King's Dr 39 H7
**Kingston** 38 D6
Kingston St 38 E5
King St 39 G5
**Kinning Pk** 38 B6
Kinning St 38 D6
Kyle St 39 G2

**L**
La Belle Allee 38 C2
La Belle Pl 38 C2
Ladywell St 39 J4
Laidlaw St 38 D6
Laird Pl 39 J7
Lambhill Quad 38 B6
Lambhill St 38 B6
Lanark St 39 H5
Lancefield Quay 38 C4
Lancefield St 38 C4
Landressy Pl 39 J7
Landressy St 39 J7
Langshot St 38 A6
Lansdowne Cres 38 C1
Lansdowne Cres La 38 C1
Larbert St 39 F2
**Laurieston** 39 F6
Laurieston Rd 39 F7
Lendel Pl 38 A6
Lilybank Gdns 38 A1
Lilybank Gdns La 38 A1
Lilybank Ter 38 B1
Lister St 39 H2
Little Dovehill 39 H5
Little St 38 C4
London Rd 39 G5
Lorne St 38 B5
Lumsden St 38 A3
Lymburn St 38 B2
Lynedoch Cres 38 C2
Lynedoch Cres La 38 C2

Lynedoch Pl 38 C2
Lynedoch St 38 C2
Lynedoch Ter 38 D2

**M**
Mcalpine St 38 D5
McAslin Ct 39 H3
Mcaslin St 39 H3
McCulloch St 38 C7
Mcfarlane St 39 H5
McIntosh Ct 39 J4
McIntosh St 39 J4
Mcintyre St 38 D4
MacKeith St 39 J7
MacKinlay St 39 E7
Maclean Sq 38 B5
Maclean St 38 B5
Maclennan St 38 A6
Macleod St 39 H4
McNeil Gdns 39 H7
McNeil St 39 G7
McPhail St 39 J7
McPhater St 39 F2
Mair St 38 B5
Maitland St 39 F2
Malta Ter 39 F7
Manresa Pl 39 E1
Marine Cres 38 C5
Marine Gdns 38 C5
Marlow St 38 C7
Martha St 39 G3
Mart St 39 G5
Mary St 39 F1
Mauchline St 38 E7
Mavisbank Gdns 38 B5
Maxwell Av 38 C7
Maxwell Ct 38 B7
Maxwell Dr 38 B7
Maxwell Gdns 38 A7
Maxwell Grn 38 B7
Maxwell La 38 C7
Maxwell Oval 38 C7
Maxwell Rd 38 C7
Megan Gate 39 F5
Megan St 39 J7
Melbourne St 39 J5
Melrose St 38 D1
**Merchant City** 39 G4
Merchant La 39 G5
Metropole La 39 F5
Middlesex Gdns 38 B6
Middlesex St 38 B6
Middleton St 38 A5
Midland St 39 E4
Midwharf St 39 F1
Miller St 39 F4
Millroad Dr 39 J5
Millroad Gdns 39 J5
Millroad St 39 H5
Milnpark Gdns 38 B6
Milnpark St 38 B6
Milton St 39 F2
Minerva St 38 B3
Minerva Way 38 B3
Mitchell La 39 F4
Mitchell St 39 F4
Moffat St 39 G7
Moir St 39 H5
Molendinar St 39 H5
Moncur St 39 H5
Montague St 38 C1
Monteith Pl 39 H6
Monteith Row 39 H5
Montrose St 39 G4
Moore St 39 J5
Morrison Ct 39 F4
Morrison St 38 D5
Mosque Av 39 F6
Muslin St 39 J7

**N**
Naburn Gate 39 F7
Nairn St 38 A2
Napiershall La 38 D1
Napiershall Pl 38 D1

Napiershall St 38 D1
Nelson Mandela Pl 39 F4
Nelson St 38 E5
Netherby Dr 38 A7
New City Rd 38 D2
Newton St 38 D2
Newton Ter La 38 C3
New Wynd 39 G5
Nicholas St 39 H4
Nicholson St 39 F6
Norfolk Ct 39 F6
Norfolk St 39 F6
North Canal Bk 39 F4
North Canal Bk St 39 F1
North Claremount St 38 C2
North Ct 39 F4
North Ct La 39 F4
North Dr 39 F4
North Frederick Path 39 G3
North Frederick St 39 G4
North Gower St 38 A6
North Hanover St 39 G4
North Portland St 39 G4
North St 38 D2
North Wallace St 39 G2

**O**
Oakfield Av 38 B1
Oakfield La 38 B1
Oak St 38 D4
Old Dumbarton Rd 38 A2
Old Rutherglen Rd 39 G6
Old Wynd 39 G5
Oregon Pl 39 G7
Orr St 39 J6
Osborne St 39 F5
Oswald St 39 E5
Otago La 38 C1
Otago La N 38 C1
Otago St 38 B1
Overnewton Pl 38 B3
Overnewton Sq 38 A3
Overnewton St 38 A2
Oxford La 39 F5
Oxford St 39 E5

**P**
Pacific Dr 38 A5
Pacific Quay 38 A4
Paisley Rd 38 D5
Paisley Rd W 38 C5
Palmerston Pl 38 B3
Parine St 39 G5
Park Av 38 C1
Park Circ 38 C2
Park Circ La 38 C2
Park Circ Pl 38 C2
Park Dr 38 C1
Park Gdns 38 C2
Park Gdns La 38 C2
Park Gate 38 C2
Parkgrove Ter 38 B2
Parkgrove Ter La 38 B2
Park Quad 38 C2
Park Rd 38 C1
Park St S 38 C2
Park Ter 38 C2
Park Ter E La 38 C2
Park Terrace La 38 C2
Parsonage Row 39 H4
Parsonage Sq 39 H4
Parson St 39 H3
Paterson St 38 D6
Payne St 39 F1
Pembroke St 38 C3
Percy St 38 A6
Perth St 38 D4
Piccadilly St 38 D4
Pine Pl 39 G7
Pinkston Dr 39 H2
Pinkston Rd 39 H1
Pitt St 38 E4
Plantation Pk Gdns 38 A5
Plantation Sq 38 B5
**Port Dundas** 39 F1
Port Dundas La 39 F3

Port Dundas Rd 39 F2
**Port Eglinton** 38 D7
Portman St 38 C6
Port St 38 C3
Portugal St 39 F6
Possil Rd 39 E1
Professors Sq 38 B1
Provanhill St 39 J2

**Q**
Queen Elizabeth Gdns 39 G7
Queens Cres 38 D1
Queen St 39 F4

**R**
Radnor St 38 B2
Raglan St 38 E1
Regent Moray St 38 A2
Renfield La 38 E4
Renfield St 39 F4
Renfrew Ct 39 F3
Renfrew La 39 F3
Renfrew St 38 D2
Renton St 39 F2
Rhymer St 39 J2
Richmond St 39 G4
Ritchie St 38 E7
Riverview Dr 38 D5
Riverview Gdns 38 E5
Riverview Pl 38 D5
Robertson La 38 E4
Robertson St 38 E5
Rodney St 39 E1
Ropework La 39 F5
Rose St 39 E3
Ross St 39 H5
Rottenrow 39 G3
Rottenrow E 39 H4
Royal Bk Pl 39 F4
Royal Cres 38 B3
Royal Ex Ct 39 F4
Royal Ex Sq 39 F4
Royal Ter 38 B2
Royal Ter La 38 B2
**Royston** 39 J2
Roystonhill 39 J2
Royston Rd 39 J2
Royston Sq 39 J2
Rupert St 38 D1
Rutland Ct 38 C5
Rutland Cres 38 C5
Rutland Pl 38 B5

**S**
St. Andrews Cres 38 C7
St. Andrew's La 39 G5
St. Andrews Rd 38 C7
St. Andrews Sq 39 G5
St. Andrews St 39 G5
St. Clair St 38 D1
**St. Enoch** 39 F5
St. Enoch Sq 39 F4
St. Francis Rigg 39 G7
St. Georges Rd 38 D2
St. Georges Rd 38 D2
St. James Rd 39 G3
St. John's Ct 38 B7
St. John's Quad 38 C7
St. Josephs Vw 39 J2
St. Luke's Pl 39 F6
St. Luke's Ter 39 F6
St. Margaret's Pl 39 G5
St. Marys La 39 F4
St. Mungo Av 39 G3
St. Mungo Pl 39 H3
St. Ninian Ter 39 F6
St. Peters La 38 E4
St. Peters St 38 E2
St. Rollox Brae 39 J1
St. Valentine Ter 39 G7
St. Vincent Cres 38 B3
St. Vincent Cres La 38 B3
St. Vincent La 38 E3
St. Vincent Pl 39 F4
St. Vincent St 38 C3
St. Vincent Ter 38 C3

Salisbury La 39 F7
Salisbury St 39 F7
Salkeld St 38 E7
Saltmarket 39 G5
Sandiefield Rd 39 F7
Sandyford Pl La 38 C3
Sandyford St 38 A3
Saracen Head Rd 39 H5
Sauchiehall La 38 E3
Sauchiehall St 38 B2
Savoy St 39 J7
Sawmillfield St 39 E1
Scotland St 38 C6
Scotland St W 38 B6
Scott St 38 E3
Seamore St 38 D1
Seaward La 38 C5
Seaward Pl 38 C6
Seaward St 38 C6
Shaftesbury St 38 D3
Shamrock St 38 E2
Shields Rd 38 C6
Shipbank La 39 G5
Shuttle St 39 G4
**Sighthill** 39 H1
Silverfir St 39 G7
Silvergrove St 39 J6
Snowdon St 39 G7
Somerset Pl Ms 38 C2
South Ex Ct 39 F4
South Frederick St 39 G4
Southpark Av 38 B1
Southpark La 38 B1
South Portland St 39 F5
Southside Cres 39 F7
South Woodside Rd 38 C1
Spiers Wf 39 F1
Spoutmouth 39 H5
Springburn Rd 39 J2
Springfield Ct 39 F4
Springfield Quay 38 C5
Spring Wynd 39 G7
Stafford St 39 G2
Stanley St 38 C6
Stanley St La 38 C6
Steel St 39 G5
Stevenson St 39 J6
Stewart St 39 F2
Stirlingfauld Pl 39 F7
Stirling Rd 39 H3
Stobcross Rd 38 A3
Stobcross St 38 C4
Stockwell Pl 39 F5
Stockwell St 39 F5
Stromness St 38 E7
Suffolk St 39 H5
Surrey St 39 F7
Sussex St 38 B6
Sutherland La 38 A1
Swan St 39 G2
Sydney St 39 J5

**T**
Taylor Pl 39 H3
Taylor St 39 H4
Templeton St 39 J6
Teviot St 38 A3
Thistle St 39 G6
Thistle Ter 39 F7
Thornbank St 38 A3
Thurso St 38 A2
Tobago Pl 39 J5
Tobago St 39 J6
Toll La 38 C5
Tontine La 39 G5
Torness St 38 A1
Tower St 38 B6
**Townhead** 39 G2
Townsend St 39 F2
**Tradeston** 39 E6
Tradeston St 38 E6
Trongate 39 G5
Tullis Ct 39 J7
Tullis St 39 J7
Tunnel St 38 B4
Tureen St 39 J5

Turnbull St 39 G5
Turnlaw St 39 H7
Turriff St 39 E7
Tyndrum St 39 F2

**U**
Union Pl 39 F4
Union St 39 F4
Unity Pl 38 E1
University Av 38 A1
University Gdns 38 A1
University Pl 38 A1

**V**
Vermont St 38 B6
Victoria Br 39 F5
Viewfield La 38 B1
Vinter St 39 F1
Virginia Pl 39 G4
Virginia St 39 G4

**W**
Waddell Ct 39 G6
Waddell St 39 G7
Wallace St 38 D5
Walls St 39 G4
Walmer Cres 38 A6
Warnock St 39 J3
Warroch St 38 D5
Washington St 38 D5
Waterloo La 39 E4
Waterloo St 38 E4
Waterside Pl 39 H7
Waterside St 39 G5
Watson St 39 G5
Watt St 38 C6
Weaver St 39 H4
Wellcroft Pl 39 E7
Wellington La 38 E4
Wellington St 38 E4
Wellpark St 39 J4
Westbank La 38 B1
Westbank Quad 38 B1
West Campbell St 38 E4
West End Pk St 38 C2
West George La 38 E3
West George St 38 E3
West Graham St 38 E2
West Greenhill Pl 38 B3
West Nile St 39 F4
West Prince's La 38 C1
West Princes St 38 C1
West Regent La 39 E3
West Regent St 39 E3
West St 38 D7
Whitehall St 38 D4
William St 38 D3
Willowbank Cres 38 C1
Willowbank St 38 C2
Wilson St 39 G4
Windsor St 38 D1
Windsor Ter 38 D1
Wishart St 39 J4
Woodlands Dr 38 C1
Woodlands Gate 38 C2
Woodlands Rd 38 C1
Woodlands Ter 38 C2
Woodrow Circ 38 A7
Woodrow Pl 38 A7
Woodrow Rd 38 A7
Woodside Cres 38 D2
Woodside Pl 38 C2
Woodside Pl La 38 C2
Woodside Ter 38 C2
Woodside Ter La 38 C2

**Y**
**Yorkhill** 38 B2
Yorkhill Par 38 A2
Yorkhill St 38 A3
York St 38 E5

# Leeds street index

**A**
Abbey St 40 C3
Abbott Ct 40 A3
Abbott Rd 40 A4
Abbott Vw 40 A3
Admiral St 41 E7
Aire St 40 D4
Albion Pl 41 E3

Albion St 41 E3
Alexander St 40 E3
Alexandra Gro 40 B1
Alexandra Rd 40 A1
Alma St 41 H2
Anderson Av 41 H1
Anderson Mt 41 H1
Apex Vw 40 E6

Apex Way 41 E6
Appleton Cl 41 J3
Appleton Ct 41 J3
Appleton Sq 41 J3
Appleton Way 41 J3
Archery Pl 40 D1
Archery Rd 40 D1
Archery St 40 E1

Archery Ter 40 E1
Armley Rd 40 A3
Armouries Rd 41 G5
Artist St 40 B4
Ascot Ter 41 J4
Ashley Av 41 J1
Ashley Rd 41 J1
Ashley Ter 41 J1

Ashton Av 41 J1
Ashton Gro 41 J1
Ashton Mt 41 J1
Ashton Pl 41 J1
Ashton Ter 41 J1
Ashton Vw 41 J1
Ashville Vw 40 A1
Assembly St 41 F4

Atkinson St 41 G6
Autumn Av 40 B1
Autumn Gro 40 B1
Autumn Pl 40 B1
Autumn St 40 B1
Autumn Ter 40 B1
Avenue, The 41 G4
Aysgarth Cl 41 J4

Aysgarth Dr 41 J4
Aysgarth Pl 41 J4
Aysgarth Wk 41 J4

**B**

Back Ashville Av 40 A1
Back Hyde Ter 40 C2
Back Row 40 E5
Balm Pl 40 C6
Balm Wk 40 C6
Bank St 41 E4
Baron Cl 40 C7
Barrack St 41 F1
Barran Ct 41 H1
Barton Gro 40 D7
Barton Mt 40 D7
Barton Pl 40 C7
Barton Rd 40 C7
Barton Ter 40 D7
Barton Vw 40 C7
Bath Rd 40 D5
Bayswater Vw 41 H1
Beamsley Gro 40 A1
Beamsley Mt 40 A1
Beamsley Pl 40 A1
Beamsley Ter 40 A1
Beckett St 41 H3
Bedford St 40 E3
Beech Gro Ter 40 D1
Belgrave St 41 E3
Belinda St 41 H7
Belle Vue Rd 40 B2
Bell St 41 G3
Belmont Gro 40 D2
Benson St 41 F1
Benyon Pk Way 40 A7
Berking Av 41 J3
Bertrand St 40 C6
Bexley Av 41 H1
Bexley Gro 41 J1
Bexley Mt 41 H1
Bexley Pl 41 H1
Bexley Rd 41 J1
Bexley Ter 41 J1
Bingley St 40 C3
Bishopgate St 40 E4
Bismarck Dr 40 E7
Bismarck St 40 E7
Black Bull St 41 F5
Blackman La 40 E1
Blandford Gdns 40 D1
Blandford Gro 40 D1
Blayds St 41 H4
Blayd's Yd 41 E4
Blenheim Av 40 E1
Blenheim Ct 40 E1
Blenheim Cres 40 E1
Blenheim Gro 40 E1
Blenheim Sq 40 E1
Blenheim Vw 40 D1
Blenheim Wk 40 D1
Blundell St 40 D2
Boar La 40 E4
Bodley Ter 40 A2
Bond St 40 E3
Boundary Pl 41 G1
Boundary St 41 G1
Bourse, The 41 E4
Bowling Grn Ter 40 D6
Bowman La 41 F4
Bow St 41 G4
Bracken Ct 40 A6
Braithwaite St 40 C5
Brancepeth Pl 40 B4
Brandon Rd 40 C2
Brandon St 40 B4
Branksome Pl 40 B1
Brick St 41 G4
Bridge Ct 40 C5
Bridge End 41 E4
Bridge Rd 40 C5
Bridge St 41 F3
Bridgewater Rd 41 H6
Briggate 41 E4
Brignall Garth 41 J2
Brignall Way 41 H2
Bristol St 41 G2
Britannia St 40 D4
Broadway Av 40 A1
Brookfield St 41 G6
Brown Av 40 B7
Brown La E 40 B6
Brown La W 40 A6
Brown Pl 40 B7
Brown Rd 40 B7
Bruce Gdns 40 B4
Bruce Lawn 40 B4
Brunswick Ct 41 F3
Brunswick Ter 41 E2
Brussels St 41 G4
Buckton Cl 40 C7
Buckton Mt 40 C7
Buckton Vw 40 C7
**Burley** 40 A1

Burley Lo Pl 40 B2
Burley Lo Rd 40 A1
Burley Lo St 40 B2
Burley Lo Ter 40 B1
Burley Pl 40 A2
Burley Rd 40 A1
Burley St 40 C3
**Burmantofts** 41 H3
Burmantofts St 41 G3
Burton Row 41 E7
Burton St 41 E7
Burton Way 41 J2
Butterfield St 41 H4
Butterley St 41 F6
Butts Ct 41 E3
Byron St 41 F2

**C**

Cain Cl 41 H4
Call La 41 F4
Calls, The 41 F4
Calverley St 40 D2
Cambrian St 40 D7
Cambrian Ter 40 D7
Canal Pl 40 B4
Canal St 40 A3
Canal Wf 40 D4
Carberry Pl 40 A1
Carberry Rd 40 A1
Carberry Ter 40 A1
Carlisle Rd 41 G5
Carlton Carr 41 E1
Carlton Ct 40 A7
Carlton Gdns 41 E1
Carlton Gate 41 E1
Carlton Gro 41 E1
Carlton Hill 41 E1
Carlton Pl 41 E1
Carlton Ri 41 E1
Carlton Twrs 41 F1
Carlton Vw 41 E1
Castle St 40 D3
Castleton Cl 40 B4
Castleton Rd 40 A3
Cautley Rd 41 J5
Cavalier App 41 H5
Cavalier Cl 41 H5
Cavalier Ct 41 H5
Cavalier Gdns 41 H5
Cavalier Gate 41 H5
Cavalier Ms 41 H5
Cavalier Vw 41 H5
Cavendish Rd 40 D1
Cavendish St 40 C3
Cemetery Rd 40 C7
Central Rd 41 F4
Central St 40 D3
Chadwick St 41 F5
Chadwick St S 41 G5
Chantrell Ct 41 F4
Charles Av 41 J5
Charlton Gro 41 J4
Charlton Pl 41 J4
Charlton Rd 41 J4
Charlton St 41 J4
Cherry Pl 41 G2
Cherry Row 41 G2
Chesney Av 41 F7
Chiswick St 40 A2
Chorley La 40 D2
Churchill Gdns 40 E1
Church La 41 F4
City Sq 40 E4
City Wk 40 E5
Claremont Av 40 C2
Claremont Gro 40 C2
Claremont Vw 40 C2
Clarence Rd 41 G5
Clarendon Pl 40 C1
Clarendon Rd 40 C1
Clarendon Way 40 D2
Clark Av 41 J4
Clark Cres 41 J4
Clark Gro 41 J5
Clark La 41 H5
Clark Mt 41 J4
Clark Rd 41 J5
Clark Row 41 J5
Clark Ter 41 J4
Clark Vw 41 J5
Clay Pit La 41 E2
Cleveleys Av 40 C7
Cleveleys Mt 40 C7
Cleveleys Rd 40 C7
Cleveleys St 40 C7
Cleveleys Ter 40 C7
Cloberry St 40 C1
Close, The 41 G4
Cloth Hall St 41 F4
Clyde App 40 A5
Clyde Gdns 40 B5
Clyde Vw 40 A5
Coleman St 40 B5
Colenso Gdns 40 C7

Colenso Mt 40 C7
Colenso Pl 40 C7
Colenso Rd 40 C7
Colenso Ter 40 C7
Colville Ter 40 D7
Commercial St 41 E3
Compton Av 41 J1
Compton Cres 41 J1
Compton Gro 41 J1
Compton Mt 41 J1
Compton Pl 41 J1
Compton Rd 41 J1
Compton St 41 J1
Compton Ter 41 J1
Compton Vw 41 J1
Concordia St 41 E4
Concord St 41 F2
Consort St 40 C2
Consort Ter 40 C2
Consort Vw 40 B2
Consort Wk 40 C2
Constance Gdns 40 E1
Constance Way 40 E1
Cookridge St 40 E3
Copley Hill 40 A5
Copley Hill Way 40 A6
Copley St 40 A5
Copperfield Av 41 J5
Copperfield Cres 41 J5
Copperfield Gro 41 J5
Copperfield Mt 41 J5
Copperfield Pl 41 J5
Copperfield Row 41 J5
Copperfield Ter 41 J5
Copperfield Vw 41 J5
Copperfield Wk 41 J5
Copperfiield Dr 41 J5
Cotton St 41 G4
Coupland Pl 40 D7
Coupland Rd 40 D7
Cowper Av 41 J1
Cowper Cres 41 J1
Cowper Rd 41 J1
Cromer Pl 40 C1
Cromer Rd 40 C1
Cromer St 40 C1
Cromer Ter 40 C2
Cromwell Mt 41 G2
Cromwell St 41 G3
Crosby Pl 40 C6
Crosby Rd 40 C7
Crosby St 40 C6
Crosby Ter 40 C6
Crosby Vw 40 C6
Cross Aysgarth Mt 41 H4
Cross Belgrave St 41 F3
Cross Catherine St 41 H4
**Cross Grn** 41 J6
Cross Grn App 41 J6
Cross Grn Av 41 H5
Cross Grn Cl 41 J6
Cross Grn Cres 41 H5
Cross Grn Dr 41 J6
Cross Grn Garth 41 J6
Cross Grn La 41 H5
Cross Grn Ri 41 J6
Cross Grn Way 41 J6
Cross Ingram Rd 41 F7
Cross Kelso Rd 40 C2
Cross Mitford Rd 40 A4
Cross Stamford St 41 F2
Cross York St 41 F4
Crown Ct 41 F4
Crown Pt Rd 41 F5
Crown St 41 F4
Croydon St 40 B5
Cudbear St 41 F5
Czar St 40 C5

**D**

Danby Wk 41 H4
David St 40 D5
Dene Ho Ct 40 E1
Denison Rd 40 C3
Dent St 41 H4
Derwent Pl 40 D5
Devon Cl 40 D1
Devon Rd 40 D1
Dewsbury Rd 41 E6
Dial St 41 H5
Disraeli Gdns 40 E7
Disraeli Ter 40 E7
Dock St 41 F4
Dolly La 41 G2
Dolphin Ct 41 H4
Dolphin St 41 H4
Domestic Rd 40 B6
Domestic St 40 C5
Donisthorpe St 41 G6
Drive, The 41 G4
Driver Ter 40 B5
Dudley Way 41 E3
Duke St 41 F3
Duncan St 41 E4

Duncombe St 40 C3
Duxbury Ri 40 E1
Dyer St 41 F3

**E**

East Fld St 41 H4
Eastgate 41 F3
East King St 41 G4
East Par 40 E3
East Pk Dr 41 J4
East Pk Gro 41 J4
East Pk Mt 41 J4
East Pk Par 41 J4
East Pk Pl 41 J4
East Pk Rd 41 J4
East Pk St 41 J4
East Pk Ter 41 J4
East Pk Vw 41 J4
East St 41 G4
Easy Rd 41 H5
Ebor Mt 40 B1
Ebor Pl 40 B1
Ebor St 40 B1
Edgware Av 41 H1
Edgware Gro 41 H1
Edgware Mt 41 H1
Edgware Pl 41 H1
Edgware Row 41 H1
Edgware St 41 H1
Edgware Ter 41 H1
Edgware Vw 41 H1
Edward St 41 F3
Edwin Rd 40 B1
Eighth Av 40 A5
Elland Rd 40 C7
Elland Ter 40 D6
Ellerby La 41 H5
Ellerby Rd 41 G4
Elmtree La 41 G7
Elmwood La 41 F2
Elmwood Rd 41 E2
Elsworth St 40 A4
Enfield Av 41 G1
Enfield St 41 G1
Enfield Ter 41 G1
Euston Gro 40 B7
Euston Mt 40 B7
Euston Ter 40 B7
Everleigh St 41 J3

**F**

Far Cft Ter 40 A5
Fewston Av 41 H5
Fewston Ct 41 J5
Finsbury Rd 40 D2
First Av 40 A4
Firth St 41 G2
Firth Ter 41 G2
Fish St 41 F3
Flax Pl 41 G4
Florence Av 41 J1
Florence Gro 41 J1
Florence Mt 41 J1
Florence Pl 41 J1
Florence St 41 J1
Folly La 40 D7
Forster St 41 G6
Foundry St
  (Holbeck) 40 D5
Foundry St
  (Quarry Hill) 41 G4
Fountain St 40 D3
Fourteenth Av 40 A5
Fourth Ct 40 C5
Fox Way 41 H6
Fraser St 41 J2
Frederick Av 41 J5
Front Row 40 D5
Front St 40 D5

**G**

Gardeners Ct 41 G7
Gargrave App 41 H3
Gargrave Pl 41 H2
Garth, The 41 G4
Garton Av 41 J4
Garton Gro 41 J4
Garton Rd 41 J4
Garton Ter 41 J4
Garton Vw 41 J4
Gelderd Pl 40 B5
Gelderd Rd 40 A7
George St 41 F3
Gibraltar
  Island Rd 41 H7
Gilpin Pl 40 A5
Gilpin St 40 A5
Gilpin Ter 40 A5
Gilpin Vw 40 A5
Glasshouse St 41 G6
Gledhow Mt 41 H1
Gledhow Pl 41 H1
Gledhow Rd 41 H1
Gledhow Ter 41 H1

Glencoe Vw 41 J5
Glensdale Gro 41 J4
Glensdale Mt 41 J4
Glensdale Rd 41 J4
Glensdale St 41 J4
Glensdale Ter 41 J4
Glenthorpe Av 41 J3
Glenthorpe Cres 41 J3
Glenthorpe Ter 41 J3
Globe Rd 40 C4
Gloucester Ter 40 A4
Goodman St 41 G6
Gotts Rd 40 C4
Gower St 41 F3
Grace St 40 D3
Grafton St 41 F2
Grange Cl 41 G7
Grange Rd 41 G7
Grant Av 41 G1
Granville Rd 41 H2
Grape St 41 F7
Grasmere Cl 40 A5
Grassmere Rd 40 A5
Great George St 40 D3
Great Wilson St 40 E5
Greek St 40 E3
Greenfield Rd 41 H4
Green La 40 A5
Grosvenor Hill 41 E1

**H**

Hall Gro 40 B1
Hall La 40 A4
Hall Pl 41 H4
Hanover Av 40 C2
Hanover La 40 D3
Hanover Mt 40 C2
Hanover Sq 40 C2
Hanover Wk 40 C3
Harewood St 41 F3
Harold Av 40 A1
Harold Gro 40 A1
Harold Mt 40 A1
Harold Pl 40 A1
Harold Rd 40 A1
Harold St 40 A1
Harold Ter 40 A1
Harold Vw 40 A1
Harold Wk 40 A1
Harper St 41 F4
Harrison St 41 F3
Hartwell Rd 40 B1
Haslewood Cl 41 H3
Haslewood Ct 41 H3
Haslewood Dene 41 H3
Haslewood Dr 41 H3
Haslewood Ms 41 J3
Haslewood Pl 41 H3
Haslewood Sq 41 H3
Hawkins Dr 41 E1
Headrow, The 40 D3
Heaton's Ct 41 E4
Hedley Chase 40 A4
Hedley Gdns 40 A4
Hedley Grn 40 A4
High 41 G7
High Ct 41 F4
High Ct La 41 F4
Hillary Pl 40 D1
Hillidge Rd 41 F7
Hillidge Sq 41 F7
Hill Top Pl 40 B1
Hill Top St 40 B1
Hirst's Yd 41 F4
**Holbeck** 40 D5
Holbeck La 40 C5
Holbeck Moor Rd 40 C6
Holdforth Cl 40 A4
Holdforth Gdns 40 A4
Holdforth Grn 40 A4
Holdforth Pl 40 A4
Holmes St 41 E5
Holroyd St 41 G1
Hope Rd 41 G3
Howden Gdns 40 B1
Howden Pl 40 B1
Hudson Rd 41 J1
Hudswell Rd 41 F7
**Hunslet** 41 G7
Hunslet
  Grn Way 41 F7
Hunslet Hall Rd 40 E7
Hunslet La 41 F5
Hunslet Rd 41 F4
Hyde Pk Cl 40 B1
Hyde Pk Rd 40 B1
Hyde Pl 40 C2
Hyde St 40 C2
Hyde Ter 40 C2

**I**

Infirmary St 40 E3
Ingram Cl 40 C6
Ingram Cres 40 B7

Ingram Gdns 40 C6
Ingram Rd 40 C7
Ingram Row 40 E5
Ingram St 40 E5
Ingram Vw 40 C6
Inner Ring Rd 40 E2
Ivory St 41 F6

**J**

Jack La 40 D6
Jenkinson Cl 40 D6
Jenkinson Lawn 40 D6
John Smeaton
  Viaduct 41 G6
Joseph St 41 G7
Junction St 41 F5

**K**

Keeton St 41 H3
Kelsall Av 40 B1
Kelsall Gro 40 B2
Kelsall Pl 40 B1
Kelsall Rd 40 B1
Kelsall Ter 40 B1
Kelso Gdns 40 C1
Kelso Rd 40 C1
Kelso St 40 C2
Kendal Bk 40 C2
Kendal Cl 40 C2
Kendal Gro 40 C2
Kendal La 40 C2
Kendell St 41 F4
Kenneth St 40 B6
Kepler Gro 41 H1
Kepler Mt 41 H1
Kepler Ter 41 H1
Kidacre St 41 F5
Kildare Ter 40 B5
King Charles St 41 E3
King Edward St 41 F3
Kings Av 40 B2
King's Rd 40 B1
Kingston Ter 40 D1
King St 40 D4
Kippax Pl 41 H4
Kirkgate 41 F4
Kirkstall Rd 40 A2
Kitson Rd 41 G6
Kitson St 41 H4
Knowsthorpe Cres 41 H5
Knowsthorpe La 41 J6

**L**

Ladybeck Cl 41 F3
Lady La 41 F3
Lady Pit La 40 D7
Lands La 41 E3
Lane, The 41 G4
Larchfield Rd 41 G6
Latchmore Rd 40 A7
Laura St 40 C5
Lavender Wk 41 H4
Leathley Rd 41 F6
Leathley St 41 F6
Leicester Cl 40 E1
Leicester Gro 40 E1
Leicester Pl 40 D1
Leighton St 40 D3
Leodis Ct 40 D5
Leylands Rd 41 G2
Lifton Pl 40 C1
Lincoln Grn Rd 41 G2
Lincoln Rd 41 G2
Lindsey Ct 41 H2
Lindsey Gdns 41 H2
Lindsey Rd 41 H2
Lisbon St 40 D3
Little King St 40 E4
Little Queen St 40 D4
Little Woodhouse St 40 D2
Livinia Gro 40 E1
Lodge St 40 D1
Lofthouse Pl 40 E1
Londesboro Gro 41 J4
Long Causeway 41 H6
Long Cl La 41 H4
Lord St 40 C5
Lord Ter 40 B5
Lovell Pk Cl 41 F2
Lovell Pk Gate 41 F2
Lovell Pk Hill 41 F2
Lovell Pk Rd 41 F2
Lovell Pk Vw 41 F2
Lower Basinghall St 40 E3
Lower Brunswick St 41 F2
Low Flds Av 40 B7
Low Flds Rd 40 A7
Low Flds Way 40 B7
Low Fold 41 G5
Low Rd 41 G5
Low Whitehouse Row 41 G6
Ludgate Hill 41 F3
Lyddon Ter 40 C1
Lydgate 41 J2

Lydia St 41 F3

**M**
Mabgate 41 G3
Mabgate Grn 41 G3
Macauley St 41 G3
Maitland Pl 40 D7
Maltings Rd 41 F7
Malvern Gro 40 D7
Malvern Ri 40 D7
Malvern Rd 40 C7
Malvern St 40 C7
Malvern Vw 40 C7
Manor Rd 40 D5
Manor St 41 G1
Mark La 41 E3
Marlborough Gdns 40 D1
Marlborough Gro 40 D1
Marlborough St 40 C3
Marlborough Twrs 40 C3
Marshall St 40 D5
Marsh La 41 G4
Maude St 41 F4
May Ter 41 H5
Meadowcroft Ms 41 H4
Meadow La 41 E5
Meadow Rd 40 E6
Melbourne St 41 F2
Merrion Pl 41 F3
Merrion St 41 E3
Merrion Way 41 E2
Meynell App 40 C6
Middleton Av 41 J2
Milford Pl 40 A2
Millgarth St 41 F3
Mill Grn 40 B5
Mill Hill 41 E4
Mill St 41 G4
Millwright St 41 G2
Milner Gdns 41 H5
Milnes St 40 B5
Mitford Rd 40 A4
Mitford Vw 40 A4
Moor Cres 41 E7
Moor Cres Chase 41 E7
Moorland Av 40 B1
Moorland Rd 40 B1
Moor Rd 41 E7
Moorside Maltings 41 E7
Moor Vw 40 D6
Moorville Cl 40 D7
Moorville Ct 40 D7
Moorville Gro 40 D7
Moorville Rd 40 D7
Mount Preston St 40 C2
Mulberry St 41 F6
Mullins Ct 41 H5
Mushroom St 41 G2

**N**
Naseby Garth 41 G2
Naseby Ter 41 H3
National Rd 41 H6
Navigation Wk 41 F4
Neptune St 41 G4
Neville St 40 E4
New Briggate 41 F3
New Craven Gate 41 F6
New La 40 E5
New Mkt St 41 F4
New Princess St 40 D6
New Sta St 40 E4
New York Rd 41 G3
New York St 41 F4
Nickleby Rd 41 J3

Nile St 41 F3
Nineveh Gdns 40 D6
Nineveh Par 40 D6
Nineveh Rd 40 C6
Nippet La 41 H3
Normanton Gro 40 C7
Normanton Pl 40 D7
Nortech Cl 41 G1
Northcote Cres 40 E7
Northcote Dr 40 D7
Northcote Grn 40 D7
North Ct 41 F3
Northern St 40 D4
North St 41 F3

**O**
Oak Rd 40 A4
Oatland Cl 41 F1
Oatland Ct 41 F1
Oatland Dr 41 F1
Oatland Gdns 41 F1
Oatland Grn 41 F1
Oatland Hts 41 F1
Oatland La 41 E1
Oatland Rd 41 E1
Oatland Twrs 41 F1
O'Grady Sq 41 H4
Old Mill La 41 H7
Oval, The 41 G7
Oxford Pl 40 D3
Oxford Row 40 D3
Oxley St 41 J4
Oxton Mt 41 J3
Oxton Way 41 J3

**P**
Parade, The 41 G4
Park Cross St 40 D3
Parkfield St 41 E6
Park La 40 C3
Park Par 41 H5
Park Pl 40 D3
Park Row 40 E3
Park Sq E 40 D3
Park Sq N 40 D3
Park Sq S 40 D3
Park Sq W 40 D3
Park St 40 D3
Park Vw Rd 40 A1
Pearson St 41 F6
Penny La Way 41 F7
Pilot St 41 G2
Pitt Row 41 E4
Place's Rd 41 H4
Plaid Row 41 H3
Playhouse Sq 41 G3
Pleasant Mt 40 C6
Pleasant Pl 40 C6
Pleasant Ter 40 C6
Pontefract Av 41 J4
Pontefract La 41 H3
Pontefract La Cl 41 H4
Pontefract St 41 H4
Portland Cres 40 E2
Portland Gate 40 E2
Portland St 40 D3
Portland Way 40 E2
Pottery Rd 41 F7
Prosper St 41 G7
Providence Pl 41 E2
Pym St 41 G6

**Q**
Quarry Hill 41 G3
Quebec St 40 D3

Queen Sq 41 E2
Queens Rd 40 B1
Queen St 40 D4

**R**
Radnor St 40 B5
Railway St 41 G4
Raincliffe Gro 41 J3
Raincliffe Rd 41 J3
Raincliffe St 41 J3
Recreation Cres 40 C7
Recreation Gro 40 C7
Recreation Mt 40 C7
Recreation Pl 40 C7
Recreation Row 40 C7
Recreation St 40 C7
Recreation Ter 40 C7
Recreation Vw 40 C7
Rectory St 41 H2
Redshaw Rd 40 A5
Regent St 41 G3
Regent Ter 40 B1
Rhodes Ter 40 A5
Richmond Hill App 41 H4
Richmond Hill Cl 41 H4
Richmond St 41 G4
Rickard St 40 C5
Rider St 41 G3
Rigton App 41 H3
Rigton Cl 41 H3
Rigton Dr 41 H3
Rigton Grn 41 H3
Rigton Lawn 41 H3
Rigton Ms 41 H3
Rillbank La 40 B2
Roscoe St 41 G1
Rosebank Gdns 40 B2
Rosebank Rd 40 B2
Rosebud Wk 41 G1
Roseville Rd 41 G1
Roseville St 41 H1
Rossington St 40 E3
Roundhay Rd 41 G1
Roxby Cl 41 H2
Royal Pk Av 40 B1
Royal Pk Gro 40 B1
Royal Pk Rd 40 A1
Royal Pk Ter 40 B1
Ruby St 41 G2
Runswick Av 40 C6
Runswick Pl 40 C6
Runswick St 40 C6
Runswick Ter 40 C6
Russell St 40 E3
Rydall Pl 40 C6
Rydall St 40 C6
Rydall Ter 40 C6

**S**
Sackville St 41 F1
St. Andrew's St 40 C3
St. Barnabas Rd 40 E5
St. Georges Rd 40 D2
St. Helen's St 41 G6
St. Hilda's Av 41 J5
St. Hilda's Cres 41 H5
St. Hilda's Gro 41 J5
St. Hilda's Mt 41 J5
St. Hilda's Pl 41 J5
St. Hilda's Rd 41 J5
St. John's Av 40 C1
St. John's Cl 40 B1
St. John's Gro 40 B1
St. John's Rd 40 B2
St. Luke's Cescent 40 D7

St. Luke's Cres 40 D7
St. Luke's Grn 40 D7
St. Luke's Rd 40 D7
St. Luke's Ter 40 D7
St. Mark's Av 40 D1
St. Mark's Rd 40 D1
St. Mark's St 40 D1
St. Mary's Cl 40 A5
St. Mary's St 41 G3
St. Matthew's St 40 C6
St. Matthias St 40 A1
St. Matthias Ter 40 A1
St. Paul's St 40 D3
St. Peter's Ct 41 E7
St. Peter's Pl 41 G3
St. Peter's Sq 41 G3
St. Stephen's Ct 41 H3
St. Stephen's Rd 41 H3
Salem Pl 41 F5
Sandlewood Cl 40 D6
Sandlewood Grn 40 D6
Sardinia St 41 F6
Saville Grn 41 J3
Saxton La 41 G4
Sayner La 41 G5
Sayner Rd 41 F5
Scargill Cl 41 H2
Scarth Av 41 J1
Second Av 40 A4
Seminary St 40 D2
Severn Way 41 H7
Shafton La 40 C6
Shafton Pl 40 C6
Shafton St 40 C6
Shafton Vw 40 C6
Shakespeare App 41 H2
Shakespeare Av 41 H2
Shakespeare Cl 41 J2
Shakespeare Gdns 41 J2
Shakespeare Lawn 41 H2
Shakespeare St 41 J1
Shannon Rd 41 H3
Shannon St 41 G3
Sheaf St 41 F5
Sheepscar Ct 41 F1
Sheepscar Gro 41 F2
Sheepscar St N 41 F1
Sheepscar St S 41 F1
Siddal St 40 D5
Sidney St 41 F3
Silver St 40 D5
Skinner La 41 F2
Skinner St 40 C3
Somers St 40 D3
South Accommodation Rd 41 G6
South Par 40 E3
Sovereign St 40 E4
Spence La 40 B5
Spenceley St 40 D1
Spinney, The 41 H4
Spinneyfield Ct 41 H4
Spring Cl Av 41 H5
Spring Cl Gdns 41 H5
Spring Cl St 41 H5
Spring Cl Wk 41 H5
Springfield Mt 40 C2
Spring Gro Ter 40 A1
Spring Gro Vw 40 B1
Spring Gro Wk 40 A1
Springwell Ct 40 C5
Springwell Rd 40 C5
Springwell St 40 C5
Springwell Vw 40 C5
Stafford St 41 G7

Stanley Av 41 J1
Stanley Pl 41 J1
Stanley Rd 41 J1
Stanley Ter 40 D7
Stocks Hill 40 C6
Stoney Rock Gro 41 J2
Stoney Rock La 41 H2
Stott Rd 40 A4
Studio Rd 40 B2
Sutton St 40 C6
Sweet St 40 D5
Sweet St W 40 C5
Swinegate 41 E4
Sydenham Rd 40 B5
Sydenham St 40 B5

**T**
Telephone Pl 41 G2
Templar La 41 F3
Templar Pl 41 F3
Templar St 41 F3
Temple Vw Gro 41 J4
Temple Vw Pl 41 J4
Temple Vw Rd 41 J3
Temple Vw Ter 41 J4
Thealby Cl 41 G3
Thealby Lawn 41 G2
Thealby Pl 41 G3
Third Av 40 A5
Thirsk Row 40 D4
Thoresby Pl 40 D3
Thornleigh Gdns 41 J5
Thornleigh Gro 41 J5
Thornleigh Mt 41 J5
Thornleigh St 41 J5
Thornleigh Vw 41 J5
Thornville Pl 40 B1
Thornville Rd 40 A1
Thornville Row 40 B1
Thornville St 40 B1
Thornville Vw 40 B1
Tilbury Av 40 C7
Tilbury Gro 40 C7
Tilbury Mt 40 C7
Tilbury Par 40 C7
Tilbury Rd 40 C7
Tilbury Ter 40 C7
Tilbury Vw 40 C7
Tong Rd 40 A5
Top Moor Side 40 C6
Torre Cl 41 J3
Torre Dr 41 J2
Torre Rd 41 H3
Tower Ho St 41 F2
Trafalgar St 41 F3
Trent Rd 41 J3
Trent St 40 D6
Trinity St 41 E3
Triumph Cl 40 C5
Turlow Ct 41 G4

**U**
Union Pl 40 D5
Union St 41 F3
University Rd 40 C1
Upper Accommodation Rd 41 H3
Upper Basinghall St 40 E3
Upper N St 40 E2
Upper Westlock Av 41 J2

**V**
Vernon Rd 40 D2
Vernon St 40 E2
Vicar La 41 F3

Victoria Rd 40 E5
Victoria Sq 40 D3
Victoria St 40 C2
Victoria Ter 40 C2
Village Ter 40 A1
Vinery Mt 41 J4
Vinery Pl 41 J4
Vinery St 41 J3
Vinery Ter 41 J4

**W**
Wade La 41 E3
Walford Gro 41 J3
Walford Rd 41 J3
Walford Ter 41 J3
Walter Cres 41 H4
Walter St 40 A2
Walton St 40 D5
Washington St 40 B3
Water La 40 C5
Waterloo Rd 41 G7
Waterloo St 41 F4
Waverley Garth 40 D7
Weaver St 40 A2
Welbeck Rd 41 J4
Well Cl Ri 41 E1
Wellington Br St 40 C3
Wellington Pl 40 C4
Wellington Rd 40 B4
Wellington St 40 D4
Wesley Pl 41 H4
Westfield Cres 40 B2
Westfield Rd 40 B2
Westfield Ter 40 B2
Westgate 40 D3
Westlock Av 41 J2
West St 40 C3
West Vale 40 A6
Wharf St 41 F4
Whitehall Rd 40 B5
Whitehouse St 41 G7
Whitelock St 41 F2
Whitfield Av 41 G7
Whitfield Gdns 41 G7
Whitfield Pl 41 G7
Whitfield Sq 41 G7
Whitfield Way 41 G7
Willis St 41 H4
Willoughby Ter 40 C6
Willow App 40 A2
Willow Av 40 A2
Willow Cl 40 B2
Willow Garth 40 A2
Willow Rd 40 A2
Willow Ter Rd 40 D2
Wilmington St 41 F1
Winchester St 40 A4
Winfield Gro 40 E1
Winfield Pl 40 E1
Winfield Ter 40 E1
Wintoun St 41 F2
Wolseley Rd 40 A1
Woodhouse La 40 D1
Woodhouse Sq 40 D3
Woodsley Grn 40 B1
Woodsley Rd 40 B2
Wormald Row 41 E3
Wortley La 40 B5
Wortley Pk 40 A5

**Y**
Yarn St 41 H6
York Pl 40 D3
York Rd 41 H3
York St 41 F4

## Liverpool street index

**A**
Abercromby Sq 43 F4
Abney Cl 43 H5
Acorn Ct 43 E7
Acton Way 43 H5
Adderley St 43 H3
Addison St 42 C2
Addison Way 42 C2
Adelaide Pl 42 D1
Adelaide Rd 43 G4
Adele Thompson Dr 43 F6
Agnes Way 43 H4
Aigburth St 43 G5
Ainsworth St 42 E4
Albany Rd 43 G3
Albert Edward Rd 43 G3
Albert St 43 G4
Alderson Rd 43 J6
Alexandra Cl 43 G2

Alexandra Rd 43 J5
Alex Cl 43 F7
Alfred Ms 42 D6
Alfred St 43 J5
Altcar Av 43 J6
Alt St 43 G6
Amberley St 43 F6
Amelia Cl 43 F2
Amethyst Cl 43 G1
Anchorage, The 42 C7
Angela St 43 G5
Anglezark Cl 43 H3
Anglican Ct 42 E6
Archbishop Warlock Ct 42 B1
Argyle St 42 C5
Arley St 42 C1
Arnold Cres 43 F7
Arnside Rd 43 H4

Arrad St 43 E5
Arundel Av 43 J7
Arundel Cl 43 G7
Asbridge St 43 G7
Ashton St 43 F3
Ashwell St 42 D6
Askham Cl 43 G6
Aspen Gro 43 H7
Atlantic Pt 42 C2
Atwell St 43 G1

**B**
Back Colquitt St 42 D5
Back Guildford St 43 F1
Back Kelvin Gro 43 G7
Back Leeds St 42 B2
Baker St 43 G2
Baker Way 43 F2
Balmoral Rd 43 J1

Balm St 43 H3
Baltimore St 42 E5
Bannerman St 43 J5
Barnet Cl 43 H5
Basnett St 42 C4
Bath St 42 A3
Battenberg St 43 G3
Bayhorse La 43 E3
Beaconsfield St 43 G7
Beaufort St 42 D7
Beaumont St 43 G6
Beau St 42 D1
Beckwith St 42 C5
Bective St 43 J5
Bedford Cl 43 F5
Bedford St S 43 F6
Beech St 43 J3
Benson St 42 D4
Bentley Rd 43 G7

Beresford St 42 E1
Berington St 42 C1
Berkley St 43 E6
Berry St 42 D5
Berwick Cl 43 H1
Berwick St 43 H1
Bevington Bush 42 C2
Bevington Hill 42 C1
Bidder St 42 E2
Bigham Rd 43 H2
Birchfield St 42 E2
Bird St 43 J6
Birkett St 42 D2
Birstall Rd 43 J5
Birt Cl 43 G6
Bishop Sheppard Ct 42 B1
Bixteth St 42 B3
Blackburne Pl 43 E5

Blackstock St 42 C2
Blair St 42 E6
Blenheim St 42 C1
Bluefields St 43 E6
Blundell St 42 C6
Boaler St 43 G2
Bold Pl 42 D5
Bold St 42 D4
Bolton St 42 D4
Bond St 42 C1
Boothwood Cl 43 H5
Boswell St 43 H6
Botanic Grn 43 H3
Botanic Pl 43 H3
Botanic Rd 43 J3
Boundary La 43 G1
Boyton Ct 43 J5
Bradfield St 43 H3
Brae St 43 H3

Brahms Cl 43 G7
Brampton Dr 43 F5
Brassey St 42 D7
Breames Cl 43 H4
Breck Rd 43 F1
Bremner Cl 43 H4
Brick St 42 D6
Bridge Rd 43 J5
Bridgewater St 42 C6
Bridport St 42 D3
Bright St 43 F2
Brindley St 42 D7
Britannia Av 43 J6
Britten Cl 43 H7
Bronte St 42 E3
Brook St 42 B3
Brownlow Hill 42 D4
Brownlow St 43 E4
Brow Side 43 E1
Brunswick Rd 43 F3
Brunswick St 42 B4
Bryges St 43 G4
Brythen St 42 C4
Burlington St 42 C1
Burnley Cl 43 G1
Burroughs Gdns 42 C1
Burrows Ct 42 B1
Burton Cl 42 C5
Bute St 42 D2
Bute St (Edge Hill) 43 H6
Butler Cres 43 G2
Butler St 43 G1
Button St 42 C4
Byrom St 42 D3

C

Cadogan St 43 J5
Caird St 43 G2
Cairns St 43 G7
Caledonia St 43 E5
Callander Rd 43 J2
Cambria St N 43 H2
Cambria St S 43 H2
Cambridge Ct 43 E5
Cambridge St 43 E4
Camden St 42 D3
Cameo Cl 43 G1
Cameron St 43 H3
Campbell St 42 C5
Canada Boul 42 B4
Canning Pl 42 C4
Canning St 43 E5
Cantebury St 42 E2
Cantebury Way 43 E2
Cantsfield St 43 J6
Cardigan St 43 J5
Cardigan Way 43 H1
Cardwell St 43 G5
Carlingford Cl 43 G6
Carlton St 42 A1
Carmarthen Cres 42 D7
Carpenters Row 42 C5
Carruthers St 42 B2
Carstairs Rd 43 J1
Carter St 43 F6
Carver St 43 E2
Caryl St 42 D7
Castle St 42 B4
Catharine St 43 F5
Cathedral Cl 42 E6
Cathedral Gate 42 E5
Cathedral Wk 42 E4
Cawdor St 43 G7
Cazneau St 42 D1
Cedar Gro 43 H7
Celtic St 43 F7
Chadwick St 42 B2
Chaloner St 42 C6
Chandos St 43 H4
Channell Rd 43 H2
Chapel St 42 B4
Chase Way 42 E1
Chatham Pl 43 G4
Chatham St 43 F5
Chatsworth Dr 43 H5
Chaucer St 42 D2
Cheapside 42 C3
Chesney Cl 42 E7
Chesterfield St 42 E6
Chester St 42 E7
Chestnut St 43 F4
Chichester Cl 43 J5
Childwall Av 43 J6
Chisenhale St 42 B1
Chiswell St 43 H3
Christian St 42 D2
Chris Ward Cl 43 H4
Church All 42 C4
Church Mt 43 G4
Church St 42 C4
Churton Ct 43 F2
Cicely St 43 G4
Clarence St 42 E4
Claribel St 43 F7
Claughton Cl 43 H4
Claypole Cl 43 H5
Clay St 42 B1
Clearwater Cl 43 H3
Clegg St 42 D1
Clement Gdns 42 C1
Cleveland Sq 42 C5
Clifford St 42 E3
Cliff St 43 H3
Clifton Gro 42 E1
Clint Rd 43 H4
Clint Rd W 43 H4
Clint Way 43 H4
Coal St 42 D3
Cobden St 43 F2
Coburg Wf 42 C7
Cockspur St 42 C3
Coleridge St 43 H2
College La 42 C4
College St N 43 E2
College St S 43 F2
Colquitt St 42 D5
Coltart Rd 43 G7
Comberme St 43 E7
Commerce Way 43 G6
Commutation Row 42 D3
Compton Rd 43 G1
Comus St 42 D2
Concert St 42 D5
Connaught Rd 43 G3
Contance St 43 E3
Cookson St 42 D6
Cook St 42 C4
Copperas Hill 42 D4
Corinto St 42 E6
Corney St 43 H6
Cornhill 42 C5
Cornwallis St 42 D5
Corsewall St 43 J5
Cotswold St 43 H3
Cotton St 42 A1
Covent Gdn 42 B3
Cowan Dr 43 F1
Cranborne Rd 43 J6
Craven St 42 E3
Cresswell St 43 F1
Cropper St 42 D4
Crosfield Cl 43 J4
Crosfield Rd 43 H4
Crosshall St 42 C3
Crown St 43 F3
Croxteth Gro 43 H7
Croxteth Rd 43 G7
Crump St 42 D6
Cullen St 43 H6
Cumberland St 42 C3
Cunliffe St 42 C3
Custom Ho Pl 42 C5

D

Dale St 42 B4
Daniel Davies Dr 43 G6
Dansie St 43 E4
Danube St 43 H6
Darrel Dr 43 H6
Daulby St 43 F3
Davies St 42 C3
Dawber Cl 43 G1
Dawson St 42 C4
Dean Dillistone Ct 42 D6
Deane Rd 43 H3
Dean Patey Ct 42 D5
Deeley Cl 43 H4
Dell St 43 H3
Denham Dr 43 H1
Denham Way 43 H1
Dentdale Dr 42 E1
Devon St 42 E3
Dexter St 42 E7
Dial St 43 H3
Diamond St 42 C1
Dickens St 43 E7
Dickson St 42 A1
Dombey St 43 E7
Dorothy St 43 H4
Dorrit St 43 E7
Dorset Av 43 J6
Douro St 42 D1
Dovestone Cl 43 H5
Dove St 43 G6
Drury La 42 B4
Dryden St 42 D1
Dublin St 42 A1
Ducie St 43 G7
Duckinfield St 43 E4
Duke St 42 C5
Duncan St 42 D6
Dunkeld Cl 43 G2
Dunstan La 43 H5
Durden St 43 H6
Durning Rd 43 H3
Dwerryhouse St 42 D7
Dyke St 43 F1

E

Earle Rd 43 H6
Earle St 42 B3
East St 42 B3
Eaton St 42 B2
Ebenezer Rd 43 J3
Eden St 43 H6
Edgar St 42 C2
**Edge Hill** 43 G5
Edge La 43 G4
Edinburgh Rd 43 G3
Edmund St 42 B3
Egerton St 43 E6
Elaine St 43 F7
Eldonian Way 42 B1
Eldon Pl 42 C1
Eldon St 42 C1
Elizabeth St 43 F3
Elliot St 42 D4
Elm Gro 43 F4
Elm Vale 43 J1
Elstree Rd 43 J2
Ember Cres 43 F1
Embledon St 43 G6
Emerson St 43 E6
Empress Rd 43 G4
Enid St 43 F7
Epworth St 43 F3
Erin Cl 42 E7
Erskine St 43 F3
Esher Rd 43 H2
Eversley St 43 F7
Everton Brow 42 E2
Everton Rd 43 F1
Every St 43 G1
Exchange St E 42 B3
Exchange St W 42 B3

F

Fairclough St 42 D4
**Fairfield** 43 J2
Falkland St 43 E3
Falkner Sq 43 F6
Falkner St 43 E5
Fareham Rd 43 J3
Farnworth St 43 G2
Fazakerley St 42 B3
Fearnside St 43 J5
Fell St 43 H3
Fenwick St 42 B4
Fern Gro 43 H7
Fernhill Dr 43 F7
Fielding St 43 G2
Field St 42 E2
Finch Pl 43 E3
Finlay St 43 H2
Fishguard Cl 43 F1
Fitzclarence Way 43 F1
Fitzpatrick Ct 42 B1
Fitzroy Way 43 F2
Fleet St 42 D4
Fleming Ct 42 B1
Flint St 42 D6
Fontenoy St 42 C3
Ford St 42 C2
Forrest St 42 C5
Fowler Cl 43 H4
Foxhill Cl 43 F7
Fox St 42 D1
Fraser St 42 D3
Freedom Cl 43 G5
Freeman St 43 J5
Freemasons' Row 42 C2
Frost St 43 H3

G

Galloway St 43 J5
Gannock St 43 H3
Gardenside St 43 F2
Gardners Dr 43 H1
Gardner's Row 42 C2
Garrick St 43 J6
Gascoyne St 42 B2
Geneva Rd 43 J2
George Harrison Cl 43 G2
Georges Dockway 42 B4
George St 42 B3
Geraint St 43 F7
Gerard St 42 D3
Gibraltar Row 42 B3
Gibson St 43 F6
Gilbert St 42 C5
Gildarts Gdns 42 C1
Gildart St 43 E3
Gilead St 43 H3
Gill St 43 E3
Gilroy Rd 43 H2
Gladstone Rd 43 G4
Gladstone St 42 C2
Gleave Cres 43 F1
Glegg St 42 B1
Gloucester Ct 43 G2
Gloucester Pl 43 F3
Gore St 42 D7
Gower St 42 B5
Gradwell St 42 C4
Grafton Cres 42 D7
Grafton St 42 D6
Granary Wf 42 C7
Granby St 43 G6
Grantham St 43 H2
Granville Rd 43 J6
Grayson St 42 C5
Great Crosshall St 42 C3
Great George Pl 42 D6
Great George St 42 D6
Great Howard St 42 B2
Great Nelson St 42 D1
Great Newton St 43 E3
Great Orford St 43 E4
Great Richmond St 42 D2
Greek St 42 E3
Greenheys Rd 43 G7
Greenland St 42 D6
Green La 42 E4
Greenleaf St 43 H6
Greenside 43 F2
Green St 42 C1
Gregson St 43 F2
Grenville St S 42 D5
Gresley Cl 43 J4
Grierson St 43 H6
Grinfield St 43 G4
Grinshill Cl 43 F7
Grosvenor St 42 D1
Grove Pk 43 H7
Grove Rd 43 J2
Grove St 43 F6
Guelph St 43 F3
Guion St 43 H1
Gwendoline St 43 F7
Gwenfron Rd 43 G2
Gwent St 43 F7

H

Hackins Hey 42 B3
Haigh St 43 E1
Hale St 42 C3
Hall La 43 F3
Halsbury Rd 43 H2
Hampstead Rd 43 J2
Hampton St 43 E6
Hannan Rd 43 H2
Hanover St 42 C5
Harbord St 43 G4
Hardman St 42 E5
Hardy St 42 D6
Harewood St 43 G1
Harker St 42 D2
Harke St 43 H5
Harper St 43 F3
Harrington St 42 C4
Harrowby Cl 43 G6
Harrowby St 43 F6
Hartley Quay 42 B5
Hart St 42 E3
Hatherley Cl 43 G6
Hatherley St 43 F7
Hatton Gdn 42 C3
Haverston Rd 43 J2
Hawdon Ct 43 J5
Hawke St 42 D4
Hawkins St 43 H2
Hawthorn Gro 43 H4
Head St 42 E7
Heathcote Cl 43 H5
Heathfield St 42 D4
Helena St 43 H4
Helsby St 43 G4
Hendon Rd 43 J1
Henglers Cl 43 F2
Henry Edward St 42 C2
Henry St 42 C5
Hewitts Pl 42 C3
Highfield St 42 B2
Highgate St 43 G4
High St 42 B3
Hilbre St 42 D4
Hillaby Cl 43 F7
Hillside St 43 F2
Hill St 42 D7
Hinton St 43 J2
Hockenhall All 42 C3
Hodson Pl 43 F1
Holborn St 43 F3
Holden St 43 G5
Holdsworth St 43 H3
Holly Rd 43 J3
Holmes St 43 H6
Holt Rd 43 H3
Holy Cross Cl 42 C2
Homerton Rd 43 J2
Hood St 42 C3
Hope Pl 42 E5
Hope St 43 E6
Hornby Wk 42 C1
Hotham St 42 D3
Houghton St 42 D4
Houlton St 43 H3
Hughes Cl 43 J4
Hughes St 43 G1
Huntly Rd 43 J2
Hurst St 42 C5
Huskisson St 43 E6
Hutchinson St 43 G2
Hutchinson Wk 43 G2
Hygeia St 43 G1
Hyslop St 42 E7

I

Iliad St 42 D1
Ingrow Rd 43 H2
Irvine St 43 G4
Irwell St 42 B4
Islington 42 E3
Ivatt Way 43 H4

J

Jack McBain Ct 42 B1
Jade Rd 43 H1
Jamaica St 42 D6
James Clarke St 42 C1
James St 42 B4
Janet St 43 H4
Jasmine Cl 43 E1
Jenkinson St 42 E2
Jermyn St 43 G7
Jet Cl 43 H1
John Lennon Dr 43 G2
John Moores Cl 43 F5
Johnson St 42 C3
John St 42 E2
Jordan St 42 D6
Jubilee Dr 43 G3
Judges Dr 43 J1
Judges Way 43 J1
Juvenal Pl 42 D1
Juvenal St 42 D2

K

Keble St 43 G2
Kelso Rd 43 J2
Kelvin Gro 43 G7
Kempston St 42 E3
Kenley Cl 43 H1
**Kensington** 43 G3
Kensington 43 G3
Kensington St 43 G2
Kent St 42 D5
Kilshaw St 43 G1
Kimberley Cl 43 F6
Kinder St 43 F2
King Edward St 42 B3
Kinglake St 43 G4
Kings Dock St 42 C6
Kingsley Rd 43 G6
Kings Par 42 B5
Kingsway Ct 42 C1
Kingswell Cl 43 G4
Kitchen St 42 C6
Knight St 42 D5

L

Lace St 42 C3
Ladybower Cl 43 H5
Laggan St 43 H3
Lairds Pl 42 C1
Lakeland Cl 42 C5
Lambert Way 42 E3
Lamport St 42 E7
Lance Cl 43 F1
Langley St 42 E7
Langsdale St 42 E2
Langton Rd 43 J6
Lanyork Rd 42 B2
Laurel Gro 43 H7
Lavan Cl 43 F2
Lawrence Rd 43 J6
Lawton St 42 D4
Laxey St 42 E7
Leece St 42 E5
Leeds St 42 B2
Leigh St 42 C4
Leigh St (Edge Hill) 43 J4
Lemon Cl 43 J4
Lemon Gro 43 H7
Leopold Rd 43 G4
Lesseps Rd 43 H6
Lestock St 42 E6
Liffey St 43 G6
Lightwood Dr 43 H5
Lightwood St 43 H5
Lilley Rd 43 J2
Lilly Vale 43 J2
Lime Gro 43 H7
Limekiln La 42 C1
Lime St 42 D4
Lincoln Cl 43 H1
Lindley Cl 43 H5
Lindley St 43 J5
Ling St 43 H3
Lister Cres 43 J3
Lister Rd 43 J2
Little Catherine St 43 E6
Little Ct 42 B1
Little Hardman St 42 E5
Little Howard St 42 B1
Little St. Bride St 43 E5
Little Woolton St 43 F4
Liver St 42 C5
Lloyd Cl 43 F1
Lockerby Rd 43 J2
Lodge La 43 H7
London Rd 42 D3
Longfellow St 43 H6
Longstone Wk 43 G5
Lord Nelson St 42 D3
Lord St 42 C4
Lorton St 43 H6
Lothian St 43 F7
Loudon Gro 43 G7
Love La 42 B1
Lower Castle St 42 B4
Low Hill 43 F2
Lowther St 43 F6
Low Wd St 43 F3
Luke St 43 E7
Lyceum Pl 42 D4
Lydia Ann St 42 C5
Lytton St 43 F2

M

Maddrell St 42 B1
Madelaine St 43 F7
Madeley St 43 H1
Magdala St 43 H6
Maitland Cl 43 H6
Malden Rd 43 H2
Mallow Rd 43 H2
Malt St 43 G5
Malvern Rd 43 H2
Manchester St 42 C3
Manesty's La 42 C4
Manfred St 43 F3
Mann Island 42 B4
Mann St 42 D7
Mansell Rd 43 H2
Mansfield St 42 D2
Manton Rd 43 H2
Maple Gro 43 H7
Marathon Cl 43 F1
Marcot Rd 43 J1
Margaret St 43 F1
Mariners Wf 42 C7
Maritime Pl 42 E2
Maritime Way 42 C5
Marlborough St 42 C2
Marlsford St 43 H2
Marmaduke St 43 G4
Marquis St 42 E3
Marsden St 43 F2
Marsden Way 43 F2
Marshall Pl 42 C1
Martensen St 43 G4
Marvin St 43 G2
Marybone 42 C3
Maryland St 43 E5
Mason St 43 G4
Mathew St 42 C4
Maud St 43 F7
Maxton Rd 43 H2
Mayfair Cl 43 H1
May Pl 42 E4
May St 42 E4
Melda Cl 43 F2
Melville Pl 43 F5
Merlin St 43 F7
Michael Dragonette Ct 42 C1
Midghall St 42 C2
Mile End 42 C1
Millennium Pl 43 G7
Mill La 42 D3
Mill Rd 43 F1
Mill St 42 E7
Millvale St 43 H1
Milroy St 43 H4
Milverton St 43 H1
Minshull St 43 F4
Minster Ct 43 F5
Minto Cl 43 H3
Minto St 43 H3
Mirfield St 43 H2
Molyneux Rd 43 G2
Montgomery Way 43 H1
Moorfields 42 C3
Moor Pl 42 E3
Moor St 42 B4
Morden St 43 H1
Moss Gro 43 H7
Mount Pleasant 42 D4
Mount St 42 E5

|  |  | |  |  | |  |  |
|---|---|---|---|---|---|---|---|
| Mount Vernon Grn | 43 G3 | | Park La | 42 C5 | | **Q** | |
| Mount Vernon Rd | 43 F4 | | Park Pl | 42 E7 | | Queen Anne St | 42 D2 |
| Mount Vernon St | 43 F3 | | Park Rd | 43 E7 | | Queensland St | 43 G4 |
| Mozart Cl | 43 G7 | | Parkside St | 43 F2 | | Queens Sq | 42 D3 |
| Muirhead Av | 43 H1 | | Park Way | 43 F6 | | Queens Wf | 42 B6 |
| Mulberry Pl | 43 F5 | | Parliament Cl | 42 E6 | | Quorn St | 43 H3 |
| Mulberry St | 43 F5 | | Parliament St | 42 D6 | | | |
| Mulgrave St | 43 F6 | | Parr St | 42 D5 | | **R** | |
| Mulliner St | 43 J6 | | Parton St | 43 J2 | | Rachel St | 42 D1 |
| Myrtle St | 43 E5 | | Paul | | | Radstock Rd | 43 J2 |
| | | | McCartney Way | 43 H2 | | Raffles St | 42 D6 |
| **N** | | | Paul Orr Ct | 42 B1 | | Rainford Gdns | 42 C4 |
| Navigation Wf | 42 C7 | | Paul St | 42 C2 | | Rainford Sq | 42 C4 |
| Naylor St | 42 C2 | | Pavilion Cl | 43 G6 | | Ranelagh St | 42 D4 |
| Needham Rd | 43 H3 | | Pear Gro | 43 H2 | | Raven Cl | 43 F2 |
| Nelson Rd | 43 G4 | | Pearl Way | 43 G1 | | Raymond Pl | 42 C1 |
| Nelson St | 42 D6 | | Peet St | 43 H4 | | Red Cross St | 42 B4 |
| Netherfield Rd S | 42 E1 | | Pembroke Gdns | 43 E3 | | Redgrave St | 43 H3 |
| Nevin St | 43 F2 | | Pembroke Pl | 42 E3 | | Redmires Cl | 43 H5 |
| Nevison St | 43 G4 | | Pembroke St | 43 E4 | | Red Rock St | 43 G1 |
| New Bird St | 42 D6 | | Penarth Cl | 43 G5 | | Regent St | 42 A1 |
| New Grey Rock Cl | 43 G1 | | Pendine Cl | 43 H1 | | Renfrew St | 43 G3 |
| Newhall St | 42 D6 | | Penlinken Dr | 43 H1 | | Renshaw St | 42 D4 |
| New Henderson St | 42 D7 | | Penvalley Cres | 43 H1 | | Reservoir St | 43 F1 |
| Newington | 42 D4 | | Peover St | 42 D2 | | Reynolds Cl | 43 G1 |
| New Quay | 42 B3 | | Pera Cl | 43 G2 | | Rialto Cl | 43 F6 |
| New Red Rock Vw | 43 G1 | | Percy St | 43 E6 | | Rice St | 42 E5 |
| Newsham Dr | 43 H1 | | Perrygate Cl | 43 G5 | | Richardson St | 43 J6 |
| Newstead Rd | 43 H6 | | Perry St | 42 D7 | | Richmond Row | 42 D2 |
| Newton Way | 43 E4 | | Perth St | 43 G2 | | Richmond St | 42 C4 |
| Noel St | 43 H6 | | Peter's Arcade | 42 C4 | | Ridley Rd | 43 H2 |
| Norfolk St | 42 C6 | | Peter St | 42 C3 | | Rigby St | 42 B3 |
| Norman St | 43 E3 | | Phillimore Rd | 43 H2 | | Ringo Starr Dr | 43 H2 |
| Northbrook Cl | 43 G6 | | Pickop St | 42 C3 | | Ritson St | 43 G7 |
| North Brook St | 43 F6 | | Pickwick St | 43 E7 | | River Avon St | 43 H6 |
| Northcote Cl | 43 F1 | | Picton Rd | 43 J5 | | Roberts St | 42 A2 |
| North John St | 42 C3 | | Pilgrim St | 42 E5 | | Roderick St | 42 E2 |
| North St | 42 C3 | | Pimhill Cl | 43 G7 | | Rodney St | 42 E5 |
| North Vw | 43 G4 | | Pine Ms | 42 E6 | | Roe St | 42 D3 |
| Norton St | 42 D3 | | Pinetop Cl | 43 H1 | | Rokeby Cl | 42 E2 |
| Norwood Gro | 43 H1 | | Pitt St | 42 D5 | | Rokeby St | 42 E2 |
| Nuttall St | 43 H4 | | Pleasant St | 42 E4 | | Rokesmith Av | 43 H5 |
| | | | Plimsoll St | 43 H4 | | Romer Rd | 43 H2 |
| **O** | | | Plumpton St | 43 F1 | | Romilly St | 43 G2 |
| Oakes St | 43 E3 | | Pomfret St | 43 F7 | | Roscastle Cl | 43 G2 |
| Oakham St | 42 D7 | | Pomona St | 42 E4 | | Roscoe La | 42 D5 |
| O'Connell Rd | 42 C1 | | Pond Cl | 43 H1 | | Roscoe St | 42 E5 |
| Odsey St | 43 H3 | | Ponsonby St | 43 G7 | | Roscommon St | 42 D1 |
| Oil St | 42 A1 | | Porter St | 42 A1 | | Roseberry St | 43 F6 |
| Old Coll Pl | 43 H4 | | Portland Pl | 42 D1 | | Rose Hill | 42 D2 |
| Old Hall St | 42 B3 | | Portwood Cl | 43 G5 | | Rosemary Cl | 43 G4 |
| Oldham St | 42 D5 | | Pownall Sq | 42 C3 | | Rose Pl | 42 D2 |
| Old Leeds St | 42 B3 | | Pownall St | 42 C5 | | Rothsay Cl | 42 E1 |
| Olympia St | 43 G2 | | Prescot Rd | 43 J2 | | Rothwell St | 43 G1 |
| Onslow Rd | 43 J2 | | Prescot St | 43 F3 | | Royal Mail St | 42 D4 |
| Opal Cl | 43 G1 | | Preston St | 42 C3 | | Royston St | 43 G4 |
| Orange Gro | 43 H7 | | Price St | 42 C5 | | Rufford Rd | 43 J2 |
| O'Reilly Ct | 42 B1 | | Primrose Hill | 42 C3 | | Rumford Pl | 42 B3 |
| Oriel Steet | 42 C2 | | Prince Albert Ms | 42 D6 | | Rumford St | 42 B3 |
| Ormond St | 42 B3 | | Prince Edwin St | 42 D1 | | Rupert Dr | 43 F2 |
| Orphan St | 43 F5 | | Princes Av | 43 F6 | | Russel St | 42 E3 |
| Orthes St | 43 E4 | | Princes Gdns | 42 B2 | | Ryedale Cl | 43 G6 |
| Ottley St | 43 J2 | | Princes Par | 42 A3 | | | |
| Overbury St | 43 G4 | | **Princes Pk** | 43 G7 | | **S** | |
| Overton St | 43 G4 | | Princes Rd | 43 F6 | | St. Andrew St | 42 E4 |
| Oxendale Cl | 43 G6 | | Princes St | 42 C3 | | St. Anne St | 42 D2 |
| Oxford St | 43 E4 | | Prince William St | 42 D7 | | St. Bride St | 43 F5 |
| Oxford St E | 43 G4 | | Prospect St | 43 F3 | | St. James Pl | 42 D6 |
| | | | Providence Cres | 42 D7 | | St. James Rd | 42 E6 |
| **P** | | | Prussia St | 42 B3 | | St. James St | 42 D6 |
| Paddington | 43 F4 | | Pudsey St | 42 D3 | | St. John's La | 42 D3 |
| Page Wk | 42 E2 | | Pumpfields Rd | 42 B2 | | St. Josephs Cres | 42 D2 |
| Paisley St | 42 A2 | | Pythian Cl | 43 G2 | | St. Martins Ms | 42 D1 |
| Pall Mall | 42 B2 | | Pythian St | 43 F2 | | St. Michaels Gro | 43 H1 |
| Paradise St | 42 C5 | | | | | St. Nicholas Pl | 42 A4 |
| Parker St | 42 D4 | | | | | | |

|  |  | |  |  | |  |  |
|---|---|---|---|---|---|---|---|
| St. Stephen's Pl | 42 C2 | | Strand St | 42 B4 | | **V** | |
| Salisbury Rd | 43 J6 | | Strathmore Rd | 43 H1 | | Vandries St | 42 A1 |
| Salisbury St | 42 E1 | | Strauss Cl | 43 H7 | | Vandyke St | 43 H6 |
| Salthouse Quay | 42 B5 | | Suffolk St | 42 D5 | | Vauxhall Rd | 42 C2 |
| Saltney St | 42 A1 | | Sugnall St | 43 E5 | | Vernon St | 42 C3 |
| Sandhead St | 43 J5 | | Summer Seat | 42 C1 | | Verulam Cl | 43 G6 |
| Sandino St | 42 E7 | | Surrey St | 42 C5 | | Victoria St | 42 C4 |
| Sandon St | 42 F5 | | Sutcliffe St | 43 H2 | | Village St | 43 E1 |
| Saxon Cl | 43 G1 | | Sweeting St | 42 B4 | | Vincent Ct | 42 D5 |
| Saxony Rd | 43 G3 | | Swindale Cl | 43 G6 | | Vining St | 43 F7 |
| Scholar St | 43 J6 | | Swiss Rd | 43 J2 | | Virgil St | 42 D1 |
| Schomberg St | 43 G2 | | | | | Voelas St | 43 G7 |
| School La | 42 C4 | | **T** | | | Vronhill Cl | 43 G7 |
| Scotland Rd | 42 D2 | | Tabley St | 42 C6 | | Vulcan St | 42 A1 |
| Seaport Rd | 43 G7 | | Tace Cl | 43 F6 | | | |
| Seddon St | 42 C5 | | Tagus Cl | 43 G7 | | **W** | |
| Seel St | 42 C4 | | Tamar Cl | 43 F1 | | Wainwright Cl | 43 H5 |
| Sefton Pk Rd | 43 H7 | | Tarleton St | 42 C4 | | Wakefield St | 42 D2 |
| Sefton St | 42 C6 | | Tatlock St | 42 C1 | | Waldron Cl | 42 C2 |
| Selborne Cl | 43 F6 | | Tavy Rd | 43 F1 | | Walker St | 43 F2 |
| Selborne St | 43 F6 | | Teck St | 43 G3 | | Wall St | 42 C4 |
| Selsey Cl | 43 H5 | | Teign Cl | 43 F1 | | Walsh Cl | 42 C1 |
| Severs St | 43 G1 | | Tempest Hey | 42 B3 | | Wapping | 42 C5 |
| Seymour St | 42 E3 | | Temple Ct | 42 C4 | | Ward St | 42 D3 |
| Shakespeare Cl | 43 G1 | | Temple La | 42 C3 | | Warwick St | 42 E7 |
| Shallcross Pl | 43 G1 | | Temple St | 42 C3 | | Waterloo Quay | 42 A2 |
| Shaws All | 42 C5 | | Tenterden St | 42 C1 | | Water St | 42 B4 |
| Shaw St | 43 E1 | | Thackeray Pl | 43 F7 | | Watkinson St | 42 C6 |
| Sheil Rd | 43 H1 | | Thames St | 43 G7 | | Watmough St | 42 E1 |
| Shenstone St | 43 G4 | | Thomas St Way | 42 C5 | | Wavertree Boul | 43 J4 |
| Shepherd's Fold Cl | 43 G7 | | Thorburn St | 43 H4 | | Wavertree Rd | 43 G4 |
| Sherwood St | 42 B1 | | Thornes Rd | 43 G2 | | Webb Cl | 43 H4 |
| Shimmin St | 43 G4 | | Tichbourne Way | 43 F2 | | Webb St | 43 H6 |
| Sidney Pl | 43 H5 | | Tideswell Cl | 43 H5 | | Webster Rd | 43 J6 |
| Silkstone Cl | 43 H5 | | Timpron St | 43 H5 | | Webster St | 42 C3 |
| Simpson St | 42 C6 | | Titchfield St | 42 C1 | | Wedgewood St | 43 H3 |
| Sim St | 42 E2 | | Tithebarn St | 42 B3 | | Wendell St | 43 H6 |
| Sirdar Cl | 43 H5 | | Tobin Cl | 42 C1 | | Wentworth Dr | 43 F1 |
| Sir Thomas St | 42 C3 | | Toft St | 43 H3 | | West Derby Rd | 43 G2 |
| Skelhorne St | 42 D4 | | Tom Mann Cl | 42 C3 | | West Derby St | 43 F3 |
| Slater St | 42 D5 | | Tordelow Cl | 43 F1 | | Westmorland Dr | 42 C2 |
| Smithdown La | 43 F4 | | Tower Gdns | 42 B4 | | Whitcroft Rd | 43 J2 |
| Smithdown Rd | 43 H6 | | Trafalgar Way | 43 F2 | | Whitechapel | 42 C4 |
| Smithfield St | 42 C3 | | Trowbridge St | 42 E4 | | Whitefield Rd | 43 G1 |
| Soho Pl | 42 E2 | | Trueman St | 42 C3 | | Whitefield Way | 43 G1 |
| Soho St | 42 E2 | | Tudor St N | 43 H2 | | White Rock Ct | 43 G1 |
| Solomon St | 42 H3 | | Tudor St S | 43 H2 | | White Rock St | 43 G1 |
| Solway St E | 43 H6 | | Tulloch St | 43 G2 | | Whithorn St | 43 J5 |
| Solway St W | 43 G6 | | Tunnel Rd | 43 H5 | | Whitland Rd | 43 J1 |
| South Chester St | 42 E7 | | Tunstall St | 43 J6 | | Whitley St | 42 B1 |
| Southern Cres | 42 D7 | | Tweed Cl | 43 H1 | | Whittier St | 43 H6 |
| South Ferry Quay | 42 C7 | | Twomey Cl | 42 C1 | | Wightman St | 43 G2 |
| South Hunter St | 42 E5 | | | | | Wilde St | 42 D3 |
| South John St | 42 C4 | | **U** | | | Wilfer Cl | 43 H5 |
| Sparling St | 42 C6 | | Underley St | 43 J6 | | William Brown St | 42 D3 |
| Spekeland Rd | 43 H5 | | Union Ct | 42 C4 | | William Henry St | 42 E2 |
| Spencer St | 43 F1 | | Union St | 42 B3 | | Williamson St | 42 C4 |
| Spindle Cl | 43 F1 | | Upper Baker St | 43 G2 | | Wimpole St | 43 H3 |
| Spofforth Rd | 43 J5 | | Upper Beau St | 42 D1 | | Windsor St | 43 E6 |
| Sprainger St | 42 B1 | | Upper Bute St | 42 E1 | | Windsor Vw | 43 H6 |
| Springfield | 42 D2 | | Upper Duke St | 42 D5 | | Winifred St | 43 H4 |
| Squires St | 43 G4 | | Upper Frederick St | 42 C5 | | Winter St | 43 F2 |
| Stafford St | 42 E3 | | Upper Hampton St | 43 F6 | | Wolstenholme Sq | 42 D5 |
| Stamford St | 43 H3 | | Upper Harrington St | 42 D7 | | Woodside St | 43 H4 |
| Standish St | 42 C3 | | Upper Hill St | 43 E7 | | Wood St | 42 D4 |
| Stanhope St | 42 D7 | | Upper Hope Pl | 43 E5 | | Wordsworth St | 43 H6 |
| Stanier Way | 43 H4 | | Upper Mann St | 42 D7 | | Wrayburn Cl | 43 H5 |
| Stanley St | 42 C3 | | Upper Mason St | 43 G4 | | Wrenbury Cl | 43 H3 |
| Star St | 42 D7 | | Upper Newington | 42 D4 | | Wynnstay St | 43 G7 |
| Steinberg Ct | 42 B1 | | Upper Parliament St | 42 D6 | | | |
| Sterndale Cl | 43 H5 | | Upper Pitt St | 42 D6 | | **Y** | |
| Stockdale Cl | 42 C2 | | Upper Pownall St | 42 C5 | | Yanwath St | 43 H6 |
| Stone St | 42 B1 | | Upper Stanhope St | 43 E6 | | York St | 42 C5 |
| Stowell St | 42 E5 | | Upper Warwick St | 43 F7 | | | |
| Strada Way | 43 E2 | | Upper William St | 42 B1 | | | |
| Strand, The | 42 B4 | | Uxbridge St | 43 H5 | | | |

## London street index

|  |  | |  |  | |  |  |
|---|---|---|---|---|---|---|---|
| **A** | | | Albemarle St W1 | 44 B4 | | Amen Ct EC4 | 45 H2 |
| Abbey Orchard St SW1 | 44 D6 | | Albemarle Way EC1 | 45 H1 | | America St SE1 | 45 J5 |
| Abingdon St SW1 | 44 E6 | | Albert Barnes Ho SE1 | 45 J7 | | Andrew Borde St WC2 | 44 D2 |
| Achilles Way W1 | 44 A5 | | Albion Pl EC1 | 45 H1 | | Andrewes Ho EC2 | 45 J2 |
| Adam & Eve Ct W1 | 44 C2 | | Albion Way EC1 | 45 J2 | | Andrewes Crosse WC2 | 45 G3 |
| Adams Row W1 | 44 A4 | | Aldburgh Ms W1 | 44 A2 | | Angel Ct SW1 | 44 C5 |
| Adam St WC2 | 45 E4 | | Aldermanbury EC2 | 45 J2 | | Angel St EC1 | 45 J2 |
| Addington St SE1 | 45 F6 | | Aldermanbury Sq EC2 | 45 J2 | | Apothecary St EC4 | 45 H3 |
| Addle Hill EC4 | 45 H3 | | Aldersgate St EC1 | 45 J2 | | Apple Tree Yd SW1 | 44 C4 |
| Adelaide St WC2 | 44 E4 | | Aldford St W1 | 44 A4 | | Apsley Way W1 | 44 A5 |
| Adeline Pl WC1 | 44 D2 | | Aldwych WC2 | 45 F3 | | Aquinas St SE1 | 45 G4 |
| Adelphi Ter WC2 | 45 E4 | | Alfred Ms W1 | 44 D1 | | Archer St W1 | 44 D3 |
| Agar St WC2 | 44 E4 | | Alfred Pl WC1 | 44 D1 | | Arches, The WC2 | 45 E4 |
| Air St W1 | 44 C4 | | Allington St SW1 | 44 C7 | | Archibald Ms W1 | 44 A4 |
| Alaska St SE1 | 45 G5 | | All Souls Pl W1 | 44 B2 | | Arch St SE1 | 45 J7 |
| Albany W1 | 44 C4 | | Ambassador's Ct SW1 | 44 C5 | | Argyll St W1 | 44 C2 |
| Albany Ctyd W1 | 44 C4 | | Ambrosden Av SW1 | 44 C7 | | Aria Ho WC2 | 45 E2 |
| | | | Amen Cor EC4 | 45 H3 | | Arlington St SW1 | 44 C4 |

|  |  | |  |  | |  |  |
|---|---|---|---|---|---|---|---|
| Arne St WC2 | 45 E3 | | Avonmouth St SE1 | 45 J6 | | Baltic St W EC1 | 45 J1 |
| Arneway St SW1 | 44 D7 | | Avon Pl SE1 | 45 J6 | | Banbury Ct WC2 | 44 E3 |
| Arrol Ho SE1 | 45 J7 | | Aybrook St W1 | 44 A2 | | Bank End SE1 | 45 J4 |
| Artillery Mans SW1 | 44 D6 | | Aylesbury St EC1 | 45 H1 | | Banks Ho SE1 | 45 J7 |
| Artillery Pl SW1 | 44 D7 | | Ayres St SE1 | 45 J5 | | Bankside SE1 | 45 J4 |
| Artillery Row SW1 | 44 D7 | | | | | Bankside Lofts SE1 | 45 H4 |
| Arundel Gt Ct WC2 | 45 F3 | | **B** | | | Banner St EC1 | 45 J1 |
| Arundel St WC2 | 45 F3 | | Babmaes St SW1 | 44 D4 | | **Barbican EC2** | 45 J2 |
| Ashenden SE17 | 45 J7 | | Back Hill EC1 | 45 G1 | | Barbican, The EC2 | 45 J2 |
| Ashentree Ct EC4 | 45 G3 | | Bainbridge St WC1 | 44 D2 | | Barbon Cl WC1 | 45 E1 |
| Ashland Pl W1 | 44 A1 | | Baker's Ms W1 | 44 A2 | | Barge Ho St SE1 | 45 G4 |
| Ashley Gdns SW1 | 44 C7 | | Baker's Row EC1 | 45 G1 | | Barkham Ter SE1 | 45 G6 |
| Ashley Pl SW1 | 44 C7 | | Baker's Yd EC1 | 45 G1 | | Barley Mow Pas EC1 | 45 H1 |
| Astbury Ho SE11 | 45 G7 | | Balderton St W1 | 44 A3 | | Barlow Pl W1 | 44 B4 |
| Audley Sq W1 | 44 A4 | | Baldwin's Gdns EC1 | 45 G1 | | Barnard's Inn EC1 | 45 G2 |
| Austral St SE11 | 45 H7 | | Balfour Ms W1 | 44 A4 | | Barons Pl SE1 | 45 G6 |
| Ave Maria La EC4 | 45 H3 | | Balfour Pl W1 | 44 A4 | | Barrett St W1 | 44 A3 |
| Avery Row W1 | 44 B3 | | Baltic St E EC1 | 45 J1 | | Barter St WC1 | 45 E2 |

Bartholomew Cl EC1 **45** J2
Bartholomew Pl EC1 **45** J2
Bartlett Ct EC4 **45** G2
Bartletts Pas EC4 **45** G2
Barton St SW1 **44** E6
Bastion Highwalk EC2 **45** J1
Bateman's Bldgs W1 **44** D3
Bateman St W1 **44** D3
Bath Ct EC1 **45** G1
Bath Ter SE1 **45** J7
Bayley St WC1 **44** D2
Baylis Rd SE1 **45** G6
Beak St W1 **44** C3
Bear All EC4 **45** H2
Bear Gdns SE1 **45** J4
Bear La SE1 **45** H4
Bear St WC2 **44** D3
Beauchamp St EC1 **45** G2
Beaumont Ms W1 **44** A1
Beaumont St W1 **44** A1
Bedford Av WC1 **44** D2
Bedfordbury WC2 **44** E3
Bedford Ct WC2 **44** E4
Bedford Pl WC1 **44** E1
Bedford Row WC1 **45** F1
Bedford Sq WC1 **44** D2
Bedford St WC2 **44** E3
Bedford Way WC1 **44** D1
Bedlam Ms SE11 **45** G7
Beech St EC2 **45** J1
Beeston Pl SW1 **44** B7
Belgrave Ms N SW1 **44** A6
Belgrave Ms S SW1 **44** A6
Belgrave Ms W SW1 **44** A6
Belgrave Pl SW1 **44** A6
Belgrave Sq SW1 **44** A6
Belgrave Yd SW1 **44** B7
**Belgravia SW1** **44** A7
Bell Wf La EC4 **45** J4
Bell Yd WC2 **45** G2
Belvedere Bldgs SE1 **45** H6
Belvedere Pl SE1 **45** H6
Belvedere Rd SE1 **45** F5
Benjamin St EC1 **45** H1
Bennet's Hill EC4 **45** H3
Bennet St SW1 **44** C4
Bennetts Yd SW1 **44** D7
Bentinck Ms W1 **44** A2
Bentinck St W1 **44** A2
Berkeley Sq W1 **44** B4
Berkeley St W1 **44** B4
Bernard St WC1 **44** E1
Berners Ms W1 **44** C2
Berners Pl W1 **44** C2
Berners St W1 **44** C2
Berwick St W1 **44** D3
Betterton St WC2 **44** E3
Bingham Pl W1 **44** A1
Binney St W1 **44** A3
Birdcage Wk SW1 **44** C6
Bird St W1 **44** A3
Bishop's Ct EC4 **45** H2
Bishop's Ct WC2 **45** G2
Bishops Ter SE11 **45** G7
Bittern St SE1 **45** J6
Blackburne's Ms W1 **44** A3
Blackfriars Br EC4 **45** H3
Blackfriars Br SE1 **45** H3
Blackfriars Ct EC4 **45** H3
Black Friars La EC4 **45** H3
Blackfriars Pas EC4 **45** H3
Blackfriars Rd SE1 **45** H6
Bleeding Heart Yd EC1 **45** G2
Blenheim St W1 **44** B3
Bloomfield Pl W1 **44** B3
**Bloomsbury WC1** **44** D2
Bloomsbury Ct WC1 **45** E2
Bloomsbury Pl WC1 **45** E1
Bloomsbury Sq WC1 **45** E2
Bloomsbury St WC1 **44** D2
Bloomsbury Way WC1 **44** E2
Blore Ct W1 **44** D3
Blue Ball Yd SW1 **44** C5
Bolsover St W1 **44** B1
Bolt Ct EC4 **45** G3
Bolton St W1 **44** B4
Book Ms WC2 **44** D3
Booth La EC4 **45** J3
Booth's Pl W1 **44** C2
**Borough, The SE1** **45** J6
Borough High St SE1 **45** J6
Borough Rd SE1 **45** H6
Borough Sq SE1 **45** J6
Boscobel Pl SW1 **44** A7
Boswell Ct WC1 **45** E1
Boswell St WC1 **45** E1
Boundary Row SE1 **45** H5
Bourchier St W1 **44** D3
Bourdon Pl W1 **44** B3
Bourdon St W1 **44** B3
Bourlet Cl W1 **44** C2

Bourne Est EC1 **45** G1
Bouverie St EC4 **45** G3
Bow Chyd EC4 **45** J3
Bow La EC4 **45** J3
Bow St WC2 **45** E3
Boyce St SE1 **45** F5
Boyfield St SE1 **45** H6
Boyle St W1 **44** C3
Brackley St EC1 **45** J1
Brad St SE1 **45** G5
Bread St EC4 **45** J3
Bream's Bldgs EC4 **45** G2
Bressenden Pl SW1 **44** B6
Brewer's Grn SW1 **44** D6
Brewers Hall Gdns EC2 **45** J2
Brewer St W1 **44** C3
Briant Est SE1 **45** G7
Briant Ho SE1 **45** F7
Brick Ct EC4 **45** G3
Brick St W1 **44** B5
Bride Ct EC4 **45** H3
Bride La EC4 **45** H3
Bridewell Pl EC4 **45** H3
Bridford Ms W1 **44** B1
Bridge Pl SW1 **44** B7
Bridge St SW1 **44** E6
Bridgewater Sq EC2 **45** J1
Bridgewater St EC2 **45** J1
Bridle La W1 **44** C3
Brinton Wk SE1 **45** H5
Briset St EC1 **45** H1
Britton St EC1 **45** H1
Broadbent St W1 **44** B3
Broad Ct WC2 **45** E3
Broad Sanctuary SW1 **44** D6
Broadstone Pl W1 **44** A2
Broad Wk W1 **44** A4
Broadwall SE1 **45** G4
Broadway SW1 **44** D6
Broadwick St W1 **44** C3
Broad Yd EC1 **45** H1
Brockham St SE1 **45** J6
Broken Wf EC4 **45** J3
Bromley Pl W1 **44** C1
Brooke's Ct EC1 **45** G1
Brookes Mkt EC1 **45** G1
Brooke St EC1 **45** G2
Brook's Ms W1 **44** B3
Brook St W1 **44** A3
Brown Hart Gdns W1 **44** A3
Browning Ms W1 **44** A2
Brownlow Ms WC1 **45** F1
Brownlow St WC1 **45** F2
Brunswick Sq WC1 **45** E1
Bruton La W1 **44** B4
Bruton Pl W1 **44** B4
Bruton St W1 **44** B4
Brydges Pl WC2 **44** E4
Buckingham Arc WC2 **45** E4
Buckingham Gate SW1 **44** C6
Buckingham Ms SW1 **44** C6
Buckingham Pl SW1 **44** C6
Buckingham St WC2 **45** E4
Buckley St SE1 **45** G5
Bucknall St WC2 **44** D2
Bull Inn Ct WC2 **45** E4
Bulstrode Pl W1 **44** A2
Bulstrode St W1 **44** A2
Burdett St SE1 **45** G6
Burgon St EC4 **45** H3
Burleigh St WC2 **45** F3
Burlington Arc W1 **44** C4
Burlington Gdns W1 **44** C4
Burrell St SE1 **45** H4
Burrows Ms SE1 **45** H5
Bury Pl WC1 **44** E2
Bury St SW1 **44** C4
Butler Pl SW1 **44** D6
Byng Pl WC1 **44** D1
Bywell Pl W1 **44** C2

**C**

Cadogan La SW1 **44** A7
Cahill St EC1 **45** J1
Caleb St SE1 **45** J5
Cambridge Circ WC2 **44** D3
Candover St W1 **44** C2
Cannon St EC4 **45** J3
Canon Row SW1 **44** E6
Canterbury Ho SE1 **45** F6
Canvey St SE1 **45** H4
Capener's Cl SW1 **44** A6
Capper St WC1 **44** C1
Carburton St W1 **44** B1
Carey La EC2 **45** J2
Carey St WC2 **45** F3
Carlisle La SE1 **45** F7
Carlisle Pl SW1 **44** C7
Carlisle St W1 **44** D3
Carlos Pl W1 **44** A4
Carlton Gdns SW1 **44** D5

Carlton Ho Ter SW1 **44** D5
Carlton St SW1 **44** D4
Carmelite St EC4 **45** G3
Carnaby St W1 **44** C3
Carpenter St W1 **44** B4
Carrington St W1 **44** B5
Carteret St SW1 **44** D6
Carter La EC4 **45** H3
Carthusian St EC1 **45** J1
Carting La WC2 **45** E4
Castle Baynard St EC4 **45** H3
Castlebrook Cl SE11 **45** H7
Castle La SW1 **44** C6
Castle Yd SE1 **45** H4
Cathedral Piazza SW1 **44** C7
Cathedral Wk SW1 **44** C6
Catherine Pl SW1 **44** C6
Catherine St WC2 **45** F3
Catherine Wheel Yd SW1 **44** C5
Catton St WC1 **45** F2
Cavendish Ms N W1 **44** B1
Cavendish Ms S W1 **44** B1
Cavendish Pl W1 **44** B2
Cavendish Sq W1 **44** B2
Caxton St SW1 **44** C6
Cecil Ct WC2 **44** D4
Centaur St SE1 **45** F6
Centrepoint WC1 **44** D2
Chadwick St SW1 **44** D7
Chancel St SE1 **45** H4
Chancery La WC2 **45** G2
Chandos Pl WC2 **44** E4
Chandos St W1 **44** B2
Chapel Pl W1 **44** B3
Chapel St SW1 **44** A6
Chaplin Cl SE1 **45** G5
Chapone Pl W1 **44** D3
Chapter Ho Ct EC4 **45** J3
Charing Cross SW1 **44** D4
Charing Cross Rd WC2 **44** D2
Charles II St SW1 **44** D4
Charles St W1 **44** B4
Charlotte Ms W1 **44** C1
Charlotte Pl W1 **44** C2
Charlotte St W1 **44** C1
Charterhouse, The EC1 **45** H1
Charterhouse Bldgs EC1 **45** H1
Charterhouse Ms EC1 **45** H1
Charterhouse Sq EC1 **45** H1
Charterhouse St EC1 **45** G2
Cheapside EC2 **45** J3
Chenies Ms WC1 **44** D1
Chenies St WC1 **44** D1
Chequer St EC1 **45** J1
Cherry Tree Wk EC1 **45** J1
Chesham Cl SW1 **44** A7
Chesham Ms SW1 **44** A6
Chesham Pl SW1 **44** A7
Chesham St SW1 **44** A7
Cheshire Ct EC4 **45** G3
Chester Cl SW1 **44** A6
Chesterfield Gdns W1 **44** B4
Chesterfield Hill W1 **44** B4
Chesterfield St W1 **44** B4
Chester Ms SW1 **44** B6
Chester Sq SW1 **44** B7
Chester Sq Ms SW1 **44** B7
Chester St SW1 **44** A6
Chichely St SE1 **45** F5
Chichester Rents WC2 **45** G2
Chiltern St W1 **44** A1
Ching Ct WC2 **44** E3
Chiswell St EC1 **45** J1
Chitty St W1 **44** C1
Christ Ch Pas EC1 **45** H2
Church Entry EC4 **45** H3
Church Pl SW1 **44** C4
Churchyard Row SE11 **45** H7
Clare Mkt WC2 **45** F3
Clarges Ms W1 **44** B4
Clarges St W1 **44** B4
Clarke's Ms W1 **44** A1
Clement's Inn WC2 **45** F3
Clement's Inn Pas WC2 **45** F3
Clennam St SE1 **45** J5
**Clerkenwell EC1** **45** H1
Clerkenwell Grn EC1 **45** G1
Clerkenwell Rd EC1 **45** G1
Cleveland Ms W1 **44** C1
Cleveland Pl SW1 **44** C4
Cleveland Row SW1 **44** C5
Cleveland St W1 **44** C1
Clifford's Inn Pas EC4 **45** G3
Clifford St W1 **44** C4
Clink St SE1 **45** J4
Clipstone Ms W1 **44** C1

Clipstone St W1 **44** B1
Cliveden Pl SW1 **44** A7
Cloak La EC4 **45** J3
Cloth Ct EC1 **45** H2
Cloth Fair EC1 **45** H2
Cloth St EC1 **45** J1
Coach & Horses Yd W1 **44** B3
Coburg Cl SW1 **44** C7
Cock La EC1 **45** H2
Cockpit Steps SW1 **44** D6
Cockpit Yd WC1 **45** F1
Cockspur Ct SW1 **44** D4
Cockspur St SW1 **44** D4
Coin St SE1 **45** G4
Cole St SE1 **45** J6
Coley St WC1 **45** F1
College Hill EC4 **45** J3
College Ms SW1 **44** E6
College St EC4 **45** J3
Collinson St SE1 **45** J6
Collinson Wk SE1 **45** J6
Colnbrook St SE1 **45** H7
Colombo St SE1 **45** H5
Colonnade WC1 **44** E1
Colville Pl W1 **44** C2
Computer Pass EC2 **45** J2
Concert Hall App SE1 **45** F5
Conduit Ct WC2 **44** E3
Conduit St W1 **44** B3
Cons St SE1 **45** G5
Constitution Hill SW1 **44** B5
Conway Ms W1 **44** C1
Conway St W1 **44** C1
Cooper Cl SE1 **45** G6
Copeland Ho SE11 **45** F7
Copperfield St SE1 **45** H5
Coptic St WC1 **44** E2
Coral St SE1 **45** G6
Coram St WC1 **44** E1
Cork St W1 **44** C4
Cork St Ms W1 **44** C4
Corner Ho St WC2 **44** E4
Cornwall Rd SE1 **45** G4
Cosmo Pl WC1 **45** E1
Cosser St SE1 **45** G6
Cottesloe Ms SE1 **45** G6
County St SE1 **45** J7
Covent Gdn WC2 **45** E3
Covent Gdn Mkt WC2 **45** E3
Coventry St W1 **44** D4
Cowcross St EC1 **45** H1
Cowley St SW1 **44** E6
Craig's Ct SW1 **44** E4
Cramer St W1 **44** A2
Cranbourn St WC2 **44** D3
Crane Ct EC4 **45** G3
Cranfield Row SE1 **45** G6
Craven Pas WC2 **44** E4
Craven St WC2 **44** E4
Crawford Pas EC1 **45** G1
Creed La EC4 **45** H3
Crescent Row EC1 **45** J1
Cripplegate St EC2 **45** J1
Cromwell Twr EC2 **45** J1
Cross Keys Cl W1 **44** A2
Cross Keys Sq EC1 **45** J2
Crown Ct EC2 **45** J3
Crown Ct WC2 **45** E3
Crown Office Row EC4 **45** G3
Crown Pas SW1 **44** C5
Cubitts Yd WC2 **45** E3
Cuddington SE17 **45** J7
Culross St W1 **44** A4
Cursitor St EC4 **45** G2
Curzon Gate W1 **44** A5
Curzon Sq W1 **44** A5
Curzon St W1 **44** A5
Cut, The SE1 **45** G5
Cypress Pl W1 **44** C1

**D**

Dacre St SW1 **44** D6
Dane St WC1 **45** F2
Dansey Pl W1 **44** D3
Dante Pl SE11 **45** H7
Dante Rd SE11 **45** H7
D'Arblay St W1 **44** C3
Dartmouth St SW1 **44** D6
Davidge St SE1 **45** H6
Davies Ms W1 **44** B3
Davies St W1 **44** B3
Deacon Way SE17 **45** J7
Dean Bradley St SW1 **44** E7
Deanery Ms W1 **44** A4
Deanery St W1 **44** A4
Dean Farrar St SW1 **44** D6
Dean Ryle St SW1 **44** E7
Deans Ct EC4 **45** H3
Deans Ms W1 **44** B2
Dean Stanley St SW1 **44** E7
Dean St W1 **44** D2
Dean's Yd SW1 **44** D6

Dean Trench St SW1 **44** E7
Denman St W1 **44** D4
Denmark Pl WC2 **44** D2
Denmark St WC2 **44** C3
Derby Gate SW1 **44** E5
Derby St W1 **44** A5
Dering St W1 **44** B3
Devereux Ct WC2 **45** G3
Devonshire Cl W1 **44** B1
Devonshire Ms N W1 **44** B1
Devonshire Ms S W1 **44** B1
Devonshire Ms W W1 **44** B1
Devonshire Pl W1 **44** A1
Devonshire Pl Ms W1 **44** A1
Devonshire Row Ms W1 **44** B1
Devonshire St W1 **44** A1
De Walden St W1 **44** A2
Diadem Ct W1 **44** D3
Dickens Ms EC1 **45** H1
Dickens Sq SE1 **45** J6
Disney Pl SE1 **45** J5
Disney St SE1 **45** J5
Distaff La EC4 **45** J3
Doby Ct EC4 **45** J3
Dodson St SE1 **45** G6
Dolben St SE1 **45** H5
Dombey St WC1 **45** F1
Doon St SE1 **45** G5
Dorrington St EC1 **45** G1
Dorrit St SE1 **45** J5
Dorset Bldgs EC4 **45** H3
Dorset Ms SW1 **44** B6
Dorset Ri EC4 **45** H3
Doughty Ms WC1 **45** F1
Dover St W1 **44** B4
Dover Yd W1 **44** B4
Downing St SW1 **44** E5
Down St W1 **44** B5
Down St Ms W1 **44** B5
Doyce St SE1 **45** J5
D'Oyley St SW1 **44** A7
Drake St WC1 **45** F2
Draper Ho SE1 **45** H7
Drury La WC2 **45** E3
Dryden St WC2 **45** E3
Duchess Ms W1 **44** B2
Duchess St W1 **44** B2
Duchy Pl SE1 **45** G4
Duchy St SE1 **45** G4
Duck La W1 **44** D3
Dufferin St EC1 **45** J1
Dufour's Pl W1 **44** C3
Dugard Way SE11 **45** H7
Duke of Wellington Pl SW1 **44** A5
Duke of York St SW1 **44** C4
Duke's Ms W1 **44** A2
Duke St SW1 **44** C4
Duke St W1 **44** A2
Duke's Yd W1 **44** A3
Duncannon St WC2 **44** E4
Dunns Pas WC1 **45** E2
Dunstable Ms W1 **44** A1
Durham Ho St WC2 **45** E4
Dyer's Bldgs EC1 **45** G2
Dyott St WC1 **44** E2

**E**

Eagle Ct EC1 **45** H1
Eagle Pl SW1 **44** C4
Eagle St WC1 **45** F2
Earlham St WC2 **44** D3
Earnshaw St WC2 **44** D2
Easley's Ms W1 **44** A2
Eastcastle St W1 **44** C2
East Harding St EC4 **45** G2
East Pas EC1 **45** H1
East Poultry Av EC1 **45** H2
Eaton Gate SW1 **44** A7
Eaton La SW1 **44** B7
Eaton Ms N SW1 **44** A7
Eaton Ms S SW1 **44** A7
Eaton Ms W SW1 **44** A7
Eaton Pl SW1 **44** A7
Eaton Row SW1 **44** B6
Eaton Sq SW1 **44** B6
Eaton Ter SW1 **44** A7
Eaton Ter Ms SW1 **44** A7
Ebury Ms SW1 **44** B7
Ebury Ms E SW1 **44** B7
Ebury Sq SW1 **44** B7
Ebury St SW1 **44** B7
Eccleston Br SW1 **44** B7
Eccleston Ms SW1 **44** A7
Eccleston Pl SW1 **44** B7
Eccleston St SW1 **44** B7
Edwards Ms W1 **44** A3
Elba Pl SE17 **45** J7
Elephant & Castle SE1 **45** H7
Elephant Rd SE17 **45** J7
Elizabeth Ct SW1 **44** D7
Elizabeth St SW1 **44** A7
Ellington Ho SE1 **45** J6

Elliotts Row SE11 **45** H7
Elm Ct EC4 **45** G3
Elm St WC1 **45** F1
Elverton St SW1 **44** D7
Ely Ct EC1 **45** G2
Ely Pl EC1 **45** G2
Embankment Pier WC2 **45** F4
Embankment Pl WC2 **45** E4
Emerald St WC1 **45** F1
Emerson St SE1 **45** J4
Emery Hill St SW1 **44** C7
Emery St SE1 **45** G6
Endell St WC2 **44** E2
Errol St EC1 **45** J1
Essex Ct EC4 **45** G3
Essex St WC2 **45** G3
Euston Rd NW1 **44** B1
Evelyn Yd W1 **44** D2
Ewer St SE1 **45** J5
Excel Ct WC2 **44** D4
Exchange Ct WC2 **45** E4
Exeter St WC2 **45** E3
Exton St SE1 **45** G5
Eyre St Hill EC1 **45** G1

**F**

Falconberg Ct W1 **44** D2
Falconberg Ms W1 **44** D2
Falcon Ct EC4 **45** G3
Falmouth Rd SE1 **45** J6
Fann St EC1 **45** J1
Fann St EC2 **45** J1
Fareham St W1 **44** D2
Farm St W1 **44** B4
Farnham Pl SE1 **45** H5
Farringdon La EC1 **45** G1
Farringdon St EC4 **45** H2
Faulkner's All EC1 **45** H1
Ferrybridge Ho SE11 **45** F7
Fetter La EC4 **45** G3
Field Ct WC1 **45** F2
Fisher St WC1 **45** E2
Fitzalan St SE11 **45** G7
Fitzhardinge St W1 **44** A2
Fitzmaurice Pl W1 **44** B4
Fitzroy Ct W1 **44** C1
Fitzroy Ms W1 **44** C1
Fitzroy Sq W1 **44** C1
Fitzroy St W1 **44** C1
Fives Ct SE11 **45** H7
Flaxman Ct W1 **44** D3
Fleet St EC4 **45** G3
Flitcroft St WC2 **44** D2
Floral St WC2 **44** E3
Florin Ct EC1 **45** J1
Foley St W1 **44** C2
Fore St EC2 **45** J2
Fortune St EC1 **45** J1
Forum Magnum Sq SE1 **45** F5
Foster La EC2 **45** J2
Foubert's Pl W1 **44** C3
Fountain Ct EC4 **45** G3
Fountain Sq SW1 **44** B7
Fox & Knot St EC1 **45** H1
Francis St SW1 **44** C7
Frazier St SE1 **45** G6
Friars Cl SE1 **45** H5
Friar St EC4 **45** H3
Friary Ct SW1 **44** C5
Friday St EC4 **45** J3
Frith St W1 **44** D3
Fulwood Pl WC1 **45** F2
Furnival St EC4 **45** G2
Fynes St SW1 **44** D7

**G**

Gabriel's Wf SE1 **45** G4
Gage St WC1 **45** E1
Galen Pl WC1 **45** E2
Gambia St SE1 **45** H5
Ganton St W1 **44** C3
Garbutt Pl W1 **44** A1
Garden Row SE1 **45** H6
Gardners La EC4 **45** J3
Garlick Hill EC4 **45** J3
Garrick St WC2 **44** E3
Garrick Yd WC2 **44** E3
Gate Ho Sq SE1 **45** J4
Gate St WC2 **45** F2
Gaunt St SE1 **45** H6
Gayfere St SW1 **44** E7
Gaywood Est SE1 **45** H7
Gaywood St SE1 **45** H7
Gees Ct W1 **44** A3
George Ct WC2 **45** E4
George Mathers Rd SE11 **45** H7
George Yd W1 **44** A3
Geraldine St SE11 **45** H7
Gerald Ms SW1 **44** A7
Gerald Rd SW1 **44** A7
Gerrard Pl W1 **44** D3

Gerrard St W1 44 D3
Gerridge St SE1 45 G6
Gilbert Pl WC1 44 E2
Gilbert St W1 44 A3
Gildea St W1 44 B2
Gillingham Row SW1 44 C7
Gillingham St SW1 44 B7
Giltspur St EC1 45 H2
Gladstone St SE1 45 H6
Glasshill St SE1 45 H5
Glasshouse St W1 44 C4
Glasshouse Yd EC1 45 J1
Globe St SE1 45 J6
Globe Yd W1 44 B3
Godliman St EC4 45 J3
Golden Jubilee Br SE1 45 F5
Golden Jubilee Br
  WC2 45 E4
Golden La EC1 45 J1
Golden La Est EC1 45 J1
Golden Sq W1 44 C3
Goldsmith St EC2 45 J2
Goodge Pl W1 44 C2
Goodge St W1 44 C2
Goodwins Ct WC2 44 E3
Gordon Sq WC1 44 D1
Gosfield St W1 44 C1
Goslett Yd WC2 44 D3
Goswell Rd EC1 45 J1
Gough Sq EC4 45 G2
Gower Ms WC1 44 D2
Grafton Ms W1 44 C1
Grafton St W1 44 B4
Grafton Way W1 44 C1
Grafton Way WC1 44 C1
Granby Pl SE1 45 G6
Grand Av EC1 45 H1
Grange Ct WC2 45 F3
Grantham Pl W1 44 B5
Granville Pl W1 44 A3
Grape St WC2 44 E2
Gray's Inn WC1 45 F1
Gray's Inn Pl WC1 45 F2
Gray's Inn Sq WC1 45 G1
Gray St SE1 45 G6
Gray's Yd W1 44 A3
Great Arthur Ho EC1 45 J1
Great Castle St W1 44 B2
Great Chapel St W1 44 D2
Great Coll St SW1 44 E6
Great Dover St SE1 45 J6
Great George St SW1 44 D6
Great Guildford St
  SE1 45 J4
Great James St WC1 45 F1
Great Marlborough St
  W1 44 C2
Great New St EC4 45 G2
Great Ormond St
  WC1 45 E1
Great Peter St SW1 44 D7
Great Portland St W1 44 B1
Great Pulteney St W1 44 C3
Great Queen St WC2 45 E3
Great Russell St W1 44 D2
Great St. Thomas
  Apostle EC4 45 J3
Great Scotland Yd
  SW1 44 E5
Great Smith St SW1 44 D6
Great Suffolk St SE1 45 H5
Great Sutton St EC1 45 H1
Great Titchfield St W1 44 C2
Great Trinity La EC4 45 J3
Great Turnstile WC1 45 F2
Great Windmill St W1 44 D3
Greek Ct W1 44 D3
Greek St W1 44 D3
Green Arbour Ct EC1 45 H2
Greencoat Pl SW1 44 C7
Greencoat Row SW1 44 C7
Greenham Cl SE1 45 G6
Greenhill's Rents EC1 45 H1
Green's Ct W1 44 D3
Greenwell St W1 44 B1
Greet St SE1 45 G5
Grenville St WC1 45 E1
Gresham St EC2 45 J2
Gresse St W1 44 D2
Greville St EC1 45 G2
Greycoat Pl SW1 44 C7
Greycoat St SW1 44 D7
Greyfriars Pas EC1 45 H2
Greystoke Pl EC4 45 G2
Grindal St SE1 45 G6
Groom Pl SW1 44 A6
Grosvenor Cotts SW1 44 A7
Grosvenor Cres SW1 44 A6
Grosvenor Cres Ms
  SW1 44 A6
Grosvenor Est SW1 44 D7
Grosvenor Gdns SW1 44 B6
Grosvenor Gdns Ms E
  SW1 44 B6

Grosvenor Gdns Ms N
  SW1 44 B7
Grosvenor Gdns Ms S
  SW1 44 B7
Grosvenor Hill W1 44 B3
Grosvenor Pl SW1 44 A6
Grosvenor Sq W1 44 A3
Grosvenor St W1 44 B3
Grotto Pas W1 44 A1
Groveland Ct EC4 45 J3
Guildhall Yd EC2 45 J2
Guildhouse St SW1 44 C7
Guilford Pl WC1 45 F1
Guilford St WC1 45 F1
Gunpowder Sq EC4 45 G2
Gutter La EC2 45 J2

H
Half Moon Ct EC1 45 J2
Half Moon St W1 44 B4
Halkin Arc SW1 44 A6
Halkin Ms SW1 44 A6
Halkin Pl SW1 44 A6
Halkin St SW1 44 A6
Hallam Ms W1 44 B1
Hallam St W1 44 B1
Hamilton Ms W1 44 B5
Hamilton Pl W1 44 A5
Ham Yd W1 44 D3
Hand Ct WC1 45 F2
Hanging Sword All
  EC4 45 G3
Hanover Pl WC2 45 E3
Hanover Sq W1 44 B3
Hanover St W1 44 B3
Hanson St W1 44 C1
Hanway Pl W1 44 D2
Hanway St W1 44 D2
Hare Ct EC4 45 G3
Hare Pl EC4 45 G3
Harewood Av W1 44 B3
Harley Pl W1 44 B2
Harley St W1 44 B2
Harmsworth Ms SE11 45 H7
Harp All EC4 45 H2
Harper Rd SE1 45 J6
Harpur Ms WC1 45 F1
Harpur St WC1 45 F1
Hat & Mitre Ct EC1 45 H1
Hatfields SE1 45 G4
Hatton Gdn EC1 45 G1
Hatton Pl EC1 45 G1
Hatton Wall EC1 45 G1
Haunch of Venison Yd
  W1 44 B3
Hay Hill W1 44 B4
Hayles St SE11 45 H7
Haymarket SW1 44 D4
Haymarket Arc SW1 44 D4
Hayne St EC1 45 H1
Hay's Ms W1 44 B4
Hayward's Pl EC1 45 H1
Headfort Pl SW1 44 A6
Heddon St W1 44 C3
Hedger St SE11 45 H7
Hen & Chicken Ct
  EC4 45 G3
Henrietta Pl W1 44 B3
Henrietta St WC2 45 E3
Herald's Pl SE11 45 H7
Herbal Hill EC1 45 G1
Hercules Rd SE1 45 F7
Herrick St SW1 44 D7
Hertford St W1 44 B4
High Holborn WC1 45 E2
High Timber St EC4 45 J3
Hills Pl W1 44 C3
Hill St W1 44 A4
Hind Ct EC4 45 G3
Hinde St W1 44 A2
Hindon Ct SW1 44 C7
Hobart Pl SW1 44 B6
Holbein Pl EC1 45 G2
Holborn WC2 45 F2
Holborn Circ EC1 45 G2
Holborn Pl WC1 45 F2
Holborn Viaduct EC1 45 G2
Holland St SE1 45 H4
Hollen St W1 44 D2
Holles St W1 44 B2
Holmes Ter SE1 45 G5
Holsworthy Sq WC1 45 F1
Holyoak Rd SE11 45 H7
Honey La EC2 45 J3
Hood Ct EC4 45 G3
Hop Gdns WC2 44 E4
Hopkins St W1 44 C3
Hopton's Gdns SE1 45 H4
Hopton St SE1 45 H4
Hornbeam Cl SE11 45 G7
Horse & Dolphin Yd
  W1 44 D3
Horseferry Rd SW1 44 D7
Horse Guards Av SW1 44 E5

Horse Guards Rd SW1 44 D5
Horsemongers Ms
  SE1 45 J6
Horse Ride SW1 44 D5
Hosier La EC1 45 H2
Houghton St WC2 45 F3
Howick Pl SW1 44 C7
Howland Ms E W1 44 C1
Howland St W1 44 C1
Hudson's Pl SW1 44 B7
Huggin Ct EC4 45 J3
Huggin Hill EC4 45 J3
Hulme Pl SE1 45 J6
Hungerford Br SE1 45 E4
Hungerford Br WC2 45 E4
Hungerford La WC2 44 E4
Huntley St W1 44 C1
Hunt's Ct WC2 44 D4
Hutton St EC4 45 G3
Hyde Pk Cor W1 44 A5

I
India Pl WC2 45 F3
Ingestre Pl W1 44 C3
Ingram Cl SE11 45 F7
Inigo Pl WC2 44 E3
Inner Temple La EC4 45 G3
Invicta Plaza SE1 45 H4
Ireland Yd EC4 45 H3
Irving St WC2 44 D4
Isaac Way SE1 45 J5
Isabella St SE1 45 H5
Ivybridge La WC2 45 E4

J
Jacob's Well Ms W1 44 A2
James St W1 44 A2
James St WC2 45 E3
Jermyn St SW1 44 C4
Jerusalem Pas EC1 45 H1
Jervis Ct W1 44 B3
Joan St SE1 45 H5
Jockey's Flds WC1 45 F1
Johanna St SE1 45 G6
John Adam St WC2 45 E4
John Carpenter St
  EC4 45 H3
John Milton Pass EC2 45 J3
John Princes St W1 44 B2
John's Ms WC1 45 F1
John St WC1 45 F1
Jones St W1 44 B4
Jubilee Mkt Hall WC2 45 E3
Juxon St SE11 45 F7

K
Kean St WC2 45 F3
Keeley St WC2 45 F3
Kell St SE1 45 H6
Kemble St WC2 45 F3
Kemp's Ct W1 44 C3
Kendall Pl W1 44 A2
Kennet Wf La EC4 45 J3
Kennington Rd SE1 45 G6
Kennington Rd SE11 45 G7
Kenrick Pl W1 44 A1
Keppel Row SE1 45 J5
Keppel St WC1 44 D1
Keyworth Pl SE1 45 H6
Keyworth St SE1 45 H6
King Charles St SW1 44 D5
King Edward St EC1 45 J2
King Edward Wk SE1 45 G6
Kinghorn St EC1 45 J2
King James Ct SE1 45 H6
King James St SE1 45 H6
Kingly Ct W1 44 C3
Kingly St W1 44 C3
Kings Bench St SE1 45 H5
Kings Bench Wk EC4 45 G3
Kingscote St EC4 45 H3
King's Ms WC1 45 F1
Kings Pl SE1 45 J6
King's Reach Twr SE1 45 G4
King's Scholars' Pas
  SW1 44 C7
King St EC2 45 J3
King St SW1 44 C5
King St WC2 45 E3
Kingsway WC2 45 F2
Kinnerton St SW1 44 A6
Kirby St EC1 45 G1
Kirkman Pl W1 44 D2
Kirk St WC1 45 F1
Knightrider St EC4 45 J3

L
Lambeth SE1 45 F7
Lambeth Br SE1 45 E7
Lambeth Br SW1 45 E7
Lambeth Hill EC4 45 J3
Lambeth Palace Rd
  SE1 45 F7
Lambeth Pier SE1 45 E7

Lambeth Rd SE1 45 F7
Lambeth Rd SE11 45 F7
Lambeth Twrs SE11 45 G7
Lambeth Wk SE1 45 F7
Lambeth Wk SE11 45 F7
Lambs Conduit Pas
  WC1 45 F1
Lamb's Conduit St
  WC1 45 F1
Lamlash St SE11 45 H7
Lamp Office Ct WC1 45 F1
Lancashire Ct W1 44 B3
Lancaster Pl WC2 45 F3
Lancaster St SE1 45 H6
Lanesborough Pl
  SW1 44 A5
Langham Pl W1 44 B2
Langham St W1 44 B2
Langley Ct WC2 44 E3
Langley St WC2 44 E3
Lansdowne Row W1 44 B4
Lansdowne Ter WC1 45 E1
Lant St SE1 45 J5
Lauderdale Twr EC2 45 J1
Launcelot St SE1 45 G6
Lavington St SE1 45 H5
Lawrence La EC2 45 J3
Laystall St EC1 45 G1
Laytons Bldgs SE1 45 J5
Lazenby Ct WC2 44 E3
Leake St SE1 45 F5
Leather La EC1 45 G2
Lees Pl W1 44 A3
Leicester Ct WC2 44 D3
Leicester Pl WC2 44 D3
Leicester Sq WC2 44 D4
Leicester St WC2 44 D3
Leigh Hunt St SE1 45 J5
Leigh Pl EC1 45 G1
Leopards Ct EC1 45 G1
Leo Yd EC1 45 H1
Lewisham St SW1 44 D6
Lexington St W1 44 C3
Library St SE1 45 H6
Lily Pl EC1 45 G1
Limeburner La EC4 45 H3
Lincoln's Inn WC2 45 F2
Lincoln's Inn Flds
  WC2 45 F2
Lindsey St EC1 45 H1
Lisle St WC2 44 D3
Litchfield St WC2 44 D3
Little Argyll St W1 44 C3
Little Britain EC1 45 J2
Little Chester St SW1 44 A6
Little Coll St SW1 44 E6
Little Dean's Yd SW1 44 E6
Little Dorrit Ct SE1 45 J5
Little Essex St WC2 45 G3
Little George St SW1 44 E6
Little Newport St WC2 44 D3
Little New St EC4 45 G2
Little Portland St W1 44 C2
Little Russell St WC1 44 E2
Little St. James's St
  SW1 44 C5
Little Sanctuary SW1 44 D6
Little Smith St SW1 44 D6
Little Titchfield St W1 44 C2
Little Trinity La EC4 45 J3
Little Turnstile WC1 45 F2
Livonia St W1 44 C3
Lollard St SE11 45 F7
Loman St SE1 45 H5
Lombard La EC4 45 G3
London Cen Mkts
  EC1 45 H1
London Rd SE1 45 H6
London Silver Vaults
  WC2 45 G2
London Trocadero,
  The W1 44 D4
London Wall EC2 45 J2
Long Acre WC2 44 E3
Long La EC1 45 H1
Longridge Ho SE1 45 J7
Long's Ct WC2 44 D3
Longstone Ct SE1 45 J6
Longville Rd SE11 45 H7
Long Yd WC1 45 F1
Lord N St SW1 44 E7
Love La EC2 45 J2
Lover's Wk W1 44 A4
Lower Belgrave St
  SW1 44 B7
Lower Grosvenor Pl
  SW1 44 B6
Lower James St W1 44 C3
Lower John St W1 44 C3
Lower Marsh SE1 45 G6
Lower Rd SE1 45 G5
Lowndes Cl SW1 44 A7
Lowndes St SW1 44 A6
Lowndes Pl SW1 44 A7

Ludgate Bdy EC4 45 H3
Ludgate Circ EC4 45 H3
Ludgate Hill EC4 45 H3
Ludgate Sq EC4 45 H3
Lumley Ct WC2 45 E4
Lumley St W1 44 A3
Luxborough St W1 44 A1
Lyall Ms SW1 44 A7
Lyall Ms W SW1 44 A7
Lyall St SW1 44 A7
Lygon Pl SW1 44 B7

M
McAuley Cl SE1 45 G6
Macclesfield St W1 44 D3
McCoid Way SE1 45 J6
Macfarren Pl NW1 44 A1
Macklin St WC2 45 E2
Mac's Pl EC4 45 G2
Magpie All EC4 45 G3
Maiden La SE1 45 J4
Maiden La WC2 45 E3
Maidstone Bldgs Ms
  SE1 45 J5
Malet Pl WC1 44 D1
Malet St WC1 44 D1
Mall, The SW1 44 C5
Maltravers St WC2 45 F3
Manchester Ms W1 44 A2
Manchester Sq W1 44 A2
Manchester St W1 44 A2
Mandeville Pl W1 44 A2
Manette St W1 44 D3
Mansfield Ms W1 44 B2
Mansfield St W1 44 B2
Maple Pl W1 44 C1
Maple St W1 44 C1
Margaret Ct W1 44 C2
Margaret St W1 44 B2
Marigold All SE1 45 H4
Market Ct EC2 44 A2
Market Ms W1 44 B5
Market Pl W1 44 C2
Marlborough Ct W1 44 C3
Marlborough Rd SW1 44 C5
Marshall St W1 44 C3
Marshalsea Rd SE1 45 J5
Marsham St SW1 44 D7
Martin Ho SE1 45 J7
Martlett Ct WC2 45 E3
Marylebone High St
  W1 44 A1
Marylebone La W1 44 B3
Marylebone Ms W1 44 B2
Marylebone Pas W1 44 C2
Marylebone St W1 44 A2
Masons Arms Ms W1 44 B3
Mason's Yd SW1 44 C4
Matthew Parker St
  SW1 44 D6
Matthews Yd WC2 44 E3
Maunsel St SW1 44 D7
Mayfair W1 44 B4
Mayfair Pl W1 44 B4
Mays Ct WC2 44 E4
Meadow Row SE1 45 J7
Mead Row SE1 45 G6
Meard St W1 44 D3
Medway St SW1 44 D7
Melbourne Pl WC2 45 F3
Memel Ct EC1 45 J1
Memel St EC1 45 J1
Mepham St SE1 45 F5
Mercer St WC2 44 E3
Merrick Sq SE1 45 J6
Metro Cen Hts SE1 45 J7
Meymott St SE1 45 H5
Middlesex Pas EC1 45 H2
Middle St EC1 45 J1
Middle Temple EC4 45 G3
Middle Temple La
  EC4 45 G3
Middleton Pl W1 44 C2
Midford Pl W1 44 C1
Milcote St SE1 45 H6
Milford La WC2 45 F3
Milk St EC2 45 J3
Millbank SW1 44 E7
Millbank Ct SW1 44 E7
Millennium Br EC4 45 J3
Millennium Br SE1 45 J3
Miller Wk SE1 45 G5
Millman Ms WC1 45 F1
Millman St WC1 45 F1
Milroy Wk SE1 45 H4
Minera Ms SW1 44 A7
Mint St SE1 45 J5
Mitre Ct EC2 45 J2
Mitre Rd SE1 45 G5
Monck St SW1 44 D7
Monkton St SE11 45 G7
Monkwell Sq EC2 45 J2

Monmouth St WC2 44 E3
Montague Pl WC1 44 D1
Montague St EC1 45 J2
Montague St WC1 44 E1
Montreal Pl WC2 45 F3
Montrose Pl SW1 44 A6
Moor St W1 44 D3
Morley St SE1 45 G6
Morpeth Ter SW1 44 C7
Mortimer Mkt WC1 44 C1
Mortimer St W1 44 C2
Morton Pl SE1 45 G7
Morwell St WC1 44 D2
Mount Pleasant WC1 45 F1
Mount Row W1 44 B4
Mount St W1 44 A4
Mount St Ms W1 44 B4
Moxon St W1 44 A2
Museum St WC1 44 E2

N
Nag's Head Ct EC1 45 J1
Nassau St W1 44 C2
Neal St WC2 44 E3
Neal's Yd WC2 44 E3
Neathouse Pl SW1 44 C7
Nelson Sq SE1 45 H5
Newall Ho SE1 45 J6
New Bond St W1 44 B3
New Br St EC4 45 H3
Newburgh St W1 44 C3
New Burlington Ms
  W1 44 C3
New Burlington Pl
  W1 44 C3
New Burlington St
  W1 44 C3
Newbury St EC1 45 J2
Newcastle Cl EC4 45 H2
New Cavendish St W1 44 B1
New Change EC4 45 J3
New Compton St
  WC2 44 D3
New Fetter La EC4 45 G2
Newgate St EC1 45 H2
New Globe Wk SE1 45 J4
Newington SE1 45 J7
Newington Causeway
  SE1 45 H7
New Inn Pas WC2 45 F3
New Kent Rd SE1 45 J7
Newman Pas W1 44 C2
Newman's Row WC2 45 F2
Newman St W1 44 C2
Newman Yd W1 44 C2
Newnham Ter SE1 45 G6
New N St WC1 45 F1
New Oxford St WC1 44 D2
Newport Ct WC2 44 D3
Newport Pl WC2 44 D3
New Row WC2 44 E3
New Sq WC2 45 F2
New Sq EC4 45 G3
Newton St WC2 45 E2
New Turnstile WC1 45 F2
Nicholson St SE1 45 H5
Nightingale Ms SE11 45 G7
Noble St EC2 45 J2
Noel St W1 44 C3
Norfolk Row SE1 45 F7
Norris St SW1 44 D4
North Audley St W1 44 A3
North Cres WC1 44 D1
Northington St WC1 45 F1
North Ms WC1 45 F1
Northumberland Av
  WC2 44 E4
Northumberland St
  WC2 44 E4
Norwich St EC4 45 G2
Nottingham Ct WC2 44 E3
Nottingham Pl W1 44 A1
Nottingham St W1 44 A1
Nottingham Ter NW1 44 A1

O
Oakden St SE11 45 G7
Oakey La SE1 45 G6
Oat La EC2 45 J2
Odhams Wk WC2 45 E3
Ogle St W1 44 C1
Old Bailey EC4 45 H3
Old Barrack Yd SW1 44 A5
Old Bond St W1 44 B4
Old Brewers Yd WC2 44 E3
Old Bldgs WC2 45 G2
Old Burlington St W1 44 C3
Oldbury Pl W1 44 A1
Old Cavendish St W1 44 B2
Old Compton St W1 44 D3
Old Fish St Hill EC4 45 J3
Old Fleet La EC4 45 H2

Old Gloucester St WC1 45 E1
Old Mitre Ct EC4 45 G3
Old N St WC1 45 F1
Old Palace Yd SW1 44 E6
Old Paradise St SE11 45 F7
Old Pk La W1 44 A5
Old Pye St SW1 44 D6
Old Queen St SW1 44 D6
Old Seacoal La EC4 45 H2
Old Sq WC2 45 F2
O'Meara St SE1 45 J5
Onslow St EC1 45 G1
Ontario St SE1 45 H7
Orange St WC2 44 D4
Orange Yd W1 44 D3
Orchard St W1 44 A3
Orde Hall St WC1 45 F1
Orient St SE11 45 H7
Ormond Cl WC1 45 E1
Ormond Ms WC1 45 E1
Ormond Yd SW1 44 C4
Osnaburgh St NW1 44 B1
Ossington Bldgs W1 44 A1
Oswin St SE11 45 H7
Outer Circle NW1 44 A1
Oxendon St SW1 44 D4
Oxford Circ Av W1 44 C3
Oxford St W1 44 C2
Oxo Twr Wf SE1 45 G4

P
Paddington St W1 44 A1
Pageantmaster Ct EC4 45 H3
Page St SW1 44 D7
Palace Pl SW1 44 C6
Palace St SW1 44 C6
Pall Mall SW1 44 C5
Pall Mall E SW1 44 D4
Palmer St SW1 44 D6
Pancras La EC4 45 J3
Panton St SW1 44 D4
Panyer All EC4 45 J3
Paris Gdn SE1 45 H4
Park Cres W1 44 B1
Park Cres Ms E W1 44 B1
Park Cres Ms W W1 44 B1
Parker Ms WC2 45 E2
Parker St WC2 45 E2
Park La W1 44 A5
Park Pl SW1 44 C5
Park Sq Ms NW1 44 B1
Park St SE1 45 J4
Park St W1 44 A3
Parliament Sq SW1 44 E6
Parliament St SW1 44 E6
Parliament Vw Apts SE1 45 F7
Passing All EC1 45 H1
Pastor St SE11 45 H7
Paternoster Row EC4 45 J3
Paternoster Sq EC4 45 H3
Paul's Wk EC4 45 H3
Peabody Est EC1 45 J1
Peabody Est SE1 45 G5
Peabody Est SW1 44 C7
Peabody Sq SE1 45 H6
Peabody Trust SE1 45 J5
Pearman St SE1 45 G6
Pear Pl SE1 45 G5
Pear Tree Ct EC1 45 G1
Pemberton Row EC4 45 G2
Pembroke Cl SW1 44 A6
Penhurst Pl SE1 45 F7
Pepper St SE1 45 J5
Percy Ms W1 44 D2
Percy Pas W1 44 D2
Percy St W1 44 D2
Perkin's Rents SW1 44 D6
Perkins Sq SE1 45 J4
Perrys Pl W1 44 D2
Peters Hill EC4 45 J3
Peter's La EC1 45 H1
Peter St W1 44 C3
Petty France SW1 44 C6
Phipp's Ms SW1 44 B7
Phoenix St WC2 44 D3
Piccadilly W1 44 B5
Piccadilly Arc SW1 44 C4
Piccadilly Circ W1 44 C4
Piccadilly Pl W1 44 C4
Pickering St EC1 45 J6
Picton Pl W1 44 A3
Pilgrim St EC4 45 H3
Pineapple Ct SW1 44 C6
Pitt's Head Ms W1 44 A5
Playhouse Yd EC4 45 H3
Plaza Shop Cen, The W1 44 C2
Pleydell Ct EC4 45 G3
Pleydell St EC4 45 G3
Plough Pl EC4 45 G2

Plumtree Ct EC4 45 G2
Pocock St SE1 45 H5
Poland St W1 44 C3
Pollen St W1 44 B3
Polperro Ms SE11 45 G7
Pontypool Pl SE1 45 H5
Pooles Bldgs EC1 45 G1
Poppins Ct EC4 45 H3
Porter St SE1 45 J4
Portland Ms W1 44 C3
Portland Pl W1 44 B1
Portman Ms S W1 44 A3
Portman St W1 44 A3
Portpool La EC1 45 G1
Portsmouth St WC2 45 F3
Portugal St WC2 45 F3
Powis Pl WC1 45 E1
Pratt Wk SE11 45 F7
Price's St SE1 45 H5
Priest Ct EC2 45 J2
Primrose Hill EC4 45 G3
Prince's Arc SW1 44 C4
Princes Pl SW1 44 C4
Princess St SE1 45 H7
Princes St W1 44 B3
Princeton St WC1 45 F1
Printers Inn Ct EC4 45 G2
Printer St EC4 45 G2
Procter St WC1 45 F2
Providence Ct W1 44 A3
Prudent Pas EC2 45 J2
Puddle Dock EC4 45 H3

Q
Quadrant Arc W1 44 C4
Quality Ct WC2 45 G2
Queen Anne Ms W1 44 B2
Queen Anne's Gate SW1 44 D6
Queen Anne St W1 44 B2
Queenhithe EC4 45 J3
Queen's Head Pas EC4 45 J2
Queen Sq WC1 45 E1
Queen Sq Pl WC1 45 E1
Queen St EC4 45 J3
Queen St W1 44 B4
Queen St Pl EC4 45 J4
Queen's Wk SW1 44 C5
Queen's Wk, The SE1 45 F4
Queens Yd WC1 44 C1
Queen Victoria St EC4 45 H3
Quilp St SE1 45 J5

R
Ramillies Pl W1 44 C3
Ramillies St W1 44 C3
Rathbone Pl W1 44 D2
Rathbone St W1 44 C2
Raymond Bldgs WC1 45 F1
Ray St EC1 45 G1
Ray St Br EC1 45 G1
Redcross Way SE1 45 J5
Red Lion Ct EC4 45 G2
Red Lion Sq WC1 45 F2
Red Lion St WC1 45 F1
Red Pl W1 44 A3
Reeves Ms W1 44 A4
Regency Pl SW1 44 D7
Regency St SW1 44 D7
Regent Pl W1 44 C3
Regent St SW1 44 D4
Regent St W1 44 B2
Remnant St WC2 45 F2
Renfrew Rd SE11 45 H7
Rennie St SE1 45 H4
Rex Pl W1 44 A4
Richardson's Ms W1 44 C1
Richbell Pl WC1 45 F1
Richmond Bldgs W1 44 D3
Richmond Ms W1 44 D3
Richmond Ter SW1 44 E5
Ridgmount Gdns WC1 44 D1
Ridgmount Pl WC1 44 D1
Ridgmount St WC1 44 D1
Riding Ho St W1 44 C2
Risborough St SE1 45 H5
Rising Sun Ct EC1 45 H2
River Ct SE1 45 H4
Robert Adam St W1 44 A2
Roberts Ms SW1 44 A7
Robert St WC2 45 E4
Rochester Row SW1 44 C7
Rochester St SW1 44 D7
Rockingham Est SE1 45 J7
Rockingham St SE1 45 J7
Rodney Pl SE17 45 J7
Rodney Rd SE17 45 J7
Roger St WC1 45 F1
Rolls Bldgs EC4 45 G2
Rolls Pas EC4 45 G2
Romilly St W1 44 D3

Romney Ms W1 44 A1
Romney St SW1 44 D7
Roscoe St EC1 45 J1
Rose All SE1 45 J4
Rose & Crown Ct EC2 45 J2
Rose & Crown Yd SW1 44 C4
Rosebery Av EC1 45 G1
Rosebery Sq EC1 45 G1
Rose St EC4 45 H2
Rose St WC2 44 E3
Rotary St SE1 45 H6
Rotherham Wk SE1 45 H5
Rotten Row W1 44 A5
Roupell St SE1 45 G5
Royal Arc W1 44 C4
Royal Ms, The SW1 44 B6
Royal Opera Arc SW1 44 D4
Royal St SE1 45 F6
Royalty Ms W1 44 D3
Rugby St WC1 45 F1
Rupert Ct W1 44 D3
Rupert St W1 44 D3
Rushworth St SE1 45 H5
Russell Ct SW1 44 C5
Russell Sq WC1 45 E1
Russell St WC2 45 E3
Russia Row EC2 45 J3
Rutherford St SW1 44 D7
Rutland Pl EC1 45 J1
Ryder Ct SW1 44 C4
Ryder St SW1 44 C4
Ryder Yd SW1 44 C4

S
Sackville St W1 44 C4
Saddle Yd W1 44 B4
Saffron Hill EC1 45 G1
Saffron St EC1 45 G1
Sail St SE11 45 F7
St. Albans Ct EC2 45 J2
St. Albans St SW1 44 D4
St. Alphage Gdns EC2 45 J2
St. Andrew's Hill EC4 45 H3
St. Andrew St EC4 45 G2
St. Anne's Ct W1 44 D3
St. Ann's La SW1 44 D6
St. Ann's St SW1 44 D6
St. Anselm's Pl W1 44 B3
St. Brides Av EC4 45 H3
St. Bride St EC4 45 H2
St. Christopher's Pl W1 44 A2
St. Clement's La WC2 45 F3
St. Cross St EC1 45 G1
St. Ermin's Hill SW1 44 D6
St. Georges Circ SE1 45 H6
St. Georges Ct EC4 45 H2
St. Georges Ms SE1 45 G6
St. Georges Rd SE1 45 G6
St. George St W1 44 B3
St. Giles High St WC2 44 D2
St. Giles Pas WC2 44 D3
St. James's Ct SW1 44 C6
St. James's Mkt SW1 44 D4
St. James's Palace SW1 44 C5
St. James's Pk SW1 44 D5
St. James's Pl SW1 44 C5
St. James's Sq SW1 44 C4
St. James's St SW1 44 C4
St. John's La EC1 45 H1
St. John's Path EC1 45 H1
St. John's Pl EC1 45 H1
St. John's Sq EC1 45 H1
St. John St EC1 45 H1
St. Margaret's Ct SE1 45 J5
St. Margaret's St SW1 44 E6
St. Martin's La WC2 44 E3
St. Martin's-le-Grand EC1 45 J2
St. Martin's Ms WC2 44 E4
St. Martin's Pl WC2 44 E4
St. Martin's St WC2 44 D4
St. Mary's Gdns SE11 45 G7
St. Mary's Wk SE11 45 G7
St. Matthew St SW1 44 D7
St. Olaves Gdns SE11 45 G7
St. Paul's Chyd EC4 45 H3
St. Vincent St W1 44 A2
Salisbury Ct EC4 45 H3
Salisbury Sq EC4 45 H3
Sanctuary, The SW1 44 D6
Sanctuary St SE1 45 J6
Sandell St SE1 45 G5
Sandland St WC1 45 F2
Saperton Wk SE11 45 F7
Sardinia St WC2 45 F3
Savile Row W1 44 C3
Savoy Bldgs WC2 45 F4
Savoy Ct WC2 45 E4
Savoy Hill WC2 45 F4
Savoy Pl WC2 45 E4

Savoy Row WC2 45 F3
Savoy St WC2 45 F3
Savoy Way WC2 45 F4
Sawyer St SE1 45 J5
Scala St W1 44 C1
Scoresby St SE1 45 H5
Scotland Pl SW1 44 E4
Scovell Cres SE1 45 J6
Scovell Rd SE1 45 J6
Secker St SE1 45 G5
Sedding St SW1 44 A7
Sedley Pl W1 44 B3
Sekforde St EC1 45 H1
Serjeants Inn EC4 45 G3
Serle St WC2 45 F2
Sermon La EC4 45 J3
Seymour Ms W1 44 A2
Shaftesbury Av W1 44 D3
Shaftesbury Av WC2 44 D3
Shakespeare Twr EC2 45 J1
Shavers Pl SW1 44 D4
Sheffield St WC2 45 F3
Shelton St WC2 44 E3
Shepherd Mkt W1 44 B4
Shepherd's Pl W1 44 A3
Shepherd St W1 44 B5
Sheraton St W1 44 D3
Sherlock Ms W1 44 A1
Sherwood St W1 44 C3
Shoe La EC4 45 G2
Shorts Gdns WC2 44 E3
Short St SE1 45 G5
Shropshire Pl WC1 44 C1
Sicilian Av WC1 45 E2
Sidford St SE1 45 F7
Sidney St SE1 45 H6
Silex St SE1 45 H6
Silk St EC2 45 J1
Silver Pl W1 44 C3
Silvester St SE1 45 J6
Skinners La EC4 45 J3
Slingsby Pl WC2 44 E3
Smart's Pl WC2 45 E2
Smeaton Ct SE1 45 J7
Smithfield St EC1 45 H2
Smith's Ct W1 44 C3
Smith Sq SW1 44 E7
Smokehouse Yd EC1 45 H1
Snow Hill EC1 45 H2
Snow Hill Ct EC1 45 H2
Soho Sq W1 44 D2
Soho St W1 44 D2
Southampton Bldgs WC2 45 G2
Southampton Pl WC1 45 E2
Southampton Row WC1 45 E1
Southampton St WC2 45 E3
South Audley St W1 44 A4
South Cres WC1 44 D2
South Eaton Pl SW1 44 A7
South Molton La W1 44 B3
South Molton St W1 44 B3
South Sq WC1 45 G2
South St W1 44 A4
Southwark Br EC4 45 J4
Southwark Br SE1 45 J4
Southwark Br Rd SE1 45 H6
Southwark St SE1 45 H4
Spanish Pl W1 44 A2
Spenser St SW1 44 C6
Spring Gdns SW1 44 D4
Spur Rd SE1 45 G5
Spur Rd SW1 44 C6
Stable Yd SW1 44 C5
Stable Yd Rd SW1 44 C5
Stacey St WC2 44 D3
Stafford Pl SW1 44 C6
Stafford St W1 44 C4
Staining La EC2 45 J2
Stamford St SE1 45 G5
Stangate SE1 45 F6
Stanhope Gate W1 44 A4
Stanhope Row W1 44 B5
Staple Inn WC1 45 G2
Staple Inn Bldgs WC1 45 G2
Star Yd WC2 45 G2
Station App SE1 45 F5
Stedham Pl WC1 44 E2
Stephen Ms W1 44 D2
Stephen St W1 44 D2
Stew La EC4 45 J3
Stillington St SW1 44 C7
Stone Bldgs WC2 45 F2
Stonecutter St EC4 45 H2
Stones End St SE1 45 J6
Store St WC1 44 D2
Storey's Gate SW1 44 D6
Strand WC2 44 E4
Strand WC2 44 D4
Strand La WC2 45 F3
Stratford Pl W1 44 B3

Stratton St W1 44 B4
Streatham St WC1 44 D2
Strutton Grd SW1 44 D6
Stukeley St WC1 45 E2
Stukeley St WC2 45 E2
Sturge St SE1 45 J5
Sudrey St SE1 45 J6
Suffolk Pl SW1 44 D4
Suffolk St SW1 44 D4
Sullivan Rd SE11 45 G7
Summers St EC1 45 G1
Sumner St SE1 45 H4
Surrey Row SE1 45 H5
Surrey St WC2 45 F3
Sutton La EC1 45 H1
Sutton Row W1 44 D2
Sutton's Way EC1 45 J1
Sutton Wk SE1 45 F5
Swallow Pl W1 44 B3
Swallow St W1 44 C4
Swan St SE1 45 J6
Swiss Ct W1 44 D4
Sycamore St EC1 45 J1

T
Tachbrook Ms SW1 44 C7
Tallis St EC4 45 G3
Tanswell Est SE1 45 G6
Tanswell St SE1 45 G6
Tarn St SE1 45 J7
Tavistock St WC2 45 E3
Telford Ho SE1 45 J7
Temple Av EC4 45 G3
Temple La EC4 45 G3
Temple Pl WC2 45 F3
Temple W Ms SE11 45 H7
Tenison Ct W1 44 C3
Tenison Way SE1 45 G5
Tenterden St W1 44 B3
Terminus Pl SW1 44 B7
Thavies Inn EC1 45 G2
Thayer St W1 44 A2
Theed St SE1 45 G5
Theobald's Rd WC1 45 F1
Thirleby Rd SW1 44 C7
Thomas Doyle St SE1 45 H6
Thorney St SW1 44 E7
Thornhaugh Ms WC1 44 D1
Thornhaugh St WC1 44 D1
Thrale St SE1 45 J5
Three Barrels Wk EC4 45 J4
Three Cups Yd WC1 45 F2
Three Kings Yd W1 44 B3
Tilney St W1 44 A4
Tiverton St SE1 45 J7
Took's Ct EC4 45 G2
Tothill St SW1 44 D6
Tottenham Ct Rd W1 44 C1
Tottenham Ms W1 44 C1
Toulmin St SE1 45 J6
Tower Ct WC2 44 E3
Tower Royal EC4 45 J3
Tower St WC2 44 D3
Trafalgar Sq SW1 44 D4
Trafalgar Sq WC2 44 D4
Trebeck St W1 44 B4
Treveris St SE1 45 H5
Trig La EC4 45 J3
Trinity Ch Sq SE1 45 J6
Trinity St SE1 45 J6
Trio Pl SE1 45 J6
Trump St EC2 45 J3
Trundle St SE1 45 J5
Tudor St EC4 45 G3
Tufton St SW1 44 D6
Turk's Head Yd EC1 45 H1
Turnagain La EC4 45 H2
Turnmill St EC1 45 G1
Tweezer's All WC2 45 G3
Twyford Pl WC2 45 F2
Tyler's Ct W1 44 D3

U
Ufford St SE1 45 G5
Ulster Pl NW1 44 B1
Ulster Ter NW1 44 B1
Union Jack Club SE1 45 G5
Union St SE1 45 H5
University St WC1 44 C1
Upper Belgrave St SW1 44 A6
Upper Brook St W1 44 A3
Upper Grosvenor St W1 44 A4
Upper Grd SE1 45 G4
Upper James St W1 44 C3
Upper John St W1 44 C3
Upper Marsh SE1 45 F6
Upper St. Martin's La WC2 44 E3

Upper Tachbrook St SW1 44 C7
Upper Thames St EC4 45 H3
Upper Wimpole St W1 44 B1

V
Valentine Pl SE1 45 H5
Valentine Row SE1 45 H6
Vandon Pas SW1 44 C6
Vandon St SW1 44 C6
Vane St SW1 44 C7
Vauxhall Br Rd SW1 44 C7
Vere St W1 44 B3
Vernon Pl WC1 45 E2
Verulam Bldgs WC1 45 F1
Verulam St WC1 45 G1
Vesage Ct EC1 45 G2
Victoria Embk EC4 45 F4
Victoria Embk SW1 44 E5
Victoria Embk WC2 45 F4
Victoria Pl SW1 44 B7
Victoria Sq SW1 44 B6
Victoria Sta SW1 44 B7
Victoria St SW1 44 C7
Vigo St W1 44 C4
Villiers St WC2 44 E4
Vincent Sq SW1 44 C7
Vincent St SW1 44 D7
Vine Hill EC1 45 G1
Vine St W1 44 C4
Vine St Br EC1 45 G1
Vine Yd SE1 45 J5
Vintners Ct EC4 45 J3
Virgil St SE1 45 F6
Viscount St EC1 45 J1

W
Waithman St EC4 45 H3
Walcot Sq SE11 45 G7
Walcott St SW1 44 C7
Walkers Ct W1 44 D3
Wallis All SE1 45 J5
Wallside EC2 45 J2
Walnut Tree Wk SE11 45 G7
Walworth Rd SE1 45 J7
Walworth Rd SE17 45 J7
Wardens Gro SE1 45 J5
Wardour Ms W1 44 C3
Wardour St W1 44 D3
Wardrobe Ter EC4 45 H3
Warner St EC1 45 G1
Warner Yd EC1 45 G1
Warren Ms W1 44 C1
Warren St W1 44 B1
Warwick Ct WC1 45 F2
Warwick Ho St SW1 44 D4
Warwick La EC4 45 H3
Warwick Pas EC4 45 H2
Warwick Row SW1 44 B6
Warwick Sq EC4 45 H2
Warwick St W1 44 C3
Warwick Yd EC1 45 J1
Watergate EC4 45 H3
Watergate Wk WC2 45 E4
Waterhouse Sq EC1 45 G2
Waterloo Br SE1 45 F4
Waterloo Br WC2 45 F4
Waterloo Pl SW1 44 D4
Waterloo Rd SE1 45 G5
Waterloo Sta SE1 45 G5
Water St WC2 45 F3
Watling Ct EC4 45 J3
Watling St EC4 45 J3
Waverton St W1 44 A4
Webber Row SE1 45 G6
Webber St SE1 45 G5
Wedgwood Ho SE11 45 G7
Wedgwood Ms W1 44 D3
Weighhouse St W1 44 A3
Welbeck St W1 44 B2
Welbeck Way W1 44 B2
Well Ct EC4 45 J3
Weller St SE1 45 J5
Wellington St WC2 45 E3
Wells Ms W1 44 C2
Wells St W1 44 C2
Wesley St W1 44 A2
West Cen St WC1 44 E2
West Eaton Pl SW1 44 A7
West Eaton Pl Ms SW1 44 A7
West Halkin St SW1 44 A6
West Harding St EC4 45 G2
Westminster SW1 44 C6
Westminster Br SE1 45 E6
Westminster Br SW1 45 E6
Westminster Br Rd SE1 45 F6
Westminster Gdns SW1 44 E7
Westmoreland St W1 44 A2

West One Shop Cen W1 44 A3
West Poultry Av EC1 45 H2
West Smithfield EC1 45 H2
West Sq SE11 45 H7
West St WC2 44 D3
Weymouth Ms W1 44 B1
Weymouth St W1 44 A2
Wheatley St W1 44 A2
Whetstone Pk WC2 45 F2
Whichcote St SE1 45 G5
Whitcomb St WC2 44 D4
Whitefriars St EC4 45 G3

Whitehall SW1 44 E4
Whitehall Ct SW1 44 E5
Whitehall Gdns SW1 44 E5
Whitehall Pl SW1 44 E5
White Hart St EC4 45 H2
White Horse All EC1 45 H1
White Horse Ms SE1 45 G6
White Horse St W1 44 B5
White Lion Hill EC4 45 H3
White Lyon Ct EC2 45 J1
Whitfield Pl W1 44 C1
Whitfield St W1 44 D2
Whitgift St SE11 45 F7

Whittlesey St SE1 45 G5
Whitworth Ho SE1 45 J7
Wicksteed Ho SE1 45 J7
Wigmore Pl W1 44 B2
Wigmore St W1 44 A3
Wilcox Pl SW1 44 C7
Wild Ct WC2 45 F2
Wild St WC2 45 E3
Wilfred St SW1 44 C6
William IV St WC2 44 E4
Willoughby St WC1 44 E2
Willow Pl SW1 44 C7
Wilton Cres SW1 44 A6

Wilton Ms SW1 44 A6
Wilton Pl SW1 44 A6
Wilton Rd SW1 44 B7
Wilton Row SW1 44 A6
Wilton St SW1 44 B6
Wilton Ter SW1 44 A6
Wimpole Ms W1 44 B1
Wimpole St W1 44 B2
Wincott St SE11 45 G7
Windmill St W1 44 D2
Windmill Wk SE1 45 G5
Windsor Pl SW1 44 C7
Wine Office Ct EC4 45 G2

Winnett St W1 44 D3
Winsley St W1 44 C2
Woburn Sq WC1 44 D1
Wollaston Cl SE1 45 J7
Woodstock Ms W1 44 A2
Woodstock St W1 44 B3
Wood St EC2 45 J3
Wootton St SE1 45 G5

**Y**
Yarmouth Pl W1 44 B5
York Bldgs WC2 45 E4
York Gate NW1 44 A1

York Pl WC2 45 E4
York Rd SE1 45 F5
Yorkshire Grey Yd WC1 45 F2
York Ter E NW1 44 A1
York Ter W NW1 44 A1

**Z**
Zoar St SE1 45 J4

## Manchester street index

**A**
Abingdon St 47 E4
Academy Wk 46 D7
Ackers St 47 F7
Acton Sq 46 A3
Adair St 47 G4
Addington St 47 F2
Addison Cl 47 G7
Adelphi St 46 B3
Aden Cl 47 J4
Adlington St 47 H5
Adstone Cl 47 J3
Adswood St 47 J3
Airton Cl 47 H1
Aked Cl 47 J7
Albion Pl 46 A3
Albion St 46 D5
Albion Way 46 A3
Alderman Sq 47 J4
Aldred St 46 A3
Alexander Gdns 46 C1
Alexandra St 46 C1
Alfred James Cl 47 H2
Alker Rd 47 J2
Alley St 46 E3
Almond St 47 G1
Altair Pl 46 B1
Amory St 47 G5
Anaconda Dr 46 C2
**Ancoats** 47 G3
Ancoats Gro 47 H4
Ancroft St 46 C7
Angela St 46 C6
Angel St 47 F2
Angora Cl 46 B2
Angora Dr 46 B2
Anita St 47 G3
Anne Nuttall St 46 B6
Anscombe Cl 47 H1
Antares Av 46 B1
Apsley Gro 47 H6
Aquarius St 47 E7
Archway 46 D7
**Ardwick** 47 J5
Ardwick Grn N 47 G5
Ardwick Grn S 47 G5
Arlington St 46 C2
Arnott Cres 46 E7
Artillery St 46 D4
Arundel St 46 C5
Asgard Dr 46 B5
Asgard Grn 46 B5
Ashlar Dr 47 J4
Ashley St 47 F2
Ashton New Rd 47 J3
Ashton Old Rd 47 H5
Aspin La 47 F2
Atherton St 46 C4
Atkinson St 46 D4
Atwood St 47 E5
Auburn St 47 F4
Audlem Cl 47 J2
Augustus St 47 E1
Avenham Cl 46 D7
Aytoun St 47 F4

**B**
Back Acton St 47 F4
Back Ashley St 47 F2
Back Bk St 47 F1
Back Br St 46 D3
Back China La 47 F3
Back Coll Land 46 D3
Back George St 47 E4
Back Hampson St 47 H1
Back Hulme St 46 B3
Back Junct St 47 G4
Back Piccadilly 47 F3
Back Pool Fold 46 E3
Back Red Bk 47 F1
Back St. George's Rd 47 G2
Back S Par 46 D3
Back Thomas St 47 F3
Back Turner St 47 F3
Badby Cl 47 J3
Bainbridge Cl 47 J7
Baird St 47 G4
Bale St 46 E4
Balloon St 47 E2
Balmforth St 46 C5
Balsam Cl 47 G6
Bangor St 46 C7
Bankmill Cl 47 G6
Bank Pl 46 B3
Bank St 46 B3
Baptist St 47 F2
Barbeck Cl 47 J2
Baring St 47 G5
Barker St 46 D1
Barlow Pl 47 G6
Barlow's Cft 46 D3
Barnett Dr 46 C2
Barrack St 46 B6
Barrhill Cl 46 C6
Barrow St 46 B3
Barton St 46 D5
Basildon Cl 47 J7
Beamish Cl 47 G6
Beattock St 46 C6
Beaufort St 46 C5
Beaver St 47 E5
Beckhampton Cl 47 H7
Bednal Av 47 J1
Beechcroft Cl 47 H2
Belfort Dr 46 A5
Bendix St 47 F2
Bengal St 47 G2
Bennett St 47 J6
Bentinck St 46 B6
Bent St 47 E1
Berkshire Rd 47 J1
Berry St 47 G5
Beswick Row 47 E2
Beswick St 47 H3
Betley St 47 G4
Bevan Cl 47 J4
Bilbrook St 47 F1
Billing Av 47 G5
Binns Pl 47 G3
Birchin La 47 F3
Birchvale Cl 46 D6
Birt St 47 H1
Bishopsgate 46 E4
Blackburn Pl 46 A4
Blackburn St 46 B2
Blackfriars Rd 46 C2
Blackfriars St 46 D3
Blackhill Cl 47 G6
Blackley St 46 B7
Blacklock St 46 E1
Blantyre St 46 C5
Bletchley Cl 47 H7
Blind La 47 J5
Blisworth Cl 47 J3
Bloom St 47 F4
Blossom St 46 D2
Blossom St (Ancoats) 47 G3
Blucher St 46 A4
Blyton St 47 F7
Boad St 47 G4
Bollington Rd 47 H2
Bombay St 47 F5
Bond St 47 G5
Bonsall St 46 D7
Boond St 46 C2
Boond St (Ancoats) 47 H3
Booth St 47 E4
Booth St (Salford) 46 D3
Booth St E 47 F6
Booth St W 47 E7
Bootle St 46 D4
Botham Cl 46 E7
Bothwell Rd 47 G2
Boundary La 47 F6
Boundary St E 47 F6
Boundary St W 47 E6
Bourdon St 47 J2
Bow La 46 E4
Bow St 46 D4
Brackley Av 46 B6
Bradford Rd 47 H3
Bradleys Ct 47 F3
Braley St 47 G5
Bramble Av 46 A5
Bramwell Dr 47 G6
Brancaster Rd 47 F5
Branson St 47 J3
Brazennose St 46 D4
Brazil St 47 F5
Brennan Cl 47 E7
Brewer St 47 F3
Brian Redhead Ct 47 C6
Brickley St 47 E1
Brick St 47 F3
Briddon St 46 D1
Bridgeford St 47 F7
Bridge St 46 D3
Bridge St W 46 D3
Bridgewater Pl 47 E3
Bridgewater St 46 D5
Bridgewater St (Salford) 46 C1
Bridgewater Viaduct 46 D5
Briggs St 46 C2
Brighton Pl 47 F7
Brighton St 47 F1
Brindle Pl 47 E7
Brocade Cl 46 B2
Brock St 47 G3
Bromley St 47 F1
Bronte St 47 E7
Brook St 47 F5
Brotherton Cl 46 B6
Brotherton Dr 46 C2
Browfield Av 46 A5
Brown Cross St 46 C3
Browning St 46 B7
Browning St (Salford) 46 C3
Brown St 46 E4
Brunel Av 46 A3
**Brunswick** 47 G7
Brunswick St 47 F7
Bryant Cl 47 H7
Brydon Av 47 H5
Buckfield Av 46 A5
Bugle St 46 D5
Bunsen St 47 F3
Burlington St 47 E7
Burnell Cl 47 H2
Burstock St 47 F1
Burton St 47 G1
Burton Wk 46 B2
Bury St 46 C2
Butler La 47 H2
Butler St 47 H2
Butter La 46 D3
Buxton St 47 G5
Byrcland Cl 47 J5
Byron St 46 D4

**C**
Cable St 47 F2
Cabot St 47 G6
Cakebread St 47 G5
Calder St 46 B5
Calico Cl 46 B2
Camberwell St 47 E1
Cambrian St 47 J2
Cambridge St 46 E5
Cambridge St (Salford) 46 C1
Camelford Cl 47 E7
Cameron St 46 D5
Canal St 47 F4
Cannon St 46 B2
Canon Ct 46 E3
Canon Grn Dr 46 C2
Carding Gro 46 C2
Cardroom Rd 47 G3
Carey Cl 46 C1
Carib St 46 D7
Carmel Av 46 A5
Carmel Cl 46 A5
Carnarvon St 46 E1
Caroline St 46 C1
Carpenters La 47 F3
Carriage St 46 C7
Carruthers St 47 H3
Cassidy Cl 47 G2
Castle St 46 C5
Caterham St 47 J4
Cathedral App 46 E2
Cathedral Gates 46 E3
Cathedral St 46 E3
Cathedral Yd 46 E3
Catlow La 46 D1
Catlow St 46 D1
Cavalier St 47 J3
Cavanagh Cl 47 H7
Cavell St 47 F3
Cavendish St 46 E6
Cawdor St 46 B6
Caxton St 46 D3
Caygill St 46 D2
Cedar Pl 46 B1
Central St 46 E4
Chadderton St 47 F2
Chain St 47 E4
Chancel Av 46 A5
Chancellor La 47 H5
Chancery La 46 E4
Change Way 46 C2
Chapelfield Rd 47 H5
Chapel St 46 C3
Chapeltown St 47 G4
Chapel Walks 46 E3
Charles St 47 E5
Charlotte St 47 E4
Charlton Pl 47 G5
Charnley Cl 47 J2
Charter St 46 D1
Chase St 47 F1
Chatford Cl 46 C1
Chatham St 47 F4
Chatley St 46 E1
Cheapside 46 E3
Cheetham Hill Rd 47 E2
Cheetwood St 46 D1
Chepstow St 46 E5
Cherryton Wk 47 G7
Chesshyre Av 47 J3
Chester Rd 46 B6
Chester St 46 E6
Chevassut St 46 C6
Cheviot St 46 E1
Chevril Cl 46 D7
Chichester Rd 46 D7
Chiffon Way 46 B2
China La 47 F4
Chippenham Rd 47 H3
Chorlton Rd 46 C7
Chorlton St 47 F4
Chorlton St (Old Trafford) 46 A7
Christchurch Av 46 A3
Churchgate Bldgs 47 G4
Church St 47 F3
Cinder St 47 G2
Cipher St 47 G2
City Rd 46 B7
City Rd E 46 D6
Clarence St 46 D6
Clarendon St 46 D6
Clare St 47 G5
Clarion St 47 G2
Clayburn Rd 46 D6
Cleminson St 46 B3
Cleworth St 46 B6
Clifford St 47 F6
Clifton Gro 46 B7
Clifton St 46 B7
Clive St 47 F2
Cloak St 47 F5
Cloughfield Av 46 A5
Clowes St 46 D3
Cobourg St 47 F4
Coburg Av 46 B1
Cockcroft Rd 46 A2
Cockspur St 46 D3
Coleshill St 47 J1
Colin Murphy Rd 46 C6
College Land 46 D3
Collier St 46 E2
Collier St (Salford) 46 D2
Collingham St 47 F1
Collyhurst Rd 47 G1
Colman Gdns 46 A5
Comet St 47 G4
Commercial St 46 D5
Comus St 46 A4
Concert La 47 E4
Congou St 47 G4
Cooper St 46 E4
Coop St 47 F3
Copeman Cl 47 G7
Copperas St 47 F3
Coral St 47 G6
Cork St 47 J4
Cornbrook 46 B6
**Cornbrook** 47 E4
Cornbrook Ct 46 B7
Cornbrook Gro 46 B7
Cornbrook Pk Rd 46 B6
Cornbrook St 46 B7
Cornell St 47 G2
Coronation Sq 47 H5
Coronation St 46 A4
Corporation St 46 E3
Cottenham La 46 C1
Cottenham St 47 G6
Cotter St 47 G5
Cotton St 47 G3
Cottingham Rd 47 J7
County St 46 E4
Coupland St 46 E7
Coupland St E 47 F7
Coverdale Cres 47 H6
Cowan St 47 J3
Cowburn St 46 E1
Cow La 46 B4
Crabbe St 46 E1
Cranbourne St 46 A4
Crane St 47 H5
Cranfield Cl 47 J2
Craven St 46 B4
Crediton Cl 46 E7
Cresbury St 47 H5
Crescent, The 46 A2
Cross Keys St 47 F2
Crossley Ct 47 J3
Cross St 46 E4
Cross St (Salford) 46 D3
Crown La 47 F2
Crown St 46 C5
Crown St (Salford) 46 C2
Culmington Cl 46 C7
Cumberland St 46 B1
Cumbrian Cl 47 G6
Cunard Cl 47 G6
Cygnus Av 46 B1
Cyrus St 47 J3

**D**
Dainton St 47 J5
Daintry Cl 46 D6
Dalberg St 47 H6
Dale St 47 F3
Dalley Av 46 B1
Dalton Ct 47 G1
Dalton St 47 G1
Damask Av 46 B2
Danebank Wk 47 G6
Danecroft Cl 47 H7
Danson St 47 J2
Dantzic St 47 E3
Dark La 47 H5
Dartford Cl 47 J7
Darton Av 47 J2
Darwen St 46 A4
Davy St 47 G1
Dawson St 46 B5
Dean Rd 46 D2
Deansgate 46 D4
Dean St 47 F3
Deanwater Cl 47 G6
Dearden St 46 D6
Dearmans Pl 46 D3
Deer St 47 G4
Denewell Cl 47 H7
Denver Av 47 J1
Derby St 47 E1
Derwent St 46 B5
Devas St 47 F7
Devine Cl 46 B2
Devonshire St 47 H7
Devonshire St N 47 J6
Devonshire St S 47 H7
Dewhurst St 46 D1
Dickinson St 46 E4
Dilston Cl 47 H7
Dinsdale Cl 47 J2
Dinton St 46 B6
Dobson Cl 47 H7
Dolefield 46 D3
Dolphin Pl 47 H6
Dolphin St 47 H6
Donald St 47 F5
Dorsey St 47 F3
Dover St 47 F7
Downing St 47 G5
Downley Dr 47 H3
Drayton Wk 46 B7
Droitwich Rd 47 H1
Dryden St 47 G7
Dryhurst Wk 47 E7
Ducie St 47 F4
Duke Pl 46 C5
Duke St 46 C5
Duke St (Salford) 46 D2
Dulwich St 47 F1
Duncan St 46 A4
Dun Cl 46 B3
Dunham St 46 D7
Dunlop St 46 D3
Durant St 47 F2
Durling Av 47 H6
Dutton St 46 E1
Dyche St 47 F2
Dyer St 46 A5

**E**
Eagle St 47 F2
Eastburn Av 47 H1
Eastfield Av 47 J2
Eastleigh Dr 47 H1
East Mkt St 46 C3
East Newton St 47 H2
Eastnor Cl 46 B7
East Ordsall La 46 B4
Eastpark Cl 47 H6
East Philip St 46 D1
East Union St 46 B7
Ebden St 47 F4
Ebenezer St 46 E6
Echo St 47 F5
Eden Cl 46 E7
Edgehill St 47 F3
Edge St 47 F3
Edward St 46 D1
Egerton Rd 46 C5
Egerton St 46 C5
Elbe St 47 H5
Eliza St 46 C6
Ellesmere St 46 B6
Ellis St 46 D7
Elsworth St 47 E1

| Street | Grid | Street | Grid | Street | Grid | Street | Grid | Street | Grid | Street | Grid |
|---|---|---|---|---|---|---|---|---|---|---|---|
| Elton St | 46 C1 | Great George St | 46 B3 | Hulme St | 46 D6 | Little Holme St | 47 J3 | Mouncey St | 47 E5 | Parsonage Way | 46 A5 |
| Elton's Yd | 46 C1 | Great Jackson St | 46 C5 | Hulme St (Salford) | 46 B3 | Little John St | 46 C4 | Mount Carmel Cres | 46 A5 | Paton St | 47 F4 |
| Elverdon Cl | 46 D7 | Great John St | 46 C4 | Humberstone Av | 46 D6 | Little Lever St | 47 F3 | Mount St | 46 E4 | Pattishall Cl | 47 J4 |
| Empire St | 46 E1 | Great | | Hunmanby Av | 46 D6 | Little Nelson St | 47 F2 | Mount St (Salford) | 46 C2 | Peak St | 47 G3 |
| Empress St | 46 A7 | Marlborough St | 47 E5 | Hunt's Bk | 46 E2 | Little Peter St | 46 D5 | Mozart Cl | 47 H2 | Peary St | 47 G1 |
| Encombe Pl | 46 B3 | Greek St | 47 F6 | Hyde Gro | 47 G7 | Little Pit St | 47 G3 | Mullberry St | 46 D4 | Peel Mt | 46 A1 |
| Epping St | 46 E6 | Green Gate | 46 D2 | Hyde Pl | 47 H7 | Little Quay St | 46 D4 | Munday St | 47 H3 | Pegasus Sq | 46 B1 |
| Epsley Cl | 47 E7 | Greengate W | 46 C2 | Hyde Rd | 47 H6 | Liverpool Rd | 46 C4 | Munster St | 47 E2 | Pembroke Cl | 47 H7 |
| Epworth St | 47 H4 | Grenham Av | 46 B6 | Hyde St | 46 C7 | Livesey St | 47 G1 | Murrey St | 47 G3 | Pencroft Way | 47 F7 |
| Errington Dr | 46 B1 | Griffiths Cl | 46 C1 | | | Lizard St | 47 F3 | Museum St | 46 E4 | Penfield Cl | 47 F5 |
| Erskine St | 46 C7 | Groom St | 47 F6 | **I** | | Lloyd St | 46 D4 | Muslin St | 46 B4 | Percy Dr | 46 A6 |
| Essex St | 46 E4 | Grosvenor Gdns | 46 C1 | Inchley Rd | 47 F6 | Lloyd St N | 47 F7 | Myrtle Pl | 46 A1 | Percy St | 46 C7 |
| Essex Way | 46 C7 | Grosvenor Sq | 46 C1 | Instow Cl | 47 H7 | Lockett St | 46 D1 | | | Peru St | 46 B2 |
| Etruria Cl | 47 J7 | Grosvenor St | 47 F6 | Ionas St | 46 C1 | Lockton Cl | 47 G5 | **N** | | Peter St | 46 D4 |
| Evans St | 46 D2 | Guide Post Sq | 47 H7 | Irk St | 47 F1 | Lomax St | 47 G3 | Nancy St | 46 B6 | Phoenix St | 47 E3 |
| Everard St | 46 B5 | Gunson St | 47 H2 | Iron St | 47 J2 | London Rd | 47 F4 | Nansen St | 47 J5 | Phoenix Way | 46 D7 |
| Every St | 47 H4 | Gun St | 47 G3 | Irwell Pl | 46 A3 | Longacre St | 47 G4 | Naples St | 47 F2 | Piccadilly | 47 F3 |
| Exford Cl | 47 H2 | Gurner Av | 46 A6 | Irwell St | 46 D1 | Long Millgate | 46 E2 | Nash St | 46 C7 | Pickford St | 47 G3 |
| Eyre St | 47 E7 | Gurney St | 47 J3 | Irwell St (Salford) | 46 C3 | Longworth St | 46 D4 | Nathan Dr | 46 C2 | Picton Cl | 46 C2 |
| | | | | Islington Way | 46 B3 | Loom St | 47 G2 | Naval St | 47 G3 | Picton St | 46 C1 |
| **F** | | **H** | | | | Lordsmead St | 46 C6 | Naylor St | 47 H1 | Piercy Av | 46 B1 |
| Fairbrother St | 46 A6 | Hackleton Cl | 47 J3 | **J** | | Lord St | 46 E1 | Neild St | 47 G5 | Piercy St | 47 H3 |
| Fairfield St | 47 G5 | Hadfield St | 46 B7 | Jackson Cres | 46 C6 | Lostock St | 47 H2 | Neill St | 46 C1 | Pigeon St | 47 G3 |
| Fair St | 47 G4 | Half St | 46 D2 | Jackson's Row | 46 D4 | Lowcock St | 46 C4 | Nelson St | 47 J1 | Pimblett St | 46 E1 |
| Falkland Av | 47 J1 | Hall St | 46 E4 | James Henry Av | 46 A4 | Lower Byrom St | 46 C4 | Nether St | 47 G5 | Pine St | 47 E4 |
| Faraday St | 47 F3 | Halmore Rd | 47 H2 | James St | 47 J1 | Lower Chatham St | 46 E6 | New Allen St | 47 G2 | Pin Mill Brow | 47 H5 |
| Farnborough Rd | 47 H1 | Halsbury Cl | 47 J7 | James St (Salford) | 46 B3 | Lower Mosley St | 46 D5 | Newbeck St | 47 F2 | Pittbrook St | 47 J5 |
| Farrell St | 46 C1 | Halston St | 46 D7 | Jenkinson St | 47 F6 | Lower Moss La | 46 C6 | New Br St | 46 D2 | Plymouth Gro | 47 G7 |
| Farwood Cl | 46 B7 | Hamerton Rd | 47 G1 | Jersey St | 47 G3 | Lower Ormond St | 47 E5 | Newcastle St | 46 E6 | Plymouth Vw | 47 G7 |
| Faulkner St | 47 E4 | Hamilton Gro | 46 B7 | Jerusalem Pl | 46 D4 | Lower Vickers St | 47 J2 | New Cath St | 46 E3 | Pochin St | 47 J1 |
| Federation St | 47 E2 | Hamilton St | 46 B7 | Jessamine Av | 46 B1 | Lowndes Wk | 47 G6 | Newcombe St | 46 E1 | Poland St | 47 G2 |
| Fennel St | 46 E2 | Hampson St | 47 H1 | Jessel Cl | 47 G6 | Loxford St | 46 E6 | New Elm St | 46 C4 | Polebrook Av | 47 H7 |
| Fenn St | 46 C7 | Hamsell Rd | 47 G6 | Joddrell St | 46 D4 | Lucy St | 46 B7 | New Gartside St | 46 D4 | Police St | 46 D3 |
| Fenwick St | 47 E6 | Handsworth St | 47 J5 | John Clynes Av | 47 H1 | Ludgate Hill | 47 F2 | New Islington | 47 H3 | Pollard St | 47 H4 |
| Ferdinan St | 47 H1 | Hanging Ditch | 46 E3 | John Dalton St | 46 D3 | Ludgate St | 47 F2 | New Mkt | 46 E3 | Pollard St E | 47 H3 |
| Fernbrook Cl | 47 J7 | Hanover St | 47 E2 | Johnson Sq | 47 H1 | Luna street | 47 F3 | New Mkt St | 46 E3 | Polygon Av | 47 H7 |
| Fernie St | 47 E1 | Hanworth Cl | 47 G6 | Johnson St | 46 B7 | Lund St | 46 A7 | New Mt St | 47 F2 | Polygon St | 47 G6 |
| Fernleigh Dr | 46 B7 | Harding St | 47 J4 | Johnson St (Salford) | 46 C3 | Lupton St | 46 C3 | New Quay St | 46 C4 | Pomona Strand | 46 A6 |
| Fern St | 47 E1 | Harding St (Salford) | 46 D2 | John St | 47 F3 | Lyceum Pl | 47 E6 | Newton St | 47 F3 | Poplar St | 47 J5 |
| Ferry St | 47 J4 | Hardman Sq | 46 D4 | John St | | | | New Union St | 47 G3 | Poplin Dr | 46 D2 |
| Filby Wk | 47 J1 | Hardman St | 46 D4 | (Lower Broughton) | 46 C1 | **M** | | New Vine St | 46 D6 | Portland St | 47 E5 |
| Firbeck Dr | 47 H2 | Hardshaw Cl | 47 G6 | John St (Salford) | 46 D2 | Maidford Cl | 47 J3 | New Wakefield St | 47 E5 | Portsmouth St | 47 G7 |
| Firefly Cl | 46 B3 | Harehill Cl | 47 G5 | Joiner St | 47 F3 | Major St | 47 E4 | New Welcome St | 46 D6 | Port St | 47 F3 |
| Fire Sta Sq | 46 A3 | Hare St | 47 F3 | Jordan St | 46 D5 | Makin St | 47 E5 | New Windsor | 46 A3 | Portugal St | 47 G2 |
| Fir St | 47 H1 | Hargreave's St | 47 F1 | Joynson Av | 46 B1 | Mallard St | 47 E5 | Nicholas St | 47 E4 | Portugal St E | 47 G4 |
| Fitzwilliam St | 46 C1 | Harkness St | 47 H6 | Julia St | 46 D1 | Mallow St | 46 C6 | Nine Acre Dr | 46 A6 | Postal St | 47 G3 |
| Flatley Cl | 47 E7 | Harold St | 46 B7 | Jury St | 46 D1 | Malta St | 47 H3 | Niven St | 47 G5 | Postbridge Cl | 47 H7 |
| Flora Dr | 46 C1 | Harriett St | 47 H2 | Justin Cl | 47 F6 | Malt St | 46 B6 | North Bailey St | 46 C3 | Potato Wf | 46 C5 |
| Ford St | 47 H6 | Harrison St | 47 H4 | Jutland St | 47 G4 | Malvern St | 46 B7 | Northdown Av | 46 B6 | Poynton St | 46 E6 |
| Ford St (Salford) | 46 C3 | Harrison St (Salford) | 46 C1 | | | Manchester St | 46 A7 | North George St | 46 B2 | Price St | 47 J3 |
| Foundry La | 47 F3 | Harris St | 46 D1 | **K** | | Mancunian Way | 46 C6 | North Hill St | 46 C2 | Primrose St | 47 G2 |
| Fountain St | 47 E4 | Harry Hall Gdns | 46 B1 | Kale St | 47 G6 | Mangle St Street | 47 F3 | North Phoebe St | 46 A4 | Prince's Br | 46 C4 |
| Four Yards | 46 E4 | Harter St | 47 E4 | Kays Gdns | 46 C3 | Manor St | 47 G5 | North Star Dr | 46 B3 | Princess Rd | 46 D6 |
| Frances St | 47 G6 | Hartfield Cl | 47 G6 | Keele Wk | 47 H1 | Manson Av | 46 B6 | Northumberland Cl | 46 A7 | Princess St | 46 E4 |
| Francis St | 46 D1 | Hart St | 47 F4 | Kelling Wk | 46 C6 | Maplin Cl | 47 G6 | Northumberland | | Princess St | |
| Frederick St | 46 C3 | Hatter St | 47 F2 | Kelvin St | 47 F3 | Marble St | 47 E3 | Cres | 46 A7 | (Cornbrook) | 46 B6 |
| Freeman Sq | 47 E7 | Hatton Av | 46 B1 | Kennedy St | 46 E4 | Marcer Rd | 47 H4 | North Western St | 47 G5 | Pritchard St | 47 F5 |
| Freya Gro | 46 A5 | Haverlock Dr | 46 B1 | Kenwright St | 47 F2 | Marchmont Cl | 47 H7 | North W Services Rd | 46 D3 | Providence St | 47 H4 |
| Frobisher Cl | 47 J7 | Haymarket Cl | 47 H7 | Kincardine Rd | 47 F6 | Market St | 46 E3 | Norton St | 46 D2 | Pryme St | 46 C5 |
| Frost St | 47 J3 | Heath Av | 46 B1 | King Edward St | 46 A5 | Markfield Av | 47 J7 | Norway St | 47 J4 | Pump St | 47 J3 |
| Fulmer Dr | 47 H2 | Helga St | 47 H1 | Kingham Dr | 47 H2 | Markham Cl | 47 J4 | Nuneaton Dr | 47 H1 | Purslow Cl | 47 J3 |
| | | Hellidon Cl | 47 H6 | Kingsfold Av | 47 H1 | Marple St | 46 C7 | Nuttall St | 46 A7 | | |
| **G** | | Helmet St | 47 H5 | Kingsland Cl | 47 H1 | Marsden St | 46 E3 | | | **Q** | |
| Gaitskell Cl | 47 J4 | Henry St | 47 G3 | King St | 46 D3 | Marshall St | 47 F2 | **O** | | Quay St | 46 C4 |
| Galgate Cl | 46 C6 | Henry St | | King St (Salford) | 46 D2 | Marshall St (Ardwick) | 47 H6 | Oakford Av | 47 G1 | Quay St (Salford) | 46 D3 |
| Garden La | 46 D3 | (Old Trafford) | 46 A7 | King St W | 46 D3 | Marsworth Dr | 47 H3 | Oak St | 47 F3 | Queen St | 46 D4 |
| Garden St | 46 D2 | Hewitt St | 46 D5 | Kirkgate Cl | 47 H2 | Mary France St | 46 C6 | Old Bk St | 46 E3 | Queen St (Salford) | 46 D2 |
| Garden Wall Cl | 46 A5 | Heyrod St | 47 G4 | Kirkhaven Sq | 47 J1 | Mary St | 46 D1 | Old Birley St | 46 D7 | Quenby St | 46 C6 |
| Garforth Av | 47 H1 | Higher Ardwick | 47 H6 | Kirkstall Sq | 47 G7 | Mason St | 47 F2 | Oldbury Cl | 47 H2 | Quendon Av | 46 C1 |
| Gartside St | 46 D4 | Higher Cambridge St | 47 E6 | Kirkwood Dr | 47 H1 | Mason St (Salford) | 46 C3 | Old Elm St | 47 G6 | | |
| Garwood St | 46 D6 | Higher Chatham St | 47 E6 | | | Massey St | 46 B3 | Oldfield Rd | 46 A5 | **R** | |
| Gateaton St | 46 E3 | Higher Ormond St | 47 F6 | **L** | | Mayan Av | 46 B2 | Oldham Rd | 47 F3 | Rachel St | 47 H5 |
| Gaythorn St | 46 B3 | Higher Oswald St | 47 F2 | Lackford Dr | 47 H1 | Mayes St | 47 E2 | Oldham St | 47 F3 | Radium St | 47 G2 |
| George Leigh St | 47 F3 | Higher York St | 47 F6 | Lamb La | 46 C3 | Mayo St | 47 H5 | Old Medlock St | 46 C4 | Ralli Cts | 46 C3 |
| George Parr Rd | 46 D7 | High St | 47 E3 | Lamport Cl | 47 F5 | Mays St | 47 F2 | Old Mill St | 47 G3 | Randerson St | 47 G5 |
| George St | 47 E4 | Hillcourt St | 47 F6 | Lanchester St | 47 J2 | Meadow Rd | 46 B1 | Old Mt St | 47 F2 | Rankin Cl | 46 D7 |
| Georgette Dr | 46 D2 | Hillfield Cl | 47 J7 | Landos Rd | 47 H2 | Medlock St | 46 D5 | Old Trafford | 46 A7 | Raven St | 47 H5 |
| Gibbs St | 46 B3 | Hillkirk St | 47 J3 | Langholme Cl | 46 C6 | Melbourne St | 46 C6 | Old York St | 46 C6 | Reather Wk | 47 H1 |
| Gibson Pl | 47 E1 | Hilton St | 47 F3 | Langport Av | 47 J7 | Mellor St | 47 H2 | Oliver St | 47 F7 | Red Bk | 47 E2 |
| Girton St | 46 C1 | Hinton St | 47 G2 | Langston St | 46 D1 | Melville St | 46 C3 | Ordsall Dr | 46 A6 | Redfern St | 47 E2 |
| Glasshouse St | 47 G2 | Hodson St | 46 C2 | Lanstead Dr | 47 J5 | Merrill St | 47 H3 | Ordsall La | 46 A5 | Redhill St | 47 G3 |
| Gleden St | 47 J2 | Holdgate Cl | 46 D7 | Lauderdale Cres | 47 H7 | Middlewood St | 46 B4 | Oregon Cl | 47 G6 | Red Lion St | 47 F3 |
| Glenbarry Cl | 47 G7 | Holkham Cl | 47 H3 | Laystall St | 47 G3 | Midland St | 47 H5 | Orion Pl | 46 B1 | Regent Sq | 46 A5 |
| Glenbarry St | 47 J5 | Holland St | 47 H2 | Layton St | 47 J2 | **Miles Platting** | | Ormsgill St | 46 D7 | Reilly St | 46 D6 |
| Gloucester St | 46 E5 | Holly Bk Cl | 46 B6 | Leaf St | 46 D6 | Milk St | 47 F3 | Orsett Cl | 47 H1 | Reservoir St | 46 D2 |
| Gloucester St (Salford) | 46 A5 | Holly St | 47 J4 | Leak St | 46 B6 | Millbank St | 47 G4 | Osborne St | 47 G1 | Reyner St | 47 E4 |
| Goadsby St | 47 F2 | Holt Town | 47 J3 | Ledburn Ct | 46 C6 | Millbeck St | 47 E6 | Oswald St | 47 E2 | Rial Pl | 47 E7 |
| Gold St | 47 F4 | Honey St | 47 F1 | Left Bk | 46 C4 | Miller St | 47 F2 | Oswald St (Ancoats) | 47 H4 | Ribston St | 46 C7 |
| Gordon St | 46 C1 | Hood St | 47 G3 | Lena St | 47 F4 | Mill Grn St | 47 H5 | Overbridge Rd | 46 D1 | Rice St | 46 C5 |
| Gore St | 47 F4 | Hooper St | 47 J5 | Leslie Hough Way | 46 A1 | Millhall Cl | 47 C7 | Oxford Rd | 47 E5 | Richmond St | 47 F4 |
| Gore St (Salford) | 46 C3 | Hope St | 47 F4 | Lever St | 47 F3 | Millhead Av | 47 J2 | Oxford St | 46 E4 | Richmond St | |
| Gorton St | 46 D2 | Hope St (Salford) | 46 A3 | Lewis St | 47 J1 | Millow St | 47 E2 | | | (Salford) | 46 C2 |
| Goulden St | 47 F2 | Hornby St | 46 D1 | Leycroft St | 47 G4 | Milnrow Cl | 47 F5 | **P** | | Ridgefield | 46 D3 |
| Gould St | 47 F1 | Hornchurch St | 46 C7 | Lidbrook Wk | 47 J7 | Milton St | 46 C1 | Paddock St | 47 G5 | Ridgeway St E | 47 H3 |
| Grafton St | 47 G7 | Horne Dr | 47 H3 | Lime Bk St | 47 J5 | Mincing St | 47 F2 | Palfrey Pl | 47 H6 | Ridgway St | 47 H3 |
| Granby Row | 47 F5 | Houldsworth St | 47 F3 | Lime Gro | 47 F7 | Minshull St | 47 F4 | Pall Mall | 47 E3 | Riga St | 47 F2 |
| Granshaw St | 47 J2 | Hoyle St | 47 H5 | Limekiln La | 47 H5 | Minshull St S | 47 F4 | Palmerston St | 47 H4 | Rigel Pl | 46 B1 |
| Gratrix Av | 46 A6 | Huddart Cl | 46 A5 | Linby St | 46 C6 | Mistletoe Grn | 46 C2 | Parish Vw | 46 A4 | Rigel St | 47 H2 |
| Gravell La | 46 D2 | Hughes St | 47 J5 | Lind St | 47 J3 | Moorhead St | 47 G2 | Parker St | 47 F3 | Rimworth Dr | 47 H1 |
| Grear Ducie St | 46 E2 | Hull Sq | 46 B2 | Linen Ct | 46 B2 | Morbourne Cl | 47 J7 | Park Pl | 47 E1 | Ringstead Dr | 47 G1 |
| Great Ancoats St | 47 F3 | **Hulme** | | Linsley St | 46 D2 | Mosley St | 47 E4 | Park St | 46 E1 | Ripley Cl | 47 H4 |
| Great Bridgewater St | 46 D5 | Hulme Ct | 46 C6 | Linton Cl | 47 H4 | Mosscott Wk | 47 G5 | Park St (Salford) | 46 B3 | River Pl | 46 D5 |
| Great Clowes St | 46 C1 | Hulme Hall Rd | 46 B5 | Litcham Cl | 47 F5 | Mosshall Cl | 46 C7 | Parsonage | 46 D3 | Riverside | 46 B2 |
| Great Ducie St | 46 D1 | Hulme Pl | 46 B3 | Little Ancoats St | 47 F3 | Moulton St | 46 D1 | Parsonage La | 46 D3 | River St | 46 D6 |

River St (Ardwick) 47 H5
Robert St 46 E1
Roby St 47 F4
Rochdale Rd 47 F2
Rockdove Av 46 D6
Rocket Way 46 C3
Rockingham Cl 47 J7
Rodney St 47 H2
Rodney St (Salford) 46 C3
Roe St 47 G2
Roger St 47 F1
Rolla St 46 D2
Rolleston Av 47 H2
Rolls Cres 46 C7
Roman St 47 F3
Rome Rd 47 G2
Rondin Cl 47 J5
Rondin Rd 47 J5
Rope Wk 46 D2
Rosamond Dr 46 C3
Rosamond St W 47 E6
Rosewell Cl 47 J1
Rostron Av 47 J6
Rowendale St 46 D5
Royce Rd 46 C6
Roydale St 47 J2
Royds Cl 47 J7
Ruby St 47 E7
Rudcroft Cl 47 G6
Rudman Dr 46 A5
Rugby St 46 D1
Runcorn St 46 B6

S
Sackville St 47 E4
Sagar St 46 D1
St. Andrew's Sq 47 H4
St. Andrew's St 47 G4
St. Ann's Sq 46 D3
St. Ann St 46 D3
St. Bartholomew's Dr 46 A4
St. Chad's St 47 E1
St. Clement's Dr 46 A5
St. George's 46 B6
St. Ignatius Wk 46 A5
St. James's Sq 46 E4
St. James St 47 E4
St. John St 46 D4
St. Mary's Gate 46 E3
St. Mary's
  Parsonage 46 D3
St. Mary's St 46 C3
St. Michael's Sq 47 F2
St. Nicholas Rd 46 C6
St. Philip's St 46 B3
St. Simon St 46 C1
St. Stephen's Cl 47 H7
St. Stephen St 46 C3
St. Thomas St 47 F1
St. Vincent St 47 H3
St. Wilfrids St 46 C6
Salford 46 A4
Salford App 46 D3
Salmon St 47 F3
Saltford Av 47 H3
Salutation St 46 E7
Samouth Cl 47 H2
Sam Swire St 46 D7
Samuel Ogden St 47 F5
Sanctuary, The 46 D7
Sandal St 47 J2
Sandford St 46 C1
Sand St 47 G1
Sawley Rd 47 J1
Scarsdale St 46 A1
School Ct 47 G3
School St 47 F2
School St (Salford) 46 C1
Scotland 47 E2
Scotporth Cl 46 C6
Sefton Cl 47 G6
Senior St 46 D2
Seymour Cl 46 A7
Sharp St 47 F2
Shaw Cres 46 E2
Shawgreen Cl 46 C6
Shawheath Cl 46 C6
Shearsby Cl 46 D7
Sheffield St 47 G4
Sherborne St 46 D1
Sherbourne St W 46 D1
Sherratt St 47 G2
Shetland Rd 47 H1
Shilford Dr 47 G2
Shortcroft St 46 D5
Short St 47 F3
Short St (Salford) 46 C1
Shrewsbury St 46 B7
Shudehill 47 F3
Sidney St 47 F6
Sidney St (Salford) 46 C3
Silkin Cl 47 F6
Silk St 47 G2
Silk St (Salford) 46 B2

Silvercroft St 46 C5
Silver St 47 F4
Simeon St 47 F2
Simms Cl 46 B3
Simpson St 47 F2
Sirius Pl 46 B1
Skerry Cl 47 G6
Skip Pl 47 E1
Slate Av 47 H3
Sleaford Cl 47 H1
Smallridge Cl 47 H2
Smith St 46 A6
Smithy La 46 D3
Snell St 47 H4
Soar St 47 F3
Sorrel St 46 C6
Southall St 46 D4
Southall St
  (Strangeways) 46 D1
Southend Av 46 B7
Southern St 46 D5
Southgate 46 D3
South Hall St 46 B5
South King St 46 D3
Southmill St 46 E4
South Pump St 47 F4
South W Services Rd 46 C4
Sparkle St 47 G4
Spa St 47 F7
Spaw St 46 C3
Spear St 47 F3
Spectator St 47 H3
Springfield La 46 D2
Springfield Sq 46 D4
Spring Gdns 47 E4
Spruce St 46 C7
Stalham Cl 47 H1
Stanley Rd 46 B7
Stanley St 47 F1
Stanley St (Salford) 46 C4
Stansby Gdns 47 J7
Station App (for
  Oxford Road
  Station) 47 E5
Station App (for
  Piccadilly Station) 47 F4
Staverton Cl 47 G6
Stephen St 46 E1
Stevenson Pl 47 F3
Stevenson Sq 47 F3
Stevenson St 46 B3
Stockland Cl 47 F6
Stockport Rd 47 H6
Stocks St 47 E1
Stocks St E 47 E1
Stonall Av 46 C6
Stonelow Cl 46 E6
Stone St 46 C5
Store St 47 F4
Stracey St 47 J2
Strawberry Hill 46 A1
Stretford Rd 46 B7
Style St 47 F2
Sudbury Cl 46 B7
Sudell St 47 G2
Sussex St 46 B1
Swan St 47 F2
Swiftsure Av 46 B3
Syndall Av 47 H6
Syndall St 47 H6

T
Talgarth Rd 47 G1
Tamar Ct 46 B7
Tame St 47 H4
Tariff St 47 F3
Tasle All 46 D4
Tatton St 46 B6
Tatton St (Salford) 46 A5
Taunton St 47 J3
Tavery Cl 47 H3
Tebutt St 47 G2
Teer St 47 J3
Temperance St 47 G5
Tewkesbury Rd 47 J2
Thirsk St 47 G5
Thomas St 47 F3
Thompson St 47 F2
Thompson St
  (Strangeways) 46 D1
Thomson St 47 H7
Thor Grn 46 B5
Thornage Dr 47 H1
Thorncross Cl 46 B6
Thornden Rd 47 J1
Thornley Brow 47 E2
Thornton St 47 H1
Tib La 46 E4
Tib St 47 F3
Tidewell Av 47 H2
Tidworth Av 47 H3
Tinsley Cl 47 J2
Tivoli St 46 D4
Todd St 47 E2

Tomlinson St 46 D7
Tonge St 47 J5
Tonman St 46 D4
Torquay Cl 47 H7
Towcester Cl 47 J3
Town Hall La 46 E3
Trafford Bk Rd 46 A7
Trafford Ct 46 C6
Trafford Pl 46 B7
Trafford St 46 D5
Travis St 47 G5
Trentham St 46 B6
Trinity Way 46 B5
Tristam Cl 47 G6
Troutbeck Av 47 H3
Trumpet St 46 D5
Tudbury Way 46 C2
Tudbury St 47 H4
Tuer St 47 F7
Turner St 47 F3
Turner St
  (Old Trafford) 46 A6
Tutbury St 47 H4
Twillbrook Dr 46 D2

U
Union St 47 F3
Union St (Ardwick) 47 H5
University Rd 46 A2
University Rd W 46 A2
Upper Brook St 47 F6
Upper Cyrus St 47 J3
Upper Helena St 47 J2
Upper Kirby St 47 H3
Upper Moss La 46 C7
Upper Wf St 46 B3

V
Varley St 47 J1
Vauxhall St 47 G1
Velour Cl 46 B1
Vesta St 47 H3
Viaduct St 47 J4
Viaduct St (Salford) 46 D2
Vickers St 47 J1
Victoria Br St 46 D3
Victoria Sta App 46 E2
Victoria St 46 E3
Victor St 47 G1
Victor St (Salford) 46 C3
Virgil St 46 B6

W
Wadeford Cl 47 G2
Wadeson Rd 47 G5
Wadlow Cl 46 C2
Walker's Cft 46 E2
Wallness 46 A1
Wallness La 46 A1
Warde St 46 C7
Wardle St 47 J2
Warford St 47 F1
Warmington Dr 47 J7
Warwick St 47 F3
Warwick St (Hulme) 46 D7
Waterloo St 47 E4
Water St 46 B5
Water St (Ardwick) 47 H5
Watkin Cl 47 G7
Watkin St 46 C1
Watson St 46 D5
Weald Cl 47 G6
Weir St 46 D7
Welland Cl 46 B7
Wellhead Cl 46 E7
Wellington Grn 46 C7
Wellington St 46 C2
Well St 47 E3
West Bk St 46 A4
West Charles St 46 A3
West Crown Av 46 A4
West Hope St 46 A3
West King St 46 C2
Westminster St 46 B6
West Mosley St 47 E4
Weston St 47 J3
West Pk St 46 A5
Weybridge Rd 47 H3
Whalley St 47 H2
Wheater's Cres 46 B1
Wheater's St 46 B1
Wheater's Ter 46 B1
Whimberry Cl 46 A5
Whitchurch St 46 D1
Whitekirk Cl 47 G6
White St 46 B7
Whitfield St 47 E1
Whittle's Cft 47 G4
Whittle St 47 F3
Whitworth St 47 F5
Whitworth St W 46 D5
Wilberforce Cl 46 D7
Wilfred St 46 D1
William Chadwick Cl 47 H1
Williamson St 47 F1

William St 47 H5
Wilmott St 46 E6
Wilson St 47 H7
Wilton Pl 46 B3
Wilton St 47 F6
Winder Dr 47 H3
Windmill Av 46 A5
Windmill St 46 D4
Winfell Dr 47 J2
Winscombe Dr 47 H1
Winser St 47 E5
Winstanley Rd 47 H2
Withy Gro 47 E3
Woden's Av 46 A5
Woden St 46 B5
Woodlark Cl 46 B3
Wood St 46 D4
Woodward Pl 47 H3
Woodward St 47 H3
Woollam Pl 46 C4
Worrall St 46 A5
Worsley St 46 B5
Worsley St (Salford) 46 D3
Wright St 46 A7
Wroe St 46 B3
Wyatt Av 46 A5
Wynne St 46 A1
Wyre St 47 G5

Y
Yew St 46 C7
Yorkshire St 46 D3
York St 47 E3
York St (Hulme) 46 C6
York St (off Charles
  Street) 47 E5
York St E 47 F6

Z
Zion Cres 46 D7

**Tourist Information Centre: 23 Union Street**
**Tel: 01224 288828**

| | | | |
|---|---|---|---|
| Albert Quay | C3 | Hutcheon Street | B2 |
| Albert Street | B2 | Justice Mill Lane | B3 |
| Albury Road | B3 | King's Crescent | C1 |
| Albyn Place | A3 | King Street | C1 |
| Argyll Place | A2 | Langstane Place | B3 |
| Ashgrove Road | A1 | Leadside Road | B2 |
| Ashgrove Road West | A1 | Leslie Terrace | B1 |
| Ash-hill Drive | A1 | Links Road | C2 |
| Ashley Road | A3 | Linksfield Road | C1 |
| Back Hilton Road | A1 | Loch Street | B2 |
| Baker Street | B2 | Maberly Street | B2 |
| Beach Boulevard | C2 | Market Street | C3 |
| Bedford Place | B1 | Menzies Road | C3 |
| Bedford Road | B1 | Merkland Road East | C1 |
| Beechgrove Terrace | A2 | Mid Stocket Road | A2 |
| Belgrave Terrace | A2 | Mile-end Avenue | A2 |
| Berryden Road | B1 | Miller Street | C2 |
| Blaikie's Quay | C3 | Mount Street | B2 |
| Bon-Accord Street | B3 | Nelson Street | C2 |
| Bonnymuir Place | A2 | North Esplanade East | C3 |
| Bridge Street | B2 | North Esplanade West | C3 |
| Brighton Place | A3 | Orchard Street | C1 |
| Cairncry Road | A1 | Osborne Place | A3 |
| Canal Road | B1 | Palmerston Road | C3 |
| Carden Place | A3 | Park Road | C1 |
| Carlton Place | A3 | Park Street | C2 |
| Causewayend | B1 | Pittodrie Place | C1 |
| Chapel Street | B2 | Pittodrie Street | C1 |
| Claremont Street | A3 | Powis Place | B1 |
| Clifton Road | A1 | Powis Terrace | B1 |
| College Bounds | B1 | Queens Road | A3 |
| College Street | C3 | Queens Terrace | A3 |
| Commerce Street | C2 | Regent Quay | C2 |
| Commercial Quay | C3 | Rosehill Crescent | A1 |
| Constitution Street | C2 | Rosehill Drive | A1 |
| Cornhill Drive | A1 | Rosemount Place | A2 |
| Cornhill Road | A1 | Rose Street | B2 |
| Cornhill Terrace | A1 | Rubislaw Terrace | B3 |
| Cotton Street | C2 | St. Swithin Street | A3 |
| Cromwell Road | A3 | Schoolhill | B2 |
| Desswood Place | A3 | Seaforth Road | C1 |
| Devonshire Road | A3 | Sinclair Road | C3 |
| Elmbank Terrace | B1 | Skene Square | B2 |
| Esslemont Avenue | B2 | Skene Street | B2 |
| Ferryhill Road | B3 | South Crown Street | B3 |
| Fonthill Road | B3 | South Esplanade West | C3 |
| Forest Road | A3 | Spital | C1 |
| Forest Avenue | A3 | Springbank Terrace | B3 |
| Fountainhall Road | A2 | Spring Gardens | B2 |
| Froghall Terrace | B1 | Stanley Street | A3 |
| Gallowgate | C2 | Sunnybank Road | B1 |
| George Street | B1 | Sunnyside Road | B1 |
| Gillespie Crescent | A1 | Union Glen | B3 |
| Gladstone Place | A3 | Union Grove | A3 |
| Golf Road | C1 | Union Street | B2 |
| Gordondale Road | A2 | Urquhart Road | C2 |
| Great Southern Road | B3 | Victoria Bridge | C3 |
| Great Western Road | A3 | Victoria Road | C3 |
| Guild Street | C3 | Walker Road | C3 |
| Hamilton Place | A2 | Waterloo Quay | C2 |
| Hardgate | B3 | Waverley Place | B3 |
| Hilton Drive | A1 | Well Place | C3 |
| Hilton Place | A1 | Westburn Drive | A1 |
| Hilton Street | A1 | Westburn Road | A2 |
| Holburn Road | B3 | West North Street | C2 |
| Holburn Street | B3 | Whitehall Place | A2 |
| Holland Street | B1 | Whitehall Road | A2 |
| | | Willowbank Road | B3 |

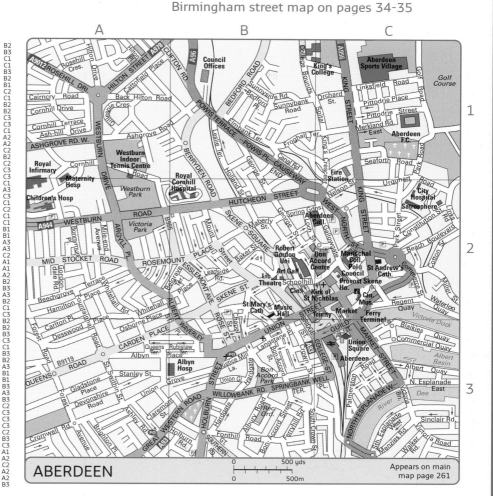

ABERDEEN

0    500 yds
0    500m

Appears on main map page 261

**Tourist Information Centre: Abbey Chambers, Abbey Churchyard**
**Tel: 0906 711 2000**

| | | | |
|---|---|---|---|
| Ambury | A3 | Pierrepont Street | B3 |
| Archway Street | C3 | Pulteney Gardens | C3 |
| Argyle Street | B2 | Pulteney Mews | C1 |
| Avon Street | A2 | Pulteney Road | C2 |
| Barton Street | A2 | Queen Street | A2 |
| Bath Street | B2 | Quiet Street | A1 |
| Bathwick Hill | C1 | Rossiter Road | B3 |
| Beau Street | B2 | Royal Crescent | A1 |
| Bennett Street | A1 | St. James's Parade | A2 |
| Bridge Street | B2 | St. John's Road | A2 |
| Broad Quay | A3 | St. Marks Road | B3 |
| Broad Street | B1 | Sawclose | A2 |
| Broadway | C3 | Southgate Street | B3 |
| Brock Street | A1 | Spring Crescent | C3 |
| Chapel Row | A2 | Stall Street | B2 |
| Charles Street | A2 | Sutton Street | C1 |
| Charlotte Street | A1 | Sydney Place | C1 |
| Cheap Street | B2 | The Circus | A1 |
| Claverton Street | B3 | Union Street | B2 |
| Corn Street | A3 | Upper Borough Walls | A2 |
| Daniel Street | C1 | Walcot Street | B1 |
| Darlington Street | C1 | Wells Road | A3 |
| Dorchester Street | B3 | Westgate Buildings | A2 |
| Edward Street | C1 | Westgate Street | A2 |
| Excelsior Street | C3 | Wood Street | A1 |
| Ferry Lane | C2 | York Street | B2 |
| Gay Street | A1 | | |
| George Street | A1 | | |
| Grand Parade | B2 | | |
| Great Pulteney Street | C1 | | |
| Green Park Road | A2 | | |
| Green Street | B1 | | |
| Grove Street | B1 | | |
| Henrietta Gardens | C1 | | |
| Henrietta Mews | C1 | | |
| Henrietta Road | B1 | | |
| Henrietta Street | B1 | | |
| Henry Street | B2 | | |
| High Street | B2 | | |
| Holloway | A3 | | |
| James Street West | A2 | | |
| John Street | A1 | | |
| Kingsmead East | A2 | | |
| Kingsmead Square | A2 | | |
| Lansdown Road | A1 | | |
| Laura Place | B1 | | |
| Lime Grove | C2 | | |
| Lime Grove Gardens | C2 | | |
| Lower Borough Walls | B2 | | |
| Lower Bristol Road | A3 | | |
| Magdalen Avenue | A3 | | |
| Manvers Street | B3 | | |
| Milk Street | A2 | | |
| Milsom Street | B1 | | |
| Monmouth Place | A1 | | |
| Monmouth Street | A2 | | |
| Newark Street | B3 | | |
| New Bond Street | B2 | | |
| New King Street | A2 | | |
| New Orchard Street | B2 | | |
| New Street | A2 | | |
| North Parade | B2 | | |
| North Parade Road | C2 | | |
| Old King Street | A1 | | |
| Orange Grove | B2 | | |
| Paragon | B1 | | |

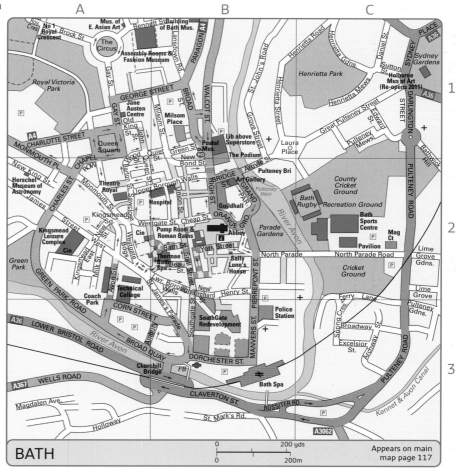

BATH

0    200 yds
0    200m

Appears on main map page 117

**BLACKPOOL**

0 ___ 300 yds
0 ___ 300m

Appears on main map page 191

**Tourist Information Centre: 1 Clifton Street**
**Tel: 01253 478222**

|  |  |  |  |
|---|---|---|---|
| Abingdon Street | A2 | Manor Road | C3 |
| Adelaide Street | A2 | Market Street | A2 |
| Albert Road | A3 | Mather Street | C1 |
| Ascot Road | C1 | Mere Road | C2 |
| Ashburton Road | A1 | Milbourne Street | B2 |
| Ashton Road | B3 | Mount Street | A1 |
| Bank Hey Street | A2 | New Bonny Street | A3 |
| Banks Street | A1 | Newcastle Avenue | C2 |
| Beech Avenue | C2 | Newton Drive | C2 |
| Birchway Avenue | C1 | Oxford Road | B3 |
| Bonny Street | A3 | Palatine Road | B3 |
| Boothley Road | B1 | Park Road | B3 |
| Breck Road | C3 | Peter Street | B2 |
| Bryan Road | C2 | Pleasant Street | A1 |
| Buchanan Street | B2 | Portland Road | C3 |
| Butler Street | B1 | Princess Parade | A2 |
| Caunce Street | B2/C1 | Promenade | A1 |
| Cecil Street | B1 | Queens Square | A2 |
| Central Drive | A3 | Queen Street | A2 |
| Chapel Street | A3 | Rathlyn Avenue | C1 |
| Charles Street | B2 | Reads Avenue | B3 |
| Charnley Road | A3 | Regent Road | B2 |
| Church Street | B2 | Ribble Road | B3 |
| Clifford Road | A1 | Ripon Road | B3 |
| Clifton Street | A2 | St. Albans Road | C3 |
| Clinton Avenue | B3 | Salisbury Road | C3 |
| Cocker Square | A1 | Seasiders Way | A3 |
| Cocker Street | A1 | Selbourne Road | B1 |
| Coleridge Road | B1 | Somerset Avenue | C3 |
| Collingwood Avenue | C1 | South King Street | B2 |
| Cookson Street | B2 | Stirling Road | C1 |
| Coopers Way | B1 | Talbot Road | A2/B1 |
| Coronation Street | A3 | Talbot Square | A2 |
| Corporation Street | A2 | Topping Street | A2 |
| Cumberland Avenue | C3 | Victory Road | B1 |
| Deansgate | A2 | Wayman Road | C2 |
| Devonshire Road | B1 | Westmorland Avenue | C3 |
| Devonshire Square | C2 | West Park Drive | C2 |
| Dickson Road | A1 | Whitegate Drive | C2/C3 |
| Egerton Road | A1 | Woodland Grove | C3 |
| Elizabeth Street | B1 | Woolman Road | B3 |
| Exchange Street | A1 | Yates Street | A1 |
| Forest Gate | C2 | | |
| Gainsborough Road | B3 | | |
| George Street | B2/B1 | | |
| Gloucester Avenue | C3 | | |
| Gorse Road | C3 | | |
| Gorton Street | B1 | | |
| Granville Road | B2 | | |
| Grosvenor Street | B2 | | |
| High Street | A1 | | |
| Hollywood Avenue | C2 | | |
| Hornby Road | A3 | | |
| Hounds Hill | A3 | | |
| King Street | A1 | | |
| Knowsley Avenue | C3 | | |
| Larbreck Avenue | C1 | | |
| Laycock Gate | C1 | | |
| Layton Road | C1 | | |
| Leamington Road | B2 | | |
| Leicester Road | B2 | | |
| Lincoln Road | B2 | | |
| Liverpool Road | B2 | | |
| London Road | C1 | | |
| Lord Street | A1 | | |
| Manchester Road | C1 | | |

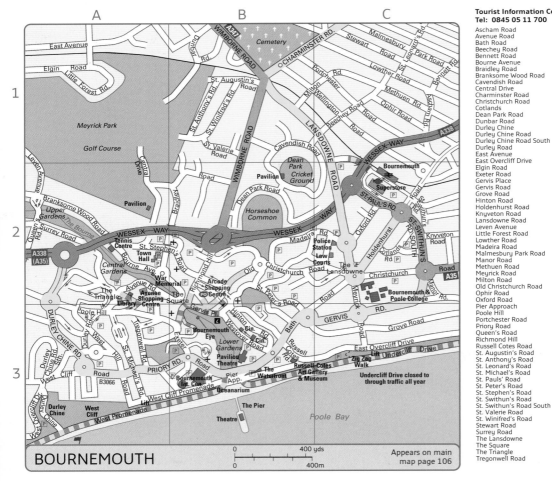

**BOURNEMOUTH**

0 ___ 400 yds
0 ___ 400m

Appears on main map page 106

**Tourist Information Centre: Westover Road**
**Tel: 0845 05 11 700**

|  |  |  |  |
|---|---|---|---|
| Ascham Road | C1 | Undercliff Drive | C3 |
| Avenue Road | A2 | Wellington Road | C1 |
| Bath Road | B3 | Wessex Way | A2/C1 |
| Beechey Road | C1 | West Cliff Promenade | A3 |
| Bennett Road | C1 | West Cliff Road | A3 |
| Bourne Avenue | A2 | West Hill Road | A3 |
| Braidley Road | B2 | West Overcliff Drive | A3 |
| Branksome Wood Road | A2 | West Promenade | A3 |
| Cavendish Road | B1 | Westover Road | B3 |
| Central Drive | A1 | Wimborne Road | B2 |
| Charminster Road | B1 | | |
| Christchurch Road | C2 | | |
| Cotlands | C2 | | |
| Dean Park Road | B2 | | |
| Dunbar Road | B1 | | |
| Durley Chine | A3 | | |
| Durley Chine Road | A3 | | |
| Durley Chine Road South | A3 | | |
| Durley Road | A3 | | |
| East Avenue | A1 | | |
| East Overcliff Drive | C3 | | |
| Elgin Road | A1 | | |
| Exeter Road | B3 | | |
| Gervis Place | B3 | | |
| Gervis Road | C3 | | |
| Grove Road | C3 | | |
| Hinton Road | B3 | | |
| Holdenhurst Road | C2 | | |
| Knyveton Road | C2 | | |
| Lansdowne Road | B1 | | |
| Leven Avenue | A1 | | |
| Little Forest Road | A1 | | |
| Lowther Road | C1 | | |
| Madeira Road | B2 | | |
| Malmesbury Park Road | C1 | | |
| Manor Road | C2 | | |
| Methuen Road | C1 | | |
| Meyrick Road | C2 | | |
| Milton Road | B1 | | |
| Old Christchurch Road | B2 | | |
| Ophir Road | C1 | | |
| Oxford Road | C2 | | |
| Pier Approach | B3 | | |
| Poole Hill | A3 | | |
| Portchester Road | C1 | | |
| Priory Road | A3 | | |
| Queen's Road | A2 | | |
| Richmond Hill | B2 | | |
| Russell Cotes Road | B3 | | |
| St. Augustin's Road | B1 | | |
| St. Anthony's Road | B1 | | |
| St. Leonard's Road | C1 | | |
| St. Michael's Road | A3 | | |
| St. Pauls' Road | C2 | | |
| St. Peter's Road | B2 | | |
| St. Stephen's Road | A2 | | |
| St. Swithun's Road | C2 | | |
| St. Swithun's Road South | C2 | | |
| St. Valerie Road | B1 | | |
| St. Winifred's Road | B1 | | |
| Stewart Road | C1 | | |
| Surrey Road | A2 | | |
| The Lansdowne | C2 | | |
| The Square | B2 | | |
| The Triangle | A2 | | |
| Tregonwell Road | A3 | | |

**Tourist Information Centre: City Hall, Centenary Square**
**Tel: 01274 433678**

| | |
|---|---|
| Akam Road | A1 |
| Ann Place | A3 |
| Ashgrove | A3 |
| Balme Street | B1 |
| Bank Street | B2 |
| Baptist Place | A1 |
| Barkerend Road | C1 |
| Barry Street | A2 |
| Bolling Road | C3 |
| Bolton Road | C1 |
| Brearton Street | A1 |
| Bridge Street | B2 |
| Britannia Street | B3 |
| Broadway | B2 |
| Burnett Street | C2 |
| Caledonia Street | B3 |
| Canal Road | B1 |
| Captain Street | C1 |
| Carlton Street | A2 |
| Carter Street | C3 |
| Centenary Square | B2 |
| Chain Street | A1 |
| Channing Way | B2 |
| Chapel Street | C2 |
| Charles Street | B2 |
| Cheapside | B2 |
| Chester Street | A3 |
| Churchbank | C2 |
| Claremont | C1 |
| Croft Street | B3 |
| Darfield Street | A1 |
| Darley Street | B1 |
| Drake Street | B2 |
| Drewton Road | A1 |
| Dryden Street | C3 |
| Duke Street | B1 |
| Dyson Street | A1 |
| East Parade | C2 |
| Edmund Street | A3 |
| Edward Street | C3 |
| Eldon Place | A1 |
| Fairfax Street | C3 |
| Filey Street | C2 |
| Fitzwilliam Street | C3 |
| Fountain Street | A1 |
| George Street | C2 |
| Godwin Street | B2 |
| Gracechurch Street | A1 |
| Grafton Street | A3 |
| Grattan Road | A2 |
| Great Horton Road | A3 |
| Grove Terrace | A3 |
| Guy Street | C3 |
| Hall Ings | B2 |
| Hall Lane | C3 |
| Hallfield Road | A1 |
| Hamm Strasse | B1 |
| Hammerton Street | C2 |
| Hanover Square | A1 |
| Harris Street | C2 |
| Heap Lane | B2 |
| Houghton Place | A1 |
| Howard Street | A3 |
| Hustlergate | B2 |
| Ivegate | B2 |
| James Street | B2 |

| | |
|---|---|
| John Street | A2 |
| Kirkgate | B2 |
| Leeds Road | C2 |
| Little Horton Lane | A3 |
| Lower Kirkgate | B2 |
| Lumb Lane | A1 |
| Manchester Road | B3 |
| Manningham Lane | A1 |
| Mannville Terrace | A3 |
| Manor Row | B1 |
| Melbourne Place | A3 |
| Midland Road | B1 |
| Moody Street | C3 |
| Morley Street | A3 |
| Neal Street | A3 |
| Nelson Street | B3 |
| North Parade | B1 |
| North Street | C1 |
| North Wing | C1 |
| Nuttall Road | C1 |
| Otley Road | C1 |
| Paradise Street | A1 |
| Park Road | B3 |
| Peckover Street | C2 |
| Prince's Way | B2 |
| Prospect Street | C3 |
| Radwell Drive | A3 |
| Rawson Place | B1 |
| Rawson Road | A1 |
| Rebecca Street | A1 |
| Rouse Fold | C3 |
| Russell Street | A3 |
| Salem Street | B1 |
| Sawrey Place | A3 |
| Sedgwick Close | A1 |
| Sharpe Street | B3 |
| Shipley Airedale Road | C1 |
| Simes Street | A1 |
| Snowden Street | A1 |
| Sunbridge Road | A1 |
| Sylhet Close | A1 |
| Ternhill Grove | B3 |
| Tetley Street | A2 |
| The Tyrls | B2 |
| Thornton Road | B2 |
| Trafalgar Street | A1 |
| Trinity Road | A3 |
| Tumbling Hill Street | A2 |
| Valley Road | B1 |
| Vaughan Street | A1 |
| Vicar Lane | C2 |
| Vincent Street | A2 |
| Wakefield Road | C3 |
| Wapping Road | C1 |
| Water Lane | A2 |
| Westgate | A1 |
| Wigan Street | A2 |

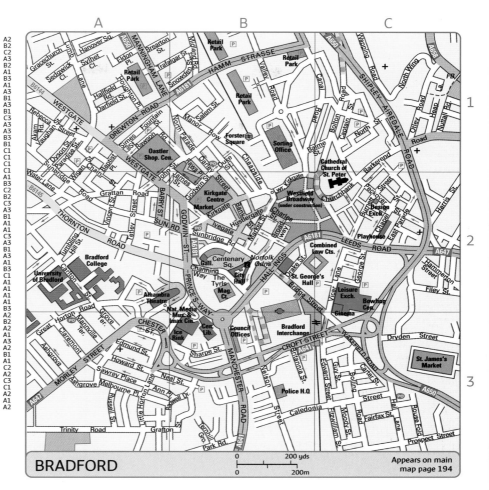

BRADFORD

0   200 yds
0   200m

Appears on main
map page 194

**Tourist Information Centre: Royal Pavilion Shop,**
**4-5 Pavilion Buildings  Tel: 0906 711 2255**

| | |
|---|---|
| Addison Road | A1 |
| Albion Hill | C2 |
| Beaconsfield Road | B1 |
| Brunswick Square | A2 |
| Buckingham Place | B1 |
| Buckingham Road | B2 |
| Carlton Hill | C2 |
| Cheapside | B2 |
| Church Street | B2 |
| Churchill Square | B3 |
| Clifton Hill | A2 |
| Clyde Road | B1 |
| Davigdor Road | A1 |
| Ditchling Rise | B1 |
| Ditchling Road | C1 |
| Dyke Road | B2 |
| Dyke Road Drive | B1 |
| Eastern Road | C3 |
| Edward Street | C3 |
| Elm Grove | C1 |
| Fleet Street | B2 |
| Florence Road | B1 |
| Freshfield Road | C3 |
| Furze Hill | A2 |
| Gloucester Road | B2 |
| Grand Junction Road | B3 |
| Hamilton Road | B1 |
| Hanover Street | C2 |
| Highdown Road | A1 |
| Holland Road | A2 |
| Hollingdean Road | C1 |
| Howard Place | B1 |
| Islingword Road | C1 |
| John Street | C2 |
| King's Road | A3 |
| Lansdowne Road | A2 |
| Lewes Road | C1 |
| London Road | B1 |
| Lyndhurst Road | A1 |
| Madeira Drive | C3 |
| Marine Parade | C3 |
| Montefiore Road | A1 |
| Montpelier Road | A2 |
| New England Road | B1 |
| New England Street | B1 |
| Nizells Avenue | A1 |
| Norfolk Terrace | A2 |
| North Road | B2 |
| North Street | B2 |
| Old Shoreham Road | A1 |
| Old Steine | C3 |
| Park Crescent Terrace | C1 |
| Park Street | C2 |
| Port Hall Road | A1 |
| Preston Circus | B1 |
| Preston Road | B1 |
| Preston Street | A3 |
| Prince's Crescent | C1 |
| Queen's Park Road | C2 |
| Queen's Road | B2 |
| Richmond Place | C2 |
| Richmond Road | C1 |
| Richmond Street | C2 |
| Richmond Terrace | C2 |
| St. James's Street | C3 |
| Somerhill Road | A2 |

| | |
|---|---|
| Southover Street | C2 |
| Springfield Road | B1 |
| Stafford Road | A1 |
| Stanford Road | B1 |
| Sussex Street | C2 |
| Terminus Road | B2 |
| The Lanes | B3 |
| The Upper Drive | A1 |
| Trafalgar Street | B2 |
| Union Road | C1 |
| Upper Lewes Road | C1 |
| Upper North Street | A2 |
| Upper Rock Gardens | C3 |
| Viaduct Road | B1 |
| Victoria Road | A2 |
| Waterloo Street | A2 |
| Wellington Road | C1 |
| West Drive | C2 |
| West Street | B3 |
| Western Road | A2 |
| Wilbury Crescent | A1 |
| York Avenue | A2 |
| York Place | C2 |

BRIGHTON

0   200 yds
0   200m

Appears on main
map page 109

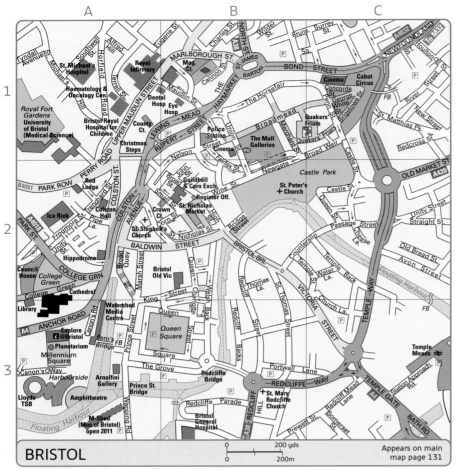

BRISTOL

| | | |
|---|---|---|
| 0 | | 200 yds |
| 0 | | 200m |

Appears on main
map page 131

**Tourist Information Centre:  Explore@Bristol, Anchor Road**
**Tel:  0906 711 2191**

| | | | | |
|---|---|---|---|---|
| Alfred Hill | A1 | Redcliffe Bridge | B3 |
| Anchor Road | A3 | Redcliffe Parade | B3 |
| Avon Street | C2 | Redcliff Hill | B3 |
| Baldwin Street | A2 | Redcliff Mead Lane | C3 |
| Bath Road | C3 | Redcliff Street | B2 |
| Bond Street | B1 | Redcross Street | C1 |
| Bridge Street | B2 | River Street | C1 |
| Brigstowe Street | C1 | Rupert Street | A1 |
| Bristol Bridge | B2 | St. James Barton | B1 |
| Broadmead | B1 | St. Matthias Park | C1 |
| Broad Quay | A2 | St. Michael's Hill | A1 |
| Broad Street | B2 | St. Nicholas Street | B2 |
| Broad Weir | C1 | St. Thomas Street | B2 |
| Brunswick Square | B1 | Small Street | A2 |
| Cannon Street | B1 | Somerset Street | C3 |
| Canon's Road | A3 | Southwell Street | A1 |
| Canon's Way | A3 | Station Approach Road | C3 |
| Castle Street | C2 | Straight Street | C2 |
| Charles Street | B1 | Surrey Street | C1 |
| Cheese Lane | C2 | Temple Back | C2 |
| Christmas Steps | A1 | Temple Gate | C3 |
| Church Lane | C2 | Temple Street | B2 |
| College Green | A2 | Temple Way | C2 |
| College Avenue | A2 | Terrell Street | A1 |
| Colston Street | A2 | The Grove | A3 |
| Concorde Street | C1 | The Haymarket | B1 |
| Corn Street | C1 | The Horsefair | B1 |
| Countership | B2 | Thomas Lane | B2 |
| Eugene Street | A1 | Trenchard Street | A2 |
| Fairfax Street | B1 | Tyndall Avenue | A1 |
| Frogmore Street | A2 | Union Street | B1 |
| George White Street | C1 | Unity Street | A2 |
| High Street | B2 | Unity Street | C2 |
| Horfield Road | A1 | Upper Maudlin Street | A1 |
| Houlton Street | C1 | Victoria Street | B2 |
| John Street | B2 | Wapping Road | A3 |
| King Street | A2 | Water Lane | C2 |
| Lewins Mead | A1 | Welsh Back | B2 |
| Lower Castle Street | C2 | Wilder Street | B1 |
| Lower Maudlin Street | B1 | Wine Street | B2 |
| Marlborough Street | B1 | | |
| Marsh Street | A2 | | |
| Merchant Street | B1 | | |
| Nelson Street | B1 | | |
| Newfoundland Street | C1 | | |
| Newgate | B2 | | |
| New Street | C1 | | |
| North Street | B1 | | |
| Old Bread Street | C2 | | |
| Old Market Street | C2 | | |
| Park Row | A2 | | |
| Park Street | A2 | | |
| Passage Street | C2 | | |
| Penn Street | C1 | | |
| Pero's Bridge | A3 | | |
| Perry Road | A2 | | |
| Pipe Lane | A2 | | |
| Portwall Lane | B3 | | |
| Prewett Street | B3 | | |
| Prince Street | A3 | | |
| Prince Street Bridge | C1 | | |
| Quakers' Friars | B1 | | |
| Queen Charlotte Street | B2 | | |
| Queen Square | A3 | | |
| Queen Street | C2 | | |
| Redcliff Backs | B3 | | |

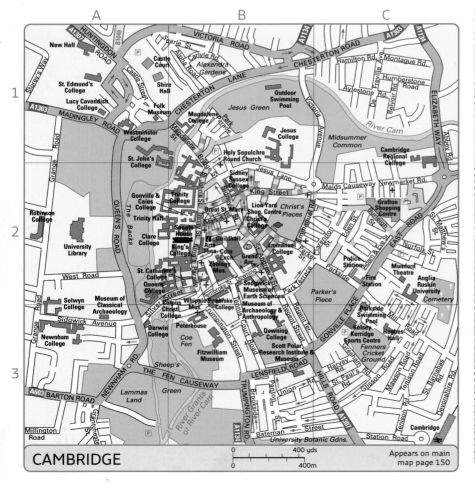

CAMBRIDGE

| | | |
|---|---|---|
| 0 | | 400 yds |
| 0 | | 400m |

Appears on main
map page 150

**Tourist Information Centre:  Wheeler Street**
**Tel:  0871 226 8006**

| | | | | |
|---|---|---|---|---|
| Adam and Eve Street | C2 | Tenison Road | C3 |
| Alpha Road | B1 | Tennis Court Road | B2 |
| Aylestone Road | C1 | Trinity Street | B2 |
| Barton Road | A3 | Trumpington Road | B3 |
| Bateman Street | B3 | Trumpington Street | B3 |
| Belvoir Road | C1 | Union Road | B3 |
| Brookside | B3 | Victoria Avenue | B1 |
| Burleigh Street | C2 | Victoria Road | B1 |
| Carlyle Road | B1 | West Road | A2 |
| Castle Street | A1 | | |
| Chesterton Lane | B1 | | |
| Chesterton Road | B1 | | |
| Clarendon Street | C2 | | |
| De Freville Avenue | C1 | | |
| Devonshire Road | C3 | | |
| Downing Street | B2 | | |
| East Road | C2 | | |
| Eden Street | C2 | | |
| Elizabeth Way | C1 | | |
| Emmanuel Road | B2 | | |
| Fen Causeway, The | A3 | | |
| Glisson Road | C3 | | |
| Gonville Place | C3 | | |
| Granchester Street | A3 | | |
| Grange Road | A3 | | |
| Gresham Road | C3 | | |
| Hamilton Road | C1 | | |
| Harvey Road | C3 | | |
| Hills Road | C3 | | |
| Humberstone Road | C1 | | |
| Huntingdon Road | A1 | | |
| Jesus Lane | B2 | | |
| King's Parade | B2 | | |
| King Street | B2 | | |
| Lensfield Road | B3 | | |
| Madingley Road | A1 | | |
| Magdalene Bridge Street | B1 | | |
| Maids Causeway | C2 | | |
| Market Street | B2 | | |
| Mawson Road | C3 | | |
| Millington Road | A3 | | |
| Mill Road | C3 | | |
| Montague Road | C1 | | |
| Newmarket Road | C2 | | |
| Newnham Road | A3 | | |
| Norfolk Street | C2 | | |
| Panton Street | B3 | | |
| Parker Street | B2 | | |
| Park Parade | B1 | | |
| Parkside | C2 | | |
| Park Terrace | B2 | | |
| Pembroke Street | B2 | | |
| Queen's Road | A2 | | |
| Regent Street | B2 | | |
| Regent Terrace | B2 | | |
| St. Andrew's Street | B2 | | |
| St. Barnabas Road | C3 | | |
| St. John's Street | B2 | | |
| St. Matthew's Street | C2 | | |
| St. Paul's Road | C3 | | |
| Searce Street | A1 | | |
| Sidgwick Avenue | A3 | | |
| Sidney Street | B2 | | |
| Silver Street | A3 | | |
| Station Road | C3 | | |
| Storey's Way | A1 | | |

**Tourist Information Centre: 12-13 Sun Street, The Buttermarket**
**Tel: 01227 378100**

| | | | |
|---|---|---|---|
| Best Lane | B2 | Watling Street | B2 |
| Borough Northgate | B1 | Whitehall Gardens | A2 |
| Broad Street | C1 | Whitehall Road | A2 |
| Burgate | B2 | Wincheap | A3 |
| Castle Row | A3 | York Road | A3 |
| Castle Street | A3 | | |
| College Road | C1 | | |
| Cossington Road | C3 | | |
| Craddock Road | C1 | | |
| Dover Street | C2 | | |
| Edgar Road | C1 | | |
| Ersham Road | C3 | | |
| Forty Acres Road | A1 | | |
| Gordon Road | A3 | | |
| Havelock Street | C1 | | |
| Hawk's Lane | B2 | | |
| High Street | B2 | | |
| Ivy Lane | C2 | | |
| King Street | B1 | | |
| Kirby's Lane | A1 | | |
| Lansdown Road | B3 | | |
| Longport | C2 | | |
| Lower Bridge Street | C2 | | |
| Lower Chantry Lane | C2 | | |
| Marlowe Avenue | B3 | | |
| Martyrs' Field Road | A3 | | |
| Mead Way | A2 | | |
| Military Road | C1 | | |
| Monastery Street | C2 | | |
| New Dover Road | C3 | | |
| North Holmes Road | C1 | | |
| North Lane | A1 | | |
| Nunnery Fields | C3 | | |
| Oaten Hill | C3 | | |
| Old Dover Road | C3 | | |
| Orchard Street | A1 | | |
| Oxford Road | B3 | | |
| Palace Street | B2 | | |
| Pin Hill | A3 | | |
| Pound Lane | A1 | | |
| Puckle Lane | C3 | | |
| Rheims Way | A2 | | |
| Rhodaus Town | B3 | | |
| Roper Road | A1 | | |
| Rose Lane | B2 | | |
| St. Dunstan's Street | A1 | | |
| St. George's Lane | B2 | | |
| St. George's Place | C2 | | |
| St. George's Street | B2 | | |
| St. Gregory's Road | C1 | | |
| St. Margarets Street | B2 | | |
| St. Peter's Lane | B1 | | |
| St. Peter's Place | A2 | | |
| St. Peter's Street | A1 | | |
| St. Radigund's Street | B1 | | |
| St. Stephen's Road | B1 | | |
| Simmonds Road | A3 | | |
| Station Road East | A3 | | |
| Station Road West | A1 | | |
| Stour Street | A2 | | |
| The Causeway | B1 | | |
| The Friar's | B2 | | |
| Tourtel Road | C1 | | |
| Tudor Road | A3 | | |
| Union Street | C1 | | |
| Upper Bridge Street | B3 | | |

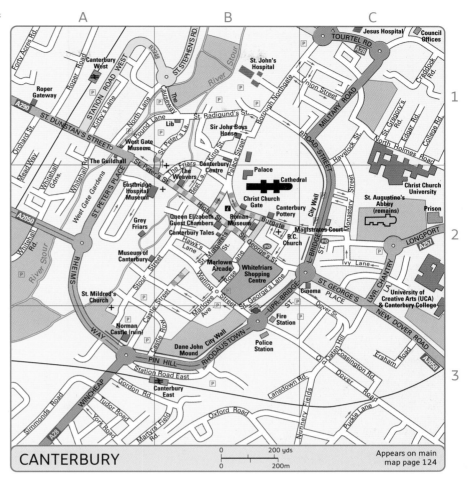

CANTERBURY

0 — 200 yds
0 — 200m

Appears on main
map page 124

**Tourist Information Centre: The Old Library, Trinity Street**
**Tel: 0870 1211 258**

| | | | |
|---|---|---|---|
| Adam Street | C3 | Moira Terrace | C2 |
| Albany Road | C1 | Moy Road | C1 |
| Allerton Street | A3 | Museum Avenue | B1 |
| Arran Place | C1 | Neville Street | A2 |
| Arran Street | C1 | Newport Road | C2 |
| Basil Place | B1 | Newport Road Lane | C2 |
| Bedford Street | C1 | Ninian Park Road | A3 |
| Boulevard de Nantes | B2 | North Road | A1 |
| Bridge Street | B3 | Oxford Lane | C2 |
| Brook Street | A3 | Park Grove | B2 |
| Bute Street | B3 | Park Place | B1 |
| Bute Terrace | B3 | Park Street | B3 |
| Castle Street | A2 | Partridge Road | C1 |
| Cathays Terrace | B1 | Penarth Road | B3 |
| Cathedral Road | A2 | Pendyris Street | A3 |
| Celerity Drive | C3 | Pitman Street | A2 |
| Central Link | C3 | Planet Street | C2 |
| Charles Street | B2 | Queen Street | B2 |
| Churchill Way | C2 | Rhymney Street | B1 |
| City Road | C1 | Richard Street | B1 |
| Clare Road | A3 | Richmond Road | C1 |
| Clare Street | A2 | Ryder Street | A2 |
| Claude Road | C1 | St. Mary Street | B3 |
| Coburn Street | B1 | St. Peters Street | C2 |
| College Road | B2 | Salisbury Road | B1 |
| Colum Road | A1 | Schooner Way | C3 |
| Corbett Road | B1 | Senghennydd Road | B1 |
| Cornwall Street | A3 | Stafford Road | A3 |
| Cottrell Road | C1 | Strathnairn Street | C1 |
| Cowbridge Road East | A2 | Stuttgarter Strasse | B3 |
| Craddock Street | A3 | Taffs Mead Embankment | B3 |
| Craiglee Drive | C3 | Talbot Street | A2 |
| Croft Street | C1 | Thesiger Street | B1 |
| Crwys Road | C1 | The Parade | C2 |
| Cufartha Street | C1 | The Walk | C1 |
| De Burgh Street | A2 | Tudor Street | A3 |
| Despenser Street | A3 | Tyndall Street | C3 |
| Duke Street | B2 | Wedmore Road | A3 |
| Dumfries Place | C2 | Wells Street | A3 |
| Ellen Street | C3 | West Grove | C2 |
| Elm Street | C1 | Westgate Street | B2 |
| Fanny Street | B1 | Windsor Place | B2 |
| Fitzhamon Embankment | A3 | Windsor Road | C2 |
| Flora Street | B1 | Wood Street | B3 |
| Glossop Road | C1 | Woodville Road | B1 |
| Gordon Road | C1 | Wordsworth Avenue | C2 |
| Greyfriars Road | B2 | Working Street | B2 |
| Hamilton Street | A2 | Wyeverne Road | B1 |
| Harriet Street | B1 | | |
| Herbert Street | C3 | | |
| High Street | B2 | | |
| Hirwain Street | B1 | | |
| Keppoch Street | C1 | | |
| Kingsway | B2 | | |
| Lewis Street | A2 | | |
| Longcross Street | C2 | | |
| Maindy Road | A1 | | |
| Mardy Street | A3 | | |
| Mark Street | A2 | | |
| Merches Gardens | A3 | | |
| Merthyr Street | B1 | | |
| Meteor Street | C3 | | |
| Mill Lane | B3 | | |
| Minny Street | B1 | | |
| Miskin Street | B1 | | |
| Moira Place | C2 | | |

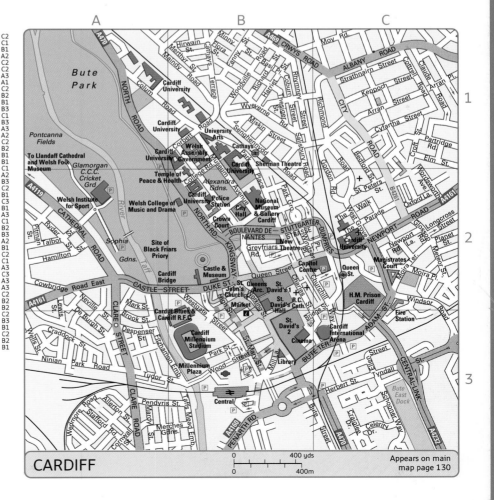

CARDIFF

0 — 400 yds
0 — 400m

Appears on main
map page 130

# Carlisle   Cheltenham

**CARLISLE**

Appears on main map page 210

**Tourist Information Centre: Old Town Hall, Green Market**
**Tel: 01228 625600**

| | | | | |
|---|---|---|---|---|
| Abbey Street | B2 | Lancaster Street | C3 |
| Aglionby Street | C2 | Lime Street | B3 |
| Albion Street | C3 | Lindon Street | C3 |
| Alexander Street | C3 | Lismore Place | C2 |
| Alfred Street | C2 | Lismore Street | C2 |
| Ashley Street | A2 | London Road | C3 |
| Bank Street | B2 | Lonsdale | B2 |
| Bassenthwaite Street | A3 | Lorne Crescent | B3 |
| Bedford Road | A3 | Lorne Street | B3 |
| Botchergate | B3 | Lowther Street | B2 |
| Brampton Road | B1 | Marlborough Gardens | B1 |
| Bridge Lane | A2 | Mary Street | B3 |
| Bridge Street | A2 | Metcalfe Street | B3 |
| Broad Street | C2 | Milbourne Street | B2 |
| Brook Street | C3 | Morton Street | A2 |
| Brunswick Street | C2 | Myddleton Street | C2 |
| Byron Street | A2 | Nelson Street | A3 |
| Caldcotes | A2 | Newcastle Street | A2 |
| Carlton Gardens | B1 | Norfolk Road | A3 |
| Castle Street | B2 | Norfolk Street | A3 |
| Castle Way | B2 | Peel Street | A2 |
| Cavendish Terrace | B1 | Petteril Street | C2 |
| Cecil Street | C2 | Port Road | A2 |
| Charlotte Street | B3 | Portland Place | C3 |
| Chatsworth Square | C2 | Rickergate | B2 |
| Chiswick Street | C2 | Rigg Street | A2 |
| Church Lane | B1 | River Street | B3 |
| Church Road | B1 | Robert Street | B3 |
| Church Street | A2 | Rome Street | B3 |
| Clifton Street | A3 | Rydal Street | C3 |
| Close Street | C3 | St. George's Crescent | B1 |
| Collingwood Street | B3 | St. James Road | A3 |
| Colville Street | A3 | St. Nicholas Street | C3 |
| Crown Street | B3 | Scawfell Road | A3 |
| Currock Road | B3 | Scotch Street | B2 |
| Currock Street | B3 | Scotland Road | B1 |
| Dale Street | B3 | Shaddongate | A2 |
| Denton Street | B3 | Silloth Street | A2 |
| Dunmail Drive | A3 | Skiddaw Road | A3 |
| East Dale Street | B3 | Spencer Street | C2 |
| East Norfolk Street | B3 | Stanhope Road | A2 |
| Eden Bridge | B1 | Strand Road | C2 |
| Edward Street | C3 | Sybil Street | C3 |
| Elm Street | B3 | Tait Street | C3 |
| English Street | B2 | Talbot Road | A3 |
| Etterby Street | B1 | Trafalgar Street | B3 |
| Finkle Street | B2 | Viaduct Estate Road | B2 |
| Fisher Street | B2 | Victoria Place | C2 |
| Fusehill Street | C3 | Victoria Viaduct | B3 |
| Georgian Way | B2 | Warwick Road | B2 |
| Goschen Road | A3 | Warwick Square | C2 |
| Graham Street | B3 | Water Street | B3 |
| Granville Road | A2 | Weardale Road | A3 |
| Greta Avenue | A3 | West Tower Street | B2 |
| Grey Street | C3 | West Walls | B2 |
| Hardwicke Circus | B1 | Westmorland Street | B3 |
| Hart Street | C2 | Wigton Road | A2 |
| Hartington Place | C2 | Willow Holme Road | A1 |
| Hawick Street | A2 | | |
| Howard Place | C2 | | |
| Infirmary Street | A2 | | |
| James Street | B3 | | |
| John Street | A2 | | |
| Junction Street | A2 | | |
| Kendal Street | A2 | | |
| King Street | C3 | | |

**CHELTENHAM**

Appears on main map page 146

**Tourist Information Centre: 77 Promenade**
**Tel: 01242 522878**

| | | | | |
|---|---|---|---|---|
| Albany Road | A3 | Portland Street | B2 |
| Albert Road | C1 | Prestbury Road | C1 |
| Albion Street | B2 | Princes Road | A3 |
| All Saints Road | C2 | Priory Street | C3 |
| Andover Road | A3 | Promenade | B2 |
| Arle Avenue | A1 | Rodney Road | B2 |
| Ashford Road | A3 | Rosehill Street | C3 |
| Bath Parade | B2 | Royal Well Road | B2 |
| Bath Road | B3 | St. George's Place | B2 |
| Bayshill Road | A2 | St. George's Road | A2 |
| Berkeley Street | B2 | St. James Street | B2 |
| Brunswick Street | B1 | St. Johns Avenue | B2 |
| Carlton Street | C2 | St. Margaret's Road | B1 |
| Central Cross Drive | C1 | St. Paul's Road | B1 |
| Christchurch Road | A2 | St. Paul's Street North | B1 |
| Churchill Drive | C3 | St. Paul's Street South | B1 |
| Clarence Road | B1 | St. Stephen's Road | A3 |
| College Lawn | B3 | Sandford Mill Road | C3 |
| College Road | B3 | Sandford Road | B3 |
| Cranham Road | C3 | Sherborne Street | C2 |
| Douro Road | A2 | Southgate Drive | C3 |
| Dunalley Street | B1 | Strickland Road | C3 |
| Eldon Road | C2 | Suffolk Road | A3 |
| Evesham Road | C1 | Suffolk Square | A3 |
| Fairview Road | C2 | Sun Street | A1 |
| Folly Lane | B1 | Swindon Road | A1 |
| Gloucester Road | A2 | Sydenham Road | C2 |
| Grafton Road | A3 | Sydenham Villas Road | C3 |
| Hales Road | C3 | Tewkesbury Road | A1 |
| Hanover Street | B1 | Thirlestaine Road | B3 |
| Hayward's Road | C3 | Tivoli Road | A3 |
| Henrietta Street | B2 | Townsend Street | A1 |
| Hewlett Road | C2 | Vittoria Walk | B3 |
| High Street | B1 | Wellington Road | C1 |
| Honeybourne Way | A1 | West Drive | B1 |
| Hudson Street | B1 | Western Road | A2 |
| Imperial Square | B2 | Whaddon Road | C1 |
| Keynsham Road | B3 | Winchcombe Street | B2 |
| King Alfred Way | C3 | Windsor Street | C1 |
| King's Road | C2 | | |
| Lansdown Crescent | A3 | | |
| Lansdown Road | A3 | | |
| London Road | C3 | | |
| Lypiatt Road | A3 | | |
| Malvern Road | A2 | | |
| Market Street | A1 | | |
| Marle Hill Parade | B1 | | |
| Marle Hill Road | B1 | | |
| Millbrook Street | A1 | | |
| Montpellier Spa Road | B3 | | |
| Montpellier Street | A3 | | |
| Montpellier Terrace | A3 | | |
| Montpellier Walk | A3 | | |
| New Street | A2 | | |
| North Place | B2 | | |
| North Street | B2 | | |
| Old Bath Road | C3 | | |
| Oriel Road | B2 | | |
| Overton Road | A2 | | |
| Painswick Road | A3 | | |
| Parabola Road | A2 | | |
| Park Place | A3 | | |
| Park Street | A1 | | |
| Pittville Circus | C1 | | |
| Pittville Circus Road | C2 | | |
| Pittville Lawn | C1 | | |

## Chester

Tourist Information Centre: Town Hall, Northgate Street
Tel: 01244 402111

| | |
|---|---|
| Bath Street | C2 |
| Bedward Row | A2 |
| Black Diamond Street | B1 |
| Black Friars | A3 |
| Bold Square | B2 |
| Boughton | C2 |
| Bouverie Street | A1 |
| Bridge Street | B2 |
| Brook Street | B1 |
| Canal Street | A1 |
| Castle Drive | A3 |
| Charles Street | B1 |
| Cheyney Road | A1 |
| Chichester Street | A1 |
| City Road | C2 |
| City Walls Road | A2 |
| Commonhall Street | A2 |
| Cornwall Street | B1 |
| Crewe Street | C1 |
| Cuppin Street | A3 |
| Dee Hills Park | C2 |
| Dee Lane | C2 |
| Deva Terrace | C2 |
| Duke Street | B3 |
| Eastgate Street | B2 |
| Edinburgh Way | C3 |
| Egerton Street | B1 |
| Elizabeth Crescent | C3 |
| Foregate Street | B2 |
| Forest Street | B2 |
| Francis Street | C1 |
| Frodsham Street | B2 |
| Garden Lane | A1 |
| George Street | B1 |
| Gloucester Street | B1 |
| Grey Friars | A3 |
| Grosvenor Park Terrace | C2 |
| Grosvenor Road | A3 |
| Grosvenor Street | A3 |
| Handbridge | B3 |
| Hoole Road | B1 |
| Hoole Way | B1 |
| Hunter Street | A2 |
| King Street | A2 |
| Leadworks Lane | C2 |
| Lightfoot Street | C1 |
| Louise Street | A1 |
| Love Street | B2 |
| Lower Bridge Street | B3 |
| Lower Park Road | C3 |
| Mill Street | C2 |
| Milton Street | B1 |
| Newgate Street | B2 |
| Nicholas Street | A2 |
| Nicholas Street Mews | A2 |
| Northern Pathway | C3 |
| Northgate Avenue | B1 |
| Northgate Street | A2 |
| Nun's Road | A3 |
| Old Dee Bridge | B3 |
| Pepper Street | B3 |
| Phillip Street | C1 |
| Prince's Avenue | C1 |
| Princess Street | A2 |
| Queen's Avenue | C1 |
| Queen's Drive | C3 |

| | |
|---|---|
| Queen's Park Road | B3 |
| Queen's Road | C1 |
| Queen Street | B2 |
| Raymond Street | A1 |
| Russel Street | C2 |
| St. Anne Street | B1 |
| St. George's Crescent | C3 |
| St. John's Road | C3 |
| St. John Street | B2 |
| St. Martins Way | A1 |
| St. Oswalds Way | B1 |
| St. Werburgh Street | B2 |
| Seller Street | C2 |
| Sibell Street | C1 |
| Souter's Lane | B3 |
| Stanley Street | A2 |
| Station Road | C1 |
| Steam Mill Street | C2 |
| Talbot Street | B1 |
| The Bars | C2 |
| The Groves | B3 |
| Trafford Street | B1 |
| Union Street | B2 |
| Upper Northgate Street | A1 |
| Vicar's Lane | B2 |
| Victoria Crescent | C3 |
| Victoria Place | B2 |
| Victoria Road | A1 |
| Walker Street | C1 |
| Walpole Street | A1 |
| Walter Street | B1 |
| Watergate Street | A2 |
| Water Tower Street | A2 |
| Weaver Street | A2 |
| White Friars | A3 |
| York Street | B2 |

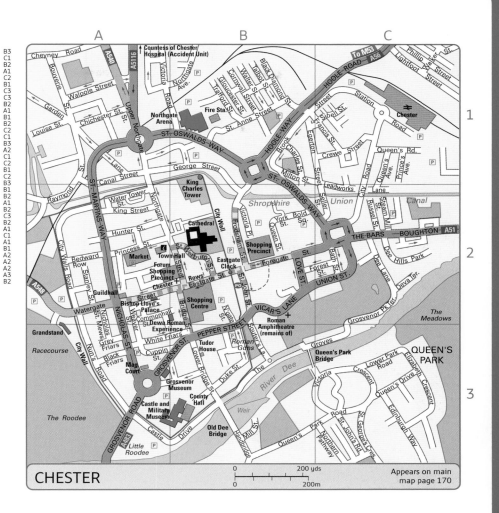

**CHESTER**

0 — 200 yds / 0 — 200m

Appears on main
map page 170

## Coventry

Tourist Information Centre: St. Michael's Tower, Coventry
Cathedral   Tel: 024 7622 7264

| | |
|---|---|
| Abbott's Lane | A1 |
| Acacia Avenue | C3 |
| Albany Road | A3 |
| Alma Street | C2 |
| Asthill Grove | B3 |
| Barker's Butts Lane | A1 |
| Barras Lane | A2 |
| Berry Street | C1 |
| Bishop Street | B1 |
| Blythe Road | C1 |
| Bond Street | A2 |
| Bramble Street | C2 |
| Bretts Close | C1 |
| Broadway | A3 |
| Burges | B2 |
| Butts Road | A2 |
| Cambridge Street | C1 |
| Canterbury Street | C1 |
| Clifton Street | C1 |
| Colchester Street | C1 |
| Cornwall Road | C3 |
| Corporation Street | B2 |
| Coundon Road | A1 |
| Coundon Street | A1 |
| Cox Street | C2 |
| Croft Road | A2 |
| Drapers Fields | B1 |
| Earl Street | B2 |
| East Street | C2 |
| Eaton Road | B3 |
| Fairfax Street | B2 |
| Far Gosford Street | C2 |
| Foleshill Road | B1 |
| Fowler Road | A1 |
| Gordon Street | A3 |
| Gosford Street | C2 |
| Greyfriars Road | A2 |
| Gulson Road | C2 |
| Hales Street | B2 |
| Harnall Lane East | C1 |
| Harnall Lane West | B1 |
| Harper Road | C2 |
| Harper Street | B2 |
| Hertford Street | B2 |
| Hewitt Avenue | A1 |
| High Street | B2 |
| Hill Street | B2 |
| Holyhead Road | A2 |
| Hood Street | C2 |
| Howard Street | B1 |
| Jordan Well | B2 |
| King William Street | C1 |
| Lamb Street | B2 |
| Leicester Row | B1 |
| Leigh Street | C1 |
| Little Park Street | B3 |
| London Road | C3 |
| Lower Ford Street | C2 |
| Market Way | B2 |
| Meadow Street | A2 |
| Michaelmas Road | A3 |
| Middleborough Road | A1 |
| Mile Lane | B3 |
| Mill Street | A1 |
| Minster Road | A2 |
| Much Park Street | B2 |

| | |
|---|---|
| New Union Street | B2 |
| Norfolk Street | A2 |
| Oxford Street | C2 |
| Park Road | B3 |
| Parkside | B3 |
| Primrose Hill Street | C1 |
| Priory Street | B2 |
| Puma Way | B3 |
| Quarryfield Lane | C3 |
| Queen's Road | A3 |
| Queen Street | C1 |
| Queen Victoria Road | A2 |
| Quinton Road | B3 |
| Radford Road | A1 |
| Raglan Street | C2 |
| Regent Street | A3 |
| Ringway Hill Cross | A2 |
| Ringway Queens | A2 |
| Ringway Rudge | A2 |
| Ringway St. Johns | B3 |
| Ringway St. Nicholas | B1 |
| Ringway St. Patricks | B3 |
| Ringway Swanswell | B2 |
| Ringway Whitefriars | C2 |
| St. Nicholas Street | B1 |
| Sandy Lane | B1 |
| Seagrave Road | C3 |
| Silver Street | B1 |
| Sky Blue Way | C2 |
| South Street | C2 |
| Spencer Avenue | A3 |
| Spon Street | A2 |
| Srathmore Avenue | C3 |
| Stoney Road | B3 |
| Stoney Stanton Road | B1 |
| Swanswell Street | B1 |
| The Precinct | B2 |
| Tomson Avenue | A1 |
| Trinity Street | B2 |
| Upper Hill Street | A2 |
| Upper Well Street | B2 |
| Vauxhall Street | C2 |
| Vecqueray Street | C2 |
| Victoria Street | C1 |
| Vine Street | C1 |
| Warwick Road | A3 |
| Waveley Road | A2 |
| Westminster Road | A3 |
| White Street | B1 |
| Windsor Street | A2 |
| Wright Street | C1 |

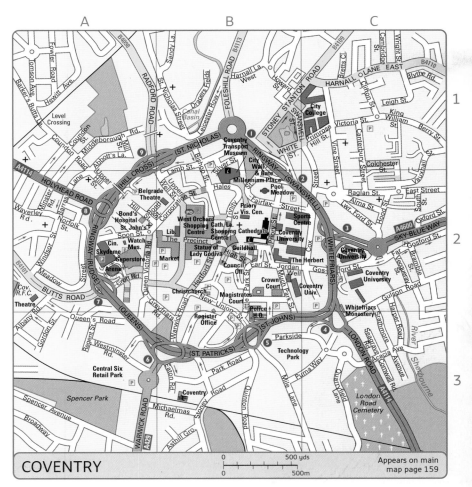

**COVENTRY**

0 — 500 yds / 0 — 500m

Appears on main
map page 159

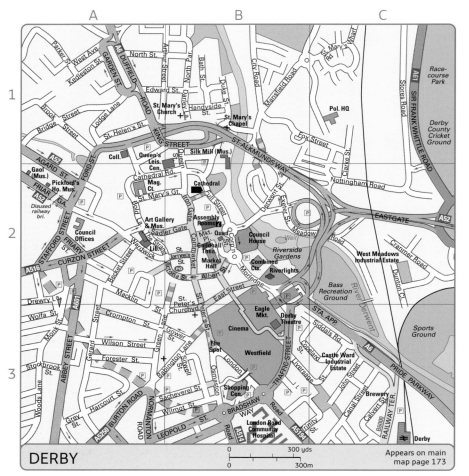

| | | | | |
|---|---|---|---|---|
| Abbey Street | A3 | Pride Parkway | C3 |
| Agard Street | A1 | Queen Street | B1 |
| Albert Street | B2 | Railway Terrace | C3 |
| Arthur Street | A1 | Sacheverel Street | A3 |
| Babington Lane | A3 | Sadler Gate | B2 |
| Bath Street | B1 | St. Alkmunds Way | B1 |
| Becket Street | A2 | St. Helen's Street | A1 |
| Bold Lane | A2 | St. James Street | B2 |
| Bradshaw Way | B3 | St. Mary's Gate | A2 |
| Bridge Street | A1 | St. Mary's Wharf Road | C1 |
| Brook Street | A1 | St. Peter's Churchyard | B3 |
| Burton Road | A3 | St. Peter's Street | B2 |
| Calvert Street | C3 | Siddals Road | C3 |
| Canal Street | C3 | Sir Frank Whittle Road | C1 |
| Cathedral Road | A2 | Sitwell Street | B3 |
| City Road | B1 | Stafford Street | A2 |
| Clarke Street | C2 | Station Approach | C2 |
| Copeland Street | B3 | Stockbrook Street | A3 |
| Cornmarket | B2 | Stores Road | C1 |
| Corporation Street | B2 | The Strand | A2 |
| Crammer Road | C2 | Traffic Street | B3 |
| Crompton Street | A3 | Trinity Street | B3 |
| Curzon Street | A2 | Victoria Street | A2 |
| Darley Lane | B1 | Wardwick | A2 |
| Derwent Street | B2 | West Avenue | A1 |
| Drewry Lane | A2 | Wilmot Street | A3 |
| Duffield Road | A1 | Wilson Street | A3 |
| Duke Street | B1 | Wolfa Street | A3 |
| Dunton Close | A3 | Woods Lane | A3 |
| Eastgate | C2 | | |
| East Street | B2 | | |
| Edward Street | A1 | | |
| Exeter Street | B2 | | |
| Ford Street | A2 | | |
| Forester Street | A3 | | |
| Fox Street | B1 | | |
| Friar Gate | A2 | | |
| Friary Street | A2 | | |
| Full Street | B2 | | |
| Garden Street | A1 | | |
| Gerard Street | A3 | | |
| Gower Street | B3 | | |
| Green Lane | A3 | | |
| Grey Street | A3 | | |
| Handyside Street | B1 | | |
| Harcourt Street | A3 | | |
| Iron Gate | B2 | | |
| John Street | C3 | | |
| Kedleston Street | A1 | | |
| King Street | A1 | | |
| Leopold Street | A3 | | |
| Liversage Street | B3 | | |
| Lodge Lane | A1 | | |
| London Road | B3 | | |
| Macklin Street | A2 | | |
| Mansfield Road | B1 | | |
| Market Place | B2 | | |
| Meadow Road | B2 | | |
| Monk Street | A3 | | |
| Morledge | B2 | | |
| Normanton Road | A3 | | |
| North Parade | B1 | | |
| North Street | A1 | | |
| Nottingham Road | C2 | | |
| Osmaston Road | B3 | | |
| Parker Street | A1 | | |

Appears on main map page 173

DERBY

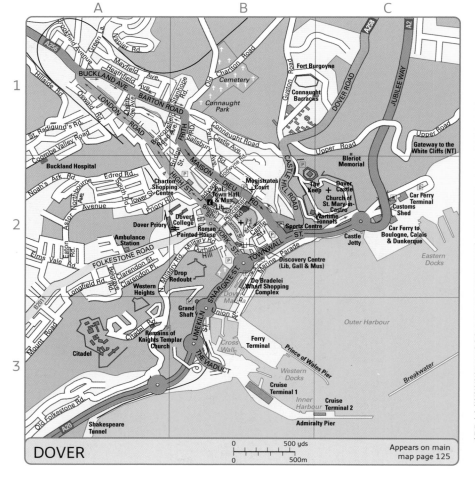

| | | | |
|---|---|---|---|
| Astor Avenue | A2 | | |
| Barton Road | A1 | | |
| Beaconsfield Avenue | A1 | | |
| Beaconsfield Road | A1 | | |
| Belgrave Road | A2 | | |
| Biggin Street | B2 | | |
| Bridge Street | B2 | | |
| Brookfield Avenue | A1 | | |
| Buckland Avenue | A1 | | |
| Cannon Street | B2 | | |
| Canons Gate Road | B2 | | |
| Castle Avenue | B1 | | |
| Castle Hill Road | B2 | | |
| Castle Street | B2 | | |
| Cherry Tree Avenue | A1 | | |
| Citadel Road | A3 | | |
| Clarendon Place | A2 | | |
| Clarendon Street | A2 | | |
| Connaught Road | B1 | | |
| Coombe Valley Road | A2 | | |
| Dover Road | C1 | | |
| Durham Hill | B2 | | |
| Eaton Road | A2 | | |
| Edred Road | A2 | | |
| Elms Vale Road | A2 | | |
| Folkestone Road | A2 | | |
| Frith Road | B1 | | |
| Godwyne Road | B2 | | |
| Green Lane | A1 | | |
| Guston Road | B1 | | |
| Heathfield Avenue | A1 | | |
| High Street | B2 | | |
| Hillside Road | A1 | | |
| Jubilee Way | C1 | | |
| Ladywell | B2 | | |
| Limekiln Street | B3 | | |
| London Road | A1 | | |
| Longfield Road | A2 | | |
| Maison Dieu Road | B2 | | |
| Marine Parade | B2 | | |
| Mayfield Avenue | A1 | | |
| Military Road | B2 | | |
| Mount Road | A3 | | |
| Napier Road | A1 | | |
| Noah's Ark Road | A2 | | |
| Northbourne Avenue | A2 | | |
| North Military Road | A2 | | |
| Old Charlton Road | B1 | | |
| Old Folkestone Road | A3 | | |
| Oswald Road | A1 | | |
| Park Avenue | B1 | | |
| Pencester Road | B2 | | |
| Priory Hill | A2 | | |
| St. Radigund's Road | A1 | | |
| Salisbury Road | B1 | | |
| Snargate Street | B3 | | |
| South Road | A2 | | |
| Stanhope Road | B1 | | |
| The Viaduct | B3 | | |
| Tower Street | A2 | | |
| Townwall Street | B2 | | |
| Union Street | B3 | | |
| Upper Road | C1 | | |
| York Street | B2 | | |

Appears on main map page 125

DOVER

**Tourist Information Centre: Discovery Point, Discovery Quay**
**Tel: 01382 527527**

| | |
|---|---|
| Adelaide Place | A1 |
| Albany Terrace | A1 |
| Albert Street | C2 |
| Alexander Street | B1 |
| Ann Street | B2 |
| Arbroath Road | C2 |
| Arklay Street | C1 |
| Arklay Terrace | C1 |
| Arthurstone Terrace | C2 |
| Barrack Road | A2 |
| Blackness Road | A2 |
| Blinshall Street | A2 |
| Brewery Lane | A2 |
| Brook Street | A2 |
| Broughty Ferry Road | C2 |
| Brown Street | A2 |
| Bruce Street | A1 |
| Byron Street | A1 |
| Canning Street | B1 |
| City Square | B3 |
| Clepington Road | C1 |
| Constitution Road | B2 |
| Constitution Street | B1 |
| Court Street | C1 |
| Cowgate Street | B2 |
| Dens Road | B1 |
| Douglas Street | A2 |
| Dudhope Street | A1 |
| Dudhope Terrace | C1 |
| Dundonald Street | C1 |
| Dura Street | C2 |
| East Dock Street | C2 |
| East Marketgait | B2 |
| Fairbairn Street | B1 |
| Greenmarket | B3 |
| Guthrie Street | A2 |
| Hawkhill | A2 |
| High Street | B3 |
| Hill Street | B1 |
| Hilltown | B1 |
| Kenmore Terrace | A1 |
| Killin Avenue | A1 |
| Kinghorne Road | A1 |
| King Street | B2 |
| Larch Street | A2 |
| Law Crescent | A1 |
| Lawside Avenue | A1 |
| Law Street | A1 |
| Leng Street | A1 |
| Lochee Road | A2 |
| Lower Princes Street | C2 |
| Mains Road | B1 |
| Main Street | B1 |
| Meadowside | B2 |
| Morgan Street | C2 |
| Murraygate | B2 |
| Nelson Street | B2 |
| Nethergate | A3 |
| North Marketgait | A2 |
| Perth Road | A3 |
| Polepark Road | A2 |
| Princes Street | C2 |
| Riverside Drive | A3 |
| Roseangle | A3 |
| Rosebank Road | B2 |
| Seagate | B2 |

| | |
|---|---|
| South Marketgait | B3 |
| South Tay Street | A3 |
| Strathmartine Road | B1 |
| Tannadice Street | B1 |
| Tay Road Bridge | B3 |
| Trades Lane | B2 |
| Upper Constitution Street | A1 |
| Victoria Road | B2 |
| Victoria Street | C2 |
| Ward Road | A2 |
| West Marketgait | A2 |
| West Port | A2 |
| William Street | C2 |

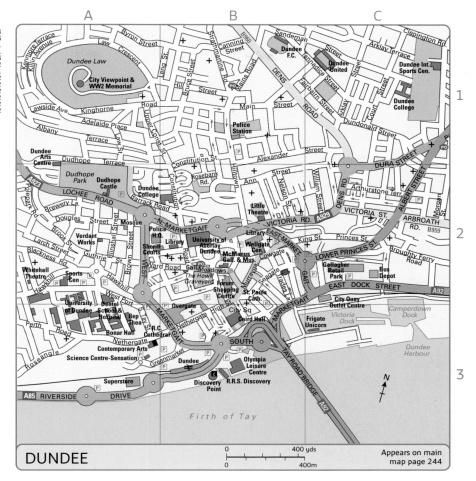

**DUNDEE**

0 ___ 400 yds
0 ___ 400m

Appears on main
map page 244

**Tourist Information Centre: 2 Millennium Place**
**Tel: 0191 384 3720**

| | |
|---|---|
| Aykley Heads | A1 |
| Church Street | B3 |
| Clay Lane | A3 |
| Claypath | B2 |
| Crossgate | B2 |
| Crossgate Peth | A3 |
| Darlington Road | A3 |
| Dryburn Road | A1 |
| Durham Road | A1 |
| Fieldhouse Lane | A1 |
| Framwelgate | B2 |
| Framwelgate Peth | B1 |
| Framwelgate Waterside | B2 |
| Gilesgate | C2 |
| Great North Road | A1 |
| Green Lane | C2 |
| Grove Street | B3 |
| Hallgarth Street | C3 |
| Hawthorn Terrace | A2 |
| Leazes Road | B2 |
| Margery Lane | B3 |
| Market Place | B2 |
| Millburngate Bridge | B2 |
| Newcastle Road | A1 |
| New Elvet | B2 |
| North Bailey | B2 |
| North End | A1 |
| North Road | B2 |
| Old Elvet | C2 |
| Pity Me Bypass | A1 |
| Potters Bank | A3 |
| Quarryheads Lane | B3 |
| Providence Row | B2 |
| Redhills Lane | A2 |
| St. Monica Grove | A2 |
| Sidegate | B2 |
| Silver Street | B2 |
| South Bailey | B3 |
| South Road | B3 |
| South Street | B3 |
| Southfield Way | A1 |
| Stockton Road | B3 |
| Sutton Street | B2 |
| The Avenue | A3 |
| Toll House Road | A2 |
| Western Hill | A2 |
| Whinney Hill | C3 |
| Whitesmocks | A1 |

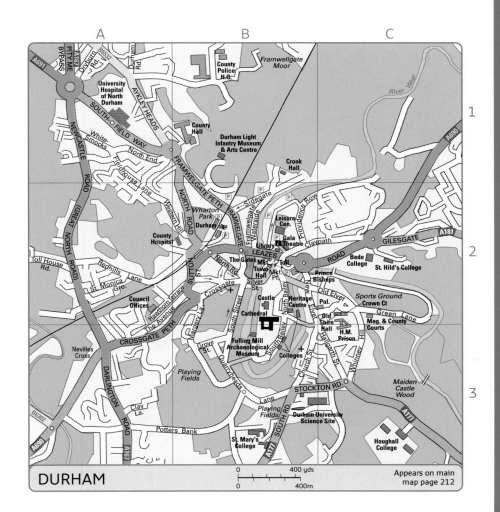

**DURHAM**

0 ___ 400 yds
0 ___ 400m

Appears on main
map page 212

Edinburgh street map on pages 36-37

EASTBOURNE

Appears on main map page 110

Appears on main map page 110

**Tourist Information Centre: 3 Cornfield Road**
**Tel: 0871 663 0031**

|  |  |
|---|---|
| Arlington Road | A2 |
| Arundel Road | B1 |
| Ashford Road | B2/C2 |
| Avondale Road | C1 |
| Bedforwell Road | B1 |
| Belmore Road | C1 |
| Blackwater Road | B3 |
| Borough Lane | A1 |
| Bourne Street | C2 |
| Carew Road | A1/B1 |
| Carlisle Road | A3 |
| Cavendish Avenue | C1 |
| Cavendish Place | C2 |
| College Road | B3 |
| Commercial Road | B2 |
| Compton Place Road | A2 |
| Compton Street | B3 |
| Cornfield Terrace | B2 |
| Denton Road | A3 |
| Devonshire Place | B2 |
| Dittons Road | A2 |
| Dursley Road | C2 |
| Enys Road | B1 |
| Eversfield Road | B1 |
| Fairfield Road | A3 |
| Firle Road | C1 |
| Furness Road | B3 |
| Gaudick Road | A3 |
| Gilbert Road | C1 |
| Gildredge Road | B2 |
| Gorringe Road | B1 |
| Grand Parade | C3 |
| Grange Road | B3 |
| Grassington Road | B3 |
| Grove Road | B2 |
| Hartfield Road | B1 |
| Hartington Place | C2 |
| High Street | A1 |
| Hyde Gardens | B2 |
| King Edward's Parade | B3 |
| Langney Road | C2 |
| Lewes Road | B1 |
| Marine Parade | C2 |
| Mark Lane | B2 |
| Meads Road | A3 |
| Melbourne Road | C1 |
| Mill Gap Road | A1 |
| Mill Road | A1 |
| Moat Croft Road | A1 |
| Moy Avenue | C1 |
| Ratton Road | A1 |
| Royal Parade | C2 |
| Saffrons Park | A3 |
| Saffrons Road | A2 |
| St. Anne's Road | A1 |
| St. Leonard's Road | B2 |
| Seaside | C2 |
| Seaside Road | C2 |
| Selwyn Road | A1 |
| Silverdale Road | B3 |
| South Street | B2 |
| Southfields Road | A2 |
| Station Parade | B2 |
| Susan's Road | C2 |
| Sydney Road | C2 |
| Terminus Road | B2 |
| The Avenue | B2 |
| The Goffs | A1 |
| Trinity Trees | C2 |
| Upper Avenue | B1 |
| Upperton Lane | B2 |
| Upperton Road | A1 |
| Watts Lane | A1 |
| Whitley Road | A1 |
| Willingdon Road | A1 |
| Winchcombe Road | C1 |

EXETER

Appears on main map page 102

Appears on main map page 102

**Tourist Information Centre: Dix's Field**
**Tel: 01392 665700**

|  |  |
|---|---|
| Albion Street | A3 |
| Alphington Street | A3 |
| Barnfield Road | B2 |
| Bartholomew Street West | A2 |
| Bedford Street | B2 |
| Belmont Road | C1 |
| Blackboy Road | C1 |
| Blackall Road | B1 |
| Bonhay Road | A2 |
| Buller Road | A3 |
| Church Road | A3 |
| Clifton Hill | C1 |
| Clifton Road | C2 |
| Clifton Street | C2 |
| College Road | C2 |
| Commercial Road | B3 |
| Cowick Street | A3 |
| Cowley Bridge Road | A1 |
| Danes Road | B1 |
| Denmark Road | C2 |
| Devonshire Place | C1 |
| Dix's Field | B2 |
| East Grove Road | C3 |
| Elmside | C1 |
| Exe Street | A2 |
| Fore Street | B2 |
| Haldon Road | A2 |
| Haven Road | B3 |
| Heavitree Road | C2 |
| Hele Road | A1 |
| High Street | B2 |
| Holloway Street | B3 |
| Hoopern Street | B1 |
| Howell Road | B1 |
| Iddesleigh Road | C1 |
| Iron Bridge | A2 |
| Isca Road | B3 |
| Jesmond Road | C1 |
| Longbrook Street | B1 |
| Looe Road | A1 |
| Lyndhurst Road | C3 |
| Magdalen Road | C2 |
| Magdalen Street | B3 |
| Marlborough Road | C3 |
| Matford Avenue | C3 |
| Matford Lane | C3 |
| Mount Pleasant Road | C1 |
| New Bridge Street | A3 |
| New North Road | A1/B1 |
| North Street | B2 |
| Okehampton Road | A3 |
| Okehampton Street | A3 |
| Old Tiverton Road | C1 |
| Oxford Road | C1 |
| Paris Street | B2 |
| Paul Street | B2 |
| Pennsylvania Road | B1 |
| Portland Street | C2 |
| Prince of Wales Road | A1 |
| Princesshay | B2 |
| Prospect Park | C1 |
| Queen's Road | A3 |
| Queen Street | B2 |
| Radford Road | C3 |
| Richmond Road | A2 |
| St. David's Hill | A1 |
| St. James' Road | C1 |
| St. Leonard's Road | C3 |
| Sidwell Street | B2 |
| Southernhay East | B2 |
| South Street | B2 |
| Spicer Road | C2 |
| Station Road | A1 |
| Streatham Drive | A1 |
| Streatham Rise | A1 |
| The Quay | B3 |
| Thornton Hill | B1 |
| Topsham Road | B3 |
| Velwell Road | A1 |
| Victoria Street | C1 |
| Water Lane | B3 |
| Well Street | C1 |
| West Avenue | B1 |
| Western Road | A2 |
| Western Way | C2 |
| Wonford Road | C3 |
| York Road | B1 |

## Folkestone

**Tourist Information Centre: Discover Folkestone, 20 Bouverie Place. Tel: 01303 258594**

| | |
|---|---|
| Alder Road | B2 |
| Archer Road | C2 |
| Bathurst Road | A2 |
| Beatty Road | C1 |
| Black Bull Road | B2 |
| Bournemouth Road | B2 |
| Bouverie Road West | A3 |
| Bradstone Road | B2 |
| Broadfield Road | A2 |
| Broadmead Road | B2 |
| Brockman Road | B2 |
| Canterbury Road | C1 |
| Castle Hill Avenue | B3 |
| Cheriton Gardens | B3 |
| Cheriton Road | A2/B2 |
| Cherry Garden Avenue | A1 |
| Christ Church Road | B3 |
| Churchill Avenue | B1 |
| Clifton Crescent | A3 |
| Coniston Road | A1 |
| Coolinge Road | B2 |
| Cornwallis Avenue | A2 |
| Dawson Road | B2 |
| Dixwell Road | A3 |
| Dolphins Road | B1 |
| Dover Hill | C1 |
| Dover Road | C1 |
| Downs Road | B1 |
| Earles Avenue | A3 |
| Foord Road | B2 |
| Godwyn Road | A3 |
| Grimston Avenue | A3 |
| Grimston Gardens | A3 |
| Guildhall Street | B2 |
| Guildhall Street North | B2 |
| Harbour Way | C2 |
| Hill Road | C1 |
| Ivy Way | C1 |
| Joyes Road | C1 |
| Linden Crescent | B2 |
| Links Way | A1 |
| Lower Sandgate Road | A3 |
| Lucy Avenue | A1 |
| Manor Road | B3 |
| Marine Parade | B3 |
| Marshall Street | C1 |
| Mead Road | B2 |
| Old High Street | C3 |
| Park Farm Road | B1 |
| Pavilion Road | B2 |
| Radnor Bridge Road | C2 |
| Radnor Park Avenue | A2 |
| Radnor Park Road | B2 |
| Radnor Park West | A2 |
| Sandgate Hill | A3 |
| Sandgate Road | B3 |
| Shorncliffe Road | A2 |
| Sidney Street | C2 |
| The Leas | B3 |
| The Stade | C3 |
| The Tram Road | C2 |
| Tontine Street | C2 |
| Turketel Road | A3 |
| Tyson Road | C1 |
| Wear Bay Crescent | C2 |
| Wear Bay Road | C1 |
| Westbourne Gardens | A3 |
| Wingate Road | B1 |
| Wood Avenue | C1 |
| Wilton Road | A2 |

**FOLKESTONE**

0  200 yds
0  200m

Appears on main map page 125

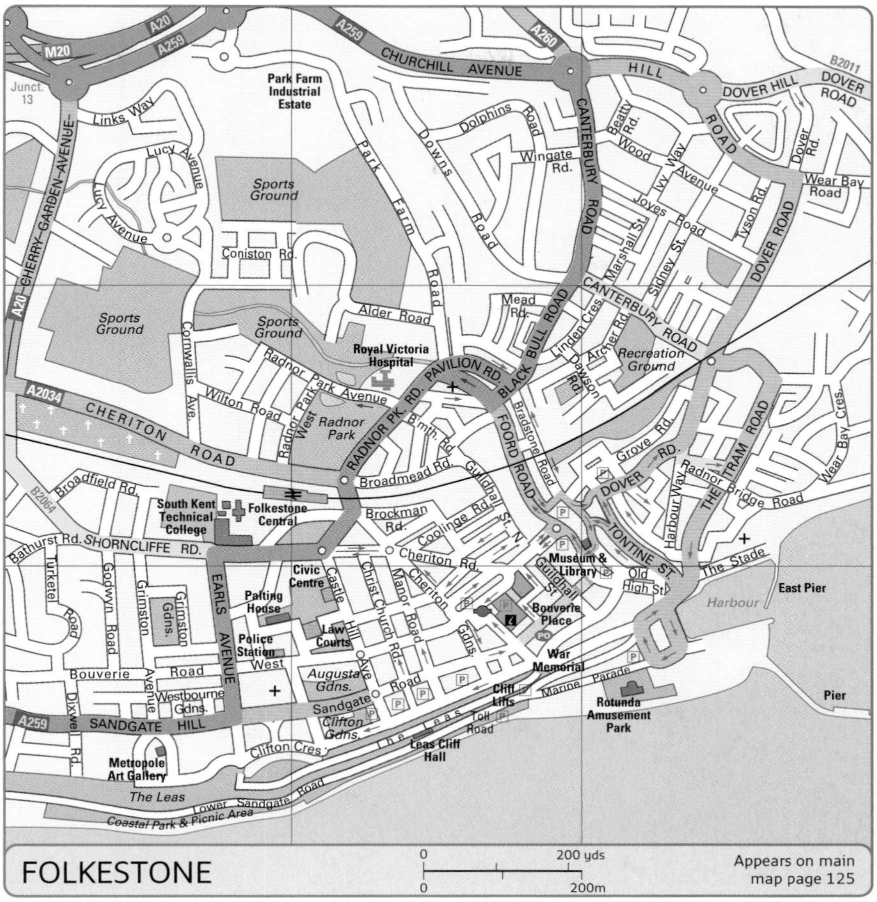

## Gloucester

**Tourist Information Centre: 28 Southgate Street Tel: 01452 396572**

| | |
|---|---|
| Adelaide Street | B3 |
| Alexandra Road | B1 |
| Alfred Street | C2 |
| Alma Place | A3 |
| Alvin Street | B1 |
| Archdeacon Street | A1 |
| Argyll Road | C1 |
| Askwith Road | C3 |
| Barnwood Road | C1 |
| Barton Street | B2 |
| Black Dog Way | B1 |
| Bristol Road | A3 |
| Brunswick Road | B2 |
| Bruton Way | B2 |
| Calton Road | B3 |
| Castle Meads Way | A1 |
| Cecil Road | A3 |
| Cheltenham Road | C1 |
| Churchill Road | A3 |
| Clifton Road | A3 |
| Conduit Street | B3 |
| Coney Hill Road | C3 |
| Dean's Way | B1 |
| Denmark Road | B1 |
| Derby Road | B2 |
| Estcourt Road | B1 |
| Eastern Avenue | C3 |
| Eastgate Street | B2 |
| Frampton Road | A3 |
| Gouda Way | A1 |
| Great Western Road | B2 |
| Greyfriars | B2 |
| Hatherley Road | B3 |
| Heathville Road | B1 |
| Hempsted Lane | A2 |
| Henry Road | B1 |
| High Street | B3 |
| Hopewell Street | B3 |
| Horton Road | C2 |
| Howard Street | B3 |
| India Road | C2 |
| King Edward's Avenue | B3 |
| Kingsholm Road | B1 |
| Lansdown Road | B1 |
| Linden Road | A3 |
| Llanthony Road | A2 |
| London Road | B1 |
| Lower Westgate Street | A1 |
| Marlborough Road | C3 |
| Merevale Road | C1 |
| Metz Way | B2 |
| Midland Road | B3 |
| Millbrook Street | B2 |
| Myers Road | C2 |
| Northgate Street | B2 |
| Oxford Road | B1 |
| Oxstalls Lane | C1 |
| Painswick Road | C3 |
| Park Road | B2 |
| Parkend Road | B3 |
| Pitt Street | B1 |
| Quay Street | A2 |
| Regent Street | B3 |
| Robinson Road | A3 |
| Ryecroft Street | B3 |
| St. Ann Way | A3 |
| St. Oswald's Road | A1 |
| Secunda Way | A3 |
| Severn Road | A2 |
| Seymour Road | A3 |
| Southgate Street | A2 |
| Spa Road | A2 |
| Stanley Road | B3 |
| Station Road | B2 |
| Stroud Road | A3 |
| The Quay | A2 |
| Tredworth Road | B3 |
| Trier Way | A3 |
| Upton Street | B3 |
| Vicarage Road | C3 |
| Victoria Street | B2 |
| Wellington Street | B2 |
| Weston Road | A3 |
| Westgate Street | A1 |
| Wheatstone Road | B3 |
| Willow Avenue | C3 |
| Worcester Street | B1 |

**GLOUCESTER**

0  500 yds
0  500m

Appears on main map page 132

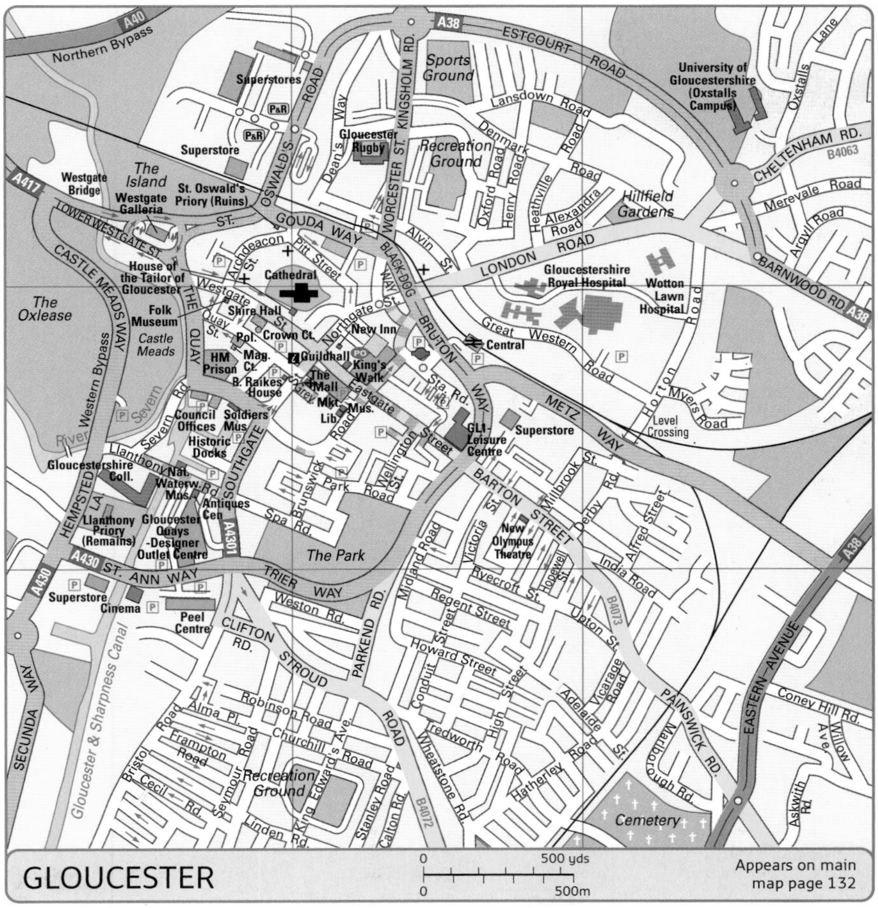

GUILDFORD

0    200 yds
0    200m

Appears on main
map page 121

**Tourist Information Centre: 14 Tunsgate**
**Tel: 01483 444333**

| | | | |
|---|---|---|---|
| Abbot Road | C3 | Portsmouth Road | B3 |
| Artillery Road | B1 | Poyle Road | C3 |
| Artillery Terrace | B1 | Quarry Street | B2 |
| Bedford Road | B1 | Queens Road | C1 |
| Bridge Street | B2 | Rookwood Court | A3 |
| Bright Hill | C2 | Rupert Road | A2 |
| Brodie Road | C2 | Sand Terrace | B1 |
| Bury Fields | B3 | Semaphore Road | C3 |
| Bury Street | B3 | South Hill | C2 |
| Castle Hill | C3 | Springfield Road | C1 |
| Castle Square | C2 | Station Approach | C1 |
| Castle Street | B2 | Station View | A1 |
| Chertsey Street | C1 | Stoke Road | C1 |
| Cheselden Road | C2 | Swan Lane | B2 |
| Commercial Road | B2 | Sydenham Road | C2 |
| Dapdune Court | B1 | Testard Road | A2 |
| Dapdune Road | B1 | The Bars | B2 |
| Dapdune Wharf | B1 | The Mount | A3 |
| Dene Road | C1 | Tunsgate | C2 |
| Denmark Road | C1 | Upperton Road | A2 |
| Denzil Road | A2 | Victoria Road | C1 |
| Drummond Road | B1 | Walnut Tree Close | A1 |
| Eagle Road | C1 | Warwicks | C3 |
| Eastgate Gardens | C1 | Wharf Road | B1 |
| Falcon Road | C1 | Wherwell Road | A2 |
| Farnham Road | A2 | William Road | B1 |
| Flower Walk | B3 | Wodeland Avenue | A3 |
| Fort Road | C3 | Woodbridge Road | B1 |
| Foxenden Road | C1 | York Road | B1 |
| Friary Bridge | B2 | | |
| Friary Street | B2 | | |
| Genyn Road | A2 | | |
| George Road | B1 | | |
| Great Quarry | C3 | | |
| Guildford Park Avenue | A1 | | |
| Guildford Park Road | A2 | | |
| Harvey Road | C2 | | |
| Haydon Place | B1 | | |
| High Pewley | C3 | | |
| High Street | B2/C2 | | |
| Laundry Road | B1 | | |
| Lawn Road | B3 | | |
| Leap Lane | B2 | | |
| Leas Road | B1 | | |
| Ludlow Road | A2 | | |
| Mareschal Road | A3 | | |
| Margaret Road | B1 | | |
| Market Street | B2 | | |
| Martyr Road | B2 | | |
| Mary Road | B1 | | |
| Millbrook | B3 | | |
| Millmead | B2 | | |
| Millmead Terrace | B3 | | |
| Mount Pleasant | A3 | | |
| Mountside | A3 | | |
| Nether Mount | A3 | | |
| Nightingale Road | C1 | | |
| North Place | B1 | | |
| North Street | B2 | | |
| Onslow Road | C1 | | |
| Onslow Street | B2 | | |
| Oxford Road | C2 | | |
| Pannells Court | C2 | | |
| Park Road | B1 | | |
| Park Street | B2 | | |
| Pewley Hill | C2 | | |

HARROGATE

0    150 yds
0    150m

Appears on main
map page 194

**Tourist Information Centre: Royal Baths, Crescent Road**
**Tel: 0845 389 3223**

| | | | |
|---|---|---|---|
| Ainsty Road | C1 | Regent Grove | C1 |
| Albert Street | B2 | Regent Parade | C1 |
| Alexandra Road | B1 | Regent Street | C1 |
| Arthington Avenue | B2 | Regent Terrace | C1 |
| Beech Grove | A3 | Ripon Road | A1 |
| Belford Road | B2 | Robert Street | B3 |
| Bower Road | B1 | St. James Drive | C3 |
| Bower Street | B2 | St. Mary's Walk | A3 |
| Cambridge Street | B2 | Skipton Road | C1 |
| Cavendish Avenue | C3 | South Park Road | B3 |
| Chelmsford Road | B2 | Springfield Avenue | A1 |
| Cheltenham Mount | B1 | Spring Grove | A1 |
| Chudleigh Road | C1 | Spring Mount | A1 |
| Clarence Drive | A2 | Station Avenue | B2 |
| Claro Road | C1 | Station Parade | B2 |
| Cold Bath Road | A3 | Stray Rein | B3 |
| Commercial Street | B1 | Stray Walk | C3 |
| Coppice Drive | A1 | Studley Road | B1 |
| Cornwall Road | A2 | Swan Road | A2 |
| Crescent Gardens | A2 | The Grove | C1 |
| Dragon Avenue | B1 | Tower Street | B3 |
| Dragon Parade | B1 | Trinity Road | B3 |
| Dragon Road | B1 | Valley Drive | A2 |
| Duchy Road | A1 | Victoria Avenue | B2 |
| East Parade | B2 | Victoria Road | A3 |
| East Park Road | B2 | West End Avenue | A3 |
| Franklin Mount | B1 | West Park | B2 |
| Franklin Road | B1 | Woodside | B2 |
| Gascoigne Crescent | C1 | York Place | B3 |
| Glebe Avenue | A2 | York Road | A2 |
| Glebe Road | A3 | | |
| Grove Park Terrace | C1 | | |
| Grove Road | B1 | | |
| Harcourt Drive | C2 | | |
| Harcourt Road | C1 | | |
| Heywood Road | A3 | | |
| Hollins Road | A1 | | |
| Homestead Road | B2 | | |
| James Street | B2 | | |
| Kent Road | A1 | | |
| King's Road | A2 | | |
| Knaresborough Road | C2 | | |
| Lancaster Road | A3 | | |
| Leeds Road | B3 | | |
| Lime Grove | C1 | | |
| Lime Street | C1 | | |
| Mayfield Grove | B1 | | |
| Montpellier Hill | A2 | | |
| Montpellier Street | A2 | | |
| Mowbray Square | C1 | | |
| North Park Road | C2 | | |
| Oatlands Drive | C3 | | |
| Otley Road | A3 | | |
| Oxford Street | B2 | | |
| Park Chase | C1 | | |
| Park Drive | B3 | | |
| Park Parade | C2 | | |
| Park Road | A3 | | |
| Park View | B2 | | |
| Parliament Street | A2 | | |
| Princes Villa Road | B2 | | |
| Providence Terrace | B1 | | |
| Queen Parade | C2 | | |
| Queen's Road | A3 | | |
| Raglan Street | B2 | | |
| Regent Avenue | C1 | | |

**Tourist Information Centre: Queens Square, Priory Meadow**
**Tel: 0845 274 1001**

| | | | |
|---|---|---|---|
| Albert Road | B3 | St. Margaret's Road | A3 |
| All Saints Street | C2 | St. Mary's Road | B2 |
| Amherst Road | A2 | St. Mary's Terrace | B2 |
| Ashburnham Road | C2 | St. Thomas's Road | C2 |
| Ashford Road | A1 | Thanet Way | A1 |
| Ashford Way | A1 | The Bourne | C2 |
| Baldslow Road | B2 | Upper Park Road | A2 |
| Beaconsfield Road | B1 | Vicarage Road | B2 |
| Bembrook Road | C2 | Warrior Square | A3 |
| Bohemia Road | A2 | Wellington Road | B2 |
| Braybrooke Road | B2 | White Rock | A3 |
| Broomsgrove Road | C1 | Woodbrook Road | B1 |
| Cambridge Road | A3 | Wykeham Road | A2 |
| Castle Hill Road | B3 | | |
| Castle Street | B3 | | |
| Chiltern Drive | C1 | | |
| Church Road | A3 | | |
| Collier Road | C2 | | |
| Cornwallis Terrace | A3 | | |
| Croft Road | C2 | | |
| De Cham Road | A3 | | |
| Denmark Place | B3 | | |
| Downs Road | B1 | | |
| East Parade | C3 | | |
| Elphinstone Road | B1 | | |
| Eversfield Place | A3 | | |
| Falaise Road | A3 | | |
| Farley Bank | C1 | | |
| Fearon Road | B1 | | |
| Fellows Road | C1 | | |
| Frederick Road | C1 | | |
| Freshwater Avenue | A1 | | |
| George Street | C3 | | |
| Harold Place | B3 | | |
| Harold Road | C2 | | |
| High Street | C2 | | |
| Hillside Road | A1 | | |
| Hoad's Wood Road | B1 | | |
| Hughenden Road | B1 | | |
| Laton Road | B1 | | |
| Linley Drive | B1 | | |
| Linton Road | A2 | | |
| Lower Park Road | A2 | | |
| Magdalen Road | A3 | | |
| Malvern Way | C1 | | |
| Marine Parade | C3 | | |
| Milward Road | B2 | | |
| Mount Pleasant Road | B1 | | |
| Old London Road | C2 | | |
| Park Avenue | A1 | | |
| Park Crescent | A1 | | |
| Park View | A1 | | |
| Park Way | A1 | | |
| Parker Road | B1 | | |
| Parkstone Road | A1 | | |
| Pelham Place | B3 | | |
| Priory Avenue | B2 | | |
| Priory Road | C2 | | |
| Queen's Road | B2 | | |
| Robertson Street | B3 | | |
| Rock-a-Nore Road | C3 | | |
| St. George's Road | C2 | | |
| St. Helen's Down | B1 | | |
| St. Helen's Park Road | B2 | | |
| St. Helen's Road | A1 | | |
| St. John's Road | A3 | | |

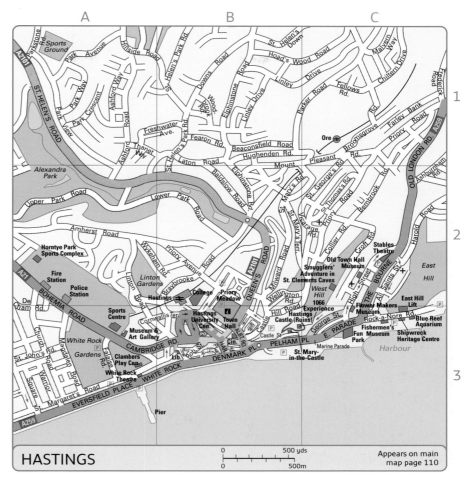

HASTINGS

0    500 yds

0    500m

Appears on main
map page 110

**Tourist Information Centre: 1 King Street**
**Tel: 01432 268430**

| | | | |
|---|---|---|---|
| Aubrey Street | B2 | Vaughan Street | C2 |
| Barrs Court Road | C1 | Victoria Street | A2 |
| Barton Road | A2 | West Street | B2 |
| Barton Yard | A2 | Widemarsh Street | B2 |
| Bath Street | C2 | Wye Street | B3 |
| Belmont Avenue | A3 | | |
| Berrington Street | B2 | | |
| Bewell Street | B2 | | |
| Blackfriars Street | B1 | | |
| Blueschool Street | B1 | | |
| Brewers Passage | B2 | | |
| Bridge Street | B2 | | |
| Broad Street | B2 | | |
| Canonmoor Street | A1 | | |
| Cantilupe Street | C2 | | |
| Castle Street | B2 | | |
| Catherine Street | B1 | | |
| Central Avenue | C2 | | |
| Church Street | B2 | | |
| Commercial Road | C1 | | |
| Commercial Street | B2 | | |
| Coningsby Street | B1 | | |
| East Street | B2 | | |
| Edgar Street | B1 | | |
| Eign Gate | B2 | | |
| Eign Street | A2 | | |
| Ferrers Street | B2 | | |
| Friars Street | A2 | | |
| Gaol Street | C2 | | |
| Green Street | C3 | | |
| Grenfell Road | C3 | | |
| Greyfriars Avenue | A3 | | |
| Greyfriars Bridge | B2 | | |
| Grove Road | C3 | | |
| Harold Street | C3 | | |
| High Street | B2 | | |
| High Town | B2 | | |
| King Street | B2 | | |
| Kyrle Street | C2 | | |
| Maylord Street | B2 | | |
| Mill Street | C3 | | |
| Monkmoor Street | C1 | | |
| Moorfield Street | A1 | | |
| Moor Street | B1 | | |
| Mostyn Street | A1 | | |
| Nelson Street | C3 | | |
| Newmarket Street | B1 | | |
| Park Street | C3 | | |
| Penhaligon Way | A1 | | |
| Plough Lane | A1 | | |
| Portland Street | A1 | | |
| Quay Street | B2 | | |
| Ryeland Street | A2 | | |
| St. Guthlac Street | C2 | | |
| St. James Road | C3 | | |
| St. Martin's Avenue | B3 | | |
| St. Martin's Street | B3 | | |
| St. Owen Street | C2 | | |
| Station Approach | C1 | | |
| Station Road | A2 | | |
| Stonebow Road | C1 | | |
| Symonds Street | C2 | | |
| The Atrium | B1 | | |
| Turner Street | C3 | | |
| Union Street | B2 | | |
| Union Walk | C1 | | |

HEREFORD

0    250 yds

0    250m

Appears on main
map page 145

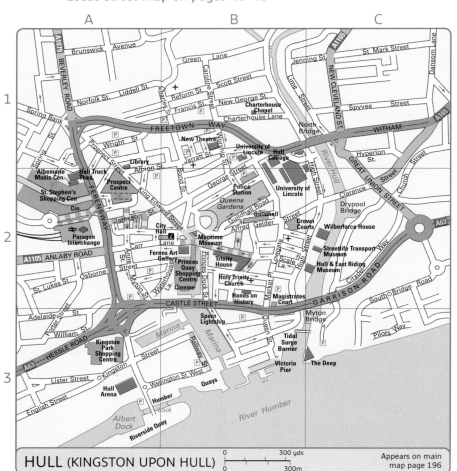

HULL (KINGSTON UPON HULL)

0 ___ 300 yds
0 ___ 300m

Appears on main
map page 196

INVERNESS

0 ___ 300 yds
0 ___ 300m

Appears on main
map page 266

**Tourist Information Centre: 7-9 Every Street, Town Hall Square**
**Tel: 0844 888 5181**

| | | | |
|---|---|---|---|
| Abbey Street | B1 | Market Place South | B2 |
| Albion Street | B2 | Market Street | B2 |
| All Saints Road | A2 | Mill Lane | A3 |
| Aylestone Road | B3 | Millstone Lane | B2 |
| Bassett Street | A1 | Montreal Road | C1 |
| Bath Lane | A2 | Morledge Street | C2 |
| Bedford Street North | C1 | Narborough Road | A3 |
| Belgrave Gate | B1 | Narborough Road North | A3 |
| Bell Lane | C1 | Nelson Street | C3 |
| Belvoir Street | B2 | Newarke Close | A3 |
| Braunstone Gate | A2 | Newarke Street | B2 |
| Burgess Street | B1 | Northgate Street | A1 |
| Burleys Way | B1 | Ottawa Road | C1 |
| Byron Street | B1 | Oxford Street | B2 |
| Cank Street | B2 | Pasture Lane | A1 |
| Castle Street | A2 | Peacock Lane | B2 |
| Charles Street | C2 | Pocklingtons Walk | B2 |
| Christow Street | C1 | Prebend Street | C3 |
| Church Gate | B1 | Princess Road East | C3 |
| Clarence Street | B1 | Pringle Street | A1 |
| Clyde Street | C1 | Queen Street | C2 |
| College Street | C2 | Regent Road | B3 |
| Colton Street | C2 | Regent Street | C3 |
| Conduit Street | C2 | Repton Street | A1 |
| Crafton Street East | C1 | Rutland Street | C2 |
| Cravan Street | A1 | Samuel Street | C2 |
| De Montfort Street | C3 | Sanvey Gate | A1 |
| Deacon Street | B3 | Saxby Street | C3 |
| Dryden Street | B1 | Slater Street | A1 |
| Duns Lane | A2 | Soar Lane | A1 |
| Dunton Street | A1 | South Albion Street | C2 |
| Eastern Boulevard | A3 | Southampton Street | C2 |
| Friar Lane | B2 | Sparkenhoe Street | C2 |
| Friday Street | B1 | St. George Street | C2 |
| Frog Island | A1 | St. George's Way | C2 |
| Gallowtree Gate | B2 | St. John's Street | B1 |
| Gaul Street | A3 | St. Margaret's Way | A1 |
| Glebe Street | C2 | St. Matthew's Way | C1 |
| Gotham Street | C3 | St. Nicholas Circle | A2 |
| Granby Street | B2 | Swain Street | C2 |
| Grange Lane | B3 | Swan Street | A1 |
| Grasmere Street | A3 | Taylor Road | C1 |
| Great Central Street | A1 | Thames Street | B1 |
| Halford Street | B2 | The Gateway | A3 |
| Havelock Street | B3 | The Newarke | A2 |
| Haymarket | B1 | Tigers Way | B3 |
| High Street | B2 | Tower Street | B3 |
| Highcross Street | A1 | Tudor Road | A1 |
| Hobart Street | C2 | Ullswater Way | A3 |
| Horsfair Street | B2 | University Road | C3 |
| Humberstone Gate | B2 | Upperton Road | A3 |
| Humberstone Road | C1 | Vaughan Way | A1 |
| Infirmary Road | B3 | Vestry Street | C2 |
| Jarrom Street | A3 | Walnut Street | A3 |
| Jarvis Street | A2 | Waterloo Way | C3 |
| Kamloops Crescent | C1 | Welford Road | B2 |
| Kent Street | C1 | Wellington Street | B2 |
| King Richard's Road | A2 | West Street | B3 |
| King Street | B2 | Western Boulevard | A3 |
| Lancaster Road | B3 | Western Road | A3 |
| Lee Street | B1 | Wharf Street North | C1 |
| Lincoln Street | C2 | Wharf Street South | C1 |
| London Road | C3 | Wilberforce Road | A3 |
| Loseby Lane | B2 | Windermere Street | A3 |
| Lower Brown Street | B2 | Woodboy Street | C1 |
| Manitoba Road | C1 | Yeoman Street | B2 |
| Mansfield Street | B1 | York Road | B2 |

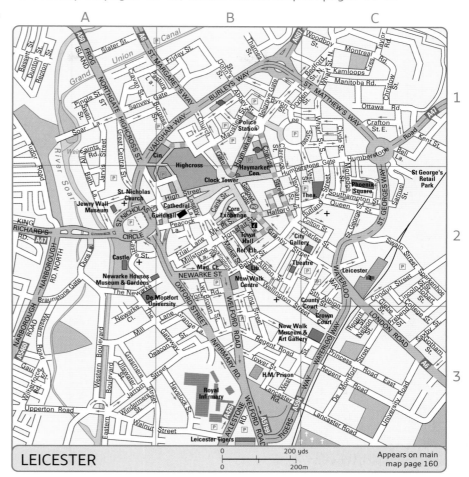

**LEICESTER**

0 — 200 yds
0 — 200m

Appears on main
map page 160

**Tourist Information Centre: 9 Castle Hill**
**Tel: 01522 873000**

| | | | |
|---|---|---|---|
| Alexandra Terrace | A2 | Spa Road | C3 |
| Baggholme Road | C2 | St. Anne's Road | C2 |
| Bailgate | B1 | St. Giles Avenue | C1 |
| Beaumont Fee | B2 | St. Mark Street | B3 |
| Beevor Street | A3 | St. Mary's Street | B3 |
| Brayford Way | A3 | St. Rumbold Street | C2 |
| Brayford Wharf North | A2 | Stamp End | C3 |
| Broadgate | B2 | Steep Hill | B2 |
| Broadway | B1 | The Avenue | A2 |
| Bruce Road | C1 | Tritton Road | A3 |
| Burton Road | A1 | Union Row | B2 |
| Canwick Road | B3 | Upper Lindum Street | C2 |
| Carholme Road | A2 | Upper Long Leys Road | A1 |
| Carline Road | A1 | Vere Street | B1 |
| Carr Street | A2 | Vine Street | C2 |
| Cheviot Street | C2 | Waterside North | B3 |
| Church Lane | B1 | Waterside South | B3 |
| Clasketgate | B2 | West Parade | A2 |
| Croft Street | B2 | Westgate | B1 |
| Cross Street | B3 | Wigford Way | B2 |
| Curle Avenue | C1 | Wilson Street | A1 |
| Drury Lane | B2 | Winn Street | C2 |
| East Gate | B2 | Wragby Road | C2 |
| Firth Road | A3 | Yarborough Road | A1 |
| George Street | C3 | | |
| Great Northern Terrace | B3 | | |
| Greetwell Close | C1 | | |
| Greetwell Road | C2 | | |
| Gresham Street | A2 | | |
| Hampton Street | A2 | | |
| Harvey Street | A2 | | |
| High Street | B3 | | |
| John Street | C2 | | |
| Langworthgate | B1 | | |
| Lee Road | C1 | | |
| Lindum Road | B2 | | |
| Lindum Terrace | C2 | | |
| Long Leys Road | A1 | | |
| Mainwaring Road | C1 | | |
| Mill Road | A1 | | |
| Milman Road | C2 | | |
| Monks Road | C2 | | |
| Monson Street | B3 | | |
| Moor Street | A2 | | |
| Mount Street | A1 | | |
| Nettleham Road | B1 | | |
| Newland | A2 | | |
| Newland Street West | A2 | | |
| Newport | B1 | | |
| Northgate | B1 | | |
| Orchard Street | A2 | | |
| Pelham Bridge | B3 | | |
| Portland Street | B3 | | |
| Portland Street | B3 | | |
| Pottergate | B2 | | |
| Queensway | C1 | | |
| Rasen Lane | B1 | | |
| Richmond Road | A2 | | |
| Ripon Street | B3 | | |
| Rope Walk | A3 | | |
| Rosemary Lane | B2 | | |
| Ruskin Avenue | C1 | | |
| Saltergate | B2 | | |
| Sewell Road | C2 | | |
| Silver Street | B2 | | |
| Sincil Bank | B3 | | |

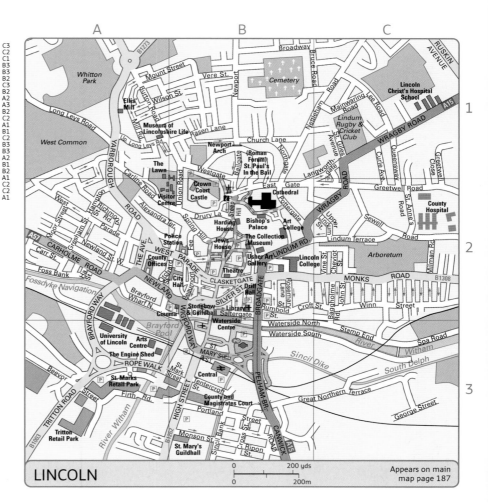

**LINCOLN**

0 — 200 yds
0 — 200m

Appears on main
map page 187

# Middlesbrough  Milton Keynes

Manchester street map on pages 46-47

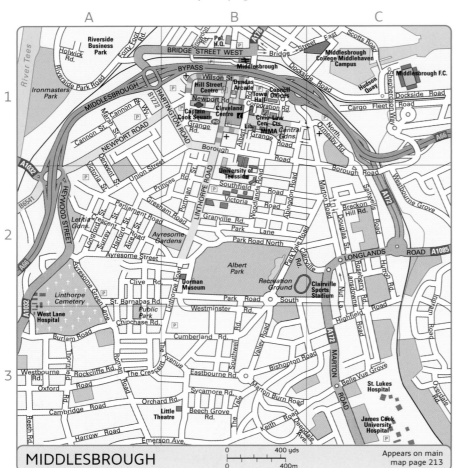

**MIDDLESBROUGH**

| | |
|---|---|
| 0 | 400 yds |
| 0 | 400m |

Appears on main
map page 213

**Tourist Information Centre: Town Hall, Albert Road
Tel: 01642 729700**

| | | | | |
|---|---|---|---|---|
| Abingdon Road | B2 | Roman Road | A3 |
| Aire Street | A2 | Roseberry Road | C2 |
| Albert Road | B1 | Saltwells Road | C2 |
| Ayresome Green Lane | A2 | Scotts Road | C1 |
| Ayresome Street | A2 | Sheperdson Way | C1 |
| Beech Grove Road | B3 | Snowdon Road | B1 |
| Belle Vue Grove | C3 | Southfield Road | B2 |
| Bishopton Road | B3 | Southwell Road | B3 |
| Borough Road | B1/C3 | St. Barnabas Road | A2 |
| Breckon Hill Road | C2 | Surrey Street | A2 |
| Bridge Street East | B1 | Sycamore Road | B3 |
| Bridge Street West | B1 | The Avenue | B3 |
| Burlam Road | A3 | The Crescent | A3 |
| Cambridge Road | A3 | The Vale | B3 |
| Cannon Park Way | A1 | Thornfield Road | A3 |
| Cannon Street | A1 | Union Street | A2 |
| Cargo Fleet Road | C1 | Valley Road | B3 |
| Chipchase Road | A3 | Victoria Road | B2 |
| Clairville Road | B2 | Victoria Street | A1 |
| Clive Road | A2 | Westbourne Grove | C2 |
| Corporation Road | B1 | Westbourne Road | A3 |
| Crescent Road | A2 | Westminster Road | B3 |
| Cumberland Road | B3 | Wilson Street | B1 |
| Deepdale Avenue | B3 | Woodlands Road | B2 |
| Derwent Street | A1 | | |
| Dockside Road | B1/C1 | | |
| Douglas Street | C2 | | |
| Eastbourne Road | B3 | | |
| Emerson Avenue | B3 | | |
| Forty Foot Road | A1 | | |
| Grange Road | B1 | | |
| Granville Road | B2 | | |
| Gresham Road | A2 | | |
| Harford Street | A2 | | |
| Harrow Road | A3 | | |
| Hartington Road | A1 | | |
| Heywood Street | A2 | | |
| Highfield Road | C3 | | |
| Holwick Road | A1 | | |
| Hudson Quay | C1 | | |
| Hutton Road | C2 | | |
| Ingram Road | C2 | | |
| Keith Road | B3 | | |
| Lansdowne Road | C2 | | |
| Linthorpe Road | B3 | | |
| Longford Street | A2 | | |
| Longlands Road | C2 | | |
| Marsh Street | A1 | | |
| Marton Burn Road | B3 | | |
| Marton Road | C2/C3 | | |
| Newport Road | A1/B1 | | |
| North Ormesby Road | C1 | | |
| Nut Lane | C2 | | |
| Orchard Road | A3 | | |
| Overdale Road | C3 | | |
| Oxford Road | A3 | | |
| Park Lane | B2 | | |
| Park Road North | B2 | | |
| Park Road South | B2 | | |
| Park Vale Road | B2 | | |
| Parliament Road | A2 | | |
| Portman Street | B2 | | |
| Princes Road | A2 | | |
| Reeth Road | A3 | | |
| Riverside Park Road | A1 | | |
| Rockcliffe Road | A3 | | |

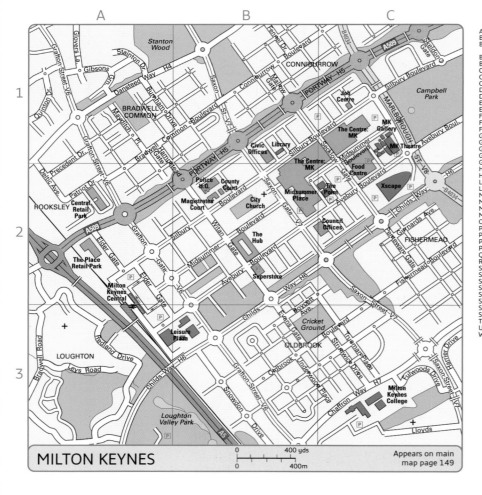

**MILTON KEYNES**

| | |
|---|---|
| 0 | 400 yds |
| 0 | 400m |

Appears on main
map page 149

| | | |
|---|---|---|
| Avebury Boulevard | B2/C1 |
| Boycott Avenue | B3 |
| Bradwell Common Boulevard | A1 |
| Bradwell Road | A3 |
| Burnham Drive | A1 |
| Chaffron Way | C3 |
| Childs Way | A3/C2 |
| Conniburrow Boulevard | B1 |
| Dansteed Way | A1 |
| Deltic Avenue | A2 |
| Elder Gate | A2 |
| Evans Gate | B3 |
| Fennel Drive | B1 |
| Fishermead Boulevard | C2 |
| Fulwoods Drive | C3 |
| Gibsons Green | A1 |
| Glovers Lane | A1 |
| Grafton Gate | A2 |
| Grafton Street | A1/B3 |
| Gurnards Avenue | C2 |
| Hampstead Gate | A1 |
| Harrier Drive | C3 |
| Leys Road | A3 |
| Lloyds | C3 |
| Mallow Gate | B1 |
| Marlborough Street | C1 |
| Mayditch Place | A1 |
| Midsummer Boulevard | B2/C1 |
| Oldbrook Boulevard | B3 |
| Patriot Drive | A2 |
| Pentewan Gate | C2 |
| Portway | B2/C1 |
| Precedent Drive | A2 |
| Quinton Drive | A1 |
| Redland Drive | A3 |
| Saxon Gate | B2 |
| Saxon Street | B1/C3 |
| Secklow Gate | C1 |
| Silbury Boulevard | B2/C1 |
| Skeldon Gate | C1 |
| Snowdon Drive | B3 |
| Stainton Drive | A1 |
| Strudwick Drive | C3 |
| Trueman Place | C3 |
| Underwood Place | B3 |
| Witan Gate | B2 |

**Tourist Information Centre: 8-9 Central Arcade**
**Tel: 0191 277 8000**

| | |
|---|---|
| Albert Street | C2 |
| Ancrum Street | A1 |
| Argyle Street | C2 |
| Askew Road | C3 |
| Barrack Road | A1 |
| Barras Bridge | B1 |
| Bath Lane | A2 |
| Bigg Market | B2 |
| Blackett Street | B2 |
| Byron Street | C1 |
| Chester Street | C1 |
| City Road | C2 |
| Claremont Road | B1 |
| Clarence Street | C2 |
| Clayton Street | A2 |
| Clayton Street West | A3 |
| Corporation Street | A2 |
| Coulthards Lane | C3 |
| Crawhall Road | C2 |
| Dean Street | B2 |
| Diana Street | A2 |
| Elswick East Terrace | A3 |
| Eskdale Terrace | C1 |
| Essex Close | A3 |
| Falconar Street | C1 |
| Forth Banks | B3 |
| Forth Street | B3 |
| Gallowgate | A2 |
| Gateshead Highway | C3 |
| George Street | A3 |
| Gibson Street | C2 |
| Grainger Street | B2 |
| Grantham Road | C1 |
| Grey Street | B2 |
| Hanover Street | B3 |
| Hawks Road | C3 |
| Helmsley Road | C1 |
| High Street | C3 |
| Hillgate | C3 |
| Howard Street | C2 |
| Hunters Road | A1 |
| Ivy Close | A3 |
| Jesmond Road | C1 |
| Jesmond Road West | B1 |
| John Dobson Street | B2 |
| Kelvin Grove | C1 |
| Kyle Close | A3 |
| Lambton Street | C3 |
| Mansfield Street | A2 |
| Maple Street | A3 |
| Maple Terrace | A3 |
| Market Street | B2 |
| Melbourne Street | C2 |
| Mill Road | C3 |
| Neville Street | A3 |
| New Bridge Street | C2 |
| Newgate Street | B2 |
| Northumberland Road | B2 |
| Northumberland Street | B1 |
| Oakwellgate | C3 |
| Orchard Street | B3 |
| Oxnam Crescent | A1 |
| Park Terrace | B1 |
| Percy Street | B2 |
| Pilgrim Street | B2 |
| Pipewellgate | B3 |

| | |
|---|---|
| Pitt Street | A2 |
| Portland Road | C1 |
| Portland Terrace | C1 |
| Pottery Lane | A3 |
| Quarryfield Road | C3 |
| Quayside | C3 |
| Queen Victoria Road | B1 |
| Railway Street | A3 |
| Redheugh Bridge | A3 |
| Richardson Road | A1 |
| Rye Hill | A3 |
| St. James Boulevard | A3 |
| St. Mary's Place | B1 |
| St. Thomas Street | B1 |
| Sandyford Road | B1/C1 |
| Scotswood Road | A3 |
| Skinnerburn Road | B3 |
| South Shore Road | C3 |
| Stanhope Street | A2 |
| Starbeck Avenue | C1 |
| Stodart Street | C1 |
| Stowell Street | A2 |
| Strawberry Place | A2 |
| Summerhill Grove | A2 |
| Swing Bridge | B3 |
| The Close | B3 |
| Tyne Bridge | C3 |
| Union Street | C2 |
| Warwick Street | C1 |
| Wellington Street | A2 |
| West Street | C3 |
| Westgate Road | A2 |
| Westmorland Road | A3 |
| Windsor Terrace | B1 |
| York Street | A2 |

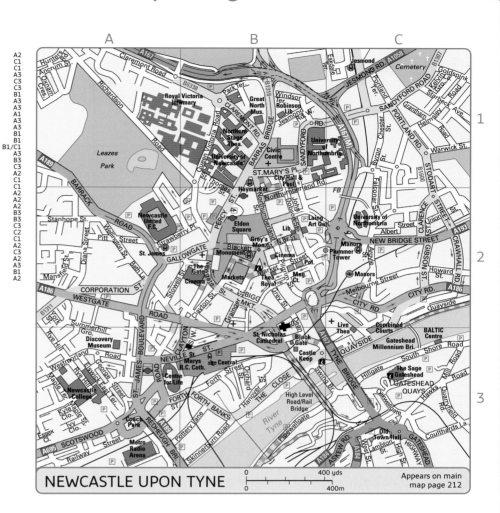

NEWCASTLE UPON TYNE

Appears on main map page 212

**Tourist Information Centre: The Forum, Millennium Plain**
**Tel: 01603 213999**

| | |
|---|---|
| Albion Way | C3 |
| All Saints Green | B3 |
| Ashby Street | B3 |
| Bakers Road | A1 |
| Bank Plain | B2 |
| Barker Street | A1 |
| Barn Road | A2 |
| Barrack Street | B1 |
| Bedford Street | B2 |
| Ber Street | B3 |
| Bethel Street | A2 |
| Bishopbridge Road | C2 |
| Bishopgate | C2 |
| Botolph Street | B1 |
| Brazen Gate | B3 |
| Britannia Road | C1 |
| Brunswick Road | A3 |
| Bullclose Road | B1 |
| Canary Way | C3 |
| Carrow Hill | C3 |
| Carrow Road | C3 |
| Castle Meadow | B2 |
| Chapel Field Road | A2 |
| Chapelfield North | A2 |
| City Road | B3 |
| Clarence Road | C3 |
| Colegate | B1 |
| Coslany Street | A2 |
| Cowgate | B1 |
| Dereham Road | A2 |
| Duke Street | B1 |
| Earlham Road | A2 |
| Edward Street | B1 |
| Elm Hill | B2 |
| Fishergate | B1 |
| Gas Hill | C1 |
| Grapes Hill | A2 |
| Grove Avenue | A3 |
| Grove Road | A3 |
| Grove Walk | A3 |
| Gurney Road | C1 |
| Hall Road | B3 |
| Hardy Road | C3 |
| Heathgate | C1 |
| Heigham Street | A1 |
| Horns Lane | B3 |
| Ipswich Road | A3 |
| Ketts Hill | C1 |
| King Street | B3 |
| Koblenz Avenue | C3 |
| Lothian Street | A1 |
| Lower Clarence Road | C2 |
| Magdalen Street | B1 |
| Magpie Road | B1 |
| Market Avenue | B2 |
| Marlborough Road | B1 |
| Mountergate | B2 |
| Mousehold Street | C1 |
| Newmarket Road | A3 |
| Newmarket Street | A3 |
| Oak Street | A1 |
| Orchard Street | A1 |
| Palace Street | B2 |
| Pitt Street | B1 |
| Pottergate | A2 |
| Prince of Wales Road | B2 |

| | |
|---|---|
| Queens Road | B3 |
| Rampant Horse Street | B2 |
| Recorder Road | C2 |
| Red Lion Street | B2 |
| Riverside | C3 |
| Riverside Road | C2 |
| Rosary Road | C2 |
| Rose Lane | B2 |
| Rouen Road | B3 |
| Rupert Street | A3 |
| Russell Street | A1 |
| St. Andrew's Street | B2 |
| St. Augustine's Street | A1 |
| St. Benedict's Street | A2 |
| St. Crispin's Road | A1 |
| St. Faiths Lane | B2 |
| St. George's Street | B1 |
| St. Giles Street | A2 |
| St. James Close | C1 |
| St. Leonards Road | C2 |
| St. Martin's Road | A1 |
| St. Stephen's Road | A3 |
| St. Stephen's Street | B3 |
| Silver Road | B1 |
| Silver Street | B1 |
| Southwell Road | B3 |
| Surrey Street | B3 |
| Sussex Street | A1 |
| Theatre Street | A2 |
| Thorn Lane | B3 |
| Thorpe Road | C2 |
| Tombland | B2 |
| Trinity Street | A3 |
| Troy Street | A2 |
| Union Street | A3 |
| Unthank Road | A3 |
| Vauxhall Street | A3 |
| Victoria Street | A3 |
| Wensum Street | B1 |
| Wessex Street | A3 |
| Westwick Street | A1 |
| Wherry Road | C3 |
| Whitefriars | B1 |
| Wodehouse Street | B1 |
| York Street | A3 |

NORWICH

Appears on main map page 178

NOTTINGHAM

0   400 yds
0   400m

Appears on main
map page 173

**Tourist Information Centre:  1-4 Smithy Row**
**Tel:  08444 77 56 78**

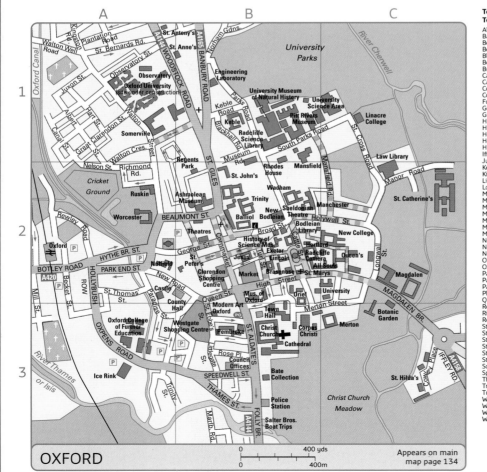

OXFORD

0   400 yds
0   400m

Appears on main
map page 134

**Tourist Information Centre:  15-16 Broad Street**
**Tel:  01865 726871**

**Tourist Information Centre: Lower City Mills, West Mill Street**
**Tel: 01738 450600**

| | |
|---|---|
| Abbot Crescent | A3 |
| Abbot Street | A3 |
| Albany Terrace | A1 |
| Atholl Street | B1 |
| Balhousie Street | B1 |
| Barossa Place | B1 |
| Barossa Street | B1 |
| Barrack Street | B1 |
| Bowerswell Road | C2 |
| Caledonian Road | B2 |
| Canal Street | B2 |
| Cavendish Avenue | A3 |
| Charlotte Street | B1 |
| Clyde Place | A3 |
| Darnhall Drive | A3 |
| Dundee Road | C2 |
| Dunkeld Road | A1 |
| Edinburgh Road | B3 |
| Feus Road | A1 |
| Friar Street | A3 |
| George Street | C2 |
| Glasgow Road | A2 |
| Glover Street | A2 |
| Gowrie Street | C1 |
| Gray Street | A2 |
| Graybank Road | A2 |
| Hay Street | B1 |
| High Street | B2 |
| Isla Road | C1 |
| Jeanfield Road | A2 |
| King's Place | B3 |
| King James Place | B3 |
| King Street | B2 |
| Kinnoull Street | B1 |
| Kinnoull Terrace | C2 |
| Knowelea Place | A3 |
| Leonard Street | B2 |
| Lochie Brae | C1 |
| Long Causeway | A1 |
| Main Street | C1 |
| Manse Road | C2 |
| Marshall Place | B3 |
| Melville Street | B1 |
| Mill Street | B1 |
| Milne Street | B2 |
| Murray Crescent | A3 |
| Needless Road | A3 |
| New Row | B2 |
| North Methven Street | B1 |
| Park Place | A3 |
| Perth Bridge | C1 |
| Pickletullum Road | A2 |
| Pitcullen Terrace | C1 |
| Pitheavlis Crescent | A3 |
| Princes Street | C3 |
| Priory Place | B3 |
| Queen Street | A3 |
| Queens Bridge | C2 |
| Raeburn Park | A3 |
| Riggs Road | A2 |
| Rose Crescent | A2 |
| Rose Terrace | B1 |
| St. Catherines Road | A1 |
| St. John Street | C2 |
| St. Leonard's Bank | B3 |
| Scott Street | B2 |

| | |
|---|---|
| Shore Road | C3 |
| South Methven Street | B2 |
| South Street | B2 |
| Strathmore Street | C1 |
| Stuart Avenue | A3 |
| Tay Street | C2 |
| Victoria Street | B2 |
| Watergate | C2 |
| Whitefriars Crescent | A2 |
| Whitefriars Street | A2 |
| William Street | B2 |
| Wilson Street | A3 |
| Young Street | A3 |
| York Place | A2 |

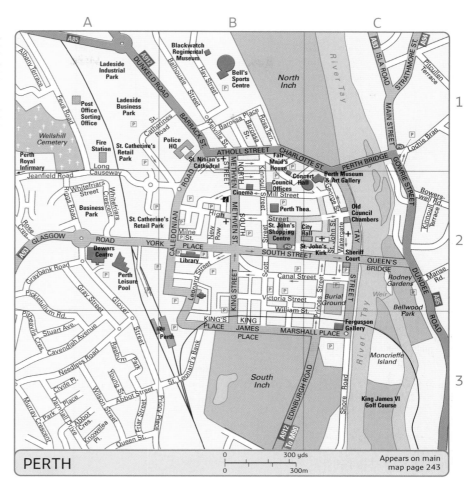

**PERTH**

Appears on main map page 243

**Tourist Information Centre: Plymouth Mayflower Centre,**
**3-5 The Barbican   Tel: 01752 306330**

| | |
|---|---|
| Alexandra Road | C1 |
| Alma Road | A1 |
| Armada Street | B2 |
| Armada Way | B2 |
| Ashford Road | C1 |
| Barbican Approach | C3 |
| Beaumont Road | C2 |
| Beechwood Avenue | B1 |
| Belgrave Road | C1 |
| Bretonside | B2 |
| Buckwell Street | B3 |
| Camden Street | B2 |
| Cattledown Road | C3 |
| Cecil Street | A2 |
| Central Park Avenue | A1 |
| Charles Street | B2 |
| Citadel Road | A3 |
| Clarence Place | A2 |
| Cliff Road | A3 |
| Clifton Place | B1 |
| Clovelly Road | C3 |
| Cobourg Street | B2 |
| Coleridge Road | C1 |
| Connaught Avenue | C1 |
| Cornwall Street | B2 |
| Dale Road | B1 |
| De-La-Hay Avenue | A1 |
| Desborough Road | C2 |
| Drake Circus | B2 |
| East Street | A3 |
| Ebrington Street | B2 |
| Elliot Street | A3 |
| Embankment Road | C2 |
| Exeter Street | B2 |
| Ford Park Road | B1 |
| Furzehill Road | C1 |
| Gdynia Way | C3 |
| Glen Park Avenue | B1 |
| Grand Parade | A3 |
| Greenbank Avenue | C2 |
| Greenbank Road | C1 |
| Grenville Road | C2 |
| Harwell Street | A2 |
| Hill Park Crescent | B1 |
| Hoe Road | B3 |
| Houndiscombe Road | B1 |
| James Street | B2 |
| King Street | A2 |
| Knighton Road | C2 |
| Lipson Hill | C1 |
| Lipson Road | C2 |
| Lisson Grove | C1 |
| Lockyer Street | B3 |
| Looe Street | B2 |
| Madeira Road | B3 |
| Manor Road | A2 |
| Martin Street | A3 |
| Mayflower Street | B2 |
| Millbay Road | A3 |
| Mount Gould Road | C1 |
| Mutley Plain | B1 |
| New George Street | B2 |
| North Cross | B2 |
| North Hill | B2 |
| North Road East | B2 |
| North Road West | A2 |

| | |
|---|---|
| North Street | B2 |
| Notte Street | B3 |
| Oxford Street | A2 |
| Pentillie Road | B1 |
| Ponsonby Road | A1 |
| Princess Street | B3 |
| Queen's Road | C1 |
| Royal Parade | B2 |
| Salisbury Road | C2 |
| Saltash Road | A1 |
| Seaton Avenue | B1 |
| Seymour Avenue | C2 |
| Southside Street | B3 |
| Stoke Road | A2 |
| Stuart Road | A1 |
| Sutton Road | C2 |
| Sydney Street | A2 |
| Teats Hill Road | C3 |
| The Crescent | A3 |
| Tothill Avenue | C2 |
| Tothill Road | C2 |
| Union Street | A2 |
| Vauxhall Street | B3 |
| West Hoe Road | A3 |
| Western Approach | A2 |
| Whittington Street | A1 |
| Wilton Street | A2 |
| Wyndham Street | A2 |

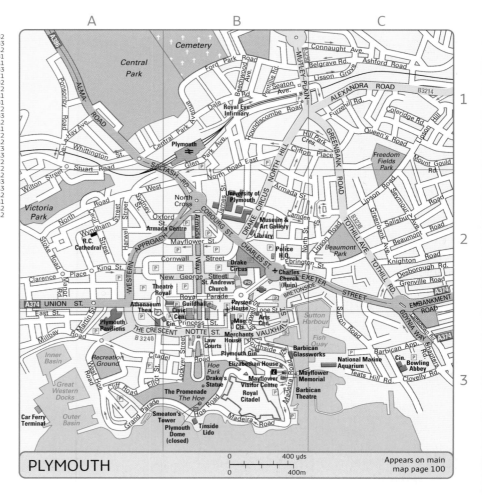

**PLYMOUTH**

Appears on main map page 100

## PORTSMOUTH

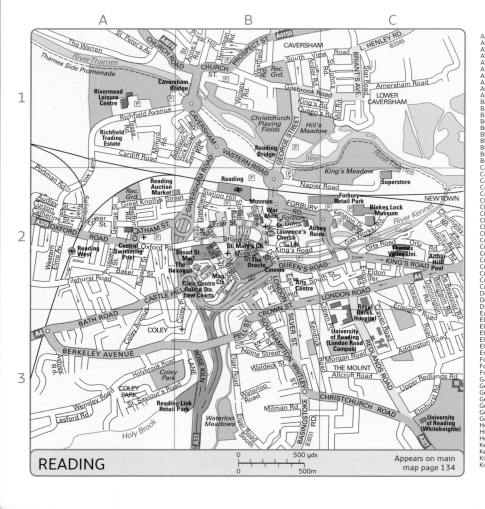

**Tourist Information Centre: The Hard**
**Tel: 023 9282 6722**

|  |  | |  |  |
|---|---|---|---|---|
| Albany Road | C3 | | Penny Street | A3 |
| Albert Grove | C3 | | Queen's Crescent | C3 |
| Alfred Road | B2 | | Queen Street | A2 |
| Anglesea Road | B2 | | Raglan Street | C2 |
| Arundel Street | C2 | | Railway View | C2 |
| Astley Street | B3 | | St. Andrews Road | C3 |
| Bailey's Road | C2 | | St. Edward's Road | B3 |
| Bellevue Terrace | B3 | | St. George's Road | A2 |
| Belmont Street | C3 | | St. James Road | B3 |
| Bishop Street | A1 | | St. James Street | B2 |
| Blackfriars Road | C2 | | St. Paul's Road | B3 |
| Bradford Road | C2 | | St. Thomas's Street | A3 |
| Britain Street | A2 | | Somers Road | C2 |
| Broad Street | A3 | | Southsea Terrace | B3 |
| Burnaby Road | B2 | | Station Street | C2 |
| Cambridge Road | B3 | | Stone Street | B3 |
| Canal Walk | C2 | | Sultan Road | C1 |
| Castle Road | B3 | | Sussex Street | B3 |
| Church Road | C1 | | The Hard | A2 |
| Church Street | C1 | | Turner Road | C1 |
| Clarendon Street | C1 | | Unicorn Road | B1 |
| College Street | A2 | | Upper Arundel Street | C2 |
| Commercial Road | B2 | | Victoria Road North | C3 |
| Cottage Grove | C3 | | Warblington Street | A3 |
| Crasswell Street | C1 | | Watts Road | C1 |
| Cross Street | A1 | | White Hart Road | A3 |
| Cumberland Street | A1 | | Wingfield Street | C1 |
| Duke Crescent | C1 | | Winston Churchill Avenue | B2 |
| Edinburgh Road | B2 | | York Place | B2 |
| Eldon Street | B3 | | | |
| Elm Grove | C3 | | | |
| Flathouse Road | C1 | | | |
| Fyning Street | C1 | | | |
| Green Road | B3 | | | |
| Greetham Street | C2 | | | |
| Grosvenor Street | C3 | | | |
| Grove Road South | C3 | | | |
| Gunwharf Road | A3 | | | |
| Hampshire Terrace | B3 | | | |
| Havant Road | A2 | | | |
| High Street | A3 | | | |
| Holbrook Road | C1 | | | |
| Hope Street | B1 | | | |
| Hyde Park Road | C2 | | | |
| Isambard Brunel Road | B2 | | | |
| Kent Road | B3 | | | |
| Kent Street | A1 | | | |
| King Charles Street | A3 | | | |
| King's Road | B3 | | | |
| King's Terrace | B3 | | | |
| King Street | B3 | | | |
| Lake Road | C1 | | | |
| Landport Terrace | B3 | | | |
| Lombard Street | A3 | | | |
| Margate Road | C3 | | | |
| Market Way | B1 | | | |
| Melbourne Place | C2 | | | |
| Museum Road | B3 | | | |
| Nelson Road | C1 | | | |
| Norfolk Street | B3 | | | |
| Northam Street | C2 | | | |
| Outram Road | C3 | | | |
| Pain's Street | C3 | | | |
| Paradise Street | C2 | | | |
| Park Road | B2 | | | |
| Pembroke Road | A3 | | | |

Appears on main map page 107

## READING

|  |  | |  |  |
|---|---|---|---|---|
| Addington Road | C3 | | Lesford Road | A3 |
| Addison Road | A1 | | London Road | C2 |
| Alexandra Road | C2 | | London Street | B2 |
| Allcroft Road | C3 | | Lower Henley Road | C1 |
| Alpine Street | B3 | | Mill Road | C1 |
| Amersham Road | C1 | | Milford Road | A1 |
| Amity Road | A2 | | Milman Road | B3 |
| Ardler Road | B1 | | Minster Street | B2 |
| Ashley Road | A3 | | Morgan Road | C3 |
| Audley Street | A2 | | Napier Road | B2 |
| Baker Street | A2 | | Orts Road | C2 |
| Basingstoke Road | B3 | | Oxford Road | A2 |
| Bath Road | A3 | | Pell Street | B3 |
| Bedford Road | A2 | | Portman Road | A1 |
| Berkeley Avenue | A3 | | Priest Hill | B1 |
| Blagrave Street | B2 | | Prospect Street *Caversham* | B1 |
| Blenheim Road | C2 | | Prospect Street *Reading* | A2 |
| Briant's Avenue | C1 | | Queen's Road *Caversham* | B1 |
| Bridge Street | B2 | | Queen's Road *Reading* | B2 |
| Broad Street | B2 | | Richfield Avenue | A1 |
| Cardiff Road | A1 | | Rose Kiln Lane | B3 |
| Castle Hill | A2 | | Russell Street | A2 |
| Castle Street | B2 | | St. Anne's Road | B1 |
| Catherine Street | A2 | | St. John's Road | C1 |
| Caversham Road | B2 | | St. Mary's Butts | B2 |
| Chatham Street | A2 | | St. Peters Avenue | A1 |
| Cheapside | B2 | | St. Saviours Road | A3 |
| Cholmeley Road | C2 | | Silver Street | B3 |
| Christchurch Road | C3 | | South Street | B2 |
| Church Road | A1 | | Southampton Street | B3 |
| Church Street | B1 | | South View Road | B1 |
| Coley Avenue | A3 | | Star Road | C1 |
| Coley Place | B2 | | Station Hill | B2 |
| Cow Lane | A2 | | Station Road | B2 |
| Craven Road | C3 | | Swansea Road | B1 |
| Crown Place | C2 | | Tessa Place | A1 |
| Crown Street | B3 | | The Warren | A1 |
| Cumberland Road | C2 | | Tilehurst Road | A2 |
| Curzon Street | A2 | | Upper Redlands Road | C3 |
| De Beauvoir Road | C2 | | Vastern Road | B1 |
| Donnington Road | C2 | | Waldelk Street | B3 |
| Duke Street | B2 | | Waterloo Road | B3 |
| East Street | B2 | | Wensley Road | A3 |
| Eldon Road | C2 | | Western Elms Avenue | A2 |
| Eldon Terrace | C2 | | Westfield Road | B1 |
| Elgar Road | B3 | | West Street | B2 |
| Elgar Road South | B3 | | Whitley Street | B3 |
| Elmhurst Road | C3 | | Wolsey Road | B1 |
| Erleigh Road | C3 | | York Road | B1 |
| Fobney Street | B2 | | | |
| Forbury Road | B2 | | | |
| Friar Street | B2 | | | |
| Gas Work Road | B1 | | | |
| George Street *Caversham* | B1 | | | |
| George Street *Reading* | A2 | | | |
| Gosbrook Road | B1 | | | |
| Gower Street | A2 | | | |
| Great Knollys Street | A2 | | | |
| Greyfriars Road | B2 | | | |
| Hemdean Road | B1 | | | |
| Hill Street | B3 | | | |
| Holybrook Road | A3 | | | |
| Kenavon Drive | C2 | | | |
| Kendrick Road | C3 | | | |
| King's Road *Caversham* | B1 | | | |
| King's Road *Reading* | B2 | | | |

Appears on main map page 134

**Tourist Information Centre:  Fish Row**
**Tel: 01722 334956**

| | |
|---|---|
| Albany Road | B1 |
| Ashley Road | A1 |
| Avon Terrace | A1 |
| Barnard Street | C2 |
| Bedwin Street | B1 |
| Belle Vue Road | B1 |
| Bishops Walk | B3 |
| Blackfriars Way | C3 |
| Blue Boar Row | B2 |
| Bourne Avenue | C1 |
| Bourne Hill | C1 |
| Bridge Street | B2 |
| Brown Street | B2 |
| Butcher Row | B2 |
| Carmelite Way | B3 |
| Castle Street | B1 |
| Catherine Street | B2 |
| Chipper Lane | B2 |
| Churchfields Road | A2 |
| Churchill Way East | C2 |
| Churchill Way North | B1 |
| Churchill Way South | C3 |
| Churchill Way West | A1 |
| Clifton Road | A1 |
| College Street | C1 |
| Crane Bridge Road | A2 |
| Crane Street | B2 |
| De Vaux Place | B3 |
| Devizes Road | A1 |
| Elm Grove Road | C2 |
| Endless Street | B1 |
| Estcourt Road | C1 |
| Exeter Street | B3 |
| Fairview Road | C1 |
| Fisherton Street | A2 |
| Fowlers Hill | C2 |
| Fowlers Road | C2 |
| Friary Lane | C3 |
| Gas Lane | A1 |
| Gigant Street | C2 |
| Greencroft Street | C1 |
| Hamilton Road | B1 |
| High Street | B2 |
| Ivy Street | B2 |
| Kelsey Road | C1 |
| Laverstock Road | C2 |
| Manor Road | C1 |
| Marsh Lane | A1 |
| Meadow Road | A1 |
| Milford Hill | C2 |
| Milford Street | B2 |
| Mill Road | A2 |
| Millstream Approach | B1 |
| Minster Street | B2 |
| New Canal | B2 |
| New Street | B2 |
| North Walk | B3 |
| Park Street | C1 |
| Pennyfarthing Street | B2 |
| Queens Road | B1 |
| Rampart Road | C2 |
| Rollestone Street | B1 |
| St. Ann Street | C3 |
| St. John's Street | B2 |
| St. Marks Road | C1 |
| St. Paul's Road | A1 |

| | |
|---|---|
| Salt Lane | B2 |
| Scots Lane | B2 |
| Silver Street | B2 |
| Southampton Road | C3 |
| Swaynes Close | B1 |
| Tollgate Road | C2 |
| Trinity Street | C2 |
| Wain-a-long Road | C1 |
| West Walk | B3 |
| Wilton Road | A1 |
| Winchester Street | B2 |
| Windsor Road | A2 |
| Wyndham Road | B1 |
| York Road | A1 |

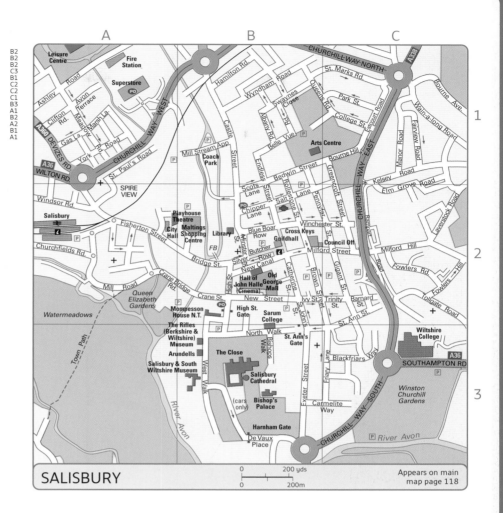

SALISBURY

Appears on main map page 118

0   200 yds
0   200m

**Tourist Information Centre:  Brunswick Shopping Centre,**
**Unit 15a, Westborough  Tel: 01723 383636**

| | |
|---|---|
| Aberdeen Walk | B2 |
| Albion Road | B3 |
| Ashville Avenue | A2 |
| Avenue Road | A3 |
| Belmont Road | B3 |
| Candler Street | A2 |
| Castle Road | B2 |
| Chatsworth Gardens | A1 |
| Columbus Ravine | A2 |
| Commercial Street | A3 |
| Cross Street | B2 |
| Dean Road | A2 |
| Eastborough | B2 |
| Esplanade | B3 |
| Falconers Rd | B2 |
| Falsgrave Road | A3 |
| Foreshore Road | B2 |
| Franklin Street | A2 |
| Friargate | B2 |
| Friarsway | B2 |
| Garfield Road | A2 |
| Gladstone Road | A2 |
| Gladstone Street | A2 |
| Gordon Street | A2 |
| Grosvenor Road | B3 |
| Highfield | A3 |
| Hoxton Road | A2 |
| Longwestgate | C2 |
| Manor Road | A2 |
| Marine Drive | C1 |
| Mayville Avenue | A2 |
| Moorland Road | A1 |
| New Queen Street | B1 |
| Newborough | B2 |
| North Marine Road | B1 |
| North Street | B2 |
| Northstead Manor Drive | A1 |
| Northway | A2 |
| Norwood Street | A2 |
| Oak Road | A3 |
| Peasholm Crescent | A1 |
| Peasholm Drive | A1 |
| Peasholm Road | A1 |
| Prince Of Wales Terrace | B3 |
| Princess Street | C2 |
| Prospect Road | A2 |
| Queen Street | B2 |
| Queen's Parade | B1 |
| Raleigh Street | A2 |
| Ramshill Road | B3 |
| Roscoe Street | A3 |
| Rothbury Street | A2 |
| Royal Albert Drive | B1 |
| Royal Avenue | B3 |
| Sandside | C2 |
| Seamer Road | A3 |
| St. James Road | A3 |
| St. John's Avenue | A3 |
| St. John's Road | A3 |
| St. Thomas Street | B2 |
| Tollergate | B1 |
| Trafalgar Road | A1 |
| Trafalgar Square | B1 |
| Trafalgar Street West | A2 |
| Trinity Road | A3 |
| Valley Bridge Parade | B3 |

| | |
|---|---|
| Valley Bridge Road | B2 |
| Valley Road | A3 |
| Vernon Road | B2 |
| Victoria Park Mount | A1 |
| Victoria Road | A3 |
| Victoria Street | B2 |
| West Street | B3 |
| Westborough | A3 |
| Westbourne Grove | B3 |
| Westover Road | A3 |
| Westwood | B3 |
| Westwood Road | A3 |
| Weydale Avenue | A1 |
| Wykeham Street | A3 |

SCARBOROUGH

Appears on main map page 204

0   400 yds
0   400m

## SHEFFIELD

Tourist Information Centre: 14 Norfolk Row
Tel: 0114 221 1900

| | | | |
|---|---|---|---|
| Allen Street | B1 | Hanover Square | A3 |
| Angel Street | C1 | Hanover Street | A3 |
| Arundel Gate | B2 | Hanover Way | A3 |
| Arundel Lane | C3 | Harmer Lane | C2 |
| Arundel Street | B3 | Haymarket | C1 |
| Bailey Lane | B1 | Headford Street | A3 |
| Bailey Street | B1 | High Street | C1 |
| Bank Street | C1 | Hodgson Street | A3 |
| Barker's Pool | B2 | Hollis Croft | B1 |
| Beet Street | A1 | Howard Street | C2 |
| Bellefield Street | A1 | Hoyle Street | A1 |
| Bishop Street | B3 | Leadmill Road | C3 |
| Blonk Street | C1 | Leopold Street | B2 |
| Boston Street | B3 | Mappin Street | A2 |
| Bower Street | B1 | Margaret Street | B3 |
| Bramwell Street | A1 | Mary Street | B3 |
| Bridge Street | C1 | Matilda Street | B3 |
| Broad Lane | A2 | Meadow Street | A1 |
| Broad Street | C1 | Milton Street | A3 |
| Broomhall Street | A3 | Moore Street | A3 |
| Broomhall Place | A3 | Napier Street | A3 |
| Broomspring Lane | A2 | Netherthorpe Road | A1 |
| Brown Street | C3 | Norfolk Street | C2 |
| Brunswick Street | A2 | Nursery Street | C1 |
| Campo Lane | B1 | Pinstone Street | B2 |
| Carver Street | B2 | Pond Hill | C2 |
| Castle Square | C1 | Pond Hill | C2 |
| Castle Street | C1 | Pond Street | C2 |
| Castlegate | C1 | Portobello Street | A2 |
| Cavendish Street | A2 | Queen Street | B1 |
| Cemetery Road | A3 | Queens Road | C3 |
| Charles Street | B2/C2 | Rockingham Street | B2 |
| Charlotte Road | B3 | St. Mary's Gate | B3 |
| Charter Road | B3 | St. Mary's Road | B3 |
| Charter Row | B3 | St. Philip's Road | A1 |
| Charter Square | B1 | Scotland Street | B1 |
| Church Street | B1 | Sheaf Gardens | C3 |
| Clarke Street | A3 | Sheaf Square | C2 |
| Commercial Street | C1 | Sheaf Street | C2 |
| Copper Street | B1 | Shepherd Street | B1 |
| Corporation Street | B1 | Shoreham Street | C3 |
| Devonshire Street | A2 | Shrewsbury Road | C3 |
| Division Street | B2 | Sidney Street | B3 |
| Dover Street | A1 | Snig Hill | C1 |
| Duchess Road | C3 | Snow Lane | B1 |
| Earl Street | B3 | Solly Street | A1 |
| Earl Way | B3 | South Lane | B3 |
| East Parade | C1 | Spring Street | B1 |
| Ecclesall Road | A3 | Suffolk Road | C3 |
| Edmund Road | C3 | Sunny Bank | A3 |
| Edward Street | A1 | Surrey Street | A3 |
| Eldon Street | B2 | Surrey Street | B2 |
| Exchange Street | C1 | Tenter Street | B1 |
| Exeter Drive | A3 | The Moor | B3 |
| Eyre Lane | C2 | Thomas Street | A3 |
| Eyre Street | B3 | Townhead Street | B1 |
| Farm Road | C3 | Trafalgar Street | B2 |
| Fawcett Street | A1 | Trippet Lane | B2 |
| Filey Street | A2 | Upper Allen Street | A1 |
| Fitzwilliam Street | A2 | Upper Hanover Street | A2 |
| Flat Street | C1 | Victoria Street | A2 |
| Furnace Hill | B1 | Waingate | C1 |
| Furnival Gate | B2 | Wellington Street | B2 |
| Furnival Square | B2 | West Bar | B1 |
| Furnival Street | B2 | West Street | B2 |
| Garden Street | A1 | Westbar Green | B1 |
| Gell Street | A2 | Weston Street | A1 |
| Gibraltar Street | B1 | William Street | A3 |
| Glossop Road | A2 | Young Street | B3 |

Appears on main map page 186

## SOUTHAMPTON

Tourist Information Centre: 9 Civic Centre Road
Tel: 023 8083 3333

| | | | |
|---|---|---|---|
| Above Bar Street | B2 | Queensway | B3 |
| Albert Road North | C3 | Radcliffe Road | C1 |
| Argyle Road | B1 | Roberts Road | A1 |
| Bedford Place | A1 | St. Andrews Road | B1 |
| Belvidere Road | C2 | St. Mary's Road | B1 |
| Bernard Street | B3 | St. Mary Street | B2 |
| Brintons Road | B1 | Shirley Road | A1 |
| Britannia Road | C1 | Solent Road | A2 |
| Briton Street | B3 | Southern Road | A2 |
| Burlington Road | A1 | South Front | B2 |
| Canute Road | B3 | Terminus Terrace | B3 |
| Castle Way | B2 | Town Quay | A3 |
| Central Bridge | B3 | Trafalgar Road | B3 |
| Central Road | B3 | West Quay Road | A2 |
| Chapel Road | B2 | West Road | B3 |
| Civic Centre Road | A2 | Western Esplanade | A2 |
| Clovelly Road | B1 | Wilton Avenue | A1 |
| Commercial Road | A1 | | |
| Cranbury Avenue | B1 | | |
| Cumberland Place | A1 | | |
| Denzil Avenue | B1 | | |
| Derby Road | C1 | | |
| Devonshire Road | A1 | | |
| Dorset Street | B1 | | |
| East Park Terrace | B1 | | |
| East Street | B2 | | |
| Endle Street | C2 | | |
| European Way | B3 | | |
| Golden Grove | B2 | | |
| Graham Road | B1 | | |
| Harbour Parade | A2 | | |
| Hartington Road | C1 | | |
| Henstead Road | A1 | | |
| Herbert Walker Avenue | A2 | | |
| High Street | B2 | | |
| Hill Lane | A1 | | |
| Howard Road | A1 | | |
| James Street | B2 | | |
| Kent Street | C1 | | |
| Kingsway | B2 | | |
| Landguard Road | A1 | | |
| London Road | B1 | | |
| Lyon Street | B1 | | |
| Marine Parade | C2 | | |
| Marsh Lane | B2 | | |
| Melbourne Street | C2 | | |
| Millbank Street | C1 | | |
| Milton Road | A1 | | |
| Morris Road | A1 | | |
| Mount Pleasant Road | B1 | | |
| Newcombe Road | A1 | | |
| New Road | B2 | | |
| Northam Road | C1 | | |
| North Front | B2 | | |
| Northumberland Road | C1 | | |
| Ocean Way | B3 | | |
| Onslow Road | B1 | | |
| Orchard Lane | B3 | | |
| Oxford Avenue | B1 | | |
| Oxford Street | B3 | | |
| Palmerston Road | B2 | | |
| Peel Street | C1 | | |
| Platform Road | B3 | | |
| Portland Terrace | A2 | | |
| Pound Tree Road | B2 | | |
| Princes Street | C1 | | |

Appears on main map page 106

## Stoke-on-Trent

**Tourist Information Centre: Victoria Hall, Bagnall Street, Hanley  Tel: 01782 236000**

|  |  |
|---|---|
| Albion Street | B1 |
| Ashford Street | B2 |
| Avenue Road | B2 |
| Aynsley Road | B2 |
| Bedford Road | B2 |
| Bedford Street | A2 |
| Belmont Road | A1 |
| Beresford Street | B2 |
| Berry Hill Road | C2 |
| Boon Avenue | A3 |
| Botteslow Street | C1 |
| Boughey Road | B3 |
| Broad Street | B1 |
| Bucknall New Road | C1 |
| Bucknall Old Road | C1 |
| Cauldon Road | B2 |
| Cemetery Road | A2 |
| Church Street | B3 |
| Clough Street | A1 |
| College Road | B2 |
| Commercial Road | C1 |
| Copeland Street | B3 |
| Dewsbury Road | C3 |
| Eagle Street | C1 |
| Eastwood Road | C1 |
| Elenora Street | B3 |
| Etruria Road | A1 |
| Etruria Vale Road | A1 |
| Etruscan Street | A2 |
| Festival Way | A1 |
| Forge Lane | A1 |
| Garner Street | A2 |
| Glebe Street | B3 |
| Greatbatch Avenue | A3 |
| Hanley | B1 |
| Hartshill Road | A3 |
| Hill Street | A3 |
| Honeywall | A3 |
| Howard Place | B2 |
| Ivy House Road | C1 |
| Leek Road | B3 |
| Lichfield Street | C1 |
| Liverpool Road | B3 |
| Lordship Lane | B3 |
| Lytton Street | B3 |
| Manor Street | C3 |
| Marsh Street | B1 |
| Newlands Street | B2 |
| North Street | A2 |
| Old Hall Street | B1 |
| Oxford Street | A3 |
| Parliament Row | B1 |
| Potteries Way | B1 |
| Potters Way | C1 |
| Prince's Road | A3 |
| Quarry Avenue | A3 |
| Quarry Road | A3 |
| Queen's Road | A3 |
| Queensway | A2 |
| Rectory Road | B2 |
| Regent Road | B2 |
| Richmond Street | A3 |
| Ridgway Road | B2 |
| Seaford Street | B2 |
| Shelton New Road | A2 |
| Shelton Old Road | A3 |
| Snow Hill | B2 |
| Stafford Street | B1 |
| Station Road | B3 |
| Stoke | B3 |
| Stoke Road | B3 |
| Stone Street | A3 |
| Stuart Road | C2 |
| Sun Street | B1 |
| The Parkway | B2 |
| Trentmill Road | C2 |
| Victoria Road | C2 |
| Warner Street | B1 |
| Waterloo Street | C1 |
| Wellesley Street | B2 |
| Wellington Road | C1 |
| West Avenue | A3 |
| Westland Street | A3 |
| Yoxall Avenue | A3 |

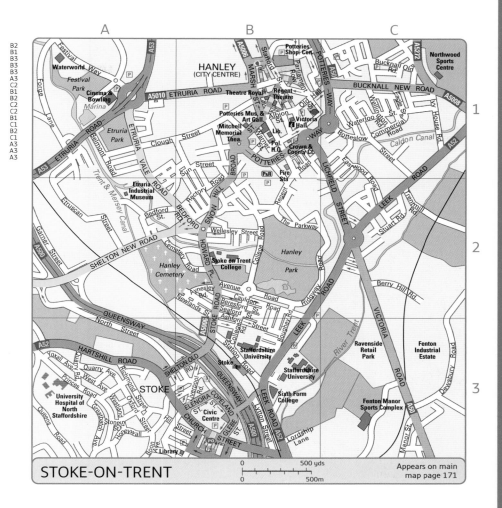

STOKE-ON-TRENT

0        500 yds
0        500m

Appears on main map page 171

## Stratford-upon-Avon

**Tourist Information Centre: Bridgefoot  Tel: 0870 160 7930**

|  |  |
|---|---|
| Albany Road | A2 |
| Alcester Road | A1 |
| Arden Street | A1 |
| Avonside | B3 |
| Banbury Road | C2 |
| Bancroft Place | C2 |
| Birmingham Road | A1 |
| Brewery Street | B1 |
| Bridgefoot | C2 |
| Bridge Street | B2 |
| Bridgeway | C2 |
| Bridgetown Road | C3 |
| Broad Street | A3 |
| Broad Walk | A3 |
| Bull Street | A3 |
| Chapel Lane | B2 |
| Chapel Street | B2 |
| Cherry Orchard | A3 |
| Chestnut Walk | A2 |
| Church Street | B2 |
| Clopton Bridge | C2 |
| Clopton Road | B1 |
| College Lane | B3 |
| College Street | B3 |
| Ely Street | B2 |
| Evesham Place | A3 |
| Evesham Road | A3 |
| Great William Street | B1 |
| Greenhill Street | A2 |
| Grove Road | A2 |
| Guild Street | B1 |
| Henley Street | B1 |
| High Street | B2 |
| Holtom Street | A3 |
| John Street | B1 |
| Kendall Avenue | B1 |
| Maidenhead Road | B1 |
| Mansell Street | A1 |
| Meer Street | B2 |
| Mill Lane | B3 |
| Mulberry Street | B1 |
| Narrow Lane | A3 |
| New Street | B3 |
| Old Town | B3 |
| Old Town Square | B3 |
| Old Tramway Walk | C3 |
| Orchard Way | A3 |
| Payton Street | B1 |
| Red Lion Court | B2 |
| Rother Street | A2 |
| Ryland Street | B3 |
| St. Andrews Crescent | A2 |
| St. Gregory's Road | B1 |
| Sanctus Drive | A3 |
| Sanctus Road | A3 |
| Sanctus Street | A3 |
| Sandfield Road | A3 |
| Scholar's Lane | A2 |
| Seven Meadow Road | A3 |
| Shakespeare Street | B1 |
| Sheep Street | B2 |
| Shipston Road | C3 |
| Shottery Road | A2 |
| Shrieve's Walk | B2 |
| Southern Lane | B3 |
| Station Road | A1 |
| Swan's Nest Lane | C2 |
| The Waterways | A1 |
| Tiddington Road | C2 |
| Trinity Street | B3 |
| Tyler Street | B1 |
| Union Street | B2 |
| Warwick Court | B1 |
| Warwick Crescent | C1 |
| Warwick Road | C1 |
| Waterside | B2 |
| Welcombe Road | C1 |
| Westbourne Grove | A2 |
| Western Road | A1 |
| West Street | A3 |
| Wharf Road | A1 |
| Windsor Street | B2 |
| Wood Street | B2 |

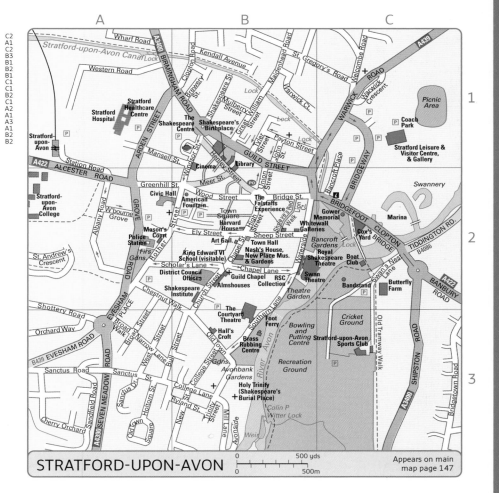

STRATFORD-UPON-AVON

0        500 yds
0        500m

Appears on main map page 147

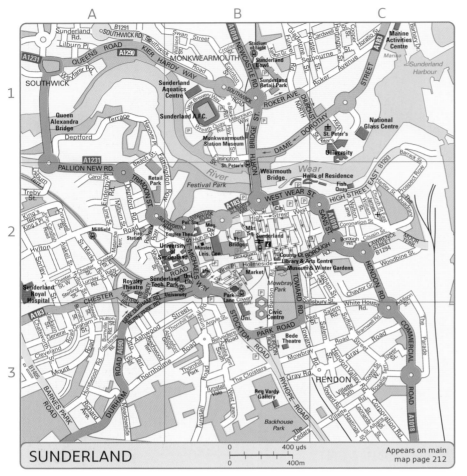

SUNDERLAND

Appears on main
map page 212

**Tourist Information Centre:  50 Fawcett Street**
**Tel:  0191 553 2000**

| | | | |
|---|---|---|---|
| Abbotsford Grove | B3 | Lime Street | A2 |
| Addison Street | C3 | Livingstone Road | B2 |
| Aiskell Street | A2 | Lumley Road | A2 |
| Argyle Street | B3 | Matamba Terrace | A2 |
| Ashwood Street | A3 | Milburn Street | A2 |
| Azalea Terace South | B3 | Millennium Way | B1 |
| Barnes Park Road | A3 | Moor Terrace | C2 |
| Barrack Street | C1 | Mount Road | A3 |
| Beach Street | A2 | Mowbray Road | B3 |
| Beechwood Terrace | A3 | New Durham Road | A3 |
| Belvedere Road | B3 | Newcastle Road | B1 |
| Black Road | B1 | North Bridge Street | B2 |
| Borough Road | B2/C2 | Otto Terrace | A3 |
| Bramwell Road | C3 | Pallion New Road | A2 |
| Brougham Street | B2 | Park Lane | B2 |
| Burdon Road | B3 | Park Road | B3 |
| Burn Park Road | A3 | Peel Street | B3 |
| Burnaby Street | A3 | Prospect Row | C2 |
| Burnville Road | A3 | Queens Road | A1 |
| Carol Street | A2 | Raby Road | A2 |
| Chatsworth Street | A3 | Railway Row | A3 |
| Chaytor Grove | C2 | Roker Avenue | B1/C1 |
| Chester Road | A2 | Rosalie Terrace | C3 |
| Chester Street | A2 | Ryhope Road | B3 |
| Church Street East | C2 | St. Albans Street | C3 |
| Church Street North | B1 | St. Leonards Street | C3 |
| Cleveland Road | A3 | St. Marks Road | A2 |
| Commercial Road | C3 | St. Mary's Way | B2 |
| Cooper Street | C1 | St. Michaels Way | B2 |
| Coronation Street | A2 | St. Peter's Way | C1 |
| Corporation Road | C3 | Salem Road | C3 |
| Cousin Street | C2 | Salem Street | C3 |
| Cromwell Street | A2 | Salisbury Street | B2 |
| Crozier Street | B1 | Sans Street | C2 |
| Dame Dorothy Street | B1 | Selbourne Street | B1 |
| Deptford Road | A2 | Silksworth Row | A2 |
| Deptford Terrace | A1 | Sorley Street | A2 |
| Durham Road | A3 | Southwick Road | A1 |
| Easington Street | B1 | Southwick Road | B1 |
| Eden House Road | A3 | Stewart Street | A3 |
| Eglinton Street | B1 | Stockton Road | B3 |
| Enderby Road | A2 | Suffolk Street | C3 |
| Farringdon Row | A1 | Sunderland Road | A1 |
| Forster Street | C1 | Swan Street | B1 |
| Fox Street | A3 | Tatham Street | C2 |
| Fulwell Road | B1 | The Cedars | B3 |
| General Graham Street | A3 | The Cloisters | B3 |
| Gladstone Street | B1 | The Parade | C3 |
| Gray Road | B3/C3 | The Quadrant | C2 |
| Hanover Place | A1 | The Royalty | A2 |
| Hartington Street | C1 | Thornhill Park | B3 |
| Hartley Street | C2 | Thornhill Terrace | B3 |
| Hastings Street | C3 | Thornholme Road | A3 |
| Hay Street | B1 | Toward Road | B2/C3 |
| Hendon Road | C2 | Tower Street | C3 |
| Hendon Valley Road | C3 | Tower Street West | C3 |
| High Street East | C2 | Trimdon Street | A2 |
| High Street West | B2 | Tunstall Road | B3 |
| Holmeside | B2 | Tunstall Vale | B3 |
| Horatio Street | C1 | Vaux Brewery Way | B1 |
| Hurstwood Road | A3 | Villette Road | C3 |
| Hutton Street | A3 | Vine Place | B2 |
| Hylton Road | A2 | Wallace Street | B1 |
| Hylton Road | A2 | West Lawn | B3 |
| Jackson Street | A3 | West Wear Street | B2 |
| James William Street | C2 | Western Hill | A2 |
| Kenton Grove | B1 | Wharncliffe Street | A2 |
| Kier Hardy Way | A1 | White House Road | C3 |
| King's Place | A2 | Woodbine Street | C2 |
| Lawrence Street | C2 | Wreath Quay Road | B1 |

SWANSEA

Appears on main
map page 128

**Tourist Information Centre:  Plymouth Street**
**Tel:  01792 468321**

| | | | |
|---|---|---|---|
| Aberdyberthi Street | C1 | Mount Pleasant | B2 |
| Albert Row | B3 | Mumbles Road | A3 |
| Alexandra Road | B2 | Neath Road | C1 |
| Argyle Street | A3 | Nelson Street | B3 |
| Baptist Well Place | B1 | New Cut Road | C2 |
| Baptist Well Street | B1 | New Orchard Street | B1 |
| Beach Street | A3 | Nicander Parade | A2 |
| Belgrave Lane | A3 | Norfolk Street | A2 |
| Belle Vue Way | B2 | North Hill Road | B1 |
| Berw Road | A1 | Orchard Street | B2 |
| Berwick Terrace | B1 | Oxford Street | A3 |
| Bond Street | A3 | Oystermouth Road | A3 |
| Brooklands Terrace | A2 | Page Street | B2 |
| Brunswick Street | A3 | Pant-y-Celyn Road | A2 |
| Brynymor Crescent | A3 | Park Terrace | B1 |
| Brynymor Road | A3 | Pedrog Terrace | A1 |
| Burrows Place | C3 | Penlan Crescent | A2 |
| Cambrian Place | C3 | Pentre Guinea Road | C1 |
| Cang Crescent | A1 | Pen-y-Craig Road | A1 |
| Carlton Terrace | B2 | Picton Terrace | A2 |
| Carmarthen Road | B1 | Powys Avenue | A1 |
| Castle Street | B2 | Princess Way | B2 |
| Clarence Terrace | B3 | Quay Parade | C2 |
| Colbourne Terrace | B1 | Rhondda Street | A2 |
| Constitution Hill | A2 | Rose Hill | A2 |
| Creidiol Road | A1 | St. Elmo Avenue | C1 |
| Cromwell Street | A2 | St. Helen's Avenue | A3 |
| Cwm Road | C1 | St. Helen's Road | A3 |
| De La Beche Street | B2 | St. Mary Street | B2 |
| Delhi Street | C2 | Singleton Street | B3 |
| Dillwyn Street | B3 | Somerset Place | C3 |
| Dyfatty Street | B1 | South Guildhall Road | A3 |
| Dyfed Avenue | A2 | Strand | C2 |
| Earl Street | C1 | Taliesyn Road | A2 |
| East Burrows Road | C3 | Tan-y-Marian Road | A2 |
| Eigen Crescent | A1 | Tegid Road | A1 |
| Emlyn Road | A1 | Teilo Crescent | A1 |
| Fabian Way | C2 | Terrace Road | A2 |
| Fairfield Terrace | A2 | The Kingsway | B2 |
| Ffynone Drive | A2 | Townhill Road | A1 |
| Ffynone Road | A2 | Trawler Road | B3 |
| Foxhole Road | C1 | Villiers Street | C1 |
| Glamorgan Street | B3 | Vincent Street | A3 |
| Gors Avenue | A1 | Walter Road | A3 |
| Granagwen Road | B1 | Watkin Street | B2 |
| Grove Place | B2 | Waun-Wen Road | B1 |
| Gwent Road | A1 | Wellington Street | B3 |
| Gwili Terrace | A1 | West Way | B3 |
| Hanover Street | A2 | Westbury Street | A3 |
| Heathfield | A2 | Western Street | A3 |
| Hewson Street | A2 | William Street | B3 |
| High Street | B2 | Windmill Terrace | C1 |
| High View | B1 | York Street | C3 |
| Islwyn Road | A1 | | |
| Kilvey Road | C1 | | |
| Kilvey Terrace | C2 | | |
| King Edward's Road | A3 | | |
| King's Road | A2 | | |
| Llangyfelach Road | B1 | | |
| Long Ridge | B1 | | |
| Mackworth Street | C2 | | |
| Maesteg Street | C1 | | |
| Mansel Street | A2 | | |
| Mayhill Road | A1 | | |
| Milton Terrace | B2 | | |
| Morris Lane | C2 | | |

**Tourist Information Centre: 37 Regent Street**
**Tel: 01793 530328**

| Street | Grid | | Street | Grid |
|---|---|---|---|---|
| Albion Street | A3 | | Upham Road | C3 |
| Bath Road | B3 | | Victoria Road | C2 |
| Beatrice Street | B1 | | Westcott Place | A3 |
| Beckhampton Street | C2 | | Western Street | C3 |
| Birch Street | A2 | | William Street | A3 |
| Bridge Street | B2 | | York Road | C2 |
| Broad Street | C1 | | | |
| Canal Walk | B2 | | | |
| Caulfield Road | C1 | | | |
| Church Place | A2 | | | |
| Cirencester Way | C1 | | | |
| Clifton Street | B3 | | | |
| Commercial Road | B2 | | | |
| County Road | C1 | | | |
| Cricklade Street | C3 | | | |
| Curtis Street | B2 | | | |
| Dean Street | A2 | | | |
| Drove Road | C3 | | | |
| Eastcott Hill | B3 | | | |
| Edmund Street | B2 | | | |
| Elmina Road | C1 | | | |
| Euclid Street | C2 | | | |
| Faringdon Road | A2 | | | |
| Farnsby Street | B2 | | | |
| Fleet Street | B2 | | | |
| Fleming Way | B2 | | | |
| Gladstone Street | C1 | | | |
| Goddard Avenue | B3 | | | |
| Great Western Way | A1 | | | |
| Grosvenor Road | A3 | | | |
| Groundwell Road | C2 | | | |
| Hawksworth Way | A1 | | | |
| High Street | C3 | | | |
| Holbrook Way | B2 | | | |
| Hythe Road | B3 | | | |
| Islington Street | B2 | | | |
| Jennings Street | A2 | | | |
| Kemble Drive | A1 | | | |
| Kent Road | B3 | | | |
| Kingshill Street | A3 | | | |
| Lansdown Road | B3 | | | |
| Manchester Road | B1 | | | |
| Market Street | B2 | | | |
| Milford Street | B2 | | | |
| Milton Road | B2 | | | |
| Morris Street | A1 | | | |
| Newburn Crescent | A2 | | | |
| Newcombe Drive | A1 | | | |
| North Star Avenue | B1 | | | |
| Ocotal Way | C1 | | | |
| Okus Road | A3 | | | |
| Park Lane | A2 | | | |
| Penzance Drive | A2 | | | |
| Plymouth Street | C2 | | | |
| Princes Street | C2 | | | |
| Queen Street | B2 | | | |
| Radnor Street | A3 | | | |
| Redcliffe Street | A2 | | | |
| Regent Street | B2 | | | |
| Rodbourne Road | A1 | | | |
| Rosebery Street | C1 | | | |
| Spring Gardens | C2 | | | |
| Stafford Street | B3 | | | |
| Station Road | B1 | | | |
| Swindon Road | B3 | | | |
| The Parade | B2 | | | |

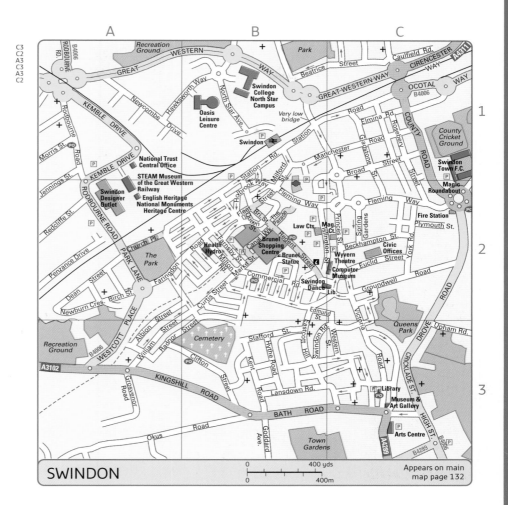

SWINDON

Appears on main map page 132

**Tourist Information Centre: Vaughan Parade**
**Tel: 0870 70 70 010**

| Street | Grid | | Street | Grid |
|---|---|---|---|---|
| Abbey Road | B2 | | Thurlow Road | B1 |
| Ash Hill Road | B1 | | Tor Hill Road | B2 |
| Avenue Road | A2 | | Torbay Road | A3 |
| Bampfylde Road | A2 | | Torwood Gardens Road | C3 |
| Barton Road | A1 | | Torwood Street | C3 |
| Belgrave Road | A2 | | Union Street | B2 |
| Belmont Road | C1 | | Upton Hill | B1 |
| Braddons Hill Road East | C2 | | Upton Road | A1 |
| Bridge Road | A2 | | Vanehill Road | C3 |
| Bronshill Road | B1 | | Victoria Parade | C3 |
| Brunswick Square | B1 | | Walnut Road | A3 |
| Carlton Road | C1 | | Warbro Road | C1 |
| Cary Parade | C3 | | Warren Road | B2 |
| Cedars Road | C2 | | Windsor Road | C1 |
| Chestnut Avenue | A2 | | | |
| Cockington Lane | A3 | | | |
| Croft Road | B2 | | | |
| Crownhill Park | A1 | | | |
| Dunmere Road | C1 | | | |
| East Street | A1 | | | |
| Ellacombe Church Road | C1 | | | |
| Ellacombe Road | B1 | | | |
| Falkland Road | A2 | | | |
| Falkland Road | A2 | | | |
| Fleet Street | B2 | | | |
| Forest Road | B1 | | | |
| Goshen Road | A2 | | | |
| Hatfield Road | B1 | | | |
| Hennapyn Road | A3 | | | |
| Higher Warberry Road | C2 | | | |
| Hillesdon Road | C2 | | | |
| Kenwyn Road | C1 | | | |
| Lower Warberry Road | C2 | | | |
| Lucius Street | A2 | | | |
| Lymington Road | B1 | | | |
| Mallock Road | A2 | | | |
| Market Street | B2 | | | |
| Marnham Road | C1 | | | |
| Meadfoot Lane | C3 | | | |
| Meadfoot Road | C3 | | | |
| Middle Warberry Road | C2 | | | |
| Mill Lane | A2 | | | |
| Newton Road | A1 | | | |
| Old Mill Road | A2 | | | |
| Old Mill Road | A3 | | | |
| Parkfield Road | B1 | | | |
| Parkhill Road | C3 | | | |
| Prince's Road | C2 | | | |
| Princes Road East | C2 | | | |
| Quinta Road | C1 | | | |
| Rathmore Road | A3 | | | |
| Reddenhill Road | C1 | | | |
| Rosehill Road | C2 | | | |
| Sanford Road | A2 | | | |
| Seaway Lane | A3 | | | |
| Shedden Hill | B2 | | | |
| Sherwell Lane | A2 | | | |
| Solsbro Road | A3 | | | |
| South Street | A2 | | | |
| St. Lukes Road | B2 | | | |
| St. Marychurch Road | B2 | | | |
| St. Michael's Road | A1 | | | |
| Stitchill Road | C2 | | | |
| Strand | C3 | | | |
| Teignmouth Road | A1 | | | |
| The King's Drive | A2 | | | |

TORQUAY

Appears on main map page 101

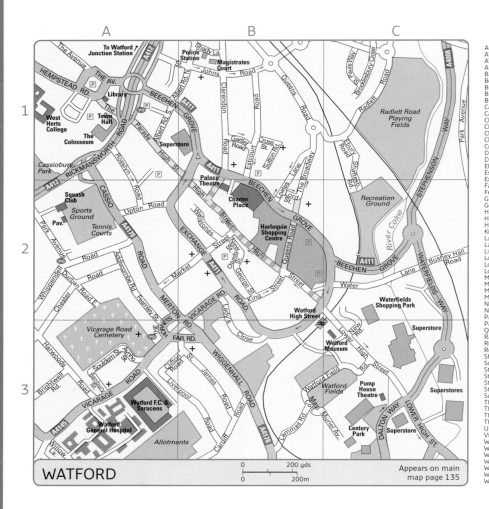

**WATFORD**

0   200 yds
0   200m

Appears on main map page 135

| | |
|---|---|
| Addiscombe Road | A2 |
| Albert Road North | A1 |
| Albert Road South | A1 |
| Aynho Street | A3 |
| Banbury Street | A3 |
| Beechen Grove | A1/C2 |
| Brightwell Road | A3 |
| Brocklesbury Close | C1 |
| Bushey Hall Road | C2 |
| Cardiff Road | B3 |
| Cassio Road | A2 |
| Chester Road | A2 |
| Church Street | B2 |
| Clarendon Road | B1 |
| Clifton Road | A3 |
| Cross Street | B1 |
| Dalton Way | C3 |
| Durban Road East | A2 |
| Ebury Road | C1 |
| Estcourt Road | B1 |
| Exchange Road | A2 |
| Farraline Road | A3 |
| Fearnley Street | A2 |
| Garlet Road | B1 |
| George Street | B2 |
| Harwoods Road | A3 |
| Hempsted Road | A1 |
| High Street | A1/B2 |
| King Street | B2 |
| Lady's Close | B2 |
| Lammas Road | B3 |
| Liverpool Road | A3 |
| Loates Lane | B2 |
| Lord Street | B2 |
| Lower High Street | C3 |
| Market Street | A2 |
| May Cottages | B3 |
| Merton Road | A2 |
| Muriel Avenue | B3 |
| New Road | C3 |
| New Street | B2 |
| Park Avenue | C1 |
| Park Avenue | A2 |
| Queens Road | B1/B2 |
| Radlett Road | C1 |
| Rickmansworth Road | A2 |
| Rosslyn Road | A1 |
| Shaftesbury Road | C1 |
| Souldern Street | A3 |
| St. James Road | B3 |
| St. Johns Road | A1 |
| St. Pauls Way | C1 |
| Stephenson Way | C2 |
| Sutton Road | B1 |
| The Avenue | A1 |
| The Broadway | B2 |
| The Hornets | A3 |
| The Parade | A1 |
| Upton Road | A2 |
| Vicarage Road | A3/B2 |
| Water Lane | C2 |
| Waterfields Way | C2 |
| Watford Field Road | B3 |
| Wellstones | B2 |
| Whippendell Road | A2 |
| Wiggenhall Road | B3 |
| Willow Lane | A3 |

**WESTON-SUPER-MARE**

0   400 yds
0   400m

Appears on main map page 115

**Tourist Information Centre: Beach Lawns**
**Tel: 01934 888800**

| | |
|---|---|
| Addicott Road | B3 |
| Albert Avenue | B3 |
| Alexandra Parade | B2 |
| Alfred Street | B2 |
| All Saints Road | B1 |
| Amberey Road | C3 |
| Arundell Road | B1 |
| Ashcombe Gardens | C1 |
| Ashcombe Road | C2 |
| Atlantic Road | A1 |
| Baker Street | B2 |
| Beach Road | B3 |
| Beaconsfield Road | B2 |
| Birnbeck Road | A1 |
| Boulevard | B2 |
| Brendon Avenue | C1 |
| Bridge Road | C2 |
| Brighton Road | B3 |
| Bristol Road | B1 |
| Carlton Street | B2 |
| Cecil Road | B1 |
| Clarence Road North | B3 |
| Clarendon Road | C2 |
| Clevedon Road | B3 |
| Clifton Road | B3 |
| Drove Road | C3 |
| Earlham Grove | C2 |
| Ellenborough Park North | B3 |
| Ellenborough Park South | B3 |
| Exeter Road | B3 |
| George Street | B2 |
| Gerard Road | B1 |
| Grove Park Road | B1 |
| High Street | B2 |
| Highbury Road | A1 |
| Hildesheim Bridge | B2 |
| Hill Road | C1 |
| Jubilee Road | B2 |
| Kenn Close | C3 |
| Kensington Road | C3 |
| Knightstone Road | A1 |
| Langford Road | C3 |
| Lewisham Grove | C2 |
| Locking Road | C2 |
| Lower Bristol Road | C1 |
| Lower Church Road | A1 |
| Manor Road | C1 |
| Marchfields Way | C3 |
| Marine Parade | B3 |
| Meadow Street | B2 |
| Milton Road | B1 |
| Montpelier | B1 |
| Neva Road | B2 |
| Norfolk Road | C3 |
| Oxford Street | B2 |
| Queen's Road | B1 |
| Rectors Way | C3 |
| Regent Street | B2 |
| Ridgeway Avenue | B3 |
| Royal Crescent | A1 |
| St. Paul's Road | B3 |
| Sandford Road | C2 |
| Severn Road | B3 |
| Shrubbery Road | A1 |
| South Road | A1 |
| Southside | B1 |

| | |
|---|---|
| Stafford Road | C2 |
| Station Road | B2 |
| Sunnyside Road | B3 |
| Swiss Road | C2 |
| The Centre | B2 |
| Trewartha Park | C1 |
| Upper Church Road | A1 |
| Walliscote Road | B3 |
| Waterloo Street | B2 |
| Whitecross Road | B3 |
| Winterstoke Road | C3 |

**Tourist Information Centre:  Guildhall, High Street**
**Tel:  01962 840500**

| Alison Way | A1 |
| Andover Road | A1 |
| Archery Lane | A2 |
| Bar End Road | C3 |
| Barfield Close | C3 |
| Beaufort Road | A3 |
| Beggar's Lane | C2 |
| Blue Ball Hill | C2 |
| Bridge Stret | C2 |
| Broadway | B2 |
| Canon Street | B3 |
| Chesil Street | C3 |
| Christchurch Road | A3 |
| City Road | A1 |
| Clifton Hill | A2 |
| Clifton Road | A1 |
| Clifton Terrace | A2 |
| Colebrook Street | B2 |
| College Street | B3 |
| College Walk | B3 |
| Compton Road | A3 |
| Cranworth Road | A1 |
| Culver Road | B3 |
| Domum Road | C3 |
| Durngate | C2 |
| East Hill | C3 |
| Eastgate Street | C2 |
| Easton Lane | C1 |
| Ebden Road | C1 |
| Edgar Road | A3 |
| Elm Road | A1 |
| Fairfield Road | A1 |
| Friarsgate | B2 |
| Gordon Road | B1 |
| Great Minster Street | B2 |
| Hatherley Road | A1 |
| High Street | B2 |
| Hyde Abbey Road | B1 |
| Hyde Close | B1 |
| Hyde Street | B1 |
| Jewry Street | B2 |
| King Alfred Place | B1 |
| Kingsgate Street | B3 |
| Little Minster Street | B2 |
| Lower Brook Street | B2 |
| Magdalen Hill | C2 |
| Market Lane | B2 |
| Middle Brook Street | B2 |
| Middle Road | A2 |
| Milland Road | C3 |
| North Walls | A1 |
| Parchment Street | B2 |
| Park Avenue | B1 |
| Peninsula Square | A2 |
| Portal Road | C3 |
| Quarry Road | C3 |
| Romans' Road | A3 |
| Romsey Road | A2 |
| St. Catherine's Road | C3 |
| St. Cross Road | A3 |
| St. George's Street | B2 |
| St. James Lane | A2 |
| St. James Villas | A3 |
| St. John's Street | C2 |
| St. Michael's Road | A3 |
| St. Paul's Hill | A1 |

| St. Peter Street | B2 |
| St. Swithun Street | B3 |
| St. Thomas Street | B3 |
| Saxon Road | B1 |
| Silver Hill | B2 |
| Southgate Street | A3 |
| Staple Gardens | B2 |
| Station Road | A1 |
| Step Terrace | A2 |
| Stockbridge Road | A1 |
| Sussex Street | A2 |
| Swan Lane | B1 |
| Symond's Street | B3 |
| Tanner Street | B2 |
| The Square | B2 |
| Tower Street | A2 |
| Union Street | C2 |
| Upper Brook Street | B2 |
| Upper High Street | A2 |
| Wales Street | C2 |
| Water Lane | C2 |
| Wharf Hill | C3 |
| Worthy Lane | A1 |

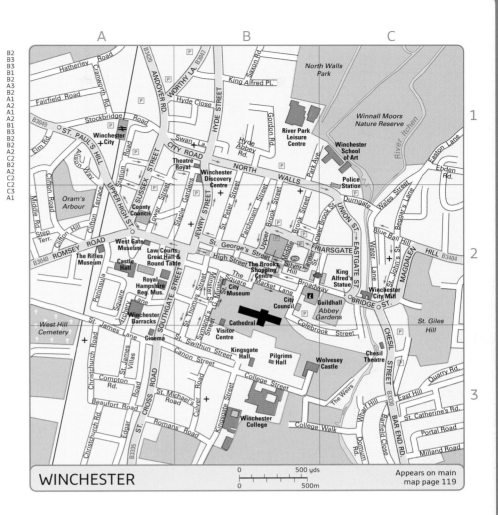

WINCHESTER

0    500 yds
0    500m

Appears on main
map page 119

**Tourist Information Centre:  Old Booking Hall, Central Station**
**Tel:  01753 743900**

| Adelaide Square | C3 |
| Albert Street | A2 |
| Alexandra Road | B3 |
| Alma Road | B2/B3 |
| Arthur Road | B2 |
| Barry Avenue | B1 |
| Bexley Street | B2 |
| Bolton Avenue | B3 |
| Bolton Crescent | B3 |
| Bolton Road | B3 |
| Bulkeley Avenue | A3 |
| Castle Hill | C2 |
| Charles Street | B2 |
| Clarence Crescent | B2 |
| Clarence Road | A2 |
| College Crescent | A3 |
| Dagmar Road | B2 |
| Datchet Road | C1 |
| Frances Road | B3 |
| Goslar Way | A2 |
| Goswell Road | B2 |
| Green Lane | A2 |
| Grove Road | B2 |
| Helston Lane | A2 |
| High Street (Eton) | B1 |
| High Street (Windsor) | C2 |
| Imperial Road | A3 |
| King Edward VII Avenue | C1 |
| Kings Road | C3 |
| Meadow Lane | B1 |
| Mill Lane | A1 |
| Osborne Road | B3 |
| Oxford Road | B2 |
| Park Street | C2 |
| Parsonage Lane | A2 |
| Peascod Street | B2 |
| Peel Close | A3 |
| Princess Avenue | A3 |
| Romney Lock Road | C1 |
| St. Leonards Road | B3 |
| St. Marks Road | B2 |
| Sheet Street | C2 |
| South Meadow Lane | B1 |
| Springfield Road | A3 |
| Stovell Road | A1 |
| Thames Street | C1 |
| The Long Walk | C3 |
| Upcroft | A3 |
| Vansittart Road | B2 |
| Victoria Street | B2 |
| Victor Road | B3 |
| Westmead | A3 |
| Windsor & Eton Relief Road | A2 |
| York Avenue | A3 |
| York Road | A3 |

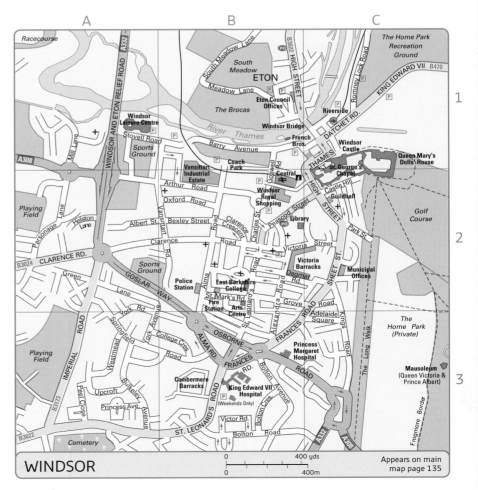

WINDSOR

0    400 yds
0    400m

Appears on main
map page 135

## WORCESTER

Appears on main map page 146

**Tourist Information Centre: The Guildhall, High Street**
**Tel: 01905 726311**

## YORK

Appears on main map page 195

**Tourist Information Centre: De Grey Rooms, Exhibition Square**
**Tel: 01904 550099**

## Key to map symbols

🅿 Short stay car park  🅿 Mid stay car park  🅿 Long stay car park  🅿 Other car park  ▭ Airport terminal building

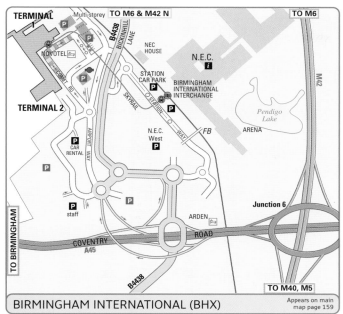

BIRMINGHAM INTERNATIONAL (BHX)

Appears on main map page 159

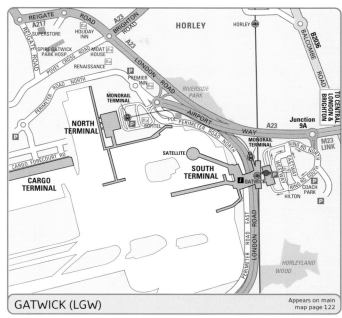

GATWICK (LGW)

Appears on main map page 122

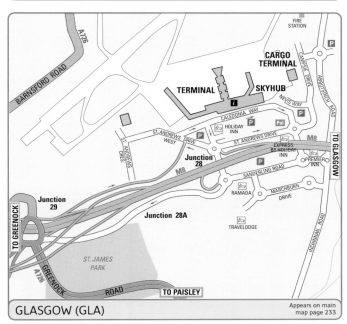

GLASGOW (GLA)

Appears on main map page 233

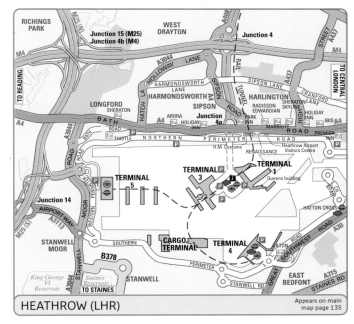

HEATHROW (LHR)

Appears on main map page 135

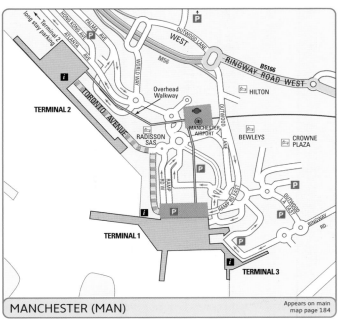

MANCHESTER (MAN)

Appears on main map page 184

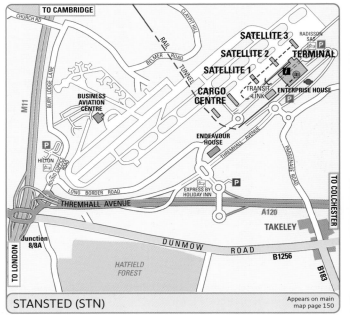

STANSTED (STN)

Appears on main map page 150

## Symbols used on the map

| | |
|---|---|
| M5 | Motorway |
| M6 Toll | Toll motorway |
| 8 — 9 | Motorway junction with full / limited access (in congested areas there is just a numbered symbol) |
| Maidstone / Birch / Sarn | Motorway service area with off road / full / limited access |
| A556 | Primary route dual / single carriageway |
| S | 24 hour service area on primary route |
| **Peterhead** | Primary route destination — Primary route destinations are places of major traffic importance linked by the primary route network. They are shown on a green background on direction signs. |
| A30 | 'A' road dual / single carriageway |
| B1403 | 'B' road dual / single carriageway |
| | Minor road |
| | Road with restricted access |
| | Roads with passing places |
| | Road proposed or under construction |
| 33 | Multi-level junction with full / limited access (with junction number) |
| | Roundabout |
| 4 | Road distance in miles between markers |
| | Road tunnel |
| | Steep hill (arrows point downhill) |
| Toll | Level crossing / Toll |
| St. Malo 8hrs | Car ferry route with journey times |
| | Railway line / station / tunnel |
| South Downs Way | National Trail / Long Distance Route |

| | |
|---|---|
| 30 / V | Fixed safety camera — Speed limit shown by a number within the camera, a V indicates a variable limit. |
| 30 — 30 | Fixed average-speed safety camera — Speed limit shown by a number within the camera. |
| ✈ | Airport with / without scheduled services |
| H | Heliport |
| P&R | Park and Ride site operated by bus / rail (runs at least 5 days a week) |
| | Built up area |
| □ □ ▫ | Town / Village / Other settlement |
| **Hythe** | Seaside destination |
| ─·─·─ | National boundary |
| KENT | County / Unitary Authority boundary and name |

| | metres |
|---|---|
| 0 150 300 500 700 900 | |
| water 0 490 985 1640 2295 2950 feet | |

Land height reference bar

| | |
|---|---|
| | Heritage Coast |
| | National Park |
| | Regional / Forest Park boundary |
| | Woodland |
| Danger Zone | Military range |
| 468 · 941 ▲ | Spot / Summit height (in metres) |
| | Lake / Dam / River / Waterfall |
| | Canal / Dry canal / Canal tunnel |
| | Beach / Lighthouse |
| SEE PAGE 3 | Area covered by urban area map |

## Reading our maps

**Park & Ride** Sites are shown that operate at least 5 days a week. Bus operated sites have a yellow symbol and rail operated sites a pink symbol.

**Distances** Blue numbers give distances in miles between junctions shown with a blue marker

**Multi-level junctions** Non-motorway junctions where slip roads are used to access the main roads

**Motorway service area**

**World Heritage site** Places of interest defined by UNESCO as special on a world scale.

**Places of interest** Blue symbols indicate places of interest. See the section to the right for the different types of feature represented on the map.

**Safety Camera** The number inside the camera shows the speed limit at the camera location.

**More detailed maps** Green boxes indicate busy built-up-areas where more detailed mapping is available.

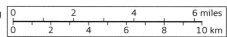

## Places of interest

A selection of tourist detail is shown on the mapping. It is advisable to check with the local tourist information centre regarding opening times and facilities available.

Any of the following symbols may appear on the map in maroon ★ which indicates that the site has World Heritage status.

| | |
|---|---|
| *i* | Tourist information centre (open all year) |
| *i* | Tourist information centre (open seasonally) |
| m | Ancient monument |
| | Aquarium |
| | Aqueduct / Viaduct |
| | Arboretum |
| 1643 | Battlefield |
| | Blue flag beach |
| ▲ ⊞ | Camp site / Caravan site |
| | Castle |
| | Cave |
| | Country park |
| | County cricket ground |
| | Distillery |
| ✝ | Ecclesiastical feature |
| | Event venue |
| | Farm park |
| | Garden |
| ⌐ | Golf course |
| | Historic house |
| | Historic ship |
| ⚽ | Major football club |
| £ | Major shopping centre / Outlet village |
| | Major sports venue |
| | Motor racing circuit |
| | Mountain bike trail |
| | Museum / Art gallery |
| | Nature reserve (NNR indicates a National Nature Reserve) |
| | Racecourse |
| | Rail Freight Terminal |
| | Ski slope (artificial / natural) |
| | Spotlight nature reserve (Best sites for access to nature) |
| | Steam railway centre / preserved railway |
| | Surfing beach |
| | Theme park |
| | University |
| | Vineyard |
| | Wildlife park / Zoo |
| ★ | Other interesting feature |
| (NT) (NTS) | National Trust / National Trust for Scotland property |

## Map scale

A scale bar appears at the bottom of every page to help with distances.

```
0          2          4        6 miles
0     2     4     6     8    10 km
```

England, Wales & Southern Scotland are at a scale of 1:200,000 or 3.2 miles to 1 inch
Northern Scotland is at a scale of 1:263,158 or 4.2 miles to 1 inch.

## Map pages

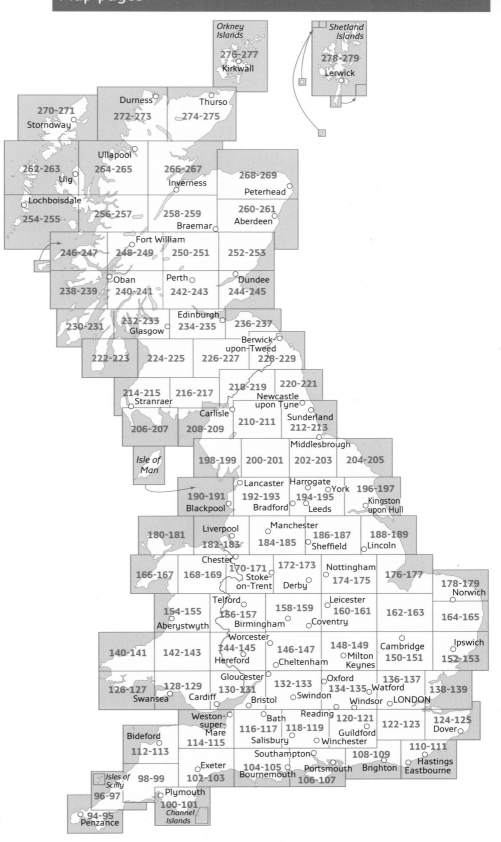

Orkney Islands 276-277 Kirkwall
Shetland Islands 278-279 Lerwick
270-271 Stornoway
Durness 272-273
Thurso 274-275
Ullapool 264-265 Uig
262-263
266-267 Inverness
268-269 Peterhead
Lochboisdale 256-257
254-255
258-259 Braemar
260-261 Aberdeen
246-247
Fort William 248-249
250-251
252-253
Oban 240-241
238-239
Perth 242-243
Dundee 244-245
230-231
Edinburgh 232-233 Glasgow
234-235
236-237
222-223
224-225
226-227
Berwick-upon-Tweed 228-229
Stranraer 214-215
216-217
218-219
Newcastle upon Tyne 220-221
Carlisle 206-207
208-209
210-211
Sunderland 212-213
Isle of Man 198-199
200-201
Middlesbrough 202-203
204-205
Lancaster 190-191 Blackpool
192-193 Bradford
Harrogate York 194-195 Leeds
196-197 Kingston upon Hull
180-181
Liverpool 182-183
Manchester 184-185
186-187 Sheffield
188-189 Lincoln
Chester 166-167
168-169
170-171 Stoke-on-Trent
172-173 Derby
Nottingham 174-175
176-177
178-179 Norwich
Telford 154-155 Aberystwyth
156-157 Birmingham
158-159
Leicester 160-161 Coventry
162-163
164-165
140-141
142-143
Worcester 144-145 Hereford
146-147 Cheltenham
148-149 Milton Keynes
Cambridge 150-151
Ipswich 152-153
126-127 Swansea
128-129 Cardiff
Gloucester 130-131
132-133 Bristol
Oxford 134-135 Swindon
136-137 Watford Windsor LONDON
138-139
Weston-super-Mare 114-115
Bideford 112-113
Bath 116-117
118-119 Salisbury
Reading 120-121 Guildford Winchester
122-123
124-125 Dover
Southampton 104-105 Bournemouth
102-103 Exeter
106-107 Portsmouth
108-109 Brighton
110-111 Hastings Eastbourne
Isles of Scilly 98-99
96-97
Plymouth 100-101 Channel Islands
94-95 Penzance

A    B    C    D

1

2

Portreath
Harbour
Godrevy - Portreath
Heritage Coast          Crane        Portre
Islands

Godrevy          Navax
Island          Point
Penwith                                    Tehidy
Heritage          Barbara                Gwithian
Coast          Hepworth                              Red
Carn Naun          Museum          St          Coombe
Pt          The          Ives          Kehelland      Camborne
The                Island          Bay                    A30    Min
Carracks          Tate          St Ives          Gwithian                Trevarnon          60
St Ives                          60    Camborne
Gurnard's                          Port of          Phillack          Connor          Barripper
Head          Trendrine          Carbis          Hayle          Downs
Zennor          Hill    B3306    Bay    Longstone          4    Copperhouse          Angarrack          Penponds
247          Halsetown          Lelant          Hayle 7    Carnhell          Praze-
Treen          Towednack                                        Green          Beeble
Porthmeor          12          Amalebra          Canon's Town          St Erth          Gwinear          Wall          Crow
Pendeen          Chysauster Ancient    Nancledra          Trencrom          Whitecross    A30    Praze
Watch          Village          Castle          Hill          St    3    Kerthen          Paul's          Fraddam    B3303
Lower Boscaswell          New          Gate    (NT)          Erth          Wood          Green          Leedstown
Levant Steam          Mill    Chysauster          Crowlas          Tregonning &          Townshend          B3280          Trenwheal
Engine (NT)    Morvah          252          Ludgvan          Gwinear Mining          Re
Trewellard    Pendeen          Boswarthan          4          District with Trewavas          Godolphin    B3302    Godolphin
Botallack    Carnyorth    B3306          Heamoor    Gulval          Longrock    Relubbus          House (NT)    Cross          Crown
Kenidjack    St Just Mining District    Madron          (H)          Penzance          Goldsithney    Trescowe    Tregonning          Pollardras
Cape          Newbridge    Trengwainton          Trevarrack          Marazion          Perran Downs    Hill 194          Crown
Cornwall          7    (NT)          A30          St Michael's          Rosudgeon          Newtown          Germoe
The Brisons    Bosavern          Tremethick          Chyandour          Mount (NT)          Kennegay          Ashton
Carn Leskys    St Just          Cross          St Clement's    Perranuthnoe    Downs    Tresowes Green          Sithne
Kelynack          Grumbla    Sancreed          Buryas Bridge          Prussia Cove          10    Carleen    A394
Penwith          Carn Euny          Tredavoe          Cudden          Praa Sands          Breage    Hels
Heritage          Ancient          Brane    Lower          Newlyn          Point          Rinsey          Trewavas Head          The Flam
Coast          Village          Drift          M O U N T S          Porthleven    Expedi
LAND'S END    Crows-          9    Kerris          Paul    Whitesand          an-wra                Mousehole
Bay          St Buryan          Boleigh    Lamorna          Berep
Sennen          Sennen          St Clement's          Gunwal
Cove          7          Isle
LAND'S    Trevescan          Lamorna Cove
Longships    END          Trethewey          Burial          The Lizard
Land's          Minack          Chamber          Penwith Heritage Coast          Heritage Coast
End          Theatre          Po
Porthcurno    Treen          Poldhu
Gwennap Head    Porthcurno Sands    St          Cribba Head
Levan    Logan          Mulli
Rock          Mulli

Mullion Is

Predanna

3

4

5

Wolf Rock

0    2    4    6 miles
0    2    4    6    8    10 km

B    C    D

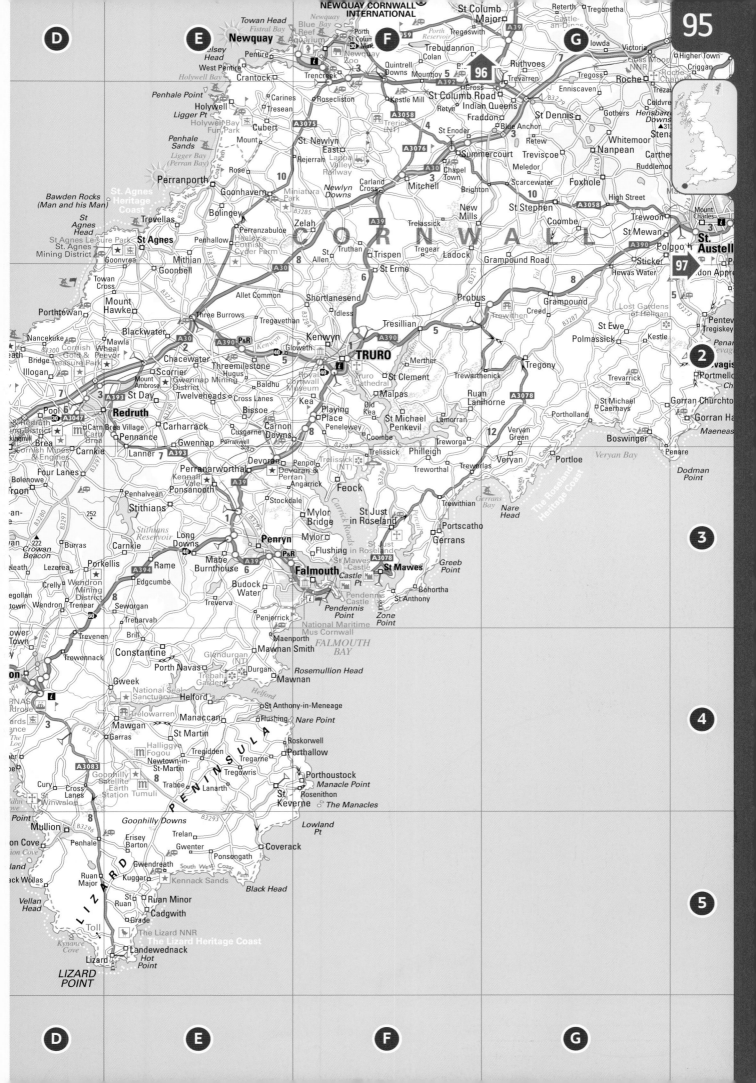

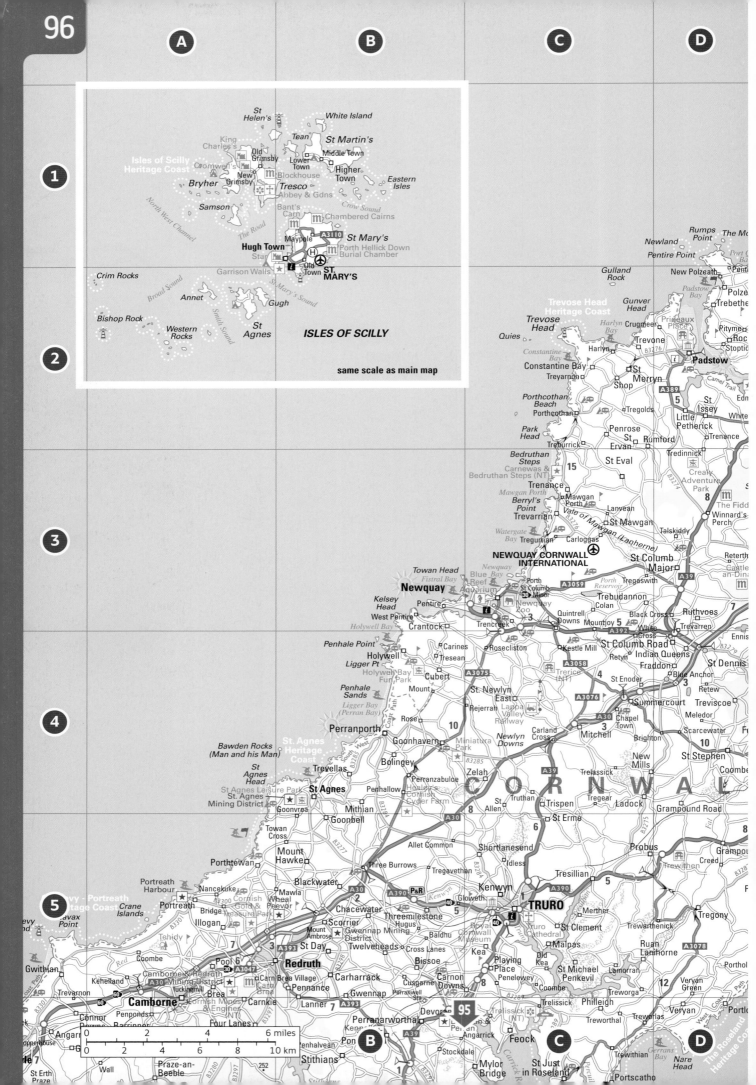

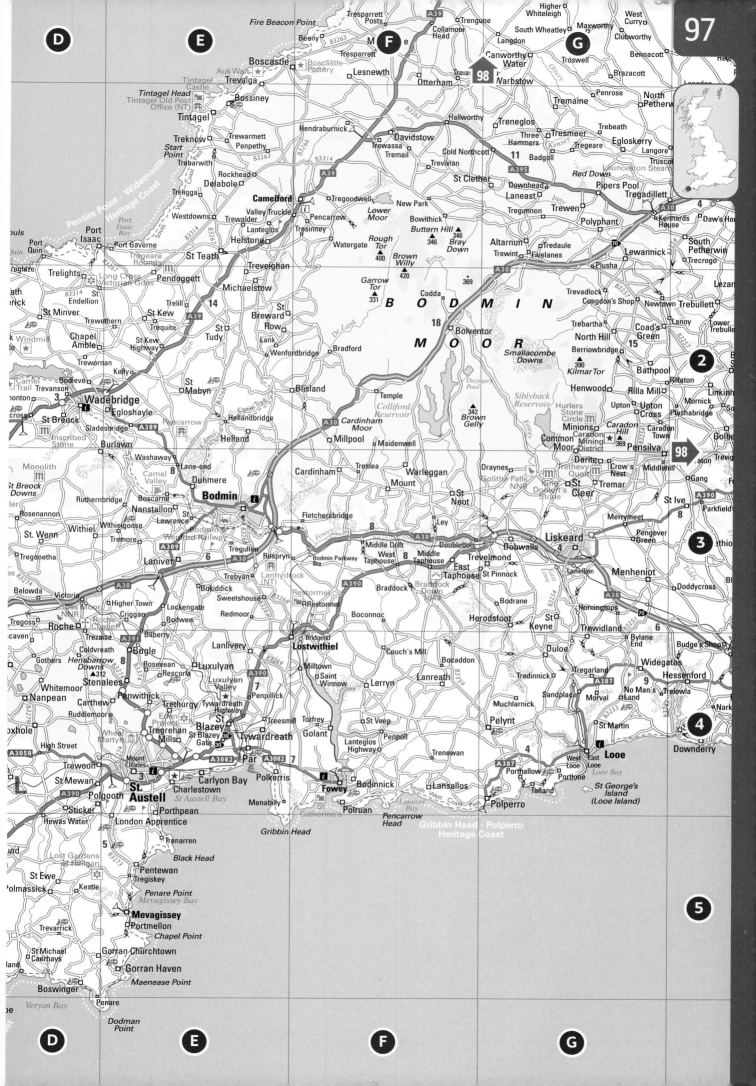

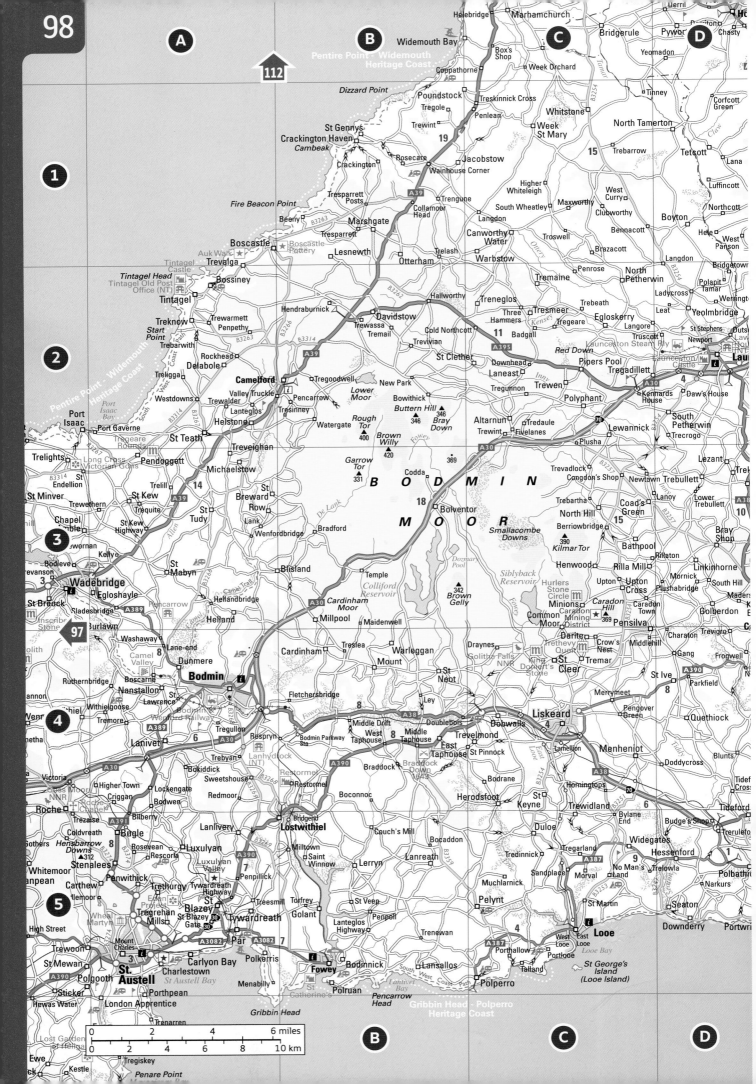

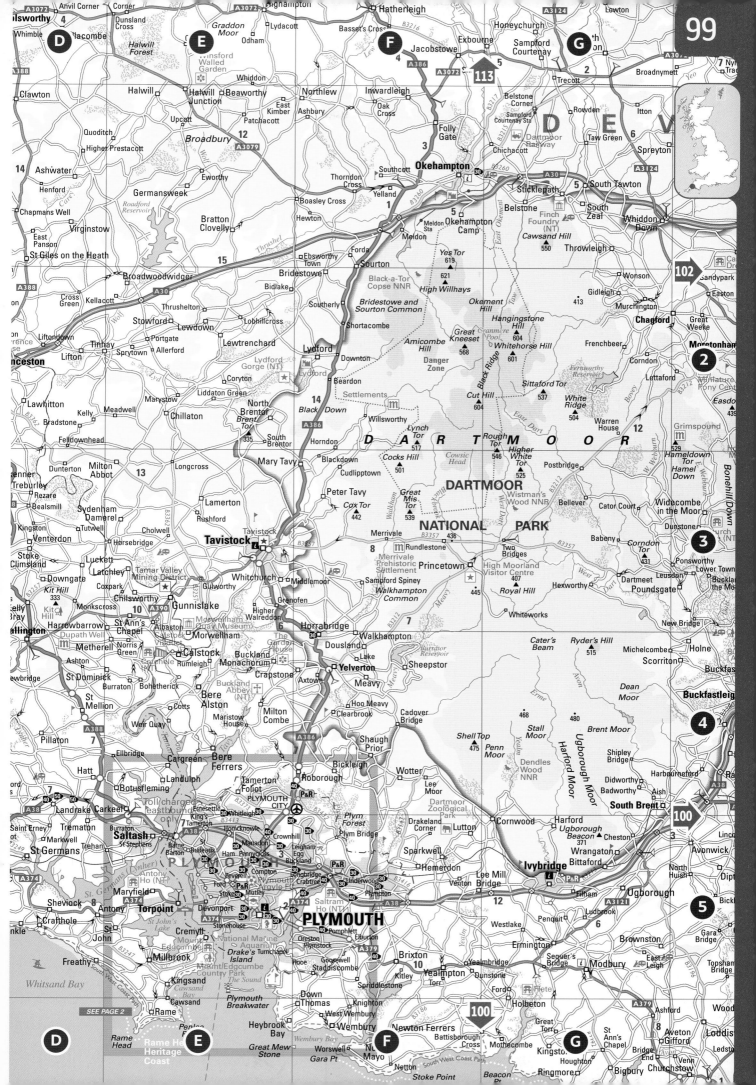

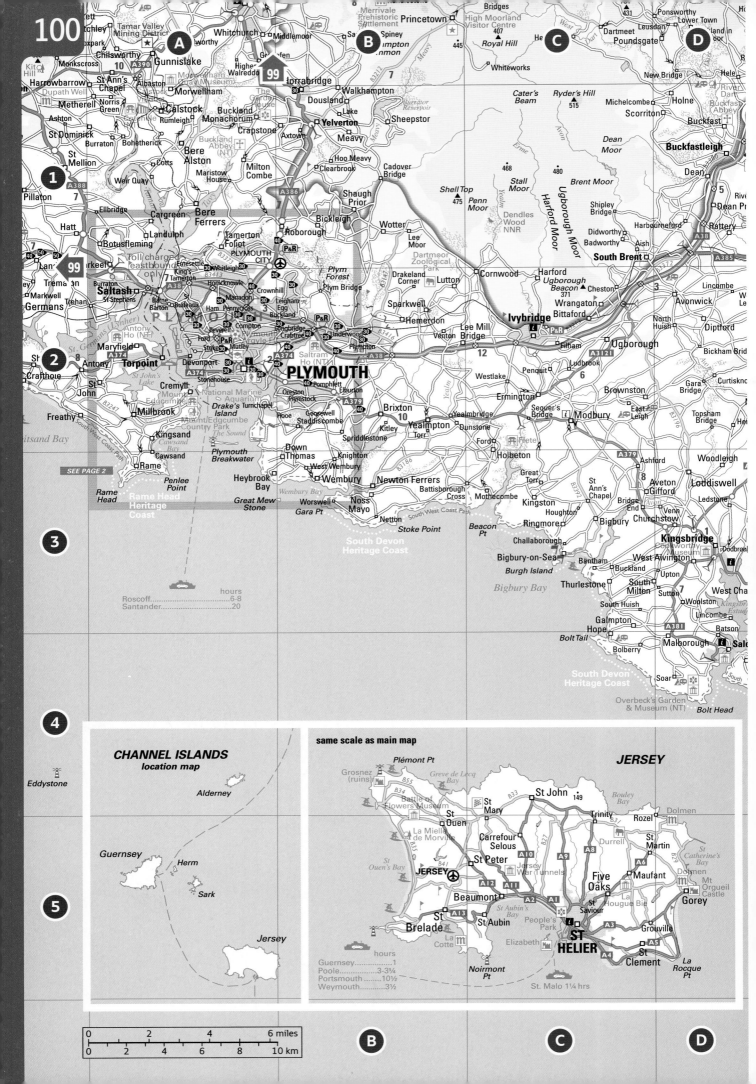

**A**  **B**  **C**  **D**

Kit Hill
Harrowbarrow
St Ann's Chapel
Monkscross
Chilsworthy
Gunnislake
Whitchurch
Middlemoor
Merrivale Prehistoric Settlement
Princetown
High Moorland Visitor Centre
Bridges
Ponsworthy
Leusdon
Lower Town
Dartmeet
Poundsgate
New Bridge
Hele
Holne
Buckfast

Tamar Valley Mining District
Metherell
Calstock
Morwellham
Morwellham Quay Museum
Higher Walreddon
Horrabridge
Walkhampton
Dousland
Lake
Sheepstor
Burrator Reservoir
Cater's Beam
Ryder's Hill
515
Michelcombe
Scorriton

Ashton
St Dominick
Burraton
Bohetherick
Rumleigh
Buckland Monachorum
Crapstone
Yelverton
Meavy
Hoo Meavy
Clearbrook
Shaugh Prior
Cadover Bridge
Wotter
Lee Moor
Dartmoor Zoological Park
Shell Top
Penn Moor
Stall Moor
480
Brent Moor
Harford Moor
Ugborough Moor
371
Shipley Bridge
Didworthy
Harbourneford
Badworthy
Aish
Buckfastleigh
Dean Moor
Dean
Dean Prior
Rattery

Pillaton
St Mellion
Ellbridge
Cargreen
Bere Ferrers
Bere Alston
Milton Combe
Maristow House
Bickleigh
Roborough
Plym Forest
Plym Bridge
Sparkwell
Hemerdon
Cornwood
Lutton
Drakeland Corner
Ugborough Beacon
Cheston
Wrangaton
Bittaford
Ivybridge
North Huish
Diptford
Avonwick

Hatt
Botusfleming
Landulph
Tamerton Foliot
Whitleigh
PLYMOUTH CITY
Leigham
Egg Buckland
Lee Mill Bridge
Venton
Filham
Ugborough
Bickham Bri

Lan
Trema on
Markwell
Germans
Saltash
St Stephens
Barne Barton
Budeaux
Ham
Pennycross
Compton
Crownhill
Mannamead
Underwood
Plympton
Westlake
Ludbrook
Penquit
Gara Bridge
Curtiskno

Antony
Torpoint
Devonport
Ford
Stoke
Mutley
Peverell
Crabtree
PLYMOUTH
Saltram Ho (NT)
Ermington
Sequer's Bridge
Modbury
Topsham Bridge

Crafthole
St John
Maryfield
Cremyll
Mount Edgcumbe
Stonehouse
Oreston
Plymstock
Elburton
Brixton
Yealmbridge
Torr
Dunstone
Ford
Holbeton
Kingston
Houghton
Aveton Gifford
Loddiswell
Ledstone

Freathy
Millbrook
Kingsand
Cawsand
Rame
Down Thomas
Knighton
West Wembury
Wembury
Newton Ferrers
Battisborough Cross
Mothecombe
Ringmore
Bigbury
Churchstow
Venn
East Allington
Kingsbridge

Penlee Point
Heybrook Bay
Worswell
Gara Pt
Noss Mayo
Netton
Stoke Point
Beacon Pt
Challaborough
Bigbury-on-Sea
Burgh Island
Bantham
Buckland
Upton
West Alvington
Dodbrook

SEE PAGE 2
Rame Head Heritage Coast
Great Mew Stone
Wembury Bay
South West Coast Path
South Devon Heritage Coast
Bigbury Bay
Thurlestone
South Milton
Sutton
Woolston
Lincombe
West Cha

hours
Roscoff..............................6-8
Santander...........................20

Hope
Galmpton
Bolt Tail
Bolberry
South Huish
Malborough
Batson
Soar
South Devon Heritage Coast
Overbeck's Garden & Museum (NT)
Bolt Head

**CHANNEL ISLANDS**
location map

Eddystone

Alderney

Guernsey
Herm
Sark

Jersey

same scale as main map

*JERSEY*

Plémont Pt
Grosnez (ruins)
Greve de Lecq Bay
St John
Bouley Bay
Dolmen
Rozel
Battle of Flowers Museum
St Mary
Trinity
Durrell
St Martin
La Mielle de Morville
St Ouen
Carrefour Selous
St Peter
Maufant
Dolmen
Mt Orgueil Castle
St Catherine's Bay
St Ouen's Bay
Jersey War Tunnels
Five Oaks
Gorey
JERSEY
Beaumont
St Aubin
St Saviour
La Hougue Bie
St Brelade
People's Park
Grouville
La Cotte
St Aubin's Bay
ST HELIER
St Clement
La Rocque Pt
Elizabeth
Noirmont Pt
St. Malo 1¼ hrs

hours
Guernsey...............1
Poole..............3-3¾
Portsmouth........10½
Weymouth..........3½

0    2    4    6 miles
0  2  4  6  8  10 km

**B**  **C**  **D**

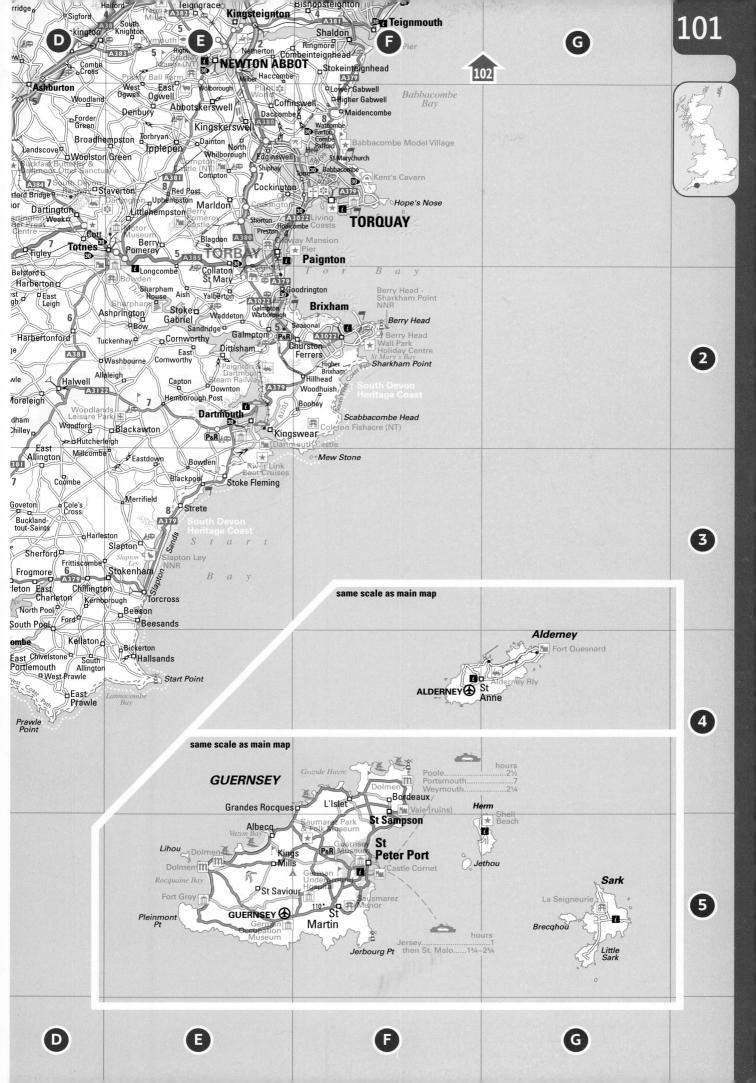

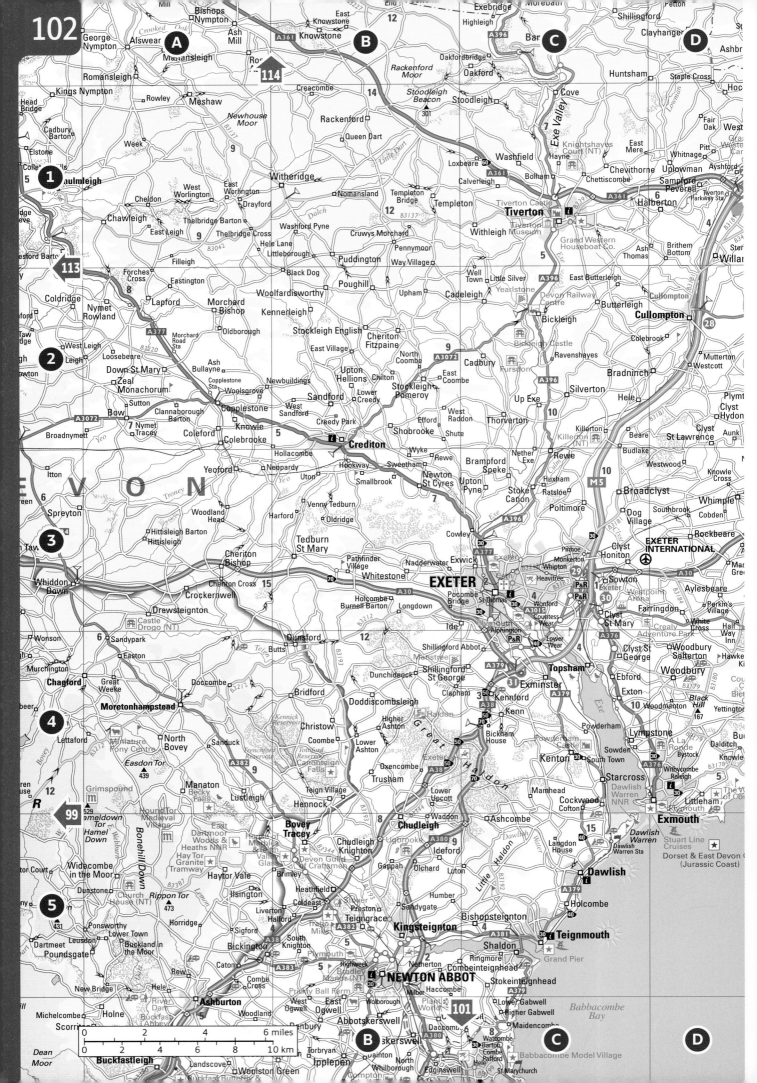

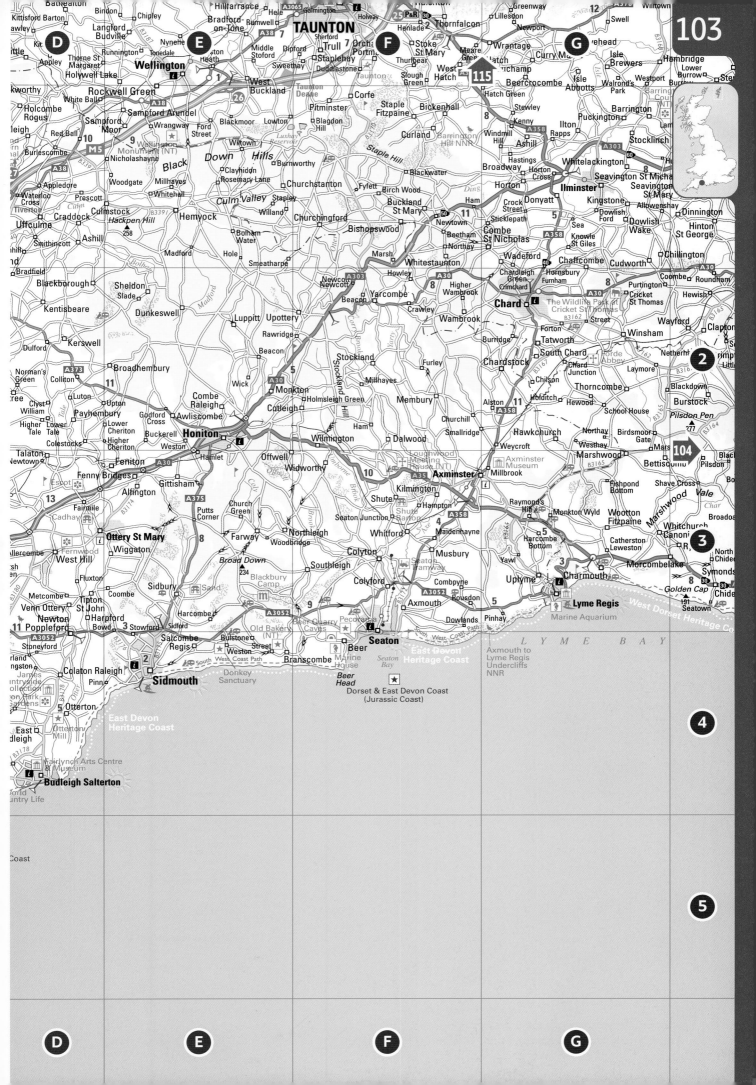

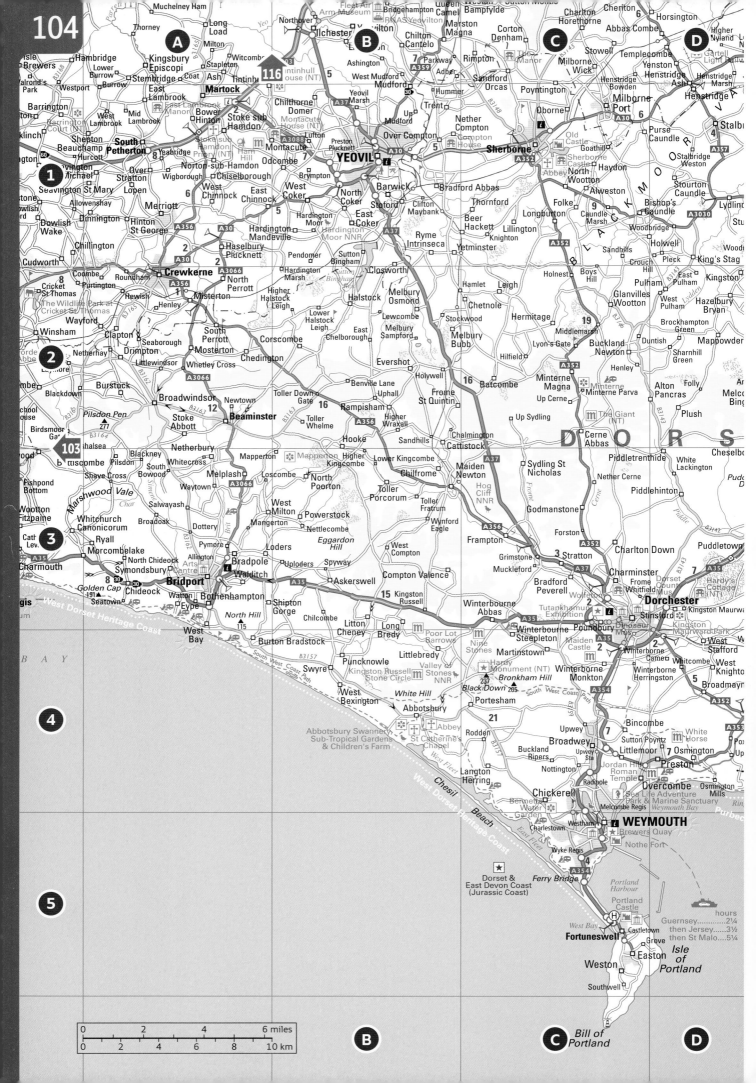

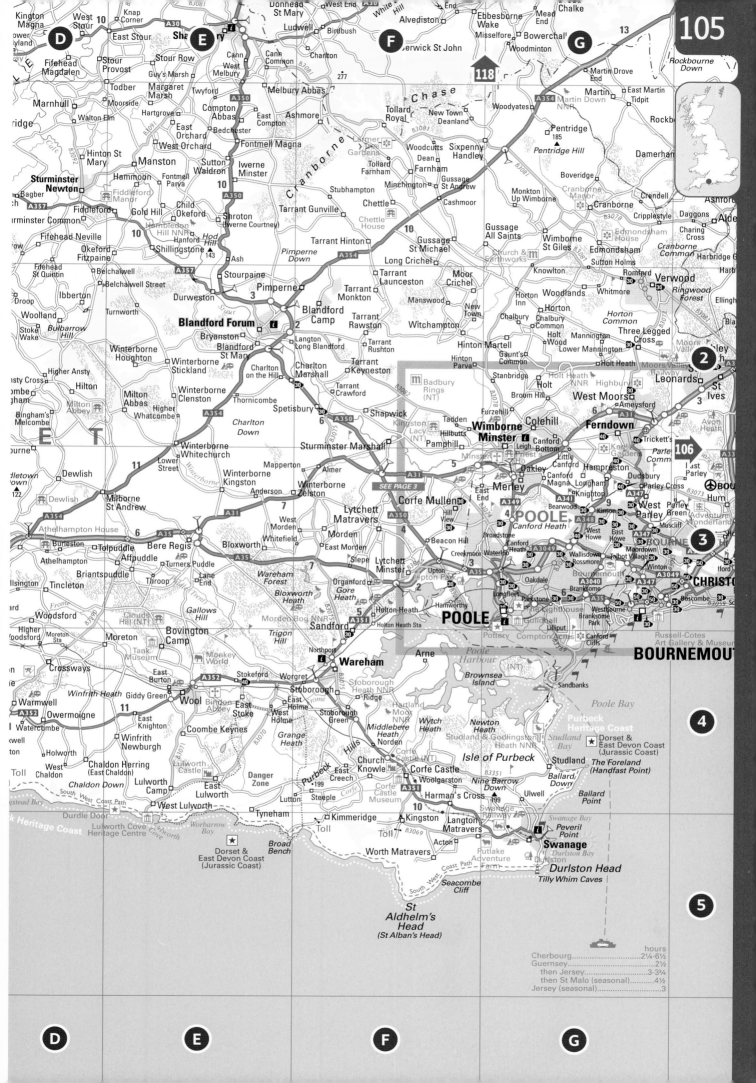

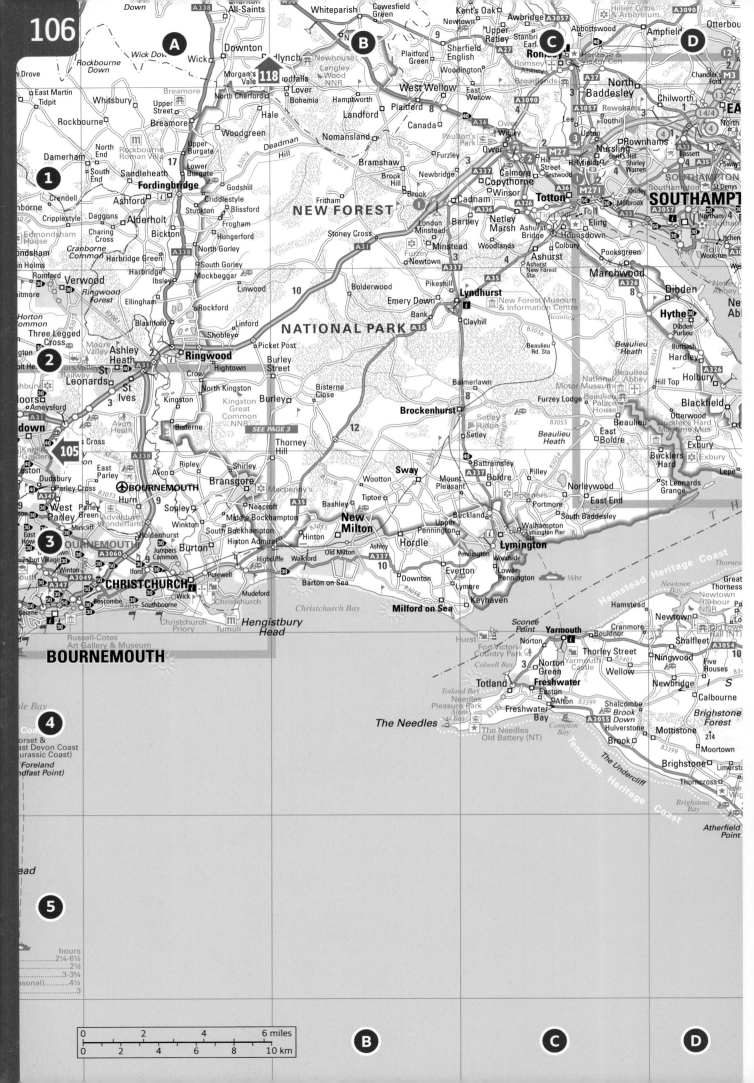

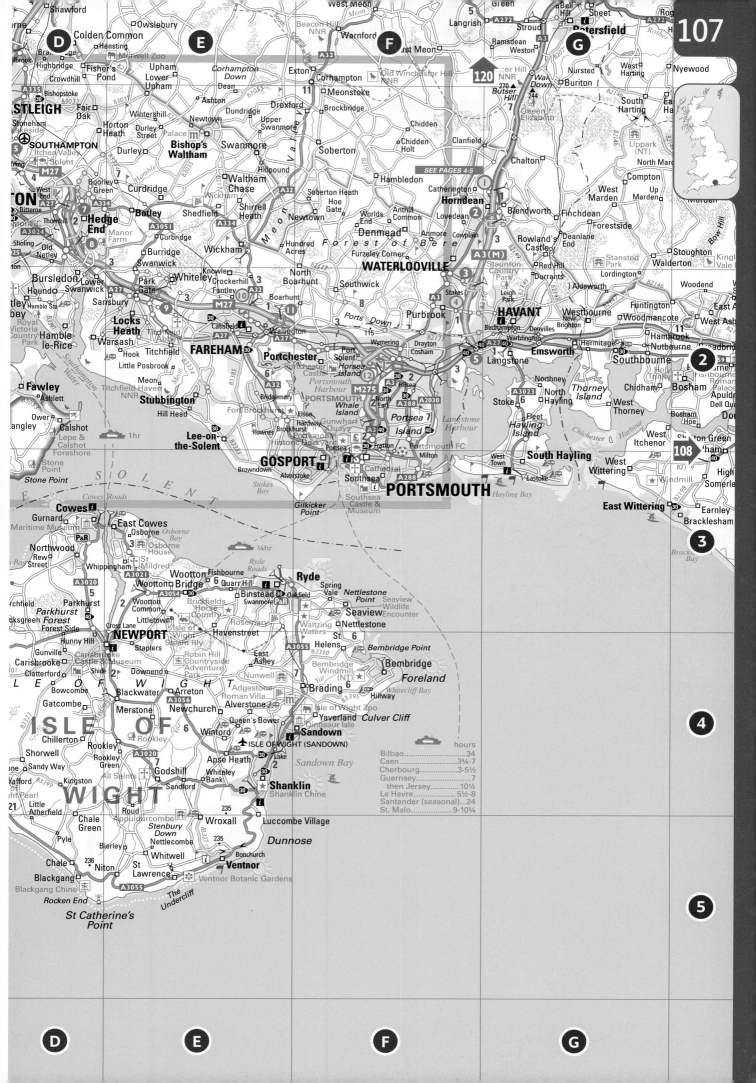

SEE PAGES 4-5

| | hours |
|---|---|
| Bilbao | 34 |
| Caen | 3¾-7 |
| Cherbourg | 3-5½ |
| Guernsey | 7 |
| then Jersey | 10½ |
| Le Havre | 5½-8 |
| Santander (seasonal) | 24 |
| St. Malo | 9-10¾ |

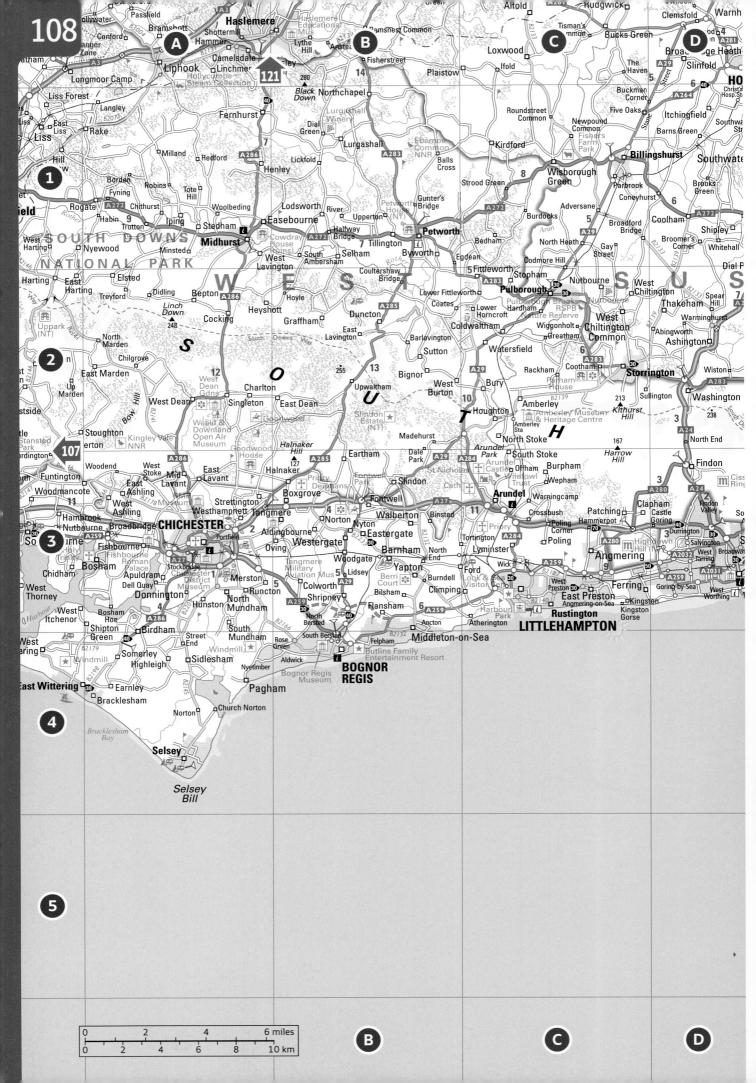

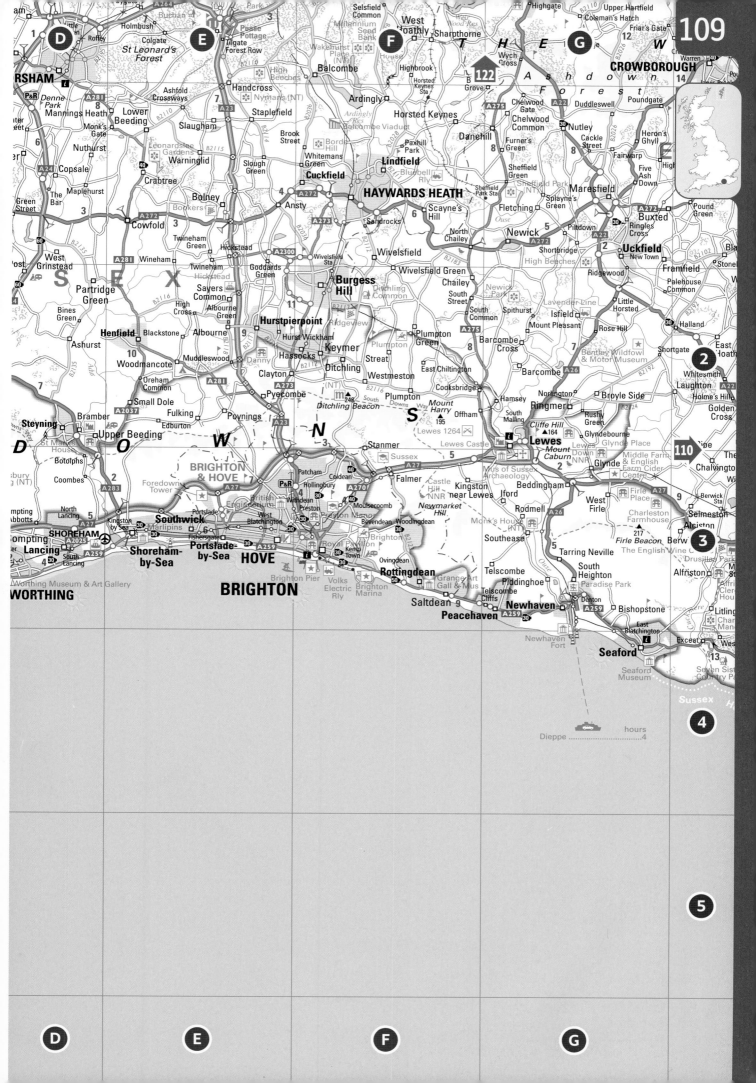

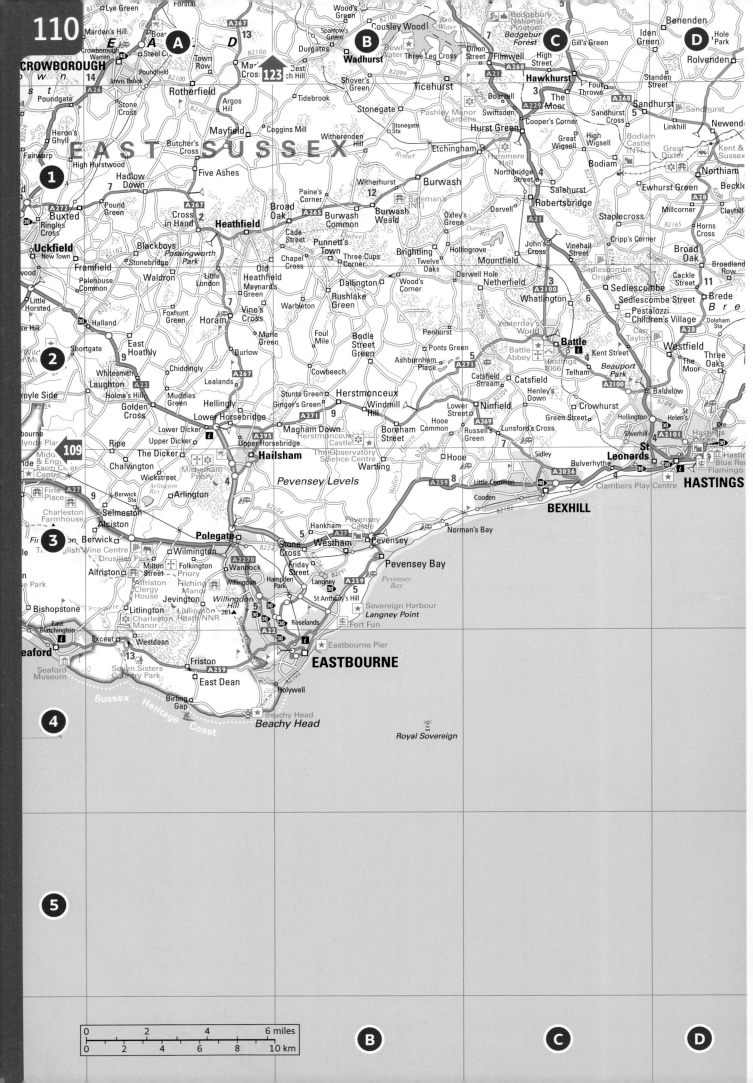

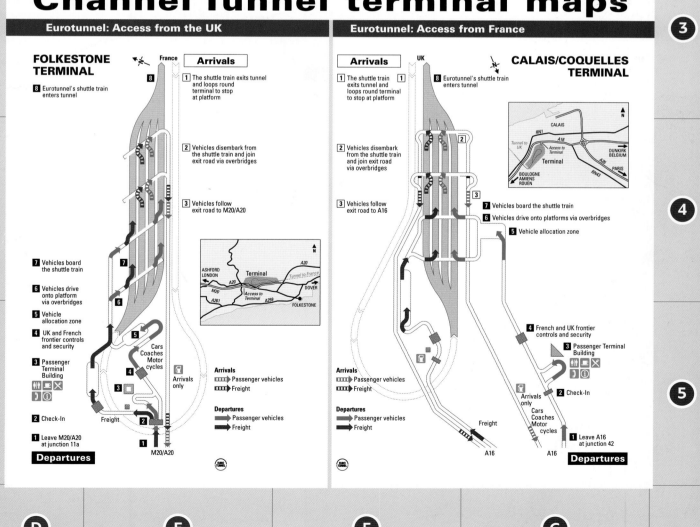

# Channel Tunnel terminal maps

## Eurotunnel: Access from the UK

### FOLKESTONE TERMINAL

France

**Arrivals**

8 Eurotunnel's shuttle train enters tunnel

1 The shuttle train exits tunnel and loops round terminal to stop at platform

2 Vehicles disembark from the shuttle train and join exit road via overbridges

3 Vehicles follow exit road to M20/A20

7 Vehicles board the shuttle train

6 Vehicles drive onto platform via overbridges

5 Vehicle allocation zone

4 UK and French frontier controls and security

3 Passenger Terminal Building

2 Check-In

1 Leave M20/A20 at junction 11a

**Departures**

Cars Coaches Motor cycles

Arrivals only

Freight

M20/A20

**Arrivals**
▭▭▭▸ Passenger vehicles
▭▭▭▸ Freight

**Departures**
▸ Passenger vehicles
▸ Freight

ASHFORD LONDON — A20 — Terminal — Tunnel to France
A261 — Access to Terminal — A259 — DOVER — FOLKESTONE

## Eurotunnel: Access from France

### CALAIS/COQUELLES TERMINAL

UK

**Arrivals**

8 Eurotunnel's shuttle train enters tunnel

1 The shuttle train exits tunnel and loops round terminal to stop at platform

2 Vehicles disembark from the shuttle train and join exit road via overbridges

3 Vehicles follow exit road to A16

7 Vehicles board the shuttle train

6 Vehicles drive onto platforms via overbridges

5 Vehicle allocation zone

4 French and UK frontier controls and security

3 Passenger Terminal Building

2 Check-In

1 Leave A16 at junction 42

**Departures**

Arrivals only

Cars Coaches Motor cycles

Freight

A16

A16

CALAIS — RN1 — A16 — DUNKIRK BELGIUM
Tunnel to UK — Access to Terminal — Terminal — A26 — PARIS
BOULOGNE AMIENS ROUEN — RN43

**Arrivals**
▭▭▭▸ Passenger vehicles
▭▭▭▸ Freight

**Departures**
▸ Passenger vehicles
▸ Freight

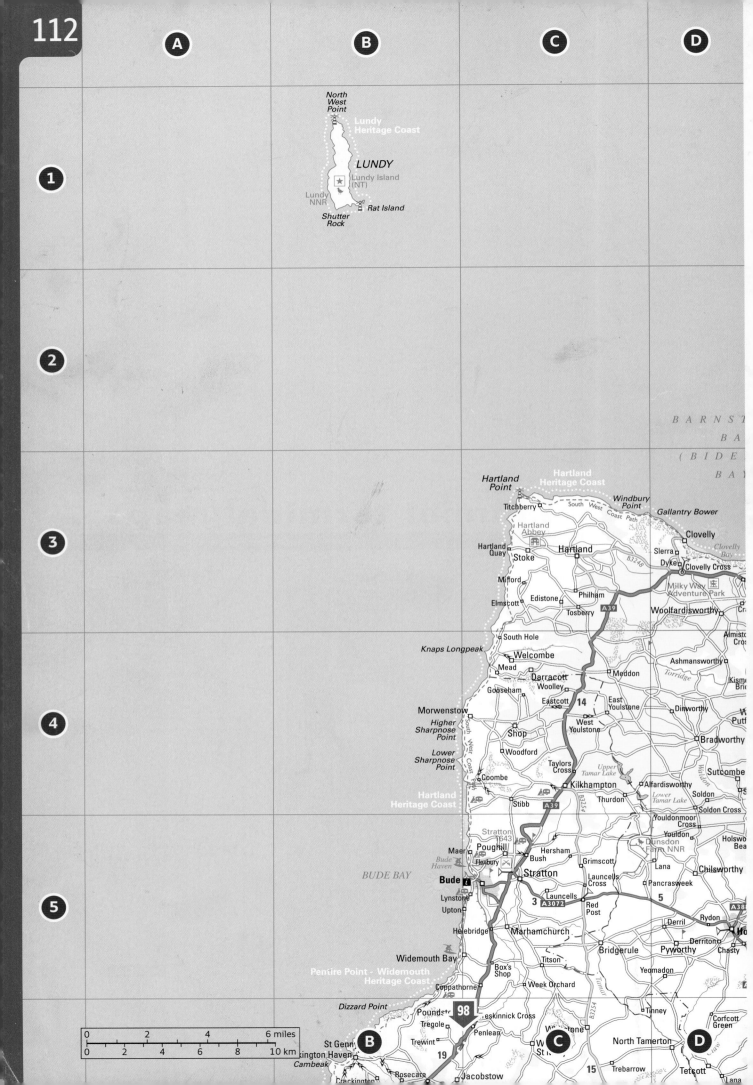

A   B   C   D

1

2

*BARNST*
*BA*
*( B I D E*
*BA Y*

3

4

5

*North*
*West*
*Point*

**Lundy**
**Heritage Coast**

*LUNDY*

Lundy Island
(NT)

*Lundy*
*NNR*

*Rat Island*

*Shutter*
*Rock*

*Hartland*
*Point*

**Hartland**
**Heritage Coast**

*Windbury*
*Point*

*Gallantry Bower*

Titchberry

*South*  *West*  *Coast*  *Path*

Clovelly

*Hartland*
*Abbey*

Hartland

*Clovelly*
*Bay*

Hartland
Quay

Stoke

Sierra

Dyke    Clovelly Cross

Milford

*Milky Way*
*Adventure Park*

Elmscott

Edistone

Philham

Woolfardisworthy

Tosberry

A39

*Almisto*
*Cross*

Cra

South Hole

Ashmansworthy

Kismi
Bri

*Knaps Longpeak*

Welcombe

*Torridge*

Mead

Darracott

Meddon

Gooseham

Woolley

Eastcott

14

East
Youlstone

Dinworthy

Putf

Morwenstow

West
Youlstone

Bradworthy

*Higher*
*Sharpnose*
*Point*

Shop

*South*  *West*  *Coast*  *Path*

Woodford

*Lower*
*Sharpnose*
*Point*

Taylors
Cross

*Upper*
*Tamar Lake*

Sutcombe

Coombe

Kilkhampton

Alfardisworthy

*Walton*

Soldon

**Hartland**
**Heritage Coast**

Stibb

A39

B3254

Thurdon

*Lower*
*Tamar Lake*

Soldon Cross

Youldonmoor
Cross

Stratton
1643

Youldon

*Dunsdon*
*Farm NNR*

Holswo
Bea

Maer

Poughill

Hersham
Bush

Grimscott

Lana

Chilsworthy

*Bude*
*Haven*

Flexbury

Stratton

Launcells
Cross

Pancrasweek

**Bude**

*BUDE BAY*

Launcells

5

Lynstone

3   A3072

Red
Post

Derril

Rydon

A38

Upton

Derriton

Ho

Helebridge

Marhamchurch

Bridgerule

Pyworthy

Chasty

Widemouth Bay

Titson

Yeomadon

**Peniire Point - Widemouth**
**Heritage Coast**

Box's
Shop

Week Orchard

*Tamar*

*Dizzard Point*

Coppathorne

Tinney

Corfcott
Green

**98**

Poundst

eskinnick Cross

W
tone

North Tamerton

St Genn

B    19

Tregole

Penlean

W
St

15

Trebarrow

Tetcott

kington Haven

Trewint

C

D

*Cambeak*

Lana

Crackington

Rosecare

Jacobstow

A    B    C    D

1

2

129

GLAMORG

Pitcot
Llysworney   Llanblethian   St   Llantrit
Llandow   Llandough   Tre-A
Wick   Nash   Llanmihangel   The
Sigingstone   Herberts   St Mary   Llantw
Monkton   Church
Marcross   Llanmaes   Eglwys-Brewis   Llanbethery   Llancadle
Llantwit   Flemingston
**Major**   Boverton   St Athan   Fonmon
Nash Point   St   Gileston
Donats   West Aberthaw   East
Glamorgan Heritage Coast   Aberthaw
Breaksea
Pt

B R I S T O L

BristolBay

Lynton &
Lynmouth   Lynmouth
Cliff Railway   Bay   Foreland Point
The Valley   Countisbury
of Rocks   Cove
**Lynton**
e Coast   **Lynmouth**   Exmoor Heritage Coast
Woody   Countisbury   Selworthy
Bay   Watersmeet Rd (NT)   Culbone   Porlock   Beacon
East Lyn   South West Coast Path   Weir   Porlock   308
Toll   Bay   South West Coast Path   B
Barbrook   Wilsham   387   Culbone Hill   West   Bossington
West   Malmsmead   413   11   Porlock   Lynch   North Hill
Lyn   Brendon   Oare   Toll   **Porlock**   Allerford   Selworthy   Holnicote Estate (NT)   **Minehead**
A39   Hillsford   Holnicote   Woodcombe   Butlins Family
Bridge   Tippacott   Hawkcombe   Hindon   Bratton   Entertainment Resort
Cheriton   Woods NNR   A39   8   Periton   Dunster Sta   Blue Anchor
10   Furzehill   9   Brendon   Luccombe   Horner   Tivington   Alcombe   Bay
Shallowford   B3223   Common   South Common   Stoke Pero   Dunkery &   Wootton   Knowle   **Dunster**   Marsh Street   Blue
Challacombe   480   Hoaroak   Horner Woods   Courtenay   Carhampton   Dunster   Anchor
Common   Hill   EXMOOR   NNR   Ranscombe   Cowbridge   Watermill   Chape
Swincombe   473   Dunkery Hill   Burrow   Dunster Castle   (NT)   Cleeve
Challacombe   Pinkworthy   444   Dunkery Beacon   7   & Gardens (NT)   Old Cleeve
Bar   Pond   Dry   519   Bickham   Timberscombe   A39   7
Ba   Dure Down   B3358   9   Hill   EXMOOR   Codsend   Croydon   Withycombe   Bilbrook
Leworthy   Shoulsbarrow   Moors   Hill   Cleeve
113   Common   Quarme   365   Abbey   Torre
9   Barle   10   Edgcott   Cutcombe   Rodhuish   Beggearn Hus
Fullaford   B3223   B3224   Wheddon   Luxborough   Lower Roadwater
11   Simonsbath   Exford   Luckwell   Cross   Roadwater
Lydcott   409   Bridge   Triscombe   Lype Hill   Kingsbridge   Nettleco
Span   Long   Exe   Great   423   Treborough
Whitefield   Head   NATIONAL   Holcombe   Blacklands   Nurcot   North Quarme   BRENDON   Leighland
4   493   436   PARK   Chapel
ayford   North   Withypool   Exe   HILLS   Rale
High   Radworthy   Common   Withypool   Winsford   West Howetown   Withiel
Bray   Worth Hill   Hill   Winsford   Florey
Charles   North Heasley   Kinsford Water   426   Exton   Gupworthy
East   Dane's Brook   Knaplock   Bridgetown
Buckland   South Radworthy   Tarr Steps   B3223   Brompton   S O M E R
Heasley Mill   Woodland   Tarr   Week   Regis   Woolcotts   Clatworthy
NNR   Steps   Higher   15   Reservoir
Twitchen   Molland   Liscombe   Combe
Common   Hawkridge   Barle   317   Coombe E
North   Hartford   Upton   B3190   Huish Champflower
A361   Molton   Molland   A396   Wimbleball   Heydo
A399   Lake   Haddon   Skilgate   Chipstable
Quince   2   West Anstey   **Dulverton**   Hill   Bury   Raddington
Honey   50   4   Battleton   Waterrow
Farm   Newtown   Yeo Mill   East   Nightcott   Brushford   Timewell   12
5   Bish   Anstey   Exebridge   Petton
**South**   Mill   Bishops   Upcott   Morebath   Shillingford
Clapworthy   **Molton**   B3227   Nympton   Oldways   Sowerhill   Highleigh   A396   Clayhanger
8   End   12   A396   Bampton
George   Alswear   Ash Mill   Knowstone   Highleigh   Ashb
Nympton   A361   Knowstone   Oakfordbridge
Mariansleigh   Rose   Rackenford   Oakford   Huntsham   Staple Cross
Romansleigh   Ash   Moor   102   Hoc
Kings Nympton   Rowley   Meshaw   Creacombe   Stoodleigh   Cove   West
Head   14   Beacon   301   Knightshayes   East
Bridge   Rackenf   Court (NT)   Mere   Pitt
Cadbury   Washfield   Hayne   Whitnage
Barton   B    Loxbeare   60   C   D
Elstone
Colleton Mills   9

0    2    4    6 miles
0  2  4  6  8  10 km

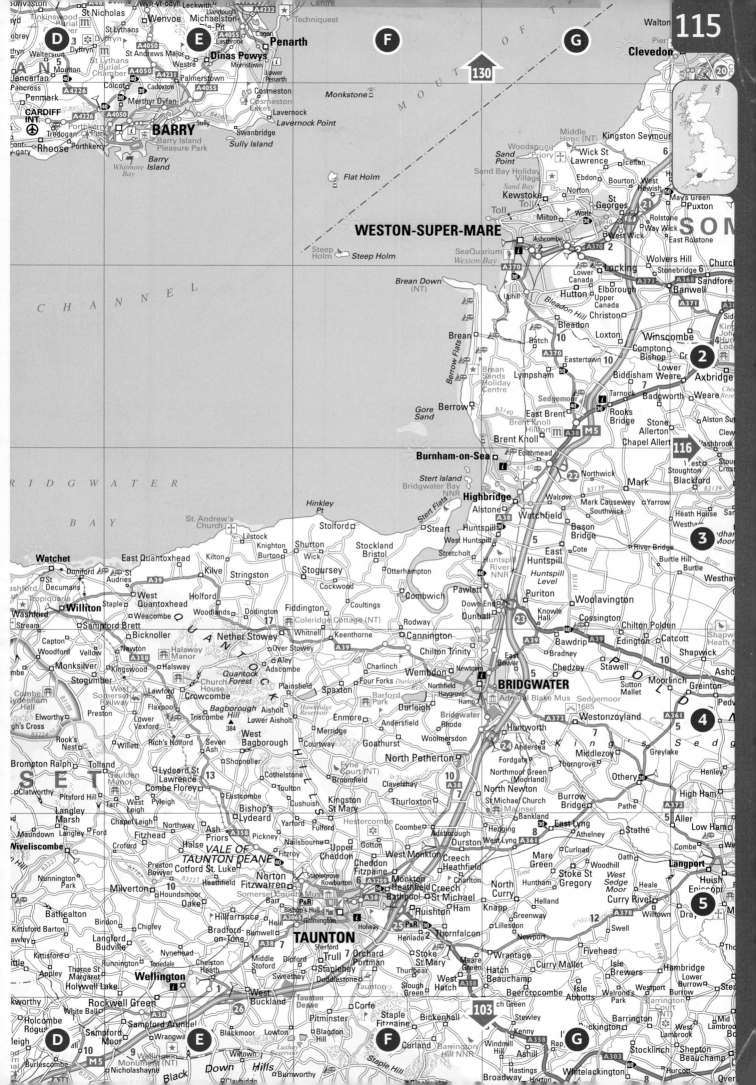

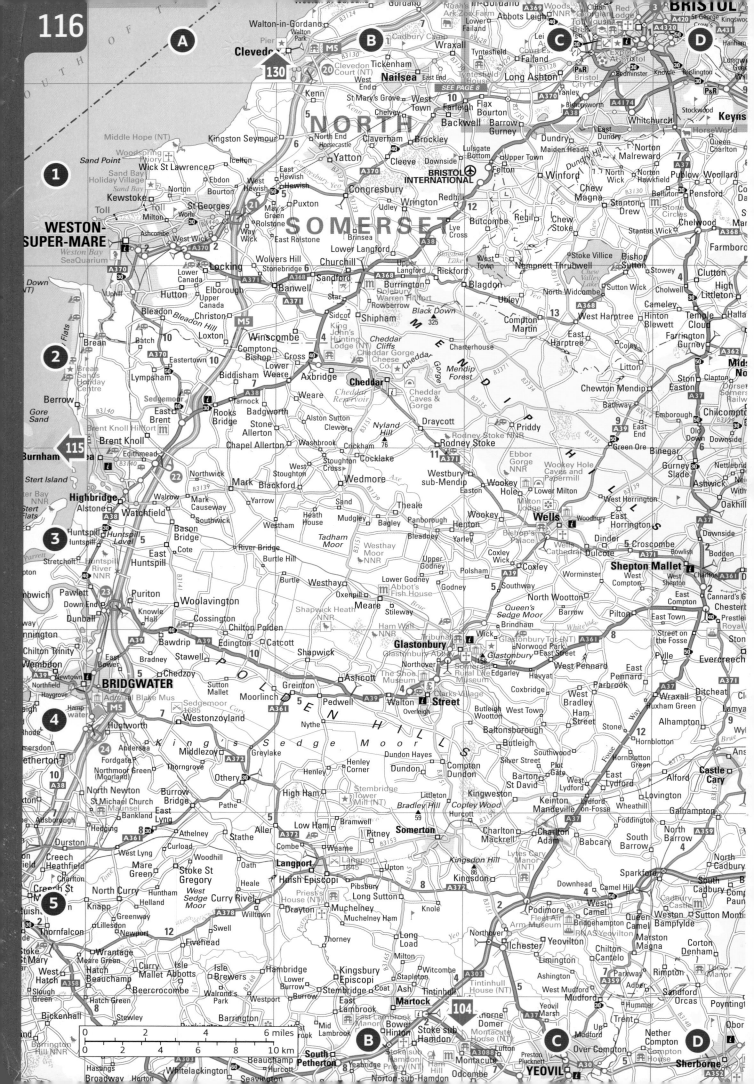

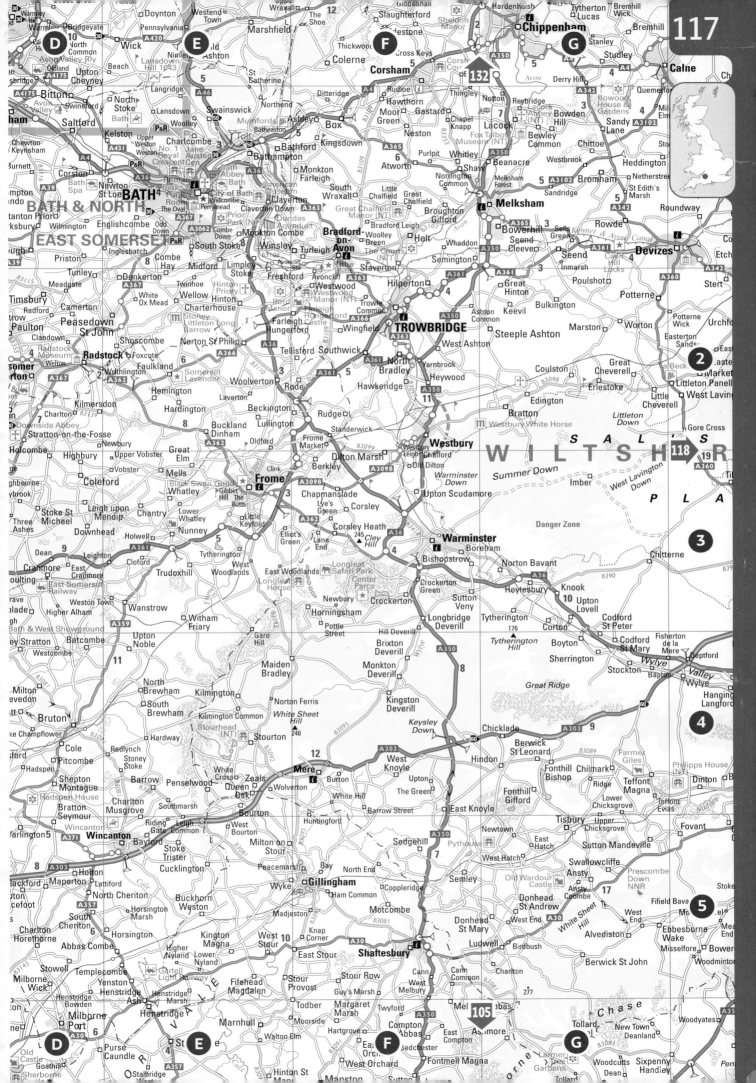

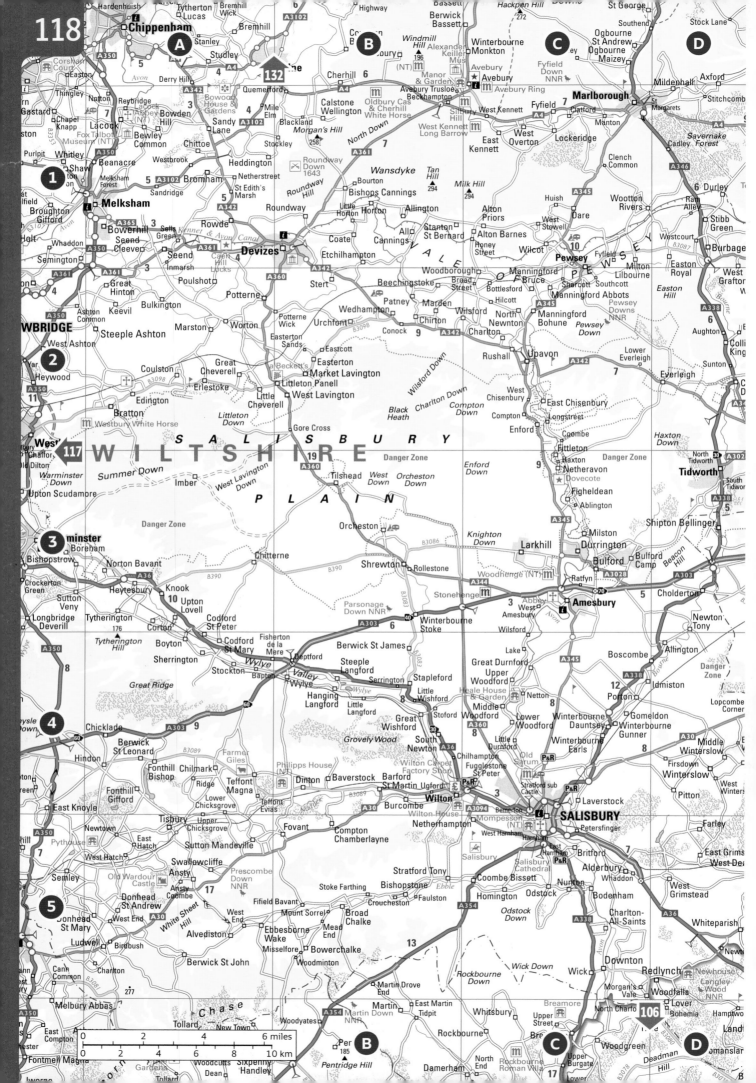

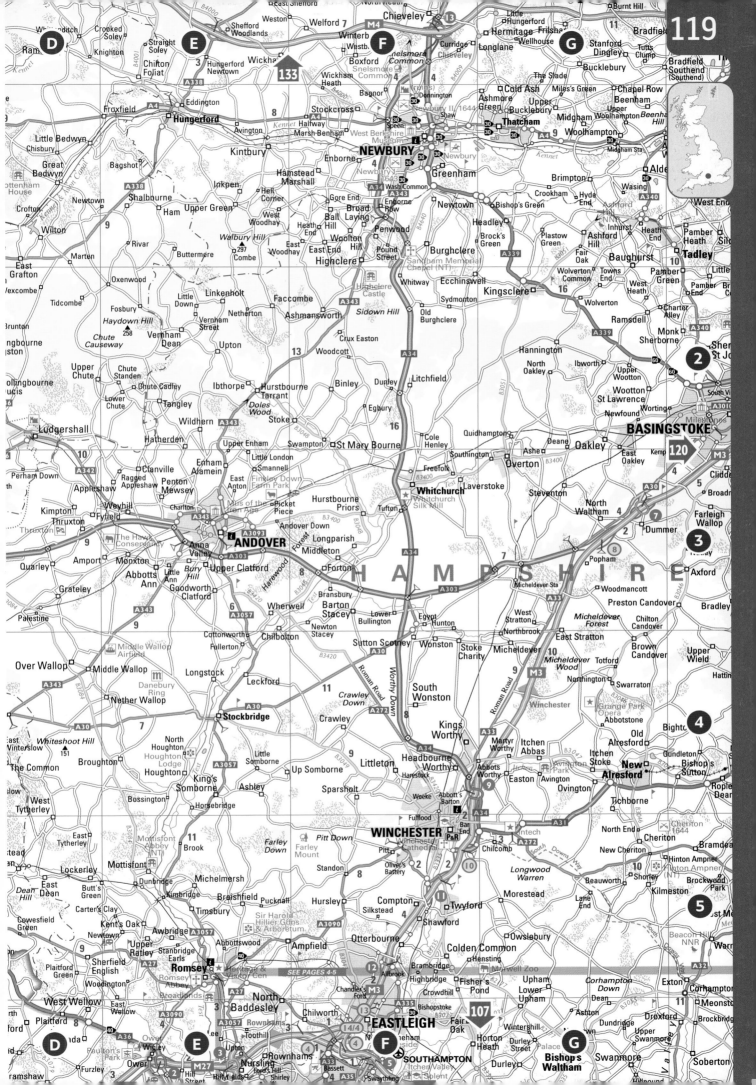

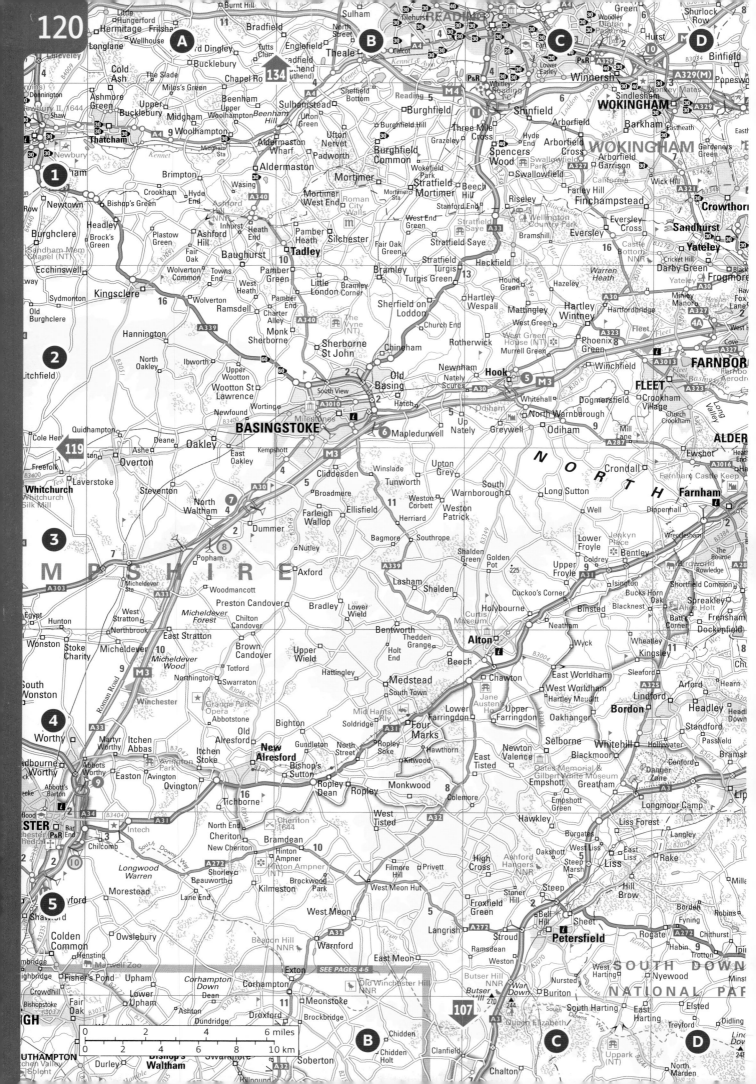

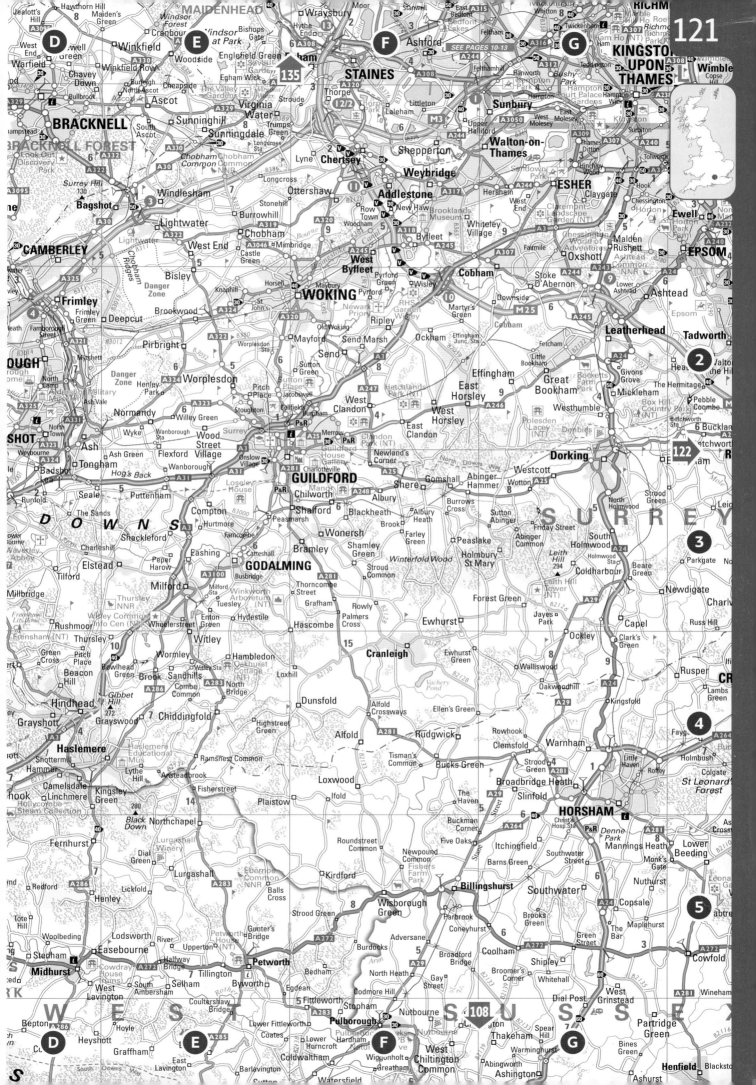

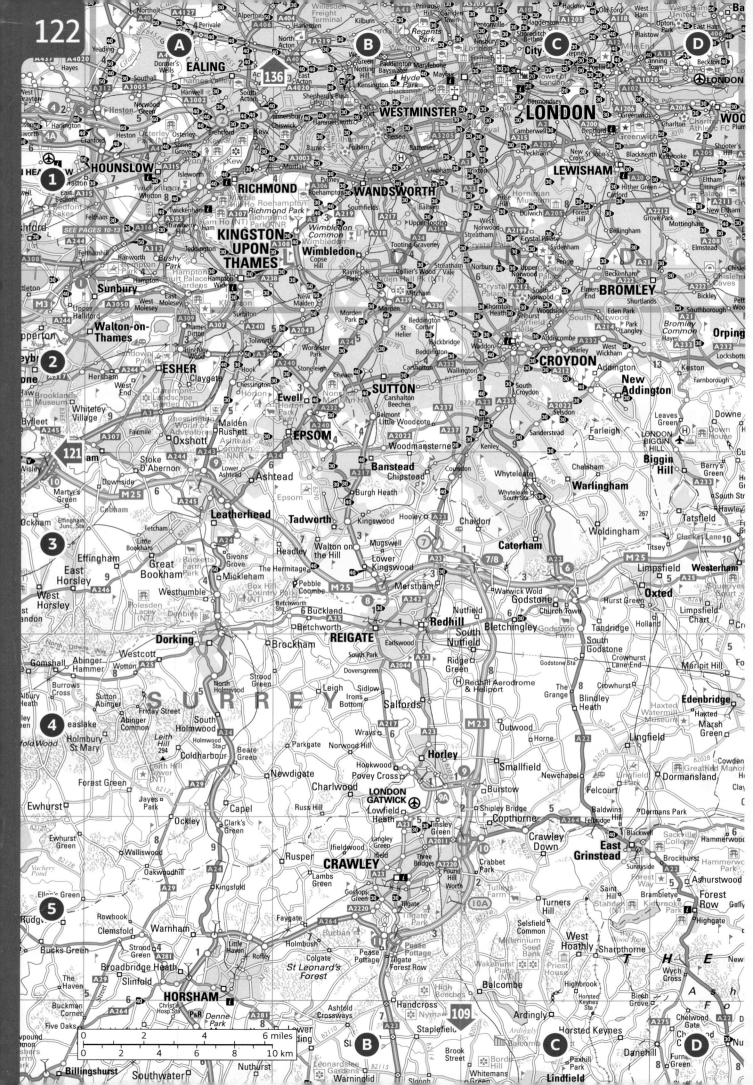

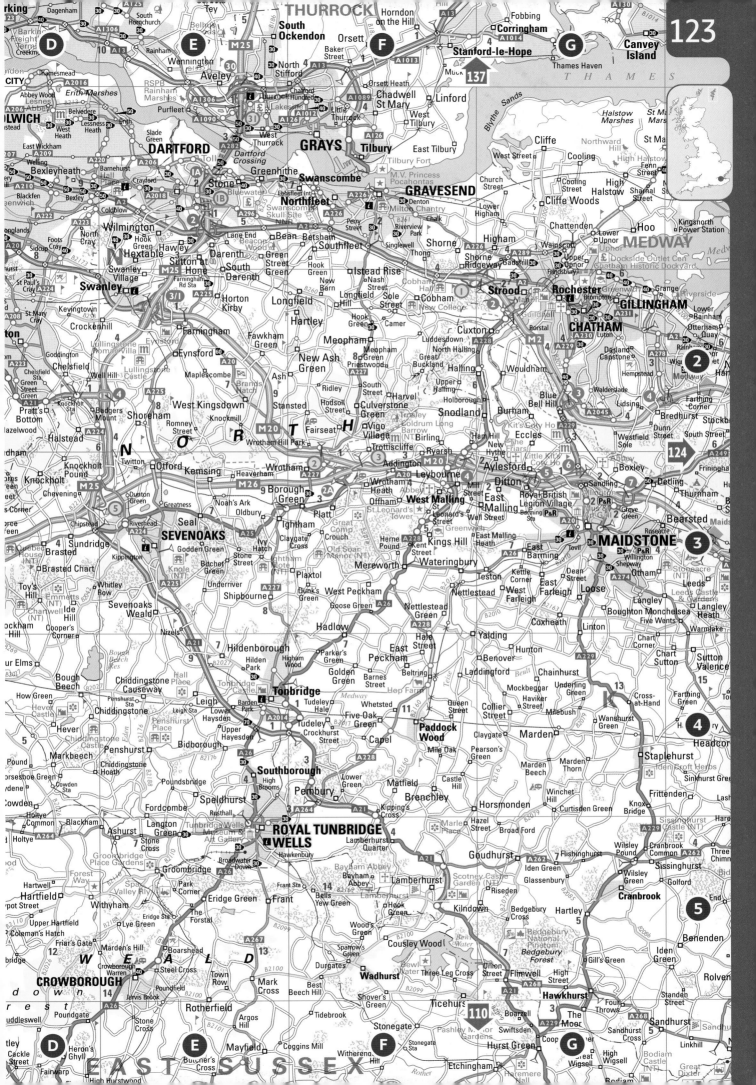

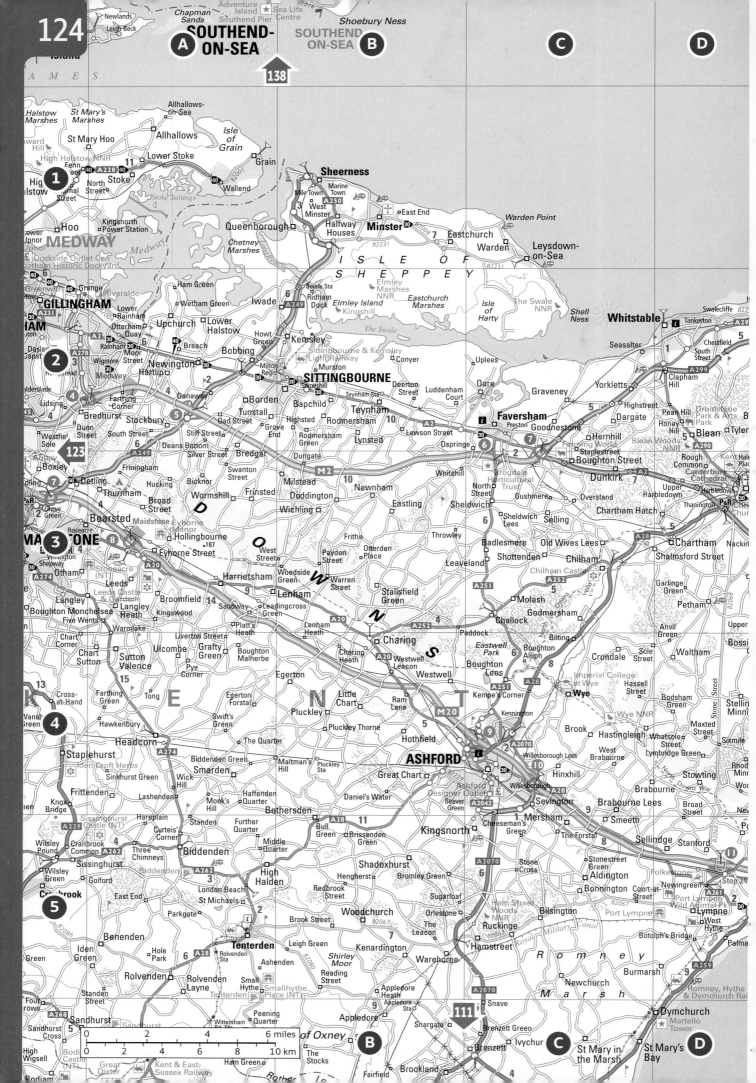

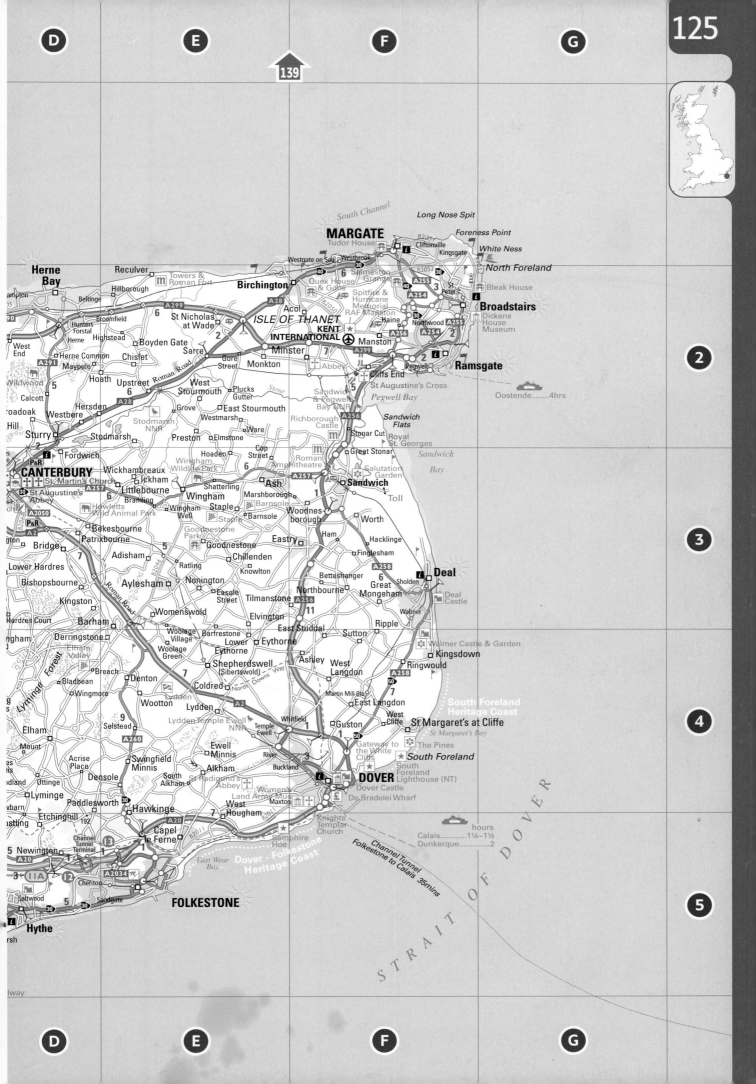

139

South Channel
Long Nose Spit
Foreness Point
**MARGATE**
Tudor House
White Ness
Cliftonville
Kingsgate
North Foreland
Westgate on Sea
Westbrook
Salmestone Grange
Quex House & Gdns
St Peter's
**Herne Bay**
Reculver
Towers & Roman Fort
Hillborough
**Birchington**
Spitfire & Hurricane Memorial RAF Manston
Bleak House
**Broadstairs**
Beltinge
Broomfield
St Nicholas at Wade
Acol
*ISLE OF THANET*
Haine
Dickens House Museum
West End
Hunters Forstal
Highstead
Boyden Gate
**KENT INTERNATIONAL**
Manston
Northwood
Herne
Sarre
Minster
**Ramsgate**
Herne Common
Maypole
Chislet
Gore Street
Monkton
Abbey
Pegwell
Wildwood
Hoath
Upstreet
Roman Road
West Stourmouth
Plucks Gutter
Sandwich & Pegwell Bay NNR
St Augustine's Cross
Calcott
Hersden
Grove
East Stourmouth
Westmarsh
*Pegwell Bay*
Oostende........4hrs
Broadoak
Westbere
Ware
Preston
Elmstone
Richborough Castle
*Sandwich Flats*
Hill
Stodmarsh
Hoaden
Stonar Cut
Great Stonar
Sturry
Fordwich
Stodmarsh NNR
Cop Street
Roman Amphitheatre
Royal St. Georges
*Sandwich Bay*
**CANTERBURY**
St Martin's Church
Wingham Wildlife Park
Salutation Garden
St Augustine's Abbey
Wickhambreaux
Ickham
Shatterling
**Ash**
Marshborough
**Sandwich**
Littlebourne
Bramling
**Wingham**
Staple
Barnsole
*Toll*
Howletts Wild Animal Park
Wingham Well
Staple
Barnsole
Woodnesborough
Bekesbourne
Patrixbourne
Goodnestone Park
Eastry
Worth
Bridge
Goodnestone
Chillenden
Ham
Hacklinge
Adisham
Knowlton
Finglesham
Lower Hardres
Ratling
Nonington
Betteshanger
**Deal**
Bishopsbourne
Aylesham
Easole Street
Tilmanstone
Northbourne
Sholden
Kingston
Womenswold
Elvington
Great Mongeham
Deal Castle
Hardres Court
Barham
Woolage Village
Barfrestone
Lower Eythorne
East Studdal
Ripple
Walmer
Derringstone
Woolage Green
Shepherdswell (Sibertswold)
Ashley
West Langdon
Sutton
Walmer Castle & Garden
Elham
Breach
Denton
Coldred
Kingsdown
Ringwould
Bladbean
Wingmore
Martin Mill Sta
East Langdon
Mount
Wootton
Lydden
Whitfield
West Cliffe
*South Foreland Heritage Coast*
Acrise Place
Lydden Temple Ewell NNR
Temple Ewell
Guston
St Margaret's at Cliffe
Ottinge
Selstead
Ewell Minnis
West Cliffe
*St Margaret's Bay*
Lyminge
Densole
Alkham
River
The Pines
Paddlesworth
Swingfield Minnis
St Radigund's Abbey
Buckland
Gateway to the White Cliffs
South Foreland Lighthouse (NT)
Etchinghill
Hawkinge
South Alkham
Women's Land Army Mus
West Hougham
**Dover**
South Foreland
Newington
Channel Tunnel Terminal
Capel le Ferne
Maxton
Dover Castle
De Bradelei Wharf
Cheriton
Knights Templar Church
*Dover - Folkestone Heritage Coast*
Samphire Hoe
Calais........1¼–1½
Dunkerque.............2
Saltwood
Sandgate
*East Wear Bay*
*Channel Tunnel Folkestone to Calais 35mins*
**Hythe**
**FOLKESTONE**

*STRAIT OF DOVER*

D E F G

2

3

4

5

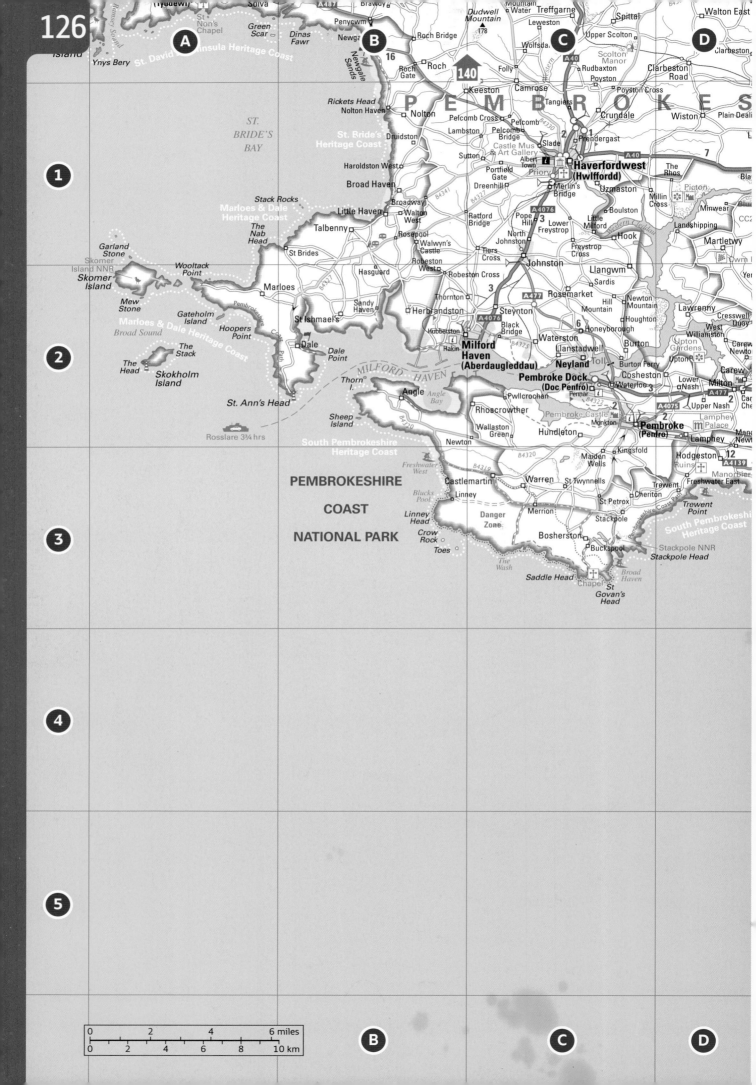

ST. BRIDE'S BAY

PEMBROKESHIRE
COAST
NATIONAL PARK

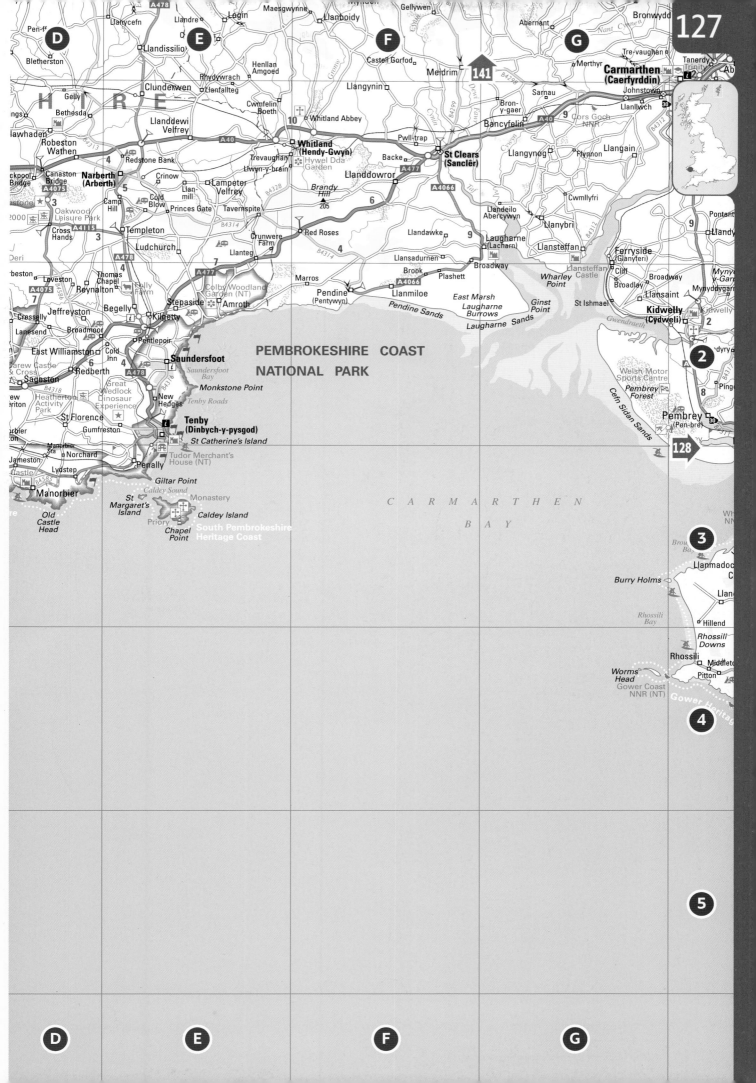

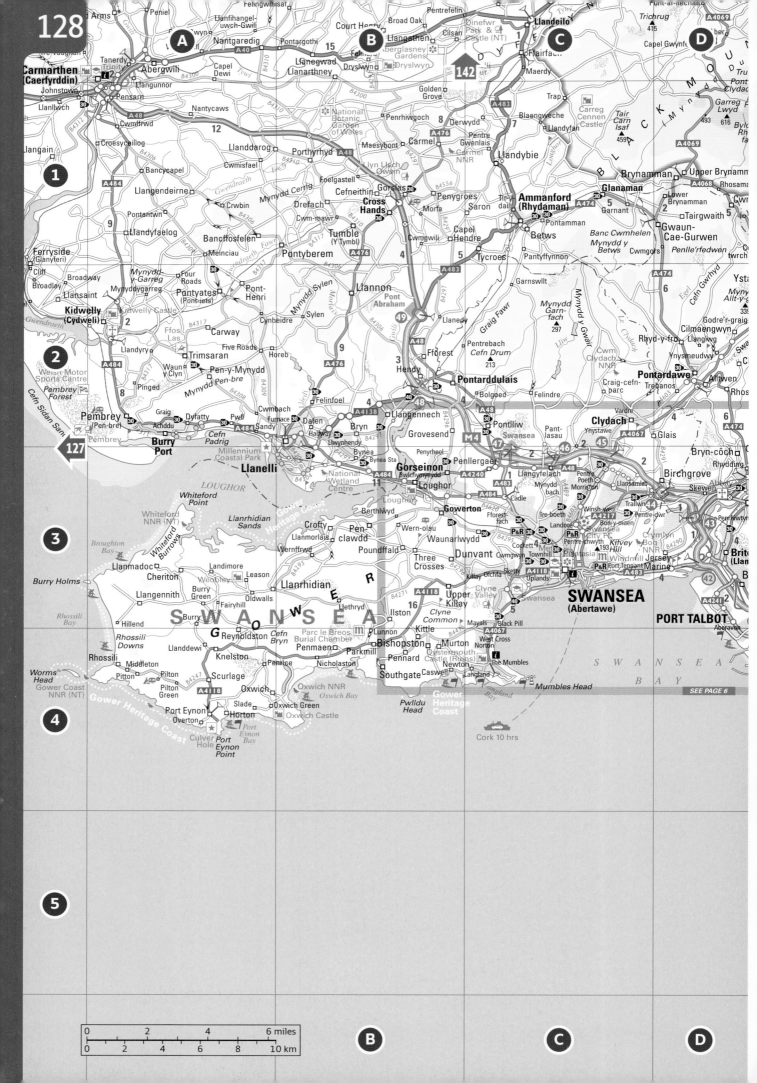

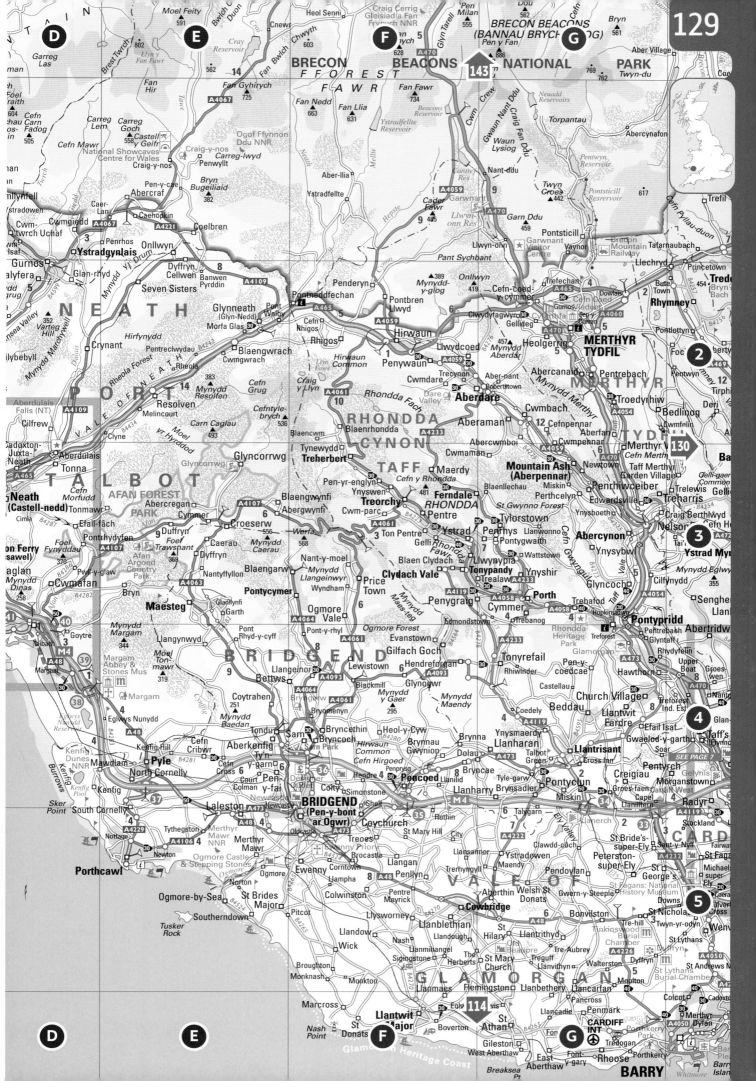

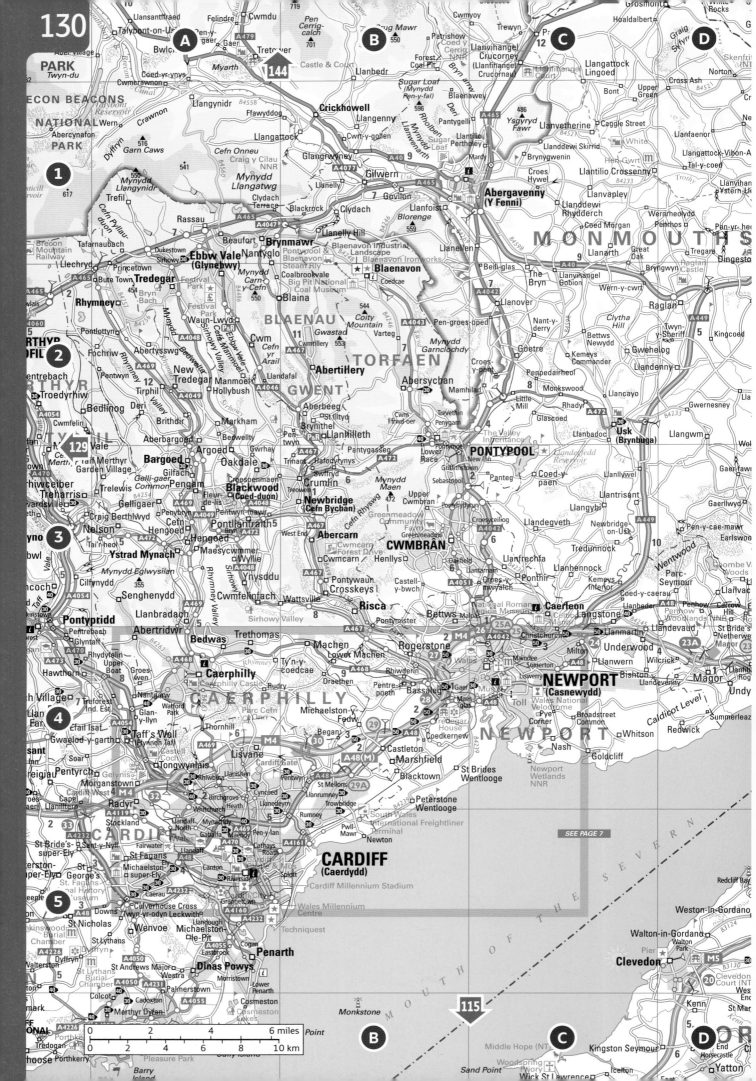

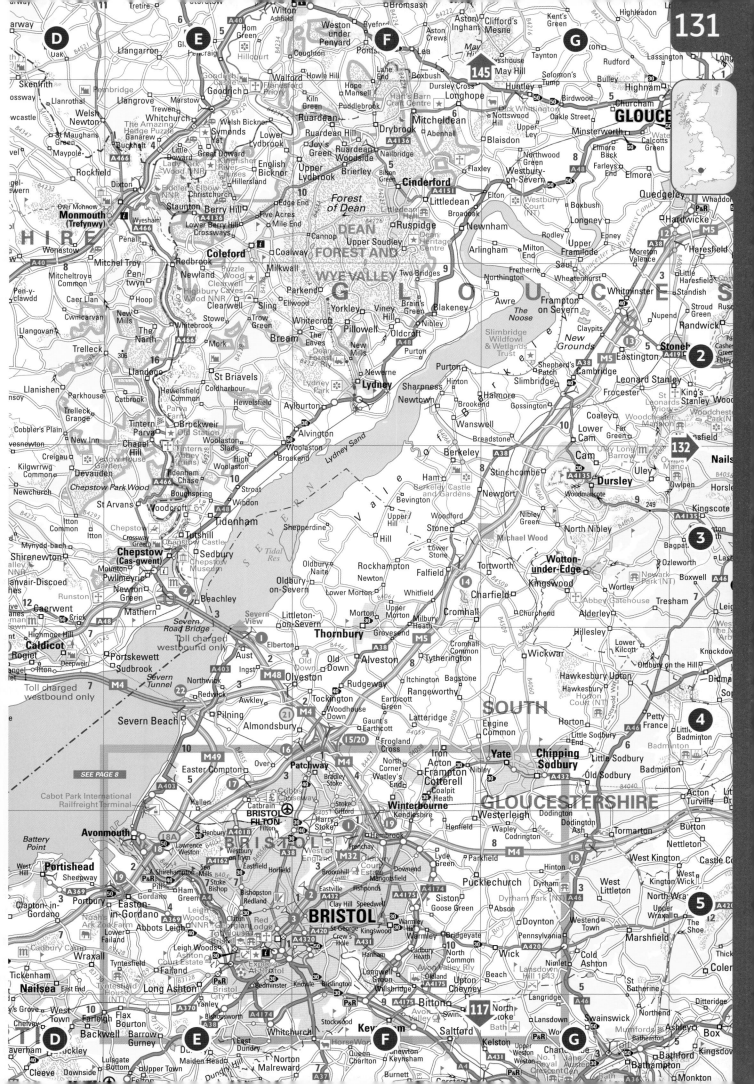

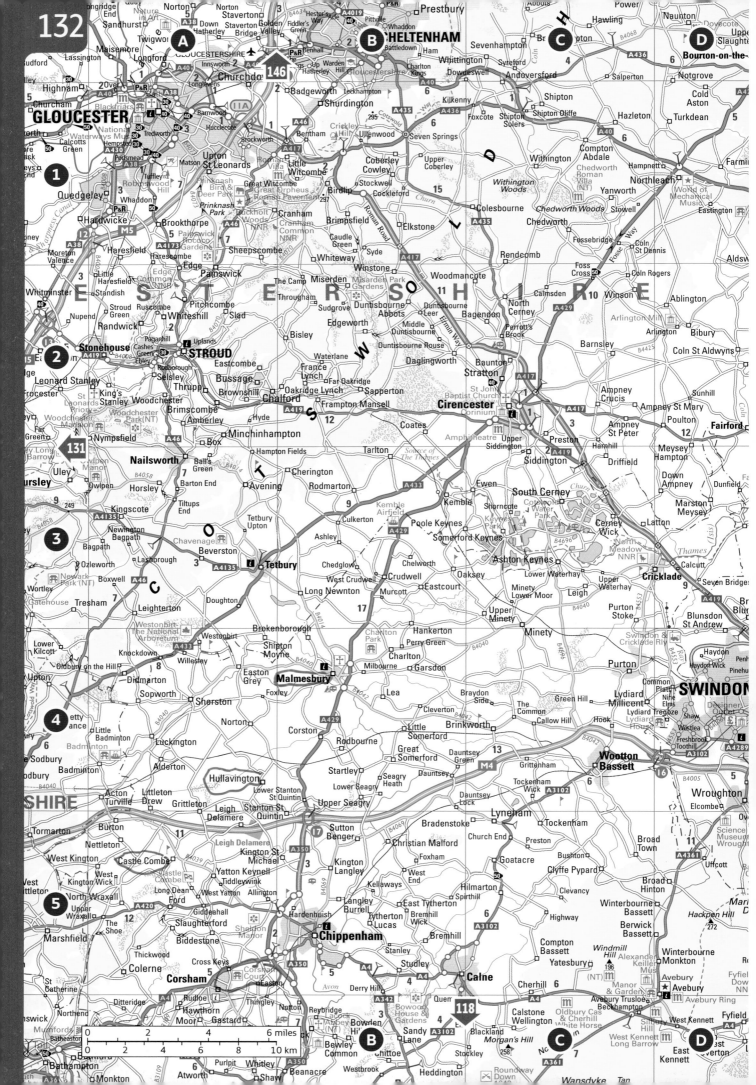

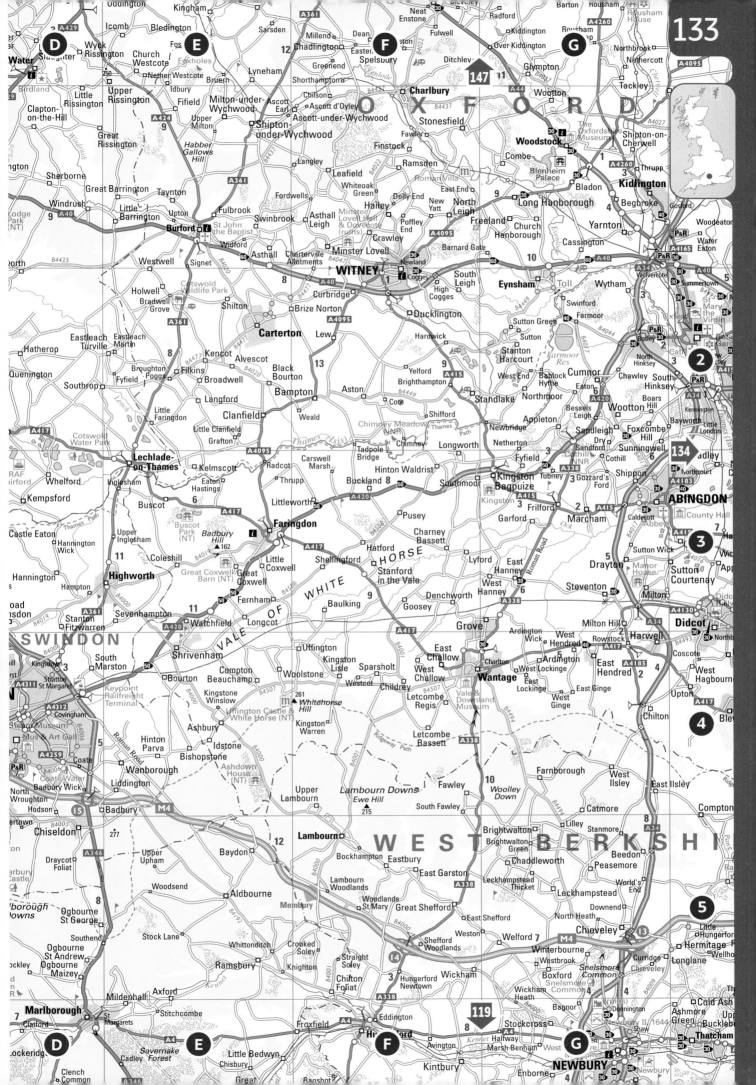

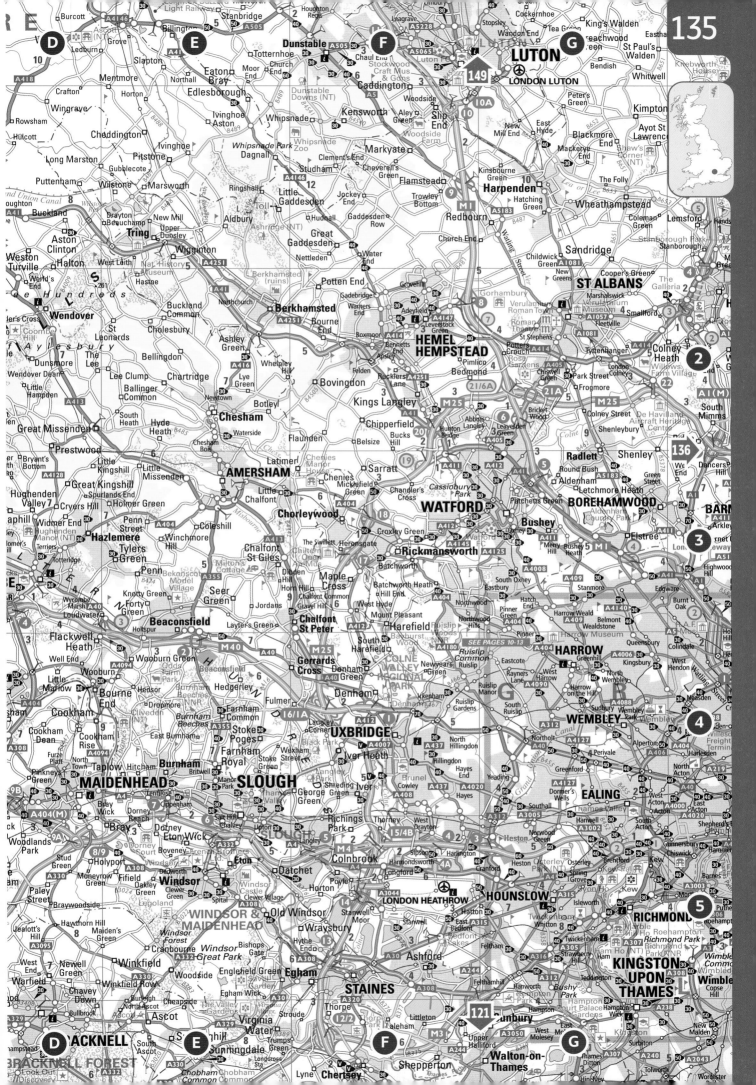

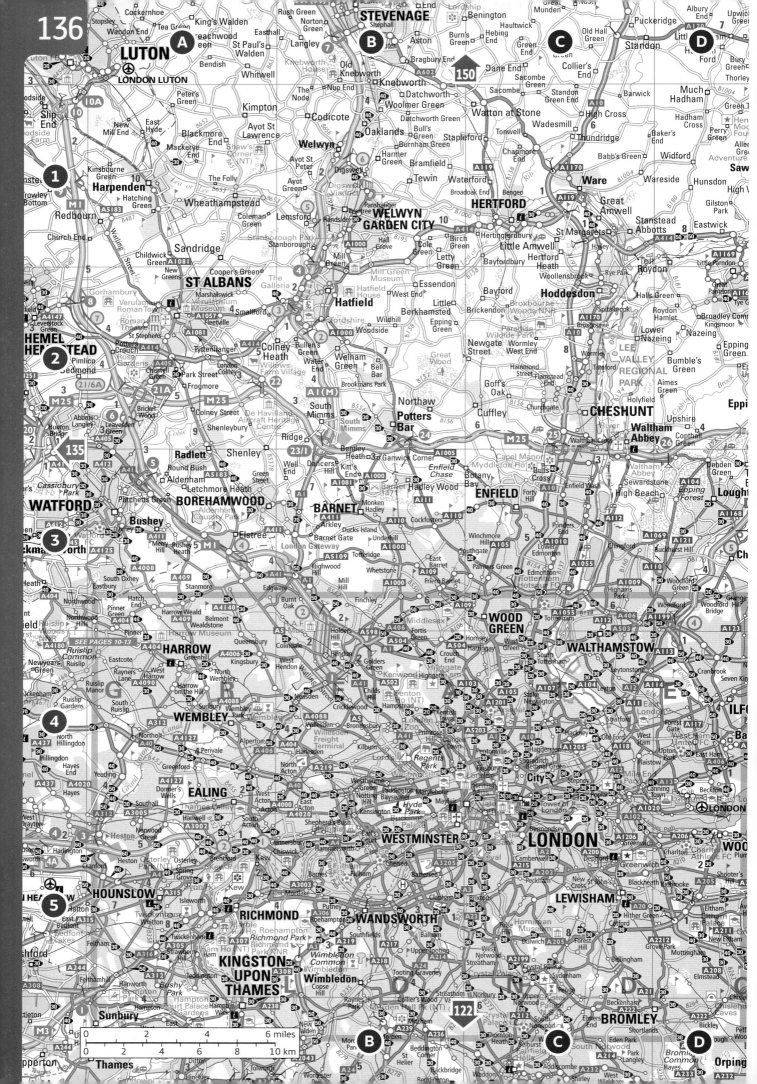

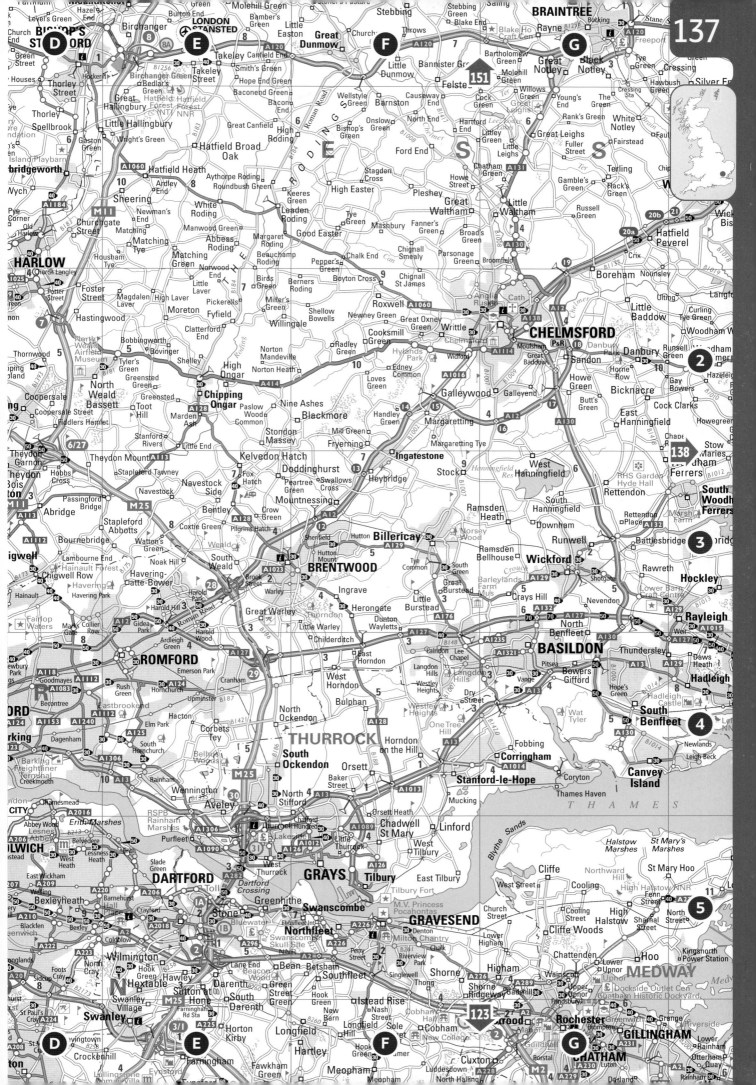

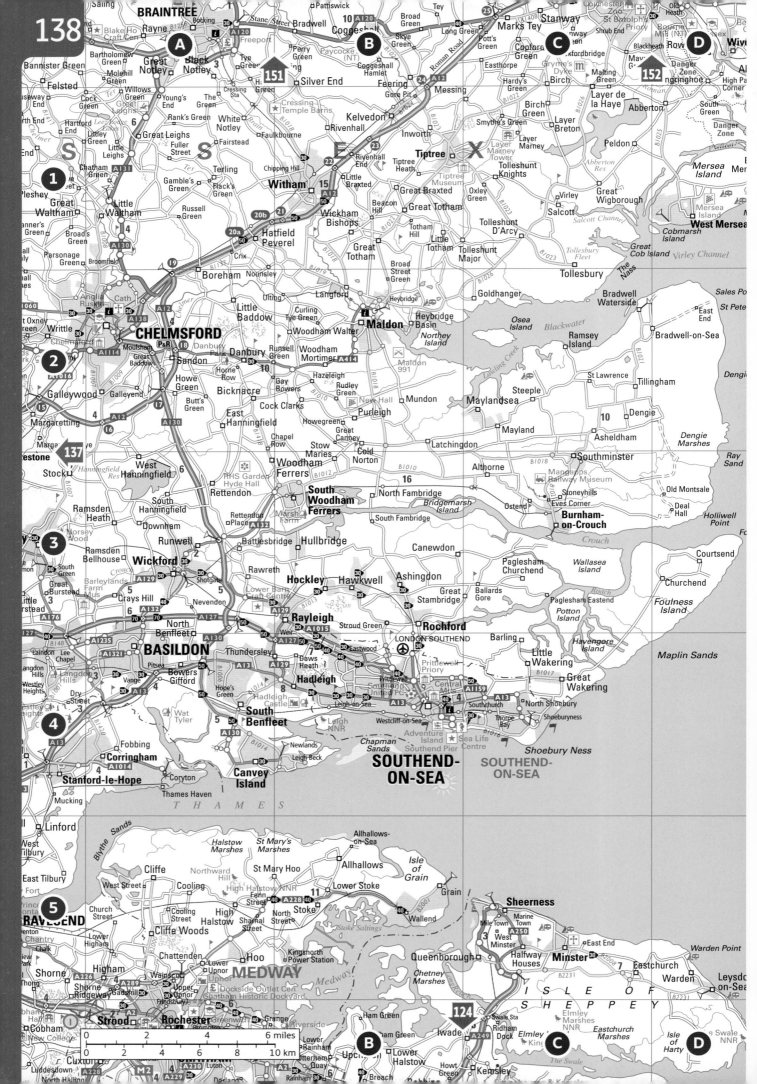

Chatto
Gardens
Balls
Green
Raven's Green
Tendring
Thorpe Green
Beaumont
Island
The Naze

**D** ating
Great Bentley
Weeley
**E** 10
Thorpe-le-Soken
Hamford Water NN'
Kirby le Soken
**F** Walton on the Naze
New Walton Pier
**G**

enhoe
A133
Aingers Green
Weeley Heath
B1414
Kirby Cross
B1033

resford
Thorrington
Row Heath
9
Great Holland
Great Holland
**Frinton-on-Sea**

**Brightlingsea**
B1029
Little Clacton
Clacton Common
Holland-on-Sea
Sandy Point

East
sea
Hurst Green
Priory
Great Clacton
Gunfleet Sand
B1027
30
30
30
30

Cudmore Grove
Point Clear
St Osyth
**CLACTON-ON-SEA**

Mersea Flats
St Osyth Marsh
Jaywick
Clacton Pier
30

Colne Point
Seawick

153

int
r's Flat

e Flat

**2**

Foulness Sands

oulness Point

**3**

**4**

**5**

South Channel
Long Nose Spit

MARGATE
Tudor House
Cliftonville
Foreness Point
White Ness
Kingsgate

Westgate on Sea
Westbrook
North Forela

Herne Bay
Reculver
Towers & Roman Fort
Birching
125
Quex House & Gdns
Salmeston Grange
Spitfire & Hurri Mem RAF M
A255
St Peter's
Bleak House
Dickens House Museum

**D** hitstable
Swalecliffe
mpton
Beltinge
Hillborough
6
A28
40
Acol
30
Northwood
A254
**Broadstairs**

Shell Ness
Tankerton
Hunters Forstal
Broomfield
Highstead
**F** as at Wade
2
**ISLE OF THANET**
**G**
A256
2

Seasalter
Chestfield
5
Herne
Bovden Gate
**KENT INTERNATIONAL**
Manston

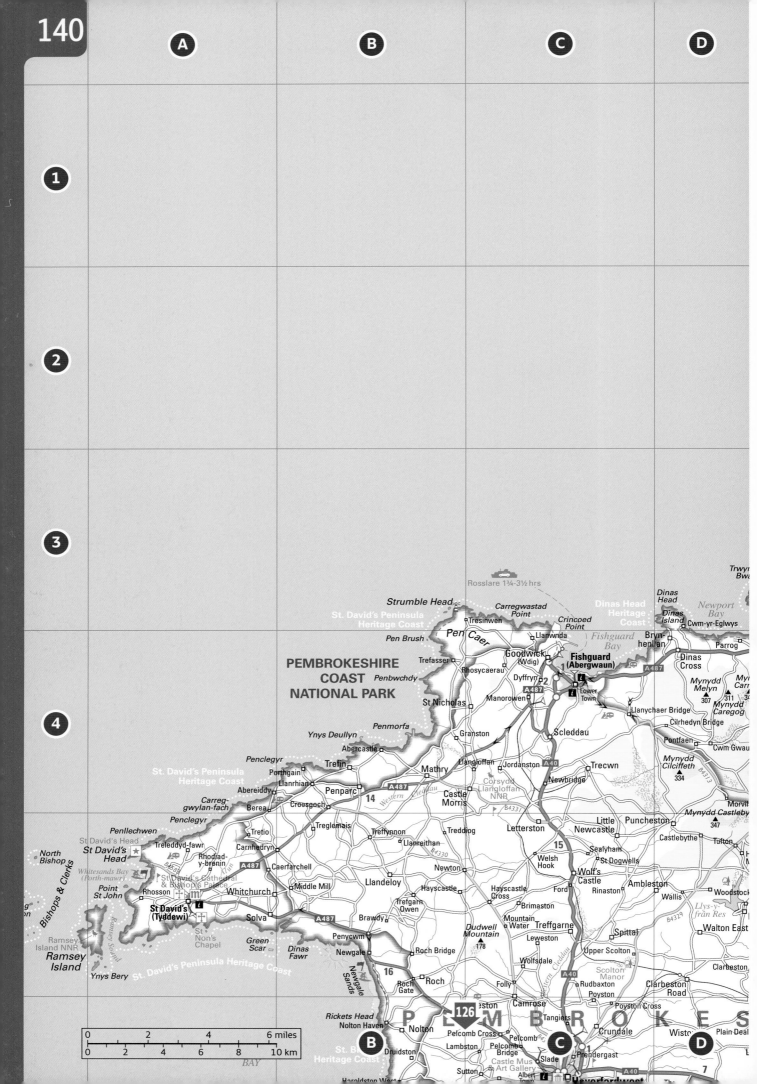

A     B     C     D

1

2

3

Rosslare 1¾-3½ hrs

Strumble Head

*St. David's Peninsula Heritage Coast*

Carregwastad Point

Crincoed Point

*Trwyn Bwa*

Dinas Head Heritage Coast

Dinas Head

*Newport Bay*

Tresinwen

Pen Brush

Llanwnda

*Fishguard Bay*

Dinas Island

Cwm-yr-Eglwys

Bryn-henllan

**PEMBROKESHIRE COAST NATIONAL PARK**

Pen Caer

Goodwick (Wdig)

**Fishguard (Abergwaun)**

Dinas Cross

Parrog

Trefasser

Rhosycaerau

Penbwchdy

Dyffryn

Lower Town

A487

*Mynydd Melyn* 307

*Myn Carr*

311

St Nicholas

Manorowen

Llanychaer Bridge

*Mynydd Caregog*

Penmorfa

Granston

Scleddau

Cilrhedyn Bridge

4

*Ynys Deullyn*

Abercastle

Pontfaen

*Cwm Gwau*

Penclegyr

Trefin

Mathry

Llangloffan

Jordanston

A40

Trecwn

*Mynydd Cilciffeth* 334

B4313

Porthgain

Llanrhian

Penparc

A487

*Western Cleddau*

Castle Morris

B4331

Corsydd Llangloffan NNR

Newbridge

Abereiddy

Berea

Croesgoch

14

*Mynydd Castlebyt*

347

Carreg-gwylan-fach

Penclegyr

Treglemais

Treffynnon

Treddiog

Letterston

Little Newcastle

Castlebythe

Tufton

St David's Head

Tretio

Llanreithan

B4330

15

Sealyham

St Dogwells

Ambleston

Woodstock

*North Bishop*

St David's Head

Treleddyd-fawr

Carnhedryn

Newton

Welsh Hook

Wolf's Castle

Ford

Rinaston

Wallis

*Llys-y-frân Res*

Rhodiad-y-brenin

A487

Caerfarchell

Hayscastle

Hayscastle Cross

Brimaston

*Whitesands Bay (Porth-mawr)*

St David's Cathedral & Bishop's Palace

Middle Mill

Llandeloy

Mountain Water

Treffgarne

Spittal

Walton East

*Point St John*

Rhosson

Whitchurch

Trefgarn Owen

Brawdy

Leweston

Upper Scolton

**St David's (Tyddewi)**

Solva

A487

Penycwm

*Dudwell Mountain* 178

Wolfsdale

Clarbeston

Ramsey Island NNR

*St Non's Chapel*

*Green Scar*

*Dinas Fawr*

Newgale

Roch Bridge

Rudbaxton

Scolton Manor

Clarbeston Road

*Ramsey Island*

*Ramsey Sound*

16

Roch Gate

Roch

Folly

Poyston

**Ramsey Island**

*Ynys Bery*

*St David's Peninsula Heritage Coast*

*Newgale Sands*

126

Camrose

Tangiers

Poyston Cross

*Rickets Head*

Nolton Haven

Nolton

**P E M B R O K E S**

B

C

Crundale

Wiston

Plain-Deal

Pelcomb Cross

Pelcomb

Lambston

Pelcomb Bridge

Slade

Prendergast

A40

*Bishops & Clerks*

Druidston

Castle Mus Art Gallery

Sutton

7

St B Heritage Coast

*BAY*

Haroldston West

**Haverfordwest**

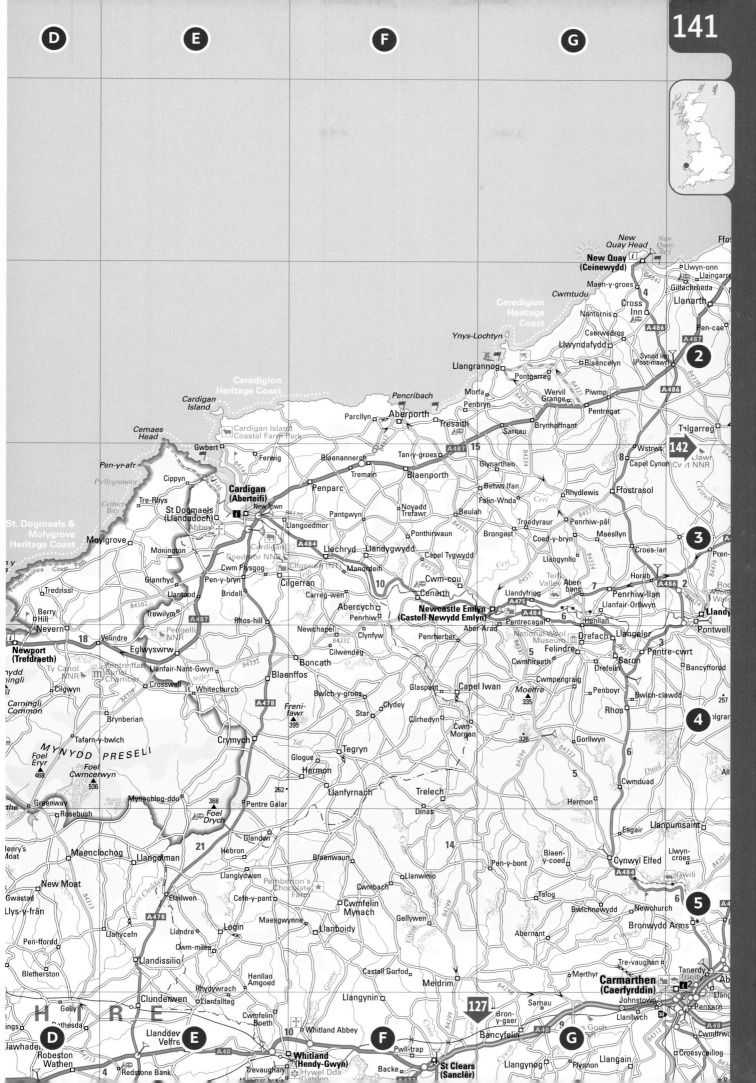

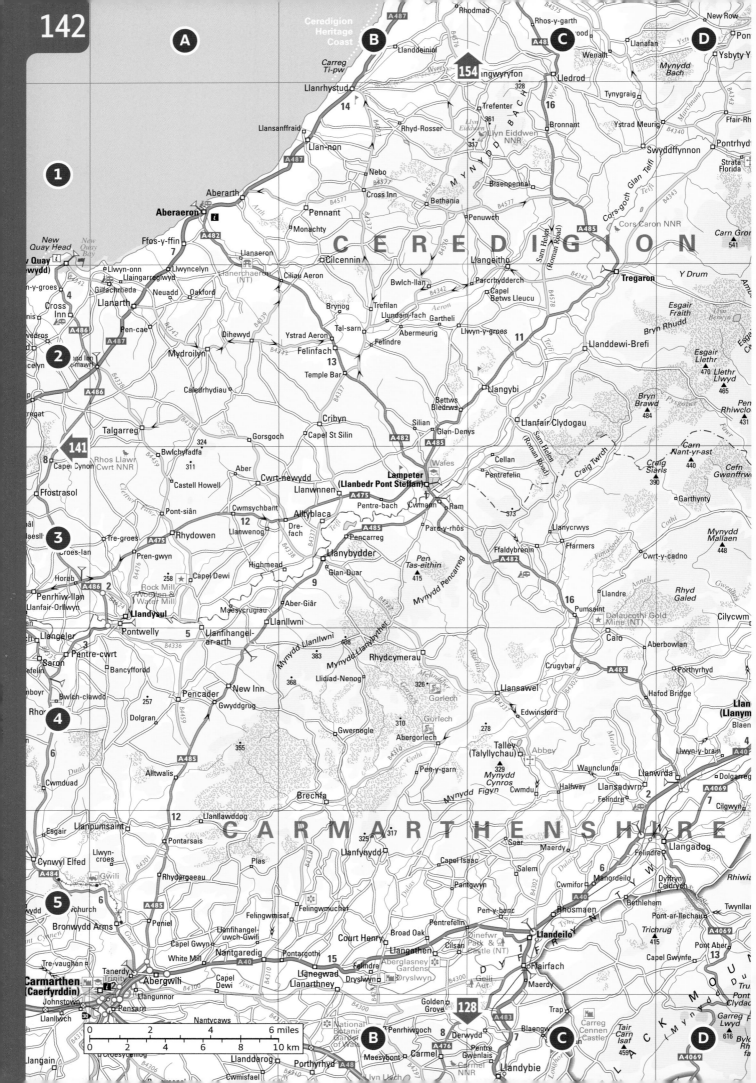

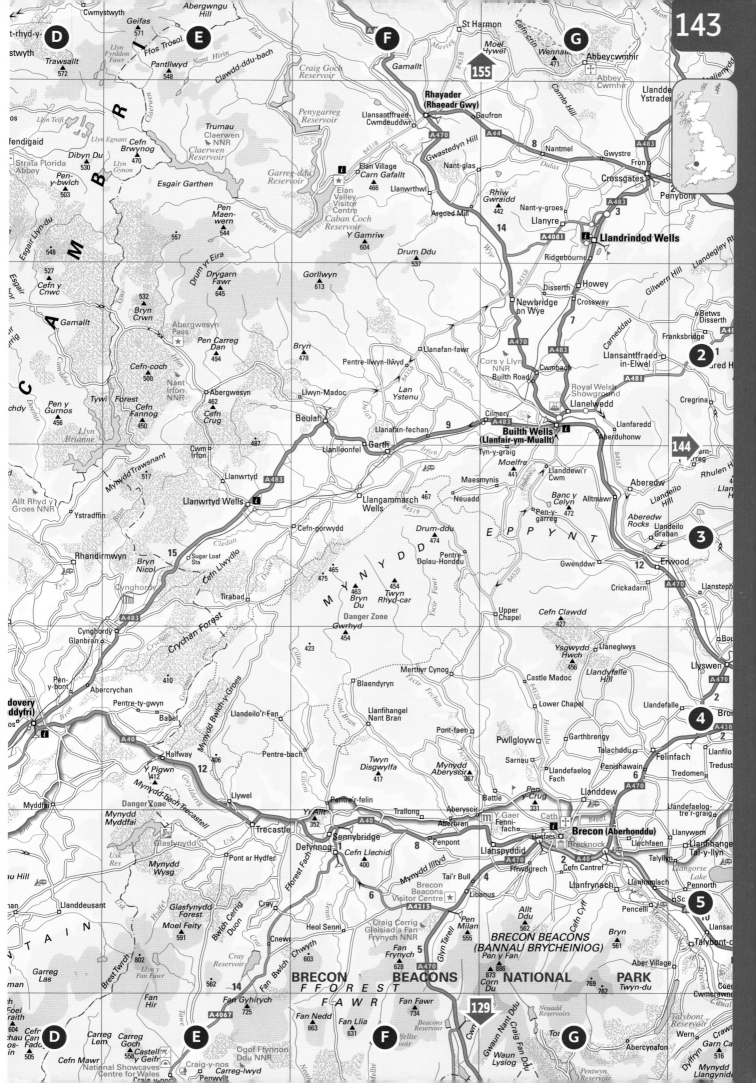

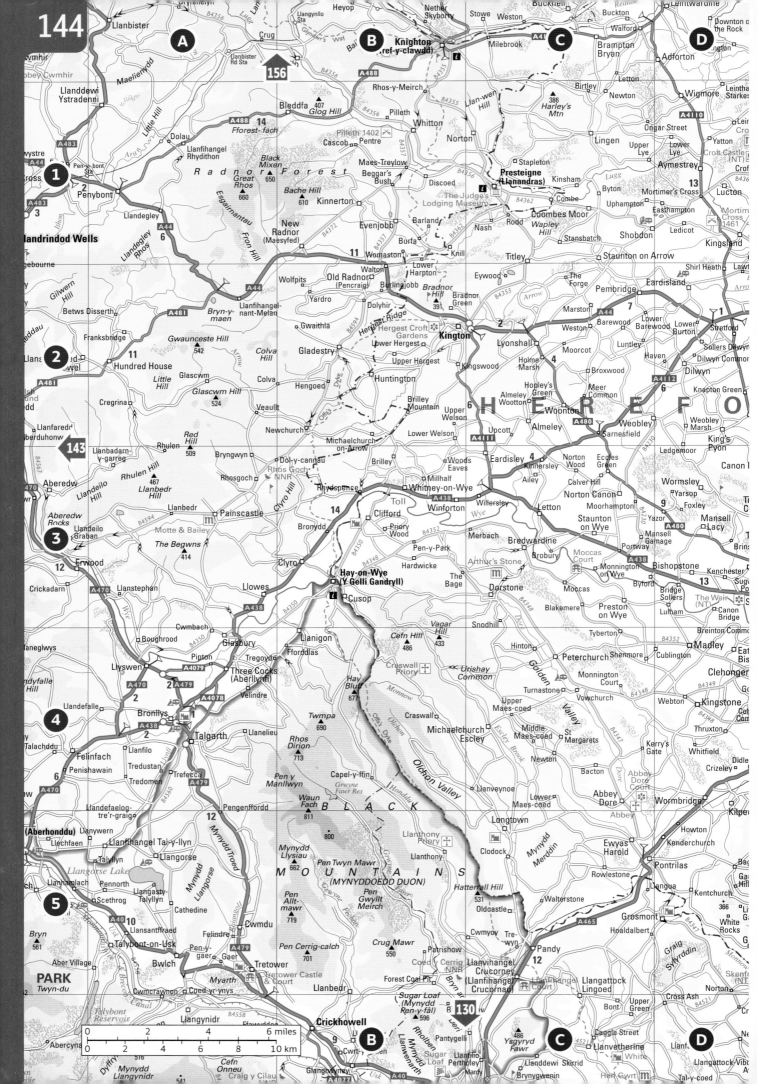

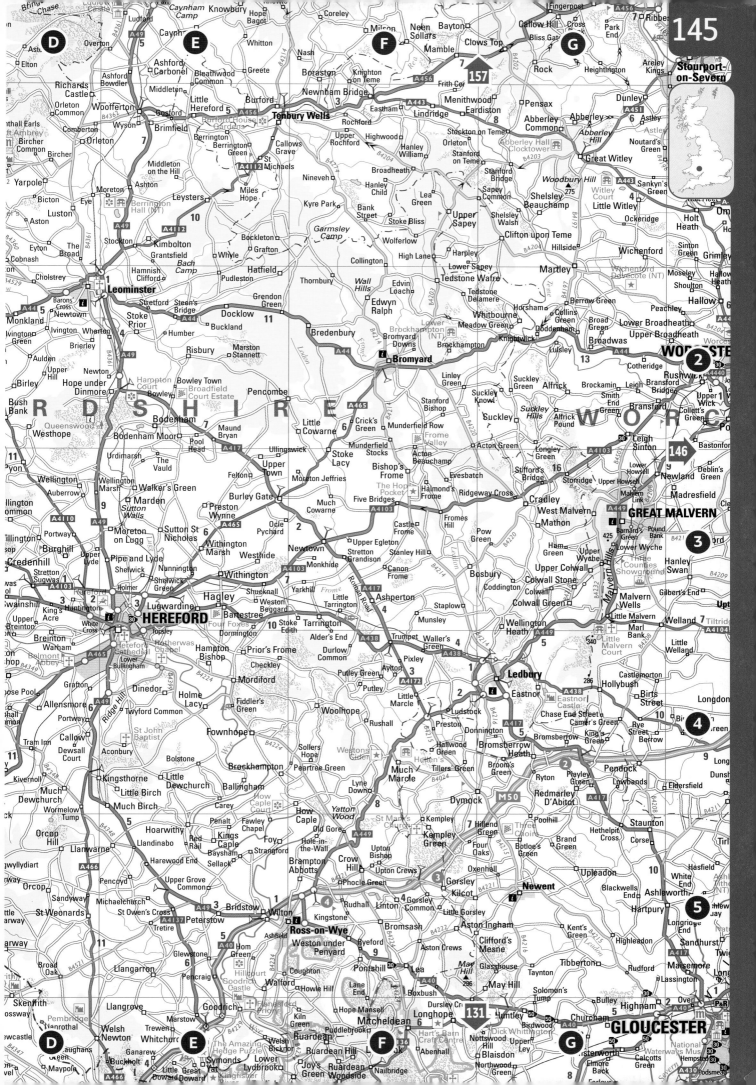

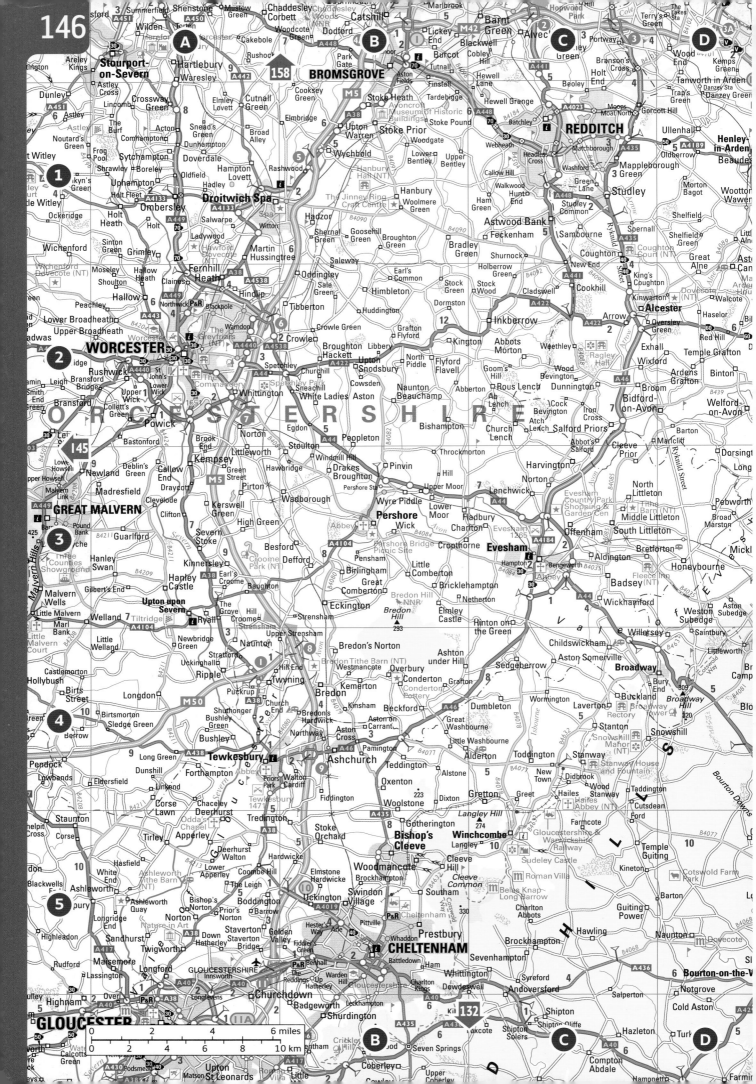

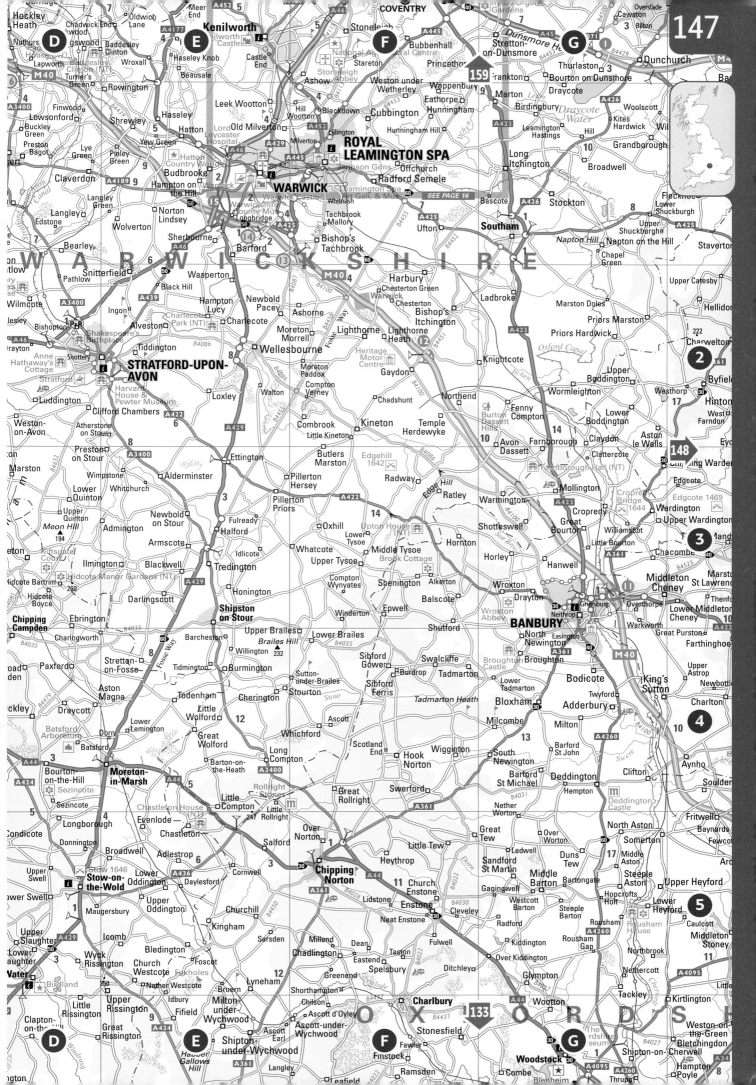

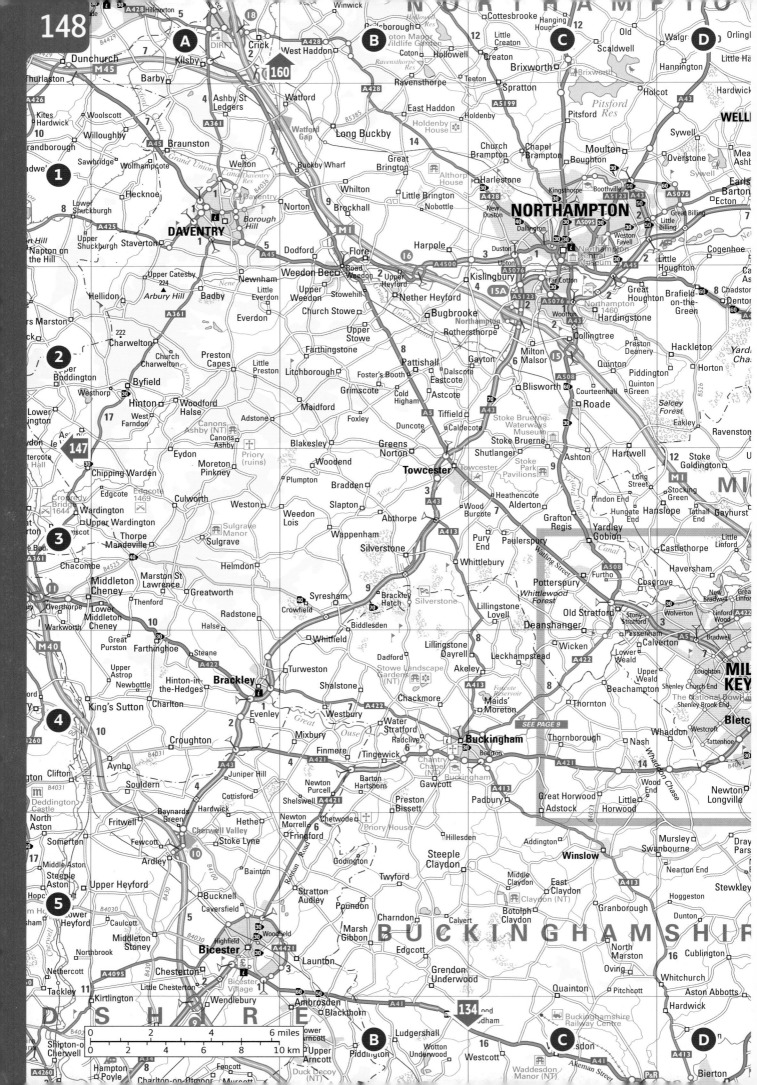

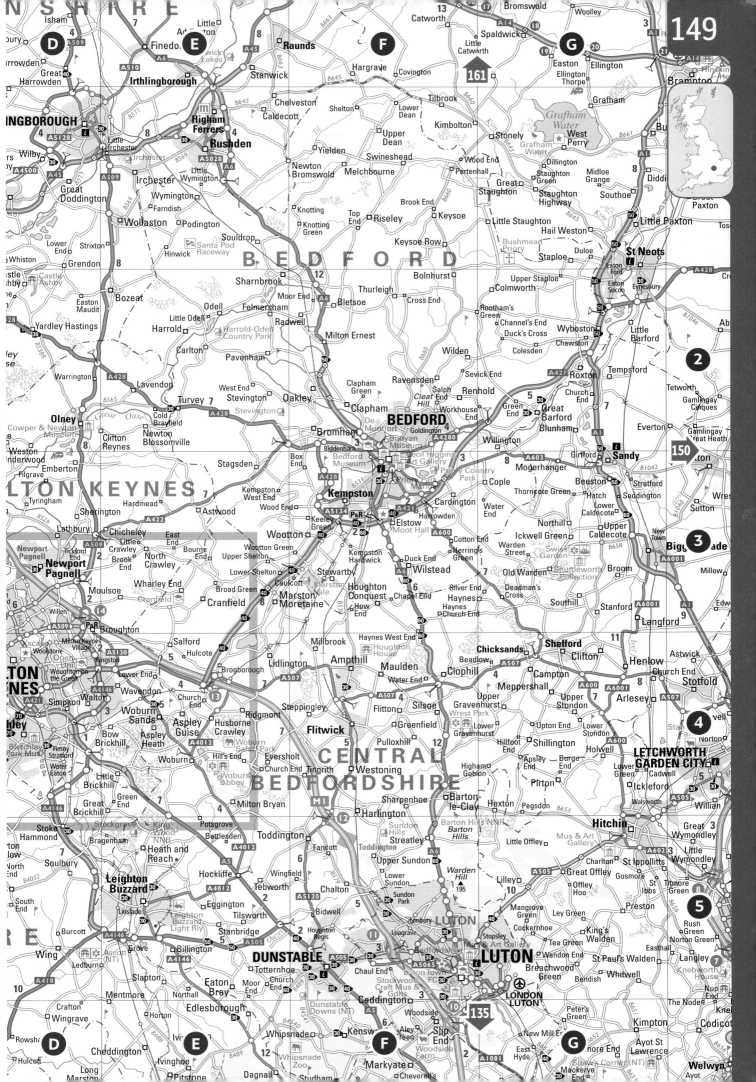

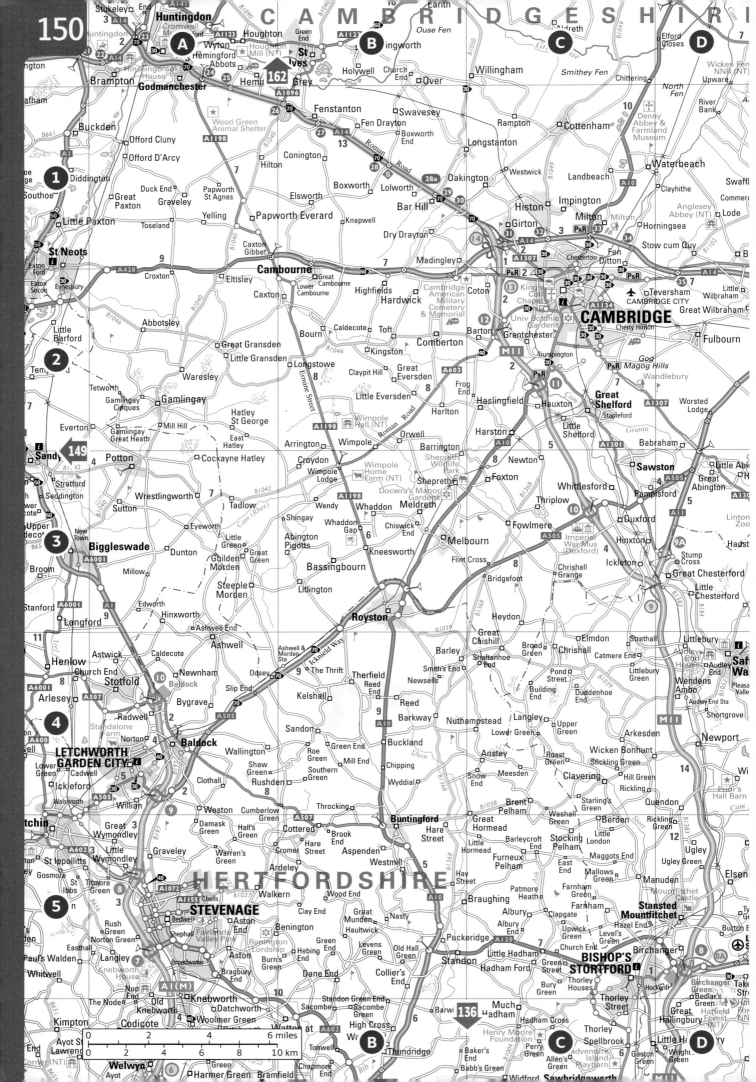

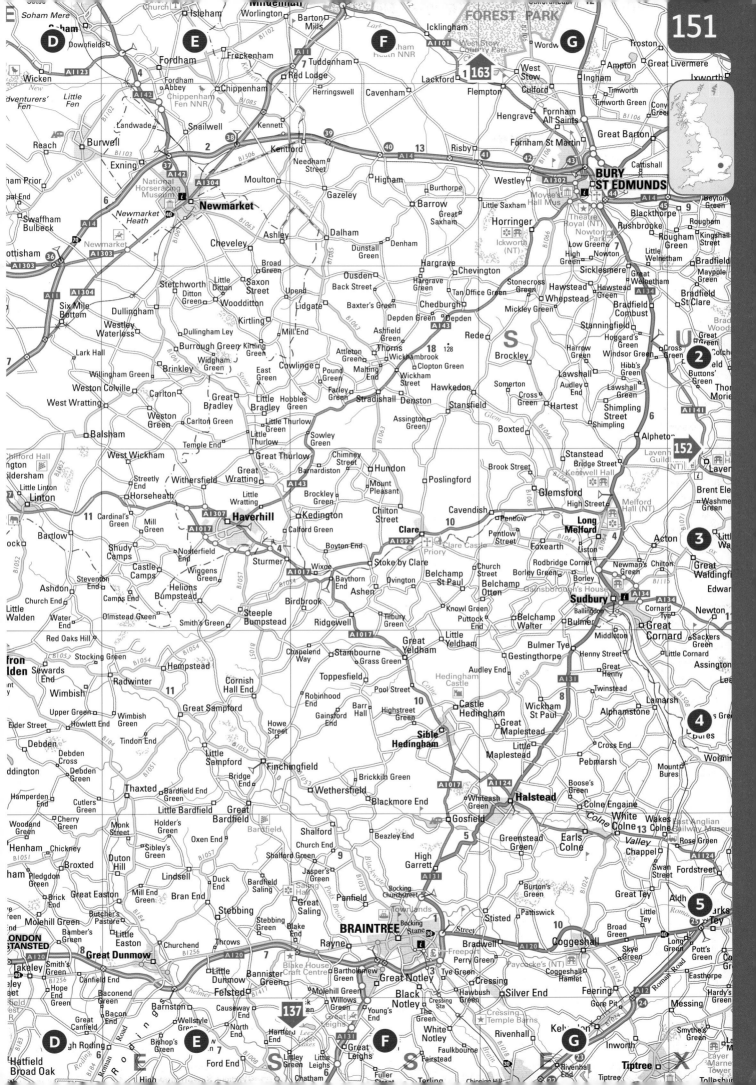

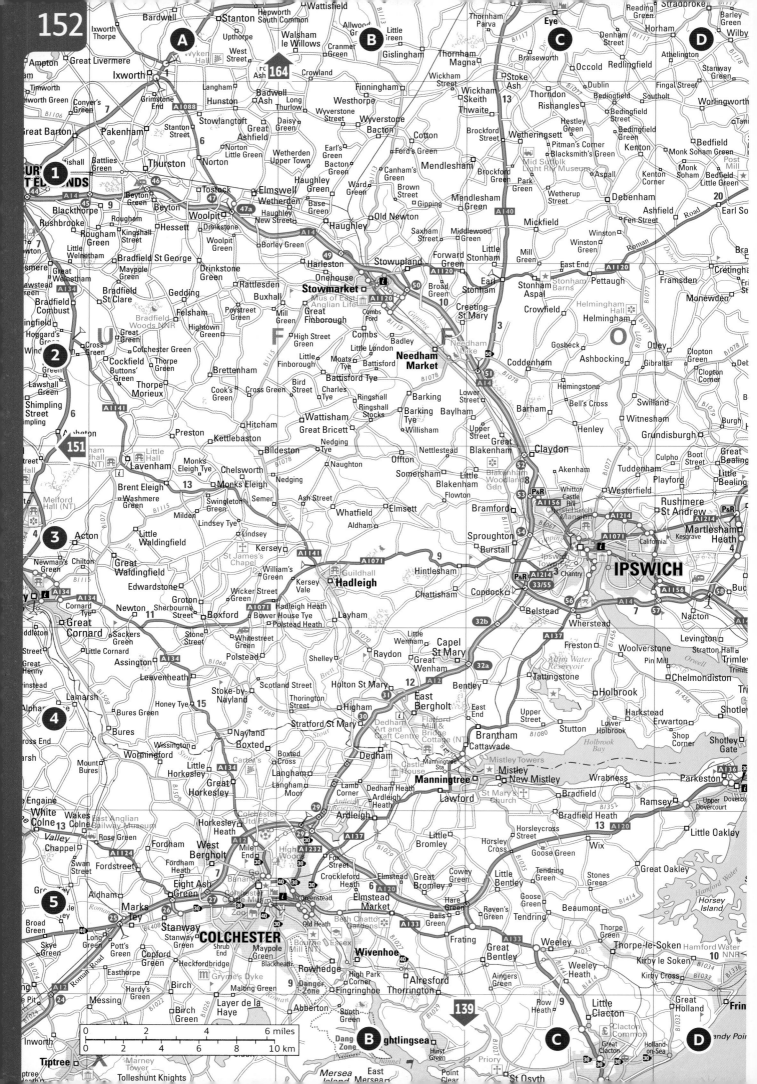

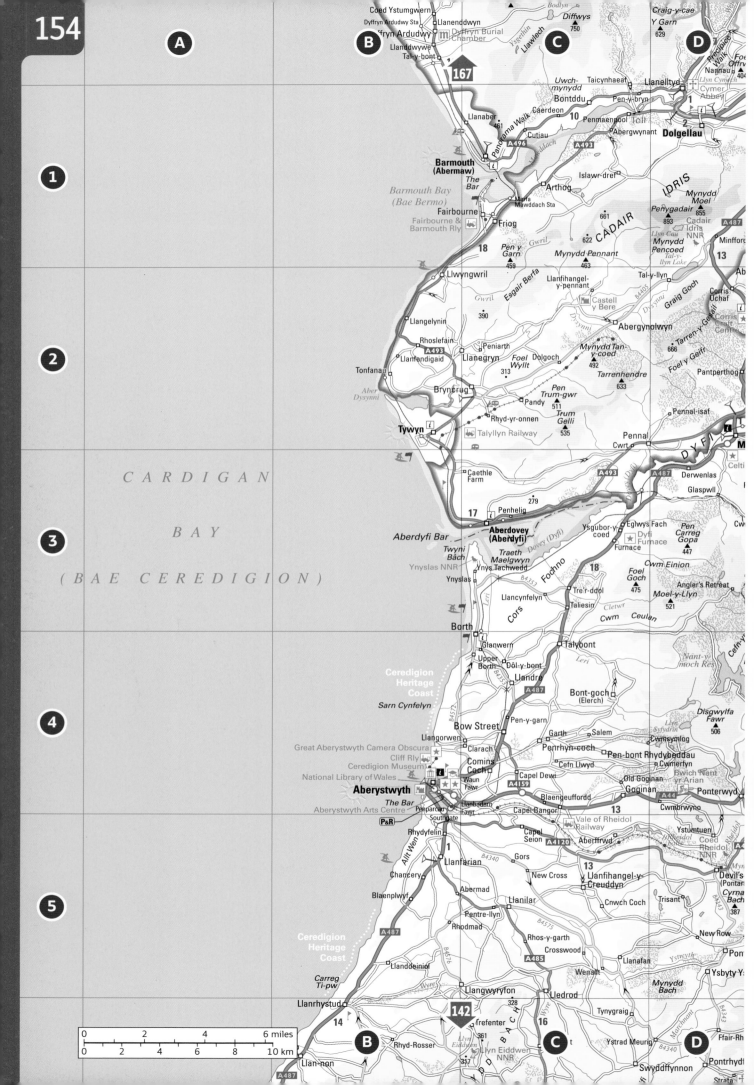

Coed Ystumgwern
Dyffryn Ardudwy Sta
ffryn Ardudwy
Llanddwywe
Tal-y-bont
Llanenddwyn
Dyffryn Burial Chamber

**A**  **B**  **C**  **D**

Bodlyn
Diffwys
750
Craig-y-cae
Y Garn
629

**167**

Uwch-mynydd
Taicynhaeat
Bontddu
Pen-y-bryn
Llanelltyd
Cymer Abbey

Llanaber
461
Cutiau
Caerdeon
10
Penmaenpool Toll
Abergwynant
**Dolgellau**

**Barmouth (Abermaw)**
The Bar
Arthog
Islawr-dref
**IDRIS**
Mynydd Moel

**Barmouth Bay (Bae Bermo)**
Morfa Mawddach Sta
Penygadair
855
893
Cadair Idris NNR

Fairbourne
Fairbourne & Barmouth Rly
Friog
661
**CADAIR**
Llyn Cau
Mynydd Pencoed
Tal-y-llyn Lake
Minffordd

18
Pen y Garn
459
Gwril
622
Mynydd Pennant
463

**C A R D I G A N**

Llwyngwril
Llanfihangel-y-pennant
Tal-y-llyn
Corris Uchaf
Corris Craft Centre

Castell y Bere
Graig Goch
Tarren-y-Gesail

Llangelynin
390
Abergynolwyn

**B A Y**

Rhoslefain
Peniarth
Foel Wyllt
Dolgoch
Mynydd Tan-y-coed
492
Tarren-y-Gesail
666
Foel y Geifr

Tonfanau
Llanfendigaid
Llanegryn
313
633
Pantperthog

Aber Dysynni
Bryncrug
Pen Trum-gwr
511
Pennal-isaf

**( B A E   C E R E D I G I O N )**

**Tywyn**
Pandy
Trum Gelli
535
Pennal
**DYFI**
**M**

Rhyd-yr-onnen
Talyllyn Railway
Cwrt

Caethle Farm
Derwenlas
Celti

**3**
Penhelig
279
**A493**
**A487**
Glaspwll

Aberdyfi Bar
17
**Aberdovey (Aberdyfi)**
Ysgubor-y-coed
Eglwys Fach
Pen Carreg Gopa
447

Twyni Bach
Traeth Maelgwyn
Dovey (Dyfi)
Fochno
Dyfi Furnace
Furnace

Ynyslas NNR
Ynys Tachwedd
18
Foel Goch
475
Cwm Einion
Moel-y-Llyn
521
Angler's Retreat

Ynyslas
**B4353**
Tre'r-ddol

Llancynfelyn
Taliesin
Cletwr
Cwm
Ceulan

Cors
Borth

**4**
Glanwern
Talybont
Nant-y-moch Res

Upper Borth
Dôl-y-bont

Ceredigion Heritage Coast
Llandre
Bont-goch (Elerch)
Disgwylfa Fawr
506

Sarn Cynfelyn
**A487**

Bow Street
Pen-y-garn
Garth
Salem
Cwmsymlog

Great Aberystwyth Camera Obscura
Llangorwen
Penrhyn-coch
Pen-bont Rhydybeddau

Cliff Rly
Clarach
Cefn Llwyd
Cwmerfyn
Bwlch Nant yr Arian

Ceredigion Museum
Comins Coch
Capel Dewi
Old Goginan
**A44**

National Library of Wales
Waun Fawr
Capel Bangor
**A4159**
Goginan
Ponterwyd

**Aberystwyth**
Llanbadarn Fawr
Blaengeuffordd
13
Cwmbrwyno

The Bar
Penparcau
Vale of Rheidol Railway
Ystumtuen
Coed Rheidol NNR

Aberystwyth Arts Centre
Southgate
Capel Seion
Aberffrwd
**Devil's (Pontar**

**P&R**
Rhydyfelin
**A4120**
Cyrnau Bach

**5**
Llanfarian
Gors
13
Trisant
387

Chancery
New Cross
Llanfihangel-y-Creuddyn
New Row

Blaenplwyf
Abermad
Llanilar
Cnwch Coch
Mynydd Bach

Ceredigion Heritage Coast
Pentre-llyn
Rhos-y-garth
Ystbyty Y

Carreg Ti-pw
Rhodmad
Crosswood
**A485**
Llanafan

Llanddeiniol
Wenallt
Pontrh

**14**
Llangwyryfon
328
Lledrod
16
Tynygraig

Llanrhystud
**142**
Trefenter
361

Ffair-Rh

Rhyd-Rosser
Ystrad Meurig
**B4340**
Swyddffynnon

Llan-non
Llyn Eiddwen NNR
317
Strata

**B**  **C**  **D**

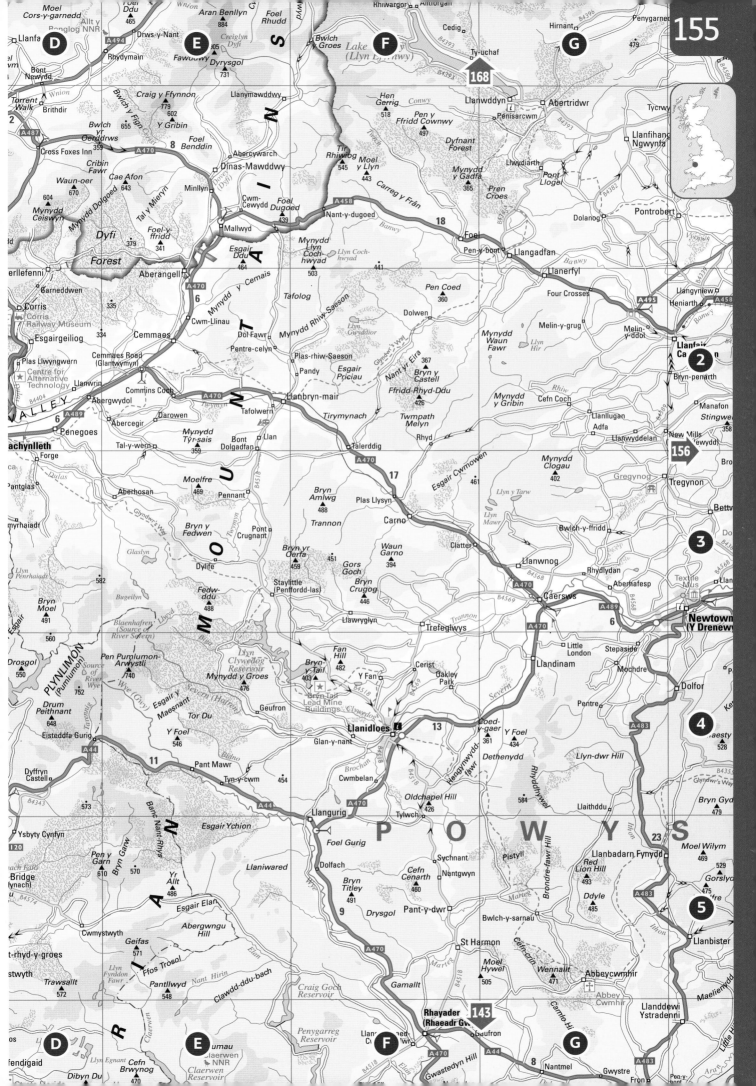

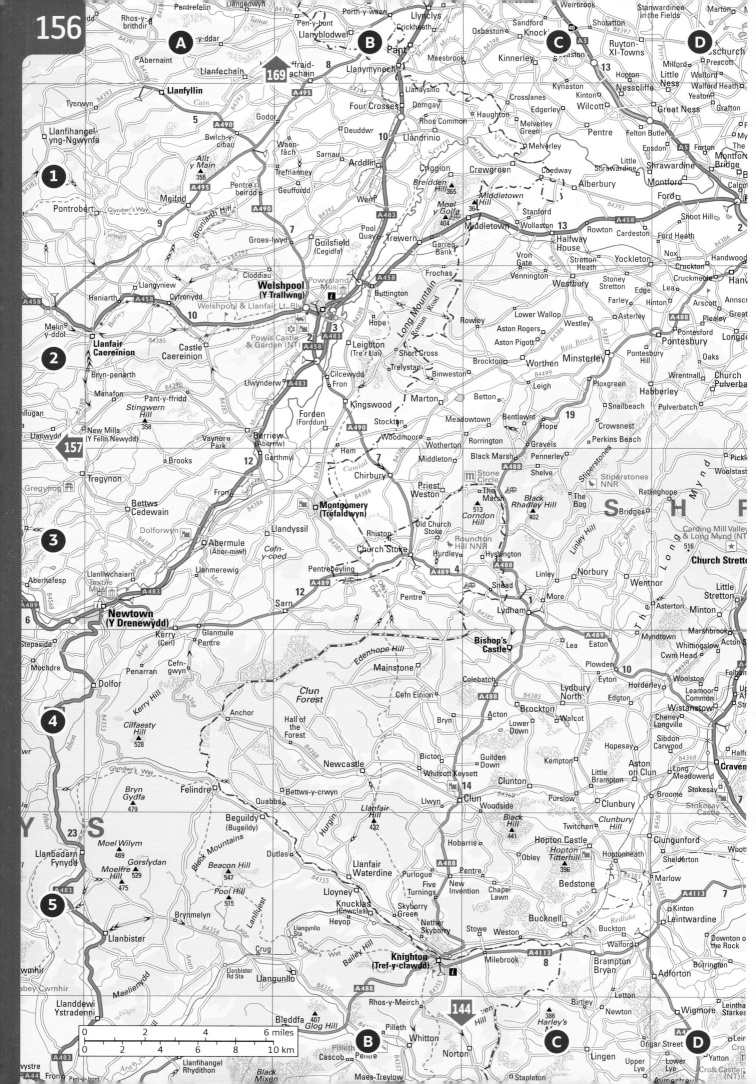

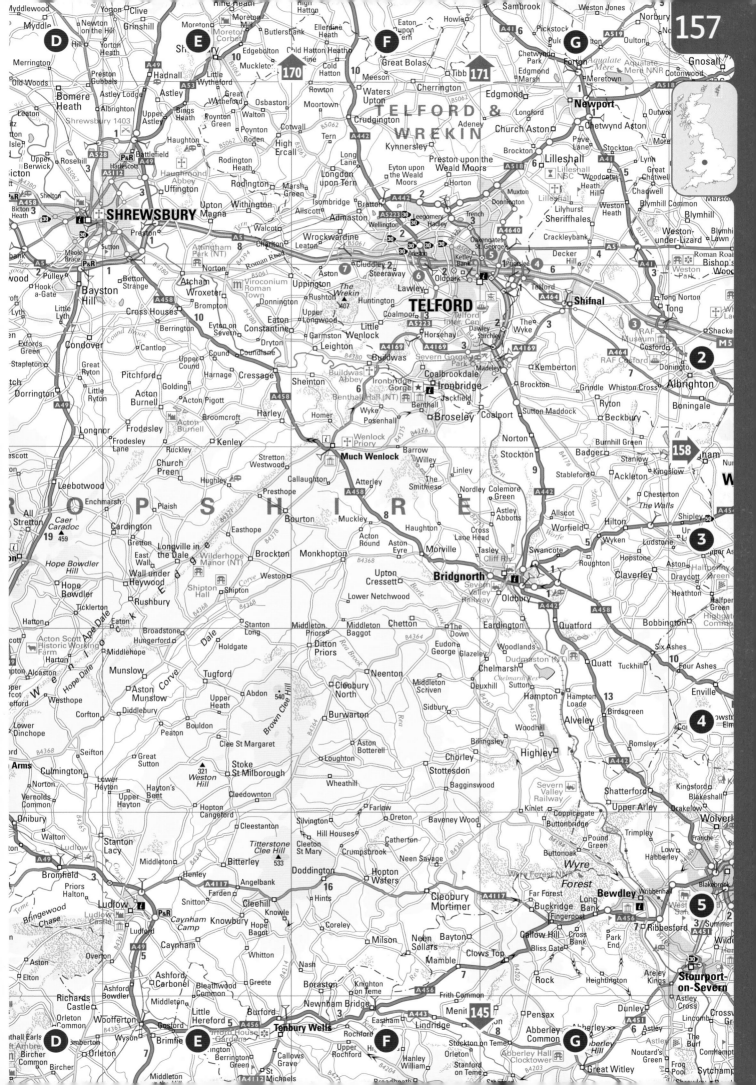

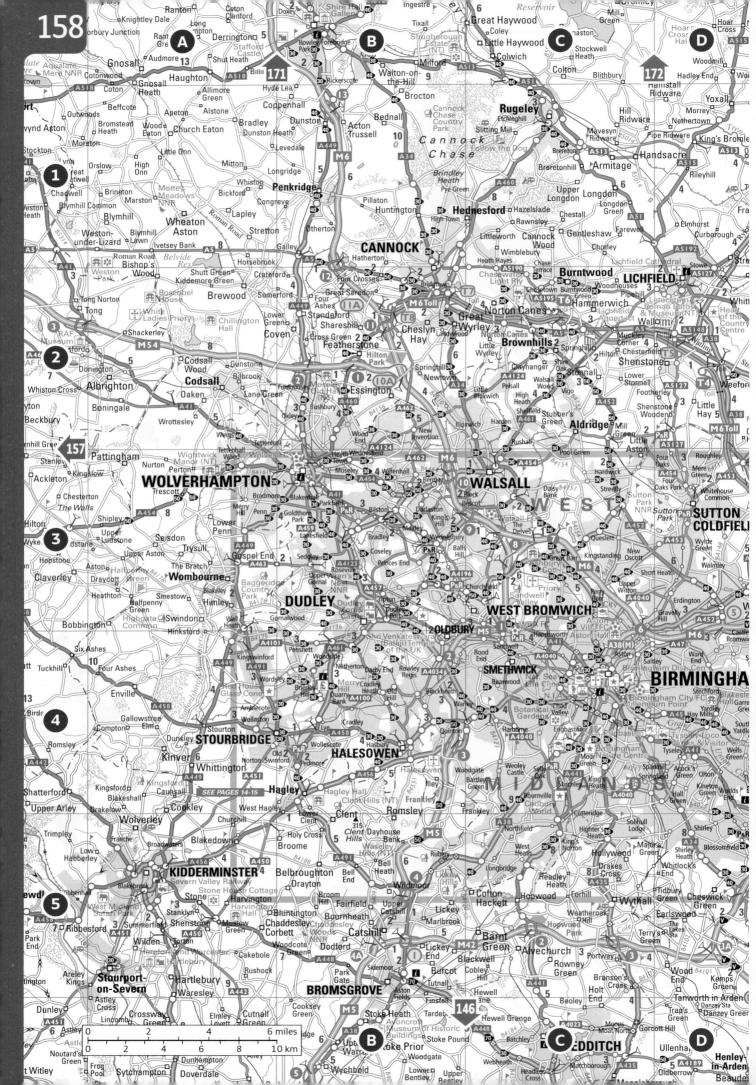

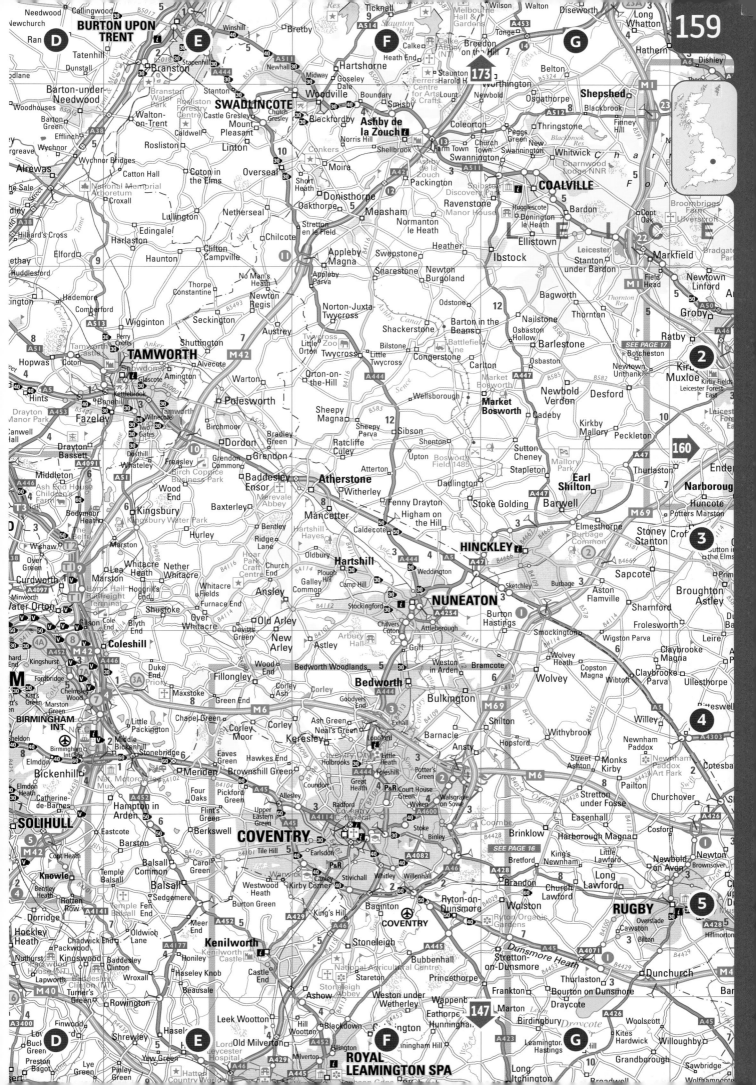

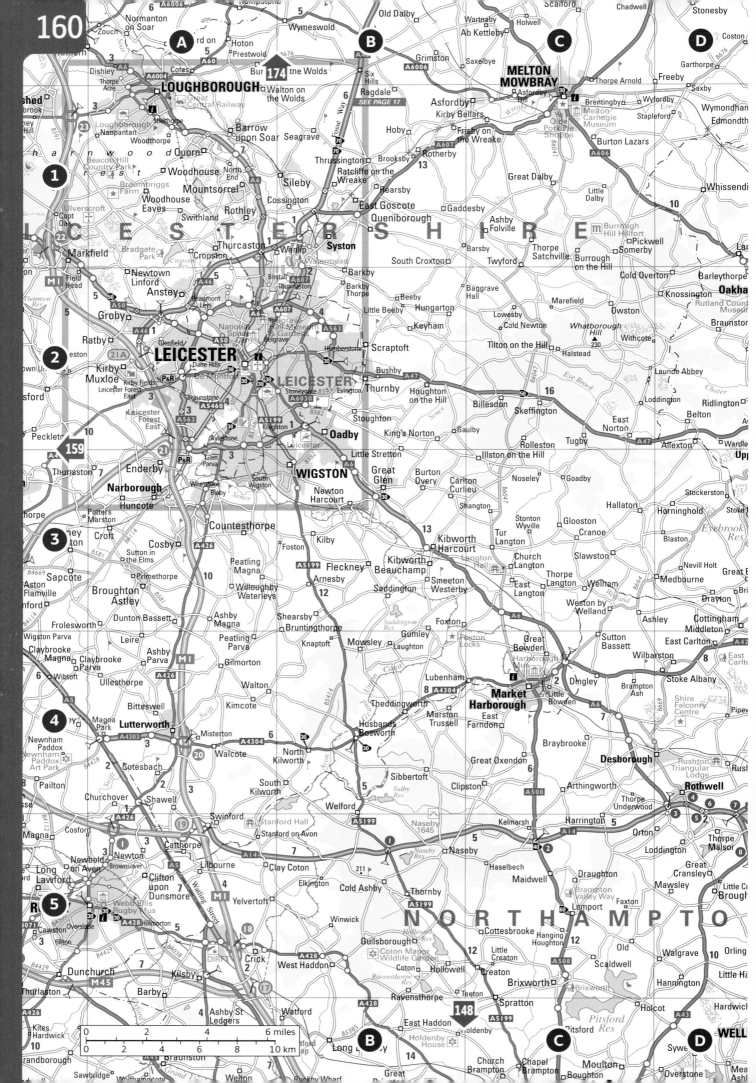

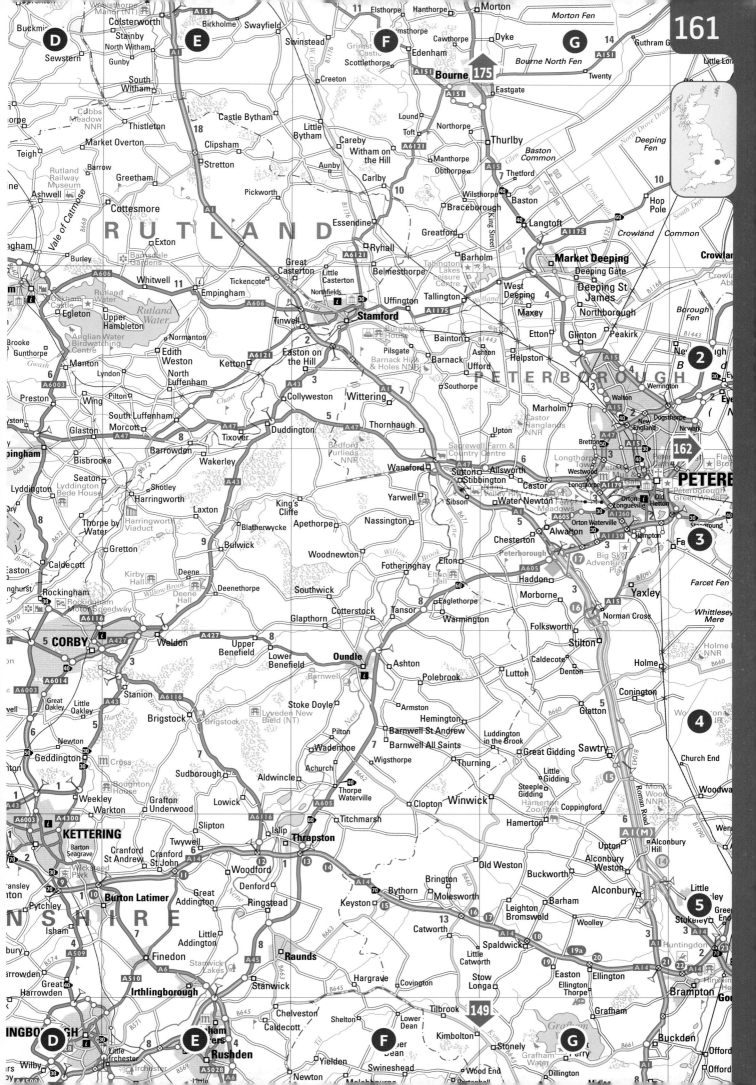

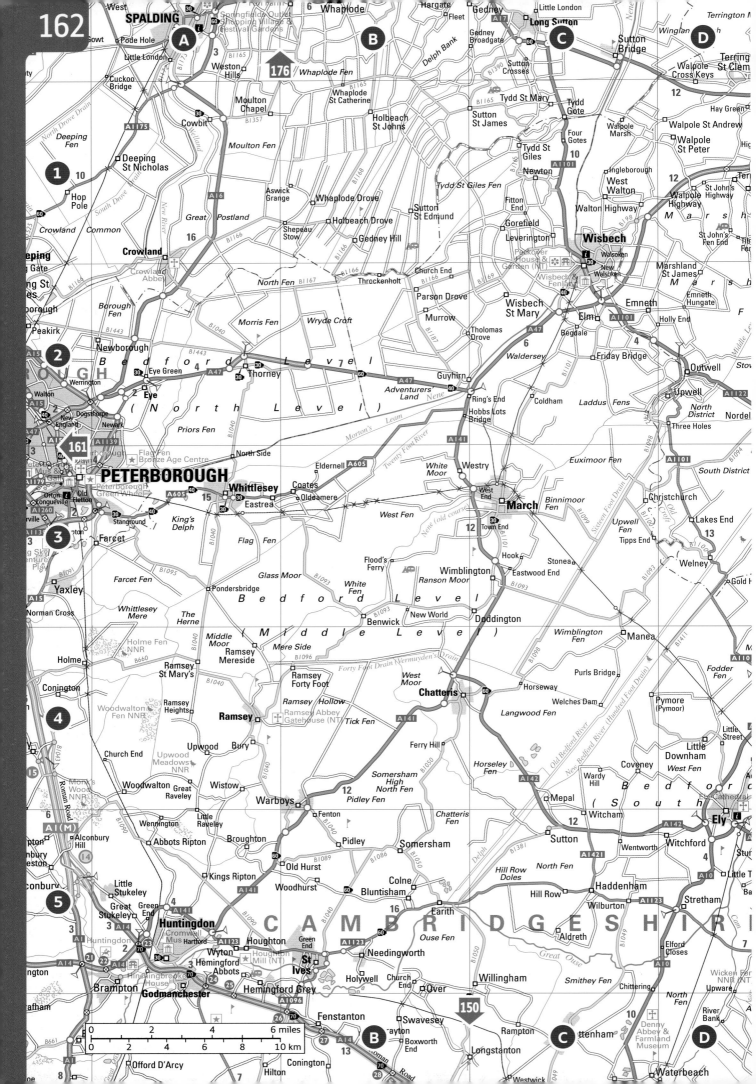

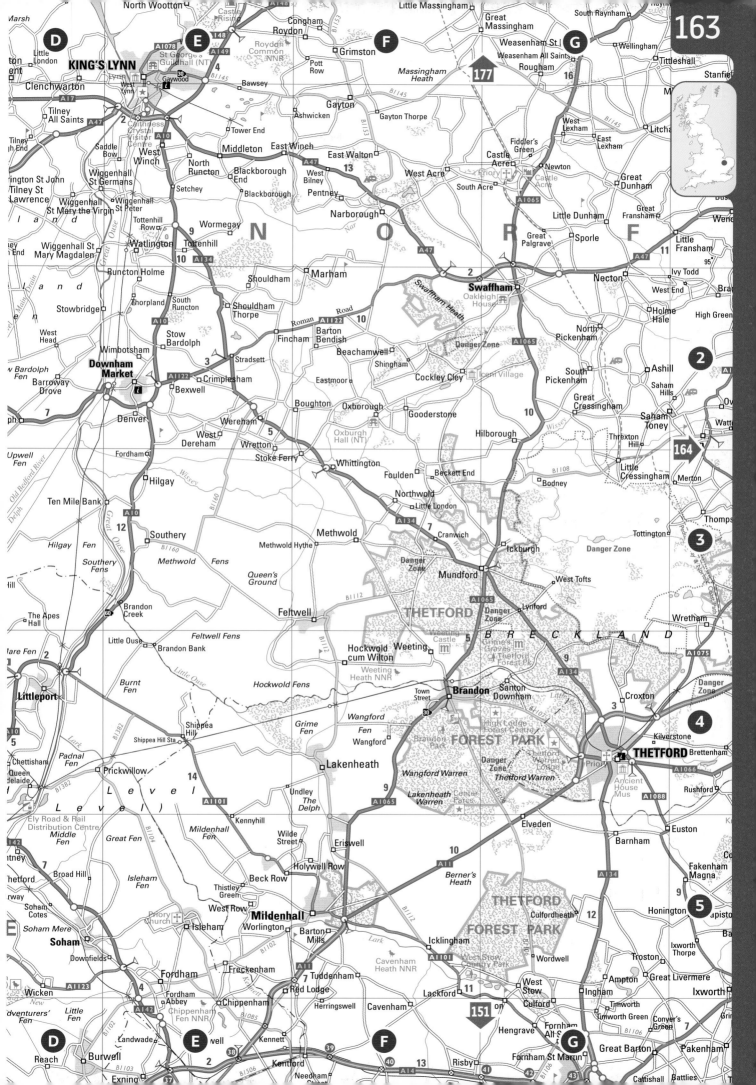

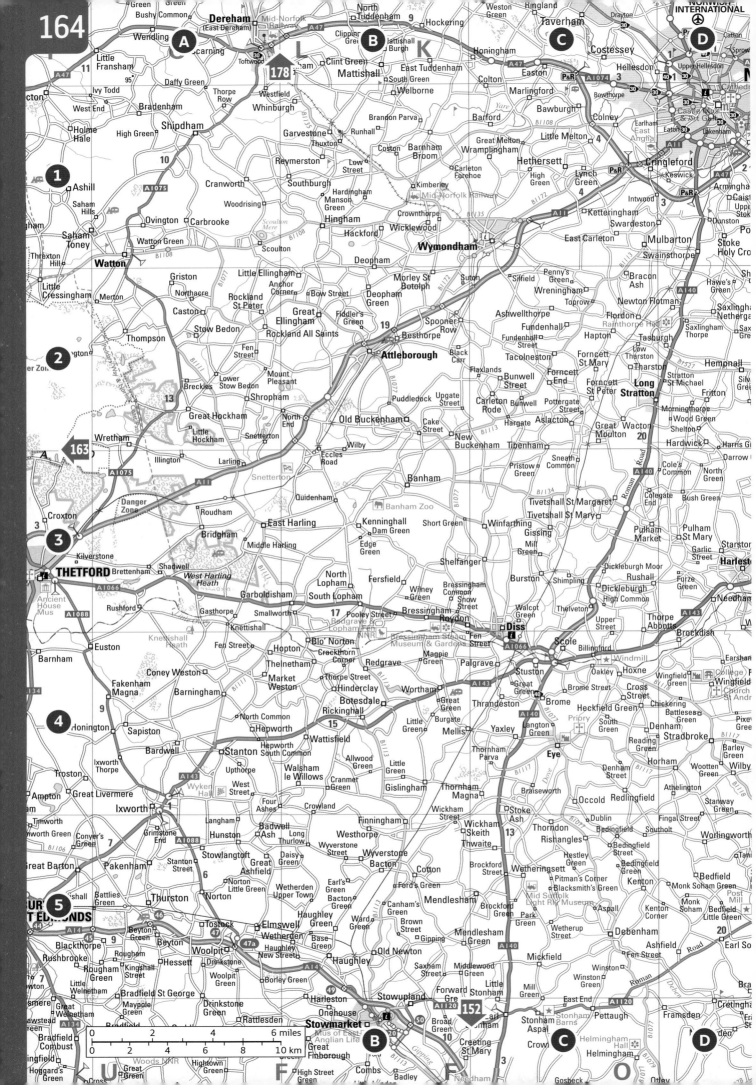

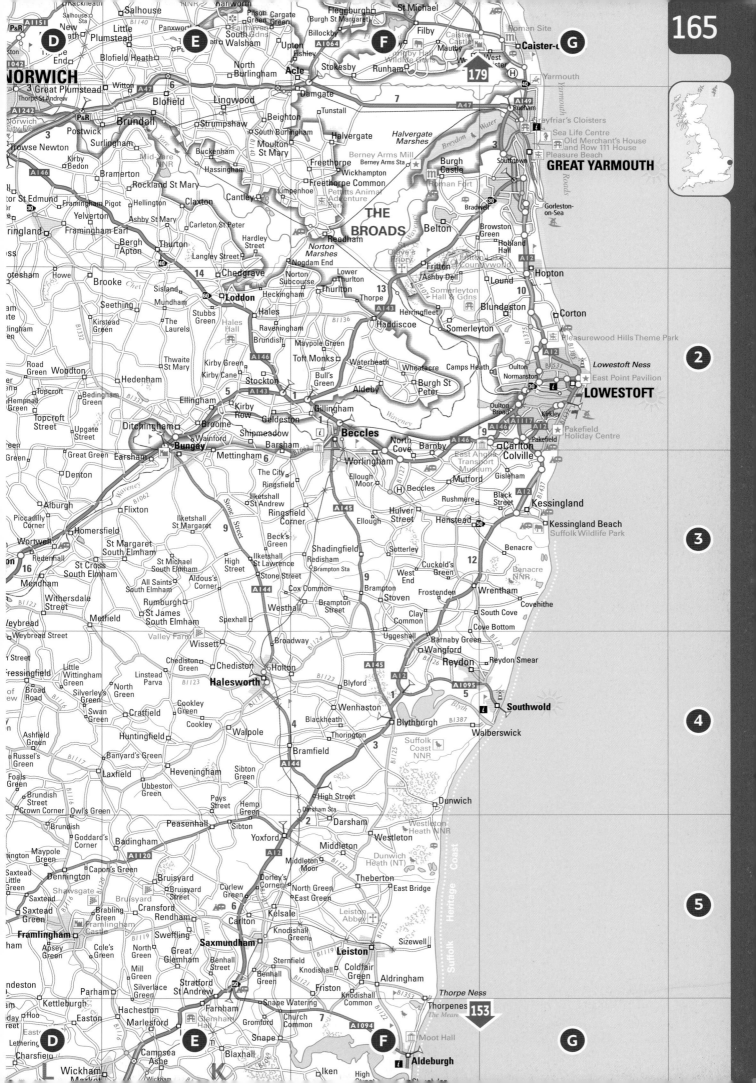

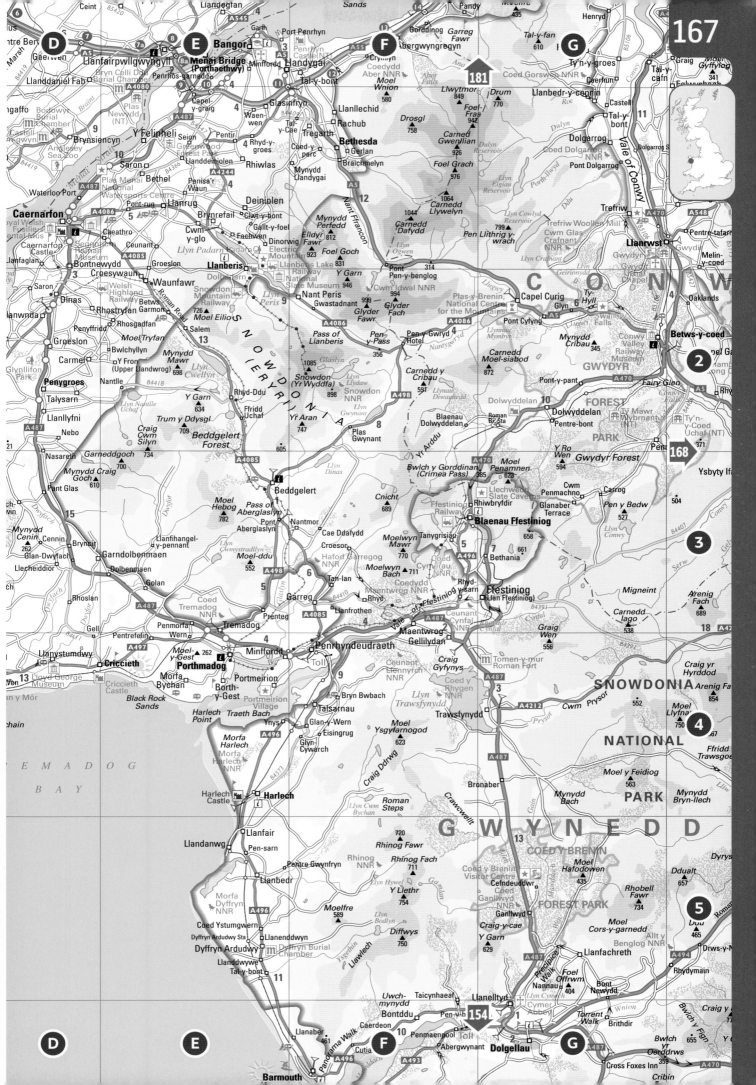

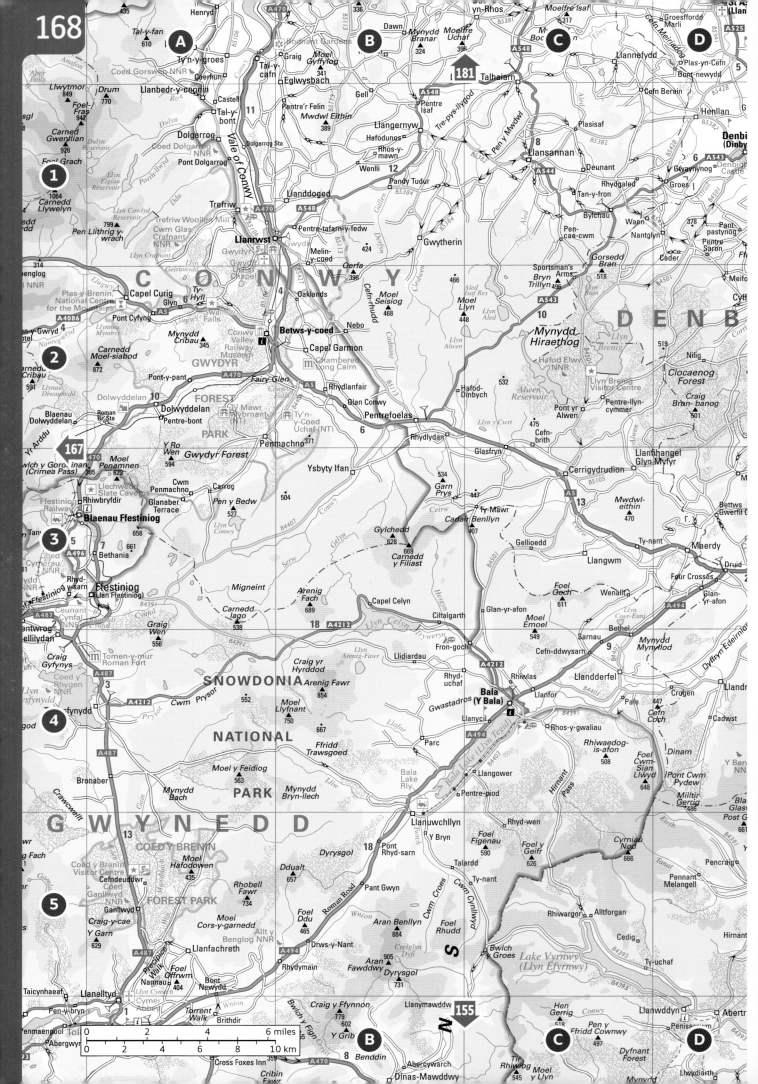

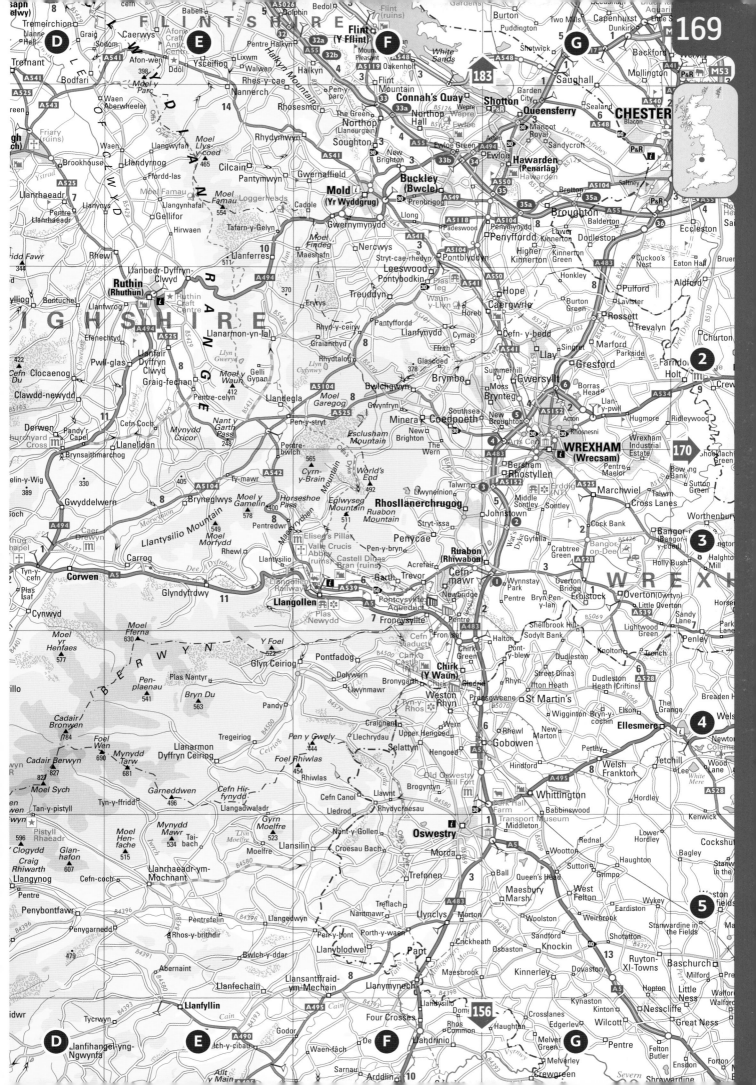

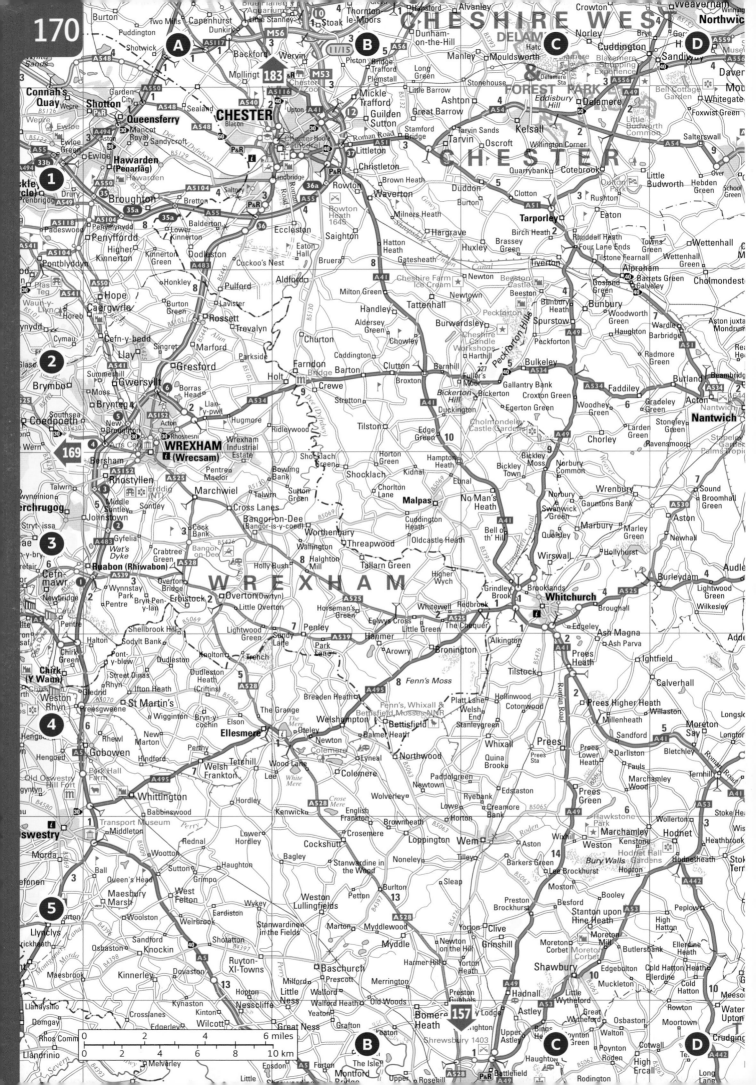

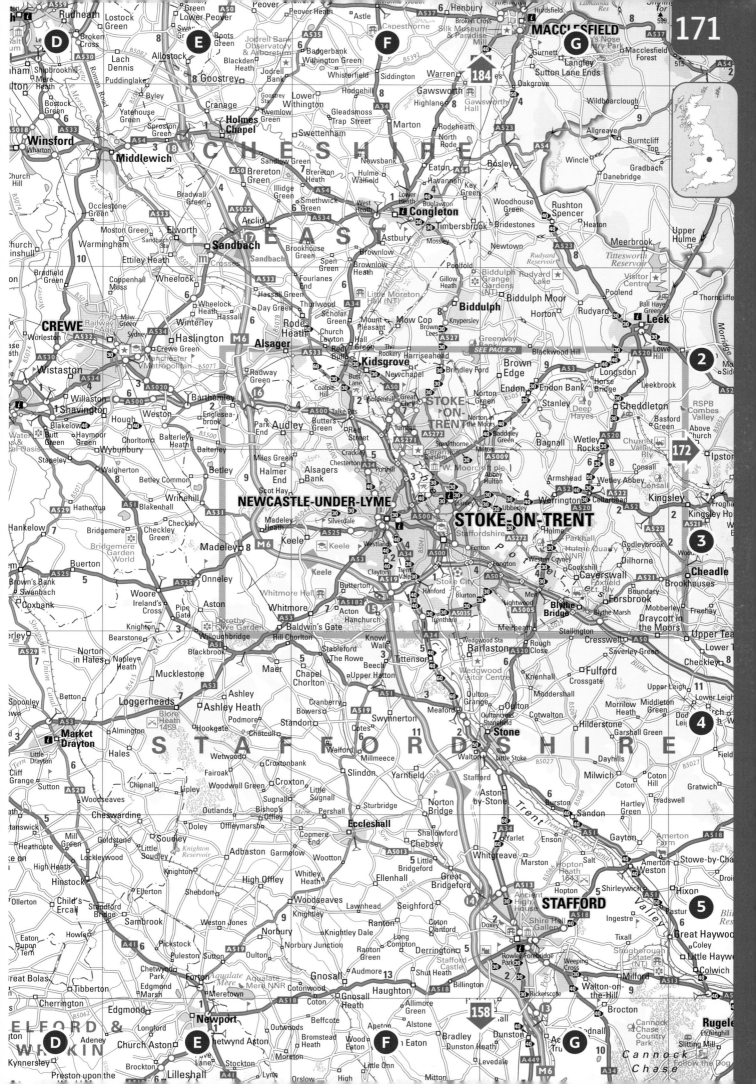

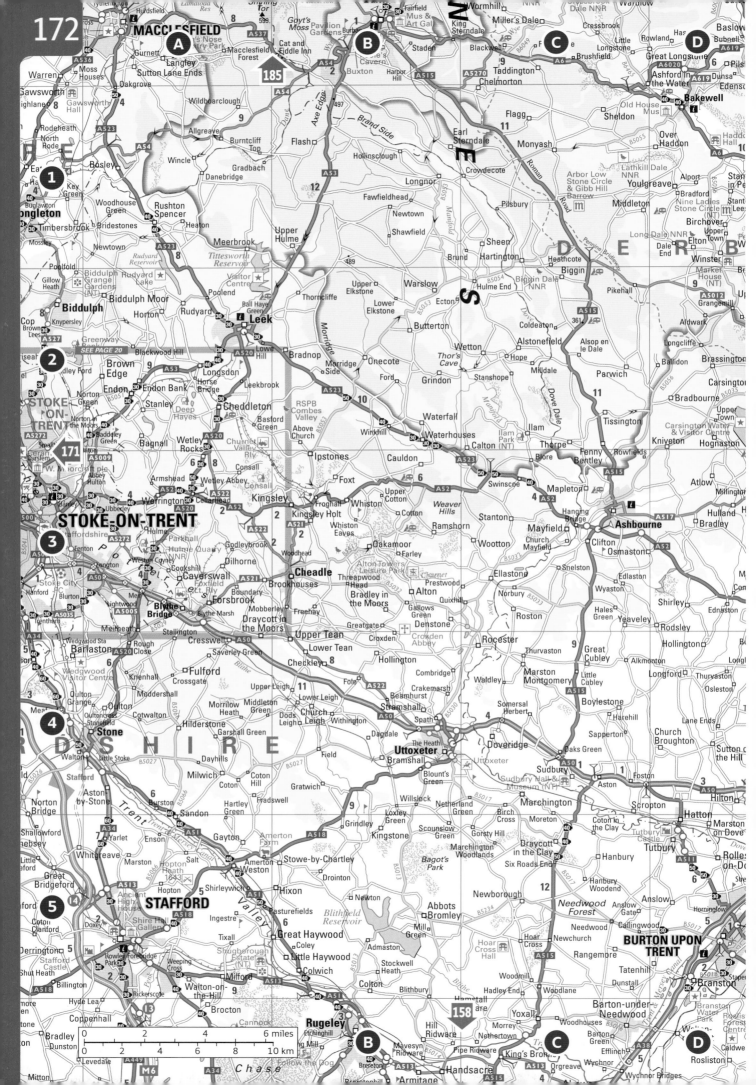

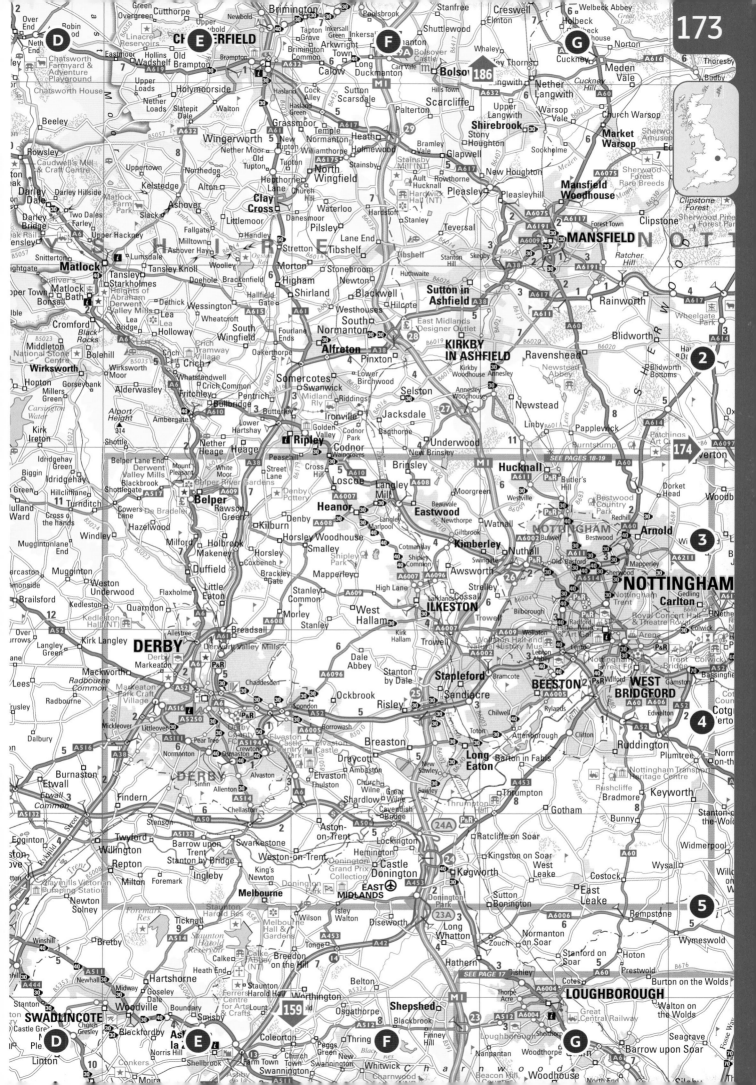

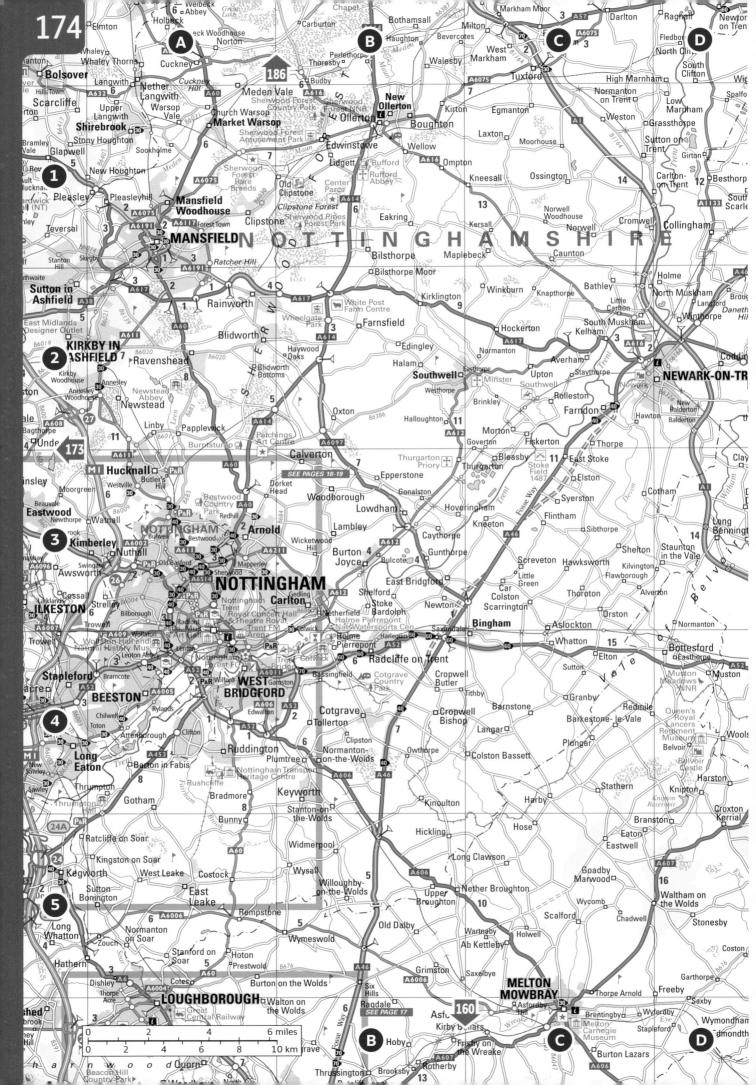

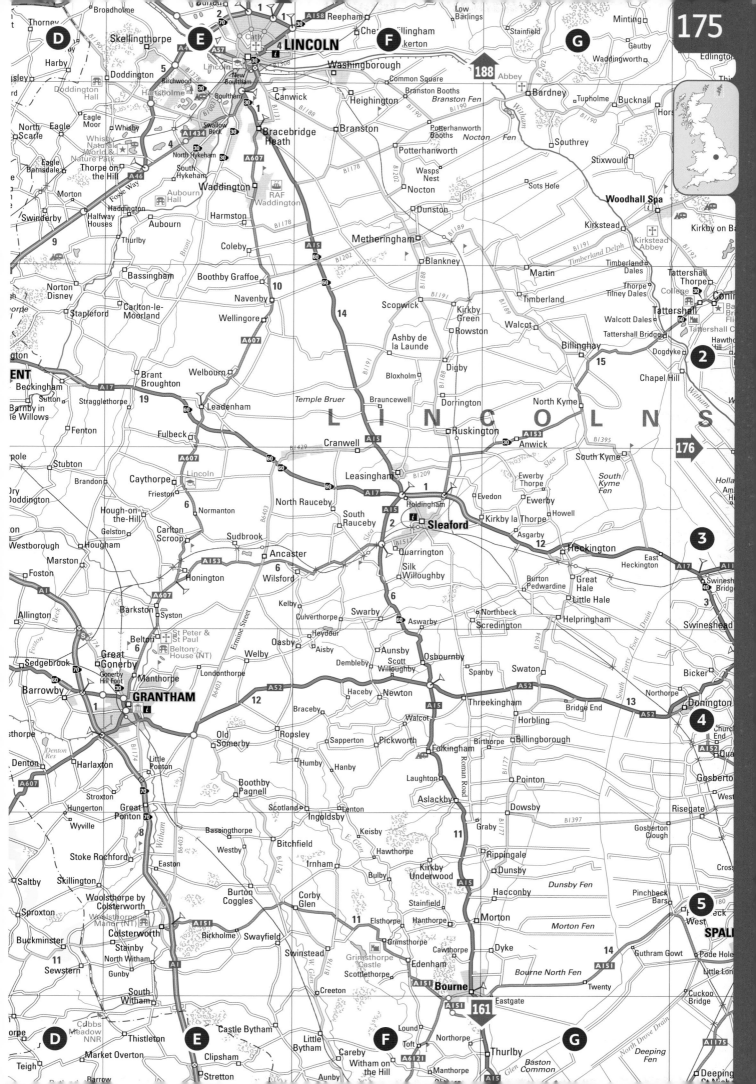

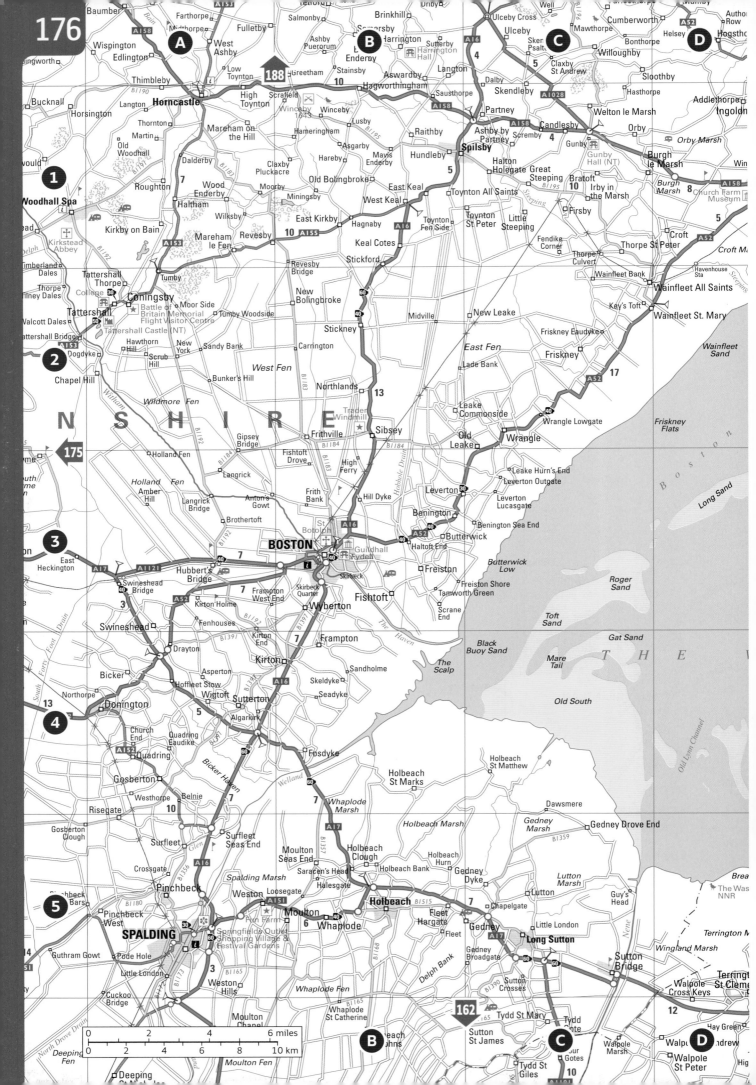

D St Leonards
189

Ingoldmells Point
Fantasy Island
Butlins Family Entertainment Resort
Skegness Water Leisure Park
Seathorne

**Skegness**
Natureland Seal Sanctuary

Seacroft

Gibraltar Point NNR
Gibraltar
*Gibraltar Pt*

*L y n n   D e e p s*

*D e e p s*

E

F

G

2

North Norfolk Heritage Coast

Scolt Head Island NNR

*Holkham Bay*

*Brancaster Bay*

Norton

Creek

3

Holme Dunes NNR

Brancaster Staithe
Burnham Deepdale
Burnham Norton
Burnham Overy Staithe
Holkham Bay NNR

**Wells-ne**

Holme next the Sea
Thornham A149
Titchwell
Brancaster

Burnham Overy Town
Holkham
Holkham Hall

17

**Burnham Market**

Burnham Thorpe

Peddars Way & Norfolk Coast Path

Sea Life Centre
Ringstead

Creake Abbey

Wells & Walsingham Lt. Rly

Wight

**Hunstanton**

Summerfield

B1155

North Creake

Egmere
Shirehall Museum

Shrine of Our Lady of Walsingham

*W A S H*

*Seal Sand*

Norfolk Lavender
40

Heacham
Eaton
Sedgeford

Docking
B1454

Stanhoe

South Creake

North Barsh
Slipper Chapel
Houg St Gi
East Barsham

4

West Barsham

13
Snettisham

B1440

Southgate
A149
Ingoldisthorpe
Shernborne

Fring

Bircham Newton

Great Bircham
Bircham Tofts
Bagthorpe

Barmer

Syderstone

Sculthorpe

B1454

*Peter Black Sand*

Dersingham

Anmer

Houghton Hall

Tattersett A148
Coxford
Dunton
Shereford

178
**Faken**

Fakenh

*Bulldog Sand*

Dersingham Bog NNR
Sandringham House
Sandringham
Wolferton
West Newton

New Houghton

East Rudham
17
West Rudham
Tatterford
Helhoughton

Hempton

Toftrees

Colkirk
A1065

st Sand
h

Ongar Hill

St Mary Magdalene Chapel
Flitcham
Harpley
West Raynham
East Raynham

5

Whissonsett

Castle Rising
Hillington
Little Massingham
Great Massingham
South Raynham

Horningtoft

North Wootton
B1153

Weasenham St Peter
Wellingham
Godwick

Marsh

Trinity Hospital
Congham
Roydon
Grimston
Weasenham All Saints
Rougham
Tittleshall

16
Stanfie

*Massingham Heath*

Little London

**KING'S LYNN**
St George's Guildhall (NT)
4
A1078
A148
Roydon Common NNR
Pott Row

163

Clenchwarton
Lynn
West Lynn
30
Gaywood
B1145
Bawsey
Gayton
Ashwicken
n Thorpe

Mileham

Litcham
Bitteri

Tilney nts
A47
2
Caithness Crystal Visitor Centre
A10
Tower End
Middleton
East Winch
East Walton

Castle Acre
Fiddler's Green
East Lexham

Longh

Tilney h End
Saddle Bow
West Winch
North

East Walton
A47
13
Newton
Beeston

D

E

F

G

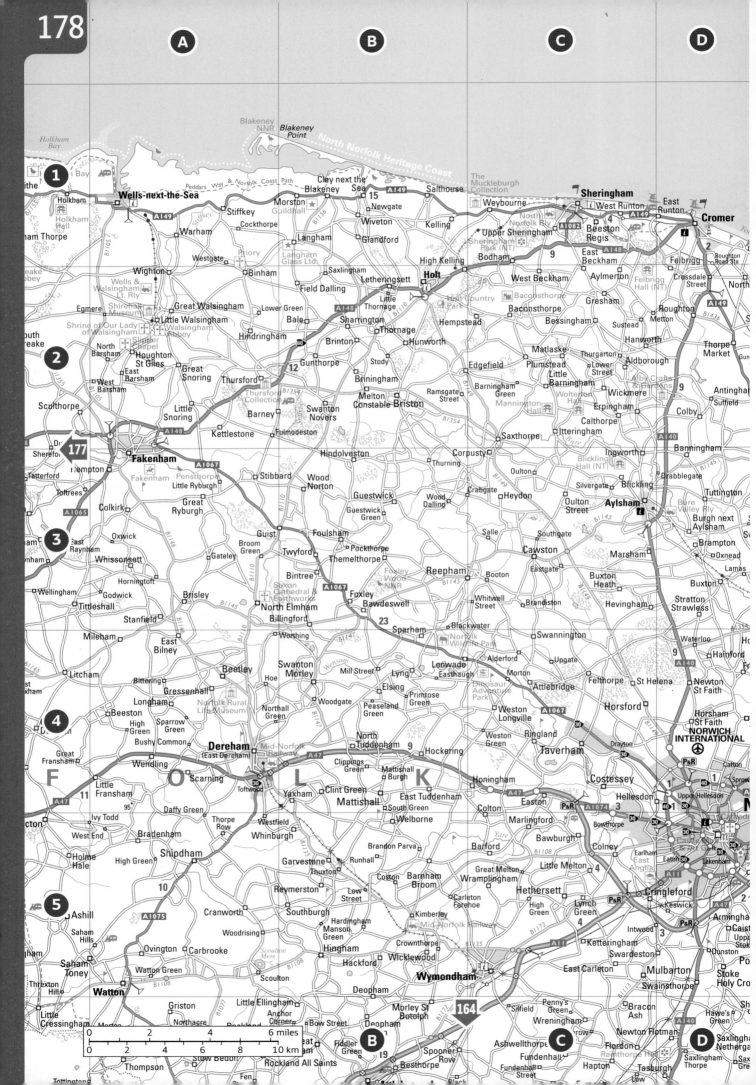

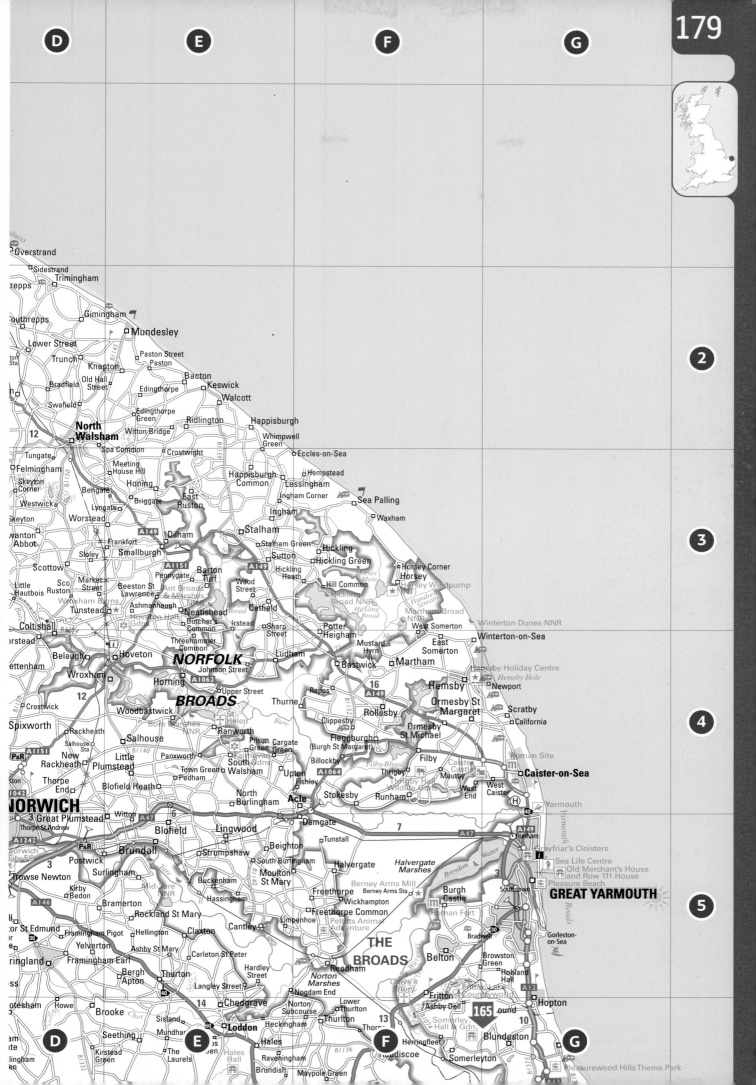

D     E     F     G

**2**

**3**

**4**

**5**

Overstrand
Sidestrand
Trimingham
Crepps
Southrepps
Gimingham
Mundesley
Lower Street
Trunch
Paston Street
Paston
Knapton
Bradfield
Old Hall Street
Bacton
Edingthorpe
Keswick
Swafield
Edingthorpe Green
Walcott
North Walsham
Witton Bridge
Ridlington
Happisburgh
12
Spa Common
Crostwight
Whimpwell Green
Eccles-on-Sea
Tungate
Felmingham
Meeting House Hill
Honing
Happisburgh Common
Hempstead
Lessingham
Skeyton Corner
Bengate
Briggate
East Ruston
Ingham Corner
Sea Palling
Westwick
Lyngate
Worstead
Ingham
Waxham
Skeyton
Swanton Abbot
Frankfort
Dilham
Stalham
Stalham Green
Hickling
Horsey Corner
Sloley
Smallburgh
Sutton
Hickling Green
Horsey
Scottow
Market Street
Barton Turf
Hickling Heath
Hill Common
Horsey Mere
Horsey Windpump
Little Hautbois
Sco Ruston
Beeston St Lawrence
Ant Broads & Marshes
Wood Street
Catfield
Hickling Broad NNR
Hundred Stream
Tunstead
Ashmanhaugh
Neatishead
Irstead
Sharp Street
Potter Heigham
Martham Broad NNR
West Somerton
Winterton Dunes NNR
Coltishall
Hoveton Hall Gdns
Butcher's Common
Ludham
Mustard Hyrn
Martham
Winterton-on-Sea
Belaugh
Threehammer Common
Johnson Street
Bastwick
East Somerton
Hoveton
**NORFOLK**
Horning
Wroxham
Upper Street
Repps
16
Hemsby
Newport
Hemsby Holiday Centre
Hemsby Hole
Crostwick
12
**BROADS**
Woodbastwick
Thurne
Rollesby
Ormesby St Margaret
Scratby
Spixworth
Rackheath
Salhouse
Clippesby
Ormesby St Michael
California
Salhouse Sta
Pilson Green
Cargate Green
Fleggburgh (Burgh St Margaret)
Filby
Roman Site
New Rackheath
Little Plumstead
Panxworth
Town Green
South Walsham
Upton
Billockby
Filby Broad
Thrigby
Thrigby Hall Wildlife Gdns
Mautby
Caister Castle
Caister-on-Sea
Thorpe End
Blofield Heath
Pedham
Fishley
A1064
Stokesby
Runham
West End
West Caister
**NORWICH**
Great Plumstead
Witton
North Burlingham
Acle
Damgate
7
Yarmouth
Runham
Thorpe St Andrew
Blofield
Lingwood
Tunstall
Greyfriar's Cloisters
Brundall
Strumpshaw
Beighton
Sea Life Centre
Postwick
Surlingham
South Burlingham
Halvergate
Halvergate Marshes
Old Merchant's House and Row 111 House
Pleasure Beach
Trowse Newton
Kirby Bedon
Bramerton
Moulton St Mary
Berney Arms Mill
Berney Arms Sta
Burgh Castle
Southtown
Framingham Pigot
Rockland St Mary
Hassingham
Freethorpe
Wickhampton
Roman Fort
**GREAT YARMOUTH**
Yelverton
Hellington
Claxton
Cantley
Limpenhoe
Freethorpe Common
Pettits Animal Adventure Park
Bradwell
Gorleston-on-Sea
Framingham Earl
Ashby St Mary
Carleton St Peter
**THE BROADS**
Belton
Browston Green
Hobland Hall
Bergh Apton
Thurton
Hardley Street
Reedham
Olave's Priory
Fritton
Ashby Dell
Fritton Lake Countryworld
Hopton
Howe
Langley Street
Norton Marshes
Nogdam End
Lower Thurlton
Somerley Hall & Gdn.
165
10
Brooke
Chedgrave
14
Norton Subcourse
Thurlton
13
Blundeston
Seething
Sisland
Loddon
Heckingham
Hales
Somerleyton
Pleasurewood Hills Theme Park

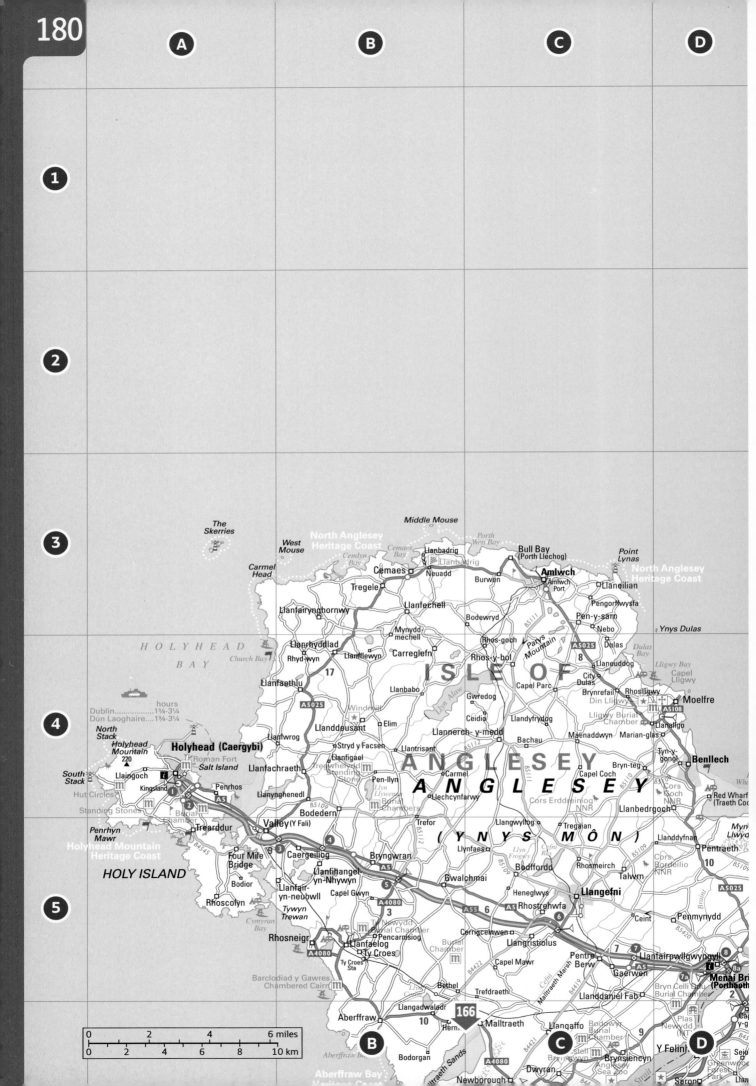

A     B     C     D

1

2

3

Middle Mouse

North Anglesey
Heritage Coast

*West
Mouse*

The
Skerries

Porth
Wen Bay

Llanbadrig
Llanbadrig

Bull Bay
(Porth Llechog)

Point
Lynas

*Carmel
Head*

Cemlyn
Bay

*Cemaes
Bay*

Cemaes

Neuadd

Amlwch

Amlwch
Port

North Anglesey
Heritage Coast

Tregele

Burwen

Llaneilian

Llanfairynghornwy

Llanfechell

Bodewyrd

Pengorffwysfa

Pen-y-sarn

Mynydd-
mechell

Nebo

*Ynys Dulas*

*HOLYHEAD*

Llanrhyddlad

Rhos-goch

Parys
Mountain

A5025

Dulas

*Dulas
Bay*

*BAY*

Church Bay

Rhyd-wyn

Llanfflewyn

Carreglefn

Rhos-y-bol

8

Llaneuddog

*Lligwy Bay*

17

Capel Parc

Dulas

Capel
Lligwy

4

Llanfaethlu

A5025

Llanbabo

ISLE OF

Brynrefail

Rhoslligwy

Moelfre

North
Stack

Dublin.................. 1¾-3¼
Dún Laoghaire....1¾-3¼
hours

Windmill

Gwredog

Din Lligwy

Lligwy Burial
Chamber

A5108

Holyhead
Mountain
220

Llanddeusant

Elim

Ceidio

Llandyfrydog

Llannerch-y-medd

Bachau

Maenaddwyn

Marian-glas

Llanallgo

*South
Stack*

Llaingoch

Holyhead (Caergybi)

Llanfwrog

Llantrisant

ANGLESEY

Tyn-y-
gongl

Benllech

Roman Fort
Salt Island

Llanfigael

Tregwehelydd
Standing
Stone

ANGLESEY

Bryn-teg

Hut Circles

Kingsland

Llanfachraeth

Pen-llyn

Llechcynfarwy

Capel Coch

B5110

*Standing Stones*

Burial
Chamber

Llyn
Llywenan

Burial
Chambers

Cors
Goch
NNR

Red Wharf
(Traeth Coch)

*Penrhyn
Mawr*

Penrhos

Llanynghenedl

ANGLESEY

Llanbedrgoch

Holyhead Mountain
Heritage Coast

Trearddur

B4545

Bodedern

B5109

Trefor

(YNYS MÔN)

Myn
Llwy

Valley (Y Fali)

Llangwyllog

Tregaian

Llanddyfnan

Pentraeth

HOLY ISLAND

Four Mile
Bridge

Caergeiliog

Bryngwran

Llynfaes

*Llyn
Frogwy*

Bodffordd

Rhosmeirch

Cors
Bodeilio
NNR

10

Bodior

A5

Gwalchmai

Heneglwys

Talwrn

A5025

*Cymyran
Bay*

Llanfair-
yn-neubwll

Capel Gwyn

A4080

3

A55

A5

Rhostrehwfa

Llangefni

Rhoscolyn

Tywyn
Trewan

Ty Newydd
Burial Chamber

Cerrigceinwen

Ceint

Penmynydd

Rhosneigr

Pencarnisiog

Burial
Chamber

Llangristiolus

Penmynydd

A4080

Llanfaelog

Ty Croes

Capel Mawr

Pentre
Berw

Llanfairpwllgwyngyll

Bethel

A5

Gaerwen

Ty Croes
Sta

Barclodiad y Gawres
Chambered Cairn

Bryn Celli Ddu
Burial Chamber

Menai Bri
(Porthaeth

Bryn Celli Ddu
Burial Chamber

Trefdraeth

Llanddaniel Fab

Plas
Newydd
(NT)

Langadwaladr

166

Malltraeth

Llangaffo

Bodowyr
Burial
Chamber

9

Y Felin

Aberffraw

10

Hern

B4421

Anglesey
Sea Zoo

Greenwo
Forest
Park

*Aberffraw Bay*

Bodorgan

*Malltraeth Sands*

A4080

Brynsiencyn

Newborough

Dwyran

Sejo

B

C

D

0    2    4    6 miles
0  2  4  6  8  10 km

D   E   F   G

182

2

3

4

5

Great Orme
Heritage Coast
*Great Ormes Head*
Great Orme
Cabin
Lift
Venue
Cymru
Great Orme
Country Park
Gogarth
Great Orme
Tramway
Toll
**Llandudno**
*Little Ormes Head*
B5115
Penrhyn-side
**Penrhyn Bay** (Bae Penrhyn)
Rhos-on-Sea
A546
Glanwydden
*Conwy
Sands*

*C O N W Y
B A Y*

Red
*rf Bay*
St Seiriol's
Well
Mariandyrys
Glan-yr-afon
Caim
Penmon
Penmon Priory
(ruins)
Llanddona
Llangoed
*Dutchman
Bank*
Aberconwy House (NT)
17
**Llandudno
Junction**
Degany
5
Esgyryn
A470
**Mochdre**
19
A547
**Colwyn Bay**
(Bae Colwyn)
20
21
A55
22
10
23
Llanddulas
A547   Aber
*Abergele
Roads*
Bay
Llan-faes
Beaumaris
Castle
**Beaumaris**
(Biwmares)
Llansadwrn
4   A545
Llandegfan
*Penrhos*
*Swatch*
Dwygyfylchi
16a
**Penmaenmawr**
16
Capelulo
Suspension
Bridge (NT)
**Conwy**
Conwy Castle
18
Llansanffraid
Glan Conwy
Bryn-y-maen
Llanelian-
yn-Rhos
Dolwen
Llysfaen
Rhyd-y-foe
Be
yn-Rhos
B5381
*Lavan
Sands*
15
14
Penmaenan
362
*Foel Lus*
*Moelfre*
435
Mochdre
Mynydd
Llanelian
336
324
Moelfre Uchaf
396
**Bangor**
Garth
Penrhyn
Castle
(NT)
A55
3
Crymlyn
Goredinog
Garreg
Fawr
Abergwyngregyn
*Nant-y-Pandy*
Henryd
*Tal-y-fan*
610
Rowen
Pentrefelin
Graig
Moel
Gyffylog
341
Trofarth
Mynydd
Branar
Pentre
Isaf
Llanfair Talhaiarn
A548
*idge*
A4087
Minffordd
Llandygai
12
Tal-y-bont
Glasinfryn
3
Llanllechid
Rachub
Tregarth
Coed-y-parc
Rhiwlas
Braichmelyn
*Moel
Wnion*
580
Drosgl
758
Llwytmor
926
*Drum*
770
Llanbedr-y-cennin
Ty'n-y-groes
Caerhun
Coed Gorswen
NNR
B5106
Coed
Tal-y-
cafn
A470
11
Bodnant
Gdns (NT)
Eglwysbach
Castell
Tal-y-bont
*Mwdwl
Eithin*
389
Gell
*Elwy*
Pen
Pentre
ngernyw
dunos
Rhos-
y-mawn
Wenlli
*Pen y Mwdwl*
Pen-
Rhyd
Pentir
Coed-y-parc
Gerlan
**Bethesda**
Carned Gwenllian
842
*Dulyn
Res*
Aber
Falls
*Aber
Res*
849
Coed Dolgarrog
NNR
Pont Dolgarrog
Dolgarrog Sta
Vale of
168
**S N O W D O N I A**

A     B     C     D

1

2

◁ 181

3

*L I V E R P O O L*

*B A Y*

Birkenhead to   hours
Belfast.........................8
Douglas.............2½–4¼
Liverpool to   hours
Dublin.........................8

East
Hoyle
Bank

Meols
Sta

Mockb

West
Hoyle
Bank

Hoylake

Manor Road Sta
Hoylake Sta

4

Royal
Liverpool

Hilbre Island

West Kirby Sta

Grange

Frankby

4   A553

A5139

Prestatyn
Sands
Holiday
Centre

Welsh Channel

Talacre

Point of
Ayr

Llawndy

West Kirby

Caldy

Irb
Hi

B5140

A540

Thurstaston

Prestatyn

Gronant

Gwespyr

Mostyn Bank

Flynnongroyw

Dawpool
Bank

Sky
Tower

A548

Efrith

Rhyl

SeaQuarium

Rhyl Sun Centre

Kinmel Bay
(Bae Cinmel)

30

30

B5119

2

A525

Bodrhyddan
Hall

Meliden
(Gallt Melyd)

Tan-yr-
allt

Gwaenysgor

Gop
Hill 8

Llanasa

Pen-y-ffordd

Trelogan

Gyrn

Mostyn

Mostyn Quay

Glan-y-don

18

A548

40

Llannerch-y-Môr

Holywell Bank

Greenfield Valley

Towyn

Plas
Llwyd

Morfa
Rhuddlan

Pensarn

Rhuddlan

Dyserth

Ochr-
y-foel

Trelawnyd

Axton

Whitford
(Chwitffordd)

A5151

Maen
Achwyfan

Lloc

Roman   Road

Gorsedd

A5026

Basingwerk
Abbey

Carmel

Greenfield
(Maes-Glas)

St Winifred's Holy Well & Chap

'wyn Bay
(Colwyn)

22

10

Llanddulas

23

A547

Abergele

Rhyd-y-foel

23a

A55

Trelawnyd

Marian
Cwm

Cwm

Helyg

Road

1

31

Pantasaph

Pantasaph
Friary

Calcoed

Babell

Brynford

Dolphin

Holywell (Treffynnon)

5

Walwen

A5026

Bagillt
Bank

Whelston

Bagillt

A548

Bedol

Llysfaen

24

A55

St George

24a

Pengwern

A525

B5429

Rhuallt

28

29

A55

30

Pen-y-
cefn

Roman

Dawn

Betws
yn-Rhos

6

Bodelwyddan

26

27

St Asaph
(Llanelwy)

27a

C L

Pen-y-
cefn

Afon-wen

Ysceifiog

Lixwm

Walwen

Pentre Halkyn

32

32b

Mount Pleasant

A5119

Flint
(Y Fflint)

FLINTSHIRE

32a

A55

B5723

Moelfre Isaf

Cefn Meiriadog

B5381

Tremeirchion

Graig

Sodom

Caerwys

Moel
y Parc
398

Ddôl

Afonwen
Craft and
Antique
Centre

Lixwm

Rhes-y-cae

Halkyn

Dolphin

Pen-y-
parc

Fli
Mo

Moelfre Uchaf

Dawn
324

Mynydd
Branar

396

Cefn
Berain

Llannefydd

Plas-yn-Cefn

Trefnant

Lannerch
Hall

A541

Bodfari

168

Wheeler

n

Moel
Llys-y-coed
465

Nannerch

14

Halkyn Mountain

Rhosesmor

The Green

'rthop

Soughton

A541

Flint

Pen-y-
Mo

Llanfair Talhaiarn

A548

Bont-newydd

Trefant

A543

Green

A525

A544

Tre-pys-llyyod

Llan

Pentre
Isaf

B5382

Pen

Alled

0   2   4   6 miles
0   2   4   6   8   10 km

B

Denbigh
(Dinbych)

A543

V A L E   O F   C L W Y D

Friary
(ruins)

Waen

Llangwyfan

C

Moel
Llys-y-coed

D

Rhydymwyn

Llansannan

Llandyrnog

A541

Cilcain

Llansannan

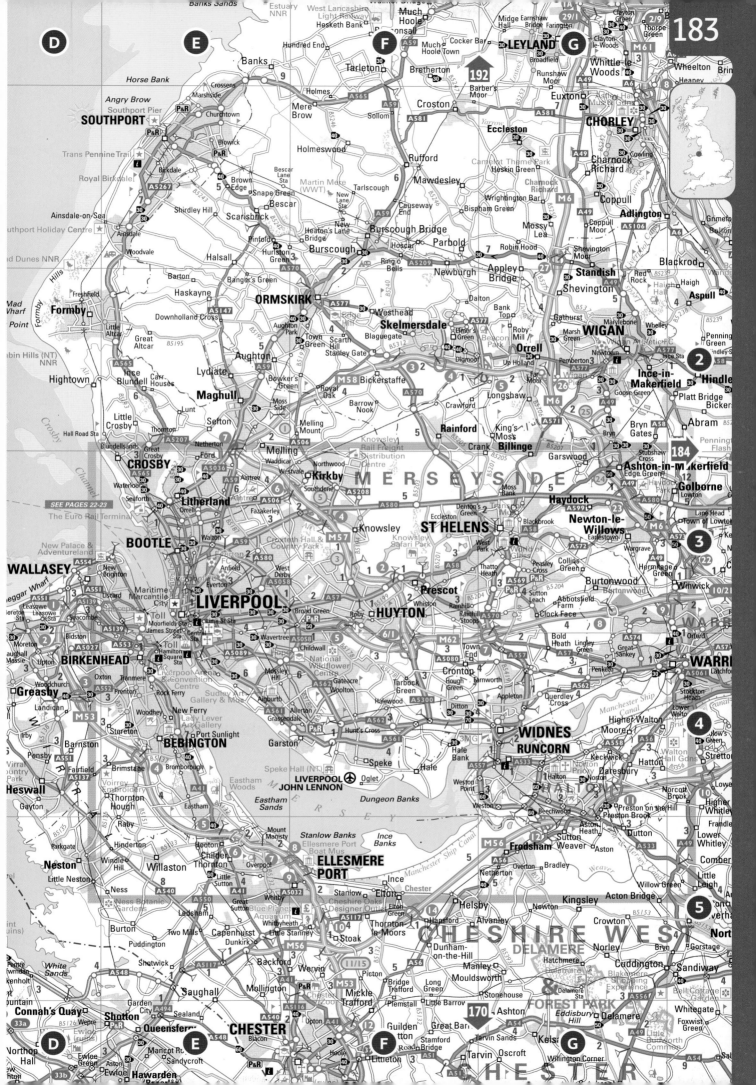

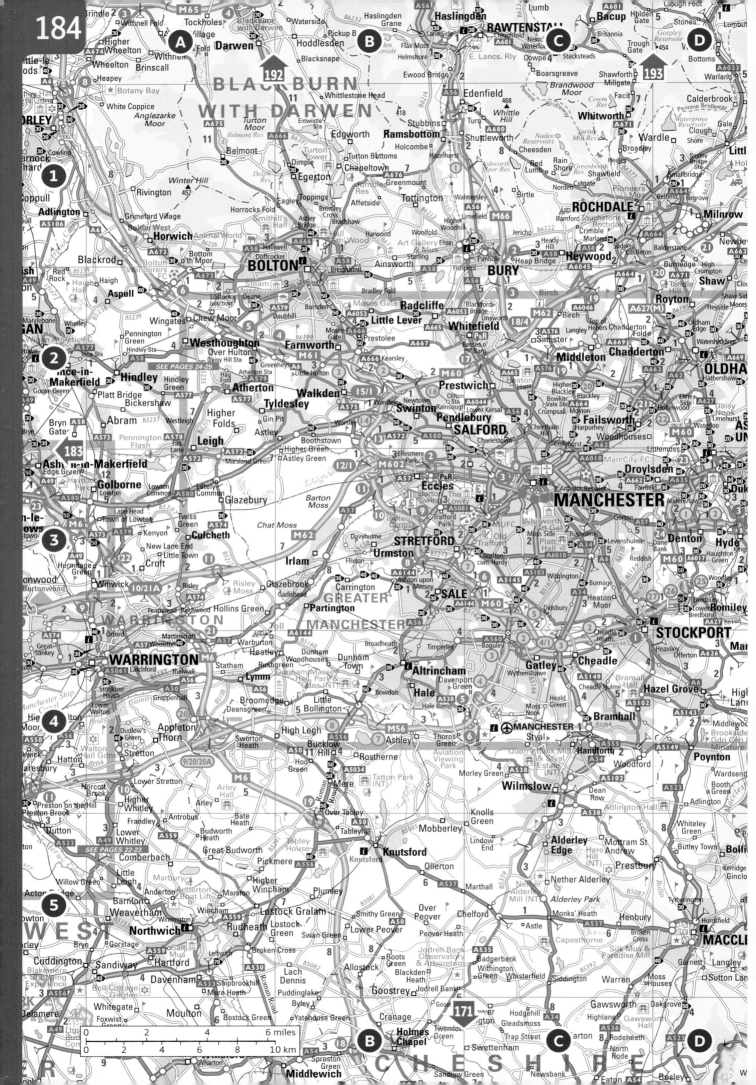

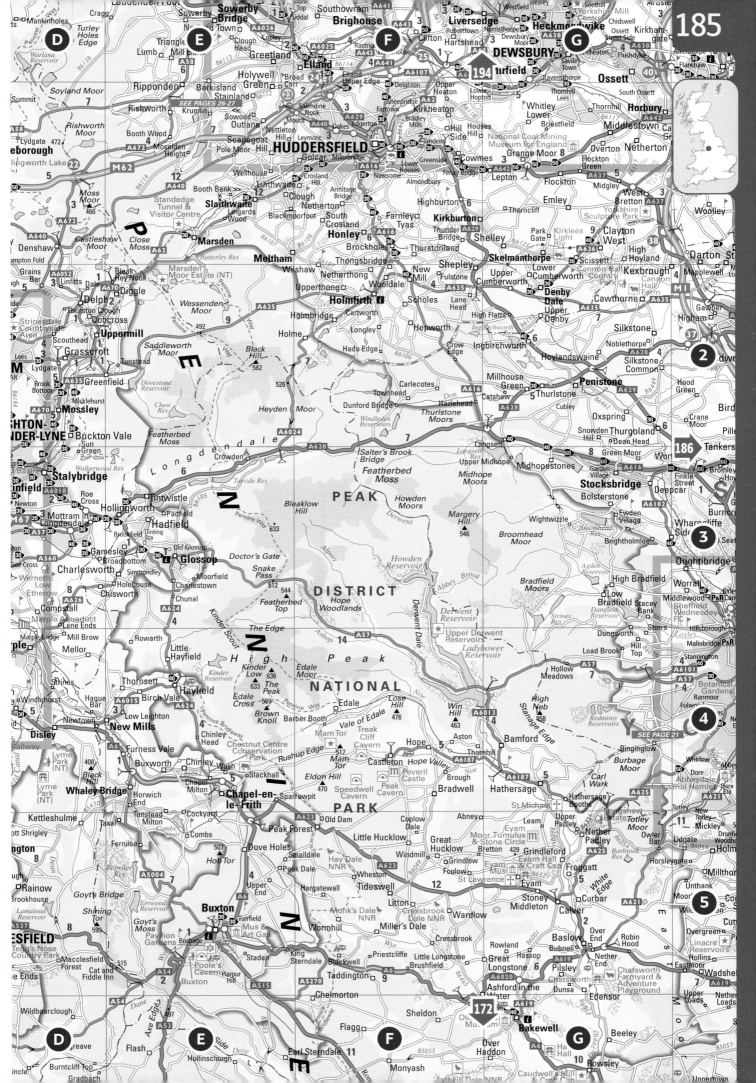

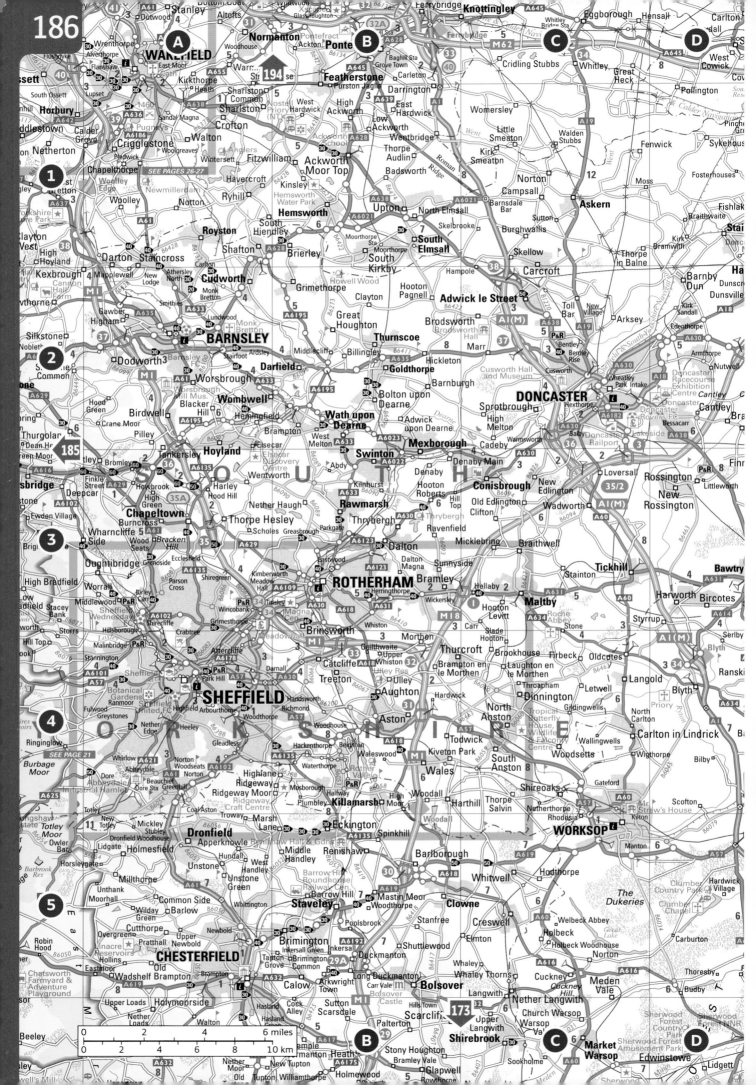

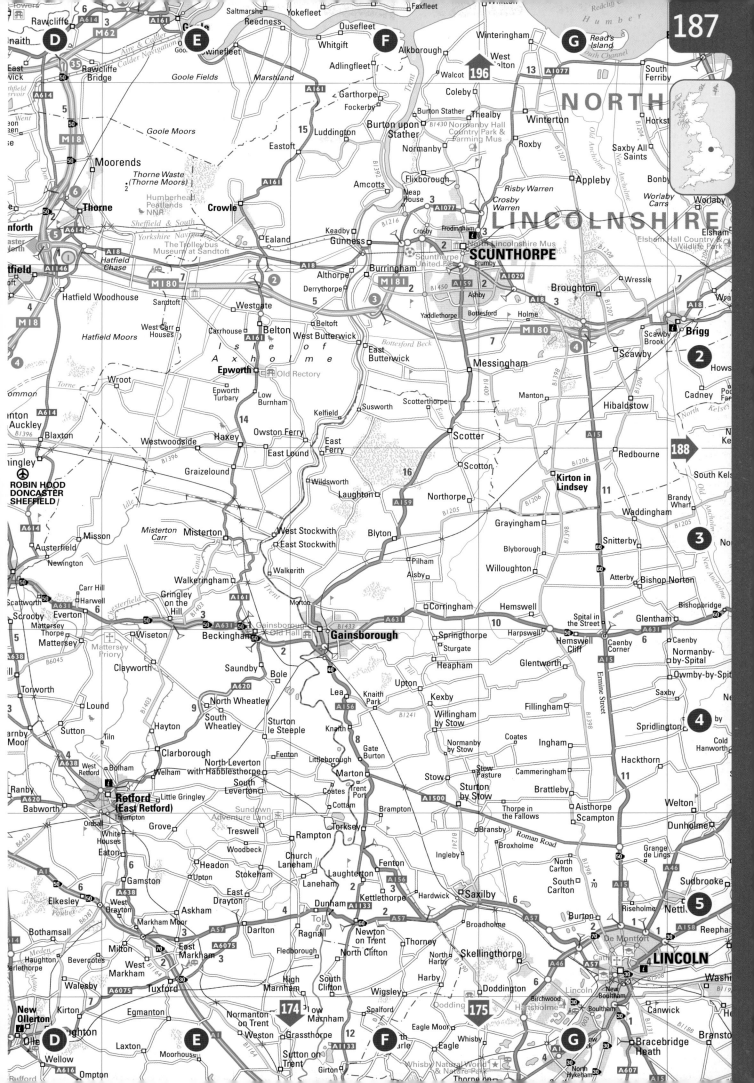

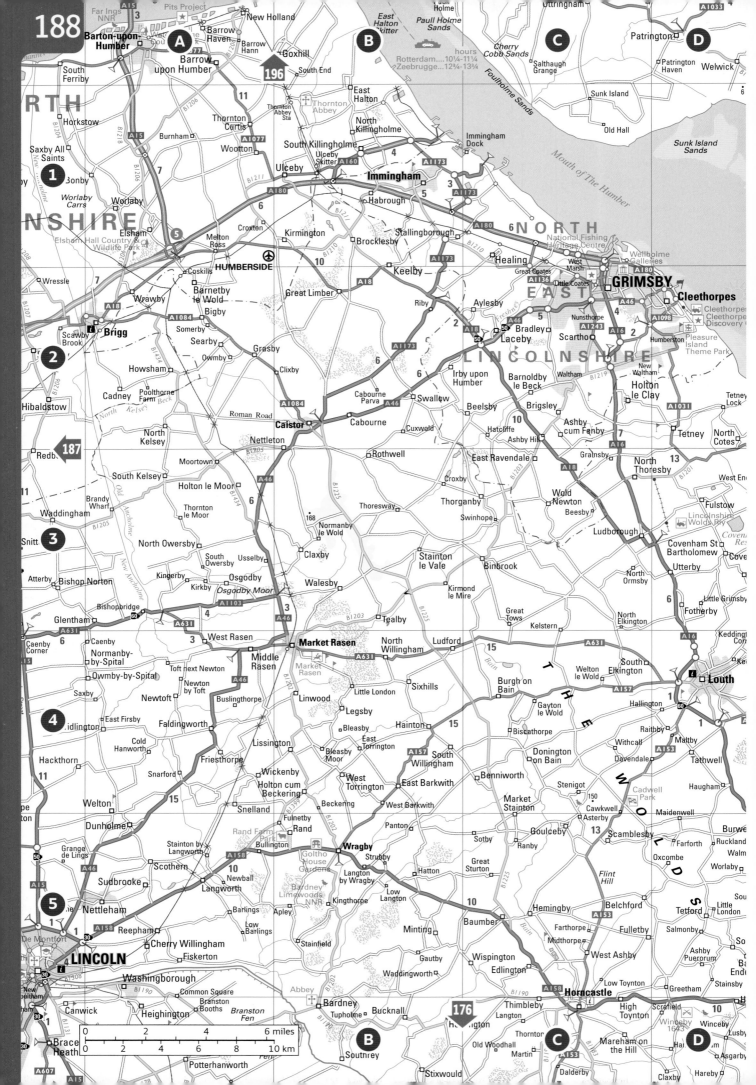

D Holmpton
Out Newton
7 Weeton
Skeffling
Easington
197
Skeffling Clays
Kilnsea
Spurn Heritage Coast
Kilnsea Clays
Spurn NNR
Spurn Head
Spurn Head

E

F

G

2

s Coast Light Rly
Centre

Marshchapel
Eskham
Wragholme
Grainthorpe
Ludney
Conisholme
South Somercotes
nham St Mary
Yarburgh
South Somercotes Fen Houses
Alvingham
North Cockerington
South Cockerington
ddington
Grimoldby
Stewton
Manby
Little Carlton
Legbourne
Little Cawthorpe
North Reston
South Reston
Gayton le Marsh
Strubby
Woodthorpe
Muckton
Authorpe
Tothill
Withern
Maltby le Marsh
Beesby
Claythorpe
Saleby
Belleau
Aby
Greenfield
sgate
White Pit
Swaby
South Thoresby
Ketsby
th Ormsby
Calceby
Driby
Rigsby
Haugh
Brinkhill
mersby
Harrington
Sutterby
Ulceby Cross
Ulceby
Skendleby Psalter
ag
Harrington Hall
rby
Langton
Dalby
Aswardby
Sausthorpe
Skendleby
gworthingham
D
nby
Hundleby
Spilsby
Mavis Enderby
Partney
Ashby by Partney
Scremby
Gunby
Halton Holegate
E
sby
Gunby Hall (NT)
Orby
Orby Marsh

Donna Nook
Donna Nook NNR
Meals
North Somercotes
Church End
Skidbrooke North End
A1031
Saltfleet
Skidbrooke
Saltfleetby St Clements
12
Saltfleetby - Theddlethorpe NNR
Saltfleetby All Saints
Saltfleetby St Peter
Theddlethorpe St Helen
Theddlethorpe All Saints
A1031
Great Carlton
Mablethorpe
A1104
3
Thorpe
4 Trusthorpe
A52
Sutton on Sea
Sutton le Marsh
Sandilands
Hannah
6
Ragnaby
Markby
A52
Thoresthorpe
A1104
A1111
Asserby
The Grange
5
Anderby Creek
Bilsby
Ailby
Thurlby
Huttoft
Alford
Farlesthorpe
Anderby
Mumby
B1449
Bilsby Field
Mawthorpe
Cumberworth
Authorpe Row
Well
Bonthorpe
Helsey
Hogsthorpe
Chapel St Leonards
Willoughby
A16
4
Claxby St Andrew
Sloothby
10
A1028
Welton le Marsh
Hasthorpe
A52
Addlethorpe
Ingoldmells
177
Ingoldm Point
Fantasy Island
Burgh le Marsh
Winthorpe
Seathorne
Butlins Family Entertainment Resort
Skegness Water Leisure Park
F
G

3

4

5

A157
A16
B1200
B1373
A157
A16

2
3
4
5
8
11
3
5
6
5

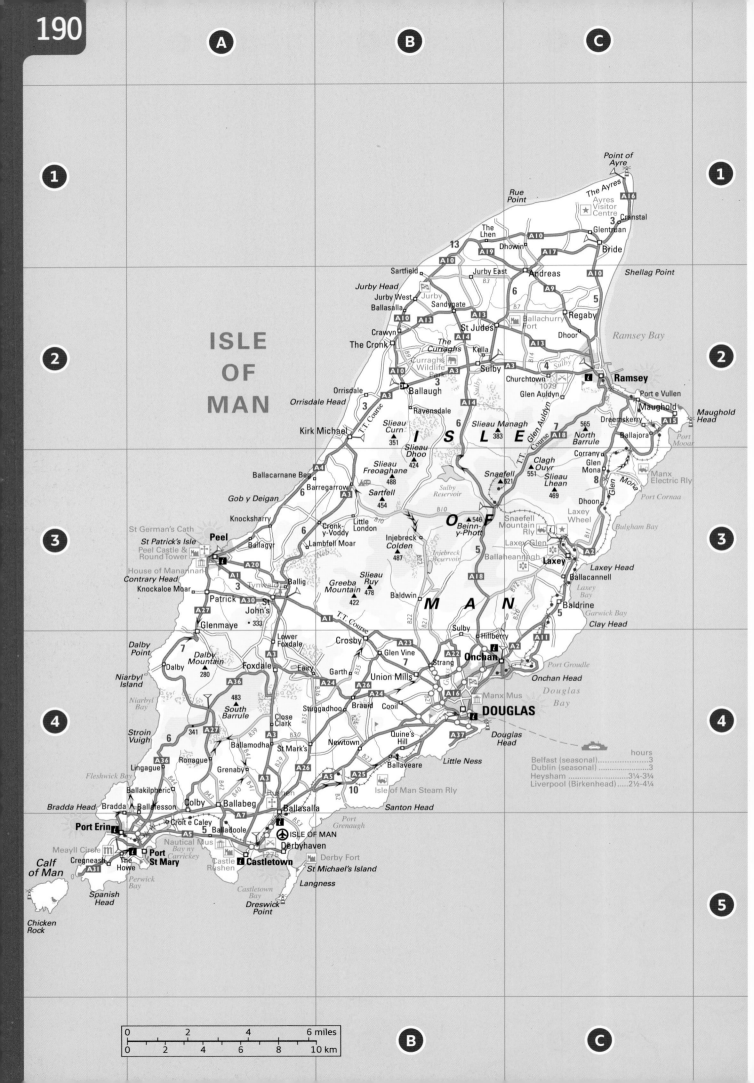

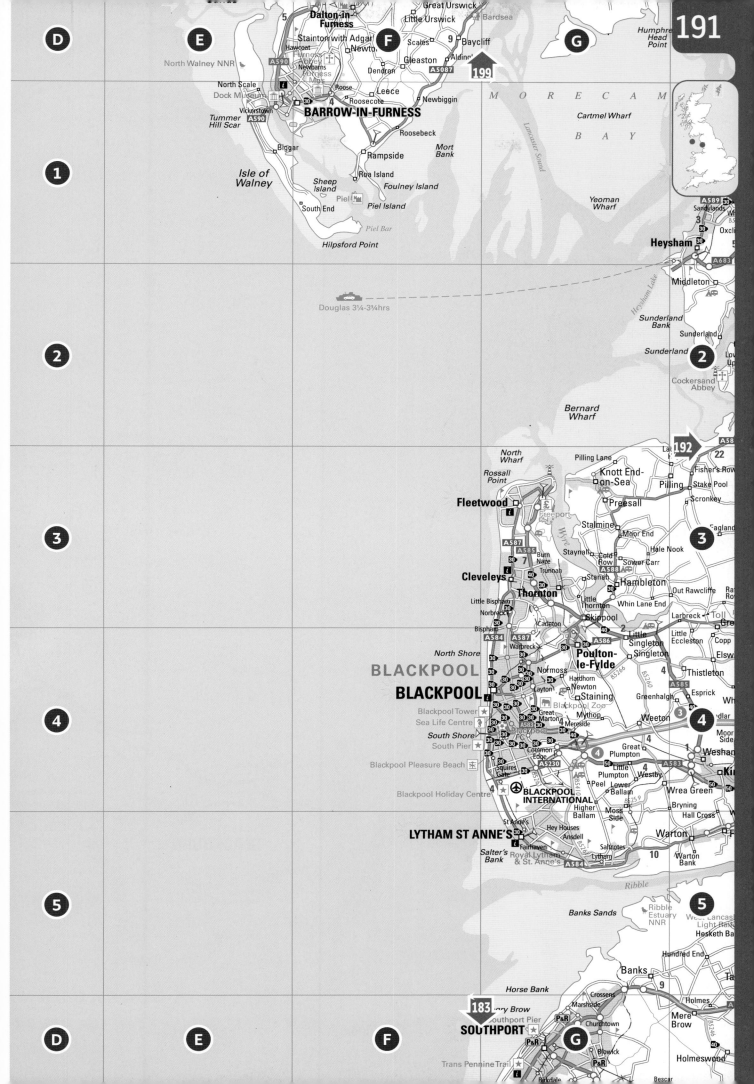

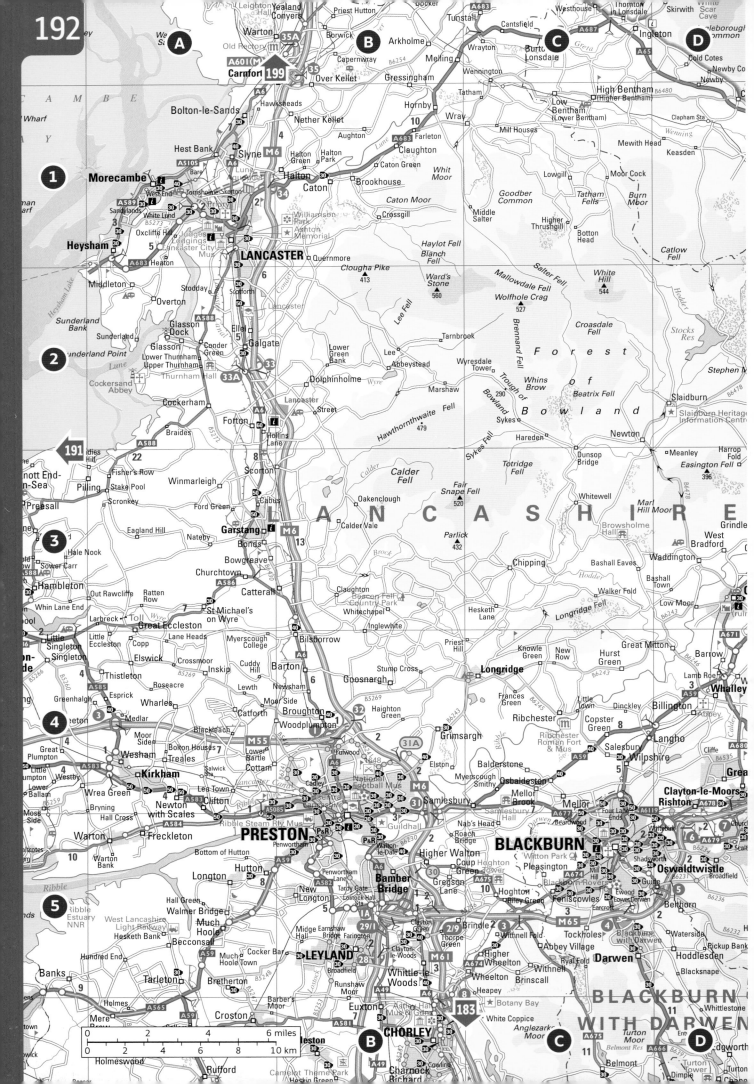

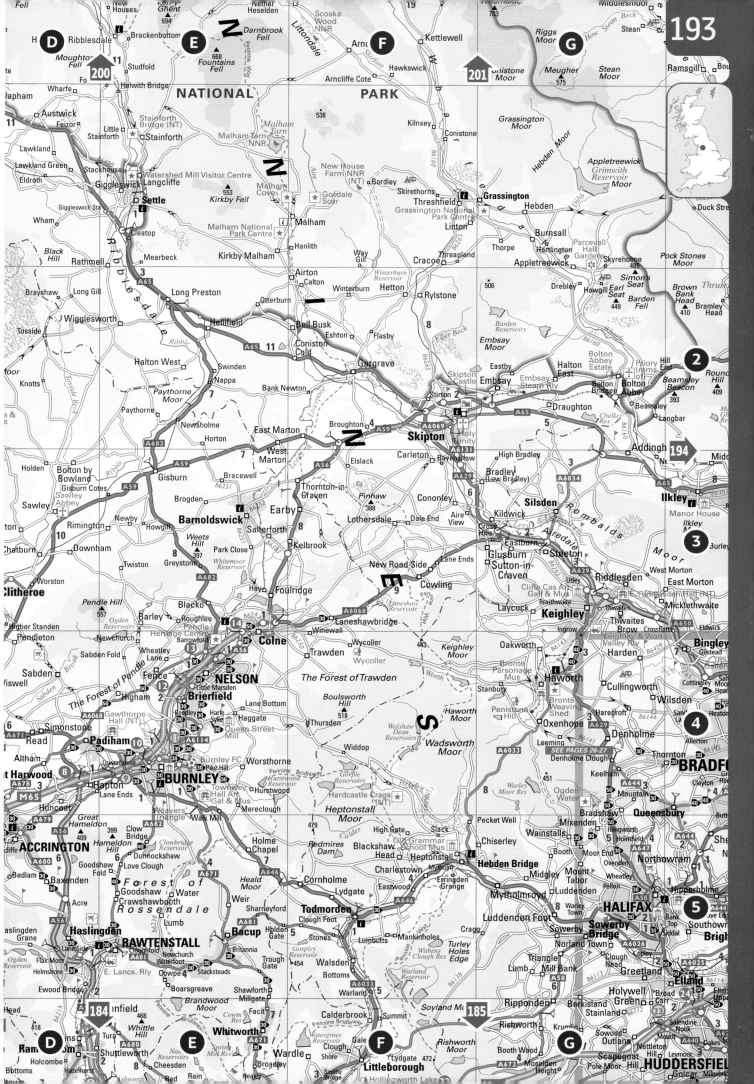

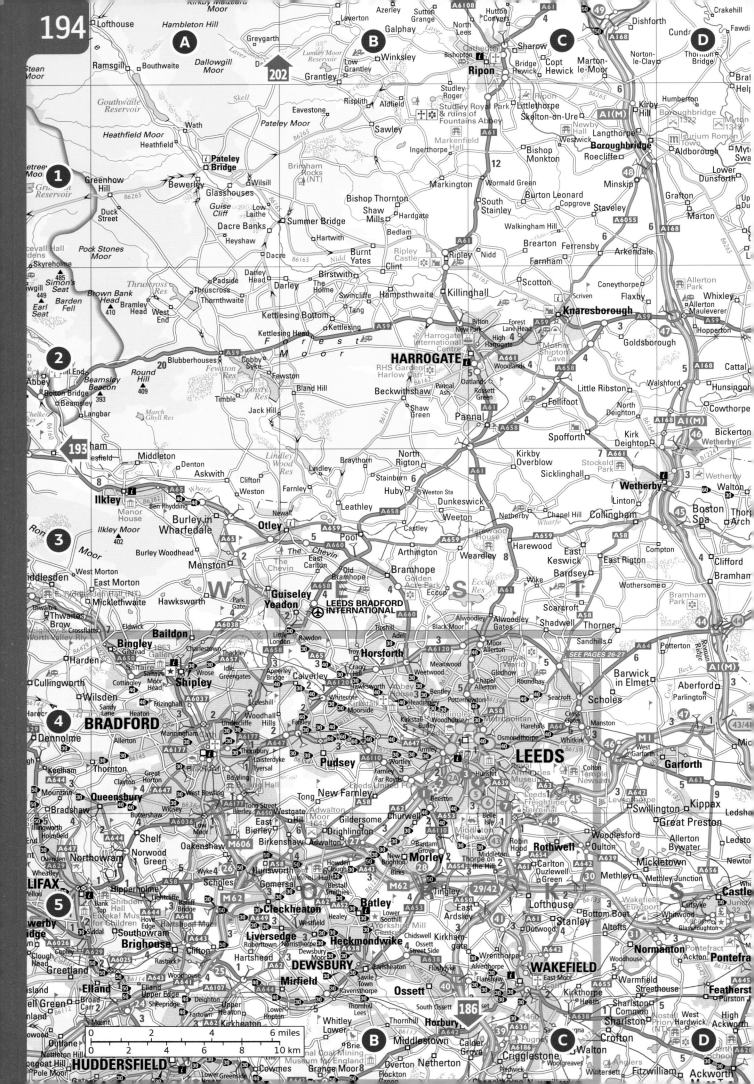

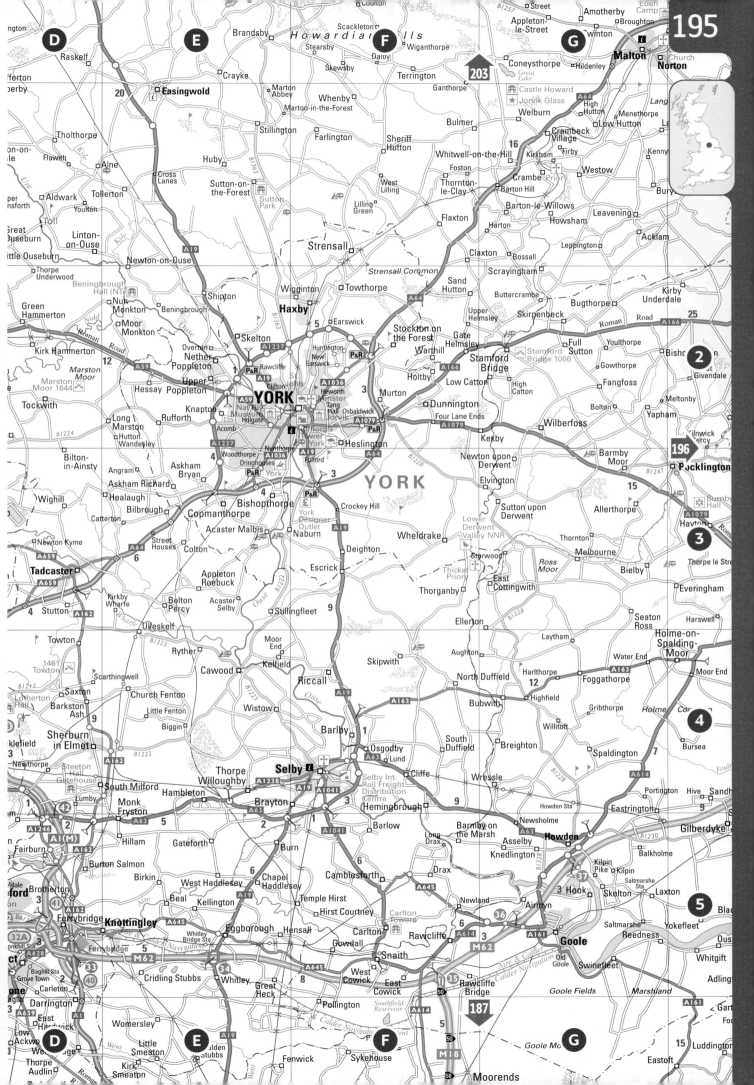

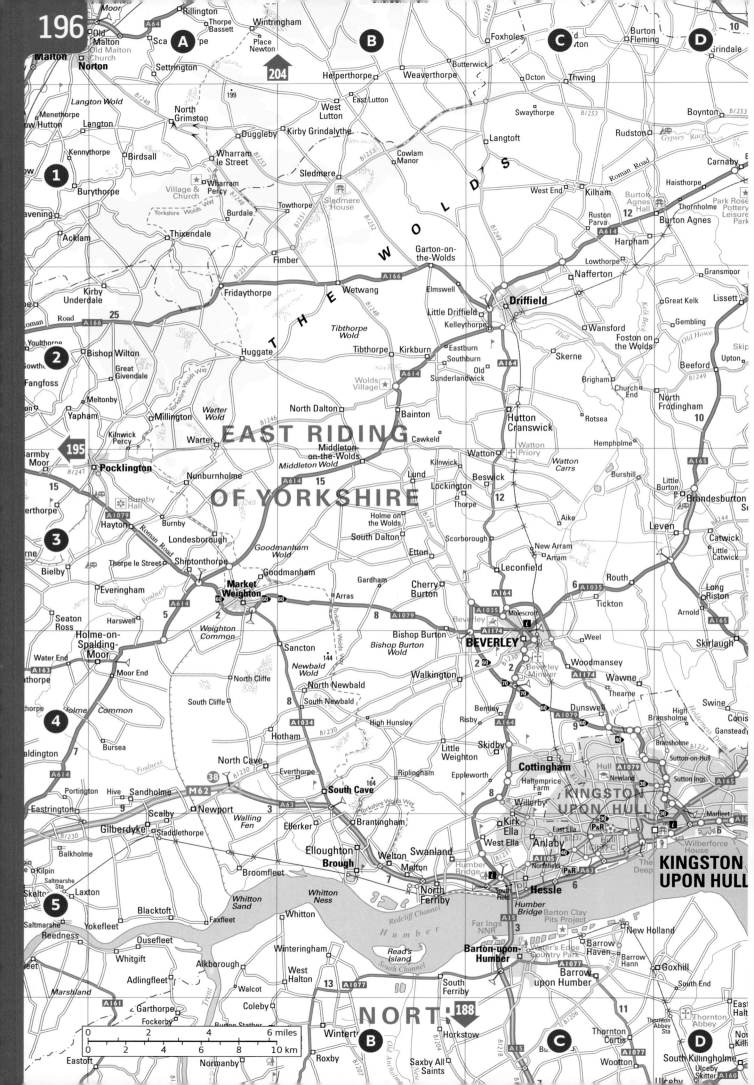

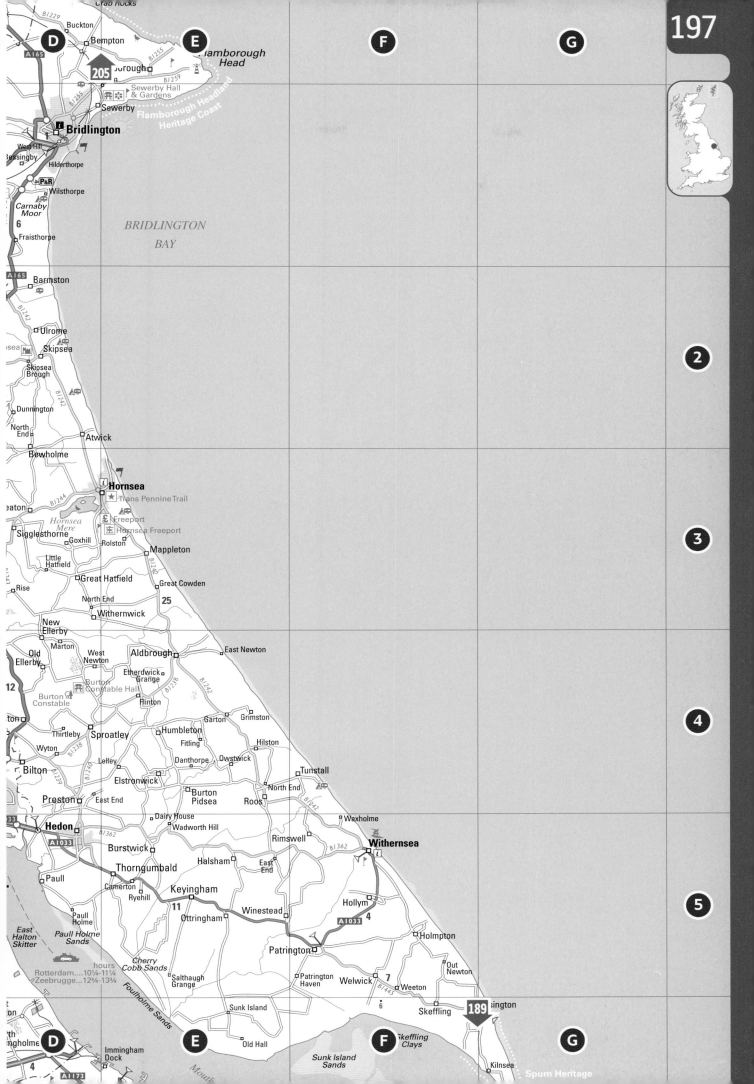

**D**  **E**  **F**  **G**

B1229
Crab Rocks
Buckton
Bempton
B1255
**Flamborough Head**
A165
**205**
orough
B1259
Sewerby Hall & Gardens
Flamborough Headland Heritage Coast
Sewerby
**Bridlington**
West Hill
Bessingby
Hilderthorpe
**P&R**
Wilsthorpe
*Carnaby Moor*
6
Fraisthorpe

*BRIDLINGTON BAY*

A165
Barmston
B1242
Ulrome
Skipsea
Skipsea Brough
B1242
Dunnington
North End
Atwick
Bewholme

**2**

B1244
**Hornsea**
★ Trans Pennine Trail
eaton
*Hornsea Mere*
£ Freeport
Hornsea Freeport
Sigglesthorne  Goxhill
Rolston
Little Hatfield  Mappleton
Rise
Great Hatfield
Great Cowden
North End  **25**
Withernwick
New Ellerby
Marton
Old Ellerby  West Newton  Aldbrough
East Newton
Etherdwick Grange
**12**
Burton Constable Hall
B1238
B1242
Burton Constable
Flinton
Thirtleby  Humbleton
Garton
Grimston
Sproatley
Fitling
ton  Hilston
Wyton
Lelley  Danthorpe  Owstwick
Bilton  Elstronwick
Tunstall
B1239
East End  North End
Preston  Burton Pidsea  Roos
B1242
Dairy House  Waxholme
**33**  **Hedon**
B1362  Wadworth Hill
A1033  Rimswell
Burstwick  Halsham  B1362  **Withernsea**
Thorngumbald  East End
Paull  Camerton
Keyingham  Hollym
Ryehill
**11**  Winestead  **4**
Ottringham  A1033
Paull Holme
*East Halton Skitter*  Paull Holme Sands
Holmpton
*Cherry Cobb Sands*
Patrington
Salthaugh Grange
Out Newton
hours
Rotterdam....10¼-11¼
Zeebrugge...12¾-13¾
*Foulholme Sands*
Patrington Haven  Welwick  **7**  Weeton
B1445
6
Sunk Island
Skeffling  **189**  sington
Old Hall
*Sunk Island Sands*
*Skeffling Clays*
Kilnsea
Immingham Dock
ngholme
A1173
4
Mouth
**Spurn Heritage**

**2**  **3**  **4**  **5**

**D**  **E**  **F**  **G**

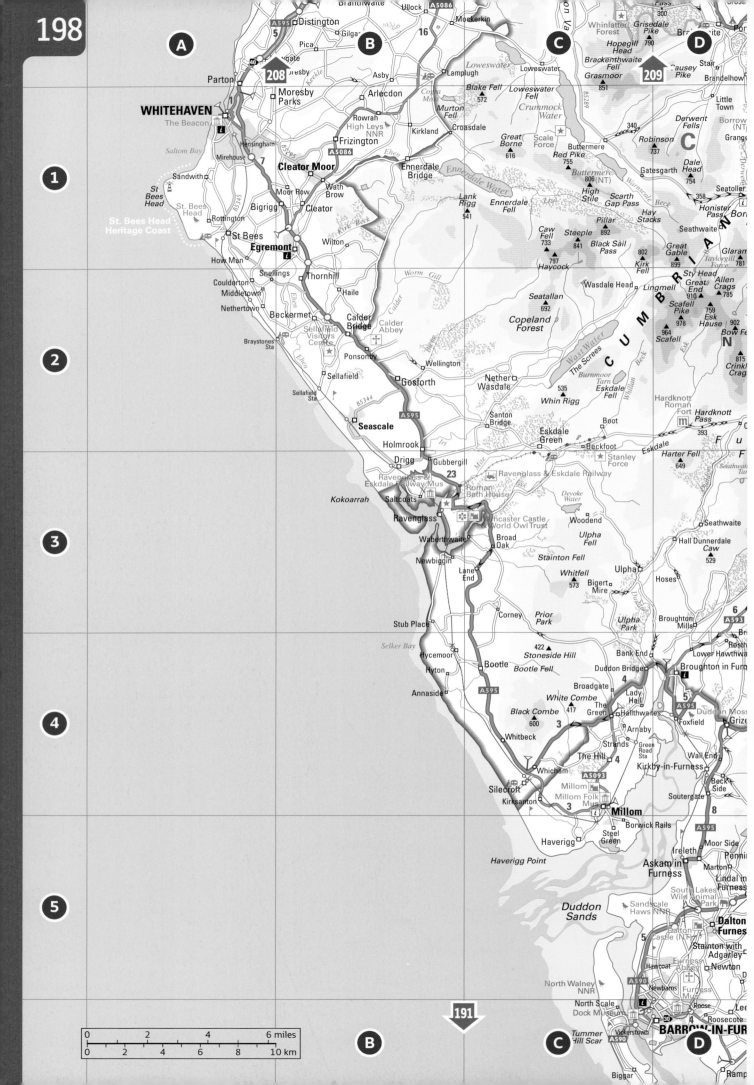

208
209
191

A  B  C  D

1  2  3  4  5

**WHITEHAVEN**
The Beacon
Saltom Bay
St Bees Head
St. Bees Head
Heritage Coast
St Bees Head
St. Bees Head
Sandwith
Parton
Moresby Parks
Distington
Pica
Keekle
Moresby
Hensingham
Mirehouse
Rottington
How Man
St Bees
Bigrigg
Moor Row
**Cleator Moor**
Wath Brow
Cleator
Wilton
**Egremont**
Snellings
Thornhill
Haile
Coulderton
Middletown
Nethertown
Beckermet
Braystones Sta
Sellafield Visitors Centre
Calder Bridge
Calder Abbey
Ponsonby
Sellafield
Sellafield Sta
Gosforth
Wellington
**Seascale**
Holmrook
Drigg
Gubbergill
23
Kokoarrah
Saltcoats
**Ravenglass**
Ravenglass & Eskdale Railway Mus
Roman Bath House
Muncaster Castle World Owl Trust
Waberthwaite
Newbiggin
Broad Oak
Lane End
Stub Place
Corney
Prior Park
Selker Bay
Hycemoor
Hyton
Bootle
Bootle Fell
Annaside
Stoneside Hill
Bank End
Duddon Bridge
Broadgate
White Combe
Black Combe
The Green
Hallthwaites
Whitbeck
Arnaby
Strands
Green Road Sta
Whicham
The Hill
Kirkby-in-Furness
**Silecroft**
Kirksanton
Millom Folk Mus
**Millom**
Borwick Rails
Haverigg
Steel Green
Moor Side
Ireleth
Askam in Furness
Haverigg Point
Marton
Lindal in Furness
Duddon Sands
Sandscale Haws NNR
South Lakes Wild Animal Park
**Dalton in Furness**
Stainton with Adgarley
Newton
Furness Abbey
Hawcoat
North Walney NNR
North Scale
Dock Museum
North Scale
Newbarns
Furness Mus
**BARROW-IN-FUR...**
Tummer Hill Scar
Vickerstown
Roosecote
Biggar

Ullock
Mockerkin
A5086
5
A595
16
Gilgarran
Asby
Arlecdon
Rowrah
High Leys NNR
Kirkland
A5086
Frizington
Ennerdale Bridge
Croasdale
Lamplugh
Loweswater
Loweswater
Cogra Moss
Murton Fell
Blake Fell 572
Loweswater Fell
Crummock Water
Scale Force
Whinlatter Forest
Hopegill Head
Brackenthwaite Fell
Grasmoor 851
Grisedale Pike 790
Causey Pike
Stair
Brandelhow
Little Town
Derwent Fells
Robinson 737
Gatesgarth
Dale Head 754
Borrowdale
Grange
Seatoller
Honister Pass
Seathwaite
Great Borne 616
Red Pike 755
Buttermere (NT)
High Stile 806 (NT)
Scarth Gap Pass
Hay Stacks
Pillar 892
Steeple 841
Black Sàil Pass
802
Kirk Fell
Great Gable 899
Glaram... 781
Taylorgill Force
358
Ennerdale Water
Ennerdale
Bridge
Lank Rigg 541
Ennerdale Fell
Caw Fell 733
797
Haycock
Wasdale Head
Lingmell
Sty Head
Great End 910
Allen Crags 785
Scafell Pike 978
759
Esk Hause
902
Bow Fell
964
Scafell
815
Crinkle Crags
Worm Gill
Copeland Forest
Seatallan 692
Nether Wasdale
Whin Rigg
535
The Screes
Wast Water
Burnmoor Tarn
Eskdale Fell
Hardknott Roman Fort
Hardknott Pass 393
Santon Bridge
Eskdale Green
Beckfoot
Eskdale
Harter Fell 649
Boot
Stanley Force
Ravenglass & Eskdale Railway
Devoke Water
Woodend
Ulpha Fell
Stainton Fell
Whitfell 573
Bigert Mire
Ulpha
Hoses
Seathwaite
Hall Dunnerdale
Caw 529
Broughton Mills
Lower Hawthwa...
Broughton in Furn...
Foxfield
Grize...
Wall End
Beck Side
Soutergate
A595
A5093
A5093
A590
A590
Balton Castle (NF)

Sellafield Visitors Centre
B5345
B5344
B5289
Warnscale Beck
Lingmell Beck
Mite
Irt
Esk
Whillan Beck
Duddon
Ehen
Calder
Bleng
Keekle

0  2  4  6 miles
0  2  4  6  8  10 km

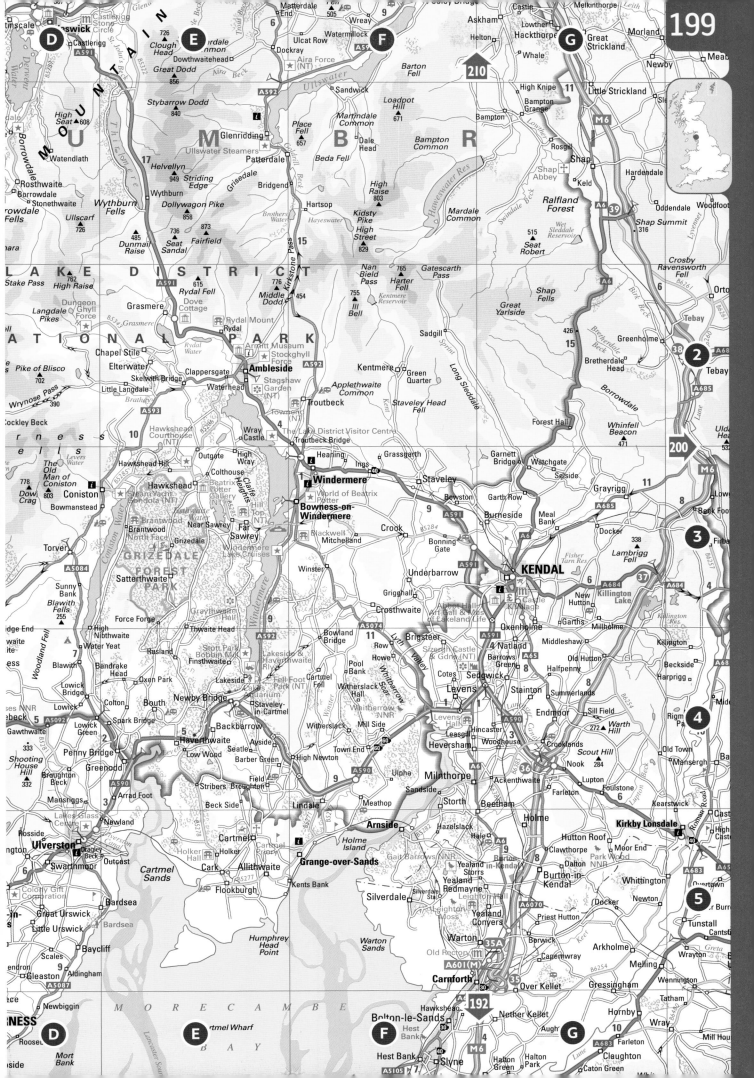

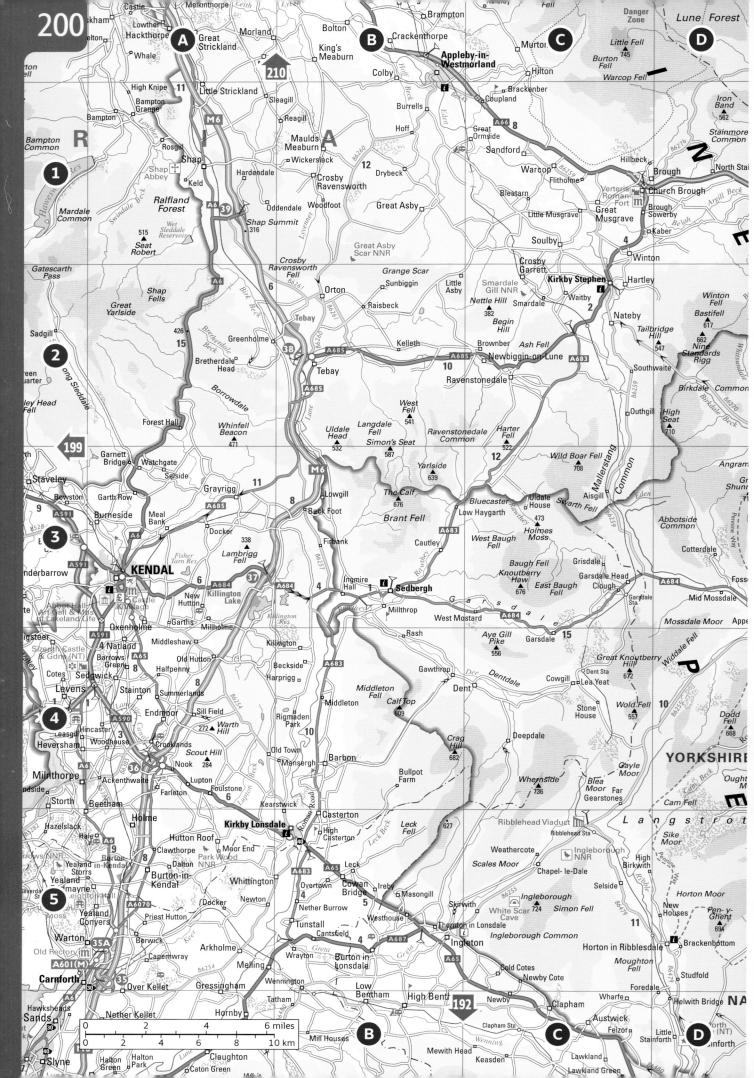

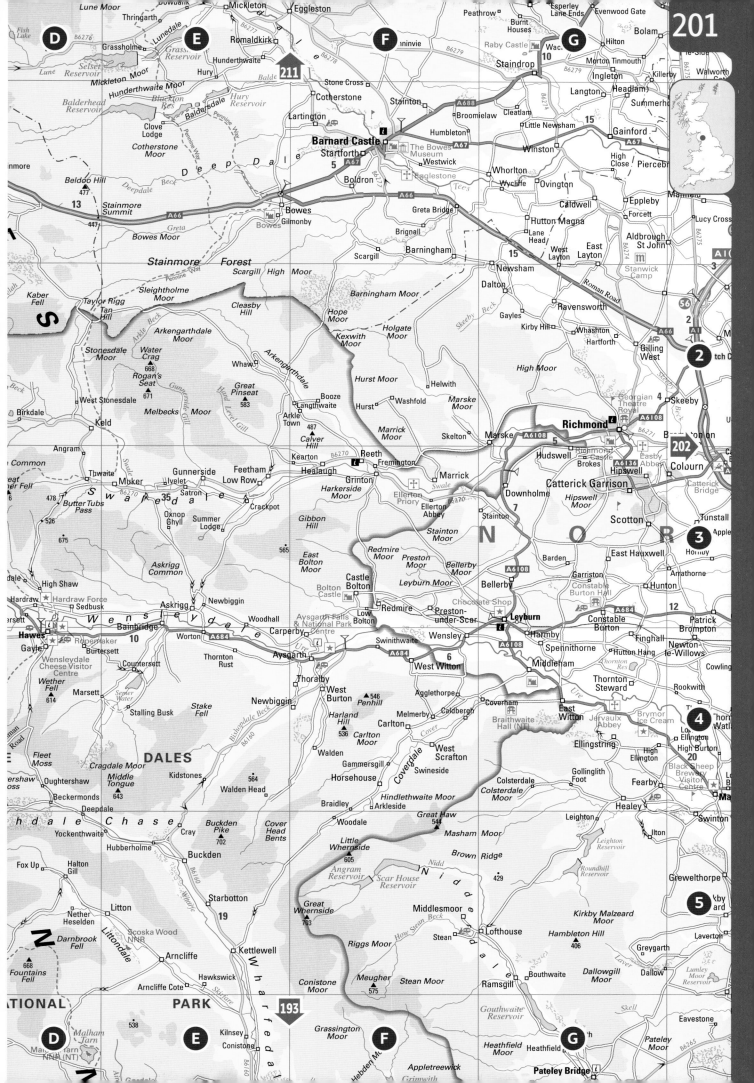

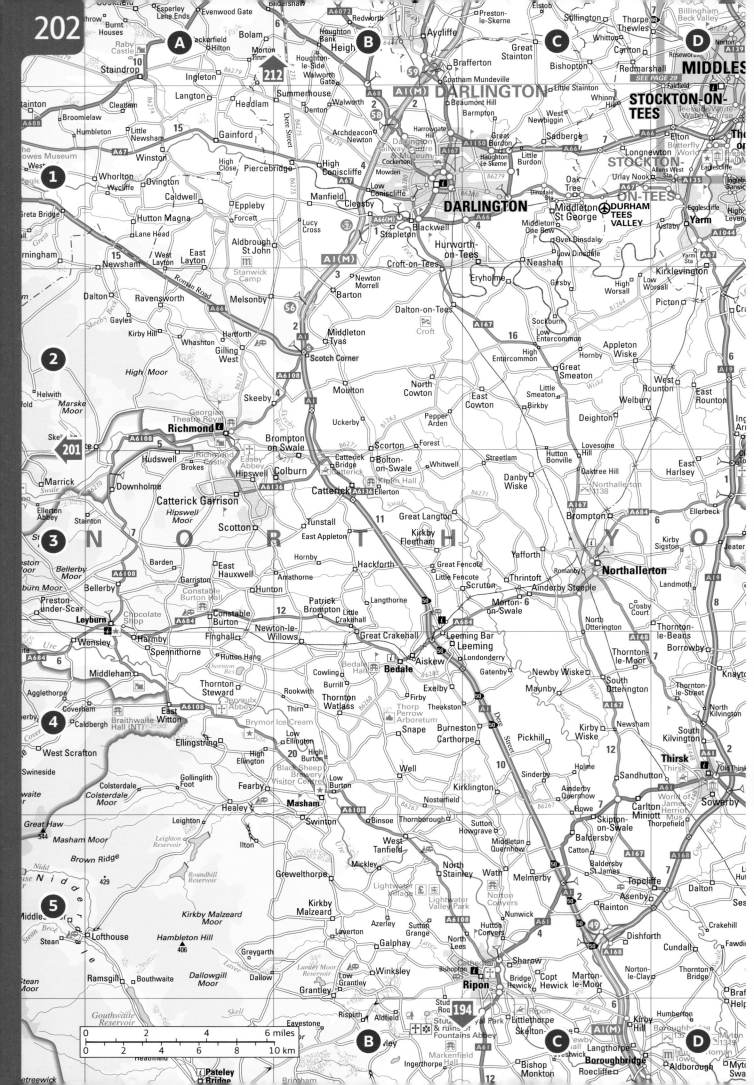

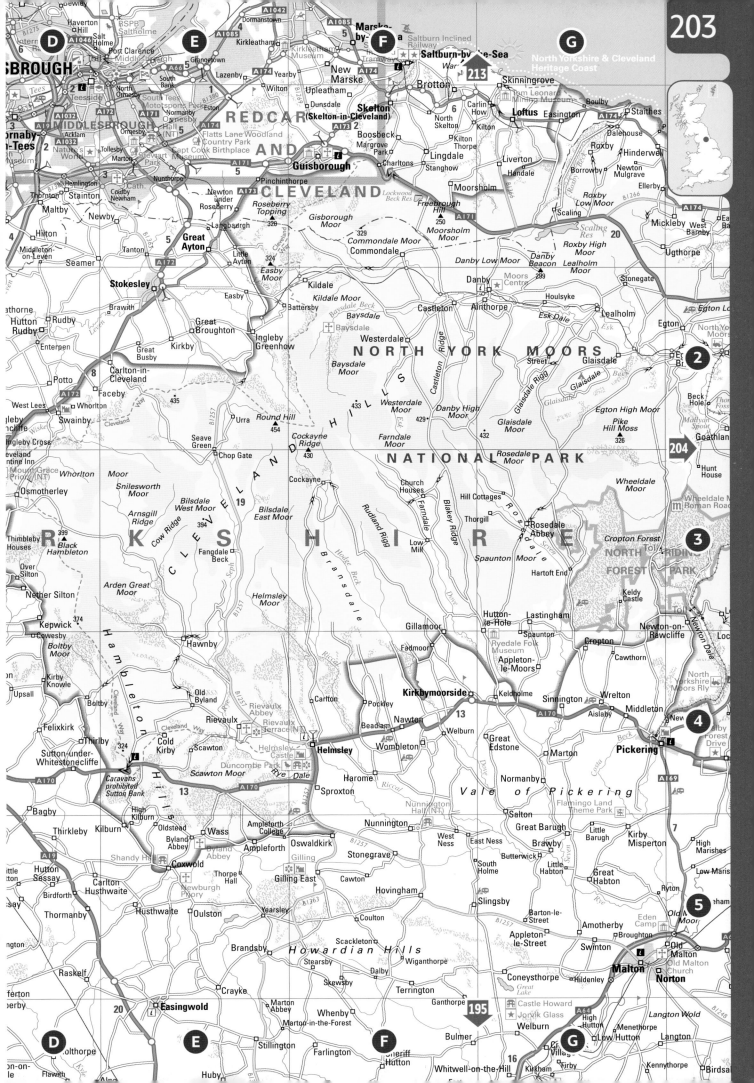

D  E  F  G

205

2

3

4

5

e & Cleveland

*Ness Rocks*
fe & Marine Sanctuary
*North Bay*
Miniature Railway

Scarborough Castle

**SCARBOROUGH**
carborough Art Gall
*South Bay*
Spa Complex
*Black Rocks*

P&R

Osgodby

*Cayton Bay*

ld

Cayton  7

*The Wyke*

Lebberston

Gristhorpe

*Filey Brigg*

*Hertford*

A165

*i*  Filey

A1039

Folkton  6  Muston

West
Flotmanby

*Filey
Bay*

Hunmanby

*Reighton
Sands*

Reighton

Speeton

*Crab Rocks*

B1229

Buckton

Wold
Newton

Burton
Fleming

10

Bempton

B1255

*Flamborough
Head*

Grindale

A165

Flamborough

B1259

Thwing

Marton

Sewerby Hall
& Gardens

B1253

Boynton

B1252

Sewerby

Flamborough Headland
Heritage Coast

197

E  Bridlington  F  G

udston

*Gypsey Race*

Carnaby

West Hill

Bessingby

Hilderthorpe

B1253

Road

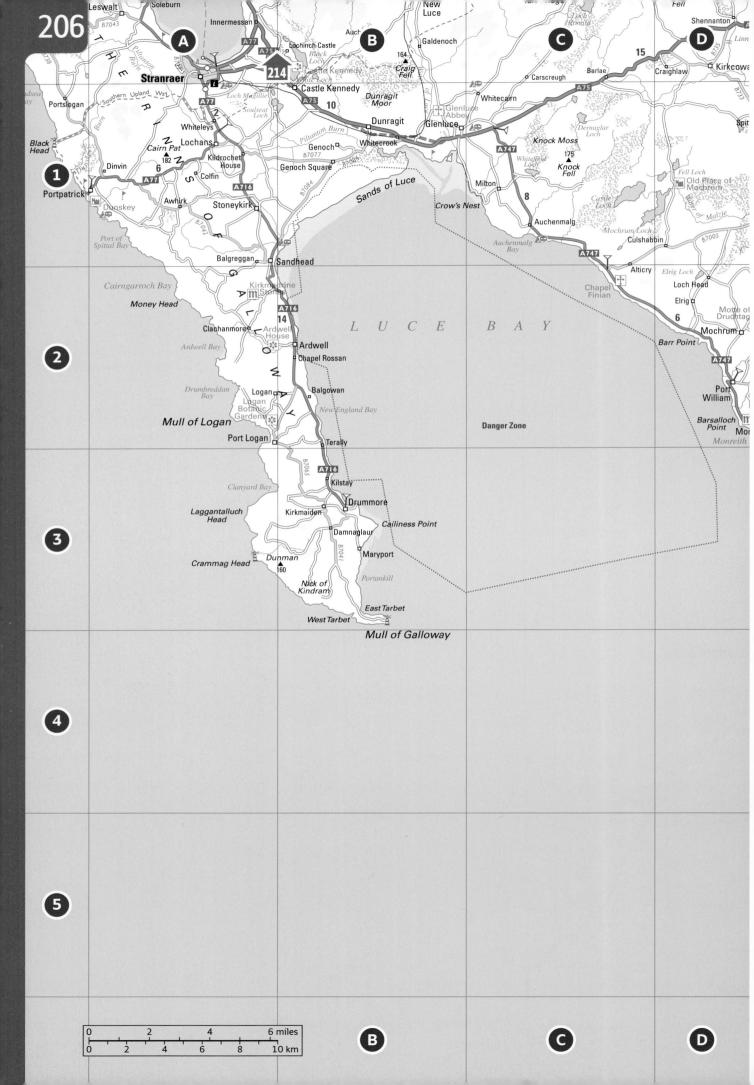

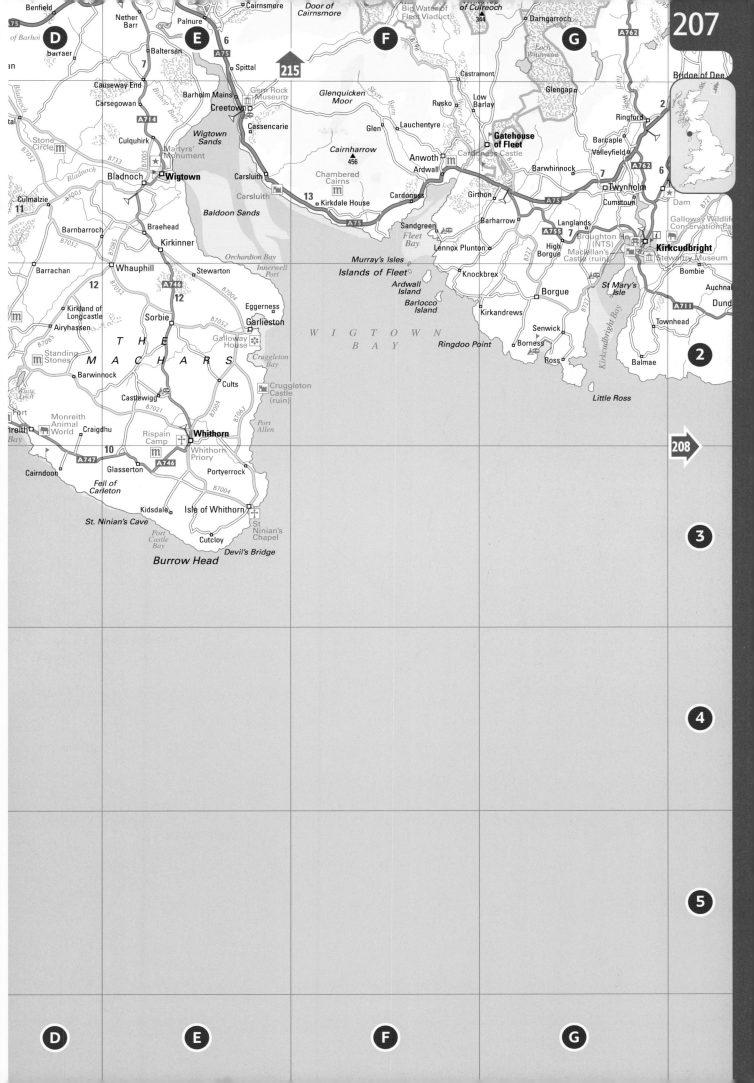

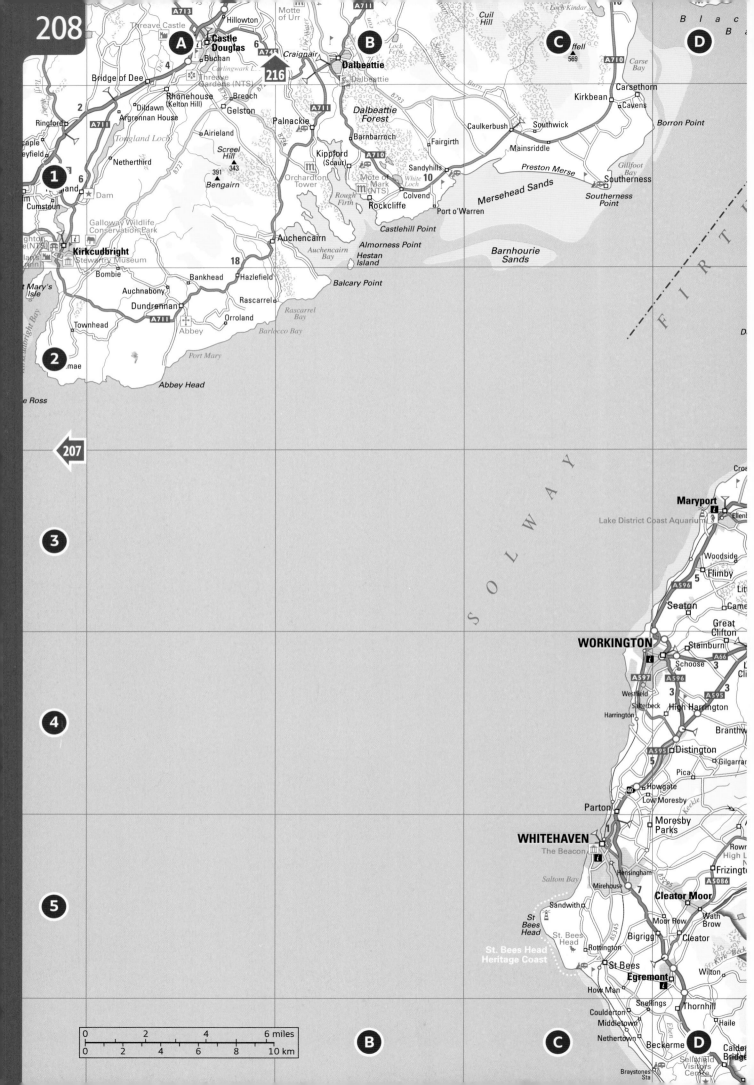

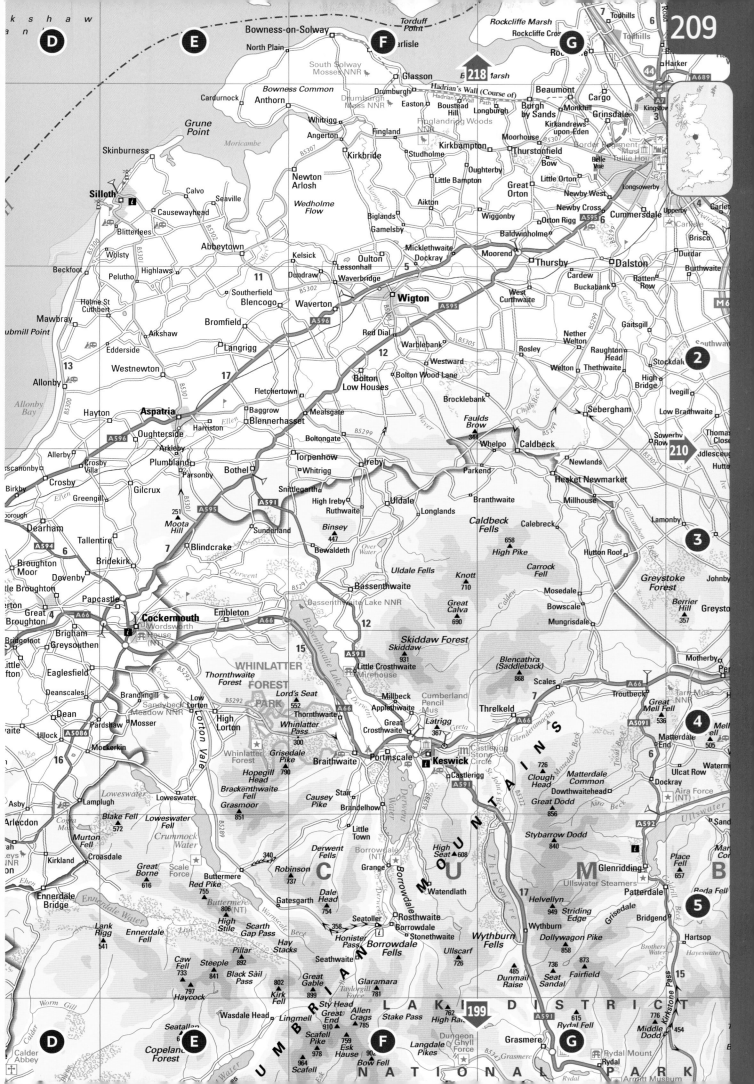

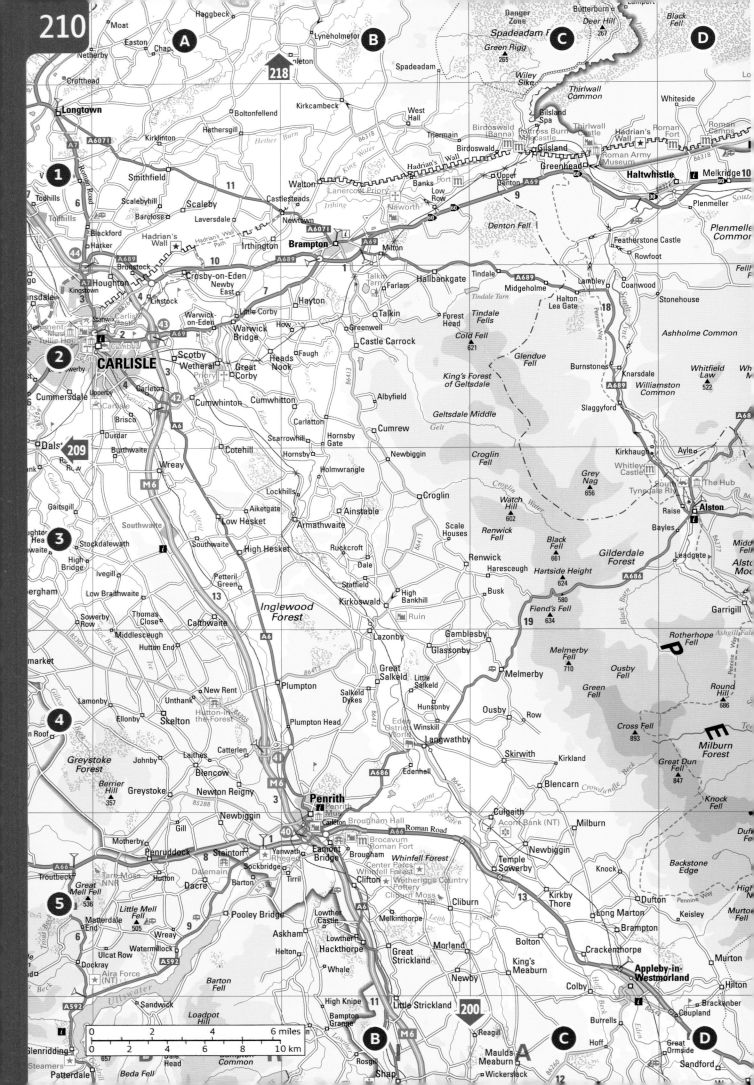

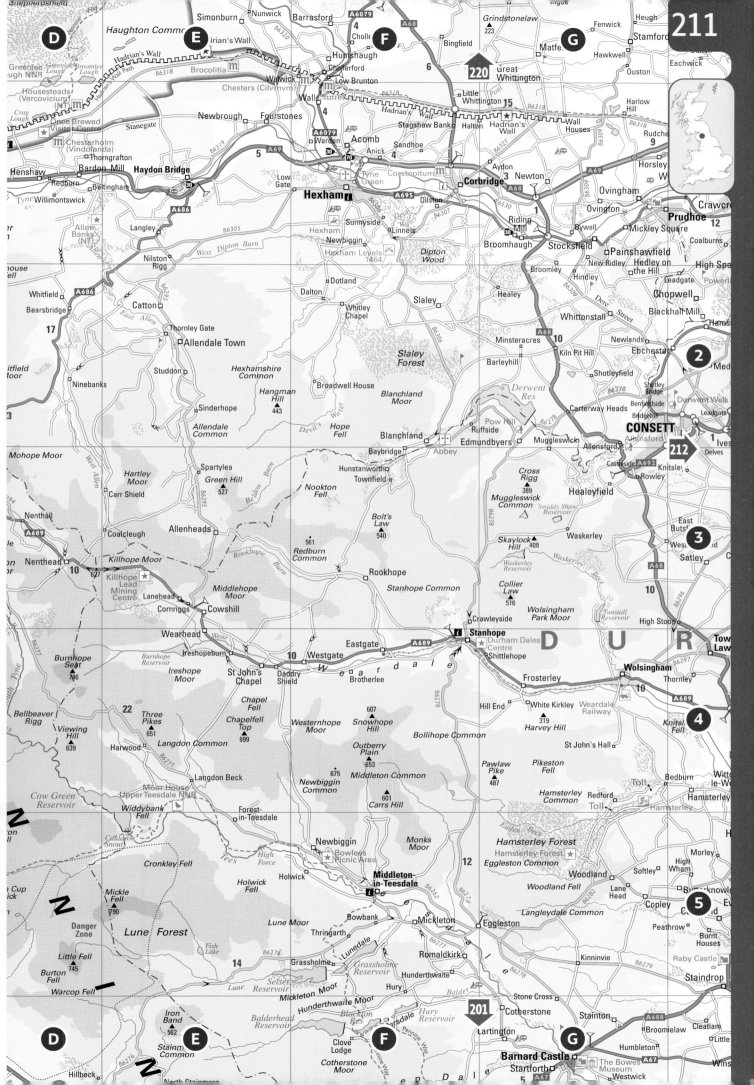

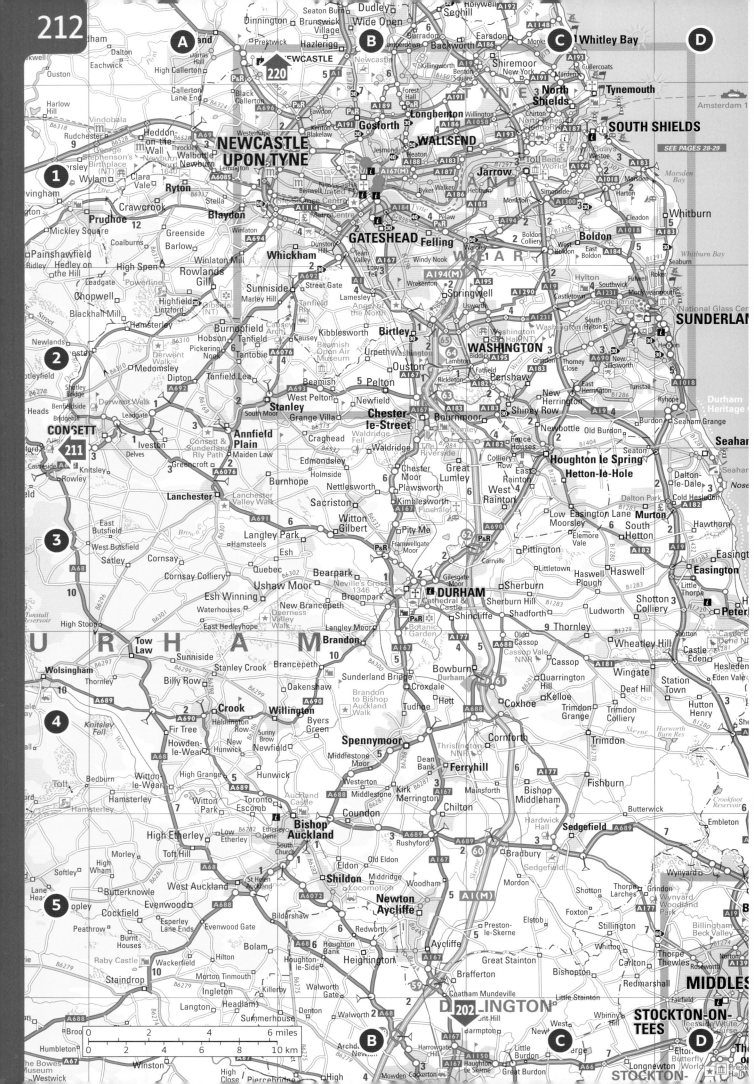

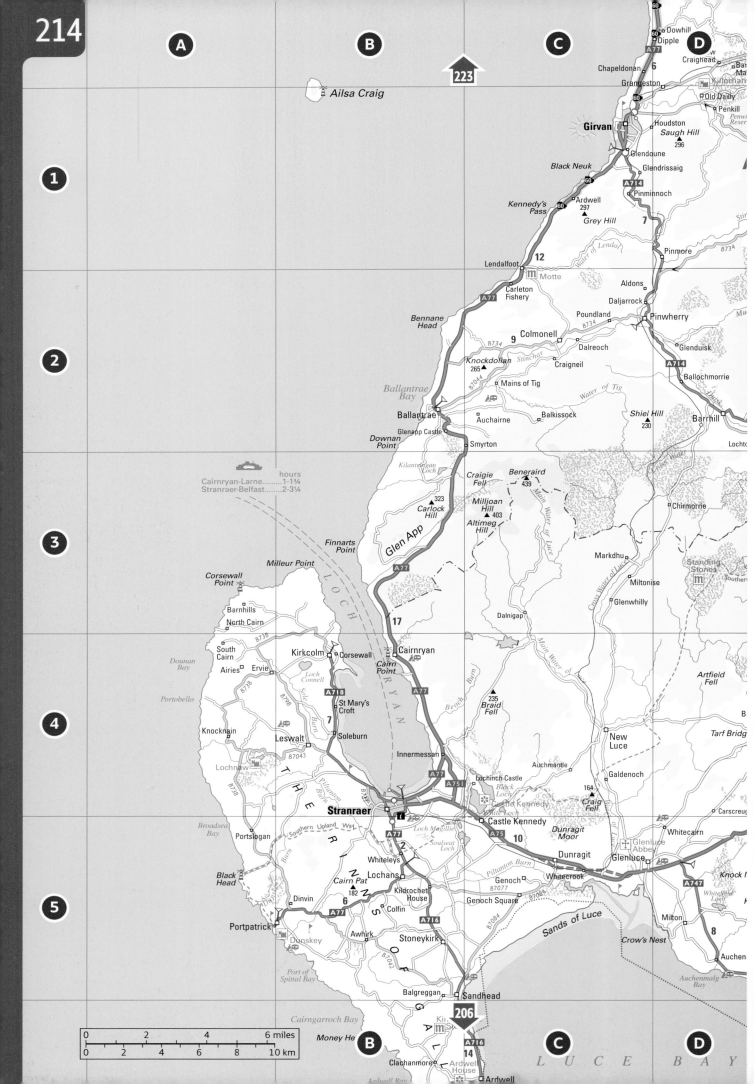

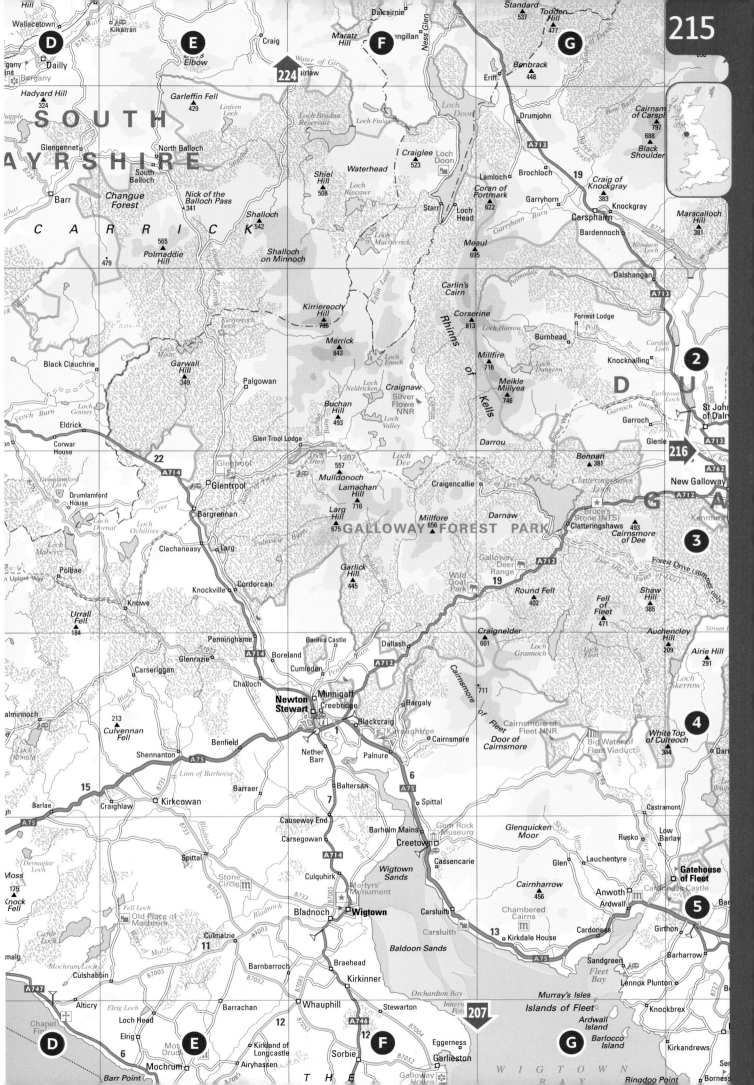

D

E

F

G

Wallacetown

Hill

Kilkerran

B714

Craig

Dalcairnie

Maratz
Hill

Ness Glen

Standard
537

Todden
Hill
477

Dangillan

Dailly

Bargany

224

Fairlaw

Water of Girvan

Water of Deugh

Bonbrack
448

Cairnsm
of Carsph

Hadyard Hill
324

Hill
ins

Garleffin Fell
429

Linfern
Loch

Loch Bradan
Reservoir

Loch Finlas

Eriff

Drumjohn

797

688

Black
Shoulder

Glengennet

North Balloch

South Balloch

Chapple
voir

SOUTH

AYRSHIRE

Waterhead

Shiel
Hill
508

Craiglee
523

Loch
Doon

Loch Doon

Lamloch

Coran of
Portmark
622

Brochloch

Garryhorn

19

Craig of
Knockgray
383

Knockgray

Barr

Changue
Forest

Nick of the
Balloch Pass
341

Shalloch
542

Loch
Riecawr

Starr

Loch
Head

Carsphairn

Bardennoch

Marscalloch
Hill
381

CARRICK

Loch Macaterick

Meaul
695

Garryhorn Burn

Kendoon
Loch

565

Polmaddie
Hill

479

Shalloch
on Minnoch

Carlin's
Cairn

Polmaddy Burn

Dalshangan

A713

Black Clauchrie

Cree

Kirriereoch
Hill
786

Corserine
813

Loch Harrow

Burnhead

Forest Lodge

Polharrow Burn

Carsfad
Loch

Garwall
Hill
349

Loch
Moan

Kirriereoch
Loch

Merrick
843

Palgowan

Loch
Neldricken

Loch
Enoch

Rhinns of Kells

Millfire
716

St Loch
Dungeon

Meikle
Millyea
746

Knocknalling

2

D

Feoch Burn

Eldrick

Loch
Goosey

Craignaw
Silver
Flowe
NNR

Loch
Valley

Buchan
Hill
493

Buchan Burn

Garroch Burn

Garroch

Earlstoun
Loch

St John
of Dalry

Corwar
House

22

A714

Glentrool

Glen Trool Lodge

Loch
Dee

1307
557

Mulldonoch

Darrou

Bennan
381

Clatteringshaws
Loch

Glenle

216

A713

A762

New Galloway

Drumlamford
House

Loch
Dornal

Loch
Ochiltree

Bargrennan

Larg
Hill
716

Lamachan
Hill
716

Millfore
656

Darnaw

Bruce's
Stone (NTS)

Clatteringshaws

Cairnsmore
of Dee

493

A712

Kenmure

Loch
Maberry

Polbae

Clachaneasy

Larg

Cree

Palnure Burn

675

GALLOWAY FOREST PARK

A712

Forest Drive (summer only)

3

Upland Way

Knowe

Knockville

Cordorcan

Garlick
Hill
445

Galloway
Deer
Range

19

Round Fell
402

Fell
of
Fleet
471

Shaw
Hill
385

Urrall
Fell
184

Black Burn

Penninghame

Garlies Castle

Boreland

Dallash

Wild
Goat
Park

601

Craignelder

Loch
Grannoch

Loch
Fleet

Auchencloy
Hill
209

Stroan

Airie Hill
291

Glenrazie

A714

A7022

Cumloden

A712

Cairnsmore of Dee

Loch
Skerrow

Carseriggan

Challoch

Minnigaff

Newton
Stewart

Creebridge

Bargaly

711

Culvennan
Fell

213

Benfield

Blackcraig

Kirroughtree

Cairnsmøre

Cairnsmore of
Fleet NNR

Big Water of
Fleet Viaduct

White Top
of Culreoch
344

Dar

Shennanton

A75

Nether
Barr

Palnure

Door of
Cairnsmore

Barlae

15

Craighlaw

Kirkcowan

Barraer

Baltersan

A75

6

Spittal

Castramont

Low
Barlay

B725

Linn of Barhoise

7

Spittal

Glenquicken
Moor

Rusko

Dernaglar
Loch

175

Knock
Fell

Spittal

Causeway End

Carsegowan

Barholm Mains

Gem Rock
Museum

Creetown

Cassencarie

Glen

Lauchentyre

Gatehouse
of Fleet

Moss

Stone
Circle

B733

Culquhirk

Martyrs'
Monument

Cairnharrow
456

Anwoth

Ardwall

Cardoness Castle

5

Old Place of
Mochrum

Bladnoch

Wigtown

Wigtown
Sands

Carsluith

Chambered
Cairns

Cardoness

Girthon

Barharrow

11

Culmalzie

Carsluith

13

Kirkdale House

Sandgreen

Lennox Plunton

B7027

Barnbarroch

Braehead

Baldoon Sands

Fleet
Bay

Castle
Loch

A747

Alticry

Elrig Loch

Barrachan

Whauphill

Stewarton

Orchardton Bay

Murray's Isles

207

Islands of Fleet

Knockbrex

malg

Loch Head

Elrig

12

B7052

Sorbie

A746

Eggerness

Ardwall
Island

Barlocco
Island

Chapel
Finn

Mot
Drud

Mochrum

Kirkland of
Longcastle

12

A746

B7004

Galloway
House

Garlieston

WIGTOWN

BAY

Kirkandrews

Barr Point

Airyhassen

Ringdoo Point

Bornes

D

6

E

F

G

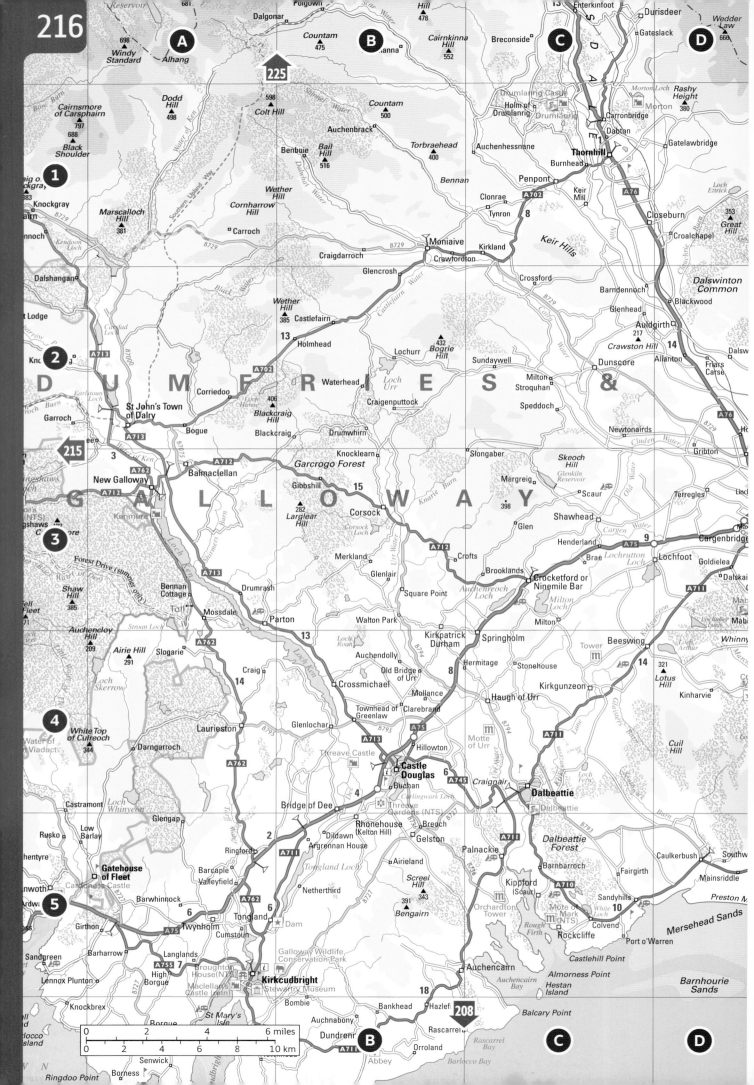

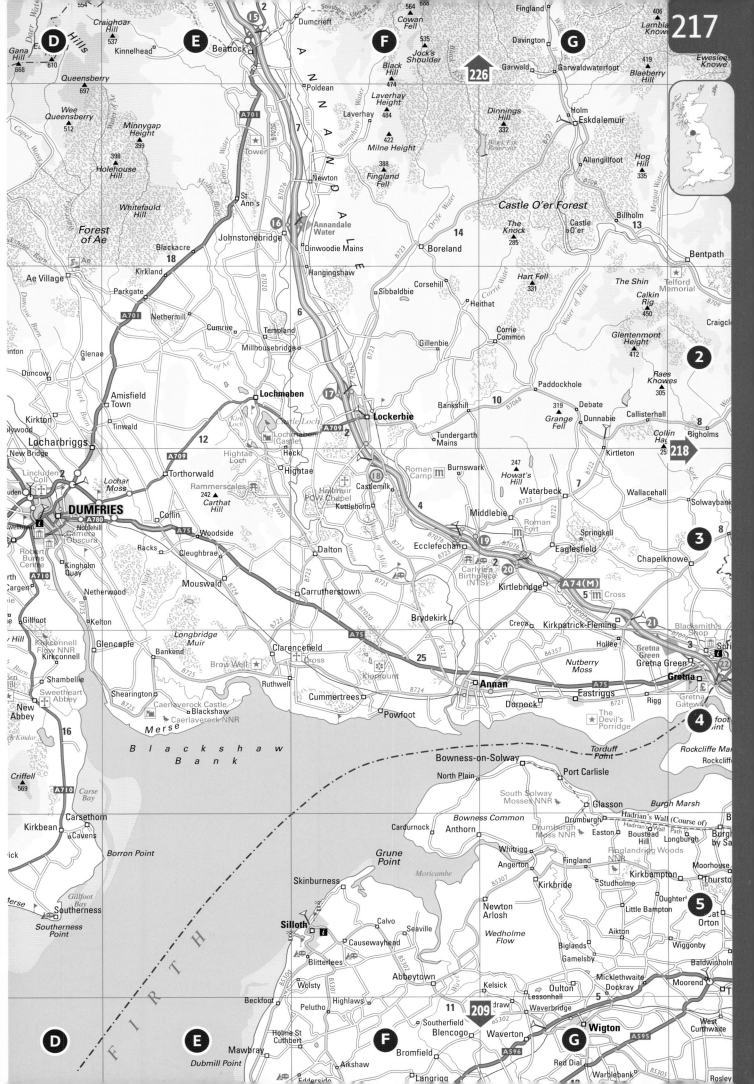

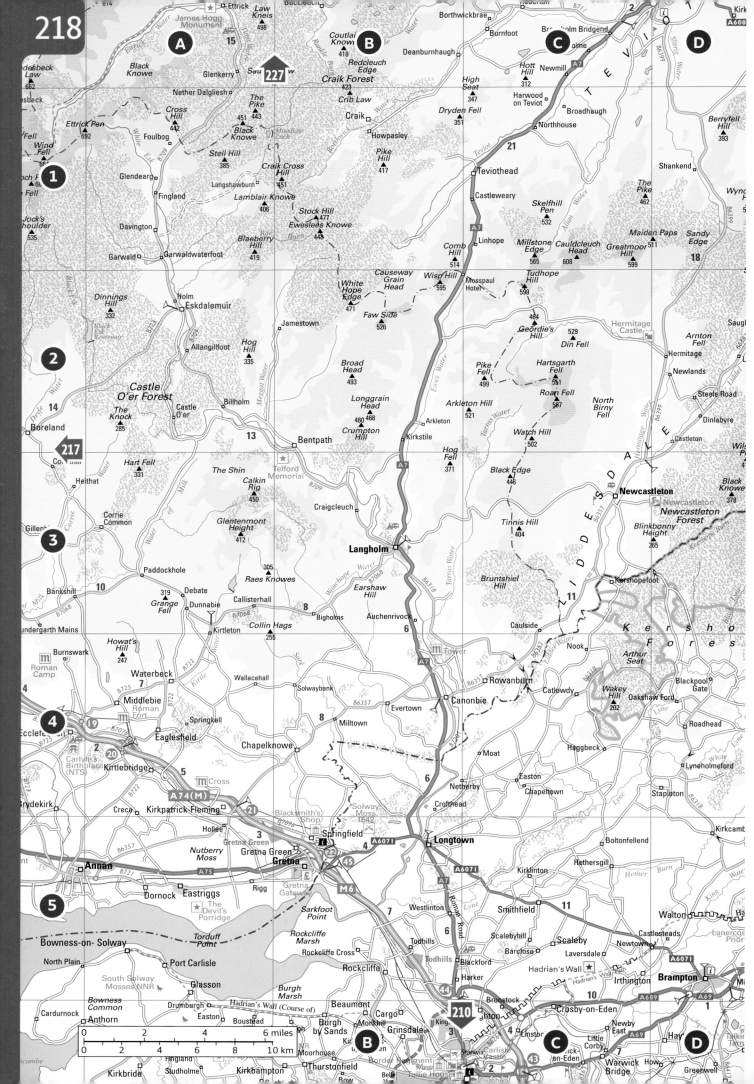

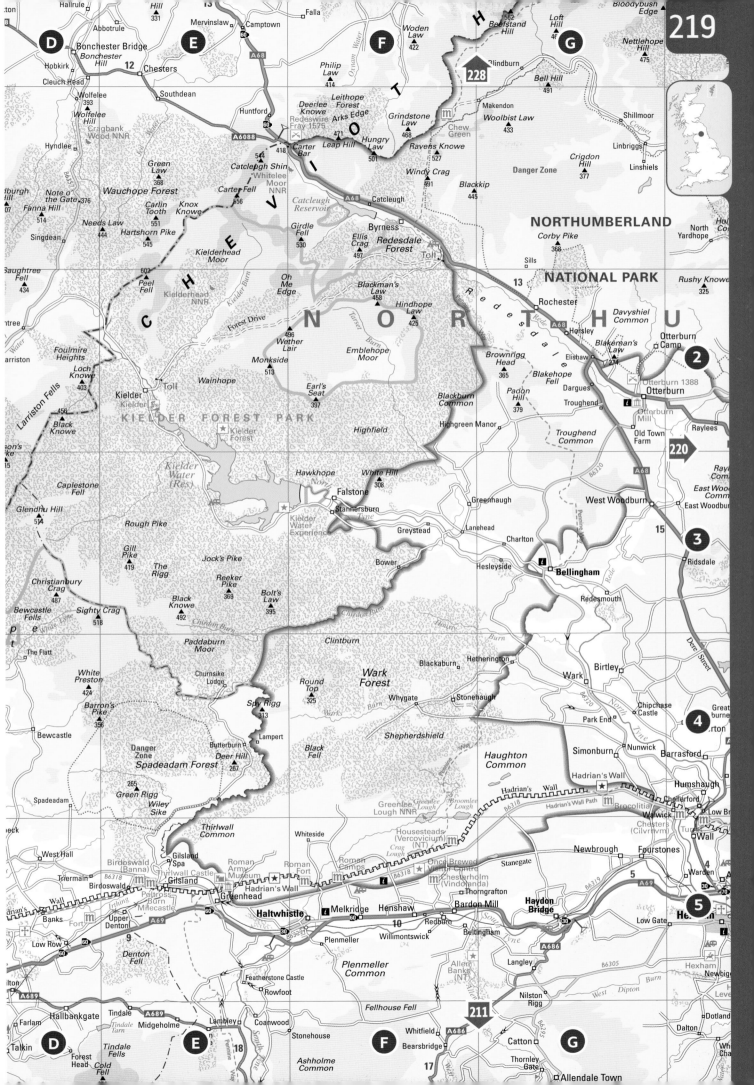

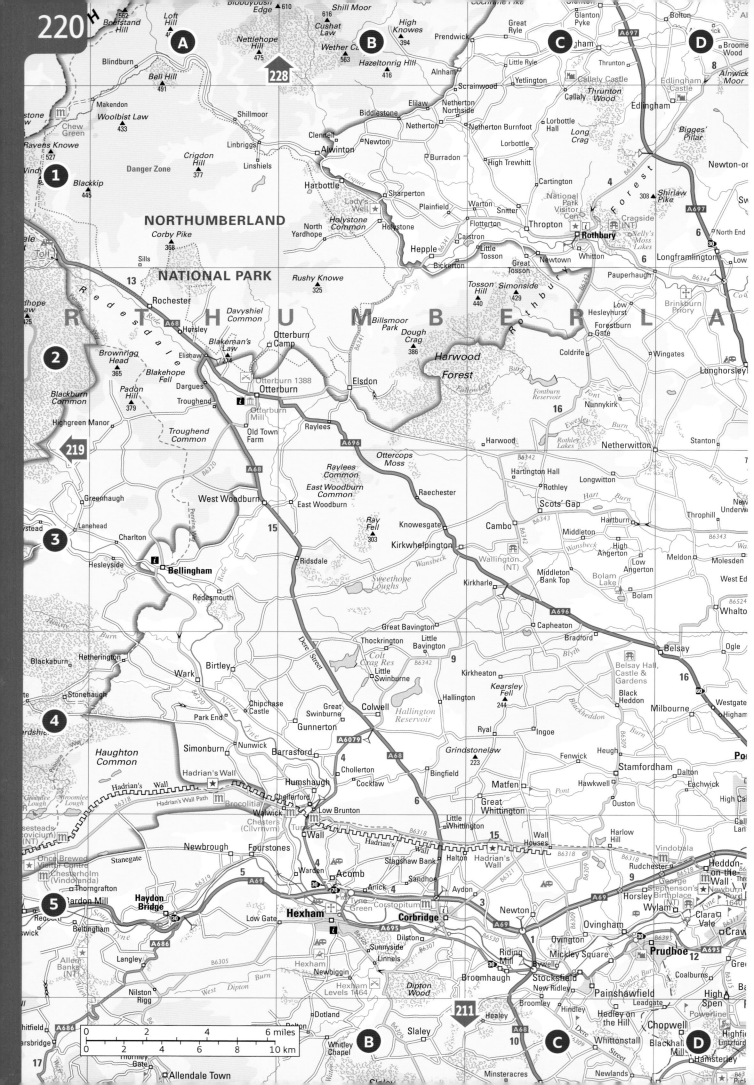

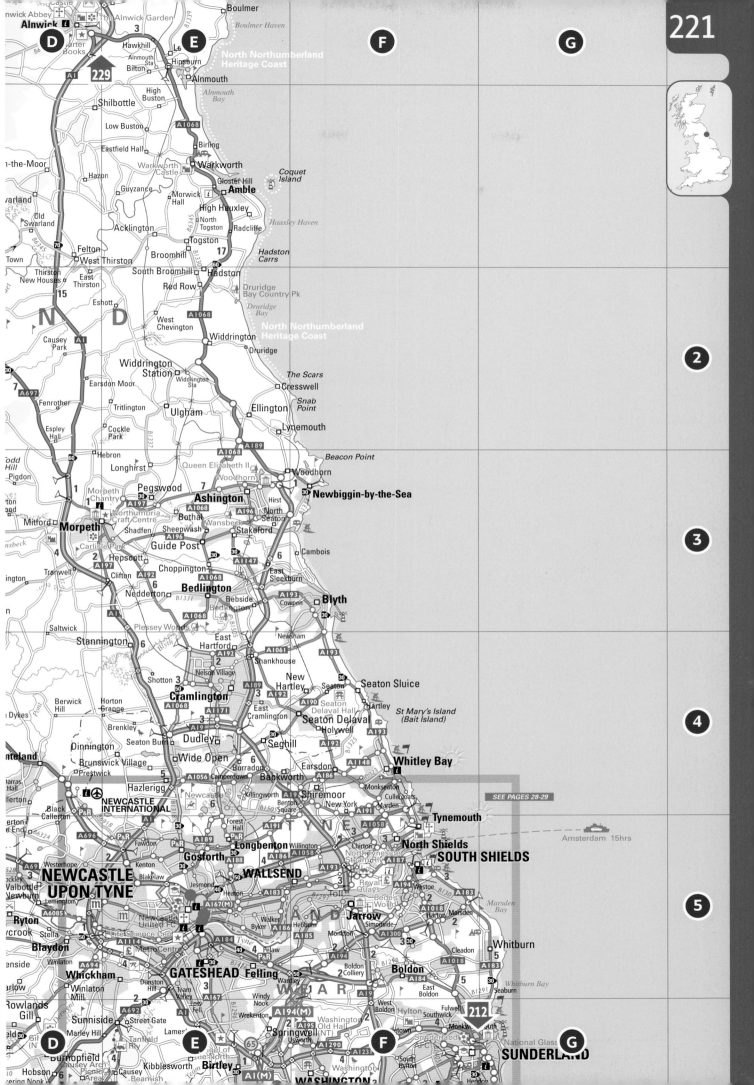

D · E · F · G

Alnwick Abbey
Alnwick
Carter Books
A1 229
Hawkhill
Bilton
Alnmouth Sta.
Hipsburn
Alnmouth
North Northumberland Heritage Coast
Boulmer
Boulmer Haven

Shilbottle
High Buston
Low Buston
Eastfield Hall
A1068
Birling
Warkworth Castle
Warkworth
Gloster Hill
Coquet Island

-the-Moor
Hazon
Guyzance
Morwick Hall
Amble
High Hauxley
North Togston
Radcliffe
Hauxley Haven

Old Swarland
Acklington
Togston
17
Hadston Carrs

Town
Felton
West Thirston
Broomhill
South Broomhill
Hadston
Druridge Bay Country Pk
Druridge Bay
North Northumberland Heritage Coast

15
Thirston New Houses
East Thirston
Red Row
Widdrington

N · D
Eshott
West Chevington
A1068
Widdrington
Druridge

Causey Park
Widdrington Station
Widdrington Sta
The Scars
Cresswell

Fenrother
Earsdon Moor
Tritlington
Ulgham
Ellington
Snab Point

Espley Hall
Cockle Park
Lynemouth

Hebron
Longhirst
A1068
Queen Elizabeth II
Woodhorn
Beacon Point

Pigdon
Morpeth Chantry
Pegswood
A197
Ashington
A1068
Hirst
North Seaton
Newbiggin-by-the-Sea

Mitford
Morpeth
Northumbria Craft Centre
Shadfen
Bothal
Sheepwash
A196
Stakeford
Wansbeck
Cambois

Carlisle Park
Guide Post
A196

Hepscott
A197
Choppington
A1068
East Sleekburn

Tranwell
Clifton
A192
Bedlington
Bebside
Cowpen
Blyth

Nedderton
B1331
Bedlington
A1068

Saltwick
Plessey Woods
A193

Stannington
East Hartford
Newsham

Berwick Hill
A192
Shankhouse

Horton Grange
Shotton
Nelson Village
A189
New Hartley
Seaton
Seaton Sluice

Brenkley
Cramlington
A1068
A192
Seaton Delaval Hall
Hartley
St Mary's Island (Bait Island)

Dinnington
Seaton Burn
A1171
East Cramlington
Dudley
Seghill
A192
Seaton Delaval
Holywell

Brunswick Village
Prestwick
A1056
Wide Open
Burradon
Earsdon
A186
A148
Whitley Bay

Hazlerigg
Camperdown
Backworth
Monkseaton

NEWCASTLE INTERNATIONAL
Newcastle
Killingworth
A19
Shiremoor
New York
A191
Marden
Cullercoats
SEE PAGES 28-29

Black Callerton
Forest Hall
A191
TYNE
A1058
Tynemouth
Amsterdam 15hrs

Westerhope
Longbenton
A188
Willington
Chirton
North Shields
SOUTH SHIELDS

Kenton
Gosforth
A193
North Tyneside Steam Rly
A187
Westoe

NEWCASTLE UPON TYNE
Blakelaw
Jesmond
WALLSEND
A194
B130
A183

Ryton
Heaton
Walker
A183
Royal Quays
Bede's World

Newburn
Lemington
Byker
Jarrow
Simonside
Harton
Marsden Bay

Blaydon
Life Science Cen
MetroCentre
Pelaw
Monkton
A1300
Cleadon
Whitburn

Whickham
Dunston Hill
GATESHEAD
Felling
Wardley
A184
Windy Nook
Boldon Colliery
Boldon
A1018
A183

Winlaton Mill
Team Valley
Low Fell
A167
WEAR
Boldon
East Boldon
Seaburn
Whitburn Bay

Rowlands Gill
Sunniside
Street Gate
A692
Wrekenton
A194(M)
West Boldon
Hylton
Southwick
Fulwell
212

Marley Hill
Lamesley
Washington Old Hall (NT)
A1290
SUNDERLAND

Burnopfield
Angel of the North
65
Springwell
Usworth
South Hylton
National Glass

Hobson
Causey Arch Picnic Area
Kibblesworth
Causey
Birtley
A1(M)
Washington
Hendon

WASHINGTON

2 · 3 · 4 · 5

A

B

C

D

Ardmore
Point
Ardmore

Eilean
a' Chuirn

Eilean
'Chride

2¼ hrs

West
Tarbert
Bay

East
Tarbert
Bay

Tarbert

Bhan
100
Ardailly

Druimyeon
Bay

Corriechrevie

Ballo

Auchinafaud

Loch
Ciaran

Escart
Farm

Crossaig

Loch Garasdale

Gigha

Ardminish

Rhunahaorine
Point

Ardminish
Bay

A83

Rhunahaorine

248

Cruach Mhic-
Gougain

Cnoc an t-
Samhlaidh

264

Cour Bay

Cour

16

Craro
Island

Ardmore
Gardens

¼ hr

Narachan
Hill
285

Cnoc
Reamhar
203

Sunadale

Grob Bagh

Tayinloan

Cara Island

Killean

Deucheran Hill
329

Grogport

Whitefarland

Mull
of Cara

Beacharr

Cruach Mhic-an-t- Saoir
364
Cruach nan Gabhar
354

Carradale
Forest

Muasdale

Achaglass

Diollaid
Mhòr
362

33

Glenacardoch
Point

Belloch

A83

Glenbarr

Arnicle

Beinn
Bhreac
426

Beinn
an
Tuirc
454

Rhonadale

Dippen

Torrisdale

Carradale

Carradale
Garden

Carradale
Bay

2

Bellochantuy Bay

Bellochantuy

Bord Mòr
408

Meall
Buidhe
374

Abbey
(ruins)

Whitestone

Saddell

Saddell Bay

Killocraw

Corrylach

Lussa
Loch

Saddell Forest

Sgreadan Hill
397

N

13

Bunlarie

Tangy
Loch

Tangy

Skeroblingarry

Drumgarve
Calliburn

Glen Lussa

Ballochgair

Ugadale Point

3

Machrihanish Bay

Westport

Low Ballevain

Kilchenzie

East Darlochan

A83

Peninver

Ardnacross
Bay

CAMPBELTOWN

Kilmichael

Drumore

Campbeltown
(Ceann Loch
Chille Chiarain)

Davaar Island

Machrihanish

Machrihanish
Water

Dalivaddy

Witchburn

Mus

Davaar

Drumlemble

B843

6

Chiscan

Knocknaha

Kilchrist

Kilkerran

Glenramskill

New Orleans

Earadale Point

The
Slate
385

Conie

Oatfield

K

Beinn
Ghuilean
352

Cnoc
Moy
446

Water

Killellan

10

Arinarach
Hill
312

Feochaig

Ru Stafnish

Rubha
Dùin Bhàin

Largybaan

273

Cnoc
Reamhar

Glen Breackerie

Cnoc
Odhar
277

Brecklate

Conie Glen

Glen Kerran

Sheanachie

Strone
Glen

Keprigan

Kildavie

Beinn
na Lice
428

South Point

Carrine

Garveld

Feorlan

Southend

Keil

Macharioch

Polliwilline Bay

Mull
of Kintyre

Carskey Bay

Borgadelmore Point

Sanda Sound

Sheep Island

Sanda
Island

0     2     4     6 miles

0   2   4   6   8   10 km

B

C

D

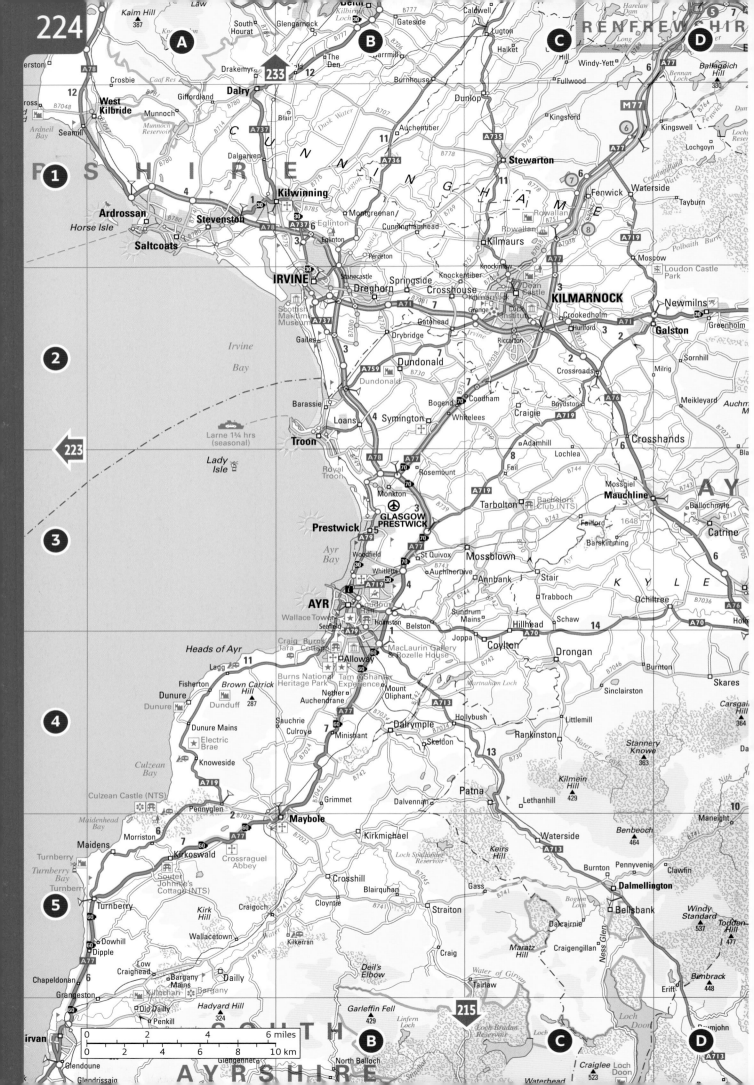

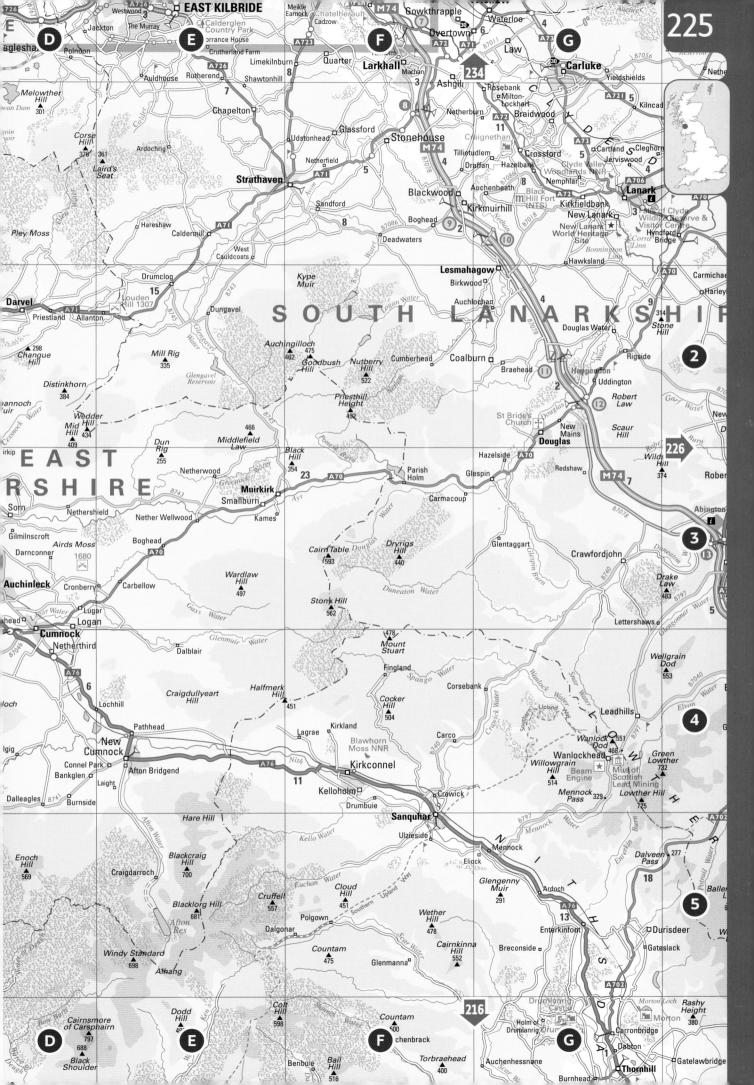

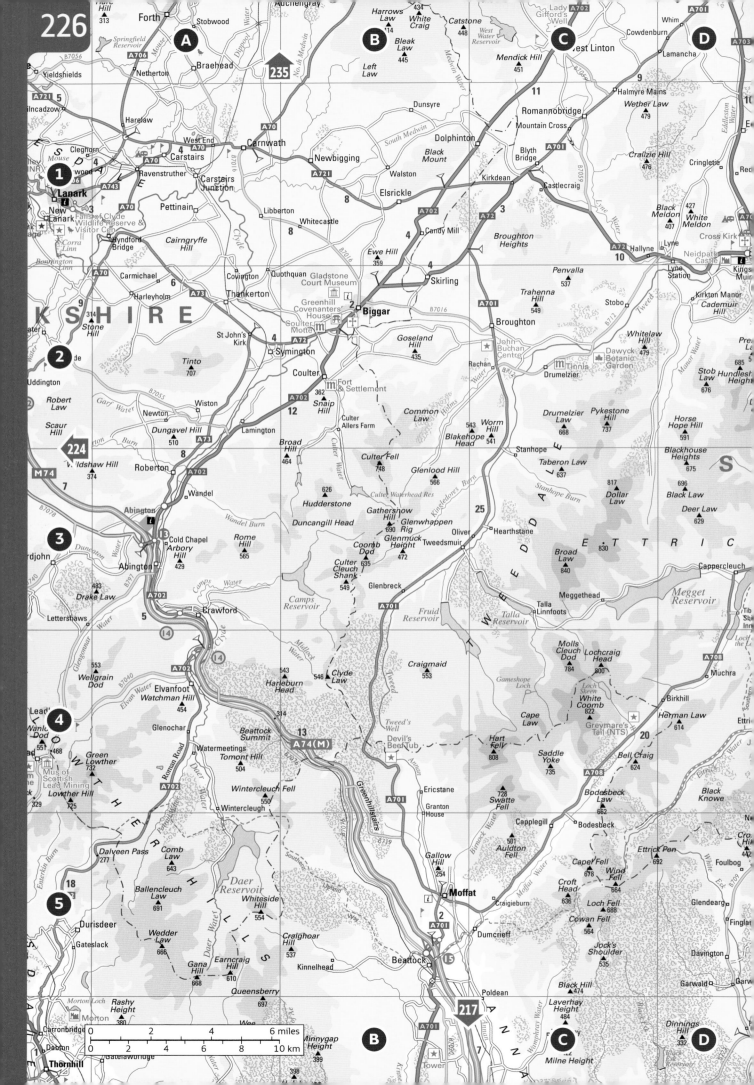

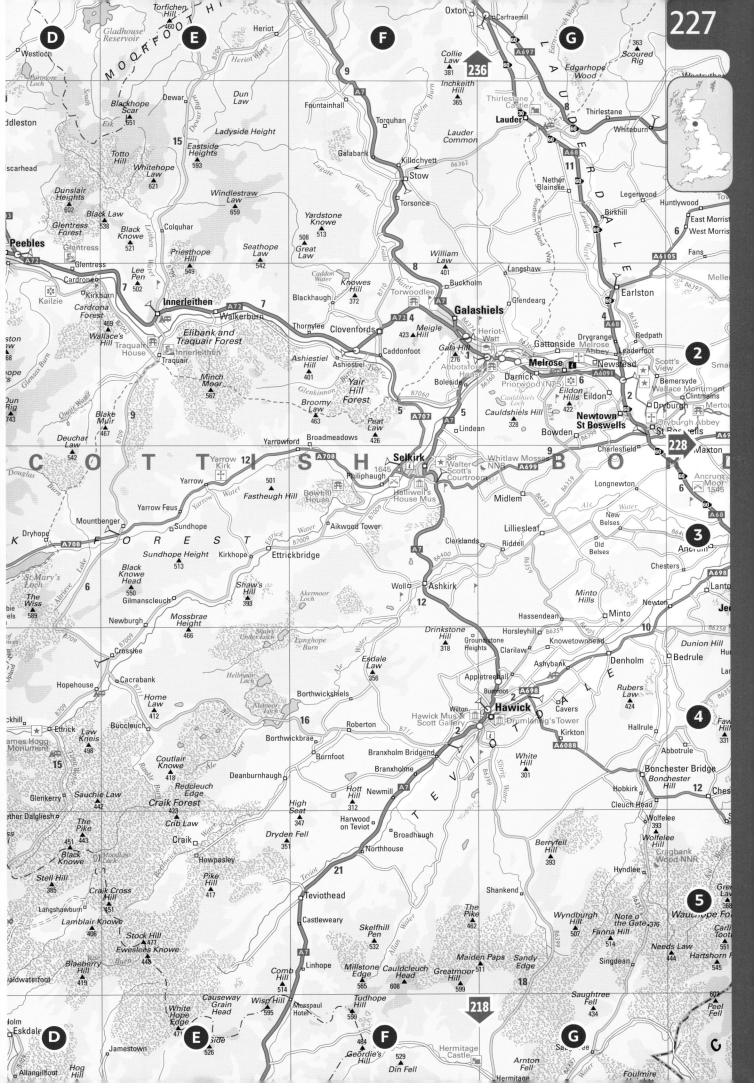

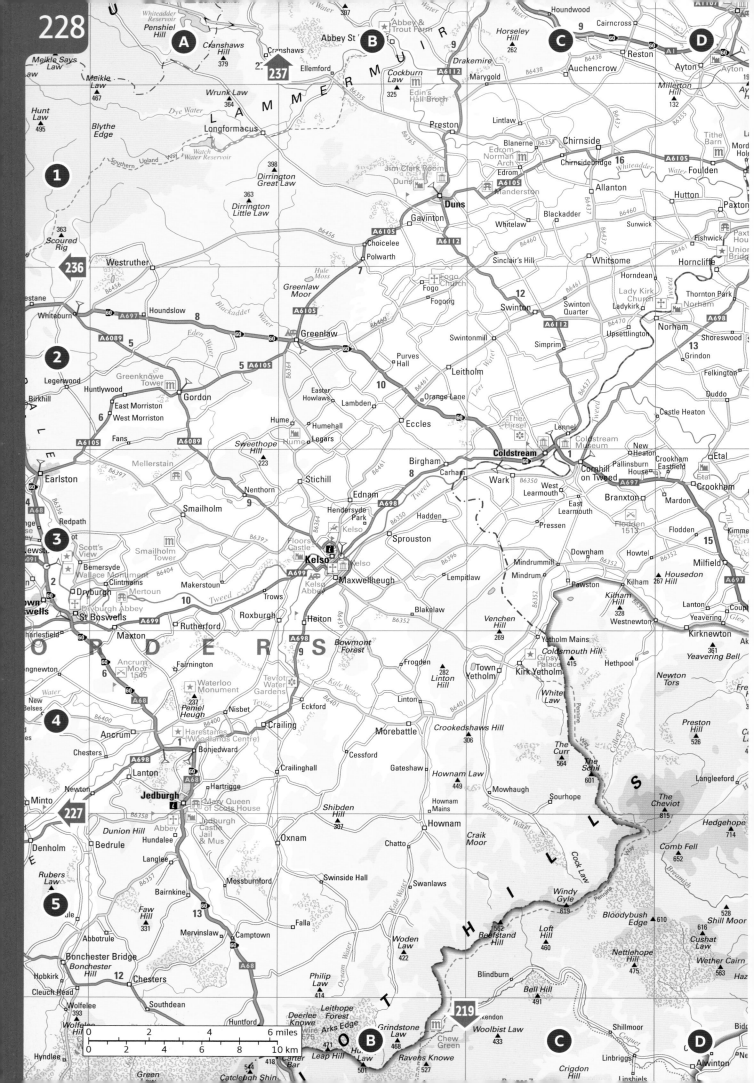

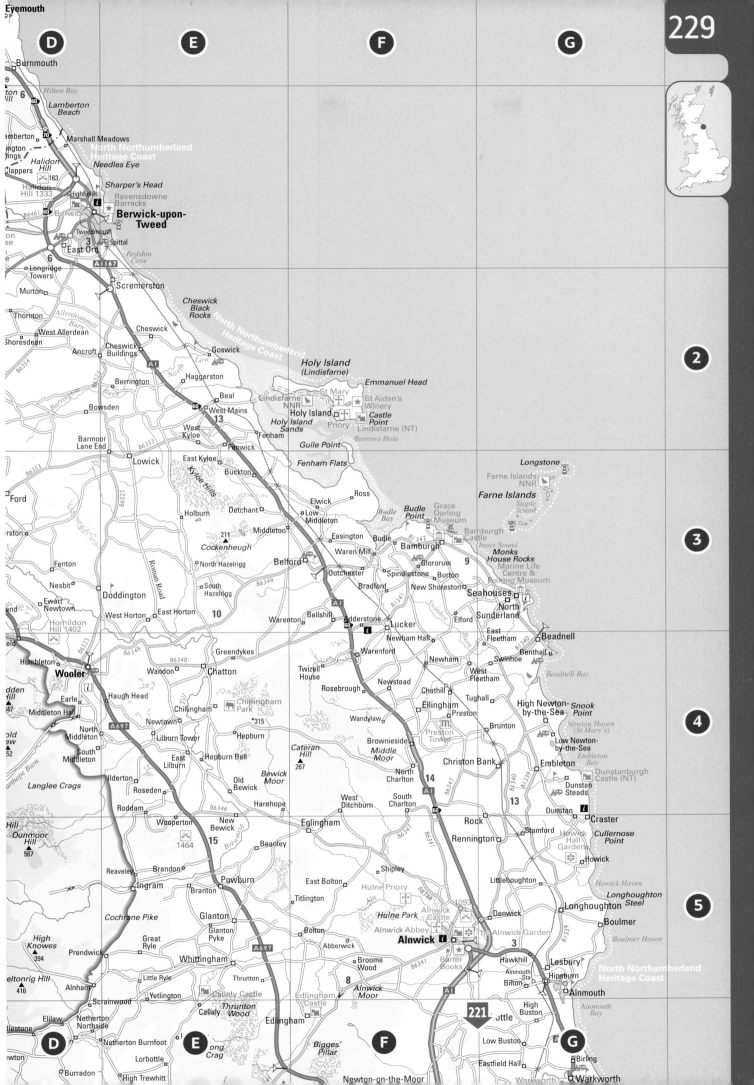

A  B  C  D

**COLONSAY**

Port Mòr
Scalasaig
Machrins
Loch Staosnaig
Kilchattan
Balerominbdubh
238
Sguide an Leanna
Garvard
Rubha Dubh
Port L
Balerominmore
Eilean Mhucaig
Rubha Bàn
Dubh Eilean
Priory
Oronsay
Eilean nan Ron
Caolas Mòr
Eilean Ghaoideamal

Shian Bay

1

1¼ hrs (seasonal)

A

Sgeir Mhòr a' Bhrein- phuirt
Rubh' an t- Sàilein

Loch Tarbert
Rubh' a' Chrois-aoinidh

Rubh' a' Mhàil
Rubha Bholsa
Glenbatrick
Scrinadle
506
Beinn Bhreac
439
Beinn Tarsuir
416

Sgarbh Breac
364
283
Margadale Hill
Giur-bheinn
316
Bunnahabhain
Ardnahoe
Loch Staoisha
Balulive
Keills
Port Askaig
Feolin Ferry

Beinn an Oir
785
Jura Forest
Beinn Shiantaidh
755
a' Beinn Chaolais
734
Loch a' Chnuic Bhric
Paps of Jura
Gleann Asdale
Loch an t-Siob
Corran
Knockro

2

Na Peileirean
Nave Island
Ardnave Point
Gortantaoid Point
Killinallan Point
Killinallan
Beinn Bhreac
286
Loch Gruinart
Ardnave
Tayovullin
Kilnave
Carraig Bhàn
Ton Mhòr
Sanaigmore
Loch Finlaggan
Loch Cam
Ballygrant
8
Kilmeny
Loch Ballygrant
Loch Lossit

Glas Bheinn
561
Feolin
Keils
Dubh Bheinn
530
Craighouse
342
Brat Bheinn
Cabrach
Ardfin
Jura House
Am Fraoch Eilean
Brosdale Island
Sannaig
Crackaig
Rubha na Tràille

3

Eilean Mòr
Braigo
Leckgruinart
Rubha Lamanais
Smaull
Ballinaby
Carnduncan
Aoradh
Grainel
Craigens
Saligo Bay
B8017
I S L A Y
Coul Point
Machrie
Aruadh
Foreland
Lyrabus
B8018
Loch Gorm
Rockside
Conisby
Blackrock
Islay House
Kilchoman
Moin'a'choire
Esknish
Redhouses
Machir Bay
Bruichladdich
Bridgend
Cachlaidh Mhòr
Neriby
Barr
Cattadale
Kilchiaran
Gartnatra
Bowmore
Ronnachmore
Cruach
Cluanach
Kilchiaran Bay
Port Charlotte
15
Gearach
Gartbreck
Tormisdale
Carn
Beinn Tart a' Mhill
232
Nerabus
Lossit
Kelsay
Laggan
Rubha na Faing
Easter Ellister
A847
Portnahaven
Port Wemyss
Orsay
Rinns Point
Lossit Bay
RINNS OF ISLAY
Loch Indaal
Laggan
Dutch
13
A846
ISLAY
Glenegedale
Machrie
Loch Uraraidh
Beinn Uraraidh
454
Kilennan
Beinn Bhan
471
Beinn Bheigeir
491
Ardtalla
Rubha Liath
Kintour
Loch Uigeadail
Sgorr Bhogachain
Beinn Sholum
347
Kildalton Church & Crosses
Ardmore Point
Ardmore

Redhouses
Esknish
8
A846
Sgorr nam Faoileann
429
Beinn na Caillich
337
Glas Bheinn
471
McArthur's Head
Proaig
2 hrs
Claggain Bay
Trudernish

5

Machrie
Kintra
Rubha Mòr
Leorin
Leorin Lochs
Maol Buidhe
165
Cornabus
Laggan Bay
THE OA
Lower Killeyan
Risabus
Carnmore
Inerval
Loch Kinnabus
Mull of Oa
Port Chubaird
The Ard
Texa
Port Ellen
A846
Lagavulin
Laphroaig
Ardbeg
Rubha na Gainmhich
Eilean a' Chuirn
Eilean Bhride
2¼ hrs
Caolas an Eilein
Rubha nan Leacan

0   2   4   6 miles
0  2  4  6  8  10 km

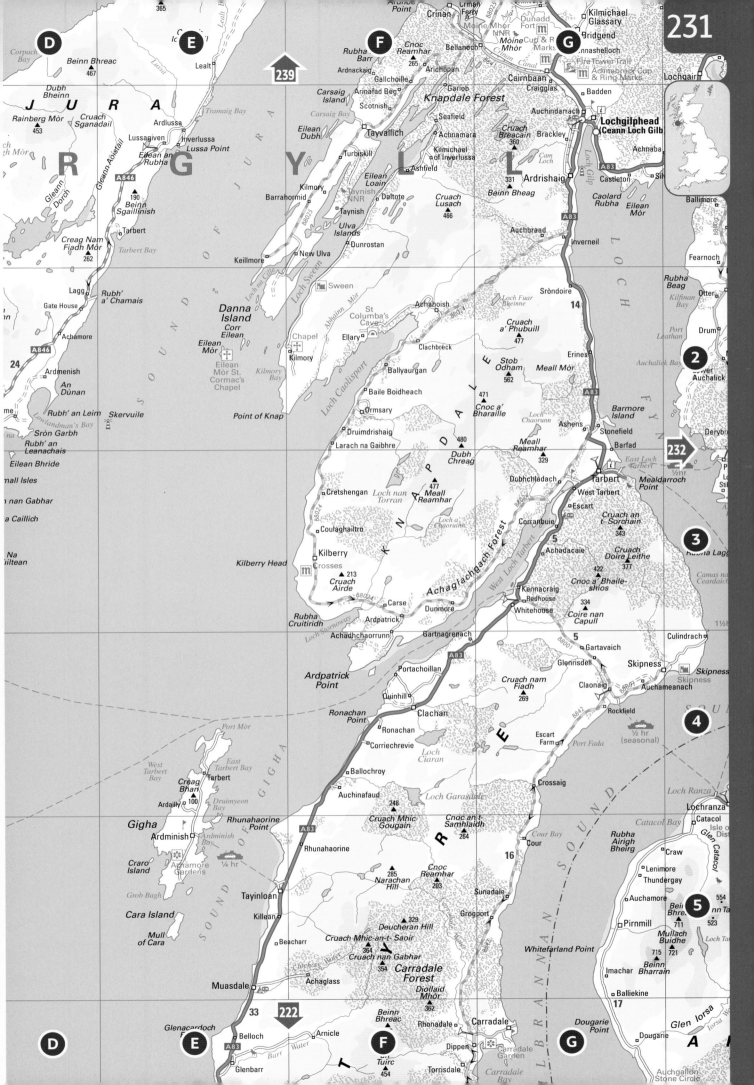

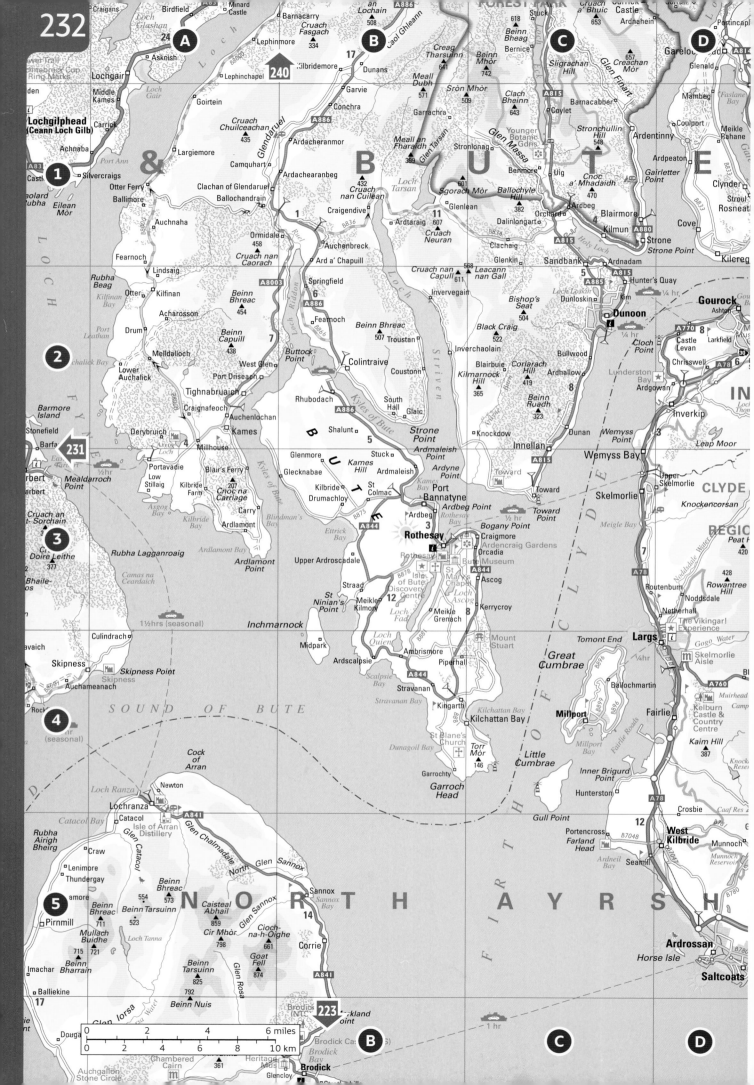

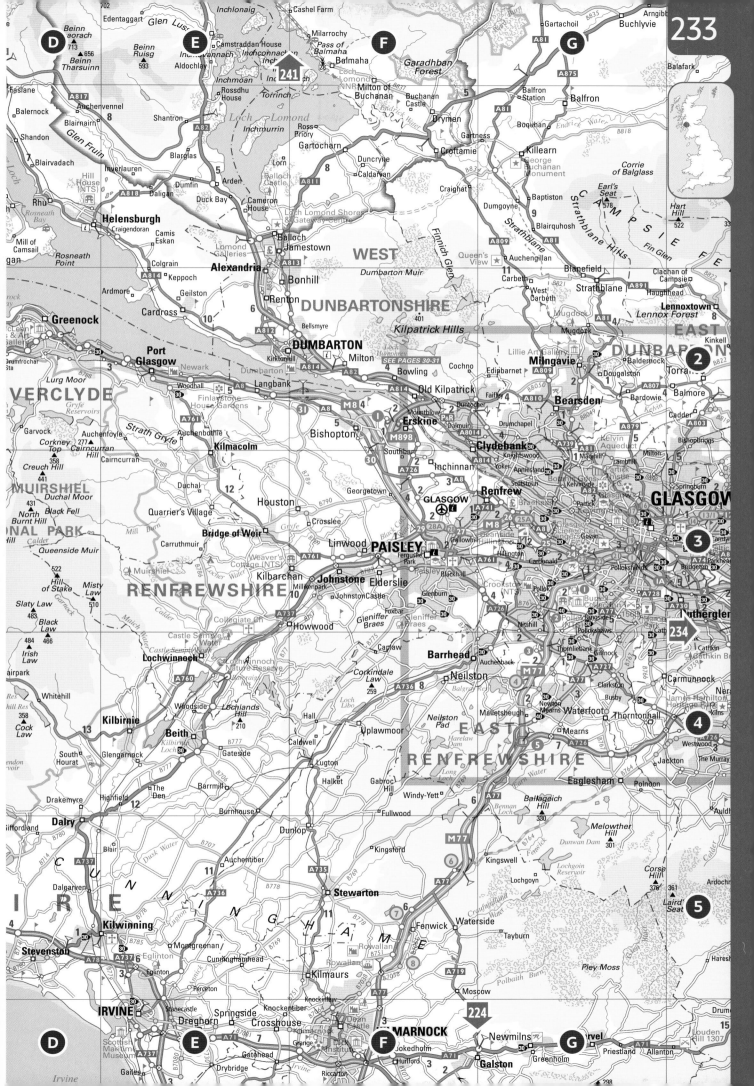

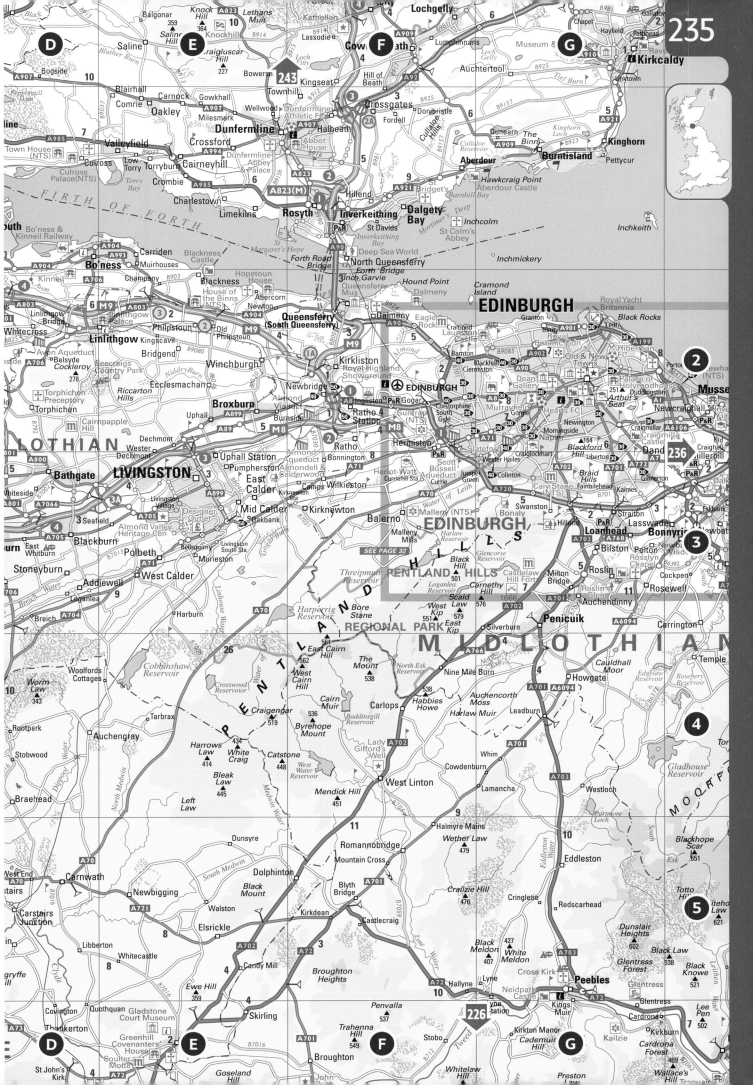

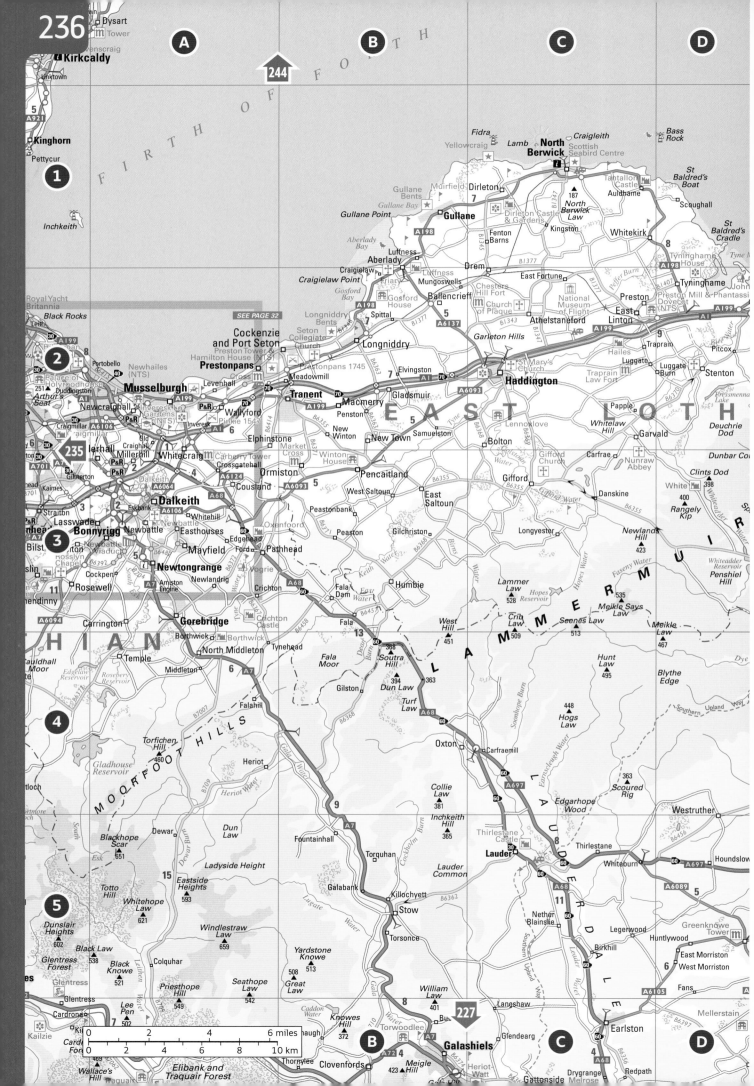

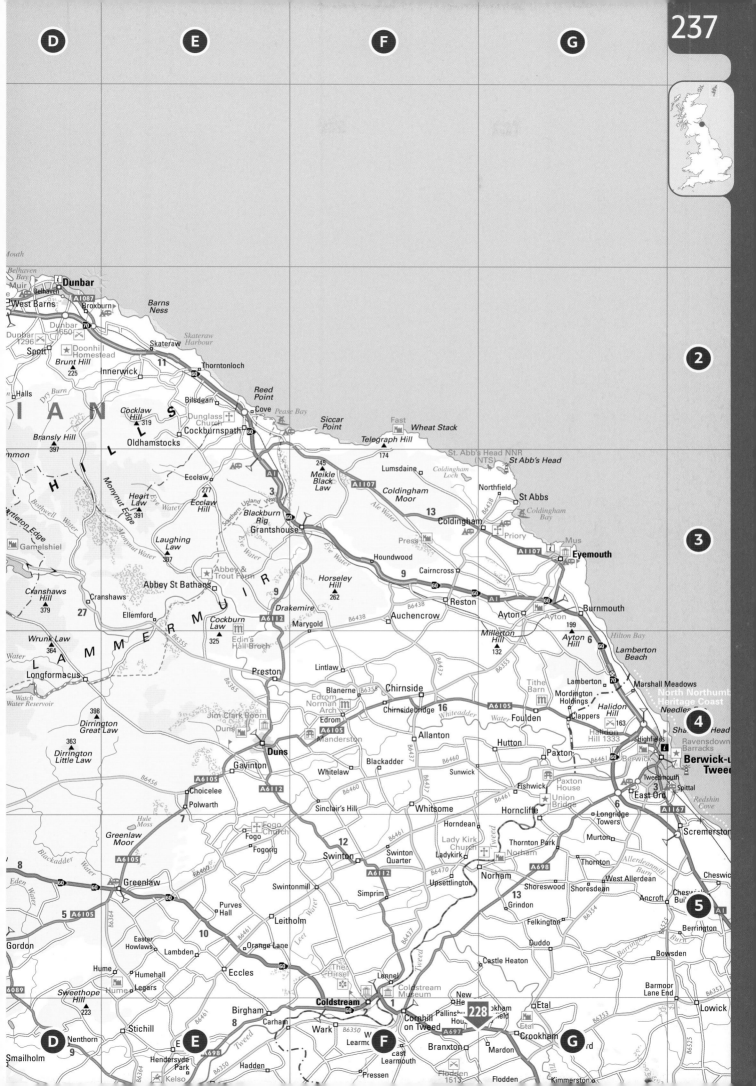

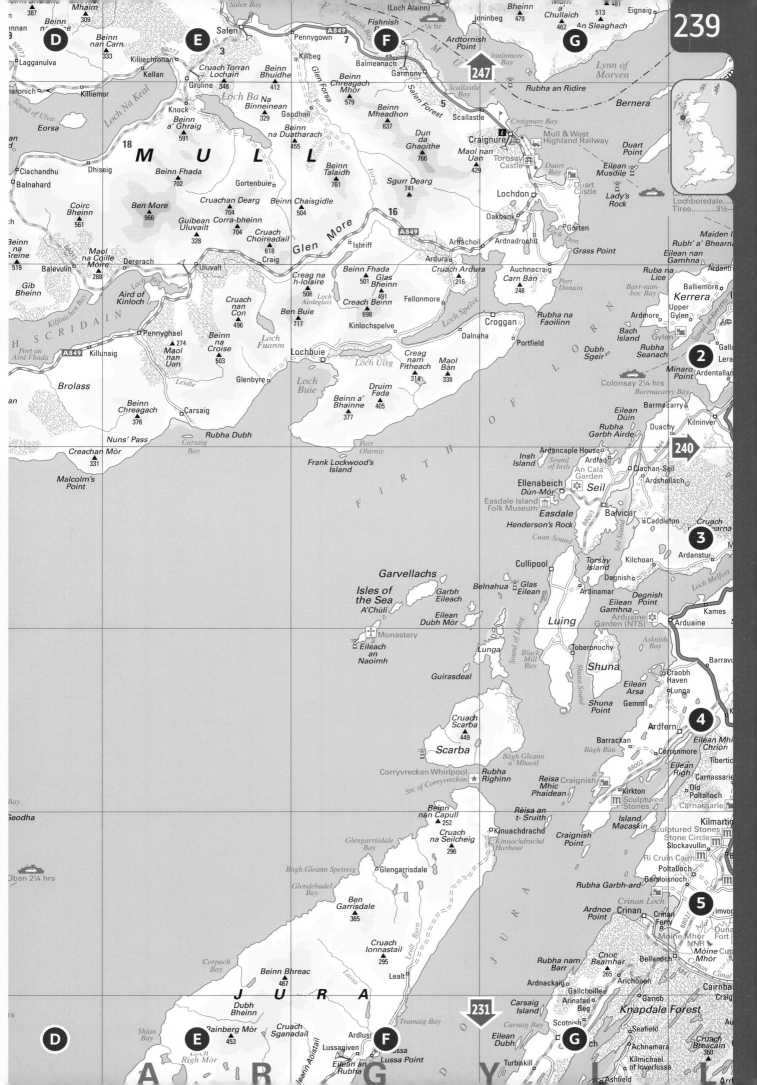

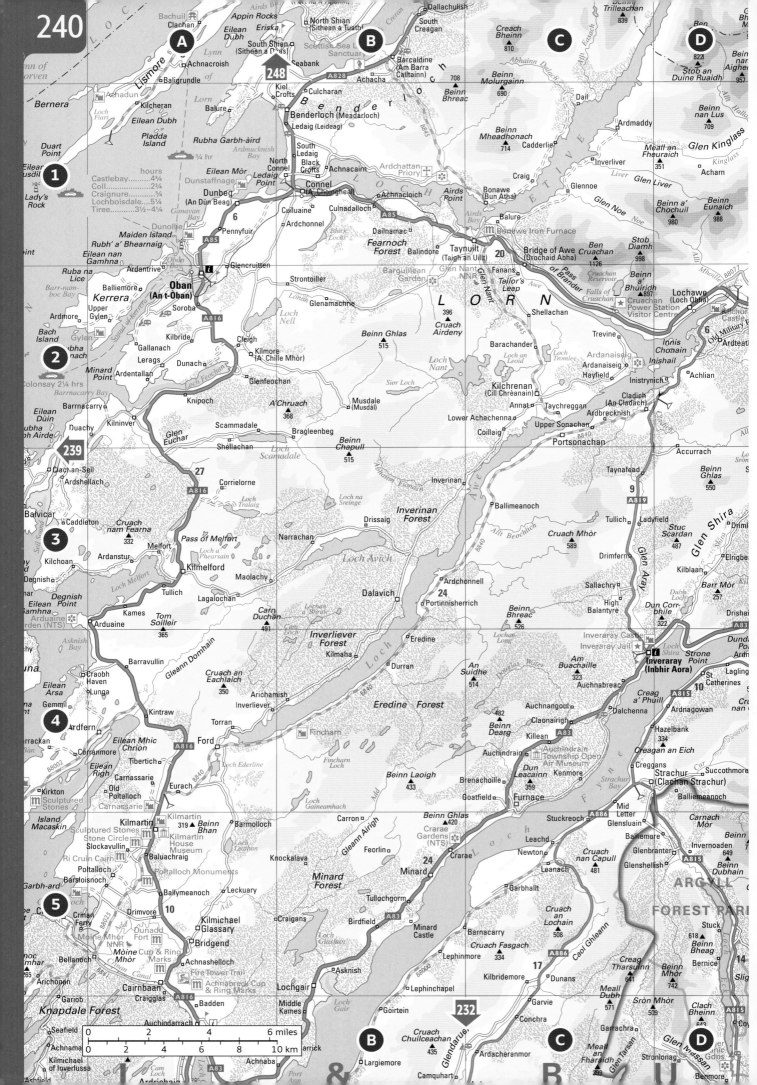

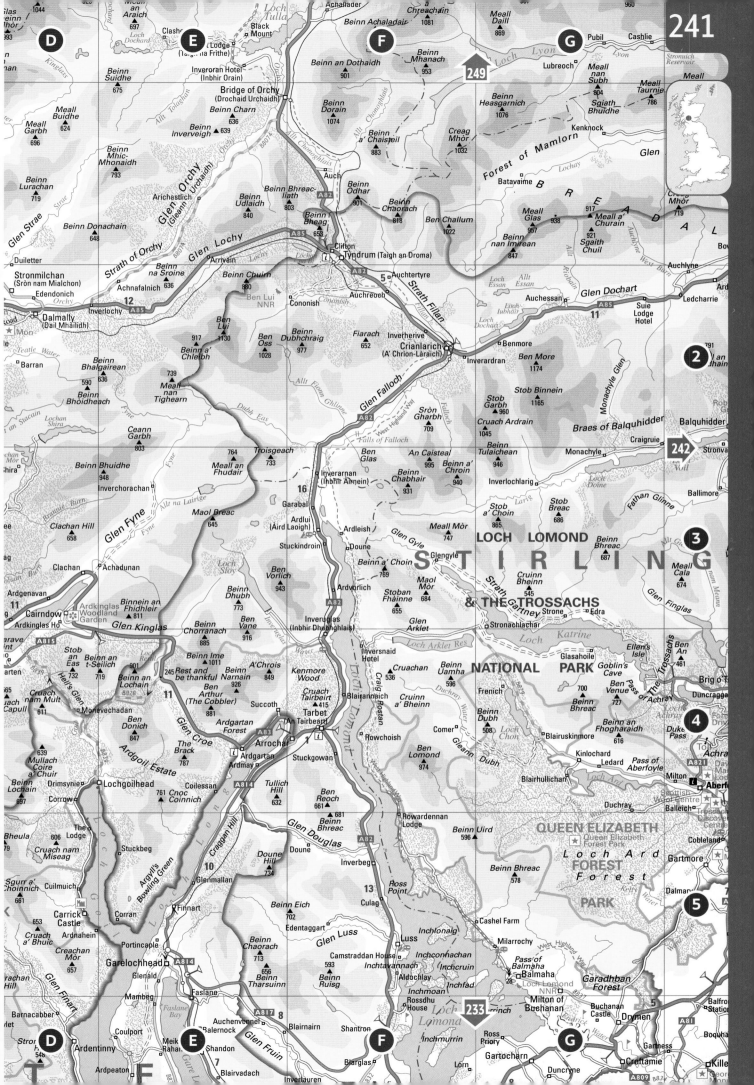

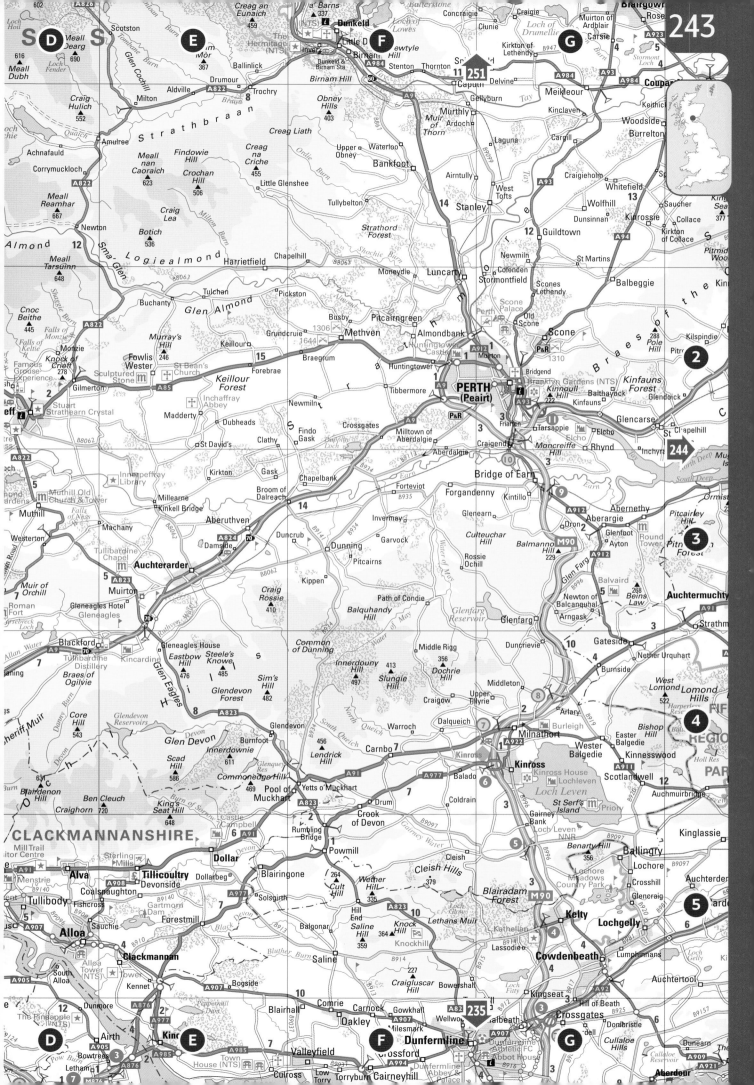

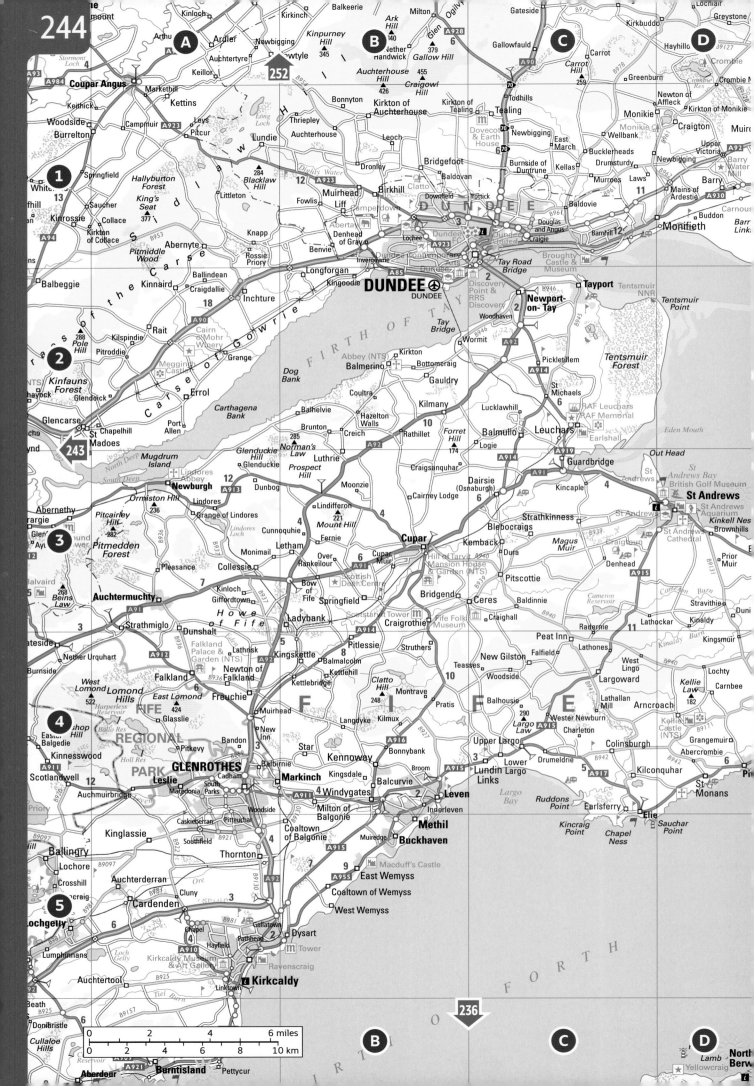

Carmyll
Denhead of
birlot
Guy
D
St Vigeans
E
Meg's
Craig
Carlingheugh
Bay
F
G
Arbirlot
B9127
The Deil's Heid
Mill
Bonnyton
Easter
Knox
A92
Elliot
Arbroath Abbey
Arbroath
253
drum
Salmond's Muir
6
A92
East Haven
2
Panbride
Carnoustie
stie
s
Buddon Ness

Bell Rock
(Inchcape)

2

Buddo Ness
Boarhills
Babbet Ness

3

10 A917
Kingsbarns
Cambo
Estate
Cambo
Ness
North
Carr
Kenly Water
no
Tullybothy Craigs
Wormiston
Craighead
Kippo Burn
Fife Ness
B946
Airdrie
B9171
Crail
Spalefield
4 A917
West Ness

4

Innergellie
Kilrenny
Cellardyke
Anstruther
Scottish Fisheries Museum
ttenweem

North Ness
Isle of May NNR
Isle of May
Chapel
South Ness

5

237

Craig
D
Bass Rock
E
F
G
rick
Scottish
Seabird
Centre

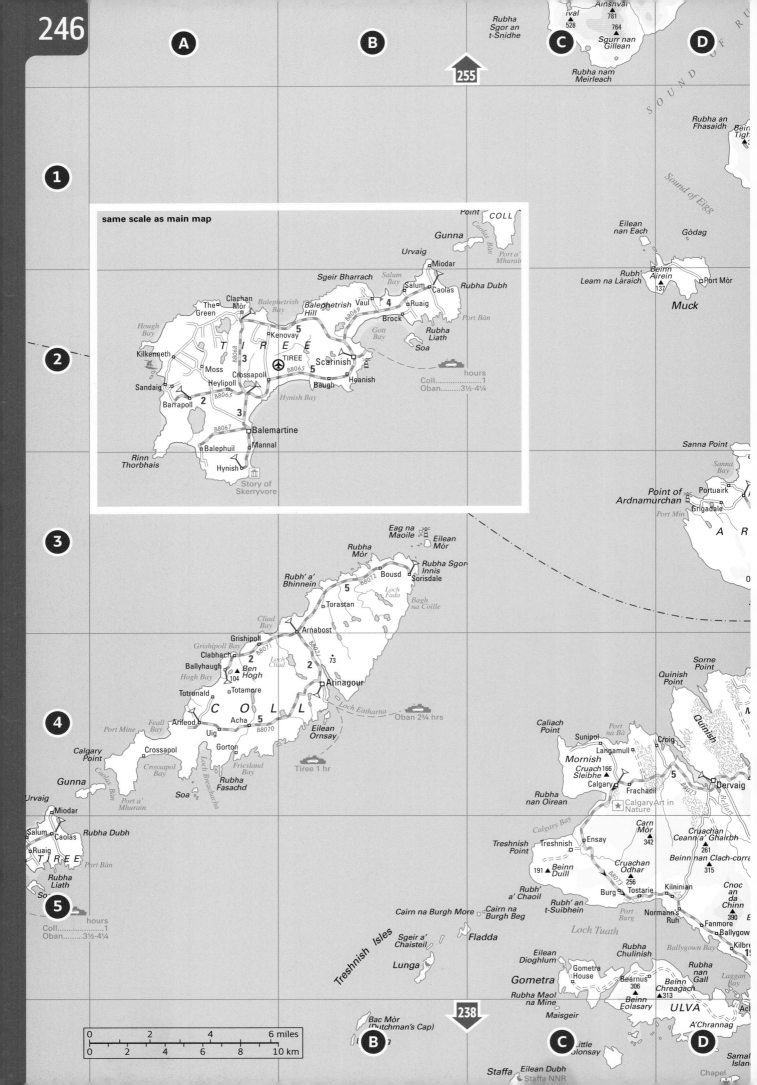

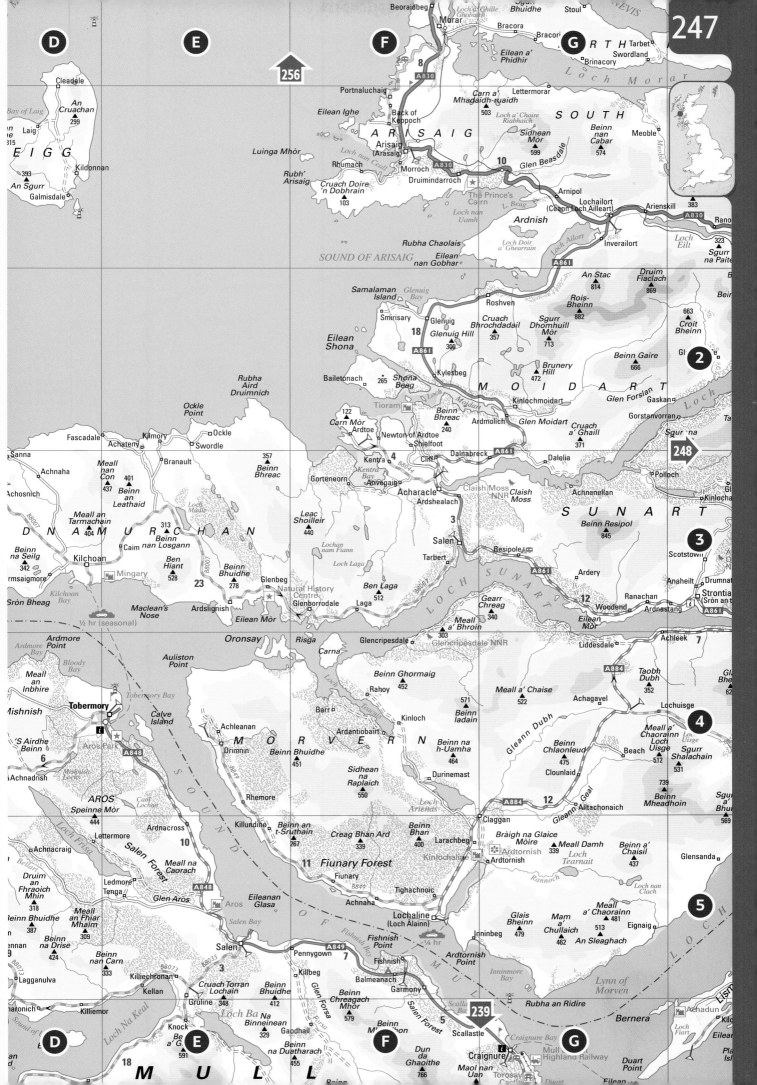

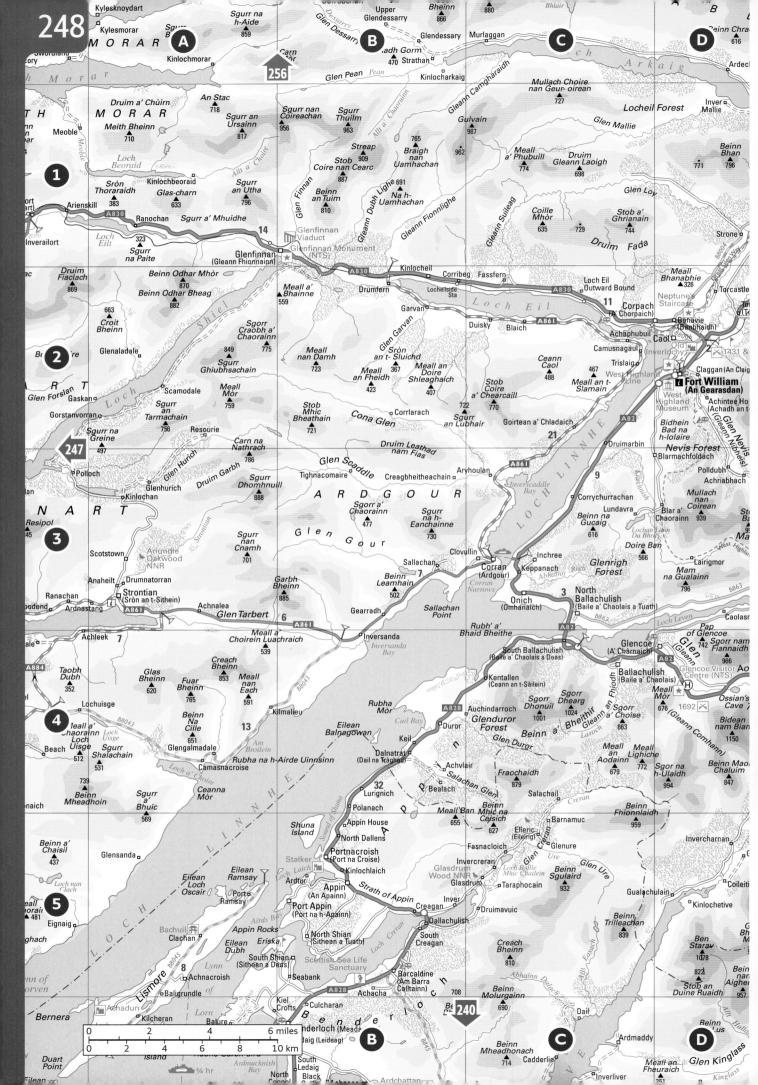

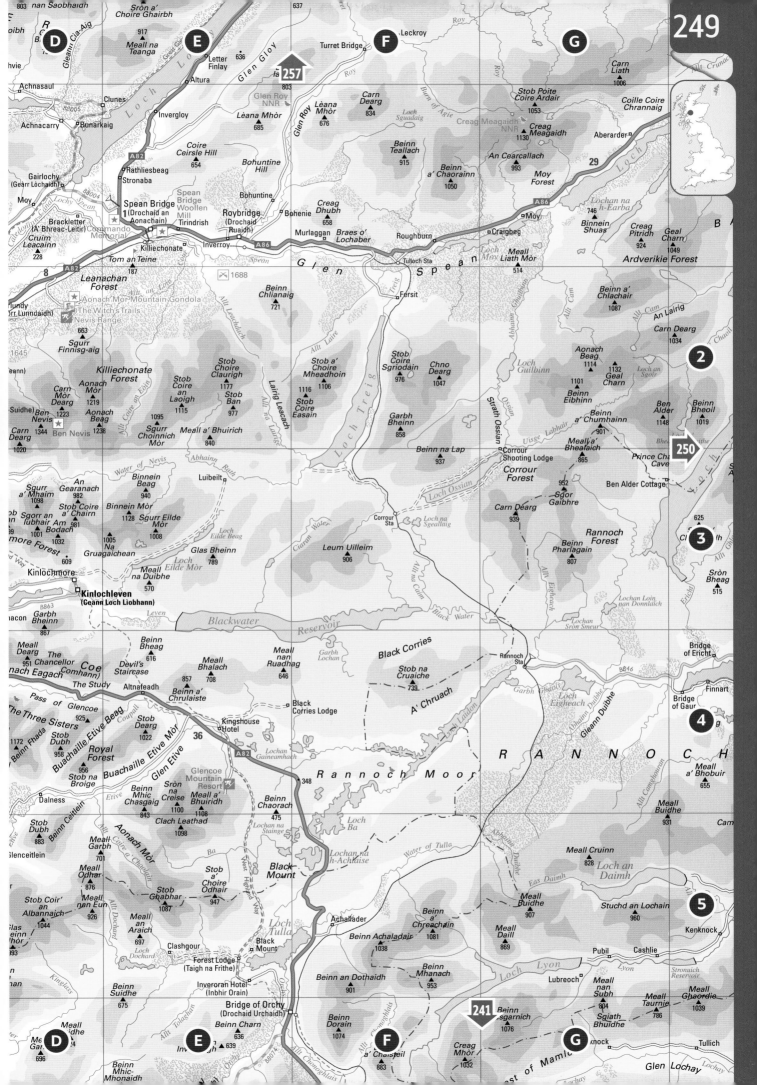

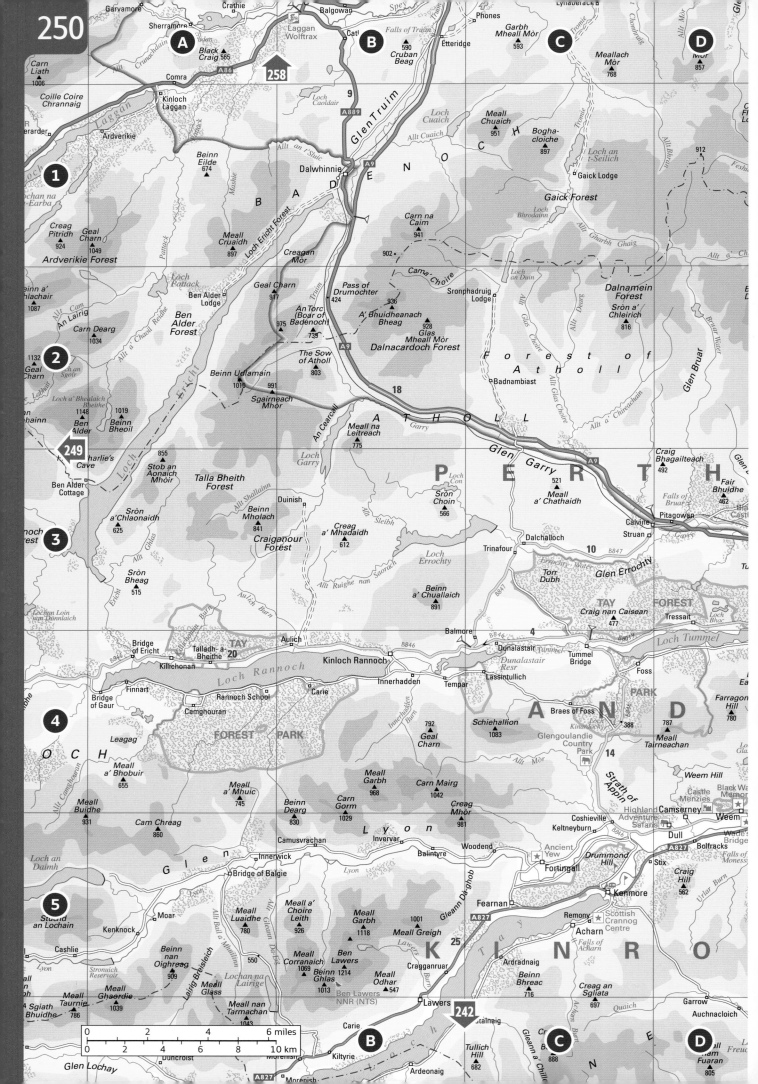

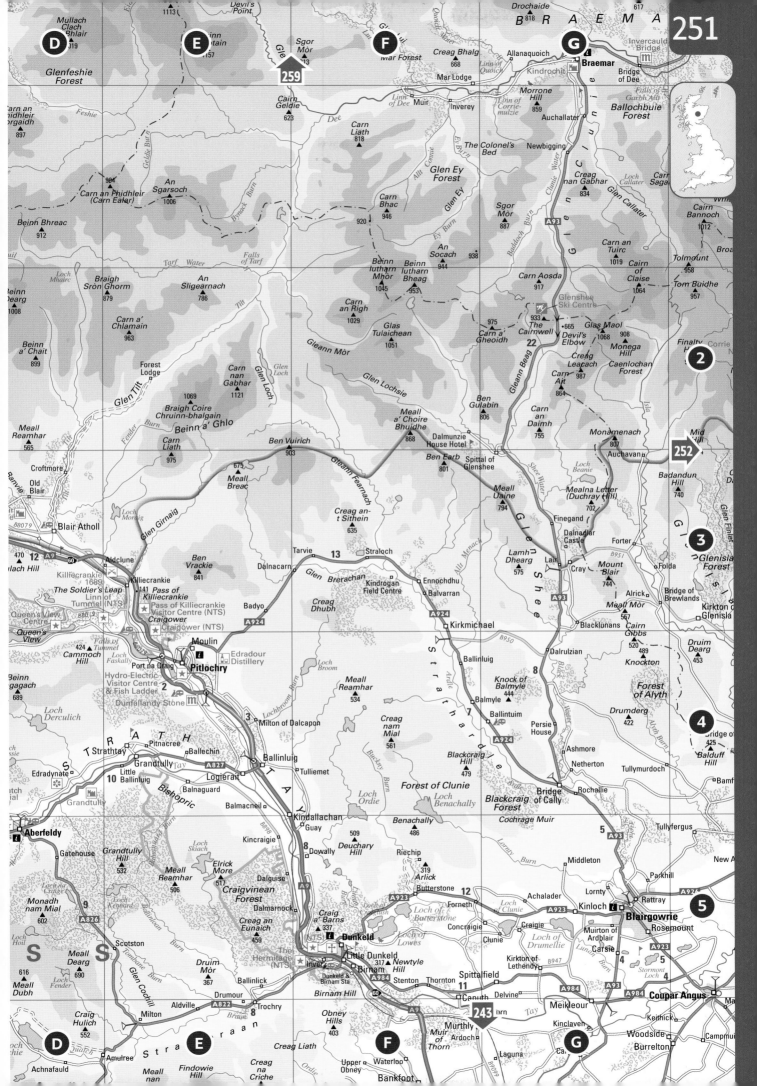

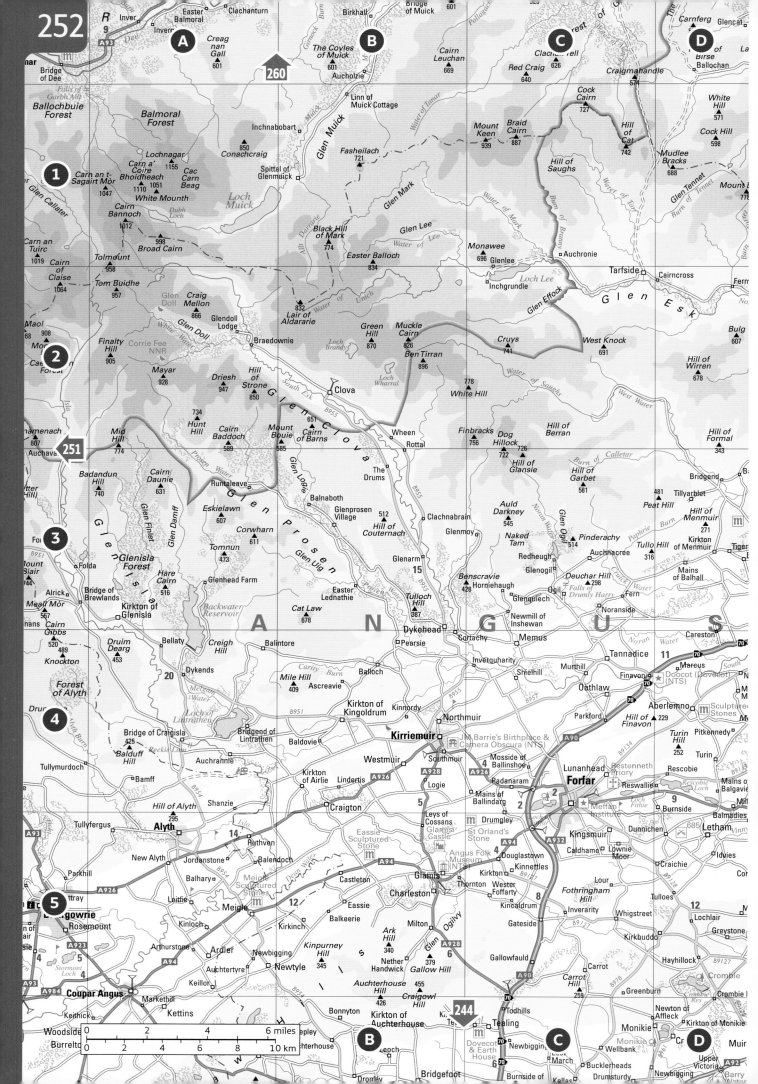

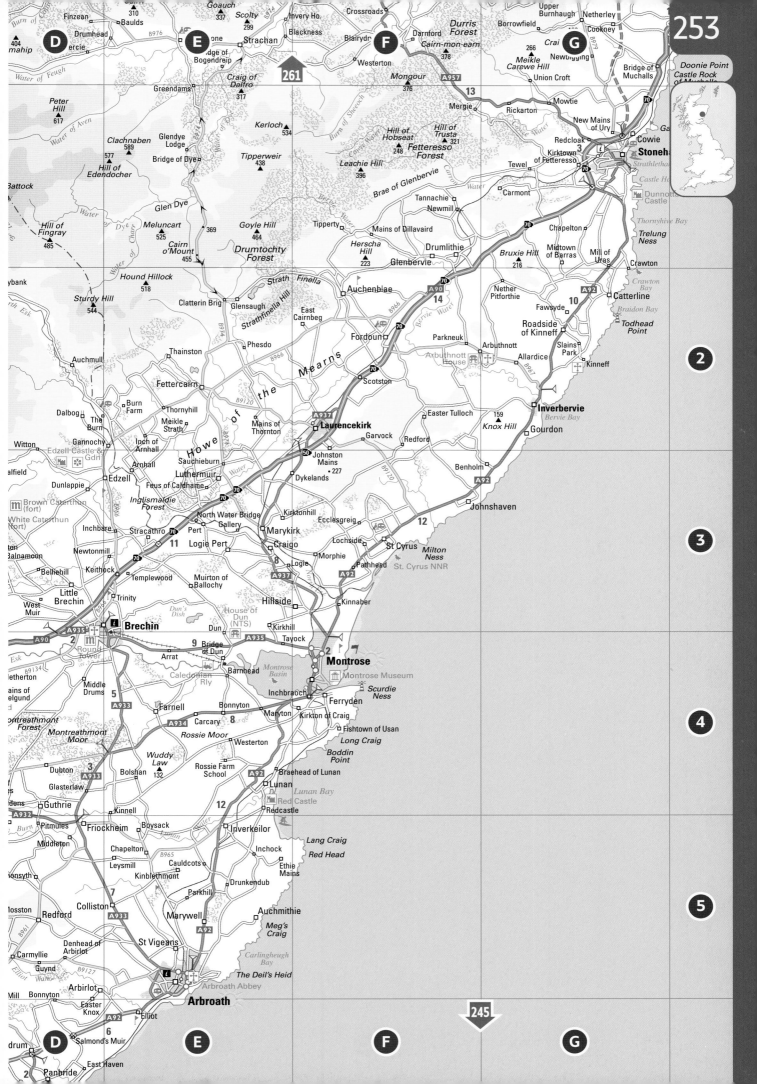

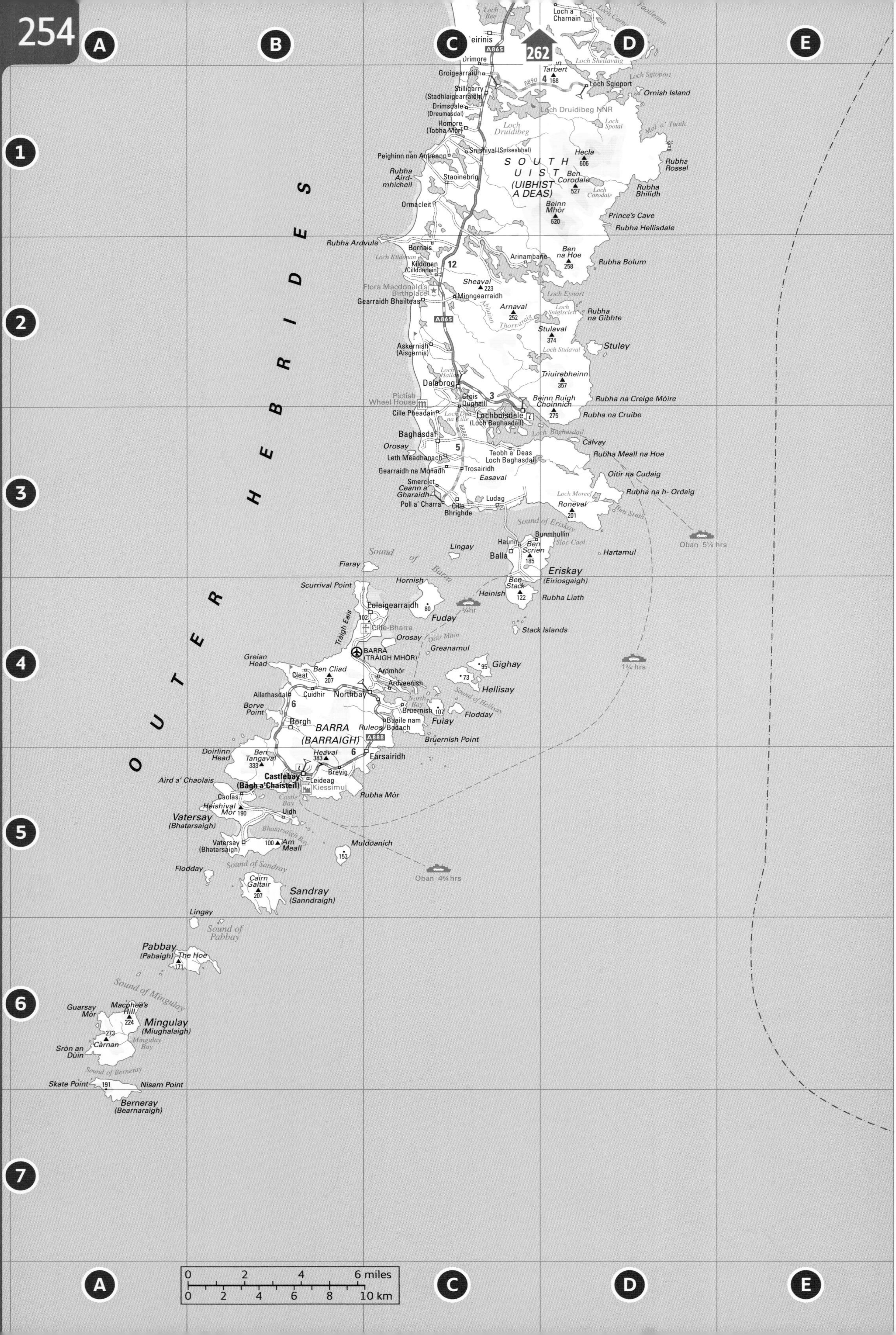

A
B
C
D
E
1
2
3
4
5
6
7
262
Loch Bee
Eirinis
A865
Loch a Charnain
Loch Carnan
Faoileann
Drimore
Tarbert
168
Loch Sheilavaig
Groigearraidh
Loch Sgioport
B890
Loch Sgioport
Ornish Island
Stilligarry (Stadhlaigearraidh)
Drimsdale (Dreumasdal)
Loch Druidibeg NNR
Homore (Tobha Mòr)
Loch Druidibeg
Loch Spotal
Mol a' Tuath
Snishival (Sniseabhal)
Peighinn nan Aoireann
Hecla
606
SOUTH UIST (UIBHIST A DEAS)
Rubha Rossel
Rubha Aird-mhicheil
Staoinebrig
Ben Corodale
527
Loch Corodale
Rubha Bhilidh
Ormacleit
Beinn Mhòr
620
Prince's Cave
Rubha Hellisdale
Rubha Ardvule
Bornais
Loch Kildonan
Kildonan (Cilldonnain)
12
Arinambane
Ben na Hoe
258
Rubha Bolum
Flora Macdonald's Birthplace
Sheaval
223
Gearraidh Bhailteas
Minngearraidh
Loch Eynort
Arnaval
252
Abhainn Thornaraig
Loch Snigisclett
Rubha na Gibhte
A865
Stulaval
374
Askernish (Aisgernis)
Loch Stulaval
Stuley
Loch Hallan
Triuirebheinn
357
Dalabrog
Pictish Wheel House
Crois Dughaill
3
Beinn Ruigh Choinnich
Rubha na Creige Mòire
Cille Pheadair
Loch Dùn na Cille
Lochboisdale (Loch Baghasdail)
275
Rubha na Cruibe
B888
Baghasdal
Loch Baghasdail
Calvay
Orosay
5
Taobh a' Deas Loch Baghasdail
Rubha Meall na Hoe
Leth Meadhanach
Gearraidh na Monadh
Trosairidh
Oitir na Cudaig
Smerclet
Easaval
Ceann a' Gharaidh
Loch Moreef
Rubha na h- Ordaig
Poll a' Charra
Cille Bhrighde
Ludag
Roneval
201
Bun Sruth
Sound of Eriskay
Bunmhullin
Oban 5¼ hrs
Haunn
Ben Scrien
Sloc Caol
Lingay
Hartamul
Sound of Barra
Balla
185
Fiaray
Eriskay (Eiriosgaigh)
Hornish
Ben Stack
Scurrival Point
Heinish
122
Rubha Liath
Eolaigearraidh
80
¾hr
Fuday
Tràigh Eais
102
Cille-Bharra
Stack Islands
Orosay
Oitir Mhòr
BARRA (TRAIGH MHÒR)
Greanamul
Greian Head
95
Gighay
1¾ hrs
Ben Cliad
207
Ardmhòr
Cleat
73
Ardveenish
Hellisay
Allathasdal
Cuidhir
Northbay
Sound of Hellisay
North Bay
Borve Point
6
Bruernish
107
Flodday
Fuiay
Borgh
BARRA (BARRAIGH)
Ruleos
Buaile nam Bodach
A888
Bruernish Point
Doirlinn Head
Ben Tangaval
333
Heaval
383
6
Earsairidh
Brevig
Castlebay (Bàgh a' Chaisteil)
Aird a' Chaolais
Leideag
Kiessimul
Caolas
Castle Bay
Rubha Mòr
Heishival Mòr
190
Uidh
Vatersay (Bhatarsaigh)
Bhatarsaigh Bay
Vatersay (Bhatarsaigh)
100
Am Meall
Muldoanich
153
Sound of Sandray
Flodday
Oban 4¾ hrs
Cairn Galtair
207
Sandray (Sanndraigh)
Lingay
Sound of Pabbay
Pabbay (Pabaigh)
The Hoe
171
Sound of Mingulay
Guarsay Mòr
Macphee's Hill
224
Mingulay (Miughalaigh)
273
Càrnan
Mingulay Bay
Sròn an Dùin
Sound of Berneray
Skate Point
191
Nisam Point
Berneray (Bearnaraigh)
OUTER HEBRIDES
0 2 4 6 miles
0 2 4 6 8 10 km

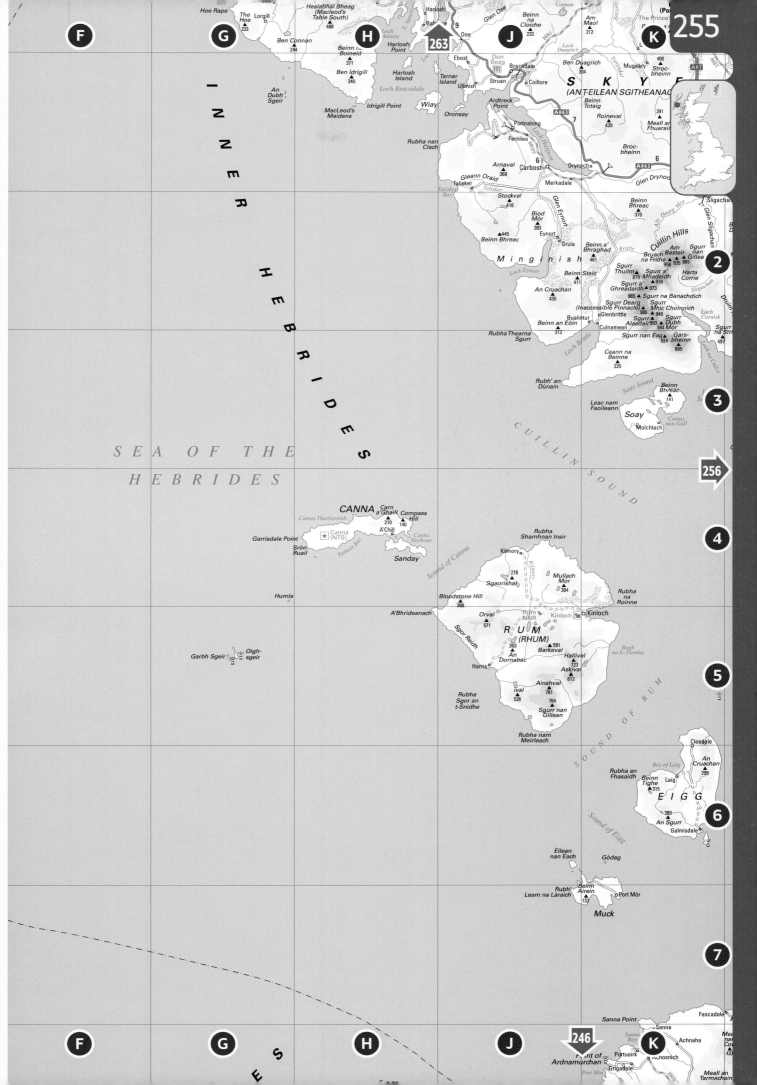

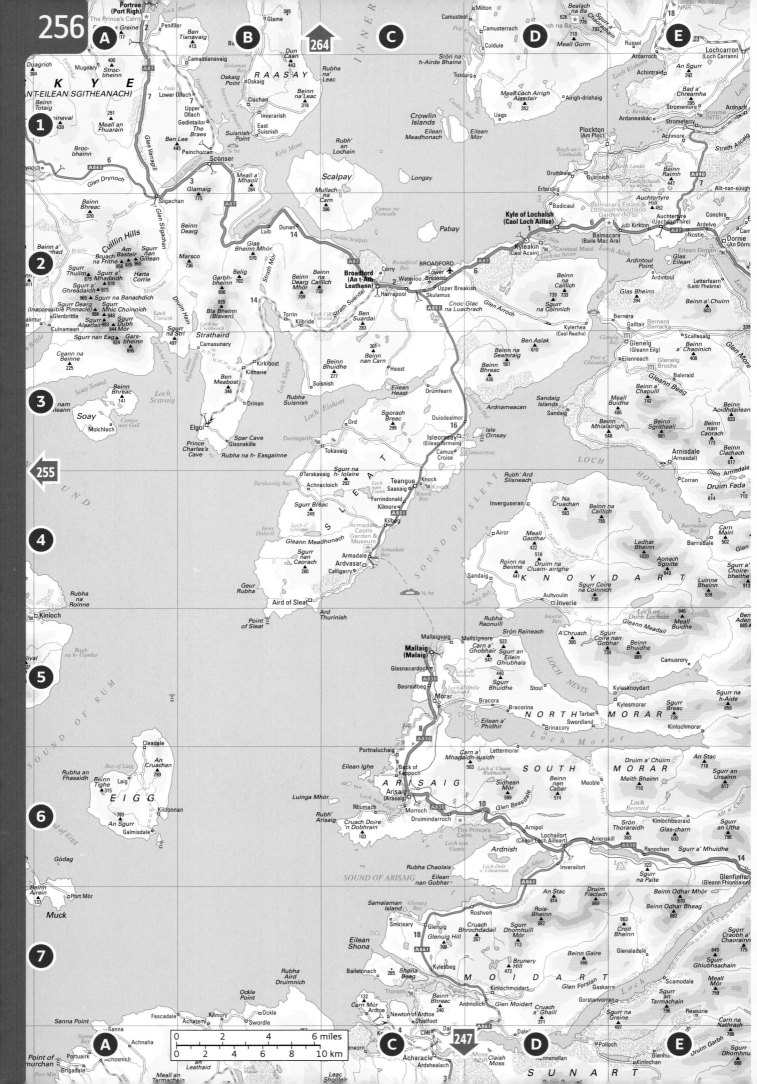

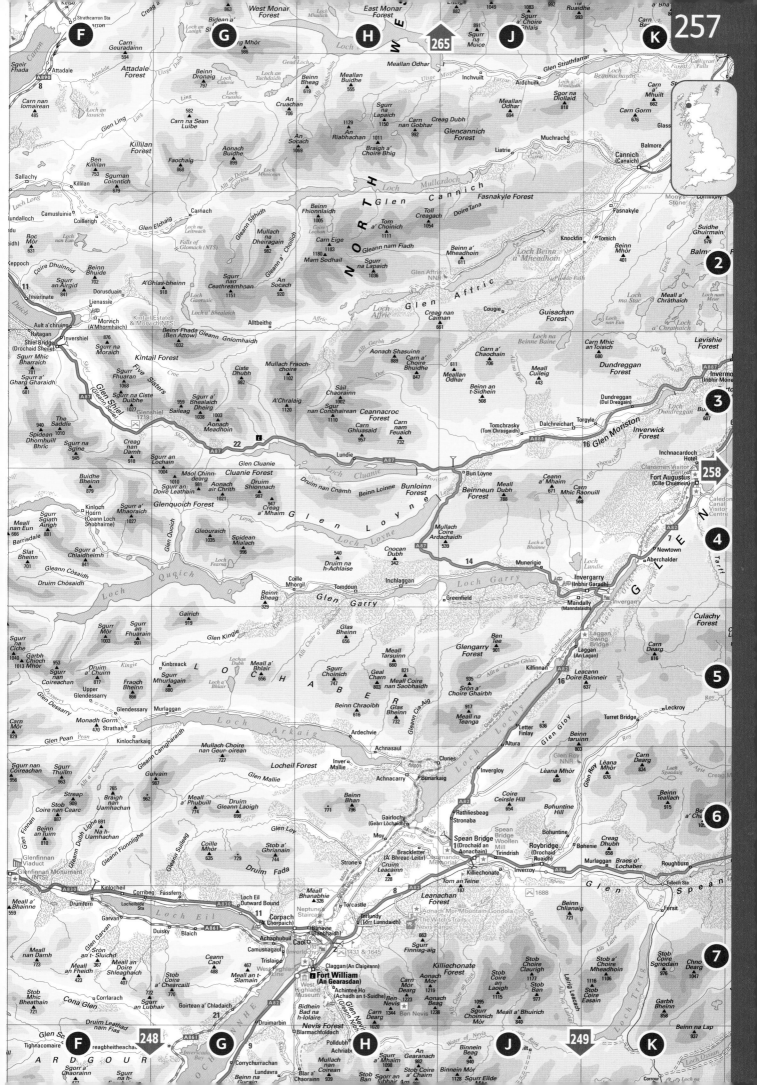

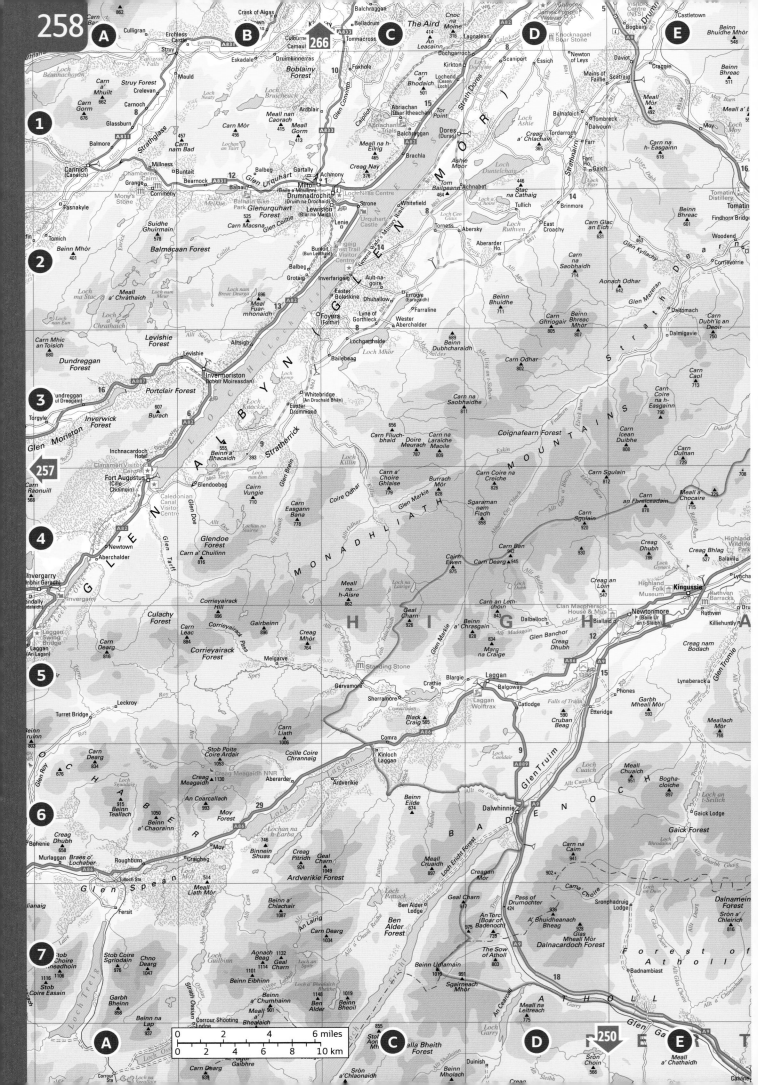

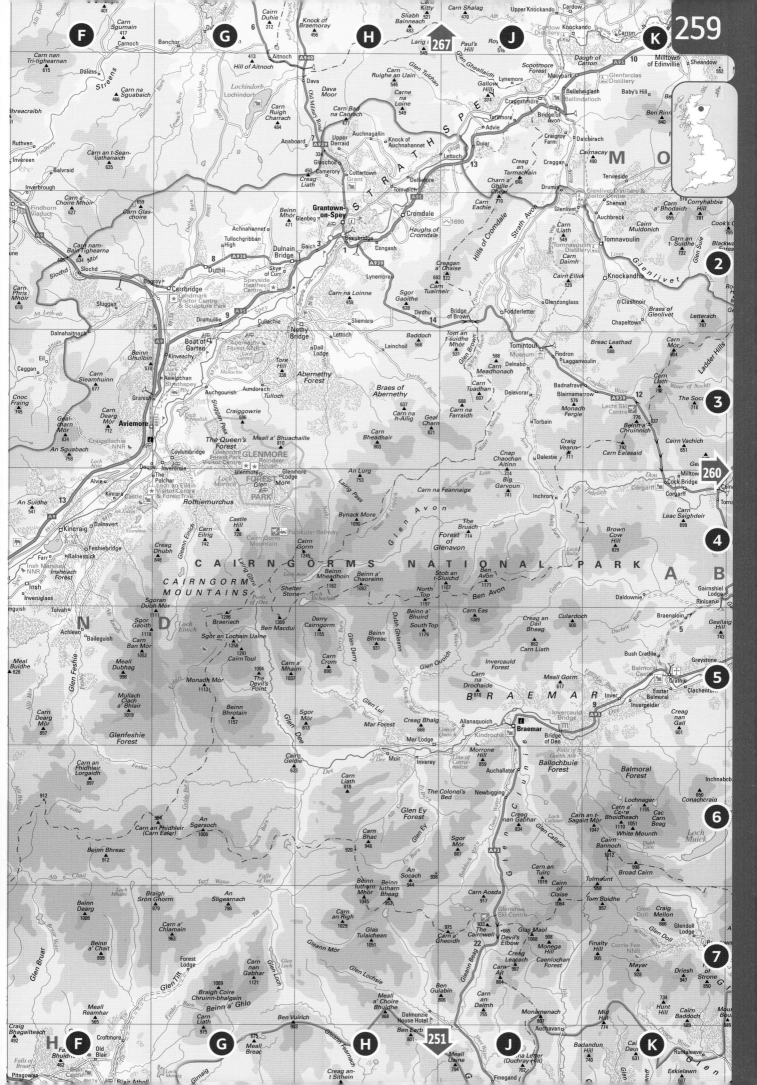

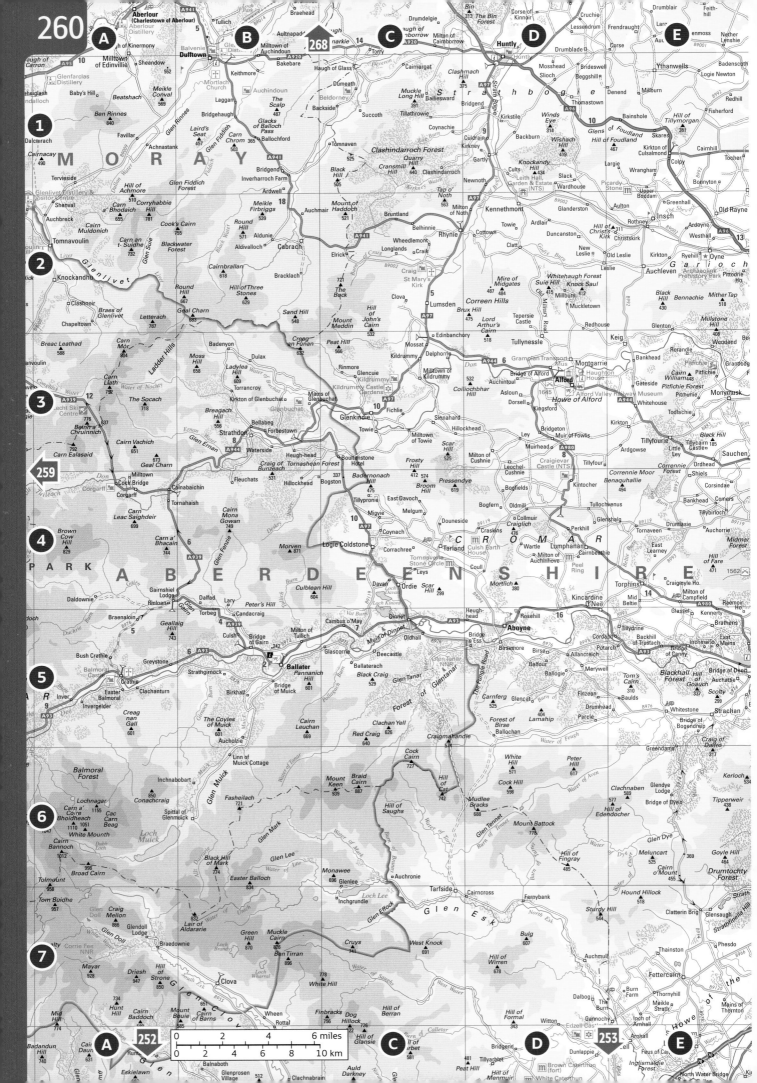

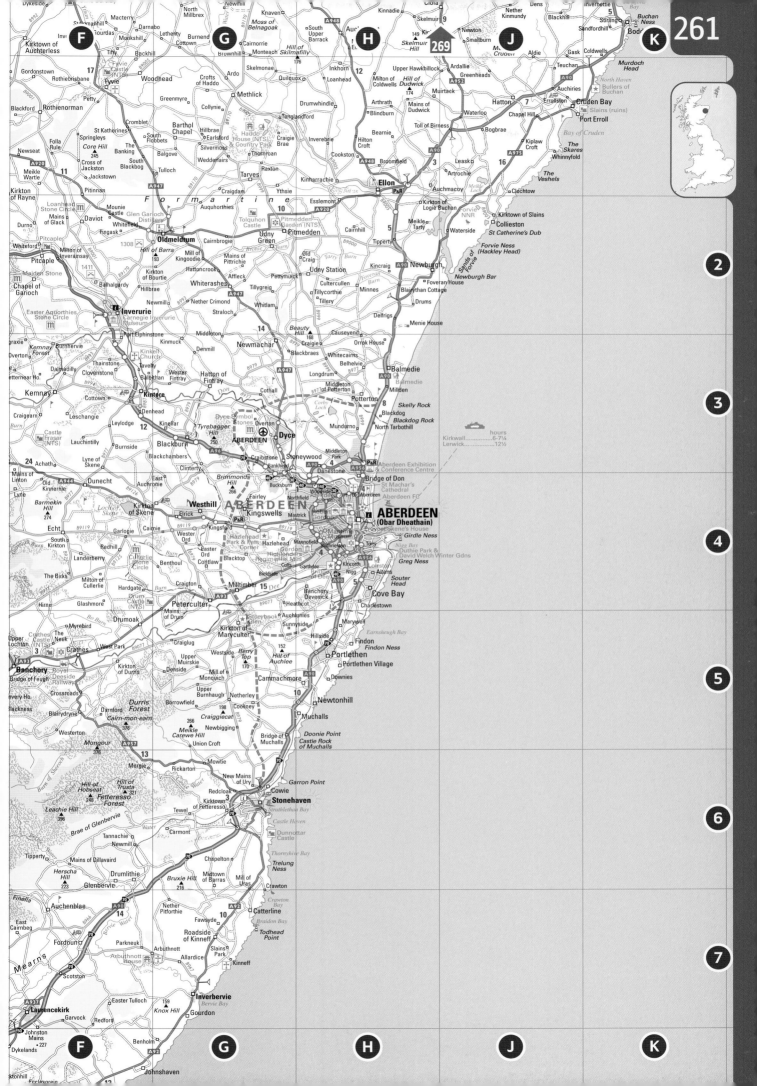

A    B    C    D    E

1

2

3

# E I L E A N S I A R
## (WESTERN ISLES)

*Gasker*

*Huisinis*

*Nish Point*

*Horsanish*

*Taransay Glorigs*

*Aird Vanish*

*Rubha Sgeirigin*

*Rubha Màs a' Chnuic*

*Toe Head*

*Shillay*

*Chaipaval* 339 365

*Tràigh na Cleavag*

*Northton (Taobh Tuath)*

*Beinn a' Charnain* 196

*Pabbay*

*Baile-na-Cill*

*Quinish*

*Carminish Islands*

*Ensay*

*Berneray (Eilean Bhearnaraigh)*

*Killegray*

*Massacamber*

*Bòrve Hill* 85

*Ruisigearraidh*

*Borgh*

*Haskeir Island*

*Haskeir Eagach*

*Boreray*

*Sound of Pabbay*

*Caolas u' Mhorain*

*Groay*

*Otternish*

*HARRIS*

*Sound of Berneray*

*Loch*

*1 hr*

*Huilish Point*

*Veilish Point*

*Lingay*

*Port nan Long*

*Baile Mhic Phail*

*Aird Thormaid*

*Stromay*

*Hermetray*

*Griminis Point*

*Vallay*

*Oronsay*

*Scolpaig*

*Vallay Strand*

*Sollas (Solas)*

*Grenitote (Greibetobht)*

*Beinn Mhòr* 190

*Leac na Hoe*

*Scarts Rock*

*Balelone (Baile Lìon)*

*Malaclett*

*Middlequarter (Ceathramh Meadhanach)*

*Trumaisgearraidh*

*Maari* 180 171

*A865*

*Keallasay Mòr*

*A865*

*Baile Mhartainn*

12

*Crogary Mòr*

*Keallasay Beg*

*Lochportain*

*Manish Point*

*Tigh a' Gearraidh*

*Loch Hosta*

*Hosta*

**N O R T H   U I S T
(UIBHIST A TUATH)**

*Loch nan Geireann*

*Blathaisbhal*

4

*Loch Aulasary*

*Loch na Dubhcha*

*Causamul*

*Aird an Rùnair*

*Baile Raghaill*

*Hogha Gearraidh*

*Loch Fada*

*Loch Skealtar*

*Lochmaddy (Loch na Madadh)*

*Loch na Madadh*

*Rubha Port Scolpaig*

*Ceann a' Bhàigh*

*Cladach Chnoc a Lin*

*Marrival* 230

*Loch Scadavay*

*Knockintorran (Cnoc an Torrain)*

8

*Oitir Mhòr*

*Loch nan Eun*

*North Lee* 250

*Deasker*

*Batemore (Baile Mòr)*

*Cladach a' Chaolais*

*Loch a' Bharpa*

8

*South Lee* 281

*Rubha Raouill*

*Cladach Chircebost*

*Loch Huna*

*A867*

*Loch Eford*

*Loch Hunder*

*Huskeiran*

*Sound of Monach*

*Kirkibost Island*

*Langais*

*Loch Scadavay*

*Rubha Mhic Gille- mhicheil*

5

*Shillay*

*Ceann Iar*

*Hearnish*

*Stockay*

*Clachan-a-Luib*

*Carnach*

*Loch(e)port (Locheuphort)*

*Saighdinis*

*Monach Islands (Heisker Islands)*

*Samhla*

*Cladach a Bhale Shear*

*Loch Obisary*

*Eigneig Mhòr*

*Monach Islands NNR*

*Ceann Ear*

*Teanamachar*

*Teampull na Trionaid*

*Carinish (Cairinis)*

5

*Eaval* 347

*Eigneig Bheag*

*Scrot Mòr*

*Baleshare (Bhaleshear)*

*Loch Caravat*

*Eachkamish*

*Baile Glas*

*Floddaybeg*

*Oitir Mhòr*

*Grimsay (Griomsaigh)*

*Bàgh Mòr*

*Beinn a' Charnain* 115

*Floddaymore*

4

*BENBECULA (BALIVANICH)*

*Uachdar*

*Eilean Flodaigh*

*Ceannaridh*

*Ronay (Ronaigh)*

*Balivanich (Baile a'Mhanaich)*

*Gramisdale (Gramsdal)*

*Beinn Rodagrich* 89

6

*Aird*

*Rubha na Rodagrich*

*Baile nan Cailleach*

*Loch Olavat*

*Ruveal* 124

*Griminish (Griminis)*

6

**B E N B E C U L A
(BEINN NA FAOGHLA)**

*Torlum*

*Loch Uisgebhagh*

*Loch Olavat*

*Uiskevagh (Uisgebhagh)*

*Linaclate (Lìonacleit)*

*Rubha Cam nan Gall*

*Gualann*

*Creagorry (Creag Ghoraidh)*

*Hacklet (Haclait)*

*Hornish Point*

*Carnan*

*Ardivachar Point*

*Baile Gharbhaidh*

*Iochdar*

*Aird a' Mhachair*

*Clachan*

*Bualadubh*

*Peters Port (Port Pheadair)* 102

*Wiay*

7

*A865*

*Bàgh nam Faoileann*

*Geirinis*

*Loch a Charnain*

*Loch Bee*

*Loch Sheilavaig*

*Loch Carnan*

*Drimore*

254

*Garry...*

*Loch Sgioport*

*Ornish Island*

*Drimsdale (Dreumasdal)*

*Loch Druidibeg NNR*

*Homore*

*Loch Druidibeg*

*Loch Spotal*

*Mol a' Tuath*

0   2   4   6 miles
0   2   4   6   8   10 km

A    C    D    E

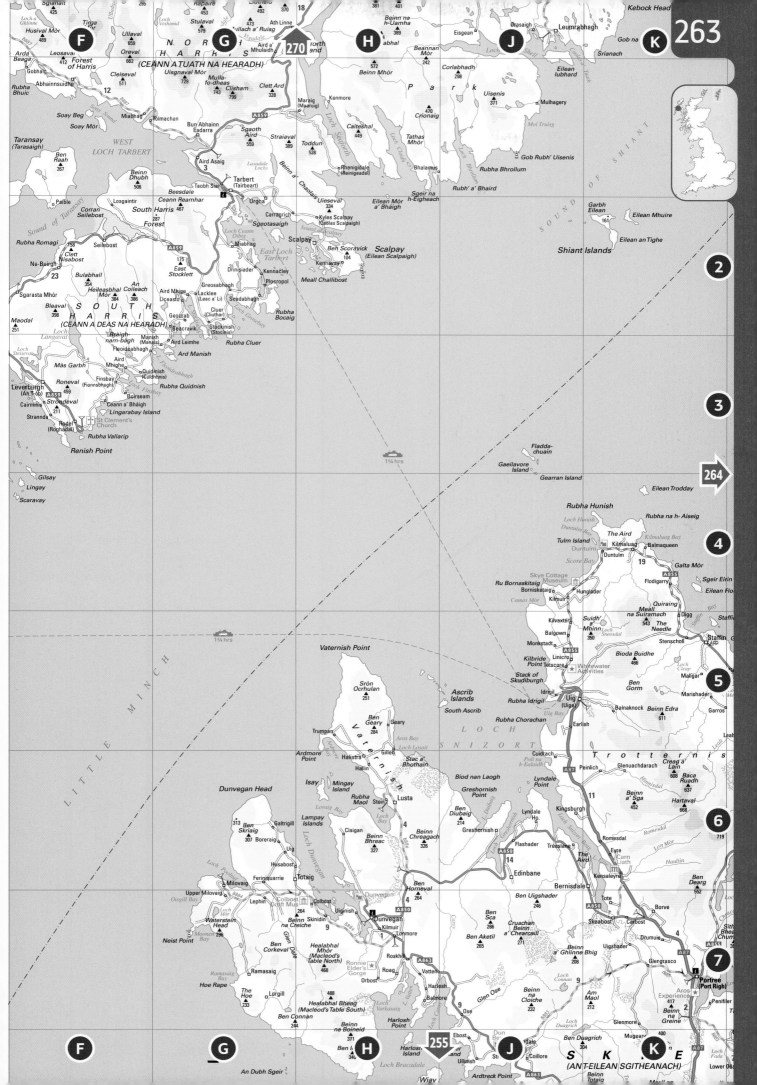

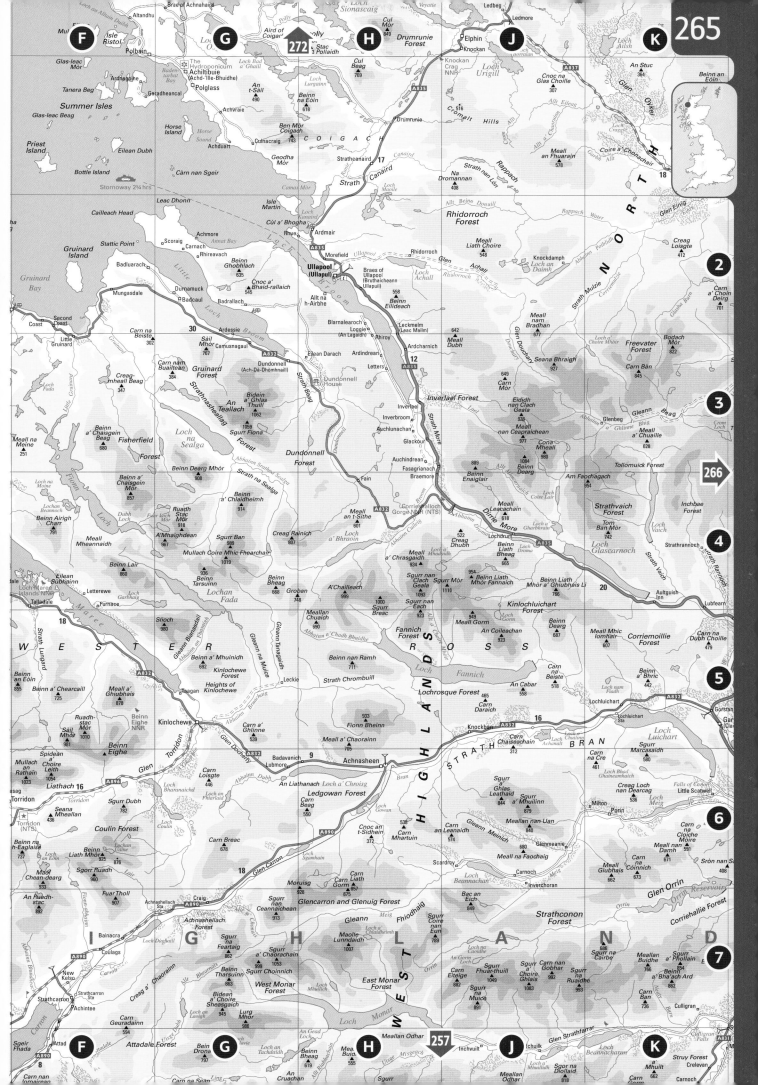

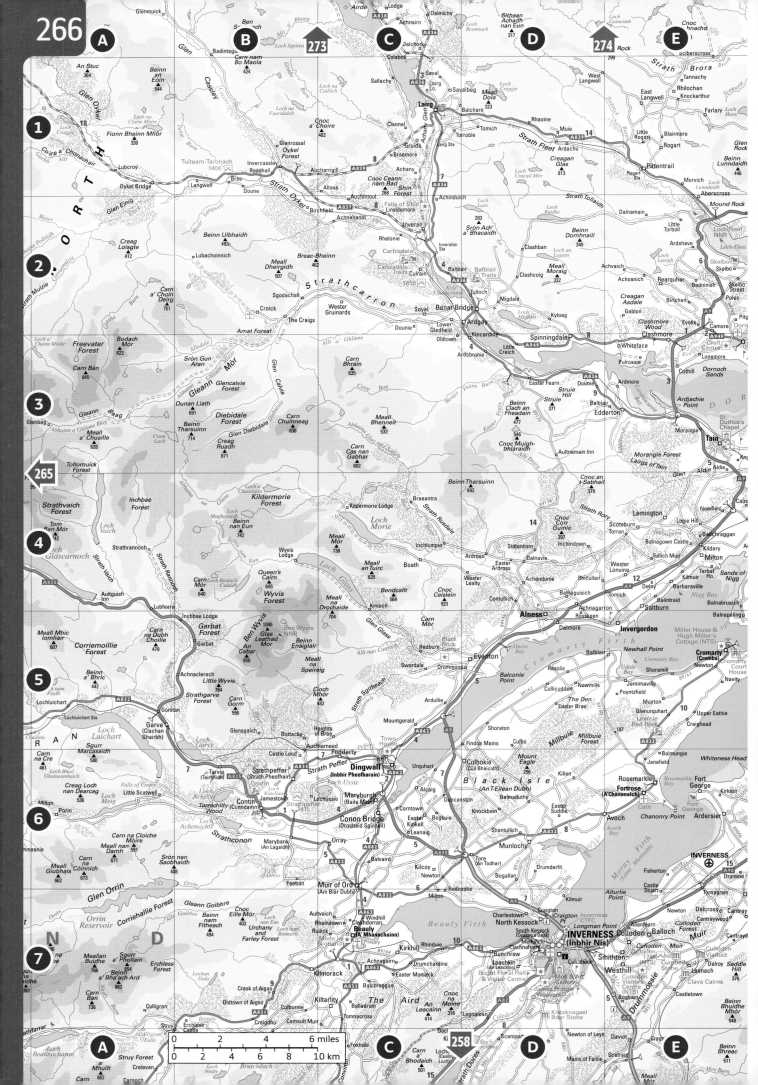

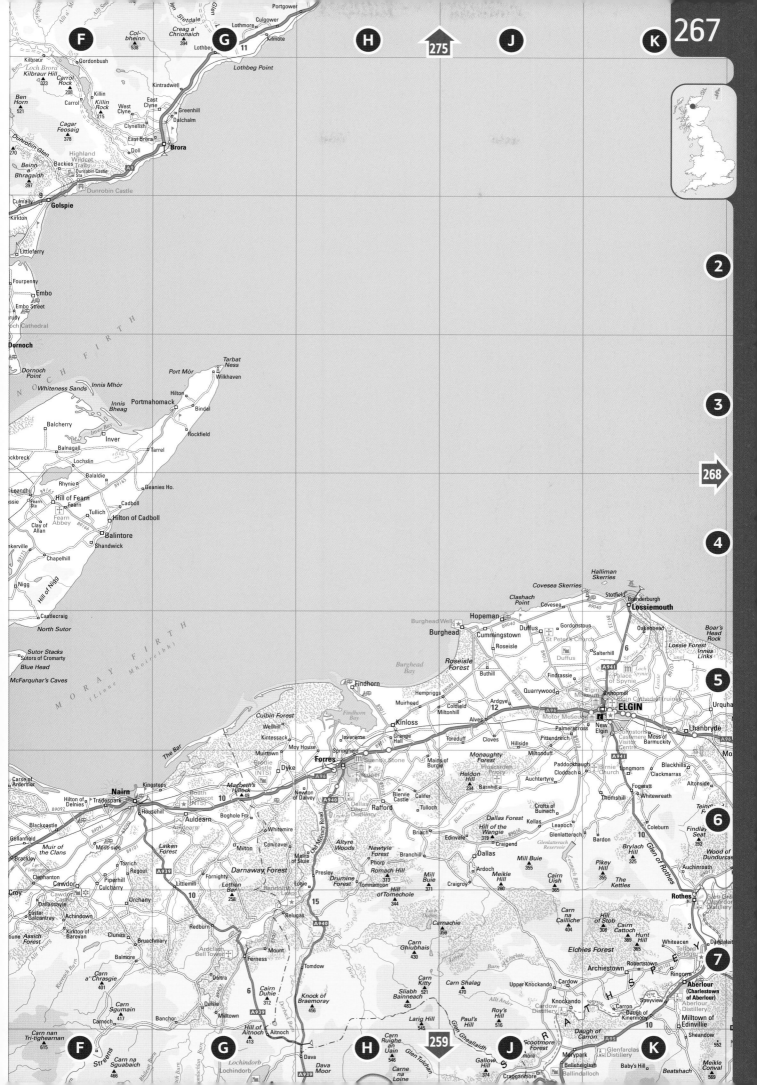

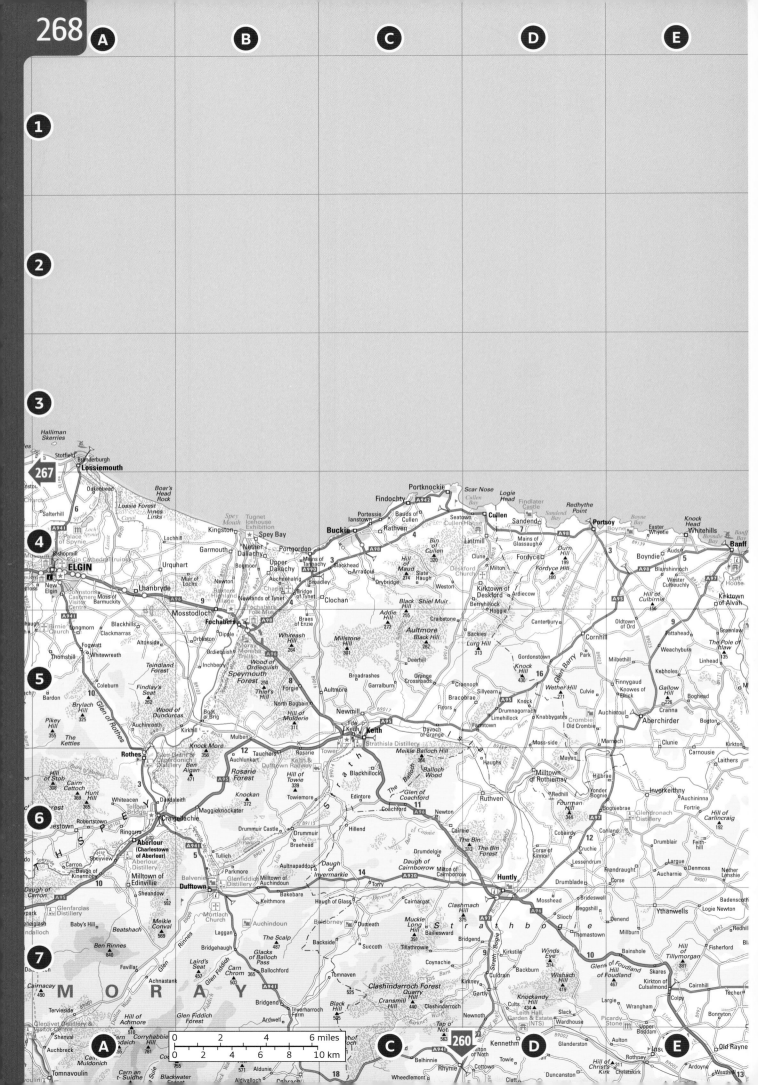

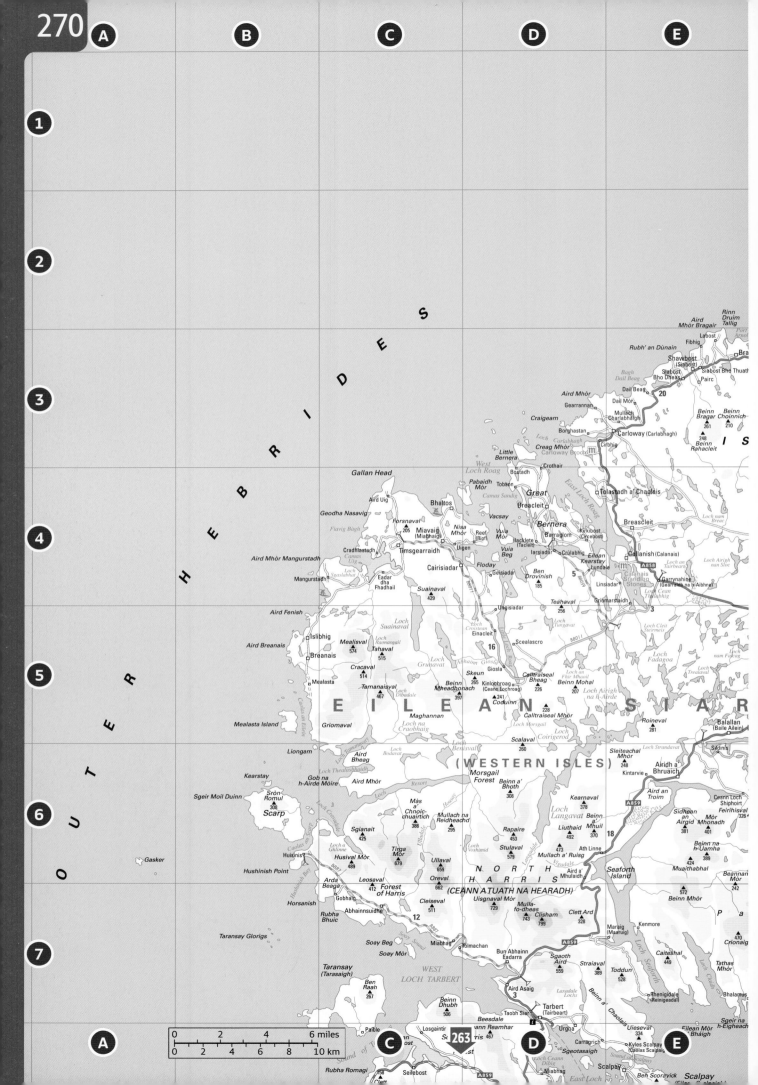

A  B  C  D  E

1

2

3

**HEBRIDES**

Aird Mhòr Bragair
Rinn Druim Tallig
Port Arnol
Labost
Fibhig
Rubh' an Dùnain
Shawbost (Siabost)
Bra
Siabost Bho Dheas
Siabost Bho Thuath
Pairc
Bagh Dail Beag
Dail Beag
20
Aird Mhòr
Dail Mòr
Gearrannan
Beinn Bragar 261
Beinn Choinnich 210
Craigeam
Mullach Charlabhaigh
Borghastan
Carloway (Carlabhagh)
248
Beinn Rahacleit
Is
Little Bernera
Creag Mhòr
Carloway Broch
Cirbhig

4

Gallan Head
West Loch Roag
Pabaidh Mòr
Tobson
Great
Tolastadh a' Chaolais
Aird Uig
Bhaltos
Camas Sandig
Bernera
Breacleit
Geodha Nasavig
Forsnaval
Vacsay
Breascleit
Fliuvig Bàgh
205
Miavaig (Miabhaig)
Nisa Mhòr
Reef (Riof)
Hacklete (Tacleit)
Kirkibost (Circebost)
Callanish (Calanais)
Aird Mhòr Mangurstadh
Cradhlastadh
Timsgearraidh
Uigen
Iarsiadar
Barraglom
Eilean Kearstay Lundale
Loch Airigh nan Sloc
Camas Uig
Cairisiadar
Floday
Vuia Beg
Crùlabhig
Calanais Standing Stones
Loch an Tairbhearts
Mangurstadh
Eadar dha Fhadhail
Geisiadar
Ben Drovinish 185
5
Garrynahine (Gearraidh na h-Aibhne)
Linsiadar
Loch Seaslabhat
Suainaval 429
Ungisiadar
Teahaval 256
Griomarstaidh
3

5

Aird Fenish
Loch Suainaval
Loch Croistean
Einacleit
Loch Tungavat
Loch Cleit Stearmeis
Islibhig
Loch Raonasgail
Mealisval 574
Tahaval 515
16
Scealascro
Loch Fadagoa
Aird Breanais
Breanais
Loch Grunavat
Skeun 265
Calltraiseal Bheag
Beinn Mohal 207
Loch nam Falcag
Cracaval 514
Giosla
Kinlochroag (Ceann Lochroag)
Loch an Fhir Mhaoil
Loch Airigh na h-Airde
Loch Trealaval
Mealasta
Tamanaisval 467
Loch Dibadale
Beinn Mheadhonach 397
Coduinn 241
228
Calltraiseal Mhòr
Roineval 281
Mealasta Island
Griomaval
Maghannan
**EILEAN**
Loch Morsgail
**SIAR**
Balallan (Baile Ailein)
Caolas an Eilein
Loch na Craobhaig
Loch Coirigerod
Scalaval 260
Sildinis

6

Liongam
Loch Tamanavay
Aird Bheag
Loch Bodavat
Loch Beinisval
**(WESTERN ISLES)**
Sleiteachal Mhòr 248
Loch Strandavat
Airidh a' Bhruaich
Kearstay
Gob na h-Airde Mòire
Aird Mhòr
Morsgail Forest
Kintarvie
Aird an Troim
Sgeir Moil Duinn
Loch Thealasbhaidh
Resort
Beinn a' Bhoth 308
Kearnaval 378
A859
Ceann Loch Shiphoirt
Feirihisval 326
Sròn Romul 308
Loch Cromlaig
Màs a' Chnoic-chuairtich 386
Mullach na Reidheachd 295
Loch Langavat
18
Sidhean an Airgid 381
Mòr Mhonadh 401
Scarp
Sgianait 425
Rapaire 453
Liuthaid 492
Beinn Mhuil 370
Huisinis
Tirga Mòr 679
Loch Voshimid
Stulaval 579
Ath Linne
Beinn na h-Uamha 424 389
Gasker
Husival Mòr 489
Ullaval 659
Mullach a' Ruisg
**NORTH**
Muaithabhal
Hushinish Point
Leosaval
Oreval 662
Aird a' Mhulaidh
Seaforth Island
Beannan Mòr 242
Arda Beaga
Forest of Harris 412
**HARRIS**
P a
Horsanish
Gobhaig
Cleiseval 511
Uisgnaval Mòr 729
Mulla-fo-dheas 743
Clisham 799
Clett Ard 328
Beinn Mhòr 572
Abhainnsuidhe
**(CEANN A TUATH NA HEARADH)**
Rubha Bhuic
12
Maraig (Maaruig)
Kenmore
470 Crionaig

7

Taransay Glorigs
Soay Beg
Miabhag
Bun Abhainn Eadarra
Sgaoth Aird 559
Straiaval 389
Toddun 528
Caiteshal 449
Tathas Mhòr
Soay Mòr
Tolmachan
A859
Taransay (Tarasaigh)
**WEST LOCH TARBERT**
Aird Asaig
Laxadale Lochs
Rhenigidale (Reinigeadal)
Beinn Dhubh 506
Taobh Siar
Tarbert (Tairbeart)
Bhalamus
Ben Raah 267
Beesdale
Uieseval 334
Eilean Mòr h-Eigheach
Paible
Losgaintir
Ceann Reamhar
Urgha
Carragrich
Sgeir na h-Eigheach
Rubha Romagi
Seilebost
**263**
Miabhag
Kyles Scalpay (Caolas Scalpaigh)
Clett
Sgeotasaigh
Scalpay
Ben Scoravick
East Loch

A  B  C  D  E

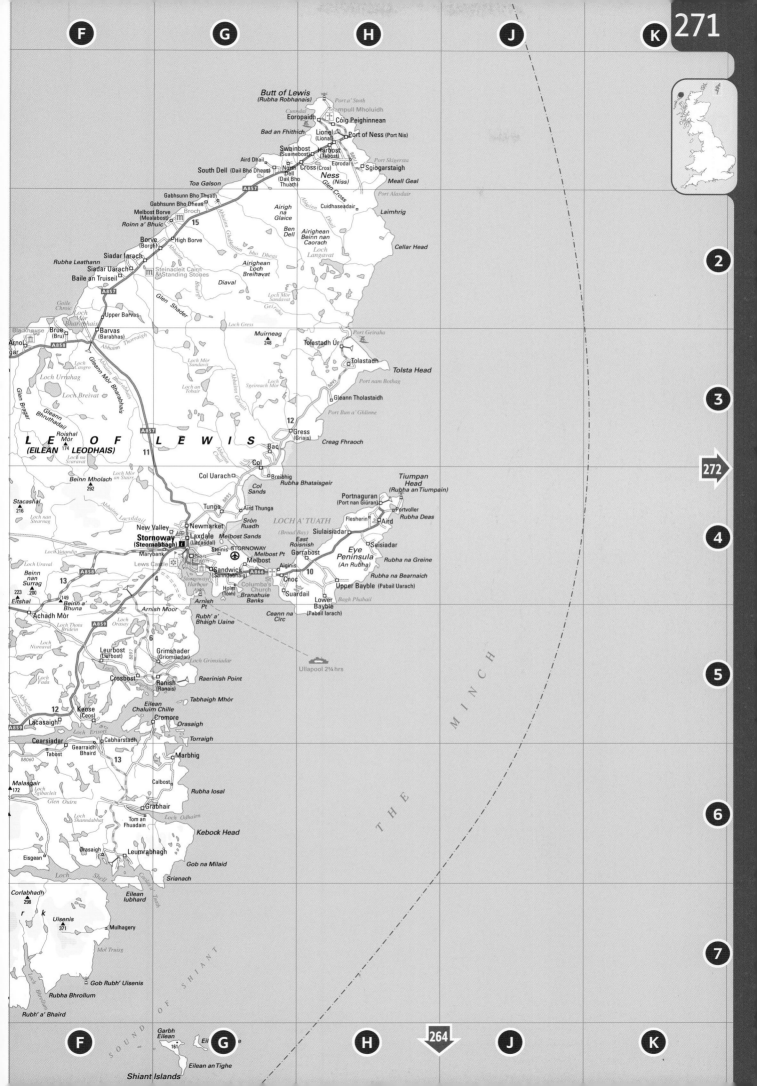

Butt of Lewis
(Rubha Robhanais)
Port a' Stoth
Teampull Mholuidh
Eoropaidh
Còig Peighinnean
Cunndal
Bad an Fhithich
Lional
(Lional)
Port of Ness (Port Nis)
Swainbost
(Suainebost)
Harbost
(Tàbost)
Eorodal
Aird Dhail
Cross (Cros)
Sgiogarstaigh
South Dell (Dail Bho Dheas)
Dell
(Dail Bho Thuath)
Ness
(Niss)
Meall Geal
Toa Galson
Port Skigersta
A857
Glen Cross
Abhainn Dhail
Port Alasdair
Gabhsunn Bho Thuath
Gabhsunn Bho Dheas
Cuidhaseadair
Melbost Borve
(Mealabost)
Broch
Roinn a' Bhuic
15
Airigh
na
Glaice
Laimhrig
Airighean Dhail
Borve
(Borgh)
High Borve
Ben
Dell
Airighean
Beinn nan
Caorach
Cellar Head
Siadar Iarach
Abhainn Ghabhsainn
Loch bho Dheas
Loch
Langavat
Rubha Leathann
Siadar Uarach
Steinacleit Cairn
& Standing Stones
Airighean
Loch
Breihavat
Baile an Truiseil
A857
Diaval
Glen Shader
Loch Mòr
Sandavat
Goile Chròic
Abhainn Bhiastaigh
Loch Gèiridha

Blackhouse
Loch
Mòr
Bharabhais
Upper Barvas
Loch Gress
Loch Mòr
Sandavit
Muirneag
248
Loch
Sgeireach Mòr
Port Geiraha
Tolastadh Ùr
Brùe
(Bru)
Barvas
(Barabhas)
Tolastadh
Arnol
A858
Abhainn Thorraigh
Tolsta Head
Loch Urrahag
Abhainn an Tobair
Port nam Bothag
Loch Casgro
Gleann Mòr Bharabhais
Abhainn Ghriais
B895
Gleann Tholastaidh
Glen Bragar
Gleann Bhruthadail
LE OF LEWIS
(EILEAN LEODHAIS)
Roishal
Mòr
174
Loch na
Scaravat
A857
11
Abhainn Chuil
Port Bun a' Ghlinne

Gress
(Griais)
12
Creag Fhraoch
Beinn Mholach
292
Loch Mòr
an Stairr
Bac
Stacashal
216
Col
Loch nan
Stearnag
Col Uarach
Breibhig
Rubha Bhataisgeir
Tiumpan
Head
(Rubha an Tiumpain)
Abhainn Lacsddail
Col
Sands
Portnaguran
(Port nan Giúran)
Portvoller

New Valley
Newmarket
Tunga
Aird Thunga
Sròn
Ruadh
LOCH A' TUATH
(Broad Bay)
Flesherin
Rubha Deas
Stornoway
(Steornabhagh)
Laxdale
(Lacasdal)
Melbost Sands
Aird
Loch Màndip
Marybank
Steinis
Melbost Pt
Siulaisiadar
East
Roisnish
Seisiadar
Beinn
nan
Surrag
13
149
200
Lews Castle
STORNOWAY
Melbost
Garrabost
Eye
Peninsula
(An Rubha)
Rubha na Greine

Loch Shiantaidh
Eitshal
Beinn a'
Bhuna
4
Eilean
Sandwick
(Sanndabhaig)
A866
Aiginis
10
Rubha na Bearnaich
Achadh Mòr
A859
Loch Thota
Bridein
6
Loch
Orasay
Holm
(Tolm)
St
Columba's
Church
Branahuie
Banks
Cnoc
Suardail
Upper Bayble (Pabail Uarach)
Loch
Nisreaval
Arnish
Pt
Rubh' a'
Bhàigh Uaine
Ceann na
Circ
Lower
Bayble
(Pabail Iarach)
Bagh Phabail
Leurbost
(Liurbost)
B897
Grimshader
(Griomsiadar)
Loch Grimsiadar
Ullapool 2¾ hrs
Loch
Fada
Crosbost
Raerinish Point

Loch
Leurbost
Ranish
(Ranais)
12
Keose
(Ceos)
Tabhaigh Mhòr
Eilean
Chaluim Chille
Lacasaigh
A859
Cromore
Orasaigh
Cearsiadar
Cabharstadh
Torraigh
Tabost
Gearraidh
Bhaird
13
Marbhig
B8060
Malasgair
172
Loch
Sgibacleit
Calbost
Glen Ouirn
Rubha Iosal

Grabhair
Tom an
Fhuadain
Loch Odhairn
Loch
Shanndabhai
Kebock Head
Orasaigh
Leumrabhagh
Eisgean
Gob na Milaid
Corlabhadh
298
Eilean
Iubhard
Srianach
Loch Shell
Cooks Lag
Uisenis
371
Mulhagery

r
k
Mòl Truish
Gob Rubh' Uisenis
Rubha Bhrollum
Rubh' a' Bhaird
SOUND OF SHIANT
THE MINCH
Garbh
Eilean
161
Eil
e
Eilean an Tighe
Shiant Islands

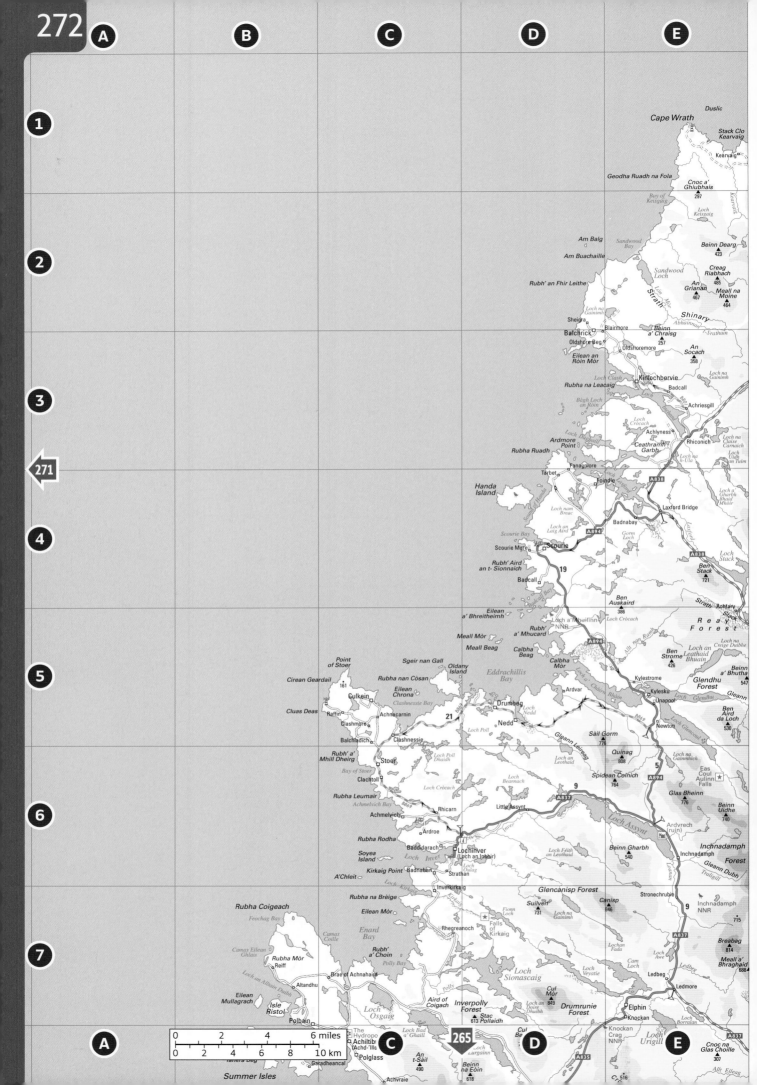

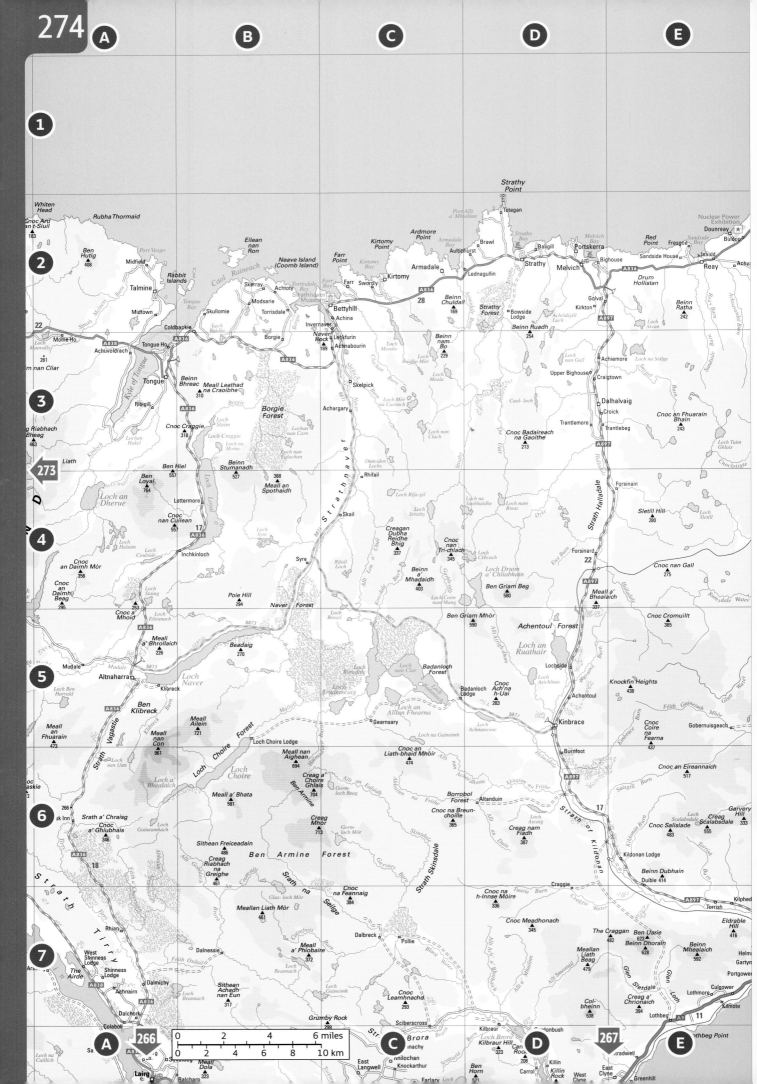

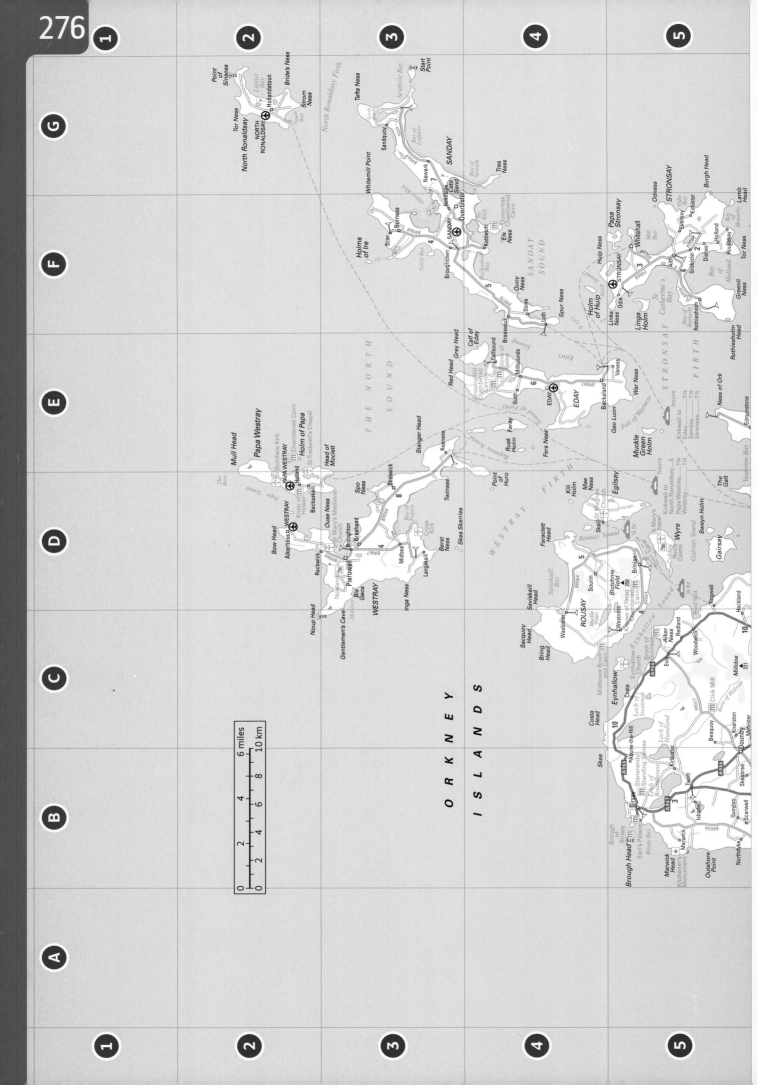

ORKNEY ISLANDS

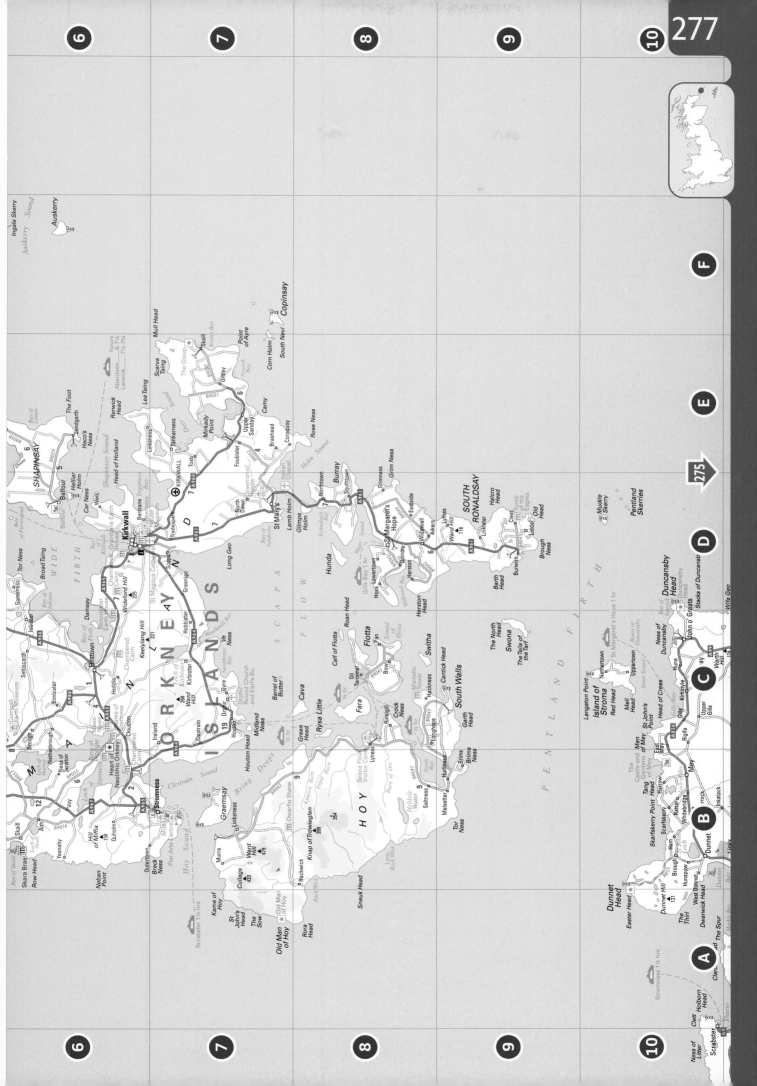

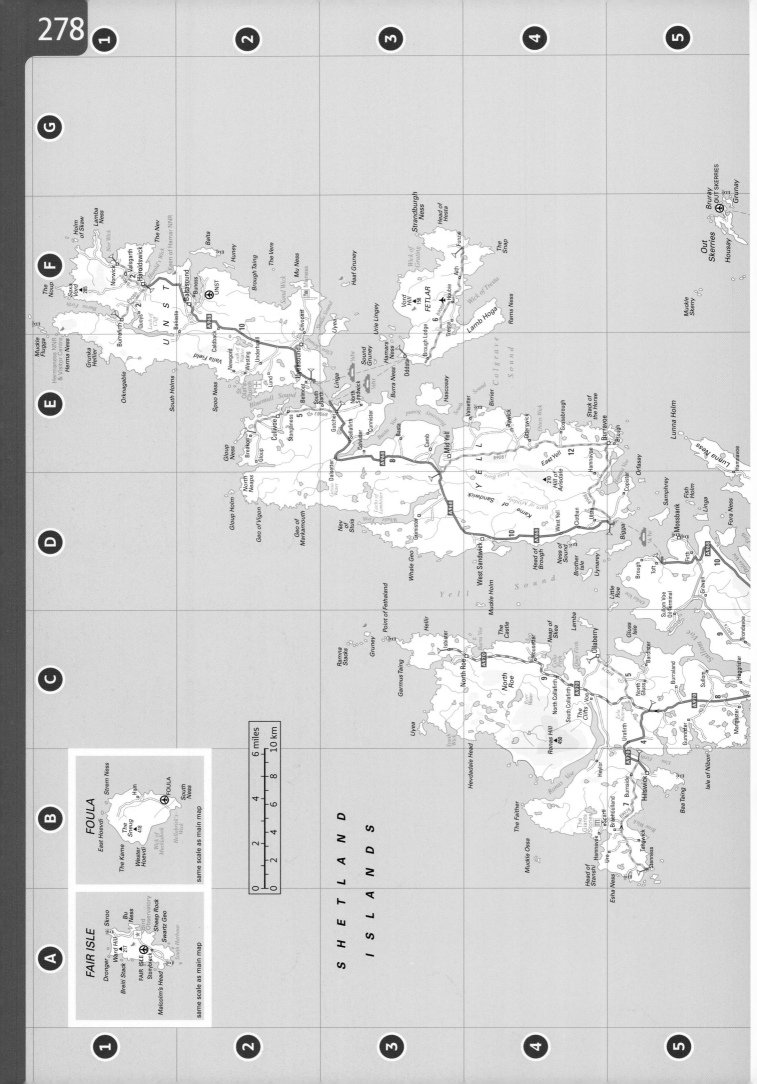

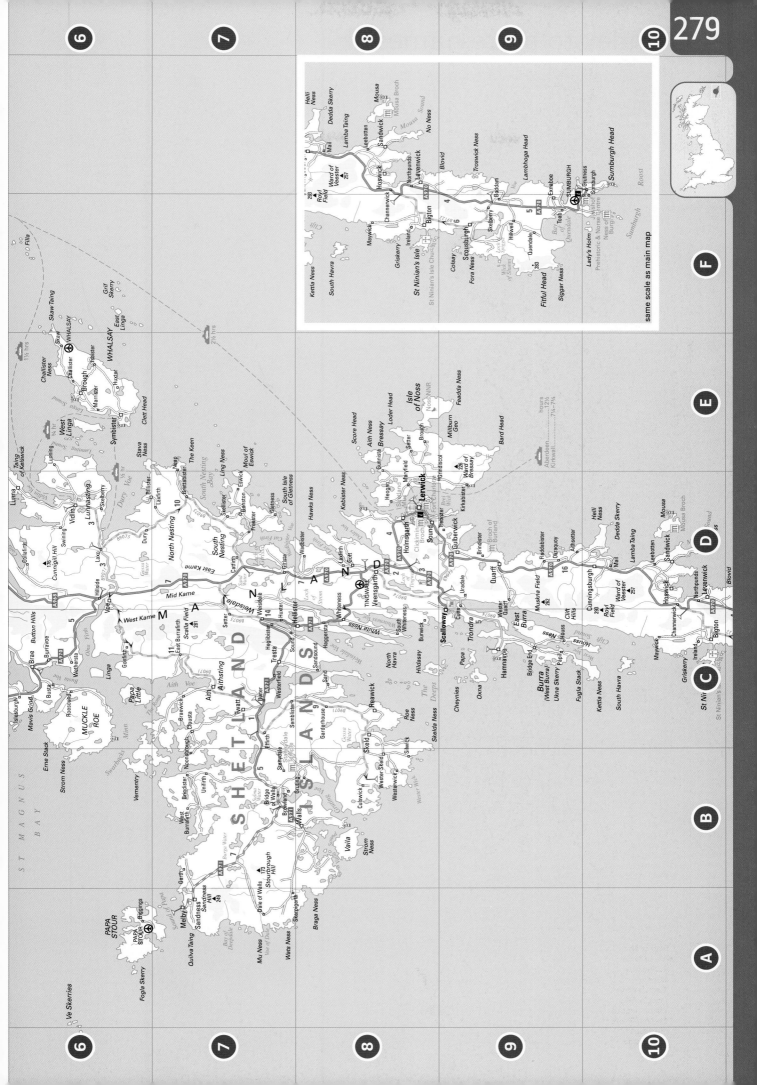

Place and place of interest names are followed by a **page number** and a grid reference in black type. The feature can be found on the map somewhere within the grid square shown.

Where two or more places have the same name the abbreviated *county* or *unitary authority* names are shown to distinguish between them. A list of these abbreviated names appears below.

The top 1000 most visited places of interest are shown within the index in blue type. Their postcode information is supplied after the county names to aid integration with satnav systems.

| 1 | Bath & North East Somerset |
|---|---|
| 2 | Blaenau Gwent |
| 3 | Bournemouth |
| 4 | Bracknell Forest |
| 5 | Bridgend |
| 6 | Bristol |
| 7 | Caerphilly |
| 8 | Cardiff |
| 9 | Clackmannanshire |
| 10 | Darlington |
| 11 | Dundee |
| 12 | East Dunbartonshire |
| 13 | East Renfrewshire |
| 14 | Glasgow |
| 15 | Halton |
| 16 | Hartlepool |
| 17 | Inverclyde |
| 18 | Luton |
| 19 | Merthyr Tydfil |
| 20 | Middlesbrough |
| 21 | Monmouthshire |
| 22 | Neath Port Talbot |
| 23 | Newport |
| 24 | North Lanarkshire |
| 25 | Plymouth |
| 26 | Poole |
| 27 | Portsmouth |
| 28 | Reading |
| 29 | Redcar And Cleveland |
| 30 | Renfrewshire |
| 31 | Rhondda Cynon Taff |
| 32 | Slough |
| 33 | South Gloucestershire |
| 34 | Southampton |
| 35 | Stockton-on-tees |
| 36 | Telford & Wrekin |
| 37 | Torfaen |
| 38 | Vale Of Glamorgan |
| 39 | Warrington |
| 40 | West Dunbartonshire |
| 41 | Windsor & Maidenhead |
| 42 | Wokingham |

| | |
|---|---|
| *A&B* | Argyll & Bute |
| *Aber* | Aberdeenshire |
| *B&H* | Brighton & Hove |
| *B&NESom* | Bath & North East Somerset |
| *B'burn* | Blackburn with Darwen |
| *B'pool* | Blackpool |
| *BGwent* | Blaenau Gwent |
| *Bed* | Bedford |
| *Bourne* | Bournemouth |
| *BrackF* | Bracknell Forest |
| *Bucks* | Buckinghamshire |
| *Caerp* | Caerphilly |
| *Cambs* | Cambridgeshire |
| *Carmar* | Carmarthenshire |
| *CenBeds* | Central Bedfordshire |
| *Cere* | Ceredigion |
| *Chanl* | Channel Islands |
| *ChesE* | Cheshire East |
| *ChesW&C* | Cheshire West & Chester |
| *Corn* | Cornwall |
| *Cumb* | Cumbria |
| *D&G* | Dumfries & Galloway |
| *Darl* | Darlington |
| *Denb* | Denbighshire |
| *Derbys* | Derbyshire |
| *Dur* | Durham |
| *EAyr* | East Ayrshire |
| *EDun* | East Dunbartonshire |
| *ELoth* | East Lothian |
| *ERenf* | East Renfrewshire |
| *ERid* | East Riding of Yorkshire |
| *ESuss* | East Sussex |
| *Edin* | Edinburgh |
| *ESiar* | Eilean Siar (Western Isles) |
| *Falk* | Falkirk |
| *Flints* | Flintshire |
| *Glas* | Glasgow |
| *Glos* | Gloucestershire |
| *GtLon* | Greater London |
| *GtMan* | Greater Manchester |
| *Gwyn* | Gwynedd |
| *Hants* | Hampshire |
| *Hart* | Hartlepool |
| *Here* | Herefordshire |
| *Herts* | Hertfordshire |
| *High* | Highland |
| *Hull* | Kingston upon Hull |
| *Invcly* | Inverclyde |
| *IoA* | Isle of Anglesey |
| *IoM* | Isle of Man |
| *IoS* | Isles of Scilly |
| *IoW* | Isle of Wight |
| *Lancs* | Lancashire |
| *Leic* | Leicester |
| *Leics* | Leicestershire |
| *Lincs* | Lincolnshire |
| *MK* | Milton Keynes |
| *MTyd* | Merthyr Tydfil |
| *Med* | Medway |
| *Mersey* | Merseyside |

| | |
|---|---|
| *Middl* | Middlesbrough |
| *Midlo* | Midlothian |
| *Mon* | Monmouthshire |
| *N'hants* | Northamptonshire |
| *N'umb* | Northumberland |
| *NAyr* | North Ayrshire |
| *NELincs* | North East Lincolnshire |
| *NLan* | North Lanarkshire |
| *NLincs* | North Lincolnshire |
| *NPT* | Neath Port Talbot |
| *NSom* | North Somerset |
| *NYorks* | North Yorkshire |
| *Norf* | Norfolk |
| *Nott* | Nottingham |
| *Notts* | Nottinghamshire |
| *Ork* | Orkney |
| *Oxon* | Oxfordshire |

| | |
|---|---|
| *P&K* | Perth & Kinross |
| *Pembs* | Pembrokeshire |
| *Peter* | Peterborough |
| *Plym* | Plymouth |
| *Ports* | Portsmouth |
| *R&C* | Redcar & Cleveland |
| *RCT* | Rhondda Cynon Taff |
| *Read* | Reading |
| *Renf* | Renfrewshire |
| *Rut* | Rutland |
| *S'end* | Southend-on-Sea |
| *SAyr* | South Ayrshire |
| *SGlos* | South Gloucestershire |
| *SLan* | South Lanarkshire |
| *SYorks* | South Yorkshire |

| | |
|---|---|
| *ScBord* | Scottish Borders |
| *Shet* | Shetland |
| *Shrop* | Shropshire |
| *Slo* | Slough |
| *Som* | Somerset |
| *Soton* | Southampton |
| *Staffs* | Staffordshire |
| *Stir* | Stirling |
| *Stock* | Stockton-on-Tees |
| *Stoke* | Stoke-on-Trent |
| *Suff* | Suffolk |
| *Surr* | Surrey |
| *Swan* | Swansea |
| *Swin* | Swindon |
| *T&W* | Tyne & Wear |
| *Tel&W* | Telford & Wrekin |
| *Thur* | Thurrock |

| | |
|---|---|
| *VGlam* | Vale of Glamorgan |
| *W&M* | Windsor & Maidenhead |
| *W'ham* | Wokingham |
| *WBerks* | West Berkshire |
| *WDun* | West Dunbartonshire |
| *WLoth* | West Lothian |
| *WMid* | West Midlands |
| *WSuss* | West Sussex |
| *WYorks* | West Yorkshire |
| *Warks* | Warwickshire |
| *Warr* | Warrington |
| *Wilts* | Wiltshire |
| *Worcs* | Worcestershire |
| *Wrex* | Wrexham |

1853 Gallery *WYorks*
BD18 3LA **26** C1

**A**
Ab Kettleby **174** C5
Ab Lench **146** C2
Abbas Combe **117** E5
Abberley **145** G1
Abberley Common **145** G1
Abberton *Essex* **138** D1
Abberton *Worcs* **146** B2
Abberwick **229** F5
Abbess Roding **137** E1
Abbey Dore **144** C4
Abbey Hulton **171** G3
Abbey St. Bathans **237** E3
Abbey Village **192** C5
Abbey Wood **137** D5
Abbeycwmhir **155** G5
Abbeydale **186** A4
Abbeystead **192** B5
Abbotrule **228** A5
Abbots Bickington **113** D4
Abbots Bromley **172** B5
Abbots Langley **135** F2
Abbots Leigh **131** E5
Abbots Morton **146** C2
Abbots Ripton **162** A5
Abbot's Salford **146** C2
Abbots Worthy **119** F4
Abbotsbury **104** B4
Abbotsbury Swannery,
Subtropical Gardens &
Children's Farm *Dorset*
DT3 4JG **104** B4
Abbotsfield Farm **183** G3
Abbotsham **113** E3
Abbotskerswell **101** E1
Abbotsley **150** B3
Abbotstone **119** G4
Abbots Ann **119** F4
Abbott's Barton **119** F4
Abbottswood **119** E5
Abdon **157** E4
Abdy **186** B3
Abenhall **131** F1
Aber **142** A3
Aber Village **144** A5
Aberaeron **142** A1
Aberaman **129** G2
Aberangell **155** E2
Aber-Arad **141** G3
Aberarder **249** G1
Aberarder House **258** D2
Aberargie **243** G3
Aberarth **142** A1
Aberavon **129** E2
Aber-banc **141** G3
Aberbargoed **130** A2
Aberbeeg **130** B2
Aberbowlan **142** C4
Aberbran **143** F5
Abercanaid **129** G2
Abercarn **130** B3
Abercastle **140** B4
Abercegir **155** E2
Aberchalder **257** K4
Aberchirder **268** E5
Abercorn **235** E2
Abercraf **129** E1
Abercregan **129** E2
Abercrombie **244** D4
Abercrychan **143** D4
Abercwmboi **129** G2
Abercych **141** F3
Abercynafon **129** G1
Abercynon **129** G3
Abercywarch **155** E1
Aberdalgie **243** F2
Aberdare **129** F2
Aberdaron **166** A4
Aberdeen (Obar Dheathain)
**261** H4
Aberdeen Airport **261** G3
Aberdeen Art Gallery *AB10*
1FQ **63** Aberdeen
Aberdeen Exhibition &
Conference Centre
*Aberdeen* AB23 8BL
**261** H3
Aberdesach **166** D2
Aberdour **235** F1
Aberdovey (Aberdyfi)
**154** C2
Aberduhonw **143** G2
Aberdulais **129** D3
Aberedw **143** G3
Abereiddy **140** A4
Abererch **166** C4
Aberfan **129** G2
Aberfeldy **251** D5
Aberffraw **166** C1
Aberffrwd **154** C5
Aberford **194** D4
Aberfoyle **242** A4
Abergavenny (Y Fenni)
**130** B1
Abergele **182** A5
Aber-Giâr **142** B3
Abergorlech **142** B4
Abergwesyn **143** E2
Abergwili **142** A5
Abergwydol **155** D2
Abergwynant **154** C1
Abergwynfi **129** E2
Abergwyngregyn **181** E5
Abergwynolwyn **154** C2
Aberhafesp **155** G3
Aberhosan **155** E3
Aberkenfig **129** E3
Aberlady **236** B1
Aberlemno **252** D4
Aberllefenni **155** D2
Aber-Ilia **129** F1
Aberlour (Charlestown of
Aberlour) **267** K7
Abermad **154** B5
Abermeurig **142** B2
Abermule (Aber-miwl)
**156** A3
Abernaint **169** E5
Abernant *Carmar* **141** G5
Aber-nant *RCT* **129** G2
Abernethy **243** G3
Abernyte **244** A1
Aberporth **141** F2
Abersoch **166** C5
Abersky **258** C2
Abersoch **166** C5
Aberthin **129** G5
Abertillery **130** B2
Abertridwr *Caerp* **130** A4
Abertridwr *Powys* **155** G1
Abertysswg **130** A2
Aberuthven **243** E3
Aberyscir **143** F5
Aberystwyth **154** B4
Aberystwyth Arts Centre
*Cere* SY23 3DE **154** B4
Abhainnsuidhe **270** C7
Abingdon **133** G3
Abinger Common **121** G3
Abinger Hammer **121** F3
Abington **226** A3
Abington Pigotts **150** B3
Abingworth **108** D2
Ablington *Glos* **132** D2
Ablington *Wilts* **118** C3
Abney **185** F5
Above Church **172** B2
Aboyne **260** D5
Abram **184** B2
Abriachan (Obar Itheachan)
**258** C1
Abridge **137** D3
Abronhill **234** B2
Abson **131** G5
Abthorpe **148** B3
Abune-the-Hill **276** B5
Aby **189** E5
Acaster Malbis **195** E3
Acaster Selby **195** E3
Accrington **193** D5
Accurrach **240** D2
Acha **246** A4
Achadacaie **231** G3
Achadunan **241** E3
Achagavel **247** G4
Achaglass **231** F5
Achahoish **231** F2
Achalader **251** G5
Achallader **249** F5
Achamore **232** B4
Achandunie **266** D4
Achany **266** C1
Achaphubuil **248** C2
Acharacle **247** F3
Achargary **274** C3
Acharn *A&B* **240** D1
Acharn *P&K* **250** D5
Acharonich **239** D1
Acharosson **232** A2
Achateny **247** E2
Achath **261** F3
Achavanich **275** G4
Achddu **128** A2
Achduart **265** G1
Achentoul **274** D5
Achfary **272** E5
Achgarve **264** C2
Achiemore *High* **273** F2
Achiemore *High* **274** D3
Achies **275** G3
A'Chill **255** H4
Achiltibuie (Achd-'Ille-
Bhuidhe) **265** G1
Achina **274** C2
Achindown **267** F7
Achinduich **266** C2
Achingills **275** G2
Achintee *High* **265** F2
Achintraid **256** E1
Achlean **259** F5
Achleanan **247** E4
Achleek **247** G4
Achlian **240** D2
Achlyness **272** E3
Achmelvich **272** B6
Achmony **258** C1
Achmore *High* **256** E1
Achmore *High* **265** G2
Achmore *Stir* **242** A1
Achnaba **232** A1
Achnabat **258** C1
Achnabourin **274** C3
Achnacarin **240** B1
Achnacarnin **272** C5
Achnacarry **240** C1
Achnaclerach **266** B5
Achnacloich *A&B* **240** B1
Achnacloich *High* **256** B4
Achnaclyth **275** F5
Achnacraig **247** D4
Achnacroish **248** A5
Achnadrish **246** D4
Achnafalnich **241** E2
Achnafauld **243** D1
Achnagarron **266** C7
Achnagarron **266** D4
Achnaha *High* **247** F5
Achnaha *High* **247** D3
Achnahanat **266** C2
Achnahannet **259** G2
Achnairn **259** H7
Achnalea **248** B4
Achnamara **231** F1
Achnanellan **247** G3
Achnasaul **249** D1
Achnasheen **265** H6
Achnashelloch **240** A5
Achnastank **259** K1
Achorn **275** G5
Achosnich *High* **266** E2
Achosnich *High* **246** D3
Achreamie **275** F2
Achriabhach **248** D3
Achriesgill **272** E3
Achtoty **273** J2
Achurch **161** F4
Achuvoldrach **273** H3
Achvaich **266** D2
Achvarasdal **274** E2
Achvlair **248** B4
Achvraie **265** G1
Ackenthwaite **199** G4
Ackergill **275** J3
Acklam *Middl* **203** D1
Acklam *NYorks* **195** G1
Ackleton **157** G3
Acklington **221** E1
Ackton **194** D5
Ackworth Moor Top **186** B1
Acle **179** F4
Acock's Green **158** D4
Acol **125** F2
Acomb *N'umb* **211** F1
Acomb *York* **195** E2
Aconbury **145** E4
Acre **193** D5
Acrefair **169** F3
Acrise Place **125** D4
Acton *ChesE* **170** D2
Acton *Dorset* **105** F5
Acton *GtLon* **136** A4
Acton *Shrop* **156** C4
Acton *Staffs* **171** F3
Acton *Suff* **151** G3
Acton *Worcs* **146** A1
Acton *Wrex* **170** A2
Acton Beauchamp **145** F2
Acton Bridge **183** G5
Acton Burnell **157** E2
Acton Green **145** F2
Acton Pigott **157** E2
Acton Round **157** F3
Acton Scott **157** D4
Acton Trussell **158** B1
Acton Turville **132** A4
Adamhill **224** C2
Adbaston **171** E5
Adber **116** C5
Adderbury **147** G4
Adderley **171** D4
Adderstone **229** F3
Addiewell **235** D3
Addingham **193** G3
Addington *Bucks* **148** C5
Addington *GtLon* **122** C2
Addington *Kent* **123** F3
Addiscombe **122** C2
Addlestone **121** F1
Addlethorpe **176** D1
Adel **194** B4
Aden Country Park *Aber*
AB42 5FQ **269** H6
Adeney **157** G1
Adeyfield **135** F2
Adfa **155** G2
Adforton **156** D5
Adisham **125** E3
Adlestrop **147** E5
Adlingfleet **196** A5
Adlington *ChesE* **184** D4
Adlington *Lancs* **183** G1
Admaston *Staffs* **172** B5
Admaston *Tel&W* **157** F1
Admington **147** E3
Adsborough **115** F5
Adscombe **115** E4
Adstock **148** C4
Adstone **148** A2
Adventure Island *S'end*
SS1 1EE **138** B4
Adventure Wonderland
*Dorset* BH23 6BA **3** D2
Adversane **121** F5
Advie **259** J1
Adwalton **194** B5
Adwell **134** B3
Adwick le Street **186** C2
Adwick upon Dearne
**186** B2
Adziel **269** H5
Ae Village **217** D2
Afan Argoed Country Park
*NPT* SA13 3HG **129** E3
Affetside **184** B1
Affleck **261** G2
Affpuddle **105** E3
Afon Wen **166** C4
Afon-wen **182** C5
Afonwen Craft & Antique
Centre *Flints* CH7 5UB
**182** C5
Africa Alive! *Suff* NR33 7TF
**165** G3
Afton **106** C4
Afton Bridgend **225** E4
Agglethorpe **201** F4
Aigburth **183** E4
Aiginis **271** G4
Aike **196** C3
Aikerness **276** D2
Aikers **277** D8
Aiketgate **210** B3
Aikshaw **209** E2
Aikton **209** F1
Ailsworth **161** G3
Ailby **189** E5
Ailey **144** C3
Ailsworth **161** G3
Aimes Green **136** D2
Aingers Green **152** C5
Ainsdale **183** E1
Ainsdale-on-Sea **183** E1
Ainstable **210** B3
Ainsworth **184** B1
Ainthorpe **203** G2
Aintree **183** E3
Aird *ESiar* **262** C6
Aird *ESiar* **271** H4
Aird a' Mhachair **262** C7
Aird a' Mhulaidh **270** D6
Aird Asaig **270** D7
Aird Dhail **271** G1
Aird Leimhe **263** G3
Aird Mhige **263** G2
Aird Mhighe **263** F3
Aird of Sleat **256** B4
Aird Thunga **271** G4
Aird Uig **270** C4
Airdrie **234** B3
Airdrie *NLan* **234** B3
Airds **266** D3
Aird View **193** F3
Airidh a' Bhruaich **270** E6
Airieland **216** B5
Airies **214** A4
Airigh-drishaig **256** D1
Airmyn **195** G5
Airntully **243** F1
Airor **256** D4
Airth **234** C1
Airton **193** F2
Airyhassen **207** D2
Aisby *Lincs* **187** F3
Aisby *Lincs* **175** F4
Aisgill **200** C3
Aish *Devon* **100** C1
Aish *Devon* **101** D2
Aisholt **115** E4
Aiskew **202** B4
Aislaby *NYorks* **204** B2
Aislaby *NYorks* **203** G4
Aislaby *Stock* **202** D1
Aisthorpe **187** G5
Aith *Ork* **277** B6
Aith *Ork* **276** F5
Aith *Shet* **279** C7
Aith *Shet* **278** F3
Aithsetter **279** D9
Aitnoch **259** G1
Akeld **229** D4
Akeley **148** C4
Akenham **152** C3
Albaston **99** E3
Albecq **101** E5
Alberbury **156** C1
Albert Park *TS1 3LB*
**78** Middlesbrough
Albert Town **126** C1
Albourne **109** E2
Albourne Green **109** E2
Albrighton *Shrop* **158** A2
Albrighton *Shrop* **157** D1
Alburgh **165** D3
Albury *Herts* **150** C5
Albury *Oxon* **134** B3
Albury *Surr* **121** F3
Albury End **150** C5
Albury Heath **121** F3
Alby Hill **178** C2
Alcaig **266** C6
Alcaston **157** D4
Alcester **146** C2
Alciston **110** A3
Alcombe **114** C3
Alconbury **161** G5
Alconbury Hill **161** G5
Alconbury Weston **161** G5
Aldborough *Norf* **178** C2
Aldborough *NYorks*
**194** D1
Aldbourne **133** E5
Aldbrough **197** E4
Aldbrough St. John **202** B1
Aldbury **135** E1
Aldclune **251** E3
Aldeburgh **153** F2
Aldeby **165** F2
Aldenham **136** A3
Aldenham Country Park
*Herts* WD6 3AT **136** A3
Alderbury **118** C5
Alderford **178** C4
Alderholt **106** A3
Alderley **131** G3
Alderley Edge **184** C5
Aldermaston **119** G1
Aldermaston Wharf **120** B1
Alderminster **147** E3
Alderney **101** G4
Alderney Airport **101** F4
Alder's End **145** F4
Aldersey Green **170** B2
Aldershot **121** D2
Alderton *Glos* **146** B4
Alderton *N'hants* **148** C3
Alderton *Suff* **153** E3
Alderton *Wilts* **132** A4
Alderwasley **173** E2
Aldfield **194** B1
Aldford **170** B2
Aldham *Essex* **152** A5
Aldham *Suff* **152** B3
Aldie *Aber* **269** J6
Aldie *High* **266** E3
Aldingbourne **108** B3
Aldingham **199** D5
Aldington *Kent* **124** C5
Aldington *Worcs* **146** C3
Aldivalloch **260** B2
Aldochlay **241** F5
Aldons **214** C2
Aldous's Corner **165** E3
Aldreth **162** C5
Aldridge **158** C2
Aldringham **153** F1
Aldsworth *Glos* **146** B4
Aldsworth *WSuss* **107** G2
Aldunie **260** B2
Aldville **243** E1
Aldwark *Derbys* **172** D2
Aldwark *NYorks* **195** D1
Aldwick **108** B4
Aldwincle **161** F4
Aldworth **134** A5
Alexandra Palace *GtLon*
N22 7AY **12** A1
Alexandria **233** E2
Aley **115** E4
Aley Green **135** F1
Alfardisworthy **112** C4
Alfington **103** E3
Alfold **121** F4
Alfold Crossways **121** F4
Alfington **103** E3
Alfold **121** F4
Alfold Bars **121** F4
Alford *Aber* **260** D3
Alford *Lincs* **189** E5
Alford *Som* **116** C4
Alfreton **173** F2
Alfrick **145** G2
Alfrick Pound **145** G2
Alfriston **110** A3
Algarkirk **176** A4
Alhampton **116** D4
Alkborough **196** A5
Alkerton **147** F3
Alkham **125** E4
Alkington **170** C4
Alkmonton **172** C4
All Cannings **118** B1
All Saints South Elmham
**165** E3
All Stretton **157** D3
Allaleigh **101** E2
Allanaquoich **259** J5
Allancreich **260** D5
Allanfearn **266** E7
Allangillfoot **218** A2
Allanton *D&G* **216** D2
Allanton *EAyr* **225** E2
Allanton *NLan* **234** C4
Allanton *ScBord* **237** F4
Allanton *SLan* **234** B4
Allardice **253** F2
Allathasdal **254** B4
Allbrook **119** F5
Allendale Town **211** E2
Allenheads **211** E3
Allen's Green *Herts* **137** D1
Allensford **211** G2
Allensmore **145** D4
Allenton **173** E4
Aller **116** B5
Allerby **209** D3
Allercombe **102** D3
Allerford *Devon* **99** E2
Allerford *Som* **114** C3
Allerston **204** B4
Allerthorpe **195** G3
Allerton *Mersey* **183** F4
Allerton *WYorks* **194** A4
Allerton Bywater **194** D5
Allerton Mauleverer **194** D2
Allesley **159** E5
Allestree **173** E4
Allet Common **96** B5
Allexton **160** D2
Allgreave **171** G1
Allhallows **124** A1
Allhallows-on-Sea **124** A1
Alligin Shuas **264** E6
Allimore Green **158** A1
Allington *Dorset* **104** A3
Allington *Lincs* **175** D3
Allington *Lincs* **176** B1
Allington *Wilts* **118** B1
Allington *Wilts* **132** A5
Allithwaite **199** F5
Allnabad **273** G4
Allonby **209** D3
Allonby **209** D3
Allostock **184** B5
Alloway **224** B5
Allowenshay **103** G1
Allscot **157** G2
Allscott **157** F1
Allt na h-Airbhe **265** H2
Alltachonaich **247** G4
Alltbeithe **257** G2
Alltforgan **168** C5
Alltmawr **143** G3
Alltnacaillich **273** G4
Allt-nan-sùugh **257** F1
Alltsigh **258** B3
Alltwalis **142** A4
Alltwen **128** D2
Alltyblaca **142** B3
Allwood Green **164** B4
Almeley **144** C2
Almeley Wootton **144** C2
Almer **105** F3
Almington **171** E4
Alminstone Cross **113** D3
Almiston Cross **113** D3
Almondbank **243** F2
Almondbury **185** F1
Almondell & Calderwood
Country Park *WLoth*
EH52 5PE **235** D3
Almondsbury **131** F4
Alne **195** D1
Alness **266** D5
Alnham **229** D5
Alnmouth **229** G5
Alnwick **229** F5
Alnwick Garden, The *N'umb*
NE66 1YU **229** F5
Alperton **136** A4
Alphamstone **151** G4
Alpheton **151** G2
Alphington **102** C3
Alport **172** D1
Alpraham **170** C2
Alresford **152** B5
Alrewas **159** D1
Alrick **251** G3
Alsager **171** E2
Alsagers Bank **171** F3
Alsop en le Dale **172** C2
Alston *Cumb* **210** D3
Alston *Devon* **103** G2
Alston Sutton **116** B2
Alstone *Glos* **146** B4
Alstone *Som* **116** A3
Alstone *Staffs* **158** A1
Alstonefield **172** C2
Alswear **114** A5
Alt **184** D2
Altandhu **272** B7
Altanduin **274** D6
Altarnun **97** G1
Altass **266** C1
Altens **261** H4
Alterwall **275** H2
Altham **193** D4
Althorne **138** C3
Althorp House *N'hants*
NN7 4HQ **148** B1
Althorpe **187** F2
Alticry **215** D5
Altnafeadh **249** E4
Altnaharra **273** H5
Altofts **194** C5
Alton *Derbys* **173** E1
Alton *Hants* **120** C4
Alton *Staffs* **172** B3
Alton Barnes **118** C1
Alton Pancras **104** D2
Alton Priors **118** C1
Alton Towers Leisure Park
*Staffs* ST10 4DB **172** B3
Alton Water Reservoir *Suff*
IP9 2RY **152** C4
Altonside **267** K6
Altrincham **184** B4
Altura **257** J5
Alva **243** D5
Alvanley **183** F5
Alvaston **173** E4
Alvechurch **158** C5
Alvecote **159** E2
Alvediston **118** A5
Alveley **157** G4
Alverdiscott **113** F3
Alverstoke **107** F3
Alverstone **107** E4
Alverthorpe **194** C5
Alverton **174** C3
Alves **267** J5
Alvescot **133** E3
Alveston *SGlos* **131** F4
Alveston *Warks* **147** E2
Alvie **259** F4
Alvingham **189** D3
Alvington **131** F2
Alwalton **161** G3
Alweston **104** C1
Alwington **113** E3
Alwinton **220** B1
Alwoodley **194** C3
Alwoodley Gates **194** C3
Alyth **252** A5
Amalebra **94** B3
Ambaston **173** F4
Amber Hill **176** A3
Ambergate **173** E2
Amberley *Glos* **132** A2
Amberley *WSuss* **108** C2
Amble **221** E1
Amblecote **158** A4
Ambleside **199** E2
Ambleston **140** D5
Ambrismore **232** B4
Ambrosden **134** B1
Amcotts **187** F1
Amersham **135** E3
Amerton **171** G5
Amerton Farm *Staffs*
ST18 0LA **171** G5
Amesbury **118** C3
Ameysford **105** G2
Amington **159** E2
Amisfield Town **217** E2
Amlwch **180** C3
Amlwch Port **180** C3
Ammanford
(Rhydaman) **128** C1
Amotherby **203** G5
Ampfield **119** E5
Ampleforth **203** E5
Ampleforth College **203** E5
Ampney Crucis **132** C2
Ampney St. Mary **132** C2
Ampney St. Peter **132** C2
Amport **119** E3
Ampthill **149** F3
Ampton **163** G5
Amroth **127** E2
Amulree **243** D1
Anaboard **259** H1
Anaheilt **248** B3
Ancaster **175** E3
Anchor **156** A4
Anchor Corner **164** B2
Ancroft **237** G5
Ancrum **228** A4
Ancton **108** B3
Anderby **189** F5
Anderby Creek **189** F5
Andersea **116** A4
Andersfield **115** F4
Anderson **105** E3
Anderton **184** A5
Anderton Boat Lift
*ChesW&C*
CW9 6FW **184** A5
Andover **119** E3
Andover Down **119** E3
Andoversford **132** C1
Andreas **190** C2
Anelog **166** A4
Anfield **183** E3
Angarrack **95** E3
Angarrick **95** E4
Angelbank **157** E5
Angerton **209** F1
Angle **126** B2
Anglers Country
Park *WYorks*
WF4 2EB **186** A1
Angler's Retreat **154** D3
Anglesey
(Ynys Môn) **180** B4
Anglesey Abbey *Cambs*
CB25 9EJ **150** D1
Angmering **108** C3
Angmering-on-Sea **108** C3
Angram *NYorks* **195** E3
Angram *NYorks* **201** D3
Anick **211** F1
Anie **242** A3
Animal World & Butterfly
House *GtMan*
BL1 5UG **184** B1
Ankerville **267** F4
Anlaby **196** C5
Anmer **177** F5
Anmore **107** F1
Annan **217** F4
Annaside **198** B4
Annat *A&B* **240** C2
Annat *High* **264** E6
Annbank **224** C3
Anne Hathaway's
Cottage *Warks*
CV37 9HH **147** D2
Annesley **173** G2
Annesley
Woodhouse **173** F2
Annfield Plain **212** A2
Anniesland **233** G3
Annscroft **157** D2
Ansdell **191** G5
Ansford **116** C4
Ansley **159** F4
Anslow **172** D5
Anslow Gate **172** C5
Ansteadbrook **121** E4
Anstey *Herts* **150** C4
Anstey *Leics* **160** A2
Anston **186** C4
Anstruther **245** D4
Ansty *Warks* **159** F4
Ansty *Wilts* **118** A5
Ansty *WSuss* **109** E1
Ansty Coombe **118** A5
Ansty Cross **105** D2
Anthill Common **107** F1
Anthorn **209** E1
Antingham **179** D2
Anton's Gowt **176** A3
Antony **99** D5
Antrobus **184** A5
Anvil Corner **113** D5
Anvil Green **124** D4
Anwick **175** G2
Anwoth **215** G5
Aonach Mòr Mountain
Gondola & Nevis Range
Ski Centre *High*
PH33 6SW **249** D2
Aoradh **230** A3
Apethorpe **161** F3
Apeton **158** A1
Apley **188** B5
Apperknowle **186** A5
Apperley **146** A5
Apperley Bridge **194** A4
Appersett **201** D3
Appin (An Apainn) **248** B5
Appin House **248** B5
Appleby **187** G1
Appleby Magna **159** F1
Appleby Parva **159** F2
Appleby-in-
Westmorland **210** C5
Applecross **264** D7
Appledore *Devon* **113** E2
Appledore *Devon* **103** D1
Appledore *Kent* **111** E1
Appledore Heath **124** B5
Appleford **134** A3
Appleshaw **119** E3
Applethwaite **209** F4
Appleton *Halton* **183** G4
Appleton *Oxon* **133** G3
Appleton Roebuck **195** E3
Appleton Thorn **184** A4
Appleton Wiske **202** C2
Appleton-le-Moors **203** G4
Appleton-le-Street **203** G5
Appletreehall **227** G4
Appletreewick **193** G1
Appley **115** D5
Appley Bridge **183** G2
Apse Heath **107** E4
Apsey Green **153** D1
Apsley **135** F2
Apsley End **149** G4
Apuldram **108** A3
Arbeia Roman Fort &
Museum *T&W*
NE33 2BB **28** E1
Arbirlot **253** D5
Arborfield **120** C1
Arborfield Cross **120** C1
Arborfield Garrison **120** C1
Arbourthorne **186** A4
Arbroath **253** E5
Arbuthnott **253** F2
Archdeacon
Newton **202** B1
Archiestown **267** K7
Arclid **171** E1
Ard a' Chapuill **232** B1
Ardacheranbeg **232** B1
Ardacheranmor **232** B1
Ardachoil **239** G1
Ardachu **266** D1
Ardailly **231** F4
Ardalanish **238** C3
Ardallie **261** J1
Ardanaiseig **240** C2
Ardaneaskan **256** E1
Ardanstur **240** A3
Ardantiobairt **247** F4
Ardantrive **240** A2
Ardarroch **264** E7
Ardbeg *A&B* **232** B1
Ardbeg *A&B* **230** C5
Ardbeg *A&B* **232** C1
Ardblair **258** C1
Ardbrecknish **240** C2
Ardcharnich **265** H3
Ardchiavaig **238** C3
Ardchonnel **240** B3
Ardchonnell **240** B3
Ardchrishnish **238** D2
Ardchronie **266** D3
Ardchuilk **257** J1
Ardchullarie More **242** A3
Ardchyle **242** A2
Arddlin **156** B1
Ardechive **257** H5
Ardeley **150** B5
Ardelve **256** E2
Arden **233** E1
Ardencaple House **239** G3
Ardens Grafton **146** D2
Ardentallan **240** A2
Ardentinny **232** C1
Ardeonaig **242** B1
Ardersier **266** E6
Ardery **247** G3
Ardessie **265** G3
Ardfad **239** G3
Ardfern **240** A4
Ardfin **230** C3
Ardgartan **241** E4
Ardgay **266** D2
Ardgenavan **241** D3
Ardgour (Corran) **248** C3
Ardgowan **232** D2
Ardgowse **260** E3
Ardgye **267** J5
Ardhallow **232** C2
Ardheslaig **264** D6
Ardiecow **268** D4
Ardinamar **239** G3
Ardindrean **265** H3
Ardingly **109** F1
Ardington **133** G4
Ardington Wick **133** G4
Ardintoul **256** E2
Ardkinglas House **241** D3
Ardlair **260** D2
Ardlamont **232** A3
Ardleigh **152** B5
Ardleigh Green **137** E4
Ardleigh Heath **152** B4
Ardler **252** A5
Ardley **148** A5
Ardley End **137** E1
Ardlui (Àird Laoigh) **241** F3
Ardlussa **231** E1
Ardmaddy **240** C1
Ardmair **265** H2
Ardmaleish **232** B3
Ardmay **241** E4
Ardmenish **231** D2
Ardmhòr **254** C4
Ardminish **231** E5
Ardmolich **247** G2

Ardmore *A&B* **230** C4
Ardmore *A&B* **239** G2
Ardmore *A&B* **233** E2
Ardmore *High* **266** E3
Ardnackaig **239** G5
Ardnadam **232** C1
Ardnagoine **265** F1
Ardnagowan **240** D4
Ardnahein **241** D5
Ardnarff **256** E1
Ardnastang **248** A3
Ardnave **230** A2
Ardno **241** D4
Ardo **261** G1
Ardoch *D&G* **225** G5
Ardoch *Moray* **267** J6
Ardoch *P&K* **243** F1
Ardochrig **234** A5
Ardoyne **260** E2
Ardpatrick **231** F3
Ardpeaton **232** D1
Ardradnaig **250** C5
Ardroe **272** C6
Ardross **266** D4
Ardrossan **232** D5
Ardscalpsie **232** B4
Ardshave **266** E2
Ardshealach **247** F3
Ardshellach **239** G3
Ardsley **186** A2
Ardslignish **247** E3
Ardtalla **230** C4
Ardtalnaig **242** B1
Ardtaraig **232** B1
Ardteatle **240** D2
Ardtoe **247** F2
Ardtornish **247** G5
Ardtrostan **242** B2
Ardtur **248** B5
Arduaine **240** A3
Ardura **239** F1
Ardvar **272** D5
Ardvasar **256** C4
Ardveenish **254** C4
Ardveich **242** B2
Ardverikie **250** A1
Ardvorlich *A&B* **241** F3
Ardvorlich *P&K* **242** B2
Ardwall **215** G5
Ardwell *D&G* **206** B2
Ardwell *Moray* **260** B1
Ardwell *SAyr* **214** C1
Ardwick **184** C3
Areley Kings **158** A5
Arford **120** D4
Argaty **242** C4
Argoed **130** A3
Argoed Mill **143** F1
Argos Hill **110** A1
Argrennan House **216** B5
Argyll & Sutherland
  Highlanders Museum
  *Stir* FK8 1EH **242** C5
Arichamish **240** B4
Arichastlich **241** E1
Arichonan **239** G5
Aridhglas **238** C2
Arienskill **247** G1
Arileod **246** A4
Arinacrinachd **264** D6
Arinafad Beg **231** F1
Arinagour **246** B4
Arinambane **254** C2
Arisaig (Àrasaig) **247** F1
Arivegaig **247** F3
Arkendale **194** C1
Arkesden **150** C4
Arkholme **199** G5
Arkle Town **201** F2
Arkleby **209** E3
Arkleside **201** F4
Arkleton **218** B2
Arkley **136** B3
Arksey **186** C2
Arkwright Town **186** B5
Arlary **243** G4
Arle **146** B5
Arlecdon **208** D5
Arlesey **149** G4
Arleston **157** F1
Arley **184** A4
Arlingham **131** G1
Arlington *Devon* **113** G1
Arlington *ESuss* **110** A3
Arlington *Glos* **132** D2
Arlington Beccott **113** G1
Armadale *High* **272** C2
Armadale *High* **256** C4
Armadale *WLoth*
  **234** D3
Armathwaite **210** B3
Arminghall **179** D5
Armitage **158** C1
Armitage Bridge **185** F1
Armley **194** B4
Armscote **147** E3
Armshead **171** G3
Armston **161** F4
Armthorpe **186** D2
Arnaby **198** C4
Arncliffe **201** E5
Arncliffe Cote **201** E5
Arncroach **244** D4
Arne **105** F4
Arnesby **160** B3
Arngask **243** G3
Arngibbon **242** B5
Arngomery **242** B5
Arnhall **253** E3
Arnicle **222** C2
Arnipol **247** G1
Arnisdale
  (Àrnasdal) **256** E3
Arnish **264** B7
Arniston Engine **236** A3
Arnol **271** F2
Arnold *ERid* **196** D3
Arnold *Notts* **173** G3
Arnolfini Gallery
  BS1 4QA **66** Bristol
Arnprior **242** B5
Arnside **199** F5

Aros Experience *High*
  IV51 9EU **263** K7
Arowry **170** B4
Arrad Foot **199** E4
Arradoul **268** C4
Arram **196** C3
Arran **223** E2
Arras **196** B3
Arrat **253** E4
Arrathorne **202** B3
Arreton **107** E4
Arrington **150** B2
Arrivain **241** E1
Arrochar **241** F4
Arrow **146** C2
Arscaig **273** H7
Arscott **156** D2
Arthington **194** B3
Arthingworth **160** C4
Arthog **154** C1
Arthrath **261** H1
Arthurstone **252** A5
Artrochie **261** J1
Aruadh **230** A3
Arundel **108** C3
Arundel Castle *WSuss*
  BN18 9AB **108** C3
Arundel Cathedral (R.C.)
  *WSuss*
  BN18 9AY **108** C3
Aryhoulan **248** C3
Asby **209** D4
Ascog **232** C3
Ascot **121** E1
Ascott **147** F4
Ascott d'Oyley **133** F1
Ascott Earl **133** E1
Ascott-under-
  Wychwood **133** F1
Ascreavie **252** B4
Asenby **202** D5
Asfordby **160** C1
Asfordby Hill **160** C1
Asgarby *Lincs* **176** B1
Asgarby *Lincs* **175** G3
Ash *Dorset* **105** E1
Ash *Kent* **125** E3
Ash *Kent* **123** F2
Ash *Som* **116** B5
Ash *Surr* **121** D2
Ash Barton **113** F5
Ash Bullayne **102** A2
Ash Green *Surr* **121** E3
Ash Green *Works* **159** F4
Ash Magna **170** C4
Ash Mill **114** A5
Ash Parva **170** C4
Ash Priors **115** E5
Ash Street **152** B3
Ash Thomas **102** D1
Ash Vale **121** D2
Ashampstead **134** A5
Ashbocking **152** C2
Ashbourne **172** C3
Ashbrittle **115** D5
Ashburnham Place **110** B2
Ashburton **101** D1
Ashbury *Devon* **99** F1
Ashbury *Oxon* **133** E4
Ashby **187** E2
Ashby by Partney **176** C1
Ashby cum Fenby **188** C2
Ashby de la Launde **175** F2
Ashby de la Zouch **159** F1
Ashby Dell **165** F2
Ashby Folville **160** C1
Ashby Hill **188** C2
Ashby Magna **160** A3
Ashby Parva **160** A4
Ashby Puerorum **188** D5
Ashby St. Ledgers **148** A1
Ashby St. Mary **179** E5
Ashchurch **146** B4
Ashcombe *Devon* **102** C5
Ashcombe *NSom* **116** A1
Ashcott **116** B4
Ashdon **151** D3
Ashe **119** G3
Asheldham **138** C2
Ashen **151** F3
Ashenden **124** A5
Ashendon **134** C1
Ashens **231** G2
Ashfield *A&B* **231** F1
Ashfield *Here* **145** E5
Ashfield *Stir* **242** C4
Ashfield *Suff* **152** D1
Ashfield Green *Suff* **165** D4
Ashfield Green *Suff* **151** F2
Ashfold Crossways **109** E1
Ashford *Devon* **100** C3
Ashford *Devon* **113** F2
Ashford *Hants* **106** A1
Ashford *Kent* **124** C4
Ashford *Surr* **135** F5
Ashford Bowdler **157** E5
Ashford Carbonel **157** E5
Ashford Hill **119** G1
Ashford in the
  Water **185** F5
Ashgill **234** B4
Ashiestiel **227** F2
Ashill *Devon* **103** D1
Ashill *Norf* **163** G2
Ashill *Som* **116** A5
Ashingdon **138** B3
Ashington
  *WSuss* **108** D2
Ashkirk **227** F2
Ashlett **107** D2
Ashleworth **146** A5
Ashleworth Quay **146** A5
Ashley *Cambs* **151** E1
Ashley *ChesE* **184** B4
Ashley *Devon* **113** G4
Ashley *Glos* **132** B3
Ashley *Hants* **119** E3
Ashley *Hants* **106** B4
Ashley *Kent* **125** F4
Ashley *N'hants* **160** C3
Ashley *Staffs* **171** E3
Ashley *Wilts* **117** F1
Ashley Down **131** E5
Ashley Green **135** E2
Ashley Heath
  *Dorset* **106** A2

Ashley Heath
  *Staffs* **171** E4
Ashmanhaugh **179** E3
Ashmansworth **119** F2
Ashmansworthy **112** D4
Ashmolean Museum
  *Oxon* OX1 2PH
  **80** Oxford
Ashmore *Dorset* **105** F4
Ashmore *P&K* **251** G4
Ashmore Green **119** G1
Ashorne **147** F2
Ashover **173** E1
Ashover Hay **173** E1
Ashow **159** F5
Ashperton **145** F3
Ashprington **101** E2
Ashreigney **113** G4
Ashridge Estate *Herts*
  HP4 1LX **135** E1
Ashtead **121** F2
Ashton *ChesW&C* **170** C1
Ashton *Corn* **94** D4
Ashton *Corn* **99** F4
Ashton *Hants* **107** E1
Ashton *Here* **145** E1
Ashton *Invcly* **232** D2
Ashton *N'hants* **161** F4
Ashton *N'hants* **148** C3
Ashton *Peter* **161** G2
Ashton Common **117** F2
Ashton Court Estate
  *NSom* BS41 9JN **8** B3
Ashton Keynes **132** C3
Ashton under Hill **146** B4
Ashton upon
  Mersey **184** B3
Ashton-in-
  Makerfield **183** G3
Ashton-under-Lyne **184** D3
Ashurst *Hants* **106** C1
Ashurst *Kent* **123** E5
Ashurst *WSuss* **109** E3
Ashurst Bridge **106** C1
Ashurstwood **122** D5
Ashwater **99** D1
Ashwell *Herts* **150** A4
Ashwell *Rut* **161** D1
Ashwell End **150** A4
Ashwellthorpe **164** C2
Ashwick **116** D3
Ashwicken **163** F1
Ashybank **227** G4
Askam in Furness **198** D5
Askern **186** C1
Askernish
  (Aisgernis) **254** C2
Askerswell **104** B3
Askett **134** C2
Askham *Cumb* **210** B5
Askham *Notts* **187** E5
Askham Bryan **195** E3
Askham Richard **195** E3
Asknish **240** B5
Askrigg **201** E3
Askwith **194** A3
Aslackby **175** F4
Aslacton **164** C2
Aslockton **174** C3
Asloun **260** D3
Aspall **152** C1
Aspatria **209** E2
Aspenden **150** B5
Asperton **176** A4
Aspley Guise **149** E4
Aspley Heath **149** E4
Aspull **184** A2
Asselby **195** G5
Asserby **189** E5
Assington **152** A4
Assington Green **151** F2
Astbury **171** F1
Astcote **148** B2
Asterby **188** C5
Asterley **156** C2
Asterton **156** D3
Asthall **133** E1
Asthall Leigh **133** F1
Astle **184** C5
Astley *GtMan* **184** B2
Astley *Shrop* **157** E1
Astley *Warks* **159** F4
Astley *Worcs* **145** G1
Astley Abbotts **157** G3
Astley Bridge **184** B1
Astley Cross **146** A1
Astley Green **184** B3
Astley Lodge **157** E1
Aston *ChesE* **170** D3
Aston *ChesW&C* **183** G5
Aston *Derbys* **185** F4
Aston *Derbys* **172** C4
Aston *Flints* **170** A1
Aston *Here* **157** D5
Aston *Here* **145** D1
Aston *Here* **145** E1
Aston *Herts* **150** A5
Aston *Oxon* **133** F2
Aston *Shrop* **170** C5
Aston *Shrop* **158** A3
Aston *Staffs* **171** E3
Aston *SYorks* **186** B4
Aston *Tel&W* **157** F2
Aston *W'ham* **134** C4
Aston *WMid* **158** C4
Aston Abbotts **148** D5
Aston Botterell **157** F4
Aston Cantlow **146** D2
Aston Clinton **135** D1
Aston Crews **145** F5
Aston Cross **146** B4
Aston Eyre **157** F3
Aston Fields **146** B1
Aston Flamville **159** G3
Aston Heath **183** G5
Aston Ingham **145** F5
Aston juxta
  Mondrum **171** D2
Aston le Walls **147** G2
Aston Magna **147** D4
Aston Munslow **157** E4
Aston on Carrant **146** B4
Aston on Clun **156** C4
Aston Pigott **156** C2
Aston Rogers **156** C2
Aston Rowant **134** C3
Aston Sandford **134** C2
Aston Somerville **146** C4

Aston Subedge **146** D3
Aston Tirrold **134** A4
Aston Upthorpe **134** A4
Aston-on-Trent **173** F5
Astwick **150** A4
Astwood **149** E3
Astwood Bank **146** C1
Aswarby **175** F3
Aswardby **189** D5
Aswick Grange **162** B1
Atcham **157** E2
Ath Linne **270** D6
Athelhampton **105** D3
Athelington **164** D4
Athelney **116** A5
Athelstaneford **236** C2
Atherfield Green **107** D5
Atherington *Devon* **113** F3
Atherington *WSuss* **108** C3
Athersley North **186** A2
Atherstone **159** F3
Atherstone on Stour **147** E2
Atherton **184** A2
Atlow **172** D3
Attadale **257** F1
Attenborough **173** G4
Atterby **187** G3
Attercliffe **186** A4
Atterley **157** F3
Atterton **159** F3
Attingham Park
  *Shrop* SY4 4TP **157** E1
Attleborough *Norf*
  **164** B2
Attleborough
  *Warks* **159** F3
Attlebridge **178** C4
Attleton Green **151** F2
Atwick **197** D2
Atworth **117** F1
Auberrow **145** D3
Aubourn **175** E1
Auch **241** E1
Auchairne **214** C2
Auchallater **251** G1
Auchameanach **231** G5
Auchamore **231** G5
Aucharnie **268** E6
Aucharrigill **266** B1
Auchattie **260** E5
Auchavan **251** G3
Auchbraad **231** G1
Auchbreck **259** K2
Auchenback **233** G4
Auchenblae **253** F2
Auchenbothie **233** E2
Auchenbrack **216** B1
Auchenbreck **232** B1
Auchencairn **216** B5
Auchencrow **237** F3
Auchendinny **235** G3
Auchendolly **216** B4
Auchenfoyle **233** E2
Auchengallin **233** G1
Auchengray **235** D4
Auchenhalrig **268** B4
Auchenharvie **233** E5
Auchenheath **234** C5
Auchenhessnane **216** C1
Auchenlochan **232** A2
Auchenmalg **214** D5
Auchenrivock **218** B3
Auchentiber **233** E5
Auchenvennel **233** D1
Auchessan **241** G2
Auchgourish **259** G3
Auchinafaud **231** F4
Auchincruive **224** B3
Auchindarrach **231** G1
Auchindarroch **248** C4
Auchindrain **240** C4
Auchindrean **265** H3
Auchininna **268** E6
Auchinleck **224** D3
Auchinloch **234** A2
Auchinner **242** B3
Auchinroath **267** K6
Auchintoul *Aber* **260** D3
Auchintoul *Aber* **268** E5
Auchintoul *High* **266** C2
Auchiries **261** J1
Auchleven **260** E2
Auchlochan **225** G2
Auchlunachan **265** H3
Auchlunies **261** G5
Auchlyne **242** A2
Auchmacoy **261** H1
Auchmair **260** B2
Auchmantle **214** C4
Auchmithie **253** E5
Auchmuirbridge **244** A4
Auchnabony **216** B6
Auchnabreac **240** C4
Auchnacloich **242** D1
Auchnacraig **239** G1
Auchnacree **252** C3
Auchnafree **242** D1
Auchnagallin **259** H1
Auchnagatt **269** H6
Auchnaha **232** A1
Auchnangoul **240** C4
Aucholzie **260** B5
Auchorrie **260** E4
Auchrannie **252** A4
Auchraw **242** A2
Auchreoch **241** F2
Auchronie **252** C1
Auchterarder **243** E3
Auchtercairn **264** E4
Auchterderran **244** A5
Auchterhouse **244** B1
Auchtermuchty **244** A3
Auchterneed **266** B6
Auchtertool **244** A5
Auchtertyre *Angus* **252** A5
Auchtertyre (Uachdar Thire)
  *High* **256** E2
Auchtertyre *Moray* **267** J6
Auchtertyre *Stir* **241** F2
Auchtubh **242** A2
Auckengill **275** J2
Auckley **186** D2
Audenshaw **184** D3
Audlem **171** D3
Audley **171** E2
Audley End *Essex* **150** D4

Audley End *Essex* **151** G4
Audley End *Suff* **151** G2
Audmore **171** F1
Auds **268** E4
Aughton *ERid* **195** G4
Aughton *Lancs* **183** E2
Aughton *Lancs* **192** B1
Aughton *SYorks* **186** B4
Aughton *Wilts* **118** D2
Aughton Park **183** F2
Auldearn **267** G6
Aulden **145** D2
Auldgirth **216** D2
Auldhame **236** C1
Auldhouse **234** A4
Aulich **250** B4
Ault a'chruinn **257** F2
Ault Hucknall **173** F1
Aultanrynie **273** F5
Aultbea
  (An t-Allt Beithe) **264** E3
Aultgrshan **264** D3
Aultguish Inn **265** K4
Aultibea **275** F6
Aultiphurst **274** D2
Aultmore **268** C5
Ault-na-goire **258** C2
Aultnamain Inn **266** D3
Aultnapaddock **268** B6
Aulton **260** E2
Aultvaich **266** C7
Aultvoulin **256** D4
Aunby **161** F1
Aundorach **259** G3
Aunk **102** D2
Aunsby **175** F3
Auquhorthies **261** G2
Aust **131** E4
Austerfield **187** D3
Austrey **159** E2
Austwick **193** D1
Authorpe **189** E4
Authorpe Row **189** F5
Avebury **132** D5
Avebury Trusloe **118** B1
Aveley **137** E4
Avening **132** A3
Averham **174** C2
Avery Hill **136** D5
Aveton Gifford **100** C3
Aviation Viewing Park
  *GtMan* M90 1QX **25** E6
Avielochan **259** G3
Aviemore **259** F3
Avington *Hants* **119** G4
Avington *WBerks* **119** E1
Avoch **266** D6
Avon **106** A3
Avon Dassett **147** G2
Avon Heath Country Park
  *Dorset* BH24 2DA **3** E1
Avon Valley Railway *SGlos*
  BS30 6HD **8** B4
Avonbridge **234** D2
Avoncliff **117** F2
Avonmouth **131** E5
Avonwick **100** D2
Awbridge **119** E5
Awhirk **214** B5
Awkley **131** E4
Awliscombe **103** E2
Awre **131** G2
Awsworth **173** F3
Axbridge **116** B2
Axford *Hants* **120** B3
Axford *Wilts* **133** E5
Axminster **103** F3
Axmouth **103** F3
Axton **182** C4
Axtown **100** B1
Aycliffe **212** B5
Aydon **211** G1
Aylburton **131** F2
Ayle **210** D3
Aylesbeare **102** D3
Aylesbury **134** D1
Aylesby **188** C2
Aylesford **123** G3
Aylesham **125** E3
Aylestone **160** A2
Aylmerton **178** C2
Aylsham **178** C3
Aylton **145** F4
Aymestrey **144** D1
Aynho **148** A4
Ayot Green **136** B1
Ayot St. Lawrence **136** A1
Ayot St. Peter **136** B1
Ayr **224** B3
Aysgarth **201** F3
Aysgarth Falls & National
  Park Centre *NYorks*
  DL8 3TH **201** F4
Ayshford **102** D1
Ayside **199** E4
Ayston **161** D2
Aythorpe Roding **137** E1
Ayton *P&K* **243** G3
Ayton *ScBord* **237** G3
Aywick **278** E4
Azerley **202** B5

# B
Babbacombe **101** F1
Babbacombe Model Village
  *Torbay* TQ1 3LA **101** F1
Babbinswood **170** A4
Babb's Green **136** C1
Babcary **116** C5
Babel **143** E4
Babell **182** C5
Babeny **99** G3
Bablock Hythe **133** G2
Babraham **150** D2
Babworth **187** D4
Baby's Hill **259** K1
Bac **271** G3
Bachau **180** C4
Back of Keppoch **247** F1
Back Street **151** F2
Backaland **276** E4
Backaskaill **276** D2
Backbarrow **199** E4
Backburn **260** D1
Backe **127** E1
Backfolds **269** J5
Backford **183** F5
Backhill **261** F1

Backhill of
  Clackriach **269** H6
Backhill of Trustach **260** E5
Backies *High* **267** F1
Backies *Moray* **268** B5
Backlass **275** H3
Backside **260** C1
Backwell **116** B1
Backworth **221** E4
Bacon End **137** E1
Baconend Green **137** E1
Baconsthorpe **178** C2
Bacton *Here* **144** C4
Bacton *Norf* **179** E2
Bacton *Suff* **152** B1
Bacton Green **152** B1
Bacup **193** E5
Badachro **264** D4
Badanloch Lodge **274** C5
Badavanich **265** H6
Badbea **275** F7
Badbury **133** D4
Badbury Wick **133** D4
Badby **148** A2
Badcall *High* **272** C4
Badcall *High* **272** E3
Badcaul **265** G2
Baddeley Green **171** G2
Baddesley Clinton **159** D5
Baddesley Clinton *Works*
  B93 0DQ **159** D5
Baddesley Ensor **159** E3
Baddidarach **272** C6
Badenscoth **261** F1
Badenyon **260** B3
Badgall **97** G1
Badger **157** G3
Badgerbank **184** C5
Badgers Mount **123** D2
Badgeworth **132** B1
Badgworth **116** A2
Badicaul **256** D2
Badingham **153** E1
Badintagairt **273** H7
Badlesmere **124** C3
Badley **152** B2
Badlipster **275** H4
Badluarach **265** F2
Badminton **132** A4
Badnaban **272** C6
Badnabay **272** D4
Badnafrave **259** K3
Badnagie **275** G5
Badnambiast **250** D3
Badninish **266** E2
Badrallach **265** G2
Badsey **146** C3
Badshot Lea **121** D3
Badsworth **186** B1
Badwell Ash **152** A1
Badworthy **100** C1
Badyo **251** E3
Bag Enderby **189** D5
Bagber **105** D1
Bagby **203** D4
Bagendon **132** C1
Baggeridge Country Park
  *Staffs* DY3 4HB **14** A2
Bagginswood **157** F4
Baggrave Hall **160** B2
Baggrow **209** E3
Bàgh Mòr **262** D6
Baghasdal **254** C3
Bagillt **182** D5
Baginton **159** F5
Baglan **128** D3
Bagley *Shrop* **170** B5
Bagley *Som* **116** B3
Bagmore **120** B3
Bagnall **171** G2
Bagnor **119** F1
Bagpath **132** A3
Bagshot *Surr* **121** E1
Bagshot *Wilts* **119** E1
Bagstone **131** F4
Bagthorpe *Norf* **177** F4
Bagthorpe *Notts* **173** F2
Baguley **184** C4
Bagworth **159** G2
Bagwyllydiart **144** D5
Baildon **194** A4
Baile an Truiseil **271** F2
Baile Boidheach **231** F2
Baile Gharbhaidh **262** C7
Baile Glas **262** D6
Baile Mhartainn **262** C4
Baile Mhic Phail **262** D4
Baile Mòr **238** C2
Baile nan Cailleach **262** C6
Baile Raghaill **262** C5
Bailebeag **258** C3
Baileguish **259** F5
Baile-na-Cille **262** C4
Baileyhead **218** C3
Bailiesward **260** C1
Bailiff Bridge **194** A5
Baillieston **234** A3
Bainbridge **201** E3
Bainsford **234** C1
Bainshole **260** E1
Bainton *ERid* **196** B2
Bainton *Oxon* **148** A5
Bainton *Peter* **161** G2
Bairnkine **228** A5
Baker Street **137** F4
Baker's End **136** C1
Bakewell **172** D1
Bala (Y Bala) **168** C4
Balachuirn **264** B7
Balado **243** F4
Balafark **242** B5
Balaldie **267** F4
Balallan
  (Baile Ailein) **270** E5
Balavil *High* **258** E4
Balbeg *High* **258** B1
Balbeg *High* **258** B2
Balbeggie **243** G2
Balbirnie **244** A4
Balbithan **261** F3
Balblair *High* **266** E5
Balblair *High* **266** C5
Balby **186** C2
Balcharn **266** C1
Balcherry **267** F3

Balchers **269** F5
Balchladich **272** C5
Balchraggan *High* **266** C7
Balchraggan *High* **258** C1
Balchrick **272** D3
Balcombe **122** C5
Balcurvie **244** B4
Baldernock **233** G2
Baldersby **202** C5
Baldersby
  St. James **202** C5
Balderstone
  *GtMan* **184** D1
Balderstone *Lancs* **192** C4
Balderton
  *ChesW&C* **170** A1
Balderton *Notts* **174** D2
Baldhu **96** B5
Baldinnie **244** C3
Baldock **150** A4
Baldon Row **134** A2
Baldovan **244** B1
Baldovie *Angus* **252** B4
Baldovie *Dundee* **244** C1
Baldrine **190** C3
Baldslow **110** C2
Baldwin **190** B3
Baldwinholme **209** G1
Baldwin's Gate **171** E3
Baldwins Hill **122** C5
Bale **178** B2
Balelone
  (Baile Lion) **262** C4
Balemartine **246** A2
Balemore
  (Baile Mòr) **262** C5
Balendoch **252** A5
Balephuil **246** A2
Balerno **235** F3
Balernock **233** D1
Baleromindubh **238** C5
Baleromore **238** C5
Baleshare
  (Bhaleshear) **262** C5
Balevulin **239** D2
Balfield **252** D3
Balfour *Aber* **260** D5
Balfour *Ork* **277** D6
Balfron **233** G1
Balfron Station **233** G1
Balgonar **243** F5
Balgove **261** G1
Balgowan *D&G* **206** B2
Balgowan *High* **258** D5
Balgown **263** J5
Balgreen **269** F5
Balgreggan **214** B5
Balgy **264** E6
Balhaldie **242** D4
Balhalgardy **261** F2
Balham **136** B5
Balhary **252** A5
Balhelvie **244** B2
Balhousie **244** C4
Baliasta **278** F2
Baligill **274** D2
Baligrundle **248** A5
Balindore **240** B1
Balintore *Angus* **252** A4
Balintore *High* **267** F4
Balintraid **266** E4
Balintyre **250** B5
Balivanich (Baile
  a'Mhanaich) **262** C6
Balkeerie **252** B5
Balkholme **195** G5
Balkissock **214** C2
Ball **170** A5
Ball Haye Green **171** G2
Ball Hill **119** F1
Balla **254** C3
Ballabeg **190** A4
Ballacannell **190** C3
Ballacarnane Beg **190** A3
Ballachulish (Baile a'
  Chaolais) **248** C4
Balladoole **190** A5
Ballafesson **190** A4
Ballagyr **190** A3
Ballajora **190** C2
Ballakilpheric **190** A4
Ballamodha **190** A4
Ballantrae **214** B2
Ballards Gore **138** C3
Ballasalla *IoM* **190** A5
Ballasalla *IoM* **190** B2
Ballater **260** B5
Ballaterach **260** C5
Ballaugh **190** B2
Ballaveare **190** B4
Ballchraggan **266** E4
Ballechin **251** F4
Balleich **242** A4
Ballencrieff **236** B2
Ballidon **172** D2
Balliekine **231** G5
Balliemeanoch **240** D4
Balliemore *A&B* **240** D5
Balliemore *A&B* **240** A2
Ballig **190** A3
Ballimeanoch **240** C3
Ballimore *A&B* **232** A1
Ballimore *Stir* **242** A3
Ballinaby **230** A3
Ballindean **244** A2
Ballingdon **151** G3
Ballinger Common **135** E2
Ballingham **145** E4
Ballingry **243** G5
Ballinlick **251** E5
Ballinluig *P&K* **251** F4
Ballinluig *P&K* **251** F4
Ballintuim **251** G4
Balloch *Angus* **252** B4
Balloch *High* **266** E7
Balloch *High* **258** E1
Balloch *NLan* **234** B2
Balloch *WDun* **233** E1
Ballochan **260** D5
Ballochandrain **232** A1
Ballochford **260** B1
Ballochgair **222** C3
Ballochmartin **232** C4
Ballochmorrie **214** D2
Ballochmyle **224** D3
Ballochroy **231** F4
Balls Cross **121** E5
Balls Green *Essex* **152** B5

Ball's Green *Glos* 132 A3
Balls Hill 158 B3
Ballyaurgan 231 F2
Ballygown 246 D5
Ballygrant 230 B3
Ballyhaugh 246 A4
Ballymeanoch 240 A5
Ballymichael 223 E2
Balmacara
 (Baile Mac Ara) 256 E2
Balmaclellan 216 A3
Balmacneil 251 E4
Balmadies 253 D5
Balmae 207 G2
Balmaha 241 G5
Balmalcolm 244 B4
Balmaqueen 263 K4
Balmeanach *A&B* 247 F5
Balmeanach *A&B* 238 D1
Balmedie 261 H3
Balmedie Country Park
 *Aber* AB23 8XG 261 H3
Balmer Heath 170 B4
Balmerlawn 106 C2
Balminnoch 215 D4
Balmoral *EDun* 234 A2
Balmore *High* 267 F7
Balmore *High* 257 K1
Balmore *High* 263 H7
Balmore *P&K* 250 C4
Balmullo 244 C2
Balmungie 266 E6
Balmyle 251 F4
Balnaboth 252 B3
Balnabruaich 266 E4
Balnacra 265 F7
Balnafoich 258 D1
Balnagall 267 F3
Balnagown Castle 266 E4
Balnaguard 251 E4
Balnaguisich 266 D4
Balnahard *A&B* 238 D5
Balnahard *A&B* 239 D1
Balnain 258 B1
Balnakeil 273 F2
Balnamoon 252 D3
Balnapaling 266 E5
Balnespick 89 F4
Balquhidder 242 A2
Balsall 159 E5
Balsall Common 159 E5
Balsall Heath 158 C4
Balscote 147 F3
Balsham 151 D2
Baltasound 278 F2
Balterley 171 E2
Balterley Heath 171 E2
Baltersan 215 F4
Balthangie 269 G5
Balthayock 243 F2
Baltonsborough 116 C4
Baluachraig 240 A5
Balulive 230 C3
Balure *A&B* 240 C1
Balure *A&B* 240 A1
Balvaird 266 C6
Balvarran 251 F3
Balvicar 239 G3
Balvraid *High* 256 E3
Balvraid *High* 259 F1
Bamber Bridge 192 B5
Bamber's Green 151 D5
Bamburgh 229 F3
Bamburgh Castle *N'umb*
 NE69 7DF 229 F3
Bamff 252 A4
Bamford *Derbys* 185 G4
Bamford *GtMan* 184 C1
Bampton *Cumb* 199 G1
Bampton *Devon* 114 C5
Bampton *Oxon* 133 F2
Bampton Grange 199 G1
Banavie
 (Banbhaidh) 248 D2
Banbury 147 G3
Banbury Museum *Oxon*
 OX16 2PQ 147 G4
Bancffosfelen 128 A1
Banchor 267 G7
Banchory 261 F5
Banchory Devenick 261 H4
Bancycapel 128 A1
Bancyfelin 127 G1
Bancyffordd 142 A4
Bandon 244 A4
Bandrake Head 199 G4
Banff 268 E4
Bangor 181 D5
Bangor-on-Dee (Bangor-
 is-y-coed) 170 A3
Bangor's Green 183 E2
Banham 164 B3
Banham Zoo *Norf*
 NR16 2HE 164 B3
Bank 106 B2
Bank End 198 C4
Bank Newton 193 F2
Bank Street 145 F1
Bank Top *Lancs* 183 G2
Bank Top *WYorks* 194 A5
Bankend 217 E4
Bankfoot 243 F1
Bankglen 225 D4
Bankhead *Aber* 260 E3
Bankhead *Aber* 260 E4
Bankhead
 Aberdeen 261 G3
Bankhead *D&G* 208 A2
Bankland 116 A5
Banknock 234 B2
Banks *Cumb* 210 B1
Banks *Lancs* 191 G5
Bankshill 217 F2
Banningham 178 D3
Bannister Green 151 E5
Banstead 122 B3
Bantam Grove 194 B5
Banton 234 B2
Banwell 116 A2
Banwen Pyrddin 129 E2
Banyard's Green 165 E4
Bapchild 124 B2
Baptiston 233 G1
Bapton 118 A4

Bar End 119 F5
Bar Hill 150 B1
Barachander 240 C2
Barassie 224 B2
Barbaraville 266 E4
Barber Booth 185 F4
Barber Green 199 E4
Barber's Moor 183 F1
Barbican Arts & Conference
 Centre *GtLon*
 EC2Y 8DS 45 J1
Barbon 200 B4
Barbridge 170 D2
Barbrook 114 A3
Barby 160 A5
Barcaldine (Am Barra
 Calltainn) 248 B5
Barcaple 216 A5
Barchester 210 A1
Barclose 210 A1
Barcombe 109 G2
Barcombe Cross 109 G2
Barden 202 A3
Barden Park 123 E4
Bardennoch 215 G1
Bardfield End Green 151 E4
Bardfield Saling 151 E5
Bardister 278 C5
Bardney 175 G1
Bardon *Leics* 159 G1
Bardon *Moray* 267 K6
Bardon Mill 211 D1
Bardowie 233 G2
Bardsea 199 D5
Bardsey 194 C3
Bardsey Island
 (Ynys Enlli) 166 A5
Bardwell 164 A4
Bare 192 A1
Barewood 144 C2
Barfad 231 G3
Barford *Norf* 178 C5
Barford *Warks* 147 E1
Barford St. John 147 G4
Barford St. Martin 118 B4
Barford St. Michael 147 G4
Barfrestone 125 E3
Bargaly 215 F4
Bargany Mains 224 A5
Bargeddie 234 A3
Bargoed 130 A3
Bargrennan 215 E3
Barham *Cambs* 161 G5
Barham *Kent* 125 E3
Barham *Suff* 152 C2
Barharrow 216 A5
Barholm 161 F1
Barholm Mains 215 F5
Barkby 160 B2
Barkby Thorpe 160 B2
Barkers Green 170 C5
Barkestone-le-Vale 174 C4
Barkham 120 C1
Barking *GtLon* 136 D4
Barking *Suff* 152 B2
Barking Tye 152 B2
Barkisland 193 G5
Barkston 175 E3
Barkston Ash 195 D4
Barkway 150 B4
Barlae 215 D4
Barland 144 B1
Barlaston 171 F4
Barlavington 108 B2
Barlborough 186 B5
Barlby 195 F4
Barlestone 159 G2
Barley *Herts* 150 B4
Barley *Lancs* 193 E3
Barley Green 164 D4
Barleycroft End 150 C5
Barleyhill 211 G2
Barleythorpe 160 D2
Barling 138 C4
Barlings 188 A5
Barlow *Derbys* 186 A5
Barlow *NYorks* 195 F5
Barlow *T&W* 212 A1
Barmby Moor 195 G3
Barmby on the
 Marsh 195 F5
Barmer 177 G4
Barmolloch 240 A5
Barmoor Lane End 229 E3
Barmouth
 (Abermaw) 154 C1
Barmpton 202 C1
Barmston 197 D2
Barnaby Green 165 F4
Barnacabber 232 C1
Barnacarry 240 B5
Barnack 161 F2
Barnacle 159 F4
Barnamuc 248 C5
Barnard Castle 201 F1
Barnard Gate 133 G1
Barnardiston 151 F3
Barnard's Green 146 A2
Barnbarroch *D&G* 215 E5
Barnbarroch *D&G* 216 C5
Barnburgh 186 B2
Barnby 165 F3
Barnby Dun 186 D2
Barnby in
 the Willows 175 D2
Barnby Moor 187 D4
Barndennoch 216 C2
Barne Barton 100 A2
Barnehurst 137 E5
Barnes 136 B5
Barnes Street 123 F4
Barnet 136 B3
Barnet Gate 136 B3
Barnetby le Wold 188 A2
Barney 178 A2
Barnham *Suff* 163 G5
Barnham *WSuss* 108 B3
Barnham Broom 178 B5
Barnhead 253 E4
Barnhill *ChesW&C* 170 B2
Barnhill *Dundee* 244 C1
Barnhill *Moray* 267 J6
Barnhills 214 A3
Barningham *Dur* 201 F1
Barningham *Suff* 164 A4
Barningham Green 178 C2
Barnoldby le Beck 188 C2
Barnoldswick 193 E3

Barns Green 121 G5
Barnsdale Bar 186 C1
Barnsley *Glos* 132 C2
Barnsley *SYorks* 186 A2
Barnsole 125 E3
Barnstaple 113 F2
Barnston *Essex* 137 F1
Barnston *Mersey* 183 D4
Barnstone 174 C4
Barnt Green 158 C5
Barnton *ChesW&C* 184 A5
Barnton *Edin* 235 F2
Barnwell All Saints 161 F4
Barnwell Country Park
 *N'hants*
 PE8 5PB 161 F4
Barnwell St. Andrew 161 F4
Barnwood 132 A1
Barons' Cross 145 D2
Barr *A&B* 230 B3
Barr *High* 247 F4
Barr *SAyr* 215 D1
Barr *Som* 115 E5
Barr Hall 151 E4
Barra (Barraigh) 254 B4
 Airport 254 B4
Barrachan 207 D2
Barrackan 239 G4
Barraer 215 E4
Barraglom 270 D4
Barran 241 D2
Barrapoll 246 A2
Barrasford 220 B4
Barravullin 240 A4
Barregarrow 190 B3
Barrets Green 170 C2
Barrhead 233 F4
Barrhill 214 D2
Barrington *Cambs* 150 B3
Barrington *Som* 103 G1
Barripper 94 D3
Barrisdale 256 E4
Barrmill 233 E4
Barrnacarry 240 A2
Barrock 275 H1
Barrow *Glos* 146 A5
Barrow *Lancs* 192 D4
Barrow *Rut* 161 D1
Barrow *Shrop* 157 F2
Barrow *Som* 117 E5
Barrow *Som* 116 C3
Barrow *Suff* 151 F1
Barrow Gurney 116 C2
Barrow Hann 196 C5
Barrow Haven 196 C5
Barrow Hill 186 B5
Barrow Nook 183 F2
Barrow Street 117 F4
Barrow upon
 Humber 196 C5
Barrow upon Soar 160 A1
Barrow upon Trent 173 E5
Barroway Drove 163 D2
Barrowby 175 D4
Barrowcliff 204 D4
Barrowden 161 E2
Barrowford 193 E4
Barrow-in-Furness 191 F1
Barrows Green 199 G4
Barry *Angus* 244 D1
Barry *VGlam* 115 E1
Barry Island Pleasure
 Park *VGlam*
 CF62 5TR 115 E1
Barsby 160 B1
Barsham 165 E3
Barskimming 224 C3
Barsloisnoch 240 A5
Barston 159 E5
Barter Books,
 Alnwick *N'umb*
 NE66 2NP 229 F5
Bartestree 145 E3
Barthol Chapel 261 G1
Bartholomew Green 151 F5
Bartholmley 171 E2
Bartley 106 C1
Bartley Green 158 C4
Bartlow 151 D3
Barton *Cambs* 150 C2
Barton *ChesW&C* 170 B2
Barton *Cumb* 210 A5
Barton *Glos* 146 C5
Barton *Lancs* 192 B4
Barton *Lancs* 183 E2
Barton *NYorks* 202 B2
Barton *Oxon* 134 A2
Barton *Torbay* 101 F1
Barton *Warks* 146 D2
Barton Bendish 163 F2
Barton End 132 A3
Barton Green 159 D1
Barton Hartshorn 148 B4
Barton Hill 195 G1
Barton in Fabis 173 G4
Barton in the Beans 159 F2
Barton Mills 163 F5
Barton on Sea 106 B3
Barton St. David 116 C4
Barton Seagrave 161 D5
Barton Stacey 119 F3
Barton Town 113 G1
Barton Turf 179 E3
Bartongate 147 G5
Barton-le-Clay 149 F4
Barton-le-Street 203 G5
Barton-le-Willows 195 G1
Barton-on-
 the-Heath 147 E4
Barton-under-
 Needwood 159 D1
Barton-upon-
 Humber 196 C5
Barvas
 (Barabhas) 271 F2
Barway 162 D5
Barwell 159 G3
Barwhinnock 216 A5
Barwick *Herts* 136 C1
Barwick *Som* 104 B1
Barwick in Elmet 194 C4
Barwinnock 207 D2
Baschurch 170 B5
Bascote 147 G1
Base Green 152 B1
Basford Green 171 G2

Bashall Eaves 192 C3
Bashall Town 192 D3
Bashley 106 B3
Basildon *Essex* 137 G4
Basildon *WBerks* 134 B5
Basingstoke 120 B2
Baslow 185 G5
Bason Bridge 116 A3
Bassaleg 130 B4
Bassenthwaite 209 F3
Basset's Cross 113 F5
Bassett 106 C1
Bassingbourn 150 B3
Bassingfield 174 B4
Bassingham 175 E2
Bassingthorpe 175 E5
Basta 278 E3
Baston 161 G1
Bastonford 146 A2
Bastwick 179 F4
Batavaime 241 G1
Batch 116 A2
Batchley 146 C1
Batchworth 135 F3
Batchworth Heath 135 F3
Batcombe
 *Dorset* 104 C2
Batcombe *Som* 117 D4
Bate Heath 184 A5
Bath 117 E1
Bath Abbey *B&NESom*
 BA1 1LT 63 Bath
Bathampton 117 E1
Bathealton 115 D5
Batheaston 117 E1
Bathford 117 E1
Bathgate 235 D3
Bathley 174 C2
Bathpool *Corn* 97 G2
Bathpool *Som* 115 F5
Bathway 116 C2
Batley 194 B5
Batsford 147 D4
Batson 100 D4
Battersby 203 E2
Battersea 136 B5
Battersea Cats & Dogs
 Home *GtLon*
 SW8 4AA 13 A5
Battersea Park Children's
 Zoo *GtLon*
 SW11 4NJ 13 A5
Battisborough
 Cross 100 C3
Battisford 152 B2
Battisford Tye 152 B2
Battle *ESuss* 110 C2
Battle *Powys* 143 G4
Battle Abbey *ESuss*
 TN33 0AD 110 C2
Battledown 146 B5
Battlefield 157 E1
Battlesbridge 137 G3
Battlesden 149 E5
Battlesea Green 164 D4
Battleton 114 C5
Battles Green 152 C1
Battramsley 106 C3
Batt's Corner 120 D3
Bauds of Cullen 268 C4
Baugh 246 B2
Baughton 146 A3
Baughurst 119 G1
Baulds 260 E5
Baulking 133 F3
Baumber 188 C5
Baunton 132 C2
Baveney Wood 157 F5
Baverstock 118 B4
Bawburgh 178 C5
Bawdeswell 178 B3
Bawdrip 116 A4
Bawdsey 153 E3
Bawdsey Manor 153 E4
Bawsey 163 E1
Bawtry 187 D3
Baxenden 193 D5
Baxterley 159 E3
Baxter's Green 151 F2
Baxters Highland
 Village *Moray*
 IV32 7LD 268 B4
Bay 117 F3
Baybridge 211 F3
Baycliff 199 D5
Baydon 133 E5
Bayford *Herts* 136 C1
Bayford *Som* 117 E5
Bayfordbury 136 C1
Bayham Abbey 123 F5
Bayles 210 C3
Baylham 152 C2
Baynards Green 148 A5
Baysham 145 E5
Bayston Hill 157 D2
Bayswater 136 B4
Baythorn End 151 F3
Bayton 157 F5
Bayworth 134 A2
Beach *High* 247 G4
Beach *SGlos* 131 G5
Beachampton 148 C4
Beachamwell 163 F2
Beacharr 231 E5
Beachley 131 E3
Beacon *Devon* 103 E2
Beacon *Devon* 103 F2
Beacon Fell Country
 Park *Lancs*
 PR3 2NL 192 B3
Beacon Hill *Dorset* 105 F3
Beacon Hill *Essex* 138 B1
Beacon Hill *Surr* 121 D4
Beacon Hill Country Park
 *Leics* LE12 8SR 17 A2
Beacon Park,
 Up Holland *Lancs*
 WN8 7RU 183 G2
Beacon's Bottom 134 C3
Beaconsfield 135 E3
Beacravik 263 G2
Beadlam 203 F4
Beadlow 149 G4
Beadnell 229 G4
Beaford 113 F4
Beal *Nthumb* 229 E2
Beal *NYorks* 195 D5
Bealach 248 B4

Beale Park *WBerks*
 RG8 9NH 134 B5
Bealsmill 99 D3
Beambridge 170 D2
Beamhurst 172 B4
Beaminster 104 A2
Beamish 212 B2
Beamish, North of England
 Open Air Museum
 *Dur* DH9 0RG 29 A1
Beamsley 193 G2
Bean 137 E5
Beanacre 118 A1
Beanley 229 E5
Beaquoy 276 C5
Beardon 99 F2
Beardwood 192 C5
Beare 102 C2
Beare Green 121 G3
Bearley 147 D1
Bearnock 258 B1
Bearnus 246 C5
Bearpark 212 B3
Bearsbridge 211 D2
Bearsden 233 G2
Bearsted 123 G3
Bearstone 171 E4
Bearwood *Poole* 105 G3
Bearwood *WMid* 158 C4
Beatles Story
 *Mersey* L3 4AD 42 B5
Beattock 226 B3
Beauchamp Roding 137 E2
Beauchief 186 A4
Beaudesert 147 D1
Beaufort 130 A1
Beaulieu 106 C2
Beaulieu: National Motor
 Museum, Abbey & Palace
 House *Hants*
 SO42 7ZN 4 A5
Beauly (A' Mhanachainn)
 266 C7
Beaumaris (Biwmares)
 181 E5
Beaumont *Chanl* 100 C5
Beaumont *Cumb* 209 G1
Beaumont *Essex* 152 C5
Beaumont Hill 202 B1
Beaumont Leys 160 A2
Beausale 159 E5
Beauvale 173 F3
Beauworth 119 G5
Beaver Green 124 B4
Beaworthy 99 E1
Beazley End 151 F5
Bebington 183 E4
Bebside 221 E3
Beccles 165 F2
Beccles Heliport 165 F3
Becconsall 192 A5
Beck Foot 200 B3
Beck Hole 204 B2
Beck Row 163 E5
Beck Side *Cumb* 198 D4
Beck Side *Cumb* 199 E4
Beckbury 157 G2
Beckenham 122 C2
Beckering 188 B4
Beckermet 198 B2
Beckett End 163 F3
Beckfoot *Cumb* 198 D2
Beckfoot *Cumb* 209 D2
Beckford 146 B4
Beckhampton 118 B1
Beckingham *Lincs* 175 D2
Beckingham *Notts* 187 E4
Beckington 117 F2
Beckley *ESuss* 111 D1
Beckley *Oxon* 134 A1
Beck's Green 165 E3
Beckside 200 B4
Beckton 136 D4
Beckwithshaw 194 B2
Becontree 137 D4
Bedale 202 B4
Bedburn 211 G4
Bedchester 105 E1
Beddau 129 G4
Beddgelert 167 E3
Beddington 122 B2
Beddington Corner 122 B2
Bedfield 152 D1
Bedfield Little
 Green 152 D1
Bedford 149 F3
Bedgebury Cross 123 G5
Bedgrove 134 C1
Bedham 121 F5
Bedhampton 107 G2
Bedingfield 152 C1
Bedingfield Green 152 C1
Bedingham Green 165 D2
Bedlam *Lancs* 193 D5
Bedlam *NYorks* 194 B1
Bedlam Street 109 E2
Bedlar's Green 150 D5
Bedlington 221 E3
Bedlinog 129 G2
Bedminster 131 E5
Bedmond 135 F2
Bednall 158 B1
Bedol 182 D5
Bedrule 228 A5
Bedstone 156 C5
Bedwas 130 A4
Bedwell 150 A5
Bedwellty 130 A2
Bedworth 159 F4
Bedworth
 Woodlands 159 F4
Beeby 160 B2
Beech *Hants* 120 B4
Beech *Staffs* 171 F4
Beech Hill 120 B1
Beechingstoke 118 B2
Beechwood 183 G4
Beecraigs Country
 Park *WLoth*
 EH49 6PL 235 D2
Beedon 133 G5
Beeford 196 D2
Beeley 173 D1
Beelsby 188 C2
Beenham 119 G1

Beeny 98 B1
Beer 103 F4
Beer Hackett 104 C1
Beercrocombe 116 A5
Beesands 101 E3
Beesby *Lincs* 189 E4
Beesby *NELincs* 188 C3
Beeson 101 E3
Beeston *CenBeds* 149 G3
Beeston *ChesW&C* 170 C2
Beeston *Norf* 178 A4
Beeston *Notts* 173 G4
Beeston *WYorks* 194 B4
Beeston Regis 178 C1
Beeston
 St. Lawrence 179 E3
Beeswing 216 C4
Beetham *Cumb* 199 F5
Beetham *Som* 103 F1
Beetley 178 A4
Beffcote 158 A1
Began 130 B4
Begbroke 133 G1
Begdale 162 C2
Begelly 127 E2
Beggar's Bush 144 B1
Beggearn Huish 114 D4
Beggshill 260 D1
Beguildy (Bugeildy) 156 A5
Beighton *Norf* 179 E5
Beighton *SYorks* 186 B4
Beili-glas 130 C2
Beith 233 E4
Bekesbourne 125 D3
Bekonscot Model Village
 *Bucks* HP9 2PL 135 E3
Belaugh 179 D4
Belbroughton 158 B5
Belchalwell 105 D2
Belchalwell Street 105 D2
Belchamp Otten 151 G3
Belchamp St. Paul 151 F3
Belchamp Walter 151 G3
Belchford 188 C5
Belfield 184 D1
Belford 229 F3
Belgrave 160 A2
Belhaven 237 D2
Belhelvie 261 H3
Belhinnie 260 C2
Bell Bar 136 B2
Bell Busk 193 F2
Bell End 158 B5
Bell Heath 158 B5
Bell Hill 120 B5
Bell o' th' Hill 170 C3
Bellabeg 260 B3
Belladrum 266 C7
Bellanoch 240 A5
Bellaty 252 A4
Belle Isle 194 C5
Belle Vue 209 G1
Belleau 189 E5
Bellehiglash 259 J1
Bellerby 202 A3
Bellever 99 G3
Bellfields 121 E2
Belliehill 253 D3
Bellingdon 135 E2
Bellingham *GtLon* 136 C5
Bellingham *N'umb* 220 A3
Belloch 222 B2
Bellochantuy 222 B2
Bell's Cross 152 C2
Bellsbank 224 C5
Bellshill *N'umb* 229 F3
Bellshill *NLan* 234 B3
Bellside 234 C4
Bellsmyre 233 F2
Bellsquarry 235 E3
Belluton 116 C2
Belmaduthy 266 D6
Belmesthorpe 161 F1
Belmont *B'burn* 184 A1
Belmont *GtLon* 122 B2
Belmont *GtLon* 136 A3
Belmont *Shet* 278 E2
Belnie 176 A4
Belowda 97 D3
Belper 173 E3
Belper Lane End 173 E3
Belsay 220 D3
Belsford 101 D2
Belsize 135 F2
Belstead 152 C3
Belston 224 B3
Belstone 99 G1
Belstone Corner 99 G1
Belsyde 235 D2
Belthorn 192 D5
Beltinge 125 D2
Beltingham 211 D1
Belton *Leics* 173 F5
Belton *Lincs* 175 E4
Belton *NLincs* 187 E2
Belton *Norf* 179 F5
Belton *Rut* 160 D2
Belton House *Lincs*
 NG32 2LS 175 E4
Beltring 123 F4
Belvedere 137 D5
Belvoir 174 D4
Bembridge 107 F4
Bemersyde 227 G2
Bemerton 118 C4
Bempton 205 E5
Ben Alder Cottage 249 G3
Ben Alder Lodge 250 A2
Ben Rhydding 194 A3
Benacre 165 G3
Benbecula (Beinn na
 Faoghla) 262 D6
Benbecula (Balivanich)
 Airport 262 D6
Benbuie 216 B1
Benderloch
 (Meadarloch) 240 B1
Bendish 149 G5
Benenden 124 A5
Benfield 215 E4
Benfieldside 211 G2
Bengate 179 E3
Bengeo 136 C1
Bengeworth 146 C3
Benhall 146 B5
Benhall Green 153 E1

Benhall Street 153 E1
Benholm 253 G2
Beningbrough 195 E2
Benington *Herts* 150 A5
Benington *Lincs* 176 B3
Benington Sea End 176 C3
Benllech 180 D4
Benmore *A&B* 232 C1
Benmore *Stir* 241 G2
Bennacott 98 C1
Bennan Cottage 216 A3
Bennett End 134 C2
Bennetts End 135 F2
Benniworth 188 C4
Benover 123 G4
Benson 134 B3
Benston 279 D7
Benthall *N'umb* 229 G4
Benthall *Shrop* 157 F2
Bentham 132 B1
Benthoul 261 G4
Bentlawnt 156 C2
Bentley *ERid* 196 C4
Bentley *Essex* 137 E3
Bentley *Hants* 120 C3
Bentley *Suff* 152 C4
Bentley *SYorks* 186 C2
Bentley *Warks* 159 E3
Bentley *WMid* 158 B3
Bentley *WYorks* 194 B4
Bentley Heath
 *Herts* 136 B3
Bentley Heath
 *WMid* 159 D5
Bentley Rise 186 C2
Benton 113 G2
Benton Square 221 F4
Bentpath 218 B2
Bentworth 120 B3
Benvie 244 B1
Benville Lane 104 B2
Benwell 212 B1
Benwick 162 B3
Beoley 146 C1
Beoraidbeg 256 C5
Bepton 108 A2
Berden 150 C5
Bere Alston 100 A1
Bere Ferrers 100 A1
Bere Regis 105 E3
Berea 140 A4
Berepper 95 D4
Bergh Apton 179 E5
Berinsfield 134 A3
Berkeley 131 F3
Berkhamsted 135 E2
Berkley 117 F3
Berkswell 159 E5
Bermondsey 136 C5
Bernera 256 E2
Berneray (Eilean
 Bhearnaraigh) 262 E3
Berners Roding 137 F2
Bernice 240 D5
Bernisdale 263 K6
Berrick Prior 134 B3
Berrick Salome 134 B3
Berriedale 275 G6
Berriew (Aberriw) 156 A2
Berrington
 *N'umb* 229 E2
Berrington *Shrop* 157 E2
Berrington *Worcs* 145 E1
Berrington Green 145 E1
Berriowbridge 97 G2
Berrow *Som* 115 G2
Berrow *Worcs* 145 G4
Berrow Green 145 G2
Berry Cross 113 E4
Berry Down Cross 113 F1
Berry Hill *Glos* 131 E1
Berry Hill *Pembs* 141 D3
Berry Pomeroy 101 E1
Berryhillock 268 C4
Berrynarbor 113 F1
Berry's Green 122 D3
Bersham 170 A3
Berstane 277 D6
Berthlwyd 128 B3
Berwick 110 A3
Berwick Bassett 132 D5
Berwick Hill 221 D4
Berwick St. James 118 B4
Berwick St. John 118 A5
Berwick St. Leonard 118 A4
Berwick-upon-
 Tweed 237 G4
Bescar 183 E1
Bescot 158 C3
Besford *Shrop* 170 C5
Besford *Worcs* 146 B3
Bessacarr 186 D2
Bessels Leigh 133 G2
Besses o' th' Barn 184 C2
Bessingby 197 D1
Bessingham 178 C2
Best Beech Hill 123 F5
Besthorpe *Norf* 164 B2
Besthorpe *Notts* 174 D1
Bestwood 173 G3
Bestwood Country Park
 *Notts* NG6 8UF 19 G1
Beswick *ERid* 196 C3
Beswick *GtMan* 184 C3
Betchworth 122 B3
Bethania *Cere* 142 B1
Bethania *Gwyn* 168 A3
Bethel *Gwyn* 167 E1
Bethel *Gwyn* 168 C4
Bethel *IoA* 180 B5
Bethersden 124 B5
Bethesda *Gwyn* 167 F1
Bethesda *Pembs* 127 D1
Bethlehem 142 C4
Bethnal Green 136 C4
Betley 171 E3
Betley Common 171 E3
Betsham 137 F5
Betteshanger 125 F3
Bettiscombe 103 G3
Bettisfield 170 B4
Betton *Shrop* 156 C2
Betton *Shrop* 171 D4
Betton Strange 157 E2
Bettws *Bridgend* 129 F4
Bettws *Newport* 130 B3
Bettws Bledrws 142 B2
Bettws Cedewain 156 A3

Bettws Gwerfil
Goch **168** D3
Bettws Newydd **130** C2
Bettws-y-crwyn **156** B4
Bettyhill **274** C1
Betws **128** C1
Betws Disserth **144** A4
Betws Garmon **167** E2
Betws Ifan **141** G3
Betws-y-coed **168** A2
Betws-yn-Rhos **182** A5
Beulah *Cere* **141** F3
Beulah *Powys* **143** F2
Bevendean **109** F3
Bevercotes **187** D5
Beverley **196** C4
Beverston **132** A3
Bevington **131** F3
Bewaldeth **209** F3
Bewcastle **219** D4
Bewdley **157** G5
Bewerley **194** A1
Bewholme **197** D2
*Bewl Water ESuss*
*TN3 8JH* **123** F5
Bexhill **110** C3
Bexley **137** D5
Bexleyheath **137** D5
Bexwell **163** E2
Beyton **152** A1
Beyton Green **152** A1
Bhalamus **270** E7
Bhaltos **270** C4
Biallaid **258** E5
Bibury **132** D2
Bicester **148** A5
Bickenhall **103** F1
Bickenhill **159** D4
Bicker **176** A4
Bickershaw **184** A2
Bickerstaffe **183** F2
Bickerton
*ChesW&C* **170** C2
Bickerton *Devon* **101** E4
Bickerton *N'umb* **220** B1
Bickerton *NYorks* **195** D2
Bickford **158** A1
Bickham **114** C3
Bickham Bridge **100** D3
Bickham House **102** C4
Bickingcott *Devon* **113** F2
Bickington *Devon* **102** A5
Bickleigh *Devon* **100** B1
Bickleigh *Devon* **102** C2
Bickleton **113** F2
Bickley **122** D2
Bickley Moss **170** C3
Bickley Town **170** C3
Bicknacre **137** G2
Bicknoller **115** E4
Bickton **106** A4
Bicton *Here* **145** D1
Bicton *Shrop* **156** D1
Bicton *Shrop* **156** B4
Bicton Heath **157** D1
*Bicton Park Gardens*
*Devon EX9 7BJ* **103** D4
Bidborough **123** E4
Biddenden **124** A4
Biddenden Green **124** A4
Biddenham **149** F3
Biddestone **132** A5
Biddick **212** C2
Biddisham **116** A2
Biddlesden **148** B3
Biddlestone **220** B1
Biddulph **171** F2
Biddulph Moor **171** G2
Bideford **113** E3
Bidford-on-Avon **146** D2
Bidlake **99** E2
Bidston **183** D3
Bidwell **149** F5
Bieldside **261** G4
Bierley *IoW* **107** E5
Bierley *WYorks* **194** A4
Bierton **134** D1
*Big Pit National Coal*
*Museum Torfaen*
*NP4 9XP* **130** B2
Big Sand **264** D4
*Big Sheep, The Devon*
*EX39 5AP* **113** E3
*Big Sky Adventure Play*
*Peter PE2 7BU* **161** G2
Bigbury **100** C3
Bigbury-on-Sea **100** C3
Bigby **188** A2
Bigert Mire **198** D3
Biggar *Cumb* **191** E1
Biggar *SLan* **226** B2
Biggin *Derbys* **173** D3
Biggin *Derbys* **172** C2
Biggin *NYorks* **195** E4
Biggin Hill **122** D2
Biggin Hill Airport **122** D2
Biggings **279** A6
Biggleswade **149** G3
Bigholms **218** B3
Bighouse **274** D2
Bighton **120** B4
Biglands **209** F1
Bignor **108** B3
Bigrigg **208** D3
Bigton **279** C10
Bilberry **97** E4
Bilborough **173** G3
Bilbrook *Som* **114** D3
Bilbrook *Staffs* **158** A2
Bilbrough **195** E3
Bilbster **275** H3
Bilby **186** B4
Bildershaw **212** A5
Bildeston **152** A3
Billesdon **160** C2
Billericay **137** F3
Billesdon **160** C2
Billesley **146** D2
Billholme **218** A4
Billinge **183** G3
Billingford *Norf* **164** C4
Billingford *Norf* **178** B3
Billingham **213** D5
Billinghay **175** G2
Billingborough **175** G4
Billingley **186** B2

Billingshurst **121** F5
Billingsley **157** G4
Billington *CenBeds* **149** E5
Billington *Lancs* **192** D4
Billington *Staffs* **171** F5
Billister **279** D6
Billockby **179** F4
Billy Row **212** A4
Bilsborrow **192** B4
Bilsby **189** E5
Bilsby Field **189** E5
Bilsdean **237** D3
Bilsham **108** B3
Bilsington **124** C5
Bilson Green **131** F1
Bilsthorpe **174** B1
Bilsthorpe Moor **174** B2
Bilston *Midlo* **235** G3
Bilston *WMid* **158** B3
Bilstone **159** F2
Bilting **124** C4
Bilton *ERid* **197** D4
Bilton *N'umb* **229** G5
Bilton *NYorks* **194** C2
Bilton *Warks* **159** G5
Bilton-in-Ainsty **195** D3
Bimbister **277** C6
Bincombe **104** C4
Bindal **267** G3
Bindon **115** E5
Binegar **116** D3
Bines Green **109** D2
Binfield **134** C5
Binfield Heath **134** C5
Bingfield **220** B4
Bingham **174** C4
*Bingham's*
*Melcombe* **105** D2
Bingley **194** A4
Bings Heath **157** E1
Binham **178** A2
Binley *Hants* **119** F2
Binley *WMid* **159** F5
Binniehill **234** C2
Binsoe **202** B5
Binstead **107** E3
Binsted *Hants* **120** C4
Binsted *WSuss* **108** B3
Binton **146** D2
Bintree **178** B3
Binweston **156** C2
Birch *Essex* **152** A5
Birch *GtMan* **184** C2
Birch Cross **172** C4
Birch Green *Essex* **138** C1
Birch Green *Herts* **136** B1
Birch Grove **109** G1
Birch Heath **170** C1
Birch Vale **185** E4
Birch Wood **103** F1
Bircham Newton **177** F4
Bircham Tofts **177** F4
Birchanger **150** D5
Bircher **145** D1
Bircher Common **145** D1
Birchfield **266** E2
Birchgrove *Cardiff* **130** A4
Birchgrove *Swan* **128** D3
Birchington **125** F2
Birchmoor **159** E2
Birchover **172** D1
Birchwood *Lincs* **175** E1
Birchwood *Warr* **184** A3
Bircotes **186** B3
Bird Street **152** B2
Birdbrook **151** F3
Birdforth **203** D5
Birdham **108** A3
Birdingbury **147** G1
*Birdland, Bourton-on-*
*the-Water Glos*
*GL54 2BN* **147** D5
Birdlip **132** B1
Birdoswald **210** C1
Birds Green **137** E2
Birdsall **196** A1
Birdsgreen **157** G4
Birdsmoor Gate **103** G2
Birdston **234** A2
Birdwell **186** A2
Birdwood **131** G1
*Birdworld, Farnham Hants*
*GU10 4LD* **120** D3
Birgham **228** B3
Birichen **266** E2
Birkby *Cumb* **209** D3
Birkby *NYorks* **202** D2
Birkdale *Mersey* **183** E1
Birkdale *NYorks* **201** D2
Birkenhead **183** E4
Birkenhills **269** F6
Birkenshaw **194** B5
Birkhall **260** B5
Birkhill *Angus* **244** B1
Birkhill *ScBord* **236** C5
Birkhill *ScBord* **226** D4
Birkholme **175** E5
Birkin **195** E5
Birks **194** B5
Birkwood **225** G3
Birley **157** D5
Birley Carr **186** A3
Birling *Kent* **123** F2
Birling *N'umb* **221** E1
Birling Gap **110** A4
Birlingham **146** B3
Birmingham **158** C4
*Birmingham Botanical*
*Gardens WMid*
*B15 3TR* **34** B7
*Birmingham City Museum*
*& Art Gallery WMid*
*B3 3DH* **35** E4
*Birmingham International*
*Airport* **159** D4
Birnam **251** F5
Birsay **276** B5
Birse **260** D5
Birsemore **260** D5
Birstall **160** A2
Birstall Smithies **194** B5
Birstwith **194** B2
Birthorpe **175** G4
Birtle **184** C1
Birtley *Here* **144** C1

Birtley *N'umb* **220** A4
Birtley *T&W* **212** B2
Birts Street **145** G4
Birtsmorton **146** A4
Bisbrooke **161** D3
Biscathorpe **188** C4
Bish Mill **114** A5
Bisham **135** D4
Bishampton **146** B2
Bishop Auckland **212** B5
Bishop Burton **196** B3
Bishop Middleham **212** C4
Bishop Monkton **194** C1
Bishop Norton **187** G3
Bishop Sutton **116** C2
Bishop Thornton **194** B1
Bishop Wilton **195** G2
Bishopbridge **188** A3
Bishopbriggs **234** A2
Bishopmill **267** K5
Bishops Cannings **118** B1
Bishop's *Essex* **137** F1
Bishop's Castle **156** C4
Bishop's Caundle **104** C1
Bishop's Cleeve **146** B5
Bishop's Frome **145** F3
Bishops Gate **135** E5
Bishop's Green
*Essex* **137** F1
Bishop's Green
*Hants* **119** G1
Bishop's Hull **115** F5
Bishop's Itchington **147** F2
Bishop's Lydeard **115** E5
Bishop's Norton **146** A5
Bishops Nympton **114** A5
Bishop's Offley **171** E5
Bishop's Sutton **120** B4
Bishop's Tachbrook **147** F1
Bishop's Tawton **113** F2
Bishop's Waltham **107** E1
Bishop's Wood **158** A2
Bishopsbourne **125** D3
Bishopsteignton **102** C5
Bishopstoke **107** D1
Bishopston *Bristol* **131** E5
Bishopston *Swan* **128** B4
Bishopstone *Bucks* **134** D1
Bishopstone *ESuss* **109** G3
Bishopstone *Here* **144** D3
Bishopstone *Swin* **133** E4
Bishopstone *Wilts* **118** B5
Bishopstrow **117** F3
Bishopswood **103** F1
Bishopsworth **116** C1
Bishopthorpe **195** E3
Bishopton *Darl* **212** C5
Bishopton *NYorks* **202** B5
Bishopton *Renf* **233** F2
Bishopton *Warks* **147** D2
Bishton **130** C4
Bisley *Glos* **132** B2
Bisley *Surr* **121** E2
Bispham **191** G3
Bispham Green **183** F1
Bissoe **96** B5
Bisterne **106** A2
Bisterne Close **106** B2
Bitchet Green **123** E3
Bitchfield **175** E5
Bittadon **113** F1
Bittaford **100** C2
Bittering **178** A4
Bitterley **157** E5
Bitterne **107** D1
Bitteswell **160** A4
Bitton **117** D1
Bix **134** C4
Bixter **279** C7
Blaby **160** A3
Black Bourton **133** E2
Black Bridge **126** C2
Black Callerton **212** A1
Black Carr **164** B2
Black Clauchrie **215** D2
Black Corries Lodge **249** E4
*Black Country Living*
*Museum WMid*
*DY1 4SQ* **14** B2
Black Crofts **240** B1
Black Cross **96** B3
Black Dog **102** B2
Black Heddon **220** C4
Black Hill **147** E2
Black Marsh **156** C3
Black Moor **194** B3
Black Mount **249** E5
Black Notley **151** F5
*Black Park Country*
*Park Bucks*
*SL3 6DR* **135** F4
Black Pill **128** C3
*Black Sheep Brewery*
*Visitor Centre NYorks*
*HG4 4EN* **202** B4
Black Street **165** G3
Blackacre **217** E1
Blackadder **237** F4
Blackawton **101** E2
Blackborough
*Devon* **103** E2
Blackborough *Norf* **163** E1
Blackborough End **163** E1
Blackboys **110** A1
Blackbraes *Aber* **261** G3
Blackbraes *Falk* **234** D2
Blackbrook *Derbys* **173** E3
Blackbrook *Leics* **159** G1
Blackbrook *Mersey* **183** G3
Blackbrook *Staffs* **171** E4
Blackbrook *Surr* **121** G3
Blackburn *Aber* **261** G3
Blackburn *B'burn* **192** C5
Blackburn *WLoth* **235** D3
Blackcastle **267** F6
Blackchambers **261** F3
Blackcraig *D&G* **215** F4
Blackcraig *D&G* **216** B3
Blackden Heath **184** B5
Blackdog **261** H3
Blackdown *Devon* **99** F3
Blackdown *Dorset* **103** G2
Blackdown *Warks* **147** F1

Blacker Hill **186** A2
Blackfen **137** D5
Blackfield **106** D2
Blackford *Aber* **261** F1
Blackford *Cumb* **218** B5
Blackford *P&K* **243** D3
Blackford *Som* **117** D5
Blackford *Som* **116** B3
Blackford Bridge **184** C2
Blackfordby **159** F1
Blackgang
*IoW PO38 2HN* **107** D5
Blackhall *Edin* **235** G2
Blackhall *Renf* **233** F3
Blackhall Colliery **213** D4
Blackhall Mill **212** A2
Blackhall Rocks **213** D4
Blackham **123** E5
Blackhaugh **227** F2
Blackheath *Essex* **152** B5
Blackheath *GtLon* **136** C5
Blackheath *Suff* **165** F4
Blackheath *Surr* **121** F3
Blackheath *WMid* **158** B4
Blackhill *Aber* **269** J5
Blackhill *Aber* **269** J6
Blackhillock **268** C6
Blackhills **267** K6
Blackland **118** B1
Blacklands **114** B4
Blackleach **192** A4
Blackley **184** C2
Blacklunans **251** G3
Blackmill **129** F4
Blackmoor *Hants* **120** C4
Blackmoor *Som* **103** E1
Blackmoor Gate **113** G1
Blackmore **137** E2
Blackmore End
*Essex* **151** F4
Blackmore End
*Herts* **136** A1
Blackness *Aber* **260** E5
Blackness *Falk* **235** E2
Blackness *High* **275** H5
Blacknest **120** C3
Blackney **104** A3
Blacko **193** E3
Blackpole **146** A2
Blackpool *B'pool* **191** G4
Blackpool *Devon* **101** E3
Blackpool Bridge **127** D1
Blackpool Gate **218** C3
*Blackpool International*
*Airport* **191** G4
*Blackpool Piers B'pool*
*FY4 1BB* **191** G4
*Blackpool Pleasure*
*Beach B'pool*
*FY4 1PL* **191** G4
*Blackpool Tower*
*FY1 4BJ* **64** Blackpool
*Blackpool Zoo*
*B'pool FY3 8PP* **191** G4
Blackridge **234** C3
Blackrock *A&B* **230** B3
Blackrock *Mon* **130** B1
Blackrod **184** A1
Blackshaw *Devon* **171** E2
Blackshaw Head **193** F5
Blacksmith's Green **152** C1
Blacksnape **192** D5
Blackstone **109** E2
Blackthorn **134** B1
Blackthorpe **152** A1
Blacktoft **196** A5
Blacktop **261** G4
Blacktown **130** B4
Blackwater
*Corn* **96** B5
Blackwater
*Hants* **120** D2
Blackwater *IoW* **107** E4
Blackwater *Norf* **178** B3
Blackwater *Som* **103** F1
Blackwaterfoot **223** E3
Blackwell *Darl* **202** B1
Blackwell *Derbys* **185** F5
Blackwell *Derbys* **173** E1
Blackwell *Warks* **147** E3
Blackwell *Worcs* **158** B5
Blackwell *WSuss* **122** C5
Blackwells End **145** G5
Blackwood (Coed-duon)
*Caerp* **130** A3
Blackwood *D&G* **216** D2
Blackwood *SLan* **234** B5
Blackwood Hill **171** G2
Blacon **170** A1
Bladbean **125** D4
Bladnoch **215** F5
Bladon **133** G1
Blaen Clydach **129** F3
Blaenannerch **141** F3
Blaenau
Dolwyddelan **167** F2
Blaenau Ffestiniog **167** F3
Blaenavon **130** B2
Blaenawey **130** B1
Blaencelyn **141** G2
Blaencwm **129** F2
Blaendyryn **143** F3
Blaenffos **141** E4
Blaengarw **129** F3
Blaengeuffordd **154** C4
Blaengweche **128** C1
Blaengwrach **129** E2
Blaengwynfi **129** E3
Blaenllechau **129** G3
Blaenos **143** D4
Blaenpennal **142** C1
Blaenplwyf **154** B5
Blaenporth **141** F3
Blaenrhondda **129** F2
Blaenwaun **141** F5
Blaen-y-coed **141** G5
Blagdon *NSom* **116** B2
Blagdon *Torbay* **101** E1
Blagdon Hill **103** F1
Blagill **210** C3
Blaguegate **183** F2
Blaich **248** C2
Blaina **130** A2
Blair **233** E5
Blair Atholl **251** D3
Blair Castle *P&K*
*PH18 5TL* **251** D3
Blair Drummond **242** C5

*Blair Drummond Safari &*
*Adventure Park Stir*
*FK9 4UR* **242** C5
Blairannaich **241** F4
Blairbuie **232** C2
Blairgowrie **251** G5
Blairhall **235** E1
Blairhoyle **242** B4
Blairhullichan **241** G4
Blairingone **243** E5
Blairkip **224** D2
Blairlogie **242** D5
Blairmore *A&B* **232** C1
Blairmore *High* **266** E1
Blairmore *High* **272** D2
Blairnairn **259** K3
Blairquhan **224** B5
Blairquhosh **233** G1
Blair's Ferry **232** A2
Blairshinnoch **268** E4
Blairuskinmore **241** G4
Blairvadach **233** E1
Blairydryne **261** F5
Blairythan Cottage **261** H2
Blaisdon **131** G1
Blake End **151** F5
*Blake House Craft*
*Centre Essex*
*CM7 6RA* **151** F5
Blakebrook **158** A5
Blakedown **158** A5
Blakelaw *ScBord* **228** B3
Blakelaw *T&W* **212** B1
Blakeley **158** A3
Blakelow **171** D2
Blakemere **144** C3
*Blakemere Shopping*
*Experience ChesW&C*
*CW8 2EB* **183** G5
Blakeney *Glos* **131** F2
Blakeney *Norf* **178** B1
Blakenhall
*ChesE* **171** E3
Blakenhall *WMid* **158** B3
Blakeshall **158** A4
Blakesley **148** B2
Blanchland **211** F2
Bland Hill **194** B2
Blandford Camp **105** F2
Blandford Forum **105** E2
Blandford St. Mary **105** E2
Blanefield **233** G2
Blanerne **237** F3
Blankney **175** F1
Blantyre **234** A4
Blar a' Chaorainn **248** D3
Blargie **258** D2
Blarglas **233** E1
Blarmachfoldach **248** C3
Blarnalearoch **265** H2
Blashford **106** A2
Blaston **160** D3
Blathaisbhal **262** D4
Blatherwycke **161** E3
Blawith **199** D4
Blaxhall **153** E2
Blaxton **187** D2
Blaydon **212** A1
Bleadney **116** B3
Bleadon **116** A2
Bleak Hey Nook **185** E2
Blean **124** D2
Bleasby *Lincs* **188** B4
Bleasby *Notts* **174** C3
Bleasby Moor **188** B4
Bleatarn **200** C1
Bleathwood
Common **145** E1
Blebocraigs **244** C3
Bleddfa **144** C1
Bledington **147** E5
Bledlow **134** C2
Bledlow Ridge **134** C3
Blencarn **210** C4
Blencogo **209** E2
Blencow **210** A4
Blendworth **107** G1
*Blenheim Palace Oxon*
*OX20 1PX* **133** G2
Blennerhasset **209** E2
Blervie Castle **267** H6
Bletchingdon **134** A1
Bletchingley **122** C3
Bletchley *MK* **149** D4
Bletchley *Shrop* **170** D4
Bletherston **141** D5
Bletsoe **149** F2
Blewbury **134** A4
Blickling **178** C3
*Blickling Hall Norf*
*NR11 6NF* **178** C3
Blidworth **173** G2
Blidworth Bottoms **173** G2
Blindburn *Aber* **261** H1
Blindburn *N'umb* **228** B3
Blindcrake **209** E3
Blindley Heath **122** C4
Blisland **97** G1
Bliss Gate **157** G5
Blissford **106** A1
Blisworth **148** C2
Blithbury **172** B5
Blitterlees **209** E1
Blo' Norton **164** B4
Blockley **146** D4
Blofield **179** E5
Blofield Heath **179** E4
Blore **172** C3
Blossomfield **158** D5
Blount's Green **172** B4
Blowick **183** E1
Bloxham **147** G4
Bloxholm **175** F2
Bloxwich **158** B2
Bloxworth **105** E3
Blubberhouses **194** A2
Blue Anchor *Corn* **96** D4
Blue Anchor *Som* **114** D3
Blue Bell Hill **123** G2
*Blue Planet Aquarium,*
*Ellesmere Port*
*ChesW&C*
*CH65 9LF* **183** F5
*Blue Reef Aquarium*
*ESuss' TN34 3DW*
**75** Hastings

*Blue Reef Aquarium,*
*Newquay Corn*
*TR7 1DU* **96** C3
*Blue Reef Aquarium,*
*Southsea Ports*
*PO5 3PB* **5** G6
*Blue Reef Aquarium,*
*Tynemouth T&W*
*NE30 4JF* **28** E1
*Bluebell Railway WSuss*
*TN22 3QL* **109** F1
Bluewater **137** E5
Blundellsands **183** E3
Blundeston **165** G2
Blunham **149** G2
Blunsdon
St. Andrew **132** D4
Bluntington **158** A5
Bluntisham **162** B5
Blunts **98** D1
Blurton **171** F3
Blyborough **187** G3
Blyford **165** F4
Blymhill **158** A1
Blymhill Common **157** G1
Blymhill Lawn **158** A1
Blyth *N'umb* **221** F3
Blyth *Notts* **186** D4
Blyth Bridge **235** F5
Blyth End **159** E4
Blythburgh **165** F4
Blythe Bridge **171** G3
Blythe Marsh **171** G3
Blyton **187** F3
Boarhills **245** D3
Boarhunt **107** F2
Boars Hill **133** G2
Boarsgreave **193** E5
Boarshead **123** E5
Boarstall **134** B1
Boarzell **110** C1
Boasley Cross **99** F1
Boat o' Brig **268** B5
Boat of Garten **259** G3
Boath **266** C4
Bobbing **124** A2
Bobbington **158** A3
Bobbingworth **137** E2
Bocaddon **97** F3
Bochastle **242** B4
*Bocketts Farm Park*
*Surr KT22 9BS* **121** G2
Bockhampton **133** F5
Bocking **151** F5
Bocking
Churchstreet **151** F5
Bockleton **145** E1
Boconnoc **97** F3
Boddam *Aber* **269** K6
Boddam *Shet* **279** F9
Boddington **146** A5
Bodelwyddan **182** B5
Bodenham *Here* **145** E1
Bodenham *Wilts* **118** C5
Bodenham Moor **145** E2
Bodesbeck **226** C5
Bodewryd **180** C3
Bodfari **182** B5
Bodffordd **180** C5
Bodfuan **166** C4
Bodham **178** C1
Bodiam **110** C1
*Bodiam Castle ESuss*
*TN32 5UA* **110** C1
Bodicote **147** G4
Bodieve **97** D2
Bodinnick **97** F4
Bodior **180** A5
Bodle Street Green **110** B2
*Bodleian Library*
*Oxon OX1 3BG*
**80** OX1
Bodmin **97** E3
*Bodnant Garden Conwy*
*LL28 5RE* **181** G5
Bodney **163** G3
Bodorgan **166** C1
Bodrane **97** G3
Bodsham Green **124** D4
Bodymoor Heath **159** D3
Bogallan **266** D6
Bogbain **266** E7
Bogbrae **261** J1
Bogbuie **266** C6
Bogend **224** B2
Bogfern **260** D4
Bogfields **260** D4
Bogfold **269** G5
Boghall *Aber* **268** E5
Boghall *EAyr* **225** E3
Boghall *SLan* **234** C5
Boghole Farm **267** G6
Bogmoor **268** B4
Bogniebrae **268** D6
Bognor Regis **108** B3
Bograxie **261** F3
Bogroy **259** G2
Bogside **243** E5
Bogston **260** B4
Bogton **268** E5
Bogue **216** A2
Bohemia **106** B1
Bohenie **249** E1
Bohetherick **100** A1
Bohortha **95** F3
Bohuntine **249** E1
Boirseam **263** F3
Bojewyan **94** A3
Bokiddick **97** E3
Bolam *Dur* **212** A5
Bolam *N'umb* **220** C3
*Bolam Lake Country*
*Park N'umb*
*NE20 0HE* **220** C3
Bolberry **100** C4
Bold Heath **183** G4
Bolderwood **106** B2
Boldon **212** C1
Boldre **106** C3
Boldron **201** F1
Bole **187** E4
Bolehill **173** D2
Boleigh **94** B4
Bolenowe **95** D3

Boleside **227** F2
Bolfracks **250** B5
Bolgoed **128** C2
Bolham *Devon* **102** C1
Bolham *Notts* **187** E4
Bolham Water **103** E1
Bolingey **96** B4
Bollington **184** D5
Bolney **109** E1
Bolnhurst **149** F2
Bolshan **253** E4
Bolsover **186** B5
Bolsterstone **185** G3
Bolstone **145** E4
Boltby **203** D4
Bolter End **134** C3
Bolton *Cumb* **210** C5
Bolton *ELoth* **236** C2
Bolton *ERid* **195** G2
Bolton *GtMan* **184** B2
Bolton *N'umb* **229** F5
*Bolton Abbey*
*NYorks*
*BD23 6EX* **193** G2
Bolton Abbey Estate
*NYorks*
*BD23 6EX* **193** G2
Bolton Bridge **193** G2
Bolton by Bowland **193** D3
Bolton Houses **192** A4
Bolton Low Houses **209** F2
*Bolton Museum &*
*Art Gallery GtMan*
*BL1 1SE* **184** B2
Bolton Percy **195** E3
*Bolton Priory NYorks*
*BD23 6EX* **193** G2
Bolton upon
Dearne **186** B2
Bolton Wood Lane **209** F2
Boltonfellend **210** A1
Boltongate **209** F2
Bolton-le-Sands **192** A1
Bolton-on-Swale **202** B3
Bolventor **97** F2
Bombie **208** A2
Bomere Heath **157** D1
Bonar Bridge **266** D2
Bonawe (Bun Atha) **240** C1
Bonby **188** A1
Boncath **141** F4
Bonchester Bridge **227** G4
Bonchurch **107** E5
Bondleigh **113** G5
Bonds **192** A3
Bonehill **159** D2
Bo'ness **235** D1
Bonhill **233** E2
Boningale **158** A2
Bonjedward **228** A4
Bonkle **199** F3
Bonning Gate **199** F3
Bonnington *Edin* **235** F3
Bonnington *Kent* **124** C5
Bonnybank **244** B4
Bonnybridge **234** C1
Bonnykelly **269** G5
Bonnyrigg **236** A3
Bonnyton *Aber* **260** E1
Bonnyton *Angus* **245** D1
Bonnyton *Angus* **253** E4
Bonnyton *Angus* **244** B1
Bonsall **173** D2
Bont **130** C1
Bont Dolgadfan **155** E2
Bont Newydd **168** A5
Bontddu **154** C1
Bont-goch (Elerch) **154** C4
Bonthorpe **189** E5
Bont-newydd
*Conwy* **182** B5
Bontnewydd *Gwyn* **167** D1
Bontuchel **169** D2
Bonvilston **129** G5
Bon-y-maen **128** C3
Boode **113** F2
Boohay **101** F2
Booker **134** C3
Booley **170** C5
Boor **264** E3
Boorley Green **107** E1
Boosbeck **203** F1
Boose's Green **151** G4
Boot **198** C2
Boot Street **152** D3
Booth **193** G5
Booth Bank **185** E1
Booth Green **184** D4
Booth Wood **185** E1
Boothby Graffoe **175** E2
Boothby Pagnell **175** E4
Boothstown **184** B2
Boothville **148** C1
Bootle *Cumb* **198** C3
Bootle *Mersey* **183** E3
Booton **178** C3
Boots Green **184** B5
Booze **201** F2
Boquhan **233** G1
Boraston **157** F5
Bordeaux **101** F4
Borden *Kent* **124** A2
Borden *WSuss* **120** C5
Bordley **193** F1
Bordon **120** C4
Boreham *Essex* **137** G2
Boreham *Wilts* **117** F3
Boreham Street **110** B2
Borehamwood **136** A3
Boreland *D&G* **217** F1
Boreland *D&G* **215** G3
Boreland *Stir* **242** A1
Boreley **146** A1
Boreraig **263** G6
Borgh *ESiar* **262** E3
Borgh *ESiar* **254** B4
Borghastan **270** D3
Borgie **273** J3
Borgue *D&G* **207** G2
Borgue *High* **275** G6
Borley **151** G3
Borley Green *Essex* **151** G3
Borley Green *Suff* **152** A1
Bornais **254** C1
Borness **207** G2
Bornisketaig **263** J4
Borough Green **123** F3
Boroughbridge **194** C1
Borras Head **170** A2
Borrowash **173** F4

Borrowby *NYorks* 203 G1
Borrowby *NYorks* 202 D4
Borrowdale 209 F5
Borrowfield 261 G5
Borstal 123 G3
Borth 154 C4
Borthwick 236 A4
Borthwickbrae 227 F4
Borthwickshiels 227 F4
Borth-y-Gest 167 F2
Borve *High* 263 K7
Borve (Borgh)
*ESiar* 271 G2
Borwick 199 G5
Borwick Rails 198 C5
Bosavern 94 A3
Bosbury 145 F3
Boscarne 97 E3
Boscastle 98 A1
Boscastle Pottery *Corn*
PL35 OHE 98 B1
Boscombe *Bourne* 106 A3
Boscombe *Wilts* 118 D4
Bosham 108 A3
Bosham Hoe 108 A4
Bosherston 126 C3
Bosley 171 G1
Bossall 195 G1
Bossiney 97 E1
Bossingham 125 D4
Bossington *Hants* 119 E4
Bossington *Som* 114 B3
Bostadh 270 D4
Bostock Green 171 D1
Boston 176 B3
Boston Spa 194 D3
Boswarthan 94 B3
Boswinger 97 D5
Bosworth Battlefield
Country Park *Leics*
CV13 0AD 159 G2
Botallack 94 A3
Botanic Garden
*Oxon* OX1 4AZ
80 Oxford
Botany Bay *Lancs*
PR6 9AF 184 A1
Botcheston 159 G2
Botesdale 164 B4
Bothal 221 E3
Bothamsall 187 D5
Bothel 209 E3
Bothenhampton 104 A3
Botley *Bucks* 135 E2
Botley *Hants* 107 E1
Botley *Oxon* 133 G4
Botloe's Green 145 G5
Botolph Claydon 148 C5
Botolph's Bridge 124 D5
Bottacks 266 B5
Bottesford *Leics* 174 D4
Bottesford *NLincs* 187 F2
Bottisham 150 D1
Bottlesford 118 C2
Bottom Boat 194 C4
Bottom of Hutton 192 A5
Bottom o'th'Moor 184 A1
Bottomcraig 244 B2
Bottoms 193 F5
Botton Head 192 C1
Botusfleming 100 A1
Botwnnog 166 B4
Bough Beech 123 D4
Boughrood 144 A4
Boughspring 131 E3
Boughton *N'hants* 148 C1
Boughton *Norf* 163 F2
Boughton *Notts* 174 B1
Boughton Aluph 124 C4
Boughton Lees 124 C4
Boughton Malherbe 124 A4
Boughton
Monchelsea 123 G3
Boughton Street 124 C3
Boulby 203 G1
Bouldnor 106 C4
Bouldon 157 E4
Boulge 153 D2
Boulmer 229 G5
Boulston 126 C1
Boultenstone Hotel 260 C3
Boultham 175 E1
Boundary *Derbys* 159 F1
Boundary *Staffs* 171 G3
Bourn 150 B2
Bourne 175 F5
Bourne End *Bucks* 135 D4
Bourne End
*CenBeds* 149 E3
Bourne End *Herts* 135 F2
Bournebridge 137 E3
Bournemouth 105 G3
Bournemouth
Airport 106 A4
Bournemouth International
Centre BH2 5BH 64
Bournemouth
Bournheath 158 B5
Bournmoor 212 C2
Bournville 158 C4
Bourton *Bucks* 148 C4
Bourton *Dorset* 117 E4
Bourton *NSom* 116 A1
Bourton *Oxon* 133 E4
Bourton *Shrop* 157 E3
Bourton *Wilts* 118 B1
Bourton on
Dunsmore 159 G5
Bourton-on-the-Hill 147 D4
Bourton-on-
the-Water 147 D5
Bousd 246 B3
Boustead Hill 209 F1
Bouth 199 E4
Bouthwaite 202 A5
Bovain 242 A1
Boveney 135 E5
Boveridge 105 G1
Boverton 114 C1
Bovey Tracey 102 B5
Bovingdon 135 F2
Bovinger 137 E2
Bovington Camp 105 E4
Bow *Cumb* 209 G1
Bow *Devon* 102 A2

Bow *Devon* 101 E2
Bow *Ork* 277 D8
Bow Brickhill 149 E4
Bow of Fife 244 B3
Bow Street *Cere* 154 C4
Bow Street *Norf* 164 B2
Bowbank 211 F5
Bowburn 212 C4
Bowcombe 107 D4
Bowd 103 E3
Bowden *Devon* 101 E3
Bowden *ScBord* 227 G2
Bowden Hill 118 A3
Bowdon 184 B4
Bower 219 F3
Bower Hinton 104 A1
Bower House Tye 152 A3
Bowerchalke 118 B5
Bowerhill 118 A1
Bowermadden 275 H2
Bowers 171 F4
Bowers Gifford 137 G4
Bowershall 243 F5
Bowertower 275 H2
Bowes 201 E1
Bowgreave 192 A3
Bowhousebog 234 C4
Bowithick 97 F1
Bowker's Green 183 F2
Bowland Bridge 199 F4
Bowley 145 E2
Bowley Town 145 E2
Bowlhead Green 121 E4
Bowling *WDun* 233 F2
Bowling *WYorks* 194 A4
Bowling Bank 170 A3
Bowlish 116 D3
Bowmanstead 199 E3
Bowmore 230 B3
Bowness-on-
Solway 218 A5
Bowness-on-
Windermere 199 F3
Bowscale 209 G3
Bowsden 237 G5
Bowside Lodge 274 D2
Bowston 199 F3
Bowthorpe 178 C5
Bowtrees 234 D1
Box *Glos* 132 A2
Box *Wilts* 117 F1
Box End 149 F3
Boxbush *Glos* 131 G1
Boxbush *Glos* 145 F5
Boxford *Suff* 152 A3
Boxford *WBerks* 133 G5
Boxgrove 108 B3
Boxley 123 G3
Boxmoor 135 F2
Box's Shop 112 C5
Boxted *Essex* 152 A4
Boxted *Suff* 151 G2
Boxted Cross 152 A4
Boxwell 132 A3
Boxworth 150 B1
Boxworth End 150 B1
Boyden Gate 125 E2
Boydston 224 C2
Boylestone 172 C4
Boyndie 268 E4
Boynton 196 D1
Boys Hill 104 C2
Boysack 253 E5
Boyton *Corn* 98 D1
Boyton *Suff* 153 E3
Boyton *Wilts* 118 A4
Boyton Cross 137 F2
Boyton End 151 F3
Bozeat 149 E2
Braaid 190 B4
Braal Castle 275 G2
Brabling Green 153 D1
Brabourne 124 C4
Brabourne Lees 124 C4
Brabster 275 J2
Bracadale 255 J1
Braceborough 161 F1
Bracebridge Heath 175 E1
Braceby 175 F4
Bracewell 193 E3
Brachla 258 C1
Brackenber 200 C1
Brackenbottom 200 D5
Brackenfield 173 E2
Brackens 269 F5
Bracklach 260 B2
Bracklamore 269 G5
Bracklesham 108 A4
Brackletter (A' Bhreac-
Leitir) 249 D1
Brackley *A&B* 231 F1
Brackley *High* 267 F6
Brackley *N'hants* 148 A4
Brackley Gate 173 E3
Brackley Hatch 148 B3
Bracknell 121 D1
Braco 242 D4
Bracobrae 268 D5
Bracon Ash 164 C2
Bracora 256 D5
Bracorina 256 D5
Bradbourne 172 D2
Bradbury 212 C5
Bradda 190 A4
Bradden 148 B3
Braddock 97 F3
Bradenham *Bucks* 134 D3
Bradenham *Norf* 178 A5
Bradenstoke 132 C5
Bradfield *Devon* 103 D2
Bradfield *Essex* 152 C4
Bradfield *WBerks* 134 B5
Bradfield Combust 151 G2
Bradfield Green 171 D2
Bradfield Heath 152 C5
Bradfield St. Clare 152 A2
Bradfield St. George 152 A1
Bradfield Southend
(Southend) 134 A5
Bradford *Corn* 97 F2
Bradford *Derbys* 172 D1
Bradford *Devon* 113 E5
Bradford *N'umb* 229 F3
Bradford *N'umb* 220 C4

Bradford *WYorks* 194 A4
Bradford Abbas 104 B1
*Bradford Cathedral
Church of St. Peter
WYorks* BD1 4EH
65 Bradford
Bradford Leigh 117 F1
Bradford Peverell 104 C3
Bradford-on-Avon 117 F1
Bradford-on-Tone 115 E5
*Bradgate Park Leics
LE6 0HE* 17 B3
Bradiford 113 F2
Brading 107 F4
Bradley *ChesW&C* 183 G5
Bradley *Derbys* 172 D3
Bradley *Hants* 120 B3
Bradley *NELincs* 188 C2
Bradley (Low Bradley)
*NYorks* 193 G3
Bradley *Staffs* 158 A1
Bradley *WMid* 158 B1
Bradley Fold 184 B2
Bradley Green
*Warks* 159 E2
Bradley Green
*Worcs* 146 B1
Bradley in the
Moors 172 B3
Bradley Mills 185 F1
Bradley Stoke 131 F4
Bradmore *Notts* 173 G4
Bradmore *WMid* 158 A3
Bradney 116 A4
Bradninch 102 D2
Bradnop 172 B2
Bradnor Green 144 B2
Bradpole 104 A3
Bradshaw *GtMan* 184 B1
Bradshaw *WYorks* 193 G4
Bradstone 99 D2
Bradwall Green 171 E1
Bradwell *Derbys* 185 F4
Bradwell *Devon* 113 E1
Bradwell *Essex* 151 G5
Bradwell *MK* 148 D4
Bradwell *Norf* 179 G5
Bradwell Grove 133 E2
Bradwell Waterside 138 C2
Bradwell-on-Sea 138 D2
Bradworthy 112 D4
Brae *D&G* 216 C3
Brae *High* 266 B1
Brae *Shet* 279 C6
Brae of Achnahaird 272 C7
Braeantra 266 C4
Braedownie 252 A2
Braefoot 269 F6
Braegrum 243 F2
Braehead *D&G* 215 F5
Braehead *Glas* 233 G3
Braehead *Moray* 268 B6
Braehead *Ork* 277 E7
Braehead *Ork* 276 D3
Braehead *SLan* 225 G2
Braehead *SLan* 235 D4
Braehead of Lunan 253 E4
Braehoulland 278 B5
Braeleny 242 B3
Braemar 259 J5
Braemore *High* 266 C1
Braemore *High* 275 F5
Braemore *High* 265 H4
Braenaloin 259 J5
Braes of Enzie 268 B5
Braes of Foss 250 C4
Braes of Ullapool
(Bruthaichean Ullapuil)
265 H2
Braeswick 276 F4
Braeval 242 A4
Braewick 279 C7
Brafferton *Darl* 212 B5
Brafferton *NYorks* 202 D5
Brafield-on-the-
Green 148 D2
Bragar 270 E3
Bragbury End 150 A5
Bragenham 149 E5
Bragleenbeg 240 B2
Braichmelyn 167 F1
Braides 192 A3
Braidley 201 F4
Braidwood 234 C5
Braigo 230 A3
Brailsford 173 D3
Brain's Green 131 F2
Braintree 151 F5
Braiseworth 164 C4
Braishfield 119 E5
Braithwaite *Cumb* 209 F4
Braithwaite
*SYorks* 186 D1
Braithwaite
*WYorks* 193 G3
Braithwell 186 C3
Bramber 109 D2
Brambletye 122 D5
Brambridge 119 F5
Bramcote *Notts* 173 G4
Bramcote *Warks* 159 G4
Bramdean 120 B5
Bramerton 179 D5
Bramfield *Herts* 136 B1
Bramfield *Suff* 165 E4
Bramford 152 C3
Bramhall 184 C4
Bramham 194 D3
Bramhope 194 B3
Bramley *Hants* 120 B2
Bramley *Surr* 121 F3
Bramley *SYorks* 186 B3
Bramley Corner 120 B2
Bramley Head 194 A2
Bramley Vale 173 F1
Bramling 125 E3
Brampford Speke 102 C3
Brampton *Cambs* 162 A5
Brampton *Cumb* 210 B1
Brampton *Cumb* 210 C3
Brampton *Derbys* 186 A5
Brampton *Lincs* 187 F5
Brampton *Norf* 178 D3
Brampton *Suff* 165 F3
Brampton *SYorks* 186 B2
Brampton Abbotts 145 F5
Brampton Ash 160 C4
Brampton Bryan 156 C5

Brampton en le
Morthen 186 B4
Brampton Street 165 F3
*Brampton Valley Way
Country Park N'hants*
NN6 9DG 160 C5
Bramshaw 106 B1
Bramshill 120 C1
Bramshott 120 D4
Bramwell 116 B5
Bran End 151 E5
Branault 247 E3
Brancaster 177 F3
Brancaster Staithe 177 F3
Brancepeth 212 B4
Branchill 267 H6
Brand Green 145 G5
Brandelhow 209 F4
Branderburgh 267 K4
Brandesburton 196 D3
Brandeston 152 D1
Brandis Corner 113 E5
Brandiston 178 C3
Brandlingill 209 E4
Brandon *Dur* 212 B4
Brandon *Lincs* 175 E3
Brandon *N'umb* 229 E5
Brandon *Suff* 163 F4
Brandon *Warks* 159 G5
Brandon Bank 163 E4
Brandon Creek 163 E3
*Brandon Park Suff*
IP27 0SU 163 F4
Brandon Parva 178 B5
*Brandon to Bishop
Auckland Walk Dur*
DH7 7RJ 212 B4
Brandsby 203 E5
Brandy Wharf 188 A3
Brane 94 B4
Branksome 105 G3
Branksome Park 105 G3
Bransbury 119 F3
Bransby 187 F5
Branscombe 103 E4
Bransford 145 G2
Bransford Bridge 146 A2
Bransgore 106 A3
Bransholme 196 D4
Branson's Cross 158 C5
Branston *Leics* 174 D5
Branston *Lincs* 175 F1
Branston *Staffs* 172 D5
Branston Booths 175 F1
*Branston Water Park Staffs*
DE14 3EZ 172 D5
Brant Broughton 175 E2
Brantham 152 C4
Branthwaite *Cumb* 209 F3
Branthwaite *Cumb* 209 D4
Brantingham 196 B5
Branton *N'umb* 229 E5
Branton *SYorks* 186 D2
Brantwood 199 E3
Branxholm
Bridgend 227 F4
Branxholme 227 F4
Branxton 228 C3
Brassey Green 170 C1
Brassington 172 D2
Brasted 123 D3
Brasted Chart 123 D3
Brathens 260 E5
Bratoft 176 C1
Brattleby 187 G4
Bratton *Som* 114 B3
Bratton *Tel&W* 157 F1
Bratton *Wilts* 118 A2
Bratton Clovelly 99 E1
Bratton Fleming 113 G2
Bratton Seymour 117 D5
Braughing 150 B5
Brauncewell 175 F2
Braunston *N'hants* 148 A1
Braunstone 160 A2
Braunston *Rut* 160 D2
Braunton 113 E2
Brawby 203 G5
Brawdy 140 B5
Brawith 203 E2
Brawl 274 D2
Brawlbin 275 F3
Bray 135 E5
Bray Shop 98 D3
Bray Wick 135 D5
Braybrooke 160 C4
Braydon Side 132 C4
Brayford 113 G2
Brayshaw 193 D2
Braythorn 194 B3
Brayton 195 F4
Braywoodside 135 D5
Brazacott 98 C1
Brea 96 A5
Breach *Kent* 125 D4
Breach *Kent* 124 A2
Breachwood Green 149 G5
Breacleit 270 D4
Breaden Heath 170 B4
Breadsall 173 E4
Breadstone 131 G2
Breage 94 D4
Breakon 278 E2
Bream 115 F2
Breamore 106 A1
Brean 115 F2
Breanais 270 B5
Brearton 194 C1
Breascleit 270 E4
Breaston 173 F4
Brechfa 142 B4
Brechin 253 E3
Breckles 164 A2
Brecon
(Aberhonddu) 143 G5
*Brecon Beacons Visitor
Centre Powys*
LD3 8ER 143 F5
Breconside 225 G5
Bredbury 184 D3
Brede 110 D2
Bredenbury 145 F2
Bredfield 153 D2
Bredgar 124 A2
Bredhurst 123 G2
Bredon 146 B4

Bredon's Hardwick 146 B4
Bredon's Norton 146 B4
Bredwardine 144 C3
Breedon on the Hill 173 F5
Breibhig 271 G2
Breich 235 D3
Breightmet 184 B2
Breighton 195 G4
Breinton 145 D4
Breinton Common 145 D4
Bremhill 132 B5
Bremhill Wick 132 B5
Brenachoille 240 C4
Brenchley 123 F4
Brendon *Devon* 114 A3
Brendon *Devon* 113 D4
Brendon *Devon* 113 D5
Brenkley 221 E4
Brent Eleigh 152 A3
Brent Knoll 116 A2
Brent Pelham 150 C4
Brentford 136 A5
Brentingby 160 C1
Brentwood 137 E4
Brenzett 111 F1
Brenzett Green 111 F1
Breoch 216 B5
Brereton 158 C1
Brereton Green 171 E1
Brereton Heath 171 E1
Breretonhill 158 C1
Bressay 279 E8
Bressingham 164 B3
Bressingham
Common 164 B3
*Bressingham Steam
Museum & Gardens
Norf* IP22 2AA 164 B3
Bretby 173 D5
Bretford 159 G5
Bretforton 146 C3
Bretherdale Head 199 G2
Bretherton 192 A5
Brettabister 279 D7
Brettenham *Norf* 164 A3
Brettenham *Suff* 152 A2
Bretton *Derbys* 185 F5
Bretton *Flints* 170 A1
Bretton *Peter* 161 G2
Brevig 254 B5
Brewood 158 A2
Briach 267 H6
Briantspuddle 105 E3
Brick End 151 D5
Brickendon 136 C2
Bricket Wood 136 A2
*Brickfields Horse Country
IoW* PO33 3TH 107 E3
Brickkiln Green 151 E4
Bricklehampton 146 B3
Bride 190 C1
Bridekirk 209 E3
Bridell 141 E3
Bridestones 171 G1
Bridestowe 99 F1
Brideswell 260 D1
Bridford 102 B4
Bridge *Corn* 96 A5
Bridge *Kent* 125 D3
Bridge End *Cumb* 198 D4
Bridge End *Devon* 100 C3
Bridge End *Essex* 151 E4
Bridge End *Lincs* 175 G4
Bridge End *Shet* 279 C9
Bridge Hewick 202 C5
Bridge of Allan 242 C5
Bridge of Avon 259 J1
Bridge of Awe
(Drochaid Abha) 240 C1
Bridge of Balgie 250 A5
Bridge of
Bogendreip 260 E5
Bridge of
Brewlands 251 G3
Bridge of Brown 259 J2
Bridge of Cally 251 G4
Bridge of Canny 260 E5
Bridge of Craigisla 252 A4
Bridge of Dee *Aber* 259 J5
Bridge of Dee *Aber* 260 E5
Bridge of Dee *D&G* 216 B4
Bridge of Don 261 H4
Bridge of Dun 253 E4
Bridge of Dye 253 E1
Bridge of Earn 243 G3
Bridge of Ericht 250 A4
Bridge of Feugh 260 E5
Bridge of Forss 275 F2
Bridge of Gairn 260 B5
Bridge of Gaur 250 A4
Bridge of Muchalls 261 G5
Bridge of Muick 260 B5
Bridge of Orchy (Drochaid
Urchaidh) 241 E1
Bridge of Tynet 268 B4
Bridge of Walls 279 B7
Bridge of Weir 233 E3
Bridge Reeve 113 G4
Bridge Sollers 144 D3
Bridge Street 151 G3
Bridge Trafford 183 F5
Bridgefoot *Angus* 244 B1
Bridgefoot *Cumb* 209 D4
Bridgehampton 116 C5
Bridgehaugh 260 B1
Bridgehill 211 G2
Bridgemary 107 E2
Bridgemere 171 E3
Bridgend *A&B* 230 B3
Bridgend *A&B* 240 A1
Bridgend *Aber* 260 D1
Bridgend *Aber* 269 F6
Bridgend *Angus* 252 D3
Bridgend
(Aberhonddu) 143 G5
Bridgend
(Pen-y-bont ar
Ogwr) *Bridgend* 129 F5
Bridgend *Corn* 97 F4
Bridgend *Cumb* 199 F1
Bridgend *Fife* 244 B3
Bridgend *Moray* 260 B1
Bridgend *P&K* 243 G2
Bridgend *WLoth* 235 E2

Bridgeton *Aber* 260 D3
Bridgeton *Glas* 234 A3
Bridgetown *Corn* 98 D2
Bridgetown *Som* 114 C4
*Bridgewater Hall,
Manchester GtMan*
M2 3WS 46 E4
Bridgeyate 131 F5
Bridgham 164 A3
Bridgnorth 157 G3
*Bridgnorth Cliff
Railway Shrop*
WV16 4AH 157 G3
Bridgtown 158 B2
Bridgwater 115 F4
Bridlington 197 D1
Bridport 104 A3
Bridstow 145 E5
Brierfield 193 E4
Brierley *Glos* 131 F1
Brierley *Here* 145 D2
Brierley *SYorks* 186 B1
Brierley Hill 158 B4
Brierton 213 D5
Briestfield 185 G1
Brig o'Turk 242 A4
Brigg 188 A2
Briggate 179 E3
Briggswath 204 B2
Brigham *Cumb* 209 D3
Brigham *ERid* 196 C2
Brighouse 194 A5
Brighstone 106 D4
Brightgate 173 D2
Brighthampton 133 F2
Brightholmlee 185 G3
Brightling 110 B1
Brightlingsea 139 D1
Brighton *B&H* 109 F3
Brighton *Corn* 96 D4
*Brighton Centre, The
B&H* BN1 2GR
65 Brighton
*Brighton Museum &
Art Gallery B&H*
BN1 1EE 65 Brighton
*Brighton Pier B&H*
BN2 1TW 65 Brighton
Brightons 234 D2
Brightwalton 133 G5
Brightwalton Green 133 G5
Brightwell 152 D3
Brightwell Baldwin 134 B3
Brightwell
Upperton 134 B3
Brightwell-cum-
Sotwell 134 A3
Brignall 201 F1
Brigsley 188 C2
Brigsteer 199 F4
Brigstock 161 E4
Brill *Bucks* 134 B1
Brill *Corn* 95 E4
Brilley 144 B3
Brilley Mountain 144 B2
Brimaston 140 C5
Brimfield 145 E1
Brimington 186 B5
Brimington
Common 186 B5
Brimley 102 B5
Brimpsfield 132 B1
Brimpton 119 G1
Brims 277 B9
Brimscombe 132 A2
Brimstage 183 E4
Brinacory 256 D5
Brindham 116 C3
Brindister *Shet* 279 D9
Brindister *Shet* 279 B7
Brindle 192 B5
Brindley Ford 171 F2
Brineton 158 A1
Bringhurst 160 D3
Brington 161 F5
Brinian 276 D5
Briningham 178 B2
Brinkhill 189 D5
Brinkley *Cambs* 151 E2
Brinkley *Notts* 174 C2
Brinklow 159 G5
Brinkworth 132 C4
Brinmore 258 D2
Brinscall 192 B5
Brinscombe 116 B2
Brinsea 116 B1
Brinsley 173 F3
Brinsop 144 D3
Brinsworth 186 B3
Brinton 178 B2
Brisco 210 A2
Brisley 178 A3
Brislington 131 F5
Brissenden Green 124 B5
Bristol 131 E5
*Bristol Cathedral
BS1 5TJ* 66 Bristol
*Bristol City Museum &
Art Gallery Bristol
BS8 1RL* 8 B3
Bristol Filton
Airport 131 E4
Bristol International
Airport 116 C1
*Bristol Zoo Bristol
BS8 3HA* 8 B3
Briston 178 B2
*Britain At War Experience
GtLon* SE1 2TF 12 C4
Britannia 193 E5
Britford 118 C5
Brithdir *Caerp* 130 A2
Brithdir *Gwyn* 155 D1
Brithem Bottom 102 D1
British Empire &
Commonwealth Museum
BS1 6QH 66 Bristol
*British Library
(St. Pancras) GtLon*
NW1 2DB 12 B4
*British Museum GtLon*
WC1B 3DG 44 E2
Briton Ferry
(Llansawel) 128 D3
Britwell 135 E4
Britwell Salome 134 B3
Brixham 101 F2
Brixton *Devon* 100 B2
Brixton *GtLon* 136 C5

Brixton Deverill 117 F4
Brixworth 160 C5
*Brixworth Country Park
N'hants*
NN6 9DG 160 C5
Brize Norton 133 E2
Broad Alley 146 A1
Broad Blunsdon 133 D3
Broad Campden 147 D4
Broad Carr 185 E1
Broad Chalke 118 B5
Broad Ford 123 G5
Broad Green
*Cambs* 151 E2
Broad Green
*CenBeds* 149 E3
Broad Green *Essex* 151 G5
Broad Green *Essex* 150 C4
Broad Green
*Mersey* 183 F3
Broad Green *Suff* 152 B2
Broad Green *Worcs* 145 G2
Broad Haven 126 B1
Broad Hill 163 D5
Broad Hinton 132 D5
Broad Laying 119 F1
Broad Marston 146 D3
Broad Oak *Carmar* 142 B5
Broad Oak *Cumb* 198 C3
Broad Oak *ESuss* 110 D2
Broad Oak *ESuss* 110 B1
Broad Oak *Here* 145 D5
Broad Street *ESuss* 111 D2
Broad Street *Kent* 124 A3
Broad Street *Kent* 124 D5
Broad Street *Wilts* 118 C2
Broad Street Green 138 B2
Broad Town 132 C5
Broadbottom 185 D3
Broadbridge 108 A3
Broadbridge Heath 121 G4
Broadclyst 102 C3
Broadfield *Lancs* 192 B5
Broadfield *Lancs* 192 B5
Broadford (An t-Ath
Leathann) 256 C2
Broadford Airport 256 C2
Broadford Bridge 121 F5
Broadgate 198 C4
Broadhaugh 227 F5
Broadhaven 275 J3
Broadheath *GtMan* 184 B4
Broadheath *Worcs* 145 F1
Broadhembury 103 E2
Broadhempston 101 E1
Broadholme 187 F5
Broadland Row 110 D2
Broadlay 127 G2
Broadley *Lancs* 184 C1
Broadley *Moray* 268 B4
Broadley Common 136 D2
Broadmayne 104 D4
Broadmeadows 227 F2
Broadmere 120 B3
Broadmoor 127 D2
Broadnymett 102 A2
Broadoak *Dorset* 104 A3
Broadoak *Glos* 131 F1
Broadoak *Kent* 125 D2
Broadoak End 136 C1
Broadrashes 268 C5
Broad's Green 137 F1
Broadsea 269 H4
Broadstairs 125 F2
Broadstone *Poole* 105 G3
Broadstone *Shrop* 157 E4
Broadstreet
Common 130 C4
Broadwas 145 G2
Broadwater *Herts* 150 A5
Broadwater *WSuss* 108 D3
Broadwater Down 123 E5
Broadwaters 158 A5
Broadway *Carmar* 127 G2
Broadway *Carmar* 127 F1
Broadway *Pembs* 126 B1
Broadway *Som* 103 G1
Broadway *Suff* 165 E4
Broadway *Worcs* 146 C4
Broadwell *Glos* 147 E5
Broadwell *Oxon* 133 E2
Broadwell *Warks* 147 G1
Broadwell House 211 F3
Broadwey 104 C4
Broadwindsor 104 A2
Broadwood Kelly 113 G5
Broadwoodwidger 99 E2
Brobury 144 C3
Brocastle 129 F5
Brochel 264 B7
Brochloch 215 G1
Brock 246 B3
Brockamin 145 G2
Brockbridge 107 F1
Brockdish 164 D4
Brockenhurst 106 B2
Brockford Green 152 C1
Brockford Street 152 C1
Brockhall 148 B1
Brockham 121 G3
Brockhampton
*Glos* 146 C5
Brockhampton
*Glos* 146 B5
Brockhampton
*Here* 145 E4
Brockhampton
*Here* 145 F4
Brockhampton
Green 104 D2
Brockholes 185 F1
Brockhurst *Hants* 107 E2
Brockhurst *WSuss* 122 D5
Brocklebank 209 G2
Brocklesby 188 B1
Brockley *NSom* 116 B1
Brockley *Suff* 151 G2
Brock's Green 119 F1
Brockton *Shrop* 157 E3
Brockton *Shrop* 157 F2
Brockton *Shrop* 157 E2
Brockton *Shrop* 156 C4
Brockton *Tel&W* 157 G1
Brockweir 131 E2
Brockwood Park 120 B5
Brockworth 132 A1

285

Brocton 158 B1
Brodick 223 F2
Brodsworth 186 C2
Brogborough 149 E4
Brogyntyn 169 F4
Broken Cross
ChesE 184 C5
Broken Cross
ChesW&C 184 A5
Brokenborough 132 B4
Brokes 202 A3
Bromborough 183 E4
Brome 164 C4
Brome Street 164 C4
Bromeswell 153 E2
Bromfield Cumb 209 E2
Bromfield Shrop 157 D5
Bromham Bed 149 F2
Bromham Wilts 118 A1
Bromley GtLon 122 D2
Bromley SYorks 186 A3
Bromley Cross 184 B1
Bromley Green 124 B5
Brompton Med 123 G5
Brompton NYorks 202 C3
Brompton NYorks 204 C3
Brompton Shrop 157 E2
Brompton on Swale 202 B3
Brompton Ralph 115 D4
Brompton Regis 114 C4
Bromsash 145 F5
Bromsberrow 145 G4
Bromsberrow
Heath 145 G4
Bromsgrove 158 B5
Bromstead Heath 158 A1
Bromyard 145 F2
Bromyard Downs 145 F2
Bronaber 168 A4
Brondesbury 136 B4
Brongest 141 G3
Bronington 170 B4
Bronllys 144 A4
Bronnant 142 C1
Brontë Weaving Shed
WYorks
BD22 8EP 193 E4
Bronwydd Arms 142 A5
Bronydd 144 B3
Bron-y-gaer 127 G1
Brongyarth 169 F4
Brook Carmar 127 F2
Brook Hants 106 B1
Brook Hants 119 E5
Brook IoW 106 C4
Brook Kent 124 C4
Brook Surr 121 E4
Brook Surr 121 F3
Brook Bottom 185 D2
Brook End Bed 149 F1
Brook End Herts 150 B5
Brook End MK 149 E2
Brook End Worcs 146 A3
Brook Hill 106 B1
Brook Street Essex 137 E3
Brook Street Kent 124 B5
Brook Street Suff 151 G3
Brook Street WSuss 109 F1
Brooke Norf 165 D2
Brooke Rut 160 D2
Brookend Glos 131 E3
Brookend Glos 131 E3
Brookfield 185 E3
Brookhampton 134 B3
Brookhouse Denb 169 D1
Brookhouse Lancs 192 B1
Brookhouse SYorks 186 B3
Brookhouse Green 171 F1
Brookhouses 171 G3
Brookland 111 E1
Brooklands D&G 216 C3
Brooklands Shrop 170 C3
Brooklands Museum Surr
KT13 0QN 121 F1
Brookmans Park 136 B2
Brooks 156 A3
Brooks Green 121 G5
Brooksby 160 B1
Brookside Miniature
Railway ChesE
SK12 1BZ 25 G6
Brookthorpe 132 A1
Brookwood 121 E2
Broom CenBeds 149 G3
Broom Fife 244 B4
Broom Warks 146 C2
Broom Green 178 A3
Broom Hill Dorset 105 G2
Broom Hill Worcs 158 B5
Broom of Dalreach 243 F3
Broomcroft 157 E2
Broome Norf 165 E2
Broome Shrop 156 D4
Broome Worcs 158 B5
Broome Wood 229 F5
Broomedge 184 B4
Broomer's Corner 121 G5
Broomfield Aber 261 H1
Broomfield Essex 137 G2
Broomfield Kent 125 D2
Broomfield Kent 124 A3
Broomfield Som 115 F4
Broomfleet 196 A5
Broomhall Green 170 D3
Broomhaugh 211 G1
Broomhead 269 H4
Broomhill Bristol 131 F5
Broomhill N'umb 221 E1
Broomielaw 201 F1
Broomley 211 G1
Broompark 212 B3
Broom's Green 145 G4
Brora 267 G1
Broseley 157 F2
Brotherlee 211 F4
Brotherton 195 D5
Brotton 203 F1
Broubster 275 F2
Brough Cumb 200 C1
Brough Derbys 185 F4
Brough ERid 196 B5
Brough High 275 H1
Brough Notts 174 D2
Brough Ork 277 C6
Brough Shet 279 E8

Brough Shet 278 D5
Brough Shet 279 E6
Brough Shet 278 E5
Brough Lodge 278 E3
Brough Sowerby 200 C1
Broughall 170 C3
Brougham 210 B5
Brougham Hall Cumb
CA10 2DE 210 B5
Broughton Bucks 149 D1
Broughton Cambs 162 A5
Broughton Flints 170 A1
Broughton Hants 119 E4
Broughton Lancs 192 B4
Broughton MK 149 D2
Broughton N'hants 160 D5
Broughton NLincs 187 G2
Broughton NYorks 203 G5
Broughton NYorks 193 F2
Broughton Ork 276 D3
Broughton Oxon 147 G4
Broughton ScBord 226 C2
Broughton VGlam 129 F5
Broughton Astley 160 A3
Broughton Beck 199 D4
Broughton Gifford 117 F1
Broughton Green 146 B2
Broughton Hackett 146 B2
Broughton in
Furness 198 D4
Broughton Mills 198 D3
Broughton Moor 209 D3
Broughton Poggs 133 E2
Broughtown 276 F3
Broughty Ferry 244 C1
Browland 279 B7
Brown Candover 119 G4
Brown Edge Lancs 183 E1
Brown Edge Staffs 171 G2
Brown Heath 170 B1
Brown Lees 171 F2
Brown Street 152 B1
Browndown 107 E3
Brownheath 170 B5
Brownhill 269 G6
Brownhills Fife 244 D3
Brownhills WMid 158 C2
Brownieside 229 F4
Brownlow 171 F1
Brownlow Heath 171 F1
Brown's Bank 170 C3
Brownsea Island Dorset
BH13 7EE 105 G4
Brownshill 132 A2
Brownshill Green 159 F4
Brownsover 160 A5
Brownston 100 C2
Browston Green 179 F5
Broxa 204 C3
Broxbourne 136 C2
Broxburn ELoth 237 D2
Broxburn WLoth 235 E2
Broxholme 187 G5
Broxted 151 D5
Broxton 170 B2
Broxwood 144 C3
Broyle Side 109 G2
Bruachmary 267 F7
Bruan 275 J5
Brue (Brù) 271 F3
Bruera 170 B1
Bruern 147 E5
Bruernish 254 C4
Bruichladdich 230 A3
Bruisyard 153 E1
Bruisyard Street 153 E1
Brumby 187 G1
Brund 172 C1
Brundall 179 E5
Brundish Norf 165 E2
Brundish Suff 153 D1
Brundish Street 165 D4
Brunstock 210 A2
Brunswick Village 221 E4
Bruntingthorpe 160 B3
Bruntland 260 C2
Brunton Fife 244 B2
Brunton N'umb 229 F4
Brunton Wilts 118 D2
Brushfield 185 F5
Brushford Devon 113 G5
Brushford Som 114 C5
Bruton 117 D4
Bryanston 105 E2
Bryant's Bottom 135 D3
Brydekirk 217 F3
Brymbo 169 F2
Brymor Ice Cream NYorks
HG4 4PG 202 A4
Brympton 104 B1
Bryn Caerp 130 A3
Bryn Carmar 128 B2
Bryn ChesW&C 184 A5
Bryn GtMan 183 G2
Bryn NPT 129 E3
Bryn Shrop 156 B4
Bryn Bach Country
Park BGwent
NP22 3AY 130 A2
Bryn Bwbach 167 F4
Bryn Gates 183 G2
Bryn Pen-y-lan 170 A3
Brynamman 128 D1
Bryncae 129 F4
Bryncethin 129 F4
Bryncir 167 D3
Bryncoch Bridgend 129 F4
Bryn-côch NPT 128 D3
Bryncroes 166 B4
Bryncrug 154 C2
Bryneglwys 169 E3
Brynford 182 C5
Bryngwran 180 B5
Bryngwyn Mon 130 C2
Bryngwyn Powys 144 A3
Bryn-henllan 140 D4
Brynhoffnant 141 G2
Bryning 192 A4
Brynithel 130 B2
Brynmawr BGwent 130 A1
Bryn-mawr Gwyn 166 B4
Brynmenyn 129 F4
Brynna 129 F4
Brynnau Gwynion 129 F4
Brynog 142 B2

Bryn-penarth 156 A2
Brynrefail Gwyn 167 E1
Brynrefail IoA 180 C4
Brynsadler 129 G4
Brynsaithmarchog 169 D2
Brynsiencyn 167 D1
Bryn-teg IoA 180 C4
Brynteg Wrex 170 A2
Bryn-y-cochin 170 A4
Brynygwenin 130 C1
Bryn-y-maen 181 G5
Buaile nam Bodach 254 C4
Bualadubh 262 C7
Bualintur 255 K2
Bualnaluib 264 E2
Bubbenhall 159 F5
Bubnell 185 G5
Bubwith 195 G4
Buccleuch 227 E4
Buchan 216 B4
Buchanan Castle 233 F1
Buchanhaven 269 K6
Buchanty 243 E2
Buchlyvie 242 A5
Buckabank 209 G2
Buckby Wharf 148 B1
Buckden Cambs 149 G1
Buckden NYorks 201 E5
Buckenham 179 E5
Buckerell 103 E2
Buckfast 100 D1
Buckfast Abbey Devon
TQ11 0EE 100 D1
Buckfastleigh 100 D1
Buckhaven 244 B5
Buckholm 227 F2
Buckholt 131 E1
Buckhorn Weston 117 E5
Buckhurst Hill 136 D3
Buckie 268 C4
Buckies 275 G2
Buckingham 148 C3
Buckingham Palace GtLon
SW1A 1AA 44 B6
Buckland Bucks 135 D1
Buckland Devon 100 C3
Buckland Glos 146 C4
Buckland Hants 106 C3
Buckland Here 145 E2
Buckland Herts 150 B4
Buckland Kent 125 F4
Buckland Oxon 133 F3
Buckland Surr 122 B3
Buckland Brewer 113 E3
Buckland Common 135 E2
Buckland Dinham 117 E2
Buckland Filleigh 113 E5
Buckland in the
Moor 102 A5
Buckland
Monachorum 100 A1
Buckland Newton 104 C2
Buckland Ripers 104 C4
Buckland St. Margaret
(Fleggburgh) 179 F4
Buckland St. Mary 103 F1
Buckland-tout-
Saints 101 D3
Bucklebury 134 A5
Bucklerheads 244 C1
Bucklers Hard 106 D3
Bucklesham 152 D3
Buckley (Bwcle) 169 F1
Buckley Green 147 D1
Bucklow Hill 184 B4
Buckman Corner 121 G5
Buckminster 175 D5
Bucknall Lincs 175 G1
Bucknall Oxon 148 A5
Bucknell Shrop 156 C5
Buckridge 157 G5
Buck's Cross 112 D3
Bucks Green 121 F4
Bucks Hill 135 F2
Buck's Horn Oak 120 D3
Buck's Mills 113 D3
Buckspool 126 C3
Buckton ERid 205 E5
Buckton Here 156 C5
Buckton N'umb 229 E3
Buckton Vale 185 D2
Buckworth 161 G5
Budby 186 D5
Buddon 244 D1
Bude 112 C5
Budge's Shop 98 D5
Budlake 102 C2
Budle 229 F3
Budleigh Salterton 103 D4
Budock Water 95 E3
Budworth Heath 184 A5
Buerton 171 D3
Bugbrooke 148 B2
Buglawton 171 F1
Bugle 97 E4
Bugthorpe 195 G2
Building End 150 C4
Buildwas 157 F2
Builth Road 143 G2
Builth Wells (Llanfair-
ym-Muallt) 143 G2
Bulby 175 F5
Bulcote 174 B3
Buldoo 274 C2
Bulford 118 C3
Bulford Camp 118 C3
Bulkeley 170 C2
Bulkington Warks 159 F4
Bulkington Wilts 118 A2
Bulkworthy 113 D4
Bulkington Wilts 118 A2
Bull Bay
(Porth Llechog) 180 C3
Bull Green 124 C5
Bullbridge 173 E2
Bullbrook 121 D1
Bullen's Green 136 B2
Bulley 131 G1
Bullington 188 A5
Bullpot Farm 200 B4
Bulls Cross 136 C3
Bull's Green Herts 136 B1
Bull's Green Norf 165 F2
Bullwood 232 C2
Bulmer Essex 151 G3
Bulmer NYorks 195 F1
Bulmer Tye 151 G4
Bulphan 137 F4
Bulstone 103 E4

Bulverhythe 110 C3
Bulwark 269 H6
Bulwell 173 G3
Bulwick 161 E3
Bumble's Green 136 D2
Bun Abhainn
Eadarra 270 D7
Bun Loyne 257 J4
Bunacaimb 247 D1
Bunarkaig 249 D1
Bunbury 170 C2
Bunbury Heath 170 C2
Bunchrew 266 D7
Bundalloch 256 D2
Bunessan 238 C2
Bungay 165 E3
Bunker's Hill 176 A2
Bunlarie 222 C2
Bunloit
(Bun Leothaid) 258 C2
Bunmhullin 254 C3
Bunnahabhain 230 C3
Bunny 173 G5
Buntait 257 K1
Buntingford 150 B5
Bunwell 164 C2
Bunwell Street 164 C2
Burbage Derbys 185 E5
Burbage Leics 159 G3
Burbage Wilts 118 D1
Burbage Common Leics
LE10 3DD 159 G3
Burchett's Green 134 D4
Burcombe 118 B4
Burcot Oxon 134 A3
Burcot Worcs 158 B5
Burcott 149 D5
Burdale 196 A1
Burdocks 121 F5
Burdon 212 C2
Burdrop 147 F4
Bure Valley Railway Norf
NR11 6BW 178 D3
Bures 152 A4
Bures Green 152 A4
Burfa 144 B1
Burford Oxon 133 E1
Burford Shrop 145 E1
Burg 246 C5
Burgate 164 B4
Burgates 120 C5
Burge End 149 G4
Burgess Hill 109 F2
Burgh 153 D2
Burgh by Sands 209 G1
Burgh Castle 179 F5
Burgh Heath 122 B3
Burgh le Marsh 176 C1
Burgh next
Aylsham 178 D3
Burgh on Bain 188 C4
Burgh St. Margaret
(Fleggburgh) 179 F4
Burgh St. Peter 165 F2
Burghclere 119 F1
Burghead 267 J5
Burghfield 120 B1
Burghfield
Common 120 B1
Burghfield Hill 120 B1
Burghill 145 D3
Burghwallis 186 C1
Burham 123 G2
Buriton 120 C5
Burland 97 D3
Burleigh 121 E1
Burlescombe 103 D1
Burleston 105 D3
Burley Hants 106 B2
Burley Rut 161 D1
Burley WYorks 194 B4
Burley Gate 145 E3
Burley in
Wharfedale 194 A3
Burley Street 106 B2
Burley Woodhead 194 A3
Burleydam 170 D3
Burlingjobb 144 B2
Burlow 110 A2
Burlton 170 B5
Burmarsh 124 D5
Burmington 147 E4
Burn 195 E5
Burn Farm 253 E2
Burn Naze 191 G3
Burn of Cambus 242 C4
Burnage 184 C3
Burnaston 173 D4
Burnby 196 A3
Burncross 186 A3
Burndell 108 B3
Burnden 184 B2
Burnedge 184 D1
Burneside 199 G3
Burness 276 F3
Burneston 202 C4
Burnett 117 D1
Burnfoot High 274 D6
Burnfoot P&K 243 E4
Burnfoot ScBord 227 F4
Burnfoot ScBord 227 F4
Burnham Bucks 135 E4
Burnham NLincs 188 A1
Burnham Deepdale 177 G3
Burnham Green 136 B1
Burnham Market 177 G3
Burnham Norton 177 G3
Burnham Overy
Staithe 177 G3
Burnham Overy
Town 177 G3
Burnham Thorpe 177 G3
Burnham-on-
Crouch 138 C3
Burnham-on-Sea 116 A3
Burnhaven 269 K6
Burnhead D&G 215 G2
Burnhead D&G 216 C1
Burnhervie 261 F3
Burnhill Green 157 G2
Burnhope 212 A3
Burnhouse 233 E4
Burniston 204 D3
Burnley 193 E4
Burnmouth 237 G3
Burnopfield 212 A2

Burn's Green 150 B5
Burns National Heritage
Park SAyr
KA7 4PQ 224 B4
Burnsall 193 G1
Burnside Aber 261 F3
Burnside Angus 252 D4
Burnside EAyr 225 D4
Burnside Fife 243 G4
Burnside Shet 278 B5
Burnside WLoth 235 E2
Burnside of
Duntrune 244 C1
Burnstones 210 C2
Burnswark 217 F3
Burnt Hill 134 A5
Burnt Houses 212 A5
Burnt Oak 136 B3
Burnt Yates 194 B1
Burntcliff Top 171 G1
Burntisland 235 G1
Burntwood 158 C2
Burntwood Green 158 C2
Burnworthy 103 E1
Burpham Surr 121 F2
Burpham WSuss 108 C3
Burra 279 C9
Burradon N'umb 220 B1
Burradon T&W 221 E4
Burrafirth 278 F1
Burraland 278 C5
Burras 95 D3
Burraton Corn 100 A1
Burraton Corn 100 A1
Burravoe Shet 278 E5
Burravoe Shet 279 C6
Burray 277 D8
Burrells 200 B1
Burrelton 244 A1
Burridge Devon 103 G2
Burridge Hants 107 E1
Burrill 202 B4
Burringham 187 F2
Burrington Devon 113 G4
Burrington Here 156 D5
Burrington NSom 116 B2
Burrough Green 151 E2
Burrough on the
Hill 160 C1
Burrow Som 114 C3
Burrow Som 104 A1
Burrow Bridge 116 A4
Burrowhill 121 E1
Burrows Cross 121 F3
Burry 95 D3
Burry Green 128 A3
Burry Port 128 A2
Burscough 183 F1
Burscough Bridge 183 F1
Bursea 196 A4
Burshill 196 C3
Bursledon 107 D2
Burslem 171 F3
Burstall 152 B3
Burstock 104 A2
Burston Norf 164 C3
Burston Staffs 171 G4
Burstow 122 C4
Burstwick 197 E5
Burtersett 201 D4
Burthorpe 151 F1
Burthwaite 210 A3
Burtle 116 B3
Burtle Hill 116 A3
Burton ChesW&C 183 E5
Burton ChesW&C 170 C1
Burton Dorset 106 A3
Burton Lincs 187 G5
Burton N'umb 229 F3
Burton Pembs 126 C2
Burton Som 115 E3
Burton Wilts 132 A5
Burton Wilts 117 F4
Burton Agnes 196 C1
Burton Bradstock 104 A4
Burton Coggles 175 E5
Burton End 150 D5
Burton Ferry 126 C2
Burton Fleming 205 D5
Burton Green
Wrex 159 F5
Burton Green Wrex 170 A2
Burton Hastings 159 G4
Burton in Lonsdale 200 B5
Burton Joyce 174 B3
Burton Latimer 161 E5
Burton Lazars 160 C1
Burton Leonard 194 C1
Burton on the
Wolds 173 G5
Burton Overy 160 B3
Burton Pedwardine 175 G3
Burton Pidsea 197 E4
Burton Salmon 195 D5
Burton Stather 187 F1
Burton upon
Stather 187 F1
Burton upon Trent 172 D5
Burton-in-Kendal 199 G5
Burton's Green 151 G5
Burtonwood 183 G3
Burwardsley 170 C2
Burwarton 157 F4
Burwash 110 B1
Burwash Common 110 B1
Burwash Weald 110 B1
Burwell Cambs 151 E1
Burwell Lincs 189 D5
Burwen 180 C3
Burwick Ork 277 D9
Bury Cambs 162 A4
Bury GtMan 184 C1
Bury Som 114 C5
Bury WSuss 108 C2
Bury End 146 C4
Bury Green 150 C5
Bury St. Edmunds 151 G1
Buryas Bridge 94 B4
Burythorpe 195 G1
Busby ERenf 233 G3
Busby P&K 243 F2
Buscot 133 E3

Bush 112 C5
Bush Bank 145 D2
Bush Crathie 259 K5
Bush Green 164 D3
Bushbury 158 B2
Bushby 160 B2
Bushey 136 A3
Bushey Heath 136 A3
Bushley 146 A4
Bushley Green 146 A4
Bushton 132 C5
Bushy Common 178 A4
Business Design Centre,
Islington GtLon
N1 0QH 12 B3
Busk 210 C3
Buslingthorpe 188 A4
Bussage 132 A2
Busta 279 C6
Butcher's Common 179 E3
Butcher's Cross 110 A1
Butcher's Pasture 151 E5
Butcombe 116 C1
Bute 232 B3
Bute Town 130 A2
Buthill 267 J5
Butleigh 116 C4
Butleigh Wootton 116 C4
Butler's Cross 134 D2
Butler's Hill 173 G3
Butlers Marston 147 F3
Butlersbank 170 C5
Butley 153 E2
Butley Abbey 153 E3
Butley Low Corner 153 E3
Butley Mills 153 E2
Butley Town 184 D5
Butt Green 171 D2
Butt Lane 171 F2
Butterburn 219 E4
Buttercrambe 195 G2
Butterknowle 212 A5
Butterleigh 102 C2
Butterley 173 F2
Buttermere Cumb 209 E5
Buttermere Wilts 119 E1
Butters Green 171 F2
Butterstone 251 F5
Butterton Staffs 172 B2
Butterton Staffs 171 F3
Butterwick Dur 212 C5
Butterwick Lincs 176 B3
Butterwick NYorks 204 C5
Butterwick NYorks 203 G5
Buttington 156 B2
Buttonoak 157 G5
Buttons' Green 152 A2
Butts 102 B4
Butt's Green Essex 137 G2
Butt's Green
Hants 119 D5
Buttsash 106 D2
Buxted 109 G1
Buxton Derbys 185 E5
Buxton Norf 178 D3
Buxton Heath 178 C3
Buxworth 185 E4
Bwlch 144 A4
Bwlch-clawdd 141 G4
Bwlch-derwin 167 D3
Bwlchgwyn 169 F2
Bwlch-llan 142 B2
Bwlchnewydd 141 G5
Bwlchtocyn 166 C5
Bwlch-y-cibau 156 A1
Bwlch-y-ddar 169 E5
Bwlchyfadfa 142 A3
Bwlch-y-ffridd 155 G3
Bwlch-y-groes 141 F4
Bwlchyllyn 167 E2
Bwlch-y-sarnau 155 G5
Byers Green 212 B4
Byfield 148 A2
Byfleet 121 F1
Byford 144 C3
Bygrave 150 A4
Byker 221 E4
Byland Abbey 203 E5
Bylane End 97 G4
Bylchau 168 C1
Byley 171 E1
Bynea 128 B3
Byness 219 F1
Bystock 102 D4
Bythorn 161 F5
Byton 144 C1
Bywell 211 G1
Byworth 121 E5

# C

Cabharstadh 271 F5
Cabourne 188 B2
Cabourne Parva 188 B2
Cabrach A&B 230 C3
Cabrach Moray 260 B2
Cabus 192 A3
Cackle Street
ESuss 110 D2
Cackle Street
ESuss 109 G1
Cacrabank 227 E4
Cadboll 267 F4
Cadbury 102 C2
Cadbury Barton 113 G4
Cadbury Heath 131 F5
Cadbury World WMid
B30 1JR 15 E5
Cadder 234 A2
Cadderlie 240 C1
Caddington 135 F1
Caddleton 239 G3
Caddonfoot 227 F2
Cade Street 110 B1
Cadeby Leics 159 G2
Cadeby SYorks 186 C2
Cadeleigh 102 C2
Cader 168 D2
Cadgwith 95 E5
Cadham 244 A4
Cadishead 184 B3
Cadle 128 C3
Cadley Lancs 192 B4
Cadley Wilts 118 D1
Cadmore End 134 C3

Cadnam 106 B1
Cadney 188 A2
Cadole 169 F1
Cadover Bridge 100 B1
Cadoxton 115 E3
Cadoxton-Juxta-
Neath 129 D3
Cadwell 149 G4
Cadwst 168 D4
Cadzow 234 B4
Cae Ddafydd 167 F3
Caeathro 167 E1
Caehopkin 129 E1
Caen 275 F7
Caenby 188 A4
Caenby Corner 187 G4
Caer Llan 131 D2
Caerau Bridgend 129 E3
Caerau Cardiff 130 A5
Caerdeon 154 C1
Caerfarchell 140 A5
Caergeiliog 180 B5
Caergwrle 170 A2
Caerhun 181 F5
Caer-Lan 129 E1
Caerleon 130 C3
Caernarfon 167 D1
Caernarfon Castle Gwyn
LL55 2AY 167 D1
Caerphilly 130 A4
Caersws 155 G3
Caerwedros 141 G2
Caerwent 131 D3
Caerwys 182 C5
Caethle Farm 154 C3
Caggan 259 F3
Caggle Street 130 C1
Caim High 247 E3
Caim IoA 181 E4
Caio 142 C2
Cairisiadar 270 C4
Cairminis 263 F3
Cairnargat 260 C1
Cairnbaan 240 A5
Cairnbeathie 260 D4
Cairnbrogie 261 G2
Cairnbulg 269 J4
Cairncross Angus 252 D2
Cairncross ScBord 237 F3
Cairncurran 233 E3
Cairndoon 207 D3
Cairndow 241 D3
Cairness 269 J4
Cairney Lodge 244 B3
Cairneyhill 235 E1
Cairngorm Mountain High
PH22 1RB 259 G4
Cairnhill Aber 261 H2
Cairnhill Aber 260 H1
Cairnie Aber 261 G4
Cairnie Aber 268 C6
Cairnorrie 269 G6
Cairnryan 214 B4
Cairnsmore 215 F4
Caister-on-Sea 179 G4
Caistor 188 B2
Caistor St. Edmund 178 D5
Caistron 220 B1
Caithness Crystal Visitor
Centre Norf
PE30 4NE 163 E1
Cake Street 164 B2
Cakebole 158 A5
Calbost 271 G6
Calbourne 106 D4
Calceby 189 D5
Calcoed 182 C5
Calcot 134 B2
Calcot Kent 125 D2
Calcott Shrop 156 D1
Calcotts Green 131 G1
Calcutt 132 D3
Caldarvan 233 F1
Caldback 278 F2
Caldbeck 209 G3
Caldbergh 201 F4
Caldecote Cambs 150 B2
Caldecote Cambs 161 G4
Caldecote Herts 150 A4
Caldecote N'hants 148 B2
Caldecote Warks 159 F3
Caldecott N'hants 149 E1
Caldecott Oxon 133 G3
Caldecott Rut 161 D3
Calder Bridge 198 B2
Calder Grove 186 A1
Calder Mains 275 F3
Calder Vale 192 B3
Calderbank 234 B3
Calderbrook 184 D1
Caldercruix 234 C3
Calderglen 234 A4
Calderglen Country Park
SLan G75 0QZ 31 E7
Caldermill 234 A4
Caldey Island 127 E3
Caldhame 252 C5
Caldicot 131 D4
Caldwell Derbys 159 E4
Caldwell ERenf 233 F4
Caldwell NYorks 202 A1
Caldy 182 D4
Calebreck 209 G3
Caledrhydiau 142 A2
Calford Green 151 E3
Calfsound 276 E4
Calgary 246 C4
Califer 267 H6
California Falk 234 D2
California Norf 179 G4
California Suff 152 D3
California Country Park
W'ham
RG40 4HT 120 C1
Calke 173 E5
Calke Abbey Derbys
DE73 7LE 173 E5
Calkill 264 C6
Callally 220 C1
Callander 242 B4
Callanish (Calanais) 270 E4
Callaughton 157 F3
Callerton Lane End 212 A1
Calliburn 222 C3
Calligarry 256 C4
Callington 99 D4
Callingwood 172 C5
Callisterhall 218 A3

Callow **145** D4
Callow End **146** A3
Callow Hill *Wilts* **132** C4
Callow Hill *Worcs* **157** G5
Callow Hill *Worcs* **146** C5
Callows Grave **145** E1
Calmore **106** C1
Calmsden **132** C2
Calne **132** B5
Calow **186** B5
Calrossie **266** E4
Calshot **107** D2
Calstock **100** A1
Calstone
   Wellington **118** B1
Calthorpe **178** C2
Calthwaite **210** A3
Calton *NYorks* **193** F2
Calton *Staffs* **172** C2
Calveley **170** B2
Calver **185** G5
Calver Hill **144** C3
Calverhall **170** D4
Calverleigh **102** C1
Calverley **194** B4
Calvert **148** B5
Calverton *MK* **148** C4
Calverton *Notts* **174** B3
Calvine **250** C3
Calvo **209** E1
Cam **131** G3
Camasnacroise **248** A4
Camastianavaig **256** B1
Camasunary **256** C5
Camault Muir **266** C7
Camb **278** E3
Camber **111** E2
Camberley **121** D1
Camberwell **136** C5
Camblesforth **195** F5
Cambo **220** C3
Cambois **221** F3
Camborne **95** D3
Cambourne **150** B2
Cambridge *Cambs* **150** C2
Cambridge *Glos* **131** G2
Cambridge American
   Military Cemetery &
   Memorial *Cambs*
   CB23 7PH **150** B2
Cambridge City
   Airport **150** C2
Cambridge University
   Botanic Garden *Cambs*
   CB2 1JF **150** C2
Cambus **234** D5
Cambus o'May **260** C5
Cambusbarron **242** C5
Cambuskenneth **242** D5
Cambuslang **234** A3
Cambusnethan **234** C4
Camden Town **136** B4
Camel Hill **116** C5
Camel Trail *Corn*
   PL27 7AL **97** D2
Cameley **116** D2
Camelford **97** F1
Camelon **234** C1
Camelot Theme Park
   *Lancs* PR7 5LP **183** G1
Camelsdale **121** D4
Camer **123** F2
Cameron House **233** E1
Camerory **259** H1
Camer's Green **145** G4
Camerton
   *B&NESom* **117** D2
Camerton *Cumb* **208** D3
Camerton *ERid* **197** E5
Camghouran **250** A4
Camis Eskan **233** E1
Cammachmore **261** H5
Cammeringham **187** G4
Camore **266** E2
Camp Hill *Pembs* **127** F2
Camp Hill *Warks* **159** F3
Campbeltown (Ceann Loch
   Chille Chiarain) **222** C3
Campbeltown
   Airport **222** B3
Camperdown **221** E4
Camperdown Country
   Park *Dundee*
   DD2 4TF **244** B1
Campmuir **244** A1
Camps **235** F3
Camps End **151** E3
Camps Heath **165** G2
Campsall **186** C1
Campsea Ashe **153** E2
Campton **149** G4
Camptown **228** A5
Camquhart **232** A1
Camrose **140** C5
Camserney **250** D5
Camstraddan
   House **241** F5
Camus Croise **256** C3
Camus-luinie **257** F2
Camusnagaul *High* **248** C2
Camusnagaul *High* **265** G3
Camusrory **256** E5
Camusteel **264** D7
Camusurich **242** B1
Camusvrachan **250** B5
Canada **106** B1
Canaston Bridge **127** D1
Candacraig **260** B5
Candlesby **176** C1
Candy Mill **235** G5
Cane End **134** B5
Canewdon **138** B3
Canfield End **151** D5
Canford Bottom **105** G2
Canford Cliffs **105** G4
Canford Heath **105** G3
Canford Magna **105** G3
Canham's Green **152** B1
Canisbay **275** J1
Canley **159** F5
Cann **117** F5
Cann Common **117** F5
Canna **255** H4
Cannard's Grave **116** D3
Cannich (Canaich) **257** K1
Canning Town **136** D4
Cannington **115** F4

Cannock **158** B2
Cannock Wood **158** C1
Cannon Hall Country Park
   *SYorks* S75 4AT **185** G2
Cannon Hall Farm *SYorks*
   S75 4AT **185** G2
Cannon Hill Park *WMid*
   B13 8RD **15** E4
Cannop **131** F1
Canon Bridge **144** D3
Canon Frome **145** F3
Canon Pyon **145** D3
Canonbie **218** B4
Canons Ashby **148** A2
Canon's Town **94** C3
Canterbury *Aber* **268** D5
Canterbury *Kent* **124** D3
Canterbury Cathedral
   *Kent* CT1 2EH
   **67** Canterbury
Canterbury Tales, The
   *Kent* CT1 2TG
   **67** Canterbury
Cantley *Norf* **179** E5
Cantley *SYorks* **186** D2
Cantlop **157** E2
Canton **130** A5
Cantray **266** E7
Cantraydoune **266** E7
Cantraywood **266** E7
Cantsfield **200** B5
Canvey Island **137** G4
Canwell Hall **158** D2
Canwick **175** E1
Canworthy Water **98** C1
Caol **248** D2
Caolas *A&B* **246** B2
Caolas *ESiar* **254** B5
Caolasnacon **248** D3
Capel *Kent* **123** F4
Capel *Surr* **121** G3
Capel Bangor **154** C4
Capel Betws Lleucu **142** C2
Capel Carmel **166** A5
Capel Celyn **168** B3
Capel Coch **180** C4
Capel Curig **168** A2
Capel Cynon **142** A5
Capel Dewi *Carmar* **142** A5
Capel Dewi *Cere* **154** C4
Capel Dewi *Cere* **142** A3
Capel Garmon **168** B2
Capel Gwyn
   *Carmar* **142** A5
Capel Gwyn *IoA* **180** B5
Capel Gwynfe **142** D5
Capel Hendre **128** B1
Capel Isaac **142** B5
Capel Iwan **141** F4
Capel le Ferne **125** E3
Capel Llanilltern **129** G4
Capel Mawr **180** C5
Capel Parc **180** C4
Capel St. Andrew **153** E3
Capel St. Mary **152** B4
Capel St. Silin **142** B2
Capel Seion **154** C5
Capel Tygwydd **141** F3
Capeluchaf **166** D3
Capel-y-ffin **144** B4
Capel-y-graig **167** E1
Capenhurst **183** E5
Capernwray **199** G5
Capheaton **220** C3
Caplaw **233** F4
Capon's Green **153** D1
Cappercleuch **226** D3
Capplegill **226** C5
Capstone **123** G2
Capton *Devon* **101** E2
Capton *Som* **115** D4
Caputh **251** F5
Car Colston **174** C3
Caradon Town **97** G2
Carbellow **225** E3
Carberth **233** F2
Carbis Bay **94** C3
Carbost *High* **263** K7
Carbost *High* **255** J1
Carbrain **234** B2
Carbrooke **178** A5
Carburton **186** D5
Carcary **253** E4
Carco **225** F4
Carcroft **186** C1
Cardenden **244** A5
Cardeston **156** C1
Cardew **209** G2
Cardiff
   (Caerdydd) **130** A5
Cardiff Bay Visitor Centre
   *Cardiff* CF10 4PA **7** C4
Cardiff Castle & Museum
   CF10 3RB **67** Cardiff
Cardiff International
   Airport **115** D1
Cardiff Millennium
   Stadium CF10 1GE
   **67** Cardiff
Cardigan (Aberteifi) **141** E3
Cardinal's Green **151** E3
Cardington *Bed* **149** F3
Cardington *Shrop* **157** E3
Cardinham **97** F3
Cardno **269** H4
Cardonald **233** G3
Cardoness **215** G5
Cardow **267** J7
Cardrona **227** D2
Cardross **233** E2
Cardurnock **209** E1
Careby **161** F1
Careston **252** D4
Carew **126** D2
Carew Cheriton **126** D2
Carew Newton **126** D2
Carey **145** E4
Carfin **234** B4
Carfrae **236** C3
Carfraemill **236** C4
Cargate Green **179** E4
Cargen **217** F3
Cargenbridge **217** D3
Cargill **243** G1
Cargo **209** G1
Cargreen **100** A1
Carham **228** B3

Carhampton **114** D3
Carharrack **96** B5
Carie *P&K* **250** B4
Carie *P&K* **242** B1
Carines **96** B4
Carinish (Cairinis) **262** D5
Carisbrooke **107** D4
Carisbrooke Castle &
   Museum *IoW*
   PO30 1XY **107** D4
Cark **199** E5
Carkeel **100** A1
Carland Cross **96** C4
Carlatton **210** B2
Carlby **161** F1
Carlecotes **185** F2
Carleen **94** D4
Carleton *Cumb* **210** A2
Carleton *Cumb* **210** B5
Carleton *Lancs* **191** G3
Carleton *NYorks* **193** F3
Carleton *WYorks* **195** D5
Carleton Fishery **214** C2
Carleton Forehoe **178** B5
Carleton Rode **164** C2
Carleton St. Peter **179** E5
Carlin How **203** G1
Carlisle **210** A2
Carlisle Cathedral
   *Cumb* CA3 8TZ
   **68** Carlisle
Carlisle Park,
   Morpeth *N'umb*
   NE61 1YD **221** D3
Carloggas **96** C3
Carlops **235** F4
Carloway
   (Càrlabhagh) **270** E3
Carlton *Bed* **149** E2
Carlton *Cambs* **151** E2
Carlton *Leics* **159** F2
Carlton *Notts* **174** B3
Carlton *NYorks* **195** F5
Carlton *NYorks* **201** E4
Carlton *NYorks* **203** F4
Carlton *Stock* **212** C1
Carlton *Suff* **153** E1
Carlton *SYorks* **186** A1
Carlton *WYorks* **194** C5
Carlton Colville **165** G2
Carlton Curlieu **160** B3
Carlton Green **151** E2
Carlton Husthwaite **203** D5
Carlton in Lindrick **186** C4
Carlton Miniott **202** C4
Carlton Scroop **175** E3
Carlton-in-
   Cleveland **203** E2
Carlton-le-
   Moorland **175** E2
Carlton-on-Trent **174** D1
Carluke **234** C4
Carlyon Bay **97** E4
Carmacoup **225** F3
Carmarthen
   (Caerfyrddin) **142** A5
Carmel *Carmar* **128** B1
Carmel *Flints* **182** C5
Carmel *Gwyn* **167** D2
Carmel *IoA* **180** B4
Carmichael **234** C2
Carmont **253** G1
Carmunnock **233** G4
Carmyle **234** A3
Carmyllie **253** D5
Carn **230** A4
Carn Brea Village **96** A5
Carn Dearg **264** D4
Carnaby **196** D1
Carnach *High* **257** G2
Carnach *High* **265** G2
Carnach *ESiar* **262** D6
Carnan **264** C7
Carnassarie **240** A4
Carnbee **244** D4
Carnbo **243** F4
Carndu **256** E2
Carnduncan **230** A3
Carnforth **199** F5
Carnhedryn **140** B5
Carnhell Green **94** D4
Carnichal **269** H5
Carnie **261** G4
Carnkie *Corn* **95** E4
Carnkie *Corn* **95** E3
Carnmore **230** B5
Carno **155** F3
Carnoch *High* **257** K1
Carnoch *High* **265** J6
Carnoch *High* **267** F7
Carnock **235** E1
Carnon Downs **96** C5
Carnousie **268** E5
Carntyne **234** A3
Carnwath **235** E5
Carnyorth **94** A3
Carol Green **159** E5
Carperby **201** F4
Carr **186** C3
Carr Hill **187** D3
Carr Houses **183** E1
Carr Shield **211** E3
Carr Vale **186** B5
Carradale **222** D2
Carragrich **263** G2
Carrbridge **259** G2
Carrefour Selous **100** C5
Carreglefn **180** B4
Carreg-wen **141** E3
Carrhouse **187** E2
Carrick **232** A1
Carrick Castle **241** D5
Carriden **235** E1
Carrine **222** B5
Carrington *GtMan* **184** B3
Carrington *Lincs* **176** B2
Carrington *Midlo* **236** A3
Carroch **216** A1
Carrog *Conwy* **168** A3
Carrog *Denb* **169** E3
Carroglen **242** C2
Carrol **267** F1
Carron *A&B* **240** B5
Carron *Falk* **234** C1
Carron *Moray* **267** K7
Carron Bridge **234** B1
Carronbridge **216** C1
Carronshore **234** C1

Carrot **252** C5
Carrow Hill **130** D3
Carrutherstown **217** F3
Carruthmuir **233** E2
Carrville **212** C3
Carry **232** A3
Carsaig **239** E2
Carscreugh **214** D4
Carse **231** F2
Carse of Ardersier **267** F6
Carsegowan **215** F5
Carseriggan **215** E4
Carsethorn **217** D5
Carsgoe **275** G2
Carshalton **122** B2
Carshalton Beeches **122** B2
Carsie **251** G5
Carsington **173** D2
Carsington Water *Derbys*
   DE6 1ST **172** D2
Carskey **222** B5
Carsluith **215** F5
Carsphairn **215** G1
Carstairs **234** D5
Carstairs Junction **235** D5
Carswell Marsh **133** F3
Carter's Clay **119** E5
Carterton **133** E2
Carterway Heads **211** G2
Carthew **97** E4
Carthorpe **202** C4
Cartington **220** C1
Cartland **234** C2
Cartmel **199** E5
Cartmel Fell **199** F4
Cartworth **185** F2
Carway **128** A2
Cascades Adventure
   Pool *Devon*
   EX33 1NZ **113** E2
Cascob **144** B1
Cashel Farm **241** G5
Cashes Green **132** A2
Cashlie **249** G5
Cashmoor **105** F1
Caskieberran **244** A4
Cassencarie **215** F5
Cassington **133** G1
Cassop **212** C4
Castell **168** A1
Castell Gorfod **141** F5
Castell Howell **142** A3
Castellau **129** G4
Castell-y-bwch **130** B3
Casterton **200** B5
Castle Acre **163** G1
Castle Ashby **149** E2
Castle Bolton **201** F3
Castle Bromwich **158** D4
Castle Bytham **161** E1
Castle Caereinion **156** A2
Castle Camps **151** E3
Castle Carrock **210** B2
Castle Cary **116** D4
Castle Combe **132** A5
Castle Donington **173** F5
Castle Douglas **216** B4
Castle Drogo *Devon*
   EX6 6PB **102** A3
Castle Eaton **132** D3
Castle Eden **212** D4
Castle Eden Dene National
   Nature Reserve *Dur*
   SR8 1NJ **212** D4
Castle End **159** E5
Castle Frome **145** F3
Castle Gate **94** B3
Castle Goring **108** D3
Castle Green **121** E1
Castle Gresley **159** E1
Castle Heaton **237** G5
Castle Hedingham **151** F4
Castle Hill *Kent* **123** F4
Castle Hill *Suff* **152** C3
Castle Howard *NYorks*
   YO60 7DA **195** G1
Castle Kennedy **214** C5
Castle Leod **266** B6
Castle Levan **232** C2
Castle Madoc **143** G4
Castle Morris **140** C4
Castle O'er **218** A2
Castle Rising **177** E5
Castle Semple Water
   Country Park *Renf*
   PA12 4HJ **233** E4
Castle Stuart **266** E7
Castlebay (Bàgh
   a'Chaisteil) **254** B5
Castlebythe **140** D5
Castlecary **234** B1
Castlecraig *High* **267** F5
Castlecraig *ScBord* **235** F5
Castlefairn **216** B2
Castleford **194** D5
Castlehill *D&G* **217** F2
Castlehill *Glas* **234** A4
Castlemorton **145** G4
Castlerigg **209** F4
Castleside **211** G3
Castlethorpe **148** C3
Castleton *A&B* **231** G1
Castleton *Aber* **269** F5
Castleton *Angus* **252** B5
Castleton *Derbys* **185** F4
Castleton *GtMan* **184** C1
Castleton *Newport* **130** B4
Castleton *NYorks* **203** F2
Castleton *ScBord* **218** D2
Castletown *Dorset* **104** C5
Castletown *High* **275** G2
Castletown *High* **266** E7
Castletown *IoM* **190** A6
Castletown *T&W* **212** C2
Castleweary **227** F5
Castlewigg **207** E2
Castley **194** B3
Caston **164** A2
Castor **161** G3
Caswell **128** B4
Cat & Fiddle Inn **185** E5
Catacol **232** A5
Catbrain **131** E4
Catbrook **131** E2
Catchall **94** B4
Catcleugh **219** F1

Catcliffe **186** B4
Catcott **116** A4
Caterham **122** C3
Catfield **179** E3
Catfirth **279** D7
Catford **136** C5
Catforth **192** A4
Cathays **130** A5
Cathcart **233** G3
Cathedine **144** A5
Catherine-de-
   Barnes **159** D4
Catherington **107** F1
Catherston
   Leweston **103** G3
Catherton **157** F5
Cathkin **234** A4
Catisfield **107** E2
Catlodge **258** D5
Catlowdy **218** C4
Catmere End **150** C4
Catmore **133** G4
Caton *Devon* **102** A5
Caton *Lancs* **192** B1
Caton Green **192** B1
Cator Court **99** F2
Catrine **224** D3
Catsfield **110** C2
Catsfield Stream **110** C2
Catshaw **185** G2
Catshill **158** B5
Cattadale **230** B3
Cattal **194** D2
Cattawade **152** B4
Catterall **192** B3
Catterick **202** B3
Catterick Bridge **202** B3
Catterick Garrison **202** A3
Catterlen **210** A4
Catterline **253** G2
Catterton **195** E3
Catteshall **121** E3
Catthorpe **160** A5
Cattishall **151** G1
Cattistock **104** B2
Catton *N'umb* **211** E2
Catton *Norf* **178** D4
Catton *NYorks* **202** C5
Catton Hall **159** E1
Catwick **196** D3
Catworth **161** F5
Caudle Green **132** B1
Caudwell's Mill & Craft
   Centre *Derbys*
   DE4 2EB **173** D1
Caulcott *CenBeds* **149** F3
Caulcott *Oxon* **148** A5
Cauldcots **253** E5
Cauldhame *Stir* **242** B5
Cauldhame *Stir* **242** B4
Cauldon **172** B3
Caulkerbush **217** D5
Caulside **218** C3
Caundle Marsh **104** C1
Caunsall **158** A4
Caunton **174** C1
Causeway End
   *D&G* **215** F4
Causeway End
   *Essex* **137** F1
Causeway End
   *Lancs* **183** F1
Causewayhead
   *Cumb* **209** E1
Causewayhead
   *Stir* **242** D5
Causey **251** E5
Causey Arch Picnic Area
   *Dur* NE16 5EG. **28** A4
Causey Park **221** D2
Causeyend **261** H3
Cautley **200** B3
Cavendish **151** G3
Cavendish Bridge **173** F5
Cavenham **151** F1
Cavens **217** D5
Cavers **227** G4
Caversfield **148** A5
Caversham **134** C5
Caverswall **171** G3
Cawdor **267** F6
Cawkeld **196** B2
Cawkwell **188** C4
Cawood **195** E4
Cawsand **100** A3
Cawston *Norf* **178** C3
Cawston *Warks* **159** G5
Cawthorne **185** G2
Cawthorpe **175** F5
Cawton **203** F5
Caxton **150** B2
Caxton Gibbet **150** A1
Caynham **157** E5
Caythorpe *Lincs* **175** E3
Caythorpe *Notts* **174** B3
Cayton **205** D4
CC2000 Pembs
   SA67 8DD **127** D1
Ceallan **262** D6
Ceann a' Bhàigh
   *ESiar* **262** C5
Ceann a' Bhàigh
   *ESiar* **263** F3
Ceann Loch
   Shiphoirt **270** E6
Ceannacroc **258** D6
Cearsiadar **271** F6
Cedig **168** C5
Cefn Berain **168** C1
Cefn Canol **169** F4
Cefn Cantref **143** G5
Cefn Coch *Denb* **169** E2
Cefn Coch *Powys* **155** G2
Cefn Cribwr **129** E4
Cefn Cross **129** E4
Cefn Einion **156** B4
Cefn Hengoed **130** A3
Cefn Llwyd **154** C4
Cefn Rhigos **129** F2
Cefn-brith **168** C2
Cefn-coch **169** E5
Cefn-coed-y-
   cymmer **129** G2
Cefn-ddwysarn **168** C4
Cefneithin **128** B1
Cefn-ddeuddwr **168** A5
Cefn-coed-y-
   cymmer **129** G2

Chapeltown *SYorks* **186** A3
Chapmans Well **99** D1
Chapmanslade **117** F3
Chapmore End **136** C1
Chappel **151** G5
Charaton **98** D4
Chard **103** G2
Chard Junction **103** G2
Chardleigh Green **103** G1
Chardstock **103** G2
Charfield **131** G3
Charing **124** B4
Charing Cross **106** A1
Charing Heath **124** B4
Charingworth **147** E4
Charlbury **133** F1
Charlcombe **117** E1
Charlecote **147** E2
Charles **113** G2
Charles Tye **152** B2
Charlesfield **227** G3
Charleston **252** B5
Charlestown *Aber* **269** J4
Charlestown
   *Aberdeen* **261** H4
Charlestown *Corn* **97** E4
Charlestown
   *Derbys* **185** E3
Charlestown
   *Dorset* **104** C5
Charlestown *Fife* **235** E1
Charlestown
   *GtMan* **184** C2
Charlestown *High* **264** E6
Charlestown *High* **266** D7
Charlestown
   *WYorks* **194** A4
Charlestown
   *WYorks* **193** F5
Charlestown of Aberlour
   (Aberlour) **267** K7
Charlesworth **185** E3
Charleton **244** C4
Charlinch **115** F4
Charlottetville **121** F3
Charlton *GtLon* **136** D5
Charlton *Hants* **119** E3
Charlton *Herts* **149** G5
Charlton *N'hants* **148** A4
Charlton *N'umb* **220** A3
Charlton *Oxon* **133** G3
Charlton *Som* **117** D2
Charlton *Som* **116** D3
Charlton *Som* **115** F5
Charlton *Tel&W* **157** F1
Charlton *Wilts* **118** A5
Charlton *Wilts* **132** B4
Charlton *Wilts* **118** C2
Charlton *Worcs* **146** C3
Charlton *WSuss* **108** A2
Charlton Abbots **146** C5
Charlton Adam **116** C5
Charlton Down **104** C3
Charlton
   Horethorne **117** D5
Charlton Kings **146** B5
Charlton Mackrell **116** C5
Charlton Marshall **105** E2
Charlton Musgrove **117** E5
Charlton on the Hill **105** E2
Charlton-All-Saints **118** C5
Charlton-on-
   Otmoor **134** A1
Charltons **203** F1
Charlwood **122** B4
Charminster **104** C3
Charmouth **103** G3
Charndon **148** B5
Charney Bassett **133** F3
Charnock Richard **183** G1
Charsfield **153** D2
Chart Corner **123** G4
Chart Sutton **124** A4
Charter Alley **119** G2
Charterhouse **116** B2
Charterville
   Allotments **133** F2
Chartham **124** D3
Chartham Hatch **124** D3
Chartridge **135** E2
Chartwell
   *Kent* TN16 1PS **123** D4
Charvil **134** C5
Charwelton **148** A2
Chase End Street **145** G4
Chase Terrace **158** C2
Chasetown **158** C2
Chastleton **147** E5
Chasty **112** D5
Chatburn **193** D3
Chatcull **171** E4
Chatelherault Country
   Park *SLan*
   ML3 7UE **31** G6
Chatham **123** G2
Chatham Green **137** G1
Chatham Historic
   Dockyard *Med*
   ME4 4TZ **123** G2
Chathill **229** F4
Chatsworth Farmyard &
   Adventure Playground
   *Derbys*
   DE45 1PP **185** G5
Chatsworth House *Derbys*
   DE45 1PP **185** G5
Chattenden **137** G5
Chatteris **162** B4
Chattisham **152** B3
Chatto **228** B5
Chatton **229** E4
Chaul End **149** F5
Chavey Down **121** D1
Chawleigh **102** A1
Chawley **133** G2
Chawston **149** G2
Chawton **120** C4
Chazey Heath **134** B5
Cheadle *GtMan* **184** C4
Cheadle *Staffs* **172** B3
Cheadle Heath **184** C4
Cheadle Hulme **184** C4
Cheam **122** B2
Cheapside **121** E1
Chearsley **134** C1
Chebsey **171** F5
Checkendon **134** B4

Checkley *ChesE* 171 E3
Checkley *Here* 145 E4
Checkley *Staffs* 172 B4
Checkley Green 171 E3
Chedburgh 151 F2
Cheddar 116 B2
*Cheddar Caves & Gorge
Som BS27 3QF* 116 B2
Cheddington 135 E1
Cheddleton 171 G2
Cheddon Fitzpaine 115 F5
Chedglow 132 B3
Chedgrave 165 E2
Chedington 104 A2
Chediston 165 E4
Chediston Green 165 E4
Chedworth 132 C1
Chedzoy 116 A4
Cheesden 184 C1
Cheeseman's Green 124 C5
Cheetham Hill 184 C2
Cheglinch 113 E1
Cheldon 102 A1
Chelford 184 C5
Chellaston 173 E4
Chells 150 A5
Chelmarsh 157 F4
Chelmondiston 152 D4
Chelmorton 172 C1
Chelmsford 137 G2
*Chelmsford Cathedral
Essex CM1 1TY* 137 G2
Chelmsley Wood 159 D4
Chelsea 136 B5
Chelsfield 123 D3
Chelsham 122 C3
Chelston Heath 115 E5
Chelsworth 152 A3
Cheltenham 146 B5
Chelveston 149 E1
Chelvey 116 B1
Chelwood 116 D1
Chelwood Common 109 G1
Chelwood Gate 109 G1
Chelworth 132 B3
Cheney Longville 156 D4
Chenies 135 F3
Chepstow
(Cas-gwent) 131 E3
Cherhill 132 C5
Cherington *Glos* 132 B3
Cherington *Warks* 147 E4
Cheriton *Devon* 114 A2
Cheriton *Hants* 119 G5
Cheriton *Kent* 125 D5
Cheriton *Pembs* 126 C3
Cheriton *Swan* 128 A3
Cheriton Bishop 102 A3
Cheriton Cross 102 A3
Cheriton Fitzpaine 102 B2
Cherrington 171 E5
Cherry Burton 196 B3
Cherry Green 151 D5
Cherry Hinton 150 C4
Cherry Willingham 188 A5
Chertsey 121 F1
Cheselbourne 105 D3
Chesham 135 E2
Chesham Bois 135 E2
*Cheshire Farm Ice Cream,
Tattenhall ChesW&C
CH3 9NE* 170 B2
Cheshunt 136 C2
Cheslyn Hay 158 B2
Chessington 121 E1
*Chessington World of
Adventures GtLon
KT9 2NE* 121 E1
Chestall 158 C1
Chester 170 B1
*Chester Cathedral
ChesW&C CH1 2HU*
69 Chester
Chester Moor 212 B3
*Chester Zoo ChesW&C
CH2 1LH* 183 F5
Chesterblade 117 D3
Chesterfield
*Derbys* 186 A5
Chester-le-Street 212 B2
Chesters *ScBord* 228 A5
Chesters *ScBord* 228 A4
Chesterton *Cambs* 150 C1
Chesterton *Cambs* 161 G3
Chesterton *Oxon* 148 A5
Chesterton *Shrop* 157 G3
Chesterton *Staffs* 171 F3
Chesterton *Warks* 147 F2
Chesterton Green 147 F2
Chestfield 124 D2
Cheston 101 D4
Cheswardine 171 E5
Cheswick 229 E2
Cheswick Buildings 229 E2
Cheswick Green 158 D5
Chetnole 104 C2
Chettiscombe 102 C1
Chettisham 162 D4
Chettle 105 F1
Chetton 157 F3
Chetwode 148 B5
Chetwynd Aston 157 G1
Chetwynd Park 171 E5
Cheveley 151 E1
Chevening 123 D3
Cheverell's Green 135 F1
*Chevin Forest Park WYorks
LS21 3JL* 194 B3
Chevington 151 F2
Chevithorne 102 C1
Chew Magna 116 C1
Chew Moor 184 A2
Chew Stoke 116 C1
Chewton
Keynsham 116 D1
Chewton Mendip 116 C2
Chicacott 99 G1
Chicheley 149 E3
Chichester 108 A3
*Chichester Cathedral WSuss
PO19 1PX* 108 A3
Chickerell 104 C4
Chickering 164 D4
Chicklade 118 A4
Chickney 151 D5
Chicksands 149 G4
Chidden 107 F1

Chidden Holt 107 F1
Chiddingfold 121 E4
Chiddingly 110 A2
Chiddingstone 123 D4
Chiddingstone
Causeway 123 E4
Chiddingstone
Hoath 123 D4
Chideock 104 A3
Chidham 107 G2
Chidswell 194 B5
Chieveley 133 G5
Chignall St. James 137 F2
Chignall Smealy 137 F1
Chigwell 136 D3
Chigwell Row 137 D3
Chilbolton 119 E3
Chilcomb 119 G5
Chilcombe 104 B3
Chilcote 159 E1
Child Okeford 105 E1
Childer Thornton 183 E5
Childerditch 137 F4
Childrey 133 F4
Child's Ercall 171 D5
Childs Hill 136 B4
Childswickham 146 C4
Childwall 183 F4
Childwick Green 136 A1
Chilfrome 104 B3
Chilgrove 108 A2
Chilham 124 C3
Chilhampton 118 B4
Chilla 113 E5
Chillaton 99 E2
Chillenden 125 E3
Chillerton 107 D4
Chillesford 153 E2
Chilley 101 D2
Chillingham 229 E4
Chillington *Devon* 101 D3
Chillington *Som* 103 G1
Chilmark 118 A4
Chilson *Oxon* 133 F1
Chilson *Som* 103 G2
Chilsworthy *Corn* 99 E3
Chilsworthy *Devon* 112 D5
Chilthorne Domer 104 B2
Chilton *Bucks* 134 B1
Chilton *Devon* 102 B2
Chilton *Dur* 212 B5
Chilton *Oxon* 133 G4
Chilton *Suff* 151 G3
Chilton Candover 119 G4
Chilton Cantelo 116 C5
Chilton Foliat 133 F5
Chilton Lane 212 C5
Chilton Polden 116 A4
Chilton Street 151 F3
Chilton Trinity 115 F4
Chilvers Coton 159 F3
Chilwell 173 G4
Chilworth *Hants* 106 D1
Chilworth *Surr* 121 F3
Chimney 133 F2
Chimney Street 151 F3
Chineham 120 B2
Chingford 136 C3
Chinley 185 E4
Chinley Head 185 E4
Chinnor 134 C2
Chipchase Castle 220 A4
Chipley 115 E5
Chipnall 171 E4
Chippenham
*Cambs* 151 E1
Chippenham *Wilts* 132 B5
Chipperfield 135 F2
Chipping *Herts* 150 B4
Chipping *Lancs* 192 C3
Chipping Campden 147 D4
Chipping Hill 138 B1
Chipping Norton 147 F5
Chipping Ongar 137 E2
Chipping Sodbury 131 G4
Chipping Warden 147 G3
Chipstable 114 D5
Chipstead *Kent* 123 D3
Chipstead *Surr* 122 B3
Chirbury 156 B3
Chirk (Y Waun) 169 F4
Chirk Green 169 F4
Chirmorrie 214 D3
Chirnside 237 F4
Chirnside 237 F4
Chirnsidebridge 237 F4
Chirton *T&W* 212 C1
Chirton *Wilts* 118 B2
Chisbury 119 E1
Chiscan 222 B4
Chiselborough 104 A1
Chiseldon 133 D5
Chiserley 193 G5
Chislehampton 134 A3
Chislehurst 136 D5
Chislet 125 E2
Chiswell 136 A2
Chiswell Green 136 A2
Chiswick 136 B5
Chiswick End 150 B3
Chisworth 185 D3
Chithurst 120 D5
Chittering 162 C5
Chitterne 118 A3
Chittlehamholt 113 G3
Chittlehampton 113 G3
Chittoe 118 A1
Chivelstone 101 D4
Chivenor 113 F2
Chobham 121 E1
Choicelee 237 E4
Cholderton 118 D3
Cholesbury 135 E2
Chollerford 220 B4
Chollerton 220 B4
Cholmondeston 170 D2
Cholsey 134 A4
Cholstrey 145 D2
Cholwell
*B&NESom* 116 D2
Cholwell *Devon* 99 E3
Chop Gate 203 E3
Choppington 221 E3
Chopwell 212 A2
Chorley *ChesE* 170 C2
Chorley *Lancs* 183 G1
Chorley *Shrop* 157 F4
Chorley *Staffs* 158 C1
Chorleywood 135 F3
Chorlton 171 E2

Chorlton Lane 170 B3
Chorlton-cum-
Hardy 184 C3
Chowley 170 B2
Chrishall 150 C4
Chrishall Grange 150 C3
Chrisswell 232 D2
Christ Church *Oxon
OX1 1DP* 80 Oxford
Christchurch
*Cambs* 162 C3
Christchurch
*Dorset* 106 A3
Christchurch
*Newport* 130 C4
Christian Malford 132 B5
Christmas Common 134 C3
Christon 116 A2
Christon Bank 229 G4
Christow 102 B4
Christskirk 260 E2
Chryston 234 A2
Chudleigh 102 B5
Chudleigh Knighton 102 B5
Chulmleigh 113 G4
Chunal 185 E3
Church 192 D5
Church Aston 157 G1
Church Brampton 148 C1
Church Brough 200 C1
Church Broughton 172 D4
Church Charwelton 148 A2
Church Common 153 E2
Church Crookham 120 D2
Church Eaton 158 A1
Church End
*CenBeds* 149 G4
Church End
*CenBeds* 149 E5
Church End
*CenBeds* 149 G2
Church End
*CenBeds* 149 E4
Church End
*CenBeds* 149 E4
Church End *ERid* 196 C2
Church End *Essex* 138 C3
Church End *Essex* 151 E5
Church End *Essex* 151 F5
Church End *Glos* 146 A4
Church End *Hants* 120 B1
Church End *Herts* 136 A1
Church End *Herts* 150 C5
Church End *Lincs* 176 A4
Church End *Lincs* 189 D5
Church End *Warks* 159 E3
Church End *Wilts* 132 C5
Church Enstone 147 F5
Church Fenton 195 E4
Church Green 103 E3
Church Gresley 159 E1
Church
Hanborough 133 G1
Church Hill
*ChesW&C* 170 D1
Church Hill *Derbys* 173 F1
Church Houses 203 F3
Church Knowle 105 F4
Church Laneham 187 F5
Church Langley 137 D2
Church Langton 160 C3
Church Lawford 159 G5
Church Lawton 171 F2
Church Leigh 172 B4
Church Lench 146 C2
Church Mayfield 172 C3
Church Minshull 171 D1
Church Norton 108 A4
*Church of St. Mary-
in-Castro Kent
CT16 1HU* 70 Dover
Church Preen 157 E3
Church Pulverbatch 156 D2
Church Stoke 156 B3
Church Stowe 148 B2
Church Street
*Essex* 151 F3
Church Street *Kent* 137 G5
Church Stretton 157 D3
Church Town *Leics* 159 F1
Church Town *Surr* 122 C3
Church Village 130 A4
Church Warsop 173 G1
Church Westcote 147 E5
Church Wilne 173 F4
Churcham 131 G1
Churchdown 132 A1
Churchend *Essex* 138 D3
Churchend *Essex* 151 E5
Churchend *SGlos* 131 G3
Churchfield 158 C3
Churchgate 136 C2
Churchgate Street 137 D1
Churchill *Devon* 113 F1
Churchill *Devon* 103 F2
Churchill *NSom* 116 B2
Churchill *Oxon* 147 E5
Churchill *Worcs* 146 B2
Churchill *Worcs* 158 A5
*Churchill Museum &
Cabinet War Rooms
GtLon SW1A 2AQ* 44 D5
Churchingford 103 F1
Churchover 160 A4
Churchstanton 103 E1
Churchstow 100 D3
Churchtown *Devon* 113 G1
Churchtown *IoM* 190 C2
Churchtown *Lancs* 192 A3
Churchtown
*Mersey* 183 E1
Churnsike Lodge 219 E4
Churston Ferrers 101 F2
Churt 121 D4
Churton 170 B2
Churwell 194 B5
Chute Cadley 119 E2
Chute Standen 119 E2
Chwilog 166 D4
Chyandour 94 B3
Chysauster 94 B3
Cilan Uchaf 166 B5
Cilcain 169 E1
Cilcennin 142 B1

Cilcewydd 156 B2
Cilfrew 129 D2
Cilfynydd 129 G3
Cilgerran 141 E3
Cilgwyn *Carmar* 142 D4
Cilgwyn *Pembs* 141 D4
Ciliau Aeron 142 B1
Cille Bhrighde 254 C5
Cille Pheadair 254 C5
Cilmaengwyn 128 D2
Cilmery 143 F2
Cilrhedyn 141 F4
Cilrhedyn Bridge 140 D4
Cilsan 142 B5
Ciltalgarth 168 B3
Cilwendeg 141 F4
Cilybebyll 128 D2
Cilycwm 143 D3
Cimla 128 D3
Cinderford 131 F1
Cippenham 135 E4
Cippyn 141 E3
Cirbhig 270 D3
Cirencester 132 C2
City *GtLon* 136 C4
City *VGlam* 129 F5
City Airport 136 D4
City Dulas 180 C4
Clabhach 246 A4
Clachaig 232 C1
Clachan *A&B* 241 D3
Clachan *A&B* 248 A5
Clachan *A&B* 231 F4
Clachan *High* 256 B1
Clachan *ESiar* 262 C1
Clachan Mòr 246 A2
Clachan of
Campsie 234 A2
Clachan of
Glendaruel 232 A1
Clachan-a-Luib 262 D5
Clachandhu 239 D1
Clachaneasy 215 E3
Clachanmore 206 A2
Clachan-Seil 239 G3
Clachanturn 259 K5
Clachbreck 231 F2
Clachnabrain 252 B3
Clachnaharry 266 D7
Clachtoll 272 C6
Clackmannan 243 E5
Clackmarras 267 K6
*Clacton Pier Essex
CO15 1QX* 139 E1
Clacton-on-Sea 139 E1
Cladach a Bhale
Shear 262 D5
Cladach a' Chaolais 262 C5
Cladach Chirceboist 262 C5
Cladach Chnoc a
Lin 262 C5
Cladich
(An Cladach) 240 C2
Cladswell 146 C2
Claggan (An Claigeann)
*High* 248 D2
Claggan *High* 247 G5
Claigan 263 H6
Claines 146 A2
Clandown 117 D2
Clanfield *Hants* 107 G1
Clanfield *Oxon* 133 E2
Clannaborough
Barton 102 A2
Clanville 119 E3
Claonaig 231 G4
Claonairigh 240 C4
Claonel 266 C1
Clapgate 150 C5
Clapham *Bed* 149 F2
Clapham *Devon* 102 B4
Clapham *GtLon* 136 B5
Clapham *NYorks* 192 D1
Clapham *WSuss* 108 C3
Clapham Green 149 F2
Clapham Hill 124 D2
Clappers 237 G4
Clappersgate 199 E2
Clapton *Som* 104 A2
Clapton *Som* 116 D2
Clapton-in-
Gordano 131 D5
Clapton-on-the-Hill 133 D1
Clapworthy 113 G3
Clara Vale 212 A1
Clarbeston 140 D5
Clarbeston Road 140 D5
Clarborough 187 E4
Clardon 275 H2
Clare 151 F3
*Clare Castle Country Park
Suff CO10 8NJ* 151 F3
Clarebrand 216 B4
*Claremont Landscape
Garden Surr
KT10 9JG* 121 G1
Clarencefield 217 E4
Clanlaw 227 G2
Clark's Green 121 G4
Clarkston 233 G4
Clashban 266 D2
Clashcoig 266 D2
Clashdorran 266 C7
Clashgour 249 E5
Clashindarroch 260 C1
Clashmore *High* 266 E3
Clashmore *High* 272 C5
Clashnessie 272 C5
Clashnoir 259 K2
Clatford 118 C1
Clathy 243 E2
Clatt 260 D2
Clatter 155 F3
Clattercote 147 G3
Clatterford 107 D4
Clatterford End 137 E2
Clatterin Brig 253 E2
Clatteringshaws 215 G3
Clatworthy 115 D4
Claughton *Lancs* 192 B1
Claughton *Lancs* 192 B3
Clavelshay 115 F4
Claverdon 147 D1
Claverham 116 B1

Clavering 150 C4
Claverley 157 G3
Claverton 117 E1
Claverton Down 117 E1
Clawdd-côch 129 G5
Clawdd-newydd 169 D2
Clawfin 224 D5
Clawthorpe 199 G5
Clawton 99 D1
Claxby 188 B3
Claxby Pluckacre 176 B1
Claxby St. Andrew 189 E5
Claxton *Norf* 179 E5
Claxton *NYorks* 195 F1
Claxton Grange 213 D5
Clay Common 165 F3
Clay Coton 160 A5
Clay Cross 173 E1
Clay End 150 B5
Clay Hill 131 F5
Clay of Allan 267 G4
Claybrooke Magna 159 G4
Claybrooke Parva 159 G4
Claydene 123 D4
Claydon *Oxon* 147 G2
Claydon *Suff* 152 C3
Claygate *Kent* 123 G4
Claygate *Surr* 121 G1
Claygate Cross 123 F3
Clayhanger *Devon* 114 D5
Clayhanger *WMid* 158 C2
Clayhidon 103 E1
Clayhill *ESuss* 110 D1
Clayhill *Hants* 106 C2
Clayhithe 150 D1
Clayock 275 D1
Claypit Hill 150 B2
Claypole 174 D3
Claythorpe 189 E5
Clayton *Staffs* 171 F3
Clayton *SYorks* 186 B2
Clayton *WSuss* 109 E2
Clayton *WYorks* 194 A4
Clayton Green 192 B5
Clayton West 185 G1
Clayton-le-Moors 192 D4
Clayton-le-Woods 192 B5
Clayworth 187 E4
Cleadale 247 D1
Cleadon 212 C1
Clearbrook 100 B1
Clearwell 131 E2
Cleasby 202 B1
Cleat *Ork* 277 D9
Cleat *ESiar* 254 B4
Cleatlam 202 A1
Cleatop 193 E1
Cleator 208 D5
Cleator Moor 208 D5
Cleckheaton 194 A5
Clee St. Margaret 157 E4
Cleedownton 157 E4
Cleehill 157 E5
Cleestanton 157 E5
Cleethorpes 188 D2
*Cleethorpes Discovery
Centre NELincs
DN35 0AG* 188 D2
Cleeton St. Mary 157 F5
Cleeve *NSom* 116 B1
Cleeve *Oxon* 134 B5
Cleeve Hill 146 B5
Cleeve Prior 146 C3
Cleghorn 234 C5
Clehonger 145 D4
Cleigh 240 A2
Cleish 243 F5
Cleland 234 B4
Clement's End 135 F1
Clemsfold 121 G4
Clench Common 118 C1
Clenchwarton 177 D5
Clennell 220 B1
Clent 158 B5
*Clent Hills
Worcs DY9 9JR* 14 B5
Cleobury Mortimer 157 F5
Cleobury North 157 F4
Clephanton 267 F6
Clerklands 227 G3
Clermiston 235 F2
Clestrain 277 C7
Cleuch Head 227 G4
Clevancy 132 C5
Clevedon 130 D5
*Cleveland Tontine
Inn* 202 D3
Cleveley 147 F5
Cleveleys 191 G3
Clevelode 146 A3
Cleverton 132 B4
Clewer 116 B2
Clewer Green 135 E5
Clewer Village 135 E5
Cley next the Sea 178 B1
Cliburn 210 B5
Cliddesden 120 B3
Cliff *Carmar* 127 G2
Cliff *High* 247 F3
Cliff End 111 D2
Cliff Grange 170 D4
Cliffe *Lancs* 192 D4
Cliffe *Med* 137 G5
Cliffe *NYorks* 195 F4
Cliffe Woods 137 G5
Clifford *Here* 144 B3
Clifford *WYorks* 194 D3
Clifford Chambers 147 D2
Clifford's Mesne 145 F5
*Clifford's Tower
YO1 9SA* 90 York
Cliffs End 125 F2
Clifton *Bristol* 131 E5
Clifton *CenBeds* 149 G4
Clifton *Cumb* 210 B5
Clifton *Derbys* 172 C3
Clifton *Devon* 113 F1
Clifton *Lancs* 192 A4
Clifton *N'umb* 221 E3
Clifton *Nott* 173 G4
Clifton *NYorks* 194 B3
Clifton *Oxon* 147 G4
Clifton *Stir* 241 F1
Clifton *SYorks* 186 C3
Clifton *Worcs* 146 A3
Clifton *WYorks* 194 A5

Clifton *York* 195 E2
Clifton Campville 159 E1
Clifton Hampden 134 A3
Clifton Maybank 104 B1
*Clifton Park Museum
SYorks* S65 2AA 21 D1
Clifton Reynes 149 E2
Clifton upon
Dunsmore 160 A5
Clifton upon Teme 145 G1
Cliftonville 125 F1
Climping 108 C3
Climpy 234 D4
Clink 117 E3
Clint 194 B2
Clint Green 178 B4
Clinterty 261 G3
Clintmains 228 A3
Clippesby 179 F4
Clippings Green 178 B4
Clipsham 161 E1
Clipston *N'hants* 160 C4
Clipston *Notts* 174 B4
Clipstone 173 G2
Clitheroe 192 D3
Clive 170 C5
Clivocast 278 F2
Clixby 188 B3
Clocaenog 169 D2
Clochan 268 C4
Clochtow 261 J1
Clock Face 183 G3
Clockhill 269 G6
Cloddach 267 J6
Cloddiau 156 A2
Clodock 144 C5
Cloford 117 E3
Cloichran 242 B1
Clola 269 J6
Clonrae 216 C2
Clophill 149 F4
Clopton 161 F4
Clopton Corner 152 D2
Clopton Green *Suff* 151 F2
Clopton Green *Suff* 152 D2
Close Clark 190 A4
Closeburn 216 C2
Closworth 104 B1
Clothall 150 A4
Clothan 278 D4
Clotton 170 C1
Clough *Cumb* 200 C3
Clough *GtMan* 184 D1
Clough *GtMan* 184 C1
Clough *WYorks* 185 E1
Clough Foot 193 F5
Clough Head 193 G5
Cloughfold 193 E5
Cloughton 204 D3
Cloughton
Newlands 204 D3
Clounlaid 247 G4
Clousta 279 C7
Clouston 277 C6
Clova *Aber* 260 D3
Clova *Angus* 252 B2
Clove Lodge 201 E1
Clovelly 112 D3
*Clovelly Cross 112 D3
*Clovelly Village Devon
EX39 5TA* 112 D3
Clovenfords 227 F2
Clovenstone 261 F3
Cloves 267 J5
Clovullin 248 C2
Clow Bridge 193 E5
Clowne 186 B5
Clows Top 157 F5
Cloyntie 224 B5
Cluanach 230 B4
Clubworthy 98 C1
Cluddley 157 F1
Cluer (Cliuthar) 263 G2
*Clumber Country Park
Notts* S80 3AZ 186 D5
Clun 156 B4
Clunas 267 F7
Clunbury 156 C4
Clunderwen 127 E1
Clune *High* 258 E1
Clune *Moray* 268 D4
Clunes 249 E1
Clungunford 156 C5
Clunie *Aber* 268 E5
Clunie *P&K* 251 G5
Clunton 156 C4
Cluny 244 A5
Clutton *B&NESom* 116 D2
Clutton *ChesW&C* 170 B2
Clwt-y-bont 167 E1
Clwydyfagwyr 129 G2
Clydach *Mon* 130 B1
Clydach *Swan* 128 C2
Clydach Terrace 130 A1
Clydach Vale 129 F3
Clydebank 233 F2
Clydey 141 F4
Clyffe Pypard 132 C5
Clynder 232 D1
Clyne 129 E2
Clynelish 267 F1
Clynfyw 141 F4
Clynnog-fawr 166 D3
Clyro 144 B3
Clyst Honiton 102 C3
Clyst Hydon 102 D2
Clyst St. George 102 C4
Clyst St. Lawrence 102 D2
Clyst St. Mary 102 C3
Clyst William 103 D2
Cnewr 143 E4
Cnoc 271 G4
Cnwch Coch 154 C5
Coachford 268 C6
Coad's Green 97 G2
Coal Aston 186 A5
Coalbrookdale 157 F2
Coalbrookvale 130 A2
Coalburn 225 G2
Coalburns 212 A1
Coalcleugh 211 E3
Coaley 131 G2
Coalmoor 157 F2
Coalpit Heath 131 F4
Coalpit Hill 171 F2
Coalport 157 G2

Coalsnaughton 243 E5
Coaltown of
Balgonie 244 B5
Coaltown of
Wemyss 244 B5
Coalville 159 G1
Coalway 131 E1
Coast 265 F2
Coat 116 B5
Coatbridge 234 B3
Coate *Swin* 133 D4
Coate *Wilts* 118 B1
Coates *Cambs* 162 B2
Coates *Glos* 132 B2
Coates *Lincs* 187 G4
Coates *Notts* 187 F4
Coates *WSuss* 108 B2
Coatham 213 E5
Coatham
Mundeville 212 B5
Cobairdy 268 D6
Cobbaton 113 G3
Cobbler's Plain 131 D2
Cobby Syke 194 A2
Cobden 102 D3
Coberley 132 B1
Cobhall Common 145 D4
Cobham *Kent* 123 F3
Cobham *Surr* 121 G1
Cobleland 242 A5
Cobley Hill 158 C5
Cobnash 145 D2
Coburty 269 H4
Cochno 233 F2
Cock Alley 173 F1
Cock Bank 170 A3
Cock Bevington 146 C2
Cock Bridge 259 K4
Cock Clarks 138 C2
Cock Green 137 G1
Cock Marling 111 D2
Cockayne 203 F3
Cockayne Hatley 150 A3
Cockburnspath 237 E2
Cockenzie & Port
Seton 236 B2
Cocker Bar 192 B5
Cockerham 192 A2
Cockermouth 209 E3
Cockernhoe 149 G5
Cockerton 202 B1
Cockett 128 C3
Cockfield *Dur* 212 A5
Cockfield *Suff* 152 A2
Cockfosters 136 B3
Cocking 108 A2
*Cockington Country
Park Torbay
TQ2 6XA* 101 E1
Cocklake 116 B3
Cocklaw 220 B4
Cockle Park 221 E2
Cockleford 132 B1
Cockley Beck 198 D2
Cockley Cley 163 F2
Cockpen 236 A3
Cockpole Green 134 C4
Cockshutt 170 B5
Cockthorpe 178 A1
Cockwood *Devon* 102 C4
Cockwood *Som* 115 F3
Cockyard 185 E4
Codda 97 F2
Coddenham 152 C2
Coddington
*ChesW&C* 170 B2
Coddington *Here* 145 G3
Coddington *Notts* 174 D2
Codford St. Mary 118 A4
Codford St. Peter 118 A4
Codicote 136 B1
Codmore Hill 108 C2
Codnor 173 F3
Codnor Park 173 F3
Codrington 131 G5
Codsall 158 A2
Codsall Wood 158 A2
Coed Morgan 130 C1
Coed Ystumgwern 167 E5
Coedcae 130 B2
Coedely 129 G4
Coedkernew 130 B4
Coedpoeth 169 F2
Coedway 156 C1
Coed-y-bryn 141 G3
Coed-y-caerau 130 C3
Coed-y-paen 130 C3
Coed-y-parc 167 E1
Coed-yr-ynys 144 A5
Coelbren 129 E1
Coffinswell 101 E1
Cofton 102 C4
Cofton Hackett 158 C5
Cogan 130 A5
Cogenhoe 148 D2
Cogges 133 F2
Coggeshall 151 G5
Coggeshall Hamlet 151 G5
Coggins Mill 110 A1
Cóig Peighinnean 271 H1
Coilantogle 242 A4
Coilleitir 248 D5
Coillessan 241 E4
Coillaig 240 C1
Coille Mhorgil 257 G4
Coille-righ 257 F2
Coillore 255 J1
Coity 129 F4
Col 271 G4
Col Uarach 271 G4
Colaboll 273 H7
Colan 96 C3
Colaton Raleigh 103 D3
Colbost 263 H7
Colburn 202 B3
Colbury 106 C1
Colby *Cumb* 210 C5
Colby *IoM* 190 A4
Colby *Norf* 178 D2
Colchester 152 A5
*Colchester Castle Museum
Essex CO1 1TJ* 152 A5
Colchester Green 152 A2
*Colchester Zoo Essex
CO3 0SL* 152 A5
Colcot 115 E1

Cold Ash 119 G1
Cold Ashby 160 B5
Cold Ashton 131 G5
Cold Aston 132 D1
Cold Blow 127 E1
Cold Brayfield 149 E2
Cold Cotes 200 C5
Cold Hanworth 188 A4
Cold Harbour 134 B4
Cold Hatton 170 D5
Cold Hatton Heath 170 D5
Cold Hesledon 212 D3
Cold Inn 127 E2
Cold Higham 148 B2
Cold Kirby 203 E4
Cold Newton 160 C2
Cold Northcott 97 G1
Cold Norton 138 B2
Cold Overton 160 D2
Cold Row 191 G3
Coldbackie 273 J2
Coldblow 137 E5
Coldean 109 F3
Coldeast 102 B5
Coldeaton 172 C4
Colden Common 119 F5
Coldfair Green 153 F1
Coldham 162 C2
Coldharbour Glos 131 E2
Coldharbour Surr 121 G3
Coldingham 237 E3
Coldrain 243 F4
Coldred 125 E4
Coldrey 120 C3
Coldridge 113 G5
Coldrife 220 C2
Coldstream 228 C3
Coldvreath 97 D4
Coldwaltham 108 C2
Coldwells 269 K6
Cole 117 D4
Cole End 159 D4
Cole Green 136 B1
Cole Henley 119 F2
Colebatch 156 C4
Colebrook 102 D2
Colebrooke 102 A2
Coleburn 267 K6
Coleby Lincs 175 E1
Coleby NLincs 187 F1
Coleford Devon 102 A2
Coleford Glos 131 D1
Coleford Som 117 D3
Colegate End 164 C3
Colehill 105 G2
Coleman Green 136 A1
Coleman's
    Hatch 122 D5
Colemere 170 B4
Colemore 120 C4
Colemore Green 157 G3
Colenden 243 G2
Coleorton 160 A1
Colerne 132 A5
Cole's Common 164 D3
Cole's Cross 101 E3
Cole's Green 153 D1
Colesbourne 132 C1
Colesden 149 G2
Coleshill Bucks 135 E3
Coleshill Oxon 133 E3
Coleshill Warks 159 E4
Colestocks 103 D2
Coley B&NESom 116 C2
Coley Staffs 172 B5
Colfin 214 B5
Colgate 122 B5
Colgrain 233 E2
Colindale 136 B4
Colinsburgh 244 C4
Colinton 235 G3
Colintraive 232 B2
Colkirk 178 A3
Coll 246 A4
Collace 244 A1
Collafirth 279 D6
Collamoor Head 98 B1
Collaton St. Mary 101 E1
Collessie 244 A3
Colleton Mills 113 G4
Collett's Green 146 A2
Collier Row 137 E3
Collier Street 123 G4
Collier's End 150 B5
Collier's Wood 136 B5
Colliery Row 212 C3
Colliston 261 J2
Collin 217 E3
Collingbourne
    Ducis 118 D2
Collingbourne
    Kingston 118 D2
Collingham Notts 174 D1
Collingham WYorks 194 C3
Collington 145 F1
Collingtree 148 C2
Collins End 134 B5
Collins Green
    Warr 183 G3
Collins Green
    Worcs 145 G2
Colliston 253 E5
Colliton 103 D2
Collmuir 260 D4
Collycroft 159 F4
Collyhurst 184 C2
Collynie 261 G1
Collyweston 161 G2
Colmonell 214 C2
Colmworth 149 G2
Coln Rogers 132 C2
Coln St. Aldwyns 132 D2
Coln St. Dennis 132 C1
Colnabaichin 259 K4
Colnbrook 135 F5
Colne Cambs 162 B5
Colne Lancs 193 E4
Colne Engaine 151 G4
Colney 178 C5
Colney Heath 136 B2
Colney Street 136 A2
Colonsay 238 C5
Colonsay House 238 C5
Colpy 260 E1
Colquhar 236 A5

Colsterdale 202 A4
Colsterworth 175 E5
Colston Bassett 174 C4
Colston Hall
    BS1 5AR 66 Bristol
Coltfield 267 J5
Colthouse 199 E3
Coltishall 179 D4
Colton Cumb 199 E4
Colton Norf 178 C5
Colton NYorks 195 E3
Colton Staffs 172 B5
Colton WYorks 194 C4
Colva 144 B2
Colvend 216 C5
Colvister 278 E3
Colwall 145 G3
Colwall Green 145 G3
Colwall Stone 145 G3
Colwell 220 B4
Colwich 172 B5
Colwick 174 B3
Colwinston 129 F5
Colworth 108 B3
Colwyn Bay
    (Bae Colwyn) 181 G5
Colyford 103 F3
Colyton 103 F3
Combe Here 144 C1
Combe Oxon 133 G1
Combe Som 116 B5
Combe WBerks 119 E1
Combe Common 121 E4
Combe Cross 102 A5
Combe Down 117 E1
Combe Florey 115 E4
Combe Hay 117 E2
Combe Martin 113 F1
Combe Pafford 101 F1
Combe Raleigh 103 E2
Combe St. Nicholas 103 G1
Combeinteignhead 102 B5
Comberbach 184 A5
Comberford 159 D2
Comberton Cambs 150 B2
Comberton Here 145 D1
Combpyne 103 F3
Combridge 172 B4
Combrook 147 F2
Combs Derbys 185 E5
Combs Suff 152 B2
Combs Ford 152 B2
Combwich 115 F3
Comer 241 F4
Comers 260 E4
Comhampton 146 A1
Comins Coch 154 C4
Commercial End 151 D1
Commins Coch 155 E2
Common Edge 191 G4
Common Moor 97 G2
Common Platt 132 D4
Common Side 186 A5
Common Square 188 A5
Commondale 203 F1
Commonside 172 D3
Compstall 185 D3
Compton Devon 101 E1
Compton Hants 119 F5
Compton Plym 100 A2
Compton Staffs 158 A4
Compton Surr 121 E3
Compton WBerks 134 A5
Compton Wilts 118 C2
Compton WYorks 194 D3
Compton Abbas 105 E1
Compton Abdale 132 C1
Compton Bassett 132 C5
Compton
    Beauchamp 133 E4
Compton Bishop 116 A2
Compton
    Chamberlayne 118 B5
Compton Dando 116 D1
Compton Dundon 116 B4
Compton Martin 116 C2
Compton
    Pauncefoot 116 D5
Compton Valence 104 B3
Compton Verney 147 F2
Compton Wynyates 147 F3
Comra 258 C2
Comrie Fife 235 E1
Comrie P&K 242 C1
Conchra A&B 232 B1
Conchra High 256 E2
Concraigie 251 G5
Conder Green 192 A2
Conderton 146 B4
Condicote 146 D5
Condorrat 234 B2
Condover 157 D2
Coney Weston 164 A4
Coneyhurst 121 G5
Coneysthorpe 203 G5
Coneythorpe 194 C2
Conford 120 D4
Congash 259 H2
Congdon's Shop 97 G2
Congerstone 159 F2
Congham 177 F5
Congleton 171 F1
Congresbury 116 B1
Congreve 158 B1
Conicavel 267 G6
Coningsby 176 A2
Conington Cambs 161 G4
Conington Cambs 150 B1
Conisbrough 186 C3
Conisby 230 A3
Conisholme 189 E3
Coniston Cumb 199 E3
Coniston ERid 197 D4
Coniston Cold 193 F2
Conistone 193 F1
Conkers, Swadlincote Leics
    DE12 6GA 159 F1
Conland 268 E6
Connah's Quay 169 F1
Connel
    (A' Choingheal) 240 B1
Connel Park 225 E4
Connor Downs 94 C3

Conock 118 B2
Conon Bridge (Drochaid
    Sgùideil) 266 C6
Cononish 241 F2
Cononley 193 F3
Cononsyth 253 D5
Consall 171 G3
Consett 212 A2
Constable Burton 202 A3
Constantine 95 E4
Constantine Bay 96 C2
Contin
    (Cunndainn) 266 B6
Contlaw 261 G4
Contullich 266 D4
Conwy 181 F5
Conwy Castle Conwy
    LL32 8LD 181 F5
Conyer 124 B2
Conyer's Green 151 G1
Cooden 110 C3
Coodham 224 C2
Cooil 190 B4
Cookbury 113 E5
Cookbury Wick 113 D5
Cookham 135 D4
Cookham Dean 135 D4
Cookham Rise 135 D4
Cookhill 146 C2
Cookley Suff 165 E4
Cookley Worcs 158 A4
Cookley Green
    Oxon 134 B3
Cookley Green Suff 165 E4
Cooksbridge 109 F2
Cooksey Green 146 B1
Cookshill 171 G3
Cooksmill Green 137 F2
Cookston 261 H1
Coolham 121 G5
Cooling 137 G5
Cooling Street 137 G5
Coombe Corn 97 D4
Coombe Corn 112 C1
Coombe Corn 96 A5
Coombe Corn 96 C5
Coombe Devon 101 D3
Coombe Devon 102 B4
Coombe Devon 103 E2
Coombe Som 115 F5
Coombe Som 104 A2
Coombe Wilts 118 C2
Coombe Bissett 118 C5
Coombe Country Park
    Warks CV3 2AB 16 D3
Coombe End 114 D5
Coombe Hill 146 A5
Coombe Keynes 105 E4
Coombes 109 D3
Coombes Moor 144 C1
Cooper's Corner
    ESuss 110 C1
Cooper's Corner
    Kent 123 D4
Cooper's Green 136 A2
Coopersale 137 D2
Coopersale Street 137 D2
Cootham 108 C2
Cop Street 125 E3
Copdock 152 C3
Copford Green 152 A5
Copgrove 194 C1
Copister 278 D5
Cople 149 G2
Copley Dur 211 G5
Copley WYorks 193 G5
Coplow Dale 185 F5
Copmanthorpe 195 E3
Copmere End 171 F5
Copp 192 A4
Coppathorne 112 C5
Coppenhall 158 B1
Coppenhall Moss 171 E2
Copperhouse 94 C3
Coppicegate 157 G4
Coppingford 161 G4
Copplestone 102 A2
Coppull 183 G1
Coppull Moor 183 G1
Copsale 121 G5
Copse Hill 122 B2
Copster Green 192 C4
Copston Magna 159 G4
Copt Heath 159 D5
Copt Hewick 202 C5
Copt Oak 159 G1
Copthall Green 136 D2
Copthorne 122 C5
Copy Lake 113 G4
Copythorne 106 C1
Coralhill 269 J4
Corbets Tey 137 E4
Corbiegoe 275 J3
Corbridge 211 F1
Corby 161 D4
Corby Glen 175 E5
Cordach 260 E5
Cordorcan 215 E3
Coreley 157 F5
Corfcott Green 98 D1
Corfe 103 F1
Corfe Castle 105 F4
Corfe Castle Dorset
    BH20 5EZ 105 F4
Corfe Mullen 105 F3
Corfton 157 D4
Corgarff 259 K4
Corhampton 120 B5
Corley 159 F4
Corley Ash 159 E4
Corley Moor 159 F4
Corn Exchange Cambs
    CB2 3QB 66 Cambridge
Cornabus 230 B5
Cornard Tye 152 A3
Corndon 99 G2
Corney 198 C3
Cornforth 212 C4
Cornhill 268 D5
Cornhill on Tweed 228 C3
Cornholme 193 F5
Cornish Gold & Treasure
    Park Corn
    TR16 4HN 96 A5
Cornish Hall End 151 E4

Cornquoy 277 E7
Cornriggs 211 F3
Cornsay 212 A3
Cornsay Colliery 212 A3
Corntown High 266 C6
Corntown VGlam 129 F5
Cornwell 147 E5
Cornwood 100 C2
Cornworthy 101 E2
Corpach
    (A' Chorpaich) 248 D2
Corpusty 178 C3
Corrachree 260 C4
Corran A&B 241 E5
Corran High 256 E1
Corran (Ardgour)
    High 248 C3
Corranbuie 231 G3
Corranmore 239 G4
Corrany 190 C2
Corribeg 248 B2
Corrie 223 B5
Corrie Common 218 A3
Corriecravie 223 E3
Corriedoo 216 A2
Corriekinloch 273 F6
Corrielorne 240 A3
Corrievorrie 258 E2
Corrimony 257 K1
Corringham Lincs 187 F3
Corringham Thur 137 G4
Corris 155 D2
Corris Uchaf 154 D2
Corrlarach 248 B2
Corrour Shooting
    Lodge 249 G3
Corrow 241 D4
Corry 256 C2
Corrychurrachan 248 C3
Corrylach 222 C2
Corrymuckloch 243 D1
Corsback 275 H1
Corscombe 104 B2
Corse Aber 268 E6
Corse Glos 145 G5
Corse Lawn 146 A4
Corse of Kinnoir 268 D6
Corsebank 225 G4
Corsegight 269 G5
Corsehill 217 F2
Corsewall 214 B4
Corsham 132 A5
Corsindae 260 E4
Corsley 117 E3
Corsley Heath 117 E3
Corsock 216 B3
Corston B&NESom 117 D1
Corston Wilts 132 B4
Corstorphine 235 F2
Cortachy 252 B4
Corton Suff 165 G2
Corton Wilts 118 A3
Corton Denham 116 D5
Corwar House 215 D2
Corwen 169 D3
Coryton Devon 99 E2
Coryton Thur 137 G4
Cosby 160 A3
Coscote 134 A4
Coseley 158 B3
Cosford Shrop 157 G2
Cosford Warks 160 A5
Cosgrove 148 C3
Cosham 107 F2
Cosheston 126 D2
Coshieville 250 C5
Coskills 188 A1
Cosmeston 115 E1
Cosmeston Lakes Country
    Park VGlam
    CF64 5UY 115 E1
Cossall 173 F3
Cossington Leics 160 B1
Cossington Som 116 A3
Costa 276 C5
Costessey 178 C4
Costock 173 G5
Coston Leics 174 D5
Coston Norf 178 B5
Cote Oxon 133 F2
Cote Som 116 A3
Cotebrook 170 C1
Cotehill 210 A2
Cotes Cumb 199 F4
Cotes Leics 173 G5
Cotes Staffs 171 F4
Cotesbach 160 A4
Cotford St. Luke 115 E5
Cotgrave 174 B4
Cothall 261 G3
Cotham 174 C3
Cothelstone 115 E4
Cotheridge 145 G2
Cotherstone 201 F1
Cothill 133 G3
Cotleigh 103 F2
Cotmanhay 173 F3
Coton Cambs 150 C2
Coton N'hants 160 B5
Coton Staffs 171 G4
Coton Staffs 159 D2
Coton Staffs 171 F5
Coton Clanford 171 F5
Coton Hill 171 G4
Coton in the Clay 172 C5
Coton in the Elms 159 E1
Cotonwood Shrop 170 C4
Cotonwood Staffs 171 F5
Cott 101 D1
Cottam Lancs 192 A4
Cottam Notts 187 F4
Cottartown 259 H1
Cottenham 150 C1
Cotterdale 200 D3
Cottered 150 B5
Cotteridge 158 C5
Cotterstock 161 F3
Cottesmore 161 E1
Cottingham ERid 196 C4
Cottingham
    N'hants 160 D4
Cottingley 194 A4

Cottisford 148 A4
Cotton Staffs 172 B3
Cotton Suff 152 B1
Cotton End 149 F3
Cottonworth 119 E4
Cottown Aber 260 D2
Cottown Aber 269 G6
Cottown Aber 261 F3
Cotts 100 A1
Cottwood 113 G4
Cotwall 157 F1
Cotwalton 171 G4
Couch's Mill 97 F4
Coughton Here 145 E5
Coughton Warks 146 C1
Cougie 257 J2
Coulaghailtro 231 F3
Coulags 265 F7
Coulby Newham 203 E1
Coulderton 198 A2
Coull 260 D4
Coulport 232 D1
Coulsdon 122 B3
Coulston 118 A2
Coulter 226 B2
Coultershaw Bridge 108 B2
Coultings 115 F3
Coulton 203 F5
Coultra 244 B2
Cound 157 E2
Coundlane 157 E2
Coundon Dur 212 B5
Coundon WMid 159 F4
Countersett 201 E4
Countess Wear 102 C3
Countesthorpe 160 A3
Countisbury 114 A3
Coup Green 192 B5
Coupland Cumb 200 C1
Coupar Angus 252 A5
Coupland N'umb 228 D3
Cour 231 G5
Court Colman 129 E4
Court Henry 142 B5
Court House Green 159 F4
Court-at-Street 124 C5
Courtauld Institute of Art
    Gallery GtLon
    WC2R 0RN 45 F3
Courteenhall 148 C2
Courtsend 138 D3
Courtway 115 F4
Cousland 236 A3
Cousley Wood 123 F5
Coustonn 232 B2
Cove A&B 232 D1
Cove Devon 102 C1
Cove Hants 120 D2
Cove High 264 D5
Cove ScBord 237 E2
Cove Bay 261 H4
Cove Bottom 165 F3
Covehithe 165 G3
Coven 158 B2
Coveney 162 C4
Covenham
    St. Bartholomew 188 D3
Covenham St. Mary 188 D3
Coventry 159 F5
Coventry Airport 159 F5
Coventry Cathedral WMid
    CV1 5AB 69 Coventry
Coventry Transport Museum
    WMid CV1 1JD
    69 Coventry
Coverack 95 E4
Coverham 202 A4
Covesea 267 J4
Covingham 133 D4
Covington Cambs 161 F5
Covington SLan 226 A2
Cowan Bridge 200 B5
Cowbeech 110 B2
Cowbit 162 B1
Cowbridge Som 114 D3
Cowbridge VGlam 129 F5
Cowden 123 D4
Cowden Pound 123 D4
Cowdenbeath 243 G5
Cowdenburn 235 G4
Cowers Lane 173 E3
Cowes 107 D3
Cowesby 203 D4
Cowesfield Green 119 D5
Cowey Green 152 B5
Cowfold 109 E1
Cowgill 200 D4
Cowie Aber 253 G1
Cowie Stir 234 C1
Cowlam Manor 196 B1
Cowley Devon 102 C3
Cowley Glos 132 B1
Cowley GtLon 135 F4
Cowley Oxon 134 A2
Cowling Lancs 183 G1
Cowling NYorks 202 B4
Cowlinge 151 F2
Cowmes 185 F1
Cowpe 193 E5
Cowpen 221 E3
Cowpen Bewley 213 D5
Cowplain 107 F1
Cowsden 146 B2
Cowshill 211 E3
Cowthorpe 194 D2
Cox Common 165 E3
Coxbank 171 E3
Coxbench 173 E3
Coxbridge 116 C4
Coxford 177 G5
Coxheath 123 G3
Coxhoe 212 C4
Coxley 116 C3
Coxley Wick 116 C3
Coxpark 99 E3
Coxtie Green 137 E3
Coxwold 203 E5
Coychurch 129 F5
Coylet 232 C1
Coylton 224 C4
Coylumbridge 259 G3
Coynach 260 C4
Coynachie 260 C1
Coytrahen 129 E4
Crabbet Park 122 C5
Crabgate 178 B3
Crabtree Plym 100 B2
Cranna 268 E5

Crabtree SYorks 186 A4
Crabtree WSuss 109 E1
Crabtree Green 170 A3
Crackaig 230 D3
Crackenthorpe 210 C5
Crackington 98 B1
Crackington Haven 98 B1
Crackley 171 F2
Crackleybank 157 G1
Crackpot 201 E3
Crackthorn Corner 164 B4
Cracoe 193 F1
Craddock 103 D1
Cradhlastadh 270 C4
Cradley Here 145 G3
Cradley WMid 158 B4
Cradley Heath 158 B4
Crafthole 99 D5
Crafton 135 D1
Cragg 193 G5
Cragg Hill 194 B4
Craggan Moray 259 J1
Craggan P&K 242 D3
Cragganmore 259 J1
Cragganruar 250 B5
Craggie High 258 E1
Craggie High 274 D7
Craghead 212 B2
Cragside Aber 259 K5
Craibstone
    Aberdeen 261 G3
Craibstone Moray 268 C5
Craichie 252 D5
Craig A&B 240 C1
Craig A&B 239 E1
Craig D&G 216 A4
Craig High 264 D5
Craig High 265 G7
Craig SAyr 224 B5
Craig Berthlwyd 129 G3
Craigans 240 A5
Craigbeg 249 G1
Craig-cefn-parc 128 C2
Craigcleuch 218 B3
Craigculter 269 H5
Craigdallie 244 A2
Craigdam 261 G1
Craigdarroch D&G 216 B1
Craigdarroch EAyr 225 E5
Craigdhu D&G 207 D2
Craigdhu High 266 B7
Craigearn 261 F3
Craigellachie 267 K7
Craigencallie 215 G3
Craigend Moray 267 J6
Craigend P&K 243 G2
Craigendive 232 B1
Craigendoran 233 E1
Craigens A&B 261 H3
Craigie Aber 261 H3
Craigie Dundee 244 C1
Craigie P&K 251 E5
Craigie SAyr 224 C2
Craigie Brae 261 G1
Craigieburn 226 C5
Craigiehill 235 F2
Craigielaw 236 A2
Craiglockhart 235 G2
Craiglug 261 G3
Craigmaud 269 G5
Craigmillar 235 G2
Craigmore 232 C3
Craigmyle House 260 D4
Craignafeoch 232 A2
Craignant 169 F4
Craignavie 242 A1
Craigneil 214 C1
Craigneuk 234 B4
Craignure 239 G1
Craigo 253 E3
Craigoch 224 A5
Craigow 243 F4
Craigrothie 244 B3
Craigroy 267 J6
Craigruie 241 G2
Craigsanquhar 244 B3
Craigton Aberdeen 261 G4
Craigton Angus 253 D5
Craigton Angus 252 B4
Craigton High 266 D7
Craigton Stir 234 A1
Craigtown 274 D3
Craig-y-nos 129 E1
Craik Aber 260 D2
Craik ScBord 227 E5
Crail 245 E4
Crailing 228 A4
Crailinghall 228 A4
Crakehill 202 D5
Crakemarsh 172 B4
Crambe 195 G1
Crambeck Village 195 G1
Cramlington 221 E4
Cramond 235 F2
Cranage 171 E1
Cranberry 171 F4
Cranborne 105 G1
Cranbourne 135 E5
Cranbrook GtLon 136 D4
Cranbrook Kent 123 G5
Cranbrook
    Common 123 G5
Crane Moor 186 A3
Cranfield 149 E3
Cranford Devon 112 D3
Cranford St. Andrew 161 E5
Cranford St. John 161 E5
Cranham Glos 132 A1
Cranham GtLon 137 E4
Crank 183 G3
Cranleigh 121 F4
Cranmer Green 164 B4
Cranmore IoW 106 C4
Cranmore Som 117 D3

Crannoch 268 C5
Cranoe 160 C3
Cransford 153 E1
Cranshaws 237 D3
Cranstal 190 C1
Crantock 96 B3
Cranwell 175 F3
Cranwich 163 F3
Cranworth 178 A5
Craobh Haven 239 G4
Crapstone 100 B1
Crarae 240 B5
Crask Inn 273 H6
Crask of Aigas 266 B7
Craskins 260 D4
Craster 229 G5
Craswall 144 B4
Crateford 158 B2
Cratfield 165 E4
Crathes 261 F5
Crathie Aber 259 K5
Crathie High 258 C5
Crathorne 202 D2
Craven Arms 156 D4
Craw 231 G5
Crawcrook 212 A1
Crawford Lancs 183 F2
Crawford SLan 226 A3
Crawfordjohn 225 G3
Crawfordton 216 B1
Crawick 225 F4
Crawley Devon 103 F2
Crawley Hants 119 F4
Crawley Oxon 133 F1
Crawley WSuss 122 B5
Crawley Down 122 C5
Crawleyside 211 F3
Crawshawbooth 193 E5
Crawton 253 G2
Crawyn 190 B2
Cray NYorks 201 E5
Cray P&K 251 G3
Cray Powys 143 E5
Crayford 137 E5
Crayke 203 E5
Crays Hill 137 G3
Cray's Pond 134 B4
Crazies Hill 134 C4
Creacombe 102 B1
Creagan 248 C5
Creagbheitheachain
    248 B3
Creagorry
    (Creag Ghoraidh) 262 C7
Creag Adventure
    Park Devon
    Devon EX5 1DR 102 C3
Creamore Bank 170 C4
Creaton 160 C5
Creca 218 A4
Credenhill 145 D3
Crediton 102 B2
Creebridge 215 F4
Creech Heathfield 115 F5
Creech St. Michael 115 F5
Creed 96 C4
Creedy Park 102 B2
Creekmoor 105 F3
Creekmouth 137 D4
Creeting St. Mary 152 B2
Creeton 175 F5
Creetown 215 F5
Creggans 240 C4
Cregneash 190 A5
Cregrina 144 A2
Creich 244 A2
Creigiau 129 G4
Crelevan 257 K1
Crelly 95 D3
Cremyll 100 A2
Crendell 105 G1
Cressage 157 E2
Cressbrook 185 F5
Cresselly 127 D2
Cressing 151 F5
Cresswell N'umb 221 E2
Cresswell Staffs 171 G4
Cresswell Quay 127 D2
Creswell 186 C5
Cretingham 152 D2
Cretshengan 231 F3
Crewe ChesE 171 E2
Crewe ChesW&C 170 B2
Crewe Green 171 E2
Crewgreen 156 C1
Crewkerne 104 A2
Crew's Hole 131 F5
Crewton 173 E4
Crianlarich (A' Chrion-
    Làraich) 241 F2
Cribbs Causeway 131 E4
Cribyn 142 B2
Criccieth 167 D4
Crich 173 E2
Crich Carr 173 E2
Crich Common 173 E2
Crich Tramway Village
    Derbys DE4 5DP 173 E2
Crichie 269 H6
Crichton 236 A3
Crick Mon 131 D3
Crick N'hants 160 A5
Crickadarn 143 G3
Cricket Hill 120 D1
Cricket St. Thomas 103 G2
Crickham 116 B3
Crickheath 169 F5
Crickhowell 130 B1
Cricklade 132 D3
Cricklewood 136 B4
Crickley Hill Country Park
    Glos GL4 8JY 132 B1
Crick's Green 145 F2
Criddlestyle 106 A1
Cridling Stubbs 195 E5
Crieff 243 D2
Crieff Visitor Centre &
    Caithness Glass P&K
    PH7 4HQ 243 D2
Criftins (Dudleston
    Heath) 170 A4
Criggan 97 E3
Criggion 156 B1
Crigglestone 186 A1
Crimble 184 C1
Crimchard 103 G2
Crimdon Park 213 D4

Crimond **269** J5
Crimonmogate **269** J5
Crimplesham **163** E2
Crinan **239** G5
Crinan Ferry **239** G5
Cringleford **105** G1
Cringleford *Here* **117** F3
Crinow **127** E1
Cripplestyle **105** G1
Cripp's Corner **110** C1
Crix **137** G1
Crizeley **144** D4
Croalchapel **216** D1
Croasdale **209** D5
Crock Street **103** G1
Crockenhill **123** E2
Crocker End **134** C4
Crockerhill **107** E2
Crockernwell **102** A3
Crockerton **117** F3
Crockerton Green **117** F3
Crocketford
   (Ninemile Bar) **216** C3
Crockey Hill **195** F3
Crockham Hill **122** D3
Crockhurst Street **123** F4
Crockleford Heath **152** B5
Croes Hywel **130** C1
Croesau Bach **169** F5
Croeserw **129** E3
Croesgoch **140** B4
Croes-lan **141** G4
Croesor **157** F1
Croespenmaen **130** A3
Croesyceiliog
   *Carmar* **128** A1
Croesyceiliog
   *Torfaen* **130** C3
Croes-y-mwyalch **130** C3
Croes-y-pant **130** C2
Croesywaun **167** E2
Croford **115** E5
Croft *Here* **145** D1
Croft *Leics* **160** A3
Croft *Lincs* **176** D1
Croft *Warr* **184** A3
Croftamie **233** F1
Crofthead **218** B4
Croftmore **251** D3
Crofton *Wilts* **133** E5
Crofton *WYorks* **186** A1
Croft-on-Tees **202** B2
Crofts **216** B3
Crofts of Benachielt **275** G5
Crofts of Buinach **267** J6
Crofts of Haddo **261** G1
Crofty **128** B3
Crogen **168** D4
Croggan **239** G2
Croglin **210** B3
Croick *High* **266** B2
Croick *High* **274** D3
Croig **246** D4
Crois Dughaill **254** C3
Croit e Caley **190** A5
Cromarty (Cromba) **266** E5
Crombie **235** E1
Crombie Country Park
   *Angus* DD5 3QL **252** D5
Crombie Mill **244** D1
Cromblet **261** F1
Cromdale **259** H2
Cromer *Herts* **150** A4
Cromer *Norf* **178** D1
Cromford **173** D2
Cromhall **131** F3
Cromhall Common **131** F4
Cromore **271** G5
Crompton Fold **185** D1
Cromwell **174** C1
Cronberry **225** E3
Crondall **120** C3
Cronk-y-Voddy **190** B3
Cronton **183** F4
Crook *Cumb* **199** F3
Crook of Devon **243** F4
Crooked Soley **133** F5
Crookedholm **224** C2
Crookham *N'umb* **228** D3
Crookham *WBerks* **119** G1
Crookham Eastfield **228** D3
Crookham Village **120** C2
Crooklands **199** G4
Cropredy **147** G3
Cropston **160** A1
Cropthorne **146** B3
Cropton **203** G4
Cropwell Bishop **174** B4
Cropwell Butler **174** B4
Crosbie **232** D5
Crosbost **271** F5
Crosby *IoM* **190** B4
Crosby *Mersey* **183** E3
Crosby *NLincs* **187** F1
Crosby Court **202** C3
Crosby Garrett **200** C3
Crosby
   Ravensworth **200** B1
Crosby Villa **209** D3
Crosby-on-Eden **210** A2
Croscombe **116** C3
Crosemere **170** B5
Crosland Hill **185** F1
Cross *Som* **116** B2
Cross (Cros) *ESiar* **271** H1
Cross Ash **130** D1
Cross Bank **157** G5
Cross End *Bed* **149** F2
Cross End *Essex* **151** G4
Cross Foxes Inn **155** D1
Cross Gates **194** C4
Cross Green *Devon* **99** D2
Cross Green *Staffs* **158** B2
Cross Green *Suff* **152** A2
Cross Green *Suff* **151** G2
Cross Green *Suff* **151** G2
Cross Hands
   *Carmar* **128** A1
Cross Hands
   *Pembs* **127** D1
Cross Hill **173** E5
Cross Hills **193** G3
Cross Houses **157** E3
Cross in Hand **110** A1
Cross Inn *Cere* **141** G2
Cross Inn *Cere* **142** B1

Cross Inn *RCT* **129** G4
Cross Keys **132** A5
Cross Lane **107** E3
Cross Lane Head **157** G3
Cross Lanes *Corn* **96** B5
Cross Lanes *Corn* **95** D4
Cross Lanes *NYorks* **195** E4
Cross Lanes *Wrex* **170** A3
Cross of Jackston **261** F1
Cross o'th'hands **173** D3
Cross Street **164** B4
Crossaig **231** G4
Crossapol **246** A2
Crossapoll **246** A2
Cross-at-Hand **123** G4
Crossbush **108** C3
Crosscanonby **209** D3
Crossdale Street **178** D2
Crossens **183** E1
Crossflatts **194** A3
Crossford *D&G* **216** C2
Crossford *Fife* **235** E1
Crossford *SLan* **234** C5
Crossgate *Lincs* **176** A5
Crossgate *Staffs* **171** G4
Crossgate **235** F1
Crossgatehall **236** A3
Crossgates *Fife* **235** F1
Crossgates *NYorks* **204** D4
Crossgates *P&K* **243** F2
Crossgates *Powys* **143** G1
Crossgill **192** B1
Crosshands **224** C2
Crosshill *Fife* **243** G5
Crosshill *SAyr* **224** B5
Crosshouse **224** B2
Crosskeys **130** B3
Crosskirk **275** F1
Crosslanes **156** C1
Crosslee *Renf* **233** F3
Crosslee *ScBord* **227** E4
Crossmichael **216** B4
Crossmoor **192** A4
Crossroads *Aber* **261** F5
Crossroads *EAyr* **224** C2
Crossway *Mon* **130** D1
Crossway *Powys* **143** G2
Crossway Green
   *Mon* **131** E3
Crossway Green
   *Worcs* **146** A1
Crossways *Dorset* **105** D4
Crossways *Glos* **131** E1
Crosswell **141** E4
Crosthwaite **199** F3
Croston **183** F1
Crostwick **179** D4
Crostwight **179** E3
Crothair **270** D4
Crouch **123** F3
Crouch End **136** B4
Crouch Hill **104** D1
Croucheston **118** B5
Croughton **148** A4
Crovie **269** G4
Crow **106** A2
Crow Edge **185** F2
Crow Green **137** E3
Crow Hill **145** F5
Crowan **96** A3
Crowborough **123** E5
Crowborough
   Warren **123** E5
Crowcombe **115** E4
Crowdecote **172** C1
Crowden **185** E3
Crowdhill **119** F5
Crowell **134** C3
Crowfield *N'hants* **148** B3
Crowfield *Suff* **152** C2
Crowhurst *ESuss* **110** C2
Crowhurst *Surr* **122** C4
Crowhurst Lane End **122** C4
Crowland *Lincs* **162** A1
Crowland *Suff* **164** B4
Crowlas **94** C3
Crowle *NLincs* **187** E1
Crowle *Worcs* **146** B2
Crowle Green **146** B2
Crowmarsh Gifford **134** B4
Crown Corner **165** E4
Crownhill **100** A2
Crownthorpe **178** B5
Crowntown **94** D3
Crow's Nest **97** G3
Crows-an-wra **94** A4
Crowsnest **156** C2
Crowthorne **120** D1
Crowton **183** G5
Croxall **159** E1
Croxby **188** B3
Croxdale **212** B4
Croxden **172** B4
Croxley Green **135** F3
Croxteth Country Park
   *Mersey* L12 0HB **22** C2
Croxteth Hall *Mersey*
   L12 0HB **22** C2
Croxton *Cambs* **150** A2
Croxton *NLincs* **188** A1
Croxton *Norf* **178** A3
Croxton *Staffs* **171** E4
Croxton Green **170** C2
Croxton Kerrial **174** D5
Croxtonbank **171** E4
Croy *High* **266** E7
Croy *NLan* **234** B2
Croyde **113** E2
Croyde Bay **113** E2
Croydon *Cambs* **150** B3
Croydon *GtLon* **122** C2
Cruach **230** B4
Cruchie **268** D6
Cruckmeole **156** D2
Cruckton **156** D1
Cruden Bay **261** J1
Crudgington **157** F1
Crudwell **132** B3
Crug **156** A5
Crugmeer **96** D2
Crugybar **142** C4
Crùlabhig **270** D4
Crumlin **130** B3
Crumpsall **184** C2
Crumpsbrook **157** F5
Crundale *Kent* **124** C4
Crundale *Pembs* **126** C1
Crunwere Farm **127** E1
Crutherland Farm **234** A4

Cruwys Morchard **102** B1
Crux Easton **119** F2
Crwbin **128** A1
Cryers Hill **135** D3
Crymlyn **181** E5
Crymych **141** E4
Crynant **129** E3
Crystal Palace **136** C5
Crystal Palace Park
   *GtLon* SE20 8DT **13** C7
Cuaig **264** D6
Cubbington **147** F1
Cubert **96** B4
Cubley **185** G2
Cublington *Bucks* **148** D5
Cublington *Here* **144** D4
Cuckfield **109** F1
Cucklington **117** E5
Cuckney **186** C5
Cuckold's Green **165** F3
Cuckoo Bridge **176** A5
Cuckoo's Corner **120** C3
Cuckoo's Nest **170** A1
Cuddesdon **134** A2
Cuddington *Bucks* **134** C1
Cuddington
   *Ches W&C* **183** G5
Cuddington Heath **170** B3
Cuddy Hill **192** A4
Cudham **122** D3
Cudliptown **99** F3
Cudmore Grove Country
   Park *Essex*
   CO5 8UE **139** D1
Cudworth *Som* **103** G1
Cudworth *SYorks* **186** A2
Cuerdley Cross **183** G4
Cuffley **136** C2
Cuidhaseadair **271** H2
Cuidhir **254** B4
Cuidrach **263** J6
Cuilmuich **241** D5
Cuil-uaine **240** B1
Culag **241** D5
Culbo **266** D5
Culbokie
   (Cùil Bhàicidh) **266** D6
Culbone **114** B3
Culburnie **266** B7
Culcabock **266** D7
Culcharry **267** F6
Culcheth **184** A3
Culdrain **260** D1
Culduie **264** D7
Culford **151** G1
Culfordheath **163** G5
Culgaith **210** C5
Culgower **274** E7
Culham **134** A3
Culindrach **232** A4
Culkein **272** C5
Culkerton **132** B3
Cullachie **259** G2
Cullen **268** D4
Cullercoats **221** F4
Cullicudden **266** D5
Culligran **265** K7
Cullingworth **193** G4
Cullipool **239** G3
Culliyoe **278** E3
Culloch **242** C3
Culloden **266** E7
Cullompton **102** D2
Culmaily **267** F2
Culmalzie **215** E5
Culmington **157** D4
Culmstock **103** E1
Culnacraig **265** G1
Culnadalloch **240** B1
Culnaknock **264** B5
Culnamean **255** K2
Culpho **152** D3
Culquhirk **215** F5
Culrain **266** C2
Culroy **224** B4
Culsh **260** B5
Culshabbin **215** E5
Culswick **279** B8
Culverhouse Cross **130** A5
Culverstone Green **123** F2
Culverthorpe **175** F3
Culvie **268** D5
Culworth **148** A3
Culzean Castle &
   Country Park *SAyr*
   KA19 8LE **224** A4
Cumberhead **234** C5
Cumberlow Green **150** B4
Cumbernauld **234** B2
Cumberworth **189** F5
Cuminestown **269** G6
Cumloden **215** F4
Cummersdale **209** G1
Cummertrees **217** F4
Cummingstown **267** J5
Cumnock **225** D3
Cumnor **133** G2
Cumrew **210** B2
Cumrue **217** E2
Cumstoun **216** A5
Cumwhinton **210** A2
Cumwhitton **210** B2
Cundall **202** D5
Cunninghamhead **233** E5
Cunningsburgh **279** D10
Cunnister **278** E3
Cunnoquhie **244** B3
Cupar **244** B3
Cupar Muir **244** B3
Curbar **185** G5
Curborough **158** D1
Curbridge *Hants* **107** E1
Curbridge *Oxon* **133** F2
Curdridge **107** E1
Curdworth **159** D3
Curland **103** F1
Curlew Green **153** E1
Curling Tye Green **138** B2
Curload **116** A5

Curridge **133** G5
Currie **235** F3
Curry Mallet **116** A5
Curry Rivel **116** A5
Curteis' Corner **124** A5
Curtisden Green **123** G4
Curtisknowle **100** D2
Cury **95** D4
Cusgarne **96** B5
Cushnie **269** F4
Cushuish **115** E4
Cusop **144** B3
Cusworth **186** C2
Cutcombe **114** C4
Cutgate **184** C1
Cuthill **266** E3
Cutiau **154** C1
Cutlers Green **151** D4
Cutnall Green **146** A1
Cutsdean **146** C4
Cutsyke **194** D5
Cutthorpe **186** A5
Cutts **279** D9
Cuttyhill **269** J5
Cuxham **134** B3
Cuxton **123** G2
Cuxwold **188** B2
Cwm *Denb* **182** B5
Cwm *Ffrwd-oer* **130** B2
Cwm Gwaun **140** D4
Cwm Head **156** D4
Cwm Irfon **143** E3
Cwm Penmachno **168** A3
Cwm Plysgog **141** E3
Cwmafan **129** G3
Cwmaman **129** G3
Cwmann **142** B3
Cwmbach *Carmar* **141** F5
Cwmbach *Carmar* **128** A3
Cwmbach *Powys* **144** A4
Cwmbach *Powys* **143** G2
Cwmbelan **155** F4
Cwmbrân **130** B3
Cwmbrwyno **154** D4
Cwmcarn **130** B3
Cwmcarvan **131** D2
Cwm-Cewydd **155** E1
Cwmcrawnon **130** A1
Cwmdare **129** F2
Cwmdu *Carmar* **142** C4
Cwmdu *Powys* **144** A4
Cwmduad **141** G4
Cwmerfyn **154** D4
Cwmfelin *Boeth* **127** E1
Cwmfelin *Mynach* **141** F5
Cwmfelinfach **130** A3
Cwmffrwd **128** A1
Cwmgiedd **129** D1
Cwmgors **128** D1
Cwmgwili **128** B1
Cwmgwrach **129** E2
Cwmgwyn **128** C3
Cwmhiraeth **141** G4
Cwmifor **142** C5
Cwmisfael **128** A1
Cwm-Llinau **155** E2
Cwmllyfri **127** G1
Cwmllynfell **128** D1
Cwm-mawr **128** B1
Cwm-Morgan **141** F4
Cwm-parc **129** F3
Cwmpengraig **141** G4
Cwmpennar **129** G2
Cwmsychbant **142** A3
Cwmsymlog **154** C4
Cwmtillery **130** B2
Cwm-twrch Isaf **129** D1
Cwm-twrch Uchaf **129** D1
Cwm-y-glo **167** E1
Cwmyoy **144** C5
Cwm-yr-Eglwys **140** D3
Cwmyrhaiadr **155** D3
Cwmystwyth **155** D5
Cwrt **154** C2
Cwrt-newydd **142** A3
Cwrt-y-cadno **142** C3
Cwrt-y-gollen **130** B1
Cyffylliog **169** D2
Cyfronydd **156** A2
Cymau **169** F2
Cymmer *NPT* **129** E3
Cymmer *RCT* **129** G4
Cyncoed **130** A4
Cynghordy **143** E4
Cynheidre **128** A2
Cynwyd **169** D3
Cynwyl Elfed **141** G5

# D

Dabton **216** C1
Daccombe **101** F1
Dacre *Cumb* **210** A5
Dacre *NYorks* **194** A1
Dacre Banks **194** A1
Daddry Shield **211** E4
Dadford **148** B4
Dadlington **159** G3
Dafen **128** B2
Daffy Green **178** A5
Dagdale **172** B4
Dagenham **137** D4
Daggons **106** A1
Daglingworth **132** B2
Dagnall **135** E1
Dail **240** C1
Dail Beag **270** E3
Dail Mòr **270** E3
Dailly **224** A5
Dailnamac **240** B1
Dainton **101** E1
Dairsie (Osnaburgh) **244** C3
Dairy House **197** E5
Daisy Bank **158** C3
Daisy Green **152** B1
Dalabrog **262** C7
Dalavich **240** B3
Dalblair **225** E4
Dalbog **253** D2
Dalbreck **274** C7
Dalbury **173** D4

Dalby *IoM* **190** A4
Dalby *Lincs* **176** C1
Dalby *NYorks* **203** F5
Dalby Forest Drive *NYorks*
   YO18 7LT **204** B3
Dalcairnie **224** C5
Dalchalloch **250** C3
Dalchalm **267** G1
Dalchenna **240** C4
Dalchirach **259** J1
Dalchork **273** H7
Dalchreichart **257** J3
Dalchruin **242** C3
Dalcross **266** E7
Dalderby **176** A1
Daldownie **259** K4
Dale *Cumb* **210** B3
Dale *GtMan* **185** D2
Dale *Pembs* **126** B2
Dale Abbey **173** E4
Dale End *Derbys* **172** D1
Dale End *NYorks* **193** F3
Dale Head **199** F3
Dale of Walls **279** A7
Dale Park **108** B2
Dalehouse **203** G1
Dalelia **247** G3
Daless **259** H2
Dalestie **259** J3
Dalganachan **275** F4
Dalgarven **233** D5
Dalgety Bay **235** F1
Dalgig **225** E5
Dalginross **242** C2
Dalgonar **225** F5
Dalguise **251** E5
Dalhalvaig **274** D3
Dalham **151** F1
Daligan **233** E1
Dalinlongart **232** C1
Dalivaddy **222** B3
Daljarrock **214** C2
Dalkeith **236** A3
Dallam **183** G4
Dallas **267** J6
Dallaschyle **267** F7
Dallash **215** F4
Dalleagles **225** D4
Dallinghoo **153** D2
Dallington *ESuss* **110** B2
Dallington *N'hants* **148** C1
Dallow **202** A5
Dalmadilly **261** F3
Dalmarnock **251** F5
Dalmary **242** A5
Dalmellington **224** C5
Dalmeny **235** F2
Dalmichy **273** H7
Dalmigavie **258** D2
Dalmore **266** D5
Dalmuir **233** F2
Dalmunzie House
   Hotel **251** F2
Dalnabreck **247** G3
Dalnacarn **251** F3
Dalnaglar Castle **251** G3
Dalnaha **239** F2
Dalnahaitnach **259** F3
Dalnamain **266** E2
Dalnatrat
   (Dail na Tràghad) **248** B4
Dalnavert **259** F4
Dalnavie **266** D4
Dalness **249** E4
Dalnessie **273** J7
Dalnigap **214** C3
Dalqueich **243** F4
Dalreoch **214** C2
Dalriech **242** C1
Dalroy **266** E7
Dalrulzian **251** G4
Dalry **233** D5
Dalrymple **224** B4
Dalscote **148** B2
Dalserf **234** B4
Dalsetter **278** E3
Dalshangan **215** G2
Dalskairth **216** D3
Dalston **209** G1
Dalswinton **216** D1
Daltomach **258** E2
Dalton *Cumb* **199** G5
Dalton *D&G* **217** F3
Dalton *Lancs* **183** F2
Dalton *N'umb* **220** D4
Dalton *N'umb* **211** F2
Dalton *NYorks* **202** D5
Dalton *NYorks* **202** A2
Dalton *SYorks* **186** B3
Dalton Magna **186** B3
Dalton Piercy **213** D4
Dalton-in-Furness **198** D5
Dalton-le-Dale **212** D3
Dalton-on-Tees **202** B2
Daltote **231** F1
Daltra **242** G7
Dalveich **242** B2
Dalvennan **224** B4
Dalvourn **258** D1
Dalwhinnie **250** B1
Dalwood **103** F2
Dam Green **164** B3
Damask Green **150** A5
Damerham **106** A1
Damgate **179** F5
Damnaglaur **206** B3
Damside **243** F3
Danaway **124** A2
Danbury **137** G2
Danby **203** G2
Danby Wiske **202** C2
Dancers Hill **136** B3
Dandaleith **267** K7
Danderhall **236** A3
Dane Bank **184** D3
Dane End **150** B5
Dane Hills **160** A2
Danebridge **171** G1
Danehill **109** G1
Danesmoor **173** F1
Danestone **261** H3
Daniel's Water **124** B4
Danskine **236** C3
Danthorpe **197** E4

Danzey Green **146** D1
Darby End **158** B4
Darby Green **120** D1
Darenth **137** E5
Daresbury **183** G4
Darfield **186** B2
Dargate **124** C2
Dargues **220** A2
Darite **97** G3
Darland **123** G2
Darlaston **158** B3
Darley **194** B2
Darley Bridge **173** D1
Darley Dale **173** D1
Darley Head **194** A2
Darlingscott **147** D3
Darlington **202** B1
Darliston **170** C4
Darlton **187** E5
Darnabo **269** F6
Darnall **186** A4
Darnconner **225** D3
Darnford **261** F5
Darngarroch **216** A4
Darnick **227** G3
Darowen **155** E2
Darra **269** F6
Darracott **112** C4
Darras Hall **221** D4
Darrington **186** B1
Darrow Green **165** D3
Darsham **153** F1
Dartfield **269** J5
Dartford **137** E5
Dartington **101** D1
Dartington Cider Press
   Centre *Devon*
   TQ9 6TQ **101** D1
Dartington Crystal Ltd.
   *Devon*
   EX38 7AN **113** E4
Dartmeet **99** G3
Dartmouth **101** E2
Darton **186** A1
Darvel **225** D2
Darwell **110** B2
Darwen **192** C5
Datchet **135** E5
Datchworth **136** B1
Datchworth Green **136** B1
Daubhill **184** A2
Daugh of
   Kinermony **267** K7
Dauntsey **132** B4
Dauntsey Green **132** B4
Dauntsey Lock **132** B4
Dava **259** H1
Davaar **222** C4
Davan **260** C4
Davenham **184** A5
Davenport Green **184** C4
Daventry **148** A1
Daventry Country Park
   *N'hants*
   NN11 2JB **148** A1
David Marshall Lodge
   *Stir* FK8 3SX **242** A4
Davidstow **97** F1
Davington **226** D5
Daviot *Aber* **261** F2
Daviot *High* **258** E1
Davoch of Grange **268** C5
Davyhulme **184** B3
Dawley **157** F2
Dawlish **102** C5
Dawn **181** G5
Daws Heath **138** B4
Daw's House **98** D2
Dawsmere **176** C4
Day Green **171** E2
Dayhills **171** G4
Dayhouse Bank **158** B5
Daylesford **147** E5
Ddôl **182** C5
Deadman's Cross **149** G3
Deadwaters **234** B5
Deaf Hill **212** C4
Deal **125** F3
Deal Hall **138** D3
Dean *Cumb* **209** D4
Dean *Devon* **100** D1
Dean *Dorset* **105** F1
Dean *Hants* **107** E1
Dean *Oxon* **147** F5
Dean *Som* **117** D3
Dean Bank **212** B4
Dean Castle & Country
   Park *EAyr*
   KA3 1XB **224** C2
Dean Cross **113** F1
Dean Gallery *Edin*
   EH4 3DS **36** B4
Dean Head **185** G2
Dean Prior **100** D1
Dean Row **184** C4
Deane *GtMan* **184** A2
Deane *Hants* **119** G2
Deanland **105** F1
Deanlane End **107** G1
Deans Bottom **124** A2
Deanscales **209** D4
Deansgreen **184** A4
Deanshanger **148** C4
Deanston **242** C4
Dearham **209** D3
Debach **152** D2
Debate **218** A3
Debden **151** D4
Debden Cross **151** D4
Debden Green
   *Essex* **151** D4
Debden Green
   *Essex* **136** D3
Debenham **152** C1
Deblin's Green **146** A3
Dechmont **235** D2
Decker Hill **157** G1
Deddington **147** G4
Dedham **152** B4
Dedham Heath **152** B4
Dedworth **135** E5
Deecastle **260** C5
Deene **161** E3
Deenethorpe **161** E3

Deep, The HU1 4DP
   **76** Kingston upon Hull
Deep Sea World, North
   Queensferry *Fife*
   KY11 1JR **235** F1
Deepcar **185** G3
Deepcut **121** E2
Deepdale *Cumb* **200** C4
Deepdale *NYorks* **201** D5
Deeping Gate **161** G2
Deeping St. James **161** G2
Deeping
   St. Nicholas **162** A1
Deepweir **131** D4
Deerhill **268** C5
Deerhurst **146** A5
Deerhurst Walton **146** A5
Deerness Valley Walk
   *Dur* DH7 7RJ **212** A3
Deerton Street **124** B2
Defford **146** B3
Defynnog **143** F5
Deganwy **181** F5
Degnish **239** G3
Deighton *NYorks* **202** C2
Deighton *WYorks* **185** F1
Deighton *York* **195** F3
Deiniolen **167** E1
Delabole **97** E1
Delamere **170** C1
Delavorar **259** J3
Delfrigs **261** H2
Dell Lodge **259** H3
Dell Quay **108** A3
Delliefure **259** H1
Delly End **133** F2
Delnabo **259** J3
Delny **266** E4
Delph **185** D2
Delphorrie **260** C3
Delves **212** A3
Delvine **251** G5
Dembleby **175** F4
Denaby **186** B3
Denaby Main **186** B3
Denbies Wine Estate
   *Surr* RH5 6AA **121** G2
Denbigh (Dinbych) **168** D1
Denbury **101** E1
Denby **173** E3
Denby Dale **185** G2
Denby Pottery *Derbys*
   DE5 8NX **18** C1
Denchworth **133** F3
Dendron **198** D5
Denend **260** E1
Denford **161** E5
Dengie **138** C2
Denham *Bucks* **135** F4
Denham *Suff* **164** C4
Denham *Suff* **151** F1
Denham Green **135** F4
Denham Street **164** C4
Denhead *Aber* **261** J3
Denhead *Fife* **244** C3
Denhead of
   Arbirlot **253** D5
Denhead of Gray **244** B1
Denholm **227** G4
Denholme **193** G4
Denholme Clough **193** G4
Denio **166** C4
Denmead **107** F1
Denmill **261** G3
Denmore **261** H3
Denmoss **268** E6
Dennington **153** D1
Denny **234** B1
Dennyloanhead **234** C1
Denshaw **185** D1
Denside **261** G5
Densole **125** E4
Denston **151** F2
Denstone **172** B3
Dent **200** C4
Denton *Cambs* **161** G4
Denton *Darl* **202** B1
Denton *ESuss* **109** G3
Denton *GtMan* **184** D3
Denton *Kent* **125** E4
Denton *Kent* **137** F5
Denton *Lincs* **175** D4
Denton *N'hants* **148** D2
Denton *Norf* **165** D3
Denton *NYorks* **194** A3
Denton *Oxon* **134** A2
Denton's Green **183** F3
Denver **163** E2
Denville **107** G2
Denwick **229** G5
Deopham **178** B5
Deopham Green **164** B2
Depden **151** F2
Depden Green **151** F2
Deptford *GtLon* **136** C5
Deptford *Wilts* **118** B4
Derby **173** E4
Derby City Museum & Art
   Gallery DE1 1BS
   **70** Derby
Derbyhaven **190** A5
Dereham
   (East Dereham) **178** A4
Dererach **239** E2
Deri **130** A2
Derril **112** D5
Derringstone **125** E4
Derrington **171** F5
Derriton **112** D5
Derry **242** B2
Derry Hill **132** B5
Derrythorpe **187** F2
Dersingham **177** E4
Dervaig **246** D4
Derwen **169** D2
Derwenlas **154** D3
Derwent Walk Country Park
   *Dur* NE16 3BN **28** A3
Derwydd **128** C1
Derybruich **232** A2
Desborough **160** D4
Desford **159** G2
Detchant **229** E3
Detling **123** G3
Dethick **173** D2
Detling **123** G3
Deuddwr **156** B1
Deunant **168** C1
Deuxhill **157** F4

Devauden **131** D3
Devil's Bridge
(Pontarfynach) **154** D5
Devitts Green **159** E3
Devizes **118** B1
Devon Guild of Craftsmen
*Devon*
TQ13 9AF **102** B5
Devonport **100** A2
Devonside **243** E5
Devoran **95** E3
Dewar **236** A5
Dewlish **105** D3
Dewsall Court **145** D4
Dewsbury **194** B5
Dewsbury Moor **194** B5
Dhiseig **239** D1
Dhoon **190** C3
Dhoor **190** C2
Dhowin **190** C1
Dhuhallow **258** C2
Dial Green **121** E5
Dial Post **109** D2
Dibden **106** D2
Dibden Hill **135** E3
Dibden Purlieu **106** D2
Dick Institute *EAyr*
KA1 3BU **224** C2
Dickleburgh **164** C3
Dickleburgh Moor **164** C3
Didbrook **146** C4
Didcot **134** A3
Diddington **149** G1
Diddlebury **157** E4
Didley **145** D4
Didling **108** A2
Didmarton **132** A4
Didsbury **184** C3
Didworthy **100** C1
Digby **175** F2
Digg **263** K5
Diggle **185** E2
Digmoor **183** F2
Digswell **136** B1
Dihewyd **142** A2
Dildawn **216** B5
Dilham **179** E3
Dilhorne **171** G3
Dillington **149** G1
Dilston **211** F1
Dilton Marsh **117** F3
Dilwyn **144** D2
Dilwyn Common **144** D2
Dimple **184** B1
Dinas *Carmar* **141** F4
Dinas *Gwyn* **165** D2
Dinas *Gwyn* **166** B4
Dinas Cross **140** D4
Dinas *Powys* **130** A5
Dinas-Mawddwy **155** E1
Dinckley **192** C4
Dinder **116** C3
Dinedor **145** E4
Dingestow **131** D1
Dingley **160** C4
Dingwall (Inbhir
Pheofharain) **266** C6
Dinlabyre **218** D2
Dinnet **260** D5
Dinnington *Som* **104** A1
Dinnington *SYorks* **186** C4
Dinnington *T&W* **221** E4
Dinorwig **167** E1
Dinosaur Adventure Park
*Norf* NR9 5JW **178** C4
Dinosaur Museum,
Dorchester *Dorset*
DT1 1EW **104** C3
Dinton *Bucks* **134** C1
Dinton *Wilts* **118** B4
Dinton Pastures Country
Park *W'ham*
RG10 0TH **134** C5
Dinvin **214** B5
Dinwoodie Mains **217** F1
Dinworthy **112** D4
Dipford **115** F5
Dippen *A&B* **222** C2
Dippen *NAyr* **223** F3
Dippenhall **120** D3
Dipple *Moray* **268** B5
Dipple *SAyr* **224** A5
Diptford **100** D2
Dipton **212** A2
Dirdhu **259** H2
Dirleton **236** C1
Discoed **144** B1
Discovery Museum
*T&W* NE1 4JA
79 Newcastle upon Tyne
Diseworth **173** F5
Dishes **276** F5
Dishforth **202** C5
Dishley **173** G5
Disley **185** D4
Diss **164** C3
Disserth **143** G2
Distington **208** D4
Ditcheat **116** D4
Ditchingham **165** E2
Ditchley **147** F5
Ditchling **109** F2
Ditteridge **117** F1
Dittisham **101** E2
Ditton *Halton* **183** F4
Ditton *Kent* **123** G3
Ditton Green **151** E2
Ditton Priors **157** F4
Dixton *Glos* **146** B4
Dixton *Mon* **131** E1
Dobcross **185** D2
Dobwalls **97** G3
Doccombe **102** A4
Dochgarroch **258** D1
Dock Museum, Barrow-in-
Furness *Cumb*
LA14 2PW **191** E1
Dockenfield **120** D3
Docker *Cumb* **199** G3
Docker *Lancs* **199** G5
Docking **177** G3
Docklow **145** E2
Dockray *Cumb* **209** G4
Dockray *Cumb* **209** F1
Dodbrooke **100** D3
Doddenham **145** G2
Doddinghurst **137** E3

Doddington *Cambs* **162** C3
Doddington *Kent* **124** B3
Doddington *Lincs* **187** G5
Doddington
*N'umb* **229** D3
Doddington *Shrop* **157** F5
Doddiscombsleigh **102** B4
Doddycross **98** D4
Dodford *N'hants* **148** B1
Dodford *Worcs* **158** B5
Dodington *SGlos* **131** G4
Dodington *Som* **115** F3
Dodington Ash **131** G5
Dodleston **170** A1
Dods Leigh **172** B4
Dodscott **113** F4
Dodworth **186** A2
Doehole **173** E2
Doffcocker **184** A1
Dog Village **102** C3
Dogdyke **176** A2
Dogmersfield **120** C2
Dogsthorpe **162** A2
Dol Fawr **155** E2
Dolanog **155** G1
Dolau *Powys* **144** A1
Dolau *RCT* **129** G4
Dolbenmaen **167** E3
Doley **171** E5
Dolfach **155** F5
Dolfor **156** A4
Dolgarreg **142** D4
Dolgarrog **168** A1
Dolgellau **154** D1
Dolgoch **154** C2
Dolgran **142** A4
Doll **267** F1
Dollar **243** E5
Dollarbeg **243** E5
Dolphin **182** C5
Dolphinholme **192** B2
Dolphinton **235** F5
Dolton **113** F4
Dolwen *Conwy* **181** G5
Dolwen *Powys* **155** F2
Dolwyddelan **168** A2
Dôl-y-bont **154** C4
Dol-y-cannau **144** A3
Dolyhir **144** B2
Dolywern **169** F4
Domgay **156** B1
Donaghadee **286** E3
Doncaster Racecourse
Exhibition Centre
*SYorks* DN2 6BB **186** D2
Donhead
St. Andrew **118** A5
Donhead St. Mary **118** A5
Donibristle **235** F1
Doniford **115** D3
Donington *Lincs* **176** A4
Donington *Shrop* **158** A2
Donington le Heath **159** G1
Donington on Bain **188** C4
Donisthorpe **159** F1
Donkey Sanctuary,
Salcombe Regis *Devon*
EX10 0NU **103** E4
Donna Nook **189** E3
Donnington *Glos* **147** D5
Donnington *Here* **145** G4
Donnington *Shrop* **157** E2
Donnington *Tel&W* **157** F1
Donnington *WBerks* **119** F1
Donnington *WSuss* **108** A3
Donyatt **103** E1
Dorchester *Dorset* **104** C3
Dorchester *Oxon* **134** A3
Dorchester Abbey *Oxon*
OX10 7HH **134** A3
Dordon **159** E3
Dore **186** A4
Dores (Duras) **258** C1
Dorket Head **173** G3
Dorking **121** G3
Dorley's Corner **153** E1
Dormans Park **122** C4
Dormansland **122** D4
Dormanstown **213** E5
Dormer's Wells **136** A4
Dormington **145** E3
Dormston **146** B2
Dorn **147** E4
Dorney **135** E5
Dorney Reach **135** E5
Dornie
(An Dòrnaidh) **256** E2
Dornoch **266** E3
Dornock **218** A5
Dorrery **275** F3
Dorridge **159** D5
Dorrington *Lincs* **175** F2
Dorrington *Shrop* **157** D2
Dorsell **260** D3
Dorsington **146** D3
Dorstone **144** C3
Dorton **134** B1
Dorusduain **257** F2
Dosthill **159** E3
Dotland **211** F2
Dottery **104** A3
Doublebois **97** F3
Dougalston **233** G2
Doughton **132** A3
Douglas *IoM* **190** B4
Douglas *SLan* **225** G2
Douglas & Angus **244** C1
Douglas Water **225** G2
Douglastown **252** C5
Doulting **116** D3
Dounby **276** B5
Doune *A&B* **241** F5
Doune *A&B* **241** F3
Doune *High* **266** B1
Doune *High* **266** B1
Doune *Stir* **242** C4
Dounepark **269** F4
Douneside **260** C4
Dounie *High* **266** D3
Dounie *High* **266** C2
Dounreay **274** E2
Dousland **100** B1
Dovaston **170** A5
Dove Holes **185** E5
Dovenby **209** D3
Dovendale **188** D4
Dover **125** F4

Dover Castle *Kent*
CT16 1HU **70** Dover
Dovercourt **152** D4
Doverdale **146** A1
Doveridge **172** C4
Doversgreen **122** B4
Dowally **251** F5
Dowdeswell **146** C5
Dowhill **224** A5
Dowlais **129** G2
Dowland **113** F4
Dowlands **103** F3
Dowlish Ford **103** G1
Dowlish Wake **103** G1
Down Ampney **132** C3
Down End **116** A3
Down Hatherley **146** A5
Down St. Mary **102** A2
Down Thomas **100** B3
Downderry **98** D5
Downe **122** D2
Downend *IoW* **107** E4
Downend *SGlos* **131** F5
Downend *WBerks* **133** G5
Downfield **244** B1
Downfields **163** E5
Downgate **99** F2
Downham *Essex* **137** G3
Downham *Lancs* **193** D3
Downham *N'umb* **228** C3
Downham Market **163** E2
Downhead *Corn* **97** G1
Downhead *Som* **117** D3
Downhead *Som* **116** D3
Downholland Cross **183** E2
Downholme **202** A3
Downies **261** H5
Downley **135** D3
Downs **130** A5
Downside *NSom* **116** B1
Downside *Som* **116** D3
Downside *Som* **116** D2
Downside *Surr* **121** G2
Downton *Devon* **99** F3
Downton *Devon* **101** E2
Downton *Hants* **106** B3
Downton *Wilts* **118** C5
Downton on the
Rock **156** D5
Dowsby **175** F4
Dowthwaitehead **209** G4
Doxey **171** G5
Doynton **131** G5
Drabblegate **178** D3
Draethen **130** B4
Draffan **234** B5
Dragley Beck **199** D5
Drakeland Corner **100** B2
Drakelow **158** A4
Drakemyre **233** D4
Drakes Broughton **146** B3
Drakes Cross **158** C5
Draughton *N'hants* **160** C5
Draughton *NYorks* **193** G2
Drax **195** F5
Draycot Foliat **133** D5
Draycote **147** G1
Draycott *Derbys* **173** F4
Draycott *Glos* **147** D5
Draycott *Shrop* **158** A3
Draycott *Som* **116** B2
Draycott *Worcs* **146** B3
Draycott in the
Clay **172** C5
Draycott in the
Moors **171** G4
Drayford **102** A1
Draynes **97** G3
Drayton *Leics* **160** D3
Drayton *Lincs* **176** A4
Drayton *Norf* **178** D4
Drayton *Oxon* **147** G3
Drayton *Oxon* **133** G3
Drayton *Ports* **107** F2
Drayton *Som* **116** A5
Drayton *Warks* **147** D2
Drayton *Worcs* **158** B5
Drayton Bassett **159** D2
Drayton Beauchamp
**135** E1
Drayton Manor Park *Staffs*
B78 3TW **159** D2
Drayton Parslow **148** D5
Drayton
St. Leonard **134** A3
Drebley **193** G2
Dreemskerry **190** C2
Dreenhill **126** C1
Drefach *Carmar* **141** G4
Drefach *Carmar* **128** B1
Dre-fach *Cere* **142** B3
Drefelin **141** G4
Dreghorn **224** B2
Drem **236** C2
Drewsteignton **102** A3
Driby **189** D5
Driffield *ERid* **196** C2
Driffield *Glos* **132** C3
Drigg **198** B3
Drighlington **194** B5
Drimfern **240** C2
Drimlee **240** D3
Drimnin **247** E4
Drimpton **104** A2
Drimsdale
(Dreumasdal) **254** C1
Drimsynie **241** D4
Drimvore **240** A5
Drinan **256** B3
Dringhouses **195** E2
Drinisiadar **263** G2
Drinkstone **152** A1
Drinkstone Green **152** A1
Drishaig **241** D3
Drissaig **240** B3
Drointon **172** B5
Droitwich Spa **146** A1
Dron **243** G3
Dronfield **186** A5
Dronfield
Woodhouse **186** A5
Drongan **224** C4
Dronley **244** B1
Droop **105** D2
Dropmore **135** E4
Droxford **107** F1
Droylsden **184** D3

Druid **168** D3
Druidston **126** B1
Druimarbin **248** C2
Druimavuic **248** C5
Druimdrishaig **231** F2
Druimindarroch **247** F1
Druimkinnerras **258** B1
Drum *A&B* **232** B3
Drum *P&K* **243** F3
Drumachloy **232** B3
Drumbeg **272** D5
Drumblade **268** D6
Drumblair **268** E6
Drumbuie *D&G* **225** F4
Drumbuie *High* **256** D1
Drumburgh **209** F1
Drumchapel **233** G2
Drumchardine **266** C7
Drumchork **264** E3
Drumclog **225** E2
Drumdelgie **268** C6
Drumderfit **266** D6
Drumeldrie **244** C4
Drumelzier **226** C2
Drumfearn **256** C3
Drumfearn **248** B2
Drumgarve **222** C3
Drumgley **252** C4
Drumguish **258** E5
Drumhead **260** E5
Drumin **259** J1
Drumine **266** E6
Drumjohn **215** G3
Drumlamford
House **215** D3
Drumlasie **260** E4
Drumlemble **222** B4
Drumlithie **253** F1
Drummond *High* **266** D5
Drummond *Stir* **242** B4
Drummore **206** B3
Drummuir **268** B6
Drummuir Castle (Druim na
Drochaid) **258** C3
Drumnagorrach **268** D5
Drumnatorran **248** A3
Drumoak **261** F5
Drumore **222** C3
Drumour **243** E1
Drumpellier Country Park
*NLan* ML5 1RX **31** G3
Drumrash **216** B4
Drumrunie **265** H1
Drums **261** H2
Drumsturdy **244** C1
Drumuie **263** K7
Drumuillie **259** G2
Drumvaich **242** B4
Drumwhindle **261** H1
Drumwhirn **216** B4
Drunkendub **253** E5
Druridge **221** E2
Druridge Bay Country
Park *N'umb*
NE61 5BX **221** E2
Drury **169** F1
Drusillas Park *ESuss*
BN26 5QS **110** A3
Dry Doddington **174** D3
Dry Drayton **150** B1
Dry Harbour **264** C6
Dry Sandford **133** G2
Dry Street **137** F4
Drybeck **200** B1
Drybridge *Moray* **268** C4
Drybridge *NAyr* **224** B2
Drybrook **131** F1
Dryburgh **227** G2
Drygrange **227** G2
Dryhope **227** D3
Drymen **233** F1
Drymuir **269** H6
Drynoch **255** K1
Dryslwyn **142** B5
Dryton **157** E2
Duachy **240** A2
Dubford **269** F4
Dubhchladach **231** G3
Dubheads **243** E2
Dublin **152** C1
Duchal **233** E3
Duchray **241** G4
Duck Bay **233** G1
Duck End *Bed* **149** F3
Duck End *Cambs* **150** A1
Duck End *Essex* **151** F5
Duck Street **194** A1
Duckington **170** B2
Ducklington **133** F2
Duckmanton **186** B5
Duck's Cross **149** G2
Ducks Island **136** B3
Duddenhoe End **150** C4
Duddingston **235** G2
Duddington **161** E2
Duddleswell **109** G1
Duddlewick **157** F4
Duddo **237** G5
Duddon **170** C1
Duddon Bridge **198** C4
Dudleston **170** A4
Dudleston Heath
(Criftins) **170** A4
Dudley *T&W* **221** E4
Dudley *WMid* **158** B3
Dudley Port **158** B3
Dudley Zoo & Castle
*WMid* DY1 4QB **14** B3
Dudlow's Green **184** A4
Dudsbury **105** G3
Duffield **173** E3
Duffryn **129** E3
Dufftown **260** B1
Duffus **260** F3
Dufton **210** C5
Duggleby **196** B1
Duiar **259** J1
Duible **274** E6
Duiletter **241** D2
Duinish **250** B3
Duirinish **256** D1
Duisdealmor **256** D3
Duisky **248** C2
Duke End **159** E4

Dukestown **130** A1
Dukinfield **184** D3
Dulas **180** C4
Dulax **260** B3
Dulcote **116** C3
Dulford **103** D2
Dull **250** D5
Dullatur **234** B2
Dullingham **151** E2
Dullingham Ley **151** E2
Dulnain Bridge **259** G2
Duloe *Bed* **149** G2
Duloe *Corn* **97** G4
Dulsie **267** G7
Dulverton **114** C5
Dulwich **136** C5
Dulwich Picture Gallery
*GtLon* SE21 7AD **13** C7
Dumbarton **233** E2
Dumbleton **146** C4
Dumcrieff **226** C5
Dumeath **260** C1
Dumfin **233** E1
Dumfries **217** D3
Dumgoyne **233** G1
Dummer **119** G3
Dun **253** E4
Dunach **240** A1
Dunalastair **250** C4
Dunan *A&B* **232** C2
Dunan *High* **256** B2
Dunans **240** C5
Dunball **116** A3
Dunbar **237** D2
Dunbeath **275** G5
Dunbeg
(An Dùn Beag) **240** A1
Dunblane **242** C4
Dunbog **244** A3
Dunbridge **119** E5
Duncanston *Aber* **260** D2
Duncanston *High* **266** C6
Dunchideock **102** B4
Dunchurch **159** G5
Duncote **148** B2
Duncow **217** D2
Duncraggan **242** A4
Duncrievie **243** G4
Duncroist **242** A1
Duncrub **243** F3
Duncryne **233** F1
Duncton **108** B2
Dundee **244** C1
Dundee Contemporary Arts
*DD1 4DY* **71** Dundee
Dundon **116** B4
Dundon Hayes **116** B4
Dundonald **224** B2
Dundonnell (Ach-Dà-
Dhòmhnaill) **265** G3
Dundraw **209** F2
Dundreggan
(Dul Dreagain) **257** K3
Dundrennan **208** A2
Dundridge **107** E1
Dundry **116** C1
Dunearn **235** G1
Dunecht **261** F4
Dunfermline **235** E1
Dunfield **132** D3
Dunford Bridge **185** F2
Dungate **124** B3
Dungavel **225** E2
Dungworth **185** G3
Dunham **187** F5
Dunham Massey Hall,
Park & Gardens *GtMan*
WA14 4SJ **24** C6
Dunham Town **184** B4
Dunham
Woodhouses **184** B4
Dunham-on-the-
Hill **183** F5
Dunhampton **146** A1
Dunholme **188** A5
Dunino **244** D3
Dunipace **234** C1
Dunira **242** C2
Dunkeld **251** F5
Dunkerton **117** E2
Dunkeswell **103** E2
Dunkeswick **194** C3
Dunkirk *ChesW&C* **183** E5
Dunkirk *Kent* **124** C3
Dunk's Green **123** F3
Dunlappie **253** D3
Dunley *Hants* **119** F2
Dunley *Worcs* **145** G1
Dunlop **233** F5
Dunloskin **232** C2
Dunmere **97** E3
Dunmore *A&B* **231** F3
Dunmore *Falk* **234** C1
Dunn **275** G3
Dunn Street **123** G2
Dunnabie **218** A3
Dunnet **275** H1
Dunnichen **252** D5
Dunning **243** F3
Dunnington *ERid* **197** D2
Dunnington *Warks* **146** C2
Dunnington *York* **195** F2
Dunnockshaw **193** E5
Dunoon **232** C2
Dunragit **214** C5
Dunrostan **231** F1
Duns **237** E4
Duns Tew **147** G5
Dunsa **185** G5
Dunsby **175** G5
Dunscore **216** C2
Dunscroft **187** D2
Dunsdale **203** F1
Dunsden Green **134** C5
Dunsfold **121** F4
Dunsford **102** B4
Dunshalt **244** A3
Dunshill **146** A4
Dunsinnan **243** G1
Dunsland Cross **113** E5
Dunsley *NYorks* **204** B1
Dunsley *Staffs* **158** A4
Dunsmore **135** D2
Dunsop Bridge **192** C3
Dunstable **149** F5
Dunstable Downs *CenBeds*
LU6 2GY **149** F5

Dunstall **172** C5
Dunstall Green **151** F1
Dunstan **229** G5
Dunstan Steads **229** G4
Dunster **114** C3
Dunster Castle & Gardens
*Som* TA24 6SL **114** C3
Dunston *Lincs* **175** F1
Dunston *Norf* **178** D5
Dunston *Staffs* **158** B1
Dunston Heath **158** B1
Dunston Hill **212** B1
Dunstone *Devon* **102** A5
Dunstone *Devon* **100** B2
Dunsville **196** C4
Dunswell **196** C4
Dunsyre **235** E5
Dunterton **99** D3
Duntisbourne
Abbots **132** B2
Duntisbourne Leer **132** B2
Duntisbourne
Rouse **132** B2
Duntish **104** C2
Duntocher **233** F2
Dunton *Bucks* **148** D5
Dunton *CenBeds* **150** A3
Dunton *Norf* **177** G3
Dunton Bassett **160** A3
Dunton Green **123** E3
Dunton Waylets **137** F3
Duntulm **263** K4
Dunure **224** A4
Dunure Mains **224** A4
Dunvant **128** B3
Dunvegan **263** H7
Dunvegan Castle *High*
IV55 8WF **263** H7
Dunwich **165** F4
Dura **244** C3
Durdar **210** A2
Durgan **95** E4
Durgates **123** F5
Durham **212** B3
Durham Cathedral
DH1 3EH **71** Durham
Durham Dales Centre *Dur*
DL13 2FJ **211** G4
Durham Tees Valley
Airport **202** C1
Durinemast **247** F4
Durisdeer **225** G5
Durleigh **115** F4
Durley *Hants* **107** E1
Durley *Wilts* **118** D1
Durley Street **107** E1
Durlow Common **145** F4
Durlston Country
Park *Dorset*
BH19 2JL **105** G5
Durnamuck **265** G2
Durness **273** G2
Durno **261** F2
Duror **248** B4
Durran *A&B* **240** B4
Durran *High* **275** G2
Durrants **107** G2
Durrington *Wilts* **118** C3
Durrington *WSuss* **108** D3
Dursley **131** G3
Dursley Cross **131** F1
Durston **115** F5
Durweston **105** E2
Dury **279** D6
Duston **148** C1
Duthie Park & David Welch
Winter Gardens *Aberdeen*
AB11 7TH **261** H4
Duthil **259** G2
Dutlas **156** B5
Duton Hill **151** E5
Dutson **98** D2
Dutton **183** G5
Duxford **150** C3
Dwygyfylchi **181** F5
Dwyran **166** D2
Dyce **261** G3
Dyfatty **128** A2
Dyffryn *Bridgend* **129** E3
Dyffryn *Pembs* **140** C4
Dyffryn *VGlam* **129** G5
Dyffryn Ardudwy **167** E5
Dyffryn Castell **155** D4
Dyffryn Ceidrych **142** D5
Dyffryn Cellwen **129** E1
Dyke *Devon* **112** D3
Dyke *Lincs* **175** G5
Dyke *Moray* **267** G6
Dykehead *Angus* **252** B3
Dykehead *NLan* **234** C4
Dykehead *Stir* **242** A5
Dykelands **253** F3
Dykends **252** A4
Dykeside **269** F6
Dylan Thomas Centre
*SA1 1RR* **86** Swansea
Dylife **155** E3
Dymchurch **111** G1
Dymock **145** G4
Dyrham **131** G5
Dyrham Park *SGlos*
SN14 8ER **8** F2
Dysart **244** B5
Dyserth **182** B5

Eardisley **144** C3
Eardiston *Shrop* **170** A5
Eardiston *Worcs* **145** F1
Earith **162** B5
Earl Shilton **159** G3
Earl Soham **152** D1
Earl Sterndale **172** B1
Earl Stonham **152** C2
Earle **229** D4
Earlestown **183** G3
Earley **134** C5
Earlham **178** D5
Earlish **263** J5
Earls Barton **149** D1
Earls Colne **151** G5
Earl's Common **146** B2
Earl's Court **136** B5
Earls Court Exhibition
Centre *GtLon*
SW5 9TA **11** E5
Earl's Croome **146** A3
Earl's Green **152** B1
Earlsdon **159** F5
Earlsferry **244** C4
Earlsford **261** G1
Earlsheaton **194** B5
Earlston **227** G2
Earlswood *Mon* **131** D3
Earlswood *Surr* **122** B4
Earlswood *Warks* **158** D5
Earnley **108** A4
Earnshaw Bridge **192** B5
Earsairidh **254** C5
Earsdon **221** F4
Earsdon Moor **221** D2
Earsham **165** E3
Earsham Street **164** D4
Earswick **195** F2
Eartham **108** B3
Earthcott Green **131** F4
Easby **203** E2
Easdale **239** G3
Easebourne **121** D5
Easenhall **159** G5
Eashing **121** E3
Easington *Bucks* **134** B1
Easington *Dur* **212** D3
Easington *ERid* **189** D1
Easington *N'umb* **229** F3
Easington *Oxon* **134** B3
Easington *Oxon* **147** G4
Easington *R&C* **203** G1
Easington Colliery **212** D3
Easington Lane **212** C3
Easingwold **195** E1
Easole Street **125** E3
Eassie **252** B5
East Aberthaw **114** D1
East Acton **136** B4
East Allington **101** D3
East Anstey **114** C5
East Anton **119** E3
East Appleton **202** B3
East Ardsley **194** B5
East Ashey **107** E4
East Ashling **108** A3
East Auchronie **261** G4
East Ayton **204** C4
East Barkwith **188** B4
East Barming **123** G3
East Barnby **204** B1
East Barnet **136** B3
East Barsham **178** A2
East Beckham **178** C2
East Bedfont **135** F5
East Bergholt **152** B4
East Bierley **194** A5
East Bilney **178** A4
East Blatchington **109** G4
East Boldon **212** C1
East Boldre **106** C2
East Bolton **229** F5
East Bower **116** A4
East Brent **116** A2
East Bridge **153** F1
East Bridgford **174** B3
East Brora **267** G1
East Buckland **113** G2
East Budleigh **103** D4
East Burnham **135** E4
East Burra **279** C9
East Burrafirth **279** C7
East Burton **105** E4
East Butsfield **212** A3
East Butterleigh **102** C2
East Butterwick **187** F2
East Cairnbeg **253** F2
East Calder **235** E3
East Carleton **178** C5
East Carlton
*N'hants* **160** D4
East Carlton
*WYorks* **194** B3
East Carlton Countryside
Park *N'hants*
LE16 8YF **160** D4
East Chaldon (Chaldon
Herring) **105** D4
East Challow **133** F4
East Charleton **101** D3
East Chelborough **104** B2
East Chiltington **109** F2
East Chinnock **104** A1
East Chisenbury **118** C2
East Clandon **121** F2
East Claydon **148** C5
East Clyne **267** G1
East Clyth **275** H5
East Compton
*Dorset* **105** E1
East Compton
*Som* **116** D3
East Coombe **102** B2
East Cornworthy **101** E2
East Cottingwith **195** G3
East Cowes **107** E3
East Cowton **202** C2
East Cramlington **221** E4
East Cranmore **117** D3
East Creech **105** F4
East Croachy **258** C2
East Darlochan **222** B3
East Davoch **260** C4
East Dean *ESuss* **110** A4
East Dean *Hants* **119** D5
East Dean *WSuss* **108** A3

East Dereham
(Dereham) **178** A4
East Down **113** F1
East Drayton **187** E5
East Dundry **116** C1
East Ella **196** C5
East End *ERid* **197** D4
East End *ERid* **197** E5
East End *Essex* **138** D2
East End *Hants* **119** F1
East End *Hants* **119** E1
East End *Hants* **106** C3
East End *Herts* **150** C5
East End *Kent* **124** A5
East End *Kent* **124** B1
East End *MK* **149** E5
East End *NSom* **131** D5
East End *Oxon* **133** F1
East End *Poole* **105** F3
East End *Som* **116** C2
East End *Suff* **152** C4
East End *Suff* **152** C2
East Farleigh **123** G3
East Farndon **160** C4
East Ferry **187** F3
East Firsby **188** A4
East Fleetham **229** G4
East Fortune **236** C2
East Ginge **133** G4
East Garston **133** F5
East Goscote **160** B1
East Grafton **119** E1
East Green *Suff* **153** F1
East Green *Suff* **151** E2
East Grimstead **118** B5
East Grinstead **122** C5
East Guldeford **111** E1
East Haddon **148** B1
East Hagbourne **134** A4
East Halton **188** B3
East Ham **136** D4
East Hanney **133** G3
East Hanningfield **137** G2
East Hardwick **186** A5
East Harling **164** A3
East Harlsey **202** D3
East Harnham **118** C5
East Harptree **116** C2
East Hartford **221** E4
East Harting **107** G1
East Hatch **118** A5
East Hatley **150** A2
East Hauxwell **202** A3
East Haven **245** D1
East Heckington **175** G3
East Hedleyhope **212** A3
East Helmsdale **275** F7
East Hendred **133** G4
East Herrington **212** C2
East Hesleton **204** C3
East Hewish **116** B1
East Hoathly **110** A2
East Holme **105** E4
East Horndon **137** F4
East Horrington **116** C3
East Horsley **121** F2
East Horton **229** E3
East Howe **105** G3
East Huntspill **116** A3
East Hyde **136** A1
East Ilsley **133** G4
East Keal **176** B1
East Kennett **118** C1
East Keswick **194** C3
East Kilbride **234** A4
East Kimber **99** E1
East Kirkby **176** B1
East Knapton **204** B5
East Knighton **105** E4
East Knowstone **114** B5
East Knoyle **117** F4
East Kyloe **229** E3
East Lambrook **104** A1
East Lancashire Railway
*Lancs* BL9 0EY **193** E5
East Langdon **125** F4
East Langton **160** C3
East Langwell **266** E1
East Lavant **108** A3
East Lavington **108** B2
East Layton **202** A1
East Leake **173** G5
East Learmouth **228** C3
East Learney **260** E4
East Leigh *Devon* **102** A2
East Leigh *Devon* **102** A1
East Leigh *Devon* **101** D2
East Leigh *Devon* **100** C2
East Lexham **163** G1
East Lilburn **229** E4
East Linton **236** C2
East Liss **120** C5
East Lockinge **133** G4
East Looe **97** G4
East Lound **187** E2
East Lulworth **105** E4
East Lutton **196** B1
East Lydford **116** C4
East Lyn **114** A3
East Lyng **116** A5
East Mains **260** E5
East Malling **123** G3
East Malling Heath **123** F3
East March **244** C1
East Marden **108** A2
East Markham **187** E5
East Martin **105** G1
East Marton **193** F2
East Meon **120** B5
East Mere **102** C1
East Mersea **139** D1
East Mey **275** J1
East Midlands
Airport **173** F5
East Molesey **121** G1
East Moor **194** C5
East Morden **105** F3
East Morriston **236** D5
East Ness **203** E5
East Newton **197** E4
East Norton **160** C2
East Oakley **119** G2
East Ogwell **102** B5
East Orchard **105** E1
East Ord **237** G4
East Panson **99** D1
East Parley **106** A3
East Peckham **123** F4

East Pennard **116** C4
East Point Pavilion,
Lowestoft *Suff*
NR33 0AP **165** G2
East Portlemouth **100** D4
East Prawle **101** D4
East Preston **108** C3
East Pulham **104** D2
East Putford **113** D4
East Quantoxhead **115** E3
East Rainton **212** C2
East Ravendale **188** C3
East Raynham **177** G5
East Retford
(Retford) **187** E4
East Rigton **194** C3
East Rolstone **116** A1
East Rounton **202** D2
East Row **204** B1
East Rudham **177** G5
East Runton **179** D1
East Ruston **179** E3
East Saltoun **236** B3
East Shefford **133** F5
East Sleekburn **221** E3
East Somerton **179** F4
East Stockwith **187** E3
East Stoke *Dorset* **105** E4
East Stoke *Notts* **174** C3
East Stour **117** F3
East Stourmouth **125** E2
East Stratton **119** G3
East Street **116** C4
East Studdal **125** F4
East Suisnish **256** B1
East Taphouse **97** F3
East Thirston **221** D2
East Tilbury **137** F5
East Tisted **120** C4
East Torrington **188** B4
East Town **116** D3
East Tuddenham **178** B4
East Tytherley **119** D5
East Tytherton **132** B5
East Village **102** B2
East Wall **157** E3
East Walton **163** F1
East Wellow **119** E5
East Wemyss **244** B5
East Whitburn **235** D3
East Wickham **137** D5
East Williamston **127** D2
East Winch **163** E1
East Winterslow **118** D4
East Wittering **107** G3
East Witton **202** A4
East Woodburn **220** B3
East Woodhay **119** F1
East Woodlands **117** E3
East Worldham **120** C4
East Worlington **102** A1
East Youlstone **112** C4
Eastacott **113** G3
Eastburn **110** B4
Eastbourne Pier
*ESuss* BN21 3EL
**72** Eastbourne
Eastbrook **130** A5
Eastburn *ERid* **196** B2
Eastburn *WYorks* **193** G3
Eastbury *Herts* **136** B3
Eastbury *WBerks* **133** F5
Eastby **193** G2
Eastchurch **124** B1
Eastcombe *Glos* **132** A2
Eastcombe *Som* **115** E4
Eastcote *GtLon* **136** B4
Eastcote *N'hants* **148** B2
Eastcote *WMid* **159** D5
Eastcott *Corn* **112** C4
Eastcott *Wilts* **118** B2
Eastcourt **132** B3
Eastdown **101** E3
Eastend **147** F5
Easter Ardross **266** D4
Easter Balgedie **243** G4
Easter Balmoral **259** K5
Easter Boleskine **258** C2
Easter Borland **242** B4
Easter Brae **266** D5
Easter Buckieburn **234** B1
Easter Compton **131** E4
Easter Dullater **242** B4
Easter Ellister **230** A4
Easter Fearn **266** D3
Easter Galcantray **267** F7
Easter Howlaws **237** E5
Easter Kinkell **266** C6
Easter Knox **253** D5
Easter Lednathie **252** B3
Easter Moniack **266** C7
Easter Ord **261** G4
Easter Poldar **242** B5
Easter Skeld (Skeld) **279** C8
Easter Suddie **266** D6
Easter Tulloch **253** F2
Easter Whyntie **268** E4
Eastergate **108** B3
Easterhouse **234** A3
Easterton **118** B2
Easterton Sands **118** B2
Eastertown **116** A2
Eastfield *Bristol* **131** E5
Eastfield *NLan* **234** C3
Eastfield *NYorks* **204** D4
Eastfield Hall **221** E1
Eastgate *Dur* **211** F4
Eastgate *Lincs* **161** G1
Eastgate *Norf* **178** C3
Easthall **150** A5
Eastham *Mersey* **183** E4
Eastham *Worcs* **145** F1
Easthampstead **121** D1
Easthampton **144** D1
Easthaugh **178** B4
Easthatch **120** D1
Easthope **157** E3
Easthorpe *Essex* **152** A5
Easthorpe *Leics* **174** D4
Easthorpe *Notts* **174** C2
Easthouses **236** A3
Eastington *Devon* **102** A2
Eastington *Glos* **132** D1
Eastington *Glos* **131** G2
Eastleach Martin **133** E2
Eastleach Turville **133** E2
Eastleigh *Devon* **113** E3

Eastleigh *Hants* **106** D1
Eastling **124** B3
Eastmoor *Derbys* **186** A5
Eastmoor *Norf* **163** F2
Eastnor **145** G4
Eastoft **187** F1
Eastoke **107** G3
Easton *Cambs* **161** G5
Easton *Cumb* **218** C4
Easton *Cumb* **209** F1
Easton *Devon* **102** A4
Easton *Dorset* **104** C5
Easton *Hants* **119** G4
Easton *IoW* **106** C4
Easton *Lincs* **175** E5
Easton *Norf* **178** C4
Easton *Som* **116** C3
Easton *Suff* **153** D2
Easton *Wilts* **132** A5
Easton Grey **132** A4
Easton Maudit **149** D2
Easton on the Hill **161** F2
Easton Royal **118** D1
Easton-in-Gordano **131** E5
Eastrea **162** A3
Eastriggs **218** A5
Eastrington **195** G4
Eastry **125** F3
Eastside **277** D8
East-the-Water **113** E3
Eastville **131** F5
Eastwell **174** C5
Eastwick **136** D1
Eastwood *Notts* **173** F3
Eastwood *S'end* **138** B4
Eastwood *SYorks* **186** B3
Eastwood
*WYorks* **193** F5
Eastwood End **162** C3
Eathorpe **147** F1
Eaton *ChesE* **171** F1
Eaton *ChesW&C* **170** C1
Eaton *Leics* **174** C5
Eaton *Norf* **178** D5
Eaton *Norf* **177** E4
Eaton *Notts* **187** E5
Eaton *Oxon* **133** G2
Eaton *Shrop* **157** E3
Eaton *Shrop* **156** C4
Eaton Bishop **144** D4
Eaton Bray **149** E5
Eaton Constantine **157** F2
Eaton Ford **149** G2
Eaton Hall **170** B1
Eaton Hastings **133** E3
Eaton Socon **149** G2
Eaton upon Tern **171** D5
Eaves Green **159** E4
Eavestone **194** B1
Ebberston **204** B4
Ebbesborne Wake **118** A5
Ebbw Vale
(Glynebwy) **130** A2
Ebchester **212** A2
Ebdon **116** A1
Ebford **102** C4
Ebley **132** A2
Ebnal **170** B3
Ebost **255** J1
Ebrington **147** D3
Ecchinswell **119** F2
Ecclaw **237** E3
Ecclefechan **217** F3
Eccles *GtMan* **184** B3
Eccles *Kent* **123** G2
Eccles *ScBord* **237** E5
Eccles Green **144** C3
Eccles Road **164** B2
Ecclesfield **186** A3
Ecclesgreig **253** F3
Eccleshall **171** F5
Eccleshill **194** A4
Ecclesmachan **235** E2
Eccles-on-Sea **179** F3
Eccleston
*ChesW&C* **170** B1
Eccleston *Lancs* **183** G1
Eccleston *Mersey* **183** F3
Eccup **194** B3
Echt **261** F4
Eckford **228** B4
Eckington *Derbys* **186** B5
Eckington *Worcs* **146** B3
Ecton *N'hants* **148** D1
Ecton *Staffs* **172** B2
Edale **185** F4
Eday **276** E4
Eday Airfield **276** E4
Edburton **109** E2
Edderside **209** E2
Edderton **266** E3
Eddington **119** E1
Eddistone **112** C3
Eddleston **235** G5
Edenbridge **122** D4
Edendonich **241** D2
Edenfield **184** B1
Edenhall **210** B4
Edenham **175** F5
Edensor **185** G5
Edentaggart **241** F5
Edenthorpe **186** D2
Edern **166** B4
Edgarley **116** C4
Edgbaston **158** C4
Edgcott *Bucks* **148** B5
Edgcott *Som* **114** B4
Edgcumbe **96** C5
Edge *Glos* **132** A2
Edge *Shrop* **156** C2
Edge End **131** E1
Edge Green
*ChesW&C* **170** B2
Edge Green *GtMan* **183** G3
Edge Green *Norf* **164** B3
Edgebolton **170** C5
Edgefield **178** B2
Edgefield Street **178** B2
Edgehead **236** A3
Edgeley **170** C3
Edgerley **156** C1
Edgerton **185** F1

Edgeworth **132** B2
Edginswell **101** E1
Edgmond **157** G1
Edgmond Marsh **171** E5
Edgton **156** C4
Edgware **136** B3
Edgworth **184** B1
Edinample **242** B2
Edinbanchory **260** C3
Edinbane **263** J6
Edinbarnet **233** G2
Edinburgh **235** G2
Edinburgh Airport **235** F2
Edinburgh Castle *Edin*
EH1 2NG **37** E4
Edinburgh Zoo *Edin*
EH12 6TS **32** B2
Edinchip **242** A2
Edingale **159** E1
Edingley **174** B2
Edingthorpe **179** E2
Edingthorpe Green **179** E2
Edington *Som* **116** A4
Edington *Wilts* **118** A2
Edintore **268** C6
Edinvale **267** J6
Edistone **112** C3
Edith Weston **161** E2
Edithmead **116** A3
Edlaston **172** C3
Edlesborough **135** E1
Edlingham **220** D1
Edlington **188** A5
Edmondsham **105** G1
Edmondsley **212** B2
Edmondstown **129** G3
Edmondthorpe **161** D1
Edmonstone **276** E5
Edmonton *Corn* **97** D2
Edmonton *GtLon* **136** C3
Edmundbyers **211** G2
Ednam **228** B3
Ednaston **172** D3
Edney Common **137** G2
Edra **241** G2
Edradynate **251** D4
Edrom **237** F4
Edstaston **170** C4
Edstone **147** D1
Edvin Loach **145** F2
Edwalton **173** G4
Edwardstone **152** A3
Edwardsville **129** G3
Edwinsford **142** C4
Edwinstowe **174** B1
Edworth **150** A3
Edwyn Ralph **145** F2
Edzell **253** E3
Efail Isaf **129** G4
Efail-fâch **129** D3
Efailnewydd **166** C4
Efailwen **141** E5
Efenechtyd **169** E2
Effingham **121** G2
Effirth **279** C7
Efflinch **159** D1
Efford **102** B2
Egbury **119** F2
Egdean **121** E5
Egdon **146** B2
Egerton *GtMan* **184** B1
Egerton *Kent* **124** B4
Egerton Forstal **124** A4
Egerton Green **170** C2
Egg Buckland **100** A2
Eggborough **195** E5
Eggerness **207** E2
Eggesford Barton **113** G4
Eggington **173** D5
Egginton **173** D5
Egglescliffe **202** D1
Eggleston **211** F5
Egham **135** F5
Egham Wick **135** E5
Egleton **161** D2
Eglingham **229** E5
Eglinton **233** E5
Egloshayle **97** E2
Egloskerry **97** G1
Eglwys Cross **170** B3
Eglwys Fach **154** C3
Eglwys Nunydd **129** E4
Eglwysbach **181** G5
Eglwys-Brewis **114** D5
Eglwyswrw **141** E4
Egmanton **174** C1
Egmere **178** A2
Egremont **208** D5
Egton **204** B2
Egton Bridge **204** B2
Egypt **119** F4
Eigg **247** D1
Eight Ash Green **152** A5
Eignaig **247** G5
Eil **259** F3
Eilanreach **256** E3
Eildon **227** G3
Eilean Darach **265** H3
Eilean Donan Castle *High*
IV40 8DX **256** E2
Eilean Shona **247** F2
Einacleit **270** D5
Eisgean **271** F6
Eisingrug **167** F4
Eisteddfa Gurig **155** D4
Elan Valley Visitor Centre
*Powys* LD6 5HP **143** F2
Elan Village **143** F1
Elberton **131** F4
Elborough **116** A2
Elburton **100** B2
Elcho **243** G2
Elcombe **132** D4
Elder Street **151** D4
Eldernell **162** B3
Eldersfield **146** A4
Elderslie **233** F3
Eldon **212** B5
Eldrick **215** D2
Eldroth **193** D1
Eldwick **194** A3
Elemore Vale **212** C2
Elford *N'umb* **229** F3
Elford *Staffs* **159** D1
Elford Closes **162** D5
Elgin **267** K5
Elgol **256** B3

Elham **125** D4
Elie **244** C4
Elilaw **220** B1
Elim **180** B4
Eling *Hants* **106** C1
Eling *WBerks* **134** A5
Eling Tide Mill *Hants*
SO40 9HF **4** A3
Eliock **225** G3
Elishader **263** K5
Elishaw **220** B1
Elkesley **187** D5
Elkington **160** B5
Elkstone **132** B1
Elland **194** A5
Elland Upper Edge **194** A5
Ellary **231** F2
Ellastone **172** C3
Ellbridge **100** A1
Ellel **192** A2
Ellemford **237** E3
Ellenabeich **239** G3
Ellenborough **208** D3
Ellenhall **171** F5
Ellen's Green **121** F4
Ellerbeck **202** D3
Ellerby **203** G1
Ellerdine **170** D5
Ellerdine Heath **170** D5
Elleric (Eileirig) **248** C5
Ellerker **196** B5
Ellerton *ERid* **195** G3
Ellerton *NYorks* **202** B3
Ellerton *Shrop* **171** E5
Ellerton Abbey **201** F3
Ellesborough **134** D2
Ellesmere **170** A4
Ellesmere Park **184** B3
Ellesmere Port **183** F5
Ellingham *Hants* **106** A2
Ellingham *N'umb* **229** F4
Ellingham *Norf* **165** E2
Ellingstring **202** A4
Ellington *Cambs* **161** G5
Ellington *N'umb* **221** E2
Ellington Thorpe **161** G5
Elliot **245** E1
Elliot's Green **117** E3
Ellisfield **120** B3
Ellistown **159** G1
Ellon **261** H1
Ellonby **210** A4
Ellough **165** F3
Ellough Moor **165** F3
Elloughton **196** B5
Ellwood **131** E2
Elm **162** C2
Elm Park **137** E4
Elmbridge **146** B1
Elmdon *Essex* **150** C4
Elmdon *WMid* **159** D4
Elmdon Heath **159** D4
Elmers End **122** C2
Elmer's Green **183** F2
Elmesthorpe **159** G3
Elmhurst **158** D1
Elmley Castle **146** B3
Elmley Lovett **146** A1
Elmore **131** G1
Elmore Back **131** G1
Elmscott **112** C3
Elmsett **152** B3
Elmstead *Essex* **152** B5
Elmstead *GtLon* **136** D5
Elmstead Market **152** B5
Elmstone **125** E2
Elmstone
Hardwicke **146** B5
Elmswell *ERid* **196** B2
Elmswell *Suff* **152** A1
Elmton **186** C5
Elphin **272** E7
Elphinstone **236** A2
Elrick *Aber* **261** G4
Elrick *Moray* **260** C2
Elrig **206** D2
Elrigbeag **240** D3
Elsdon **220** B2
Elsecar **186** A2
Elsenham **150** D5
Elsfield **134** A1
Elsham **188** A1
Elsing **178** B4
Elslack **193** F3
Elson *Hants* **107** F2
Elson *Shrop* **170** A4
Elsrickle **235** E5
Elstead **121** E3
Elsted **108** A2
Elsthorpe **175** F5
Elstob **212** C5
Elston *Lancs* **192** B4
Elston *Notts* **174** C3
Elstone **113** G4
Elstow **149** F3
Elstree **136** B3
Elstronwick **197** E4
Elswick **192** A4
Elsworth **150** B1
Elterwater **199** E2
Eltham **136** D4
Eltisley **150** A2
Elton *Cambs* **161** F3
Elton *ChesW&C* **183** F5
Elton *Derbys* **172** D1
Elton *Glos* **131** G1
Elton *GtMan* **184** B1
Elton *Here* **157** D5
Elton *Notts* **174** C4
Elton *Stock* **202** D1
Elton Green **183** F5
Elvanfoot **226** A4
Elvaston **173** F4
Elvaston Castle Country Park
*Derbys* DE72 3EP **18** C4
Elveden **163** G5
Elvingston **236** B2
Elvington *Kent* **125** E3
Elvington *York* **195** G3
Elwick *Hart* **213** D4
Elwick *N'umb* **229** F3
Elworth **171** E1
Elworthy **115** D4
Ely *Cambs* **162** D5
Ely *Cardiff* **130** A5

Emberton Country Park
*MK* MK46 5FJ **149** D2
Embleton *Cumb* **209** E3
Embleton *Hart* **212** D5
Embleton *N'umb* **229** G4
Embo **267** F2
Embo Street **267** F2
Emborough **116** D2
Embsay **193** G2
Embsay Steam Railway
*NYorks*
BD23 6AF **193** G2
Emerson Park **137** E4
Emery Down **106** B2
Emley **185** G1
Emmington **134** C2
Emneth **162** D2
Emneth Hungate **162** D2
Empingham **161** E2
Empshott **120** C5
Empshott Green **120** C4
Emsworth **107** G2
Enborne **119** F1
Enborne Row **119** F1
Enchmarsh **157** E3
Enderby **160** A3
Endmoor **199** G4
Endon **171** G2
Endon Bank **171** G2
Enfield **136** C3
Enfield Wash **136** C3
Enford **118** C2
Engine Common **131** F4
Englefield **134** B5
Englefield Green **135** E5
Englesea-brook **171** E2
Englishbicknor **131** E1
English Frankton **170** B5
Englishcombe **117** E1
Enham Alamein **119** E3
Enmore **115** F4
Ennerdale
Bridge **209** D5
Enniscaven **97** D4
Enochdhu **251** F2
Ensay **246** C5
Ensdon **156** D1
Ensis **113** F3
Enson **171** G5
Enstone **147** F5
Enterkinfoot **225** G5
Enterpen **203** D2
Enton Green **121** E3
Enville **158** A4
Eolaigearraidh **254** C4
Eorabus **238** C2
Eorodal **271** H1
Eoropaidh **271** H1
Epney **131** G2
Epperstone **174** B3
Epping **137** D2
Epping Green
*Essex* **136** D2
Epping Green
*Herts* **136** B2
Epping Upland **136** D2
Eppleby **202** A1
Eppleworth **196** C4
Epsom **122** B2
Epwell **147** F3
Epworth **187** E2
Epworth Turbary **187** E2
Erbistock **170** A3
Erbusaig **256** D2
Erchless Castle **266** B7
Erdington **158** D3
Eredine **240** B4
Eriboll **273** G3
Ericstane **226** B4
Eridge Green **123** E5
Eriff **224** D5
Erines **231** G2
Erisey Barton **95** E5
Eriska
(Eiriosgaigh) **254** C3
Eriswell **163** F5
Erith **137** E5
Erlestoke **118** A2
Ermington **100** C2
Ernesettle **100** A1
Erpingham **178** C2
Errogie (Earagaidh) **258** C2
Errol **244** A2
Errollston **261** J1
Erskine **233** F2
Ervie **214** A4
Erwarton **152** D4
Erwood **143** G3
Eryholme **202** C2
Eryrys **169** F2
Escart **231** G3
Escart Farm **231** G4
Escomb **212** A5
Escott **115** D4
Escrick **195** F3
Esgair **141** G5
Esgairgeiliog **155** D2
Esgyryn **181** G5
Esh **212** A3
Esh Winning **212** A3
Esher **121** G1
Eshott **221** E2
Eshton **193** F2
Eskadale **258** B1
Eskbank **236** A3
Eskdale Green **198** C2
Eskdalemuir **218** A2
Eskham **189** D3
Esknish **230** B3
Esperley Lane Ends **212** A5
Espley Hall **221** D2
Esprick **192** A4
Essendine **161** F1
Essendon **136** B2
Essich **258** D1
Essington **158** B2
Esslemont **261** H2
Eston **203** E1
Eswick **279** D7
Etal **228** D3
Etchilhampton **118** B1
Etchingham **110** C1
Etchinghill *Kent* **125** D5
Etchinghill *Staffs* **158** C1
Etherdwick Grange **197** E4
Etherley Dene **212** A5
Etherow Country Park
*GtMan* SK6 5JQ **25** H5
Emberton **149** D3

Ethie Mains **253** E5
Eton **135** E5
Eton Wick **135** E5
Etteridge **258** D5
Ettiley Heath **171** E1
Ettington **147** E3
Etton *ERid* **196** B3
Etton *Peter* **161** G2
Ettrick **227** D4
Ettrickbridge **227** E3
Ettrickhill **227** D4
Etwall **173** D4
Eudon George **157** F4
Eurach **240** A4
Eureka! Museum for
Children *WYorks*
HX1 2NE **26** B4
Euston **163** G5
Euxton **183** G1
Evanstown **129** F4
Evanton **266** D5
Evedon **175** F3
Evelix **266** E2
Evenjobb **144** B1
Evenley **148** A4
Evenlode **147** E5
Evenwood **212** A5
Evenwood Gate **212** A5
Everbay **276** F5
Evercreech **116** D4
Everdon **148** A2
Everingham **196** A3
Everleigh **118** D2
Everley *High* **275** J2
Everley *NYorks* **204** C4
Eversholt **149** E4
Evershot **104** C2
Eversley **120** C1
Eversley Cross **120** C1
Everthorpe **196** B4
Everton *CenBeds* **150** A2
Everton *Hants* **106** B3
Everton *Mersey* **183** E3
Everton *Notts* **187** D3
Evertown **218** B4
Eves Corner **138** C3
Evesbatch **145** F3
Evesham **146** C3
Evesham Country Park
Shopping & Garden
Centre *Worcs*
WR11 4TP **146** C3
Evie **276** C5
Evington **160** B2
Ewart Newtown **229** D3
Ewden Village **185** G3
Ewell **122** B2
Ewell Minnis **125** E4
Ewelme **134** B3
Ewen **132** C3
Ewenny **129** F5
Ewerby **175** G3
Ewerby Thorpe **175** G3
Ewhurst **121** F3
Ewhurst Green
*ESuss* **110** C1
Ewhurst Green *Surr* **121** F4
Ewloe **170** A1
Ewloe Green **169** F1
Ewood **192** C5
Ewood Bridge **193** D5
Eworthy **99** E1
Ewshot **120** D3
Ewyas Harold **144** C5
Exbourne **113** G5
Exbury **106** D2
Exbury Gardens *Hants*
SO45 1AZ **4** B6
Exceat **110** A4
Exebridge **114** C5
Exelby **202** B4
Exeter **102** C4
Exeter Cathedral *Devon*
EX1 1HS **72** Exeter
Exeter International
Airport **102** C4
Exford **114** B4
Exfords Green **157** D2
Exhall *Warks* **146** D2
Exhall *Warks* **159** F4
Exlade Street **134** B4
Exminster **102** C4
Exmouth **102** D4
Exnaboe **279** F9
Exning **151** E1
Explore-At-Bristol
BS1 5DB **66** Bristol
Exton *Devon* **102** C4
Exton *Hants* **120** B5
Exton *Rut* **161** E1
Exton *Som* **114** C4
Exwick **102** C3
Eyam **185** G5
Eydon **148** A3
Eye *Here* **145** D1
Eye *Peter* **162** A2
Eye *Suff* **164** C5
Eye Green **162** A2
Eyemouth **237** G3
Eyeworth **150** A3
Eyhorne Street **124** A3
Eyke **153** E2
Eynesbury **149** G2
Eynort **255** J2
Eynsford **123** E2
Eynsham **133** G2
Eype **104** A3
Eyre **263** K6
Eythorne **125** E4
Eyton *Here* **145** D1
Eyton *Shrop* **156** C4
Eyton on Severn **157** E2
Eyton upon the Weald
Moors **157** F1
Eywood **144** C2

**F**

Faccombe **119** E2
Faceby **203** D2
Fachwen **167** E2
Facit **184** C1
Faddiley **170** C2
Fadmoor **203** F4
Faebait **266** B6
Faifley **233** G2
Fail **224** C3
Failand **131** E5
Failford **224** C3

Failsworth **184** C2
Fain **265** H4
Fair Isle **278** A1
Fair Isle Airstrip **278** A1
Fair Oak *Devon* **102** D1
Fair Oak *Hants* **107** D1
Fair Oak *Hants* **119** G1
Fair Oak Green **120** B1
Fairbourne **154** C1
Fairburn **195** D5
Fairfield *Derbys* **185** E5
Fairfield *GtMan* **184** D3
Fairfield *Kent* **111** E1
Fairfield *Mersey* **183** D4
Fairfield *Stock* **202** D1
Fairfield *Worcs* **158** B5
Fairfield Halls, Croydon
  *GtLon* CR9 1DG **122** C2
Fairford **132** D2
Fairgirth **216** C5
Fairhaven **191** G5
Fairhill **234** B4
Fairholm **234** B4
Fairlands Valley Park *Herts*
  SG2 0BL **150** A5
Fairley **261** G4
Fairlie **232** D4
Fairlight **111** D2
Fairlight Cove **111** D2
Fairmile *Devon* **103** D3
Fairmile *Surr* **121** G1
Fairmilehead **235** G3
Fairnington **228** A4
Fairoak **171** E4
Fairseat **123** F2
Fairstead **137** G1
Fairwarp **109** G1
Fairwater **130** A5
Fairy Cross **113** E3
Fairyhill **128** A3
Fakenham **178** A3
Fakenham Magna **164** A4
Fala **236** B3
Fala Dam **236** B3
Falahill **236** B3
Faldingworth **188** A4
Falfield *Fife* **244** C4
Falfield *SGlos* **131** F3
Falin-Wnda **141** G3
Falkenham **153** D4
Falkirk **234** D2
Falkirk Wheel *Falk*
  FK1 4RS **234** C1
Falkland **244** A4
Falla **228** B5
Fallgate **173** E1
Fallin **242** D5
Falmer **109** F2
Falmouth **95** F3
Falsgrave **204** D4
Falstone **219** F3
Famous Grouse Experience,
  Glenturret Distillery
  *P&K* PH7 4HA **243** D2
Fanagmore **272** D4
Fanans **240** C2
Fancott **149** F5
Fangdale Beck **203** E3
Fangfoss **195** G2
Fankerton **234** B1
Fanmore **246** D5
Fanner's Green **137** F1
Fans **236** D5
Fantasy Island *Lincs*
  PE25 1RH **177** D1
Far Cotton **148** C2
Far Forest **157** G5
Far Gearstones **200** C4
Far Green **131** G2
Far Moor **183** G2
Far Oakridge **132** B2
Far Royds **194** B4
Far Sawrey **199** E3
Farcet **162** A3
Farden **157** E5
Fareham **107** E2
Farewell **158** C1
Farforth **188** D5
Faringdon **133** E3
Farington **192** B5
Farlam **210** B2
Farlary **266** E1
Farleigh *NSom* **116** C1
Farleigh *Surr* **122** C1
Farleigh Hungerford **117** F2
Farleigh Wallop **120** B3
Farlesthorpe **189** E5
Farleton *Cumb* **199** G4
Farleton *Lancs* **192** A1
Farley *Derbys* **173** D1
Farley *Shrop* **156** C1
Farley *Staffs* **172** C3
Farley *Wilts* **118** D5
Farley Green *Suff* **151** F2
Farley Green *Surr* **121** F3
Farley Hill **120** C1
Farleys End **131** G1
Farlington **195** F1
Farlow **157** F4
Farm Town **159** F1
Farmborough **117** E1
Farmcote **146** C5
Farmington **132** D1
Farmoor **133** G2
Farmtown **268** D4
Farnborough
  *GtLon* **122** D2
Farnborough
  *Hants* **121** D2
Farnborough
  *Works* **147** G3
Farnborough
  *WBerks* **133** G4
Farnborough Street **121** D2
Farncombe **121** E3
Farndish **149** E1
Farndon *ChesW&C* **170** B2
Farndon *Notts* **174** C2
Farne Islands **229** G3
Farnell **253** E4
Farnham *Dorset* **105** F1
Farnham *Essex* **150** C5
Farnham *NYorks* **194** C1
Farnham *Suff* **153** E2
Farnham *Surr* **120** D3
Farnham Common **135** E4
Farnham Green **150** C5
Farnham Royal **135** E4
Farningham **123** E2
Farnley *NYorks* **194** B3
Farnley *WYorks* **194** B4
Farnley Tyas **185** F1
Farnsfield **174** B2
Farnworth
  *Halton* **183** G4
Farnworth *GtMan* **184** B2
Farnworth
  Gurney **116** D2
Farsley **194** B4
Farthing Corner **124** A2
Farthing Green **124** A4
Farthinghoe **148** A4
Farthingstone **148** B2
Farthorpe **188** C5
Fartown **185** F1
Farway **103** E3
Fasag **264** E6
Fasagrianach **265** H3
Faslane **232** D1
Fasnacloich **248** C5
Fasnakyle **257** K2
Fassfern **248** C5
Fatfield **212** C2
Fattahead **268** E5
Faugh **210** B2
Fauldhouse **234** D3
Faulkbourne **137** G1
Faulkland **117** E2
Fauls **170** C4
Faulston **118** B5
Faversham **124** C2
Favillar **259** K1
Fawdington **202** D5
Fawdon **212** B1
Fawfieldhead **172** B1
Fawkham Green **123** E2
Fawler **133** F1
Fawley *Bucks* **134** C4
Fawley *Hants* **107** D2
Fawley *WBerks* **133** F4
Fawley Chapel **145** E5
Fawsyde **253** G2
Faxfleet **196** A5
Faxton **160** C5
Faygate **122** B5
Fazakerley **183** E3
Fazeley **159** E2
Fearby **202** A4
Fearn **267** F4
Fearnan **250** C5
Fearnbeg **264** D6
Fearnhead **184** A3
Fearnmore **264** D5
Featherstone
  *Staffs* **158** B2
Featherstone
  *WYorks* **194** D5
Featherstone Castle **210** C1
Feckenham **146** C1
Feering **151** G1
Feetham **201** E3
Feizor **193** D1
Felbridge **122** C5
Felbrigg **178** D2
Felcourt **122** C4
Felden **135** F2
Felhampton **156** D4
Felindre *Carmar* **142** D5
Felindre *Carmar* **142** B5
Felindre *Carmar* **141** G4
Felindre *Carmar* **142** C4
Felindre *Cere* **142** B2
Felindre *Powys* **156** A4
Felindre *Powys* **144** A5
Felindre *Swan* **128** C2
Felinfach *Cere* **142** B2
Felinfach *Powys* **143** G4
Felinfoel **128** B2
Felingwmisaf **142** B5
Felingwmuchaf **142** B5
Felixkirk **203** D4
Felixstowe **153** E4
Felixstowe Ferry **153** E4
Felkington **237** G5
Felldownhead **99** D2
Felling **212** B1
Fellonmore **239** F2
Felmersham **149** E2
Felmingham **179** D3
Felpham **108** B4
Felsham **152** A2
Felsted **151** E5
Feltham **136** A5
Felthamhill **136** A5
Felthorpe **178** C4
Felton *Here* **145** E3
Felton *N'umb* **221** D1
Felton *NSom* **116** C1
Felton Butler **156** C1
Feltwell **163** F3
Fen Ditton **150** C1
Fen Drayton **150** B1
Fen End **159** E5
Fen Street *Norf* **164** A2
Fen Street *Norf* **164** B4
Fen Street *Suff* **164** B4
Fen Street *Suff* **152** C1
Fenay Bridge **185** F1
Fence **193** E4
Fence Houses **212** C2
Fencott **134** A1
Fendike Corner **176** C1
Fenham **229** F2
Fenhouses **176** A3
Feniscowles **192** C5
Feniton **103** D3
Fenn Street **137** G5
Fenni-fach **143** G3
Fenny Bentley **172** C2
Fenny Bridges **103** E3
Fenny Compton **147** G2
Fenny Drayton **159** F3
Fenny Stratford **149** D4
Fenrother **221** D2
Fenstanton **150** B1
Fenton *Cambs* **162** B5
Fenton *Lincs* **187** F5
Fenton *Lincs* **175** D3
Fenton *N'umb* **229** D3
Fenton *Notts* **187** E4
Fenton *Stoke* **171** F3
Fenton Barns **236** C1
Fenwick *EAyr* **233** F5
Fenwick *N'umb* **220** C4
Fenwick *N'umb* **229** E2
Fenwick *SYorks* **186** C1
Feochaig **222** C4
Feock **95** F3
Feolin **230** D3
Feolin Ferry **230** C3
Feorlan **222** B5
Feorlin **240** B5
Fergushie Park **233** F3
Feriniquarrie **263** G6
Fern **252** C3
Ferndale **129** F3
Ferndown **105** G2
Ferness **267** G7
Fernham **133** E3
Fernhill Heath **146** A2
Fernhurst **121** D5
Fernie **244** B3
Fernilea **255** J1
Fernilee **185** E5
Ferrensby **194** C1
Ferrers Centre for Arts &
  Crafts *Leics*
  LE65 1RU **173** E5
Ferrindonald **256** C4
Ferring **108** C3
Ferry Hill **162** B4
Ferrybridge **195** D5
Ferryden **253** F4
Ferryhill **212** B4
Ferryside
  (Glanyferi) **127** G1
Fersfield **164** B3
Fersit **249** E2
Ferwig **141** E3
Feshiebridge **259** F4
Fetcham **121** G2
Fetlar **278** F3
Fetterangus **269** H5
Fettercairn **253** D2
Fetternear House **261** F3
Feus of Caldhame **253** E3
Fewcott **148** A5
Fewston **194** A2
Ffairfach **142** C5
Ffair-Rhos **142** D1
Ffaldybrenin **142** C3
Ffarmers **142** C3
Ffawyddog **130** B1
Ffestiniog
  (Llan Ffestiniog) **168** A3
Ffestiniog Railway *Gwyn*
  LL49 9NF **167** F3
Ffordd-las *Denb* **169** E1
Fforddlas *Powys* **144** B4
Fforest **128** B2
Fforest-fach **128** C3
Ffos-y-ffin **142** A1
Ffridd *Denb* **182** B4
Ffrith *Flints* **169** F2
Ffrwdgrech **143** G5
Ffynnon **127** G1
Ffynnongroyw **182** C4
Fibhig **270** E3
Fichlie **260** C3
Fidden **238** C2
Fiddington *Glos* **146** B4
Fiddington *Som* **115** F3
Fiddleford **105** E1
Fiddler's Green
  *Glos* **146** B5
Fiddler's Green
  *Here* **145** E4
Fiddler's Green
  *Norf* **163** G1
Fiddler's Green
  *Norf* **164** B2
Fiddlers Hamlet **137** D2
Field **172** B4
Field Broughton **199** E4
Field Dalling **178** B2
Field Head **159** G2
Fife Keith **268** C5
Fifehead Magdalen **117** E5
Fifehead Neville **105** D1
Fifehead
  St. Quintin **105** D1
Fifield *Oxon* **133** E1
Fifield *W&M* **135** E5
Fifield Bavant **118** B5
Figheldean **118** C3
Filby **179** F4
Filey **205** F4
Filgrave **149** D3
Filham **100** C2
Filkins **133** E2
Filleigh *Devon* **113** G3
Filleigh *Devon* **102** A1
Fillingham **187** G4
Fillongley **159** F4
Filmore Hill **120** B5
Filton **131** F5
Fimber **196** A1
Finavon **252** C4
Fincham **163** E2
Finchampstead **120** C1
Finchdean **107** G1
Finchingfield **151** E4
Finchley **136** B3
Findern **173** E4
Findhorn **267** H5
Findhorn Bridge **259** F2
Findhuglen **242** C3
Findo Gask **243** F2
Findochty **268** C4
Findon *Aber* **261** H5
Findon *WSuss* **108** D3
Findon Mains **266** D5
Findon Valley **108** D3
Findrassie **267** J5
Findron **259** J3
Finedon **161** E5
Finegand **251** G3
Fingal Street **164** D4
Fingask **261** F2
Fingerpost **157** G5
Fingest **134** C3
Finghall **202** A4
Fingland *Cumb* **209** F1
Fingland *D&G* **226** D5
Fingland *D&G* **225** F4
Finglesham **125** F3
Fingringhoe **152** B5
Finkle Street **186** A3
Finlarig **242** A1
Finmere **148** B4
Finnart *A&B* **241** E5
Finnart *P&K* **250** A4
Finney Hill **159** G1
Finningham **152** B1
Finningley **187** D3
Finnygaud **268** E5
Finsbay
  (Fionnsbhagh) **263** F3
Finsbury **136** C4
Finstall **158** B5
Finsthwaite **199** E4
Finstock **133** F1
Finstown **277** C6
Fintry *Aber* **269** F5
Fintry *Stir* **234** A1
Finwood **147** D1
Finzean **260** D5
Fionnphort **238** B2
Fir Tree **212** A4
Firbank **200** B3
Firbeck **186** C4
Firby *NYorks* **202** B5
Firby *NYorks* **195** G1
Firgrove **184** D1
Firs Lane **184** A2
Firsby **176** C1
Firsdown **118** D4
Firth **278** D5
Fishbourne *IoW* **107** E3
Fishbourne *WSuss* **108** A3
Fishburn **212** C4
Fishcross **243** E5
Fisherford **260** E1
Fisher's Pond **119** F5
Fisher's Row **192** A3
Fishersgate **109** E3
Fisherstreet **121** E4
Fisherton *Here* **145** E3
Fisherton *SAyr* **224** A4
Fisherton de la
  Mere **118** A4
Fishguard
  (Abergwaun) **140** C4
Fishlake **187** D1
Fishleigh Barton **113** F4
Fishley **179** F4
Fishnish **247** F5
Fishpond Bottom **103** G3
Fishponds **131** F5
Fishpool **184** C2
Fishtoft **176** B3
Fishtoft Drove **176** B3
Fishtown of Usan **253** F4
Fishwick **237** G4
Fiskavaig **255** J1
Fiskerton *Lincs* **188** A5
Fiskerton *Notts* **174** C2
Fitling **197** E4
Fittleton **118** C3
Fittleworth **108** C2
Fitton End **162** C1
Fitz **156** D1
Fitzhead **115** E5
Fitzroy **115** E5
Fitzwilliam **186** B1
Fitzwilliam Museum
  *Cambs* CB2 1RB
  66 Cambridge
Fiunary **247** F5
Five Acres **131** E1
Five Ash Down **109** G1
Five Ashes **110** A1
Five Bridges **145** F3
Five Houses **106** D4
Five Lanes **130** D3
Five Oak Green **123** F4
Five Oaks *Chanl* **100** C5
Five Oaks *WSuss* **121** F5
Five Roads **128** A2
Five Turnings **156** B5
Five Wents **124** A3
Fivehead **116** A5
Fivelanes **97** G1
Flack's Green **137** G1
Flackwell Heath **135** D4
Fladbury **146** B3
Fladdabister **279** D9
Flagg **172** C1
Flamborough **205** F5
Flamingo Land Theme
  Park *NYorks*
  YO17 6UX **203** G4
Flamingo Park,
  Hastings *ESuss*
  TN34 3AR **110** D3
Flamstead **135** F1
Flamstead End
  **136** C2
Flansham **108** B3
Flanshaw **194** C5
Flasby **193** F2
Flash **172** B1
Flashader **263** J6
Flask Inn **204** C2
Flatts Lane Woodland
  Country Park *R&C*
  TS6 0NN **29** D4
Flaunden **135** F2
Flawborough **174** C3
Flawith **195** D1
Flax Bourton **116** C1
Flax Moss **193** D5
Flaxby **194** C2
Flaxholme **173** E3
Flaxlands **164** C2
Flaxley **131** F1
Flaxpool **115** E4
Flaxton **195** F1
Fleckney **160** B3
Flecknoe **148** A1
Fledborough **187** F5
Fleet *Hants* **120** D2
Fleet *Hants* **107** G2
Fleet *Lincs* **176** B5
Fleet Air Arm Museum
  *Som* BA22 8HT **116** C5
Fleet Hargate **176** B5
Fleetville **136** A2
Fleetwood **191** G3
Fleggburgh (Burgh St.
  Margaret) **179** F4
Flemingston **129** F5
Flemington **234** A4
Flempton **151** G1
Fleoideabhagh **263** F3
Fleshirin **271** H4
Fletchersbridge **97** F3
Fletchertown **209** F2
Fletching **109** F2
Fleuchats **260** B4
Fleur-de-lis **130** A3
Flexbury **112** C5
Flexford **121** E2
Flimby **208** D3
Flimwell **123** G5
Flint (Y Fflint) **182** D5
Flint Cross **150** C3
Flint Mountain **182** D5
Flintham **174** C3
Flinton **197** E4
Flint's Green **159** E4
Flishinghurst **123** G5
Flitcham **177** F5
Flitholme **200** C1
Flitton **149** F4
Flitwick **149** F4
Flixborough **187** F1
Flixton *GtMan* **184** B3
Flixton *NYorks* **204** D5
Flixton *Suff* **165** E3
Flockton **185** G1
Flockton Green **185** G1
Flodden **228** D3
Flodigarry **263** K4
Flood's Ferry **162** B3
Flookburgh **199** E5
Floors **268** C5
Flordon **164** C2
Flotta **277** C8
Flotterton **220** C1
Flowton **152** B3
Flushdyke **194** B5
Flushing *Aber* **269** J6
Flushing *Corn* **95** F3
Flushing *Corn* **95** E4
Fluxton **103** D3
Flyford Flavell **146** B2
Foals Green **165** D4
Fobbing **137** G4
Fochabers **268** B5
Fochriw **130** A2
Fockerby **187** F1
Fodderletter **259** J2
Fodderty **266** C6
Foddington **116** C5
Foel **155** F1
Foelgastell **128** B1
Foggathorpe **195** G4
Fogo **237** E5
Fogorig **237** E5
Foindle **272** D4
Folda **251** G3
Fole **172** B4
Foleshill **159** F4
Folke **104** C1
Folkestone **125** E5
Folkingham **175** F4
Folkington **110** A3
Folksworth **161** G4
Folkton **205** D5
Folla Rule **261** F1
Follifoot **194** C2
Folly *Dorset* **104** D2
Folly *Pembs* **140** C5
Folly Farm, Begelly *Pembs*
  SA68 0XA **127** E2
Folly Gate **99** F1
Fonmon **115** D1
Fonthill Bishop **118** A4
Fonthill Gifford **118** A4
Fontmell Magna **105** E1
Fontmell Parva **105** E1
Fontwell **108** B3
Font-y-gary **115** D1
Foolow **185** F5
Footherley **158** D2
Foots Cray **137** D5
Forbestown **260** B3
Force Forge **199** E3
Force Green **122** D3
Forcett **202** A1
Forches Cross **102** A2
Ford *A&B* **240** A4
Ford *Bucks* **134** C2
Ford *Devon* **100** C3
Ford *Devon* **113** F3
Ford *Devon* **101** D3
Ford *Glos* **146** C5
Ford *Mersey* **183** E3
Ford *Midlo* **236** A3
Ford *N'umb* **229** D3
Ford *Pembs* **140** C5
Ford *Plym* **100** A2
Ford *Shrop* **156** D1
Ford *Som* **115** D5
Ford *Staffs* **172** C1
Ford *Wilts* **132** A5
Ford *WSuss* **108** C3
Ford End **137** F1
Ford Green **192** A3
Ford Heath **156** D1
Ford Street **103** E1
Forda **99** F1
Fordcombe **123** E4
Fordell **235** F1
Forden (Fordun) **156** B2
Ford Green **120** D1
Fordgate **116** A4
Fordham *Cambs* **163** E5
Fordham *Essex* **152** A5
Fordham *Norf* **163** E3
Fordham Abbey **151** E1
Fordham Heath **152** A5
Fordhouses **158** B2
Fordingbridge **106** A1
Fordon **205** D5
Fordoun **253** F2
Ford's Green **152** B1
Fordstreet **152** A5
Fordwells **133** F1
Fordwich **125** D3
Fordyce **268** D4
Forebrae **243** E2
Forebridge **171** G5
Foredale **193** E1
Foreland **230** A3
Foremark **173** E5
Foremark Reservoir *Derbys*
  DE65 6EG **173** E5
Forest **202** B2
Forest Coal Pit **144** B5
Forest Gate **136** D4
Forest Green **121** G3
Forest Hall *Cumb* **199** G2
Forest Hall *T&W* **212** B1
Forest Hill *GtLon* **136** C5
Forest Hill *Oxon* **134** A2
Forest Lane Head **194** C2
Forest Lodge (Taigh na
  Frithe) *A&B* **249** E5
Forest Lodge *P&K* **251** F1
Forest Row **122** D5
Forest Side **107** D4
Forest Town **173** G1
Forestburn Gate **220** C2
Forest-in-Teesdale **211** E5
Forestmill **243** E5
Forestside **107** G1
Forfar **252** C4
Forfar Loch Country Park
  *Angus* DD8 1BT **252** C4
Forgandenny **243** F3
Forge **154** D3
Forgie **268** B5
Forhill **158** C5
Forncett End **164** C2
Forncett St. Mary **164** C2
Forncett St. Peter **164** C2
Forneth **251** F5
Fornham All Saints **151** G1
Fornham St. Martin **151** G1
Fornighty **267** G6
Forres **267** H6
Forrest **234** C3
Forrest Lodge **215** G2
Forsbrook **171** G3
Forse **275** H5
Forsie **275** F2
Forsinain **274** E4
Forsinard **274** D4
Forston **104** C3
Fort Augustus (Cille
  Chuimein) **257** K4
Fort Fun, Eastbourne
  *ESuss* BN22 7LQ **110** B3
Fort George **266** E6
Fort William
  (An Gearasdan) **248** D2
Forter **251** G3
Fortevoit **243** F3
Forth **234** D4
Forthampton **146** A4
Fortingall **250** C5
Fortis Green **136** B4
Forton *Hants* **119** F3
Forton *Lancs* **192** A2
Forton *Shrop* **156** D1
Forton *Som* **103** G2
Forton *Staffs* **171** E5
Fortrie **268** E6
Fortrose
  (A'Chananaich) **266** E6
Fortuneswell **104** C5
Forty Green **135** E3
Forty Hill **136** C3
Forward Green **152** B2
Fosbury **119** E2
Foscot **147** E5
Fosdyke **176** B4
Foss **250** C4
Foss Cross **132** C2
Fossdale **201** E3
Fossebridge **132** C1
Foster Street **137** D2
Fosterhouses **186** D1
Foster's Booth **148** B2
Foston *Derbys* **172** C4
Foston *Leics* **160** B3
Foston *Lincs* **175** D3
Foston *NYorks* **195** F1
Foston on the
  Wolds **196** D2
Fotherby **188** D3
Fotheringhay **161** F3
Foubister **277** E7
Foul Mile **110** B2
Foula **278** A5
Foula Airstrip **278** B1
Foulbridge **226** D5
Foulden *Norf* **163** F3
Foulden *ScBord* **237** G4
Foulness Island **138** D3
Foulridge **193** E3
Foulsham **178** B3
Foulstone **199** G4
Foulzie **269** F4
Fountainhall **236** B5
Four Ashes *Staffs* **158** B2
Four Ashes *Staffs* **158** A4
Four Ashes *Suff* **164** A4
Four Crosses
  *Denb* **168** D3
Four Crosses
  *Powys* **156** B1
Four Crosses
  *Powys* **155** G2
Four Crosses
  *Staffs* **158** B2
Four Elms **123** D4
Four Forks **115** F4
Four Gotes **162** C1
Four Lane Ends
  *B'burn* **192** D5
Four Lane Ends
  *ChesW&C* **170** C1
Four Lane Ends
  *York* **195** F2
Four Lanes **95** D3
Four Marks **120** B4
Four Mile Bridge **180** A5
Four Oaks *ESuss* **111** D1
Four Oaks *Glos* **145** F5
Four Oaks *WMid* **159** E4
Four Oaks *WMid* **158** D4
Four Oaks Park **158** D3
Four Roads **128** A2
Four Throws **110** C1
Fourlane Ends **173** E2
Fourlanes End **171** F2
Fourpenny **267** F2
Fourstones **211** E1
Fovant **118** B5
Foveran House **261** H2
Fowey **97** F4
Fowlis **244** B1
Fowlis Wester **243** E2
Fowlmere **150** C3
Fownhope **145** E4
Fox Hatch **137** E3
Fox Street **152** B5
Fox Up **201** D5
Foxbar **233** F3
Foxcombe Hill **133** G2
Foxcote *Glos* **132** C1
Foxcote *Som* **117** E2
Foxdale **190** A4
Foxearth **151** G3
Foxfield **198** D4
Foxham **132** B5
Foxhole *Corn* **97** D4
Foxhole *High* **258** C1
Foxholes **204** D5
Foxhunt Green **110** A2
Foxley *Here* **144** D3
Foxley *N'hants* **148** B2
Foxley *Norf* **178** B3
Foxley *Wilts* **132** A4
Foxt **172** B2
Foxton *Cambs* **150** C3
Foxton *Dur* **212** C5
Foxton *Leics* **160** B3
Foxton Locks *Leics*
  LE16 7RA **160** B4
Foxwist Green **170** D1
Foy **145** E5
Foyers (Foithir) **258** B2
Frachadil **246** C4
Fraddam **94** C3
Fraddon **96** D4
Fradley **159** D1
Fradswell **171** G4
Fraisthorpe **197** D1
Framfield **109** G1
Framingham Earl **179** D5
Framingham Pigot **179** D5
Framlingham **153** E1
Frampton *Dorset* **104** C3
Frampton *Lincs* **176** B4
Frampton Cotterell **131** F4
Frampton Mansell **132** B2
Frampton on
  Severn **131** G2
Frampton West
  End **176** A3
Framsden **152** D2
Framwellgate Moor **212** B3
France Lynch **132** B2
Frances Green **192** C4
Franche **158** A5
Frandley **184** A4
Frankby **182** D4
Frankfort **179** E3
Frankley **158** B4
Franksbridge **144** A2
Frankton **159** G5
Frant **123** E5
Fraserburgh **269** H4
Frating **152** B5
Fratton **107** F2
Freasley **159** E3
Freathy **99** D5
Freckenham **163** E5
Freckleton **192** A5
Freeby **174** D5
Freefolk **119** F3
Freehay **172** B3
Freeland **133** G1
Freester **279** D7
Freethorpe **179** F5
Freethorpe
  Common **179** F5
Freiston **176** B3
Freiston Shore **176** B3
Fremington *Devon* **113** F2
Fremington *NYorks* **201** F3
French Brothers Cruises
  *W&M* SL4 5JH **135** E5
Frenchay **131** F5
Frenchbeer **99** G2
Frendraught **268** E6
Frenich **241** G4
Frensham **120** D3
Fresgoe **274** E2
Freshbrook **132** D4
Freshfield **183** D2
Freshford **117** E2
Freshwater **106** C4
Freshwater Bay **106** C4
Freshwater East **126** D3
Fressingfield **165** D3
Freston **152** C4
Freswick **275** J2
Fretherne **131** G2
Frettenham **178** D4
Freuchie **244** A4
Freystrop Cross **126** C1
Friars, The, Aylesford *Kent*
  ME20 7BX **123** G3
Friars Carse **216** D2
Friar's Gate **123** D5
Friarton **243** G2
Friday Bridge **162** C2
Friday Street *ESuss* **110** B3
Friday Street *Suff* **152** D2
Friday Street *Suff* **153** E2
Friday Street *Surr* **121** G3
Fridaythorpe **196** A2
Friern Barnet **136** B3
Frieston **175** E3
Frieth **134** C3
Frilford **133** G3
Frilsham **134** A5
Frimley **121** D2
Frimley Green **121** D2

Frindsbury **123** G2
Fring **177** F4
Fringford **148** B5
Friningham **124** A3
Frinsted **124** A3
Frinton-on-Sea **139** F1
Friockheim **253** D5
Frog **154** C1
Frisby on the
  Wreake **160** B1
Friskney **176** C2
Friskney
  Eaudyke **176** C2
Friston *ESuss* **110** A4
Friston *Suff* **153** F1
Fritchley **173** E2
Frith **124** B3
Frith Bank **176** B3
Frith Common **145** F1
Fritham **106** B1
Frithelstock **113** E4
Frithelstock
  Stone **113** E4
Frithville **176** B2
Frittenden **124** A4
Frittiscombe **101** E3
Fritton *Norf* **164** D2
Fritton *Norf* **179** F5
Fritwell **148** A3
Frizinghall **194** A4
Frizington **208** D5
Frocester **131** G2
Frochas **156** B2
Frodesley **157** E2
Frodesley Lane **157** E2
Frodingham **187** F1
Frodsham **183** G5
Frog End **150** C2
Frog Pool **145** G1
Frogden **228** B4
Froggatt **185** G5
Froghall **172** B3
Frogham **106** A1
Frogland Cross **131** F4
Frogmore *Devon* **101** D3
Frogmore *Hants* **120** D2
Frogmore *Herts* **136** A2
Frogwell **98** D4
Frolesworth **160** A3
Frome **117** E3
Frome Market **117** F2
Frome St. Quintin **104** B2
Frome Whitfield **104** C3
Fromes Hill **145** F3
Fron *Gwyn* **166** C4
Fron *Powys* **156** B2
Fron *Powys* **143** F3
Fron *Powys* **156** A3
Fron Isaf **169** F4
Froncysyllte **169** F3
Fron-goch **168** C4
Frostenden **165** F3
Frosterley **211** G4
Froxfield **119** E1
Froxfield Green **120** C5
*Fruitmarket Gallery Edin*
  *EH1 1DF* **37** G4
Fryerning **137** F2
Fugglestone
  St. Peter **118** C4
Fulbeck **175** E2
Fulbourn **150** D2
Fulbrook **133** E1
Fulflood **119** F5
Fulford *Som* **115** F5
Fulford *Staffs* **171** G4
Fulford *York* **195** F3
Fulham **136** B5
Fulking **109** E2
Full Sutton **195** G2
Fullaford **113** G2
Fuller Street **137** G1
Fuller's Moor **170** B2
Fullerton **119** E4
Fulletby **188** C5
Fullwood **233** F4
Fulmer **135** F4
Fulmodeston **178** A2
Fulnetby **188** B5
Fulready **147** E3
Fulstow **188** D3
Fulwell *Oxon* **147** F5
Fulwell *T&W* **212** C2
Fulwood *Lancs* **192** B4
Fulwood *SYorks* **186** A4
*Fun Farm, Spalding Lincs*
  *PE12 6JU* **176** A5
Fundenhall **164** C2
Fundenhall
  Street **164** C2
Funtington **108** A3
Funtley **107** E2
Funzie **278** F3
Furley **103** F2
Furnace *A&B* **240** C4
Furnace *Carmar* **128** B2
Furnace *Cere* **154** C3
Furnace *High* **265** F4
Furnace End **159** E3
Furner's Green **109** G1
Furness Vale **185** E4
Furneux Pelham **150** C5
Furnham **103** G2
Further Quarter **124** A5
Furtho **148** C3
Furze Green **164** D2
Furze Platt **135** D4
Furzehill *Devon* **114** A3
Furzehill *Dorset* **105** G2
Furzeley Corner **107** F1
Furzey Lodge **106** C2
Furzley **106** B1
Fyfett **103** F1
Fyfield *Essex* **137** E2
Fyfield *Glos* **133** E2
Fyfield *Hants* **119** D3
Fyfield *Oxon* **133** G3
Fyfield *Wilts* **118** C1
Fyfield *Wilts* **118** C1
Fylingthorpe **204** C2
Fyning **120** D3
Fyvie **261** F1

# G

Gabalfa **130** A5
Gabhsunn Bho
  Dheas **271** G2

Gabhsunn Bho
  Thuath **271** G2
Gablon **266** E2
Gabroc Hill **233** F4
Gaddesby **160** B1
Gaddesden Row **135** F1
Gadebridge **135** F2
Gadshill **137** G5
Gaer *Newport* **130** B4
Gaer *Powys* **144** A5
Gaer-fawr **130** D3
Gaerllwyd **130** D3
Gaerwen **180** C5
Gagingwell **147** G5
Gaich *High* **259** H2
Gaich *High* **258** D1
Gaick Lodge **250** C1
Gailes **224** B3
Gailey **158** B1
Gainford **202** A1
Gainsborough **187** F3
Gainsford End **151** F4
Gairloch
  (Geàrrloch) **264** D4
Gairlochy (Geàrr
  Lòchaidh) **249** D1
Gairney Bank **243** G5
Gairnshiel Lodge **259** K4
Gaitsgill **209** G2
Galabank **236** B5
Galashiels **227** F2
Galdenoch **214** C4
Gale **184** D1
Galgate **192** A3
Galhampton **116** D5
Gallanach **240** A2
Gallantry Bank **170** C2
Gallatown **244** A5
Gallchoille **239** G5
Gallery **253** E3
Gallery of Modern Art,
  Glasgow *Glas*
  *G1 3AH* **39** F4
Galley Common **159** F3
Galleyend **137** G2
Galleywood **137** G2
Gallowfauld **252** C5
Gallowhill **233** F3
Gallows Green **172** B3
Gallowstree
  Common **134** B4
Gallowstree Elm **158** A4
Galltair **256** E2
Gallt-y-foel **167** E1
Gallypot Street **123** D5
Galmington **115** F5
Galmisdale **247** D1
Galmpton *Devon* **100** C3
Galmpton *Torbay* **101** E2
Galmpton
  Warborough **101** E2
Galphay **202** B5
Galston **224** C2
Galtrigill **263** G6
Gamble's Green **137** G1
Gamblesby **210** C4
Gamelsby **209** F1
Gamesley **185** E3
Gamlingay **150** A2
Gamlingay Cinques **150** A2
Gamlingay Great
  Heath **150** A2
Gammaton **113** E3
Gammaton Moor **113** E3
Gammersgill **201** F4
Gamrie **269** F4
Gamston *Notts* **187** E5
Gamston *Notts* **174** B4
Ganarew **131** E1
Gang **98** D4
Ganllwyd **168** A5
Gannochy **253** E2
Ganstead **197** D4
Ganthorpe **203** F5
Ganton **204** C5
Ganwick Corner **136** B3
Gaodhail **239** F1
Gappah **102** B5
Gara Bridge **100** D2
Garabal **241** F4
Garadheancal **265** F1
Garbat **266** B6
Garbhallt **240** C5
Garboldisham **164** B3
Garden **242** A5
Garden City **170** A1
Garden Village **185** G3
Gardeners Green **120** D1
Gardenstown **269** F4
Garderhouse **279** C8
Gardham **196** B3
Gare Hill **117** E3
Garelochhead **241** E5
Garford **133** G3
Garforth **194** D4
Gargrave **193** F2
Gargunnock **242** C5
Gariob **231** F1
Garlic Street **164** D3
Garlieston **207** E2
Garlies Castle **215** F4
Garlinge Green **124** D3
Garlogie **261** F4
Garmelow **171** F5
Garmond **269** G5
Garmony **247** F5
Garmouth **268** B4
Garmston **157** F2
Garnant **128** C2
Garndolbenmaen **167** D3
Garneddwen **155** D2
Garnett Bridge **199** G3
Garnfadryn **166** B4
Garnswllt **128** C2
Garrabost **271** H4
Garrachra **232** B1
Garras **95** E4
Garreg **167** F3
Garreg Bank **156** B1
Garret's Green **159** D4
Garrick **242** D3
Garrigill **210** D3
Garroch **215** G2
Garrochty **232** B4
Garros **263** K5
Garrow **242** D1

Garryhorn **215** G1
Garrynahine (Gearraidh na
  h-Aibhne) **270** E4
Garsdale **200** C4
Garsdale Head **200** C3
Garsdon **132** B4
Garshall Green **171** G4
Garsington **134** A2
Garstang **192** A3
Garston **183** F4
Garswood **183** G3
Gartachoil **242** A5
Gartally **258** B1
Gartbreck **230** A4
Gartcosh **234** B3
Garth *Bridgend* **129** E3
Garth *Cere* **154** C4
Garth *Gwyn* **181** D5
Garth *IoM* **190** B4
Garth *Powys* **143** F3
Garth *Shet* **279** D8
Garth *Wrex* **169** F3
Garth Row **199** G3
Garthbrengy **143** G4
Garthdee **261** H4
Gartheli **142** B2
Garthmyl **156** A3
Garthorpe *Leics* **174** D5
Garthorpe *NLincs* **187** F2
Garths **199** G3
Garthynty **142** D3
Gartincaber **242** B4
Gartloch **234** B3
Gartmore **242** A5
Gartnagrenach **231** F4
Gartness **233** G1
Gartocharn **233** F1
Garton **197** E4
Garton-on-the-
  Wolds **196** B1
Gartymore **275** F7
Garvald **236** C2
Garvamore **258** C5
Garvan **248** B2
Garvard **238** C5
Garve (Clachan
  Ghairbh) **265** K5
Garveld **222** B5
Garvie **242** B1
Garvestone **178** B5
Garvock *Aber* **253** F2
Garvock *Invcly* **233** D2
Garwald **226** D5
Garwaldwaterfoot **226** D5
Garway **145** D5
Garway Hill **144** D5
Gask *Aber* **269** J6
Gask *Aber* **269** F6
Gask *P&K* **243** E3
Gaskan **248** A2
Gass **224** C5
Gastard **117** F1
Gasthorpe **164** A3
Gaston Green **137** E1
Gatcombe **107** D4
Gate Burton **187** F4
Gate Helmsley **195** F2
Gate House **231** D2
Gateacre **183** F4
Gateford **186** C4
Gateforth **195** E5
Gatehead **224** B2
Gatehouse **251** D5
Gatehouse of Fleet **216** A5
Gatelawbridge **216** D1
Gateley **178** A3
Gatenby **202** C4
Gatesgarth **209** E5
Gateshaw **228** B4
Gateshead **212** B1
Gatesheath **170** B1
Gateside *Aber* **260** E3
Gateside *Angus* **252** C5
Gateside *Fife* **243** G4
Gateside *NAyr* **233** G4
Gateslack **225** G5
Gathurst **183** G2
Gatley **184** C4
Gattonside **227** G2
Gatwick Airport **122** B4
Gaufron **143** F1
Gaulby **160** B2
Gauldry **244** B2
Gaunt's Common **105** G2
Gaunt's Earthcott **131** F4
Gautby **188** B5
Gavinton **237** E4
Gawber **186** A2
Gawcott **148** B4
Gawsworth **184** C5
Gawthrop **200** B4
Gawthwaite **198** F4
Gay Bowers **137** G2
Gay Street **121** F5
Gaydon **147** F2
Gayhurst **149** D3
Gayle **201** D4
Gayles **202** A2
Gayton *Mersey* **183** D4
Gayton *N'hants* **148** C2
Gayton *Norf* **163** F1
Gayton *Staffs* **171** G5
Gayton le Marsh **189** E4
Gayton le Wold **188** C4
Gayton Thorpe **163** F1
Gaywood **177** E5
Gazeley **151** F1
Geanies House **267** F4
Gearach **230** A4
Gearnsary **274** C5
Gearradh **248** C2
Gearraidh Bhailteas **254** C1
Gearraidh Bhaird **271** F5
Gearraidh na
  Monadh **254** C3
Gearrannan **270** D3
Geary **263** H5
Gedding **152** B2
Geddington **161** D4
Gedgrave Hall **153** F3
Gedling **174** B3
Gedney **176** C5
Gedney Broadgate **176** C5

Gedney Drove End **176** C5
Gedney Dyke **176** C5
Gedney Hill **162** B1
Gee Cross **185** D3
Geilston **233** E2
Geirinis **262** C7
Geisiadar **270** D4
Geldeston **165** E2
Gell *Conwy* **168** B1
Gell *Gwyn* **167** D4
Gelli **129** F3
Gelli Aur Country
  Park *Carmar*
  *SA32 8LR* **142** C5
Gelli Gynan **129** E1
Gellideg **129** G3
Gellifor **169** E1
Gelligaer **130** A3
Gellilydan **167** F4
Gellioedd **168** C3
Gelly **127** D1
Gellyburn **243** F1
Gellywen **141** F5
Gelston *D&G* **216** B5
Gelston *Lincs* **175** E3
Gembling **196** D2
Gemmil **239** G4
Genoch **214** C5
Genoch Square **214** C5
Gentleshaw **158** C1
Geocrab **263** G2
George Green **135** F4
George Nympton **114** A5
Georgeham **113** E2
Georgetown **233** F3
Gerlan **167** F1
Germansweek **99** E1
Germoe **94** C4
Gerrans **95** F4
Gerrards Cross **135** F4
Gerston **275** G3
Gestingthorpe **151** G4
Geuffordd **156** B1
Geufron **155** F4
Gibbet Hill **117** E3
Gibbshill **216** B3
Gibraltar *Lincs* **177** D2
Gibraltar *Suff* **152** C3
Gibraltar Point National
  Nature Reserve *Lincs*
  *PE24 4SU* **177** D2
Gidside *T&W*
  *NE16 6BG* **212** A2
Giddeahall **132** A5
Giddy Green **105** E4
Gidea Park **137** E4
Gidleigh **99** G2
Giffnock **233** G4
Gifford **236** C3
Giffordland **233** D5
Giffordtown **244** A3
Giggleswick **193** E1
Gigha **231** F5
Gilberdyke **196** A5
Gilbert's End **146** A3
Gilchriston **236** B3
Gilcrux **209** E3
Gildersome **194** B5
Gildingwells **186** C4
Gileston **114** D1
Gilfach **130** A3
Gilfach Goch **129** F4
Gilfachrheda **142** A2
Gilgarran **208** D4
Gill **210** A4
Gillamoor **203** F4
Gillen **263** H5
Gillenbie **217** F2
Gillfoot **217** D3
Gilling East **203** F5
Gilling West **202** A2
Gillingham *Dorset* **117** F5
Gillingham *Med* **123** G5
Gillingham *Norf* **165** F2
Gillivoan **275** G5
Gillock **275** H3
Gillow Heath **171** F2
Gills **275** J1
Gill's Green **123** G5
Gilmanscleuch **227** E3
Gilmerton *Edin* **235** G3
Gilmerton *P&K* **243** D3
Gilmilnscroft **225** D3
Gilmonby **201** E2
Gilmorton **160** A4
Gilsland **210** C1
Gilsland Spa **210** C1
Gilson **159** D3
Gilston **236** B4
Gilston Park **136** D1
Gilwern **130** B1
Gimingham **179** D2
Gin Pit **184** A2
Ginclough **185** D5
Ginger's Green **110** B2
Giosla **270** D4
Gipping **152** B1
Gipsey Bridge **176** A3
Girlsta **279** D7
Girsby **202** C2
Girtford **149** G3
Girthon **216** A5
Girton *Cambs* **150** C1
Girton *Notts* **174** D1
Girvan **214** C1
Gisburn **193** E3
Gisburn Cotes **193** E3
Gisleham **165** G3
Gislingham **164** B4
Gissing **164** C3
Gittisham **103** E3
Givons Grove **121** G2
Glackour **265** H3
Gladestry **144** B2
Glaic **232** B2
Glaisdale **203** G2
Glaister **223** E2
Glame **264** B7
Glamis **252** B5
Glamis Castle *Angus*
  *DD8 1QJ* **252** B5
Glan Conwy **168** B2
Glanaber Terrace **168** A3

Glanaman **128** C1
Glanbran **143** E4
Glan-Denys **142** B2
Glanderston **260** D2
Glandford **178** B1
Glan-Duar **142** B3
Glandwr **141** E5
Glan-Dwyfach **167** D3
Glangrwyney **130** B1
Glanllynfi **129** E3
Glanmule **156** A3
Glan-rhyd *NPT* **129** D2
Glanrhyd *Pembs* **141** E3
Glanton **229** E5
Glanton Pyke **229** E5
Glanvilles Wootton **104** C2
Glanwern **154** C4
Glanwydden **181** G4
Glan-y-don **182** C5
Glan-y-llyn **130** A4
Glan-y-nant **155** F4
Glan-yr-afon
  *Gwyn* **168** C3
Glan-yr-afon
  *Gwyn* **168** D3
Glan-y-Wern **167** F4
Glapthorn **161** F3
Glapwell **173** F1
Glasahoile **241** G4
Glasbury **144** A4
Glaschoil **259** H1
Glascoed *Mon* **130** C2
Glascoed *Wrex* **169** F2
Glascorrie **260** C5
Glascote **159** E2
Glascwm **144** A2
Glasdrum **248** C5
Glasfryn **168** C2
Glasgow (Glaschu) **233** G3
Glasgow Airport **233** F3
Glasgow Botanic
  Garden *Glas*
  *G12 0UE* **30** C3
Glasgow Prestwick
  Airport **224** B3
Glasgow Royal Concert Hall
  *Glas* **G2 3NY** **39** F3
Glasgow Science Centre
  *Glas* **G51 1EA** **38** A5
Glashmore **261** F4
Glasinfryn **167** E1
Glasnacardoch **256** C5
Glasnakille **256** B3
Glaspant **141** E4
Glaspwll **154** D3
Glass Studio, Eastbourne
  Pier *ESuss*
  *BN21 3EL* **110** B4
Glassburn **257** K1
Glassel **260** E5
Glassenbury **123** G5
Glasserton **207** E3
Glassford **234** B5
Glasshouse **145** G5
Glasshouses **194** A1
Glassingall **242** C4
Glasslie **244** A4
Glasson *Cumb* **218** A5
Glasson *Lancs* **192** A2
Glasson Dock **192** A2
Glassonby **210** B4
Glasterlaw **253** D4
Glaston **161** D2
Glastonbury **116** B4
Glastonbury Abbey *Som*
  *BA6 9EL* **116** C4
Glatton **161** G4
Glazebrook **184** A3
Glazebury **184** A3
Glazeley **157** G4
Gleadless **186** A4
Gleadsmoss **171** F1
Gleann Tholastaidh **271** H3
Gleaston **199** D5
Glecknabae **232** B3
Gledhow **194** C4
Gledrid **169** F4
Glemsford **151** G3
Glen *D&G* **216** C3
Glen *D&G* **215** G3
Glen Auldyn **190** C2
Glen Mona **190** C3
Glen Parva **160** A2
Glen Trool Lodge **215** F2
Glen Village **234** C2
Glen Vine **190** B4
Glenae **217** D2
Glenald **241** F4
Glenaladale **248** A2
Glenamachrie **240** B2
Glenapp Castle **214** B2
Glenarm **252** B3
Glenbarr **222** B2
Glenbatrick **230** D2
Glenbeg *High* **247** E4
Glenbeg *High* **259** H2
Glenbeg *High* **247** E3
Glenbeich **242** B2
Glenbervie *Aber* **253** F1
Glenbervie *Falk* **234** C1
Glenboig **234** B3
Glenborrodale **247** F3
Glenbranter **240** D5
Glenbreck **226** B3
Glenbrittle **255** K2
Glenburn **233** F3
Glenbyre **239** E2
Glencaple **217** D4
Glencarse **243** G2
Glencat **260** D5
Glenceitlein **248** D5
Glencloy **223** F2
Glencoe
  (A' Chàrnaich) **248** D4
Glencoe Visitor Centre
  *High* **PH49 4LA** **248** D4
Glenconglass **259** J2
Glencraig **243** G5
Glencripesdale **247** F4
Glencrosh **216** B2
Glencruitten **240** A2
Glencuie **260** D3
Glendearg *D&G* **226** D5
Glendearg *ScBord* **227** G2
Glendessary **257** F5
Glendevon **243** E4
Glendoebeg **258** B4

Glendoick **244** A2
Glendoll Lodge **252** A2
Glendoune **214** C1
Glendrissaig **214** C1
Glenduckie **244** A3
Glendusk **214** D2
Glendye Lodge **253** E1
Gleneagles Hotel **243** E4
Gleneagles House **243** E4
Glenearn **243** G3
Glenegedale **230** B4
Glenelg
  (Gleann Eilg) **256** E3
Glenfarg **243** G3
Glenfeochan **240** A2
Glenfield **160** A2
Glenfinnan (Gleann
  Fhionnainn) **248** B1
Glenfoot **243** G3
Glengalmadale **248** A4
Glengap **216** A5
Glengarnock **233** E4
Glengarrisdale **239** F5
Glengennet **215** D2
Glengolly **275** G2
Glengorm Castle **246** D4
Glengrasco **263** K7
Glenhead **216** B4
Glenhead Farm **252** A3
Glenhurich **248** A3
Glenkerry **227** D4
Glenkin **232** C1
Glenkindie **260** C3
Glenlair **216** B3
Glenlatterach **267** K6
Glenlean **232** B1
Glenlee *Angus* **252** C2
Glenlee *D&G* **216** A2
Glenlichorn **242** C3
Glenlivet **259** J2
Glenlochar **216** B4
Glenluce **214** C5
Glenmallan **241** E5
Glenmanna **225** F5
Glenmavis **234** B3
Glenmaye **190** A4
Glenmeanie **266** J6
Glenmore *A&B* **232** B3
Glenmore *High* **265** K7
Glenmore *High* **259** G4
Glenmore Forest Park
  Visitor Centre *High*
  *PH22 1QY* **259** G3
Glenmore Lodge **259** G3
Glenmoy **252** C3
Glenmuick **273** F7
Glennoe **240** C1
Glenochar **226** A4
Glenogil **252** C3
Glenprosen
  Village **252** B3
Glenquiech **252** C3
Glenramskill **222** C4
Glenrazie **215** E4
Glenridding **209** G5
Glenrisdell **231** G4
Glenrossal **266** B1
Glenrothes **244** A4
Glensanda **248** A5
Glensaugh **253** E2
Glensgaich **266** B5
Glenshalg **260** D4
Glenshellish **240** D5
Glensluain **240** C5
Glentaggart **225** G3
Glentham **188** A3
Glenton **260** E2
Glentress **226** C2
Glentress Forest *ScBord*
  *EH45 8NB* **235** G5
Glentrool **215** E3
Glentruan **190** C1
Glentworth **187** G4
Glenuachdarach **263** K6
Glenuig **247** F2
Glenure **248** C5
Glenurquhart **266** E5
Glenwhilly **214** C3
Glespin **225** G3
Gletness **279** D7
Glewstone **145** E5
Glinton **161** G2
Glogue **141** F4
Glooston **160** C3
Glororum **229** F3
Glossop **185** E3
Gloster Hill **221** E1
Gloucester **132** A1
Gloucester Cathedral
  *Glos* **GL1 2LR**
  **73** Gloucester
Gloucester Historic
  Docks *Glos* **GL1 2ER**
  **73** Gloucester
Gloucestershire
  Airport **146** A5
Gloucestershire &
  Warwickshire Railway
  *Glos* **GL54 5DT** **146** B5
Gloup **278** E2
Gloweth **96** B5
Glusburn **193** G3
Glympton **147** G5
Glyn **168** A2
Glyn Ceiriog **169** F4
Glynarthen **141** G3
Glyncoch **129** G3
Glyncorrwg **129** E2
Glynde **109** G3
Glyndebourne **109** G3
Glyndyfrdwy **169** E3
Glynneath
  (Glyn-Nedd) **129** E2
Glynogwr **129** F4
Glyntaff **129** G3
Gnosall **171** F5
Gnosall Heath **171** F5
Go Bananas, Colchester
  *Essex* **CO1 1BX** **152** A5
Goadby **160** C3
Goadby Marwood **174** C5
Goatacre **132** C5
Goatfield **240** C4
Goathill **104** C1

Goathland **204** B2
Goathurst **115** F4
Gobernuisgeach **274** E5
Gobhaig **270** C7
Gobowen **170** A4
Godalming **121** E3
Goddard's Corner **153** D1
Goddards Green **109** E1
Godden Green **123** E3
Goddington **123** D2
Godford Cross **103** E2
Godington **148** B3
Godleybrook **171** G3
Godmanchester **162** A5
Godmanstone **104** C3
Godmersham **124** C3
Godney **116** B3
Godolphin Cross **94** D3
Godor **130** D1
Godre'r-graig **129** D2
Godshill *Hants* **106** A1
Godshill *IoW* **107** E4
Godstone **122** C3
*Godstone Farm Surr*
  *RH9 8LX* **122** C3
Godwick **178** A3
Goetre **130** C2
Goff's Oak **136** C2
Gogar **235** F2
Gogarth **181** F4
Goginan **154** C4
Goirtean a'
  Chladaich **248** C2
Goirtein **232** A1
Golan **167** E3
Golant **97** F4
Golberdon **98** D3
Golborne **184** A3
Golcar **185** F1
Gold Hill *Cambs* **162** D3
Gold Hill *Dorset* **105** E1
Goldcliff **130** C4
*Golden Acre Park*
  *WYorks*
  *LS16 8BQ* **194** B3
Golden Cross **110** A2
Golden Green **123** F4
Golden Grove **128** B1
Golden Pot **120** C3
Golden Valley
  *Derbys* **173** F2
Golden Valley *Glos* **146** B5
Goldenhill **171** F2
Golders Green **136** B4
Goldhanger **138** C2
Goldielea **216** D3
Golding **157** E2
Goldington **149** F2
Goldsborough
  *NYorks* **204** B1
Goldsborough
  *NYorks* **194** C2
Goldsithney **94** C3
Goldstone **171** E5
Goldthorn Park **158** B3
Goldthorpe **186** B2
Goldworthy **113** D3
*Goleulong 2000 Lightship,*
  *Cardiff Cardiff*
  *CF10 4PA* **7** C4
Golford **123** G5
Gollanfield **267** F6
Gollinglith Foot **202** A4
Golspie **267** F2
Golval **274** D2
Gomeldon **118** C4
Gomersal **194** B5
Gometra **246** C5
Gometra House **246** C5
Gomshall **121** F3
Gonachan Cottage **234** A1
Gonalston **174** B3
Gonerby Hill Foot **175** E4
Gonfirth **279** C6
Good Easter **137** F1
Gooderstone **163** F2
Goodleigh **113** G2
Goodmanham **196** A3
Goodmayes **137** D4
Goodnestone *Kent* **125** F3
Goodnestone *Kent* **124** C2
Goodrich **131** E1
Goodrington **101** E2
Goodshaw **193** E5
Goodshaw Fold **193** E5
Goodwick (Wdig) **140** C4
Goodworth Clatford **119** E3
Goodyers End **159** F4
Goole **195** G5
Goom's Hill **146** C2
Goonbell **96** B4
Goonhavern **96** B4
Goonvrea **96** B5
Goose Green
  *GtMan* **183** G2
Goose Green *Kent* **123** F3
Goose Green *SGlos* **131** F5
Goose Pool **145** D4
Gooseham **112** C4
Goosehill Green **146** B1
Goosewell **100** B2
Goosey **133** F3
Goosnargh **192** B4
Goostrey **184** B5
Gorcott Hill **146** C1
Gordding **181** D4
Gordon **236** D5
Gordonbush **267** F1
Gordonstoun **267** J5
Gordonstown *Aber* **268** D5
Gordonstown *Aber* **261** F1
Gore Cross **118** B2
Gore End **119** F1
Gore Pit **138** B1
Gore Street **125** E2
Gorebridge **236** A3
Gorefield **162** C1
Gorey **100** D5
Gorgie **235** G2
*Gorgie City Farm Edin*
  *EH11 2LA* **36** B7
Goring **134** B4
Goring Heath **134** B5
Goring-by-Sea **108** D3
Gorleston-on-Sea **179** G5
Gorllwyn **141** G4

Gornalwood 158 B3
Gorrachie 269 F5
Gorran Churchtown 97 D5
Gorran Haven 97 E5
Gors 154 C5
Gorsedd 182 C5
Gorseinon 128 B3
Gorseness 277 D6
Gorseybank 173 D2
Gorsgoch 142 A2
Gorslas 128 B1
Gorsley 145 F5
Gorsley Common 145 F5
Gorstage 184 A5
Gorstan 265 K5
Gorstanvorran 248 A2
Gorsty Hill 172 C5
Gorten 239 G1
Gortenbuie 239 E1
Gorteneorn 247 F3
Gorton A&B 246 A4
Gorton GtMan 184 C3
Gosbeck 152 C2
Gosberton 176 A4
Gosberton Clough 175 G5
Goseley Dale 173 E5
Gosfield 151 F5
Gosford Here 145 E1
Gosford Oxon 134 A1
Gosforth Cumb 198 B2
Gosforth T&W 212 B1
Gosland Green 170 C2
Gosmore 149 G5
Gospel End 158 A3
Gosport 107 F3
Gossabrough 278 E4
Gossington 131 G2
Gossops Green 122 B5
Goswick 229 E2
Gotham 173 G4
Gotherington 146 B5
Gothers 97 D4
Gott 279 D8
Gotton 115 F5
Goudhurst 123 G5
Goulceby 188 C5
Gourdas 269 F6
Gourdon 253 G2
Gourock 232 D2
Govan 233 G3
Goverton 174 C2
Goveton 101 D3
Govilon 130 B1
Gowanhill 269 J4
Gowdall 195 F5
Gowerton 128 B3
Gowkhall 235 E1
Gowkthrapple 234 B4
Gowthorpe 195 G2
Goxhill ERid 197 D3
Goxhill NLincs 196 D5
Goytre 129 D4
Gozzard's Ford 133 G3
Grabhair 271 F6
Graby 175 F5
Gradbach 171 G1
Grade 95 E5
Gradeley Green 170 C2
Graffham 108 B2
Grafham Cambs 149 G1
Grafham Surr 121 F3
Grafham Water Cambs PE28 0BH 149 G1
Grafton Here 145 D4
Grafton NYorks 194 D1
Grafton Oxon 133 E2
Grafton Shrop 156 D1
Grafton Worcs 145 E1
Grafton Worcs 146 B4
Grafton Flyford 146 B2
Grafton Regis 148 C3
Grafton Underwood 161 E4
Grafty Green 124 A4
Graianrhyd 169 F2
Graig Carmar 128 A2
Graig Conwy 181 G5
Graig Denb 182 B5
Graig-fechan 169 E2
Grain 124 A1
Grainel 230 A3
Grainhow 269 G6
Grains Bar 185 D2
Grainsby 188 C3
Grainthorpe 189 D3
Graizelound 187 E3
Gramisdale (Gramsdal) 262 D6
Grampound 96 D5
Grampound Road 96 D4
Granborough 148 C5
Granby 174 C4
Grand Pier, Teignmouth Devon TQ14 8BB 102 C5
Grandborough 147 G1
Grandes Rocques 101 F4
Grandtully 251 E4
Grange Cumb 209 F5
Grange EAyr 224 C2
Grange High 257 K1
Grange Med 123 G2
Grange Mersey 182 D4
Grange P&K 244 A2
Grange Crossroads 268 C5
Grange de Lings 187 G5
Grange Hall 267 H5
Grange Hill 136 D3
Grange Moor 185 G1
Grange of Lindores 244 A3
Grange Villa 212 B2
Grangemill 172 D2
Grangemouth 234 D1
Grangemuir 244 D4
Grange-over-Sands 199 F5
Grangeston 214 D1
Grangetown Cardiff 130 A5
Grangetown R&C 213 E5
Granish 259 G3
Gransmoor 196 D2
Granston 140 B4
Grantchester 150 C2
Grantham 175 E4
Grantley 202 B5
Grantlodge 261 F3
Granton 235 G2
Granton House 226 B5
Grantown-on-Spey 259 H2
Grantsfield 145 E1
Grantshouse 237 F3
Grappenhall 184 A4
Grasby 188 A2
Grasmere 199 E2
Grass Green 151 F4
Grasscroft 185 D2
Grassendale 183 E4
Grassgarth 199 F3
Grassholme 211 F5
Grassington 193 G1
Grassmoor 173 F1
Grassthorpe 174 C1
Grateley 119 D3
Gratwich 172 B4
Gravel Hill 135 F3
Graveley Cambs 150 A1
Graveley Herts 150 A5
Gravelly Hill 158 D3
Gravels 156 C2
Graven 278 D5
Graveney 124 C2
Gravesend 137 F5
Grayingham 187 G3
Grayrigg 199 G3
Grays 137 F5
Grayshott 121 D4
Grayswood 121 E4
Grazeley 120 B1
Greasbrough 186 B3
Greasby 183 D4
Great Aberystwyth Camera Obscura Cere SY23 2DN 154 B4
Great Abington 150 D3
Great Addington 161 E5
Great Alne 146 D2
Great Altcar 183 E2
Great Amwell 136 C1
Great Asby 200 B1
Great Ashfield 152 A1
Great Ayton 203 E1
Great Baddow 137 G2
Great Bardfield 151 E4
Great Barford 149 G2
Great Barr 158 C3
Great Barrington 133 E1
Great Barrow 170 B1
Great Barton 151 G1
Great Barugh 203 G5
Great Bavington 220 B3
Great Bealings 152 D3
Great Bedwyn 119 D1
Great Bentley 152 C5
Great Bernera 270 D4
Great Billing 148 D1
Great Bircham 177 F4
Great Blakenham 152 C2
Great Bolas 170 D5
Great Bookham 121 G2
Great Bourton 147 G3
Great Bowden 160 C4
Great Bradley 151 E2
Great Braxted 138 B1
Great Bricett 152 B2
Great Brickhill 149 E4
Great Bridgeford 171 F5
Great Brington 148 B1
Great Bromley 152 B5
Great Broughton Cumb 209 D3
Great Broughton NYorks 203 E2
Great Buckland 123 F2
Great Budworth 184 A5
Great Burdon 202 C1
Great Burstead 137 F3
Great Busby 203 E2
Great Cambourne 150 B2
Great Canfield 137 E1
Great Canney 138 B2
Great Carlton 189 E4
Great Casterton 161 F2
Great Chalfield 117 F1
Great Chart 124 B4
Great Chatwell 157 G1
Great Chell 171 F2
Great Chesterford 150 D3
Great Cheverell 118 A2
Great Chishill 150 C4
Great Clacton 139 E1
Great Clifton 208 D4
Great Coates 188 C2
Great Comberton 146 B3
Great Corby 210 A2
Great Cornard 151 G3
Great Cowden 197 E3
Great Coxwell 133 E3
Great Crakehall 202 B4
Great Cransley 160 D5
Great Cressingham 163 G2
Great Crosby 183 E2
Great Crosthwaite 209 F4
Great Cubley 172 C4
Great Cumbrae 232 C4
Great Dalby 160 C1
Great Doddington 149 D1
Great Doward 131 E1
Great Dunham 163 G1
Great Dunmow 151 E5
Great Durnford 118 C4
Great Easton Essex 151 E5
Great Easton Leics 160 D3
Great Eccleston 192 A3
Great Edstone 203 G4
Great Ellingham 164 B2
Great Elm 117 E3
Great Eversden 150 B2
Great Fencote 202 B3
Great Finborough 152 B2
Great Fransham 163 G1
Great Gaddesden 135 F1
Great Gidding 161 G4
Great Givendale 196 A2
Great Glemham 153 E1
Great Glen 160 B3
Great Gonerby 175 D4
Great Gransden 150 A2
Great Green Cambs 150 A3
Great Green Norf 165 D3
Great Green Suff 152 A2
Great Green Suff 164 C4
Great Green Suff 164 B4
Great Habton 203 G5
Great Hale 175 G3
Great Hall Hants SO23 8UJ 89 Winchester
Great Hallingbury 137 E1
Great Hampden 134 D2
Great Harrowden 161 D5
Great Harwood 192 D4
Great Haseley 134 B2
Great Hatfield 197 D3
Great Haywood 172 B5
Great Heath 159 F4
Great Heck 195 E5
Great Henny 151 G4
Great Hinton 118 A2
Great Hockham 164 A2
Great Holland 139 F1
Great Horkesley 152 A4
Great Hormead 150 C4
Great Horton 194 A4
Great Horwood 148 C4
Great Houghton N'hants 148 C2
Great Houghton SYorks 186 B2
Great Hucklow 185 F5
Great Kelk 196 D2
Great Kimble 134 D2
Great Kingshill 135 D3
Great Langton 202 B3
Great Leighs 137 G1
Great Limber 188 B2
Great Linford 148 D3
Great Livermere 163 G5
Great Longstone 185 G5
Great Lumley 212 B3
Great Lyth 157 D2
Great Malvern 145 G3
Great Maplestead 151 G4
Great Marton 191 G4
Great Massingham 177 F5
Great Melton 178 C5
Great Milton 134 B2
Great Missenden 135 D2
Great Mitton 192 D4
Great Mongeham 125 F3
Great Moulton 164 C2
Great Munden 150 B5
Great Musgrave 200 C1
Great Ness 156 D1
Great Notley 151 F5
Great Nurcot 114 C4
Great Oak 130 C2
Great Oakley Essex 152 C5
Great Oakley N'hants 161 D4
Great Offley 149 G5
Great Orme Tramway Conwy LL30 2HG 181 F4
Great Ormside 200 C1
Great Orton 209 G1
Great Ouseburn 194 D1
Great Oxendon 160 C4
Great Oxney Green 137 F2
Great Palgrave 163 G1
Great Parndon 136 D2
Great Paxton 150 A1
Great Plumpton 191 G4
Great Plumstead 179 E5
Great Ponton 175 E4
Great Potheridge 113 F4
Great Preston 194 C5
Great Purston 148 A4
Great Raveley 162 A4
Great Rissington 133 D1
Great Rollright 147 F4
Great Ryburgh 178 A3
Great Ryle 229 E5
Great Ryton 157 D2
Great St. Mary's Church Cambs CB2 3PQ 66 Cambridge
Great Saling 151 F5
Great Salkeld 210 B4
Great Sampford 151 E4
Great Sankey 183 G4
Great Saredon 158 B2
Great Saxham 151 F1
Great Shefford 133 F5
Great Shelford 150 C2
Great Smeaton 202 C2
Great Snoring 178 A2
Great Somerford 132 B4
Great Stainton 212 C5
Great Stambridge 138 C3
Great Staughton 149 G1
Great Steeping 176 C1
Great Stonar 125 F3
Great Strickland 210 B5
Great Stukeley 162 A5
Great Sturton 188 C5
Great Sutton ChesW&C 183 E5
Great Sutton Shrop 157 E4
Great Swinburne 220 B4
Great Tew 147 F5
Great Tey 151 G5
Great Thorness 107 D3
Great Thurlow 151 E3
Great Torr 100 C3
Great Torrington 113 E4
Great Tosson 220 C1
Great Totham Essex 138 B1
Great Totham Essex 138 B1
Great Tows 188 C3
Great Urswick 199 D5
Great Wakering 138 C4
Great Waldingfield 152 A3
Great Walsingham 178 A2
Great Waltham 137 F1
Great Warley 137 E3
Great Washbourne 146 B4
Great Weeke 102 A4
Great Welnetham 151 G2
Great Wenham 152 B4
Great Whittington 220 C4
Great Wigborough 138 C1
Great Wigsell 110 C1
Great Wilbraham 150 D2
Great Wilne 173 F4
Great Wishford 118 B4
Great Witcombe 132 B1
Great Witley 145 G1
Great Wolford 147 E4
Great Wratting 151 E3
Great Wymondley 150 A5
Great Wyrley 158 B2
Great Wytheford 157 E1
Great Yarmouth 179 G5
Great Yeldham 151 F4
Greatford 161 F1
Greatgate 172 B3
Greatham Hants 120 C4
Greatham Hart 213 D5
Greatham WSuss 108 C2
Greatness 123 E3
Greatstone-on-Sea 111 F1
Greatworth 148 A3
Green 169 D1
Green Cross 121 D4
Green End Bed 149 G2
Green End Bucks 149 E4
Green End Cambs 162 A5
Green End Cambs 162 B5
Green End Herts 150 B5
Green End Herts 150 B4
Green End Warks 159 E4
Green Hammerton 195 D2
Green Hill 132 C4
Green Lane 146 C1
Green Moor 185 G3
Green Ore 116 C2
Green Quarter 199 F2
Green Street ESuss 110 C2
Green Street Herts 136 A3
Green Street Herts 150 C5
Green Street Worcs 146 A3
Green Street WSuss 121 G5
Green Street Green GtLon 123 D2
Green Street Green Kent 137 E5
Green Tye 136 D1
Greenburn 252 C5
Greencroft 212 A3
Greendams 253 E1
Greendykes 229 E4
Greenend 147 F5
Greenfaulds 234 B2
Greenfield CenBeds 149 F4
Greenfield (Maes-Glas) Flints 182 C5
Greenfield GtMan 185 E2
Greenfield High 257 J4
Greenfield Lincs 189 E5
Greenfield Oxon 134 C3
Greenford 136 A4
Greengairs 234 B2
Greengates 194 A4
Greengill 209 E3
Greenhalgh 192 A4
Greenhall 260 E2
Greenham 119 F1
Greenhaugh 219 F3
Greenhead 210 C1
Greenheads 261 J1
Greenheys 184 B2
Greenhill GtLon 136 A4
Greenhill High 267 G1
Greenhill SYorks 186 A4
Greenhithe 137 E5
Greenholm 224 D2
Greenholme 199 G2
Greenhow Hill 194 A1
Greenigo 277 D7
Greenland 275 H2
Greenlands 134 C4
Greenlaw Aber 268 E5
Greenlaw ScBord 237 E5
Greenloaning 242 D4
Greenmeadow 130 B3
Greenmoor Hill 134 B4
Greenmount 184 B1
Greenmyre 261 G1
Greenock 233 D2
Greenodd 199 E4
Greens Norton 148 B3
Greenscares 242 C3
Greenside T&W 212 A1
Greenside WYorks 185 F1
Greenstead 152 B5
Greenstead Green 151 G5
Greensted 137 E2
Greensted Green 137 E2
Greenway Pembs 141 D4
Greenway Som 116 A5
Greenwell 210 B2
Greenwich 136 C5
Greenwood Forest Park, Y Felinheli Gwyn LL56 4QN 167 E1
Greet 146 C4
Greete 157 E5
Greetham Lincs 188 D5
Greetham Rut 161 E1
Greetland 193 G5
Gregson Lane 192 B5
Greinton 116 B4
Grenaby 190 A4
Grendon N'hants 149 D1
Grendon Warks 159 E3
Grendon Common 159 E3
Grendon Green 145 E2
Grendon Underwood 148 B5
Grenitote (Greinetobht) 262 D4
Grenofen 99 E3
Grenoside 186 A3
Greosabhagh 263 G2
Gresford 170 A2
Gresham 178 C2
Greshornish 263 J6
Gress (Griais) 271 G3
Gressenhall 178 A4
Gressingham 192 B1
Greta Bridge 201 F1
Gretna 218 B5
Gretna Green 218 B5
Gretton Glos 146 C4
Gretton N'hants 161 E3
Gretton Shrop 157 E3
Grewelthorpe 202 B5
Greygarth 202 A5
Greylake 116 A4
Greys Green 134 C4
Greysouthen 209 D4
Greystead 219 F3
Greystoke 210 A4
Greystone Aber 259 K5
Greystone Angus 252 D5
Greystone Lancs 193 E3
Greystones 186 A4
Greywell 120 C2
Gribthorpe 195 G4
Gribton 216 D2
Griff 159 F4
Griffithstown 130 B3
Grigadale 246 D3
Grigghall 199 F3
Grimeford Village 184 A1
Grimesthorpe 186 A3
Grimethorpe 186 B2
Griminish (Griminis) 262 C6
Grimister 278 D3
Grimley 146 A1
Grimmet 224 B4
Grimness 277 D8
Grimoldby 189 D4
Grimpo 170 A5
Grimsargh 192 B4
Grimsay (Griomsaigh) 262 D6
Grimsbury 147 G3
Grimsby 188 C2
Grimscote 148 B2
Grimscott 112 C5
Grimshader (Griomsiadar) 271 G5
Grimsthorpe 175 F5
Grimston ERid 197 E4
Grimston Leics 174 B5
Grimston Norf 177 F5
Grimstone 104 C3
Grimstone End 152 A1
Grindale 205 E5
Grindiscol 279 D9
Grindle 157 G2
Grindleford 185 G5
Grindleton 193 D3
Grindley 172 B5
Grindley Brook 170 C3
Grindlow 185 F5
Grindon N'umb 237 G5
Grindon Staffs 172 B2
Grindon Stock 212 C5
Grindon T&W 212 C2
Gringley on the Hill 187 E3
Grinsdale 209 G1
Grinshill 170 C5
Grinton 201 F3
Griomarstaidh 270 E4
Grisdale 200 C3
Grishipoll 246 A4
Gristhorpe 205 D4
Griston 164 A2
Gritley 277 E7
Grittenham 132 C4
Grittleton 132 A5
Grizebeck 198 D4
Grizedale 199 E3
Grizedale Forest Park Cumb LA22 0QJ 199 E3
Grobister 276 F5
Groby 160 A2
Groes 168 D1
Groes-faen 129 G4
Groesffordd 166 B4
Groesffordd Marli 182 B5
Groeslon Gwyn 167 D2
Groeslon Gwyn 167 E1
Groes-lwyd 156 B1
Groes-wen 130 A4
Grogport 231 G5
Groigearraidh 254 C1
Gromford 153 E2
Gronant 182 B4
Groombridge 123 E5
Groombridge Place Gardens Kent TN3 9QG 123 E5
Grosmont Mon 144 D5
Grosmont NYorks 204 B2
Grotaig 258 B2
Groton 152 A3
Groundistone Heights 227 F4
Grouville 100 C5
Grove Bucks 149 E5
Grove Dorset 104 C5
Grove Kent 125 E2
Grove Notts 187 E5
Grove Oxon 133 G3
Grove End 124 A2
Grove Green 123 G3
Grove Park 136 D5
Grove Town 195 D5
Grovehill 135 F2
Grovesend SGlos 131 F4
Grovesend Swan 128 B2
Gruids 266 C1
Grula 255 J2
Gruline 247 E5
Grumbla 94 B4
Grundcruie 243 F2
Grundisburgh 152 D2
Gruting 279 B8
Grutness 279 G10
Gualachulain 248 D5
Guardbridge 244 C3
Guarlford 146 A3
Guay 251 F5
Gubbergill 198 B3
Gubblecote 135 E1
Guernsey 101 F5
Guernsey Airport 101 E5
Guestling Green 111 D2
Guestling Thorn 111 D2
Guestwick 178 B3
Guestwick Green 178 B3
Guide 192 D5
Guide Post 221 E3
Guilden Down 156 C4
Guilden Morden 150 A3
Guilden Sutton 170 B1
Guildford 121 E3
Guildford House Gallery Surr GU1 3AJ 74 Guildford
Guildtown 243 G1
Guilsborough 160 B5
Guilsfield (Cegidfa) 156 B1
Guilthwaite 186 B4
Guisborough 203 F1
Guiseley 194 A3
Guist 178 B3
Guith 276 E4
Guiting Power 146 C5
Gulberwick 279 D9
Gullane 236 B1
Gullane Bents ELoth EH31 2AZ 236 B1
Gulval 94 B3
Gulworthy 99 E3
Gumfreston 127 E2
Gumley 160 B3
Gunby Lincs 175 E5
Gunby Lincs 176 C1
Gundleton 120 B4
Gunn 113 G2
Gunnersbury 136 A5
Gunnerside 201 E3
Gunnerton 220 B4
Gunness 187 F1
Gunnislake 99 E3
Gunnista 279 E8
Gunnister 278 C5
Gunstone 158 A2
Gunter's Bridge 121 E5
Gunthorpe Norf 178 B2
Gunthorpe Notts 174 B3
Gunthorpe Rut 161 D2
Gunville 107 D4
Gunwalloe 95 D4
Gupworthy 114 C4
Gurnard 107 D3
Gurnett 184 D5
Gurney Slade 116 D3
Gurnos MTyd 129 G2
Gurnos Powys 129 D2
Gushmere 124 C3
Gussage All Saints 105 G1
Gussage St. Andrew 105 F1
Gussage St. Michael 105 F1
Guston 125 F4
Gutcher 278 E3
Guthram Gowt 175 G5
Guthrie 253 D4
Guyhirn 162 B2
Guynd 253 D5
Guy's Head 176 C5
Guy's Marsh 117 F5
Guyzance 221 E1
Gwaelod-y-garth 130 A4
Gwaenysgor 182 B4
Gwaithla 144 B2
Gwalchmai 180 B5
Gwastad 140 D5
Gwastadnant 167 F2
Gwaun-Cae-Gurwen 128 D1
Gwaynynog 168 D1
Gwbert 141 E3
Gweek 95 E4
Gwehelog 130 C2
Gwenddwr 143 G3
Gwendreath 95 E5
Gwennap 96 B5
Gwenter 95 E5
Gwernaffield 169 F1
Gwernesney 130 D2
Gwernogle 142 B4
Gwernymynydd 169 F1
Gwern-y-Steeple 129 G5
Gwersyllt 170 A2
Gwespyr 182 C4
Gwinear 94 C3
Gwithian 94 C2
Gwredog 180 C4
Gwrhay 130 A3
Gwyddelwern 169 D3
Gwyddgrug 142 A4
Gwynfryn 169 F2
Gwystre 143 G1
Gwytherin 168 B1
Gyfelia 170 A3
Gyre 277 C7
Gyrn Goch 166 D3

## H

H.M.S. Belfast GtLon SE1 2JH 12 C4
H.M.S. Victory PO1 3PX 82 Portsmouth
H.M.S. Warrior PO1 3QX 82 Portsmouth
Habberley 156 C2
Habin 120 D5
Habrough 188 B1
Haccombe 102 B5
Hacconby 175 G5
Haceby 175 F4
Hacheston 153 E2
Hackbridge 122 B2
Hackenthorpe 186 B4
Hackford 178 B5
Hackforth 202 B3
Hackland 276 C5
Hacklet (Haclait) 262 D7
Hacklete (Tacleit) 270 D4
Hackleton 148 D2
Hacklinge 125 F3
Hackness NYorks 204 C3
Hackness Ork 277 C8
Hackney 136 C4
Hackthorn 187 G4
Hackthorpe 210 B5
Hacton 137 E4
Hadden 228 B3
Haddenham Bucks 134 C2
Haddenham Cambs 162 C5
Haddington ELoth 236 C2
Haddington Lincs 175 E1
Haddiscoe 165 F2
Haddo Country Park Aber AB41 7EQ 261 G1
Haddon 161 G3
Hade Edge 185 F2
Hademore 159 D2
Hadfield 185 E3
Hadham Cross 136 D1
Hadham Ford 150 C5
Hadleigh Essex 138 B4
Hadleigh Suff 152 B3
Hadleigh Castle Country Park Essex SS7 2PP 138 B4
Hadleigh Heath 152 A3
Hadley Tel&W 157 F1
Hadley Worcs 146 A1
Hadley End 172 C5
Hadley Wood 136 B3
Hadlow 123 F4
Hadlow Down 110 A1
Hadnall 170 C5
Hadspen 117 D4
Hadstock 151 D3
Hadston 221 E2
Hadzor 146 B1
Haffenden Quarter 124 A4
Hafod Bridge 142 C4
Hafod-Dinbych 168 B2
Hafodunos 168 B1
Hafodyrynys 130 B3
Haggate 193 E4
Haggbeck 218 C4
Haggersta 279 C8
Haggerston GtLon 136 C4
Haggerston N'umb 229 E2
Haggrister 278 C5
Haggs 234 B2
Hagley Here 145 E3
Hagley Worcs 158 B4
Hagnaby Lincs 176 B1
Hagnaby Lincs 189 E5
Hague Bar 185 D4
Hagworthingham 176 B1
Haigh 184 A2
Haigh Hall Country Park GtMan WN2 1PE 183 G2
Haighton Green 192 B4
Hail Weston 149 G1
Haile 198 B2
Hailes 146 C4
Hailey Herts 136 C1
Hailey Oxon 134 B4
Hailey Oxon 133 F1
Hailsham 110 A3
Haimer 275 G2
Hainault 137 D3
Hainault Forest Country Park Essex IG7 4QN 137 D3
Haine 125 F2
Hainford 178 D4
Hainton 188 B4
Haisthorpe 196 D1
Hakin 126 B2
Halam 174 B2
Halbeath 235 F1
Halberton 102 D1
Halcro 275 H2
Hale Cumb 199 G5
Hale GtMan 184 B4
Hale Halton 183 F4
Hale Hants 106 A1
Hale Surr 120 D3
Hale Bank 183 F4
Hale Barns 184 B4
Hale Nook 191 G3
Hale Street 123 F4
Hales Norf 165 E2
Hales Staffs 171 E4
Hales Green 172 C3
Hales Place 124 D3
Halesgate 176 B5
Halesowen 158 B4
Halesworth 165 E4
Halewood 183 F4
Half Way Inn 102 D3
Halford Devon 102 B5
Halford Shrop 156 D4
Halford Warks 147 E3
Halfpenny 199 G4
Halfpenny Green 158 A3
Halfway Carmar 142 C4
Halfway Carmar 128 B2
Halfway Powys 143 E4
Halfway SYorks 186 B4
Halfway WBerks 119 F1
Halfway Bridge 121 E5
Halfway House 156 C1
Halfway Houses Kent 124 B1
Halfway Houses Lincs 175 D1
Halghton Mill 170 B3
Halifax 193 G5
Halistra 263 H6
Halket 233 F4
Halkirk 275 G3
Halkyn 182 D5
Hall 233 F4
Hall Cross 192 A5
Hall Dunnerdale 198 D3
Hall Green ChesE 171 F2
Hall Green Lancs 192 A5
Hall Green WMid 158 D4
Hall Grove 136 B1
Hall of the Forest 156 B4
Halland 110 A2
Hallaton 160 C3
Hallatrow 116 D2
Hallbankgate 210 B2
Hallen 131 E4
Hallfield Gate 173 E2
Hallglen 234 C2
Hallin 263 H6
Halling 123 G2
Hallington Lincs 188 D4
Hallington N'umb 220 B4
Halliwell 184 A1
Halloughton 174 B2
Hallow 146 A2
Hallow Heath 146 A2
Hallrule 227 G4
Halls 237 D2
Halls Green Essex 136 D2
Hall's Green Herts 150 A5
Hallsands 101 E4
Hallthwaites 198 C4
Hallwood Green 145 F4
Hallworthy 97 F1
Hallyne 235 F5
Halmer End 171 E3
Halmond's Frome 145 F3
Halmore 131 F2
Halmyre Mains 235 F5
Halnaker 108 B3
Halsall 183 E1
Halse N'hants 148 A3
Halse Som 115 E5
Halsetown 94 C3
Halsham 197 E5
Halsinger 113 F2
Halstead Essex 151 G4
Halstead Kent 123 D2
Halstead Leics 160 C2
Halstock 104 B2
Halsway 115 E4
Haltemprice Farm 196 C4
Haltham 176 A1
Haltoft End 176 B3
Halton Bucks 135 D1
Halton Halton 183 G4

Halton Lancs 192 B1
Halton N'umb 211 F1
Halton East 193 G2
Halton Green 192 B1
Halton Lea Gate 210 C2
Halton Holegate 176 C1
Halton Park 192 B1
Halton West 193 E2
Haltwhistle 210 D1
Halvergate 179 F5
Halwell 101 D2
Halwill 99 E1
Halwill Junction 99 E1
Ham Devon 103 F2
Ham Glos 131 F3
Ham Glos 146 B5
Ham GtLon 136 A5
Ham High 275 H1
Ham Kent 125 F3
Ham Plym 100 A2
Ham Shet 278 B1
Ham Som 115 F5
Ham Som 103 F1
Ham Wilts 119 E1
Ham Common 117 F5
Ham Green Here 145 G3
Ham Green Kent 124 A2
Ham Green Kent 111 D1
Ham Green NSom 131 E5
Ham Green Worcs 146 C1
Ham Hill 123 F3
Ham Hill Country Park
 Som TA14 6RW 104 A1
Hambleden 134 C4
Hambledon Hants 107 F1
Hambledon Surr 121 E4
Hamble-le-Rice 107 E3
Hambleton Lancs 191 G3
Hambleton NYorks 195 E4
Hambridge 116 A5
Hambrook SGlos 131 F5
Hambrook WSuss 107 G2
Hameringham 176 B1
Hamerton 161 G3
Hamilton 234 B4
Hamlet Devon 103 E3
Hamlet Dorset 104 B2
Hammer 121 D4
Hammerpot 108 C3
Hammersmith 136 B5
Hammersmith Apollo
 GtLon W6 9QH 11 E5
Hammerwich 158 C2
Hammerwood 122 D5
Hammond Street 136 C2
Hamnavoe Shet 279 C9
Hamnavoe Shet 278 B4
Hamnavoe Shet 278 B4
Hamnavoe Shet 278 B5
Hamnish Clifford 145 E2
Hamp 115 F4
Hampden Park 110 B3
Hampden Park Stadium
 Glas G42 9BA 30 D4
Hamperden End 151 D4
Hampnett 132 C1
Hampole 186 C2
Hampreston 105 G3
Hampstead 136 B4
Hampstead
 Norreys 134 A5
Hampsthwaite 194 B2
Hampton Devon 103 F3
Hampton GtLon 121 G1
Hampton Kent 125 D2
Hampton Peter 161 G3
Hampton Shrop 157 G4
Hampton Swin 133 D3
Hampton Worcs 146 C3
Hampton Bishop 145 E4
Hampton Court Palace &
 Garden GtLon
 KT8 9AU 11 B8
Hampton Fields 132 A3
Hampton Heath 170 B3
Hampton in Arden 159 E4
Hampton Loade 157 G4
Hampton Lovett 146 A1
Hampton Lucy 147 E2
Hampton on the
 Hill 147 E1
Hampton Poyle 134 A1
Hampton Wick 121 G1
Hamptworth 106 B1
Hamsey 109 G2
Hamstall Ridware 158 D1
Hamstead 106 C3
Hamstead Marshall 119 F1
Hamsteels 212 A3
Hamsterley Dur 212 A4
Hamsterley Dur 212 A4
Hamsterley Forest Dur
 DL13 3NL 211 G5
Hamstreet 124 C5
Hamworthy 105 F3
Hanbury Staffs 172 C5
Hanbury Worcs 146 B1
Hanbury Woodend 172 C5
Hanby 175 F4
Hanchurch 171 F3
Handa Island 272 D4
Handale 203 G1
Handbridge 170 B1
Handcross 122 B5
Handforth 184 C4
Handley ChesW&C 170 B2
Handley Derbys 173 E1
Handley Green 137 F2
Handsacre 158 C1
Handside 136 B1
Handsworth SYorks 186 B4
Handsworth WMid 158 C3
Handwoodbank 156 D1
Handy Cross 135 D3
Hanford Dorset 105 E1
Hanford Stoke 171 F3
Hanging Bridge 172 C3
Hanging Houghton 160 C5
Hanging Langford 118 B4
Hangingshaw 217 F2
Hankelow 171 D3
Hankerton 132 B3
Hankham 110 B3

Hanley 171 F3
Hanley Castle 146 A3
Hanley Child 145 F1
Hanley Swan 146 A3
Hanley William 145 F1
Hanlith 193 F1
Hanmer 170 B4
Hannah 189 E5
Hannington
 Hants 119 G2
Hannington
 N'hants 160 D3
Hannington Swin 133 D3
Hannington Wick 133 D3
Hanslope 148 D3
Hanthorpe 175 F5
Hanwell GtLon 136 A4
Hanwell Oxon 147 G3
Hanwood 156 D2
Hanworth GtLon 136 A5
Hanworth Norf 178 C2
Happisburgh 179 F2
Happisburgh
 Common 179 E3
Hapsford 183 F5
Hapton Lancs 193 D4
Hapton Norf 164 C2
Harberton 101 D2
Harbertonford 101 D2
Harborne 158 C4
Harborough Magna 159 G5
Harbost (Tabost) 271 H1
Harbottle 220 B1
Harbour Park Amusements,
 Littlehampton WSuss
 BN17 5LL 108 C3
Harbourneford 100 D1
Harbridge 106 A1
Harbridge Green 106 A1
Harburn 235 E3
Harbury 147 F2
Harby Leics 174 C4
Harby Notts 187 F5
Harcombe 103 E3
Harcombe Bottom 103 G3
Harden WMid 158 C2
Harden WYorks 193 G4
Hardendale 199 G1
Hardenhuish 132 B5
Hardgate Aber 261 F4
Hardgate NYorks 194 B1
Hardham 108 C2
Hardhorn 191 G4
Hardingham 178 B5
Hardingstone 148 C2
Hardington 117 E2
Hardington
 Mandeville 104 B1
Hardington Marsh 104 B2
Hardington Moor 104 B1
Hardley 106 D2
Hardley Street 179 E5
Hardmead 149 E3
Hardstoft 173 F1
Hardway Hants 107 F2
Hardway Som 117 E4
Hardwick Bucks 148 D1
Hardwick Cambs 150 B2
Hardwick Lincs 187 F5
Hardwick N'hants 149 D1
Hardwick Norf 164 D2
Hardwick Oxon 133 F2
Hardwick Oxon 148 A5
Hardwick SYorks 186 B4
Hardwick WMid 158 C3
Hardwick Hall Derbys
 S44 5QJ 15 F7
Hardwick Hall Country Park,
 Sedgefield Dur
 TS21 2EH 212 C5
Hardwick Village 186 D5
Hardwicke Glos 146 B5
Hardwicke Glos 131 G1
Hardwicke Here 144 B3
Hardy's Green 152 B5
Hare Green 152 B5
Hare Hatch 134 D5
Hare Street Herts 150 B5
Hare Street Herts 150 B5
Hareby 176 B1
Harecroft 193 G4
Hareden 192 C2
Harefield 135 F3
Harehill 172 C4
Harehills 194 C4
Harehope 229 E4
Harelaw 234 D5
Hareplain 124 A4
Harescombe 132 A1
Haresfield 132 A1
Hareshaw NLan 234 C3
Hareshaw SLan 234 A5
Harestock 119 F4
Harewood 194 C3
Harewood End 145 E5
Harewood House WYorks
 LS17 9LG 194 C3
Harford Devon 100 C2
Harford Devon 102 B3
Hargate 164 C2
Hargatewall 185 F5
Hargrave ChesW&C 170 B1
Hargrave N'hants 161 F5
Hargrave Suff 151 F2
Hargrave Green 151 F2
Harker 218 B5
Harkstead 152 C4
Harlaston 159 E1
Harlaxton 175 D4
Harle Syke 193 E4
Harlech 167 E4
Harlech Castle Gwyn
 LL46 2YH 167 E4
Harlequin 174 B4
Harlescott 157 E1
Harlesden 136 B4
Harleston Devon 101 D3
Harleston Norf 164 D3
Harleston Suff 152 B1
Harlestone 148 C1
Harley Shrop 157 E2
Harley SYorks 186 A3
Harleyholm 226 A2
Harlington
 CenBeds 149 F4

Harlington GtLon 135 F5
Harlosh 263 H7
Harlow 136 D2
Harlow Hill 211 G1
Harlthorpe 195 G4
Harlton 150 B2
Harlyn 96 C2
Harman's Cross 105 F4
Harmby 202 A4
Harmer Green 136 B1
Harmer Hill 170 B5
Harmondsworth 135 F5
Harmston 175 E1
Harnage 157 E2
Harnham 118 C5
Harnhill 132 C2
Harold Hill 137 E3
Harold Park 137 E3
Harold Wood 137 E3
Haroldswick 278 F1
Harome 203 F4
Harpenden 136 A1
Harpford 103 D3
Harpham 196 C2
Harpley Norf 177 F5
Harpley Worcs 145 F1
Harpole 148 B1
Harprigg 200 B4
Harpsdale 275 G3
Harpsden 134 C4
Harpswell 187 G4
Harpur Hill 185 E5
Harpurhey 184 C2
Harracott 113 F3
Harrapool 256 C2
Harrietfield 243 E2
Harrietsham 124 A3
Harringay 136 C4
Harrington Cumb 208 C4
Harrington Lincs 189 D5
Harrington N'hants 160 C5
Harringworth 161 E3
Harris 255 J5
Harris Green 164 D2
Harris Museum & Art
 Gallery, Preston Lancs
 PR1 2PP 192 B5
Harriseahead 171 F2
Harriston 209 E2
Harrogate 194 C2
Harrogate International
 Centre NYorks HG1 5LA
 74 Harrogate
Harrold 149 E2
Harrold-Odell Country Park
 Bed MK43 7DS 149 E2
Harrop Fold 192 D3
Harrow GtLon 136 A4
Harrow High 275 H1
Harrow Green 151 G2
Harrow Museum GtLon
 HA2 6PX 10 A1
Harrow on the Hill 136 A4
Harrow Weald 136 A3
Harrowbarrow 99 E3
Harrowden 149 F3
Harrowgate Hill 202 B1
Harry Stoke 131 F5
Harston Cambs 150 C2
Harston Leics 174 D4
Harswell 196 A3
Hart 213 D4
Hartburn 220 C3
Hartest 151 G2
Hartfield ESuss 123 D5
Hartfield High 264 D7
Hartford Cambs 162 A5
Hartford
 ChesW&C 184 A5
Hartford Som 114 C5
Hartford End 137 F1
Hartfordbridge 120 C2
Hartforth 202 A2
Hartgrove 105 E1
Harthill ChesW&C 170 C2
Harthill NLan 234 D3
Harthill SYorks 186 B4
Hartington 172 C1
Hartington Hall 220 C3
Hartland 112 C3
Hartland Quay 112 C3
Hartlebury 158 A5
Hartlepool 213 E4
Hartlepool's Maritime
 Experience Hart
 TS24 0XZ 213 E4
Hartley Cumb 200 C2
Hartley Kent 123 F2
Hartley Kent 123 G5
Hartley N'umb 221 F4
Hartley Green 171 G5
Hartley Mauditt 120 C4
Hartley Wespall 120 B2
Hartley Wintney 120 C2
Hartlington 193 G1
Hartlip 124 A2
Hartoft End 203 G3
Harton NYorks 195 G1
Harton Shrop 157 D4
Harton T&W 212 C1
Hartpury 146 A5
Hartrigge 228 A4
Hartshead 194 A5
Hartshill 159 F3
Hartshorne 173 E5
Hartsop 199 F1
Hartwell Bucks 134 C1
Hartwell ESuss 123 D5
Hartwell N'hants 148 C2
Hartwith 194 B1
Hartwood 234 C4
Harvel 123 F2
Harvington Worcs 146 C3
Harvington Worcs 158 A5
Harwell Notts 187 D3
Harwell Oxon 133 G4
Harwich 152 D4
Harwood Dur 211 E4
Harwood GtMan 184 B1
Harwood N'umb 220 C3
Harwood on
 Teviot 227 F5
Harworth 186 D3
Harlington
 CenBeds 149 F4

Hascombe 121 F3
Haselbech 160 C5
Haselbury
 Plucknett 104 A1
Haseley 147 E1
Haseley Knob 159 E5
Haselor 146 D2
Hasfield 146 A5
Hasguard 126 B2
Haskayne 183 E2
Hasketon 153 D2
Hasland 173 E1
Hasland Green 173 E1
Haslemere 121 E4
Haslingden 193 D5
Haslingden Grane 193 D5
Haslingfield 150 C2
Haslington 171 E2
Hassall 171 E2
Hassall Green 171 E2
Hassall Street 124 C4
Hassendean 227 G3
Hassingham 179 E5
Hassocks 109 F2
Hassop 185 G5
Haster 275 J3
Hasthorpe 176 C1
Hastigrow 275 H2
Hastingleigh 124 C4
Hastings ESuss 110 D3
Hastings Som 103 G1
Hastings Fishermen's
 Museum ESuss
 TN34 3DW 75 Hastings
Hastingwood 137 D2
Hastoe 135 E2
Haswell 212 C3
Haswell Plough 212 C3
Hatch CenBeds 149 G3
Hatch Hants 120 B2
Hatch Beauchamp 116 A5
Hatch End 136 A3
Hatch Green 103 G1
Hatching Green 136 A1
Hatchmere 183 G5
Hatcliffe 188 C2
Hatfield Here 145 E2
Hatfield Herts 136 B2
Hatfield SYorks 187 D2
Hatfield Broad Oak 137 E1
Hatfield Heath 137 D1
Hatfield House Herts
 AL9 5NF 136 B2
Hatfield Peverel 137 G1
Hatfield
 Woodhouse 187 D2
Hatford 133 F3
Hatherden 119 E2
Hatherleigh 113 F5
Hathern 173 F5
Hatherop 133 D2
Hathersage 185 G4
Hathersage Booths 185 G4
Hathershaw 184 D2
Hatherton ChesE 171 D3
Hatherton Staffs 158 B1
Hatley St. George 150 A2
Hatt 99 D4
Hattingley 120 B4
Hatton Aber 261 J1
Hatton Derbys 172 C5
Hatton GtLon 136 A5
Hatton Lincs 188 B5
Hatton Shrop 157 D3
Hatton Warr 183 G4
Hatton Castle 269 F6
Hatton Country World
 Warks
 CV35 8XA 147 E1
Hatton Heath 170 B1
Hatton of Fintray 261 G3
Hattoncrook 261 G2
Haugh 189 E5
Haugh Head 229 E4
Haugh of Glass 260 C1
Haugh of Urr 216 C4
Haugham 188 D4
Haughhead 234 A2
Haughley 152 B1
Haughley Green 152 B1
Haughley New
 Street 152 B1
Haughs 268 D6
Haughton ChesE 170 C2
Haughton Notts 187 D5
Haughton Powys 156 C1
Haughton Shrop 157 F3
Haughton Shrop 157 F1
Haughton Shrop 170 A5
Haughton Staffs 171 F5
Haughton Green 184 D3
Haughton
 Le Skerne 202 C1
Haultwick 150 B5
Haunn 254 C3
Haunton 159 E1
Hauxton 150 C2
Havannah 171 F1
Havant 107 G2
Haven 144 D2
Haven Side 197 E5
Havenstreet 107 E3
Havercroft 186 A1
Haverfordwest
 (Hwlffordd) 126 C1
Haverhill 151 E3
Haverigg 198 C5
Havering Park 137 D3
Havering-atte-
 Bower 137 E3
Haversham 148 D3
Haverthwaite 199 E4
Haverton Hill 213 D5
Haviker Street 123 G4
Havyat 116 C4
Hawarden
 (Penarlâg) 170 A1
Hawbridge 146 B3
Hawbush Green 151 F5
Hawcoat 198 D5
Hawes 201 D4
Hawe's Green 164 D2
Hawick 227 G4
Hawkchurch 103 G2
Hawkedon 151 F2
Hawkenbury Kent 123 E5
Hawkenbury Kent 124 A4
Hawkeridge 117 F2

Hawkerland 103 D4
Hawkes End 159 E4
Hawkesbury 131 G4
Hawkesbury
 Upton 131 G4
Hawkhill 229 G5
Hawkhurst 123 G5
Hawkinge 125 E4
Hawkley 120 C5
Hawkridge 114 B4
Hawkshead 199 E3
Hawkshead Hill 199 E3
Hawksheads 192 A1
Hawksland 234 C5
Hawkswick 201 E5
Hawksworth
 Notts 174 C3
Hawksworth
 WYorks 194 A3
Hawkwell Essex 138 B3
Hawkwell N'umb 220 C4
Hawley Hants 121 D2
Hawley Kent 137 E5
Hawley's Corner 122 D3
Hawling 146 C5
Hawnby 203 E4
Haworth 193 G4
Hawstead 151 G2
Hawstead Green 151 G2
Hawthorn Dur 212 D3
Hawthorn Hants 120 B4
Hawthorn RCT 129 G4
Hawthorn Wilts 117 F1
Hawthorn Hill
 BrackF 135 D5
Hawthorn Hill
 Lincs 176 A2
Hawthorpe 175 F5
Hawton 174 C2
Haxby 195 F2
Haxey 187 E2
Haxted 122 D4
Haxton 118 C3
Hay Green 162 D1
Hay Mills 158 D4
Hay Street 150 B5
Haydock 183 G3
Haydon Dorset 104 C1
Haydon Swin 132 D3
Haydon Bridge 211 E1
Haydon Wick 132 D3
Hayes GtLon 135 F5
Hayes GtLon 122 D2
Hayes End 135 F4
Hayfield A&B 240 C2
Hayfield Derbys 185 E4
Hayfield Fife 244 A5
Hayfield High 275 G2
Haygrove 115 F4
Hayhillock 252 C5
Hayle 94 C3
Hayling Island 107 G2
Haymoor Green 171 D2
Hayne 102 C1
Haynes 149 G3
Haynes Church End 149 F3
Haynes West End 149 F3
Hay-on-Wye (Y Gelli
 Gandryll) 144 B3
Hayscastle 140 C5
Hayscastle Cross 140 C5
Hayton Cumb 210 C2
Hayton Cumb 209 E2
Hayton ERid 196 A3
Hayton Notts 187 E4
Hayton's Bent 157 E4
Haytor Vale 102 A5
Haytown 113 D4
Haywards Heath 109 F1
Haywood Oaks 174 B2
Hayward Gallery
 GtLon SE1 8XZ 45 F4
Hazel End 150 C5
Hazel Grove 184 D4
Hazel Street 123 F5
Hazelbank A&B 240 C4
Hazelbank SLan 234 C5
Hazelbury Bryan 104 D2
Hazeleigh 138 B2
Hazeley 120 C2
Hazelhurst 184 B1
Hazelside 225 G3
Hazelslack 199 F5
Hazelslade 158 C1
Hazelton Walls 244 B2
Hazelwood Derbys 173 E3
Hazelwood GtLon 122 D2
Hazlefield 208 A2
Hazlehead
 Aberdeen 261 G4
Hazlehead SYorks 185 F2
Hazlemere 135 D3
Hazlerigg 221 E4
Hazleton 132 C1
Hazon 221 D1
Heacham 177 E4
Head Bridge 113 G4
Headbourne
 Worthy 119 F4
Headcorn 124 A4
Headingley 194 B4
Headington 134 A2
Headlam 202 A1
Headless Cross 146 C1
Headley Hants 120 D4
Headley Hants 119 G1
Headley Surr 122 B3
Headley Down 120 D4
Headley Heath 158 C5
Headon 187 E5
Heads Nook 210 A2
Heady Hill 184 C1
Heage 173 E2
Healaugh NYorks 201 F3
Healaugh NYorks 195 E3
Heald Green 184 C4
Heale Devon 113 G1
Heale Som 116 A5
Healey Lancs 184 C1
Healey N'umb 211 G2
Healey NYorks 202 A4
Healey WYorks 194 B5
Healey's Cornish Cyder Farm
 Corn TR4 9LW 96 B4
Healing 188 C1

Hemingbrough 195 F4
Hemingby 188 C5
Hemingfield 186 A2
Hemingford Abbots 162 A5
Hemingford Grey 162 A5
Hemingstone 152 C2
Hemington Leics 173 F5
Hemington
 N'hants 161 F4
Hemington Som 117 E2
Hemley 153 D3
Hemlington 203 D1
Hemp Green 153 E1
Hempholme 196 C2
Hempnall 164 D2
Hempnall Green 164 D2
Hempriggs 267 H5
Hempriggs House 275 J4
Hempstead Essex 151 E4
Hempstead Med 123 G2
Hempstead Norf 179 F3
Hempstead Norf 178 C2
Hempsted 132 A1
Hempton Norf 178 A3
Hempton Oxon 147 G4
Hemsby 179 F4
Hemswell 187 G3
Hemswell Cliff 187 G4
Hemsworth 186 B1
Hemyock 103 E1
Henbury Bristol 131 E5
Henbury ChesE 184 C5
Henderland 216 C3
Hendersyde Park 228 B3
Hendham 100 D2
Hendon GtLon 136 B4
Hendon T&W 212 D2
Hendraburnick 97 F1
Hendre Bridgend 129 F4
Hendre Gwyn 166 C3
Hendreforgan 129 F4
Hendy 128 B2
Heneglwys 180 C5
Henfield SGlos 131 F5
Henfield WSuss 109 E2
Henford 99 D1
Hengherst 124 B5
Hengoed Caerp 130 A3
Hengoed Powys 144 B2
Hengoed Shrop 169 F4
Hengrave 151 G1
Henham 150 D5
Heniarth 156 A2
Henlade 115 F5
Henley Dorset 104 C2
Henley Shrop 157 E5
Henley Som 116 B4
Henley Som 104 A2
Henley Suff 152 C2
Henley WSuss 121 D5
Henley Corner 116 B4
Henley Park 121 E2
Henley-in-Arden 147 D1
Henley-on-Thames 134 C4
Henley's Down 110 C2
Henllan Carmar 141 G3
Henllan Denb 168 C1
Henllan Amgoed 141 E5
Hennlys 130 B3
Henlow 149 G4
Hennock 102 B4
Henny Street 151 G4
Henryd 181 F5
Henry's Moat 140 D5
Hensall 195 E5
Henshaw 211 D1
Hensingham 208 C5
Henstead 165 F3
Hensting 119 F5
Henstridge 104 D1
Henstridge Ash 104 D1
Henstridge Marsh 117 E5
Henton Oxon 134 C2
Henton Som 116 B3
Henwood 97 G2
Heogan 279 D8
Heol Senni 143 F4
Heolgerrig 129 G2
Heol-y-Cyw 129 F4
Hepburn 229 E4
Hepburn Bell 229 E4
Hepple 220 C1
Hepscott 221 E3
Hepthorne Lane 173 F1
Heptonstall 193 F5
Hepworth Suff 164 A4
Hepworth WYorks 185 F2
Hepworth South
 Common 164 A4
Herbrandston 126 B2
Hereford 145 E3
Hereford Cathedral
 Here HR1 2NG
 75 Hereford
Heriot 236 A4
Heritage Motor Centre,
 Gaydon Warks
 CV35 0BJ 147 E2
Herm 101 G5
Hermiston 235 F3
Hermitage D&G 216 B4
Hermitage Dorset 104 C2
Hermitage ScBord 218 C2
Hermitage WBerks 134 A5
Hermitage WSuss 107 G2
Hermon Carmar 184 A3
Hermon Carmar 141 G4
Hermon IoA 166 C1
Hermon Pembs 141 F4
Herne 125 D2
Herne Bay 125 D2
Herne Common 125 D2
Herne Pound 123 F3
Herner 113 F3
Hernhill 124 C2
Herodsfoot 97 G3
Herongate 137 F3
Heron's Ghyll 109 G1
Heronsgate 135 F3
Herriard 120 B3
Herringfleet 165 F2
Herring's Green 149 F3
Herringswell 151 F1
Herringthorpe 186 B3
Hersden 125 D2
Hersham Corn 112 C5
Hersham Surr 121 G1

Herstmonceux 110 B2
Herston 277 D8
Hertford 136 C1
Hertford Heath 136 C1
Hesket Newmarket 209 G3
Hesketh Bank 192 A5
Hesketh Lane 192 C3
Hesleden 212 B4
Hesleyside 220 A3
Heslington 195 F2
Hessay 195 E2
Hessenford 98 D5
Hessett 152 A1
Hessle 196 C5
Hest Bank 192 A1
Hestley Green 152 C1
Heston 136 A5
Heswall 183 D4
Hethe 148 A5
Hethelpit Cross 145 G5
Hetherington 220 A4
Hethersett 178 C5
Hethersgill 210 A1
Hethpool 228 C4
Hett 212 B4
Hetton 99 F1
Hetton-le-Hole 212 C3
Heugh 220 C4
Heugh-head Aber 260 B3
Heugh-head Aber 260 D5
Heveningham 165 E4
Hever 123 D4
Hever Castle & Gardens
  Kent
  TN8 7NG 123 D4
Heversham 199 F4
Hevingham 178 C3
Hewas Water 97 D5
Hewell Grange 146 C1
Hewell Lane 146 C1
Hewelsfield 131 E2
Hewelsfield
  Common 131 E2
Hewish NSom 116 B1
Hewish Som 104 A2
Hewood 103 G2
Heworth 195 F2
Hewton 99 F1
Hexham 211 F1
Hexham Abbey N'umb
  NE46 3NB 211 F1
Hextable 137 E5
Hexthorpe 186 C2
Hexton 149 G4
Hexworthy 99 G3
Hey 193 E3
Hey Houses 191 G5
Heybridge Essex 137 F3
Heybridge Essex 138 B2
Heybridge Basin 138 B2
Heybrook Bay 100 A3
Heydon Cambs 150 C3
Heydon Norf 178 C3
Heydour 175 F4
Heylipol 246 A2
Heylor 278 B4
Heyop 156 B5
Heysham 192 A1
Heyshaw 194 A1
Heyshott 108 A2
Heyside 184 D2
Heytesbury 118 A3
Heythrop 147 F5
Heywood GtMan 184 C1
Heywood Wilts 117 F2
Hibaldstow 187 G2
Hibb's Green 151 G2
Hickleton 186 B2
Hickling Norf 179 F3
Hickling Notts 174 B5
Hickling Green 179 F3
Hickling Heath 179 F3
Hickstead 109 E2
Hidcote Bartrim 147 D3
Hidcote Boyce 147 D3
Hidcote Manor Garden
  Glos GL55 6LR 147 D3
High Ackworth 186 B1
High Angerton 220 C3
High Balantyre 240 C3
High Bankhill 210 B3
High Beach 136 D3
High Bentham (Higher
  Bentham) 192 C1
High Bickington 113 F3
High Birkwith 200 C5
High Blantyre 234 A4
High Bonnybridge 234 C2
High Borgue 216 A5
High Borve 271 G2
High Bradfield 185 G3
High Bradley 193 G3
High Bransholme 196 D4
High Bray 113 G2
High Bridge 209 G2
High Brooms 123 E4
High Bullen 113 F3
High Burton 202 B4
High Buston 221 E1
High Callerton 221 D4
High Catton 195 G2
High Close 202 A1
High Cogges 133 F2
High Common 164 C3
High Coniscliffe 202 B1
High Crompton 184 D2
High Cross Hants 120 C5
High Cross Herts 136 C1
High Cross WSuss 109 E2
High Easter 137 F1
High Ellington 202 A4
High Entercommon 202 C2
High Ercall 157 E1
High Ferry 176 B3
High Flatts 185 G2
High Garrett 151 F5
High Gate 193 F5
High Grange 212 A4
High Green Norf 178 C5
High Green Norf 178 A4
High Green Suff 151 G1
High Green SYorks 186 A3

High Green Worcs 146 A3
High Halden 124 A5
High Halstow 137 G5
High Ham 116 B4
High Harrington 208 D4
High Harrogate 194 C2
High Hatton 170 D5
High Hauxley 221 E1
High Hawsker 204 C2
High Heath Shrop 171 D5
High Heath WMid 158 C2
High Hesket 210 A3
High Hesleden 213 D4
High Hoyland 185 G1
High Hunsley 196 B4
High Hurstwood 109 G1
High Hutton 195 G1
High Ireby 209 F3
High Kelling 178 B2
High Kilburn 203 E5
High Kingthorpe 204 B4
High Knipe 199 G3
High Lane Derbys 173 F3
High Lane GtMan 185 D4
High Lane Worcs 145 F1
High Laver 137 E2
High Legh 184 B4
High Leven 203 D1
High Littleton 116 D2
High Lodge Forest Centre
  Suff IP27 0AF 163 G4
High Lorton 209 E4
High Marishes 204 B5
High Marnham 187 F5
High Melton 186 C2
High Moor 186 B4
High Moorland Visitor
  Centre, Princetown Devon
  PL20 6QF 99 F3
High Newton 199 F4
High Newton-by-the-
  Sea 229 G4
High Nibthwaite 199 D3
High Offley 171 E5
High Ongar 137 E2
High Onn 158 A1
High Park Corner 152 B5
High Roding 137 F1
High Shaw 201 D3
High Spen 212 A1
High Stoop 212 A3
High Street Corn 97 D4
High Street Kent 123 G5
High Street Suff 153 F2
High Street Suff 165 F4
High Street Suff 165 F4
High Street Suff 151 G3
High Street Green 152 B2
High Throston 213 D4
High Town 158 B1
High Toynton 176 A1
High Trewhitt 220 C1
High Wham 212 A5
High Wigsell 110 C1
High Woods Country Park
  Essex CO4 5JR 152 B5
High Woolaston 131 E3
High Worsall 202 C2
High Wray 199 E3
High Wych 137 D1
High Wycombe 135 D3
Higham Derbys 173 E2
Higham Kent 137 G5
Higham Lancs 193 E4
Higham Suff 151 F1
Higham Suff 152 B4
Higham SYorks 186 A2
Higham Dykes 220 D4
Higham Ferrers 149 E1
Higham Gobion 149 G4
Higham on the Hill 159 F3
Higham Wood 123 E4
Highampton 113 E5
Highams Park 136 C3
Highbridge Hants 119 F5
Highbridge Som 116 A3
Highbrook 122 C5
Highburton 185 F1
Highbury 117 D3
Highclere 119 F1
Highcliffe 106 B3
Higher Alham 117 D3
Higher Ansty 105 D2
Higher Ashton 102 B4
Higher Ballam 191 G4
Higher Blackley 184 C2
Higher Brixham 101 F2
Higher Cheriton 103 E2
Higher Combe 114 C4
Higher Folds 184 A2
Higher Gabwell 101 F1
Higher Green 184 B3
Higher Halstock
  Leigh 104 B2
Higher Kingcombe 104 B3
Higher Kinnerton 170 A1
Higher Muddiford 113 F2
Higher Nyland 117 E5
Higher Prestacott 99 D1
Higher Standen 193 D3
Higher Tale 103 D2
Higher Thrushgill 192 C1
Higher Town IoS 96 C5
Higher Walreddon 99 E3
Higher Walton
  Lancs 192 B5
Higher Walton
  Warr 183 G4
Higher Wambrook 103 F2
Higher Whatcombe 105 E2
Higher Wheelton 192 C5
Higher Whiteleigh 98 C1
Higher Wincham 184 A5
Higher Woodhill 184 B1
Higher Woodsford 105 D4
Higher Wraxall 104 B3
Higher Wych 170 B3
Highfield ERid 195 G4
Highfield NAyr 233 E4
Highfield Oxon 148 A5
Highfield SYorks 186 A4
Highfield T&W 212 A2
Highfields Cambs 150 B2
Highfields N'umb 237 G4

Highgate ESuss 122 D5
Highgate GtLon 136 B4
Highgreen Manor 220 B2
Highlane ChesE 171 G1
Highlane Derbys 186 B4
Highlaws 209 E2
Highleadon 145 G5
Highleigh Devon 114 C5
Highleigh WSuss 108 A4
Highley 157 G4
Highmead 142 B3
Highmoor Cross 134 B4
Highmoor Hill 131 D4
Highnam 131 G1
Highstead 125 E2
Highsted 124 B2
Highstreet 124 C2
Highstreet Green
  Essex 151 F4
Highstreet Green
  Surr 121 E4
Hightae 217 E3
Highter's Heath 158 C5
Hightown Hants 106 A2
Hightown Mersey 183 D2
Hightown Green 152 A2
Highway 132 C5
Highweek 102 B5
Highwood 145 F1
Highwood Hill 136 B3
Highworth 133 E3
Hilborough 163 G2
Hilcote 173 F2
Hilcott 118 C2
Hilden Park 123 E4
Hildenborough 123 E4
Hildenley 203 G5
Hildersham 150 D3
Hilderstone 171 G4
Hilderthorpe 197 D1
Hilfield 104 C2
Hilgay 163 E3
Hill SGlos 131 F3
Hill Warks 147 G1
Hill Worcs 146 B3
Hill Brow 120 C5
Hill Chorlton 171 E4
Hill Common 179 F3
Hill Cottages 203 G3
Hill Croome 146 A3
Hill Deverill 117 F3
Hill Dyke 176 B3
Hill End Dur 211 G4
Hill End Fife 243 F5
Hill End Glos 146 A4
Hill End GtLon 135 F3
Hill End NYorks 193 G2
Hill Green 136 C4
Hill Head 107 E2
Hill Houses 157 F5
Hill Mountain 126 C2
Hill of Beath 235 F1
Hill of Fearn 267 F4
Hill Ridware 158 C1
Hill Row 162 C5
Hill Side 185 F1
Hill Street 106 C1
Hill Top Hants 106 D2
Hill Top SYorks 186 B3
Hill Top SYorks 185 G4
Hill View 105 F3
Hill Wootton 147 F1
Hillam 195 E5
Hillbeck 200 C1
Hillberry 190 B4
Hillborough 125 E2
Hillbrae Aber 268 E6
Hillbrae Aber 261 F3
Hillbrae Aber 261 G1
Hillbutts 105 F2
Hillclifflane 173 D3
Hillend Aber 268 C6
Hillend Fife 235 F1
Hillend Midlo 235 G2
Hillend NLan 234 C3
Hillend Swan 128 A3
Hillend Green 145 G5
Hillersland 131 E1
Hillesden 148 B5
Hillesley 131 G4
Hillfarrance 115 E5
Hillfoot End 149 G4
Hillhead Devon 101 F2
Hillhead SAyr 224 C3
Hillhead of
  Auchentumb 269 H5
Hillhead of Cocklaw 269 J6
Hilliard's Cross 159 D1
Hilliclay 275 G2
Hillingdon 135 F4
Hillington Glas 233 G3
Hillington Norf 177 F5
Hillmorton 160 A5
Hillockhead Aber 260 B4
Hillockhead Aber 260 C3
Hillowton 216 B4
Hillpound 107 E1
Hill's End 149 E4
Hills Town 173 F1
Hillsborough 185 G3
Hillside Aber 261 H5
Hillside Angus 253 F3
Hillside Moray 267 J5
Hillside Shet 279 D6
Hillside Worcs 145 G1
Hillswick 278 B5
Hillway 107 F4
Hillwell 279 F9
Hillyfields 106 C1
Hilmarton 132 C5
Hilperton 117 F2
Hilsea 107 F2
Hilston 197 E4

Hilton Cambs 150 A1
Hilton Cumb 210 D5
Hilton Derbys 172 D4
Hilton Dorset 105 D3
Hilton Dur 212 A5
Hilton High 267 G3
Hilton Shrop 157 G3
Hilton Staffs 158 C2
Hilton Stock 203 D1
Hilton Croft 261 H1
Hilton of Cadboll 267 F4
Hilton of Delnies 267 F6
Himbleton 146 B2
Himley 158 A3

Himley Hall & Park
  WMid DY3 4DF 14 A2
Hincaster 199 G4
Hinchley Wood 121 G1
Hinckley 159 G3
Hinderclay 164 B4
Hinderton 183 E5
Hinderwell 203 G1
Hindford 170 A4
Hindhead 121 D4
Hindley GtMan 184 A2
Hindley N'umb 211 G2
Hindley Green 184 A2
Hindlip 146 A2
Hindolveston 178 B3
Hindon Som 114 C3
Hindon Wilts 118 A4
Hindringham 178 A2
Hingham 178 B5
Hinksford 158 A4
Hinstock 171 D5
Hintlesham 152 B3
Hinton Glos 131 F2
Hinton Hants 106 B3
Hinton Here 144 C4
Hinton N'hants 148 A2
Hinton SGlos 131 G5
Hinton Shrop 156 D2
Hinton Admiral 106 B3
Hinton Ampner 119 G5
Hinton Blewett 116 C2
Hinton
  Charterhouse 117 E2
Hinton on the
  Green 146 C3
Hinton Parva
  Dorset 105 F2
Hinton Parva Swin 133 E4
Hinton St. George 104 A1
Hinton St. Mary 105 D1
Hinton Waldrist 133 F3
Hinton-in-the-
  Hedges 148 A4
Hints Shrop 157 F5
Hints Staffs 159 D2
Hinwick 149 E1
Hinxhill 124 C4
Hinxton 150 C3
Hinxworth 150 A3
Hipperholme 194 B4
Hipsburn 229 G5
Hipswell 202 A3
Hirn 261 F4
Hirnant 169 D5
Hirst 221 E3
Hirst Courtney 195 F5
Hirwaen 169 E1
Hirwaun 129 F2
Hiscott 113 F3
Histon 150 C1
Hitcham Bucks 135 E4
Hitcham Suff 152 A2
Hitchin 149 G5
Hither Green 136 C5
Hittisleigh 102 A3
Hittisleigh Barton 102 A3
Hive 196 A4
Hixon 172 B5
Hoaden 125 E3
Hoaldalbert 144 C5
Hoar Cross 172 C5
Hoar Park Craft Centre
  Warks
  CV10 0QU 159 E3
Hoarwithy 145 E5
Hoath 125 E2
Hobarris 156 C5
Hobbister 277 C7
Hobbles Green 151 F2
Hobbs Cross 137 D3
Hobbs Lots Bridge 162 B2
Hobkirk 227 G4
Hobland Hall 179 G5
Hobson 212 A2
Hoby 160 B1
Hockerill 150 C5
Hockering 178 B4
Hockerton 174 C2
Hockley 138 B3
Hockley Heath 159 D5
Hockliffe 149 E5
Hockwold cum
  Wilton 163 F4
Hockworthy 102 D1
Hoddesdon 136 C2
Hoddlesden 192 D5
Hodgehill 171 F1
Hodgeston 126 D3
Hodnet 170 D5
Hodnetheath 170 D5
Hodsoll Street 123 F2
Hodson 133 D4
Hodthorpe 186 C5
Hoe 178 A4
Hoe Gate 107 F1
Hoff 200 B1
Hoffleet Stow 176 A4
Hoggard's Green 151 G2
Hoggeston 148 D5
Hoggie 268 D5
Hoggrill's End 159 E3
Hogha Gearraidh 262 C4
Hoghton 192 C5
Hognaston 172 D2
Hogsthorpe 189 F5
Holbeach 176 B5
Holbeach Bank 176 B5
Holbeach Clough 176 B5
Holbeach Drove 162 B1
Holbeach Hurn 176 B5
Holbeach St. Johns 162 B1
Holbeach St. Marks 176 B4
Holbeach
  St. Matthew 176 C4
Holbeck 186 C5
Holbeck
  Woodhouse 186 C5
Holberrow Green 146 C2
Holbeton 100 C2
Holborough 123 G2
Holbrook Derbys 173 E3
Holbrook Suff 152 C4
Holbrooks 159 F4
Holburn 229 E3
Holbury 106 D2
Holcombe Devon 102 C5

Holcombe Som 117 D3
Holcombe Burnell
  Barton 102 B3
Holcombe Rogus 103 D1
Holcot 148 C1
Holden 193 D3
Holden Gate 193 E5
Holdenby 148 B1
Holdenhurst 106 A3
Holder's Green 151 E5
Holders Hill 136 B4
Holdgate 157 E4
Holdingham 175 F3
Holditch 103 G2
Hole 103 E1
Hole Park 124 A5
Holehouse 185 E3
Hole-in-the-Wall 145 F5
Holford 115 E3
Holgate 195 E2
Holker 199 E5
Holkham 177 G3
Hollacombe Devon 113 D5
Hollacombe Devon 102 B2
Hollacombe Town 113 G4
Holland Ork 276 F1
Holland Ork 276 F5
Holland Surr 122 D3
Holland Fen 176 A3
Holland Admiral 106 B3
Holland-on-Sea 139 E1
Hollandstoun 276 G2
Hollee 218 A2
Hollesley 153 E3
Hollicombe 101 F1
Hollingbourne 124 A3
Hollingrove 110 B2
Hollington Derbys 172 D4
Hollington ESuss 110 C2
Hollington Staffs 172 C3
Hollingworth 185 E3
Hollins 186 A5
Hollins Green 184 A3
Hollins Lane 192 A4
Hollinsclough 172 B1
Hollinwood GtMan 184 D2
Hollinwood Shrop 170 C4
Hollocombe 113 G4
Hollow Meadows 185 G4
Holloway 173 E2
Hollowell 160 B5
Hollybush Caerp 130 A2
Hollybush EAyr 224 B4
Hollybush Worcs 145 G4
Hollyhurst 170 C3
Hollym 197 F5
Hollywater 120 D4
Hollywood 158 C5
Holm (Tolm) 271 G4
Holm of Drumlanrig 216 C1
Holmbridge 185 F2
Holmbury St. Mary 121 G3
Holmbush 122 B5
Holme Cambs 161 G4
Holme Cumb 199 G5
Holme NLincs 187 G2
Holme Notts 174 D2
Holme NYorks 202 C4
Holme WYorks 185 F2
Holme Chapel 193 E5
Holme Hale 163 G2
Holme Lacy 145 E4
Holme Marsh 144 C2
Holme next the Sea 177 F3
Holme on the
  Wolds 196 B3
Holme Pierrepont 174 B4
Holme St. Cuthbert 209 E2
Holme-on-Spalding-
  Moor 196 A4
Holmer 145 E3
Holmer Green 135 E3
Holmes 183 F1
Holmes Chapel 171 E1
Holme's Hill 110 A2
Holmesfield 186 A5
Holmeswood 183 F1
Holmewood 173 F1
Holmfield 193 G5
Holmfirth 185 F2
Holmhead D&G 216 B2
Holmhead EAyr 225 D3
Holmpton 197 F5
Holmrook 198 B2
Holmsgarth 279 D8
Holmside 212 B3
Holmsleigh Green 103 F2
Holmston 224 B3
Holmwrangle 210 B3
Holne 100 D1
Holnest 104 C2
Holsworthy 112 D5
Holsworthy Beacon 113 D5
Holt Dorset 105 G2
Holt Norf 178 B2
Holt Wilts 117 F1
Holt Worcs 146 A1
Holt Wrex 170 B2
Holt End Hants 120 B4
Holt End Worcs 146 C1
Holt Fleet 146 A1
Holt Heath Dorset 105 G2
Holt Heath Worcs 146 A1
Holt Wood 105 G2
Holtby 195 F2
Holton Oxon 134 B2
Holton Som 117 D5
Holton Suff 165 E4
Holton cum
  Beckering 188 B4
Holton Heath 105 F3
Holton le Clay 188 C2
Holton le Moor 188 A3
Holton St. Mary 152 B4
Holtspur 135 E4
Holwell Dorset 104 C1
Holwell Herts 149 G4
Holwell Leics 174 C5
Holwell Oxon 133 E2
Holwell Som 117 E3

Holwick 211 F5
Holworth 105 D4
Holy Cross 158 B5
Holy Island IoA 180 A5
Holy Island (Lindisfarne)
  N'umb 229 F2
Holy Trinity Church,
  Skipton NYorks
  BD23 1NJ 193 F2
Holy Trinity Church,
  Stratford-upon-Avon
  Warks CV37 6BG
  85 Stratford-upon-Avon
Holybourne 120 C3
Holyfield 136 C2
Holyhead
  (Caergybi) 180 A4
Holymoorside 173 E1
Holyport 135 D5
Holystone 220 B1
Holytown 234 B3
Holywell Cambs 162 B5
Holywell Corn 96 B4
Holywell Dorset 104 B2
Holywell ESuss 110 B4
Holywell (Treffynnon)
  Flints 182 C5
Holywell N'umb 221 F4
Holywell Bay Fun Park
  Corn TR8 5PW 96 B4
Holywell Green 185 E1
Holywell Lake 115 E1
Holywell Row 163 F5
Holywood 216 D2
Hom Green 145 E5
Homer 157 F2
Homersfield 165 D3
Homington 118 C5
Homore
  (Tobha Mòr) 254 C1
Honey Hill 124 D2
Honey Street 118 C1
Honey Tye 152 A4
Honeyborough 126 C2
Honeybourne 146 D3
Honeychurch 113 G5
Honicknowle 100 A2
Honiley 159 E5
Honing 179 E3
Honingham 178 C4
Honington Lincs 175 E3
Honington Suff 164 A4
Honington Warks 147 E3
Honiton 103 E2
Honkley 170 A2
Honley 185 F1
Hoo Med 137 G5
Hoo Suff 153 D2
Hoo Green 184 B4
Hoo Meavy 100 B1
Hood Green 186 A2
Hood Hill 186 A3
Hooe ESuss 110 B3
Hooe Plym 100 B2
Hooe Common 110 B2
Hook Cambs 162 C2
Hook ERid 195 G5
Hook GtLon 121 G1
Hook Hants 120 C2
Hook Hants 107 E2
Hook Pembs 126 C1
Hook Wilts 132 C4
Hook Green Kent 123 F5
Hook Green Kent 123 E5
Hook Green Kent 137 E5
Hook Norton 147 F4
Hook-a-Gate 157 D2
Hooke 104 B3
Hookgate 171 E4
Hookway 102 B3
Hookwood 122 B4
Hoole 170 B1
Hooley 122 B3
Hoop 131 E2
Hooton 183 E5
Hooton Levitt 186 C3
Hooton Pagnell 186 B2
Hooton Roberts 186 B3
Hop Farm, The Kent
  TN12 6PY 123 F4
Hop Pocket, The Here
  WR6 5BT 145 F3
Hope Derbys 185 F4
Hope Devon 100 C4
Hope Flints 170 A2
Hope Powys 156 B2
Hope Shrop 156 C2
Hope Staffs 172 C2
Hope Bagot 157 E5
Hope Bowdler 157 D3
Hope End Green 151 D5
Hope Mansell 131 F1
Hope under
  Dinmore 145 E2
Hopehouse 227 D4
Hopeman 267 J5
Hope's Green 137 G4
Hopesay 156 C4
Hopkinstown 129 G3
Hopley's Green 144 C2
Hopperton 194 D2
Hopsford 159 G4
Hopstone 157 G3
Hopton Derbys 173 D2
Hopton Norf 165 G2
Hopton Shrop 170 C5
Hopton Shrop 170 A4
Hopton Staffs 171 G5
Hopton Suff 164 A4
Hopton Cangeford 157 E4
Hopton Castle 156 C5
Hopton Wafers 157 F5
Hoptonheath 156 C5
Hopwas 159 D2
Hopwood 158 C5
Horam 110 A2
Horbling 175 G4
Horbury 185 G1
Horden 212 D3
Horderley 156 D4
Hordle 106 B3
Hordley 170 A4
Horeb Carmar 128 A2
Horeb Cere 141 G3
Horeb Flints 169 F2

Horfield 131 E5
Horham 164 D4
Horkesley Heath 152 A5
Horkstow 187 G1
Horley Oxon 147 G3
Horley Surr 122 B4
Horn Hill 135 F3
Hornblotton 116 C4
Hornblotton Green 116 C4
Hornby Lancs 192 B1
Hornby NYorks 202 B3
Hornby NYorks 202 C2
Horncastle 176 A1
Hornchurch 137 E4
Horncliffe 237 G5
Horndean Hants 107 G1
Horndean ScBord 237 G5
Horndon 99 F3
Horndon on the Hill 137 F4
Horne 122 C4
Horne Row 137 G2
Horner 114 C3
Horniehaugh 252 C3
Horniman Museum GtLon
  SE23 3PQ 13 C7
Horning 179 E4
Horninghold 160 D3
Horninglow 172 D5
Horningsea 150 C1
Horningsham 117 F3
Horningtoft 178 A3
Horningtops 97 G3
Hornsburg 103 G1
Hornsby 210 B3
Hornsby Gate 210 B2
Hornsea 197 E3
Hornsea Freeport ERid
  HU18 1UT 197 E3
Hornsey 136 C4
Hornton 147 G3
Horrabridge 100 B1
Horridge 102 A5
Horringer 151 G1
Horrocks Fold 184 B1
Horse Bridge 171 G2
Horsebridge Devon 99 E3
Horsebridge Hants 119 E4
Horsebrook 158 A1
Horsecastle 116 B1
Horsehay 157 F2
Horseheath 151 E3
Horsehouse 201 F4
Horsell 121 E2
Horseman's Green 170 B3
Horsenden 134 C2
Horseshoe Green 123 D4
Horseway 162 C4
Horsey 179 F3
Horsey Corner 179 F3
Horsford 178 C4
Horsforth 194 B4
Horsham Worcs 145 G2
Horsham WSuss 121 G4
Horsham St. Faith 178 D4
Horsington Lincs 175 G1
Horsington Som 117 E5
Horsington Marsh 117 E5
Horsley Derbys 173 E3
Horsley Glos 132 A3
Horsley N'umb 211 G1
Horsley N'umb 220 B1
Horsley Cross 152 C5
Horsley Woodhouse 173 E3
Horsleycross Street 152 C5
Horsleygate 186 A5
Horsleyhill 227 G4
Horsmonden 123 F4
Horspath 134 A2
Horstead 179 D4
Horsted Keynes 109 F1
Horton Bucks 135 E1
Horton Dorset 105 G2
Horton Lancs 193 E2
Horton N'hants 148 D2
Horton SGlos 131 G4
Horton Shrop 170 B5
Horton Som 103 G1
Horton Staffs 171 G2
Horton Swan 128 A4
Horton Tel&W 157 F1
Horton W&M 135 F5
Horton Wilts 118 B1
Horton Cross 103 G1
Horton Grange 221 E4
Horton Green 170 B3
Horton Heath 107 D1
Horton in
  Ribblesdale 200 D5
Horton Inn 105 G2
Horton Kirby 123 F2
Horton Park Farm Surr
  KT19 8PT 121 F1
Horton-cum-
  Studley 134 B1
Horwich 184 A1
Horwich End 185 E4
Horwood 113 F3
Hoscar 183 F1
Hose 174 C5
Hoses 198 D3
Hosh 243 D2
Hosta 262 C4
Hoswick 279 D10
Hotham 196 A4
Hothfield 124 B4
Hoton 173 G5
Houbie 278 F3
Houdston 214 C1
Hough 171 F2
Hough Green 183 F4
Hougham 175 D3
Hough-on-the-Hill 175 E3
Houghton Cambs 162 A5
Houghton Cumb 210 A2
Houghton Devon 100 C3
Houghton Hants 119 E4
Houghton Pembs 126 C2
Houghton WSuss 108 C3
Houghton Bank 212 B5
Houghton Conquest 149 F3
Houghton le Spring 212 C2
Houghton on the
  Hill 160 B2
Houghton Regis 149 F5
Houghton St. Giles 178 A2

Houghton-le-Side **212** B5
Houlsyke **203** G2
Hound **107** D2
Hound Green **120** C2
Houndslow **236** D5
Houndsmoor **115** E5
Houndwood **237** F3
Hounsdown **106** C1
Hounslow **136** A5
House of Marbles & Teign Valley Glass *Devon* TQ13 9DS **102** B5
Housebay **276** F5
Househill **267** F6
Houses Hill **185** F1
Housesteads Roman Fort *N'umb* NE47 6NN **211** D1
Housetter **278** C4
Housham Tye **137** E1
Houss **279** C9
Houston **233** F3
Houstry **275** G5
Houstry of Dunn **275** H3
Houton **277** C7
Hove **109** E3
Hove Edge **194** A5
Hoveringham **174** B3
Hoveton **179** E4
Hovingham **203** F5
How **210** B2
How Caple **145** F4
How End **149** F3
How Green **123** D4
How Man **208** C5
Howbrook **186** A3
Howden **195** G5
Howden Clough **194** B5
Howden-le-Wear **212** A4
Howe *Cumb* **199** F4
Howe *High* **275** J2
Howe *Norf* **165** D2
Howe *NYorks* **202** C4
Howe Green **158** B2
Howe of Teuchar **269** F6
Howe Street *Essex* **151** F1
Howe Street *Essex* **138** C2
Howegreen **138** B2
Howell **175** G3
Howey **143** G2
Howgate *Cumb* **208** C4
Howgate *Midlo* **235** G4
Howgill *Lancs* **193** E3
Howgill *NYorks* **193** G2
Howick **229** G5
Howle **171** G5
Howle Hill **145** F5
Howlett End **151** D4
Howletts Wild Animal Park *Kent* CT4 5EL **125** D3
Howley **103** F2
Hownam **228** B5
Hownam Mains **228** B4
Howpasley **227** E5
Howsham *NLincs* **188** A1
Howsham *NYorks* **195** G1
Howt Green **124** A2
Howton **144** D5
Howwood **233** F3
Hoxa **277** D8
Hoxne **164** C4
Hoy *High* **275** J2
Hoy *Ork* **277** B8
Hoylake **182** D4
Hoyland **186** A4
Hoylandswaine **185** G2
Hoyle **108** A3
Hubberholme **201** E5
Hubberston **126** B2
Hubbert's Bridge **176** A3
Huby *NYorks* **195** E1
Huby *NYorks* **194** B3
Hucclecote **132** A1
Hucking **124** A3
Hucknall **173** G3
Huddersfield **185** F1
Huddington **146** B2
Huddlesford **158** D2
Hudnall **135** F1
Hudscott **113** G3
Hudswell **202** A3
Huggate **196** A2
Hugglescote **159** G1
Hugh Town **96** B1
Hughenden Valley **135** D3
Hughley **157** E3
Hugmore **170** B2
Hugus **96** B5
Huish *Devon* **113** F4
Huish *Wilts* **118** C1
Huish Champflower **114** D5
Huish Episcopi **116** B5
Huisinis **270** D6
Hulcote **149** E4
Hulcott **135** D1
Hull **196** D5
Hulland **172** D3
Hulland Ward **173** D3
Hullavington **132** A4
Hullbridge **138** B3
Hulme **172** A2
Hulme End **172** C2
Hulme Walfield **171** F1
Hulver Street **165** F3
Hulverstone **106** C4
Humber *Devon* **102** B5
Humber *Here* **145** E2
Humber Bridge Country Park *ERid* HU13 0LN **196** C5
Humberside Airport **188** A1
Humberston **188** D2
Humberstone **160** B2
Humberton **194** D1
Humbie **236** B3
Humbleton *Dur* **201** F1
Humbleton *ERid* **197** E4
Humbleton *N'umb* **229** D4
Humby **175** F4
Hume **237** E5
Humehall **237** E5
Hummer **104** B1
Humshaugh **220** B4
Huna **275** J1
Huncoat **193** D4
Huncote **160** A3
Hundalee **228** A5

Hundall **186** A5
Hunderthwaite **211** F5
Hundleby **176** B1
Hundleton **126** C2
Hundon **151** F3
Hundred Acres **107** E1
Hundred End **192** A5
Hundred House **144** A2
Hungarton **160** B2
Hungate End **148** C3
Hungerford *Hants* **106** A1
Hungerford *Shrop* **157** E4
Hungerford *WBerks* **119** E1
Hungerford Newtown **133** F5
Hungerton **175** D5
Hunglader **263** J4
Hunmanby **205** D5
Hunningham **147** F1
Hunningham Hill **147** F1
Hunny Hill **107** D4
Hunsdon **136** D1
Hunsingore **194** D2
Hunslet **194** C4
Hunsonby **210** B4
Hunspow **275** H1
Hunstanton **177** E3
Hunston *Suff* **163** F5
Hunston *WSuss* **108** A3
Hunsworth **194** B5
Hunt End **146** C1
Hunt House **204** B3
Huntercombe End **134** B4
Hunters Forstal **125** D2
Hunter's Inn **113** G1
Hunter's Quay **232** C2
Hunterston **232** C4
Huntford **219** E1
Huntham **116** A5
Huntingdon **162** A5
Huntingfield **165** E4
Huntingford **117** F4
Huntington *Here* **144** B2
Huntington *Here* **145** D3
Huntington *Staffs* **158** B2
Huntington *Tel&W* **157** F2
Huntington *York* **195** F2
Huntingtower **243** F2
Huntley **131** G1
Huntly **260** D1
Huntlywood **236** D5
Hunton *Hants* **119** F3
Hunton *Kent* **123** G5
Hunton *NYorks* **202** A3
Hunton Bridge **135** F2
Hunt's Cross **183** F4
Huntscott **114** C3
Huntsham **114** D5
Huntshaw **113** F3
Huntshaw Cross **113** F3
Huntshaw Water **113** F3
Huntspill **116** A3
Huntworth **116** A4
Hunwick **212** A4
Hunworth **178** B2
Hurcott *Som* **104** A2
Hurcott *Som* **103** G1
Hurdley **156** B2
Hurdsfield **184** D5
Hurley *W&M* **134** C5
Hurley *Warks* **159** E3
Hurley Bottom **134** D4
Hurlford **224** C2
Hurliness **277** B9
Hurlston Green **183** E1
Hurn **106** A3
Hursley **119** F5
Hurst *NYorks* **201** F2
Hurst *W'ham* **134** C5
Hurst Green *Essex* **139** D1
Hurst Green *ESuss* **110** C1
Hurst Green *Lancs* **193** D4
Hurst Green *Surr* **122** C3
Hurst Wickham **109** E2
Hurstbourne Priors **119** F3
Hurstbourne Tarrant **119** E2
Hurstpierpoint **109** E2
Hurstwood **193** E4
Hurtmore **121** E3
Hurworth-on-Tees **202** B1
Hury **211** F5
Husabost **263** G6
Husbands Bosworth **160** B4
Husborne Crawley **149** E4
Husthwaite **203** E5
Hutcherleigh **101** D2
Hutchwaite **173** F2
Huttoft **189** F5
Hutton *Cumb* **210** A5
Hutton *Essex* **137** F3
Hutton *Lancs* **192** B5
Hutton *NSom* **116** A2
Hutton *ScBord* **237** G4
Hutton Buscel **204** C4
Hutton Bonville **202** C2
Hutton Conyers **202** C5
Hutton Cranswick **196** C2
Hutton End **210** A4
Hutton Hang **202** A4
Hutton Henry **212** D4
Hutton Magna **202** A1
Hutton Mount **137** F3
Hutton Mulgrave **204** B2
Hutton Roof *Cumb* **199** G5
Hutton Roof *Cumb* **209** G3
Hutton Rudby **203** D2
Hutton Sessay **203** D5
Hutton Wandesley **195** E2
Hutton-le-Hole **203** G3
Huxham **102** C3
Huxham Green **116** C4
Huxley **170** C1
Huxter *Shet* **279** C7
Huxter *Shet* **279** E6
Huyton **183** F3
Hycemoor **198** B4
Hyde *Glos* **132** A2
Hyde *GtMan* **184** D3
Hyde End *W'ham* **120** C1
Hyde End *WBerks* **119** G1
Hyde Heath **135** E2
Hyde Lea **158** B1
Hydestile **121** E3
Hylands Park *Essex* CM2 8WQ **137** F2

Hyndford Bridge **234** D5
Hyndlee **227** G5
Hynish **246** A3
Hyssington **156** C3
Hythe *Hants* **106** D2
Hythe *Kent* **125** D5
Hythe End **135** F5
Hythie **269** J5
Hyton **198** B4

**I**

Ianstown **268** C4
Iarsiadar **270** D4
Ibberton **105** D2
Ible **172** D2
Ibsley **106** A2
Ibstock **159** G1
Ibstone **134** C3
Ibthorpe **119** E2
Ibworth **119** G2
Icelton **116** A1
Ickburgh **163** G3
Ickenham **135** F4
Ickford **134** B2
Ickham **125** E3
Ickleford **149** G4
Icklesham **111** D2
Ickleton **150** C4
Icklingham **163** F5
Ickwell Green **149** G3
Icomb **147** E5
Idbury **147** E5
Iddesleigh **113** F5
Ide **102** C3
Ide Hill **123** D3
Ideford **102** B5
Iden **111** E1
Iden Green *Kent* **123** G5
Iden Green *Kent* **124** A5
Idle **194** A4
Idless **96** C5
Idlicote **147** E3
Idmiston **118** C4
Idridgehay **173** D3
Idridgehay Green **173** D3
Idrigil **263** J5
Idstone **133** E4
Idvies **252** D5
Iffley **134** A2
Ifield **122** B5
Ifieldwood **122** B5
Ifold **192** A4
Iford *Bourne* **106** A3
Iford *ESuss* **109** G3
Ifton **131** D4
Ifton Heath **170** A4
Ightfield **170** C4
Ightham **123** E3
Ightham Mote *Kent* TN15 0NT **123** E3
Iken **153** F2
Ilam **172** C2
Ilchester **116** C5
Ilderton **229** E4
Ilford **136** D4
Ilfracombe **113** F1
Ilkeston **173** F3
Ilketshall St. Andrew **165** E3
Ilketshall St. Lawrence **165** E3
Ilketshall St. Margaret **165** E3
Ilkley **194** A3
Illey **158** B4
Illidge Green **171** E1
Illington **164** A3
Illingworth **193** G5
Illogan **96** A5
Illston on the Hill **160** C3
Ilmer **134** C2
Ilmington **147** E3
Ilminster **103** G1
Ilsington *Devon* **102** A5
Ilsington *Dorset* **105** D3
Ilston **128** B3
Ilton *NYorks* **202** A5
Ilton *Som* **103** G1
Imachar **231** G5
Imber **118** A3
Immeroin **242** A3
Immingham **188** B1
Immingham Dock **188** C1
Imperial War Museum, Duxford *Cambs* CB22 4QR **150** C3
Imperial War Museum, London *GtLon* SE1 6HZ **45** G7
Imperial War Museum North *GtMan* M17 1TZ **24** D3
Impington **150** C1
Ince **183** F5
Ince Blundell **183** E2
Ince-in-Makerfield **183** G2
Inch Kenneth **238** D1
Inch of Arnhall **253** E2
Inchbare **253** E3
Inchberry **268** B5
Inchbraoch **253** F4
Inchgrundle **252** C2
Inchindown **266** D4
Inchinnan **233** F3
Inchkinloch **273** J4
Inchlaggan **257** H4
Inchlumpie **266** C4
Inchmarlo **260** E5
Inchmarnock **232** B4
Inchnabobart **252** B1
Inchnacardoch Hotel **257** K3
Inchnadamph **272** E6
Inchock **253** E5
Inchrory **259** J4
Inchture **244** A2
Inchvuilt **257** J1
Inchyra **243** G2
Indian Queens **96** D4
Inerval **230** B5
Ingatestone **137** F3
Ingbirchworth **185** G2
Ingerthorpe **194** B1
Ingestre **171** G5
Ingham *Lincs* **187** G4
Ingham *Norf* **179** E3

Ingham *Suff* **163** G5
Ingham Corner **179** E3
Ingleborough **162** C1
Ingleby *Derbys* **173** E5
Ingleby *Lincs* **187** F5
Ingleby Barwick **202** D1
Ingleby Cross **202** D2
Ingleby Greenhow **203** E2
Ingleigh Green **113** G5
Inglesbatch **117** E1
Inglesham **133** E3
Ingleton *Dur* **212** A5
Ingleton *NYorks* **200** A5
Inglewhite **192** B4
Ingliston **235** F2
Ingmire Hall **200** B3
Ingoe **220** C4
Ingol **192** B4
Ingoldisthorpe **177** E4
Ingoldmells **177** D1
Ingoldsby **175** F4
Ingon **147** D2
Ingram **229** E5
Ingrave **137** F3
Ingrow **193** G4
Ings **199** F3
Ingst **131** E4
Ingworth **178** C3
Inistrynich **240** C2
Injebreck **190** B3
Inkberrow **146** C2
Inkersall **186** B5
Inkersall Green **186** B5
Inkhorn **261** H1
Inkpen **119** E1
Inkstack **275** H1
Innmarsh **118** A1
Inmarsh **118** A1
Innellan **232** C3
Innergellie **245** D4
Innerleithen **227** E2
Innerleven **244** B4
Innermessan **214** B4
Innerwick *ELoth* **237** E2
Innerwick *P&K* **250** A5
Inninbeg **247** G1
Insch **260** E2
Insh **259** F4
Inshore **273** F2
Inskip **192** A4
Instaple **116** A5
Instow **113** E3
Intake **186** C2
Intech, Winchester *Hants* SO21 1HX **119** G5
International Centre, The, Telford *Tel&W* TF3 4JH **157** G2
Intwood **178** C5
Inver *A&B* **248** B5
Inver *Aber* **259** K5
Inver *High* **267** F3
Inver *High* **275** G5
Inver *P&K* **251** F5
Inver Mallie **248** D1
Inverailort **247** G1
Inveralligin **264** E6
Inverallochy **269** J4
Inveran **266** C2
Inveraray (Inbhir Aora) **240** C4
Inverardoch Mains **242** C4
Inverardran **241** E3
Inverarish **252** C5
Inverarnan (Inbhir Àirnein) **241** F3
Inverasdale **264** D6
Inverbeg **241** F4
Inverbervie **253** G2
Inverboyndie **268** E4
Inverbroom **265** H3
Inverbrough **259** F2
Invercassley **266** B1
Inverchaolain **232** B2
Invercharnan **248** D5
Inverchorachan **241** E3
Inverchoran **265** J6
Inverdruie **259** G3
Inverebrie **261** H1
Invereen **258** E1
Inverernie **267** H5
Inveresk **236** A2
Inverey **251** J2
Inverfarigaig **258** C2
Invergarry (Inbhir Garadh) **257** K4
Invergelder **259** K5
Invergeldie **242** C2
Inverglory **249** E1
Invergordon **266** D5
Invergowrie **244** B1
Inverguseran **256** D4
Inverharroch Farm **260** B1
Inverherive **241** F2
Inverhope **273** G2
Inverie **256** D4
Inverinan **240** B3
Inverinate **257** F2
Inverkeilor **253** E5
Inverkeithing **235** F1
Inverkeithny **268** E6
Inverkip **232** C2
Inverkirkaig **272** C7
Inverlael **265** H3
Inverlauren **233** E1
Inverliever **240** C1
Inverlochlarig **241** G3
Inverlochy **241** D2
Inverlussa **231** G1
Invermay **243** F3
Invermoriston (Inbhir Moireasdan) **258** B3
Invernaver **274** C2
Inverneil **231** G1
Inverness (Inbhir Nis) **266** D7
Inverness Airport **266** E6
Invernettie **269** K6
Invernoaden **240** D5
Inveroran Hotel (Inbhir Orain) **249** E5
Inverquharity **252** C4
Inverquhomery **269** J6
Inverroy **249** E1

Inversanda **248** B4
Invershiel **257** F3
Invershore **275** H5
Inversnaid Hotel **241** F4
Inverugie **269** K6
Inveruglas (Inbhir Dhubhghlais) **241** F4
Inveruglass **259** F4
Inverurie **250** B5
Invervar **250** B5
Invervegain **232** B2
Invery House **260** E5
Inverythan **269** F6
Inwardleigh **99** F1
Inworth **138** B1
Iochdar **262** C7
Iona **238** B2
Iping **121** D5
Ipplepen **101** D5
Ipsden **134** B4
Ipstones **172** B3
Ipswich **152** C3
Irby **183** D4
Irby Hill **183** D4
Irby in the Marsh **176** C1
Irby upon Humber **188** B2
Irchester **149** E1
Ireby *Cumb* **209** F3
Ireby *Lancs* **200** B5
Ireland *Ork* **277** C7
Ireland *Shet* **279** C10
Ireland's Cross **171** E3
Ireleth **198** D5
Ireshopeburn **211** E4
Irlam **184** B3
Irnham **175** F5
Iron Acton **131** F4
Iron Cross **146** C2
Ironbridge **157** F2
Ironbridge Gorge *Tel&W* TF8 7DQ **157** F2
Irons Bottom **122** B4
Ironside **269** G5
Ironville **173** F2
Irstead **179** E3
Irthington **210** A1
Irthlingborough **161** E5
Irton **204** D4
Irvine **224** B2
Isauld **274** E2
Isbister *Ork* **277** C6
Isbister *Ork* **277** B8
Isbister *Shet* **279** E6
Isbister *Shet* **278** C3
Isfield **109** G2
Isham **161** D5
Ishriff **239** F1
Isington **120** C3
Island of Stroma **275** J1
Islawr-dref **154** C1
Islay **230** A3
Islay Airport **230** B4
Islay House **230** B3
Isle Abbotts **116** A5
Isle Brewers **116** A5
Isle of Bute Discovery Centre *A&B* PA20 0AH **232** B3
Isle of Lewis (Eilean Leodhais) **271** F3
Isle of Man **190** B3
Isle of Man Airport **190** A5
Isle of May **245** E5
Isle of Noss **279** E8
Isle of Sheppey **124** B1
Isle of Walney **191** E1
Isle of Whithorn **207** E3
Isle of Wight Pearl *IoW* PO30 4DD **106** D4
Isle of Wight (Sandown) Airport **107** E4
Isle of Wight Zoo *IoW* PO36 8QB **107** F4
Isleham **163** E5
Isleornsay (Eilean Iarmain) **256** C3
Isles of Scilly (Scilly Isles) **96** B1
Islesburgh **279** C6
Isleworth **136** A5
Isley Walton **173** F5
Islibhig **270** B5
Islip *N'hants* **161** E5
Islip *Oxon* **134** A1
Isombridge **157** F1
Istead Rise **123** F2
Itchen **106** D2
Itchen Abbas **119** G4
Itchen Stoke **119** G4
Itchen Valley Country Park *Hants* SO30 3HQ **4** C2
Itchingfield **121** G5
Itchington **131** F4
Itteringham **178** C2
Itton *Devon* **99** G1
Itton *Mon* **131** D3
Itton Common **131** D3
Ivegill **210** A3
Ivelet **201** E3
Iver **135** F4
Iver Heath **135** F4
Iveston **212** A2
Ivetsey Bank **158** A1
Ivinghoe **135** E1
Ivinghoe Aston **135** E1
Ivington **145** D2
Ivington Green **145** D2
Ivy Hatch **123** E3
Ivy Todd **163** G2
Ivybridge **100** C2
Ivychurch **111** F1
Iwade **124** B2
Iwerne Courtney (Shroton) **105** E1
Iwerne Minster **105** E1
Ixworth **164** A4
Ixworth Thorpe **164** A4

**J**

Jack Hill **194** A2
Jackfield **157** F2
Jacksdale **173** F2
Jackstown **261** F1
Jackton **233** G4

Jacobstow **98** B1
Jacobswell **121** E2
James Hamilton Heritage Park *SLan* G74 5LB **31** E1
James Pringle Weavers of Inverness *High* IV2 4RB **266** D7
Jameston **127** D3
Jamestown *D&G* **218** B2
Jamestown *High* **266** B6
Jamestown *WDun* **233** E1
Janefield **266** E6
Janetstown *High* **275** J3
Janetstown *High* **275** J3
Jarrow **212** C1
Jarvis Brook **123** E5
Jasper's Green **151** F5
Jawcraig **234** D2
Jayes Park **121** G3
Jaywick **139** E1
Jealott's Hill **135** D5
Jeater Houses **202** D3
Jedburgh **228** A4
Jeffreyston **127** D2
Jemimaville **266** E5
Jephson Gardens *Warks* CV32 4ER **16** B6
Jericho **184** C1
Jersay **234** C3
Jersey **100** C5
Jersey Airport **100** B5
Jersey Marine **128** D3
Jerviswood **234** C5
Jesmond **212** B1
Jevington **110** A3
Jinney Ring Craft Centre, The *Worcs* B60 4BU **146** B1
Jockey End **135** F1
Jodrell Bank **184** B5
Jodrell Bank Observatory & Arboretum *ChesE* SK11 9DL **184** B5
John Muir Country Park *ELoth* EH42 1UW **236** D2
John o' Groats **275** J1
Johnby **210** A4
John's Cross **110** C1
Johnshaven **253** F3
Johnson Street **179** E4
Johnston **126** C1
Johnstone **233** F3
Johnstone Castle **233** F3
Johnstonebridge **217** E1
Johnstons Cashmere Visitor Centre *Moray* IV30 4AF **267** K5
Johnstown *Carmar* **127** G1
Johnstown *Wrex* **170** A3
Joppa **224** C4
Jordans **135** E3
Jordanston **140** C4
Jordanstone **252** A5
Jorvik *YO1 9WT* **90** York
Jorvik Glass *NYorks* YO60 7DA **195** G1
Joy's Green **131** F1
Jumpers Common **106** A3
Juniper Green **235** F3
Juniper Hill **148** A4
Jura **231** D1
Jura House **230** C3
Jurby East **190** B2
Jurby West **190** B2

**K**

Kaber **200** C1
Kaimes **235** G3
Kames *A&B* **232** A2
Kames *A&B* **240** A3
Kames *EAyr* **225** E3
Kathellan *Fife* KY4 0JR **243** G5
Kea **96** C5
Keadby **187** F1
Keal Cotes **176** B1
Kearsley **184** B2
Kearstwick **200** B5
Kearton **201** F3
Kearvaig **272** E1
Keasden **192** D1
Kebholes **268** E5
Keckwick **183** G4
Keddington **188** D4
Keddington Corner **189** D4
Kedington **151** F3
Kedleston **173** E3
Keelby **188** B1
Keele **171** F3
Keeley Green **149** F3
Keelham **193** G4
Keenthorne **115** F4
Keeres Green **137** E1
Keeston **126** B1
Keevil **118** A2
Kegworth **173** F5
Kehelland **96** A5
Keig **260** E3
Keighley **193** G3
Keighley & Worth Valley Railway *WYorks* BD22 8NJ **193** G3
Keil *A&B* **222** B5
Keil *High* **248** B4
Keilhill **269** F5
Keillmore **231** E1
Keillor **243** E2
Keillour **243** E2
Keills **230** C3
Keils **230** D3
Keinton Mandeville **116** C4
Keir House **242** C5
Keir Mill **216** C1
Keisby **175** F5
Keisley **210** D5
Keiss **275** J2
Keith **268** C5
Keithick **244** A1
Keithmore **260** B1
Keithock **253** E3
Kelby **175** F3
Keld *Cumb* **199** G1
Keld *NYorks* **201** D2

Keldholme **203** G4
Keldy Castle **203** G3
Kelfield *NLincs* **187** F2
Kelfield *NYorks* **195** E4
Kelham **174** C2
Kella **190** B2
Kellacott **99** E2
Kellan **247** E5
Kellas *Angus* **244** C1
Kellas *Moray* **267** J6
Kellaton **101** D4
Kellaways **132** B5
Kelleth **200** B2
Kelleythorpe **196** C2
Kelling **178** B1
Kellington **195** E5
Kelloe **212** C4
Kelloholm **225** F4
Kelly *Corn* **97** E2
Kelly *Devon* **99** D2
Kelly Bray **99** D3
Kelmarsh **160** C5
Kelmscott **133** E3
Kelsale **153** E2
Kelsall **170** C1
Kelsay **230** A4
Kelshall **150** B4
Kelsick **209** F1
Kelso **228** B3
Kelstedge **173** E1
Kelstern **188** C3
Kelston **117** E1
Keltneyburn **250** C5
Kelton **217** D3
Kelton Hill (Rhonehouse) **216** B5
Kelty **243** G5
Kelvedon **138** B1
Kelvedon Hatch **137** E3
Kelvingrove Art Gallery & Museum *Glas* G3 8AG **38** B2
Kelvinside **233** G3
Kelynack **94** A4
Kemacott **113** G1
Kemback **244** C3
Kemberton **157** G2
Kemble **132** B3
Kemerton **146** B4
Kemeys Commander **130** C2
Kemeys Inferior **130** C3
Kemnay **261** F3
Kemp Town **109** F3
Kempe's Corner **124** C4
Kempley **145** F5
Kempley Green **145** F5
Kemps Green **158** D5
Kempsey **146** A2
Kempsford **133** D3
Kempshott **119** G3
Kempston **149** F3
Kempston Hardwick **149** F3
Kempston West End **149** E3
Kempton **156** C4
Kemsing **123** E3
Kemsley **124** B2
Kenardington **124** B5
Kenchester **144** D3
Kencot **133** E2
Kendal **199** G3
Kenderchurch **144** D5
Kendleshire **131** F5
Kenfig **129** D4
Kenfig Hill **129** E4
Kenidjack **94** A3
Kenilworth **159** E5
Kenilworth Castle *Warks* CV8 1NE **16** A4
Kenknock *P&K* **250** A5
Kenknock *Stir* **241** G1
Kenley *GtLon* **122** C2
Kenley *Shrop* **157** E2
Kenmore *A&B* **240** C4
Kenmore *High* **264** D6
Kenmore *P&K* **250** C5
Kenmore *ESiar* **270** E7
Kenn *Devon* **102** C4
Kenn *NSom* **116** B1
Kennacley **263** G2
Kennacraig **231** G3
Kennards House **97** G1
Kennavay **263** H2
Kenneggy Downs **94** C4
Kennerleigh **102** B2
Kennerty **260** E5
Kennet **243** E5
Kennethmont **260** D2
Kennett **151** E1
Kennford **102** C4
Kenninghall **164** B3
Kennington *Kent* **124** C4
Kennington *Oxon* **134** A2
Kennoway **244** B4
Kenny **103** G1
Kennyhill **163** E5
Kennythorpe **195** G1
Kenovay **246** A2
Kensaleyre **263** K6
Kensington **233** B4
Kensington Palace *GtLon* W8 4PX **10** E4
Kenstone **170** C5
Kensworth **135** F1
Kent & East Sussex Railway *Kent* TN30 6HE **124** A5
Kent International Airport **125** F2
Kent Street *ESuss* **110** C2
Kent Street *Kent* **123** F3
Kentallen (Ceann an t-Sàilein) **248** C4
Kentchurch **144** D5
Kentford **151** F1
Kentisbeare **103** D2
Kentisbury **113** G1
Kentisbury Ford **113** G1
Kentish Town **136** B4
Kentmere **199** F2
Kenton *Devon* **102** C4
Kenton *Suff* **152** C1
Kenton *T&W* **212** B1
Kenton Corner **152** D1
Kentra **247** F2
Kents Bank **199** E5
Kent's Green **145** G5
Kent's Oak **119** E5
Kenwick **170** B4

Kenwood House GtLon NW3 7JR 10 F2
Kenwyn 96 C5
Kenyon 184 A3
Keoldale 273 F2
Keose (Ceòs) 271 F5
Keppanach 248 C3
Keppoch A&B 233 E2
Keppoch High 256 E2
Keprigan 222 B4
Kepwick 203 D3
Keresley 159 F4
Kernborough 101 D3
Kerrera 240 A2
Kerridge 184 D5
Kerris 94 B4
Kerry (Ceri) 156 A3
Kerrycroy 232 C3
Kerry's Gate 144 C4
Kerrysdale 264 E4
Kersall 174 C1
Kersey 152 B3
Kersey Vale 152 B3
Kershopefoot 218 C3
Kerswell 103 D2
Kerswell Green 146 A3
Kerthen Wood 94 C3
Kesgrave 152 D3
Kessingland 165 G3
Kessingland Beach 165 G3
Kestle 97 D5
Kestle Mill 96 C4
Keston 122 D2
Keswick Cumb 209 F4
Keswick Norf 178 D5
Keswick Norf 179 E2
Ketley Bank 157 F1
Ketsby 189 D5
Kettering 161 D5
Ketteringham 178 C5
Kettins 244 A1
Kettle Corner 123 G3
Kettlebaston 152 A2
Kettlebridge 244 B4
Kettlebrook 159 E2
Kettleburgh 153 D1
Kettlehill 244 B4
Kettleholm 217 F3
Kettleness 204 B1
Kettleshulme 185 D5
Kettlesing 194 B2
Kettlesing Bottom 194 B2
Kettlesing Head 194 B2
Kettlestone 178 A2
Kettlethorpe 187 F5
Kettletoft 276 F4
Kettlewell 201 E5
Ketton 161 E2
Kevingtown 123 D2
Kew 136 A5
Kewstoke 116 A1
Kexbrough 186 A2
Kexby Lincs 187 F4
Kexby York 195 G2
Key Green 171 F1
Keyham 160 B2
Keyhaven 106 C3
Keyingham 197 E5
Keymer 109 F2
Keynsham 117 D1
Key's Toft 176 C2
Keysoe 149 F1
Keysoe Row 149 F1
Keyston 161 F5
Keyworth 174 B4
Kibblesworth 212 B2
Kibworth Beauchamp 160 B3
Kibworth Harcourt 160 B3
Kidbrooke 136 D5
Kiddemore Green 158 A2
Kidderminster 158 A5
Kiddington 147 G5
Kidlington 133 G1
Kidmore End 134 B5
Kidnal 170 B3
Kidsdale 207 E3
Kidsgrove 171 F2
Kidstones 201 E4
Kidwelly (Cydweli) 128 A2
Kiel Crofts 240 A1
Kielder 219 E2
Kielder Forest N'umb NE48 1ER 219 E2
Kielder Water N'umb NE48 1BX 219 F3
Kilbarchan 233 F3
Kilbeg 256 C4
Kilberry 231 F3
Kilbirnie 233 E4
Kilblaan 240 D3
Kilbraur 274 D7
Kilbrennan 246 D5
Kilbride A&B 240 A2
Kilbride A&B 232 B3
Kilbride High 256 B2
Kilbride Farm 232 A3
Kilbridemore 240 C5
Kilburn Derbys 173 E3
Kilburn GtLon 136 B4
Kilburn NYorks 203 E5
Kilby 160 B3
Kilchattan Bay 232 C4
Kilchenzie 222 B3
Kilcheran 240 A1
Kilchiaran 230 A3
Kilchoan A&B 239 G3
Kilchoan High 247 D3
Kilchoman 230 A3
Kilchrenan (Cill Chrèanain) 240 C2
Kilchrist 222 B4
Kilconquhar 244 C4
Kilcot 145 F5
Kilcoy 266 C6
Kilcreggan 232 D1
Kildale 203 F2
Kildary 266 E4
Kildavie 222 C4
Kildermorie Lodge 266 C4
Kildonan NAyr 223 F3
Kildonan (Cilldonnain) ESiar 254 C2
Kildonan Lodge 274 E6
Kildonnan 247 D1
Kildrochet House 214 B5
Kildrummy 260 C3
Kildwick 193 G3
Kilfinan 232 A2
Kilfinnan 257 J5
Kilgetty 127 E2
Kilgwrrwg Common 131 D3
Kilham ERid 196 C1
Kilham N'umb 228 C3
Kilkenneth 246 A2
Kilkenny 132 C1
Kilkerran A&B 222 C4
Kilkerran SAyr 224 B5
Kilkhampton 112 C4
Killamarsh 186 B4
Killay 128 C3
Killbeg 247 F5
Killean A&B 231 E5
Killean A&B 240 C4
Killearn 233 G1
Killellan 222 B4
Killen 266 D6
Killerby 212 A5
Killerton 102 C2
Killerton Devon EX5 3LE 102 C2
Killichonan 250 A4
Killiechonate 249 E1
Killiechronan 247 E5
Killiecrankie 251 E3
Killiehuntly 258 E5
Killiemor 239 D1
Killilan 257 F1
Killimster 275 J3
Killin High 267 F1
Killin Stir 242 A1
Killinallan 230 B2
Killinghall 194 B2
Killington Cumb 200 B4
Killington Devon 113 G1
Killingworth 221 E4
Killochyett 236 B5
Killocraw 222 B2
Killunaig 239 D2
Killundine 247 E5
Kilmacolm 233 E3
Kilmaha 240 B4
Kilmahog 242 B4
Kilmalieu 248 A4
Kilmaluag 263 K4
Kilmany 244 B2
Kilmarie 256 B3
Kilmarnock 224 C2
Kilmartin 240 A5
Kilmaurs 233 F5
Kilmelford 240 A3
Kilmeny 230 B3
Kilmersdon 117 D2
Kilmeston 119 G5
Kilmichael 222 B3
Kilmichael Glassary 240 A5
Kilmichael of Inverlussa 231 F1
Kilmington Devon 103 F3
Kilmington Wilts 117 E4
Kilmington Common 117 E4
Kilmorack 266 B7
Kilmore (A' Chille Mhòr) A&B 240 A2
Kilmore High 256 C4
Kilmory A&B 231 F1
Kilmory A&B 231 F2
Kilmory High 255 J4
Kilmory High 247 E2
Kilmory NAyr 223 E3
Kilmote 274 E7
Kilmuir High 263 H7
Kilmuir High 266 D7
Kilmuir High 266 E4
Kilmuir High 263 J4
Kilmun 232 C1
Kilmux 244 B4
Kiln Green Here 131 F1
Kiln Green W'ham 134 D5
Kiln Pit Hill 211 G2
Kilnave 230 A2
Kilncadzow 234 C5
Kilndown 123 G5
Kilnhurst 186 B3
Kilninian 246 D5
Kilninver 240 A2
Kilnsea 189 E1
Kilnsey 193 F1
Kilnwick 196 B3
Kilnwick Percy 196 A2
Kiloran 238 C5
Kilpatrick 223 E3
Kilpeck 144 D4
Kilphedir 274 E7
Kilpin 195 G5
Kilpin Pike 195 G5
Kilrenny 245 D4
Kilsby 160 A5
Kilspindie 244 A2
Kilstay 206 B3
Kilsyth 234 B2
Kiltarlity 266 C7
Kilton Notts 186 C5
Kilton R&C 203 F1
Kilton Som 115 E3
Kilton Thorpe 203 F1
Kiltyrie 242 B1
Kilvaxter 263 J5
Kilve 115 E3
Kilverstone 163 G4
Kilvington 174 D3
Kilwinning 233 E5
Kimberley Norf 178 B5
Kimberley Notts 173 G3
Kimberworth 186 B3
Kimble Wick 134 D2
Kimblesworth 212 B3
Kimbolton Cambs 149 F1
Kimbolton Here 145 E1
Kimbridge 119 E5
Kimcote 160 A4
Kimmeridge 105 F5
Kimmerston 229 D3
Kimpton Hants 119 D3
Kimpton Herts 136 A1
Kinaldy 244 D3
Kinblethmont 253 E5
Kinbrace 274 D5
Kinbreack 257 G5
Kinbuck 242 C4
Kincaldrum 252 C5
Kincaple 244 C3
Kincardine Fife 234 D1
Kincardine High 266 D3
Kincardine O'Neil 260 D5
Kinclaven 243 G1
Kincorth 261 H4
Kincraig Aber 261 H2
Kincraig High 259 F4
Kincraigie 251 E5
Kindallachan 251 E4
Kindrogan Field Centre 251 F3
Kinellar 261 G3
Kineton Glos 146 C5
Kineton Warks 147 F2
Kineton Green 158 D4
Kinfauns 243 G2
King Sterndale 185 E5
Kingarth 232 B4
Kingcoed 130 D2
Kingerby 188 A3
Kingham 147 E5
Kingholm Quay 217 D3
Kinghorn 235 G1
Kinglassie 244 A5
Kingoodie 244 B2
King's Acre 145 D3
King's Bank 111 D1
King's Bromley 158 D1
King's Caple 145 E5
King's Cliffe 161 F3
King's College Chapel, Cambridge Cambs CB2 1ST 150 C2
King's Coughton 146 C2
King's Green 145 G4
King's Heath 158 C4
Kings Hill Kent 123 F3
King's Hill Warks 159 F5
King's Hill WMid 158 B3
Kings Langley 135 F2
King's Lynn 177 E5
King's Meaburn 210 C5
Kings Mills 101 E5
King's Moss 183 G2
Kings Muir 227 D2
King's Newnham 159 G5
King's Newton 173 E5
King's Norton Leics 160 B2
King's Norton WMid 158 C5
Kings Nympton 113 G4
King's Pyon 144 D2
Kings Ripton 162 A5
King's Somborne 119 E4
King's Stag 104 D1
King's Stanley 132 A2
King's Sutton 147 G4
King's Tamerton 100 A2
King's Walden 149 G5
Kings Worthy 119 F4
Kingsand 100 A2
Kingsbarns 245 D3
Kingsbridge Devon 100 D3
Kingsbridge Som 114 C4
Kingsburgh 263 J6
Kingsbury GtLon 136 A4
Kingsbury Warks 159 E3
Kingsbury Episcopi 116 B5
Kingsbury Water Park Warks B76 0DY 159 E3
Kingscavil 235 E2
Kingsclere 119 G2
Kingscote 132 A3
Kingscott 113 F4
Kingscross 223 F3
Kingsdale 244 B4
Kingsdon 116 C5
Kingsdown Kent 125 F4
Kingsdown Swin 133 D4
Kingsdown Wilts 117 F1
Kingseat 243 G5
Kingsey 134 C2
Kingsfold Pembs 126 C3
Kingsfold WSuss 121 G4
Kingsford Aber 269 F6
Kingsford Aber 260 D3
Kingsford Aberdeen 261 G4
Kingsford EAyr 233 F5
Kingsford Worcs 158 A4
Kingsgate 125 F1
Kingshall Street 152 A1
Kingsheanton 113 F2
Kingshouse 242 A2
Kingshouse Hotel 249 E4
Kingshurst 159 D4
Kingskerswell 101 E1
Kingskettle 244 B4
Kingsland Here 144 D1
Kingsland IoA 180 A4
Kingsley ChesW&C 183 G5
Kingsley Hants 120 C4
Kingsley Staffs 172 B3
Kingsley Green 121 D4
Kingsley Holt 172 B3
Kingslow 157 G3
Kingsmoor 136 D2
Kingsmuir Angus 252 C5
Kingsmuir Fife 244 D4
Kingsnorth 124 C5
Kingsnorth Power Station 124 A1
Kingstanding 158 C3
Kingsteignton 102 B5
Kingsteps 267 G6
Kingsthorne 145 D4
Kingsthorpe 148 C1
Kingston Cambs 150 B2
Kingston Corn 99 D3
Kingston Devon 100 C3
Kingston Devon 103 D4
Kingston Dorset 104 D2
Kingston Dorset 105 F5
Kingston ELoth 236 C1
Kingston GtMan 184 D3
Kingston Hants 106 A2
Kingston IoW 107 D4
Kingston Kent 125 D3
Kingston MK 149 E4
Kingston Moray 268 B4
Kingston WSuss 108 C3
Kingston Bagpuize 133 G3
Kingston Blount 134 C3
Kingston by Sea 109 E3
Kingston Deverill 117 F4
Kingston Gorse 108 C3
Kingston Lacy Dorset BH21 4EA 3 A1
Kingston Lisle 133 F4
Kingston Maurward 104 D3
Kingston near Lewes 109 F3
Kingston on Soar 173 G5
Kingston Russell 104 B3
Kingston St. Mary 115 F5
Kingston Seymour 116 B1
Kingston Stert 134 C2
Kingston upon Hull 196 D5
Kingston upon Thames 121 G1
Kingston Warren 133 F4
Kingstone Here 144 D4
Kingstone Here 145 F5
Kingstone Som 103 G1
Kingstone Staffs 172 B5
Kingstone Winslow 133 E4
Kingstown 209 G1
Kingswear 101 E2
Kingswell 233 G5
Kingswells 261 G4
Kingswinford 158 A4
Kingswood Bucks 134 B1
Kingswood Glos 131 G3
Kingswood Here 144 B2
Kingswood Kent 124 A3
Kingswood Powys 156 B2
Kingswood SGlos 131 F5
Kingswood Som 115 E4
Kingswood Surr 122 B3
Kingswood Warks 159 D5
Kingthorpe 188 B5
Kington Here 144 B2
Kington Worcs 146 B2
Kington Langley 132 B5
Kington Magna 117 E5
Kington St. Michael 132 B5
Kingussie 258 E4
Kingweston 116 C4
Kinharrachie 261 H1
Kinharvie 216 D4
Kinkell 234 A2
Kinkell Bridge 243 E3
Kinknockie 269 J6
Kinlet 157 G4
Kinloch Fife 244 A3
Kinloch High 273 F5
Kinloch High 247 F4
Kinloch High 255 K5
Kinloch High 266 C4
Kinloch P&K 252 A5
Kinloch P&K 251 G5
Kinloch Hourn (Ceann Loch Shubhairne) 257 F4
Kinloch Laggan 250 A1
Kinloch Rannoch 250 B4
Kinlochan 248 A3
Kinlochard 241 G4
Kinlocharkaig 257 F5
Kinlochbeoraid 248 A1
Kinlochbervie 272 E3
Kinlocheil 248 B2
Kinlochetive 248 D5
Kinlochewe 265 G5
Kinlochlaich 248 B5
Kinlochleven (Ceann Loch Liobhann) 249 D3
Kinlochmoidart 247 G2
Kinlochmorar 256 E5
Kinlochmore 249 D3
Kinlochroag (Ceann Lochroag) 270 D5
Kinlochspelve 239 F2
Kinloss 267 H5
Kinmel Bay (Bae Cinmel) 182 A4
Kinmuck 261 G3
Kinnaber 253 F3
Kinnadie 269 H6
Kinnaird 244 A2
Kinneff 253 G2
Kinnelhead 226 B5
Kinnell Angus 253 E4
Kinnell Stir 242 A1
Kinnerley 170 A5
Kinnersley Here 144 C3
Kinnersley Worcs 146 A3
Kinnerton 144 B1
Kinnerton Green 170 A1
Kinnesswood 243 G4
Kinnettles 252 C5
Kinninvie 211 G5
Kinnordy 252 B4
Kinoulton 174 B4
Kinrara 259 F4
Kinross 243 G4
Kinrossie 243 G1
Kinsbourne Green 136 A1
Kinsham Here 144 C1
Kinsham Worcs 146 B4
Kinsley 186 B1
Kinson 105 G3
Kintarvie 270 E6
Kintbury 119 E1
Kintessack 267 G5
Kintillo 243 G3
Kintocher 260 D4
Kinton Here 156 D5
Kinton Shrop 156 C1
Kintore 261 F3
Kintour 230 C4
Kintra A&B 230 B5
Kintra A&B 238 C2
Kintradwell 267 G1
Kintraw 240 A4
Kinuachdrachd 239 G5
Kinveachy 259 G3
Kinver 158 A4
Kinwarton 146 D2
Kiplaw Croft 261 J1
Kipp 242 A3
Kippax 194 D4
Kippen P&K 243 F3
Kippen Stir 242 B5
Kippenross House 242 C4
Kippford (Scaur) 216 C5
Kipping's Cross 123 F4
Kippington 123 E3
Kirbister Ork 277 C7
Kirbister Ork 276 F5
Kirbuster 276 B5
Kirby Bedon 179 D5
Kirby Bellars 160 C1
Kirby Cane 165 E2
Kirby Corner 159 E5
Kirby Cross 152 D5
Kirby Fields 160 A2
Kirby Green 165 E2
Kirby Grindalythe 196 B1
Kirby Hill NYorks 202 A2
Kirby Hill NYorks 194 C1
Kirby Knowle 203 D4
Kirby le Soken 152 D5
Kirby Misperton 203 G5
Kirby Muxloe 160 A2
Kirby Row 165 E2
Kirby Sigston 202 D3
Kirby Underdale 196 A2
Kirby Wiske 202 C4
Kirdford 121 F5
Kirk 275 H3
Kirk Bramwith 186 D1
Kirk Deighton 194 C2
Kirk Ella 196 C5
Kirk Hallam 173 F3
Kirk Hammerton 195 D2
Kirk Ireton 173 D2
Kirk Langley 173 D4
Kirk Merrington 212 B4
Kirk Michael 190 B2
Kirk of Shotts 234 C3
Kirk Sandall 186 D2
Kirk Smeaton 186 C1
Kirk Yetholm 228 C4
Kirkabister 279 D9
Kirkandrews 207 G2
Kirkandrews-upon-Eden 209 G1
Kirkbampton 209 G1
Kirkbean 217 D5
Kirkbride 209 F1
Kirkbuddo 252 D5
Kirkburn ERid 196 B2
Kirkburn ScBord 227 D2
Kirkburton 185 F1
Kirkby Lincs 188 A3
Kirkby Mersey 183 F3
Kirkby NYorks 203 E2
Kirkby Fleetham 202 B3
Kirkby Green 175 F2
Kirkby in Ashfield 173 F2
Kirkby la Thorpe 175 F3
Kirkby Lonsdale 200 B5
Kirkby Malham 193 E1
Kirkby Mallory 159 G2
Kirkby Malzeard 202 B5
Kirkby on Bain 176 A1
Kirkby Overblow 194 C3
Kirkby Stephen 200 C2
Kirkby Thore 210 C5
Kirkby Underwood 175 F5
Kirkby Wharfe 195 E3
Kirkby Woodhouse 173 F2
Kirkby-in-Furness 198 D4
Kirkbymoorside 203 F4
Kirkcaldy 244 A5
Kirkcambeck 210 B1
Kirkcolm 214 B4
Kirkconnel 225 F4
Kirkconnell 217 D4
Kirkcowan 215 E4
Kirkcudbright 216 A5
Kirkdale House 215 G5
Kirkdean 235 F5
Kirkfieldbank 234 C5
Kirkgunzeon 216 C4
Kirkham Lancs 192 A4
Kirkham NYorks 195 G1
Kirkhamgate 194 C5
Kirkharle 220 C3
Kirkhaugh 210 C3
Kirkheaton N'umb 220 C4
Kirkheaton WYorks 185 F1
Kirkhill Angus 253 E3
Kirkhill High 266 C7
Kirkhill Moray 268 B5
Kirkhope 227 E3
Kirkibost High 256 B3
Kirkibost (Circebost) ESiar 270 D4
Kirkinch 252 B5
Kirkinner 215 F5
Kirkintilloch 234 A2
Kirkland Cumb 210 C4
Kirkland Cumb 209 D5
Kirkland D&G 216 C1
Kirkland D&G 225 F4
Kirkland D&G 217 E2
Kirkland of Longcastle 207 D2
Kirkleatham 213 E5
Kirklevington 202 D1
Kirkley 165 G2
Kirklington Notts 174 B2
Kirklington NYorks 202 C4
Kirklinton 210 A1
Kirkliston 235 F2
Kirkmaiden 206 B3
Kirkmichael P&K 251 F3
Kirkmichael SAyr 224 B5
Kirkmuirhill 234 B5
Kirknewton N'umb 228 D3
Kirknewton WLoth 235 F3
Kirkney 260 D1
Kirkoswald Cumb 210 B3
Kirkoswald SAyr 224 A5
Kirkpatrick Durham 216 B3
Kirkpatrick-Fleming 218 A4
Kirksanton 198 C4
Kirkstall 194 B4
Kirkstead 175 G1
Kirkstile Aber 260 D1
Kirkstile D&G 218 B2
Kirkstyle 275 J1
Kirkthorpe 194 C5
Kirkton A&B 239 G4
Kirkton Aber 260 E2
Kirkton Aber 268 E5
Kirkton Aber 260 E3
Kirkton Angus 252 C5
Kirkton D&G 217 D2
Kirkton Fife 244 B2
Kirkton High 258 D1
Kirkton High 266 E2
Kirkton High 266 E6
Kirkton High 274 D2
Kirkton High 256 E2
Kirkton P&K 243 E3
Kirkton ScBord 227 G4
Kirkton Manor 226 D2
Kirkton of Airlie 252 B4
Kirkton of Auchterhouse 244 B1
Kirkton of Barevan 267 F7
Kirkton of Bourtie 261 G2
Kirkton of Collace 243 G1
Kirkton of Craig 253 F4
Kirkton of Culsalmond 260 E1
Kirkton of Durris 261 F5
Kirkton of Glenbuchat 260 B3
Kirkton of Glenisla 252 A3
Kirkton of Kingoldrum 252 B4
Kirkton of Lethendy 251 G5
Kirkton of Logie Buchan 261 H2
Kirkton of Maryculter 261 G5
Kirkton of Menmuir 252 D3
Kirkton of Monikie 244 D1
Kirkton of Rayne 260 E1
Kirkton of Skene 261 G4
Kirkton of Tealing 244 C1
Kirktonhill Aber 253 E3
Kirktonhill WDun 233 E2
Kirktown 269 J5
Kirktown of Alvah 268 E4
Kirktown of Auchterless 269 F6
Kirktown of Deskford 268 D4
Kirktown of Fetteresso 253 G1
Kirktown of Slains 261 J2
Kirkwall 277 D6
Kirkwall Airport 277 D7
Kirkwhelpington 220 B3
Kirmington 188 B1
Kirmond le Mire 188 B3
Kirn 232 C2
Kirriemuir 252 B4
Kirstead Green 165 D2
Kirtlebridge 218 A4
Kirtleton 218 A3
Kirtling 151 E2
Kirtling Green 151 E2
Kirtlington 134 A1
Kirtomy 274 C2
Kirton Lincs 176 B4
Kirton Notts 174 B1
Kirton Suff 153 D4
Kirton End 176 A3
Kirton Holme 176 A3
Kirton in Lindsey 187 G3
Kiscadale 223 F3
Kislingbury 148 B2
Kismeldon Bridge 113 D4
Kit Hill Country Park Corn PL17 8AX 99 D3
Kites Hardwick 147 G1
Kitley 100 B2
Kittisford 115 D5
Kittisford Barton 115 D5
Kittle 128 B4
Kitt's End 136 B3
Kitt's Green 159 D4
Kitwood 120 B4
Kivernoll 145 D4
Kiveton Park 186 B4
Klibreck 273 H5
Knabbygates 268 D5
Knaith 187 F4
Knaith Park 187 F4
Knap Corner 117 F5
Knaphill 121 E2
Knaplock 114 B4
Knapp P&K 244 A1
Knapp Som 116 A5
Knapthorpe 174 C2
Knaptoft 160 B4
Knapton Norf 179 E2
Knapton York 195 E2
Knapton Green 144 D2
Knapwell 150 B1
Knaresborough 194 C2
Knarsdale 210 C2
Knarston 276 C5
Knaven 269 G6
Knayton 202 D4
Knebworth 150 A5
Knebworth House Herts SG3 6PY 150 A5
Knedlington 195 G5
Kneesall 174 C1
Kneesworth 150 B3
Kneeton 174 C3
Knelston 128 A4
Knenhall 171 G4
Knettishall 164 A3
Knettishall Heath Country Park Suff IP22 2TQ 164 A3
Knightacott 113 G2
Knightcote 147 G2
Knightley 171 F5
Knightley Dale 171 F5
Knighton Devon 100 B3
Knighton Dorset 104 C1
Knighton Leic 160 A2
Knighton Poole 105 G3
Knighton (Tref-y-clawdd) Powys 156 B5
Knighton Som 115 E3
Knighton Staffs 171 E5
Knighton Staffs 171 E3
Knighton Wilts 133 E5
Knighton on Teme 157 F5
Knightswood 233 G3
Knightwick 145 G2
Knill 144 B1
Knipoch 240 A2
Knipton 174 D4
Knitsley 212 A3
Kniveton 172 D2
Knock A&B 239 E1
Knock Cumb 210 C5
Knock High 256 C4
Knock Moray 268 D5
Knock of Auchnahannet 259 H1
Knockalava 240 B5
Knockally 275 G6
Knockaloe Moar 190 A3
Knockan 272 E7
Knockandhu 259 K2
Knockando 267 J7
Knockarthur 266 E1
Knockbain 266 D6
Knockban 265 J5
Knockbreck 266 E3
Knockbrex 207 F2
Knockdamph 265 J2
Knockdee 275 G2
Knockdow 232 C2
Knockdown 132 A4
Knockenkelly 223 F3
Knockentiber 224 B2
Knockfin 257 K2
Knockgray 215 G1
Knockholt 123 D3
Knockholt Pound 123 D3
Knockin 170 A5
Knockinlaw 224 C2
Knockintorran (Cnoc an Torrain) 262 C5
Knocklearn 216 B3
Knockmill 123 E2
Knocknaha 222 B4
Knocknain 214 A4
Knocknalling 215 G2
Knockrome 231 D2
Knocksharry 190 A3
Knockville 215 E3
Knockvologan 238 C3
Knodishall 153 F1
Knodishall Common 153 F1
Knodishall Green 153 F1
Knole 116 B5
Knolls Green 184 C5
Knolton 170 A4
Knook 118 A3
Knossington 160 D2
Knott End-on-Sea 191 G3
Knotting 149 F1
Knotting Green 149 F1
Knottingley 195 E5
Knotts 193 D2
Knotty Green 135 E3
Knowbury 157 E5
Knowe 215 E3
Knowes of Elrick 268 E5
Knowesgate 220 B3
Knoweside 224 A4
Knowetownhead 227 G4
Knowhead 269 H5
Knowl Green 151 F3
Knowl Hill 134 D5
Knowl Wall 171 F4
Knowle Bristol 131 F5
Knowle Devon 102 A2
Knowle Devon 113 E2
Knowle Devon 103 D4
Knowle Shrop 157 E5
Knowle Som 114 C3
Knowle WMid 159 D5
Knowle Cross 102 D3
Knowle Green 192 C4
Knowle Hall 116 A3
Knowle St. Giles 103 G1
Knowlton Dorset 105 G1
Knowlton Kent 125 E3
Knowsley 183 F3
Knowsley Safari Park Mersey L34 4AN 23 E2
Knowstone 114 B5
Knox Bridge 123 G4
Knucklas (Cnwclas) 156 B5
Knutsford 184 B5
Knypersley 171 F2
Krumlin 185 E1
Kuggar 95 E5
Kyle of Lochalsh (Caol Loch Aillse) 256 D2
Kyleakin (Caol Acain) 256 D2
Kylerhea (Ceol Reatha) 256 D2
Kyles Scalpay (Caolas Scalpaigh) 263 H2
Kylesbeg 247 F2
Kylesknoydart 256 E5
Kylesku 272 E5
Kylesmorar 256 E5
Kylestrome 272 E5
Kyloag 266 D2
Kynaston 170 A5
Kynnersley 157 F1
Kyre Park 145 F1

L

Labost 270 E3
Lacasaigh 271 F5
Lace Market Centre NG1 1HF 80 Nottingham
Laceby 188 C2
Lacey Green 134 D2
Lach Dennis 184 B5
Lackford 163 F5
Lacklee (Leac a' Li) 263 G2
Lacock 118 A1
Ladbroke 147 G2
Laddingford 123 F4
Lade Bank 176 B2
Ladies Hill 192 A3
Ladock 96 C4
Lady Hall 198 C4
Lady Lever Art Gallery Mersey CH62 5EQ 22 B4
Ladybank 244 B3
Ladycross 98 D2
Ladyfield 240 C3
Ladykirk 237 F5
Ladysford 269 H4
Ladywood 146 A1
Laga 247 F3
Lagalochan 240 A3
Lagavulin 230 C5
Lagg A&B 231 D2
Lagg NAyr 223 E3
Lagg SAyr 224 A4
Laggan A&B 230 A4
Laggan (An Lagan) High 257 J5
Laggan High 258 D5
Laggan Moray 260 B1
Laggan Stir 242 A3
Lagganulva 247 D5
Lagganvoulin 259 J3
Laglingarten 240 D4
Lagnalean 266 D7
Lagrae 225 F4
Laguna 243 G1
Laid 273 G3
Laide 265 F2
Laig 247 D1
Laight 225 E4
Lainchoil 259 H3
Laindon 137 F4

Laing Art Gallery *T&W*
    NE1 8AG
    **79** Newcastle upon Tyne
Lair **251** G3
Lairg **266** C1
Lairg Lodge **266** C1
Lairigmor **248** D3
Laisterdyke **194** A4
Laithers **268** E6
Laithes **210** A4
Lake *Devon* **113** F2
Lake *Devon* **100** B1
Lake *IoW* **107** E4
Lake *Wilts* **118** C4
Lake District Visitor Centre
    at Brockhole *Cumb*
    LA23 1LJ **199** E2
Lakenham **178** D5
Lakenheath **163** F4
Lakes Aquarium *Cumb*
    LA12 8AS **199** E4
Lakes End **162** D3
Lakes Glass Centre,
    Ulverston *Cumb*
    LA12 7LY **199** E4
Lakeside *Cumb* **199** E4
Lakeside *Thur* **137** E5
Lakeside & Haverthwaite
    Railway *Cumb*
    LA12 8AL **199** E4
Laleham **121** F1
Laleston **129** E5
Lamancha **235** G4
Lamarsh **151** G4
Lamas **178** D3
Lamb Corner **152** B4
Lamb Roe **192** D4
Lambden **237** E5
Lamberhurst **123** F5
Lamberhurst
    Quarter **123** F5
Lamberton **237** G4
Lambfell Moar **190** A3
Lambley *N'umb* **210** C2
Lambley *Notts* **174** B3
Lambourn **133** F5
Lambourn
    Woodlands **133** F5
Lambourne End **137** D3
Lambs Green **122** B5
Lambston **126** C1
Lambton **212** B2
Lamerton **99** E3
Lamesley **212** B2
Lamington *High* **266** E4
Lamington *SLan* **226** A2
Lamlash **223** F2
Lamloch **215** G1
Lamonby **210** A4
Lamorna **94** B4
Lamorran **96** C5
Lampert **219** E4
Lampeter (Llanbedr Pont
    Steffan) **142** B3
Lampeter Velfrey **127** E1
Lamphey **126** D2
Lamplugh **209** D4
Lamport **160** C5
Lamyatt **117** D4
Lana *Devon* **98** D1
Lana *Devon* **112** D5
Lanark **226** A5
Lancaster **192** A1
Lancaster Leisure Park
    *Lancs* LA1 3LA **192** A1
Lancaster Priory *Lancs*
    LA1 1YZ **192** A1
Lanchester **212** A3
Lancing **109** E3
Landbeach **150** C1
Landcross **113** E3
Landerberry **261** F4
Landewednack **95** E5
Landford **106** B1
Landhallow **275** G5
Landican **183** D4
Landimore **128** A3
Landkey **113** F2
Landmoth **202** D3
Landore **128** C3
Landrake **99** D4
Land's End *Corn*
    TR19 7AA **94** A4
Land's End Airport **94** A4
Landscove **101** D1
Landshipping **126** D1
Landulph **100** A1
Landwade **151** E1
Landywood **158** B2
Lane Bottom **193** E4
Lane End *Bucks* **134** D3
Lane End *Cumb* **198** C3
Lane End *Derbys* **173** F1
Lane End *Dorset* **105** E3
Lane End *Hants* **119** G5
Lane End *Here* **131** F1
Lane End *Kent* **137** E5
Lane End *Wilts* **117** F3
Lane Ends *Derbys* **172** D4
Lane Ends *GtMan* **185** D3
Lane Ends *Lancs* **193** D4
Lane Ends *NYorks* **193** F3
Lane Green **158** A2
Lane Head *Dur* **202** A1
Lane Head *Dur* **211** G5
Lane Head *GtMan* **184** A3
Lane Head *WYorks* **185** F2
Lane Heads **192** A4
Lane Side **193** D5
Laneast **97** G1
Lane-end **97** E3
Laneham **187** F5
Lanehead *Dur* **211** E3
Lanehead *N'umb* **219** F3
Lanesend **127** D2
Lanesfield **158** B3
Laneshawbridge **193** F3
Langais **262** C5
Langamull **246** C4
Langar **174** C4
Langbank **233** E2
Langbar **193** G2
Langbaurgh **203** E1
Langcliffe **193** E1
Langdale End **204** C3
Langdon *Corn* **98** C1

Langdon *Corn* **98** D2
Langdon Beck **211** E4
Langdon Hills **137** F4
Langdon Hills Country Park
    *Essex* SS17 9NH **137** F4
Langdon House **102** C5
Langdyke **244** B4
Langford *CenBeds* **149** G3
Langford *Essex* **138** B2
Langford *Notts* **174** D2
Langford *Oxon* **133** E2
Langford Budville **115** E5
Langham *Essex* **152** B4
Langham *Norf* **178** B1
Langham *Rut* **160** C2
Langham *Suff* **152** A1
Langham Moor **152** B4
Langho **192** C4
Langholm **218** B3
Langland **128** C4
Langlands **216** A5
Langlee **228** A5
Langleeford **228** D4
Langley *ChesE* **184** D5
Langley *Derbys* **173** F3
Langley *Essex* **150** C4
Langley *Glos* **146** C5
Langley *GtMan* **184** C2
Langley *Hants* **106** D2
Langley *Herts* **150** A5
Langley *Kent* **124** A3
Langley *N'um* **211** E1
Langley *Oxon* **133** F1
Langley *Slo* **135** F5
Langley *Som* **115** D5
Langley *Warks* **147** D1
Langley *WSuss* **120** D5
Langley Burrell **132** B5
Langley Corner **135** F4
Langley Green
    *Derbys* **173** D4
Langley Green
    *Warks* **147** E1
Langley Green
    *WSuss* **122** B5
Langley Heath **124** A3
Langley Marsh **115** D5
Langley Mill **173** F3
Langley Moor **212** B3
Langley Park *Bucks*
    SL3 6DW **135** F4
Langley Street **179** E5
Langney **110** B3
Langold **186** C4
Langore **97** G1
Langport **116** B5
Langrick **176** A3
Langrick Bridge **176** A3
Langridge
    *B&NESom* **117** E1
Langridge *Devon* **113** F3
Langridgeford **113** F3
Langrigg **209** E2
Langrish **120** C5
Langsett **185** G2
Langshaw **227** G2
Langshawburn **227** D5
Langside *Glas* **233** G3
Langside *P&K* **242** C3
Langskaill **276** D3
Langstone
    *Newport* **130** C3
Langthorne **202** B3
Langthorpe **194** C1
Langthwaite **201** F2
Langtoft *ERid* **196** C1
Langtoft *Lincs* **161** G1
Langton *Dur* **202** A1
Langton *Lincs* **189** D5
Langton *Lincs* **176** A1
Langton *NYorks* **195** G1
Langton by Wragby **188** B5
Langton Green
    *Kent* **123** E5
Langton Green *Suff* **164** C4
Langton Herring **104** C4
Langton Long
    Blandford **105** E2
Langton Matravers **105** F5
Langtree **113** E4
Langtree Week **113** E4
Langwathby **210** B4
Langwell **266** B1
Langwell House **275** G6
Langwith **186** C5
Langworth **188** A5
Lanhydrock *Corn*
    PL30 5AD **97** E3
Lanivet **97** E3
Lank **97** E2
Lanlivery **97** E4
Lanner **96** B5
Lanoy **97** G2
Lanreath **97** F4
Lansallos **97** F4
Lansdown **131** E1
Lanteglos **97** E1
Lanteglos Highway **97** F4
Lanton *N'umb* **228** D3
Lanton *ScBord* **228** A4
Lanvean **96** C3
Lapford **102** A2
Laphroaig **230** B5
Lapley **158** A1
Lapworth **159** D5
Larach na Gaibhre **231** F2
Larachbeg **247** F5
Larbert **234** C1
Larbreck **192** A3
Larden Green **170** C2
Larg **215** G3
Largie **260** E1
Largiemore **232** A1
Largoward **244** C4
Largs **232** D4
Largue **268** E6
Larguen **222** B4
Largybeg **223** F3
Largymore **223** F3
Lark Hall **151** D2
Larkfield **123** G2
Larkhall **234** B4
Larkhill **118** C3
Larklands **173** F3
Larling **164** A3
Larriston **218** D2

Lartington **201** F1
Lary **269** J4
Lasborough **132** A3
Lasham **120** B3
Lashbrook **113** E5
Lashenden **124** A4
Lassington **145** G5
Lassintullich **250** C4
Lassodie **243** G5
Lastingham **203** G3
Latchford **184** A4
Latchingdon **138** B2
Latchley **99** E3
Lately Common **184** A3
Lathbury **149** D3
Latheron **275** G5
Latheronwheel **275** G5
Lathockar **244** C4
Lathones **244** C4
Lathrisk **244** A4
Latimer **135** F3
Latteridge **131** F4
Lattiford **117** D5
Latton **132** C3
Lauchentyre **215** G5
Lauchintilly **261** F3
Lauder **236** C5
Laugharne
    (Lacharn) **127** G1
Laughterton **187** F5
Laughton *ESuss* **110** A2
Laughton *Leics* **160** B4
Laughton *Lincs* **175** F4
Laughton *Lincs* **187** F3
Laughton en le
    Morthen **186** C4
Launcells **112** C5
Launcells Cross **112** C5
Launceston **98** D2
Launde Abbey **160** C2
Launton **148** B5
Laurencekirk **253** F2
Laurieston *D&G* **216** A4
Laurieston *Falk* **234** D2
Lavendon **149** E2
Lavenham **152** A3
Laverhay **217** F1
Lavernock **115** E1
Laversdale **210** A1
Laverstock **118** C4
Laverstoke **119** F3
Laverton *Glos* **146** C4
Laverton *NYorks* **202** B5
Laverton *Som* **117** E2
Lavister **170** A2
Law **234** C4
Lawers *P&K* **242** C2
Lawers *P&K* **242** B1
Lawford *Essex* **152** B4
Lawford *Som* **115** E4
Lawhitton **99** D2
Lawkland **193** D1
Lawkland Green **193** D1
Lawley **157** F2
Lawnhead **171** F5
Lawrence Weston **131** E5
Lawrenny **126** D2
Laws **244** C1
Lawshall **151** G2
Lawshall Green **151** G2
Lawton **144** D2
Laxdale (Lacasdal) **271** G4
Laxey **190** C3
Laxfield **165** D4
Laxfirth *Shet* **279** D7
Laxfirth *Shet* **279** D8
Laxford Bridge **272** E4
Laxo **279** D6
Laxton *ERid* **195** G5
Laxton *N'hants* **161** E3
Laxton *Notts* **174** C1
Laycock **193** G3
Layer Breton **138** C1
Layer de la Haye **138** C1
Layer Marney **138** C1
Layham **152** B3
Laymore **103** G2
Layter's Green **135** E3
Laytham **195** G4
Layton **191** G4
Lazenby **213** E5
Lazonby **210** B4
Lea *Derbys* **173** E2
Lea *Here* **145** F5
Lea *Lincs* **187** F4
Lea *Shrop* **156** C4
Lea *Shrop* **156** D2
Lea *Wilts* **132** B4
Lea Bridge **173** E2
Lea Green **145** F1
Lea Marston **159** E3
Lea Town **192** A4
Lea Yeat **200** C4
Leachd **200** A2
Leachkin
    (An Leacainn) **266** D7
Leadburn **235** G4
Leaden Roding **137** E1
Leadenham **175** E2
Leaderfoot **227** G2
Leadgate *Cumb* **210** D3
Leadgate *Dur* **212** A2
Leadgate *N'umb* **212** A2
Leadhills **225** G4
Leadingcross Green **124** A3
Leafield **133** F1
Leagrave **149** F5
Leake Commonside **176** B2
Leake Hurn's End **176** C3
Lealands **110** A2
Lealholm **203** G1
Lealt *A&B* **239** F5
Lealt *High* **264** B5
Leam **185** G5
Leamington
    Hastings **147** G1
Leamington Spa **147** F1
Leamington Spa Art Gallery
    & Museum *Warks*
    CV32 4AA **16** B6
Leamoor Common **156** D4
Leanach *A&B* **240** C5
Leanach *High* **266** E7
Leanaig **266** C6
Leanoch **267** J6

Leasgill **199** F4
Leasingham **175** F3
Leask **261** J1
Leason **128** A3
Leasowe **183** D3
Leat **98** D2
Leatherhead **121** G2
Leathley **194** B3
Leaton *Shrop* **157** D1
Leaton *Tel&W* **157** F1
Leaveland **124** C3
Leavening **195** G1
Leaves Green **122** D2
Leavesden Green **136** A2
Lebberston **205** D4
Lechlade-on-
    Thames **133** E3
Leck **200** B5
Leckford **119** E4
Leckfurin **274** C3
Leckgruinart **230** A3
Leckhampstead
    *Bucks* **148** C4
Leckhampstead
    *WBerks* **133** G5
Leckhampstead
    Thicket **133** G5
Leckhampton **132** B1
Leckie *High* **265** G5
Leckie *Stir* **242** B5
Leckmelm
    (Leac Mailm) **265** H3
Leckroy **257** K5
Leckuary **240** A5
Leckwith **130** A5
Leconfield **196** C3
Ledaig (Leideag) **240** B1
Ledard **241** G4
Ledbeg **272** E7
Ledburn **149** D5
Ledbury **145** G4
Ledcharrie **242** A2
Ledgemoor **144** D2
Ledicot **144** D1
Ledmore *A&B* **247** E5
Ledmore *High* **272** E7
Lednagullin **274** D2
Ledsham *ChesW&C* **183** E5
Ledsham *WYorks* **195** D5
Ledston **194** D5
Ledstone **100** D3
Ledwell **147** G5
Lee *A&B* **238** D2
Lee *Devon* **113** E1
Lee *Hants* **106** C1
Lee *Lancs* **192** B3
Lee *Shrop* **170** B3
Lee Brockhurst **170** C5
Lee Chapel **137** F4
Lee Clump **135** E2
Lee Mill Bridge **100** B2
Lee Moor **100** B1
Lee Valley Park *Essex*
    EN9 1XQ **136** C3
Leebotten **279** D10
Leebotwood **157** D3
Leece **191** F1
Leeds *Kent* **124** A3
Leeds *WYorks* **194** B4
Leeds Art Gallery *WYorks*
    LS1 3AA **40** E3
Leeds Bradford International
    Airport **194** B3
Leeds Castle & Gardens
    *Kent* ME17 1PL **124** A3
Leedstown **94** D3
Leegomery **157** F1
Leek **171** G2
Leek Wootton **147** E1
Leekbrook **171** G2
Leeming *NYorks* **202** B4
Leeming *WYorks* **193** G4
Leeming Bar **202** B4
Lee-on-the-Solent **107** E2
Lees *Derbys* **173** D3
Lees *GtMan* **185** D2
Leeswood **169** F2
Leftwich **184** A5
Legars **237** E5
Legbourne **189** D4
Legerwood **236** C5
Legoland Windsor *W&M*
    SL4 4AY **135** E5
Legsby **188** B4
Leicester **160** A2
Leicester Forest
    East **160** A2
Leideag **254** B5
Leigh *Dorset* **104** C2
Leigh *Dorset* **105** G3
Leigh *GtMan* **184** A2
Leigh *Kent* **123** E4
Leigh *Shrop* **156** C2
Leigh *Surr* **122** B4
Leigh *Wilts* **132** C3
Leigh *Worcs* **145** G2
Leigh Beck **138** B4
Leigh Common **117** E5
Leigh Delamere **132** A5
Leigh Green **124** B5
Leigh Park **107** G2
Leigh Sinton **145** G2
Leigh upon Mendip **117** D3
Leigh Woods **131** E5
Leigham **100** B2
Leighland Chapel **114** D4
Leigh-on-Sea **138** B4
Leighterton **132** A3
Leighton *NYorks* **202** A5
Leighton
    *Powys* **156** B2
Leighton *Shrop* **157** F2
Leighton *Som* **117** E3
Leighton
    Bromswold **161** G5
Leighton Buzzard **149** E5
Leinthall Earls **144** D1
Leinthall Starkes **144** D1
Leintwardine **156** D5
Leire **160** A4
Leirinmore **273** G2
Leiston **153** F1
Leitfie **252** A5
Leith **235** G2
Leitholm **237** E5
Lelant **94** C3
Lelley **197** E4

Lemington **212** A1
Lemnas **269** G4
Lempitlaw **228** B3
Lemsford **136** B1
Lenchwick **146** C3
Lendalfoot **214** C1
Lenham **124** A3
Lenham Heath **124** B4
Lenie **258** C2
Lennel **237** F5
Lennox Plunton **216** A5
Lennoxtown **234** A2
Lent Rise **135** E4
Lenton *Lincs* **175** F4
Lenton *Nott* **173** G4
Lenton Abbey **173** G4
Lenwade **178** B4
Lenzie **234** A2
Leoch **244** B1
Leochel-Cushnie **260** D3
Leominster **145** D2
Leonard Stanley **132** A2
Leorin **230** B5
Lepe **106** D2
Lephin **263** G7
Lephinchapel **240** B5
Lephinmore **240** B5
Leppington **195** G1
Lepton **185** G1
Lerags **240** A2
Lerryn **97** F4
Lerwick **279** D8
Lesbury **229** G5
Leschangie **261** F3
Leslie *Aber* **260** D2
Leslie *Fife* **244** A4
Lesmahagow **225** G2
Lesnewth **98** B1
Lessendrum **268** D6
Lessingham **179** E3
Lessness Heath **137** D5
Lessonhall **209** F1
Leswalt **214** B4
Letchmore Heath **136** A3
Letchworth Garden
    City **150** A4
Letcombe Bassett **133** F4
Letcombe Regis **133** F4
Leth Meadhanach **254** C3
Letham *Angus* **252** D5
Letham *Falk* **234** D1
Letham *Fife* **244** B3
Lethanhill **224** C4
Lethenty **269** G6
Letheringham **153** D2
Letheringsett **178** B2
Lettaford **102** A4
Lettaford **102** A4
Letter **269** G6
Letter Finlay **257** J5
Letterewe **265** F4
Letterfearn
    (Leitir Fheàrna) **256** E2
Lettermorar **247** E2
Lettermore *A&B* **247** D5
Lettermore *High* **273** J4
Letters **265** H3
Lettershaws **225** G3
Letterston **140** C5
Lettoch *High* **259** H3
Lettoch *High* **259** J1
Letton *Here* **156** C3
Letton *Here* **144** C3
Letty Green **136** B1
Letwell **186** C4
Leuchars **244** C2
Leumrabhagh **271** F6
Leurbost (Liurbost) **271** F5
Leusdon **102** A5
Levedale **158** A1
Level's Green **150** C5
Leven *ERid* **196** D3
Leven *Fife* **244** B4
Levencorroch **223** F3
Levenhall **236** A2
Levens **199** F4
Levens Green **150** B5
Levenshulme **184** C3
Levenwick **279** D10
Leverburgh
    (An T-Òb) **263** F3
Leverington **162** C1
Leverstock Green **135** F2
Leverton **176** B3
Leverton Lucasgate **176** C3
Leverton Outgate **176** C3
Levington **152** D4
Levisham **204** B3
Levishie **258** B3
Lew **133** F2
Lewannick **97** G1
Lewcombe **104** B2
Lewdown **99** E2
Lewes **109** G2
Leweston **140** C5
Lewisham **136** C5
Lewiston
    (Blàr na Maigh) **258** C2
Lewistown **129** F4
Lewknor **134** C3
Leworthy **113** G2
Lewson Street **124** B2
Lewth **192** A4
Lewtrenchard **99** E2
Ley *Aber* **260** D3
Ley *Corn* **97** F3
Ley Green **149** G5
Leybourne **123** F3
Leyburn **202** A3
Leyland **192** B5
Leylodge **261** F3
Leymoor **185** F1
Leys *Aber* **269** J5
Leys *Aber* **260** C5
Leys *P&K* **244** A1
Leys of Cossans **252** B5
Leysdown-on-Sea **124** C5
Leysmill **253** E5
Leysters **145** E1
Leyton **136** C4
Leytonstone **136** C4
Lezant **98** D3
Lezerea **95** D3
Leziate **163** F1
Lhanbryde **267** K5
Lhanbryde **267** K5
Libanus **143** F5
Libberton **235** D5
Libbery **146** B2

Liberton **235** G3
Liceasto **263** G2
Lichfield **158** C2
Lichfield Cathedral *Staffs*
    WS13 7LD **158** C2
Lickey **158** B5
Lickey End **158** B5
Lickey Hills Country Park
    *Worcs* B45 8ER **14** C6
Lickfold **121** E5
Liddaton Green **99** E2
Liddesdale **247** G4
Liddington **133** E4
Lidgate *Derbys* **186** A5
Lidgate *Suff* **151** F2
Lidgett **174** B1
Lidlington **149** E4
Lidsey **108** B3
Lidsing **123** G2
Lidstone **147** F5
Lienassie **257** F2
Lieurary **275** F2
Liff **244** B1
Lifton **99** D2
Liftondown **99** D2
Lightcliffe **194** A5
Lighthorne **147** F2
Lighthorne Heath **147** F2
Lighthouse, The, Glasgow
    *Glas* G1 3NU **39** F4
Lighthouse, The - Poole's
    Centre for the Arts
    *Poole* BH15 1UG **3** B4
Lightwater **121** E1
Lightwater Valley Park
    *NYorks*
    HG4 3HT **202** B5
Lightwood **171** G3
Lightwood Green
    *ChesE* **170** D3
Lightwood Green
    *Wrex* **170** A3
Lilbourne **160** A5
Lilburn Tower **229** E4
Lilleshall **157** G1
Lilley *Herts* **149** G5
Lilley *WBerks* **133** G5
Lilliesleaf **227** G3
Lilling Green **195** F1
Lillingstone Dayrell **148** C4
Lillingstone Lovell **148** C3
Lillington *Dorset* **104** C1
Lillington *Warks* **147** F1
Lilliput **105** G4
Lilstock **115** E3
Lilyhurst **157** G1
Limbury **149** F5
Lime Side **184** D2
Limefield **184** C1
Limehillock **268** D5
Limehurst **184** D2
Limekilnburn **234** B4
Limekilns **235** E1
Limerigg **234** C2
Limerstone **106** D4
Limington **116** C5
Limpenhoe **179** E5
Limpley Stoke **117** E1
Limpsfield **122** D3
Limpsfield Chart **122** D3
Linaclate
    (Lionacleit) **262** C7
Linacre Reservoirs *Derbys*
    S42 7JW **186** A5
Linbriggs **220** A1
Linby **173** G2
Linchmere **121** D4
Lincluden **217** D3
Lincoln **187** G5
Lincoln Castle *Lincs*
    LN1 3AA **77** Lincoln
Lincoln Cathedral *Lincs*
    LN2 1PL **77** Lincoln
Lincomb **146** A1
Lincombe *Devon* **100** D2
Lincombe *Devon* **100** D3
Lindal in Furness **199** D5
Lindale **199** F4
Lindean **227** F2
Lindertis **252** B4
Lindfield **109** F1
Lindford **120** D4
Lindifferon **244** B3
Lindisfarne
    (Holy Island) **229** F2
Lindley **194** B3
Lindores **244** A3
Lindow End **184** C5
Lindridge **145** F1
Lindsaig **232** A2
Lindsell **151** E5
Lindsey **152** A3
Lindsey Tye **152** A3
Linfitts **185** D2
Linford *Hants* **106** A2
Linford *Thur* **137** F5
Linford Wood **148** D3
Lingague **190** A4
Lingards Wood **185** E1
Lingdale **203** F1
Lingen **144** C1
Lingfield **122** C4
Lingley Green **183** G4
Lingwood **179** E5
Linhead **268** E5
Linhope **227** E5
Linicro **263** J5
Linkend **146** A4
Linkenholt **119** E2
Linkhill **110** D1
Linkinhorne **98** D3
Linklater **277** D9
Linksness *Ork* **277** B7
Linksness *Ork* **277** E6
Linktown **244** A5
Linley *Shrop* **156** C3
Linley *Shrop* **157** F3
Linley Green **145** F2
Linlithgow **235** E2
Linlithgow Bridge **235** D2
Linn of Muick
    Cottage **252** B1

Linsiadar **270** E4
Linsidemore **266** C2
Linslade **149** E5
Linstead Parva **165** E4
Linstock **210** A1
Linthwaite **185** F1
Lintmill **268** D4
Linton *Cambs* **151** D3
Linton *Derbys* **159** E1
Linton *Here* **145** F5
Linton *Kent* **123** G3
Linton *NYorks* **193** F1
Linton *ScBord* **228** B4
Linton *WYorks* **194** C3
Linton-on-Ouse **195** D1
Lintzford **212** A2
Linwood *Hants* **106** A2
Linwood *Lincs* **188** B4
Linwood *Renf* **233** F3
Lionel (Lional) **271** H1
Liphook **120** C5
Lipley **171** E4
Liscard **183** E3
Liscombe **114** B4
Liskeard **97** G3
L'Islet **101** F4
Lismore **240** A1
Liss **120** C5
Liss Forest **120** C5
Lissett **196** D2
Lissington **188** B4
Liston **151** G3
Lisvane **130** A4
Liswerry **130** C4
Litcham **163** G1
Litchborough **148** B2
Litchfield **119** F2
Litherland **183** E3
Litlington *Cambs* **150** B3
Litlington *ESuss* **110** A3
Little Abington **151** D3
Little Addington **161** E5
Little Alne **146** D1
Little Altcar **183** E2
Little Amwell **136** C1
Little Ann **119** E3
Little Asby **200** B2
Little Assynt **272** D6
Little Aston **158** C3
Little Atherfield **107** D5
Little Ayton **203** E1
Little Baddow **137** G2
Little Badminton **132** A4
Little Ballinluig **251** E4
Little Bampton **209** F1
Little Bardfield **151** E4
Little Barford **149** G2
Little Barningham **178** C2
Little Barrington **133** E1
Little Barrow **170** B1
Little Barugh **203** G5
Little Bavington **220** B4
Little Bealings **152** D3
Little Bedwyn **119** D1
Little Beeby **160** B2
Little Bentley **152** C5
Little Berkhamsted **136** B2
Little Billing **148** D1
Little Birch **145** E4
Little Bispham **191** G3
Little Blakenham **152** C3
Little Bloxwich **158** C2
Little Bollington **184** B4
Little Bookham **121** G2
Little Bourton **147** G3
Little Bowden **160** C4
Little Bradley **151** E2
Little Brampton **156** C4
Little Braxted **138** B1
Little Brechin **253** D3
Little Brickhill **149** E4
Little Bridgeford **171** F5
Little Brington **148** B1
Little Bromley **152** B5
Little Broughton **209** D3
Little Budworth **170** C1
Little Burdon **202** C1
Little Burstead **137** F3
Little Burton **196** D3
Little Bytham **161** F1
Little Canford **105** G3
Little Carlton *Lincs* **189** D4
Little Carlton *Notts* **174** C2
Little Casterton **161** F2
Little Catwick **196** D3
Little Catworth **161** F5
Little Cawthorpe **189** D4
Little Chalfield **117** F1
Little Chalfont **135** E3
Little Chart **124** B4
Little Chesterford **151** D3
Little Chesterton **148** A5
Little Cheverell **118** A2
Little Clacton **139** E1
Little Clanfield **133** E2
Little Clifton **209** D4
Little Coates **188** C2
Little Comberton **146** B3
Little Common **110** C3
Little Compton **147** E4
Little Corby **210** A2
Little Cornard **151** G4
Little Cowarne **145** F2
Little Coxwell **133** E3
Little Crakehall **202** B3
Little Cransley **160** C5
Little Creaton **160** C5
Little Creich **266** D3
Little Cressingham **163** G3
Little Crosby **183** E2
Little Crosthwaite **209** F4
Little Cubley **172** C3
Little Dalby **160** C1
Little Dens **269** J6
Little Dewchurch **145** E4
Little Ditton **151** E2
Little Doward **131** E1
Little Downham **162** D4
Little Downham **162** D4
Little Driffield **196** C2
Little Dunham **163** G1
Little Dunkeld **251** F5
Little Dunmow **151** E5
Little Durnford **118** C4
Little Easton **151** E5

Little Eaton 173 E3
Little Eccleston 192 A4
Little Ellingham 164 B2
Little End 137 E2
Little Everdon 148 A2
Little Eversden 150 B2
Little Faringdon 133 E2
Little Fencote 202 B3
Little Fenton 195 E4
Little Finborough 152 B2
Little Fransham 178 A4
Little Gaddesden 135 E1
Little Garway 144 D5
Little Gidding 161 G4
Little Glemham 153 E2
Little Glenshee 243 E1
Little Gorsley 145 F5
Little Gransden 150 A2
Little Green *Cambs* 150 A3
Little Green *Notts* 174 C3
Little Green *Suff* 164 B4
Little Green *Suff* 164 B4
Little Green *Wrex* 170 B3
Little Grimsby 188 D3
Little Gringley 187 E4
Little Gruinard 265 F3
Little Habton 203 G5
Little Hadham 150 C5
Little Hale 175 G3
Little Hallingbury 137 D1
Little Hampden 135 D2
Little Haresfield 132 A2
Little Harrowden 161 D5
Little Haseley 134 B2
Little Hatfield 197 D3
Little Hautbois 179 D3
Little Haven *Pembs* 126 B1
Little Haven *WSuss* 121 G4
Little Hay 158 D2
Little Hayfield 185 E4
Little Haywood 172 B5
Little Heath 159 F4
Little Hereford 145 E1
Little Hockham 164 A2
Little Horkesley 152 A4
Little Hormead 150 C5
Little Horsted 109 G2
Little Horton 118 B1
Little Horwood 148 C4
Little Houghton 148 D2
Little Hucklow 185 F5
Little Hulton 184 B2
Little Hungerford 134 A5
Little Hutton 203 D5
Little Irchester 149 E1
Little Keyford 117 E3
Little Kimble 134 D2
Little Kineton 147 F2
Little Kingshill 135 D3
Little Langdale 199 E2
Little Langford 118 B4
Little Laver 137 E2
Little Lawford 159 G5
Little Leigh 184 A5
Little Leighs 137 G1
Little Lever 184 B2
Little Ley 260 E3
Little Linford 148 D3
Little Linton 151 D3
Little London *Bucks* 134 B1
Little London *Essex* 150 C5
Little London *ESuss* 110 A2
Little London *Hants* 119 E3
Little London *Hants* 120 B2
Little London *IoM* 190 B3
Little London *Lincs* 176 C5
Little London *Lincs* 176 A5
Little London *Lincs* 188 D5
Little London *Lincs* 188 B4
Little London *Norf* 177 D5
Little London *Norf* 163 F3
Little London *Oxon* 134 A2
Little London *Powys* 155 G4
Little London *Suff* 152 B2
Little London *WYorks* 194 B4
Little Longstone 185 F5
Little Lyth 157 D2
Little Malvern 145 G3
Little Maplestead 151 G4
Little Marcle 145 F4
Little Marland 113 F4
Little Marlow 135 D4
Little Marsden 193 E4
Little Massingham 177 F5
Little Melton 178 C5
Little Milford 126 C1
Little Mill 130 C2
Little Milton 134 B2
Little Missenden 135 E3
Little Musgrave 200 C1
Little Ness 156 D1
Little Neston 183 D5
Little Newcastle 140 C5
Little Newsham 202 A1
Little Oakley *Essex* 152 D5
Little Oakley *N'hants* 161 D4
Little Odell 149 E2
Little Offley 149 G5
Little Onn 158 A1
Little Orton *Cumb* 209 G1
Little Orton *Leics* 159 F2
Little Ouse 163 E4
Little Ouseburn 194 D1
Little Overton 170 A3
Little Packington 159 E4
Little Parndon 136 D1
Little Paxton 149 G1
Little Petherick 96 D2
Little Plumpton 191 G4
Little Plumstead 179 E4
Little Ponton 175 E4
Little Posbrook 107 E2
Little Potheridge 113 F4
Little Preston 148 A2
Little Raveley 162 A4
Little Ribston 194 C2
Little Rissington 133 D1
Little Rogart 266 E1
Little Rollright 147 E4
Little Ryburgh 178 A3
Little Ryle 229 E5
Little Ryton 157 D2
Little Salkeld 210 B4
Little Sampford 151 E4
Little Saxham 151 G1
Little Scatwell 265 K6
Little Shelford 150 C2
Little Shrawardine 156 C1
Little Silver 102 C2
Little Singleton 191 G4
Little Smeaton *NYorks* 186 C1
Little Smeaton *NYorks* 202 C2
Little Snoring 178 A2
Little Sodbury 131 G4
Little Sodbury End 131 G4
Little Somborne 119 E4
Little Somerford 132 B4
Little Soudley 171 E5
Little Stainforth 193 E1
Little Stainton 202 C1
Little Stanney 183 F5
Little Staughton 149 G1
Little Steeping 176 C1
Little Stoke 171 G4
Little Stonham 152 C2
Little Street 162 D4
Little Stretton *Leics* 160 B2
Little Stretton *Shrop* 156 D3
Little Strickland 199 G1
Little Stukeley 162 A5
Little Sugnall 171 F4
Little Sutton 183 E5
Little Swinburne 220 B4
Little Tarrington 145 F3
Little Tew 147 F5
Little Tey 151 G5
Little Thetford 162 D5
Little Thornage 178 B2
Little Thornton 191 G3
Little Thorpe 212 D3
Little Thurlow 151 E2
Little Thurlow Green 151 E2
Little Thurrock 137 F5
Little Torboll 266 E2
Little Torrington 113 E4
Little Tosson 220 C1
Little Totham 138 B1
Little Town *Cumb* 209 F5
Little Town *Lancs* 192 C4
Little Town *Warr* 184 A3
Little Twycross 159 F2
Little Urswick 199 D5
Little Wakering 138 C4
Little Walden 150 D3
Little Waldingfield 152 A3
Little Walsingham 178 A2
Little Waltham 137 G1
Little Warley 137 F3
Little Washbourne 146 B4
Little Weighton 196 B4
Little Welland 146 A4
Little Welnetham 151 G1
Little Wenham 152 B4
Little Wenlock 157 F2
Little Whittington 211 F1
Little Wilbraham 150 D2
Little Wishford 118 B4
Little Witcombe 132 B1
Little Witley 145 G1
Little Wittenham 134 A3
Little Wittingham Green 165 D4
Little Wolford 147 E4
Little Woodcote 122 B2
Little Wratting 151 E3
Little Wymington 149 E1
Little Wymondley 150 A5
Little Wyrley 158 C2
Little Wytheford 157 E1
Little Yeldham 151 F4
Littlebeck 204 B2
Littleborough *Devon* 102 B1
Littleborough *GtMan* 184 D1
Littleborough *Notts* 187 F4
Littlebourne 125 E3
Littlebredy 104 B4
Littlebury 150 D4
Littlebury Green 150 C4
Littledean 131 F1
Littleferry 267 F2
Littleham *Devon* 113 E3
Littleham *Devon* 102 D4
Littlehampton 108 C3
Littlehempston 101 E1
Littlehoughton 229 G5
Littlemill *EAyr* 224 C4
Littlemill *High* 267 G6
Littlemoor *Derbys* 173 E1
Littlemoor *Dorset* 104 C4
Littlemore 134 A2
Littlemoss 184 D3
Littleover 173 E4
Littleport 163 D4
Littlestead Green 134 C5
Littlestone-on-Sea 111 F1
Littlethorpe 194 C1
Littleton *ChesW&C* 170 B1
Littleton *Hants* 119 F4
Littleton *P&K* 244 A1
Littleton *Som* 116 B4
Littleton *Surr* 121 F1
Littleton Drew 132 A4
Littleton Panell 118 B2
Littleton-on-Severn 131 E3
Littletown *Dur* 212 C3
Littletown *IoW* 107 E3
Littlewick Green 134 D5
Littlewindsor 104 A2
Littleworth *Glos* 146 D4
Littleworth *Oxon* 133 F3
Littleworth *Staffs* 158 C1
Littleworth *SYorks* 186 D3
Littleworth *Worcs* 146 A3
Littley Green 137 F1
Litton *Derbys* 185 F5
Litton *NYorks* 201 E5
Litton *Som* 116 C2
Litton Cheney 104 B3
Liverpool 183 E3
Liverpool Cathedral *Mersey* L1 7AZ 42 E6
Liverpool John Lennon Airport 183 F4
Liverpool Metropolitan Cathedral (RC) *Mersey* L3 5TQ 43 E4
Liversedge 194 B5
Liverton *Devon* 102 B5
Liverton *R&C* 203 G1
Liverton Street 124 A4
Living Coasts, Torquay *Torbay* TQ1 2BG 101 F1
Livingston 235 E3
Livingston Village 235 E3
Lixwm 182 C5
Lizard 95 E5
Llaingarreglwyd 142 A2
Llaingoch 180 A4
Llaithddu 155 G4
Llampha 129 F5
Llan 155 E2
Llanaber 154 C1
Llanaelhaearn 166 C3
Llanaeron 142 A1
Llanafan 154 C5
Llanafan-fawr 143 F2
Llanafan-fechan 143 F2
Llanallgo 180 C4
Llanarmon 166 D4
Llanarmon Dyffryn Ceiriog 169 E4
Llanarmon-yn-Ial 169 E2
Llanarth *Cere* 142 A2
Llanarth *Mon* 130 C1
Llanarthney 142 B5
Llanasa 182 C4
Llanbabo 180 B4
Llanbadarn Fawr 154 B4
Llanbadarn Fynydd 155 G5
Llanbadarn-y-garreg 144 A3
Llanbadoc 130 C2
Llanbadrig 180 B3
Llanbeder 130 C3
Llanbedr *Gwyn* 167 E5
Llanbedr *Powys* 144 B5
Llanbedr *Powys* 144 A3
Llanbedr-Dyffryn-Clwyd 169 E2
Llanbedrgoch 180 D4
Llanbedrog 166 C4
Llanbedr-y-cennin 168 A1
Llanberis 167 E2
Llanbethery 114 D1
Llanbister 156 A5
Llanblethian 129 F5
Llanboidy 141 F5
Llanbradach 130 A3
Llanbryn-mair 155 E2
Llancadle 114 D1
Llancarfan 129 G5
Llancayo 130 C2
Llancynfelyn 154 C3
Llandafal 130 A2
Llandaff 130 A5
Llandaff North 130 A5
Llandanwg 167 E5
Llandawke 127 F1
Llanddaniel Fab 180 C5
Llanddarog 128 A1
Llanddeiniol 154 B5
Llanddeiniolen 167 E1
Llandderfel 168 C4
Llanddeusant *Carmar* 143 D5
Llanddeusant *IoA* 180 B4
Llanddew 143 G4
Llanddewi 128 A4
Llanddewi Rhydderch 130 C1
Llanddewi Skirrid 130 C1
Llanddewi Velfrey 127 E1
Llanddewi Ystradenni 144 A1
Llanddewi-Brefi 142 C2
Llanddewi'r Cwm 143 G3
Llanddoged 168 B1
Llanddona 181 D5
Llanddowror 127 F1
Llanddulas 182 A5
Llanddwywe 167 E5
Llanddyfnan 180 D5
Llandefaelog Fach 143 G4
Llandefaelog-tre'r-graig 144 A5
Llandefalle 144 A4
Llandegfan 181 D5
Llandegfedd Reservoir *Mon* NP4 0TA 130 C3
Llandegla 169 E2
Llandegley 144 A1
Llandegveth 130 C3
Llandegwning 166 B4
Llandeilo 142 C5
Llandeilo Abercywyn 127 G1
Llandeilo Graban 143 G3
Llandeilo'r-Fan 143 E4
Llandeloy 140 B5
Llandenny 130 D2
Llandevaud 130 D3
Llandevenny 130 D4
Llandinabo 145 E5
Llandinam 155 G4
Llandissilio 141 E5
Llandogo 131 E2
Llandough *VGlam* 130 A5
Llandough *VGlam* 129 F5
Llandovery (Llanymddyfri) 143 D4
Llandow 129 F5
Llandre *Carmar* 142 C3
Llandre *Carmar* 141 E5
Llandre *Cere* 154 C4
Llandrillo 168 D4
Llandrindod Wells 143 G1
Llandrinio 156 B1
Llandudno 181 F4
Llandudno Junction 181 F5
Llandwrog 167 D2
Llandybie 128 C1
Llandyfaelog 128 A1
Llandyfan 128 C1
Llandyfriog 141 G3
Llandyfrydog 180 C4
Llandygai 181 D5
Llandygwydd 141 F3
Llandyrnog 169 E1
Llandyry 128 A2
Llandysilio 156 B1
Llandyssil 156 A3
Llandysul 142 A3
Llanedeyrn 130 B4
Llanedy 128 B2
Llaneglwys 143 G4
Llanegryn 154 C2
Llanegwad 142 B5
Llaneilian 180 C3
Llanelian-yn-Rhos 181 G5
Llanelidan 169 E2
Llanelieu 144 A4
Llanellen 130 C1
Llanelli 128 B2
Llanelli Millennium Coastal Park *Carmar* SA15 2LF 128 A3
Llanelltyd 154 D1
Llanelly 130 B1
Llanelly Hill 130 B1
Llanelwedd 143 G2
Llanenddwyn 167 E5
Llanengan 166 B5
Llanerfyl 155 G2
Llaneuddog 180 C4
Llanfachraeth 180 B4
Llanfachreth 168 A5
Llanfaelog 180 B5
Llanfaelrhys 166 B5
Llanfaenor 130 D1
Llan-faes *IoA* 181 E5
Llanfaes *Powys* 143 G5
Llanfaethlu 180 B4
Llanfaglan 167 D1
Llanfair 167 E5
Llanfair Caereinion 156 A2
Llanfair Clydogau 142 C2
Llanfair Dyffryn Clwyd 169 E2
Llanfair Talhaiarn 182 A5
Llanfair Waterdine 156 B5
Llanfairfechan 181 E5
Llanfair-Nant-Gwyn 141 E4
Llanfair-Orllwyn 141 G3
Llanfairpwllgwyngyll 180 D5
Llanfairynghornwy 180 B3
Llanfair-yn-neubwll 180 B5
Llanfallteg 127 E1
Llanfaredd 143 G2
Llanfarian 154 B5
Llanfechain 169 E5
Llanfechell 180 B3
Llanfendigaid 154 B2
Llanferres 169 E1
Llanfflewyn 180 B4
Llanfigael 180 B4
Llanfihangel Glyn Myfyr 168 C3
Llanfihangel Nant Bran 143 F4
Llanfihangel Rhydithon 144 A1
Llanfihangel Rogiet 130 D4
Llanfihangel Tal-y-llyn 144 A5
Llanfihangel-ar-arth 142 A3
Llanfihangel-nant-Melan 144 A2
Llanfihangel-uwch-Gwili 142 A5
Llanfihangel-y-Creuddyn 154 C5
Llanfihangel-yng-Ngwynfa 155 G1
Llanfihangel-yn-Nhywyn 180 B5
Llanfihangel-y-pennant *Gwyn* 167 E3
Llanfihangel-y-pennant *Gwyn* 154 C2
Llanfilo 144 A4
Llanfoist 130 B1
Llanfor 168 C4
Llanfrechfa 130 C3
Llanfrothen 167 F3
Llanfrynach 143 G5
Llanfwrog *Denb* 169 E2
Llanfwrog *IoA* 180 B4
Llanfyllin 156 A1
Llanfynydd *Carmar* 142 B5
Llanfynydd *Flints* 169 F2
Llanfyrnach 141 F4
Llangadfan 155 G1
Llangadog 142 D5
Llangadwaladr *IoA* 166 C1
Llangadwaladr *Powys* 169 E4
Llangaffo 166 D1
Llangain 127 G1
Llangammarch Wells 143 F3
Llangan 129 F5
Llangarron 145 E5
Llangasty-Talyllyn 144 A5
Llangathen 142 B5
Llangattock 130 B1
Llangattock Lingoed 130 C1
Llangattock-Vibon-Avel 131 D1
Llangedwyn 169 E5
Llangefni 180 C5
Llangeinor 129 F4
Llangeitho 142 C2
Llangeler 141 G4
Llangelynin 154 B2
Llangendeirne 128 A1
Llangennech 128 B2
Llangennith 128 A3
Llangenny 130 B1
Llangernyw 168 B1
Llangian 166 B5
Llangiwg 128 D2
Llangloffan 140 C4
Llanglydwen 141 E5
Llangoed 181 E5
Llangoedmor 141 E3
Llangollen 169 F3
Llangollen Railway *Denb* LL20 8SN 169 F3
Llangolman 141 E5
Llangorse 144 A5
Llangorwen 154 C4
Llangovan 131 D2
Llangower 168 C4
Llangrannog 141 G2
Llangristiolus 180 C5
Llangrove 131 E1
Llangua 144 C5
Llangunllo 156 B5
Llangunnor 142 A5
Llangurig 155 F5
Llangwm *Conwy* 168 C3
Llangwm *Mon* 130 D2
Llangwm *Pembs* 126 C2
Llangwnnadl 166 B4
Llangwyfan 169 E1
Llangwyllog 180 C5
Llangwyryfon 154 C5
Llangybi *Cere* 142 C2
Llangybi *Gwyn* 166 D3
Llangybi *Mon* 130 C3
Llangyfelach 128 C3
Llangynhafal 169 E1
Llangynidr 130 A1
Llangyniew 156 A2
Llangynin 127 F1
Llangynllo 141 G3
Llangynog *Carmar* 127 G1
Llangynog *Powys* 169 D5
Llangynwyd 129 E4
Llanhamlach 143 G5
Llanharan 129 G4
Llanharry 129 G4
Llanhennock 130 C3
Llanhilleth 130 B2
Llanidloes 155 F4
Llaniestyn 166 B4
Llanigon 144 B4
Llanilar 154 C5
Llanilid 129 F4
Llanishen *Cardiff* 130 A4
Llanishen *Mon* 131 D2
Llanllawddog 142 A5
Llanllechid 167 F1
Llanlleonfel 143 F2
Llanllugan 155 G2
Llanllwch 127 G1
Llanllwchaiarn 156 A3
Llanllwni 142 A3
Llanllyfni 167 D2
Llanllywel 130 C3
Llanmadoc 128 A3
Llanmaes 114 C1
Llanmartin 130 C4
Llanmerewig 156 A3
Llanmihangel 129 F5
Llan-mill 127 E1
Llanmiloe 127 F2
Llanmorlais 128 B3
Llannefydd 182 A5
Llannerch Hall 182 B5
Llannerch-y-medd 180 C4
Llannerch-y-Môr 182 C5
Llannon *Carmar* 128 B2
Llan-non *Cere* 142 B1
Llannor 166 C4
Llanover 130 C2
Llanpumsaint 142 A5
Llanreithan 140 B5
Llanrhaeadr 169 D1
Llanrhaeadr-ym-Mochnant 169 E5
Llanrhian 140 B4
Llanrhidian 128 A3
Llanrhyddlad 180 B4
Llanrhystud 142 B1
Llanrothal 131 D1
Llanrug 167 E1
Llanrumney 130 B4
Llanrwst 168 A1
Llansadurnen 127 F1
Llansadwrn *Carmar* 142 C4
Llansadwrn *IoA* 181 D5
Llansaint 127 G2
Llansamlet 128 C3
Llansanffraid 142 B1
Llansanffraid Glan Conwy 181 G5
Llansannan 168 C1
Llansannor 129 F5
Llansantffraed 144 A5
Llansantffraed-Cwmdeuddwr 143 F1
Llansantffraed-in-Elwel 143 G2
Llansantffraid-ym-Mechain 169 F5
Llansawel 142 C4
Llansilin 169 F5
Llansoy 130 D2
Llanspyddid 143 G5
Llanstadwell 126 C2
Llansteffan 127 G1
Llanstephan 144 A3
Llantarnam 130 C3
Llanteg 127 E1
Llanthony 144 B5
Llantilio Crossenny 130 C1
Llantilio Pertholey 130 C1
Llantood 141 E3
Llantrisant *IoA* 180 B4
Llantrisant *Mon* 130 C3
Llantrisant *RCT* 129 G4
Llantrithyd 129 G5
Llantwit Fardre 129 G4
Llantwit Major 114 C1
Llantysilio 169 E3
Llanuwchllyn 168 B5
Llanvaches 130 D3
Llanvair-Discoed 130 D3
Llanvapley 130 C1
Llanvetherine 130 C1
Llanveynoe 144 C4
Llanvihangel Crucorney (Llanfihangel Crucornau) 144 C5
Llanvihangel Gobion 130 C2
Llanvihangel-Ystern-Llewern 130 D1
Llanvithyn 129 G5
Llanwarne 145 E5
Llanwddyn 155 G1
Llanwenog 142 A3
Llanwern 130 C4
Llanwinio 141 F5
Llanwnda *Gwyn* 167 D2
Llanwnda *Pembs* 140 C4
Llanwnnen 142 B3
Llanwnog 155 G3
Llanwonno 129 G3
Llanwrda 142 D4
Llanwrin 155 D2
Llanwrthwl 143 F1
Llanwrtyd 143 E3
Llanwrtyd Wells 143 E3
Llanwyddelan 155 G2
Llanyblodwel 169 F5
Llanybri 127 G1
Llanybydder 142 B3
Llanycefn 141 E5
Llanychaer Bridge 140 C4
Llanycil 168 C4
Llanycrwys 142 C3
Llanymawddwy 155 E1
Llanymynech 169 F5
Llanynghenedl 180 B4
Llanynys 169 E1
Llan-y-pwll 170 A2
Llanyre 143 G1
Llanystumdwy 167 D4
Llanywern 144 A5
Llawhaden 127 D1
Llawndy 182 C4
Llawnt 169 F4
Llawr-y-dref 166 B5
Llawryglyn 155 F3
Llay 170 A2
Llechcynfarwy 180 B4
Llecheiddior 167 D3
Llechfaen 143 G5
Llechryd *Caerp* 130 A2
Llechryd *Cere* 141 F3
Llechrydau 169 F4
Llechwedd Slate Caverns *Gwyn* LL41 3NB 168 A3
Lledrod *Cere* 154 C5
Lledrod *Powys* 169 F5
Llethryd 128 B3
Llidiad-Nenog 142 B4
Llidiardau 168 B4
Llithfaen 166 C3
Lloc 182 C5
Llong 169 F1
Llowes 144 A3
Lloyney 156 B5
Llundain-fach 142 B2
Llwydcoed 129 F2
Llwydiarth 155 G1
Llwyn 156 B4
Llwyncelyn 142 A2
Llwyn-croes 142 A5
Llwyndafydd 141 G2
Llwynderw 156 B2
Llwyndyrys 166 C3
Llwyneinion 169 F3
Llwyngwril 154 B2
Llwynhendy 128 B3
Llwyn-Madoc 143 F2
Llwynmawr 169 F4
Llwyn-onn *Cere* 142 A2
Llwyn-onn *MTyd* 129 G1
Llwyn-y-brain *Carmar* 127 E1
Llwyn-y-brain *Carmar* 142 D4
Llwyn-y-groes 142 B2
Llwynypia 129 F3
Llyn Brenig *Conwy* LL21 9TT 168 C2
Llyn Llech Owain Country Park *Carmar* SA14 7NF 128 B1
Llynclys 169 F5
Llynfaes 180 C5
Llysfaen 181 G5
Llyswen 144 A4
Llysworney 129 F5
Llys-y-frân 140 D5
Llywel 143 E4
Load Brook 185 G4
Loandhu 267 F4
Loanhead *Aber* 261 H1
Loanhead *Midlo* 235 G3
Loans 224 B2
Lobb 113 E2
Lobhillcross 99 E2
Loch a Charnain 262 D7
Loch an Eilein Visitor Centre & Forest Trail *High* PH22 1QT 259 F4
Loch Choire Lodge 273 J5
Loch Eil Outward Bound 248 C2
Loch Head *D&G* 206 D2
Loch Head *D&G* 215 F1
Loch Lomond Shores & Gateway Centre *WDun* G83 8QL 233 E1
Loch Ness Exhibition Centre *High* IV63 6TU 258 C2
Loch Sgioport 254 D1
Lochailort (Ceann Loch Ailleart) 247 G1
Lochaline (Loch Àlainn) 247 F5
Lochans 214 B5
Locharbriggs 217 D2
Lochawe (Loch Obha) 240 D2
Lochboisdale (Loch Baghasdail) 254 C3
Lochbuie 239 F2
Lochcarron (Loch Carrann) 264 E7
Lochdhu Hotel 275 F4
Lochdon 239 G1
Lochdrum 265 J4
Lochearnhead (Ceann Loch Èireann) 242 A2
Lochee 244 B1
Lochend *High* 275 H2
Lochend (Ceann Loch) *High* 258 C1
Locheport (Locheuphort) 262 D5
Lochfoot 216 D3
Lochgair 240 B5
Lochgarthside 258 C3
Lochgelly 243 G5
Lochgilphead (Ceann Loch Gilb) 231 G1
Lochgoilhead 241 E4
Lochgoyn 233 G5
Lochhill *EAyr* 225 D4
Lochhill *Moray* 267 K5
Lochinch Castle 214 C4
Lochinver (Loch an Inbhir) 272 C6
Lochlair 252 D5
Lochlane 242 D2
Lochlea 224 C2
Lochluichart 265 K5
Lochmaben 217 E2
Lochmaddy (Loch na Madadh) 262 E5
Lochore 243 G5
Lochore Meadows Country Park *Fife* KY5 8BA 243 G5
Lochportain 262 E4
Lochranza 232 A4
Lochside *Aber* 253 F3
Lochside *High* 273 G3
Lochside *High* 274 D5
Lochside *High* 275 H2
Lochslin 267 F3
Lochton 215 D2
Lochty 244 D4
Lochuisge 247 G4
Lochurr 216 B2
Lochussie 266 B6
Lochwinnoch 233 E4
Lockengate 97 E3
Lockerbie 217 F2
Lockeridge 118 C1
Lockerley 119 D5
Lockhills 210 B3
Locking 116 A2
Lockington *ERid* 196 B3
Lockington *Leics* 173 F5
Lockleywood 171 D5
Locks Heath 107 E2
Locksbottom 122 D2
Locksgreen 106 D3
Lockton 204 B4
Locomotion: The National Railway Museum at Shildon *Dur* DL4 1PQ 212 B5
Loddington *Leics* 160 C2
Loddington *N'hants* 160 D5
Loddiswell 100 D3
Loddon 165 E2
Lode 150 D1
Loders 104 A3
Lodsworth 121 E5
Lofthouse *NYorks* 202 A5
Lofthouse *WYorks* 194 C5
Loftus 203 G1
Logan *D&G* 206 A2
Logan *EAyr* 225 D3
Loganlea 235 D3
Loggerheads 171 E4
Loggerheads Country Park *Denb* CH7 5LH 169 E1
Loggie (An Lagaidh) 265 H2
Logie *Angus* 253 E3
Logie *Angus* 252 B4
Logie *Fife* 244 C2
Logie *Moray* 267 H6
Logie Coldstone 260 C4
Logie Hill 266 E4
Logie Newton 260 E1
Logie Pert 253 E3
Logierait 251 E4
Login 141 E5
Lolworth 150 B1
Lonbain 264 C6
Londesborough 196 A3
London 136 C4
London Apprentice 97 E5
London Aquarium *GtLon* SE1 7PD 45 F5
London Ashford Airport 111 F1
London Beach 124 A5
London Biggin Hill Airport 122 D2
London City Airport 136 D4
London Colney 136 A2
London Eye *GtLon* SE1 7PB 45 F5
London Gatwick Airport 122 B4
London Heathrow Airport 135 F5
London Luton Airport 149 G5
London Minstead 106 B1
London Southend Airport 138 B4
London Stansted Airport 150 D5
London Transport Museum *GtLon* WC2E 7BB 45 E3
London Wetland Centre *GtLon* SW13 9WT 11 E6
London Zoo *GtLon* NW1 4RY 12 A3
Londonderry 202 B4
Londonthorpe 175 E4
Londubh 264 E3
Lonemore 266 E3
Long Ashton 131 E5
Long Bank 157 G5
Long Bennington 174 D3
Long Bredy 104 B3
Long Buckby 148 B1
Long Clawson 174 C5
Long Compton *Staffs* 171 F5
Long Compton *Warks* 147 E4
Long Crendon 134 B2
Long Crichel 105 F1
Long Dean 132 A5
Long Downs 95 E3
Long Drax 195 F5
Long Duckmanton 186 B5
Long Eaton 173 F4
Long Gill 193 D2
Long Green *ChesW&C* 183 F5
Long Green *Essex* 152 A5
Long Green *Worcs* 146 A4
Long Hanborough 133 G1
Long Itchington 147 G1
Long Lane 157 F1
Long Lawford 159 G5
Long Load 116 B5

Long Marston
  Herts 135 D1
Long Marston
  NYorks 195 E2
Long Marston
  Warks 147 D3
Long Meadowend 156 D4
Long Melford 151 G4
Long Newnton 132 B3
Long Preston 193 E2
Long Riston 196 D3
Long Stratton 164 C2
Long Street 148 C3
Long Sutton Hants 120 C3
Long Sutton Lincs 176 C5
Long Sutton Som 116 B5
Long Thurlow 152 B1
Long Whatton 173 F5
Long Wittenham 134 A3
Longbenton 212 B1
Longborough 147 D5
Longbridge Plym 100 B2
Longbridge Warks 147 E1
Longbridge WMid 147 E1
Longbridge Deverill 117 F3
Longburgh 209 G1
Longburton 104 C1
Longcliffe 172 D2
Longcombe 101 E2
Longcot 133 E3
Longcroft 234 B2
Longcross Devon 99 E3
Longcross Surr 121 E1
Longden 156 D2
Longdon Staffs 158 C1
Longdon Worcs 146 A4
Longdon Green 158 C1
Longdon upon Tern 157 F1
Longdown 102 B3
Longdrum 261 H3
Longfield 123 F2
Longfield Hill 123 F2
Longfleet 105 E3
Longford Derbys 172 D4
Longford Glos 146 A5
Longford GtLon 135 F5
Longford Shrop 170 D4
Longford Tel&W 157 G1
Longford WMid 159 F4
Longforgan 244 B2
Longformacus 237 D4
Longframlington 220 D1
Longham Dorset 105 G3
Longham Norf 178 A4
Longhill 269 H5
Longhirst 221 E3
Longhope Glos 131 F1
Longhope Ork 277 C8
Longhorsley 220 D2
Longhoughton 229 G5
Longlands Aber 260 C2
Longlands Cumb 209 F3
Longlands GtLon 136 D5
Longlane Derbys 173 D4
Longlane WBerks 133 G5
Longleat House Wilts
  BA12 7NW 117 F3
Longleat Safari Park Wilts
  BA12 7NW 117 F3
Longlevens 132 A1
Longley 185 F2
Longley Green 145 G2
Longmanhill 269 F4
Longmoor Camp 120 C4
Longmorn 267 K6
Longnewton
  ScBord 227 G3
Longnewton Stock 202 C1
Longney 131 G1
Longniddry 236 B2
Longniddry Bents ELoth
  EH32 0PX 236 B2
Longnor Shrop 157 D2
Longnor Staffs 172 B1
Longparish 119 F3
Longridge Lancs 192 C4
Longridge Staffs 158 B1
Longridge WLoth 235 D3
Longridge End 146 A5
Longridge Towers 237 G4
Longriggend 234 C2
Longrock 94 C3
Longsdon 171 G2
Longshaw 183 G2
Longside 269 J6
Longslow 171 D4
Longsowerby 209 G1
Longstanton 150 C1
Longstock 119 E4
Longstone 94 C3
Longstowe 150 B2
Longstreet 118 C2
Longthorpe 161 G2
Longton Lancs 192 A5
Longton Stoke 171 G3
Longtown Cumb 218 B5
Longtown Here 144 C5
Longville in the
  Dale 157 E3
Longwell Green 131 F5
Longwick 134 C2
Longwitton 220 C3
Longworth 133 F3
Longyester 236 C3
Lonmay 269 J5
Lonmore 263 H7
Looe 97 G4
Look Out Discovery Park,
  Bracknell BrackF
  RG12 7QW 121 D1
Loose 123 G3
Loosebeare 102 A2
Loosegate 176 B5
Loosley Row 134 D2
Lopcombe Corner 119 D4
Lopen 104 A1
Loppington 170 B5
Lorbottle 220 C1
Lorbottle Hall 220 C1
Lordington 107 G2
Lord's Cricket Ground &
  Museum GtLon
  NW8 8QN 10 F4
Lord's Hill 106 C1
Lorgill 263 G7
Lorn 233 E1
Lornty 251 G5

Loscoe 173 F3
Loscombe 104 A3
Losgaintir 263 F2
Lossiemouth 267 K4
Lossit 230 A4
Lost Gardens of Heligan
  Corn PL26 6EN 97 D5
Lostock Gralam 184 A5
Lostock Green 184 A5
Lostock
  Junction 184 A2
Lostwithiel 97 F4
Lothbeg 274 E7
Lothersdale 193 F3
Lotherton Hall Estate
  WYorks
  LS25 3EB 195 D4
Lothmore 274 E7
Loudwater 135 E3
Loughborough 160 A1
Loughor 128 B3
Loughton Essex 136 D3
Loughton MK 148 D4
Loughton Shrop 157 F4
Louis Tussaud's Waxworks
  FY1 5AA 64 Blackpool
Lound Lincs 161 F1
Lound Notts 187 D3
Lound Suff 165 G2
Lount 159 F1
Lour 252 C5
Louth 188 C5
Love Clough 193 E5
Lovedean 107 F1
Lover 106 C2
Loversall 186 C3
Loves Green 137 F2
Lovesome Hill 202 C3
Loveston 127 D2
Lovington 116 C4
Low Ackworth 186 B1
Low Angerton 220 C3
Low Ballevain 222 B3
Low Barlay 215 G5
Low Barlings 188 C5
Low Bentham (Lower
  Bentham) 192 C1
Low Bolton 201 F3
Low Bradfield 185 G3
Low Bradley
  (Bradley) 193 G3
Low Braithwaite 210 A3
Low Brunton 220 B4
Low Burnham 187 E2
Low Burton 202 B4
Low Buston 221 E1
Low Catton 195 G2
Low Coniscliffe 202 B1
Low Craighead 224 A5
Low Dinsdale 202 C1
Low Ellington 202 B4
Low Entercommon 202 C2
Low Etherley 212 A5
Low Fell 212 B2
Low Gate 211 F1
Low Grantley 202 B5
Low Green 151 G1
Low Habberley 158 A5
Low Ham 116 B5
Low Hawsker 204 C2
Low Haygarth 200 B3
Low Hesket 210 A3
Low Hesleyhurst 220 C2
Low Hutton 195 G1
Low Kingthorpe 204 B4
Low Laithe 194 A1
Low Langton 188 B5
Low Leighton 185 E4
Low Lorton 209 E4
Low Marishes 204 A5
Low Marnham 174 D1
Low Middleton 229 F3
Low Mill 203 F3
Low Moor Lancs 192 D3
Low Moor WYorks 194 A5
Low Moorsley 212 C3
Low Moresby 208 C4
Low Newton-by-
  the-Sea 229 G4
Low Row Cumb 210 B1
Low Row NYorks 201 E3
Low Stillaig 232 A3
Low Street 178 B3
Low Tharston 164 C2
Low Torry 235 E1
Low Town 220 D1
Low Toynton 188 C5
Low Wood 199 E4
Low Worsall 202 C2
Lowbands 145 G4
Lowdham 174 B3
Lowe 170 C4
Lowe Hill 171 G2
Lower Achachenna 240 C2
Lower Aisholt 115 F4
Lower Apperley 146 A4
Lower Arncott 134 B1
Lower Ashtead 121 G2
Lower Ashton 102 B4
Lower Assendon 134 C4
Lower Auchalick 232 A2
Lower Ballam 191 G4
Lower Barewood 144 C2
Lower Bartle 192 A4
Lower Bayble
  (Pabail Iarach) 271 H4
Lower Beeding 109 E1
Lower Benefield 161 E4
Lower Bentham (Low
  Bentham) 192 C1
Lower Bentley 146 B1
Lower Berry Hill 131 E1
Lower Birchwood 173 F2
Lower Boddington 147 G2
Lower Boscaswell 94 A3
Lower Bourne 120 D3
Lower Brailes 147 F4
Lower Breakish 256 C2
Lower Bredbury 184 D3
Lower Broadheath 146 A2
Lower Brynamman 128 D1
Lower Bullingham 145 E4
Lower Bullington 119 F3
Lower Burgate 106 A1
Lower Burrow 116 B5
Lower Burton 144 D2
Lower Caldecote 149 G3

Lower Cam 131 G2
Lower Cambourne 150 B2
Lower Camster 275 H4
Lower Chapel 143 G4
Lower Cheriton 103 E2
Lower Chicksgrove 118 A4
Lower Chute 119 E2
Lower Clent 158 B4
Lower Creedy 102 B2
Lower
  Cumberworth 185 G2
Lower Darwen 192 C5
Lower Dean 149 F1
Lower Diabaig 264 D5
Lower Dicker 110 A2
Lower Dinchope 157 D4
Lower Down 156 C4
Lower Drift 94 B4
Lower Dunsforth 194 D1
Lower Earley 134 C5
Lower Edmonton 136 C3
Lower Elkstone 172 B2
Lower End Bucks 134 B2
Lower End MK 149 E4
Lower End N'hants 149 D1
Lower Everleigh 118 C2
Lower Eythorne 125 E4
Lower Failand 131 E5
Lower Farringdon 120 C4
Lower Fittleworth 108 C2
Lower Foxdale 190 A4
Lower Freystrop 126 C2
Lower Froyle 120 C3
Lower Gabwell 101 F1
Lower Gledfield 266 C2
Lower Godney 116 B3
Lower Gravenhurst 149 G4
Lower Green Essex 150 C4
Lower Green Herts 149 G4
Lower Green Kent 123 E4
Lower Green Norf 178 A2
Lower Green Staffs 158 B2
Lower Green Bank 192 B2
Lower Halstock
  Leigh 104 B2
Lower Halstow 124 A2
Lower Hardres 124 D3
Lower Harpton 144 B1
Lower Hartshay 173 E2
Lower Hartwell 134 C1
Lower Hawthwaite 198 D4
Lower Haysden 123 E4
Lower Hayton 157 E4
Lower Heath 171 F1
Lower Hergest 144 B2
Lower Heyford 147 G5
Lower Higham 137 G5
Lower Holbrook 152 C4
Lower Hopton 185 G1
Lower Hordley 170 A5
Lower Horncroft 108 C2
Lower Horsebridge 110 A2
Lower Houses 185 F1
Lower Howsell 145 G3
Lower Kersal 184 C2
Lower Kilchattan 238 C5
Lower Kilcott 131 G4
Lower Killeyan 230 A5
Lower Kingcombe 104 B3
Lower Kingswood 122 B3
Lower Kinnerton 170 A1
Lower Langford 116 B1
Lower Largo 244 C4
Lower Leigh 172 B4
Lower Lemington 147 E4
Lower Lovacott 113 F3
Lower Loxhore 113 G2
Lower Lydbrook 131 E1
Lower Lye 144 D1
Lower Machen 130 B4
Lower Maes-coed 144 C4
Lower Mannington 105 G2
Lower Middleton
  Cheney 148 A3
Lower Milton 116 C3
Lower Moor 146 B3
Lower Morton 131 F3
Lower Nash 126 D2
Lower Nazeing 136 C2
Lower Netchwood 157 F3
Lower Nyland 117 E5
Lower Oddington 147 E5
Lower Ollach 256 B1
Lower Penarth 130 A5
Lower Penn 158 A3
Lower Pennington 106 C3
Lower Peover 184 B5
Lower Pollicott 134 C1
Lower Quinton 147 D3
Lower Race 130 B2
Lower Rainham 124 A2
Lower Roadwater 114 D4
Lower Sapey 145 F1
Lower Seagry 132 B4
Lower Shelton 149 E3
Lower Shiplake 134 C5
Lower Shuckburgh 147 G1
Lower Slaughter 147 D5
Lower Soothill 194 B5
Lower Stanton
  St. Quintin 132 B4
Lower Stoke 124 A1
Lower Stondon 149 G4
Lower Stone 131 F3
Lower Stonnall 158 C2
Lower Stow Bedon 164 A2
Lower Street
  Dorset 105 E3
Lower Street ESuss 110 C2
Lower Street Norf 179 D2
Lower Street Norf 178 D2
Lower Street Suff 152 C2
Lower Stretton 184 A4
Lower Sundon 149 F5
Lower Swanwick 107 D2
Lower Swell 147 D5
Lower Tadmarton 147 G4
Lower Tale 103 D2
Lower Tean 172 B4
Lower Thurlton 165 F2
Lower Thurnham 192 A2
Lower Town Corn 95 D4
Lower Town Devon 102 A3
Lower Town IoS 96 B1
Lower Town Pembs 126 C5
Lower Trebullett 98 D3
Lower Tysoe 147 F3
Lower Upcott 102 B4

Lower Upham 107 E1
Lower Upnor 137 G5
Lower Vexford 115 E4
Lower Wallop 156 C2
Lower Walton 184 A4
Lower Waterhay 132 C3
Lower Weald 148 C4
Lower Wear 102 C4
Lower Weare 116 B2
Lower Welson 144 B2
Lower Whatley 117 E3
Lower Whitley 184 A4
Lower Wick 146 A2
Lower Wield 120 B3
Lower Winchendon (Nether
  Winchendon) 134 C1
Lower Withington 171 F1
Lower Woodend 134 D4
Lower Woodford 118 C4
Lower Wyche 145 G3
Lowerhouse 193 E4
Lowertown 277 D8
Lowesby 160 C2
Lowestoft 165 G2
Loweswater 209 E4
Lowfield Heath 122 B4
Lowgill Cumb 200 B3
Lowgill Lancs 192 C1
Lowick Cumb 199 D4
Lowick N'hants 161 E4
Lowick N'umb 229 E3
Lowick Bridge 199 D4
Lowick Green 199 D4
Lownie Moor 252 C5
Lowsonford 147 D1
Lowther 210 B5
Lowther Castle 210 B5
Lowthorpe 196 C1
Lowton Devon 113 G5
Lowton GtMan 184 A3
Lowton Som 103 E1
Lowton Common 184 A3
Loxbeare 102 C1
Loxhill 121 F4
Loxhore 113 G2
Loxley Warks 147 E2
Loxley Green 172 B4
Loxton 116 A2
Loxwood 121 F4
Lubachoinnich 266 B2
Lubenham 160 C4
Lubfearn 265 K4
Lubmore 265 G6
Lubreoch 249 G5
Luccombe 114 C3
Luccombe Village 107 E4
Lucker 229 F3
Luckett 99 D3
Luckington 132 A4
Lucklawhill 244 C2
Luckwell Bridge 114 C4
Lucton 144 D1
Lucy Cross 202 B1
Ludag 254 C3
Ludborough 188 C3
Ludchurch 127 E1
Luddenden 193 G5
Luddenden Foot 193 G5
Luddenham Court 124 B2
Luddesdown 123 F2
Luddington NLincs 187 F1
Luddington Warks 147 D2
Luddington in the
  Brook 161 G4
Ludford Lincs 188 B4
Ludford Shrop 157 E5
Ludgershall Bucks 134 B1
Ludgershall Wilts 119 D2
Ludgvan 94 C3
Ludham 179 E4
Ludlow 157 E5
Ludney 189 D3
Ludstone 158 A3
Ludwell 118 A5
Ludworth 212 C3
Luffincott 98 D1
Luffness 236 B1
Lufton 104 B1
Lugar 225 D3
Luggate 236 D2
Luggate Burn 236 D2
Luggiebank 234 B2
Lugton 233 F4
Lugwardine 145 E3
Luib 256 B2
Luibeilt 249 E3
Luing 239 G3
Lulham 144 D3
Lullington Derbys 159 E1
Lullington Som 117 E2
Lulsgate Bottom 116 C1
Lulsley 145 G2
Lulworth Camp 105 E5
Lulworth Cove & Heritage
  Centre Dorset
  BH20 5RQ 105 E5
Lumb Lancs 193 E5
Lumb WYorks 193 G5
Lumbutts 193 F5
Lumby 195 D4
Lumphanan 260 D4
Lumphinnans 243 G5
Lumsdaine 237 E3
Lumsden 260 C2
Lunan 253 E4
Lunanhead 252 C4
Luncarty 243 F2
Lund ERid 196 B3
Lund NYorks 195 F4
Lund Shet 278 E2
Lundale 270 D4
Lunderston Bay Inv/cly
  PA16 0DN 232 D2
Lunderton 269 K6
Lundie Angus 244 A1
Lundin Links 244 C4
Lundwood 186 A2
Lundy 112 A1
Lunga 240 A4
Lunna 279 D6

Lunning 279 E6
Lunnon 128 B3
Lunsford's Cross 110 C2
Lunt 183 E2
Luntley 144 C2
Luppitt 103 E2
Lupridge 100 D2
Lupset 186 A1
Lupton 199 G4
Lurgashall 121 E5
Lurignich 248 B3
Lusby 176 B1
Luss 241 F5
Lussagiven 231 E1
Lusta 263 H6
Lustleigh 102 A4
Luston 145 D1
Luthermuir 253 E3
Luthrie 244 B3
Luton Devon 103 D2
Luton Devon 102 C5
Luton Med 123 G2
Luton Airport 149 G5
Lutterworth 160 A4
Lutton Devon 100 B2
Lutton Dorset 105 F4
Lutton Lincs 176 C5
Lutton N'hants 161 G4
Luxborough 114 C4
Luxulyan 97 E4
Lybster High 275 F2
Lybster High 275 H5
Lydacott 113 E5
Lydbury North 156 C4
Lydcott 113 G2
Lydd 111 F2
Lydd-on-Sea 111 F3
Lyde Green 131 F5
Lydeard
  St. Lawrence 115 E4
Lydford 99 F2
Lydford-on-Fosse 116 C4
Lydgate GtMan 185 D1
Lydgate GtMan 185 D1
Lydgate WYorks 193 F5
Lydham 156 C3
Lydiard Millicent 132 C4
Lydiard Tregoze 132 D4
Lydiate 183 E2
Lydlinch 104 C1
Lydney 131 F2
Lydstep 127 D3
Lye 158 B4
Lye Cross 116 B1
Lye Green Bucks 135 E2
Lye Green ESuss 123 E5
Lye Green Warks 147 D1
Lye's Green 117 F3
Lyford 133 F3
Lymbridge Green 124 D4
Lyme Regis 103 G4
Lymekilns 234 A4
Lyminge 125 D4
Lymington 106 C3
Lyminster 108 C3
Lymm 184 A4
Lymore 106 B3
Lympne 124 D5
Lympsham 116 A2
Lympstone 102 C4
Lynaberack 258 E5
Lynch 114 B3
Lynch Green 178 C5
Lynchat 258 E4
Lyndale House 263 J6
Lyndhurst 106 B2
Lyndon 161 E2
Lyne Aber 261 F4
Lyne ScBord 235 G5
Lyne Surr 121 F1
Lyne Down 145 F4
Lyne of Gorthleck 258 C2
Lyne of Skene 261 F3
Lyne Station 235 G5
Lyneal 170 B4
Lynegar 275 H3
Lyneham Oxon 147 E5
Lyneham Wilts 132 C5
Lynemore High 259 H2
Lynemore Moray 259 J1
Lynemouth 221 E2
Lyness 277 C8
Lynford 163 G3
Lyng Norf 178 B4
Lyngate 179 E3
Lynmouth 114 A3
Lynn 157 G1
Lynsted 124 B2
Lynstone 112 C5
Lynton 114 A3
Lynton & Lynmouth Cliff
  Railway Devon
  EX35 6EP 114 A3
Lyon's Gate 104 C2
Lyonshall 144 C2
Lyrabus 230 A3
Lytchett Matravers 105 F3
Lytchett Minster 105 F3
Lyth 275 H2
Lytham 191 G5
Lytham St. Anne's 191 G5
Lythe 204 B1
Lythe Hill 121 E4
Lythes 277 D9
Lythmore 275 F2

## M

M.V. Princess Pocahontas
  Kent DA11 0BS 137 F5
Mabe Burnthouse 95 E3
Mabie 217 D3
Mablethorpe 189 F4
Macclesfield 184 D5
Macclesfield Forest 185 D5
Macduff 269 F4
Macedonia 244 A4
Machan 234 B4
Machany 243 D3
Machen 130 B4
Machrie A&B 230 A3
Machrie A&B 230 B5
Machrie NAyr 223 D3
Machrihanish 222 B3
Machrins 238 C5

Machynlleth 154 D2
McInroy's Point 232 D2
Mackerye End 136 A1
Mackworth 173 E4
Macmerry 236 B2
Macterry 269 F6
Madame Tussauds GtLon
  NW1 5LR 12 A1
Madderty 243 E2
Maddiston 234 D2
Madehurst 108 B2
Madeley Staffs 171 E3
Madeley Tel&W 157 G2
Madeley Heath 171 E3
Maders 98 D3
Madford 103 E1
Madingley 150 B1
Madjeston 117 F5
Madley 144 D3
Madresfield 146 A3
Madron 94 B3
Maenaddwyn 180 C4
Maenclochog 141 D5
Maendy Cardiff 130 A5
Maendy VGlam 129 G5
Maenporth 95 E4
Maentwrog 167 F3
Maen-y-groes 141 G2
Maer Corn 112 C5
Maer Staffs 171 E4
Maerdy Carmar 142 C5
Maerdy Carmar 142 C5
Maerdy Conwy 168 D3
Maerdy RCT 129 F3
Maesbrook 169 F5
Maesbury Marsh 170 A5
Maes-glas 130 B4
Maesgwynne 141 E5
Maeshafn 169 F1
Maesllyn 141 G3
Maesmynis 143 G3
Maesteg 129 E3
Maes-Treylow 144 B1
Maesybont 128 C1
Maesycrugiau 142 A3
Maesycwmmer 130 A3
Magdalen Laver 137 E2
Maggieknockater 268 B6
Maggots End 150 C5
Maghull 183 E2
Magna Park 160 A4
Magor 130 D4
Magpie Green 164 B4
Maiden Bradley 117 E4
Maiden Head 116 C1
Maiden Law 212 A3
Maiden Newton 104 B3
Maiden Wells 126 C3
Maidencombe 101 F1
Maidenhall 152 C3
Maidenhayne 103 F3
Maidenhead 135 D4
Maidens 224 A5
Maiden's Green 135 D5
Maidensgrove 134 C4
Maidenwell Corn 97 F2
Maidenwell Lincs 188 D5
Maidford 148 B2
Maids' Moreton 148 C4
Maidstone 123 G3
Maidwell 160 C5
Mail 279 D10
Maindee 130 C4
Mainland Ork 277 B6
Mainland Shet 279 C7
Mains of Ardestie 244 D1
Mains of Balgavies 252 D4
Mains of Ballindarg 252 C4
Mains of Burgie 267 H6
Mains of Culsh 269 G6
Mains of Dillavaird 253 F1
Mains of Drum 261 G4
Mains of Dudwick 261 H1
Mains of Faillie 258 E1
Mains of Feddarate 269 G6
Mains of Glack 261 F2
Mains of
  Glenbuchat 260 B3
Mains of Linton 261 F3
Mains of Melgund 252 D4
Mains of Pitfour 269 H6
Mains of Pittrichie 261 G2
Mains of Sluie 267 H6
Mains of Tannachy 268 B4
Mains of Thornton 253 E2
Mains of Tig 214 C2
Mains of Watten 275 H3
Mainsforth 212 C4
Mainsriddle 216 D5
Mainstone 156 B4
Maisemore 146 A5
Major's Green 158 D5
Makendon 220 A1
Makeney 173 E3
Makerstoun 228 A3
Malacleit 262 C4
Malborough 100 D4
Malden Rushett 121 G1
Maldon 138 C2
Malham 193 F1
Maligar 263 K5
Malinbridge 186 A4
Malleny Mills 235 F3
Mallows Green 150 C5
Malltraeth 166 D1
Mallwyd 155 E1
Malmesbury 132 B4
Malmsmead 114 A3
Malpas ChesW&C 170 B3
Malpas Corn 96 C5
Malpas Newport 130 C3
Maltby Lincs 188 D4
Maltby Stock 203 D1
Maltby SYorks 186 C3
Maltby le Marsh 189 E4
Malting End 151 F2
Malting Green 152 A5
Maltman's Hill 124 A4
Malton 203 G5

Malvern Link 145 G3
Malvern Wells 145 G3
Mambeg 232 D1
Mamble 157 F5
Mamhead 102 C4
Mamhilad 130 C2
Manaccan 95 E4
Manadon 100 A2
Manafon 156 A2
Manaton 102 A4
Manby 189 D4
Mancetter 159 F3
Manchester 184 C3
Manchester Airport 184 C4
Manchester Apollo GtMan
  M12 6AP 47 H6
Manchester Art Gallery
  GtMan M2 3JL 47 E4
Manchester Central GtMan
  M2 3GX 46 D5
Manchester Craft & Design
  Centre GtMan
  M4 5JD 47 F3
Manchester Museum
  GtMan M13 9PL 47 F7
Manchester United Museum
  & Stadium Tour Centre
  GtMan M16 0RA 24 D3
Mancot Royal 170 A1
Mandally
  (Manndalaidh) 257 J4
Manea 162 C3
Maneight 224 D5
Manfield 202 B1
Mangaster 278 C5
Mangerton 104 A3
Mangotsfield 131 F5
Mangrove Green 149 G5
Mangurstadh 270 C4
Manish (Manais) 263 G3
Mankinholes 193 F5
Manley 183 G5
Manmoel 130 A2
Mannal 246 A2
Manningford
  Abbots 118 C2
Manningford
  Bohune 118 C2
Manningford Bruce 118 C2
Manningham 194 A4
Mannings Amusement Park
  Suff IP11 2DW 153 D4
Mannings Heath 109 E1
Mannington 105 G2
Manningtree 152 C4
Mannofield 261 H4
Manor Farm Country Park
  Hants SO30 2ER 4 D3
Manor Park 135 E4
Manorbier 127 D3
Manorbier Newton 126 D2
Manordeifi 141 F3
Manordeilo 142 C5
Manorowen 140 C4
Mansell Gamage 144 C3
Mansell Lacy 144 D3
Mansergh 200 B4
Mansfield 173 G1
Mansfield
  Woodhouse 173 G1
Manson Green 178 B5
Mansriggs 199 D4
Manston Dorset 105 E1
Manston Kent 125 F2
Manston WYorks 194 C4
Manswood 105 F2
Manthorpe Lincs 161 F1
Manthorpe Lincs 175 E4
Manton NLincs 187 G2
Manton Notts 186 C5
Manton Rut 161 D2
Manton Wilts 118 C1
Manuden 150 C5
Manwood Green 137 E1
Maolachy 240 A3
Maperton 117 D5
Maple Cross 135 F3
Maplebeck 174 C1
Mapledurham 134 B5
Mapledurwell 120 B2
Maplehurst 121 G5
Maplescombe 123 E2
Mapleton 172 C3
Mapperley Derbys 173 F3
Mapperley Notts 173 G3
Mapperton Dorset 104 B3
Mapperton Dorset 105 F3
Mappleborough
  Green 146 C1
Mappleton 197 E3
Mapplewell 186 A2
Mappowder 104 D2
Mar Lodge 259 H5
Maraig (Maaruig) 270 E7
Marazion 94 C3
Marbhig 271 G6
Marbury 170 C3
Marbury Country Park
  ChesW&C
  CW9 6AT 184 A5
March 162 C3
Marcham 133 G3
Marchamley 170 C4
Marchamley Wood 170 C4
Marchington 172 C5
Marchington
  Woodlands 172 C5
Marchwiel 170 A3
Marchwood 106 C1
Marcross 114 C1
Marcus 252 D4
Marden Here 145 E3
Marden Kent 123 G4
Marden T&W 221 F4
Marden Wilts 118 B2
Marden Ash 137 E2
Marden Beech 123 G4
Marden Thorn 123 G4
Marden's Hill 123 D5
Mardon 228 D3
Mardy 130 C1
Mare Green 116 A5
Marefield 160 C2
Mareham le Fen 176 A1
Mareham on
  the Hill 176 A1
Maresfield 109 G1
Marfleet 196 D4

Marford 170 A2
Margam 129 D4
Margam Country Park
NPT SA13 2TJ 129 E4
Margaret Marsh 105 E1
Margaret Roding 137 E1
Margaretting 137 F2
Margaretting Tye 137 F2
Margate 125 F1
Margnaheglish 223 F2
Margrove Park 203 F1
Marham 163 F2
Marhamchurch 112 C5
Marholm 161 G2
Marian Cwm 182 B5
Mariandyrys 181 E4
Marian-glas 180 D4
Marionsleigh 114 A5
Marine Town 124 B1
Marishader 263 K5
Maristow House 100 A1
Mark 116 A3
Mark Causeway 116 A3
Mark Cross 123 E5
Markby 189 E5
Markdhu 214 C3
Markeaton 173 E4
Markeaton Park Craft Village
Derby DE22 3BG 18 A3
Market Bosworth 159 E2
Market Bosworth Country
Park Leics
CV13 0LP 159 G2
Market Deeping 161 G1
Market Drayton 171 D4
Market Harborough 160 C4
Market Lavington 118 B2
Market Overton 161 D1
Market Rasen 188 B4
Market Stainton 188 C5
Market Street 179 D3
Market Warsop 173 G1
Market Weighton 196 A3
Market Weston 164 A4
Markethill 244 A1
Markfield 159 G1
Markham 130 A2
Markham Moor 187 E5
Markinch 244 A4
Markington 194 B1
Marks Tey 152 A5
Marksbury 117 D1
Markwell 99 D5
Markyate 135 F1
Marl Bank 145 G3
Marland 184 C1
Marlborough 118 C1
Marlbrook 158 B5
Marlcliff 146 C2
Marldon 101 E1
Marle Green 110 A2
Marlesford 153 E2
Marley Green 170 C3
Marley Hill 212 B2
Marlingford 178 C5
Marloes 126 A2
Marlow Bucks 135 D4
Marlow Here 156 D5
Marlpit Hill 122 D4
Marlpool 173 F3
Marnhull 105 D1
Marnoch 268 D5
Marple 185 D4
Marple Bridge 185 D4
Marr 186 C2
Marrel 275 F7
Marrick 201 F3
Marrister 279 E6
Marros 127 F2
Marsden T&W 212 C1
Marsden WYorks 185 E1
Marsett 201 E4
Marsh 103 E1
Marsh Baldon 134 A3
Marsh Benham 119 F1
Marsh Farm Country Park
Essex CM3 5WP 138 B3
Marsh Gibbon 148 B5
Marsh Green
Devon 102 D3
Marsh Green
GtMan 183 G2
Marsh Green Kent 122 D4
Marsh Green
Tel&W 157 F1
Marsh Lane 186 B5
Marsh Street 114 C3
Marshall Meadows 237 G4
Marshalsea 103 G2
Marshalswick 136 A2
Marsham 178 C3
Marshaw 192 B2
Marshborough 125 F3
Marshbrook 156 D4
Marshchapel 189 D3
Marshfield
Newport 130 B4
Marshfield SGlos 131 G5
Marshgate 98 B1
Marshland
St. James 162 D2
Marshside 183 E1
Marshwood 103 G3
Marske 202 A2
Marske-by-the-Sea 213 F5
Marsland Green 184 A3
Marston ChesW&C 184 A5
Marston Here 144 C2
Marston Lincs 175 D3
Marston Oxon 134 A2
Marston Staffs 171 G5
Marston Staffs 158 A1
Marston Warks 159 E4
Marston Wilts 118 A2
Marston Doles 147 G2
Marston Green 159 D4
Marston Magna 116 C5
Marston Meysey 132 C3
Marston
Montgomery 172 C4
Marston Moretaine 149 E3
Marston on Dove 172 D5
Marston
St. Lawrence 148 A3
Marston Stannett 145 E2

Marston Trussell 160 B4
Marston Vale Millennium
Country Park CenBeds
MK43 0PR 149 F3
Marstow 131 E1
Marsworth 135 E1
Marten 119 D1
Marthall 184 B4
Martham 179 F4
Martin Hants 105 G1
Martin Lincs 175 G2
Martin Lincs 176 A1
Martin Drove End 118 B5
Martin Hussingtree 146 A1
Martin Mere Lancs
L40 0TA 183 F1
Martinhoe 113 G1
Martinscroft 184 A4
Martinstown 104 C4
Martlesham 152 D3
Martlesham Heath 152 D3
Martletwy 126 D1
Martley 145 G1
Martock 104 A1
Marton ChesE 171 F1
Marton Cumb 198 D5
Marton ERid 197 D4
Marton ERid 197 E1
Marton Lincs 187 F4
Marton Middl 203 E1
Marton NYorks 194 D1
Marton NYorks 203 G4
Marton Shrop 156 B5
Marton Shrop 170 B5
Marton Warks 147 G1
Marton Abbey 195 E1
Marton-in-the-
Forest 195 E1
Marton-le-Moor 202 C5
Martyr Worthy 119 G4
Martyr's Green 121 F2
Marwell Zoo Hants
SO21 1JH 4 D1
Marwick 276 B5
Marwood 113 F2
Mary Rose PO1 3LX
82 Portsmouth
Mary Tavy 99 F3
Marybank (An Lagaidh)
High 266 B6
Marybank ESiar 271 G4
Maryburgh
(Baile Mairi) 266 C6
Maryfield Corn 100 A2
Maryfield Shet 279 D8
Marygold 237 F4
Maryhill Aber 269 G6
Maryhill Glas 233 G3
Marykirk 253 E2
Marylebone
GtLon 136 B4
Marylebone
GtMan 183 G2
Marypark 259 J1
Maryport Cumb 208 D3
Maryport D&G 206 B3
Marystow 99 E2
Maryton 253 E4
Marywell Aber 261 H5
Marywell Aber 260 D5
Marywell Angus 253 E5
Masham 202 B4
Mashbury 137 F1
Masongill 200 B5
Mastin Moor 186 B5
Mastrick 261 H4
Matchborough 146 C1
Matching 137 E1
Matching Green 137 E1
Matching Tye 137 E1
Matfen 220 C4
Matfield 123 F4
Mathern 131 E3
Mathon 145 G3
Mathry 140 B4
Matlaske 178 C2
Matlock 173 E1
Matlock Bank 173 E1
Matlock Bath 173 D2
Matson 132 A1
Matterdale End 209 G4
Mattersey 187 D4
Mattersey Thorpe 187 D4
Mattingley 120 C2
Mattishall 178 B4
Mattishall Burgh 178 B4
Mauchline 224 C3
Maud 269 H6
Maufant 100 C5
Maugersbury 147 D5
Maughold 190 C2
Mauld 257 K1
Maulden 149 F4
Maulds Meaburn 200 B1
Maunby 202 C4
Maund Bryan 145 E2
Maundown 115 D5
Mautby 179 F4
Mavesyn Ridware 158 C1
Mavis Enderby 176 B1
Maw Green 171 E2
Mawbray 209 D2
Mawdesley 183 F1
Mawdlam 129 E4
Mawgan 95 E4
Mawgan Porth 96 C3
Mawla 96 B5
Mawnan 95 E4
Mawnan Smith 95 E4
Mawsley 160 D5
Mawthorpe 189 E5
Maxey 161 G2
Maxstoke 159 E4
Maxted Street 124 D4
Maxton Kent 125 F4
Maxton ScBord 228 A3
Maxwellheugh 228 B3
Maxworthy 98 C1
May Hill 145 E5
Mayals 128 C3
Maybole 224 B5
Mayen 268 D6
Mayfair 136 B4
Mayfield ESuss 110 A1
Mayfield Midlo 236 A3
Mayfield Staffs 172 C3
Mayford 121 E2

Mayland 138 C2
Maylandsea 138 C2
Maynard's Green 110 A2
Maypole IoS 96 B1
Maypole Kent 125 D2
Maypole Mon 131 D1
Maypole Green
Essex 152 A5
Maypole Green
Norf 165 F2
Maypole Green
Suff 153 D1
Maypole Green
Suff 152 A2
May's Green NSom 116 A1
Mays Green Oxon 134 C4
Maywick 279 C10
Mead 112 C4
Mead End 118 B5
Meadgate 117 D2
Meadle 134 D2
Meadow Green 145 G2
Meadowhall 186 A3
Meadowmill 236 B2
Meadowtown 156 C2
Meadwell 99 E2
Meaford 171 F4
Meal Bank 199 G3
Mealasta 270 B5
Meals 189 E3
Mealsgate 209 F2
Meanley 192 D3
Meanwood 194 B4
Mearbeck 193 E1
Meare 116 B3
Meare Green 115 F5
Mearns 233 G4
Mears Ashby 148 D1
Measham 159 F1
Meath Green 122 B4
Meathop 199 F4
Meavy 100 B1
Medbourne 160 D3
Meddon 112 C4
Meden Vale 173 G1
Medlar 192 A4
Medmenham 134 D4
Medomsley 212 A2
Medstead 120 B4
Meer Common 144 C2
Meer End 159 E5
Meerbrook 171 G1
Meesden 150 C4
Meeson 171 D5
Meeth 113 F5
Meeting House Hill 179 E3
Meggethead 226 C3
Meidrim 141 F5
Meifod Denb 168 D2
Meifod Powys 156 A1
Meigle 252 A5
Meikle Earnock 234 B4
Meikle Grenach 232 B3
Meikle Kilmory 232 B3
Meikle Rahane 232 D1
Meikle Strath 253 E2
Meikle Tarty 261 H2
Meikle Wartle 261 F1
Meikleour 243 G1
Meikleyard 224 D2
Meinciau 128 A1
Meir 171 G3
Meirheath 171 G3
Melbost 271 G4
Melbost Borve
(Mealabost) 271 G2
Melbourn 150 B3
Melbourne Derbys 173 E5
Melbourne ERid 195 G3
Melbury 113 D4
Melbury Abbas 105 E1
Melbury Bubb 104 B2
Melbury Osmond 104 B2
Melbury Sampford 104 B2
Melby 279 A7
Melchbourne 149 F1
Melcombe
Bingham 105 D2
Melcombe Regis 104 C4
Meldon Devon 99 F1
Meldon N'umb 220 D4
Meldreth 150 B3
Meledor 96 C4
Melfort 240 A3
Melgarve 258 B5
Melgum 260 C4
Meliden
(Gallt Melyd) 182 B4
Melincourt 129 E2
Melin-y-coed 168 B1
Melin-y-ddol 155 G2
Melin-y-grug 155 G2
Melin-y-Wig 168 D3
Melkinthorpe 210 B5
Melkridge 210 D1
Melksham 118 A1
Melksham Forest 118 A1
Melldalloch 232 A2
Melling Lancs 199 G5
Melling Mersey 183 E2
Melling Mount 183 F2
Mellis 164 C4
Mellon Charles 264 E2
Mellon Udrigle 264 E2
Mellor Lancs 192 C4
Mellor Brook 192 C4
Mells 117 E3
Melmerby Cumb 210 C4
Melmerby NYorks 201 F4
Melmerby NYorks 202 C5
Melplash 104 A3
Melrose Aber 269 F4
Melrose ScBord 227 G2
Melsetter 277 B9
Melsonby 202 A2
Meltham 185 E1
Melton ERid 196 B5
Melton Suff 153 D2
Melton
Constable 178 B2
Melton Mowbray 160 C1
Melton Ross 188 A1
Meltonby 195 G2
Melvaig 264 D3
Melverley 156 C1
Melverley Green 156 C1
Melvich 274 D2
Membury 103 F2

Memsie 269 H4
Memus 252 C4
Menabilly 97 E4
Menai Bridge
(Porthaethwy) 181 D5
Mendham 165 D3
Mendlesham 152 B1
Mendlesham Green 152 B1
Menethorpe 195 G1
Menheniot 97 G3
Menie House 261 H2
Menithwood 145 G1
Mennock 225 G5
Menston 194 A3
Menstrie 242 D5
Mentmore 135 E1
Meoble 247 F1
Meole Brace 157 D1
Meols 182 B3
Meon 107 E2
Meonstoke 107 F1
Meopham 123 F2
Meopham Green 123 F2
Mepal 162 C4
Meppershall 149 G4
Merbach 144 C3
Mercaston 173 D3
Mere ChesE 184 B4
Mere Wilts 117 F4
Mere Brow 183 F1
Mere Green 158 D3
Mere Heath 184 A5
Mereclough 193 E4
Mereside 191 G4
Meresworth 123 F3
Mergie 253 F1
Meriden 159 E4
Merkadale 255 J1
Merkinch 266 D7
Merkland 216 B3
Merley 105 G3
Merlin's Bridge 126 C1
Merridge 115 F4
Merrifield 101 E3
Merrington 170 B5
Merrion 126 C3
Merriott 104 A1
Merrivale 99 F3
Merrow 121 F2
Merry Hill Herts 136 A3
Merry Hill WMid 158 B4
Merry Hill WMid 158 A3
Merrymeet 97 G3
Mersea Island 138 C1
Mersey Ferries Mersey
CH44 6QY 42 A4
Merseyside Maritime
Museum Mersey
L3 4AQ 42 B4
Mersham 124 C5
Merstham 122 B3
Merston 108 A3
Merstone 107 E4
Merther 96 C5
Merthyr 141 G5
Merthyr Cynog 143 F4
Merthyr Dyfan 115 E1
Merthyr Mawr 129 E5
Merthyr Tydfil 129 G2
Merthyr Vale 129 G3
Merton Devon 113 F4
Merton Norf 164 A2
Merton Oxon 134 A1
Mervinslaw 228 A5
Meshaw 102 A1
Messing 138 C1
Messingham 187 F2
Metcombe 103 D3
Metfield 165 D3
Metherell 100 A1
Metheringham 175 F1
Methil 244 B5
Methlem 166 A4
Methley 194 C4
Methley Junction 194 C5
Methlick 261 G1
Methven 243 F2
Methwold 163 F3
Methwold Hythe 163 F3
MetroCentre 212 B1
Mettingham 165 E3
Metton 178 C2
Mevagissey 97 E5
Mewith Head 192 D1
Mexborough 186 B3
Mey 275 H1
Meysey Hampton 132 C3
Miabhag ESiar 263 G2
Miabhag ESiar 270 C7
Mial 264 D3
Miavaig (Miabhaig) 270 C4
Michaelchurch 145 E5
Michaelchurch
Escley 144 C4
Michaelchurch-on-
Arrow 144 B2
Michaelston-le-Pit 130 A5
Michaelston-super-
Ely 130 A5
Michaelstow-y-
Fedw 130 B4
Michaelstow 97 E2
Michcombe 100 C1
Micheldever 119 G4
Micheldever
Station 119 G4
Michelmersh 119 E5
Mickfield 152 C1
Mickle Trafford 170 B1
Micklebring 186 C3
Mickleby 204 B1
Micklefield 194 D4
Mickleham 121 G3
Micklehurst 185 D2
Mickleover 173 E4
Micklethwaite
Cumb 209 F1
Micklethwaite
WYorks 193 G3
Mickleton Glos 147 D3
Mickletown 194 C5
Mickley Derbys 186 A5
Mickley NYorks 202 B5
Mickley Green 151 G2
Mickley Square 211 G1
Mid Ardlaw 269 H4
Mid Beltie 260 E4
Mid Calder 235 E3

Mid Clyth 275 H5
Mid Hants Railway
Hants SO24 9JG 120 B4
Mid Lambrook 104 A1
Mid Lavant 108 A3
Mid Letter 240 C4
Mid Lix 242 A1
Mid Mossdale 200 D3
Mid Yell 278 E3
Midbea 276 D3
Middle Assendon 134 C4
Middle Aston 147 G5
Middle Barton 147 G5
Middle Bickenhill 159 E4
Middle
Bockhampton 106 A3
Middle Claydon 148 C5
Middle Drift 97 F3
Middle Drums 253 D4
Middle
Duntisbourne 132 B2
Middle Handley 186 B5
Middle Harling 164 A3
Middle Littleton 146 C3
Middle Maes-coed 144 C4
Middle Marwood 113 F2
Middle Mill 140 B5
Middle Quarter 124 A5
Middle Rasen 188 A4
Middle Rigg 243 F4
Middle Salter 192 C1
Middle Sontley 170 A3
Middle Stoford 115 E5
Middle Taphouse 97 F3
Middle Town 96 B1
Middle Tysoe 147 F3
Middle Wallop 119 D4
Middle Winterslow 118 D4
Middle Woodford 118 C4
Middlebie 218 A4
Middlecliff 186 B2
Middlecott 133 E5
Middleham 202 A4
Middlehill Aber 269 G6
Middlehill Corn 97 G3
Middlehope 157 E4
Middlemarsh 104 C2
Middlemoor 99 E3
Middlequarter (Ceathramh
Meadhanach) 262 D5
Middlesbrough 213 D5
Middlesceugh 210 A3
Middleshaw 199 G4
Middlesmoor 201 F5
Middlestone 212 B4
Middlestone Moor 212 B4
Middlestown 185 G1
Middleton Aber 261 G3
Middleton Angus 253 D5
Middleton Cumb 200 B4
Middleton Derbys 173 D2
Middleton Derbys 172 C1
Middleton Essex 151 G3
Middleton GtMan 184 C2
Middleton Hants 119 F3
Middleton Here 145 E1
Middleton Lancs 192 A2
Middleton Midlo 236 A4
Middleton N'hants 160 D3
Middleton N'umb 220 C3
Middleton N'umb 229 E3
Middleton Norf 163 E1
Middleton NYorks 203 G4
Middleton P&K 243 G4
Middleton P&K 251 G5
Middleton Shrop 156 B3
Middleton Shrop 157 E5
Middleton Shrop 170 A5
Middleton Suff 153 F1
Middleton Swan 128 A4
Middleton Warks 159 D3
Middleton WYorks 194 A3
Middleton WYorks 194 B5
Middleton Baggot 157 F3
Middleton Bank Top 220 C3
Middleton Cheney 147 G3
Middleton Green 171 G4
Middleton Hall 229 D4
Middleton Moor 153 F1
Middleton of
Potterton 261 H3
Middleton on the
Hill 145 E1
Middleton One Row 202 C1
Middleton Park 261 H3
Middleton Priors 157 F4
Middleton
Quernhow 202 C5
Middleton
St. George 202 C1
Middleton Scriven 157 F4
Middleton Stoney 148 A5
Middleton Tyas 202 B2
Middleton-in-
Teesdale 211 F5
Middleton-on-
Leven 203 D1
Middleton-on-Sea 108 B3
Middleton-on-the-
Wolds 196 B3
Middletown Cumb 198 A2
Middletown Powys 156 C1
Middlewich 171 E1
Middlewood ChesE 184 D4
Middlewood SYorks 186 A3
Middlewood Green 152 B1
Middlezoy 116 A4
Middridge 212 B5
Midfield 273 H2
Midford 117 E1
Midge Hall 192 B5
Midgeholme 210 C2
Midgham 119 G1
Midgley WYorks 185 G1
Midgley WYorks 193 G5
Midhopestones 185 G3
Midhurst 121 D5
Midland 120 D5
Midlem 227 G3
Midloe Grange 149 G1
Midpark 232 B4
Midsomer Norton 117 D2
Midthorpe 188 C5
Midtown High 273 H2
Midtown High 264 E3
Midtown of Barras 253 G1

Midville 176 B2
Midway 173 E5
Migdale 266 D2
Migvie 260 C4
Milarrochy 241 G5
Milber 102 B5
Milborne 268 E5
Milborne Port 104 C1
Milborne
St. Andrew 105 D3
Milborne Wick 117 D5
Milbourne
N'umb 220 D4
Milbourne Wilts 132 B4
Milburn 210 C5
Milbury Heath 131 F3
Milcombe 147 G4
Milden 152 A3
Mildenhall Suff 163 F5
Mildenhall Wilts 118 D1
Mile Elm 118 A1
Mile End Essex 152 A5
Mile End Glos 131 E1
Mile End Park GtLon
E3 4HL 12 B4
Mile Oak 123 F4
Mile Town 124 B1
Milebrook 156 C5
Milebush 123 G4
Mileham 178 A4
Miles Green 171 F3
Miles Hope 145 E1
Milesmark 235 E1
Milfield 228 D3
Milford Derbys 173 E3
Milford Devon 112 C3
Milford Shrop 170 B5
Milford Staffs 171 G5
Milford Surr 121 E3
Milford Haven
(Aberdaugleddau)
126 B2
Milford on Sea 106 B3
Milkwall 131 E2
Milky Way Adventure
Park Devon
EX39 5RY 112 D3
Mill Bank 193 G5
Mill Brow 185 D4
Mill End Bucks 134 C4
Mill End Cambs 151 E2
Mill End Herts 150 B4
Mill End Herts 150 C2
Mill End Herts 151 E5
Mill Green Cambs 151 E3
Mill Green Essex 137 F2
Mill Green Herts 136 B2
Mill Green Norf 164 C3
Mill Green Shrop 171 D5
Mill Green Staffs 172 B5
Mill Green Suff 153 D1
Mill Green Suff 152 A2
Mill Hill B'burn 192 C5
Mill Hill Cambs 150 A2
Mill Hill GtLon 136 B3
Mill Houses 192 C1
Mill Lane 120 C2
Mill of Camsail 233 D1
Mill of Colp 269 F6
Mill of Elrick 269 H6
Mill of Fortune 242 C2
Mill of Kingoodie 261 G2
Mill of Monquich 261 G5
Mill of Uras 253 G1
Mill Side 199 F4
Mill Street Kent 123 F3
Mill Street Norf 178 B4
Milland 120 D5
Millbank 269 J6
Millbeck 209 F4
Millbounds 278 F4
Millbreck 269 J6
Millbridge 120 D3
Millbrook CenBeds 149 F4
Millbrook Corn 100 A2
Millbrook Devon 103 G3
Millbrook Soton 106 C1
Millburn Aber 260 E1
Millburn Aber 260 E1
Millcombe 101 E3
Millcorner 110 D1
Milldale 172 C2
Millden 261 H3
Milldens 252 D4
Millearne 243 E3
Millend 147 F5
Millenheath 170 C4
Millersford Seed Bank,
Wakehurst Place WSuss
RH17 6TN 122 C5
Millerhill 236 A3
Miller's Dale 185 F5
Miller's Green
Derbys 173 D2
Miller's Green
Essex 137 E2
Millgate 193 E5
Millhalf 144 B3
Millhayes Devon 103 E1
Millhayes Devon 103 F2
Millholme 199 G3
Millhouse A&B 232 A2
Millhouse Cumb 209 G3
Millhouse Green 185 G2
Millhousebridge 217 F2
Millikenpark 233 F3
Millin Cross 126 C1
Millington 196 A2
Millmeece 171 F4
Millness 257 K1
Millom 198 C4
Millow 150 A3
Millpool 97 F2
Millport 232 C4
Millthorpe 186 A5
Millthrop 200 B3
Milltimber 261 G4
Milltown Aber 259 K4
Milltown Corn 97 F4
Milltown D&G 218 B4
Milltown Derbys 173 E1
Milltown Devon 113 F2
Milltown High 267 G7
Milltown of
Aberdalgie 243 F2

Milltown of
Auchindoun 260 B1
Milltown of
Craigston 269 F5
Milltown of
Edinvillie 267 K7
Milltown of
Kildrummy 260 C3
Milltown of
Rothiemay 268 D6
Milltown of Towie 260 C3
Milnacraig 252 A4
Milnathort 243 G4
Milners Heath 170 B1
Milngavie 233 G2
Milnrow 184 D1
Milnsbridge 185 F1
Milnthorpe 199 F4
Milovaig 263 G6
Milrig 224 D2
Milson 157 F5
Milstead 124 B3
Milston 118 C3
Milton Angus 252 B5
Milton Cambs 150 C1
Milton Cumb 210 B1
Milton D&G 216 B5
Milton D&G 214 D5
Milton Derbys 173 E5
Milton High 265 K6
Milton High 266 E4
Milton High 267 G6
Milton High 267 G6
Milton High 264 D7
Milton High 266 C7
Milton High 275 J3
Milton (Baile a' Mhuilinn)
High 258 B1
Milton Moray 268 D4
Milton Newport 130 C4
Milton Notts 187 E5
Milton NSom 116 A1
Milton Oxon 147 G4
Milton Oxon 133 G3
Milton P&K 243 E1
Milton Pembs 126 D2
Milton Ports 107 F3
Milton Som 116 B5
Milton Stir 242 A4
Milton Stoke 171 G2
Milton WDun 233 F2
Milton Abbas 105 D2
Milton Abbot 99 E3
Milton Bridge 235 G3
Milton Bryan 149 E4
Milton Clevedon 117 D4
Milton Combe 100 A1
Milton Country Park Cambs
CB24 6AZ 150 C1
Milton Damerel 113 D4
Milton End 131 G1
Milton Ernest 149 F2
Milton Green 170 B2
Milton Hill 133 G3
Milton Keynes 149 D4
Milton Keynes
Village 149 D4
Milton Lilbourne 118 C1
Milton Malsor 148 C2
Milton Morenish 242 B1
Milton of
Cairnborrow 268 C6
Milton of Balgonie 244 B4
Milton of Buchanan 241 G5
Milton of
Callander 242 A4
Milton of Campfield 260 E4
Milton of Campsie 234 A2
Milton of Coldwells 261 H1
Milton of Cullerie 261 F4
Milton of Cushnie 260 D3
Milton of Dalcapon 251 F4
Milton of
Inveramsay 261 F2
Milton of Noth 260 D2
Milton of Tullich 260 B5
Milton on Stour 117 E5
Milton Regis 124 A2
Milton Street 110 A3
Miltonduff 267 J5
Miltonhill 267 H5
Miltonise 214 C3
Milton-Lockhart 234 C4
Milton-under-
Wychwood 133 E1
Milverton Som 115 E5
Milverton Warks 147 F1
Milwich 171 G4
Mimbridge 121 E1
Minack Theatre Corn
TR19 6JU 94 A4
Minard 240 B5
Minard Castle 240 B5
Minchington 105 F1
Minchinhampton 132 A2
Mindrum 228 C3
Mindrummill 228 C3
Minehead 114 C3
Minera 169 F2
Minety 132 C3
Minety Lower Moor 132 C3
Minffordd Gwyn 154 D1
Minffordd Gwyn 167 E4
Minffordd Gwyn 181 D5
Miningsby 176 B1
Minions 97 G2
Minishant 224 B4
Minley Manor 120 D2
Minllyn 155 E1
Minnes 261 H2
Minngearraidh 254 C2
Minnigaff 215 F4
Minnonie 269 F4
Minskip 194 C1
Minstead 106 B1
Minster Kent 124 B1
Minster Kent 125 F2
Minster Lovell 133 F1
Minsteracres 211 G2
Minsterley 156 C2
Minsterworth 131 G1
Minterne Magna 104 C2
Minterne Parva 104 C2
Minting 188 B5
Mintlaw 269 J6
Minto 227 G3
Minton 156 D3

Minwear 126 D1
Minworth 159 D3
Miodar 246 B1
Mirbister 277 C6
Mirehouse 208 C5
Mireland 275 J2
Mirfield 194 B5
Miserden 132 B2
Miskin RCT 129 G4
Miskin RCT 129 G3
Misselfore 118 B5
Misson 187 D3
Misterton Leics 160 A4
Misterton Notts 187 E3
Misterton Som 104 A2
Mistley 152 C4
Mitcham 122 B2
Mitchel Troy 131 D1
Mitcheldean 131 F1
Mitchell 96 C4
Mitchelland 199 F3
Mitcheltroy Common 131 D2
Mitford 221 D3
Mithian 96 B4
Mitton 158 A1
Mixbury 148 B4
Mixenden 193 G5
Moar 250 A5
Moat 218 C4
Moats Tye 152 B2
Mobberley ChesE 184 B5
Mobberley Staffs 172 B3
Moccas 144 C3
Mochdre Conwy 181 G5
Mochdre Powys 155 G4
Mochrum 206 D2
Mockbeggar Hants 106 A2
Mockbeggar Kent 123 G4
Mockerkin 209 D4
Modbury 100 C2
Moddershall 171 G4
Modern Art Oxford Oxon OX1 1BP 80 Oxford
Modsarie 273 J2
Moel Famau Country Park Denb LL15 1US 169 E1
Moelfre IoA 180 D4
Moelfre Powys 169 E5
Moffat 226 B5
Mogerhanger 149 G3
Moin'a'choire 230 B3
Moine House 273 H3
Moira 159 F1
Molash 124 C3
Mol-chlach 255 K3
Mold (Yr Wyddgrug) 169 F1
Molehill Green Essex 151 D5
Molehill Green Essex 151 F5
Molescroft 196 C3
Molesden 220 D3
Molesworth 161 F5
Mollance 216 B4
Molland 114 B5
Mollington ChesW&C 183 E5
Mollington Oxon 147 G3
Mollinsburn 234 B2
Monach Islands (Heisker Islands) 262 B5
Monachty 142 B1
Monachyle 241 G3
Monevechadan 241 D4
Monewden 152 D2
Moneydie 243 F2
Moneyrow Green 135 D5
Moniaive 216 B1
Monifieth 244 D1
Monikie 244 D1
Monikie Country Park Angus DD5 3QN 244 C1
Monimail 244 A3
Monington 141 E3
Monk Bretton 186 A2
Monk Fryston 195 E5
Monk Hesleden 213 D4
Monk Sherborne 120 B2
Monk Soham 152 D1
Monk Soham Green 152 D1
Monk Street 151 E5
Monken Hadley 136 B3
Monkerton 102 C3
Monkey Mates W'ham RG41 1JA 134 C5
Monkey World, Wareham Dorset BH20 6HH 105 E4
Monkhide 145 F3
Monkhill 209 G1
Monkhopton 157 F3
Monkland 145 D2
Monkleigh 113 E3
Monknash 129 F5
Monkokehampton 113 F5
Monks Eleigh 152 A3
Monks Eleigh Tye 152 A3
Monk's Gate 109 E1
Monks' Heath 184 C5
Monk's Hill 124 A4
Monks Kirby 159 G4
Monks Risborough 134 D2
Monkscross 99 D3
Monkseaton 221 F4
Monkshill 269 F6
Monksilver 115 D4
Monkstadt 263 J5
Monkswood 130 C2
Monkton Devon 103 E2
Monkton Kent 125 E2
Monkton Pembs 126 C2
Monkton SAyr 224 B3
Monkton T&W 212 C1
Monkton VGlam 129 F5
Monkton Combe 117 E1
Monkton Deverill 117 F4
Monkton Farleigh 117 F1
Monkton Heathfield 115 F5
Monkton Up Wimborne 105 G1
Monkton Wyld 103 G3
Monkwearmouth 212 C2
Monkwood 120 B4
Monmouth (Trefynwy) 131 E1
Monnington Court 144 C4
Monnington on Wye 144 C3
Monreith 207 D2
Montacute 104 B1
Montacute House Som TA15 6XP 104 B1
Monteach 269 G6
Montford 156 D1
Montford Bridge 156 D1
Montgarrie 260 D3
Montgomery (Trefaldwyn) 156 B3
Montgreenan 233 E5
Montpellier Gallery Warks CV37 6EP 85 Stratford-upon-Avon
Montrave 244 B4
Montrose 253 F4
Monxton 119 E3
Monyash 172 C1
Monymusk 260 E3
Monzie 243 D2
Moodiesburn 234 A2
Moons Moat North 146 C1
Moonzie 244 B3
Moor Allerton 194 C4
Moor Cock 192 C1
Moor Crichel 105 F2
Moor End Bed 149 F2
Moor End CenBeds 149 E5
Moor End Cumb 199 G5
Moor End ERid 196 A4
Moor End Lancs 191 G3
Moor End NYorks 195 E4
Moor End WYorks 193 G5
Moor Green Wilts 117 F1
Moor Green WMid 158 C4
Moor Head 194 A4
Moor Monkton 195 E2
Moor Row 208 D5
Moor Side Cumb 198 D5
Moor Side Lancs 192 A4
Moor Side Lancs 192 A4
Moor Side Lincs 176 A2
Moor Street 124 A2
Moorby 176 A1
Moorcot 144 C2
Moordown 105 G3
Moore 183 G4
Moorend 209 G1
Moorends 187 D1
Moorfield 185 E3
Moorgreen 173 F3
Moorhall 186 A5
Moorhampton 144 C3
Moorhouse Cumb 209 G1
Moorhouse Notts 174 C1
Moorland (Northmoor Green) 116 A4
Moorlinch 116 A4
Moors Centre, Danby NYorks YO21 2NB 203 G2
Moors Valley Country Park Dorset BH24 2ET 106 A2
Moors Valley Railway Dorset BH24 2ET 105 G2
Moorsholm 203 F1
Moorside Dorset 105 D1
Moorside GtMan 185 D2
Moorside WYorks 194 B4
Moorthorpe 186 B1
Moortown IoW 106 D4
Moortown Lincs 188 A3
Moortown Tel&W 157 F1
Morangie 266 E3
Morar 256 C5
Morborne 161 G3
Morchard Bishop 102 A2
Morcombelake 104 A3
Morcott 161 E2
Morda 169 F5
Morden Dorset 105 F3
Morden GtLon 122 B2
Morden Hall Park GtLon SM4 5JD 11 F8
Morden Park 122 B2
Mordiford 145 E4
Mordington Holdings 237 G4
Mordon 212 C5
More 156 C3
Morebath 114 C5
Morebattle 228 B4
Morecambe 192 A1
Morefield 265 H2
Moreleigh 101 D2
Morenish 242 B1
Moresby Parks 208 C5
Morestead 119 G5
Moreton Dorset 105 E4
Moreton Essex 137 E2
Moreton Here 145 E1
Moreton Mersey 183 D4
Moreton Oxon 134 B2
Moreton Staffs 172 C4
Moreton Staffs 157 G1
Moreton Corbet 170 C5
Moreton Jeffries 145 F3
Moreton Mill 170 C5
Moreton Morrell 147 F2
Moreton on Lugg 145 E3
Moreton Paddox 147 F2
Moreton Pinkney 148 A3
Moreton Say 170 D4
Moreton Valence 131 G2
Moretonhampstead 102 A4
Moreton-in-Marsh 147 E4
Morfa Carmar 128 B1
Morfa Cere 141 G2
Morfa Bychan 167 E4
Morfa Glas 129 E2
Morfa Nefyn 166 B3
Morgan's Vale 118 C5
Morganstown 130 A4
Mork 131 E2
Morland 210 B5
Morley Derbys 173 E3
Morley Dur 212 A5
Morley WYorks 194 B5
Morley Green 184 C4
Morley St. Botolph 164 B2
Mornick 98 D3
Morningside Edin 235 G2
Morningside NLan 234 C4
Morningthorpe 164 D2
Morpeth 221 E3
Morphie 253 F3
Morrey 158 D1
Morridge Side 172 B2
Morrilow Heath 171 G4
Morriston SAyr 224 A5
Morriston Swan 128 C3
Morristown 130 A5
Morroch 247 F1
Morston 178 B1
Mortehoe 113 E1
Morthen 186 B4
Mortimer 120 B1
Mortimer West End 120 B1
Mortimer's Cross 144 D1
Mortlake 136 B5
Morton Derbys 173 F1
Morton Lincs 175 F5
Morton Lincs 187 F3
Morton Lincs 175 D1
Morton Notts 174 C2
Morton SGlos 131 F3
Morton Shrop 169 F5
Morton Bagot 146 D1
Morton on the Hill 178 C4
Morton Tinmouth 212 A5
Morton-on-Swale 202 C3
Morvah 94 B3
Morval 97 G4
Morvich (A'Mhormhaich) High 257 F2
Morvich High 266 E1
Morvil 140 D4
Morville 157 F3
Morwellham 100 A1
Morwellham Quay Museum Devon PL19 8JL 99 E3
Morwenstow 112 C4
Morwick Hall 221 E1
Mosborough 186 B4
Moscow 233 F5
Mosedale 209 G3
Moselden Height 185 E1
Moseley WMid 158 B3
Moseley Worcs 146 A2
Moses Gate 184 B2
Moss A&B 246 A2
Moss SYorks 186 C1
Moss Wrex 170 A2
Moss Bank 183 G3
Moss Houses 184 C5
Moss Nook 184 C4
Moss of Barmuckity 267 K5
Moss Side GtMan 184 C3
Moss Side Lancs 191 G4
Moss Side Mersey 183 E2
Mossat 260 C3
Mossbank 278 D5
Mossblown 224 C3
Mossburnford 228 A5
Mossdale 216 A3
Mossend 234 B3
Mosser 209 E4
Mossgiel 224 C3
Mosshead 260 D1
Mosside of Ballinshoe 252 C4
Mossley ChesE 171 F1
Mossley GtMan 185 D2
Mossley Hill 183 E4
Mosspaul Hotel 218 B2
Moss-side High 267 F6
Moss-side Moray 268 D5
Mosstodloch 268 B4
Mosston 252 D5
Mossy Lea 183 G1
Mosterton 104 A2
Moston GtMan 184 C2
Moston Shrop 170 C5
Moston Green 171 E1
Mostyn 182 C4
Motcombe 117 F5
Mothecombe 100 C3
Mother Shipton's Cave NYorks HG5 8DD 194 C2
Motherby 210 A5
Motherwell 234 B4
Mottingham 136 D5
Mottisfont 119 E5
Mottisfont Abbey Hants SO51 0LP 119 E5
Mottistone 106 D4
Mottram in Longdendale 185 D3
Mottram St. Andrew 184 C5
Mouldsworth 183 G5
Moulin 251 E4
Moulsecoomb 109 F3
Moulsford 134 A4
Moulsham 137 G2
Moulsoe 149 E3
Moulton ChesW&C 171 D1
Moulton Lincs 176 B5
Moulton N'hants 148 C1
Moulton NYorks 202 B2
Moulton Suff 151 E1
Moulton VGlam 129 G5
Moulton Chapel 162 A1
Moulton St. Mary 179 F5
Moulton Seas End 176 B5
Mounie Castle 261 F2
Mount Corn 96 B4
Mount Corn 97 F3
Mount High 267 G7
Mount Kent 125 D4
Mount WYorks 185 F1
Mount Ambrose 96 B5
Mount Bures 152 A4
Mount Charles 97 E4
Mount Edgcumbe Country Park Corn PL10 1HZ 2 B3
Mount Hawke 96 B5
Mount Manisty 183 E5
Mount Oliphant 224 B4
Mount Pleasant ChesE 171 F2
Mount Pleasant Derbys 173 E3
Mount Pleasant Derbys 159 E1
Mount Pleasant ESuss 109 G2
Mount Pleasant Flints 182 D5
Mount Pleasant GtLon 135 F3
Mount Pleasant Hants 106 C3
Mount Pleasant Norf 164 A2
Mount Pleasant Suff 151 F3
Mount Sorrel 118 B5
Mount Tabor 193 G5
Mountain 193 G4
Mountain Ash (Aberpennar) 129 G3
Mountain Cross 235 F5
Mountain Water 140 C5
Mountbenger 227 E3
Mountblairy 268 E5
Mountblow 233 F2
Mountfield 110 C1
Mountgerald 266 C5
Mountjoy 96 C3
Mountnessing 137 F3
Mounton 131 E3
Mountsorrel 160 A1
Mousa 279 D10
Mousehole 94 B4
Mouswald 217 E3
Mow Cop 171 F2
Mowden 202 B1
Mowhaugh 228 C4
Mowsley 160 B4
Mowtie 253 G1
Moxley 158 B3
Moy High 249 D1
Moy High 249 G1
Moy High 258 E1
Moy House 267 H6
Moylgrove 141 E3
Muasdale 231 E5
Much Birch 145 E4
Much Cowarne 145 F3
Much Dewchurch 145 D4
Much Hadham 136 D1
Much Hoole 192 A5
Much Hoole Town 192 A5
Much Marcle 145 F4
Much Wenlock 157 F2
Muchalls 261 H5
Muchelney 116 B5
Muchelney Ham 116 B5
Muchlarnick 97 G4
Muchra 226 D4
Muchrachd 257 J1
Muck 246 D2
Mucking 137 F4
Muckle Roe 279 C6
Muckleford 104 C3
Mucklestone 171 E4
Muckleton 170 C5
Muckletown 260 D2
Muckley 157 F3
Muckley Corner 158 C2
Muckton 189 D4
Mudale 273 H5
Muddiford 113 F2
Muddles Green 110 A2
Muddleswood 109 E2
Mudeford 106 A3
Mudford 104 B1
Mudgley 116 B3
Mugdock 233 G2
Mugdock Country Park Stir G62 8EL 30 C1
Mugeary 255 K1
Mugginton 173 D3
Muggintonlane End 173 D3
Muggleswick 211 G3
Mugswell 122 B3
Muie 266 D1
Muir 251 F1
Muir of Fowlis 260 D3
Muir of Lochs 268 B4
Muir of Ord (Am Blàr Dubh) 266 C6
Muiravonside Country Park Falk EH49 6LW 235 D2
Muirden 269 F5
Muirdrum 245 D1
Muiredge 244 B5
Muirhead Aber 260 D3
Muirhead Angus 244 B1
Muirhead Fife 244 A4
Muirhead Moray 267 H5
Muirhead NLan 234 A3
Muirhouses 235 E1
Muirkirk 225 E3
Muirmill 234 B1
Muirtack Aber 261 H1
Muirtack Aber 269 G6
Muirton High 266 E5
Muirton P&K 243 E3
Muirton P&K 243 G2
Muirton of Ardblair 251 G5
Muirton of Ballochy 253 E3
Muirtown 267 G6
Muiryfold 269 F5
Muker 201 E3
Mulbarton 178 C5
Mulben 268 B5
Mulhagery 271 F7
Mull 239 E1
Mullach Chàrlabhaigh 270 E3
Mullacott Cross 113 F1
Mullion 95 D5
Mullion Cove 95 D5
Mumby 189 F5
Munderfield Row 145 F2
Munderfield Stocks 145 F2
Mundesley 179 E2
Mundford 163 G3
Mundham 165 E2
Mundon 138 B2
Mundurno 261 H3
Munerigie 257 J4
Mungasdale 265 F2
Mungoswells 236 B2
Mungrisdale 209 G3
Munlochy 266 D6
Munnoch 232 D5
Munsley 145 F3
Munslow 157 E4
Murchington 99 G2
Murcott Oxon 134 A1
Murcott Wilts 132 B3
Murdostoun 234 C4
Murieston 235 E3
Murkle 275 G2
Murlaganmore 242 A1
Murlaggan High 257 G5
Murlaggan High 249 F1
Murra 277 B7
Murrell Green 120 C2
Murroes 244 C1
Murrow 162 B2
Mursley 148 D5
Murston 124 B2
Murthill 252 C4
Murthly 243 F1
Murton Cumb 210 D5
Murton Dur 212 C3
Murton N'umb 237 G5
Murton Swan 128 B4
Murton York 195 F2
Musbury 103 F3
Muscliff 105 G3
Musdale (Musdàl) 240 B2
Museum in Docklands GtLon E14 4AL 12 D4
Museum of Childhood, Edinburgh Edin EH1 1TG 37 G4
Museum of Childhood, London GtLon E2 9PA 12 C4
Museum of Flight ELoth EH39 5LF 236 C2
Museum of Garden History, London GtLon SE1 7LB 45 F7
Museum of London GtLon EC2Y 5HN 45 J2
Museum of Science & Industry, Manchester GtMan M3 4FP 46 C4
Museum of Transport, Glasgow Glas G3 8DP 38 A2
Musselburgh 236 A2
Mustard Hyrn 179 F4
Mustard Shop Norf NR2 1NQ 79 Norwich
Muston Leics 174 D4
Muston NYorks 205 D5
Mustow Green 158 A5
Mutford 165 F3
Muthill 243 D3
Mutley 100 A2
Mutterton 102 D2
Muxton 157 G1
Mybster 275 G3
Myddfai 143 D4
Myddle 170 B5
Myddlewood 170 B5
Mydroilyn 142 A2
Myerscough College 192 A4
Myerscough Smithy 192 C4
Mylor 95 F3
Mylor Bridge 95 F3
Mynachdy 130 A5
Mynachlog-ddu 141 E4
Myndtown 156 C4
Mynydd Llandygai 167 F1
Mynydd Mechell 180 B4
Mynydd-bach Mon 131 D3
Mynydd-bach Swan 128 C3
Mynyddygarreg 128 A2
Mynytho 166 C4
Myrebird 261 F5
Mytchett 121 D2
Mytholm 193 F5
Mytholmroyd 193 G5
Mythop 191 G4
Myton-on-Swale 194 D1
Mytton 156 D1


## N


Naast 264 E3
Nab's Head 192 C5
Na-Buirgh 263 F2
Naburn 195 E3
Nackington 125 D3
Nacton 152 D3
Nadderwater 102 B3
Nafferton 196 C2
Nailbridge 131 F1
Nailsbourne 115 F5
Nailsea 131 D5
Nailstone 159 G2
Nailsworth 132 A3
Nairn 267 F6
Nancegollan 94 D3
Nancekuke 96 A5
Nancledra 94 B3
Nanhoron 166 B4
Nannau 168 A5
Nannerch 169 E1
Nanpantan 160 A1
Nanpean 97 D4
Nanstallon 97 E3
Nant Peris 167 F2
Nant-ddu 129 G1
Nanternis 141 G2
Nantgaredig 142 A5
Nantgarw 130 A4
Nant-glas 143 F1
Nantglyn 168 D1
Nantgwyn 155 F5
Nantlle 167 E2
Nantmawr 169 F5
Nantmel 143 G1
Nantmor 167 F3
Nantwich 170 D2
Nantycaws 128 A1
Nant-y-derry 130 C2
Nant-y-dugoed 155 F1
Nantyffyllon 129 E3
Nantyglo 130 A1
Nant-y-Gollen 169 F5
Nant-y-groes 143 G1
Nant-y-moel 129 F3
Nant-y-Pandy 181 E5
Naphill 135 D3
Napley Heath 171 E4
Nappa 193 E2
Napton on the Hill 147 G1
Narberth (Arberth) 127 E1
Narborough Leics 160 A3
Narborough Norf 163 F1
Narkurs 98 D5
Narrachan 240 B3
Nasareth 167 D3
Naseby 160 B5
Nash Bucks 148 C4
Nash Here 144 C1
Nash Newport 130 C4
Nash Shrop 157 F5
Nash VGlam 129 F5
Nash Street 123 F2
Nassington 161 F3
Nasty 150 B5
Nateby Cumb 200 C2
Nateby Lancs 192 A3
Nately Scures 120 C2
National Agricultural Centre, Stoneleigh Warks CV8 2LZ 16 B5
National Army Museum GtLon SW3 4HT 13 A5
National Botanic Garden of Wales Carmar SA32 8HG 128 B1
National Coal Mining Museum for England WYorks WF4 4RH 27 F6
National Exhibition Centre WMid B40 1NT 15 H4
National Fishing Heritage Centre, Grimsby NELincs DN31 1UZ 188 C2
National Gallery GtLon WC2N 5DN 44 D4
National Gallery of Scotland Edin EH2 2EL 37 F4
National Indoor Arena, Birmingham WMid B1 2AA 34 D4
National Marine Aquarium PL4 0LF 81 Plymouth
National Maritime Museum Cornwall Corn TR11 3QY 95 F3
National Maritime Museum, Greenwich GtLon SE10 9NF 13 D5
National Media Museum WYorks BD1 1NQ 65 Bradford
National Memorial Arboretum, Alrewas Staffs DE13 7AR 159 D1
National Motorcycle Museum, Solihull WMid B92 0EJ 159 E4
National Museum Cardiff CF10 3NP 67 Cardiff
National Museum of Scotland Edin EH1 1JF 37 G5
National Portrait Gallery GtLon WC2H 0HE 44 D4
National Railway Museum YO26 4XJ 90 York
National Sea Life Centre, Birmingham WMid B1 2JB 34 D4
National Seal Sanctuary Corn TR12 6UG 95 E4
National Slate Museum, Llanberis Gwyn LL55 4TY 167 E2
National Space Centre, Leicester Leic LE4 5NS 17 C4
National Wallace Monument Stir FK9 5LF 242 D5
National War Museum, Edinburgh Edin EH1 2NG 37 E4
National Waterfront Museum SA1 3RD 86 Swansea
National Wildflower Centre, Liverpool Mersey L16 3NA 22 D3
Natland 199 G4
Natural History Museum at Tring Herts HP23 6AP 135 E1
Natural History Museum, London GtLon SW7 5BD 11 F5
Natureland Seal Sanctuary Lincs PE25 1DB 177 D1
Naughton 152 B3
Naunton Glos 146 D5
Naunton Worcs 146 A4
Naunton Beauchamp 146 B2
Navenby 175 E2
Navestock 137 E3
Navestock Side 137 E3
Navidale 275 F7
Navity 266 E5
Nawton 203 F4
Nayland 152 A4
Nazeing 136 D2
Neacroft 106 A3
Neal's Green 159 F4
Neap 279 E7
Neap House 187 F1
Near Sawrey 199 E3
Nearton End 148 D5
Neasden 136 B4
Neasham 202 C1
Neat Enstone 147 F5
Neath (Castell-nedd) 129 D3
Neatham 120 C3
Neatishead 179 E3
Nebo Cere 142 B1
Nebo Conwy 168 B2
Nebo Gwyn 167 D2
Nebo IoA 180 C3
Necton 163 G2
Nedd 272 D5
Nedderton 221 E3
Nedging 152 A3
Nedging Tye 152 B3
Needham 164 D3
Needham Lake Suff IP6 8NU 152 B2
Needham Market 152 B2
Needham Street 151 F1
Needingworth 162 B5
Needles Pleasure Park IoW PO39 0JD 106 C4
Needwood 172 C5
Neen Savage 157 F5
Neen Sollars 157 F5
Neenton 157 F4
Nefyn 166 C3
Neighbourne 116 D3
Neilston 233 F4
Neithrop 147 G3
Nelson Caerp 130 A3
Nelson Lancs 193 E4
Nelson Village 221 E4
Nemphlar 234 C5
Nempnett Thrubwell 116 C1
Nenthall 211 D3
Nenthead 211 D3
Nenthorn 228 A3
Neopardy 102 A3
Nerabus 230 A4
Nercwys 169 F1
Neriby 230 B3
Nerston 234 A4
Nesbit 229 D3
Nesfield 193 G3
Ness 183 E5
Ness Botanic Gardens ChesW&C CH64 4AY 183 E5
Ness of Tenston 277 B6
Nesscliffe 156 C1
Neston ChesW&C 183 D5
Neston Wilts 117 F1
Nether Alderley 184 C5
Nether Auchendrane 224 B4
Nether Barr 215 F4
Nether Blainslie 236 C5
Nether Broughton 174 B5
Nether Burrow 200 B5
Nether Cerne 104 C3
Nether Compton 104 B1
Nether Crimond 261 G2
Nether Dalgliesh 227 D5
Nether Dallachy 268 B4
Nether Edge 186 A4
Nether End 185 G5
Nether Exe 102 C3
Nether Glasslaw 269 G5
Nether Handwick 252 B5
Nether Haugh 186 B3
Nether Heage 173 E2
Nether Heselden 201 D5
Nether Heyford 148 B2
Nether Kellet 192 B1
Nether Kinmundy 269 J6
Nether Langwith 186 C5
Nether Lenshie 268 E6
Nether Loads 173 E1
Nether Moor 173 E1
Nether Padley 185 G5
Nether Pitforthie 253 G2
Nether Poppleton 195 E2
Nether Silton 203 D3
Nether Skyborry 156 B5
Nether Stowey 115 E4
Nether Urquhart 243 G4
Nether Wallop 119 E4
Nether Wasdale 198 C2
Nether Wellwood 225 E3
Nether Welton 209 G2
Nether Westcote 147 E5
Nether Whitacre 159 E3
Nether Winchendon (Lower Winchendon) 134 C1
Nether Worton 147 G5
Netheravon 118 C3
Netherbrae 269 F5
Netherbrough 277 C6
Netherburn 234 C5
Netherbury 104 A3
Netherby Cumb 218 B4
Netherby NYorks 194 C3
Nethercott 147 G5
Netherfield ESuss 110 C2
Netherfield Notts 174 B3
Netherfield SLan 234 B5
Netherhall 232 D3
Netherhampton 118 C5
Netherhay 104 A2
Netherland Green 172 C4
Netherley 261 G5
Nethermill 217 E2
Nethermuir 269 H6
Netherseal 159 E1
Nethershield 225 D3
Netherstreet 118 A1
Netherthird D&G 216 B5
Netherthird EAyr 225 D4
Netherthong 185 F2
Netherthorpe 186 C4
Netherton Angus 252 D4
Netherton ChesW&C 183 G5
Netherton Devon 102 B5
Netherton Hants 119 E2
Netherton Mersey 183 E2
Netherton N'umb 220 B1
Netherton NLan 234 B4
Netherton Oxon 133 G2
Netherton P&K 251 G4
Netherton SLan 234 D4
Netherton WMid 158 B4
Netherton Worcs 146 B3
Netherton WYorks 185 G1
Netherton WYorks 185 F1
Netherton Burnfoot 220 B1
Netherton Northside 220 B1
Nethertown Cumb 198 A2
Nethertown Ork 275 J1
Nethertown Staffs 158 D1
Netherwitton 220 D2
Netherwood D&G 217 D3
Netherwood EAyr 225 E3
Nethy Bridge 259 H2
Netley Abbey 107 D2
Netley Marsh 106 C1
Nettlebed 134 B4
Nettlebridge 116 D3
Nettlecombe Dorset 104 B3
Nettlecombe IoW 107 E5
Nettlecombe Som 115 D4
Nettleden 135 F1
Nettleham 188 A5
Nettlestead Kent 123 F3

Nettlestead *Suff* **152** B3
Nettlestead Green **123** F3
Nettlestone **107**
Nettlesworth **212** B3
Nettleton *Lincs* **188** B2
Nettleton *Wilts* **132** A5
Nettleton Hill **185** E1
Netton *Devon* **100** B3
Netton *Wilts* **118** C4
Neuadd *Cere* **142** A2
Neuadd *IoA* **180** B3
Neuadd *Powys* **143** F3
Nevendon **137** G3
Nevern **141** D4
Nevill Holt **160** D3
New Abbey **217** D4
New Aberdour **269** G4
New Addington **122** C2
New Alresford **119** G4
New Alyth **252** A5
New Arley **159** E3
New Arram **196** C3
New Ash Green **123** F2
New Balderton **174** D2
New Barn **123** F2
New Belses **227** G3
New Bewick **229** E4
New Bolingbroke **176** B2
New Boultham **187** G5
New Bradwell **148** D3
New Brancepeth **212** B3
New Bridge *D&G* **216** D3
New Bridge *Devon* **102** A5
New Brighton
  *Flints* **169** F1
New Brighton
  *Hants* **107** G2
New Brighton
  *Mersey* **183** E3
New Brighton
  *Wrex* **169** F2
New Brighton
  *WYorks* **194** B5
New Brinsley **173** F2
New Broughton **170** A2
New Buckenham **164** B2
New Byth **269** G5
New Cheriton **119** G5
New Cross *Cere* **154** C5
New Cross *GtLon* **136** C5
New Cumnock **225** E4
New Deer **269** G6
New Duston **148** C1
New Earswick **195** F2
New Edlington **186** C3
New Elgin **267** K5
New Ellerby **197** D4
New Eltham **136** D5
New End **146** C1
New England **161** G2
New Farnley **194** B4
New Ferry **183** E4
New Galloway **216** A3
New Gilston **244** C4
New Greens **136** A2
New Grimsby **96** A1
New Hartley **221** F4
New Haw **121** F1
New Heaton **228** C3
New Hedges **127** E2
New Herrington **212** C2
New Hinksey **134** A2
New Holland **196** C5
New Houghton
  *Derbys* **173** G1
New Houghton
  *Norf* **177** F5
New Houses **200** D5
New Hunwick **212** A4
New Hutton **199** G3
New Hythe **123** G3
New Inn *Carmar* **142** A4
New Inn *Fife* **244** A4
New Inn *Mon* **131** D2
New Inn *Torfaen* **130** B3
New Invention
  *Shrop* **156** B5
New Invention
  *WMid* **158** B3
New Kelso **265** F7
New Lanark **234** C4
New Lanark World Heritage
  Site *SLan*
  ML11 9DB **234** C5
New Lane **183** F1
New Lane End **184** A3
New Leake **176** C2
New Leeds **269** H5
New Leslie **260** D2
New Lodge **186** A2
New Longton **192** B5
New Luce **214** C4
New Mains **225** G2
New Mains of Ury **253** G1
New Malden **122** B2
New Marske **213** F5
New Marton **170** A4
New Mill *Corn* **96** B3
New Mill *Herts* **135** E1
New Mill *WYorks* **185** F2
New Mill End **136** A1
New Mills *Corn* **96** C4
New Mills *Derbys* **185** E4
New Mills *Glos* **131** F2
New Mills *Mon* **131** D2
New Mills (Y Felin Newydd)
  *Powys* **155** G2
New Milton **106** B3
New Mistley **152** C4
New Moat **141** D5
New Ollerton **174** B1
New Orleans **222** C4
New Oscott **158** C3
New Palace &
  Adventureland, New
  Brighton *Mersey*
  CH45 2JX **22** A2
New Park *Corn* **97** F1
New Park *NYorks* **194** B2
New Pitsligo **269** G5
New Polzeath **96** D2
New Quay
  (Ceinewydd) **154** C3
New Rackheath **179** D4
New Radnor
  (Maesyfed) **144** B1
New Rent **210** A4
New Ridley **211** G1

New Road Side **193** F3
New Rossington **186** D3
New Romney **111** F1
New Row *Cere* **154** D5
New Row *Lancs* **192** C4
New Sawley **173** F4
New Shoreston **229** F3
New Silksworth **212** C2
New Stevenston **234** B4
New Swannington **159** G1
New Totley **186** A5
New Town
  *CenBeds* **149** G3
New Town *Cere* **141** E3
New Town *Dorset* **105** F1
New Town *Dorset* **105** F2
New Town *ELoth* **236** B2
New Town *ESuss* **109** G1
New Town *Glos* **146** C4
New Tredegar **130** A2
New Tupton **173** E1
New Ulva **231** F1
New Valley **271** G4
New Village **186** C2
New Yatt **133** F1
New York *Lincs* **176** A2
New York *T&W* **221** F4
Newall **194** B3
Newark *Ork* **276** G3
Newark *Peter* **162** A1
Newark Castle, Newark-on-
  Trent *Notts*
  NG24 1BG **174** C2
Newark-on-Trent **174** D2
Newarthill **234** B4
Newball **188** A5
Newbarn **125** D5
Newbarns **198** D5
Newbattle **236** A3
Newbiggin *Cumb* **210** A5
Newbiggin *Cumb* **210** A5
Newbiggin *Cumb* **210** B3
Newbiggin *Cumb* **191** F1
Newbiggin *Cumb* **198** B3
Newbiggin *Dur* **211** F5
Newbiggin *N'umb* **211** G2
Newbiggin *NYorks* **201** E4
Newbiggin *NYorks* **201** E3
Newbiggin-by-the-
  Sea **221** F3
Newbigging *Aber* **261** G5
Newbigging *Aber* **251** G1
Newbigging *Angus* **244** C1
Newbigging *Angus* **244** C1
Newbigging *SLan* **235** E5
Newbiggin-on-Lune **200** C2
Newbold *Derbys* **186** A5
Newbold *Leics* **159** G1
Newbold on Avon **159** G5
Newbold on Stour **147** E3
Newbold Pacey **147** E2
Newbold Verdon **159** G2
Newborough
  (Niwbwrch) *IoA* **166** D1
Newborough *Peter* **162** A2
Newborough *Staffs* **172** C5
Newbottle *N'hants* **148** A4
Newbottle *T&W* **212** C2
Newbourne **153** E3
Newbridge (Cefn Bychan)
  *Caerp* **130** B3
Newbridge *Corn* **94** B3
Newbridge *Corn* **98** D4
Newbridge *Edin* **235** F2
Newbridge *ESuss* **109** G1
Newbridge *Hants* **106** B1
Newbridge *IoW* **106** D4
Newbridge *NYorks* **204** B3
Newbridge *Oxon* **133** G2
Newbridge *Pembs* **140** C4
Newbridge *Wrex* **169** F3
Newbridge Green **146** A4
Newbridge on Wye **143** G2
Newbridge-on-Usk **130** C3
Newbrough **211** E1
Newbuildings **102** A2
Newburgh *Aber* **269** H5
Newburgh *Aber* **261** H2
Newburgh *Fife* **244** A3
Newburgh *Lancs* **183** F1
Newburgh *ScBord* **227** E3
Newburn **212** A1
Newbury *Som* **117** D2
Newbury *WBerks* **119** F1
Newbury *Wilts* **117** F3
Newbury Park **136** D4
Newby *Cumb* **210** B5
Newby *Lancs* **193** D3
Newby *NYorks* **203** F3
Newby *NYorks* **192** D1
Newby *NYorks* **204** D4
Newby Bridge **199** E4
Newby Cote **200** C5
Newby Cross **209** G1
Newby East **210** A2
Newby Hall *NYorks*
  HG4 5AE **194** C3
Newby West **209** G1
Newby Wiske **202** C4
Newcastle
  *Bridgend* **129** E5
Newcastle *Mon* **130** D1
Newcastle *Shrop* **156** C4
Newcastle Emlyn (Castell
  Newydd Emlyn) **141** G3
Newcastle International
  Airport **221** D4
Newcastle upon
  Tyne **212** B1
Newcastleton **218** C3
Newcastle-under-
  Lyme **171** F3
Newchapel *Pembs* **141** F4
Newchapel *Staffs* **171** F2
Newchapel *Surr* **122** C4
Newchurch *Carmar* **141** F5
Newchurch *IoW* **107** E4

Newchurch *Lancs* **193** E5
Newchurch *Lancs* **193** E4
Newchurch *Mon* **131** D3
Newchurch *Powys* **144** B2
Newchurch *Staffs* **172** C5
Newcott **103** F2
Newcraighall **236** A2
Newdigate **121** G3
Newell Green **135** D5
Newenden **110** D1
Newent **145** G5
Newerne **131** F2
Newfield *Dur* **212** B4
Newfield *Dur* **212** B2
Newfield *High* **266** E4
Newfound **119** G2
Newgale **140** B5
Newgate **178** B1
Newgate Street **136** C2
Newgord **278** E2
Newhall *ChesE* **170** D3
Newhall *Derbys* **173** D5
Newham **229** F4
Newham Hall **229** F4
Newhaven **109** G3
Newhey **184** D1
Newholm **204** B1
Newhouse **234** B3
Newick **109** G1
Newingreen **124** D5
Newington *Edin* **235** G2
Newington *Kent* **125** D5
Newington *Kent* **124** A2
Newington *Notts* **187** D3
Newington *Oxon* **134** B3
Newington
  Bagpath **132** A3
Newland *Cumb* **199** E5
Newland *Glos* **131** E2
Newland *Hull* **196** C4
Newland *NYorks* **195** F5
Newland *Oxon* **133** G1
Newland *Worcs* **145** G3
Newlandrig **236** A3
Newlands *Cumb* **209** G3
Newlands *Essex* **138** B4
Newlands *N'umb* **211** G2
Newlands *ScBord* **218** D2
Newland's Corner **121** F3
Newlands of Geise **275** F2
Newlands of Tynet **268** B4
Newlyn **94** B4
Newmachar **261** G3
Newmains **234** C4
Newman's End **137** E1
Newman's Green **151** G3
Newmarket *Suff* **151** E1
Newmarket *ESiar* **271** G4
Newmill *Aber* **253** F1
Newmill *Aber* **269** G6
Newmill *Aber* **261** G2
Newmill *Moray* **268** C5
Newmill *ScBord* **227** F4
Newmill of
  Inshewan **252** C3
Newmillerdam **186** A1
Newmilldam Country Park
  *WYorks* WF2 6QP **27** H6
Newmills **266** D5
Newmilns *P&K* **243** G1
Newmilns *P&K* **243** F2
Newmilns **224** E2
Newney Green **137** F2
Newnham *Glos* **131** F1
Newnham *Hants* **120** C4
Newnham *Herts* **150** A4
Newnham *Kent* **124** B3
Newnham *N'hants* **148** A2
Newnham Bridge **145** F1
Newnham Paddox **159** G4
Newnoth **260** D1
Newport *Corn* **98** D2
Newport *ERid* **196** A4
Newport *Essex* **150** D4
Newport *Glos* **131** F3
Newport *High* **275** G6
Newport *IoW* **107** E4
Newport (Casnewydd)
  *Newport* **130** C4
Newport *Norf* **179** G4
Newport (Trefdraeth)
  *Pembs* **141** D4
Newport *Som* **116** A5
Newport *Tel&W* **157** G1
Newport Pagnell **149** D3
Newport-on-Tay **244** C2
Newpound
  Common **121** F5
Newquay **96** C3
Newquay Cornwall
  International Airport **96** C3
Newquay Zoo *Corn*
  TR7 2LZ **96** C3
Newsbank **171** F1
Newseat **261** F1
Newsells **150** B4
Newsham *Lancs* **192** B4
Newsham *N'umb* **221** F4
Newsham *NYorks* **202** A1
Newsham *NYorks* **202** C4
Newsholme *ERid* **195** G5
Newsholme *Lancs* **193** E3
Newsome **185** F1
Newstead *N'umb* **229** F4
Newstead *Notts* **173** G2
Newstead *ScBord* **227** G2
Newstead Abbey *Notts*
  NG15 8NA **173** G2
Newthorpe *Notts* **173** F3
Newthorpe *NYorks* **195** D4
Newtoft **188** A3
Newton *A&B* **240** C5
Newton *Aber* **268** C6
Newton *Aber* **269** J6
Newton *Bridgend* **129** E5
Newton *Cambs* **162** C1
Newton *Cambs* **150** C3
Newton *Cardiff* **130** B5
Newton *ChesW&C* **170** C2
Newton *ChesW&C* **170** B5
Newton *Cumb* **198** D5
Newton *D&G* **217** F1
Newton *Derbys* **173** F3
Newton *GtMan* **185** D3
Newton *Here* **144** C1
Newton *Here* **145** D2
Newton *Here* **144** C5

Newton *High* **275** J3
Newton *High* **266** E7
Newton *High* **275** H3
Newton *High* **266** C6
Newton *High* **266** E5
Newton *Lancs* **192** C5
Newton *Lancs* **199** G5
Newton *Lancs* **191** G4
Newton *Lincs* **175** F4
Newton *Moray* **268** B4
Newton *N'hants* **161** D4
Newton *N'umb* **211** G1
Newton *N'umb* **220** B1
Newton *NAyr* **232** A4
Newton *Norf* **163** G1
Newton *Notts* **174** B3
Newton *P&K* **243** D1
Newton *Pembs* **140** B5
Newton *Pembs* **126** C2
Newton *ScBord* **228** A4
Newton *SGlos* **131** F3
Newton *Shrop* **170** B4
Newton *SLan* **226** A2
Newton *Som* **115** E4
Newton *Staffs* **172** B5
Newton *Suff* **152** A3
Newton *Swan* **128** C4
Newton *Warks* **160** A5
Newton *Wilts* **118** D5
Newton *WLoth* **235** E2
Newton *WYorks* **194** D5
Newton Abbot **101** E1
Newton Arlosh **209** F1
Newton Aycliffe **212** B5
Newton Bewley **213** D5
Newton
  Blossomville **149** E2
Newton Bromswold **149** E1
Newton Burgoland **159** F2
Newton by Toft **188** A4
Newton Ferrers **100** B3
Newton Flotman **164** D2
Newton Green **131** E3
Newton Harcourt **160** B3
Newton Kyme **195** D3
Newton Longville **148** D4
Newton Mearns **233** G4
Newton Morrell
  *NYorks* **202** B2
Newton Morrell
  *Oxon* **148** B5
Newton Mountain **126** C2
Newton Mulgrave **203** G5
Newton of Affleck **244** C1
Newton of Ardtoe **247** F2
Newton of
  Balcanquhal **243** G3
Newton of Dalvey **267** H6
Newton of Falkland **244** A4
Newton of Leys **258** D1
Newton on the Hill **170** B5
Newton on Trent **187** F5
Newton Poppleford **103** D4
Newton Purcell **148** B4
Newton Regis **159** E2
Newton Reigny **210** A4
Newton St. Cyres **102** B3
Newton St. Faith **178** D4
Newton St. Loe **117** E1
Newton St. Petrock **113** E4
Newton Solney **173** D5
Newton Stacey **119** E3
Newton Stewart **215** F4
Newton Tony **118** D3
Newton Tracey **113** F3
Newton under
  Roseberry **203** E1
Newton
  Underwood **221** D3
Newton upon
  Derwent **195** G3
Newton Valence **120** C4
Newton with
  Scales **192** A4
Newtonairds **216** C2
Newtongrange **236** A3
Newtonhill **261** H5
Newton-le-Willows
  *Mersey* **183** G3
Newton-le-Willows
  *NYorks* **202** B4
Newtonmill **253** E3
Newtonmore (Baile Ùr
  an t-Slèibh) **258** E5
Newton-on-Ouse **195** E3
Newton-on-
  Rawcliffe **204** B3
Newton-on-the-
  Moor **221** D1
Newtown *Bucks* **135** E2
Newtown
  *ChesW&C* **170** C2
Newtown *Corn* **96** A5
Newtown *Corn* **94** C4
Newtown *Cumb* **210** B1
Newtown *Derbys* **185** D4
Newtown *Devon* **114** A5
Newtown *Devon* **103** D3
Newtown *Dorset* **105** F4
Newtown *Glos* **131** F2
Newtown *GtMan* **183** G2
Newtown *GtMan* **184** B2
Newtown *Hants* **107** F4
Newtown *Hants* **119** E1
Newtown *Hants* **106** B1
Newtown *Hants* **119** E5
Newtown *Hants* **107** E1
Newtown *Here* **144** C1
Newtown *Here* **145** D2
Newtown *Here* **145** D4
Newtown *High* **257** K4
Newtown *IoM* **190** B4
Newtown *IoW* **106** D3
Newtown *Oxon* **134** C4
Newtown (Y Drenewydd)
  *Powys* **156** A3
Newtown *RCT* **129** G3
Newtown *Shrop* **170** B4
Newtown *Som* **115** F4
Newtown *Som* **103** F1
Newtown *Staffs* **171** G1
Newtown *Staffs* **172** A1
Newtown *Staffs* **158** B2
Newtown *Wilts* **118** A5
Newtown *Wilts* **119** E1
Newtown Linford **160** A2

Newtown
  St. Boswells **227** G2
Newtown Unthank **159** G2
Newtown-in-Saint-
  Martin **95** E4
Newtyle **252** A5
Newyears Green **135** F4
Neyland **126** C2
Nibley *Glos* **131** F1
Nibley *SGlos* **131** F5
Nibley Green **131** G5
Nicholashayne **103** E1
Nicholaston **128** B4
Nidd **194** C1
Nigg *Aberdeen* **261** H4
Nigg *High* **267** F4
Nightcott **114** B5
Nilig **168**
Nilston Rigg **211** E1
Nimlet **131** G5
Nine Ashes **137** E2
Nine Elms **132** D4
Nine Mile Burn **235** F4
Ninebanks **211** D2
Ninemile Bar
  (Crocketford) **216** C3
Nineveh **145** F1
Ninfield **110** C2
Ningwood **106** D4
Nisbet **228** A4
Niton **107** E5
Nitshill **233** G4
Nizels **123** E3
No Man's Heath
  *ChesW&C* **170** C3
No Man's Heath
  *Warks* **159** E2
No Man's Land **97** G4
Noah's Ark **123** E3
Noak Hill **137** E3
Noblehill **217** D3
Noblethorpe **185** G2
Nobottle **148** B1
Nocton **175** F1
Noddsdale **232** D3
Nogdam End **179** E5
Noke **134** A1
Nolton **126** B1
Nolton Haven **126** B1
Nomansland
  *Devon* **102** B1
Nomansland *Wilts* **106** A3
Noneley **170** B5
Nonington **125** E3
Nook *Cumb* **218** C4
Nook *Cumb* **199** G4
Noonsbrough **279** B7
Noranside **252** C3
Norbreck **191** F3
Norbury *ChesE* **170** C3
Norbury *Derbys* **172** C3
Norbury *GtLon* **136** C5
Norbury *Shrop* **156** C3
Norbury *Staffs* **171** E5
Norbury Common **170** C3
Norbury Junction **171** E5
Norchard **127** E3
Norcott Brook **184** A4
Nordelph **163** D2
Norden *Dorset* **105** F4
Norden *GtMan* **184** C1
Nordley **157** F2
Norham **237** G5
Norland Town **193** G5
Norley **183** G5
Norleywood **106** C3
Norlington **109** G2
Norman Cross **161** G2
Normandy **121** E2
Norman's Bay **110** B3
Norman's Green **103** D2
Normanston **165** G2
Normanton *Derby* **173** E4
Normanton *Leics* **174** C2
Normanton *Lincs* **175** E2
Normanton *Notts* **174** C2
Normanton *Rut* **161** E2
Normanton
  *WYorks* **194** C5
Normanton le
  Heath **159** F1
Normanton on Soar **173** G5
Normanton on
  Trent **174** C1
Normanton-on-the-
  Wolds **174** B4
Normoss **191** G4
Norrington
  Common **117** F1
Norris Green **100** A1
Norris Hill **159** F1
Norristhorpe **194** B5
North Acton **136** B4
North Anston **186** C3
North Ascot **121** E1
North Aston **147** G5
North Baddesley **106** C1
North Balloch
  (Baile a' Chaolais a
  Tuath) **248** C5
North Balloch **215** E1
North Barrow **116** D5
North Barsham **178** A2
North Bay Miniature
  Railway *NYorks*
  YO12 6PF **204** D3
North Benfleet **137** G4
North Bersted **108** B3
North Berwick **236** C1
North Boarhunt **107** F1
North Bogbain **268** B5
North Bovey **102** A4
North Bradley **117** F2
North Brentor **99** E2
North Brewham **117** E4

Newtown
North Bridge **121** E4
North Buckland **113** E1
North Burlingham **179** E4
North Cadbury **116** D5
North Camp **121** D2
North Carlton
  *Lincs* **187** G5
North Carlton
  *Notts* **186** C4
North Cave **196** A4
North Cerney **132** C2
North Charford **106** A1
North Charlton **229** F4
North Cheriton **117** D5
North Chideock **104** A3
North Cliffe **196** A3
North Clifton **187** F5
North Cockerington **189** D3
North Coker **116** B4
North Collafirth **278** C4
North Common
  *SGlos* **131** F5
North Common
  *Suff* **164** A4
North Commonty **269** G6
North Connel **240** B1
North Coombe **102** B2
North Cornelly **129** E4
North Corner **131** F4
North Cotes **188** D2
North Cove **165** F3
North Cowton **202** B2
North Crawley **149** E3
North Cray **137** D5
North Creake **177** G4
North Curry **116** A5
North Dallens **248** B5
North Dalton **196** B2
North Dawn **277** D7
North Deighton **194** C2
North Dell (Dail Bho
  Thuath) **271** G1
North Duffield **195** F4
North Elkington **188** C3
North Elmham **178** A3
North Elmsall **186** B1
North End *Bucks* **148** D5
North End *Dorset* **117** F5
North End *ERid* **197** D4
North End *ERid* **196** D3
North End *ERid* **197** E4
North End *Essex* **137** F1
North End *Hants* **119** G5
North End *Hants* **106** A1
North End *Leics* **160** A1
North End *N'umb* **220** D1
North End *Norf* **164** B2
North End *NSom* **116** B1
North End *Ports* **107** F2
North End *WSuss* **108** D2
North End *WSuss* **108** B3
North Erradale **264** D3
North Essie **269** J5
North Fambridge **138** B3
North Ferriby **196** B5
North Frodingham **196** D2
North Gluss **278** C5
North Gorley **106** A1
North Green *Norf* **164** D3
North Green *Suff* **165** E4
North Green *Suff* **153** E1
North Green *Suff* **153** E1
North Grimston **196** A1
North Halling **123** G2
North Harby **187** F5
North Hayling **107** G2
North Hazelrigg **229** E3
North Heasley **114** A4
North Heath
  *WBerks* **133** G5
North Heath
  *WSuss* **121** F5
North Hill **97** G2
North Hillingdon **135** F4
North Hinksey **133** G2
North Holmwood **121** G3
North Houghton **119** E4
North Huish **100** D2
North Hykeham **175** E1
North Johnston **126** C1
North Kelsey **188** A2
North Kessock **266** D7
North Killingholme **188** B1
North Kilvington **202** D4
North Kilworth **160** B4
North Kingston **106** A2
North Kyme **175** G2
North Lancing **109** D3
North Lee **134** C2
North Lees **202** C5
North Leigh **133** F1
North Leverton with
  Habblesthorpe **187** E4
North Littleton **146** C3
North Lopham **164** B3
North Luffenham **161** E2
North Marden **108** A2
North Marston **148** C5
North Middleton
  *Midlo* **236** A4
North Middleton
  *N'umb* **229** E4
North Millbrex **269** G6
North Molton **114** A5
North Moreton **134** A4
North Mundham **108** A3
North Muskham **174** C2
North Newbald **196** B4
North Newington **147** G4
North Newnton **118** C2
North Newton **115** F4
North Nibley **131** G3
North Oakley **119** G2
North Ockendon **137** E4
North Ormesby **203** E1
North Ormsby **188** C3
North Otterington **202** C4
North Owersby **188** A3
North Perrott **104** A2
North Petherton **115** F4
North Petherwin **97** G1
North Piddle **146** B2
North Plain **217** F4

North Pool **101** D4
North Poorton **104** B3
North Quarme **114** C4
North Queensferry **235** F1
North Radworthy **114** A4
North Rauceby **175** F3
North Reston **189** E1
North Riding Forest Park
  *NYorks*
  YO18 7LT **204** B3
North Rigton **194** B3
North Rode **171** F1
North Roe **278** C4
North Ronaldsay **276** G2
North Ronaldsay
  Airfield **276** G2
North Runcton **163** E1
North Sandwick **278** E3
North Scale **191** E5
North Scarle **175** D1
North Seaton **221** E3
North Shian (Sithean a
  Tuath) **248** B5
North Shields **212** C1
North Shoebury **138** C4
North Side **162** A3
North Skelton **203** F1
North Somercotes **189** E3
North Stainley **202** B5
North Stainmore **200** D1
North Stifford **137** F4
North Stoke
  *B&NESom* **117** E1
North Stoke *Oxon* **134** B4
North Stoke *WSuss* **108** C2
North Stoneham **106** D1
North Street *Hants* **120** B4
North Street *Kent* **124** C3
North Street *Med* **124** A1
North Street
  *WBerks* **134** B5
North Sunderland **229** G3
North Tamerton **98** D1
North Tarbothill **261** H3
North Tawton **113** F5
North Third **234** B1
North Thoresby **188** C3
North Tidworth **118** D3
North Togston **221** E2
North Town *Devon* **113** F5
North Town *Hants* **121** D2
North Town *W&M* **135** E5
North Tuddenham **178** B4
North Uist (Uibhist a
  Tuath) **262** C4
North Walsham **179** D3
North Waltham **119** G3
North
  Warnborough **120** C2
North Water Bridge **253** E3
North Watten **275** H3
North Weald
  Bassett **137** D2
North Wembley **136** A4
North Wheatley **187** E4
North Whilborough **101** E1
North Wick **116** C1
North Widcombe **116** C2
North Willingham **188** B4
North Wingfield **173** F1
North Witham **175** E5
North Wootton
  *Dorset* **104** C1
North Wootton
  *Norf* **177** E5
North Wootton
  *Som* **116** C3
North Wraxall **132** A5
North Wroughton **132** D4
North Yardhope **220** B1
North Yorkshire Moors
  Railway *NYorks*
  YO18 7AJ **204** B4
Northacre **164** A2
Northall **149** E5
Northall Green **178** A4
Northallerton **202** C3
Northam *Devon* **113** E3
Northam *Soton* **106** D1
Northam Burrows Country
  Park *Devon*
  EX39 1XR **113** E2
Northampton **148** C1
Northaw **136** B2
Northay *Devon* **103** F1
Northay *Som* **103** F1
Northbay **254**
Northbeck **175** F3
Northborough **161** G2
Northbourne *Kent* **125** F3
Northbourne *Oxon* **134** A4
Northbridge Street **110** C1
Northbrook *Hants* **119** G4
Northbrook *Oxon* **147** G5
Northburnhill **269** G6
Northchapel **121** E5
Northchurch **135** E2
Northcote Manor **113** G4
Northcott **98** D1
Northcourt **134** A3
Northdyke **276** B5
Northedge **173** E1
Northend
  *B&NESom* **117** E1
Northend *Bucks* **134** C3
Northend *Warks* **147** F2
Northfield *Aber* **269** G4
Northfield
  *Aberdeen* **261** H4
Northfield *High* **275** J4
Northfield *Hull* **196** C5
Northfield *ScBord* **237** G3
Northfield *WMid* **158** C5
Northfields **161** F2
Northfleet **137** F5
Northhouse **227** F5
Northiam **110** D1
Northill **149** G3
Northington *Glos* **131** G2
Northington
  *Hants* **119** G4
Northlands **176** B2
Northleach **132** D1
Northleigh *Devon* **103** E3
Northleigh *Devon* **113** G3
Northlew **99** F1
Northmoor **133** G2

Northmoor Green
(Moorland) **116** A4
Northmuir **252** B4
Northney **107** G2
Northolt **136** A4
Northop
(Llaneurgain) **169** F1
Northop Hall **169** F1
Northorpe *Lincs* **176** A4
Northorpe *Lincs* **187** F3
Northorpe *Lincs* **161** F1
Northover *Som* **116** C5
Northover *Som* **116** B4
Northowram **194** A5
Northport **105** F4
Northpunds **279** D10
Northrepps **178** D2
Northton
(Taobh Tuath) **262** E3
Northumbria Craft Centre,
Morpeth *N'umb*
NE61 1PD **221** E3
Northway *Glos* **146** B4
Northway *Som* **115** E4
Northwich **184** A5
Northwick *SGlos* **131** E4
Northwick *Som* **116** A3
Northwick *Worcs* **146** A2
Northwold **163** F3
Northwood *GtLon* **135** F3
Northwood *IoW* **107** D3
Northwood *Kent* **125** F2
Northwood *Mersey* **183** F3
Northwood *Shrop* **170** B3
Northwood Green **131** G1
Northwood Hills **136** A3
Norton *Glos* **146** A5
Norton *Halton* **183** G4
Norton *Herts* **150** A4
Norton *IoW* **106** C4
Norton *Mon* **144** D5
Norton *N'hants* **148** B1
Norton *Notts* **186** C5
Norton *NSom* **116** A1
Norton *NYorks* **203** G5
Norton *Powys* **144** C1
Norton *Shrop* **157** F2
Norton *Shrop* **157** G2
Norton *Shrop* **157** D4
Norton *Stock* **212** D5
Norton *Suff* **152** A1
Norton *Swan* **128** C4
Norton *SYorks* **186** C1
Norton *SYorks* **186** A4
Norton *VGlam* **129** E5
Norton *Wilts* **132** A4
Norton *WMid* **158** C2
Norton *Worcs* **146** A2
Norton *Worcs* **146** C3
Norton *WSuss* **108** B3
Norton *WSuss* **108** A4
Norton Bavant **118** A3
Norton Bridge **171** F4
Norton Canes **158** C2
Norton Canon **144** C3
Norton Disney **175** D2
Norton Ferris **117** E4
Norton Fitzwarren **115** E5
Norton Green
*Herts* **150** A5
Norton Green *IoW* **106** C4
Norton Green
*Stoke* **171** G2
Norton Hawkfield **116** C1
Norton Heath **137** F2
Norton in Hales **171** E4
Norton in the
Moors **171** F2
Norton Lindsey **147** E1
Norton Little Green **152** A1
Norton Malreward **116** D1
Norton Mandeville **137** F2
Norton St. Philip **117** E2
Norton Subcourse **165** F2
Norton Wood **144** C3
Norton Woodseats **186** A4
Norton-Juxta-
Twycross **159** F2
Norton-le-Clay **202** D5
Norton-sub-
Hamdon **104** A1
Norwell **174** C1
Norwell Woodhouse **174** C1
Norwich **178** D5
Norwich Castle Museum &
Art Gallery *Norf*
NR1 3JU **79** Norwich
Norwich Cathedral *Norf*
NR1 4DH **79** Norwich
Norwich International
Airport **178** D4
Norwick **278** F1
Norwood End **137** E2
Norwood Green
*GtLon* **136** A5
Norwood Green
*WYorks* **194** A5
Norwood Hill **122** B4
Norwood Park **116** C4
Noseley **160** C3
Noss Mayo **100** B3
Nosterfield **202** B4
Nosterfield End **151** E3
Nostie **256** E2
Notgrove **146** D5
Nottage **129** E5
Notting Hill **136** B4
Nottingham *High* **275** H5
Nottingham *Nott* **173** G3
Nottingham Castle Museum
& Art Gallery NG1 6EL
**80** Nottingham
Nottington **104** C4
Notton *Wilts* **118** A1
Notton *WYorks* **186** A1
Nottswood Hill **131** G1
Nounsley **137** G1
Noutard's Green **145** G1
Nowton **151** G1
Nowton Park *Suff*
IP29 5LU **151** G1
Nox **156** D1
Noyadd Trefawr **141** F3
Nuffield **134** B4
Nun Monkton **195** E2
Nunburnholme **196** A3
Nuneaton **159** F3

Nuneham
Courtenay **134** A3
Nunney **117** E3
Nunnington *Here* **145** E3
Nunnington
*NYorks* **203** F5
Nunnington Park **115** D5
Nunnykirk **220** C2
Nunsthorpe **188** C2
Nunthorpe *Middl* **203** E1
Nunthorpe *York* **195** E2
Nunton **118** C5
Nunwick *N'umb* **220** A4
Nunwick *NYorks* **202** C5
Nup End **136** B1
Nupend **131** G2
Nursling **106** C1
Nursted **120** C5
Nurton **158** A2
Nutbourne *WSuss* **108** C2
Nutbourne *WSuss* **107** G2
Nutfield **122** C3
Nuthall **173** G3
Nuthampstead **150** C4
Nuthurst *Warks* **159** D5
Nuthurst *WSuss* **121** G5
Nutley *ESuss* **109** G1
Nutley *Hants* **120** B3
Nutwell **186** D2
Nyadd **242** C5
Nybster **275** J2
Nyetimber **108** A4
Nyewood **120** C5
Nymans *WSuss*
RH17 6EB **109** E1
Nymet Rowland **102** A2
Nymet Tracey **102** A2
Nympsfield **132** A2
Nynehead **115** E5
Nythe **116** B4
Nyton **108** B3

**O**

O2, The *GtLon*
SE10 0BB **13** E5
Oad Street **124** A2
Oadby **160** B2
Oak Cross **99** F1
Oak Tree **202** C1
Oakamoor **172** B3
Oakbank *A&B* **239** G1
Oakbank *WLoth* **235** E3
Oakdale *Caerp* **130** A3
Oakdale *Poole* **105** G3
Oake **115** E5
Oaken **158** A2
Oakenclough **192** B3
Oakengates **157** G1
Oakenhead **267** K5
Oakenholt **146** A1
Oakenshaw
*WYorks* **194** A5
Oakerthorpe **173** E2
Oakes **185** F1
Oakfield *IoW* **107** E3
Oakfield *Torfaen* **130** B3
Oakford *Cere* **142** A2
Oakford *Devon* **114** C5
Oakfordbridge **114** C5
Oakgrove **171** G1
Oakham **161** D2
Oakhanger **120** C4
Oakhill **116** D3
Oakington **150** C1
Oaklands *Conwy* **168** B2
Oaklands *Herts* **136** B1
Oakle Street **131** G1
Oakley *Bed* **149** F2
Oakley *Bucks* **134** B1
Oakley *Fife* **235** E1
Oakley *Hants* **119** G2
Oakley *Oxon* **134** C2
Oakley *Poole* **105** G3
Oakley *Suff* **164** C4
Oakley Green **135** E5
Oakley Park **155** F4
Oakridge Lynch **132** B2
Oaks **156** D2
Oaks Green **172** C4
Oaksey **132** B3
Oakshaw Ford **218** D4
Oakshott **120** C5
Oakthorpe **159** F1
Oaktree Hill **202** C3
Oakwell Hall & Country Park
*WYorks*
WF17 9LG **27** E4
Oakwood Leisure Park
*Pembs*
SA67 8DE **127** D1
Oakwoodhill **121** G4
Oakworth **193** G4
Oare *Kent* **124** C2
Oare *Som* **114** B3
Oare *Wilts* **118** C1
Oasby **175** F4
Oatfield **222** B4
Oath **116** A5
Oathlaw **252** C4
Oatlands **194** C2
Oban
(An t-Òban) **240** A2
Obley **156** C5
Oborne **104** C1
Obthorpe **161** F1
Occlestone Green **171** D1
Occold **164** C4
Occumster **275** H5
Oceanarium BH2 5AA
**64** Bournemouth
Ochiltree **224** D4
Ochr-y-foel **182** B5
Ochtermuthill **242** D3
Ochtertyre *P&K* **242** C2
Ochtertyre *Stir* **242** C5
Ockbrook **173** F4
Ockeridge **145** G1
Ockham **121** F2
Ockle **247** E2
Ockley **121** G4
Ocle Pychard **145** E3
Octon **204** D5
Odcombe **104** B1
Odd Down **117** E1
Oddendale **200** B1
Oddingley **146** B2
Oddington **134** A1

Odds Farm Park *Bucks*
HP10 0LX **135** E4
Oddsta **278** E3
Odell **149** E2
Odham **113** E5
Odie **276** F5
Odiham **120** C2
Odsey **150** A4
Odstock **118** C5
Odstone **159** F2
Offchurch **147** F1
Offenham **146** C3
Offerton **184** D4
Offham *ESuss* **109** F2
Offham *Kent* **123** F3
Offham *WSuss* **108** C3
Offley Hoo **149** G5
Offleymarsh **171** E5
Offord Cluny **150** A1
Offord D'Arcy **150** A1
Offton **152** B3
Offwell **103** E3
Ogbourne Maizey **133** D5
Ogbourne
St. Andrew **133** D5
Ogbourne
St. George **133** D5
Ogden Water *WYorks*
HX2 8YA **26** A3
Ogil **252** C3
Ogle **220** D4
Ogmore **129** E5
Ogmore Vale **129** F3
Ogmore-by-Sea **129** E5
Ogston Reservoir *Derbys*
DE55 6EL **173** E1
Oil Terminal **277** C8
Okeford Fitzpaine **105** E1
Okehampton **99** F1
Okehampton Camp **99** F1
Okraquoy **279** D9
Olchard **102** B5
Olchfa **128** C3
Old **160** C5
Old Aberdeen **261** H4
Old Alresford **119** G4
Old Arley **159** E3
Old Basford **173** G3
Old Basing **120** B2
Old Belses **227** G3
Old Bewick **229** E4
Old Blair **251** E2
Old Bolingbroke **176** B1
Old Bramhope **194** B3
Old Brampton **186** A5
Old Bridge of Urr **216** B4
Old Buckenham **164** B2
Old Burdon **212** C2
Old Byland **203** E4
Old Cassop **212** C4
Old Church Stoke **156** B3
Old Cleeve **114** D3
Old Clipstone **174** B1
Old Colwyn **181** G5
Old Craig **261** H2
Old Craighall **236** A2
Old Crombie **268** D5
Old Dailly **214** D1
Old Dalby **174** B5
Old Dam **185** F5
Old Deer **269** H6
Old Dilton **117** F3
Old Down *SGlos* **131** F4
Old Down *Som* **116** D2
Old Edlington **186** C3
Old Eldon **212** B5
Old Ellerby **197** D4
Old Felixstowe **153** E4
Old Fletton **161** G3
Old Ford **136** C4
Old Glossop **185** E3
Old Goginan **154** C4
Old Goole **195** G5
Old Gore **145** F5
Old Hall **188** C1
Old Hall Green **150** B5
Old Hall Street **179** E2
Old Harlow **137** D1
Old Heath **152** B5
Old Heathfield **110** A1
Old Hill **158** B4
Old Hurst **162** B5
Old Hutton **199** G4
Old Kea **96** C5
Old Kilpatrick **233** F2
Old Kinnernie **261** F4
Old Knebworth **150** A5
Old Leake **176** C2
Old Leslie **260** D2
Old Malton **204** B5
Old Milton **106** B3
Old Milverton **147** E1
Old Montsale **138** D3
Old Netley **107** D1
Old Newton **152** B1
Old Philpstoun **235** E2
Old Poltalloch **240** A4
Old Radnor
(Pencraig) **144** B2
Old Rattray **269** J5
Old Rayne **260** E2
Old Romney **111** F1
Old Royal Naval College,
Greenwich *GtLon*
SE10 9LW **13** D5
Old Scone **243** G2
Old Shields **234** C2
Old Sodbury **131** G4
Old Somerby **175** E4
Old Station, The, Tintern
Parva *Mon*
NP16 7NX **131** E2
Old Stratford **148** C3
Old Sunderlandwick **196** C2
Old Swanland **221** D1
Old Swinford **158** B4
Old Thirsk **202** D4
Old Town *Cumb* **199** G4
Old Town *IoS* **96** B1
Old Town **220** A2
Old Town Farm **220** A2
Old Tupton **173** E1
Old Warden **149** G3

Old Weston **161** F5
Old Windsor **135** E5
Old Wives Lees **124** C3
Old Woking **121** F2
Old Woodhall **176** A1
Old Woods **170** B5
Oldberrow **146** D1
Oldborough **102** A2
Oldbury *Kent* **123** E3
Oldbury *Shrop* **157** G3
Oldbury *Warks* **159** F3
Oldbury *WMid* **158** B4
Oldbury Court Estate
*Bristol* BS16 2JH **8** D2
Oldbury Naite **131** F3
Oldbury on the Hill **132** A4
Oldbury-on-Severn **131** F3
Oldcastle *Bridgend* **129** F5
Oldcastle *Mon* **144** C4
Oldcotes **186** C4
Oldcroft **131** F2
Oldeamere **162** B3
Oldfield **146** A1
Oldford **117** E2
Oldhall *Aber* **260** C5
Oldhall *High* **275** H3
Oldham **184** D2
Oldham Edge **184** D2
Oldland **131** F5
Oldmeldrum **261** G2
Oldmill **260** D4
Oldpark **157** F2
Oldridge **102** B3
Oldshore Beg **272** D3
Oldshoremore **272** E3
Oldstead **203** E5
Oldtown **203** D3
Oldtown of Aigas **266** B7
Oldtown of Ord **268** E5
Oldwalls **128** A3
Oldways End **114** B5
Oldwich Lane **159** E5
Olgrinmore **275** G3
Oliver **226** C3
Oliver's Battery **119** F5
Ollaberry **278** C4
Ollerton *ChesE* **184** B5
Ollerton *Notts* **174** B1
Ollerton *Shrop* **170** D5
Olmstead Green **151** E3
Olney **149** D2
Olrig House **275** G2
Olton **158** D4
Olveston **131** F4
Olympia *GtLon*
W14 8UX **11** E5
Ombersley **146** A1
Ompton **174** B1
Onchan **190** B4
Onecote **172** B2
Onehouse **152** B2
Ongar Hill **177** D5
Ongar Street **144** C1
Onibury **157** D5
Onich
(Omhanaich) **248** C3
Onllwyn **129** E1
Onneley **171** E3
Onslow Green **137** F1
Onslow Village **121** E3
Opinan *High* **264** A1
Opinan *High* **264** D2
Orange Lane **237** E5
Orasaigh **271** F6
Orbiston **268** B5
Orbost **263** H7
Orby **176** C1
Orcadia **232** C3
Orchard **232** C1
Orchard Portman **115** F5
Orcheston **118** B3
Orcop **145** D5
Orcop Hill **145** D5
Ord **256** C3
Ordhead **260** E4
Ordie **260** C4
Ordiequish **268** B5
Ordsall **187** D5
Ore **110** C2
Oreham Common **109** E2
Oreston **100** B2
Oreton **157** F5
Orford *Suff* **153** F3
Orford **184** A3
Organford **105** F3
Orgreave **158** D1
Orkney Islands **276** D5
Orlestone **124** B5
Orleton *Here* **145** D1
Orleton *Worcs* **145** F1
Orleton Common **145** D1
Orlingbury **161** D5
Ormacleit **254** C1
Ormesby **203** E1
Ormesby
St. Margaret **179** F4
Ormesby
St. Michael **179** F4
Ormidale **232** B1
Ormiscaig **264** E2
Ormiston **236** B3
Ormlie **275** G2
Ormsaigmore **247** D3
Ormsary **231** F2
Ormskirk **183** F2
Oronsay **230** B1
Orphir **277** C7
Orpington **123** D2
Orrell *GtMan* **183** G2
Orrell *Mersey* **183** E3
Orrisdale **190** B2
Orrok House **261** H3
Orroland **208** A2
Orsett **137** F4
Orsett Heath **137** F4
Orslow **158** A1
Orston **174** C3
Orton *Cumb* **200** B2
Orton *N'hants* **160** D5
Orton Longueville **161** G3
Orton Rigg **209** G1
Orton Waterville **161** G3
Orton-on-the-Hill **159** F2
Orwell **150** B2
Osbaldeston **192** C4

Osbaldwick **195** F2
Osbaston *Leics* **159** G2
Osbaston *Shrop* **170** A5
Osbaston *Tel&W* **157** E1
Osbaston Hollow **159** G2
Osborne House *IoW*
PO32 6JX **107** E3
Osbournby **175** F4
Oscroft **170** C1
Ose **263** J7
Osgathorpe **159** G1
Osgodby *Lincs* **188** A3
Osgodby *NYorks* **195** F4
Osgodby *NYorks* **205** D4
Oskaig **256** B1
Osleston **172** D4
Osmaston *Derby* **173** E4
Osmaston *Derbys* **172** D3
Osmington **104** D4
Osmington Mills **104** D4
Osmondthorpe **194** C4
Osmotherley **203** D3
Osnaburgh (Dairsie) **244** C3
Ospringe **124** C2
Ossett **194** B5
Ossett Street Side **194** B5
Ossington **174** C1
Ostend **178** D2
Osterley **136** A5
Osterley Park & House
*GtLon* TW7 4RB **11** B5
Oswaldkirk **203** F5
Oswaldtwistle **192** D5
Oswestry **169** F4
Oteley **170** B4
Otford **123** E3
Otham **123** G3
Otherton **158** B1
Othery **116** A4
Otley *Suff* **152** D2
Otley *WYorks* **194** B3
Otter **232** A1
Otter Ferry **232** A1
Otterbourne **119** F5
Otterburn *N'umb* **220** A1
Otterburn *NYorks* **193** E2
Otterburn Camp **220** A2
Otterden Place **124** B3
Otterham **98** B1
Otterham Quay **124** A2
Otterhampton **115** F3
Otternish **262** E4
Ottershaw **121** F1
Otterswick **278** E4
Otterton **103** D4
Otterton Mill *Devon*
EX9 7HG **103** D4
Otterwood **106** D2
Ottery St. Mary **103** D3
Ottinge **125** D4
Ottringham **197** E5
Oughterby **209** F1
Oughtershaw **201** D4
Oughterside **209** E2
Oughtibridge **186** A3
Oulston **203** E5
Oulton *Cumb* **209** F1
Oulton *Norf* **178** C2
Oulton *Staffs* **171** G4
Oulton *Staffs* **171** E5
Oulton *Suff* **165** G2
Oulton *WYorks* **194** C5
Oulton Broad **165** G2
Oulton Grange **171** G4
Oulton Street **178** C3
Oultoncross **171** G4
Ousby **210** C4
Ousdale **275** F6
Ousden **151** F2
Ousefleet **196** A5
Ouston *Dur* **212** B2
Ouston *N'umb* **220** C4
Out Newton **197** F5
Out Rawcliffe **192** A3
Out Skerries **278** F5
Outcast **199** E5
Outchester **229** F3
Outertown **277** B7
Outgate **199** E3
Outhgill **200** C2
Outlands **171** E5
Outlane **185** E1
Outwell **162** D2
Outwood *Surr* **122** C4
Outwood *WYorks* **194** B5
Outwoods **157** G1
Ouzlewell Green **194** C5
Ovenden **193** G5
Over *Cambs* **162** B5
Over *ChesW&C* **170** D1
Over *Glos* **131** G1
Over *SGlos* **131** E4
Over Burrows **173** D4
Over Compton **104** B1
Over Dinsdale **202** C1
Over End **185** G5
Over Green **159** D3
Over Haddon **172** D1
Over Hulten **184** A2
Over Kellet **192** B1
Over Kiddington **147** G5
Over Monnow **131** D1
Over Norton **147** F5
Over Peover **184** B5
Over Rankeilour **244** B3
Over Silton **203** D3
Over Stowey **115** E4
Over Stratton **104** A1
Over Tabley **184** B4
Over Wallop **119** D4
Over Whitacre **159** E3
Over Winchendon (Upper
Winchendon) **134** C1
Over Worton **147** G5
Overbister **276** F3
Overbrae **269** G5
Overbury **146** B4
Overcombe **104** C4
Overgreen **186** A5
Overleigh **116** B4
Overpool **183** E5
Overscaig Hotel **273** G6
Overseal **159** E1

Overslade **159** G5
Oversland **124** C3
Oversley Green **146** C2
Overstone **148** D1
Overstrand **178** D1
Overthorpe **147** G3
Overton *Aber* **261** F3
Overton *Aberdeen* **261** G3
Overton *ChesW&C* **183** G5
Overton *Hants* **119** G2
Overton *Lancs* **192** A2
Overton *NYorks* **195** E2
Overton *Shrop* **157** D5
Overton *Swan* **128** A4
Overton (Owrtyn)
*Wrex* **170** A3
Overton *WYorks* **185** G1
Overton Bridge **170** A3
Overtown *Lancs* **200** B5
Overtown *NLan* **234** C4
Overtown *Swin* **133** D5
Overy **134** A3
Oving *Bucks* **148** C5
Oving *WSuss* **108** B3
Ovingdean **109** F3
Ovingham **211** G1
Ovington *Dur* **202** A1
Ovington *Essex* **151** F3
Ovington *Hants* **119** G4
Ovington *N'umb* **211** G1
Ovington *Norf* **178** B5
Ower *Hants* **106** C1
Ower *Hants* **107** D2
Owermoigne **105** D4
Owler Bar **185** G5
Owlpen **131** G3
Owl's Green **153** D1
Owlswick **134** C2
Owmby **188** A2
Owmby-by-Spital **188** A4
Owslebury **119** G5
Owston **160** C2
Owston Ferry **187** F2
Owstwick **197** E4
Owthorpe **174** B4
Oxborough **163** F2
Oxcliffe Hill **192** A1
Oxcombe **188** C5
Oxen End **151** E5
Oxen Park **199** E4
Oxencombe **102** B4
Oxenhall **145** G5
Oxenholme **199** G3
Oxenhope **193** G4
Oxenpill **116** B3
Oxenton **146** B4
Oxenwood **119** E2
Oxford **134** A2
Oxford Cathedral *Oxon*
OX1 1AB **80** Oxford
Oxford Story *Oxon*
OX1 3AJ **80** Oxford
Oxford University Museum
of Natural History
*Oxon* OX1 3PW
**80** Oxford
Oxhey **136** A3
Oxhill **147** F3
Oxley **158** B2
Oxley Green **138** C1
Oxley's Green **110** B1
Oxnam **228** B5
Oxnead **178** D3
Oxnop Ghyll **201** E3
Oxshott **121** F1
Oxspring **185** G2
Oxted **122** C4
Oxton *Mersey* **183** E4
Oxton *Notts* **174** B2
Oxton *ScBord* **236** B4
Oxwich **128** A4
Oxwich Green **128** A4
Oxwick **178** A3
Oykel Bridge **265** K1
Oyne **260** E2
Ozleworth **131** G3

Palacerigg Country Park
*NLan* G67 3HU **234** B2
Pale **168** C4
Palehouse
Common **109** G2
Palestine **119** D3
Paley Street **135** D5
Palgowan **215** G2
Palgrave **164** C4
Pallinsburn House **228** C3
Palmarsh **124** D5
Palmers Cross **121** F3
Palmers Green **136** C3
Palmerscross **267** K5
Palmerstown **130** A5
Palnackie **216** C5
Palnure **215** F4
Palterton **173** F1
Pamber End **120** B2
Pamber Green **120** B2
Pamber Heath **120** B1
Pamington **146** B4
Pamphill **105** B4
Pampisford **150** C3
Pan **277** C8
Panborough **116** B3
Panbride **245** D1
Pancrasweek **112** C5
Pancross **114** C1
Pandy *Gwyn* **154** C2
Pandy *Mon* **144** C5
Pandy *Powys* **155** F2
Pandy *Wrex* **169** E4
Pandy Tudur **168** B1
Pandy'r Capel **169** D2
Panfield **151** F5
Pangbourne **134** B5
Pannal **194** C2
Pannal Ash **194** B2
Panshanger **136** B1
Pant **169** F5
Pant Glas **167** D3
Pant Gwyn **168** B5
Pant Mawr **155** E4
Pantasaph **182** C5
Panteg **130** C2
Pantglas **155** D3
Pantgwyn *Carmar* **142** B5
Pantgwyn *Cere* **141** F3
Pant-lasau **128** C2
Panton **188** B5
Pant-pastynog **168** D1
Pantperthog **154** D2
Pant-y-dwr **155** F5
Pantyffordd **169** F2
Pant-y-ffridd **156** A2
Pantyffynnon **128** C1
Pantygasseg **130** B2
Pantygelli **130** C1
Pantymwyn **169** E1
Panxworth **179** E4
Papa Stour **279** A6
Papa Stour Airstrip **279** A6
Papa Westray **276** D2
Papa Westray
Airfield **276** D2
Papcastle **209** E3
Papil **279** C9
Papple **236** C2
Papplewick **173** G2
Papworth Everard **150** A1
Papworth St. Agnes **150** A1
Par **97** E4
Paradise Park, Newhaven
*ESuss* BN9 0DH **109** G4
Paradise Wildlife Park,
Broxbourne *Herts*
EN10 7QA **136** C2
Parbold **183** F1
Parbrook *Som* **116** C4
Parbrook *WSuss* **121** F5
Parc **168** B4
Parcllyn **141** F2
Parcrhydderch **142** C2
Parc-Seymour **130** D3
Parc-y-rhôs **142** B3
Pardshaw **209** D4
Parham **153** E1
Parish Holm **225** F3
Park **268** D3
Park Close **193** E3
Park Corner *ESuss* **123** E5
Park Corner *Oxon* **134** B4
Park End *N'umb* **220** B4
Park End *Staffs* **171** E2
Park End *Worcs* **157** G5
Park Gate *Hants* **107** E1
Park Gate *Worcs* **158** B5
Park Gate *WYorks* **194** A3
Park Gate *WYorks* **185** G1
Park Green **152** C1
Park Hill **186** A4
Park Lane **170** B4
Park Langley **122** C2
Park Rose Pottery & Leisure
*ERid*
YO15 3QF **196** D1
Park Street **136** A2
Parkend *Cumb* **209** G3
Parkend *Glos* **131** F2
Parker's Green **123** F4
Parkeston **152** D4
Parkfield *Corn* **98** D4
Parkfield *SGlos* **131** F5
Parkfield *WMid* **158** B3
Parkford **252** C4
Parkgate *ChesW&C* **183** D5
Parkgate *D&G* **217** E2
Parkgate *Kent* **124** A5
Parkgate *Surr* **122** B4
Parkgate *SYorks* **186** B3
Parkham **113** D3
Parkham Ash **113** D3
Parkhead **234** A3
Parkhill *Angus* **253** D5
Parkhill *P&K* **251** G5
Parkhouse **131** D2
Parkhurst **107** D3
Parkmill **128** B4
Parkmore **268** B6
Parkneuk **253** F2
Parkside **170** A2
Parkstone **105** G3
Parkway **116** C5
Parley Cross **105** G3
Parley Green **106** A3
Parlington **194** D4
Parracombe **113** G1

Parrog 140 D4
Parson Cross 186 A3
Parson Drove 162 B2
Parsonage Green 137 F1
Parsonby 209 E3
Partick 233 G2
Partington 184 B3
Partney 176 C1
Parton *Cumb* 208 C4
Parton *D&G* 216 A3
Partridge Green 109 D2
Parwich 172 C2
Paslow Wood
  Common 137 E2
Passenham 148 C4
Passfield 120 D4
Passingford Bridge 137 E3
Paston 179 E2
Paston Street 179 E2
Pasturefields 171 G5
Patchacott 99 E1
Patcham 109 F3
Patchetts Green 136 A3
Patching 108 C3
Patchole 113 G1
Pateley Bridge 194 A1
Path of Condie 243 F3
Pathe 116 A4
Pathfinder Village 102 B3
Pathhead *Aber* 253 F3
Pathhead *EAyr* 225 E4
Pathhead *Fife* 244 A5
Pathhead *Midlo* 236 A3
Pathlow 147 D2
Patmore Heath 150 C5
Patna 224 C4
Patney 118 B2
Patrick 190 A3
Patrick Brompton 202 B3
Patrington 197 F5
Patrington Haven 197 F5
Patrishow 144 B5
Patrixbourne 125 D3
Patterdale 209 G5
Pattingham 158 A3
Pattishall 148 B2
Pattiswick 151 G5
Paul 94 B4
Paulerspury 148 C3
Paull 197 D5
Paull Holme 197 D5
Paul's Green 94 D3
Paulton 117 D2
*Paultons Park Hants*
  *SO51 6AL* 106 C1
Pauperhaugh 220 C2
Pave Lane 157 G1
Pavenham 149 E2
*Pavilion Gardens, Buxton*
  *Derbys*
  *SK17 6XN* 185 E5
Pawlett 116 A3
Pawston 228 C3
Paxford 147 D4
Paxhill Park 109 F1
Paxton 237 G4
Payden Street 124 B3
Payhembury 103 D2
Paythorne 193 E2
Peacehaven 109 G3
Peacemarsh 117 F5
Peachley 146 A2
Peak Dale 185 E5
Peak Forest 185 F5
Peakirk 161 G2
Pean Hill 124 D2
Pear Tree 173 E4
Pearsie 252 B4
Pearson's Green 123 F4
Peartree 136 B1
*Peartree Green*
  *Essex* 137 E3
Peartree Green
  *Here* 145 F4
Pease Pottage 122 B5
Peasedown St. John 117 E2
Peasehill 173 E1
Peaseland Green 178 B4
Peasemore 133 G4
Peasenhall 153 E1
Peaslake 121 F4
Peasley Cross 183 G3
Peasmarsh
  *ESuss* 111 D1
Peasmarsh *Surr* 121 E3
Peaston 236 B3
Peastonbank 236 B3
Peat Inn 244 C4
Peathill 269 H4
Peatling Magna 160 A3
Peatling Parva 160 A4
Peaton 157 E4
Pebble Coombe 122 B3
Pebmarsh 151 G4
Pebworth 146 D3
Pecket Well 193 F5
Peckforton 170 C2
Peckham 136 C5
Peckleton 159 G2
Pedham 179 E4
Pedmore 158 B4
Pedwell 116 B4
Peebles 235 G5
Peel *IoM* 190 A3
Peel *Lancs* 191 G4
Peening Quarter 111 D1
Peggs Green 159 G1
Pegsdon 149 G4
Pegswood 221 E3
Pegwell 125 F2
Peighinn nan
  Aoireann 254 C1
Peinchorran 256 B1
Peinlich 263 K6
Pelaw 212 B1
Pelcomb 126 C1
Pelcomb Bridge 126 C1
Pelcomb Cross 126 C1
Peldon 138 C1
Pellon 193 G5
Pelsall 158 C2
Pelton 212 B2
Pelutho 209 E2
Pelynt 97 G4
Pemberton 183 G2
Pembrey (Pen-bre) 128 A2

*Pembrey Country Park*
  *Carmar*
  *SA16 0EJ* 128 A2
Pembridge 144 C2
Pembroke (Penfro) 126 C2
Pembroke Dock
  (Doc Penfro) 126 C2
Pembury 123 F4
Penallt 131 E1
Penally 127 E3
Penalt 145 E5
Penare 97 D5
Penarran 156 A4
Penarth 130 A5
Pen-bont
  Rhydybeddau 154 C4
Penboyr 141 G4
Penbryn 141 F2
Pencader 142 A4
Pen-cae 142 A2
Pen-cae-cwm 168 C1
Pencaenewydd 166 D3
Pencaitland 236 B3
Pencarnisiog 180 B5
Pencarreg 142 B3
Pencarrow 97 F1
Pencelli 143 G5
Pen-clawdd 128 B3
Pencoed 129 F4
Pencombe 145 E2
Pencoyd 145 E5
Pencraig *Here* 145 E5
Pencraig *Powys* 168 D5
Pendeen 94 A3
Penderyn 129 F2
Pendine
  (Pentywyn) 127 F2
Pendlebury 184 B2
Pendleton 193 D4
Pendock 145 G4
Pendoggett 97 E2
Pendomer 104 B1
Pendoylan 129 G5
Penegoes 155 D2
Penelewey 96 C5
Pen-ffordd 141 E5
Pengam 130 A3
Penge 136 C4
Pengenffordd 144 A5
Pengorffwysfa 180 C3
Pengover Green 97 G3
Pen-groes-oped 130 C2
Pengwern 182 B5
Penhale 95 D5
Penhallow 96 B4
Penhalvaean 95 E3
Penhelig 154 C3
Penhill 133 D4
Penhow 130 D3
Penhurst 110 B2
Peniarth 154 C2
Penicuik 235 G3
Peniel 142 A5
Penifiler 263 K7
Peninver 222 C3
*Penisa'r Waun* 167 E1
Penisarcwm 155 G5
Penishawain 143 G4
Penistone 185 G2
Penjerrick 95 E3
Penketh 183 G4
Penkill 214 D1
Penkridge 158 B1
Penlean 98 C1
Penley 170 B4
Penllech 166 B4
Penllergaer 128 C3
Pen-llyn *IoA* 180 B4
Penllyn *VGlam* 129 F5
Pen-lôn 166 D1
Penmachno 168 A2
Penmaen 128 B4
Penmaenan 181 F5
Penmaenmawr 181 F5
Penmaenpool (Llyn
  Penmaen) 154 C1
Penmaen-Rhôs 181 G5
Penmark 115 D5
Penmon 181 E4
Penmorfa 167 E3
Penmynydd 180 D5
Penn *Bucks* 135 E3
Penn *WMid* 158 A3
Penn Street 135 E3
Pennal 154 C2
Pennal-isaf 154 D2
Pennan 269 G4
Pennance 96 B5
Pennant *Cere* 142 B1
Pennant *Powys* 155 E3
Pennant Melangell 168 C3
Pennar 126 C2
Pennard 128 B4
Pennerley 156 C3
Penninghame 215 E4
Pennington *Cumb* 199 D5
Pennington *Hants* 106 C3
*Pennington Flash Country*
  *Park GtMan*
  *WN7 3PA* 184 A2
Pennorth 144 A5
Pennsylvania 131 G5
Penny Bridge 199 E4
Pennycross 100 A2
Pennyfuir 240 A1
Pennygate 179 E3
Pennyghael 239 E2
Pennyglen 224 A4
Pennygown 247 F5
Pennymoor 102 B1
Penny's Green 164 C2
Pennyvenie 224 C5
Penparc *Cere* 141 F3
Penparc *Pembs* 140 B4
Penparcau 154 B4
Penpedairheol 130 A2
Penpethy 97 E1
Penpillick 97 E4
Penpol 95 F3
Penpoll 97 F4
Penponds 94 D3
Penpont *D&G* 216 C1
Penpont *Powys* 143 F5
Penprysg 129 F4
Penquit 100 C2
Penrherber 141 F4
Penrhiw 141 F3

Penrhiwceiber 129 G3
Penrhiwgoch 128 B1
Penrhiw-llan 141 G3
Penrhiw-pâl 141 G3
Penrhiwtyn 128 D3
Penrhos *Gwyn* 166 C4
Penrhos *IoA* 180 A4
Penrhos *Mon* 130 D1
Penrhos *Powys* 129 D1
Penrhos-garnedd 181 D5
Penrhyn Bay
  (Bae Penrhyn) 181 G4
*Penrhyn Castle Gwyn*
  *LL57 4HN* 181 E5
Penrhyn-coch 154 C4
Penrhyndeudraeth 167 F4
Penrhyn-side 181 G4
Penrhys 129 G3
Penrice 128 A4
Penrith 210 B5
Penrose *Corn* 96 C2
Penrose *Corn* 97 G1
Penruddock 210 A5
Penryn 95 E3
Pensarn *Carmar* 128 A1
Pensarn *Conwy* 182 A5
Pen-sarn *Gwyn* 167 E5
Pen-sarn *Gwyn* 166 D3
Pensax 145 G1
Pensby 183 D4
Penselwood 117 E4
Pensford 116 D2
Pensham 146 B3
Penshaw 212 C2
Penshurst 123 E4
Pensilva 97 G3
Pensnett 158 B4
Penston 236 B2
Pentewan 97 E5
Pentir 167 E1
Pentire 96 B3
Pentireglaze 96 D2
Pentlepoir 127 E2
Pentlow 151 G3
Pentlow Street 151 G3
Pentney 163 F1
Penton Mewsey 119 E3
Pentonville 136 C4
Pentraeth 180 D5
Pentre *Powys* 169 D5
Pentre *Powys* 155 G4
Pentre *Powys* 144 B1
Pentre *Powys* 156 B3
Pentre *Powys* 156 A4
Pentre *RCT* 129 F3
Pentre *Shrop* 156 C1
Pentre *Shrop* 156 C5
Pentre *Wrex* 169 F3
Pentre *Wrex* 170 A3
Pentre Berw 180 C5
Pentre Ffwrndan 183 D5
Pentre Galar 141 E4
Pentre Gwenlais 128 C1
Pentre Gwynfryn 167 E5
Pentre Halkyn 182 D5
Pentre Isaf 168 B1
Pentre Llanrhaeadr 169 D1
Pentre Maelor 170 A3
Pentre Meyrick 129 F5
Pentre Poeth 128 C3
Pentre Saron 168 D1
Pentre-bach *Cere* 142 B3
Pentrebach *MTyd* 129 G2
Pentre-bach *Powys* 143 F4
Pentrebach *RCT* 129 G3
Pentrebach *Swan* 128 B2
Pentre-bont 168 A2
Pentre-bwlch 169 E3
Pentrecagal 141 G3
Pentre-celyn
  *Denb* 169 E2
Pentre-celyn
  *Powys* 155 E2
Pentre-chwyth 128 C3
Pentreclwydau 129 E2
Pentre-cwrt 141 G4
Pentre-Dolau-
  Honddu 143 F3
Pentredwr *Denb* 169 E3
Pentre-dwr *Swan* 128 C3
Pentrefelin *Carmar* 142 C5
Pentrefelin *Cere* 142 C3
Pentrefelin *Conwy* 181 G5
Pentrefelin *Gwyn* 167 E4
Pentrefelin *Powys* 169 E5
Pentrefoelas 168 B2
Pentregat 141 G2
Pentreheyling 156 B3
Pentre-llwyn-
  llwyd 143 F2
Pentre-llyn 154 C5
Pentre-llyn-
  cymmer 168 C2
Pentre-piod 168 B4
Pentre-poeth 130 B4
*Pentre'r beirdd* 156 A1
Pentre'r Felin 181 E1
Pentre'r-felin 143 F4
Pentre-tafarn-y-
  fedw 168 B1
Pentre-ty-gwyn 143 E4
Pentrich 173 E2
Pentridge 105 G1
Pentwyn *Caerp* 130 A2
Pentwyn *Caerp* 130 B2
Pentwyn *Cardiff* 130 B4
Pentwyn *Mon* 130 C2
Pentwyn-mawr 130 A3
Pentyrch 130 A4
Penuwch 142 B1
Penwithick 97 E4
Penwood 119 F1
Penwortham 192 B5
Penwortham Lane 192 B5
Penwyllt 129 E1
Pen-y-banc 142 C5
Pen-y-bont
  *Carmar* 143 D4
Pen-y-bont
  *Carmar* 141 G5
Pen-y-bont *Powys* 155 G3
Pen-y-bont *Powys* 169 F5
Penybont *Powys* 144 A1
Penybontfawr 169 D5
Pen-y-bryn *Gwyn* 130 A3
Pen-y-bryn *Gwyn* 154 C1
Pen-y-bryn *Pembs* 141 E3
Pen-y-bryn *Wrex* 169 F3

Pen-y-cae *Powys* 129 E1
Penycae *Wrex* 169 F3
Pen-y-cae-mawr 130 D3
Pen-y-cefn 170 C1
Pen-y-clawdd 130 D2
Pen-y-coedcae 129 G4
Penycwm 140 C2
Pen-y-Darren 129 G2
Pen-y-fai 129 E4
Penyffordd *Flints* 170 A1
Pen-y-ffordd *Flints* 182 C4
Penyffridd 167 E2
Pen-y-gaer 144 A5
Pen-y-garn *Carmar* 142 B4
Pen-y-garn *Carmar* 154 C4
Penygarn *Torfaen* 130 B2
Penygarnedd 169 E5
Pen-y-garreg 143 G3
Pen-y-Graig *Gwyn* 166 B4
Penygraig *RCT* 129 G3
Penygroes *Carmar* 128 C2
Penygroes *Gwyn* 167 D2
Pen-y-lan 130 A2
Pen-y-Mynydd
  *Flints* 170 A1
Pen-y-parc 170 A1
Pen-y-Park 144 B3
Pen-yr-englyn 129 F3
Pen-yr-heol *Mon* 130 D1
Penyrheol *Swan* 128 B3
Pen-y-sarn 180 D3
Pen-y-stryt 169 E2
Penywaun 129 F2
Penzance 94 B3
*Penzance Heliport* 94 B3
*People's Palace & Winter*
  *Gardens Glas*
  *G40 1AT* 39 H6
Peopleton 146 B2
Peover Heath 184 B5
Peper Harow 121 E3
Peplow 170 D5
Pepper Arden 202 B2
Pepper's Green 137 F1
Perceton 233 E5
Percie 260 D5
Percyhorner 269 H4
Perham Down 119 D3
Periton 114 C3
Perivale 136 A4
Perkhill 260 D4
Perkins Beach 156 C2
Perkin's Village 102 D3
Perlethorpe 186 B5
Perran Downs 94 C3
Perranarworthal 95 E3
Perranporth 96 B4
Perranuthnoe 94 C4
Perranzabuloe 96 B4
Perrott's Brook 132 C2
Perry Barr 158 C3
Perry Crofts 159 E2
Perry Green
  *Essex* 151 G5
Perry Green *Herts* 136 D1
Perry Green *Wilts* 132 B4
Perry Street 137 F5
Perrymead 117 E1
Pershall 171 F5
Pershore 146 B3
Persie House 251 G4
Pert 253 E3
Pertenhall 149 F1
Perth (Peairt) 243 G2
Perthcelyn 129 G3
Perthy 170 A4
Perton 158 A3
Pestalozzi Children's
  Village 110 C4
Peter Tavy 99 F3
Peterborough 161 G3
Peterburn 264 D3
Peterchurch 144 C4
Peterculter 261 G4
Peterhead 269 K6
Peterlee 212 D3
Peter's Green 136 A1
Peters Marland 113 E4
Peters Port
  (Port Pheadair) 262 D7
Petersfield 120 C5
Petersfinger 118 C5
Peterstone
  Wentlooge 130 B4
Peterstow-super-
  Ely 129 G5
Peterstow 145 E5
Petham 124 D3
Petrockstowe 113 F5
Pett 111 D2
Pettaugh 152 C2
Petterill Green 210 A3
Pettinain 235 D5
Pettistree 153 D2
Petton *Devon* 114 D5
Petton *Shrop* 170 B5
Petts Wood 122 D2
Petty 261 F1
Petty France 131 G4
Pettycur 235 G1
Pettymuick 261 H2
Petworth 121 E5
Pevensey 110 B3
Pevensey Bay 110 B3
Peverell 100 A2
Pewsey 118 C1
Pheasant's Hill 134 C4
Phesdo 253 E2
Philham 112 C3
*Philharmonic Hall, Liverpool*
  *Mersey L1 9BP* 43 E5
Philiphaugh 227 F3
Phillack 94 C3
Philleigh 95 F3
Philpstoun 235 E2
Phocle Green 145 F5
Phoenix Green 120 C3
Phones 258 D1
Phorp 267 H6
*Photographer's Gallery, The,*
  *London GtLon*
  *WC2H 7HY* 44 E3
Pibsbury 116 B5
Pica 208 D4
Piccadilly Corner 165 D3

Pickerells 137 E2
Pickering 203 G4
Pickering Nook 212 A2
Picket Piece 119 E3
Picket Post 106 A2
Pickford Green 159 E4
Pickhill 202 C3
Picklescott 156 D3
Pickletillem 244 C3
Pickmere 184 A5
Pickney 115 E5
Pickstock 171 E5
Pickston *Oxon* 134 B1
Pickup Bank 192 D5
Pickwell *Devon* 113 E1
Pickwell *Leics* 160 C1
Pickworth *Lincs* 175 F4
Pickworth *Rut* 161 E1
Picton *ChesW&C* 183 F5
Picton *NYorks* 202 D2
Piddinghoe 109 G3
Piddington
  *N'hants* 148 D2
Piddington *Oxon* 134 B1
Piddlehinton 104 D3
Piddletrenthide 104 D3
Pidley 162 B5
*Piece Hall, Halifax WYorks*
  *HX1 1RE* 26 B4
Piercebridge 202 B1
Pierowall 276 D3
Pigdon 221 D3
Pike Hill 193 E4
Pikehall 172 C2
Pikeshill 106 B2
Pilgrims Hatch 137 E3
Pilham 187 F3
Pill 131 E5
Pillaton *Corn* 99 D4
Pillaton *Staffs* 158 B1
Pillerton Hersey 147 E3
Pillerton Priors 147 E3
Pilleth 144 B1
Pilley *Hants* 106 C3
Pilley *SYorks* 186 A2
Pilling 192 A3
Pilling Lane 191 G3
Pillowell 131 F2
Pilning 131 E4
Pilsbury 172 C1
Pilsdon 104 A3
Pilsgate 161 F2
Pilsley *Derbys* 173 E1
Pilsley *Derbys* 185 G5
Pilson Green 179 E4
Piltdown 109 G1
Pilton *Devon* 113 F2
Pilton *N'hants* 161 F4
Pilton *Rut* 161 E2
Pilton *Som* 116 C3
Pilton Swan 128 A4
Pilton Green 128 A4
Pimhole 184 C1
Pimlico 135 F2
Pimperne 105 F2
Pin Mill 152 D4
Pinchbeck 176 A5
Pinchbeck Bars 176 A5
Pinchbeck West 176 A5
Pincheon Green 187 D1
Pinchinthorpe 203 F1
Pindon End 148 C3
Pinehurst 132 D4
Pinfold 183 E1
Pinged 128 A2
Pinhay 103 G3
Pinhoe 102 C3
Pinkneys Green 135 D4
Pinley 147 E1
Pinley Green 147 E1
Pinminnoch 214 C1
Pinmore 214 D1
Pinn 103 E4
Pinner 136 A4
Pinner Green 136 A3
Pinvin 146 B3
Pinwherry 214 C2
Pinxton 173 E2
Pipe & Lyde 145 E3
Pipe Gate 171 E3
Pipe Ridware 158 C1
Pipehill 158 C2
Piperhall 232 B4
Piperhill 267 F6
Pipers Pool 97 G1
Pipewell 160 D4
Pippacott 113 F2
Pipton 144 A4
Pirbright 121 E2
Pirnmill 231 G5
Pirton *Herts* 149 G4
Pirton *Worcs* 146 A3
Pisgah 242 C4
Pishill 134 C4
Pistyll 166 C3
Pitagowan 250 D3
Pitblae 269 H4
Pitcairngreen 243 F2
Pitcairns 243 F3
Pitcaple 261 F2
Pitch Green 134 C2
Pitch Place *Surr* 121 E3
Pitch Place *Surr* 121 D4
Pitchcombe 132 A2
Pitchcott 148 C5
Pitchford 157 E2
Pitcombe 117 D4
Pitcot 129 E5
Pitcox 236 D2
Pitcur 244 A1
Pitfichie 260 E3
Pitgrudy 266 E2
Pitinnan 261 F1
Pitkennedy 252 D4
Pitkevy 244 A4
Pitlessie 244 A4
Pitlochry 251 E4
Pitman's Corner 152 C1
Pitmedden 261 G2
Pitminster 103 F1
Pitmuies 253 D5
Pitmunie 260 E3
Pitney 116 B5
Pitroddie 244 A2
Pitscottie 244 C3
Pitsea 137 G4
Pitsford 148 C1

Pitsford Hill 115 D4
Pitstone 135 E1
Pitt *Devon* 102 D1
Pitt *Hants* 119 F5
*Pitt Rivers Museum Oxon*
  *OX1 3PP* 80 Oxford
Pittendreich 267 J5
Pittentrail 266 E1
Pittenweem 244 D4
Pitteuchar 244 A5
Pittington 212 C3
Pittodrie House 260 E2
Pitton *Swan* 128 A4
Pitton *Wilts* 118 D4
Pittulie 269 H4
Pittville 146 B5
Pity Me 212 B3
Pityme 96 C2
Pixey Green 164 D4
Pixley 145 F4
*Place Newton* 204 B5
Plaidy 269 F5
*Plain Dealings* 127 D1
Plainfield 220 B5
Plains 234 B3
Plainsfield 115 E4
Plaish 157 E2
Plaistow *GtLon* 136 C4
Plaistow *WSuss* 121 F4
Plaitford 106 A2
Plaitford Green 119 D5
Plas 142 A5
Plas Gwynant 167 F2
Plas Isaf 169 E2
Plas Llwyd 182 A5
Plas-llwyngwern 155 D2
Plas Llysyn 155 F3
Plas Nantyr 169 E4
Plashett 127 F2
Plasisaf 168 C1
Plas-rhiw-Saeson 155 F2
Plastow Green 119 G1
Plas-yn-Cefn 182 B5
Platt 123 F3
Platt Bridge 184 A2
Platt Lane 170 C4
Platt's Heath 124 A3
Plawsworth 212 B3
Plaxtol 123 F3
Play Hatch 134 C5
Playden 111 E1
Playford 152 D3
Playing Place 96 C5
Playley Green 145 G4
Plealey 156 D2
Plean 234 C1
Pleasance 244 A3
Pleasant Valley 150 D4
Pleasington 192 C5
Pleasley 173 G1
Pleasleyhill 173 G1
*Pleasure Beach, Great*
  *Yarmouth Norf*
  *NR30 3EH* 179 G5
*Pleasure Island Theme Park*
  *NELincs*
  *DN35 0PL* 188 D2
*Pleasurewood Hills Theme*
  *Park Suff*
  *NR32 5DZ* 165 G2
Pleck *Dorset* 104 D1
Pleck *WMid* 158 B3
Pledgdon Green 151 D5
Pledwick 186 A1
Plemstall 183 F5
Plenmeller 210 D1
Pleshey 137 F1
*Plessey Woods Country*
  *Park N'umb*
  *NE22 6AN* 221 E3
Plockton (Am Ploc) 256 D1
Plocropol 263 G2
Plomer's Hill 135 D3
Plot Gate 116 C4
Plough Hill 159 F3
Plowden 156 C4
Ploxgreen 156 C2
Pluckley 124 B4
Pluckley Thorne 124 B4
Plucks Gutter 125 E2
Plumbland 209 E3
Plumbley 186 B4
Plumley 184 B5
Plumpton *Cumb* 210 A4
Plumpton *ESuss* 109 F2
Plumpton *N'hants* 148 B3
Plumpton Green 109 F2
Plumpton Head 210 B4
Plumstead *GtLon* 137 D5
Plumstead *Norf* 178 C2
Plumtree 174 B4
Plungar 174 C4
Plush 104 C2
Plusha 97 G1
Plushabridge 98 D3
Plwmp 141 G2
Plym Bridge 100 B2
Plymouth 100 A2
*Plymouth City*
  *Airport* 100 B1
*Plymouth Pavilions*
  *PL1 3LF* 81 Plymouth
Plympton 100 B2
Plymstock 100 B2
Plymtree 103 D2
Pockley 203 F4
Pocklington 196 A3
Pockthorpe 178 B3
Pocombe Bridge 102 B3
Pode Hole 176 A4
Podimore 116 C5
Podington 149 E1
Podmore 171 F4
Podsmead 132 A1
Poffley End 133 F1
Point Clear 139 D1
Pointon 175 G4
Polanach 248 B4
Polapit Tamar 98 D2
Polbae 215 D3
Polbain 272 B7
Polbathic 98 D5
Polbeth 235 E3
Poldean 217 F1
Pole Moor 185 E1
Polebrook 161 F4
Polegate 110 A3
Poles 266 E2

*Polesden Lacey Surr*
  *RH5 6BD* 121 G2
Polesworth 159 E2
Polglass 265 G1
Polgooth 97 D4
Polgown 225 F5
Poling 108 C3
Poling Corner 108 C3
*Polkemmet Country Park*
  *WLoth*
  *EH47 0AD* 234 D3
Polkerris 97 D5
Poll a' Charra 254 C3
Polla 273 F3
Pollardras 94 D3
Polldubh 248 D3
Pollie 274 C7
Pollington 186 D1
Polloch 247 G3
Pollok 233 G3
Pollokshaws 233 G3
Pollokshields 233 G3
Polmassick 97 D5
Polmont 234 D2
Polnoon 233 G4
Polperro 97 G4
Polruan 97 F4
Polsham 116 C3
Polstead 152 A4
Polstead Heath 152 A3
Poltalloch 240 A5
Poltimore 102 C3
Polton 235 G3
Polwarth 237 E4
Polyphant 97 G1
Polzeath 96 D2
Pomphlett 100 B2
Pond Street 150 C4
Ponders End 136 C3
Pondersbridge 162 A3
Ponsanooth 95 E3
Ponsonby 198 B2
Ponsongath 95 E5
Ponsworthy 102 A5
Pont Aber 142 D5
Pont Aberglaslyn 167 E3
Pont ar Hydfer 143 E5
Pont Crugnant 155 E3
Pont Cyfung 168 A1
Pont Dolgarrog 168 A1
Pont Pen-y-benglog 167 F1
Pont Rhyd-sarn 168 B5
Pont Rhyd-y-cyff 129 E4
Pont Walby 129 F2
Pont yr Alwen 168 C2
Pontamman 128 C1
Pontantwn 128 A1
Pontardawe 128 D2
Pontarddulais 128 B2
Pontargothi 142 B5
Pont-ar-llechau 142 D5
Pontarsais 142 A5
Pontblyddyn 169 F1
Pontbren Llwyd 129 F2
Pontefract 195 D5
Ponteland 221 D4
Ponterwyd 154 D4
Pontesbury 156 D2
Pontesbury Hill 156 C2
Pontesford 156 D2
Pontfadog 169 F4
Pontfaen *Pembs* 140 D4
Pont-faen *Powys* 143 F4
Pontgarreg 141 F2
Pont-Henri 128 A2
Ponthir 130 C3
Ponthirwaun 141 F3
*Pontlanfraith* 130 A3
Pontllïw 128 C2
Pontllyfni 166 D2
Pontlottyn 130 A2
Pontneddfechan 129 F2
Pontrhydfendigaid 142 D1
Pont-rhyd-y-groes 154 D5
Pontrhydyrun 130 B3
Pontrilas 144 C5
Pont-rug 167 E1
Ponts Green 110 B2
Pontshill 145 F5
Pont-siân 142 A3
Pontsticill 129 G1
Pontwelly 142 A4
*Pontyates*
  *(Pont-iets)* 128 A2
Pontyberem 128 B1
Pont-y-blew 170 A4
Pontybodkin 169 F2
Pontyclun 129 G4
Pontycymer 129 F3
Pontygwaith 129 G3
Pontymister 130 B3
Pontymoel 130 B2
Pont-y-pant 168 B2
Pontypool 130 B2
Pontypridd 129 G3
Pont-y-rhyl 129 F4
Pontywaun 130 B3
Pooksgreen 106 C1
Pool *Corn* 96 A5
Pool *WYorks* 194 B3
Pool Bank 199 F4
Pool Green 158 C2
Pool Head 145 E2
Pool of Muckhart 243 F4
Pool Quay 156 B1
Pool Street 151 F4
Poole 105 G3
*Poole Keynes* 132 B3
*Poole Pottery Poole*
  *BH15 1HJ* 3 B4
Poolend 171 G2
Poolewe 264 E3
Pooley Bridge 210 A5
Pooley Street 164 B3
Poolfold 171 F2
Poolhill 145 G5
Poolsbrook 186 B5
Poolthorne Farm 188 A2
Pope Hill 126 C1
Popeswood 120 D1
Popham 119 G3
Poplar 136 C4
Porchfield 106 D3
Porin 265 K6
Poringland 179 D5
Porkellis 95 D3

Porlock **114** B3
Porlock Weir **114** B3
Port Allen **244** A2
Port Appin (Port na h-Apainn) **248** B5
Port Askaig **230** C3
Port Bannatyne **232** B3
Port Carlisle **218** A5
Port Charlotte **230** A4
Port Clarence **213** E5
Port Driseach **232** A2
Port e Vullen **190** C2
Port Ellen **230** B5
Port Elphinstone **261** F3
Port Erin **190** A5
Port Erroll **261** J1
Port Eynon **128** A4
Port Gaverne **97** E1
Port Glasgow **233** E2
Port Henderson **264** D4
Port Isaac **97** D1
Port Logan **206** A2
Port Lympne Wild Animal Park *Kent*
  CT21 4PD **124** D5
Port Mòr **246** D2
Port Mulgrave **203** G1
Port na Craig **251** E4
Port nan Long **262** D4
Port of Menteith **242** A4
Port of Ness (Port Nis) **271** H1
Port o'Warren **216** C5
Port Penrhyn **181** D5
Port Quin **97** D1
Port Ramsay **248** A5
Port St. Mary **190** A5
Port Solent **107** F2
Port Sunlight **183** E4
Port Talbot **129** D4
Port Wemyss **230** A4
Port William **206** D2
Portachoillan **231** F4
Portavadie **232** A3
Portbury **131** E5
Portchester **107** F2
Portencross **232** C5
Portesham **104** C4
Portessie **268** C4
Portfield *A&B* **239** G2
Portfield *WSuss* **108** A3
Portfield Gate **126** C1
Portgate **99** E2
Portgordon **268** B4
Portgower **275** F7
Porth *Corn* **96** C3
Porth *RCT* **129** G3
Porth Colmon **166** A4
Porth Navas **95** E4
Porthallow *Corn* **95** E4
Porthallow *Corn* **97** G4
Porthcawl **129** E5
Porthcothan **96** C2
Porthcurno **94** A4
Porthgain **140** B4
Porthill **171** F3
Porthkerry **115** D1
Porthkerry Country Park *VGlam*
  CF62 3BY **115** D1
Porthleven **94** D4
Porthmadog **167** E4
Porthmeor **94** B3
Portholland **97** D5
Porthoustock **95** F4
Porthpean **97** E4
Porthtowan **96** A5
Porthyrhyd *Carmar* **142** D4
Porthyrhyd *Carmar* **128** B1
Porth-y-waen **169** F5
Portincaple **241** E5
Portington **195** G4
Portinnisherrich **240** B3
Portinscale **209** F4
Portishead **131** D5
Portknockie **268** C4
Portland Basin Museum *GtMan*
  OL7 0QA **25** H3
Portlethen **261** H5
Portlethen Village **261** H5
Portloe **95** G3
Portlooe **97** G4
Portmahomack **267** G3
Portmeirion **167** E4
Portmeirion Village *Gwyn*
  LL48 6ET **167** E4
Portmellon **97** E5
Portmore **106** C3
Port-na-Con **273** G2
Portnacroish (Port na Croise) **248** B5
Portnaguran (Port nan Giúran) **271** H4
Portnahaven **230** A4
Portnalong **255** J1
Portnaluchaig **247** F1
Portobello **236** A2
Porton **118** C4
Portpatrick **214** B5
Portreath **96** A5
Portree (Port Righ) **263** K7
Portscatho **95** F3
Portsea **107** F2
Portskerra **274** D2
Portskewett **131** E4
Portslade **109** E3
Portslade-by-Sea **109** E3
Portslogan **214** A5
Portsmouth **107** F3
Portsmouth Guildhall
  PO1 2AB
  **82** Portsmouth
Portsmouth Historic Dockyard PO1 3LJ
  **82** Portsmouth
Portsonachan **240** C2
Portsoy **268** D4
Portuairk **246** D3
Portvoller **271** H4
Portway *Here* **144** C3
Portway *Here* **145** D4
Portway *Here* **145** D4
Portway *Worcs* **158** C5
Portwrinkle **99** D5

Portyerrock **207** E3
Posenhall **157** F2
Poslingford **151** F3
Postbridge **99** G3
Postcombe **134** C3
Postling **124** D5
Postwick **179** D5
Potarch **260** E5
Pott Row **177** F5
Pott Shrigley **184** D1
Potten End **135** F2
Potter Brompton **204** C5
Potter Heigham **179** F4
Potter Street **137** D2
Pottergate Street **164** C2
Potterhanworth **175** F1
Potterhanworth Booths **175** F1
Potteries Museum & Art Gallery ST1 3DW
  **85** Stoke-on-Trent
Potterne **118** A2
Potterne Wick **118** B2
Potternewton **194** C4
Potters Bar **136** B4
Potters Crouch **136** A2
Potter's Green **159** F4
Potters Marston **159** G3
Potterspury **148** C3
Potterton *Aber* **261** H3
Potterton *WYorks* **194** D4
Pottle Street **117** F3
Potto **203** E1
Potton **150** A3
Pott's Green **152** A5
Poughill *Corn* **112** C5
Poughill *Devon* **102** B2
Poulshot **118** A2
Poulton **132** D2
Poulton-le-Fylde **191** G4
Pound Bank **145** G3
Pound Green *ESuss* **110** A1
Pound Green *Suff* **151** F2
Pound Green *Worcs* **157** G5
Pound Hill **122** B5
Pound Street **119** F1
Poundbury **104** C3
Poundffald **128** B3
Poundfield **123** E5
Poundgate **109** G1
Poundland **214** C2
Poundon **148** B5
Poundsbridge **123** E4
Poundsgate **99** G1
Poundstock **98** C1
Povey Cross **122** B4
Pow Green **145** G3
Powburn **229** E5
Powderham **102** C4
Powderham Castle *Devon*
  EX6 8JQ **102** C4
Powerstock **104** B3
Powfoot **217** F4
Powick **146** A2
Powis Castle & Garden *Powys*
  SY21 8RG **156** B2
Powler's Piece **113** D4
Powmill **243** F5
Poxwell **104** D4
Poyle **135** F5
Poynings **109** E2
Poyntington **117** D1
Poynton *ChesE* **184** D4
Poynton *Tel&W* **157** E1
Poynton Green **157** E1
Poyntzfield **266** D5
Poys Street **165** E4
Poyston **126** C1
Poyston Cross **126** C1
Poystreet Green **152** A2
Praa Sands **94** C4
Pratis **244** B4
Pratt's Bottom **123** D2
Praze-an-Beeble **94** D3
Predannack Wollas **95** D5
Prees **170** C4
Prees Green **170** C4
Prees Heath **170** C4
Prees Higher Heath **170** C4
Prees Lower Heath **170** C4
Preesall **191** G3
Preesgweene **169** F4
Prenbrigog **169** F1
Prendergast **126** C1
Prendwick **229** E5
Pren-gwyn **142** A3
Prenteg **167** E3
Prenton **183** E4
Prescot **183** F3
Prescott *Devon* **103** D1
Prescott *Shrop* **170** B5
Presley **267** H6
Pressen **228** C3
Prestatyn **182** B4
Prestbury *ChesE* **184** D5
Prestbury *Glos* **146** B5
Presteigne (Llanandras) **144** C1
Presthope **157** E3
Prestleigh **116** D3
Prestolee **184** B2
Preston *B&H* **109** E3
Preston *Devon* **102** B5
Preston *Dorset* **104** D4
Preston *ELoth* **236** C2
Preston *ERid* **197** D4
Preston *Glos* **145** E4
Preston *Glos* **132** C1
Preston *Herts* **149** G5
Preston *Kent* **124** C2
Preston *Kent* **125** E2
Preston *Lancs* **192** B5
Preston *N'umb* **229** F4
Preston *Rut* **161** D2
Preston *ScBord* **237** E4
Preston *Shrop* **157** E1
Preston *Som* **115** D4
Preston *Suff* **152** A2
Preston *Torbay* **101** E1
Preston *Wilts* **132** C5
Preston Bagot **147** D1
Preston Bissett **148** B4
Preston Bowyer **115** E5
Preston Brockhurst **170** C5
Preston Brook **183** G4

Preston Candover **120** B3
Preston Capes **148** A2
Preston Deanery **148** C2
Preston Gubbals **157** D1
Preston Guildhall *Lancs*
  PR1 1HT **192** B5
Preston on Stour **147** E3
Preston on the Hill **183** G4
Preston on Wye **144** C3
Preston Plucknett **104** B1
Preston upon the Weald Moors **157** F1
Preston Wynne **145** E3
Preston-le-Skerne **212** C5
Prestonpans **236** A2
Preston-under-Scar **201** F3
Prestwich **184** C2
Prestwick *N'umb* **221** D4
Prestwick *SAyr* **224** B3
Prestwold **173** G5
Prestwood *Bucks* **135** D2
Prestwood *Staffs* **172** C3
Price Town **129** F3
Prickly Ball Farm & Hedgehog Hospital *Devon*
  TQ12 6BZ **101** E1
Prickwillow **163** D4
Priddy **116** C2
Priest Hill **192** C4
Priest Hutton **199** G5
Priest Weston **156** B3
Priestcliffe **185** F5
Priestland **225** D2
Priestwood **123** F2
Primethorpe **160** A3
Primrose Green **178** B4
Primrose Hill **136** B4
Princes End **158** B3
Princes Gate **127** E1
Princes Risborough **134** D2
Princethorpe **159** G5
Princetown *Caerp* **130** A1
Princetown *Devon* **99** F3
Prior Muir **244** D3
Prior's Frome **145** E4
Priors Halton **157** D5
Priors Hardwick **147** G2
Priors Marston **147** G2
Prior's Norton **146** A5
Priors Park **146** A4
Priorslee **157** G1
Priory Country Park *Bed*
  MK41 9SH **149** F3
Priory Wood **144** B3
Priston **117** D1
Pristow Green **164** C3
Prittlewell **138** B4
Privett **120** B5
Prixford **113** F2
Proaig **230** C4
Probus **96** C5
Protstonhill **269** G4
Prudhoe **211** G1
Prussia Cove **94** C4
Publow **116** D1
Puckeridge **150** B5
Puckington **103** G1
Pucklechurch **131** F5
Pucknall **119** E5
Puckrup **146** A4
Puddinglake **171** E1
Puddington *ChesW&C* **183** E5
Puddington *Devon* **102** B1
Puddlebrook **131** F1
Puddledock **164** B2
Puddletown **105** D3
Pudleston **145** E2
Pudsey **194** B4
Pugneys Country Park *WYorks*
  WF2 7EQ **27** G6
Pulborough **108** C2
Pulborough Brooks RSPB Nature Reserve *WSuss*
  RH20 2EL **108** C2
Puldagon **275** J4
Puleston **171** E5
Pulford **170** A2
Pulham **104** D2
Pulham Market **164** C3
Pulham St. Mary **164** D3
Pulley **157** D2
Pulloxhill **149** F4
Pulrossie **266** E3
Pulverbatch **156** D2
Pumsaint **142** C3
Puncheston **140** D5
Puncknowle **104** B4
Punnett's Town **110** B1
Purbrook **107** F2
Purewell **106** A3
Purfleet **137** E5
Puriton **116** A3
Purleigh **138** B2
Purley **122** C2
Purley on Thames **134** B5
Purlogue **156** C5
Purlpit **117** F1
Purls Bridge **162** C4
Purse Caundle **104** C1
Purslow **156** C4
Purston Jaglin **186** B1
Purtington **103** G2
Purton *Glos* **131** F2
Purton *Glos* **131** F2
Purton *Wilts* **132** C4
Purton Stoke **132** C3
Purves Hall **237** E5
Pury End **148** C3
Pusey **133** F3
Putley **145** F4
Putley Green **145** F4
Putney **136** B5
Putsborough **113** E1
Puttenham *Herts* **135** D1
Puttenham *Surr* **121** D1
Puttock End **151** G3
Putts Corner **103** E3
Puxton **116** B1
Pwll **128** A2
Pwllcrochan **126** C2
Pwlldefaid **166** A5

Pwll-glas **169** E2
Pwllgloyw **143** G4
Pwllheli **166** C4
Pwll-Mawr **130** B5
Pwllmeyric **131** E3
Pwll-trap **127** F1
Pwll-y-glaw **129** D3
Pye Corner *Herts* **136** C1
Pye Corner *Kent* **124** A4
Pye Corner *Newport* **130** C4
Pye Green **158** B1
Pyecombe **109** E2
Pyle *Bridgend* **129** E4
Pyle *IoW* **107** D5
Pyleigh **115** E4
Pylle **116** D4
Pymoor (Pymore) **162** C4
Pymore (Pymore) *Cambs* **162** C4
Pymore *Dorset* **104** B3
Pyrford **121** F2
Pyrford Green **121** F2
Pyrton **134** B3
Pytchley **161** D5
Pyworthy **112** D5

## Q

Quabbs **156** B4
Quadring **176** A4
Quadring Eaudike **176** A4
Quainton **148** C5
Quarff **279** D9
Quarley **119** D3
Quarndon **173** E3
Quarr Hill **107** E3
Quarrier's Village **233** E3
Quarrington **175** F3
Quarrington Hill **212** C4
Quarry Bank **158** B4
Quarry Bank Mill & Styal Estate *ChesE*
  SK9 4LA **184** C4
Quarrybank **170** C1
Quarrywood **267** J5
Quarter **234** B4
Quatford **157** G3
Quatt **157** G3
Quebec **212** A3
Quedgeley **132** A1
Queen Adelaide **163** D4
Queen Camel **116** C5
Queen Charlton **116** D1
Queen Dart **102** B1
Queen Elizabeth Country Park, Petersfield *Hants*
  PO8 0QE **107** G1
Queen Elizabeth Forest Park *Stir* FK8 3SX **241** E4
Queen Elizabeth Hall *GtLon* SE1 8XX **45** H5
Queen Elizabeth II Conference Centre *GtLon*
  SW1P 3EE **44** D6
Queen Elizabeth II Country Park, Ashington *N'umb*
  NE63 9YF **221** E3
Queen Oak **117** E4
Queen Street **123** F4
Queenborough **124** B1
Queen's Bower **107** E4
Queen's Gallery, Buckingham Palace *GtLon* SW1A 1AA **44** B6
Queen's Hall, Edinburgh *Edin* EH8 9JG **37** H6
Queen's Head **170** A5
Queen's View Centre *P&K*
  PH16 5NR **251** D3
Queensbury *GtLon* **136** A4
Queensbury *WYorks* **194** A4
Queensferry (South Queensferry) *Edin* **235** F2
Queensferry *Flints* **170** A1
Queenswood Country Park *Here* HR6 0PY **145** D2
Queenzieburn **234** A2
Quemerford **118** B1
Quendale **279** F9
Quendon **150** D4
Queniborough **160** B1
Quenington **132** D2
Quernmore **192** B1
Queslett **158** C3
Quethiock **98** D4
Quick's Green **134** A5
Quidenham **164** B3
Quidhampton **119** G2
Quidinish (Cuidhtinis) **263** F3
Quilquox **261** H1
Quina Brook **170** C4
Quindry **277** D8
Quine's Hill **190** B4
Quinhill **231** F5
Quinton *N'hants* **148** C2
Quinton *WMid* **158** B4
Quinton Green **148** C2
Quintrell Downs **96** C3
Quixhill **172** C3
Quoditch **99** E1
Quoig **242** D2
Quoigs House **242** D4
Quoisley **170** C3
Quorn (Quorndon) **160** A1
Quorndon (Quorn) **160** A1
Quothquan **226** A2
Quoyloo **276** B5
Quoys **278** F1
Quoys of Reiss **275** J3

## R

R.A.F. Museum, Cosford *Shrop*
  TF11 8UP **157** G2
R.A.F. Museum, Hendon *GtLon*
  NW9 5LL **10** D1
R.H.S. Garden Harlow Carr *NYorks*
  HG3 1QB **194** B2
R.H.S. Garden Hyde Hall *Essex*
  CM3 8ET **137** G3

R.H.S. Garden Rosemoor *Devon*
  EX38 8PH **113** F4
R.H.S. Garden Wisley *Surr*
  GU23 6QB **121** F2
Raasay **264** B7
Rachan **226** C2
Rachub **167** E1
Rackenford **102** B1
Rackham **108** C2
Rackheath **179** D4
Racks **217** E3
Rackwick *Ork* **277** B8
Rackwick *Ork* **276** D3
Radbourne **173** D4
Radcliffe *GtMan* **184** B2
Radcliffe *N'umb* **221** E1
Radcliffe on Trent **174** B4
Radclive **148** B4
Radcot **133** E3
Raddington **114** D5
Radernie **244** C4
Radford *B&NESom* **117** D2
Radford *Nott* **173** G3
Radford *Oxon* **147** G5
Radford *WMid* **159** F4
Radford Semele **147** F1
Radipole **104** C4
Radlett **136** A3
Radley **134** A3
Radley Green **137** E2
Radmore Green **170** C2
Radnage **134** C3
Radstock **117** D2
Radstone **148** A3
Radway **147** F3
Radway Green **171** E2
Radwell *Bed* **149** F2
Radwell *Herts* **150** A4
Radwinter **151** E4
Radyr **130** A4
Raechester **220** B3
Raemoir House **260** E5
Raffin **272** C5
Rafford **267** H6
Ragdale **160** B1
Ragged Appleshaw **119** E3
Raglan **131** D1
Ragnall **187** F5
Rahoy **247** F4
Rain Shore **184** C1
Rainford **183** F2
Rainham *GtLon* **137** E4
Rainham *Med* **124** A2
Rainhill **183** G3
Rainhill Stoops **183** G3
Rainow **185** D5
Rainsough **184** B2
Rainton **202** C5
Rainworth **173** G2
Raisbeck **200** B2
Raise **210** D3
Rait **244** A2
Raithby *Lincs* **176** B1
Raithby *Lincs* **188** D4
Rake **120** D5
Raleigh's Cross **114** D4
Ram **142** B3
Ram Alley **118** D1
Ram Lane **124** B4
Ramasaig **263** G7
Rame *Corn* **95** E3
Rame *Corn* **100** A3
Rampisham **104** B2
Rampside **191** F1
Rampton *Cambs* **150** C1
Rampton *Notts* **187** F5
Ramsbottom **184** B1
Ramsbury **133** F1
Ramscraigs **275** G6
Ramsdean **120** C5
Ramsdell **119** G2
Ramsden **133** F1
Ramsden Bellhouse **137** G3
Ramsden Heath **137** G3
Ramsey *Cambs* **162** A4
Ramsey *Essex* **152** D4
Ramsey *IoM* **190** C2
Ramsey Forty Foot **162** B4
Ramsey Heights **162** A4
Ramsey Island *Essex* **138** C2
Ramsey Island *Pembs* **140** A5
Ramsey Mereside **162** A4
Ramsey St. Mary's **162** A4
Ramsgate **125** F2
Ramsgate Street **178** B2
Ramsgill **202** A5
Ramsholt **153** E3
Ramshorn **172** B3
Ramsnest Common **121** E4
Ranachan **247** G3
Ranby *Lincs* **188** C5
Ranby *Notts* **187** E5
Rand **188** B5
Rand Farm Park *Lincs*
  LN8 5NJ **188** B5
Randwick **132** A2
Rangemore **172** C5
Rangeworthy **131** F4
Ranish (Ranais) **271** G5
Rankinston **224** C4
Rank's Green **137** G1
Rannoch School **250** A4
Ranmoor **186** A4
Rannoch School **250** A4
Ranochan **248** A1
Ranscombe **114** C3
Ranskill **187** E4
Ranton **171** F5
Ranton Green **171** F5
Ranworth **179** E4
Rapness **276** E3
Rapps **103** G1
Rascarrel **208** A2
Rash **200** B4
Rashwood **146** B1
Raskelf **203** D5
Rassau **130** A1
Rastrick **194** A5
Ratagan **257** F3
Ratby **160** A2
Ratcliffe Culey **159** F3
Ratcliffe on Soar **173** F5
Ratcliffe on the Wreake **160** B1
Ratford Bridge **126** B1

Ratfyn **118** C3
Rathen **269** H4
Rathillet **244** B3
Rathliesbeag **249** E1
Rathmell **193** E1
Ratho **235** F2
Ratho Station **235** F2
Rathven **268** C4
Ratley **147** F3
Ratling **125** E3
Ratlinghope **156** D3
Ratsloe **102** C3
Rattar **275** H1
Ratten Row *Cumb* **209** G2
Ratten Row *Lancs* **192** A3
Rattery **100** D1
Rattlesden **152** A2
Rattray **251** G5
Raughton Head **209** G2
Raunds **161** E5
Ravenfield **186** B3
Ravenglass **198** B3
Ravenglass & Eskdale Railway *Cumb*
  CA18 1SW **198** C3
Raveningham **165** E2
Raven's Green **152** C5
Ravenscar **204** C2
Ravensdale **190** B2
Ravensden **149** F2
Ravenshaw **193** F3
Ravenshayes **102** C2
Ravenshead **173** G2
Ravensmoor **170** D2
Ravensthorpe *N'hants* **160** B5
Ravensthorpe *WYorks* **194** B5
Ravenstone *Leics* **159** G1
Ravenstone *MK* **149** D2
Ravenstonedale **200** C2
Ravenstruther **234** C2
Ravensworth **202** A2
Raw **204** C2
Rawcliffe *ERid* **195** F5
Rawcliffe *York* **195** F2
Rawcliffe Bridge **195** F5
Rawdon **194** B4
Rawmarsh **186** B3
Rawnsley **158** C1
Rawreth **137** G3
Rawridge **103** F2
Rawson Green **173** E3
Rawtenstall **193** E5
Rawyards **234** B3
Raxton **261** G1
Raydon **152** B4
Raylees **220** B2
Rayleigh **138** B3
Raymond's Hill **103** G3
Rayne **151** F5
Rayners Lane **136** A4
Raynes Park **122** B2
Reach **151** D1
Read **193** D4
Reading **134** C5
Reading Green **164** C4
Reading Street **124** B5
Reagill **200** B3
Real Mary King's Close, The
  *Edin* EH1 1PG **37** F4
Rearquhar **266** E2
Rearsby **160** B1
Rease Heath **170** D2
Reaster **275** H2
Reaveley **229** E5
Reawick **279** C8
Reay **274** D2
Reculver **125** E2
Red Ball **103** D1
Red Bull **171** F2
Red Dial **209** F2
Red Hill *Hants* **107** G1
Red Hill *Warks* **146** D2
Red Lodge **163** E5
Red Lumb **184** C1
Red Oaks Hill **151** D4
Red Point **264** D6
Red Post *Corn* **112** C5
Red Post *Devon* **101** D1
Red Rail **145** E5
Red Rock **183** G2
Red Roses **127** F1
Red Row **221** E2
Red Street **171** F2
Red Wharf Bay (Traeth Coch) **180** D4
Redberth **127** E2
Redbourn **136** A1
Redbourne **187** G3
Redbrook *Glos* **131** E1
Redbrook *Wrex* **170** C3
Redbrook Street **124** B5
Redburn *High* **266** C5
Redburn *High* **267** G7
Redburn *N'umb* **211** D1
Redcar **213** E4
Redcastle *Angus* **253** D5
Redcastle *High* **266** C7
Redcliff Bay **130** D5
Redcloak **253** E4
Reddingmuirhead **234** D2
Reddish **184** C3
Redditch **146** C1
Rede **151** G2
Redenhall **165** D3
Redesmouth **220** A3
Redford *Aber* **253** F2
Redford *Angus* **253** D5
Redford *Dur* **211** G4
Redford *WSuss* **121** D5
Redgrave **164** B4
Redheugh **252** C3
Redhill *Aber* **260** E1
Redhill *Aber* **261** F2
Redhill *Moray* **268** D6
Redhill *Notts* **173** G3
Redhill *NSom* **116** B1
Redhill *Surr* **122** B3
Redhill Aerodrome & Heliport **122** B4
Redhouse *A&B* **231** G3
Redhouse *Aber* **260** D2
Redhouses **230** B3
Redisham **165** F3
Redland *Bristol* **131** E5
Redland *Ork* **276** C5
Redlingfield **164** C4

Redlynch *Som* **117** E4
Redlynch *Wilts* **118** C5
Redmarley D'Abitot **145** G4
Redmarshall **212** C5
Redmile **174** C4
Redmire **201** F3
Redmoor **97** E3
Rednal **170** A5
Redpath **227** G3
Redruth **96** A5
Redscarhead **235** G5
Redshaw **225** G3
Redstone Bank **127** E1
Redwick *Newport* **130** D4
Redwick *SGlos* **131** E4
Redworth **212** B5
Reed **150** B4
Reed End **150** B4
Reedham **179** F5
Reedley **193** E4
Reedness **195** G5
Reef (Riof) **270** D4
Reepham *Lincs* **188** A5
Reepham *Norf* **178** B3
Reeth **201** F3
Regaby **190** C2
Regil **116** C1
Regoul **267** F6
Reiff **272** B7
Reigate **122** B3
Reighton **205** E5
Reisgill **275** H5
Reiss **275** J3
Rejerrah **96** C4
Releath **95** D3
Relubbus **94** C3
Relugas **267** G5
Remenham **134** C4
Remenham Hill **134** C4
Remony **250** C5
Rempstone **173** G5
Rendcomb **132** C1
Rendham **153** E1
Rendlesham **153** E2
Renfrew **233** G3
Renhold **149** F2
Renishaw **186** B5
Rennington **229** G5
Renton **233** E2
Renwick **210** B3
Repps **179** F4
Repton **173** E5
Rescobie **252** D4
Rescorla **97** E4
Resipole **247** G3
Resolis **266** D5
Resolven **129** E2
Resourie **248** A2
Respryn **97** F3
Reston **237** F3
Restormel **97** F3
Reswallie **252** D4
Reterth **96** D3
Retew **96** D4
Retford (East Retford) **187** E4
Rettendon **137** G3
Rettendon Place **137** G3
Retyn **96** C3
Revesby **176** A1
Revesby Bridge **176** B1
Rew **102** A5
Rew Street **107** D3
Rewe *Devon* **102** C3
Rewe *Devon* **102** B3
Reybridge **118** A1
Reydon **165** F4
Reydon Smear **165** G4
Reymerston **178** B5
Reynalton **127** D2
Reynoldston **128** A4
Rezare **99** D3
Rhadyr **130** C2
Rhandirmwyn **143** E3
Rhaoine **266** D1
Rhayader (Rhaeadr Gwy) **143** F1
Rhedyn **166** B4
Rheged - the Village in the Hill *Cumb*
  CA11 0DQ **210** A5
Rhegreanoch **272** C7
Rheindown **266** C7
Rhelonie **266** C2
Rhemore **247** E4
Rhenigidale (Reinigeadal) **270** D7
Rheola **129** E2
Rhes-y-cae **169** E1
Rhewl *Denb* **169** E3
Rhewl *Denb* **169** E1
Rhewl *Shrop* **170** A4
Rhian **273** H7
Rhicarn **272** C6
Rhiconich **272** E3
Rhicullen **266** D4
Rhidorroch **265** H2
Rhifail **274** C4
Rhigos **129** F2
Rhilochan **266** E1
Rhireavach **265** G2
Rhiroy **265** H3
Rhiston **156** B3
Rhiw **166** B5
Rhiwargor **168** C5
Rhiwbina **130** A4
Rhiwbryfdir **167** F3
Rhiwderin **130** B4
Rhiwinder **129** G4
Rhiwlas *Gwyn* **167** E1
Rhiwlas *Gwyn* **168** C4
Rhiwlas *Powys* **169** F4
Rhode **115** F4
Rhodes Minnis **124** D4
Rhodesia **186** C5
Rhodiad-y-brenin **140** A5
Rhodmad **154** B5
Rhonadale **222** C3
Rhonehouse (Kelton Hill) **216** B5
Rhoose **115** D1
Rhos *Carmar* **141** G4
Rhos Common **156** B1
Rhosaman **128** D2
Rhoscolyn **180** A5
Rhoscrowther **126** C2

Rho - St. J


Rhosesmor 169 F1
Rhos-fawr 166 C4
Rhosgadfan 167 E2
Rhos-goch IoA 180 C4
Rhosgoch Powys 144 A3
Rhos-hill 141 E3
Rhoshirwaun 166 A5
Rhoslan 167 D3
Rhoslefain 154 B2
Rhosllanerchrugog 169 F3
Rhoslligwy 180 C4
Rhosmaen 142 C5
Rhosmeirch 180 C5
Rhosneigr 180 B5
Rhosnesni 170 A2
Rhôs-on-Sea 181 G4
Rhossili 128 A4
Rhosson 140 A5
Rhostrehwfa 180 C5
Rhostryfan 167 D2
Rhostyllen 170 A3
Rhos-y-bol 180 C4
Rhos-y-brithdir 169 E5
Rhosycaerau 140 C4
Rhos-y-garth 154 C5
Rhos-y-gwaliau 168 C4
Rhos-y-llan 166 B4
Rhos-y-mawn 168 B1
Rhos-y-Meirch 144 B1
Rhu 233 D1
Rhuallt 182 B5
Rhubodach 232 B2
Rhuddall Heath 170 C1
Rhuddlan 182 B5
Rhue 265 H2
Rhulen 144 A3
Rhumach 247 F1
Rhunahaorine 231 F5
Rhyd Gwyn 167 F3
Rhyd Powys 155 F2
Rhydargaeau 142 A5
Rhydcymerau 142 B4
Rhyd-Ddu 167 E2
Rhydding 128 D3
Rhydgaled 168 C1
Rhydlanfair 168 B2
Rhydlewis 141 G3
Rhydlios 166 A4
Rhydlydan Conwy 168 B2
Rhydlydan Powys 155 G3
Rhydolion 166 B5
Rhydowen 142 A3
Rhyd-Rosser 142 B1
Rhydspence 144 B3
Rhydtalog 169 F2
Rhyd-uchaf 168 B4
Rhyd-wen 168 C5
Rhyd-wyn 180 B4
Rhyd-y-ceirw 169 F2
Rhyd-y-clafdy 166 C4
Rhydycroesau 169 F4
Rhydyfelin Cere 154 B5
Rhydyfelin RCT 129 G4
Rhyd-y-foel 182 A5
Rhyd-y-fro 128 D2
Rhyd-y-groes 167 E1
Rhydymain 168 B5
Rhydymwyn 169 F1
Rhyd-yr-onnen 154 C2
Rhyd-y-sarn 167 F3
Rhydywrach 127 E1
Rhyl 182 B4
Rhyl Sun Centre Denb LL18 3AQ 182 B4
Rhymney 130 A2
Rhyn 170 A4
Rhynd 243 G2
Rhynie Aber 260 C2
Rhynie High 267 F4
Ribbesford 157 G5
Ribchester 192 C4
Ribigill 273 H3
Riby 188 B2
Riccall 195 F4
Riccarton 224 C2
Richards Castle 145 D1
Richings Park 135 F5
Richmond GtLon 136 A5
Richmond NYorks 202 A2
Richmond SYorks 186 B4
Rich's Holford 115 E4
Rickarton 253 G1
Rickerscote 171 G5
Rickford 116 B2
Rickinghall 164 B4
Rickleton 212 B2
Rickling 150 C4
Rickling Green 150 D5
Rickmansworth 135 F3
Riddell 227 G3
Riddings 173 F2
Riddlecombe 113 G4
Riddlesden 193 G3
Ridge Dorset 105 F4
Ridge Herts 136 B2
Ridge Wilts 118 A4
Ridge Green 122 C4
Ridge Lane 159 E3
Ridgebourne 143 G1
Ridgeway 186 B4
Ridgeway Cross 145 G3
Ridgeway Moor 186 B4
Ridgewell 151 F3
Ridgewood 109 G1
Ridgmont 149 E4
Ridham Dock 124 B2
Riding Gate 117 E5
Riding Mill 211 G1
Ridley 123 F2
Ridleywood 170 A2
Ridlington Norf 179 E2
Ridlington Rut 160 D2
Ridsdale 220 B3
Riechip 251 F5
Rievaulx 203 E4
Rift House 213 D4
Rigg D&G 218 A5
Rigg High 264 B6
Riggend 234 B3
Rigifa 275 J1
Rigmaden Park 200 B4
Rigsby 189 E5
Rigside 225 G2
Riley Green 192 C5
Rileyhill 158 D1
Rilla Mill 97 G2
Rillaton 97 G2
Rillington 204 B5
Rimington 193 E3
Rimpton 116 D5
Rimswell 197 F5
Rinaston 140 C5
Ring o' Bells 183 F1
Ringford 216 A5
Ringinglow 185 G4
Ringland 178 C4
Ringles Cross 109 G1
Ringmer 109 G2
Ringmore Devon 100 C3
Ringmore Devon 102 C5
Ringorm 267 K7
Ring's End 162 B2
Ringsfield 165 F3
Ringsfield Corner 165 F3
Ringshall Herts 135 E1
Ringshall Suff 152 B2
Ringshall Stocks 152 B2
Ringstead N'hants 161 E5
Ringstead Norf 177 F3
Ringwood 106 A2
Ringwould 125 F4
Rinloan 259 K4
Rinmore 260 C3
Rinnigill 277 C8
Rinsey 94 C4
Ripe 110 A3
Ripley Derbys 173 E2
Ripley Hants 106 A3
Ripley NYorks 194 B1
Ripley Surr 121 F2
Riplingham 196 B4
Ripon 202 C5
Rippingale 175 G5
Ripple Kent 125 F4
Ripple Worcs 146 A4
Ripponden 185 E1
Risabus 230 B5
Risbury 145 E2
Risby ERid 196 C4
Risby Suff 151 F1
Risca 130 B3
Rise 197 D3
Riseden 123 G5
Risegate 176 A5
Riseholme 187 G5
Riseley Bed 149 F1
Riseley W'ham 120 C1
Rishangles 152 C1
Rishton 192 D4
Rishworth 185 E1
Risinghurst 134 A2
Risley Derbys 173 F4
Risley Warr 184 A3
Risplith 194 B1
Rispond 273 G2
Rivar 119 E1
Rivenhall 138 B1
Rivenhall End 138 B1
River Kent 125 E4
River WSuss 121 E5
River Bank 150 D1
River Bridge 116 A3
River Link Boat Cruises Devon TQ6 9AJ 101 E3
Riverford Bridge 101 D1
Riverhead 123 E3
Riverside 130 A5
Riverside Country Park Med ME7 2XH 124 A2
Riverton 113 G2
Riverview Park 137 F5
Riviera International Centre Torbay TQ2 5LZ 87 Torquay
Rivington 184 A1
Roa Island 191 F1
Roach Bridge 192 B5
Road Green 165 D2
Road Weedon 148 B2
Roade 148 C2
Roadhead 218 D4
Roadside High 275 G2
Roadside Ork 276 F3
Roadside of Kinneff 253 G2
Roadwater 114 D4
Roag 263 H7
Roast Green 150 C4
Roath 130 A5
Roberton ScBord 227 F4
Roberton SLan 226 A3
Robertsbridge 110 C1
Robertstown Moray 267 K7
Robertstown RCT 129 G2
Roberttown 194 A5
Robeston Cross 126 B2
Robeston Wathen 127 D1
Robeston West 126 B2
Robin Hill Countryside Adventure Park IoW PO30 2NU 107 E4
Robin Hood Derbys 185 G5
Robin Hood Lancs 183 G1
Robin Hood WYorks 194 C5
Robin Hood Doncaster Sheffield Airport 187 D3
Robin Hood's Bay 204 C2
Robinhood End 151 F4
Robins 120 D5
Robinswood Hill Country Park Glos GL4 6SX 132 A1
Roborough Devon 113 F4
Roborough Plym 100 B1
Roby 183 F3
Roby Mill 183 G2
Rocester 172 C4
Roch 140 B5
Roch Bridge 140 B5
Roch Gate 140 B5
Rochallie 251 G4
Rochdale 184 C1
Roche 97 D3
Rochester Med 123 G2
Rochester N'umb 220 A2
Rochester Cathedral Med ME1 1SX 123 G2
Rochford Essex 138 B3
Rochford Worcs 145 F1
Rock Corn 96 D2
Rock N'umb 229 G5
Rock Worcs 157 G5
Rock Ferry 183 E4
Rockbeare 102 D3
Rockbourne 106 A1
Rockcliffe Cumb 218 B5
Rockcliffe D&G 216 C5
Rockcliffe Cross 218 B5
Rockfield A&B 231 G4
Rockfield High 267 G3
Rockfield Mon 131 D1
Rockford 106 A2
Rockhampton 131 F3
Rockhead 97 E1
Rockingham 161 D3
Rockland All Saints 164 A2
Rockland St. Mary 179 E5
Rockland St. Peter 164 A2
Rockley 133 D5
Rockside 230 A3
Rockwell End 134 C4
Rockwell Green 103 E1
Rodborough 132 A2
Rodbourne 132 B4
Rodbridge Corner 151 G3
Rodd 144 C1
Roddam 229 E4
Rodden 104 C4
Rode 117 F2
Rode Heath 171 F2
Rodeheath 171 F1
Rodel (Roghadal) 263 F3
Roden 157 E1
Rodhuish 114 D4
Rodington 157 E1
Rodington Heath 157 E1
Rodley 131 G1
Rodmarton 132 B3
Rodmell 109 G3
Rodmersham 124 B2
Rodmersham Green 124 B2
Rodney Stoke 116 B2
Rodsley 172 D3
Rodway 115 F3
Roe Cross 185 D3
Roe Green 150 B4
Roecliffe 194 C1
Roehampton 136 B5
Roesound 279 C6
Roffey 121 G4
Rogart 266 E1
Rogate 120 D5
Rogerstone 130 B4
Rogiet 131 D4
Rokemarsh 134 B3
Roker 212 D2
Rollesby 179 F4
Rolleston Leics 160 C2
Rolleston Notts 174 C2
Rollestone 118 B3
Rolleston-on-Dove 172 D5
Rolston 197 E3
Rolstone 116 A1
Rolvenden 124 A5
Rolvenden Layne 124 A5
Romaldkirk 211 F5
Roman Baths & Pump Room B&NESom BA1 1LZ 63 Bath
Romanby 202 C3
Romannobridge 235 F5
Romansleigh 114 A5
Romesdal 263 K6
Romford Dorset 105 G2
Romford GtLon 137 E4
Romiley 184 D3
Romney, Hythe & Dymchurch Railway Kent TN28 8PL 124 D5
Romney Street 123 E2
Romsey 119 E5
Romsley Shrop 157 G4
Romsley Worcs 158 B5
Rona 264 C6
Ronachan 231 F4
Ronague 190 A4
Ronnachmore 230 B4
Rood End 158 C4
Rookhope 211 F3
Rookley 107 E4
Rookley Green 107 E4
Rooks Bridge 116 A2
Rook's Nest 115 D4
Rookwith 202 B4
Roos 197 E4
Roose 191 F1
Roosebeck 191 F1
Roosecote 191 F1
Rootham's Green 149 F2
Rootpark 235 D4
Ropley 120 B4
Ropley Dean 120 B4
Ropley Soke 120 B4
Ropsley 175 E4
Rora 269 J5
Rorandle 260 E3
Rorrington 156 C2
Rosarie 268 B6
Rose 96 B4
Rose Ash 114 A5
Rose Green Essex 152 A5
Rose Green WSuss 108 B4
Rose Hill 109 G2
Roseacre Kent 123 G3
Roseacre Lancs 192 A4
Rosebank 234 C5
Rosebrough 229 F4
Rosebush 141 D5
Rosecare 98 B1
Rosecliston 96 C4
Rosedale Abbey 203 G3
Roseden 229 E4
Rosehall 266 B1
Rosehearty 269 H4
Rosehill Aber 260 D5
Rosehill Shrop 157 D1
Roseisle 267 J5
Roselands 110 B3
Rosemarket 126 C2
Rosemarkie 266 E6
Rosemary Lane 103 E1
Rosemount P&K 251 G5
Rosemount SAyr 224 B3
Rosenannon 97 D3
Rosenithon 95 F4
Rosepool 126 B1
Rosevean 97 E4
Roseville 158 B3
Rosewell 235 G3
Roseworth 212 D5
Rosgill 199 G1
Roshven 247 G2
Roskhill 263 H7
Roskorwell 95 E4
Rosley 209 G2
Roslin 235 G3
Rosliston 159 E1
Rosliston Forestry Centre Derbys DE12 8JX 159 E1
Rosneath 233 D1
Ross D&G 207 G2
Ross N'umb 229 F3
Ross P&K 242 C2
Ross Priory 233 F1
Rossdhu House 233 E1
Rossett 170 A2
Rossett Green 194 C2
Rosside 199 D5
Rossie Farm School 253 E4
Rossie Ochill 243 F3
Rossie Priory 244 A1
Rossington 186 D3
Rosskeen 266 D5
Rosslyn Chapel Midlo EH25 9PU 32 D4
Rossmore 105 G3
Ross-on-Wye 145 F5
Roster 275 H5
Rostherne 184 B4
Rosthwaite Cumb 209 F5
Rosthwaite Cumb 198 D4
Roston 172 C3
Rosudgeon 94 C4
Rosyth 235 F1
Rothbury 220 C1
Rother Valley Country Park SYorks S26 5PQ 21 E3
Rotherby 160 B1
Rotherfield 123 E5
Rotherfield Greys 134 C4
Rotherfield Peppard 134 C4
Rotherham 186 B3
Rothersthorpe 148 C2
Rotherwick 120 C2
Rothes 267 K7
Rothesay 232 B3
Rothiebrisbane 261 F1
Rothiemurchus High PH22 1QH 259 G4
Rothienorman 261 F1
Rothiesholm 276 F5
Rothley Leics 160 A1
Rothley N'umb 220 C3
Rothney 260 E2
Rothwell Lincs 188 B3
Rothwell N'hants 160 D4
Rothwell WYorks 194 C5
Rotsea 196 C2
Rottal 252 B3
Rotten Row Bucks 134 C4
Rotten Row WMid 159 D5
Rottingdean 109 F3
Rottington 208 C5
Roud 107 E4
Roudham 164 A3
Rough Close 171 G4
Rough Common 124 D3
Rougham Norf 177 G5
Rougham Suff 152 A1
Rougham Green 152 A1
Roughburn 249 F1
Roughlee 193 E3
Roughley 158 D3
Roughton Lincs 176 A1
Roughton Norf 178 D2
Roughton Shrop 157 G3
Round Bush 136 A3
Roundbush Green 137 E1
Roundham 104 A2
Roundhay 194 C4
Roundstreet Common 121 F5
Roundway 118 B1
Rous Lench 146 C2
Rousay 276 D4
Rousdon 103 F3
Rousham 147 G5
Rousham Gap 147 G5
Routenburn 232 C3
Routh 196 C3
Rout's Green 134 C3
Row Corn 97 E2
Row Cumb 199 F4
Row Cumb 210 C4
Row Heath 139 E1
Row Town 121 F1
Rowanburn 218 C4
Rowardennan Lodge 241 F5
Rowarth 185 E4
Rowbarton 115 F5
Rowberrow 116 B2
Rowchoish 241 F4
Rowde 118 A1
Rowden 99 G1
Rowen 181 F5
Rowfields 172 C3
Rowfoot 210 C1
Rowhedge 152 B5
Rowhook 121 G4
Rowington 147 E1
Rowland 185 G5
Rowland's Castle 107 G1
Rowlands Gill 212 A2
Rowledge 120 D3
Rowlestone 144 C5
Rowley Devon 102 A1
Rowley Dur 211 G3
Rowley Shrop 156 C2
Rowley Park 171 G5
Rowley Regis 158 B4
Rowly 121 F3
Rowner 107 E2
Rowney Green 158 C5
Rownhams 106 C1
Rowrah 209 D5
Rowsham 135 D1
Rowsley 173 D1
Rowstock 133 G4
Rowston 175 F2
Rowthorne 173 F1
Rowton ChesW&C 170 B1
Rowton Shrop 156 C1
Rowton Tel&W 157 F1
Roxburgh 228 B3
Roxby NLincs 187 G1
Roxby NYorks 203 G1
Roxton 149 G2
Roxwell 137 F2
Royal Academy of Arts GtLon W1J 0BD 44 C4
Royal Albert Hall GtLon SW7 2AP 11 F5
Royal Albert Memorial Museum & Art Gallery Devon EX4 3RX 72 Exeter
Royal Armouries Museum, Leeds WYorks LS10 1LT 41 G5
Royal Bath & West Showground Som BA4 6QN 116 D4
Royal Botanic Garden, Edinburgh Edin EH3 5LR 36 D1
Royal Botanic Gardens, Kew GtLon TW9 3AB 11 C6
Royal British Legion Village 123 G3
Royal Centre NG1 5ND 80 Nottingham
Royal Cornwall Museum Corn TR1 2SJ 96 C5
Royal Festival Hall GtLon SE1 8XX 45 F5
Royal Highland Showground Edin EH28 8NB 32 A2
Royal Horticultural Halls GtLon SW1P 2PB 44 D7
Royal Hospital Chelsea GtLon SW3 4SR 13 A5
Royal Leamington Spa 147 F1
Royal Mews, Buckingham Palace GtLon SW1W 0QH 44 B6
Royal Naval Museum PO1 3NH 82 Portsmouth
Royal Oak 183 F2
Royal Observatory Greenwich GtLon SE10 8XJ 13 D5
Royal Opera House GtLon WC2E 9DD 45 E3
Royal Pavilion B&H BN1 1EE 65 Brighton
Royal Scots Regimental Museum, The Edin EH1 2YT 37 E5
Royal Scottish Academy Edin EH2 2EL 37 F4
Royal Tunbridge Wells 123 E5
Royal Victoria Country Park Hants SO31 5GA 4 C4
Royal Welch Fusiliers Regimental Museum Gwyn LL55 2AY 167 D1
Royal Yacht Britannia Edin EH6 6JJ 32 C1
Roybridge (Drochaid Ruaidh) 249 E1
Roydon Essex 136 D1
Roydon Norf 164 B3
Roydon Norf 177 F5
Roydon Hamlet 136 D2
Royston Herts 150 B3
Royston SYorks 186 A1
Royton 184 D2
Rozel 100 C5
Ruabon (Rhiwabon) 170 A3
Ruaig 246 B2
Ruan Lanihorne 96 C5
Ruan Major 95 D5
Ruan Minor 95 E5
Ruanaich 238 B2
Ruardean 131 F1
Ruardean Hill 131 F1
Ruardean Woodside 131 F1
Rubery 158 B5
Ruckcroft 210 B3
Ruckinge 124 C5
Ruckland 188 D5
Rucklers Lane 135 F2
Ruckley 157 E2
Rudbaxton 140 C5
Rudby 203 D2
Rudchester 212 A1
Ruddington 173 G4
Ruddlemoor 97 E4
Rudford 145 G5
Rudge 117 F2
Rudgeway 131 F4
Rudgwick 121 F4
Rudhall 145 F5
Rudheath 184 A5
Rudley Green 138 B2
Rudloe 117 F1
Rudry 130 A4
Rudston 196 C1
Rudyard 171 G2
Rudyard Lake Staffs ST13 8RT 171 G2
Rufford 183 F1
Rufford Country Park Notts NG22 9DF 174 B1
Rufforth 195 E2
Ruffside 211 F2
Rugby 160 A5
Rugby Football Union, Twickenham GtLon TW1 1DZ 11 B6
Rugeley 158 C1
Ruilick 266 C7
Ruishton 115 F5
Ruisigearraidh 262 E3
Ruislip 135 F4
Ruislip Gardens 135 F4
Ruislip Manor 136 A4
Rum 255 J5
Rumbling Bridge 243 F5
Rumburgh 165 E3
Rumford 96 C2
Rumleigh 100 A1
Rumney 130 B5
Rumwell 115 E5
Runacraig 242 A3
Runcorn 183 G4
Runcton 108 A3
Runcton Holme 163 E2
Rundlestone 99 F3
Runfold 121 D3
Runhall 178 B5
Runham Norf 179 F4
Runham Norf 179 G5
Runnington 115 E5
Runsell Green 137 G2
Runshaw Moor 183 G1
Runswick Bay 204 B1
Runtaleave 252 A3
Runwell 137 G3
Ruscombe Glos 132 A2
Ruscombe W'ham 134 C5
Rush Green GtLon 137 E4
Rush Green Herts 150 A5
Rushall Here 145 F4
Rushall Norf 164 C3
Rushall Wilts 118 C2
Rushall WMid 158 C2
Rushbrooke 151 G1
Rushbury 157 E3
Rushden Herts 150 B4
Rushden N'hants 149 E1
Rushford Devon 99 E3
Rushford Norf 164 A3
Rushgreen 184 A4
Rushlake Green 110 B2
Rushmere 165 F3
Rushmere St. Andrew 152 D3
Rushmoor 121 D3
Rushock 158 A5
Rusholme 184 C3
Rushton ChesW&C 170 C1
Rushton N'hants 160 D4
Rushton Shrop 157 F2
Rushton Spencer 171 G1
Rushwick 146 A2
Rushy Green 109 G2
Rushyford 212 B5
Ruskie 242 B4
Ruskington 175 F2
Rusko 215 G5
Rusland 199 E4
Rusper 122 B5
Ruspidge 131 F1
Russ Hill 122 B4
Russel 264 E7
Russell Green 137 G1
Russell's Green 110 C2
Russell's Water 134 C3
Russel's Green 165 D4
Rusthall 123 E5
Rustington 108 C3
Ruston 204 C4
Ruston Parva 196 C1
Ruswarp 204 B2
Rutherend 234 A4
Rutherford 228 A3
Rutherglen 234 A3
Ruthernbridge 97 E3
Ruthers of Howe 275 J2
Ruthin (Rhuthun) Denb 169 E2
Ruthin VGlam 129 F5
Ruthrieston 261 H4
Ruthven Aber 268 D6
Ruthven Angus 252 A5
Ruthven High 259 F1
Ruthven High 258 E5
Ruthvoes 96 D3
Ruthwaite 209 F3
Ruthwell 217 E4
Rutland Water Rut LE15 8QL 161 D2
Ruyton-XI-Towns 170 A5
Ryal 220 C4
Ryal Fold 192 C5
Ryall Dorset 104 A3
Ryall Worcs 146 A3
Ryarsh 123 F3
Rydal 199 E2
Ryde 107 E3
Rydon 112 D5
Rye 111 E1
Rye Foreign 111 D1
Rye Harbour 111 E2
Rye Park 136 C2
Rye Street 145 G4
Ryebank 170 C4
Ryeford 145 F5
Ryehill Aber 260 E2
Ryehill ERid 197 E5
Ryhall 161 F1
Ryhill 186 A1
Ryhope 212 D2
Rylands 173 G4
Rylstone 193 F2
Ryme Intrinseca 104 B1
Ryther 195 E4
Ryton Glos 145 G4
Ryton NYorks 203 G5
Ryton Shrop 157 G2
Ryton T&W 212 A1
Ryton-on-Dunsmore 159 F5


## S


S.S. Great Britain Bristol BS1 6TY 8 B3
Saasaig 256 C4
Sabden 193 D4
Sabden Fold 193 E4
Sackers Green 152 A4
Sacombe 136 C1
Sacombe Green 136 C1
Sacriston 212 B3
Sadberge 202 C1
Saddell 222 C2
Saddington 160 B3
Saddle Bow 163 E1
Sadgill 199 F2
Saffron Walden 150 D4
Sageston 127 D2
Saham Hills 178 A5
Saham Toney 163 G2
Saighdinis 262 D5
Saighton 170 B1
St. Abbs 237 G3
St. Agnes 96 B4
St. Aidan's Winery N'umb TD15 2RX 229 F2
St. Albans 136 A2
St. Albans Cathedral Herts AL1 1BY 136 A2
St. Allen 96 C4
St. Andrews 244 D3
St. Andrew's & Blackfriars Halls Norf NR3 1AU 79 Norwich
St. Andrews Major 130 A5
St. Anne 101 G4
St. Anne's 191 G5
St. Ann's 217 E1
St. Ann's Chapel Corn 99 E3
St. Ann's Chapel Devon 100 C3
St. Anthony 95 F3
St. Anthony-in-Meneage 95 E4
St. Anthony's Hill 110 B3
St. Arvans 131 E3
St. Asaph (Llanelwy) 182 B5
St. Athan 114 D1
St. Aubin 100 C5
St. Audries 115 E3
St. Austell 97 E4
St. Bees 208 C5
St. Blazey 97 E4
St. Blazey Gate 97 E4
St. Boswells 227 G2
St. Botolph's Church, Boston Lincs PE21 6NP 176 B3
St. Brelade 100 B5
St. Breock 97 D2
St. Breward 97 E2
St. Briavels 131 E2
St. Brides 126 B1
St. Brides Major 129 E5
St. Bride's Netherwent 130 D4
St. Brides Wentlooge 130 B4
St. Bride's-super-Ely 129 G5
St. Budeaux 100 A2
St. Buryan 94 B4
St. Catherine 117 E1
St. Catherines 240 D4
St. Clears (Sanclêr) 127 F1
St. Cleer 97 G3
St. Clement Chanl 100 C5
St. Clement Corn 96 C5
St. Clether 97 G1
St. Colmac 232 B3
St. Columb Major 96 D3
St. Columb Minor 96 C3
St. Columb Road 96 D4
St. Combs 269 J4
St. Cross South Elmham 165 D3
St. Cyrus 253 F3
St. Davids Fife 235 F1
St. David's P&K 243 E2
St. David's (Tyddewi) Pembs 140 A5
St. David's Hall CF10 1AH 67 Cardiff
St. Day 96 B5
St. Decumans 115 D3
St. Dennis 97 D4
St. Denys 106 D1
St. Dogmaels (Llandudoch) 141 E3
St. Dogwells 140 C5
St. Dominick 100 A1
St. Donats 114 C1
St. Edith's Marsh 118 A1
St. Endellion 97 D2
St. Enoder 96 C4
St. Erme 96 C5
St. Erney 99 D5
St. Erth 94 C3
St. Erth Praze 94 C3
St. Ervan 96 C2
St. Eval 96 C3
St. Ewe 97 D5
St. Fagans 130 A5
St. Fagans National History Museum Cardiff CF5 6XB 7 A4
St. Fergus 269 J5
St. Fillans 242 B2
St. Florence 127 D2
St. Gennys 98 B1
St. George Bristol 131 F5
St. George Conwy 182 A5
St. Georges NSom 116 A1
St. George's Tel&W 157 G1
St. George's VGlam 129 G5
St. George's Hall, Liverpool Mersey L1 1JJ 42 D3
St. Germans 99 D5
St. Giles' Cathedral, Edinburgh Edin EH1 1RE 37 F4
St. Giles in the Wood 113 F4
St. Giles on the Heath 99 D1
St. Harmon 155 F5
St. Helen Auckland 212 A5
St. Helena 178 C4
St. Helen's ESuss 110 D2
St. Helens IoW 107 F4
St. Helens Mersey 183 G3
St. Helier Chanl 100 C5
St. Helier GtLon 122 B2
St. Hilary Corn 94 C3
St. Hilary VGlam 129 G5
St. Hill 122 C5
St. Ibbs 149 G5
St. Illtyd 130 B2
St. Ippollitts 149 G5
St. Ishmael 127 G2
St. Ishmael's 126 B2
St. Issey 96 D2
St. Ive 98 D4
St. Ives Cambs 162 B5
St. Ives Corn 94 C2
St. Ives Dorset 106 A2
St. James South Elmham 165 E3
St. John Chanl 100 C4
St. John Corn 100 A2
St. John the Baptist Church, Cirencester Glos GL7 2NX 132 C2
St. John's GtLon 136 C5
St. John's IoM 190 A3
St. John's Surr 121 E2
St. John's Worcs 146 A2

St. John's Chapel
 Devon **113** F3
St. John's Chapel
 Dur **211** E4
St. John's Fen End **162** D1
St. John's Hall **211** E4
St. John's Highway **162** D1
St. John's Kirk **226** A2
St. John's Town of
 Dalry **216** A2
St. Judes **190** B2
St. Just **94** A3
St. Just in Roseland **95** F3
St. Katherines **261** F1
St. Keverne **95** E4
St. Kew **97** E2
St. Kew Highway **97** E2
St. Keyne **97** E3
St. Lawrence Corn **97** E3
St. Lawrence Essex **138** C2
St. Lawrence IoW **107** E5
St. Lawrence's Church,
 Eyam Derbys
 S32 5QH **185** G5
St. Leonards
 Bucks **135** E2
St. Leonards
 Dorset **106** A2
St. Leonards
 ESuss **110** D3
St. Leonard's
 Grange **106** D3
St. Leonard's Street **123** F3
St. Levan **94** A4
St. Lythans **130** A5
St. Mabyn **97** E2
St. Madoes **243** G2
St. Margaret South
 Elmham **165** E3
St. Margarets
 Here **144** C4
St. Margarets
 Herts **136** C1
St. Margarets
 Wilts **118** D1
St. Margaret's at
 Cliffe **125** F3
St. Margaret's Hope **277** D8
St. Mark's **190** A4
St. Martin Chanl **101** F5
St. Martin Chanl **100** C5
St. Martin Corn **97** G4
St. Martin Corn **95** E4
St. Martin-in-the-Fields
 Church GtLon
 WC2N 4JH **44** E4
St. Martin's IoS **96** B1
St. Martins P&K **243** G1
St. Martin's Shrop **170** A4
St. Mary **100** C5
St. Mary Bourne **119** F2
St. Mary Church **129** G5
St. Mary Cray **123** D2
St. Mary Hill **129** F5
St. Mary Hoo **137** G4
St. Mary in the
 Marsh **111** F1
St. Mary Magdalene Chapel,
 Sandringham Norf
 PE35 6EH **177** D5
St. Mary the Virgin Church,
 Holy Island N'umb
 TD15 2RX **229** F2
St. Mary the Virgin Church,
 Oxford Oxon
 OX1 4AH **134** A2
St. Mary the Virgin Church,
 Rye ESuss
 TN31 7HE **111** E2
St. Marychurch **101** F1
St. Mary's IoS **96** B1
St. Mary's Ork **277** D7
St. Mary's Airport **96** B1
St. Mary's Bay **111** F1
St. Mary's Church, Whitby
 NYorks
 YO22 4JT **204** C1
St. Mary's Croft **214** B4
St. Mary's Grove **116** B1
St. Maughans
 Green **131** D1
St. Mawes **95** F3
St. Mawgan **96** C3
St. Mellion **99** D4
St. Mellons **130** B4
St. Merryn **96** C2
St. Mewan **97** D4
St. Michael Caerhays **97** D5
St. Michael Church **116** A4
St. Michael Penkevil **96** C5
St. Michael South
 Elmham **165** E3
St. Michaels Fife **244** C2
St. Michaels Kent **124** A4
St. Michaels Worcs **145** E1
St. Michael's Church,
 Hathersage Derbys
 S32 1AJ **185** G4
St. Michael's Mount Corn
 TR17 0HT **94** C3
St. Michael's on
 Wyre **192** A3
St. Mildred's Church,
 Whippingham IoW
 PO32 6LP **107** E3
St. Minver **97** D2
St. Monans **244** D4
St. Mungo Museum of
 Religious Life & Art
 Glas G4 0RH **39** H3
St. Mungo's Cathedral,
 Glasgow Glas
 G4 0QZ **39** J3
St. Neot **97** F3
St. Neots **149** G1
St. Newlyn East **96** C4
St. Nicholas Pembs **140** B4
St. Nicholas VGlam **129** G5
St. Nicholas at
 Wade **125** E2
St. Ninians **242** C5
St. Osyth **139** E1
St. Quen **100** B5
St. Owen's Cross **145** E5
St. Paul's Cathedral,
 London GtLon
 EC4M 8AD **45** J3
St. Paul's Cray **123** D2

St. Paul's Walden **149** G5
St. Peter **100** C5
St. Peter Port **101** F5
St. Peter's **125** F2
St. Petrox **126** C3
St. Pinnock **97** G3
St. Quivox **224** B3
St. Ruan **95** E5
St. Sampson **101** F4
St. Saviour Chanl **101** E5
St. Saviour Chanl **100** C5
St. Stephen **96** D4
St. Stephens Corn **100** A2
St. Stephens Corn **98** D2
St. Stephens Herts **136** A2
St. Teath **97** E1
St. Thomas **102** C3
St. Tudy **97** E2
St. Twynnells **126** C3
St. Veep **97** F4
St. Vigeans **253** E5
St. Wenn **97** D3
St. Weonards **145** E4
St. Winnow **97** F4
St. Winwaloe's Church,
 Gunwalloe Corn
 TR12 7QE **95** D4
Saintbury **146** D4
Salachail **248** C4
Salcombe **100** D4
Salcombe Regis **103** E4
Salcott **138** C1
Sale **184** B3
Sale Green **146** B2
Saleby **189** E5
Salehurst **110** C1
Salem Carmar **142** C5
Salem Cere **154** C4
Salem Gwyn **167** E2
Salen A&B **247** G5
Salen Cere **154** C4
Salen High **247** F3
Salendine Nook **185** F1
Salesbury **192** C4
Saleway **146** B2
Salford CenBeds **149** E4
Salford GtMan **184** C3
Salford Oxon **147** E5
Salford Priors **146** C2
Salfords **122** B4
Salhouse **179** E4
Saline **243** F5
Salisbury **118** C5
Salisbury Cathedral
 Wilts SP1 2EF
 **83** Salisbury
Salkeld Dykes **210** B4
Sallachan **248** B1
Sallachy A&B **240** C3
Sallachy High **266** C3
Sallachy High **257** F1
Salle **178** C3
Sally Lunn's House
 B&NESom BA1 1NX
 **63** Bath
Salmonby **188** D5
Salmond's Muir **245** D1
Salperton **146** C5
Salph End **149** F2
Salsburgh **234** C3
Salt **171** G5
Salt Hill **135** E4
Salt Holme **213** D5
Saltaire **194** A4
Saltash **100** A2
Saltburn **266** E4
Saltburn-by-the-
 Sea **213** F5
Saltburn's Inclined
 Tramway R&C
 TS12 1DP **213** F5
Saltby **175** D5
Saltcoats Cumb **198** B3
Saltcoats NAyr **232** D5
Saltcotes **191** G5
Saltdean **109** F3
Salter **192** B2
Salterbeck **208** C4
Salterforth **193** E3
Saltergate **204** B3
Salterhill **267** K5
Salterswall **170** D1
Saltfleet **189** E3
Saltfleetby All
 Saints **189** E3
Saltfleetby
 St. Clements **189** E3
Saltfleetby St. Peter **189** E4
Saltford **117** D1
Salthaugh Grange **197** E5
Salthouse **178** B2
Saltley **158** C4
Saltmarshe **195** G5
Saltness **277** B8
Saltney **170** A1
Salton **203** G4
Saltrens **113** E3
Saltwell Park, Gateshead
 T&W NE9 5AX **28** B3
Saltwick **221** D4
Saltwood **125** D5
Salum **246** B2
Salvington **108** D3
Salwarpe **146** A1
Salwayash **104** A3
Sambourne **146** C1
Sambrook **171** E5
Samlesbury **192** C4
Sampford Arundel **103** E1
Sampford Brett **115** D3
Sampford
 Courtenay **113** G5
Sampford Moor **103** E1
Sampford Peverell **102** D1
Sampford Spiney **99** F3
Samuelston **236** B2
Sanaigmore **230** A2
Sancreed **94** B4
Sancton **196** B4
Sand Shet **279** C8
Sand Som **116** B3
Sand Hutton **195** F2
Sandaig A&B **246** A2
Sandaig High **256** D3
Sandaig High **256** D3
Sandal Magna **186** A1
Sanday **276** F2
Sanday Airfield **276** F3
Sandbach **171** E1

Sandbank **232** C1
Sandbanks **105** G4
Sandend **268** D4
Sanderstead **122** C2
Sandford Cumb **200** C1
Sandford Devon **102** B2
Sandford Dorset **105** F4
Sandford IoW **107** E4
Sandford NSom **116** B2
Sandford Shrop **170** C4
Sandford Shrop **170** C5
Sandford SLan **234** B5
Sandford Orcas **116** D5
Sandford St. Martin **147** G5
Sandfordhill **269** K6
Sandford-on-
 Thames **134** A2
Sandgarth **277** E6
Sandgate **125** E5
Sandgreen **215** G5
Sandhaven **269** H4
Sandhead **214** B5
Sandhills Dorset **104** C3
Sandhills Dorset **104** B2
Sandhills Surr **121** E4
Sandhills WYorks **194** C4
Sandhoe **211** F1
Sandholme ERid **196** A4
Sandholme Lincs **176** B4
Sandhurst BrackF **120** D1
Sandhurst Glos **146** A5
Sandhurst Kent **110** C5
Sandhurst Cross **110** C5
Sandhutton **202** C4
Sandiacre **173** F4
Sandilands **189** F4
Sandiway **184** A5
Sandleheath **106** A1
Sandleigh **133** G2
Sandling **123** G3
Sandlow Green **171** E1
Sandness **279** A7
Sandon Essex **137** G2
Sandon Herts **150** B4
Sandon Staffs **171** G5
Sandown **107** F4
Sandplace **97** G4
Sandquoy **276** G3
Sandridge Devon **101** E2
Sandridge Herts **136** A1
Sandridge Wilts **118** A1
Sandringham **177** E5
Sandrocks **109** F1
Sandsend **204** B1
Sandside **199** F4
Sandside House **274** E2
Sandsound **279** C8
Sandtoft **187** E2
Sanduck **102** A4
Sandway **124** A3
Sandwell **158** C4
Sandwich Cumb **199** F1
Sandwick Shet **279** D10
Sandwick (Sanndabhaig)
 ESiar **271** G4
Sandwith **208** C5
Sandy Carmar **128** A2
Sandy Bank **176** A1
Sandy Haven **126** B2
Sandy Lane Wilts **118** A1
Sandy Lane Wrex **170** B3
Sandy Lane
 WYorks **194** A4
Sandy Way **107** D4
Sandycroft **170** A1
Sandygate Devon **102** B5
Sandygate IoM **190** B2
Sandyhills **216** C5
Sandylands **192** A1
Sandypark **102** A4
Sandyway **145** D5
Sangobeg **273** G2
Sankyn's Green **145** G1
Sanna **247** D3
Sannaig **230** D3
Sannox **232** B5
Sanquhar **225** F5
Santon Bridge **198** C2
Santon Downham **163** G4
Sant-y-Nyll **129** G5
Sapcote **159** G3
Sapey Common **145** G1
Sapiston **164** A4
Sapperton Derbys **172** C4
Sapperton Glos **132** B2
Sapperton Lincs **175** F4
Saracen's Head **176** B5
Sarclet **275** J4
Sardis **126** C2
Sarisbury **107** E2
Sark **101** G5
Sarn Bridgend **129** F4
Sarn Powys **156** B3
Sarn Bach **166** C5
Sarn Meyllteyrn **166** B4
Sarnau Carmar **127** G3
Sarnau Cere **141** G2
Sarnau Gwyn **168** C4
Sarnau Powys **156** B1
Sarnau Powys **143** G4
Sarnesfield **144** C2
Saron Carmar **128** C1
Saron Carmar **141** G4
Saron Gwyn **167** E1
Saron Gwyn **167** D2
Sarratt **135** F2
Sarre **125** E2
Sarsden **147** E5
Sarsgrum **273** F2
Satley **212** A3
Satron **201** E3
Satterleigh **113** G3
Satterthwaite **199** E3
Sauchen **260** E3
Saucher **243** G1
Sauchie **243** D5
Sauchieburn **253** E3
Sauchrie **224** B4
Saughall **183** E5
Saughall Massie **183** D4

Saughtree **219** D2
Saul **131** G2
Saundby **187** E4
Saundersfoot **127** E2
Saunderton **134** C2
Saunton **113** E2
Sausthorpe **176** B1
Saval **266** C1
Savalbeg **266** C1
Saverley Green **171** G4
Savile Town **194** B5
Sawbridge **148** A1
Sawbridgeworth **137** D1
Sawdon **204** C4
Sawley Derbys **173** F4
Sawley Lancs **193** D3
Sawley NYorks **194** B1
Sawston **150** C3
Sawtry **161** G4
Saxby Leics **160** D1
Saxby Lincs **188** A4
Saxby All Saints **187** G1
Saxelbye **174** D5
Saxham Street **152** B1
Saxilby **187** F5
Saxlingham **178** B2
Saxlingham Green **164** D2
Saxlingham
 Nethergate **164** D2
Saxlingham Thorpe **164** D2
Saxmundham **153** E1
Saxon Street **151** E2
Saxondale **174** B4
Saxtead **153** D1
Saxtead Green **153** D1
Saxtead Little
 Green **153** D1
Saxthorpe **178** C2
Saxton **195** D4
Sayers Common **109** E2
Scackleton **203** F5
Scadabhagh **263** G2
Scaftworth **187** D3
Scagglethorpe **204** B5
Scaitcliffe **193** E4
Scalasaig **238** C5
Scalby ERid **196** A5
Scalby NYorks **204** D3
Scaldwell **160** C5
Scale Houses **210** B3
Scaleby **210** A1
Scalebyhill **210** A1
Scales Cumb **209** G4
Scales Cumb **199** D5
Scalford **174** C5
Scaling **203** G1
Scaling Dam **203** G1
Scallasaig **256** E3
Scallastle **239** G1
Scalloway **279** C9
Scalpay (Eilean
 Scalpaigh) **263** H2
Scamblesby **188** C5
Scammadale **240** A2
Scamodale **248** A2
Scampston **204** B5
Scampton **187** G5
Scaniport **258** D1
Scapa **277** D7
Scapegoat Hill **185** E1
Scar **276** F3
Scarborough **204** D4
Scarborough Sea Life &
 Marine Sanctuary
 NYorks
 YO12 6RP **204** D3
Scarcewater **96** D4
Scarcliffe **173** F1
Scarcroft **194** C3
Scardroy **265** J6
Scarff **278** B4
Scarfskerry **275** H1
Scargill **201** F1
Scarinish **246** B2
Scarisbrick **183** E1
Scarning **178** A4
Scarrington **174** C3
Scarrowhill **210** B2
Scarth Hill **183** F2
Scarthingwell **195** D4
Scartho **188** C2
Scarwell **276** B5
Scatraig **258** E1
Scaur (Kippford)
 D&G **216** C5
Scaur D&G **216** C3
Scawby **187** G2
Scawby Brook **187** G2
Scawton **203** E4
Scayne's Hill **109** F1
Scealascro **270** D5
Scethrog **144** A5
Schaw **224** C3
Scholar Green **171** F2
Scholes SYorks **186** A3
Scholes WYorks **194** C4
Scholes WYorks **185** F2
Scholes WYorks **194** A5
School Green **170** D1
School House **103** G2
Schoose **208** C4
Sciberscross **266** E1
Science Museum GtLon
 SW7 2DD **11** F5
Scilly Isles
 (Isles of Scilly) **96** B1
Scissett **185** G1
Scleddau **140** C4
Sco Ruston **179** D3
Scofton **186** D4
Scole **164** C4
Scolpaig **262** C4
Scone **243** G2
Scones Lethendy **243** G2
Sconser **256** B1
Scoor **238** D3
Scopwick **175** F2
Scoraig **265** G2
Scorborough **196** C3
Scorrier **96** B5
Scorriton **100** D1
Scorton Lancs **192** B3
Scorton NYorks **202** B2
Scot Hay **171** F3
Scotby **210** A2
Scotch Corner **202** B2
Scotch Whisky Heritage
 Centre Edin
 EH1 2NE **37** F4

Scotforth **192** A2
Scothern **188** A5
Scotland **175** F4
Scotland End **147** F4
Scotland Street **152** A4
Scotland Street School
 Museum of Education
 Glas G5 8QB **38** C6
Scotnish **231** F1
Scots' Gap **220** C3
Scotsburn **266** E4
Scotston Aber **253** F2
Scotston P&K **251** E5
Scotstoun **233** E3
Scotstown **248** A1
Scott Willoughby **175** F4
Scotter **187** F2
Scotterthorpe **187** F2
Scottish Exhibition &
 Conference Centre
 (S.E.C.C.) Glas
 G3 8YW **38** B4
Scottish National Gallery
 of Modern Art Edin
 EH4 3DR **36** B4
Scottish National Portrait
 Gallery Edin
 EH2 1JD **37** F3
Scottish Parliament Edin
 EH99 1SP **37** H4
Scottish Seabird Centre,
 North Berwick ELoth
 EH39 4SS **236** C1
Scottish Wool Centre,
 Aberfoyle Stir
 FK8 3UQ **242** A4
Scottlethorpe **175** F5
Scotton Lincs **187** F2
Scotton NYorks **202** A3
Scotton NYorks **194** C2
Scottow **179** D3
Scoughall **236** D1
Scoulton **178** A5
Scounslow Green **172** B5
Scourie **272** D4
Scourie More **272** D4
Scousburgh **279** F9
Scouthead **185** D2
Scrabster **275** G1
Scrafield **176** B1
Scrainwood **220** B1
Scrane End **176** B3
Scraptoft **160** B2
Scratby **179** G4
Scrayingham **195** G2
Scredington **175** F3
Scremby **176** C1
Scremerston **229** E2
Screveton **174** C3
Scriven **194** C2
Scronkey **192** A3
Scrooby **187** D3
Scropton **172** C4
Scrub Hill **176** A2
Scruton **202** C3
Sculcoates **196** D4
Sculthorpe **177** G4
Scunthorpe **187** F1
Scurlage **128** A4
Sea **103** G1
Sea Life Centre, Blackpool
 FY1 5AA
 **64** Blackpool
Sea Life Centre, Brighton
 B&H BN2 1TB
 **65** Brighton
Sea Life Centre, Great
 Yarmouth Norf
 NR30 3AH **179** G5
Sea Life Sanctuary,
 Hunstanton Norf
 PE36 5BH **177** E3
Sea Mills **131** E5
Sea Palling **179** F3
Seabank **248** B5
Seaborough **104** A2
Seaburn **212** D1
Seacombe **183** D3
Seacroft Lincs **177** D1
Seacroft WYorks **194** C4
Seadyke **176** B4
Seafield A&B **231** G1
Seafield SAyr **224** B3
Seafield WLoth **235** E3
Seaford **109** G4
Seaforth **183** E3
Seagrave **160** B1
Seagry Heath **132** B4
Seaham **212** D3
Seaham Grange **212** D2
Seahouses **229** G3
Seal **123** E3
Sealand **170** A1
Seale **121** E3
Sea-Life Adventure,
 Southend-on-Sea S'end
 SS1 2ER **138** C4
Sealyham **140** C5
Seamer NYorks **203** D1
Seamer NYorks **204** D4
Seamill **232** C5
SeaQuarium, Rhyl Denb
 LL18 3AF **182** A4
Searby **188** A2
Seasalter **124** C5
Seascale **198** B2
Seathorne **177** D1
Seathwaite Cumb **209** F5
Seathwaite Cumb **198** D3
Seatle **199** E4
Seatoller **209** E5
Seaton Corn **98** D5
Seaton Cumb **208** D3
Seaton Devon **103** F3
Seaton Dur **212** C2
Seaton ERid **197** D3
Seaton N'umb **221** E4
Seaton Rut **161** E2
Seaton Burn **221** E4
Seaton Carew **213** E5
Seaton Delaval **221** F4
Seaton Junction **103** F3
Seaton Ross **195** G3
Seaton Sluice **221** F4
Seaton Tramway Devon
 EX12 2NQ **103** F3
Seatown Aber **269** J5
Seatown Dorset **104** A3

Seatown Moray **268** D4
Seave Green **203** E2
Seaview **107** F3
Seaville **209** E1
Seavington
 St. Mary **104** A1
Seavington
 St. Michael **104** A1
Seawick **139** E1
Sebastopol **130** B3
Sebergham **209** G2
Seckington **159** E2
Second Coast **265** F2
Sedbergh **200** B3
Sedbury **131** E2
Sedbusk **201** D3
Seddington **149** G3
Sedgeberrow **146** C4
Sedgebrook **175** D4
Sedgefield **212** C5
Sedgeford **177** F4
Sedgehill **117** F5
Sedgemere **159** E5
Sedgley **158** B3
Sedgwick **199** G4
Sedlescombe **110** C2
Sedlescombe
 Street **110** C2
Seend **118** A1
Seend Cleeve **118** A1
Seer Green **135** E3
Seething **165** E2
Sefton **183** E2
Seghill **221** E4
Seifton **157** D4
Seighford **171** F5
Seil **239** G3
Seilebost **263** F2
Seion **167** E1
Seisdon **158** A3
Seisiadar **271** H4
Selattyn **169** F4
Selborne **120** C4
Selby **195** F4
Selham **121** E5
Selhurst **122** C2
Selkirk **227** F3
Sellack **145** E5
Sellafield **198** B2
Sellafield Visitors Centre
 Cumb
 CA20 1PG **198** B2
Sellafirth **278** E3
Sellindge **124** D5
Selling **124** C3
Sells Green **118** A1
Selly Oak **158** C4
Selmeston **110** A3
Selsdon **122** C2
Selsey **108** A4
Selsfield Common **122** C5
Selside Cumb **199** G3
Selside NYorks **200** C5
Selsley **132** A2
Selstead **125** E4
Selston **173** F2
Selworthy **114** C3
Semblister **279** C7
Semer **152** A3
Semington **117** F1
Semley **117** F5
Send **121** F2
Send Marsh **121** F2
Senghenydd **130** A3
Sennen **94** A4
Sennen Cove **94** A4
Sennybridge **143** F5
Senwick **207** G2
Sequer's Bridge **100** C2
Serpentine Gallery GtLon
 W2 3XA **11** F5
Serrington **118** B4
Sessay **203** D5
Setchey **163** E1
Setley **106** C2
Setter Shet **279** E8
Setter Shet **279** E7
Settiscarth **277** C6
Settle **193** E1
Settrington **204** B5
Seven Ash **115** E4
Seven Bridges **132** D3
Seven Kings **137** D4
Seven Sisters **129** E2
Seven Springs **132** B1
Sevenhampton
 Glos **146** C5
Sevenhampton
 Swin **133** E3
Sevenoaks **123** E3
Sevenoaks Weald **123** E3
Severn Beach **131** E4
Severn Stoke **146** A3
Severn Valley Railway
 Shrop
 DY12 1BG **157** G4
Sevick End **149** F2
Sevington **124** C4
Sewards End **151** E4
Sewardstone **136** C3
Sewerby **197** D1
Sewerby Hall & Gardens
 ERid
 YO15 1EA **197** E1
Seworgan **95** E3
Sewstern **175** D5
Seymour Villas **113** E1
Sezincote **147** D4
Sgarasta Mhòr **263** F3
Sgodachail **266** B2
Shabbington **134** B2
Shackerley **158** A2
Shackerstone **159** F2
Shackleford **121** E3
Shadfen **221** E3
Shadforth **212** C3
Shadingfield **165** F3
Shadoxhurst **124** B5
Shadsworth **192** D5
Shadwell Norf **164** A3
Shadwell WYorks **194** C3
Shaftenhoe End **150** C4
Shaftesbury **117** F5

Shafton **186** A1
Shakespeare's Birthplace
 Warks CV37 6QW
 **85** Stratford-upon-Avon
Shakespeare's Globe Theatre
 GtLon SE1 9DT **45** J4
Shalbourne **119** E1
Shalcombe **106** C4
Shalden **120** B3
Shalden Green **120** C3
Shaldon **102** C5
Shalfleet **106** D4
Shalford Essex **151** F5
Shalford Surr **121** F3
Shalford Green **151** F5
Shallowford Devon **114** A3
Shallowford Staffs **171** F5
Shalmsford Street **124** C3
Shalmstry **275** G2
Shalstone **148** B4
Shalunt **232** B2
Shambellie **217** D4
Shamley Green **121** F3
Shandon **233** D1
Shandwick **267** F4
Shangton **160** C3
Shankend **227** G5
Shankhouse **221** E4
Shanklin **107** E4
Shanklin Chine IoW
 PO37 6BW **107** E4
Shannochie **223** E3
Shantron **233** E1
Shantullich **266** D6
Shanzie **252** A4
Shap **199** G1
Shapinsay **277** E6
Shapwick Dorset **105** F2
Shapwick Som **116** B4
Sharcott **118** C2
Shard End **159** D4
Shardlow **173** F4
Shareshill **158** B2
Sharlston **186** A1
Sharlston Common **186** A1
Sharnal Street **137** G5
Sharnbrook **149** E2
Sharneyford **193** E5
Sharnford **159** G3
Sharnhill Green **104** D2
Sharow **202** C5
Sharp Street **179** E3
Sharpenhoe **149** F4
Sharperton **220** B1
Sharpham House **101** E2
Sharpness **131** F2
Sharpthorne **122** C5
Sharrington **178** B2
Shatterford **157** G4
Shatterling **125** E3
Shaugh Prior **100** B1
Shave Cross **104** A3
Shavington **171** E2
Shaw GtMan **184** D2
Shaw Swin **132** D4
Shaw WBerks **119** F1
Shaw Wilts **117** F1
Shaw Green
 NYorks **194** B2
Shaw Mills **194** B1
Shaw Side **184** D2
Shawbost
 (Siabost) **270** E3
Shawbury **170** C5
Shawell **160** A4
Shawfield GtMan **184** C1
Shawfield Staffs **172** B1
Shawford **119** F5
Shawforth **193** E5
Shawhead **216** C3
Shawtonhill **234** A5
Sheanachie **222** C4
Sheandow **259** K1
Shearington **217** E4
Shearsby **160** B3
Shebbear **113** E5
Shebdon **171** E5
Shebster **275** F2
Shedfield **107** E1
Sheen **172** C1
Sheepridge **185** F1
Sheepscombe **132** A1
Sheepstor **100** B1
Sheepwash Devon **113** E5
Sheepwash N'umb **221** E3
Sheepway **131** D5
Sheepy Magna **159** F2
Sheepy Parva **159** F2
Sheering **137** E1
Sheerness **124** B1
Sheet **120** C5
Sheffield **186** A4
Sheffield Botanic Gardens
 SYorks S10 2LN **21** B3
Sheffield Bottom **120** B1
Sheffield Green **109** G1
Sheffield Park Garden
 ESuss
 TN22 3QX **109** G1
Shefford **149** G4
Shefford Woodlands **133** F5
Sheigra **272** D2
Sheinton **157** F2
Shelderton **156** D5
Sheldon Derbys **172** C1
Sheldon Devon **103** E2
Sheldon WMid **158** D4
Sheldwich **124** C3
Sheldwich Lees **124** C3
Shelf WYorks **194** A5
Shelfanger **164** C3
Shelfield Warks **146** D1
Shelfield WMid **158** C2
Shelfield Green **146** D1
Shelford **174** B3
Shellachan A&B **240** A2
Shellachan A&B **240** B1
Shellbrook **159** F1
Shellbrook Hill **170** A3
Shelley Essex **137** E2
Shelley Suff **152** B4
Shelley WYorks **185** G1
Shellingford **133** F3
Shellow Bowells **137** F2
Shelsley
 Beauchamp **145** G1

Shelsley Walsh **145** G1
Shelswell **148** B4
Shelthorpe **160** A1
Shelton *Bed* **149** F1
Shelton *Norf* **164** D2
Shelton *Notts* **174** C3
Shelton *Shrop* **157** D1
Shelve **156** C3
Shelwick **145** E3
Shelwick Green **145** E3
Shenfield **137** F3
Shenington **147** F3
Shenley **136** A2
Shenley Brook End **148** D4
Shenley Church
End **148** D4
Shenleybury **136** A2
Shenmore **144** C4
Shennanton **215** E4
Shenstone *Staffs* **158** D2
Shenstone *Worcs* **158** A5
Shenstone
Woodend **158** D2
Shenton **159** F2
Shenval **259** H2
Shepeau Stow **162** B1
Shephall **149** A5
Shepherd's Bush **136** B5
Shepherd's Green **134** C4
Shepherd's Patch **131** G2
Shepherdswell
(Sibertswold) **125** E4
Shepley **185** F2
Shepperdstown **275** H5
Shepperdine **131** F3
Shepperton **121** F2
Shepreth **150** B3
Shepreth Wildlife Park
*Cambs SG8 6PZ* **150** B3
Shepshed **159** G1
Shepton
Beauchamp **104** A1
Shepton Mallet **116** D3
Shepton Montague **117** D4
Shepway **123** G3
Sheraton **212** D4
Sherborne *Dorset* **104** C1
Sherborne *Glos* **133** E1
Sherborne St. John **120** B2
Sherbourne **147** E1
Sherbourne Street **152** A3
Sherburn *Dur* **212** C3
Sherburn *NYorks* **204** C5
Sherburn Hill **212** C3
Sherburn in Elmet **195** D4
Shere **121** F3
Shereford **177** G5
Sherfield English **119** D5
Sherfield on
oddon **120** B2
Sherford *Devon* **101** D3
Sherford *Som* **115** F5
Sheriff Hutton **195** F1
Sheriffhales **157** G1
Sheringham **178** C1
Sheringham Park *Norf*
*NR26 8TL* **178** C1
Sherington **149** D3
Shernal Green **146** B1
Shernborne **177** F4
Sherramore **258** C3
Sherrington **118** A4
Sherston **132** A4
Sherwood **173** G3
Sherwood Forest Country
Park *Notts*
*NG21 9HN* **174** B1
Sherwood Forest Fun Park
*Notts*
*NG21 9QA* **174** B1
Sherwood Green **113** F3
Sherwood Pines Forest
Park *Notts*
*NG21 9JL* **174** B1
Shetland Islands **279** B7
Shevington **183** G2
Shevington Moor **183** G1
Sheviock **99** D5
Shide **107** E4
Shiel Bridge
(Drochaid Sheile) **257** F3
Shieldaig *High* **264** E6
Shieldaig *High* **264** E4
Shieldhill **234** C2
Shielfoot **247** F2
Shielhill **252** C4
Shiels **260** E4
Shifford **133** F2
Shifnal **157** G2
Shilbottle **221** E1
Shildon **212** B5
Shillingford
*Devon* **114** C5
Shillingford *Oxon* **134** A3
Shillingford Abbot **102** C4
Shillingford
St. George **102** C4
Shillingstone **105** E1
Shillington **149** G4
Shillmoor **220** A1
Shilstone **113** F5
Shilton *Oxon* **133** E2
Shilton *Warks* **159** G4
Shimpling *Norf* **164** C3
Shimpling *Suff* **151** G2
Shimpling Street **151** G2
Shincliffe **212** B3
Shiney Row **212** C2
Shinfield **120** C1
Shingay **150** B3
Shingham **163** F2
Shingle Street **153** E3
Shinness Lodge **273** H7
Shipbourne **123** E3
Shipbrookhill **184** A5
Shipdham **178** A5
Shipham **116** B2
Shiphay **101** E1
Shiplake **134** C5
Shiplake Row **134** C5
Shipley *N'umb* **229** F5
Shipley *Shrop* **158** A3
Shipley *WSuss* **121** G5
Shipley *WYorks* **194** A4
Shipley Bridge
*Devon* **100** C1
Shipley Bridge *Surr* **122** C4
Shipley Common **173** F3

Shipley Country Park
*Derbys*
*DE75 7GX* **18** D2
Shipmeadow **165** E2
Shippea Hill **163** E4
Shippon **133** G3
Shipston on Stour **147** E3
Shipton *Glos* **132** C1
Shipton *NYorks* **195** E2
Shipton *Shrop* **157** E3
Shipton Gorge **104** A3
Shipton Green **108** A3
Shipton Moyne **132** A4
Shipton Oliffe **132** C1
Shipton Solers **132** C1
Shipton-on-
Cherwell **133** G1
Shiptonthorpe **196** A3
Shipton-under-
Wychwood **133** E1
Shira **241** D3
Shirburn **134** B3
Shirdley Hill **183** E1
Shire Hall Gallery, Stafford
*Staffs ST16 2LD* **171** G5
Shire Oak **158** C2
Shirebrook **173** G1
Shirecliffe **186** A3
Shiregreen **186** A3
Shirehampton **131** E5
Shiremoor **221** F4
Shirenewton **131** D3
Shireoaks **186** C4
Shirl Heath **144** D2
Shirland **173** E2
Shirley *Derbys* **172** D3
Shirley *GtLon* **122** C2
Shirley *Hants* **106** A3
Shirley *Soton* **106** C1
Shirley *WMid* **158** D5
Shirley Heath **158** D5
Shirley Warren **106** C1
Shirleywich **171** G5
Shirrell Heath **107** E1
Shirwell **113** F2
Shirwell Cross **113** F2
Shiskine **223** E3
Shittlehope **211** G4
Shobdon **144** C1
Shobley **106** A2
Shobrooke **102** B2
Shocklach **170** B3
Shocklach Green **170** B3
Shoeburyness **138** C4
Sholden **125** F4
Sholing **107** D1
Shoot Hill **156** D1
Shooter's Hill **136** D5
Shop *Corn* **96** C2
Shop *Corn* **112** C4
Shop Corner **152** D4
Shopnoller **115** E4
Shore **184** D1
Shoreditch **136** C4
Shoreham **123** E2
Shoreham Airport **109** D3
Shoreham-by-Sea **109** E3
Shoremill **266** E1
Shoresdean **237** G5
Shoreswood **237** G5
Shoreton **266** D5
Shorley **119** G5
Shorncote **132** C3
Shorne **137** F5
Shorne Ridgeway **137** F5
Short Cross **156** B2
Short Green **164** B3
Short Heath
*Derbys* **159** F1
Short Heath *WMid* **158** C3
Shortacombe **99** F2
Shortbridge **109** G1
Shortfield Common **120** D3
Shortgate **109** G2
Shortgrove **150** D4
Shorthampton **147** F5
Shortlands **122** C2
Shortlanesend **96** C5
Shorton **101** E1
Shorwell **107** D4
Shoscombe **117** E2
Shotatton **170** A5
Shotesham **164** D2
Shotgate **137** G3
Shotley *N'hants* **161** E3
Shotley *Suff* **152** D4
Shotley Bridge **211** G2
Shotley Gate **152** D4
Shotleyfield **211** G2
Shottenden **124** C3
Shottermill **121** D4
Shottery **147** D2
Shotteswell **147** G3
Shottisham **153** E3
Shottle **173** E2
Shottlegate **173** E3
Shotton *Dur* **212** B5
Shotton *Dur* **212** C5
Shotton *Flints* **170** A1
Shotton *N'umb* **221** E4
Shotton Colliery **212** C3
Shotts **234** C3
Shotwick **183** E5
Shouldham **163** E2
Shouldham Thorpe **163** E2
Shoulton **146** A2
Shover's Green **123** F5
Shrawardine **156** C1
Shrawley **146** A1
Shreding Green **135** F4
Shrewley **147** E1
Shrewsbury **157** D1
Shrewton **118** B3
Shri Venkateswara (Balaji)
Temple of the United
Kingdom *WMid*
*B69 3DU* **14** C3
Shrine of Our Lady of
Walsingham (Anglican)
*Norf NR22 6EF* **178** A2
Shripney **108** B3
Shrivenham **133** E4
Shropham **164** A2
Shroton (Iwerne
Courtney) **105** E1
Shrub End **152** A5
Shucknall **145** E3

Shudy Camps **151** E3
Sixpenny Handley **105** G1
Sizewell **153** F1
Skail **274** C4
Skaill *Ork* **277** B6
Skaill *Ork* **277** E7
Skaill *Ork* **276** D1
Skares *Aber* **260** E1
Skares *EAyr* **224** D4
Skarpigarth **279** A7
Skateraw **237** E2
Skaw **279** E6
Skeabost **263** K7
Skeabrae **276** B5
Skeeby **202** B2
Skeffington **160** C2
Skeffling **189** F1
Skegby *Notts* **173** G1
Skegness **177** D2
Skegness Water Leisure
Park *Lincs*
*PE25 1JF* **177** D1
Skelberry *Shet* **279** F9
Skelberry *Shet* **279** D8
Skelbo **266** E2
Skelbo Street **266** E2
Skeldon **224** B4
Skeldyke **176** B4
Skellingthorpe **187** G5
Skellister **279** D7
Skellow **186** C1
Skelmanthorpe **185** G1
Skelmersdale **183** F2
Skelmonae **261** G1
Skelmorlie **232** C3
Skelmuir **269** H6
Skelpick **274** C3
Skelton *Cumb* **210** A4
Skelton *ERid* **195** G5
Skelton *NYorks* **195** E2
Skelton (Skelton-in-
Cleveland) *R&C* **203** F1
Skelton *York* **195** E2
Skelton-in-Cleveland
(Skelton) **203** F1
Skelton-on-Ure **194** C1
Skelwick **276** D3
Skelwith Bridge **199** E2
Skendleby **176** C1
Skendleby Psalter **189** E5
Skenfrith **145** D5
Skerne **196** C2
Skeroblingarry **222** C3
Skerray *High* **273** J2
Skerton **192** A1
Sketchley **159** G3
Sketty **128** C3
Skewen **128** D3
Skewsby **203** F5
Skeyton **178** D3
Skeyton Corner **179** D3
Skidbrooke **189** E3
Skidbrooke North
End **189** E3
Skidby **196** C4
Skilgate **114** C5
Skillington **175** D5
Skinburness **209** E1
Skinflats **234** D1
Skinidin **263** H7
Skinnet **275** G2
Skinningrove **203** G1
Skipness **197** A2
Skippool **191** G3
Skipsea **197** D2
Skipsea Brough **197** D2
Skipton **193** F2
Skipton Castle *NYorks*
*BD23 1AW* **193** F2
Skipton-on-Swale **202** D5
Skipwith **195** F4
Skirbeck **176** B3
Skirbeck Quarter **176** B3
Skirethorns **193** F1
Skirlaugh **196** D4
Skirling **226** B2
Skirmett **134** C4
Skirpenbeck **195** G2
Skirwith *Cumb* **210** C4
Skirwith *NYorks* **200** C5
Skirza **275** J2
Skittle Green **134** C2
Skomer Island **126** A2
Skulamus **256** C2
Skullomie **273** J2
Skyborry Green **156** B5
Skye **255** K1
Skye Green **151** G5
Skye of Curr **259** G2
Skyreholme **193** G1
Slack *Aber* **260** D1
Slack *WYorks* **193** F5
Slackhall **185** E4
Slackhead **268** C4
Slad **132** A2
Slade *Devon* **113** F1
Slade *Devon* **103** E2
Slade *Pembs* **126** C1
Slade *Swan* **128** A4
Slade Green **137** E5
Slade Hooton **186** C4
Sladesbridge **97** E2
Slaggyford **210** C2
Slaidburn **192** D2
Slains Park **253** G1
Slaithwaite **185** E1
Slaley **211** F2
Slamannan **234** C1
Slapton *Bucks* **149** E5
Slapton *Devon* **101** E3
Slapton *N'hants* **148** B3
Slate Haugh **268** C4
Slatepit Dale **173** E1
Slattadale **264** E4
Slaugham **109** E5
Slaughden **153** F2
Slaughterford **132** A5
Slawston **160** C3
Sleaford *Hants* **120** D4
Sleaford *Lincs* **175** F3
Sleagill **199** G3
Sleap **170** B5
Sledge Green **146** A4
Sledmere **196** B1
Sleights **204** B2

Sixmile **124** D4
Slepe **105** F3
Slerra **112** D3
Slickly **275** H2
Sliddery **223** E3
Sliemore **259** H2
Sligachan **255** K2
Slimbridge **131** G2
Slimbridge Wildfowl &
Wetlands Trust *Glos*
*GL2 7BT* **131** G2
Slindon *Staffs* **171** F4
Slindon *WSuss* **108** B3
Slinfold **121** G4
Sling **131** E2
Slingsby **203** F5
Slioch **260** D1
Slip End *CenBeds* **135** F1
Slip End *Herts* **150** A4
Slipper Chapel, Houghton
St. Giles *Norf*
*NR22 6AL* **178** A2
Slipton **161** E5
Slitting Mill **158** C1
Slochd **259** F2
Slockavullin **240** A5
Slogarie **216** A3
Sloley **179** D3
Sloothby **189** E5
Slough **135** E4
Slough Green
*Som* **115** F5
Slough Green
*WSuss* **109** E5
Slyne **192** A1
Smailholm **228** A3
Small Dole **109** E2
Small Hythe **124** A5
Smallbridge **184** D1
Smallbrook **102** B3
Smallburgh **179** E3
Smallburn *Aber* **269** J6
Smallburn *EAyr* **225** F2
Smalldale **185** E5
Smalley **173** F3
Smallfield **122** C4
Smallford **136** A2
Smallridge **103** F2
Smallthorne **171** F2
Smallworth **164** B3
Smannell **119** E3
Smardale **200** C3
Smarden **124** A4
Smaull **230** A3
Smeatharpe **103** E1
Smeeth **124** C5
Smeeton
Westerby **160** B3
Smerclet **254** C3
Smerral **275** G5
Smestow **158** A3
Smethwick **158** C4
Smethwick Green **171** F1
Sminsary **247** F2
Smisby **159** F1
Smith End Green **145** G2
Smithfield **210** A1
Smithies **186** A2
Smithincott **103** D1
Smith's End **150** B4
Smith's Green
*Essex* **151** D5
Smith's Green
*Essex* **151** E3
Smithstown **264** D4
Smithton **266** E7
Smithy Green **184** B5
Smockington **159** G4
Smugglers Adventure *ESuss*
*TN34 3HY* **75** Hastings
Smyrton **214** C2
Smythe's Green **138** C1
Snailbeach **156** C1
Snailwell **151** E1
Snainton **204** C4
Snaith **195** F5
Snape *NYorks* **202** B4
Snape *Suff* **153** E2
Snape Green **183** E1
Snape Watering **153** E2
Snarestone **159** F2
Snarford **188** A4
Snargate **111** F1
Snave **111** F1
Sneachill **146** B2
Snead **156** C3
Snead's Green **146** A1
Sneaton **204** B2
Sneatonthorpe **204** C2
Snelland **188** A4
Snellings **198** A2
Snelston **172** C3
Snetterton **164** A2
Snettisham **177** E4
Snipeshill **124** B2
Snitter **220** C1
Snitterby **187** G3
Snitterfield **147** E2
Snitton **157** D1
Snittlegarth **209** F3
Snitton **157** E1
Snodhill **144** C3
Snodland **123** G2
Snow End **150** C4
Snow Street **164** B3
Snowden Hill **185** G2
Snowdon Mountain Railway
*Gwyn*
*LL55 4TY* **167** G2
Snowshill **146** C4
Snowshill Manor *Glos*
*WR12 7JU* **146** C4
Soar *Cardiff* **130** A4
Soar *Carmar* **142** C5
Soar *Devon* **100** D4
Soay **255** K3
Soberton **107** F1
Soberton Heath **107** F1
Sockbridge **210** B5
Sockburn **202** C2
Sodom **182** B5
Sodylt Bank **170** A4
Soham **163** D5

Soham Cotes **163** D5
Soldon **112** D4
Soldon Cross **112** D4
Soldridge **120** B4
Sole Street *Kent* **124** C4
Sole Street *Kent* **123** F2
Soleburn **214** B4
Solihull **159** D5
Solihull Lodge **158** C5
Sollas (Solas) **262** D4
Sollers Dilwyn **144** D2
Sollers Hope **145** F4
Sollom **183** F1
Solomon's Tump **131** G1
Solsgirth **243** E5
Solva **140** A5
Solwaybank **218** B4
Somerby *Leics* **160** C1
Somerby *Lincs* **188** B4
Somercotes **173** F2
Somerford **132** B2
Somerford Keynes **132** C3
Somerley **108** A4
Somerleyton **165** F2
Somersal Herbert **172** C4
Somersby **188** D5
Somerset House *GtLon*
*WC2R 1LA* **45** F3
Somersham *Cambs* **162** B5
Somersham *Suff* **152** B3
Somerton *Newport* **130** C4
Somerton *Oxon* **147** G5
Somerton *Som* **116** B5
Somerton *Suff* **151** G2
Sompting **109** D3
Sompting Abbotts **109** D3
Sonning **134** C5
Sonning Common **134** C4
Sonning Eye **134** C5
Sontley **170** A3
Sookholme **173** G1
Sopley **106** A3
Sopworth **132** A4
Sorbie **207** E2
Sordale **275** G2
Sorisdale **246** B3
Sorn **225** E3
Sornhill **224** D2
Soroba **240** A2
Sortat **275** H2
Sotby **188** C5
Sots Hole **175** G1
Sotterley **165** F3
Soudley **171** E5
Soughton **169** F1
Soulbury **149** D5
Soulby **200** C3
Souldern **148** A4
Souldrop **149** E1
Sound *ChesE* **170** D3
Sound *Shet* **279** D8
Sound *Shet* **279** C7
Sourhope **228** C3
Sourin **276** D4
Sourton **99** F1
Soutergate **198** D4
South Acre **163** G1
South Alkham **125** E4
South Allington **101** D4
South Alloa **243** D5
South Ambersham **121** D5
South Anston **186** C4
South Ascot **121** E1
South Baddesley **106** C3
South Ballachulish (Baile a'
Chaolais a Deas) **248** C4
South Balloch **215** D3
South Bank **213** E5
South Barrow **116** D5
South Bellsdyke **234** D1
South Benfleet **137** G4
South Bersted **108** B3
South Blackbog **261** F1
South
Bockhampton **106** A3
South Bowood **104** A3
South Brent **100** D1
South Brentor **99** E2
South Brewham **117** E4
South Broomhill **221** E2
South Burlingham **179** E5
South Cadbury **116** D5
South Cairn **214** A4
South Carlton **187** G5
South Cave **196** B4
South Cerney **132** C3
South Chard **103** G2
South Charlton **229** F4
South Cheriton **117** D5
South Church **212** B5
South Cliffe **196** A4
South Clifton **187** F5
South Cockerington **189** D4
South Collafirth **278** C4
South Common **109** F2
South Cornelly **129** E4
South Corriegills **223** F2
South Cove **165** F3
South Creagan **248** B5
South Creake **177** G4
South Crosland **185** F1
South Croxton **160** B1
South Croydon **122** C2
South Dalton **196** B3
South Darenth **137** E5
South Dell
(Dail Bho Dheas) **271** G1
South Duffield **195** F4
South Elkington **188** C4
South Elmsall **186** B1
South End *Bucks* **149** D5
South End *Cumb* **191** E1
South End *Hants* **106** A1
South End *NLincs* **196** D5
South Erradale **264** D4
South Fambridge **138** B3
South Fawley **133** F4
South Ferriby **196** B5
South Field **196** C5
South Flobbets **261** F1
South Garth **278** E3
South Godstone **122** C3
South Gorley **106** A1
South Green *Essex* **137** F3
South Green *Essex* **138** D1
South Green *Norf* **178** B4
South Green *Suff* **164** C4

South Gyle **235** F2
South Hall **232** B2
South Hanningfield **137** G3
South Harefield **135** F4
South Harting **107** G1
South Hayling **107** G3
South Hazelrigg **229** E3
South Heath **135** E2
South Heighton **109** G3
South Hetton **212** C3
South Hiendley **186** A1
South Hill **98** D3
South Hinksey **134** A2
South Hole **112** C4
South Holme **203** F5
South Holmwood **121** G3
South Hornchurch **137** E4
South Hourat **233** D4
South Huish **100** C3
South Hykeham **175** E1
South Hylton **212** C2
South Kelsey **188** A3
South Kessock (Ceasag a
Deas) **266** D7
South Killingholme **188** B1
South Kilvington **202** D4
South Kilworth **160** B4
South Kirkby **186** B1
South Kirkton **261** F4
South Knighton **102** B5
South Kyme **175** G3
South Lakes Wild Animal
Park *Cumb*
*LA12 8JR* **198** D5
South Lancing **109** D3
South Ledaig **240** B1
South Leigh **133** F2
South Leverton **187** E4
South Littleton **146** C3
South Lopham **164** B3
South Luffenham **161** E2
South Malling **109** G2
South Marston **133** D4
South Middleton **229** D4
South Milford **195** D4
South Milton **100** C3
South Mimms **136** B2
South Molton **114** A4
South Moor **212** A2
South Moreton **134** A4
South Mundham **108** A3
South Muskham **174** C2
South Newbald **196** B4
South Newington **147** G4
South Newton **118** B4
South Normanton **173** F2
South Norwood **122** C2
South Nutfield **122** C4
South Ockendon **137** E4
South Ormsby **189** D5
South Ossett **185** G1
South Otterington **202** C4
South Owersby **188** A3
South Oxhey **136** A3
South Park **122** B4
South Parks **244** A4
South Perrott **104** A2
South Petherton **104** A1
South Petherwin **98** D2
South Pickenham **163** G2
South Pool **101** D3
South
Queensferry
(Queensferry) **235** F2
South Radworthy **114** A4
South Rauceby **175** F3
South Redbriggs **269** F6
South Reston **189** E4
South Ronaldsay **277** D9
South Ruislip **136** A4
South Runcton **163** E2
South Scarle **174** D1
South Shian
(Sithean a Deas) **248** B5
South Shields **212** C1
South Shields Museum &
Art Gallery *T&W*
*NE33 2JA* **28** E2
South Somercotes **189** E3
South Somercotes Fen
Houses **189** E3
South Stainley **194** C1
South Stoke
*B&NESom* **117** E1
South Stoke *Oxon* **134** B4
South Stoke *WSuss* **108** B3
South Street *ESuss* **109** F2
South Street
*GtLon* **122** D3
South Street *Kent* **123** F2
South Street *Kent* **124** D2
South Street *Kent* **124** A2
South Tawton **99** G1
South Thoresby **189** E5
South Tidworth **118** D3
South Tottenham **136** C4
South Town *Devon* **102** C4
South Town *Hants* **120** B4
South Uist
(Uibhist a Deas) **254** C1
South Upper
Barrack **269** H6
South View **120** B2
South Walsham **179** E4
South
Warnborough **120** C3
South Weald **137** E3
South Weston **134** C3
South Wheatley
*Corn* **98** C1
South Wheatley
*Notts* **187** E4
South Whiteness **279** C8
South Wigston **160** A3
South Wingfield **173** E2
South Witham **161** E1
South Wonston **119** F3
South Woodham
Ferrers **138** B3
South Wootton **177** E5
South Wraxall **117** F1
South Yardle **158** D4
South Zeal **99** G1
Southall **136** A4
Southam *Glos* **146** B5
Southam *Warks* **147** G1
Southampton **106** C1

Southampton Airport 107 D1
Southbar 233 F3
Southborough GtLon 122 D2
Southborough Kent 123 E4
Southbourne Bourne 106 A3
Southbourne WSuss 107 G2
Southbrook 102 D3
Southburgh 178 B5
Southburn 196 B2
Southchurch 138 C4
Southcott Devon 99 F1
Southcott Wilts 118 C2
Southcourt 134 D1
Southdean 219 E1
Southdene 183 F3
Southease 109 G3
Southend A&B 222 B5
Southend Aber 269 F6
Southend Bucks 134 C4
Southend (Bradfield Southend) WBerks 134 A5
Southend Wilts 133 D5
Southend Airport 138 B4
Southend Pier S'end SS1 1EE 138 B4
Southend-on-Sea 138 B4
Southerfield 209 E2
Southerly 99 F2
Southern Green 150 B4
Southerndown 129 E5
Southerness 217 D5
Southery 163 E3
Southfield 244 A5
Southfields 136 B5
Southfleet 137 F5
Southgate Cere 154 B4
Southgate GtLon 136 C3
Southgate Norf 178 C3
Southgate Norf 177 E4
Southgate Swan 128 B4
Southhill 149 G3
Southington 119 G3
Southleigh 103 F3
Southmarsh 117 E4
Southminster 138 C3
Southmoor 133 F3
Southmuir 252 B4
Southoe 149 G1
Southolt 152 C1
Southorpe 161 F2
Southowram 194 A5
Southport 183 E1
Southport Pier Mersey PR8 1QX 183 E1
Southrepps 179 D2
Southrey 175 G1
Southrop 133 D2
Southrope 120 B3
Southsea Ports 107 F3
Southsea Wrex 169 F2
Southtown Norf 179 G5
Southtown Ork 277 D8
Southwaite Cumb 200 C2
Southwaite Cumb 210 A3
Southwark Cathedral GtLon SE1 9DA 12 B4
Southwater 121 G5
Southwater Street 121 G5
Southway 116 C3
Southwell Dorset 104 C5
Southwell Notts 174 B2
Southwell Minster Notts NG25 0HD 174 C2
Southwick D&G 216 D5
Southwick Hants 107 F2
Southwick N'hants 161 F3
Southwick Som 116 A3
Southwick T&W 212 C2
Southwick Wilts 117 F2
Southwick WSuss 109 E3
Southwold 165 G4
Southwood 116 C4
Sowden 102 C4
Sower Carr 191 G3
Sowerby NYorks 202 D4
Sowerby WYorks 193 G5
Sowerby Bridge 193 G5
Sowerby Row 209 G2
Sowerhill 114 B5
Sowley Green 151 F2
Sowood 185 E1
Sowton 102 C3
Soyal 266 C2
Spa Common 179 D2
Spa Complex NYorks YO11 2HD 83 Scarborough
Spadeadam 219 D4
Spalding 176 A5
Spaldington 195 G4
Spaldwick 161 G5
Spalefield 245 D4
Spalford 174 D1
Spanby 175 F4
Sparham 178 B4
Spark Bridge 199 E4
Sparkford 116 D5
Sparkhill 158 C4
Sparkwell 100 B2
Sparrow Green 178 A4
Sparrowpit 185 E4
Sparrow's Green 123 F5
Sparsholt Hants 119 F4
Sparsholt Oxon 133 F4
Spartylea 211 E3
Spath 172 B4
Spaunton 203 G4
Spaxton 115 F4
Spean Bridge (Drochaid an Aonachain) 249 E1
Spean Bridge Woollen Mill High PH34 4EP 249 E1
Spear Hill 108 D2
Speddoch 216 C2
Speedwell 131 F5
Speen Bucks 134 D2
Speen WBerks 119 F1
Speeton 205 E5
Speke 183 F4
Speldhurst 123 E4
Spellbrook 137 D1
Spelsbury 147 F5
Spen Green 171 F1
Spencers Wood 120 C1
Spennithorne 202 A4
Spennymoor 212 B4
Spernall 146 C1
Spetchley 146 A2
Spetisbury 105 F2
Spexhall 165 E3
Spey Bay 268 B4
Speybridge 259 H2
Speyview 267 K7
Spilsby 176 B1
Spindlestone 229 F3
Spinkhill 186 B5
Spinnaker Tower PO1 3TN 82 Portsmouth
Spinningdale 266 D3
Spirthill 132 B5
Spital High 275 G3
Spital W&M 135 E5
Spital in the Street 187 G3
Spitalbrook 136 C2
Spitfire & Hurricane Memorial, R.A.F. Manston Kent CT12 5DF 125 F2
Spithurst 109 G2
Spittal D&G 215 F4
Spittal D&G 215 E5
Spittal ELoth 236 B2
Spittal N'umb 229 E1
Spittal Pembs 140 C5
Spittal of Glenmuick 252 B1
Spittal of Glenshee 251 G3
Spittalfield 251 G5
Spixworth 178 D4
Splayne's Green 109 G1
Splott 130 B5
Spofforth 194 C2
Spondon 173 F4
Spooner Row 164 B2
Spoonley 171 D4
Sporle 163 G1
Sportsman's Arms 168 C2
Spott 237 D2
Spratton 160 C5
Spreakley 120 D3
Spreyton 99 G1
Spriddlestone 100 B2
Spridlington 188 A4
Spring Grove 136 A5
Spring Vale 107 F3
Springburn 234 A3
Springfield A&B 232 B2
Springfield D&G 218 B5
Springfield Fife 244 B3
Springfield Moray 267 H6
Springfield P&K 243 G1
Springfield WMid 158 C4
Springhill Staffs 158 C2
Springhill Staffs 158 B2
Springholm 216 C4
Springkell 218 A4
Springleys 261 F1
Springside 224 B2
Springthorpe 187 F4
Springwell 212 B2
Sproatley 197 D4
Sproston Green 171 E1
Sprotbrough 186 C2
Sproughton 152 C3
Sprouston 228 B3
Sprowston 178 D4
Sproxton Leics 175 D5
Sproxton NYorks 203 F4
Sprytown 99 E2
Spurlands End 135 D3
Spurstow 170 C2
Spyway 104 B3
Square Point 216 B3
Squires Gate 191 G4
Sròndoire 231 G2
Sronphadruig Lodge 250 C2
Stableford Shrop 157 G3
Stableford Staffs 171 F4
Stacey Bank 185 G3
Stackhouse 193 E1
Stackpole 126 C3
Stacksteads 193 E5
Staddiscombe 100 B2
Staddlethorpe 196 A5
Staden 185 E5
Stadhampton 134 B3
Staffield 210 B3
Staffin 263 K5
Stafford 171 G5
Stagden Cross 137 F1
Stagsden 149 E3
Stagshaw Bank 211 F1
Stain 275 J2
Stainburn Cumb 208 D4
Stainburn NYorks 194 B3
Stainby 175 E5
Staincross 186 A1
Staindrop 212 A5
Staines 135 F5
Stainfield Lincs 175 F5
Stainfield Lincs 188 B5
Stainforth NYorks 193 E1
Stainforth SYorks 186 D1
Staining 191 G4
Stainland 185 E1
Stainsacre 204 C2
Stainsby Derbys 173 F1
Stainsby Lincs 188 D5
Stainton Cumb 199 G4
Stainton Cumb 210 A5
Stainton Dur 201 F1
Stainton Middl 203 D1
Stainton NYorks 202 A3
Stainton SYorks 186 C3
Stainton by Langworth 188 A5
Stainton le Vale 188 B3
Stainton with Adgarley 198 D5
Staintondale 204 C3
Stair Cumb 209 F4
Stair EAyr 224 C3
Stairfoot 186 A2
Staithes 203 G1
Stake Pool 192 A3
Stakeford 221 E3
Stakes 107 F2
Stalbridge 104 D1
Stalbridge Weston 104 D1
Stalham 179 E3
Stalham Green 179 E3
Stalisfield Green 124 B3
Stalling Busk 201 E4
Stallingborough 188 B1
Stallington 171 G4
Stalmine 191 G3
Stalybridge 185 D3
Stambourne 151 F4
Stamford Lincs 161 F2
Stamford N'umb 229 G5
Stamford Bridge ChesW&C 170 B1
Stamford Bridge ERid 195 G2
Stamfordham 220 C4
Stanah 191 G3
Stanborough 136 B1
Stanborough Park Herts AL8 6XF 136 B1
Stanbridge CenBeds 149 E5
Stanbridge Dorset 105 G2
Stanbridge Earls 119 E5
Stanbury 193 G4
Stand 234 B3
Standalone Farm, Letchworth Garden City Herts SG6 4JN 150 A4
Standburn 234 D2
Standedge Tunnel & Visitor Centre WYorks HD7 6NQ 185 E1
Standeford 158 B2
Standen 124 A5
Standen Street 124 A5
Standerwick 117 F2
Standford 120 D4
Standford Bridge 171 E5
Standish Glos 132 A2
Standish GtMan 183 G1
Standlake 133 F2
Standon Hants 119 F5
Standon Herts 150 B5
Standon Staffs 171 F4
Standon Green End 136 C1
Stane 234 C4
Stanecastle 224 B2
Stanfield 178 A3
Stanford CenBeds 149 G3
Stanford Kent 124 D5
Stanford Shrop 156 C1
Stanford Bishop 145 F2
Stanford Bridge 145 G1
Stanford Dingley 134 A5
Stanford End 120 C1
Stanford in the Vale 133 F3
Stanford on Avon 160 A5
Stanford on Soar 173 G5
Stanford on Teme 145 G1
Stanford Rivers 137 E2
Stanford-le-Hope 137 F4
Stanfree 186 B5
Stanghow 203 F1
Stanground 162 A3
Stanhoe 177 G4
Stanhope Dur 211 F4
Stanhope ScBord 226 C3
Stanion 161 E4
Stanklyn 158 A5
Stanley Derbys 173 F3
Stanley Dur 212 A2
Stanley Notts 173 F1
Stanley P&K 243 G1
Stanley Staffs 171 G2
Stanley Wilts 132 B5
Stanley WYorks 194 C5
Stanley Common 173 F3
Stanley Crook 212 A4
Stanley Gate 183 F2
Stanley Hill 145 F3
Stanleygreen 170 C4
Stanlow ChesW&C 183 F5
Stanlow Shrop 157 G3
Stanmer 109 F2
Stanmore GtLon 136 A3
Stanmore WBerks 133 G5
Stannersburn 219 F3
Stanningfield 151 G2
Stannington N'umb 221 E4
Stannington SYorks 186 A4
Stansbatch 144 C1
Stansfield 151 F2
Stanshope 172 C2
Stanstead 151 G3
Stanstead Abbotts 136 C1
Stansted 123 F2
Stansted Airport 150 D5
Stansted Mountfitchet 150 D5
Stanton Derbys 159 E1
Stanton Glos 146 C4
Stanton N'umb 220 D2
Stanton Staffs 172 C3
Stanton Suff 164 A4
Stanton by Bridge 173 E5
Stanton by Dale 173 F4
Stanton Drew 116 C1
Stanton Fitzwarren 133 D3
Stanton Harcourt 133 G2
Stanton Hill 173 F1
Stanton in Peak 172 D1
Stanton Lacy 157 D5
Stanton Lees 173 D1
Stanton Long 157 E3
Stanton Prior 117 D1
Stanton St. Bernard 118 B1
Stanton St. John 134 A2
Stanton St. Quintin 132 B5
Stanton Street 152 A1
Stanton under Bardon 159 G1
Stanton upon Hine Heath 170 C5
Stanton Wick 116 D1
Stanton-on-the-Wolds 174 B4
Stanwardine in the Fields 170 B5
Stanwardine in the Wood 170 B5
Stanway Essex 152 A5
Stanway Glos 146 C4
Stanway Green Essex 152 A5
Stanway Green Suff 164 D4
Stanwell 135 F5
Stanwell Moor 135 F5
Stanwick 161 E5
Stanwix 210 A2
Stanydale 279 B7
Staoinebrig 254 C1
Stapeley 171 D3
Stapeley Water Gardens ChesE CW5 7LH 171 D2
Stapenhill 173 D5
Staple Kent 125 E3
Staple Som 115 E3
Staple Cross 114 D5
Staple Fitzpaine 103 F1
Staplecross 110 C1
Staplefield 109 E1
Stapleford Cambs 150 C2
Stapleford Herts 136 C1
Stapleford Leics 160 D1
Stapleford Lincs 175 D2
Stapleford Notts 173 F4
Stapleford Wilts 118 B4
Stapleford Abbotts 137 D3
Stapleford Tawney 137 E3
Staplegrove 115 F5
Staplehay 115 F5
Staplehurst 123 G4
Staplers 107 E4
Staplestreet 124 C2
Stapleton Cumb 218 D4
Stapleton Here 144 C1
Stapleton Leics 159 G3
Stapleton NYorks 202 B1
Stapleton Shrop 157 D2
Stapleton Som 116 B5
Stapley 103 E1
Staploe 149 G1
Staplow 145 F3
Star Fife 244 B4
Star Pembs 141 F4
Star Som 116 B2
Starbotton 201 E5
Starcross 102 C4
Stareton 159 F5
Starkholmes 173 E2
Starling 184 B1
Starling's Green 150 C4
Starr 215 F1
Starston 164 D3
Startforth 201 F1
Startley 132 B4
Statham 184 A4
Stathe 116 A5
Stathern 174 C4
Station Town 212 D4
Staughton Green 149 G1
Staughton Highway 149 G1
Staunton Glos 131 E1
Staunton Glos 145 G5
Staunton Harold Hall 173 E5
Staunton Harold Reservoir Derbys DE73 8DN 173 E5
Staunton in the Vale 174 D3
Staunton on Arrow 144 C1
Staunton on Wye 144 C3
Staveley Cumb 199 F3
Staveley Derbys 186 B5
Staveley NYorks 194 C1
Staveley-in-Cartmel 199 E4
Staverton Devon 101 D1
Staverton Glos 146 A5
Staverton N'hants 148 A1
Staverton Wilts 117 F1
Staverton Bridge 146 A5
Stawell 116 A4
Stawley 115 D5
Staxigoe 275 J3
Staxton 204 D5
Staylittle (Penffordd-las) 155 E3
Staynall 191 G3
Staythorpe 174 C2
Stean 201 F5
Steane 148 A4
Stearsby 203 F5
Steart 115 F3
Stebbing 151 E5
Stebbing Green 151 E5
Stechford 158 D4
Stedham 121 D5
Steel Cross 123 E5
Steel Green 198 C5
Steele Road 218 D2
Steen's Bridge 145 E2
Steep 120 C5
Steep Marsh 120 C5
Steeple Dorset 105 F4
Steeple Essex 138 C2
Steeple Ashton 118 A2
Steeple Aston 147 G5
Steeple Barton 147 G5
Steeple Bumpstead 151 E3
Steeple Claydon 148 B5
Steeple Gidding 161 G4
Steeple Langford 118 B4
Steeple Morden 150 A3
Steeraway 157 F2
Steeton 193 G3
Stein 263 H6
Steinis 271 G4
Steinmanhill 269 F6
Stella 212 A1
Stelling Minnis 124 D4
Stembridge 116 B5
Stemster High 275 G2
Stemster High 275 G4
Stemster House 275 G2
Stenalees 97 E4
Stenhill 103 D1
Stenhousemuir 234 C1
Stenigot 188 C4
Stenness 278 B5
Stenscholl 263 K5
Stenson 173 E5
Stenton ELoth 236 D2
Stenton P&K 251 F5
Stepaside Pembs 127 E2
Stepaside Powys 155 G4
Stepney 136 C4
Steppingley 149 F4
Stepps 234 A3
Sternfield 153 E1
Sterridge 113 F1
Stert 118 B2
Stetchworth 151 E2
Stevenage 150 A5
Stevenston 233 D5
Steventon Hants 119 G3
Steventon Oxon 133 G3
Steventon End 151 E3
Stevington 149 E2
Stewart Park, Middlesbrough Middl TS7 8AR 29 C4
Stewartby 149 F3
Stewarton D&G 207 E2
Stewarton EAyr 233 F5
Stewkley 149 D5
Stewley 103 G1
Stewton 189 D4
Steyning 109 D2
Steynton 126 C2
Stibb 112 C4
Stibb Cross 113 E4
Stibb Green 118 D1
Stibbard 178 A3
Stibbington 161 F3
Stichill 228 B3
Sticker 97 D4
Stickford 176 B1
Sticklepath Devon 99 G1
Sticklepath Som 103 G1
Stickling Green 150 C4
Stickney 176 B2
Stiff Street 124 A2
Stiffkey 178 A1
Stifford's Bridge 145 G3
Stileway 116 B3
Stilligarry (Stadhlaigearraidh) 254 C1
Stillingfleet 195 E3
Stillington NYorks 195 E1
Stillington Stock 212 C5
Stilton 161 G4
Stinchcombe 131 G3
Stinsford 104 D3
Stirchley Tel&W 157 G2
Stirchley WMid 158 C4
Stirkoke House 275 J3
Stirling Aber 269 K6
Stirling (Sruighlea) Stir 242 C5
Stirling Castle Stir FK8 1EJ 242 C5
Stirling Visitor Centre Stir FK8 1EH 242 C5
Stirton 193 F2
Stisted 151 G5
Stitchcombe 118 D1
Stithians 95 E3
Stittenham 266 D4
Stivichall 159 F5
Stix 250 C5
Stixwould 175 G1
Stoak 183 F5
Stobo 226 C2
Stoborough 105 F4
Stoborough Green 105 F4
Stobwood 235 D4
Stock 137 F3
Stock Green 146 B2
Stock Lane 133 E5
Stock Wood 146 C2
Stockbridge Hants 119 E4
Stockbridge Stir 242 C4
Stockbridge WSuss 108 A3
Stockbury 124 A2
Stockcross 119 F1
Stockdale 95 E3
Stockdalewath 209 G2
Stockerston 160 D3
Stockgrove Country Park CenBeds LU7 0BA 149 E5
Stocking Green Essex 151 D4
Stocking Green MK 148 D3
Stocking Pelham 150 C5
Stockingford 159 F3
Stockinish (Stocinis) 263 G2
Stockland Cardiff 130 A5
Stockland Devon 103 F2
Stockland Bristol 115 F3
Stockleigh English 102 B2
Stockleigh Pomeroy 102 B2
Stockley 118 B1
Stocklinch 103 G1
Stockport 184 C3
Stocksbridge 185 G3
Stocksfield 211 G1
Stockton Here 145 E1
Stockton Norf 165 E2
Stockton Shrop 157 G3
Stockton Shrop 156 B2
Stockton Tel&W 157 G1
Stockton Warks 147 G1
Stockton Wilts 118 A4
Stockton Heath 184 A4
Stockton on Teme 145 G1
Stockton on the Forest 195 F2
Stockton-on-Tees 202 D1
Stockwell 132 B1
Stockwell Heath 172 B5
Stockwood Bristol 116 D1
Stockwood Dorset 104 B2
Stodday 192 A2
Stodmarsh 125 E2
Stody 178 B2
Stoer 272 C6
Stoford Som 104 B1
Stoford Wilts 118 B4
Stogumber 115 D4
Stogursey 115 F3
Stoke Devon 112 C3
Stoke Hants 119 F2
Stoke Hants 107 G2
Stoke Med 124 A1
Stoke Plym 100 A2
Stoke WMid 159 F5
Stoke Abbott 104 A2
Stoke Albany 160 D4
Stoke Ash 164 C4
Stoke Bardolph 174 B3
Stoke Bishop 131 E5
Stoke Bliss 145 F1
Stoke Bruerne 148 C2
Stoke by Clare 151 F3
Stoke Canon 102 C3
Stoke Charity 119 F4
Stoke Climsland 99 D3
Stoke D'Abernon 121 G2
Stoke Doyle 161 F4
Stoke Dry 161 D3
Stoke Edith 145 F3
Stoke Farthing 118 B5
Stoke Ferry 163 F3
Stoke Fleming 101 E3
Stoke Gabriel 101 E2
Stoke Gifford 131 F5
Stoke Golding 159 F3
Stoke Goldington 148 D3
Stoke Green 135 E4
Stoke Hammond 149 D5
Stoke Heath Shrop 171 D5
Stoke Heath Worcs 146 B1
Stoke Holy Cross 178 D5
Stoke Lacy 145 F3
Stoke Lyne 148 A5
Stoke Mandeville 134 D1
Stoke Newington 136 C4
Stoke on Tern 170 D5
Stoke Orchard 146 B5
Stoke Pero 114 B3
Stoke Poges 135 E4
Stoke Pound 146 B1
Stoke Prior Here 145 E2
Stoke Prior Worcs 146 B1
Stoke Rivers 113 G2
Stoke Rochford 175 E5
Stoke Row 134 B4
Stoke St. Gregory 116 A5
Stoke St. Mary 115 F5
Stoke St. Michael 117 D3
Stoke St. Milborough 157 E4
Stoke sub Hamdon 104 A1
Stoke Talmage 134 B3
Stoke Trister 117 E5
Stoke Villice 116 C1
Stoke Wake 105 D2
Stoke-by-Nayland 152 A4
Stokeford 105 E4
Stokeham 187 E5
Stokeinteignhead 102 C5
Stokenchurch 134 C3
Stokenham 101 E3
Stoke-on-Trent 171 F3
Stokesay 156 D4
Stokesby 179 F4
Stokesley 203 E2
Stolford 115 F3
Ston Easton 116 D2
Stonar Cut 125 F2
Stondon Massey 137 E2
Stone Bucks 134 C1
Stone Glos 131 F3
Stone Kent 137 E5
Stone Kent 111 E1
Stone Som 116 C4
Stone Staffs 171 G4
Stone SYorks 186 C4
Stone Worcs 158 A5
Stone Allerton 116 B2
Stone Cross Dur 201 F1
Stone Cross ESuss 110 B3
Stone Cross ESuss 110 A1
Stone Cross Kent 124 C5
Stone Cross Kent 123 E5
Stone House 200 C4
Stone Street Kent 123 E3
Stone Street Suff 165 E3
Stone Street Suff 152 A4
Stonea 162 C3
Stonebridge ESuss 110 A1
Stonebridge NSom 116 A2
Stonebridge Warks 159 E4
Stonebroom 173 F2
Stonecross Green 151 G2
Stonefield A&B 231 G2
Stonefield Staffs 171 G4
Stonegate ESuss 110 B1
Stonegate NYorks 203 G2
Stonegrave 203 F5
Stonehaugh 219 F4
Stonehaven 253 G1
Stonehenge Wilts SP4 7DE 118 C3
Stonehill 121 E1
Stonehouse ChesW&C 183 G5
Stonehouse D&G 216 C4
Stonehouse Glos 132 A2
Stonehouse N'umb 210 C2
Stonehouse Plym 100 A2
Stonehouse SLan 234 B5
Stoneleigh Surr 122 B2
Stoneleigh Warks 159 F5
Stoneley Green 170 D2
Stonely 149 G1
Stoner Hill 120 C5
Stones 193 F5
Stones Green 152 C5
Stonesby 174 D5
Stonesfield 133 F1
Stonestreet Green 124 C5
Stonethwaite 209 F5
Stoney Cross 106 B1
Stoney Middleton 185 G5
Stoney Stanton 159 G3
Stoney Stoke 117 E4
Stoney Stratton 117 D4
Stoney Stretton 156 C2
Stoneyburn 235 D3
Stoneyford 103 D4
Stoneygate 160 B2
Stoneyhills 138 C3
Stoneykirk 214 B5
Stoneywood 261 G3
Stonganess 278 E2
Stonham Aspal 152 C2
Stonham Barns Suff IP14 6AT 152 C2
Stonnall 158 C2
Stonor 134 C4
Stonton Wyville 160 C3
Stony Houghton 173 F1
Stony Stratford 148 C3
Stonybreck 278 A1
Stoodleigh Devon 102 C1
Stoodleigh Devon 113 G2
Stopham 108 C2
Stopsley 149 G5
Stoptide 96 D2
Storeton 183 E4
Stormontfield 243 G2
Stornoway (Steornabhagh) 271 G4
Stornoway Airport 271 G4
Storridge 145 G3
Storrington 108 C2
Storrs 185 G4
Storth 199 F4
Storwood 195 G3
Storybook Glen Aber AB12 5FT 261 G5
Stotfield 267 K4
Stotfold 150 A4
Stottesdon 157 F4
Stoughton Leics 160 B2
Stoughton Surr 121 E2
Stoughton WSuss 107 G1
Stoughton Cross 116 B3
Stoul 256 D5
Stoulton 146 B3
Stour Provost 117 E5
Stour Row 117 F5
Stourbridge 158 A4
Stourhead Wilts BA12 6QD 117 E4
Stourpaine 105 E2
Stourport-on-Severn 158 A5
Stourton Staffs 158 A4
Stourton Warks 147 E4
Stourton Wilts 117 E4
Stourton Caundle 104 D1
Stove 276 F4
Stoven 165 F3
Stow Lincs 187 F4
Stow ScBord 236 B5
Stow Bardolph 163 E2
Stow Bedon 164 A2
Stow cum Quy 150 D1
Stow Longa 161 G5
Stow Maries 138 B3
Stow Pasture 187 F4
Stowbridge 163 D2
Stowe Glos 131 E2
Stowe Shrop 156 C5
Stowe Staffs 158 D1
Stowe Landscape Gardens Bucks MK18 5DQ 148 B4
Stowe-by-Chartley 172 B5
Stowehill 148 B2
Stowell Glos 132 C1
Stowell Som 117 D5
Stowey 116 C2
Stowford Devon 99 E2
Stowford Devon 113 G3
Stowford Devon 103 E4
Stowlangtoft 152 A1
Stowmarket 152 B2
Stow-on-the-Wold 147 D5
Stowting 124 D4
Stowupland 152 B2
Straad 232 B3
Stracathro 253 E3
Strachan 260 E5
Strachur (Clachan Strachur) 240 C4
Stradbroke 164 D4
Stradishall 151 F2
Stradsett 163 E2
Stragglethorpe 175 E2
Straight Soley 133 F5
Straiton Edin 235 G3
Straiton SAyr 224 B5
Straloch Aber 261 G2
Straloch P&K 251 F3
Stramshall 172 B4
Strands 198 C4
Strang 190 B4
Strangford 145 E5
Strannda 263 F3
Stranraer 214 B4
Strata Florida 142 D1
Stratfield Mortimer 120 B1
Stratfield Saye 120 B1
Stratfield Turgis 120 B2
Stratford CenBeds 149 G3
Stratford Glos 146 A4
Stratford GtLon 136 C4
Stratford St. Andrew 153 E2
Stratford St. Mary 152 B4
Stratford sub Castle 118 C4
Stratford Tony 118 B5
Stratford-upon-Avon 147 E2
Stratford-upon-Avon Butterfly Farm Warks CV37 7LS 85 Stratford-upon-Avon
Strath 275 H3
Strathan High 272 C6
Strathan High 257 F5
Strathaven 234 B5
Strathblane 233 G2
Strathcanaird 265 H1
Strathcarron 265 F7
Strathclyde Country Park NLan ML1 3ED 31 G5
Strathdon 260 B3
Strathgirnock 260 B5
Strathkinness 244 C3
Strathmiglo 244 A3
Strathpeffer (Strath Pheofhair) 266 B6
Strathrannoch 265 K4
Strathtay 251 E4
Strathwhillan 223 F2
Strathy 274 D2
Strathyre 242 A3
Stratton Corn 112 C5
Stratton Dorset 104 C3
Stratton Glos 132 C2
Stratton Audley 148 B5
Stratton Hall 152 D4
Stratton St. Margaret 133 D4
Stratton St. Michael 164 D2
Stratton Strawless 178 D3
Stratton-on-the-Fosse 117 D2
Stravanan 232 B4
Stravithie 244 D3
Strawberry Hill 136 A5
Stream 115 D4
Streat 109 F2
Streatham 136 B5
Streatham Vale 136 B5
Streatley CenBeds 149 F5
Streatley WBerks 134 A4
Street Devon 103 E4
Street Lancs 192 B2
Street NYorks 203 G2
Street Som 116 B4

Street Som 103 G2
Street Ashton 159 G4
Street Dinas 170 A4
Street End 108 A4
Street Gate 212 B2
Street Houses 195 E3
Street Lane 173 E3
Street on the Fosse 116 D4
Streethay 158 D1
Streethouse 194 C5
Streetlam 202 C3
Streetly 158 C3
Streetly End 151 E3
Strefford 156 D4
Strelley 173 G3
Strensall 195 F1
Strensham 146 B3
Stretcholt 115 F3
Strete 101 E3
Stretford GtMan 184 B3
Stretford Here 144 D2
Stretford Here 145 E2
Strethall 150 C4
Stretham 162 D5
Strettington 108 A3
Stretton ChesW&C 170 B2
Stretton Derbys 173 E1
Stretton Rut 161 E1
Stretton Staffs 158 A1
Stretton Staffs 173 D5
Stretton Warr 184 A4
Stretton en le Field 159 F1
Stretton Grandison 145 F3
Stretton Heath 156 C1
Stretton Sugwas 145 D3
Stretton under Fosse 159 G4
Stretton Westwood 157 E3
Stretton-on-Dunsmore 159 G5
Stretton-on-Fosse 147 E4
Stribers 199 E4
Strichen 269 H5
Strines 185 D4
Strinesdale Countryside Area GtMan OL4 2JJ 25 H1
Stringston 115 E3
Strixton 149 E1
Stroat 131 E3
Stromeferry 256 E1
Stromemore 256 E1
Stromness 277 B7
Stronaba 249 E1
Stronachlachar 241 G3
Strone A&B 232 C1
Strone High 258 C2
Strone High 248 D1
Strone Stir 241 G3
Stronechrubie 272 E7
Stronlonag 232 C1
Stronmilchan (Sròn nam Mialchon) 241 D2
Stronsay 276 F5
Stronsay Airfield 276 F5
Strontian (Sròn an t-Sithein) 248 A3
Strontoiller 240 B2
Stronvar 242 A2
Strood 123 G2
Strood Green Surr 122 B4
Strood Green WSuss 121 F5
Strood Green WSuss 121 G4
Stroquhan 216 C2
Stroud Glos 132 A2
Stroud Hants 120 C5
Stroud Common 121 F3
Stroud Green Essex 138 B3
Stroud Green Glos 132 A2
Stroude 121 F1
Stroul 232 D1
Stroxton 175 E4
Struan High 255 J1
Struan P&K 250 C3
Strubby Lincs 189 E4
Strubby Lincs 188 B5
Strumpshaw 179 E5
Struthers 244 B4
Struy 258 B1
Stryd y Facsen 180 B4
Stryt-cae-rhedyn 169 F1
Stryt-issa 169 F3
Stuart & Waterford Crystal Factory Shop, Crieff P&K PH7 4HQ 243 D2
Stuart Line Cruises, Exmouth Devon EX8 1EJ 102 D4
Stuartfield 269 H6
Stub Place 198 B3
Stubber's Green 158 C2
Stubbington 107 E2
Stubbins 184 B1
Stubbs Green 165 E2
Stubhampton 105 F1
Stubley 186 A5
Stubshaw Cross 183 G2
Stubton 175 D3
Stuck A&B 232 B3
Stuck A&B 240 D5
Stuckbeg 241 E5
Stuckgowan 241 F4
Stuckindroin 241 F3
Stuckreoch 240 C5
Stuckton 106 A1
Stud Green 135 D5
Studdon 211 E2
Studfold 200 D5
Studham 135 F1
Studholme 209 F1
Studland 105 G4
Studland & Godlingston Heath NNR Dorset BH19 3AX 105 G4
Studley Warks 146 C1
Studley Wilts 132 B5
Studley Common 146 C1
Studley Green 134 C3
Studley Roger 202 B5
Studley Royal Park & ruins of Fountains Abbey NYorks HG4 3DY 194 B1
Stuggadhoo 190 B4
Stump Cross Essex 150 D3
Stump Cross Lancs 192 B4
Stuntney 163 D5
Stunts Green 110 B2
Sturbridge 171 F4
Sturgate 187 F4
Sturmer 151 E3
Sturminster Common 105 D1
Sturminster Marshall 105 F2
Sturminster Newton 105 D1
Sturry 125 D2
Sturton by Stow 187 F4
Sturton le Steeple 187 E4
Stuston 164 C4
Stutton NYorks 195 D3
Stutton Suff 152 C4
Styal 184 C4
Styrrup 186 D3
Suardail 271 G4
Succoth A&B 241 E4
Succoth Aber 260 C1
Succothmore 240 D4
Suckley 145 G2
Suckley Green 145 G2
Suckley Knowl 145 G2
Sudborough 161 E4
Sudbourne 153 F2
Sudbrook Lincs 175 E3
Sudbrook Mon 131 E4
Sudbrooke 188 A5
Sudbury Derbys 172 C4
Sudbury GtLon 136 A4
Sudbury Suff 151 G3
Sudbury Hall Derbys DE6 5HT 172 C4
Sudden 184 C1
Sudgrove 132 B2
Suffield Norf 178 D2
Suffield NYorks 204 C3
Sugarloaf 124 B5
Sugnall 171 E4
Sugwas Pool 145 D3
Suie Lodge Hotel 241 G2
Suisnish 256 B3
Sulby IoM 190 B2
Sulby IoM 190 B4
Sulgrave 148 A3
Sulham 134 B5
Sulhamstead 120 B1
Sullington 108 C2
Sullom 278 C5
Sullom Voe Oil Terminal 278 C5
Sully 115 E1
Sumburgh 279 F10
Sumburgh Airport 279 F9
Summer Bridge 194 B1
Summer Isles 265 F1
Summer Lodge 201 E3
Summercourt 96 C4
Summerfield Norf 177 F4
Summerfield Worcs 158 A5
Summerhill 170 A2
Summerhouse 202 B1
Summerlands 199 G4
Summerleaze 130 D4
Summertown 134 A2
Summit 184 D1
Sun Green 185 D3
Sunadale 231 G5
Sunbiggin 200 B2
Sunbury 121 G1
Sundaywell 216 C2
Sunderland Cumb 209 E3
Sunderland Lancs 192 A2
Sunderland T&W 212 C2
Sunderland Bridge 212 B4
Sunderland Museum & Winter Gardens T&W SR1 1PP 86 Sunderland
Sundhope 227 E3
Sundon Park 149 F5
Sundown Adventure Land Notts DN22 0HX 187 E5
Sundridge 123 D3
Sundrum Mains 224 C3
Sunhill 132 D2
Sunipol 246 C4
Sunk Island 188 C1
Sunningdale 121 E1
Sunninghill 121 E1
Sunningwell 133 G2
Sunniside Dur 212 A4
Sunniside T&W 212 B2
Sunny Bank 199 D3
Sunny Brow 212 A4
Sunnylaw 242 C5
Sunnyside Aber 261 G5
Sunnyside N'umb 211 F1
Sunnyside SYorks 186 B3
Sunnyside WSuss 122 C5
Sunton 118 D2
Sunwick 237 F4
Surbiton 121 G1
Surfleet 176 A5
Surfleet Seas End 176 A5
Surlingham 179 E5
Sustead 178 C2
Susworth 187 F2
Sutcombe 112 D4
Sutcombemill 112 D4
Suton 164 B2
Sutors of Cromarty 267 F5
Sutterby 189 D5
Sutterton 176 A4
Sutton Cambs 162 C5
Sutton CenBeds 150 A3
Sutton Devon 102 A2
Sutton Devon 100 D3
Sutton GtLon 122 B2
Sutton Kent 125 F4
Sutton Lincs 175 D2
Sutton Norf 179 E3
Sutton Notts 174 C4
Sutton Notts 187 D4
Sutton Oxon 133 G2
Sutton Pembs 126 C1
Sutton Peter 161 F3
Sutton Shrop 157 G4
Sutton Shrop 171 D4
Sutton Shrop 157 E1
Sutton Shrop 170 A5
Sutton Staffs 171 E5
Sutton Suff 153 E3
Sutton SYorks 186 C1
Sutton WSuss 108 B2
Sutton Abinger 121 G3
Sutton at Hone 137 E5
Sutton Bank National Park Centre NYorks YO7 2EH 203 E4
Sutton Bassett 160 C4
Sutton Benger 132 B5
Sutton Bingham 104 B1
Sutton Bonington 173 G5
Sutton Bridge 176 C5
Sutton Cheney 159 G2
Sutton Coldfield 158 D3
Sutton Courtenay 134 A3
Sutton Crosses 176 C5
Sutton Grange 202 B5
Sutton Green Oxon 133 G2
Sutton Green Surr 121 F2
Sutton Green Wrex 170 B3
Sutton Holms 105 G2
Sutton Howgrave 202 C5
Sutton in Ashfield 173 F2
Sutton in the Elms 160 A3
Sutton Ings 196 D4
Sutton Lane Ends 184 D5
Sutton le Marsh 189 F4
Sutton Leach 183 G3
Sutton Maddock 157 G2
Sutton Mallet 116 A4
Sutton Mandeville 118 A5
Sutton Montis 116 D5
Sutton on Sea 189 F4
Sutton on the Hill 172 D4
Sutton on Trent 174 C1
Sutton Poyntz 104 D4
Sutton St. Edmund 162 B1
Sutton St. James 162 C1
Sutton St. Nicholas 145 E3
Sutton Scarsdale 173 F1
Sutton Scotney 119 F4
Sutton upon Derwent 195 G3
Sutton Valence 124 A4
Sutton Veny 117 F3
Sutton Waldron 105 E1
Sutton Weaver 183 G5
Sutton Wick B&NESom 116 C2
Sutton Wick Oxon 133 G3
Sutton-in-Craven 193 G3
Sutton-on-Hull 196 D4
Sutton-on-the-Forest 195 E1
Sutton-under-Brailes 147 F4
Sutton-under-Whitestonecliffe 203 D4
Swaby 189 D5
Swadlincote 159 F1
Swaffham 163 G2
Swaffham Bulbeck 151 D1
Swaffham Prior 151 D1
Swafield 179 D2
Swainbost (Suainebost) 271 H1
Swainby 203 D2
Swainshill 145 D3
Swainsthorpe 178 D5
Swainswick 117 E1
Swalcliffe 147 F4
Swalecliffe 124 D2
Swallow 188 B2
Swallow Beck 175 E1
Swallow Falls Conwy LL24 0DW 168 A2
Swallowcliffe 118 A5
Swallowfield 120 C1
Swallows Cross 137 F3
Swampton 119 F2
Swan Green ChesW&C 184 B5
Swan Green Suff 165 D4
Swan Street 151 G5
Swanage 105 G5
Swanage Railway Dorset BH19 1HB 105 G5
Swanbach 171 D3
Swanbourne 148 D5
Swanbridge 115 E1
Swancote 157 G3
Swanland 196 B5
Swanlaws 228 B5
Swanley 123 E2
Swanley Village 123 E2
Swanmore Hants 107 E1
Swanmore IoW 107 E3
Swannington Leics 159 G1
Swannington Norf 178 C4
Swanscombe 137 F5
Swansea (Abertawe) 128 C3
Swansea Museum SA1 1SN 86 Swansea
Swanston 235 G3
Swanton Abbot 179 D3
Swanton Morley 178 B4
Swanton Novers 178 B2
Swanton Street 124 A3
Swanwick Derbys 173 F2
Swanwick Hants 107 E2
Swanwick Green 170 C3
Swarby 175 F3
Swardeston 178 D5
Swarkestone 173 E5
Swarland 221 D1
Swarraton 119 G4
Swarthmoor 199 D5
Swaton 175 G4
Swavesey 150 B1
Sway 106 B3
Swayfield 175 E5
Swaythling 106 D1
Swaythorpe 196 C1
Sweetham 102 B3
Sweethay 115 F5
Sweetshouse 97 E3
Sweffling 153 E1
Swell 116 A5
Swepstone 159 F1
Swerford 147 F4
Swettenham 171 F1
Swffryd 130 B3
Swift's Green 124 A4
Swiftsden 110 C1
Swilland 152 C2
Swillington 194 C4
Swimbridge 113 G3
Swimbridge Newland 113 F2
Swinbrook 133 E1
Swincliffe 194 B2
Swincombe 113 G1
Swinden 193 E2
Swinderby 175 D1
Swindon Staffs 158 A3
Swindon Swin 133 D4
Swindon Village 146 B5
Swine 196 D4
Swinefleet 195 G5
Swineford 117 D1
Swineshead Bed 149 F1
Swineshead Lincs 176 A3
Swineshead Bridge 176 A3
Swineside 201 F4
Swiney 275 H5
Swinford Leics 160 A5
Swinford Oxon 133 G2
Swingate 173 G3
Swingfield Minnis 125 E4
Swingleton Green 152 A3
Swinhoe 229 G4
Swinhope 188 C3
Swining 279 D6
Swinithwaite 201 F4
Swinscoe 172 C3
Swinside Hall 228 B5
Swinstead 175 F5
Swinton GtMan 184 B2
Swinton NYorks 203 G5
Swinton NYorks 202 B5
Swinton ScBord 237 F5
Swinton SYorks 186 B3
Swinton Quarter 237 F5
Swintonmill 237 F5
Swithland 160 A1
Swordale 266 C5
Swordland 256 D5
Swordle 247 E2
Swordly 274 C2
Sworton Heath 184 A4
Swyddffynnon 142 C1
Swyncombe 134 B3
Swynnerton 171 F4
Swyre 104 B4
Sychnant 155 F5
Syde 132 B1
Sydenham GtLon 136 C5
Sydenham Oxon 134 C2
Sydenham Damerel 99 E3
Syderstone 177 G4
Sydling St. Nicholas 104 C3
Sydmonton 119 F2
Sydney 171 E2
Syerston 174 C3
Sykehouse 186 D1
Sykes 192 C2
Sylen 128 B2
Symbister 279 E6
Symington SAyr 224 B2
Symington SLan 226 A2
Symonds Yat 131 E1
Symondsbury 104 A3
Synod Inn (Post-mawr) 142 A2
Syre 273 J4
Syreford 146 C5
Syresham 148 B3
Syston Leics 160 B1
Syston Lincs 175 E3
Sytchampton 146 A1
Sywell 148 D1
Sywell Country Park N'hants NN6 0QX 148 D1


## T


Taagan 265 G5
Tableyhill 184 B5
Tabost 271 F6
Tachbrook Mallory 147 F1
Tacher 275 G4
Tackley 147 G5
Tacolneston 164 C2
Tadcaster 195 D3
Tadden 105 F2
Taddington Derbys 185 F5
Taddington Glos 146 C4
Taddiport 113 E4
Tadley 120 B1
Tadlow 150 A3
Tadmarton 147 F4
Tadpole Bridge 133 F2
Tadworth 122 B3
Tafarnaubach 130 A1
Tafarn-y-bwlch 141 D4
Tafarn-y-Gelyn 169 E1
Taff Merthyr Garden Village 130 A3
Taff's Well (Ffynnon Taf) 130 A4
Tafolwern 155 E2
Taibach NPT 129 D4
Tai-bach Powys 169 E5
Taicynhaeaf 154 C1
Tain High 275 H2
Tain High 266 E3
Tai'n Lôn 166 D3
Tai'r Bull 143 F5
Tairgwaith 128 D1
Tai'r-heol 130 A3
Tairlaw 224 C5
Tai'r-ysgol 128 C3
Takeley 151 D5
Takeley Street 150 D5
Talachddu 143 G4
Talacre 182 C4
Talardd 168 B5
Talaton 103 D3
Talbenny 126 B1
Talbot Green 129 G4
Talbot Village 105 G3
Talerddig 155 F2
Talgarreg 142 A2
Talgarth 144 A4
Taliesin 154 C3
Talisker 255 J1
Talke Pits 171 F2
Talkin 210 B2
Talkin Tarn Country Park Cumb CA8 1HN 210 B2
Talla Linnfoots 226 C3
Talladale 265 F4
Talladh-a-Bheithe 250 A4
Talland 97 G4
Tallarn Green 170 B3
Tallentire 209 E3
Talley (Talyllychau) 142 C4
Tallington 161 F2
Talmine 273 H2
Talog 141 G5
Tal-sarn 142 B2
Talsarnau 167 F4
Talskiddy 96 D3
Talwrn IoA 180 C5
Talwrn Wrex 169 F3
Talwrn Wrex 170 A3
Talybont Cere 154 C4
Tal-y-bont Conwy 168 A1
Tal-y-bont Gwyn 167 E5
Tal-y-bont Gwyn 181 E5
Talybont-on-Usk 144 A5
Tal-y-Cae 167 F1
Tal-y-cafn 181 F5
Tal-y-coed 130 D1
Talygarn 129 G4
Tal-y-llyn Gwyn 154 D2
Talyllyn Powys 144 A5
Talysarn 167 D2
Tal-y-wern 155 E2
Tamavoid 242 A5
Tamerton Foliot 100 A1
Tamworth 159 E2
Tamworth Green 176 B3
Tan Office Green 151 F2
Tandem 185 F1
Tandridge 122 C3
Tanerdy 142 A5
Tanfield 212 A2
Tanfield Lea 212 A2
Tang 194 B2
Tang Hall 195 F2
Tangiers 126 C1
Tanglandford 261 G1
Tangley 119 E2
Tangmere 108 B3
Tangwick 278 B5
Tangy 222 B3
Tank Museum, Bovington Dorset BH20 6JG 105 E4
Tankerness 277 E7
Tankersley 186 A2
Tankerton 124 D2
Tan-lan 167 F3
Tannach 275 J4
Tannachie 253 F1
Tannachy 266 E1
Tannadice 252 C4
Tannington 152 D1
Tannochside 234 A3
Tansley 173 E2
Tansley Knoll 173 E2
Tansor 161 F3
Tantobie 212 A2
Tanton 203 E1
Tanworth in Arden 158 D5
Tan-y-fron 168 C1
Tan-y-graig 166 C4
Tanygrisiau 167 F3
Tan-y-groes 141 F3
Tan-y-pistyll 169 D5
Tan-yr-allt 182 B4
Taobh a' Deas Loch Baghasdail 254 C3
Taobh Siar 270 D7
Tapeley 113 E3
Taplow 135 E4
Tapton Grove 186 B5
Taransay (Tarasaigh) 270 C7
Taraphocain 248 C5
Tarbat House 266 E4
Tarbert A&B 231 G3
Tarbert A&B 231 E4
Tarbert A&B 231 E1
Tarbert High 247 F3
Tarbert (Tairbeart) ESiar 270 D7
Tarbet (An Tairbeart) A&B 241 F4
Tarbet High 256 D5
Tarbet High 272 D4
Tarbock Green 183 F4
Tarbolton 224 C3
Tarbrax 235 E4
Tardebigge 146 B1
Tardy Gate 192 B5
Tarfside 252 C2
Tarland 260 C4
Tarleton 192 A5
Tarlscough 183 F1
Tarlton 132 B3
Tarnbrook 192 B2
Tarnock 116 A2
Tarporley 170 C1
Tarr 115 E4
Tarrant Crawford 105 F2
Tarrant Gunville 105 F1
Tarrant Hinton 105 F1
Tarrant Keyneston 105 F2
Tarrant Launceston 105 F2
Tarrant Monkton 105 F2
Tarrant Rawston 105 F2
Tarrant Rushton 105 F2
Tarrel 267 F3
Tarring Neville 109 G3
Tarrington 145 F3
Tarrnacraig 223 E2
Tarsappie 243 G2
Tarskavaig 256 B4
Tarves 261 G1
Tarvie (Tairbhidh) High 266 B6
Tarvie P&K 251 F3
Tarvin 170 B1
Tarvin Sands 170 B1
Tasburgh 164 D2
Tasley 157 F3
Taston 147 F5
Tate Britain GtLon SW1P 4RG 13 B5
Tate Liverpool Mersey L3 4BB 42 B5
Tate Modern GtLon SE1 9TG 45 H4
Tate St. Ives Corn TR26 1TG 94 C2
Tatenhill 172 D5
Tathall End 148 D3
Tatham 192 C1
Tathwell 188 D4
Tatsfield 122 D3
Tattenhall 170 B2
Tattenhoe 148 D4
Tatterford 177 G5
Tattersett 177 G4
Tattershall 176 A2
Tattershall Bridge 175 G2
Tattershall Thorpe 176 A2
Tattingstone 152 C4
Tatton Park ChesE WA16 6QN 184 B4
Tatworth 103 G2
Tauchers 268 B6
Taunton 115 F5
Tavelty 261 F3
Taverham 178 C4
Tavernspite 127 E1
Tavistock 99 E3
Taw Bridge 113 G5
Taw Green 99 G1
Tawstock 113 F3
Taxal 185 E5
Tayburn 233 G5
Taychreggan 240 C2
Tayinloan 231 E5
Taylors Cross 112 C4
Taynafead 240 C3
Taynish 231 F1
Taynton Glos 145 G5
Taynton Oxon 133 E1
Taynuilt (Taigh an Uillt) 240 C1
Tayock 253 E4
Tayovullin 230 A2
Tayport 244 C2
Tayvallich 231 F1
Tea Green 149 G5
Tealby 188 B3
Tealing 244 C1
Team Valley 212 B1
Teanamachar 262 C5
Teangue 256 C4
Teasses 244 C4
Tebay 200 B2
Tebworth 149 E5
Techniquest, Cardiff Cardiff CF10 5BW 7 B4
Tedburn St. Mary 102 B3
Teddington Glos 146 B4
Teddington GtLon 136 A5
Tedstone Delamere 145 F2
Tedstone Wafre 145 F2
Teeton 160 B5
Teffont Evias 118 A4
Teffont Magna 118 A4
Tegryn 141 F4
Tehidy Country Park Corn TR14 0HA 96 A5
Teigh 161 D1
Teign Village 102 B4
Teigngrace 102 B5
Teignmouth 102 C5
Telford 157 F2
Telford Wonderland Tel&W TF3 4AY 157 G2
Telham 110 C2
Tellisford 117 F2
Telscombe 109 G3
Telscombe Cliffs 109 G3
Tempar 250 B4
Templand 217 E2
Temple Corn 97 F2
Temple Midlo 236 A4
Temple Balsall 159 E5
Temple Bar 142 B2
Temple Cloud 116 D2
Temple End 151 E2
Temple Ewell 125 E4
Temple Grafton 146 D2
Temple Guiting 146 C5
Temple Herdewyke 147 F2
Temple Hirst 195 F5
Temple Newsam WYorks LS15 0AE 27 H2
Temple Normanton 173 F1
Temple Sowerby 210 C5
Templecombe 117 E5
Templeton Devon 102 B1
Templeton Pembs 127 E1
Templeton Bridge 102 B1
Templewood 253 E3
Tempsford 149 G2
Ten Mile Bank 163 E3
Tenbury Wells 145 E1
Tenby (Dinbych-y-pysgod) 127 E2
Tendring 152 C5
Tendring Green 152 C5
Tenga 247 E5
Tenterden 124 A5
Tepersie Castle 260 D2
Terally 206 B2
Terling 137 G1
Tern 157 F1
Ternhill 170 D4
Terregles 216 D3
Terriers 135 D3
Terrington 203 F5
Terrington St. Clement 177 D5
Terrington St. John 162 D1
Terry's Green 158 D5
Tervieside 259 K1
Teston 123 G3
Testwood 106 C1
Tetbury 132 A3
Tetbury Upton 132 A3
Tetchill 170 A4
Tetcott 98 D1
Tetford 188 D5
Tetney 188 D2
Tetney Lock 188 D2
Tetsworth 134 B2
Tettenhall 158 A2
Tettenhall Wood 158 A3
Tetworth 150 A2
Teuchan 261 J1
Teversal 173 F1
Teversham 150 C2
Teviot Water Gardens ScBord TD5 8LE 228 B4
Teviothead 227 F5
Tewel 253 G1
Tewin 136 B1
Tewkesbury 146 A4
Tewkesbury Abbey Glos GL20 5RZ 146 A4
Teynham 124 B2
Thackley 194 A4
Thainston 253 E2
Thainstone 261 F3
Thakeham 108 D2
Thame 134 C2
Thames Ditton 121 G1
Thames Haven 137 G4
Thamesmead 137 D4
Thanington 124 D3
Thankerton 226 A2
Tharston 164 C2
Thatcham 119 G1
Thatto Heath 183 G3
Thaxted 151 E4
The Apes Hall 163 D3
The Bage 144 B3
The Balloch 242 D3
The Banking 261 F1
The Bar 121 G5
The Birks 261 F4
The Bog 156 C3
The Bourne 120 D3
The Bratch 158 A3
The Broad 145 D1
The Bryn 130 C2
The Burf 146 A1
The Burn 253 D2
The Butts 117 E3
The Camp 132 B2
The Chequer 170 B3
The City Bucks 134 C3
The City Suff 165 E3
The Common Wilts 118 D4
The Common Wilts 132 C4
The Craigs 266 B2
The Cronk 190 B2
The Delves 158 C3
The Den 233 E4
The Dicker 110 A3
The Down 157 F3
The Drums 252 B3
The Eaves 131 F2
The Flatt 219 D4
The Folly 136 A1
The Forge 144 C2
The Forstal ESuss 123 E5
The Forstal Kent 124 C5
The Grange Lincs 189 F5
The Grange Shrop 170 A4
The Grange Surr 122 C4
The Green A&B 246 A2
The Green Cumb 198 C4
The Green Essex 137 G1
The Green Flints 169 F1
The Green Wilts 117 F4
The Grove 146 A3
The Haven 121 F4
The Headland 213 E4
The Heath 172 B4
The Herberts 129 F5
The Hermitage 122 B3
The Hill 198 C4
The Holme 194 B2
The Howe 190 A5
The Isle 157 D1
The Laurels 165 E2
The Leacon 124 B5
The Lee 135 D2
The Leigh 146 A5
The Lhen 190 B1
The Lodge 241 D5
The Marsh 156 C3
The Moor ESuss 110 D2
The Moor Kent 110 C1
The Mumbles 128 C4
The Murray 234 A4
The Mythe 146 A4
The Narth 131 E2
The Neuk 261 F5
The Node 136 B1
The Oval 117 E1
The Polchar 259 G4
The Quarter 124 A4
The Reddings 146 B5
The Rhos 126 D1
The Rookery 171 F2
The Rowe 171 F4
The Sale 159 D1
The Sands 121 D3
The Shoe 132 A5
The Slade 134 A5
The Smithies 157 F3
The Stocks 111 E1
The Swillett 135 F3
The Thrift 150 B4
The Vauld 145 E3
The Wern 169 F2
The Wyke 157 G2
Theakston 202 C4
Thealby 187 F1
Theale Som 116 B3
Theale WBerks 134 B5
Thearne 196 C4
Theberton 153 F1
Thedden Grange 120 B4
Theddingworth 160 B4
Theddlethorpe All Saints 189 E4
Theddlethorpe St. Helen 189 E4
Thelbridge Barton 102 A1
Thelbridge Cross 102 A1
Thelnetham 164 B4
Thelveton 164 C3
Thelwall 184 A4
Themelthorpe 178 B3
Thenford 148 A3
Therfield 150 B4
Thermae Bath Spa B&NESom BA1 1SJ 63 Bath
Thetford Lincs 161 G1
Thetford Norf 163 G4
Thetford Forest Park Norf IP27 0TJ 163 G4
Thethwaite 209 G2
Theydon Bois 136 D3
Theydon Garnon 137 D3
Theydon Mount 137 D3
Thickwood 132 A5
Thimbleby Lincs 176 A1
Thimbleby NYorks 202 D3
Thingley 117 F1
Thirkleby 203 D5
Thirlby 203 D4
Thirlestane 236 C5
Thirn 202 B4
Thirsk 202 D4
Thirston New Houses 221 D2
Thirtleby 197 D4

Thistleton *Lancs* 192 A4
Thistleton *Rut* 161 E1
Thistley Green 163 E5
Thixendale 196 A1
Thockrington 220 B4
Tholomas Drove 162 B2
Tholthorpe 195 D1
Thomas Chapel 127 E2
Thomas Close 210 A3
Thomastown 260 D4
Thompson 164 A2
Thomshill 267 K6
Thong 173 F5
Thongsbridge 185 F2
Thoralby 201 F4
Thoresby 186 D5
Thoresthorpe 189 E5
Thoresway 188 B3
Thorganby *Lincs* 188 C3
Thorganby *NYorks* 195 F3
Thorgill 203 G3
Thorington 165 F4
Thorington Street 152 B4
Thorley 137 D1
Thorley Houses 150 C5
Thorley Street *Herts* 137 D1
Thorley Street *IoW* 106 C4
Thormanby 203 D5
Thornaby-on-Tees 203 D1
Thornage 178 B2
Thornborough *Bucks* 148 C4
Thornborough *NYorks* 202 B5
Thornbury *Devon* 113 D5
Thornbury *Here* 145 F2
Thornbury *SGlos* 131 F3
Thornbury *WYorks* 194 A4
Thornby 160 B5
Thorncliff 185 G1
Thorncliffe 172 B4
Thorncombe 103 G2
Thorncombe Street 121 F3
Thorncote Green 149 G3
Thorncross 106 D4
Thorndon 152 C1
Thorndon Country Park *Essex* CM13 3RZ 99 F1
Thorndon Cross 99 F1
Thorne 187 D1
Thorne St. Margaret 115 D5
Thorner 194 C4
Thorney *Bucks* 135 F5
Thorney *Notts* 187 F5
Thorney *Peter* 162 A2
Thorney *Som* 116 B5
Thorney Close 212 C2
Thorney Hill 106 B3
Thornfalcon 115 F5
Thornford 104 C1
Thorngrafton 211 D1
Thorngrove 116 A4
Thorngumbald 197 E5
Thornham 177 F3
Thornham Magna 164 C4
Thornham Parva 164 C4
Thornhaugh 161 F2
Thornhill *Cardiff* 130 A4
Thornhill *Cumb* 198 B2
Thornhill *Derbys* 185 F4
Thornhill *D&G* 216 C1
Thornhill *Soton* 107 D1
Thornhill *Stir* 242 B4
Thornhill *WYorks* 185 G1
Thornhill Lees 185 G1
Thornholme 196 B4
Thornicombe 105 E2
Thornley *Dur* 212 C4
Thornley *Dur* 212 A4
Thornley Gate 211 E2
Thornliebank 233 G4
Thornroan 261 G1
Thorns 185 E4
Thorns Green 184 B4
Thornsett 185 E4
Thornthwaite *Cumb* 209 F4
Thornthwaite *NYorks* 194 A2
Thornton *Angus* 252 B5
Thornton *Bucks* 148 C4
Thornton *ERid* 195 G3
Thornton *Fife* 244 A5
Thornton *Lancs* 191 F4
Thornton *Leics* 159 G2
Thornton *Lincs* 176 A1
Thornton *Mersey* 183 E2
Thornton *Middl* 203 D1
Thornton *N'umb* 237 G5
Thornton *P&K* 251 F5
Thornton *Pembs* 126 C2
Thornton *WYorks* 194 A4
Thornton Bridge 202 D5
Thornton Curtis 188 A1
Thornton Heath 122 C2
Thornton Hough 183 E4
Thornton in Lonsdale 200 B5
Thornton le Moor 188 A3
Thornton Park 237 G5
Thornton Rust 201 E4
Thornton Steward 202 A4
Thornton Watlass 202 B4
Thorntonhall 233 G4
Thornton-in-Craven 193 F3
Thornton-le-Beans 202 D3
Thornton-le-Clay 195 F1
Thornton-le-Dale 204 B4
Thornton-le-Moor 202 C4
Thornton-le-Moors 183 F5
Thornton-le-Street 202 D4
Thorntonloch 237 F2
Thornwood 137 D2
Thornyhill 253 E2
Thornylee 227 F2
Thoroton 174 C3
Thorp Arch 194 D3
Thorpe *Derbys* 172 C2
Thorpe *ERid* 196 B3
Thorpe *Lincs* 189 E4
Thorpe *Notts* 174 C2
Thorpe *NYorks* 193 G1
Thorpe *Surr* 121 F1
Thorpe Abbotts 164 C3
Thorpe Acre 173 G5
Thorpe Arnold 174 C5
Thorpe Audlin 186 B1
Thorpe Bassett 204 B5
Thorpe Bay 138 C4
Thorpe by Water 161 D3

Thorpe Constantine 159 E2
Thorpe Culvert 176 C1
Thorpe End 179 D4
Thorpe Green *Essex* 152 C5
Thorpe Green *Lancs* 192 B5
Thorpe Green *Suff* 152 A2
Thorpe Hall 203 E5
Thorpe Hesley 186 A3
Thorpe in Balne 186 A3
Thorpe in the Fallows 187 G4
Thorpe Langton 160 C3
Thorpe Larches 212 C5
Thorpe le Street 196 A3
Thorpe Malsor 160 D5
Thorpe Mandeville 148 A3
Thorpe Market 178 D2
Thorpe Morieux 152 A2
Thorpe on the Hill *Lincs* 175 E1
Thorpe on the Hill *WYorks* 194 C5
Thorpe Park *Surr* KT16 8PN 121 F1
Thorpe Row 178 B2
Thorpe St. Andrew 179 D5
Thorpe St. Peter 176 C1
Thorpe Salvin 186 C4
Thorpe Satchville 160 C1
Thorpe Street 164 B4
Thorpe Thewles 212 C5
Thorpe Tilney Dales 175 G2
Thorpe Underwood *N'hants* 160 C4
Thorpe Underwood *NYorks* 195 D2
Thorpe Waterville 161 F4
Thorpe Willoughby 195 E4
Thorpefield 202 D5
Thorpe-le-Soken 152 C5
Thorpeness 153 F1
Thorpland 163 E2
Thorrington 152 B5
Thorverton 102 C2
Thrandeston 164 C4
Thrapston 161 E5
Threapland 193 F1
Threapwood 170 B3
Threapwood Head 172 B3
Three Ashes 117 C3
Three Bridges 122 B5
Three Burrows 96 B5
Three Chimneys 124 A5
Three Cocks (Aberllynfi) 144 A4
Three Counties Showground *Worcs* WR13 6NW 145 G3
Three Crosses 128 C3
Three Cups Corner 110 B1
Three Hammers 97 G2
Three Holes 162 B3
Three Leg Cross 123 F5
Three Legged Cross 105 G2
Three Mile Cross 120 C1
Three Oaks 110 D2
Threehammer Common 179 E4
Threekingham 175 F4
Threemilestone 96 B5
Threlkeld 209 G4
Threshfield 193 F1
Threxton Hill 163 G2
Thriepley 244 B1
Thrigby 179 F4
Thrigby Hall Wildlife Gardens *Norf* NR29 3DR 179 F4
Thringarth 211 F5
Thringstone 159 G1
Thrintoft 202 C3
Thriplow 150 C3
Throapham 186 C4
Throckenholt 162 B2
Throcking 150 B4
Throckley 212 A1
Throckmorton 146 B3
Throop 105 E4
Throphill 220 D3
Thropton 220 C1
Througham 132 B2
Throwleigh 99 G1
Throwley 124 B3
Throws 151 E5
Thrumpton *Notts* 173 G3
Thrumpton *Notts* 187 E5
Thrumster 275 J4
Thrunton 229 E5
Thrupp *Glos* 132 A2
Thrupp *Oxon* 133 G1
Thrupp *Oxon* 133 E3
Thruscross 194 A2
Thrushelton 99 E2
Thrussington 160 B1
Thruxton *Hants* 119 D3
Thruxton *Here* 144 D4
Thrybergh 186 B3
Thrybergh Country Park *SYorks* S65 4NU 186 B3
Thulston 173 F4
Thunder Bridge 185 F1
Thundergay 231 G5
Thundersley 138 B4
Thunderton 269 J6
Thundridge 136 C1
Thurcaston 160 A1
Thurcroft 186 B4
Thurdistoft 275 H2
Thurdon 112 C4
Thurgarton *Norf* 178 C2
Thurgarton *Notts* 174 B3
Thurgoland 185 G2
Thurlaston *Leics* 160 A3
Thurlaston *Warks* 159 G5
Thurlbear 115 F5
Thurlby *Lincs* 161 G1
Thurlby *Lincs* 175 E1
Thurlby *Lincs* 189 E5
Thurleigh 149 F2
Thurlestone 100 C3
Thurloxton 115 F4
Thurlton 165 F2
Thurlwood 171 F2
Thurmaston 160 B2
Thurnby 160 B2
Thurne 179 F4
Thurnham 124 A3
Thurning *N'hants* 161 F4
Thurning *Norf* 178 B3
Thurnscoe 186 B2

Thursby 209 G1
Thursden 193 F4
Thursford 178 A2
Thursley 121 E4
Thurso (Inbhir Theòrsa) 275 G2
Thurstaston 182 D4
Thurston 152 A1
Thurston Clough 185 D2
Thurstonfield 209 G1
Thurstonland 185 F1
Thurton 179 E5
Thurvaston *Derbys* 172 D4
Thurvaston *Derbys* 172 C4
Thuster 275 H3
Thuxton 178 B5
Thwaite *NYorks* 201 D3
Thwaite *Suff* 152 C1
Thwaite Head 199 F2
Thwaite St. Mary 165 E2
Thwaites 193 G3
Thwaites Brow 193 G3
Thwing 205 D5
Tibbermore 243 F2
Tibberton *Glos* 145 G5
Tibberton *Tel&W* 171 D5
Tibberton *Worcs* 146 B2
Tibbie Shiels Inn 226 D3
Tibenham 164 C2
Tibertich 240 A3
Tibshelf 173 F1
Tibthorpe 196 B2
Ticehurst 123 F5
Tichborne 119 G4
Tickencote 161 E2
Tickenham 131 D5
Tickford End 149 D3
Tickhill 186 C3
Ticklerton 157 D3
Ticknall 173 E5
Tickton 196 C3
Tidbury Green 158 D5
Tidcombe 119 D2
Tiddington *Oxon* 134 B2
Tiddington *Warks* 147 E2
Tiddleywink 132 A5
Tidebrook 110 B1
Tideford 98 D5
Tideford Cross 98 D4
Tidenham 131 E3
Tidenham Chase 131 E3
Tideswell 185 F5
Tidmarsh 134 B5
Tidmington 147 E4
Tidpit 105 G3
Tidworth 118 D3
Tiers Cross 126 C1
Tiffield 148 B2
Tifty 269 F6
Tigerton 252 D3
Tigh a' Gearraidh 262 C4
Tighachnoic 247 F5
Tighnablair 242 C3
Tighnabruaich 232 A2
Tighnacomaire 248 B3
Tigley 101 D1
Tilbrook 149 F1
Tilbury 137 F5
Tilbury Green 151 F3
Tile Hill 159 E5
Tilehurst 134 B5
Tilford 121 D3
Tilgate 122 B5
Tilgate Forest Row 122 B5
Tilgate Park *WSuss* RH10 5PQ 122 B5
Tillathrowie 260 C1
Tillers' Green 145 F4
Tillery 261 H2
Tilley 170 C5
Tillicoultry 243 E5
Tillietudlem 225 G1
Tillingham 138 D2
Tillington *Here* 145 D3
Tillington *WSuss* 121 E5
Tillington Common 145 D3
Tillyarblet 252 D3
Tillybirloch 260 E4
Tillycairn Castle 260 E3
Tillycorthie 261 H2
Tillydrine 260 E5
Tillyfar 269 G6
Tillyfour 260 D3
Tillyfourie 260 E3
Tillygarmond 260 E5
Tillygreig 261 G2
Tillypronie 260 C4
Tilmanstone 125 F3
Tiln 187 E4
Tilney All Saints 163 D1
Tilney Fen End 162 D1
Tilney High End 163 D1
Tilney St. Lawrence 162 D1
Tilshead 118 B3
Tilstock 170 C4
Tilston 170 B2
Tilstone Fearnall 170 C1
Tilsworth 149 E5
Tilton on the Hill 160 C2
Tiltups End 132 A3
Timberland 175 G2
Timberland Dales 175 G1
Timbersbrook 171 F1
Timberscombe 114 C3
Timble 194 A2
Timewell 114 C4
Timperley 184 B4
Timsbury *B&NESom* 117 D2
Timsbury *Hants* 119 E5
Timsgearraidh 270 C4
Timworth 151 G1
Timworth Green 151 G1
Tincleton 105 D3
Tindale 210 C2
Tindon End 151 E4
Tingewick 148 B4
Tingley 194 B5
Tingrith 149 F4
Tingwall 276 D5
Tingwall (Lerwick) Airport 279 D8
Tinhay 99 D2
Tinney 98 C1
Tinshill 194 B4
Tinsley 186 B3
Tinsley Green 122 B5
Tintagel 97 E1

Tintagel Castle *Corn* PL34 0HE 97 E1
Tintern Parva 131 E2
Tintinhull 104 A1
Tintwistle 185 E3
Tinwald 217 E2
Tinwell 161 F2
Tippacott 114 A3
Tipperty *Aber* 253 F1
Tipperty *Aber* 261 H2
Tipps End 162 C2
Tiptoe 106 B3
Tipton 158 B3
Tipton St. John 103 D3
Tiptree 138 B1
Tiptree Heath 138 B1
Tiptree Museum *Essex* CO5 0RF 138 C1
Tirabad 143 E3
Tiree 246 A2
Tiree Airport 246 B2
Tirindrish 249 E1
Tirley 146 A5
Tirphil 130 A2
Tirril 210 B5
Tir-y-dail 128 C1
Tisbury 118 A5
Tisman's Common 121 F4
Tissington 172 C2
Tister 275 G2
Titchberry 112 C3
Titchfield 107 E2
Titchmarsh 161 F5
Titchwell 177 F3
Titchwell Marsh *Norf* PE31 8BB 177 F3
Tithby 174 B4
Titley 144 C2
Titlington 229 F5
Titmore Green 150 A5
Titsey 122 C3
Titson 112 C5
Tittensor 171 F4
Tittleshall 177 G5
Tiverton *ChesW&C* 170 C1
Tiverton *Devon* 102 C1
Tivetshall St. Margaret 164 C3
Tivetshall St. Mary 164 C3
Tivington 114 C3
Tixall 171 G5
Tixover 161 E2
Toab *Ork* 277 E7
Toab *Shet* 279 F9
Tobermory 247 E4
Toberonochy 239 G4
Tobson 270 D4
Tocher 260 E1
Tockenham 132 C5
Tockenham Wick 132 C4
Tockholes 192 C5
Tockington 131 F4
Tockwith 195 D2
Todber 117 E5
Toddington *CenBeds* 149 F5
Toddington *Glos* 146 C4
Todenham 147 E4
Todhills *Angus* 244 C1
Todhills *Cumb* 218 B5
Todlachie 260 E3
Todmorden 193 F5
Todwick 186 B4
Toft *Cambs* 150 B2
Toft *Lincs* 161 F1
Toft *Shet* 278 D5
Toft Hill 212 A5
Toft Monks 165 F2
Toft next Newton 188 A4
Toftcarl 275 J4
Toftrees 177 G5
Tofts 275 J2
Toftwood 178 A4
Togston 221 E1
Tokavaig 256 C3
Tokers Green 134 B5
Tolastadh 263 H1
Tolastadh a' Chaolais 270 D4
Tolastadh Ur 271 H3
Toll Bar 186 C2
Toll of Birness 261 J1
Tolland 115 E4
Tollard Farnham 105 F1
Tollard Royal 105 F1
Tollcross 234 A3
Toller Down Gate 104 B2
Toller Fratrum 104 B3
Toller Porcorum 104 B3
Toller Whelme 104 B2
Tollerton *Notts* 174 B4
Tollerton *NYorks* 195 E1
Tollesbury 138 C1
Tollesby 203 E1
Tolleshunt D'Arcy 138 C1
Tolleshunt Knights 138 C1
Tolleshunt Major 138 B1
Tolmachan 270 C7
Tolpuddle 105 D3
Tolvah 259 F5
Tolworth 121 G1
Tom an Fhuadain 271 F6
Tomatin 259 F2
Tombreck 258 D1
Tomchrasky (Tom Chrasgaidh) 257 J3
Tomdoun 257 H4
Tomdow 267 H7
Tomich *High* 257 K2
Tomich *High* 266 E4
Tomich *High* 266 D1
Tomintoul 259 J3
Tomnacross 266 C5
Tomnamoon 267 H6
Tomnaven 260 C1
Tomnavoulin 259 H1
Tomvaich 259 G1
Ton Pentre 129 F3
Tondu 129 E4
Tonfanau 154 B2
Tong *Kent* 124 A4
Tong *Shrop* 157 G2
Tong *WYorks* 194 B4
Tong Norton 157 G2
Tong Street 194 A4

Tonge 173 F5
Tongham 121 D3
Tongland 216 A5
Tongue 273 H3
Tongue House 273 H3
Tongwynlais 130 A4
Tonmawr 129 E3
Tonna 129 D3
Tonwell 136 C2
Tonypandy 129 F3
Tonyrefail 129 G4
Toot Baldon 134 A2
Toot Hill 137 E2
Toothill *Hants* 106 C1
Toothill *Swin* 132 D4
Tooting Graveney 136 B5
Top End 149 F1
Top of Hebers 184 C2
Topcliffe 202 D5
Topcroft 165 D2
Topcroft Street 165 D2
Toppesfield 151 F4
Toppings 184 B1
Toprow 164 C2
Topsham 102 C3
Topsham Bridge 100 D2
Torastan 246 B3
Torbain 259 J3
Torbeg *Aber* 260 B5
Torbeg *NAyr* 223 E3
Torbothie 234 C4
Torbryan 101 E1
Torcastle 248 D2
Torcross 101 E3
Tordarroch 258 D1
Tore (An Todhar) 266 D6
Toreduff 267 J5
Toremore *High* 259 J1
Toremore *High* 275 G5
Torfrey 97 F4
Torgyle 257 K3
Torksey 187 F5
Torlum 262 C6
Torlundy (Tòrr Lunndaidh) 248 D2
Tormarton 131 G5
Tormisdale 230 A4
Tormore 223 D2
Tornagrain 266 E6
Tornahaish 259 J4
Tornaveen 260 E4
Torness 258 C2
Toronto 212 A4
Torpenhow 209 F3
Torphichen 235 D2
Torphins 260 E4
Torpoint 100 A2
Torquay 101 F1
Torquhan 236 B5
Torran *A&B* 240 A4
Torran *High* 266 E4
Torran *High* 264 B7
Torrance 234 A2
Torrance House 234 A4
Torrancroy 260 B3
Torre *Som* 114 D3
Torre *Torbay* 101 F1
Torrich 267 F6
Torridon 264 E6
Torrin 256 B2
Torrisdale *A&B* 222 C2
Torrisdale *High* 273 J2
Torrish 274 E7
Torrisholme 192 A1
Torroble 266 C1
Torry *Aber* 268 C6
Torry *Aberdeen* 261 H4
Torryburn 235 E1
Torsonce 236 B5
Torterston 269 J6
Torthorwald 217 E3
Tortington 108 B3
Torton 158 A5
Tortworth 131 G3
Torvaig 263 K7
Torver 199 E3
Torwood 234 C1
Torworth 187 D4
Tosberry 112 C3
Toscaig 256 D1
Toseland 150 A1
Tosside 193 D2
Tostarie 246 C5
Tostock 152 A1
Totaig 263 G6
Tote 263 K7
Tote Hill 121 D5
Totegan 274 D2
Totford 119 G4
Totham Hill 138 C1
Tothill 189 E4
Totland 106 C4
Totley 186 A5
Totnes 101 E2
Toton 173 G4
Totronald 246 A4
Totscore 263 J5
Tottenham 136 C3
Tottenhill 163 E1
Tottenhill Row 163 E1
Totteridge *GtLon* 136 B3
Totternhoe 149 E5
Tottington *GtMan* 184 B1
Tottington *Norf* 163 G3
Totton 106 C1
Toulton 115 E4
Tournaig 264 B3
Toux 269 H5
Tovil 123 G3
Tow Law 212 A4
Toward 232 B3
Towcester 148 B3
Towednack 94 B3
Tower Bridge Exhibition *GtLon* SE1 2UP 12 C4
Tower End 163 E1
Tower of London *GtLon* EC3N 4AB 12 C4
Towersey 134 C2
Towie *Aber* 269 G4
Towie *Aber* 260 C3
Towie *Aber* 260 C3
Towiemore 268 B6

Town End *Cambs* 162 C3
Town End *Cumb* 199 F4
Town End *Mersey* 183 F4
Town Green *Lancs* 183 F2
Town Green *Norf* 179 E4
Town of Lowton 184 A3
Town Row 123 E5
Town Street 163 F4
Town Yetholm 228 C4
Townend 211 E3
Townfield 211 E3
Townhead *D&G* 207 G2
Townhead *SYorks* 185 F2
Townhead of Greenlaw 216 B4
Townhill *Fife* 235 F1
Townhill *Swan* 128 C3
Towns End 119 G2
Towns Green 170 D1
Townshend 94 C3
Towthorpe *ERid* 196 B1
Towthorpe *York* 195 F2
Towton 195 D4
Towyn 182 B5
Toynton All Saints 176 B1
Toynton Fen Side 176 B1
Toynton St. Peter 176 C1
Toy's Hill 123 D3
Trabboch 224 C3
Traboe 95 E4
Tradespark *High* 267 F6
Tradespark *Ork* 277 D7
Trafford Centre 184 B3
Trafford Park 184 B3
Trago Mills, Newton Abbot *Devon* TQ12 6JD 102 B3
Trallong 143 F5
Trallwn 128 C3
Tram Inn 145 D4
Tranent 236 B2
Tranmere 183 E4
Trantlebeg 274 D3
Trantlemore 274 D3
Tranwell 221 D3
Trap 128 C1
Trap Street 171 F1
Traprain 236 C2
Trap's Green 146 D1
Trawden 193 F4
Trawscoed (Crosswood) 154 C5
Trawsfynydd 168 A4
Trealaw 129 G3
Treales 192 A4
Trearddur 180 A5
Treaslane 263 J6
Tre-Aubrey 129 G5
Trebanog 129 G3
Trebanos 128 D2
Trebarrow 98 C1
Trebartha 97 G2
Trebarvah 95 E3
Trebarwith 97 E1
Trebeath 97 G1
Trebetherick 96 D2
Trebister 279 D9
Tre-boeth 128 C3
Treborough 114 D4
Trebudannon 96 C3
Trebullett 98 D3
Treburley 98 D3
Treburrick 96 C2
Trebyan 97 E3
Trecastle 143 E5
Trecrogo 98 D2
Trecwn 140 C4
Trecynon 129 F2
Tredaule 97 G1
Tredavoe 94 B4
Treddiog 140 B5
Tredegar 130 A2
Tredington *Glos* 146 B5
Tredington *Warks* 147 E3
Tredinnick *Corn* 96 C3
Tredinnick *Corn* 97 G4
Tredogan 115 D1
Tredomen 144 A4
Tredrissi 141 D3
Tredunnock 130 C3
Tredustan 144 A4
Tredworth 132 A1
Treen *Corn* 94 A4
Treen *Corn* 94 B3
Treesmill 97 E3
Treeton 186 B4
Trefasser 140 B4
Trefecca 144 A4
Trefechan 129 G2
Trefeglwys 155 F3
Trefenter 142 C1
Treffgarne 140 C5
Treffynnon 140 B5
Trefgarn Owen 140 B5
Trefil 130 A1
Trefilan 142 B2
Treflach 169 F5
Trefnanney 156 B1
Trefnant 182 B5
Trefonen 169 F5
Trefor *Gwyn* 166 C3
Trefor *IoA* 180 B4
Treforest 129 G4
Treforest Industrial Estate 130 A4
Trefriw 168 A1
Tregadillett 97 G1
Tregaian 180 C5
Tregare 130 D1
Tregarland 97 G4
Tregarne 95 E4
Tregaron 142 C2
Tregarth 167 F1
Tregaswith 96 C3
Tregavethan 96 B5
Tregear 96 C4
Tregeare 97 G1
Tregeiriog 169 E4
Tregele 180 B3
Tregidden 95 E4
Tregiskey 97 E5

Treglemais 140 B5
Tregolds 96 C2
Tregole 98 B1
Tregonetha 97 D3
Tregony 96 D5
Tregoodwell 97 F1
Tregoss 97 D3
Tregowris 95 E5
Tregoyd 144 A4
Tregrehan Mills 97 E4
Tre-groes 142 A3
Treguff 129 G5
Tregullon 97 E3
Tregunnon 97 G1
Tregurrian 96 C3
Tregynon 155 G3
Trehafod 129 G3
Trehan 100 A2
Treharris 129 G3
Treherbert 129 F3
Tre-hill 129 G5
Trekenner 98 D3
Treknow 97 E1
Trelan 95 E5
Trelash 98 B1
Trelassick 96 C4
Trelawnyd 182 B5
Trelech 141 E4
Treleddyd-fawr 140 A5
Trelewis 130 A3
Treligga 97 D2
Trelights 97 D2
Trelill 97 E2
Trelissick *Corn* TR3 6QL 95 F3
Trelleck 131 E2
Trelleck Grange 131 D2
Trelogan 182 C4
Trelowla 97 G4
Trelystan 156 B2
Tremadog 167 E3
Tremail 97 F1
Tremain 141 E3
Tremaine 97 G1
Tremar 97 G3
Trematon 99 D5
Tremeirchion 182 B5
Tremore 97 E3
Trenance *Corn* 96 C3
Trenance *Corn* 96 D2
Trenarren 97 E5
Trench *Tel&W* 157 F1
Trench *Wrex* 170 A4
Trencreek 96 C3
Trenear 95 D3
Treneglos 97 G1
Trenewan 97 F4
Trengune 98 B1
Trent 104 B1
Trent Port 187 F4
Trent Vale 171 F3
Trentham 171 F3
Trentishoe 113 G1
Trenwheal 94 D3
Treoes 129 F5
Treorchy 129 F3
Treowen 130 B3
Trequite 97 E2
Tre'r-ddol 154 C3
Trerhyngyll 129 G5
Tre-Rhys 141 E3
Trerulefoot 98 D5
Tresaith 141 F2
Tresco 96 A1
Trescott 158 A3
Trescowe 94 C3
Tresean 96 B4
Tresham 131 G3
Treshnish 246 C5
Tresillian 96 C5
Tresinney 97 F1
Tresinwen 140 B3
Treskinnick Cross 98 C1
Treslea 97 F3
Tresmeer 97 G1
Tresowes Green 94 D4
Tresparrett 98 B1
Tresparrett Posts 98 B1
Tressait 250 C3
Tresta *Shet* 278 F3
Tresta *Shet* 279 C7
Treswell 187 E5
Trethewey 94 A4
Trethomas 130 A4
Trethurgy 97 E4
Tretio 140 A5
Tretire 145 E5
Tretower 144 A5
Treuddyn 169 F2
Trevadlock 97 G2
Trevalga 98 A1
Trevalyn 170 A2
Trevanson 97 D2
Trevarnon 94 C3
Trevarrack 94 B3
Trevarren 96 D3
Trevarrian 96 C3
Trevarrick 97 D5
Tre-vaughan *Carmar* 141 G5
Trevaughan *Carmar* 127 E1
Treveighan 97 E2
Trevellas 96 B4
Trevelmond 97 G3
Trevenen 95 E3
Treverva 95 E3
Trevescan 94 A4
Trevethin 130 B2
Trevigro 98 D4
Trevine 240 C2
Treviscoe 96 D4
Trevivian 97 F1
Trevone 96 C2
Trevor 169 F3
Trewalder 97 E1
Trewarmett 97 E1
Trewarthenick 96 D5
Trewassa 97 F1
Trewellard 94 A3
Trewen *Corn* 97 G1
Trewen *Here* 131 E1
Trewennack 95 D4
Trewent 126 D3
Trewern 156 B1
Trewethern 97 E2
Trewidland 97 G4
Trewilym 141 E3

Trewint *Corn* **98** B1
Trewint *Corn* **97** G1
Trewithian **95** F3
Trewoon **97** D4
Treworga **96** C5
Treworlas **95** F3
Trewornan **97** D2
Treworthal **95** F3
Tre-wyn **144** C5
Treyarnon **96** C2
Treyford **108** A2
Trezaise **97** D4
Triangle **193** G5
Trickett's Cross **105** G2
Triermain **210** B1
Trimdon **212** C4
Trimdon Colliery **212** C4
Trimdon Grange **212** C4
Trimingham **179** D2
Trimley Lower Street **153** D4
Trimley St. Martin **153** D4
Trimley St. Mary **153** D4
Trimpley **157** G5
Trimsaran **128** A2
Trimstone **113** E1
Trinafour **250** C3
Trinant **130** B3
Tring **135** E1
Trinity *Angus* **253** E3
Trinity *Chanl* **100** C5
Trinity *Edin* **235** G2
Trisant **154** D5
Triscombe *Som* **114** C4
Triscombe *Som* **115** E4
Trislaig **248** C2
Trispen **96** C4
Tritlington **221** E2
Trochry **243** E1
Troedyraur **141** G3
Troedyrhiw **129** G2
Trofarth **181** G5
Trondavoe **278** C5
Troon *Corn* **95** D3
Troon *SAyr* **224** B2
Tropical Butterfly House, Wildlife & Falconry Centre *SYorks* S25 4EQ **21** F3
Tropical World, Roundhay *WYorks* LS8 2ER **27** G1
Trosaraidh **254** C3
Troston **163** G5
Troswell **98** C1
Trottick **244** C1
Trottiscliffe **123** F2
Trotton **120** D5
Trough Gate **193** E5
Troughend **220** A2
Troustan **232** B2
Troutbeck *Cumb* **199** F2
Troutbeck *Cumb* **209** G4
Troutbeck Bridge **199** F2
Trow Green **131** E2
Troway **186** A5
Trowbridge *Cardiff* **130** B4
Trowbridge *Wilts* **117** F2
Trowell **173** F4
Trowle Common **117** F2
Trowley Bottom **135** F1
Trows **228** A3
Trowse Newton **178** D5
Troy **194** B4
Trudernish **230** C4
Trudoxhill **117** E3
Trull **115** F5
Trumaisgearraidh **262** D4
Trumpan **263** H5
Trumpet **145** F4
Trumpington **150** C2
Trumps Green **121** E1
Trunch **179** D2
Trunnah **191** G3
Truro **96** C5
Truro Cathedral *Corn* TR1 2AF **96** C5
Truscott **98** D2
Trusham **102** B4
Trusley **173** D4
Trusthorpe **189** F4
Truthan **96** C4
Trysull **158** A3
Tubney **133** G3
Tuckenhay **101** E2
Tuckhill **157** G4
Tuckingmill **96** A5
Tuddenham *Suff* **152** C3
Tuddenham *Suff* **163** F5
Tudeley **123** F4
Tudeley Hale **123** F4
Tudhoe **212** B4
Tudweiliog **166** B4
Tuesley **121** E3
Tuffley **132** A1
Tufton *Hants* **119** F3
Tufton *Pembs* **140** D5
Tugby **160** C2
Tugford **157** E4
Tughall **229** G4
Tulchan **243** E2
Tulleys Farm *WSuss* RH10 4PE **122** C5
Tullibardine Distillery *P&K* PH4 1QG **243** E4
Tullibody **243** D5
Tullich *A&B* **240** C3
Tullich *A&B* **240** A3
Tullich *High* **267** F4
Tullich *High* **258** D2
Tullich *Moray* **268** B6
Tullich *Stir* **242** A1
Tullich Muir **266** E4
Tullie House Museum & Art Gallery *Cumb* CA3 8TP **68** Carlisle
Tulliemet **251** F4
Tulloch *Aber* **261** G1
Tulloch *High* **266** D2
Tulloch *Moray* **267** H6
Tullochgorm **240** B5
Tullochgribban High **259** G2
Tullochvenus **260** D4
Tulloes **252** D5
Tullybannocher **242** C2
Tullybelton **243** F1
Tullyfergus **252** A5
Tullymurdoch **251** G4
Tullynessle **260** D3
Tulse Hill **136** C5
Tumble (Y Tymbl) **128** B1
Tumby **176** A2
Tumby Woodside **176** A2
Tummel Bridge **250** C4
Tunbridge Wells **123** E5
Tundergarth Mains **217** F2
Tunga **271** G4
Tungate **179** D3
Tunley **117** D2
Tunstall *ERid* **197** F4
Tunstall *Kent* **124** A2
Tunstall *Lancs* **200** B5
Tunstall *Norf* **179** F5
Tunstall *NYorks* **202** B3
Tunstall *Stoke* **171** F2
Tunstall *Suff* **153** E2
Tunstall *T&W* **212** C2
Tunstead *GtMan* **185** E2
Tunstead *Norf* **179** E3
Tunstead Milton **185** E4
Tunworth **120** B3
Tupholme **175** G1
Tupsley **145** E4
Tupton **173** E1
Tur Langton **160** C3
Turbiskill **231** F1
Turclossie **269** G5
Turgis Green **120** B2
Turin **252** D4
Turkdean **132** D1
Turleigh **117** F1
Turn **184** C1
Turnastone **144** C4
Turnberry **224** A5
Turnchapel **100** A2
Turnditch **173** D3
Turner's Green **147** D1
Turners Hill **122** C5
Turners Puddle **105** E3
Turnford **136** C2
Turnworth **105** E2
Turret Bridge **257** K5
Turriff **269** F6
Turton Bottoms **184** B1
Turvey **149** E2
Turville **134** C3
Turville Heath **134** C3
Turweston **148** B4
Tutankhamun Exhibition, Dorchester *Dorset* DT1 1UW **104** C3
Tutbury **172** D5
Tutbury Castle *Staffs* DE13 9JF **172** D5
Tutnall **158** B5
Tutshill **131** E3
Tuttington **178** D3
Tutts Clump **134** A5
Tutwell **99** D3
Tuxford **187** E5
Twatt *Ork* **276** B5
Twatt *Shet* **279** C7
Twechar **234** B2
Tweedmouth **237** G4
Tweedsmuir **226** B3
Twelve Oaks **110** B1
Twelveheads **96** B5
Twemlow Green **171** E1
Twenty **175** G5
Twickenham **136** A5
Twigworth **146** A5
Twineham **109** E1
Twineham Green **109** E1
Twinhoe **117** E2
Twinstead **151** G4
Twiss Green **184** A3
Twiston **193** E3
Twitchen *Devon* **114** A4
Twitchen *Shrop* **156** C5
Twitton **123** E3
Twizell House **229** F4
Two Bridges *Devon* **99** G3
Two Bridges *Glos* **131** F2
Two Dales **173** D1
Two Gates **159** E2
Two Mills **183** E5
Twycross **159** F2
Twycross Zoo *Leics* CV9 3PX **159** F2
Twyford *Bucks* **148** B5
Twyford *Derbys* **173** E5
Twyford *Dorset* **105** E1
Twyford *Hants* **119** F5
Twyford *Leics* **160** C1
Twyford *Norf* **178** B3
Twyford *Oxon* **147** G4
Twyford *W'ham* **134** C5
Twyford Common **145** E4
Twyn Shôn-Ifan **130** A3
Twynholm **216** A5
Twyning **146** A4
Twynllanan **143** D5
Twyn-yr-odyn **130** A5
Twyn-y-Sheriff **130** D2
Twywell **161** E5
Ty Croes **180** B5
Tyberton **144** C4
Tycroes **128** C1
Tycrwyn **156** A1
Tydd Gote **162** C1
Tydd St. Giles **162** C1
Tydd St. Mary **162** C1
Tye Common **137** F3
Tye Green *Essex* **151** F5
Tye Green *Essex* **150** D5
Tye Green *Essex* **137** F1
Tye Green *Essex* **136** D2
Tyersal **194** A4
Ty-hen **166** A4
Tyldesley **184** A2
Tyle-garw **129** G4
Tyler Hill **124** D2
Tylers Green *Bucks* **135** E3
Tyler's Green *Essex* **137** E2
Tylorstown **129** G3
Tylwch **155** F5
Ty-Mawr *Conwy* **168** C3
Ty-mawr *Denb* **169** E3
Ty-nant *Conwy* **168** C3
Ty-nant *Gwyn* **168** C5
Tyndrum (Taigh an Droma) **241** F1
Tyne Green Country Park *N'umb* NE46 3RY **211** F1
Tyneham **105** E4
Tynehead **236** A4
Tynemouth **212** C1
Tynewydd **129** F3
Tyninghame **236** D2
Tynron **216** C1
Tyntesfield **131** E5
Ty'n-y-cefn **169** D3
Ty'n-y-coedcae **130** A4
Tyn-y-cwm **155** E4
Tyn-y-ffridd **169** E4
Tyn-y-garn **129** E4
Tyn-y-gongl **180** D4
Tynygraig *Cere* **142** C1
Tyn-y-graig *Powys* **143** G3
Ty'n-y-groes **181** F5
Tyrie **269** H4
Tyringham **149** D3
Tyseley **158** D4
Tythegston **129** E5
Tytherington *ChesE* **184** D5
Tytherington *SGlos* **131** F4
Tytherington *Som* **117** E3
Tytherington *Wilts* **118** A3
Tytherton Lucas **132** B5
Tyttenhanger **136** A2
Ty-uchaf **168** C5
Tywardreath **97** E4
Tywardreath Highway **97** E4
Tywyn **154** B2

## U

Uachdar **262** D6
Uags **256** D1
Ubberley **171** G3
Ubbeston Green **165** E4
Ubley **116** C2
Uckerby **202** B2
Uckfield **109** G1
Uckinghall **146** A4
Uckington **146** B5
Uddingston **234** A3
Uddington **225** G2
Udimore **111** D2
Udley **116** B1
Udny Green **261** G2
Udny Station **261** H2
Udston **234** B4
Udstonhead **234** B5
Uffcott **132** D5
Uffculme **103** D1
Uffington *Lincs* **161** F2
Uffington *Oxon* **133** F4
Uffington *Shrop* **157** E1
Ufford *Peter* **161** F2
Ufford *Suff* **153** D2
Ufton **147** F1
Ufton Green **120** B1
Ufton Nervet **120** B1
Ugborough **100** C2
Ugford **118** B4
Uggeshall **165** F3
Ugglebarnby **204** B2
Ugley **150** D5
Ugley Green **150** D5
Ugthorpe **203** G1
Uidh **254** B5
Uig *A&B* **246** A4
Uig *A&B* **232** C1
Uig (Uige) *High* **263** J5
Uig *High* **263** G6
Uigen **270** C4
Uiginish **263** H7
Uigshader **263** K7
Uisken **238** C3
Uiskevagh (Uisgebhagh) **262** D6
Ulbster **275** J4
Ulcat Row **210** A5
Ulceby *Lincs* **189** E5
Ulceby *NLincs* **188** B1
Ulceby Cross **189** E5
Ulceby Skitter **188** B1
Ulcombe **124** A4
Uldale **209** F3
Uldale House **200** C3
Uley **131** G3
Ulgham **221** E2
Ullapool (Ullapul) **265** H2
Ullenhall **146** D1
Ullenwood **132** B1
Ulleskelf **195** E4
Ullesthorpe **160** A4
Ulley **186** B4
Ulley Reservoir Country Park *SYorks* S26 3XL **21** E2
Ullingswick **145** E3
Ullinish **255** J1
Ullock **209** D4
Ullswater Steamers *Cumb* CA11 0US **209** G5
Ulpha *Cumb* **198** C3
Ulpha *Cumb* **199** F4
Ulrome **197** D2
Ulsta **278** D4
Ulting **138** B2
Uluvalt **239** E1
Ulva **238** D1
Ulverston **199** D5
Ulwell **105** G4
Ulzieside **225** F5
Umberleigh **113** G3
Unapool **272** E5
Underbarrow **199** F3
Undercliffe **194** A4
Underhill **136** B3
Underhoull **278** E2
Underling Green **123** G4
Underriver **123** E3
Underwood *Newport* **130** C4
Underwood *Notts* **173** F2
Underwood *Plym* **100** B2
Undley **163** E4
Undy **130** D4
Ungisiadar **270** D5
Unifirth **279** B7
Union Croft **261** G5
Union Mills **190** B4
Union Street **123** G5
University of Glasgow Visitor Centre *Glas* G12 8QQ **38** B1
Unst **278** F1
Unst Airport **278** F2
Unstone **186** A5
Unstone Green **186** A5
Unsworth **184** C2
Unthank *Cumb* **210** A4
Unthank *Derbys* **186** A5
Up Cerne **104** C2
Up Exe **102** C2
Up Hatherley **146** B5
Up Holland **183** G2
Up Marden **107** G1
Up Mudford **104** B1
Up Nately **120** B2
Up Somborne **119** E4
Up Sydling **104** C2
Upavon **118** C2
Upchurch **124** A2
Upcott *Devon* **99** E1
Upcott *Devon* **113** F2
Upcott *Here* **144** C2
Upcott *Som* **114** C5
Upend **151** E2
Upgate **178** C4
Upgate Street *Norf* **164** B2
Upgate Street *Norf* **165** D2
Uphall *Dorset* **104** B2
Uphall *WLoth* **235** E2
Uphall Station **235** E3
Upham *Devon* **102** B2
Upham *Hants* **119** G5
Uphampton *Here* **144** C1
Uphampton *Worcs* **146** A1
Uphempston **101** E1
Uphill **116** A2
Uplands *Glos* **132** A2
Uplands *Swan* **128** C3
Uplawmoor **233** F4
Upleadon **145** G5
Upleatham **203** F1
Uplees **124** C2
Uploders **104** B3
Uplowman **102** D1
Uplyme **103** G3
Upminster **137** E4
Upottery **103** F2
Upper Affcot **156** D4
Upper Ardroscadale **232** B3
Upper Arley **157** G4
Upper Arncott **134** B1
Upper Astley **157** E1
Upper Aston **158** A3
Upper Astrop **148** A4
Upper Barvas **271** F2
Upper Basildon **134** B5
Upper Bayble (Pabail Uarach) **271** H4
Upper Beeding **109** D2
Upper Benefield **161** E4
Upper Bentley **146** B1
Upper Berwick **157** D1
Upper Bighouse **274** D3
Upper Boat **130** A4
Upper Boddam **260** E1
Upper Boddington **147** G2
Upper Borth **154** C4
Upper Boyndlie **269** H4
Upper Brailes **147** F4
Upper Breakish **256** C2
Upper Breinton **145** D3
Upper Broadheath **146** A2
Upper Broughton **174** B5
Upper Brynamman **128** D1
Upper Bucklebury **119** G1
Upper Burgate **106** A1
Upper Burnhaugh **261** G5
Upper Caldecote **149** G3
Upper Camster **275** H4
Upper Canada **116** A2
Upper Catesby **148** A2
Upper Catshill **158** B5
Upper Chapel **143** G3
Upper Cheddon **115** F5
Upper Chicksgrove **118** A4
Upper Chute **119** D2
Upper Clatford **119** E3
Upper Coberley **132** B1
Upper Colwall **145** G3
Upper Cotton **172** B3
Upper Cound **157** E2
Upper Cumberworth **185** G2
Upper Cwmbran **130** B3
Upper Dallachy **268** B4
Upper Dean **149** F1
Upper Denby **185** G2
Upper Denton **210** C1
Upper Derraid **259** H1
Upper Derwent Reservoirs *Derbys* S33 0AQ **185** F4
Upper Diabaig **264** E5
Upper Dicker **110** A2
Upper Dovercourt **152** D4
Upper Dunsforth **194** D1
Upper Dunsley **135** E1
Upper Eastern Green **159** E4
Upper Eathie **266** E5
Upper Egleton **145** F3
Upper Elkstone **172** B2
Upper End **185** E5
Upper Enham **119** E3
Upper Farringdon **120** C4
Upper Framilode **131** G1
Upper Froyle **120** C3
Upper Gills **275** J1
Upper Glendessarry **257** F5
Upper Godney **116** B3
Upper Gornal **158** B3
Upper Gravenhurst **149** G4
Upper Green *Essex* **150** C4
Upper Green *Essex* **151** D4
Upper Green *Mon* **130** C1
Upper Green *WBerks* **119** E1
Upper Grove Common **145** E5
Upper Gylen **240** A2
Upper Hackney **173** D1
Upper Halliford **121** F1
Upper Halling **123** F2
Upper Hambleton **161** E2
Upper Harbledown **124** D3
Upper Hardres Court **125** D3
Upper Hartfield **123** D5
Upper Hatton **171** F4
Upper Hawkhillock **261** J1
Upper Hayesden **123** E4
Upper Hayton **157** E4
Upper Heath **157** E4
Upper Heaton **185** F1
Upper Hellesdon **178** D4
Upper Helmsley **195** F2
Upper Hengoed **169** F4
Upper Hergest **144** B2
Upper Heyford *N'hants* **148** B2
Upper Heyford *Oxon* **147** G5
Upper Hill *Here* **145** D2
Upper Hill *SGlos* **131** F3
Upper Horsebridge **110** A2
Upper Howsell **145** G3
Upper Hulme **172** B1
Upper Inglesham **133** E3
Upper Kilchattan **238** C5
Upper Killay **128** B3
Upper Knockando **267** J7
Upper Lambourn **133** F4
Upper Langford **116** B2
Upper Langwith **173** G1
Upper Largo **244** C4
Upper Leigh **172** B4
Upper Lochton **260** E5
Upper Loads **173** E1
Upper Lochton **260** E5
Upper Longdon **158** C1
Upper Longwood **157** F2
Upper Ludstone **158** A3
Upper Lybster **275** H5
Upper Lydbrook **131** F1
Upper Lyde **145** D3
Upper Lye **144** C1
Upper Maes-coed **144** C4
Upper Midhope **185** G3
Upper Milovaig **263** G7
Upper Milton **133** E1
Upper Minety **132** C3
Upper Moor **146** B3
Upper Morton **131** F3
Upper Muirskie **261** G5
Upper Nash **126** D2
Upper Newbold **186** A5
Upper North Dean **135** D3
Upper Norwood **136** C5
Upper Obney **243** F1
Upper Oddington **147** E5
Upper Ollach **256** B1
Upper Padley **185** G5
Upper Pennington **106** B3
Upper Pollicott **134** C1
Upper Poppleton **195** E2
Upper Quinton **147** D3
Upper Ratley **119** E5
Upper Ridinghill **269** J5
Upper Rissington **147** E5
Upper Rochford **145** F1
Upper Sanday **277** E7
Upper Sapey **145** F1
Upper Scolton **140** C5
Upper Seagry **132** B4
Upper Shelton **149** E3
Upper Sheringham **178** C1
Upper Shuckburgh **147** G1
Upper Siddington **132** C3
Upper Skelmorlie **232** D3
Upper Slaughter **147** D5
Upper Sonachan **240** C2
Upper Soudley **131** F1
Upper Stanploe **149** G2
Upper Stoke **179** D5
Upper Stondon **149** G4
Upper Stowe **148** B2
Upper Street *Hants* **106** A1
Upper Street *Norf* **179** E4
Upper Street *Norf* **164** C4
Upper Street *Suff* **152** C4
Upper Street *Suff* **152** C2
Upper Strensham **146** B4
Upper Sundon **149** F5
Upper Swanmore **107** E1
Upper Swell **147** D5
Upper Tean **172** B4
Upper Thurnham **192** A2
Upper Tillyrie **243** G4
Upper Tooting **136** B5
Upper Town *Derbys* **172** D1
Upper Town *Derbys* **173** D2
Upper Town *Derbys* **172** D2
Upper Town *Here* **145** E3
Upper Town *NSom* **116** C1
Upper Tysoe **147** F3
Upper Upham **133** E5
Upper Upnor **137** G5
Upper Victoria **244** D1
Upper Vobster **117** E3
Upper Wardington **147** G3
Upper Waterhay **132** C3
Upper Weald **148** D4
Upper Weedon **148** B2
Upper Welson **144** B2
Upper Weston **117** E1
Upper Whiston **186** B4
Upper Wick **146** A2
Upper Wield **120** B4
Upper Winchendon (Over Winchendon) **134** C1
Upper Witton **158** C3
Upper Woodford **118** C4
Upper Woolhampton **119** G1
Upper Wootton **119** G2
Upper Wraxall **132** A5
Upper Wyche **145** G3
Upperby **210** A2
Uppermill **185** D2
Upperthong **185** F2
Upperton **121** E5
Uppertown *Derbys* **173** E1
Uppertown *Ork* **275** J1
Uppingham **161** D2
Uppington **157** E2
Upsall **203** D4
Upsettlington **237** F5
Upshire **136** D2
Upstreet **125** E2
Upthorpe **164** A4
Upton *Bucks* **134** C1
Upton *Cambs* **161** G5
Upton *ChesW&C* **170** B1
Upton *Corn* **97** G2
Upton *Corn* **112** C5
Upton *Devon* **103** D2
Upton *Devon* **100** D3
Upton *Dorset* **105** F3
Upton *Dorset* **104** D4
Upton *ERid* **196** D2
Upton *Hants* **119** E2
Upton *Hants* **106** C1
Upton *Leics* **159** F3
Upton *Lincs* **187** F4
Upton *Mersey* **183** D4
Upton *N'hants* **148** C1
Upton *Norf* **179** E4
Upton *Notts* **187** E5
Upton *Notts* **174** C2
Upton *Oxon* **134** A4
Upton *Oxon* **133** E1
Upton *Pembs* **126** D2
Upton *Peter* **161** G2
Upton *Slo* **135** E5
Upton *Som* **114** C5
Upton *Som* **116** B5
Upton *Wilts* **117** F4
Upton *WYorks* **186** B1
Upton Bishop **145** F5
Upton Cheyney **117** D1
Upton Country Park *Poole* BH17 7BJ **3** A3
Upton Cressett **157** F3
Upton Crews **145** F5
Upton Cross **97** G2
Upton End **149** G4
Upton Grey **120** B3
Upton Hellions **102** B2
Upton Lovell **118** A3
Upton Magna **157** E1
Upton Noble **117** E4
Upton Park **136** D4
Upton Pyne **102** C3
Upton St. Leonards **132** A1
Upton Scudamore **117** F3
Upton Snodsbury **146** B2
Upton upon Severn **146** A3
Upton Warren **146** B1
Upwaltham **108** B2
Upware **162** D5
Upwell **162** D2
Upwey **104** C4
Upwick Green **150** C5
Upwood **162** A4
Uradale **279** D9
Urafirth **278** C5
Urbis, Manchester *GtMan* M4 3BG **47** E2
Urchany **267** F7
Urchfont **118** B2
Urdimarsh **145** E3
Ure **278** B5
Urgha **263** G2
Urlay Nook **202** D1
Urmston **184** B3
Urpeth **212** B2
Urquhart *High* **266** C6
Urquhart *Moray* **267** K5
Urquhart Castle *High* IV63 6XJ **258** C2
Urra **203** E2
Urray **266** C6
Ushaw Moor **212** B3
Usher Hall, Edinburgh *Edin* EH1 2EA **36** E5
Usk (Brynbuga) **130** C2
Usselby **188** A3
Usworth **212** C2
Utley **193** G3
Uton **102** B3
Utterby **188** D3
Uttoxeter **172** B4
Uwchmynydd **166** A5
Uxbridge **135** F4
Uyeasound **278** E2
Uzmaston **126** C1

## V

Valley (Y Fali) **180** A5
Valley Truckle **97** F1
Valleyfield *D&G* **216** A5
Valleyfield *Fife* **235** E1
Valsgarth **278** F1
Vange **137** G4
Vardre **128** C2
Varteg **130** B2
Vatersay (Bhatarsaigh) **254** B5
Vatsetter **278** E4
Vatten **263** H7
Vaul **246** B2
Vaynor **129** G1
Vaynor Park **156** A2
Veaullt **144** A2
Veensgarth **279** D8
Velindre *Pembs* **141** D4
Velindre *Powys* **144** A4
Vellow **115** D4
Veness **276** E5
Venn **100** D3
Venn Ottery **103** D3
Venngreen **113** D4
Vennington **156** C2
Venny Tedburn **102** B3
Venterdon **99** D3
Ventnor **107** E5
Ventnor Botanic Gardens *IoW* PO38 1UL **107** E5
Venton **100** B2
Venue Cymru, Llandudno *Conwy* LL30 1BB **181** F4
Vernham Dean **119** E2
Vernham Street **119** E2
Vernolds Common **157** D4
Verwood **105** G2
Veryan **95** G3
Veryan Green **96** D5
Vickerstown **191** E1
Victoria **97** D3
Victoria & Albert Museum *GtLon* SW7 2RL **11** F5
Victoria Art Gallery *B&NESom* BA2 4AT **63** Bath
Vidlin **279** D6
Viewfield **275** F2
Viewpark **234** B3
Vigo **158** C2
Vigo Village **123** F2
Villavin **113** F4
Vinehall Street **110** C1
Vine's Cross **110** A2
Viney Hill **131** F2
Virginia Water **121** E1
Virginstow **99** D1
Virley **138** C1
Vobster **117** E3
Voe *Shet* **279** D6
Voe *Shet* **278** C4
Vogrie Country Park *Midlo* EH23 4NU **32** F4
Voirrey Embroidery *Mersey* CH63 6JA **22** A5
Volks Electric Railway *B&H* BN2 1EN **109** F3
Vowchurch **144** C4
Voy **277** B6
Vron Gate **156** C2

## W

W.R. Outhwaite & Son Ropemakers *NYorks* DL8 3NT **201** D4
Waberthwaite **198** C3
Wackerfield **212** A5
Wacton **164** C2
Wadbister **279** D8
Wadborough **146** B3
Waddesdon **134** C1
Waddesdon Manor *Bucks* HP18 0JH **134** C1
Waddeton **101** E2
Waddicar **183** E3
Waddingham **187** G3
Waddington *Lancs* **192** D3
Waddington *Lincs* **175** E1
Waddingworth **188** B5
Waddon *Devon* **102** B5
Waddon *GtLon* **122** C2
Wadebridge **97** D2
Wadeford **103** G1
Wadenhoe **161** F4
Wadesmill **136** C1
Wadhurst **123** F5
Wadshelf **186** A5
Wadworth **186** C3
Wadworth Hill **197** E5
Waen *Denb* **169** E1
Waen *Denb* **168** C1
Waen Aberwheeler **169** D1
Waen-fâch **156** B1
Waen-wen **167** E1
Wag **275** F6
Wainfleet All Saints **176** C2
Wainfleet Bank **176** C2
Wainfleet St. Mary **176** C2
Wainford **165** E2
Waingroves **173** F3
Wainhouse Corner **98** B1
Wainscott **137** G5
Wainstalls **193** G5
Waitby **200** C2
Wakefield **194** C5
Wakehurst Place *WSuss* RH17 6TN **122** C5
Wakerley **161** E3
Wakes Colne **151** G5
Walberswick **165** F4
Walberton **108** B3
Walbottle **212** A1
Walcot *Lincs* **175** F4
Walcot *Lincs* **175** G2
Walcot *NLincs* **196** A5
Walcot *Shrop* **156** C4
Walcot *Tel&W* **157** E1
Walcot Green **164** C3
Walcote *Leics* **160** A4
Walcote *Warks* **146** D2
Walcott **179** E2
Walcott Dales **175** G2
Walden **201** F4
Walden Head **201** E4
Walden Stubbs **186** C1
Walderslade **123** G2
Walderton **107** G1
Walditch **104** A3
Waldley **172** C4
Waldridge **212** B3
Waldringfield **153** D3
Waldron **110** A2
Wales **186** B4
Wales Millennium Centre, Cardiff *Cardiff* CF10 5AL **130** A5
Walesby *Lincs* **188** B3
Walesby *Notts* **187** D5
Waleswood **186** B4
Walford *Here* **156** C5
Walford *Here* **145** E5
Walford *Shrop* **170** B5
Walford *Staffs* **171** F4
Walford Heath **156** D1
Walgherton **171** D3
Walgrave **160** D5
Walhampton **106** C3
Walk Mill **193** E4
Walkden **184** B2
Walker **212** B1
Walker Art Gallery, Liverpool *Mersey* L3 8EL **42** D3
Walker Fold **192** C3
Walkerburn **227** E2
Walkeringham **187** E3
Walkerith **187** E3
Walkern **150** A5
Walker's Green **145** E3
Walkford **106** B3
Walkhampton **100** B1
Walkingham Hill **194** C1
Walkington **196** B4
Walkwood **146** C1
Wall *Corn* **94** D3
Wall *N'umb* **211** F1
Wall *Staffs* **158** D2
Wall End **198** D4
Wall Heath **158** A4
Wall Houses **211** G1
Wall under Heywood **157** E3
Wallace Collection, London *GtLon* W1U 3BN **44** A2
Wallacehall **218** A4
Wallacetown **224** A5
Wallasey **183** D3
Wallaston Green **126** C2
Wallend **124** A1
Waller's Green **145** F4
Wallingford **134** B4
Wallington *GtLon* **122** B2
Wallington *Hants* **107** E2
Wallington *Herts* **150** A4
Wallington *Wrex* **170** B3
Wallingwells **186** C4
Wallis **140** D5
Wallisdown **105** G3
Walliswood **121** G4
Walls **279** B8
Wallsend **212** C1
Wallyford **236** A2
Walmer **125** F3
Walmer Bridge **192** A5
Walmersley **184** C1
Walmley **158** D3
Walmsgate **189** D5
Walpole **165** E4
Walpole Cross Keys **162** D1
Walpole Highway **162** D1
Walpole Marsh **162** C1
Walpole St. Andrew **162** D1
Walpole St. Peter **162** D1
Walrond's Park **116** A5
Walrow **116** A3
Walsall **158** C3

Walsall Arboretum
Illuminations *WMid*
WS1 2AB **14** D1
Walsall Wood **158** C2
Walsden **193** F5
Walsgrave on Sowe **159** H4
Walshford **194** D2
Walsoken **162** C1
Walston **235** E5
Walsworth **149** G4
Walter's Ash **134** D3
Walterston **129** G5
Walterstone **144** C5
Waltham *Kent* **124** D4
Waltham *NELincs* **188** C2
Waltham Abbey **136** C2
Waltham Chase **107** E1
Waltham Cross **136** C2
Waltham on the
Wolds **174** C5
Waltham
St. Lawrence **134** D5
Walthamstow **136** C4
Walton *Bucks* **134** D1
Walton *Cumb* **210** B1
Walton *Derbys* **173** E1
Walton *Leics* **160** A4
Walton *Mersey* **183** E3
Walton *MK* **149** D4
Walton *Peter* **161** G2
Walton *Powys* **144** B2
Walton *Shrop* **157** D5
Walton *Som* **116** B4
Walton *Staffs* **171** F4
Walton *Suff* **153** E2
Walton *Tel&W* **157** E2
Walton *Warks* **147** E2
Walton *WYorks* **194** A1
Walton *WYorks* **194** D3
Walton Cardiff **146** B4
Walton East **140** D4
Walton Elm **105** D1
Walton Highway **162** C1
Walton Lower Street **153** D4
Walton on the Hill **122** B3
Walton on the Naze **153** D5
Walton on the Wolds **160** A1
Walton Park *D&G* **216** B3
Walton Park *NSom* **130** D5
Walton West **126** B1
Walton-in-Gordano **130** D5
Walton-le-Dale **192** B5
Walton-on-Thames **121** G1
Walton-on-the-Hill **171** G5
Walton-on-Trent **159** E1
Walwen *Flints* **182** C5
Walwen *Flints* **182** D5
Walwick **220** B4
Walworth **202** B1
Walworth Gate **212** B5
Walwyn's Castle **126** B1
Wambrook **103** F2
Wanborough *Surr* **121** E3
Wanborough *Swin* **133** E4
Wandel **226** A3
Wandon **229** E4
Wandon End **149** G5
Wandsworth **136** B5
Wandylaw **229** F4
Wangford *Suff* **165** F4
Wangford *Suff* **163** F4
Wanlip **160** A1
Wanlockhead **225** G4
Wannock **110** A3
Wansbeck Riverside Park
*N'umb* NE63 8TX **221** E3
Wansford *ERid* **196** C2
Wansford *Peter* **161** F3
Wanshurst Green **123** G4
Wanstrow **117** E3
Wanswell **131** F2
Wantage **133** F4
Wapley **131** G5
Wappenbury **147** F1
Wappenham **148** B3
Warbleton **110** B2
Warblington **107** G2
Warborough **134** A3
Warboys **162** B4
Warbreck **191** G4
Warbstow **98** C1
Warburton **184** A4
Warcop **200** C3
Ward End **158** D4
Ward Green **152** B1
Warden *Kent* **124** C1
Warden *N'umb* **211** F1
Warden Hill **146** B5
Warden Street **149** G3
Wardhouse **260** D1
Wardington **147** G3
Wardle *ChesE* **170** D2
Wardle *GtMan* **184** D1
Wardley *GtMan* **184** B2
Wardley *Rut* **160** D2
Wardley *T&W* **212** C1
Wardlow **185** F5
Wardsend **184** D4
Wardy Hill **162** C4
Ware *Herts* **136** C1
Ware *Kent* **125** E2
Wareham **105** F4
Warehorne **124** B5
Waren Mill **229** F3
Warenford **229** F4
Warenton **229** F3
Wareside **136** C1
Waresley *Cambs* **150** A2
Waresley *Worcs* **158** A5
Warfield **135** D5
Wargrave *Mersey* **183** G3
Wargrave *W'ham* **134** C5
Warham *Here* **145** E4
Warham *Norf* **178** A1
Wark *N'umb* **220** A4
Wark *N'umb* **228** C3
Warkleigh **113** G3
Warkton **161** D5
Warkworth *N'hants* **147** G3
Warkworth *N'umb* **221** E1
Warland **193** F5
Warleggan **97** F3
Warley *Essex* **137** E3
Warley *WMid* **158** C4

Warley Town **193** G5
Warlingham **122** C3
Warmfield **194** C5
Warmingham **171** E1
Warminghurst **108** D2
Warmington *N'hants* **161** F3
Warmington *Warks* **147** G3
Warminster **117** F3
Warmlake **124** A4
Warmley **131** F5
Warmley Hill **131** F5
Warmsworth **186** C2
Warmwell **105** D4
Warndon **146** A2
Warners End **135** F2
Warnford **120** B5
Warnham **121** G4
Warningcamp **108** C3
Warninglid **109** E2
Warren *ChesE* **184** C5
Warren *Pembs* **126** C3
Warren House **99** G2
Warren Row **134** D4
Warren Street **124** B3
Warrenby **213** E5
Warren's Green **150** A5
Warrington *MK* **149** D4
Warrington *Warr* **184** A4
Warroch **243** F4
Warsash **107** D2
Warslow **172** B2
Warsop Vale **173** G1
Warter **196** A2
Warthermarske
Warthill **195** F2
Wartle **260** D4
Wartling **110** B3
Wartnaby **174** C5
Warton *Lancs* **199** G5
Warton *Lancs* **191** G4
Warton *N'umb* **220** C1
Warton *Warks* **159** E2
Warton Bank **192** A5
Warwick **147** E1
Warwick Bridge **210** A2
Warwick Castle *Warks*
CV34 4QU **16** A6
Warwick Wold **122** C3
Warwick-on-Eden **210** A2
Wasbister **276** C4
Wasdale Head **198** C2
Waseley Hills Country Park
*Worcs* B45 9AT **14** C6
Wash **185** E4
Wash Common **119** F1
Washall Green **150** C4
Washaway **97** E3
Washbourne **101** D2
Washbrook **183** H3
Washfield **102** C1
Washfold **201** E3
Washford *Som* **114** D3
Washford *Warks* **146** C1
Washford Pyne **102** B2
Washingborough **188** A5
Washington *T&W* **212** C2
Washington *WSuss* **108** D2
Washmere Green **152** A3
Wasing **119** G1
Waskerley **211** G3
Wasperton **147** E2
Wasps Nest **175** F1
Wass **203** E5
Wat Tyler Country Park *Essex*
SS16 4UH **137** G4
Watchet **115** D3
Watchfield *Oxon* **133** E3
Watchfield *Som* **116** A3
Watchgate **199** G3
Watcombe **101** F2
Watendlath **209** F5
Water **193** F5
Water Eaton *MK* **149** D4
Water Eaton *Oxon* **134** A1
Water End *Bed* **149** F4
Water End *CenBeds* **149** F4
Water End *ERid* **195** F4
Water End *Essex* **151** D3
Water End *Herts* **136** B2
Water End *Herts* **135** F1
Water Newton **161** F2
Water Orton **159** D3
Water Stratford **148** B4
Water Yeat **199** F2
Waterbeach **150** C1
Waterbeck **218** A4
Watercombe **105** D4
Waterend **143** E1
Waterfall **172** B2
Waterfoot *ERenf* **233** G4
Waterfoot *Lancs* **193** E5
Waterford **136** B1
Watergate **97** F1
Waterhead *Cumb* **199** E2
Waterhead *D&G* **216** B2
Waterheath **165** F2
Waterhill of Bruxie **269** H6
Waterhouses *Dur* **212** A3
Waterhouses *Staffs* **172** B2
Wateringbury **123** F3
Waterlane **132** A2
Waterloo *Aber* **261** J1
Waterloo *Derbys* **173** F1
Waterloo *GtMan* **184** D2
Waterloo *High* **256** C2
Waterloo *Mersey* **183** E3
Waterloo *NLan* **234** B4
Waterloo *Norf* **178** D4
Waterloo *P&K* **243** F1
Waterloo *Pembs* **126** C2
Waterloo *Poole* **105** G3
Waterloo Cross **103** D1
Waterloo Port **167** D2
Waterlooville **107** F1
Watermead Country Park
*Leics* LE7 4PF **17** C3
Watermeetings **226** A3
Watermillock **210** A5
Watermouth Castle *Devon*
EX34 9SL **113** F1
Waterperry **134** B2
Waterperry *Oxon*
OX33 1JZ **134** B2
Waterrow **115** D5
Waters Upton **157** F1
Watershed Mill Visitor Centre,
Settle *NYorks*
BD24 9LR **193** E1

Watersheddings **184** D2
Waterside *Aber* **260** B3
Waterside *Aber* **261** J2
Waterside *B'burn* **192** D5
Waterside *Bucks* **135** E2
Waterside *EAyr* **224** C5
Waterside *EAyr* **233** F5
Waterside *EDun* **234** A2
Watersmeet House *Devon*
EX35 6NT **114** A3
Waterstock **134** B2
Waterston **126** C2
Waterthorpe **186** B4
Waterworld, Hanley ST1 5PU
**85** Stoke-on-Trent
Watford *Herts* **136** A3
Watford *N'hants* **148** B1
Watford Park **130** A4
Wath *NYorks* **202** C5
Wath *NYorks* **194** A1
Wath Brow **208** D5
Wath upon Dearne **186** B2
Watley's End **131** F4
Watlington *Norf* **163** E1
Watlington *Oxon* **134** B3
Watnall **173** G2
Watten **275** H3
Wattisfield **164** B4
Wattisham **152** B2
Watton *Dorset* **104** A3
Watton *ERid* **196** C3
Watton *Norf* **178** A3
Watton at Stone **136** C1
Watton Green **178** A3
Watton's Green **137** E3
Wattston **234** B3
Wattstown **129** G3
Wattsville **130** B3
Waughtonhill **269** H5
Waun Fawr **154** C4
Waun y Clyn **128** A2
Waunarlwydd **128** C3
Waunclunda **142** C4
Waunfawr **167** E2
Waun-Lwyd **130** A2
Wavendon **149** E4
Waverbridge **209** F2
Waverton *ChesW&C* **170** B1
Waverton *Cumb* **209** F2
Wavertree **183** E4
Wawne **196** C4
Waxham **179** F3
Waxholme **197** F5
Way Gill **193** F1
Way Village **102** B1
Way Wick **116** A1
Wayford **104** A3
Waytown **104** A3
Weachyburn **268** E5
Weacombe **115** E3
Weald **133** F4
Weald & Downland Open Air
Museum *WSuss*
PO18 0EU **108** A3
Weald Country Park *Essex*
CM14 5QS **137** E3
Wealdstone **136** A3
Weardley **194** B3
Weare **116** B2
Weare Giffard **113** E3
Wearhead **211** E4
Wearne **116** B5
Weasenham
All Saints **177** G3
Weasenham St. Peter **177** G5
Weathercote **200** C5
Weatheroak Hill **158** C5
Weaverham **184** A5
Weaverthorpe **204** C5
Webheath **146** C1
Webton **144** D4
Wedderlairs **261** G1
Weddington **159** F3
Wedhampton **118** B2
Wedmore **116** B3
Wednesbury **158** B3
Wednesfield **158** B3
Weedon **134** D1
Weedon Bec **148** B2
Weedon Lois **148** B3
Weeford **158** D2
Week *Devon* **102** A1
Week *Devon* **101** D1
Week *Som* **114** C4
Week Orchard **112** C5
Week St. Mary **98** C1
Weeke **119** F4
Weekley **161** D4
Weel **196** C4
Weeley **152** C5
Weeley Heath **152** C5
Weem **250** D4
Weeping Cross **171** G5
Weethley **146** C2
Weeting **163** F4
Weeton *ERid* **197** F5
Weeton *Lancs* **191** G4
Weeton *NYorks* **194** B3
Weetwood **194** B4
Weir *Devon* **138** B4
Weir *Lancs* **193** E5
Weir Quay **100** A1
Weirbrook **170** A5
Weisdale **279** C7
Welbeck Abbey **186** C5
Welborne **178** B5
Welbourn **175** E2
Welburn *NYorks* **195** G1
Welburn *NYorks* **203** G4
Welbury **202** C2
Welby **175** E4
Welches Dam **162** C4
Welcombe **112** C4
Weldon **161** E4
Welford *N'hants* **160** B4
Welford *WBerks* **133** G5
Welford-on-Avon **146** D2
Welham *Leics* **160** C3
Welham *Notts* **187** E4
Welham Green **136** B2
Well *Hants* **120** C3
Well *Lincs* **189** E5
Well *NYorks* **202** B4
Well End *Bucks* **135** D4
Well End *Herts* **136** B3
Well Hill **123** D2
Well Street **123** F3
Well Town **102** C2

Welland **145** G3
Wellbank **244** C1
Wellesbourne **147** E2
Wellhill **267** H5
Wellhouse *WBerks* **134** A5
Wellhouse *WYorks* **185** E1
Welling **137** D5
Wellingborough **149** D1
Wellingham **177** G5
Wellingore **175** E2
Wellington *Cumb* **198** B2
Wellington *Here* **145** E3
Wellington *Som* **115** E5
Wellington *Tel&W* **157** F1
Wellington Heath **145** G3
Wellington Marsh **145** D3
Wellow *B&NESom* **117** E2
Wellow *IoW* **106** C4
Wellow *Notts* **174** B1
Wells **116** C3
Wells Cathedral *Som*
BA5 2UE **116** C3
Wells Green **159** F2
Wellsborough **159** F2
Wells-next-the-Sea **178** A1
Wellstye Green **137** F1
Wellwood **235** E1
Welney **162** D3
Welsh Bicknor **131** E1
Welsh End **170** C4
Welsh Frankton **170** A4
Welsh Hook **140** C5
Welsh Mountain Zoo *Conwy*
LL28 5UY **181** G5
Welsh Newton **131** D1
Welsh St. Donats **129** G5
Welshampton **170** B4
Welshpool
(Y Trallwng) **156** B2
Welton *B&NESom* **117** D2
Welton *Cumb* **209** G2
Welton *ERid* **196** B5
Welton *Lincs* **188** A4
Welton *N'hants* **148** A1
Welton le Marsh **176** C1
Welton le Wold **188** C4
Welwick **197** F5
Welwyn **136** B1
Welwyn Garden City **136** B1
Wem **170** C5
Wembdon **115** F4
Wembley **136** A4
Wembley *GtLon*
HA9 0WS **10** C3
Wembury **100** B3
Wembworthy **113** G4
Wemyss Bay **232** C3
Wenallt *Cere* **154** C5
Wenallt *Gwyn* **168** C2
Wendens Ambo **150** D4
Wendlebury **134** A1
Wendling **178** A4
Wendover **135** D2
Wendover Dean **135** D2
Wendron **95** D3
Wendy **150** B3
Wenfordbridge **97** E2
Wenhaston **165** F4
Wennli **168** B1
Wennington *Cambs* **162** A5
Wennington *GtLon* **137** E4
Wennington *Lancs* **200** B5
Wensley *Derbys* **173** D1
Wensley *NYorks* **201** F3
Wensleydale Cheese Visitor
Centre, Hawes *NYorks*
DL8 3RN **201** D4
Wentbridge **186** B1
Wentnor **156** C3
Wentworth *Cambs* **162** C5
Wentworth *SYorks* **186** A3
Wenvoe **130** A5
Weobley **144** C2
Weobley Marsh **144** D2
Weoley Castle **158** C4
Wepham **108** C3
Wepre **169** F1
Wepre Country Park *Flints*
CH5 4HL **169** F1
Wereham **163** E2
Wergs **158** A2
Wern *Gwyn* **167** E4
Wern *Powys* **156** B1
Wern *Powys* **130** A1
Wern *Shrop* **169** F4
Wernffrwd **128** B3
Wern-olau **128** B3
Wernrheolydd **130** C1
Wern-y-cwrt **130** C1
Werrington *Corn* **98** C2
Werrington *Peter* **161** G2
Werrington *Staffs* **171** G3
Wervil Grange **141** G2
Wervin **183** F5
Wesham **192** A4
Wessington **173** E2
West Aberthaw **114** D1
West Acre **163** F1
West Acton **136** A4
West Allerdean **237** G5
West Alvington **100** D3
West Amesbury **118** C3
West Anstey **114** B5
West Ashby **188** C5
West Ashford **113** F2
West Ashling **108** A3
West Ashton **117** F2
West Auckland **212** A5
West Ayton **204** C4
West Bagborough **115** E4
West Barkwith **188** B4
West Barnby **204** B1
West Barns **237** D2
West Barsham **178** A3
West Bay **104** A3
West Beckham **178** B2
West Benhar **234** C3
West Bergholt **152** A5
West Bexington **104** B4
West Bilney **163** F1
West Blatchington **109** E3
West Boldon **212** C1
West Bourton **117** E5
West Bowling **194** A4
West Bradford **192** D3
West Bradley **116** C4

West Bretton **185** G1
West Bridgford **173** G4
West Bromwich **158** C3
West Buckland
*Devon* **113** G2
West Buckland *Som* **115** E5
West Burton *NYorks* **201** E4
West Burton *WSuss* **108** B2
West Butsfield **211** G3
West Butterwick **187** F2
West Byfleet **121** F1
West Cairncake **269** G6
West Caister **179** G4
West Calder **235** E3
West Camel **116** C5
West Carbeth **233** G2
West Carr Houses **187** E2
West Cauldcoats **234** A5
West Chaldon **105** D4
West Challow **133** F4
West Charleton **101** D3
West Chevington **221** E2
West Chiltington **108** C2
West Chiltington
Common **108** C2
West Chinnock **104** A1
West Chisenbury **118** C2
West Clandon **121** F2
West Cliffe **125** F4
West Clyne **267** F1
West Coker **104** B1
West Compton
*Dorset* **104** B3
West Compton *Som* **116** C3
West Cowick **195** F5
West Cross **128** C4
West Crudwell **132** B3
West Curry **98** C1
West Curthwaite **209** G2
West Dean *Wilts* **119** D5
West Dean *WSuss* **108** A2
West Deeping **161** G2
West Derby **183** E3
West Dereham **163** E2
West Ditchburn **229** F4
West Down **113** F1
West Drayton *GtLon* **135** F5
West Drayton *Notts* **187** E5
West Dullater **242** A4
West Dunnet **275** H1
West Edington **221** D3
West Ella **196** C5
West End *Bed* **149** E2
West End *BrackF* **135** D5
West End *Caerp* **130** B3
West End *ERid* **196** C1
West End *Hants* **107** D1
West End *Herts* **136** B2
West End *Kent* **125** D2
West End *Lancs* **192** A1
West End *Lincs* **189** D1
West End *Norf* **179** F5
West End *Norf* **178** A5
West End *NSom* **116** B1
West End *Oxon* **133** G2
West End *Oxon* **134** A4
West End *SLan* **235** D5
West End *Suff* **165** F3
West End *Surr* **121** E1
West End *Surr* **121** E1
West End *Wilts* **132** B5
West End *Wilts* **118** A5
West End *Wilts* **118** A5
West End Green **120** B1
West Farleigh **123** G3
West Farndon **148** A2
West Felton **170** A5
West Firle **109** G3
West Fleetham **229** F4
West Flotmanby **205** D5
West Garforth **194** C4
West Ginge **133** G4
West Glen **232** A2
West Grafton **118** D1
West Green *GtLon* **136** C4
West Green *Hants* **120** C2
West Grimstead **118** D5
West Grinstead **121** G5
West Haddlesey **195** E5
West Haddon **160** B5
West Hagbourne **134** A4
West Hagley **158** B4
West Hall **210** B1
West Hallam **173** F3
West Halton **196** B5
West Ham **136** C4
West Handley **186** A5
West Hanney **133** G3
West Hanningfield **137** G3
West Hardwick **186** B1
West Harnham **118** C5
West Harptree **116** C2
West Harrow **136** A4
West Harting **120** C5
West Hatch *Som* **115** F5
West Hatch *Wilts* **118** A5
West Head **163** E2
West Heath *ChesE* **171** F1
West Heath *GtLon* **137** D5
West Heath *Hants* **121** D5
West Heath *Hants* **119** G2
West Heath *WMid* **158** C5
West Helmsdale **275** F7
West Hendon **136** B4
West Hendred **133** G4
West Heslerton **204** C5
West Hewish **116** A1
West Hill *Devon* **103** D3
West Hill *ERid* **197** D1
West Hill *NSom* **131** D5
West Hoathly **122** C5
West Holme **105** E4
West Horndon **137** F4
West Horrington **116** C3
West Horsley **121** F2
West Horton **229** E3
West Hougham **125** E5
West Howe **105** G3
West Howetown **114** C4
West Huntingfield **114** A3
West Huntspill **116** A3
West Hyde **135** F3
West Hythe **124** D5
West Ilsley **133** G4
West Itchenor **107** G2
West Keal **176** B1

West Kennett **118** C1
West Kilbride **232** D5
West Kingsdown **123** E2
West Kington **132** A5
West Kington Wick **132** A5
West Kirby **182** D4
West Knapton **204** B5
West Knighton **104** D4
West Knoyle **117** F4
West Kyloe **229** E2
West Lambrook **104** A1
West Langdon **125** F4
West Langwell **266** D1
West Lavington
*Wilts* **118** B2
West Lavington
*WSuss* **121** D5
West Layton **202** A2
West Leake **173** G5
West Learmouth **228** C3
West Lees **203** D3
West Leigh *Devon* **113** G5
West Leigh *Devon* **101** D3
West Leigh *Som* **115** E4
West Leith **135** E1
West Lexham **163** G1
West Lilling **195** F1
West Lingo **244** C4
West Linton **235** F4
West Liss **120** C5
West Littleton **131** G5
West Lockinge **133** G4
West Looe **97** G4
West Lulworth **105** E4
West Lutton **196** B1
West Lydford **116** C4
West Lyn **114** A3
West Lyng **116** A5
West Lynn **163** E1
West Mains **229** E2
West Malling **123** F3
West Malvern **145** G3
West Marden **107** G1
West Markham **187** E5
West Marsh **188** C2
West Marton **193** E2
West Melbury **117** F5
West Melton **186** B2
West Meon **120** B5
West Meon Hut **120** B5
West Mersea **138** D1
West Milton **104** A3
West Minster **124** B1
West Molesey **121** G1
West Monkton **115** F5
West Moors **105** G2
West Morden **105** F3
West Morriston **236** D5
West Morton **193** G3
West Mostard **200** C3
West Mudford **116** C5
West Muir **253** D3
West Ness **203** F5
West Newbiggin **202** C1
West Newton *ERid* **197** D4
West Newton *Norf* **177** E5
West Norwood **136** C5
West Ogwell **101** E1
West Orchard **105** E1
West Overton **118** C1
West Panson **98** D1
West Park *Aber* **261** F5
West Park *Mersey* **183** G3
West Parley **105** G3
West Peckham **123** F3
West Pelton **212** B2
West Pennard **116** C4
West Pentire **96** B3
West Perry **149** G1
West Porlock **114** B3
West Prawle **101** D4
West Preston **108** C3
West Pulham **104** D2
West Putford **113** D4
West Quantoxhead **115** E3
West Raddon **102** B2
West Rainton **212** C3
West Rasen **188** A4
West Raynham **177** G5
West Retford **187** D4
West Rounton **202** D2
West Row **163** E5
West Rudham **177** G5
West Runton **178** C1
West Saltoun **236** B3
West Sandford **102** B2
West Sandwick **278** D4
West Scrafton **201** F4
West Shepton **116** D3
West Shinness
Lodge **273** H7
West Somerset Railway *Som*
TA24 5BG **115** E4
West Somerton **179** F4
West Stafford **104** D4
West Stockwith **187** E3
West Stoke **108** A3
West Stonesdale **201** D2
West Stoughton **116** B3
West Stour **117** E5
West Stourmouth **125** E2
West Stow **163** G5
West Stow Country Park *Suff*
IP28 6HG **163** G5
West Stowell **118** C1
West Stratton **119** G3
West Street *Kent* **124** B3
West Street *Med* **137** G5
West Street *Suff* **164** A4
West Tanfield **202** B5
West Taphouse **97** F3
West Tarbert **231** G3
West Tarring **108** D3
West Thirston **221** D2
West Thorney **107** G3
West Thurrock **137** F5
West Tilbury **137** F5
West Tisted **120** B5
West Tofts *Norf* **163** G3
West Tofts *P&K* **243** G1
West Torrington **188** B4
West Town *B&NESom* **116** C1
West Town *Hants* **107** G3
West Town *NSom* **116** B1
West Town *Som* **116** C4

West Tytherley **119** D5
West Walton **162** C1
West Wellow **106** B1
West Wemyss **244** B5
West Wick **116** A1
West Wickham
*Cambs* **151** E3
West Wickham *GtLon* **122** C2
West Williamston **126** D2
West Winch **163** E1
West Winterslow **118** D4
West Wittering **107** G3
West Witton **201** F4
West Woodburn **220** A3
West Woodhay **119** E1
West Woodlands **117** E3
West Worldham **120** C4
West Worthing **108** D3
West Wratting **151** E2
West Wycombe **134** D3
West Yatton **132** B5
West Yell **278** D4
West Youlstone **112** C4
Westbere **125** D2
Westborough **174** D3
Westbourne *Bourne* **105** G3
Westbourne *WSuss* **107** G2
Westbourne Green **136** B4
Westbrook *Kent* **125** F1
Westbrook *WBerks* **133** G5
Westbrook *Wilts* **118** A1
Westbury *Bucks* **148** B4
Westbury *Shrop* **156** C2
Westbury *Wilts* **117** F2
Westbury Leigh **117** F2
Westbury on Trym **131** E5
Westbury-on-Severn **131** G1
Westbury-sub-Mendip **116** C3
Westby *Lancs* **191** G4
Westby *Lincs* **175** D5
Westcliff-on-Sea **138** B4
Westcombe **117** D4
Westcot **133** F4
Westcott *Bucks* **134** C1
Westcott *Devon* **102** D2
Westcott *Surr* **121** G3
Westcott Barton **147** G5
Westcourt **118** D1
Westcroft **148** D4
Westdean **110** A4
Westdowns **97** E1
Westend Town **131** G5
Wester Aberchalder **258** C2
Wester Badentyre **269** F5
Wester Balgedie **243** G4
Wester Culbeuchly **268** E4
Wester Dechmont **235** E2
Wester Fintray **261** G3
Wester Foffarty **252** C5
Wester Greenskares **269** F4
Wester Gruinards **266** C2
Wester Hailes **235** G3
Wester Lealty **266** D4
Wester Lonvine **266** E4
Wester Newburn **244** C4
Wester Ord **261** G4
Wester Quarff **279** D9
Wester Skeld **279** B8
Westerdale *High* **275** G4
Westerdale *NYorks* **203** F2
Westerfield *Shet* **279** C7
Westerfield *Suff* **152** C3
Westergate **108** B3
Westerham **122** D3
Westerhope **212** A1
Westerleigh **131** F5
Westerloch **275** J3
Westerton *Aber* **261** F5
Westerton *Angus* **253** E4
Westerton *Dur* **212** B4
Westerton *P&K* **243** D3
Westerwick **279** B8
Westfield *Cumb* **208** C4
Westfield *ESuss* **110** C3
Westfield *High* **275** F2
Westfield *NLan* **234** B2
Westfield *Norf* **178** A5
Westfield *WLoth* **234** D2
Westfield *WYorks* **194** B5
Westfield Sole **123** G2
Westgate *Dur* **211** F4
Westgate *N'umb* **220** A3
Westgate *NLincs* **187** E2
Westgate *Norf* **178** A1
Westgate Hill **194** B5
Westgate on Sea **125** F1
Westhall *Aber* **260** E2
Westhall *Suff* **165** F3
Westham *Dorset* **104** C5
Westham *Som* **116** B3
Westhampnett **108** A3
Westhay *Devon* **103** G2
Westhay *Som* **116** B3
Westhead **183** F2
Westhide **145** E3
Westhill *Aber* **261** G4
Westhill *High* **266** E7
Westhope *Here* **145** D2
Westhope *Shrop* **157** D4
Westhorp **148** A2
Westhorpe *Lincs* **176** A5
Westhorpe *Notts* **174** B2
Westhorpe *Suff* **152** B1
Westhoughton **184** A2
Westhouse **200** B5
Westhouses **173** F2
Westhumble **121** G2
Westing **278** D2
Westlake **100** C2
Westlands **171** F3
Westlea **132** D4
Westleigh *Devon* **113** E3
Westleigh *Devon* **103** D1
Westleigh *GtMan* **184** A2
Westleton **153** F1
Westley *Shrop* **156** C2
Westley *Suff* **151** G1
Westley Heights **137** F4
Westley Waterless **151** E2
Westlington **134** C1
Westlinton **218** B5
Westmancote **146** B4
Westmarsh **125** E2
Westmeston **109** F2

Westmill 150 B5
Westminster 136 B5
Westminster Abbey *GtLon* SW1P 3PA 44 E6
Westminster Abbey - Chapter House & Pyx Chamber *GtLon* SW1P 3PA 44 E6
Westminster Cathedral *GtLon* SW1P 2QW 44 C7
Westmuir 252 B4
Westness 276 C5
Westnewton *Cumb* 209 E2
Westnewton *N'umb* 228 D3
Westoe 212 C1
Weston *B&NESom* 117 E4
Weston *ChesE* 171 E2
Weston *Devon* 103 E4
Weston *Devon* 103 E2
Weston *Dorset* 104 C5
Weston *Halton* 183 G4
Weston *Hants* 120 C5
Weston *Here* 145 D3
Weston *Herts* 150 A4
Weston *Lincs* 176 A5
Weston *Moray* 268 C4
Weston *N'hants* 148 A3
Weston *Notts* 174 C1
Weston *NYorks* 194 A3
Weston *Shrop* 170 C4
Weston *Shrop* 157 E3
Weston *Shrop* 156 C5
Weston *Soton* 107 D1
Weston *Staffs* 171 G5
Weston *W&Berks* 135 E5
Weston Bampfylde 116 D5
Weston Beggard 145 E3
Weston by Welland 160 C3
Weston Colville 151 E2
Weston Corbett 120 B3
Weston Coyney 171 G3
Weston Favell 148 C1
Weston Green *Cambs* 151 E2
Weston Green *Norf* 178 C4
Weston Heath 157 G1
Weston in Arden 159 F4
Weston Jones 171 E5
Weston Longville 178 C4
Weston Lullingfields 170 B5
Weston Park *Staffs* TF11 8LE 158 A1
Weston Patrick 120 B3
Weston Point 183 F4
Weston Rhyn 169 F4
Weston Subedge 146 D3
Weston Town 117 E3
Weston Turville 135 D1
Weston under Penyard 145 F5
Weston under Wetherley 147 F1
Weston Underwood *Derbys* 173 D3
Weston Underwood *MK* 149 D2
Westonbirt 132 A4
Westonbirt - The National Arboretum *Glos* GL8 8QS 132 A4
Westoning 149 F5
Weston-in-Gordano 131 D5
Weston-on-Avon 147 D2
Weston-on-the-Green 134 A1
Weston-on-Trent 173 D3
Weston-super-Mare 116 A4
Weston-under-Lizard 158 A1
Westonzoyland 116 A4
Westow 195 G1
Westpoint Arena, Clyst St. Mary *Devon* EX5 1DJ 102 C3
Westport *A&B* 222 B3
Westport *Som* 116 A5
Westra 130 A5
Westray 276 D3
Westray Airfield 276 D2
Westridge Green 134 A5
Westrigg 234 D3
Westruther 236 D5
Westry 162 B3
Westside 261 G5
Westvale 183 F3
Westville 173 G3
Westward 209 F2
Westward Ho! 113 E3
Westwell *Kent* 124 B4
Westwell *Oxon* 133 E2
Westwell Leacon 124 B4
Westwick *Cambs* 150 C1
Westwick *Dur* 201 F1
Westwick *Norf* 179 D3
Westwick *NYorks* 194 C1
Westwood *Devon* 102 D3
Westwood *Peter* 161 G3
Westwood *SLan* 234 A4
Westwood *Wilts* 117 F2
Westwood Heath 159 E5
Westwoodside 187 E3
Wetham Green 124 A2
Wetheral 210 A2
Wetherby 194 D3
Wetherden 152 B1
Wetherden Upper Town 152 B1
Wetheringsett 152 C1
Wethersfield 151 F4
Wethersta 279 C6
Wetherup Street 152 C1
Wetley Abbey 171 G3
Wetley Rocks 171 G3
Wettenhall 170 D1
Wettenhall Green 170 D1
Wetton 172 C2
Wetwang 196 B2
Wetwood 171 E4
Wexcombe 119 D2
Wexham Street 135 E4
Weybourne *Norf* 178 C1
Weybourne *Surr* 121 D3
Weybread 164 D3
Weybread Street 165 D4
Weybridge 121 F3
Weycroft 103 G2
Weydale 275 G2
Weyhill 119 E3
Weymouth 104 C5

Weymouth Sea Life Adventure Park & Marine Sanctuary *Dorset* DT4 7SX 104 C4
Whaddon *Bucks* 148 C5
Whaddon *Cambs* 150 B3
Whaddon *Glos* 132 A1
Whaddon *Glos* 146 B5
Whaddon *Wilts* 118 C5
Whaddon *Wilts* 117 F1
Whaddon Gap 150 B3
Whale 210 B5
Whaley 186 C5
Whaley Bridge 185 E4
Whaley Thorns 186 C5
Whaligoe 275 J4
Whalley 192 D4
Whalley Banks 192 C4
Whalsay 279 E6
Whalsay Airport 279 E6
Whalton 220 D3
Wham 193 D1
Whaplode 176 B5
Whaplode Drove 162 B1
Whaplode St. Catherine 162 B1
Wharfe 193 D1
Wharles 192 A4
Wharley End 149 E3
Wharncliffe Side 185 G3
Wharram le Street 196 A1
Wharram Percy 196 A1
Wharton *ChesW&C* 171 D1
Wharton *Here* 145 E2
Whashton 202 A2
Whatcote 147 F3
Whateley 159 E3
Whatfield 152 B3
Whatley 117 E3
Whatlington 110 C2
Whatsole Street 124 D4
Whatstandwell 173 E2
Whatton 174 C4
Whauphill 207 E2
Whaw 201 F3
Wheatacre 165 F2
Wheatcroft 173 E2
Wheatenhurst 131 G2
Wheatfield 134 B3
Wheathampstead 136 A1
Wheathill *Shrop* 157 F4
Wheathill *Som* 116 C4
Wheatley *Hants* 120 C4
Wheatley *Oxon* 134 B2
Wheatley *W'Yorks* 193 G5
Wheatley Hill 212 C4
Wheatley Lane 193 E4
Wheatley Park 186 C2
Wheaton Aston 158 A1
Wheddon Cross 114 C4
Wheedlemont 260 C2
Wheelerstreet 121 E3
Wheelock 171 E2
Wheelock Heath 171 E2
Wheelton 192 C5
Wheen 252 B2
Wheldale 195 D5
Wheldrake 195 F3
Whelford 133 D3
Whelley 183 G2
Whelpley Hill 135 E2
Whelpo 209 F3
Whelston 182 D5
Whenby 195 F1
Whepstead 151 G2
Wherstead 152 C3
Wherwell 119 E3
Whetsted 121 F1
Whetstone *GtLon* 136 B3
Whetstone *Leics* 160 A3
Whicham 198 C4
Whichford 147 F4
Whickham 212 B1
Whiddon 113 E5
Whiddon Down 99 G1
Whifflet 234 B3
Whigstreet 252 C5
Whilton 148 B1
Whim 235 G4
Whimble 112 D5
Whimple 102 D3
Whimpwell Green 179 E3
Whin Lane End 191 G3
Whinburgh 178 B5
Whinlatter Forest *Cumb* CA12 5TW 209 E4
Whinny Hill 202 C1
Whinnyfold 261 J1
Whippingham 107 E3
Whipsnade 135 F1
Whipsnade Zoo *CenBeds* LU6 2LF 135 F1
Whipton 102 C3
Whirlow 186 A4
Whisby 175 E1
Whissendine 160 D1
Whissonsett 178 A3
Whisterfield 184 C5
Whistley Green 134 C5
Whiston *Mersey* 183 F3
Whiston *N'hants* 149 D1
Whiston *Staffs* 172 B3
Whiston *Staffs* 158 A1
Whiston *SYorks* 186 B3
Whiston Cross 157 G2
Whiston Eaves 172 B3
Whitacre Fields 159 E3
Whitacre Heath 159 E3
Whitbeck 198 C4
Whitbourne 145 G2
Whitburn *T&W* 212 D1
Whitburn *WLoth* 234 D3
Whitby *ChesW&C* 183 E5
Whitby *NYorks* 204 B1
Whitby Abbey *NYorks* YO22 4JT 204 C1
Whitby Lifeboat Museum *NYorks* YO21 3PU 204 B1
Whitbyheath 183 E5
Whitchurch *B&NESom* 116 D1
Whitchurch *Bucks* 148 D5
Whitchurch *Cardiff* 130 A4
Whitchurch *Devon* 99 E3
Whitchurch *Hants* 119 F3
Whitchurch *Here* 131 E1
Whitchurch *Pembs* 140 A5

Whitchurch *Shrop* 170 C3
Whitchurch *Warks* 147 E3
Whitchurch Canonicorum 103 G3
Whitchurch Hill 134 B5
Whitchurch-on-Thames 134 B5
Whitcombe 104 D4
Whitcott Keysett 156 B4
White Ball 103 E1
White Colne 151 G5
White Coppice 184 A1
White Cross *Corn* 96 C4
White Cross *Devon* 102 D3
White Cross *Here* 145 D3
White Cross *Wilts* 117 E4
White Cube *GtLon* N1 6PB 12 C4
White End 146 A5
White Hill 117 F4
White Houses 187 E5
White Kirkley 211 G4
White Lackington 104 D3
White Lund 192 A1
White Mill 142 A5
White Moor 173 E3
White Notley 137 G1
White Ox Mead 117 E2
White Pit 189 D5
White Post Farm Centre, Farnsfield *Notts* NG22 8HL 174 B2
White Rocks 144 D5
White Roding 137 E1
White Waltham 134 D5
Whiteacre 267 K7
Whiteash Green 151 F4
Whitebirk 192 D5
Whitebog 269 H5
Whitebridge (An Drochaid Bhàn) *High* 258 B3
Whitebrook 131 E2
Whiteburn 236 C5
Whitecairn 214 D5
Whitecairns 261 H3
Whitecastle 235 E5
Whitechapel 192 B3
Whitechurch 141 E4
Whitecote 158 B4
Whitecraig 236 A2
Whitecroft 131 F2
Whitecrook 214 C5
Whitecross *Corn* 94 C3
Whitecross *Corn* 97 D3
Whitecross *Dorset* 104 A3
Whitecross *Falk* 235 D2
Whiteface 266 E3
Whitefield *Aber* 261 F2
Whitefield *Devon* 114 A4
Whitefield *Dorset* 105 F3
Whitefield *GtMan* 184 C2
Whitefield *High* 258 C1
Whitefield *High* 275 H3
Whitefield *P&K* 243 G1
Whiteford 261 F2
Whitegate 170 D1
Whitehall *Devon* 103 E1
Whitehall *Hants* 120 C2
Whitehall *Ork* 276 F5
Whitehall *WSuss* 121 G5
Whitehaven 208 C5
Whitehill *Aber* 261 H5
Whitehill *Hants* 120 C4
Whitehill *Kent* 124 B3
Whitehill *Midlo* 236 A3
Whitehill *NAyr* 233 D4
Whitehills 268 E4
Whitehouse *A&B* 231 G3
Whitehouse *Aber* 260 E3
Whitehouse Common 158 D3
Whitekirk 236 C1
Whitelackington 103 G1
Whitelaw 237 F4
Whiteleen 275 J4
Whiteley 107 E2
Whiteley Bank 107 E4
Whiteley Green 184 D5
Whiteley Village 121 F1
Whiteleys 214 B5
Whitemans Green 109 F1
Whitemire 267 G6
Whitemoor 97 D4
Whiteness 279 C8
Whiteoak Green 133 F1
Whiteparish 118 C5
Whiterashes 261 G2
Whiterow 275 J4
Whiteshill 132 A2
Whiteside *N'umb* 210 D1
Whiteside *WLoth* 235 D3
Whitesmith 110 A2
Whitestaunton 103 F1
Whitestone *A&B* 222 C2
Whitestone *Aber* 260 E5
Whitestone *Devon* 102 B3
Whitestreet Green 152 A4
Whitestripe 269 H5
Whiteway 132 B1
Whitewell *Aber* 269 H4
Whitewell *Lancs* 192 C3
Whitewell *Wrex* 170 B3
Whiteworks 99 G3
Whitewreath 267 K6
Whitfield *Here* 144 D4
Whitfield *Kent* 125 F4
Whitfield *N'hants* 148 B4
Whitfield *N'umb* 211 D2
Whitford *Devon* 103 F3
Whitford (Chwitffordd) *Flints* 182 C5
Whitgift 196 A5
Whitgreave 171 F5
Whithorn 207 E2
Whiting Bay 223 F3
Whitkirk 194 C4
Whitlam 261 G2
Whitland (Hendy-Gwyn) 127 F1
Whitland Abbey 127 F1
Whitleigh 100 A1
Whitletts 204 B3
Whitley *NYorks* 195 E5
Whitley *Read* 120 C1
Whitley *Wilts* 117 F1

Whitley *WMid* 159 F5
Whitley Bay 221 F4
Whitley Chapel 211 F1
Whitley Heath 171 F5
Whitley Lower 185 G1
Whitley Row 123 D3
Whitlock's End 158 D5
Whitminster 131 G2
Whitmore *Dorset* 105 G2
Whitmore *Staffs* 171 F3
Whitnage 102 D1
Whitnash 147 F1
Whitnell 115 F3
Whitney-on-Wye 144 B3
Whitrigg *Cumb* 209 F1
Whitrigg *Cumb* 209 F3
Whitsbury 106 A1
Whitsome 237 F4
Whitson 130 C4
Whitstable 124 D2
Whitstone 98 C1
Whittingham 229 E5
Whittingslow 156 D4
Whittington *Derbys* 186 A5
Whittington *Glos* 146 C5
Whittington *Lancs* 200 B5
Whittington *Norf* 163 F2
Whittington *Shrop* 170 A4
Whittington *Staffs* 158 D3
Whittington *Staffs* 159 D2
Whittington *Worcs* 146 A2
Whittlebury 148 B3
Whittle-le-Woods 192 B5
Whittlesey 162 A2
Whittlestone Head 184 B1
Whitton *ChesE* 170 A5
Whitton *N'umb* 220 D1
Whitton *NLincs* 196 A5
Whitton *Powys* 144 B1
Whitton *Shrop* 157 E5
Whitton *Stock* 212 C5
Whitton *Suff* 152 C3
Whittonditch 133 E5
Whittonstall 211 G2
Whitway 119 F2
Whitwell *Derbys* 186 C5
Whitwell *Herts* 149 G5
Whitwell *IoW* 107 E5
Whitwell *NYorks* 202 B3
Whitwell *Rut* 161 E2
Whitwell Street 178 C3
Whitwell-on-the-Hill 195 G1
Whitwick 159 G1
Whitwood 194 D5
Whitworth 184 C1
Whitworth Art Gallery, Manchester *GtMan* M15 6ER 25 F4
Whixall 170 C4
Whixley 194 D2
Whorlton *Dur* 202 A1
Whorlton *NYorks* 203 D3
Whygate 219 F4
Whyle 145 E1
Whyteleafe 122 C3
Wibdon 131 E3
Wibsey 194 A4
Wibtoft 159 G4
Wichenford 145 G1
Wichling 124 B3
Wick *Bourne* 106 A3
Wick *Devon* 103 E2
Wick (Inbhir Ùige) *High* 275 J3
Wick *SGlos* 131 G5
Wick *Som* 115 F3
Wick *Som* 116 C4
Wick *VGlam* 129 F5
Wick *Wilts* 118 C5
Wick *Worcs* 146 B3
Wick *WSuss* 108 C3
Wick Airport 275 J3
Wick Hill *Kent* 124 A4
Wick Hill *W'ham* 120 C1
Wick St. Lawrence 116 A1
Wicken *Cambs* 163 D5
Wicken *N'hants* 148 C4
Wicken Bonhunt 150 C4
Wickenby 188 A4
Wicker Street Green 152 A3
Wickersley 186 B3
Wicketwood Hill 174 B3
Wickford 137 G3
Wickham *Hants* 107 E1
Wickham *WBerks* 133 F5
Wickham Bishops 138 B1
Wickham Heath 119 F1
Wickham Market 153 E2
Wickham St. Paul 151 G4
Wickham Skeith 152 B1
Wickham Street *Suff* 151 F2
Wickham Street *Suff* 152 B1
Wickhambreaux 125 E3
Wickhambrook 151 F2
Wickhamford 146 C3
Wickhampton 179 F5
Wicklewood 178 B5
Wickmere 178 C2
Wicksteed Park *N'hants* NN15 6NJ 161 D5
Wickwar 131 G4
Widcombe 117 E1
Widdington 150 D4
Widdop 193 F4
Widdrington 221 E2
Widdrington Station 221 E2
Wide Open 221 E4
Widecombe in the Moor 102 A5
Widegates 97 G4
Widemouth Bay 112 C5
Widewall 277 D8
Widford *Essex* 137 F2
Widford *Herts* 136 D1
Widford *Oxon* 133 E1
Widham 132 C4
Widmer End 135 D3
Widmerpool 174 B5
Widnes 183 G4
Widworthy 103 F3
Wigan 183 G2
Wigan Pier *GtMan* WN3 4EU 183 G2

Wiggaton 103 E3
Wiggenhall St. Germans 163 D1
Wiggenhall St. Mary Magdalen 163 D1
Wiggenhall St. Mary the Virgin 163 D1
Wiggenhall St. Peter 163 E1
Wiggens Green 151 E3
Wigginton *Herts* 135 E1
Wigginton *Oxon* 147 F4
Wigginton *Shrop* 170 A4
Wigginton *Staffs* 159 E2
Wigginton *York* 195 F2
Wigglesworth 193 F2
Wiggonby 209 G1
Wiggonholt 108 C2
Wighill 195 D3
Wighton 178 A2
Wightwizzle 185 G3
Wigley 106 C1
Wigmore *Here* 144 D1
Wigmore *Med* 124 A2
Wigsley 187 F5
Wigsthorpe 161 F4
Wigston 160 B3
Wigston Parva 159 G4
Wigthorpe 186 C4
Wigtoft 176 A4
Wigton 209 F2
Wigtown 215 F5
Wike 194 C3
Wilbarston 160 D4
Wilberfoss 195 G3
Wilburton 162 C5
Wilby *N'hants* 149 D1
Wilby *Norf* 164 B2
Wilby *Suff* 164 D4
Wilcot 118 C1
Wilcott 156 C1
Wilcrick 130 D4
Wilday Green 186 A5
Wildboarclough 171 G1
Wilde Street 163 F5
Wilden *Bed* 149 F2
Wilden *Worcs* 158 A5
Wildern 119 E2
Wildhill 136 B2
Wildmoor 158 B5
Wildsworth 187 F3
Wilford 173 G4
Wilkesley 170 D3
Wilkhaven 267 G3
Wilkieston 235 F3
Wilksby 176 A1
Willand *Devon* 102 D1
Willand *Som* 103 E1
Willaston *ChesE* 171 E2
Willaston *ChesW&C* 183 E5
Willaston *Shrop* 170 C4
Willen 149 D3
Willen Lakeside Park *MK* MK15 9HQ 9 D2
Willenhall *WMid* 158 B3
Willenhall *WMid* 159 F5
Willerby *ERid* 196 C5
Willerby *NYorks* 204 D5
Willersey 146 D4
Willersley 144 C3
Willesborough 124 C4
Willesborough Lees 124 C4
Willesden 136 B4
Willesleigh 113 F2
Willesley 132 A4
Willett 115 E4
Willey *Shrop* 157 F3
Willey *Warks* 159 G4
Willey Green 121 E2
William's Green 152 A3
Williamscot 147 G3
Williamsetter 279 C10
Williamthorpe 173 F1
Willian 150 A4
Willimontswick 211 D1
Willingale 137 E2
Willingdon 110 A3
Willingham 162 C5
Willingham by Stow 187 F4
Willingham Green 151 E2
Willington *Bed* 149 G2
Willington *Derbys* 173 D5
Willington *Dur* 212 A4
Willington *Kent* 123 G3
Willington *T&W* 212 C1
Willington *Warks* 147 E4
Willington Corner 170 C1
Willisham 152 B2
Willitoft 195 G4
Williton 115 D3
Willoughbridge 171 E3
Willoughby *Lincs* 189 E5
Willoughby *Warks* 148 A1
Willoughby Waterleys 160 A3
Willoughby-on-the-Wolds 174 B5
Willoughton 187 G3
Willow Green 184 A5
Willows Farm Village *Herts* AL2 1BB 136 A2
Willows Green 137 G1
Willsbridge 131 F5
Willslock 172 B4
Willsworthy 99 F2
Willtown 116 A5
Wilmcote 147 D2
Wilmington *B&NESom* 117 D1
Wilmington *Devon* 103 F2
Wilmington *ESuss* 110 A3
Wilmington *Kent* 137 E5
Wilmslow 184 C4
Wilnecote 159 E2
Wilney Green 164 B3
Wilpshire 192 C4
Wilsden 193 G4
Wilsford *Lincs* 175 F3
Wilsford *Wilts* 118 C3
Wilsford *Wilts* 118 C2
Wilsham 114 A3
Wilshaw 185 F2
Wilsill 194 A1
Wilsley Green 123 G5
Wilsley Pound 123 G5
Wilson 173 F5
Wilstead 149 F3
Wilsthorpe *ERid* 197 D1
Wilsthorpe *Lincs* 161 F1

Wilstone 135 E1
Wilton *Cumb* 208 D5
Wilton *Here* 145 E5
Wilton *NYorks* 204 B4
Wilton *R&C* 203 F1
Wilton *ScBord* 227 F4
Wilton *Wilts* 119 D1
Wilton *Wilts* 118 B4
Wilton House *Wilts* SP2 0BJ 118 B4
Wiltown 103 E1
Wimbish 151 D4
Wimbish Green 151 E4
Wimblebury 158 C1
Wimbledon 136 B5
Wimbledon All England Lawn Tennis & Croquet Club *GtLon* SW19 5AG 11 E7
Wimblington 162 C3
Wimborne Minster 105 G2
Wimborne Minster *Dorset* BH21 1HT 3 B2
Wimborne St. Giles 105 G1
Wimbotsham 163 D2
Wimpole 150 B2
Wimpole Home Farm *Cambs* SG8 0BW 150 B3
Wimpole Lodge 150 B3
Wimpstone 147 E3
Wincanton 117 E5
Winceby 176 B1
Wincham 184 A5
Winchburgh 235 E2
Winchcombe 146 C5
Winchelsea 111 E2
Winchelsea Beach 111 E2
Winchester 119 F5
Winchester Cathedral *Hants* SO23 9LS 89 Winchester
Winchet Hill 123 G4
Winchfield 120 C2
Winchmore Hill *Bucks* 135 E3
Winchmore Hill *GtLon* 136 C3
Wincle 171 G1
Wincobank 186 A3
Windermere 199 F3
Windermere Lake Cruises *Cumb* LA12 8AS 199 E3
Winderton 147 F3
Windhill 266 C7
Windle Hill 183 E5
Windlehurst 185 D4
Windlesham 121 E1
Windley 173 E3
Windmill 185 F5
Windmill Hill *ESuss* 110 B2
Windmill Hill *Som* 103 G1
Windmill Hill *Worcs* 146 B3
Windrush 132 D1
Windsor 135 E5
Windsor Castle *W&M* SL4 1NJ 89 Windsor
Windsor Green 151 G2
Windy Nook 212 B1
Windygates 244 B4
Windy-Yett 233 F4
Wineham 109 E1
Winestead 197 E5
Winewall 193 F4
Winfarthing 164 C3
Winford *IoW* 107 E4
Winford *NSom* 116 C1
Winforton 144 B3
Winfrith Newburgh 105 E4
Wing *Bucks* 149 D5
Wing *Rut* 161 D2
Wingate 212 C4
Wingates *GtMan* 184 A2
Wingates *N'umb* 220 C2
Wingerworth 173 E1
Wingfield *CenBeds* 149 F5
Wingfield *Suff* 164 D4
Wingfield *Wilts* 117 F2
Wingfield Green 164 D4
Wingham 125 E3
Wingmore 125 D4
Wingrave 135 D1
Winkburn 174 C2
Winkfield 135 E5
Winkfield Row 135 D5
Winkhill 172 B2
Winkleigh 113 G5
Winksley 202 B5
Winkton 106 A3
Winlaton 212 A1
Winlaton Mill 212 A1
Winless 275 J3
Winmarleigh 192 A3
Winnard's Perch 96 D3
Winnersh 134 C5
Winnington 184 A5
Winscales 208 C4
Winscombe 116 B2
Winsford *ChesW&C* 171 D1
Winsford *Som* 114 C4
Winsham *Devon* 113 E2
Winsham *Som* 103 G2
Winshill 173 D5
Winsh-wen 128 C3
Winskill 210 B4
Winslade 120 B3
Winsley 117 F1
Winslow 148 C5
Winson 132 C2
Winsor 106 C1
Winster *Cumb* 199 F3
Winster *Derbys* 172 D1
Winston *Dur* 202 A1
Winston *Suff* 152 C1
Winstone 132 B2
Winswell 113 E4
Winter Gardens FY1 1HW 64 Blackpool
Winter Gardens *NSom* BS23 1AJ 88 Weston-super-Mare
Winterborne Came 104 D4
Winterborne Clenston 105 E2
Winterborne Herringston 104 C4
Winterborne Houghton 105 E2
Winterborne Kingston 105 E3
Winterborne Monkton 104 C4

Winterborne Stickland 105 E2
Winterborne Whitechurch 105 E2
Winterborne Zelston 105 E3
Winterbourne *SGlos* 131 F4
Winterbourne *WBerks* 133 G5
Winterbourne Abbas 104 C4
Winterbourne Bassett 132 D5
Winterbourne Dauntsey 118 C4
Winterbourne Earls 118 C4
Winterbourne Gunner 118 C4
Winterbourne Monkton 132 D5
Winterbourne Steepleton 104 C4
Winterbourne Stoke 118 B4
Winterbrook 134 B4
Winterburn 193 F2
Wintercleugh 226 A4
Winteringham 196 B5
Winterley 171 E2
Wintersett 186 A1
Wintershill 107 E1
Winterslow 118 D4
Winterton 187 G1
Winterton-on-Sea 179 F4
Winthorpe *Lincs* 177 D1
Winthorpe *Notts* 174 D2
Winton *Bourne* 105 G3
Winton *Cumb* 200 C1
Wintringham 204 B5
Winwick *Cambs* 161 G4
Winwick *N'hants* 160 B5
Winwick *Warr* 184 A3
Wirksworth 173 D2
Wirksworth Moor 173 E2
Wirral Country Park *Mersey* CH61 0HN 182 D4
Wirswall 170 C3
Wisbech 162 C2
Wisbech St. Mary 162 C2
Wisborough Green 121 F5
Wiseton 187 E4
Wishaw *NLan* 234 B4
Wishaw *Warks* 159 D3
Wisley 121 F3
Wispington 188 C5
Wissett 165 E4
Wissington 152 A4
Wistanstow 156 D4
Wistanswick 171 D5
Wistaston 171 D2
Wiston *Pembs* 126 D1
Wiston *SLan* 226 A2
Wiston *WSuss* 108 D2
Wistow *Cambs* 162 A4
Wistow *NYorks* 195 E4
Wiswell 192 D4
Witcham 162 C5
Witchampton 105 F2
Witchburn 222 C3
Witchford 162 D5
Witcombe 116 B5
Witham 138 B1
Witham Friary 117 E3
Witham on the Hill 161 F1
Withcall 188 C4
Withcote 160 C2
Withdean 109 F3
Witherenden Hill 110 B1
Witherhurst 110 B1
Witheridge 102 B1
Witherley 159 F3
Withern 189 E5
Withernsea 197 F5
Withernwick 197 D3
Withersdale Street 165 D3
Withersfield 151 E3
Witherslack 199 F4
Witherslack Hall 199 F4
Withiel 97 D3
Withiel Florey 114 C4
Withielgoose 97 E3
Withington *Glos* 132 C1
Withington *GtMan* 184 C3
Withington *Here* 145 E3
Withington *Shrop* 157 E1
Withington *Staffs* 172 B4
Withington Green 184 C5
Withington Marsh 145 E3
Withleigh 102 C1
Withnell 192 C5
Withnell Fold 192 C5
Withybrook *Som* 117 D3
Withybrook *Warks* 159 G4
Withycombe 114 D3
Withycombe Raleigh 102 D4
Withyham 123 D5
Withypool 114 B4
Witley 121 E4
Witnesham 152 C2
Witney 133 F2
Wittering 161 F2
Wittersham 111 D1
Witton *Norf* 179 E5
Witton *Worcs* 146 A1
Witton Bridge 179 E2
Witton Gilbert 212 B3
Witton Park 212 A4
Witton-le-Wear 212 A4
Wiveliscombe 115 D5
Wivelsfield 109 F1
Wivelsfield Green 109 F1
Wivenhoe 152 B5
Wiveton 178 B1
Wix 152 C5
Wixford 146 C2
Wixhill 170 C5
Wixoe 151 F3
Woburn 149 E4
Woburn Safari Park *CenBeds* MK17 9QN 9 F3
Woburn Sands 149 E4
Wokefield Park 120 B1
Woking 121 F2
Wokingham 120 D1
Wolborough 102 B5
Wold Newton *ERid* 204 D5
Wold Newton *NELincs* 188 C3
Woldingham 122 C3
Wolds Village, Bainton *ERid* YO25 9EF 196 B2
Wolfelee 227 G5
Wolferlow 145 F1
Wolferton 177 E5

...e 148 A1
...G1
Wolpe...44 B2
Wolf's Castle 140 C5
Wolfsdale 140 C5
Woll 207 F3
Wollaston N'hants 149 E1
Wollaston Shrop 156 C1
Wollaston WMid 158 A4
Wollaton 173 G4
Wollerton 170 D5
Wollescote 158 B4
Wolsingham 211 G4
Wolston 159 G5
Wolsty 209 E1
Wolvercote 134 A2
Wolverhampton 158 B3
Wolverhampton Art Gallery
  WMid WV1 1DU 14 A1
Wolverley Shrop 170 B4
Wolverley Worcs 158 A5
Wolvers Hill 116 A1
Wolverton Hants 119 G2
Wolverton MK 148 D3
Wolverton Warks 147 E1
Wolverton Wilts 117 E4
Wolverton Common 119 G2
Wolvesnewton 131 D3
Wolvey 159 G4
Wolvey Heath 159 G4
Wolviston 213 D5
Womaston 144 B1
Wombleton 203 F4
Wombourne 158 A3
Wombwell 186 A2
Womenswold 125 E3
Womersley 186 C1
Wonastow 131 D1
Wonersh 121 F3
Wonford 102 C3
Wonson 99 G2
Wonston 119 F4
Wooburn 135 E4
Wooburn Green 135 E4
Wood Bevington 146 C2
Wood Burcote 148 B3
Wood Dalling 178 B3
Wood Eaton 158 A1
Wood End Bed 149 F3
Wood End Bed 149 F1
Wood End Bucks 148 C4
Wood End Herts 150 B5
Wood End Warks 159 E3
Wood End Warks 158 D5
Wood End Warks 159 E4
Wood End WMid 158 B4
Wood Enderby 176 A1
Wood Green GtLon 136 C3
Wood Green Norf 164 D2
Wood Green Animal Shelter,
  Godmanchester Cambs
  PE29 2NH 150 A1
Wood Lane 170 B4
Wood Norton 178 B3
Wood Seats 186 A3
Wood Stanway 146 C4
Wood Street 179 E3
Wood Street Village 121 E2
Woodacott 113 D5
Woodale 201 F5
Woodall 186 B4
Woodbastwick 179 E4
Woodbeck 187 E5
Woodborough Notts 174 B3
Woodborough Wilts 118 C2
Woodbridge Devon 103 E3
Woodbridge Dorset 104 D1
Woodbridge Suff 153 D3
Woodbury Devon 102 D4
Woodbury Som 116 C3
Woodbury Salterton 102 D4
Woodchester 132 A2
Woodchurch Kent 124 B5
Woodchurch Mersey 183 D4
Woodcombe 114 C3
Woodcote Oxon 134 B4
Woodcote Tel&W 157 G1
Woodcote Green 158 B5
Woodcott 119 F2
Woodcroft 131 E3
Woodcutts 105 F1
Woodditton 151 E2
Woodeaton 134 A1
Woodend Aber 260 E3
Woodend Cumb 198 C3
Woodend High 258 E2
Woodend High 247 G3
Woodend N'hants 148 B3
Woodend P&K 250 C5
Woodend WSuss 108 A3
Woodend Green 151 D5
Woodfalls 118 C5
Woodfield Oxon 148 A5
Woodfield SAyr 224 B3
Woodfoot 200 B1
Woodford Corn 112 C4
Woodford Devon 101 D2
Woodford Glos 131 F3
Woodford GtLon 136 D3
Woodford GtMan 184 C4
Woodford N'hants 161 E5
Woodford Som 115 D4
Woodford Bridge 136 D3
Woodford Green 136 D3
Woodford Halse 148 A2
Woodgate Devon 103 E1
Woodgate Norf 178 B4
Woodgate WMid 158 B4
Woodgate Worcs 146 B1
Woodgate WSuss 108 B3
Woodgreen 106 A1
Woodhall Invcly 233 E2
Woodhall NYorks 201 E3
Woodhall Hills 194 A4
Woodhall Spa 175 G1
Woodham Bucks 134 B4
Woodham Dur 212 B5
Woodham Surr 121 F1
Woodham Ferrers 137 G3
Woodham Mortimer 138 B2
Woodham Walter 138 B2
Woodhaven 244 C2
Woodhead Aber 261 H4
Woodhead Staffs 172 B3
Woodhey 183 E4
Woodhey Green 170 C2
Woodhill Shrop 157 G5
Woodhill Som 116 A5

Woodhorn 221 E3
Woodhouse Cumb 199 G4
Woodhouse Leics 160 A1
Woodhouse SYorks 186 B4
Woodhouse WYorks 194 B4
Woodhouse WYorks 194 C5
Woodhouse WYorks 194 A5
Woodhouse Down 131 F4
Woodhouse Eaves 160 A1
Woodhouse Green 131 F1
Woodhouses GtMan 184 C2
Woodhouses Staffs 159 D1
Woodhouses Staffs 158 C2
Woodhuish 101 F2
Woodhurst 162 B5
Woodingdean 119 F3
Woodington 119 E5
Woodland Devon 101 D1
Woodland Dur 211 G5
Woodland Kent 125 E3
Woodland Head 102 A3
Woodlands Dorset 105 G2
Woodlands Hants 106 C1
Woodlands NYorks 194 C2
Woodlands Shrop 157 G4
Woodlands Som 115 E3
Woodlands Leisure Park,
  Dartmouth Devon
  TQ9 7DQ 101 E2
Woodlands Park 135 D5
Woodlands St. Mary 133 F5
Woodlane 172 C5
Woodleigh 100 D3
Woodlesford 194 C5
Woodley GtMan 184 D3
Woodley W'ham 134 C5
Woodmancote Glos 132 C2
Woodmancote Glos 146 B5
Woodmancote Glos 131 G3
Woodmancote WSuss 109 E2
Woodmancote WSuss 107 G2
Woodmancott 119 G3
Woodmansey 196 C4
Woodmansterne 122 B3
Woodmanton 102 D4
Woodmill 172 C5
Woodminton 118 B5
Woodmoor 156 B2
Woodnesborough 125 F3
Woodnewton 161 F3
Woodperry 134 A1
Woodplumpton 192 B4
Woodrising 178 A5
Woodrow 105 D1
Wood's Corner 110 B2
Woods Eaves 144 B3
Wood's Green 123 F5
Woodseaves Shrop 171 D4
Woodseaves Staffs 171 E5
Woodsend 133 E5
Woodsetts 186 C4
Woodsford 105 D3
Woodside Aberdeen 261 H4
Woodside BrackF 135 E5
Woodside CenBeds 135 F1
Woodside Cumb 208 D3
Woodside Fife 244 C5
Woodside Fife 244 A4
Woodside GtLon 122 C2
Woodside Hants 106 C3
Woodside Herts 136 B2
Woodside NAyr 233 E4
Woodside P&K 243 G1
Woodside Shrop 156 C4
Woodside WMid 158 B4
Woodside Animal Farm &
  Leisure Park CenBeds
  LU1 4DG 135 F1
Woodside Green 124 B3
Woodstock Oxon 133 G1
Woodstock Pembs 140 D5
Woodthorpe Derbys 186 B5
Woodthorpe Leics 160 A1
Woodthorpe Lincs 189 E4
Woodthorpe SYorks 186 A4
Woodthorpe York 195 E3
Woodton 165 D2
Woodtown 113 E3
Woodvale 183 E1
Woodville 159 F1
Woodwall Green 171 E4
Woodwalton 162 A4
Woodwick 276 C5
Woodworth Green 170 C2
Woodyates 105 G1
Woofferton 145 E1
Wookey 116 C3
Wookey Hole 116 C3
Wookey Hole Caves &
  Papermill Som
  BA5 1BB 116 C3
Wool 105 E4
Woolacombe 113 E1
Woolage Green 125 E4
Woolage Village 125 E3
Woolaston 131 E2
Woolaston Slade 131 E2
Woolavington 116 A3
Woolbeding 121 D5
Woolcotts 114 C4
Wooldale 185 F2
Wooler 229 D4
Woolfardisworthy
  Devon 102 B2
Woolfardisworthy
  Devon 112 D3
Woolfold 184 B1
Woolfords Cottages 235 E4
Woolgarston 105 F4
Woolgreaves 186 A1
Woolhampton 119 G1
Woolhope 145 F4
Woolland 105 D2
Woollard 116 D1
Woollaton 113 E4
Woollensbrook 136 C2
Woolley B&NESom 117 E1
Woolley Cambs 161 G5
Woolley Corn 112 C4
Woolley Derbys 173 E1
Woolley WYorks 186 A1
Woolley Green W&M 135 D5
Woolley Green Wilts 117 F1
Woolmer Green 136 B1
Woolmere Green 146 B1
Woolmersdon 115 F4
Woolpit 152 A1

Woolpit Green 152 A1
Woolscott 147 G5
Woolsgrove 102 A2
Woolsthorpe 174 D4
Woolsthorpe by
  Colsterworth 175 E5
Woolston Devon 100 D3
Woolston Shrop 170 A5
Woolston Shrop 156 B3
Woolston Soton 106 D1
Woolston Warr 184 C4
Woolston Green 101 D1
Woolstone Glos 146 B4
Woolstone MK 149 D4
Woolstone Oxon 133 E4
Woolton 183 F4
Woolton Hill 119 F1
Woolverstone 152 C4
Woolverton 117 E2
Woolwich 136 D5
Woonton 144 C2
Wooperton 229 E5
Wootten Green 164 D4
Wootton Bed 149 F3
Wootton Hants 106 B3
Wootton IoW 107 E3
Wootton Kent 125 E4
Wootton N'hants 148 C2
Wootton NLincs 188 A1
Wootton Oxon 133 G1
Wootton Oxon 133 G1
Wootton Shrop 157 D5
Wootton Shrop 170 A3
Wootton Staffs 171 F5
Wootton Staffs 171 E5
Wootton Bassett 132 C4
Wootton Bridge 107 E3
Wootton Common 107 E3
Wootton Courtenay 114 C3
Wootton Fitzpaine 103 G3
Wootton Green 149 F3
Wootton Rivers 118 C1
Wootton
  St. Lawrence 119 G2
Wootton Wawen 147 D1
Worcester 146 A2
Worcester Cathedral Worcs
  WR1 2LH 90 Worcester
Worcester Park 122 B2
Worcester Woods Country Park
  Worcs WR5 2LG 146 A2
Wordsley 158 A4
Wordwell 163 G5
Worfield 157 G3
Worgret 105 F4
Work 277 D6
Workhouse End 149 G2
Workington 208 D4
Worksop 186 C5
Worlaby Lincs 188 D5
Worlaby NLincs 188 A1
World Museum Liverpool
  Mersey L3 8EN 42 D3
World of Beatrix Potter
  Attraction Cumb
  LA23 3BX 199 F3
World of James Herriot, Thirsk
  NYorks YO7 1PL 202 D4
World's End Bucks 135 D2
Worlds End Hants 107 F3
World's End WBerks 133 G5
Worlds End WMid 158 D4
Worle 116 A1
Worleston 171 D2
Worlingham 165 F3
Worlington 163 E5
Worlingworth 152 D1
Wormald Green 194 C1
Wormbridge 144 D4
Wormegay 163 E1
Wormelow Tump 145 D4
Wormhill 185 E5
Worminghall 134 B2
Wormingford 152 A4
Wormington 146 C4
Worminster 116 C3
Wormiston 245 E4
Wormit 244 B2
Wormleighton 147 G2
Wormley Herts 136 C2
Wormley Surr 121 E4
Wormley West End 136 C2
Wormshill 124 A3
Wormsley 144 D3
Worplesdon 121 E2
Worrall 186 A3
Worsbrough 186 A2
Worsley 184 B2
Worstead 179 E3
Worsted Lodge 150 D2
Worsthorne 193 E4
Worston 193 D3
Worswell 100 B3
Worth Kent 125 F3
Worth WSuss 122 B5
Worth Matravers 105 F5
Wortham 164 B4
Worthen 156 C2
Worthenbury 170 B3
Worthing Norf 178 A4
Worthing WSuss 108 D3
Worthington 173 F5
Worting 120 B2
Wortley Glos 131 G3
Wortley SYorks 186 A3
Wortley WYorks 194 B5
Worton NYorks 201 E4
Worton Wilts 118 A2
Wortwell 165 D3
Wothersome 194 D3
Wotherton 156 B2
Wotter 100 B1
Wotton 121 G3
Wotton Underwood 134 B1
Wotton-under-
  Edge 131 G3
Woughton on the
  Green 149 D4
Wouldham 123 G2
Wrabness 152 C4
Wrae 269 F5
Wrafton 113 E2
Wragby 188 B5
Wragholme 189 D3
Wramplingham 178 C5
Wrangaton 100 C2

Wrangham 260 E1
Wrangle 176 C2
Wrangle Lowgate 176 C2
Wrangway 103 E1
Wrantage 116 A5
Wrawby 188 A2
Wraxall NSom 131 D5
Wraxall Som 116 D4
Wray 192 C1
Wray Castle 199 E2
Wrays 122 B4
Wraysbury 135 F5
Wrayton 200 B5
Wrea Green 191 G4
Wreay Cumb 210 A5
Wreay Cumb 210 A3
Wrecclesham 120 D3
Wrekenton 212 B2
Wrelton 203 G4
Wrenbury 170 C2
Wrench Green 204 C4
Wreningham 164 C2
Wrentham 165 F3
Wrenthorpe 194 C5
Wrentnall 156 D2
Wressle ERid 195 G4
Wressle NLincs 187 G2
Wrestlingworth 150 A3
Wretham 164 A2
Wretton 163 F2
Wrexham (Wrecsam) 170 A3
Wrexham Arts Centre Wrex
  LL11 1AU 170 A3
Wrexham Industrial
  Estate 170 A3
Wribbenhall 157 G5
Wrightington Bar 183 G1
Wrightpark 242 B5
Wright's Green 137 E1
Wrinehill 171 E3
Wrington 116 B1
Writhlington 117 D2
Writtle 137 F2
Wrockwardine 157 F1
Wroot 187 E2
Wrose 194 A4
Wrotham 123 F3
Wrotham Heath 123 F3
Wrotham Hill Park 123 F2
Wrottesley 158 A2
Wroughton 132 D4
Wroxall IoW 107 E5
Wroxall Warks 159 E5
Wroxeter 157 E2
Wroxham 179 E4
Wroxton 147 G3
Wstrws 141 G3
Wyaston 172 C3
Wyberton 176 B3
Wyboston 149 G2
Wybunbury 171 D3
Wychbold 146 B1
Wychnor 159 D1
Wychnor Bridges 159 D1
Wyck 120 C4
Wyck Rissington 147 D5
Wycliffe 202 A1
Wycoller 193 F4
Wycoller Country Park
  Lancs BB8 8SY 193 F4
Wycomb 174 C5
Wycombe Marsh 135 D3
Wyddial 150 B4
Wye 124 C4
Wyesham 131 E1
Wyfordby 160 C1
Wyke Devon 102 B3
Wyke Dorset 117 E5
Wyke Shrop 157 F2
Wyke Surr 121 E2
Wyke WYorks 194 A5
Wyke Champflower 117 D4
Wyke Regis 104 C5
Wykeham NYorks 204 C4
Wykeham NYorks 204 B5
Wyken Shrop 157 G3
Wyken WMid 159 F4
Wykey 170 A5
Wylam 212 A1
Wylde Green 158 C3
Wyllie 130 A3
Wylye 118 B4
Wymering 107 F2
Wymeswold 174 B5
Wymington 149 E1
Wymondham Leics 161 D1
Wymondham Norf 178 C5
Wyndham 129 G5
Wynford Eagle 104 B3
Wynnstay Park 170 A3
Wynyard 212 D5
Wynyard Woodland Park
  Stock TS21 3JG 212 C5
Wyre Forest Worcs
  DY14 9XQ 157 G5
Wyre Piddle 146 B3
Wyresdale Tower 192 C2
Wysall 174 B5
Wyson 145 E1
Wythall 158 C5
Wythburn 209 G5
Wythenshawe 184 C4
Wyton Cambs 162 A5
Wyton ERid 197 D4
Wyverstone 152 B1
Wyverstone Street 152 B1
Wyville 175 D5
Wyvis Lodge 266 B4

**X**

Xscape Castleford WYorks
  WF10 4DA 194 D5

**Y**

Y Bryn 168 B5
Y Fan 155 F4
Y Felinheli 167 E1
Y Ffôr 166 C4
Y Fron (Upper
  Llandwrog) 167 E2
Yaddlethorpe 187 F2
Yafford 106 D4
Yafforth 202 C3
Yalberton 101 E2

Yalding 123 F4
Yanley 116 C1
Yanwath 210 B5
Yanworth 132 C1
Yapham 195 G2
Yapton 108 B3
Yarburgh 188 D3
Yarcombe 103 F2
Yardley 158 D4
Yardley Gobion 148 C3
Yardley Hastings 149 D2
Yardro 144 B2
Yarford 115 F5
Yarkhill 145 F3
Yarlet 171 G5
Yarley 116 C3
Yarlington 117 D5
Yarm 202 D1
Yarmouth 106 C4
Yarnacott 113 G2
Yarnbrook 117 F2
Yarnfield 171 F4
Yarnscombe 113 F3
Yarnton 133 G1
Yarpole 145 D1
Yarrow ScBord 227 E3
Yarrow Som 116 A3
Yarrow Feus 227 E3
Yarrowford 227 F3
Yarsop 144 D3
Yarwell 161 F3
Yate 131 G4
Yateley 120 D1
Yatehouse Green 171 E1
Yatesbury 132 C5
Yattendon 134 A5
Yatton Here 144 D1
Yatton NSom 116 B1
Yatton Keynell 132 A5
Yaverland 107 F4
Yawl 103 G3
Yaxham 178 B4
Yaxley Cambs 161 G3
Yaxley Suff 164 C4
Yazor 144 D3
Ye Olde Pork Pie Shoppe,
  Melton Mowbray Leics
  LE13 1NW 160 C1
Yeabridge 104 A1
Yeading 136 A4
Yeadon 194 B3
Yealand Conyers 199 G5
Yealand Redmayne 199 G5
Yealand Storrs 199 G5
Yealmbridge 100 B2
Yealmpton 100 B2
Yearby 213 F5
Yearsley 203 E5
Yeaton 156 D1
Yeaveley 172 C3
Yeavering 228 D3
Yedingham 204 B5
Yelford 133 F3
Yell 278 D4
Yelland Devon 113 E2
Yelland Devon 99 F1
Yelling 150 A1
Yellowcraig ELoth
  EH39 5DS 236 C1
Yelvertoft 160 A5
Yelverton Devon 100 B1
Yelverton Norf 179 D5
Yenston 117 E5
Yeo Mill 114 B5
Yeo Vale 113 E3
Yeoford 102 A3
Yeolmbridge 98 D2
Yeomadon 112 D5
Yeovil 104 B1
Yeovil Country Park Som
  BA20 1QZ 104 B1
Yeovil Marsh 104 B1
Yeovilton 116 C5
Yerbeston 127 D2
Yesnaby 277 B6
Yesterday's World, Battle
  ESuss TN33 0AQ 110 C2
Yetlington 229 E5
Yetminster 104 B1
Yettington 103 D4
Yetts o'Muckhart 243 F4
Yew Green 147 E1
Yielden 161 F1
Yieldshields 234 C4
Ynys 167 E4
Ynys Tachwedd 154 C3
Ynysboeth 129 G3
Ynysddu 130 A3
Ynyshir 129 G3
Ynyslas 154 C3
Ynysmaerdy 129 G4
Ynysmeudwy 128 D2
Ynystawe 128 C3
Ynyswen 129 F3
Ynysybwl 129 G3
Yockenthwaite 201 E5
Yockleton 156 C1
Yokefleet 196 A5
Yoker 233 G2
Yonder Bognie 268 E6
York 195 F2
York Castle Museum
  YO1 9SA 90 York
York Dungeon
  YO1 9RD 90 York
York Minster
  YO1 7HH 90 York
Yorkletts 124 C3
Yorkley 131 F2
Yorkshire Museum
  YO1 7FR 90 York
Yorkshire Sculpture Park
  WYorks WF4 4LG 185 G1
Yorton 170 C5
Yorton Heath 170 C5
Youldon 112 D5
Youldonmoor Cross 112 D5
Youlgreave 172 D1
Youlthorpe 195 G2
Youlton 195 D1
Young's End 137 G1
Yoxall 158 D1
Yoxford 153 E1
Ysbyty Cynfyn 155 D5
Ysbyty Ifan 168 B3
Ysbyty Ystwyth 154 D5
Ysceifiog 182 C5

Ysgubor-y-coed 154 C3
Ystalyfera 129 D2
Ystrad 129 F3
Ystrad Aeron 142 B2
Ystrad Meurig 142 D1
Ystrad Mynach 130 A3
Ystradfellte 129 F1
Ystradffin 143 D2
Ystradgynlais 129 D1
Ystradowen Carmar 128 D3
Ystradowen VGlam 129 G5
Ystumtuen 154 D5
Ythanwells 260 E1
Ythsie 261 G1

**Z**

Zeal Monachorum 102 A2
Zeals 117 E4
Zelah 96 C4
Zennor 94 B3
Zennor 130 A3
Zouch 173 G5

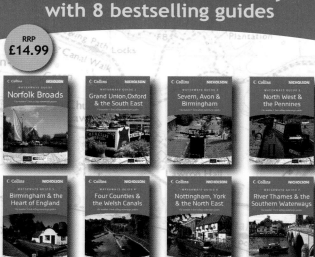

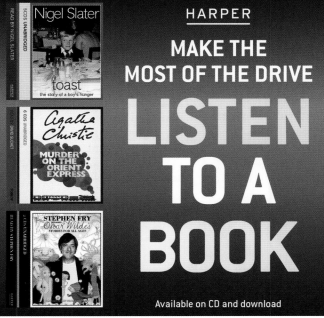